ALSO BY NEAL GABLER

Life the Movie:
How Entertainment Conquered Reality

Winchell:
Gossip, Power and the Culture of Celebrity

An Empire of Their Own:
How the Jews Invented Hollywood

Walt Disney

WALT DISNEY

THE TRIUMPH OF THE AMERICAN IMAGINATION

Neal Gabler

ALFRED A. KNOPF NEW YORK 2006

THIS IS A BORZOI BOOK
PUBLISHED BY ALFRED A. KNOPF

Published in the United States by Alfred A. Knopf,
a division of Random House, Inc., New York
and in Canada by Random House of Canada Limited, Toronto.

www.aaknopf.com

Library of Congress Cataloging-in-Publication Data
Gabler, Neal.
Walt Disney : the triumph of the American imagination / Neal Gabler.
p. cm.
Includes bibliographical references and index.
ISBN 0-679-43822-X (alk. paper)
1. Disney, Walt, 1901–1966. 2. Animators—United States—Biography.
I. Title.

NC1766.U52D5375 2006
791.43092—dc22
[B] 2006045257

Manufactured in the United States of America
First Edition

Once again, for my beloved daughters,

Laurel and Tänne,

who make all things worthwhile,
and for all those who have ever wished upon a star

I must create a system
or be enslaved by another man's;
I will not reason and compare:
my business is to create.

—WILLIAM BLAKE,
"The Marriage of Heaven and Hell"

CONTENTS

CHAPTER ILLUSTRATIONS

All images courtesy of Disney Enterprises, Inc.

INTRODUCTION

He was frozen. At least that was the rumor that emerged shortly after his death and quickly became legend: Walt Disney had been cryogenically preserved, hibernating like Snow White and Sleeping Beauty, to await the day when science could revive him and cure his disease. Though it is impossible to determine exactly, the source of the rumor may have been a tabloid named *National Spotlite*, whose correspondent claimed to have sneaked into St. Joseph's Hospital where Disney had expired, disguised himself as an orderly, picked the lock on a storage room door, and spotted Disney suspended in a metal cylinder. The story also surfaced in 1969 in a French publication, *Ici Paris*, which said it based its report on individuals close to Disney, and it was repeated in *The National Tattler*, an American scandal sheet, which added that Disney had instructed doctors to thaw him in 1975. Yet another supermarket tabloid, *Midnight*, under the headline "Walt Disney Is Being Kept Alive in Deep Freeze," quoted both a studio librarian who remembered Disney accumulating a vast file of filmed material on cryogenics and an acquaintance of Disney's who said that the producer was "obsessed" with these movies. A writer for *The Mickey Mouse Club* television show, produced under Disney auspices, seemed to corroborate the librarian's recollection by recalling that Disney had once asked him about cryogenics and that the writer had then had the studio library staff research the subject. Ward Kimball, a puckish animator at the studio, took some pride in keeping the rumor afloat. And Disney himself may have lent it credence. According to one account, just weeks after his death studio department heads were invited to a screening room with nameplates on the seats, then watched a film of Disney sitting at his desk and eerily pointing to and addressing each of them on future plans. He concluded by smiling knowingly and saying that he would be seeing them soon.

In truth, Disney's final destination was fire, not ice; he had been cremated and his ashes interred in a mausoleum in a remote corner of the Forest Lawn Cemetery in Glendale, California, not far from his studio. But the persistence of the rumor, however outlandish, testified not only to the identification of Disney with futuristic technology late in his life but to a public unwillingness to let go of him, even to the point of mythologizing him as an immortal who could not be felled by natural forces. Arguably no single figure so bestrode American popular culture as Walt Disney. By one estimate, in 1966 alone, the year of his death, 240 million people saw a Disney movie, a weekly audience of 100 million watched a Disney television show, 80 million read a Disney book, 50 million listened to Disney records, 80 million bought Disney merchandise, 150 million read a Disney comic strip, 80 million saw a Disney educational film, and nearly 7 million visited Disneyland. By another estimate, during his lifetime Disney's live-action films grossed nearly $300 million and the feature animations just under $100 million, when these were astronomical figures, and more than 60 million people had visited Disneyland. *The Saturday Evening Post* once called him the "world's most celebrated entertainer and possibly its best known non-political public figure," and *The New York Times* eulogized him as "probably the only man to have been praised by both the American Legion and the Soviet Union."

But Walt Disney's influence cannot be measured by numbers or encomia. It can only be measured by how thoroughly he reshaped the culture and the American consciousness. Disney was protean. In the late 1920s he began reinventing animation, gradually turning it from a novelty that emphasized movement and elasticity of line into an art form that emphasized character, narrative, and emotion. In doing so, he also helped reinvent graphic design by introducing the soft, round, bold, colorful forms that decades later would be adopted and adapted by a vanguard of fine artists. The critic Robert Hughes credited him with inventing Pop Art itself, not only in the look he bequeathed but also in the convergence of high art and low that he effected. "[I]t happened," Hughes wrote, "when, in *Fantasia*, Mickey Mouse clambered up to the (real) podium and shook hands with the (real) conductor Leopold Stokowski."

Beyond his animations, Disney changed the shape of American recreation with his Disneyland park. Obviously there had been amusement parks before Disneyland, but they had been grab-bag collections of various rides, games, and shows. Disney reconceptualized the amusement park as a full imaginative experience, a *theme* park, rather than a series of diversions, and just as his animation revised graphic design, his park eventually revised urban design. Detractors called the effect "Disneyfication," meaning the substitution of a synthetic world for a real one, but the urban planner James W. Rouse commended Disneyland as the "greatest piece of urban design in the United States" for the way it managed to serve its function and satisfy its guests, and architecture critic Peter Blake wrote, "[I]t seems unlikely that any American school of architecture will ever again graduate a student without first requiring him to take a field trip to Orlando, [Florida]," the site of Walt Disney World Resort, the East Coast sequel to Disneyland. In time Disneyland, with its faux environments and manipulated experiences, would become a metaphor for a whole new consciousness in which, for better or worse, the fabricated was preferred over the authentic and the real could be purged of its threats. As Robert Hughes put it, "[H]is achievement became a large shift in the limits of unreality."

Disney's influence also impregnated the American mind in subtler, less widely recognized ways. As he reinvented animation and amusement, he changed Americans' view of their own history and values. In live-action films like *So Dear to My Heart*, *Old Yeller*, and *Pollyanna*, he refined and exploited a lode of nostalgia that became identifiable enough to be called "Disneyesque," and in others like *Davy Crockett*, *Westward Ho the Wagons!*, and *Johnny Tremain* he fashioned an American past of rugged heroes and bold accomplishment that for generations turned history into boyhood adventure. By the end of his life it was the saccharine values of the nostalgic films and the sturdy patriotism of the historical ones as much as the cartoons that one associated with Disney and that made him, along with Norman Rockwell, the leading avatar of small-town, flag-waving America. At the same time, however, his forward-looking television programs depicting the future helped shape attitudes about technological change, and NASA acknowledged that Disney's early drumbeating for its program was instrumental in generating public support for space exploration. It was Disney, too, who created Tomorrowland at his Disneyland theme park and collaborated with Monsanto on a House of the Future attraction there, and Disney who advanced the ideas of monorails, "people movers," Audio-Animatronic robots, and other marvels, even to the point of designing an entire city that would, had it been built, have incorporated the latest in technology and urban planning. It made Disney at once a nostalgist and a futurist, a conservative and a visionary.

Then there was his effect on nature and conservation. By anthropomorphizing animals in his cartoons, Disney helped sensitize the public to environmental issues; with *Bambi* alone he triggered a national debate on hunting. Later when, basically for his own curiosity, he commissioned a husband-and-wife filmmaking team to shoot footage of a remote Alaskan island and then in 1948 had the film edited into a story of the seals who lived and bred there, *Seal Island*, he essentially created a new genre, the wildlife documentary, and though he would be sternly criticized in some quarters for imposing narratives on nature and turning animals into characters, his films may nevertheless have played a greater role than anything else in popular culture in educating the public on conservation and building a constituency for it.

Finally, there were Disney's accomplishments as an entrepreneur, albeit a reluctant one. He was the first motion picture mogul to realize the potential of television as an ally rather than an adversary, and his decision to make a series for the American Broadcasting Company opened the way for a rapprochement between the large screen and the small one. He was also the first to bundle television programs, feature animation, live-action films, documentaries, theme parks, music, books, comics, character merchandise, and educational films under one corporate shingle. In effect, as one observer put it, he created the first "modern multimedia corporation" and showed the way for the media conglomerates that would follow. One critic of Disney's even accused him of having dragged corporatism, in the form of the "precise, clean, insipid, mechanical image," into the daily lives of Americans and advised, "Throw him a kiss every time you get a computer letter."

Whenever someone manages to implant himself in American culture and the American psyche as deeply as Walt Disney did, analysts naturally look for explanations. In Disney's case they have pointed to the seeming innocence of his work, its gentle reassurance, its powerful sentimentality, its populism, its transport to childhood, its naïve faith in perseverance and triumph, even its appeal to atavistic images of survival in which, by one analysis, Mickey Mouse's circular shape subliminally summons breasts, babies, and fruit. One scholar has attributed Disney's popularity to his having traversed the distance between the "sentimental populism" of the Great Depression with its nudging critique of the prevailing social order and the "sentimental libertarianism" of the Cold War era that came to embrace the social order. Taking a different tack, the novelist John Gardner, a Disney advocate, located in Disney's work a lightly secularized Christian theology of hope and beneficence in which "God has things well under control" and life is fundamentally good. Essentially, as Gardner saw it, Disney had reinterpreted Christianity for mass culture.

There are certainly elements of all of these appeals in Disney's work, and its enormous popularity is undoubtedly the result of a combination of factors—indeed, of Disney's knack for splicing many disparate and even contradictory strains together. On the one hand, a Disney scholar could impute to Walt Disney a major role in the creation of a white, middle-class, Protestant ideal of childhood that turned American offspring in the 1950s into disciplined, self-sacrificing, thrifty, obedient consumers. On the other hand, another Disney scholar, citing the questioning of authority, the antagonism toward the moneyed class, the emphasis on personal liberation, the love of nature, and the advocacy of tolerance in his films, could credit him as the "primary creator of the counterculture, which the public imagination views as embracing values that are the antithesis of those that the body of his work supposedly communicated to children."

But if one source of Disney's magic was his ability to mediate between past and future, tradition and iconoclasm, the rural and the urban, the individual and the community, even between conservatism and liberalism, the most powerful source of his appeal as well as his greatest legacy may be that Walt Disney, more than any other American artist, defined the terms of wish fulfillment and demonstrated on a grand scale to his fellow Americans, and ultimately to the entire world, how one could be empowered by fantasy—how one could learn, in effect, to live within one's own illusions and even to transform the world into those illusions. "When You Wish Upon a Star," the song Disney borrowed from *Pinocchio* for his television theme, was his anthem and guiding principle. The key to his success was, as the journalist Adela Rogers St. John put it, that he "makes dreams come true," or at least gave the impression he did, and that he had "remolded a world not only nearer to his heart's desire, but to yours and mine." In numerous ways Disney struck what may be the very fundament of entertainment: the promise of a perfect world that conforms to our wishes.

He achieved this in part by managing, almost purely by instinct, to tap into archetypes that resonated with people of various ages, eras, and cultures. One of his greatest gifts was in finding the elemental and the essential of virtually every form in which he worked—its genetic code. Whether it was his fairy tales or his boy's adventures or his castle or Main Street or the *Mark Twain* Riverboat in Disneyland, each seemed to have been refined into *the* fairy tale, *the* boy's adventure, *the* castle or Main Street or riverboat of our mind's eye. In an idealized world where wish fulfillment prevailed, Disney had consistently concretized the ideal and provided the pleasure of things made simple and pure the way one imagined they should be, or at least the way one imagined they should be from childhood. He had Platonic templates in his head.

Others, virtually everyone in entertainment, attempt to tap this same reserve, but Disney understood wish fulfillment from the inside, which may be why his own longings connected so powerfully to his audience's. During a peripatetic childhood of material and emotional deprivation, at least as he remembered it, he began drawing and retreating into his own imaginative worlds. That set a pattern. His life would become an ongoing effort to devise what psychologists call a "parcosm," an invented universe, that he could control as he could not control reality. From Mickey Mouse through *Snow White and the Seven Dwarfs* through Disneyland through EPCOT, he kept attempting to remake the world in the image of his own imagination, to certify his place as a force in that world and keep reality from encroaching upon it, to recapture a sense of childhood power that he either had never felt or had lost long ago.

It was this attempt, in fact, as much as the fairy tales he used for inspiration, that forged the bond between Disney and childhood, a bond he frequently disavowed by insisting that his films were not made for children. Whether in his movies or in his theme parks, Disney always promised a fantasy in which one could exercise the privileges of childhood—privileges he never abandoned in his own life. This will to power also explained why animation was his preferred medium. In animation one took the inanimate and brought it to life, or the illusion of life. In animation one could exercise the power of a god.

No doubt because he worked in what was regarded as a juvenile idiom, and because his films seemed naïve, unselfconscious, and unpretentious, the young Walt Disney was regarded in most circles as a kind of folk artist. In the 1930s, when he became a celebrity virtually overnight, intellectuals frequently compared him to another popular artist, Charlie Chaplin, and several, including Thornton Wilder, went so far as to say that Chaplin and Disney were the only true geniuses that the movies had produced. Still, there was always something in Disney that pegged him not just as a populist but as peculiarly American, and though an early biography of him was subtitled *An American Original*, he was less original in many respects than quintessential. He had been born in the Midwest in the very heart of the country at the turn of the century and at the fulcrum of an expiring agricultural nation that looked backward to an idyllic past and an aspiring industrialized one that looked forward to a technological future, and he had a foot in each. His childhood had even been divided between the country and the city. An American Everyman, he lived the American experience and seemed to embody it in his doggedness, his idealism, his informality, and his lack of affectation, perhaps above all in his sudden rise from poverty and anonymity to the summit of success. "[H]e emerged from the very heart of the people," one admirer rhapsodized. "Only so was it possible for him to respond to our subtlest moods." Another remarked that "[o]f all the activists of public diversion, Uncle Walt was the one most precisely in the American mainstream." The synchronicity between Disney and America would become his brand. His imagination formed a double helix with the American imagination.

Obviously Disney's work had universal appeal, but in America, with its almost religious belief in possibilities, his urge to wish fulfillment was especially resonant. In both Disney's imagination and the American imagination, one could assert one's will on the world; one could, through one's own power, or more accurately through the power of one's innate goodness, achieve success. Indeed, in a typically American formulation, nothing but goodness and will mattered. Disney's best animations—*Snow White and the Seven Dwarfs*, *Pinocchio*, *Bambi*, and *Dumbo*—were archetypal expressions of this idea. In large measure, they were about the process of a child making his or her claim upon the world, about the process of overcoming obstacles to become whatever he or she wanted to be. Similarly, in both Disney's imagination and the American imagination perfection was seen as an attainable goal. In a world that was often confusing, dangerous, and even tragic, a world that seemed beyond any individual's control, Disney and America both promised not only dominance but also improvement. Disneyland was just a modern variant on the old Puritan ideal of a shining City on a Hill, as Disney's Audio-Animatronic robots were just a variant on the American dream of making oneself anew.

The helix between America and Disney was especially tight in the anxiety ridden Depression America of the 1930s, when his films seemed to capture and then soothe the national malaise. Virtually everyone interpreted *Three Little Pigs* as a Depression allegory, and many others saw in Mickey Mouse's pluck an intrepid American spirit. But among American critics the line between naïve populism and cloying sentimentality proved to be thin. Already by the end of World War II Disney's artistic reputation was in decline, and intellectuals who had been swooning just a few years earlier over his innocence and artless artfulness now complained that he had lost his touch and become a mass artist rather than a folk artist. By the end of his life, though his iconic status as America's favorite uncle was probably more unshakable than ever, his artistic status had plummeted. What had once been hailed as an unerring sense of the American temper was now attacked by critics for having transmogrified into aesthetic demagoguery and vulgarization. As one disgruntled animator put it, "Walt Disney had the innate bad taste of the American public."

In the end he was widely identified with cultural degradation—the "rallying point for the subliterates of our society," as critic Richard Schickel wrote. Almost no one took him seriously any longer, except for the undiscriminating hordes who loved his work, and one could almost have divided the country between those who subscribed to the Disney vision and those who abhorred it. "A few years ago when you mentioned Walt Disney at a respectable party . . . the standard response was a head-shake and a groan," John Gardner wrote in 1973. "Intellectuals spoke of how he butchered the classics—from *Pinocchio* to *Winnie the Pooh*—how his wildlife pictures were sadistic and coy, how the World's Fair sculptures of hippopotamuses, etc., were a national if not international disgrace." The bill of indictment was, indeed, a long one. He had infantilized the culture and removed the danger from fairy tales in the process of popularizing them for a mass market, providing, in novelist Max Apple's words, "the illusion of life without any of the mess." He had promoted treacly values that seemed anachronistic and even idiotic in a complex, modern, often tragic world and that defined him as a cultural and political troglodyte. He had usurped each person's individual imagination with a homogenized corporate one and promoted conformity, prompting one critic to declare, "The borders of fantasy are closed now." Like a capitalist Midas, he had commercialized everything he touched, reducing it all, in another antagonist's view, "to a sickening blend of cheap formulas packaged to sell . . . One feels our whole mass culture heading up the dark river to the source—that heart of darkness where Mr. Disney traffics in pastel-trinketed evil for gold and ivory." And at the same time that he was commercializing his own country, he was regarded by his detractors as perhaps the primary example of America's cultural imperialism, supplanting the myths of native cultures with his own myths just as he had supplanted the imaginations of his audience.

All of this antagonism was aimed at Disney in his role as studio head, but in his later years, and especially after his death, his personal image, at least among intellectuals, underwent a similar if somewhat more gradual transformation from beloved naïf to avaricious corporate kingpin and general villain. Much of this change was politically inspired. Ever since a cartoonists' strike in 1941 that wracked the studio and shattered its owner's utopianism, Disney had grown increasingly conservative, aligning himself with red-baiting anti-Communists and with the most reactionary elements of the Republican Party, thus putting himself in the political crosshairs. Whispered accusations of anti-Semitism and racism clearly eroded his image. But much of the criticism was also culturally inspired. His long identification with small-town, conformist America, which had been one source of his popularity, became a liability in the 1960s, when that America was itself increasingly under attack from intellectuals and political activists and was itself increasingly identified not with America's sinewy strength but with her prejudices. Disney became a symbol of an America facing backward—politically, culturally, and artistically.

One of the most important flash points in both crystallizing and advancing this revisionist view was Richard Schickel's 1968 critical study, *The Disney Version*, which portrayed Disney as mercenary and mendacious, his entire life "an illusion created by a vast machinery," so much so that even his own signature, used as the company's logo, had to be manufactured for him. (In truth, Disney's personal signature was far more flamboyantly loopy than the modified corporate version.) "Disney was a callous man, oblivious to patterns inherent in nature, art, literature," a critic wrote in an approving review of Schickel's book, delivering what rapidly became the standard intellectual verdict on Hollywood's chief fantasist. "He had a magic touch, but it turned things into gold, not art. He lacked perception and sensitivity for genuine artistic creativity, and his compulsion to control made him no respecter of the integrity of the works of others." Another biographer, drawing on the deep hostility that Disney now evoked among intellectuals, accused him of being everything from the illegitimate son of a Spanish dancer to an alcoholic to a bigot to an FBI informant. The book was subtitled *Hollywood's Dark Prince*.

By the 1950s Disney himself was well aware that as a producer he had headed up the river to the heart of commercial darkness and that as a person he had allowed himself to become lost in the corporate haze. He had created the studio; then the studio, with his complicity, created him, making him, he fully understood, as much a commodity as a man—the very sort of diffident, genial, plainspoken, unprepossessing, and childishly enthusiastic character who would have produced Walt Disney movies. Essentially, he had become his own parcosm. Though he actually possessed all of those qualities, they were now simplified, like his signature, into an image and brand. He told one prospective employee that the studio was in the business of selling the name "Walt Disney." To another associate he commented, "I'm not Walt Disney anymore. Walt Disney is a thing. It's grown to become a whole different meaning than just one man."

Though Disney was anything but a dark prince, neither was he exactly the affable illusion that had subsumed him. For all his outward sociability, associates found him deeply private, complex, often moody, and finally opaque. No one seemed to know him. "He was a difficult man to understand," said Ben Sharpsteen, who worked for him in various capacities from the late 1920s on. "He never made his motives clear. . . . When I added up thirty years of employment, I found I understood him less at the end." Bill Peet, another longtime studio hand, wrote, "I do believe I knew Walt about as well as any employee could know him," then added, "even though he was never the same two days in a row." "I've always said that if you get forty people in a room together," Walt's nephew Roy E. Disney told an interviewer, "and ask each one of them to write down who Walt was, you'd get forty different Walts."

This book is an attempt to penetrate the image and decipher the mystery of Walt Disney—to understand the psychological, cultural, economic, and social forces that acted upon him and led to his art and his empire. And because Disney was so deeply embedded in the American psyche and scene, understanding him may also enable one to understand the power of popular culture in shaping the national consciousness, the force of possibility and perfectionism as American ideals, the ongoing interplay between commerce and art, and the evolution of the American imagination in the twentieth century. In short, to understand Walt Disney, one of the most emblematic of Americans, is to understand much about the country in which he lived and which he so profoundly affected.

Walt Disney

One

ESCAPE

Elias Disney was a hard man. He worked hard, lived modestly, and worshiped devoutly. His son would say that he believed in "walking a straight and narrow path," and he did, neither smoking nor drinking nor cursing nor carousing. The only diversion he allowed himself as a young man was playing the fiddle, and even then his upbringing was so strict that as a boy he would have to sneak off into the woods to practice. He spoke deliberately, rationing his words, and generally kept his emotions in check, save for his anger, which could erupt violently. He looked hard too, his body thin and taut, his arms ropy, his blue eyes and copper-colored hair offset by his stern visage—long and gaunt, sunken-cheeked and grim-mouthed. It was a pioneer's weathered face—a no-nonsense face, the face of American Gothic.

But it was also a face etched with years of disappointment—disappointment that would shade and shape the life of his famous son, just as the Disney tenacity, drive, and pride would. The Disneys claimed to trace their lineage to the d'Isignys of Normandy, who had arrived in England with William the Conqueror and fought at the Battle of Hastings. During the English Restoration in the late seventeenth century, a branch of the family, Protestants, moved to Ireland, settling in County Kilkenny, where, Elias Disney would later boast, a Disney was "classed among the intellectual and well-to-do of his time and age." But the Disneys were also ambitious and opportunistic, always searching for a better life. In July 1834, a full decade before the potato famine that would trigger mass migrations, Arundel Elias Disney, Elias Disney's grandfather, sold his holdings, took his wife and two young children to Liverpool, and set out for America aboard the *New Jersey* with his older brother Robert and Robert's wife and their two children.

They had intended to settle in America, but Arundel Elias did not stay there long. The next year he moved to the township of Goderich in the wilderness of southwestern Ontario, Canada, just off Lake Huron, and bought 149 acres along the Maitland River. In time Arundel Elias built the area's first grist mill and a sawmill, farmed his land, and fathered sixteen children—eight boys and eight girls. In 1858 the eldest of them, twenty-five-year-old Kepple, who had come on the boat with his parents, married another Irish immigrant named Mary Richardson and moved just north of Goderich to Bluevale in Morris Township, where he bought 100 acres of land and built a small pine cabin. There his first son, Elias, was born on February 6, 1859.

Though he cleared the stony land and planted orchards, Kepple Disney was a Disney, with airs and dreams, and not the kind of man inclined to stay on a farm forever. He was tall, nearly six feet, and in his nephew's words "as handsome a man as you would ever meet." For a religious man he was also vain, sporting long black whiskers, the ends of which he liked to twirl, and jet-black oiled hair, always well coifed. And he was restless—a trait he would bequeath to his most famous descendant as he bequeathed his sense of self-importance. When oil was struck nearby in what came to be known as Oil Springs, Kepple rented out his farm, deposited his family with his wife's sister, and joined a drilling crew. He was gone for two years, during which time the company struck no oil. He returned to Bluevale and his farm, only to be off again, this time to drill salt wells. He returned a year later, again without his fortune, built himself a new frame house on his land, and reluctantly resumed farming.

But that did not last either. Hearing of a gold strike in California, he set out in 1877 with eighteen-year-old Elias and his second-eldest son, Robert. They got only as far as Kansas when Kepple changed plans and purchased just over three hundred acres from the Union Pacific Railroad, which was trying to entice people to settle at division points along the train route it was laying through the state. (Since the Disneys were not American citizens, they could not acquire land under the Homestead Act.) The area in which the family settled, Ellis County in the northwestern quadrant of Kansas about halfway across the state, was frontier and rough. Indian massacres were fresh in memory, and the Disneys themselves waited out one Indian scare by stationing themselves all night at their windows with guns. Crime was rampant too. One visitor called the county seat, Hays, the "Sodom of the Plains."

The climate turned out to be as inhospitable as the inhabitants—dry and bitter cold. At times it was so difficult to farm that the men would join the railroad crews while their wives scavenged for buffalo bones to sell to fertilizer manufacturers. Most of those who stayed on the land turned to livestock since the fields rippled with yellow buffalo grass on which sheep and cows could graze. Farming there either broke men or hardened them, as Elias would be hardened, but being as opportunistic as his Disney forebears, he had no more interest in farming than his father had. He wanted escape.

Father and son now set their sights on Florida. The winter of 1885–86 had been especially brutal in Ellis. Will Disney, Kepple's youngest son, remembered the snow drifting into ten-to-twelve-foot banks, forcing the settlers from the wagon trains heading west to camp in the schoolhouse for six weeks until the weather broke. The snow was so deep that the train tracks were cleared only when six engines were hitched to a dead locomotive with a snowplow and made run after run at the drifts, inching forward and backing up, gradually nudging through. Kepple, tired of the cruel Kansas weather, decided to join a neighbor family on a reconnaissance trip to Lake County, in the middle of Florida, where the neighbors had relatives. Elias went with him.

For Elias, Florida held another inducement besides the promise of warm weather and new opportunities. The neighbor family they had accompanied, the Calls, had a sixteen-year-old daughter named Flora. The Calls, like the Disneys, were pioneers who nevertheless disdained the hardscrabble life. Their ancestors had arrived in America from England in

1636, settling first outside Boston and then moving to upstate New York. In 1825 Flora's grandfather, Eber Call, reportedly to escape hostile Indians and bone-chilling cold, left with his wife and three children for Huron County in Ohio, where he cleared several acres and farmed. But Eber Call, like Kepple Disney, had higher aspirations. Two of his daughters became teachers, and his son, Charles, was graduated from Oberlin College in 1847 with high honors. After heading to California to find gold and then drifting through the West for several years, Charles wound up outside Des Moines, Iowa, where he met Henrietta Gross, a German immigrant. They married on September 9, 1855, and returned to his father's house in Ohio. Charles became a teacher.

Exactly why at the age of fifty-six he decided to leave Ohio in January 1879, after roughly twenty years there and ten children, is a mystery, though a daughter later claimed it was because he was fearful that one of his eight girls might marry into a neighbor family with eight sons, none of whom were sober enough for the devout teacher. Why he chose to become a farmer is equally mysterious, and why he chose Ellis, Kansas, is more mysterious still. The rough-hewn frontier town was nothing like the tranquil Ohio village he had left, and it had little to offer save for cheap land. But Ellis proved no more hospitable to the Calls than it had to the Disneys. Within a year the family had begun to scatter. Flora, scarcely in her teens, was sent to normal school in Ellsworth to be trained as a teacher, and apparently roomed with Albertha Disney, Elias's sister, though it is likely he had already taken notice of her since the families' farms were only two miles from each other.

Within a few years the weather caught up to the Calls—probably the legendary storm of January 1886. In all likelihood it was the following autumn that they left for Florida by train with Elias and Kepple Disney as company. Kepple returned to Ellis shortly thereafter. Elias stayed on with the Calls. The area where they settled, in the middle of the state, was by one account "howling wilderness" at the time. Even so, after their Kansas experience the Calls found it "beautiful" and thought their new life there would be "promising." It was known generally as Pine Island for its piney woods on the wet, high rolling land and for the rivers that isolated it, but it was dotted with new outposts. Elias settled in Acron, where there were only seven families; the Calls settled in adjoining Kismet. Charles cleared some acreage to raise oranges and took up teaching again in neighboring Norristown, while Flora became the teacher in Acron her first year and Paisley her second. Meanwhile Elias delivered mail from a horse-drawn buckboard and courted Flora.

Their marriage, at the Calls' home in Kismet on New Year's Day

1888, wedded the intrepid determination of the Disneys with the softer, more intellectual temper of the Calls—two strains of earthbound romanticism that would merge in their youngest son. The couple even looked the part, Elias's flinty gauntness contrasting with Flora's amiable roundness, as his age—he was nearly thirty at the time of the wedding—contrasted with the nineteen-year-old bride's youth. Marriage, however, didn't change his fortunes. He had bought an orange grove, but a freeze destroyed most of his crop, forcing him back into delivering the mail. In the meantime Charles Call had an accident while clearing some land of pines, never fully recovered, and died early in 1890. His death loosened the couple's bond to Florida. "Elias was very much like his father; he couldn't be contented very long in any one place," Elias's cousin, Peter Cantelon, observed. The Disney wanderlust and the need to escape would send Elias back north—this time to a nine-room house in Chicago.

He had been preceded to Chicago by someone who seemed just as blessed as Elias was cursed. Robert Disney, Elias's younger brother by two-and-a-half years, was viewed by the family as the successful one. He was big and handsome—tall, broad, and fleshy where Elias was short, slim, and wiry, and he had an expansive, voluble, glad-handing manner to match his appearance. He was the "real dandy of the family," his nephew would say. But if Robert Disney looked the very picture of a man of means, the image obscured the fact that he was actually a schemer with talents for convincing and cajoling that Elias could never hope to match. Six months after Elias married Flora, Robert had married a wealthy Boston girl named Margaret Rogers and embarked on his career of speculation in real estate, oil, and even gold mines—anything he could squeeze for a profit. He had come to Chicago in 1889 in anticipation of the 1893 Columbian Exposition, which would celebrate the four-hundredth anniversary of Columbus's discovery of America, and had built a hotel there. Elias had also come for the promise of employment from the fair, but his dreams were humbler. Living in his brother's shadow, he was hoping for work not as a magnate but as a carpenter, a skill he had apparently acquired while laboring on the railroad in his knockabout days.

The Disneys arrived in Chicago late in the spring of 1890, a few months after Charles Call's death, with their infant son, Herbert, and with Flora pregnant again. Elias rented a one-story frame cottage at 3515 South Vernon on the city's south side, an old mid-nineteenth-century farmhouse now isolated amid much more expensive residences; its chief recommendation was that it was only twenty blocks from the site of the exposition. Construction on the fair began early the next year, after Flora had given birth that December to a second son, Ray. The family enjoyed few extravagances. Elias earned only a dollar a day as a carpenter. But he was industrious and frugal, and by the fall he had saved enough to purchase a plot of land for $700 through his brother's real estate connections. By the next year he had applied for a building permit at 1249 Tripp Avenue* to construct a two-story wooden cottage for his family, which the following June would add another son, Roy O. Disney.

Though it was set within the city, the area to which they moved the spring of 1893, in the northwestern section, was primitive. It had only two paved roads and had just begun to be platted for construction, which made it a propitious place for a carpenter. Elias contracted to help build homes, and one of his sons recalled that Flora too would go out to the sites and "hammer and saw planks with the men." Still, by his wife's estimate Elias averaged only seven dollars a week. But he was a Disney, and he had not surrendered his dreams. Using Robert's contacts and leveraging his own house through mortgages, he began buying plots in the subdivision, designing residences with Flora's help and then building them—small cottages for workingmen like himself. By the end of the decade he and a contracting associate had built at least two additional homes on the same street on which he lived—one of which he sold for $2,500 and the other of which he and his partner rented out for income. In effect, under Robert's tutelage, Elias had become a real estate maven, albeit an extremely modest one.

But by this time, already in his forties, he had begun to place his hope less in success, which seemed hard-won and capricious, than in faith. Both the Disneys and the Calls had been deeply religious, and Elias and Flora's social life in Chicago now orbited the nearby Congregational church, of which they were among the most devoted members. When the congregation decided to reorganize and then voted to erect a new building just two blocks from the Disneys' home, Elias was named a trustee as well as a member of the building committee. By the time the new church, St. Paul's, was dedicated in October 1900, the family was attending services not only on Sundays but during the week. Occasionally, when the minister was absent, Elias would even take the pulpit. "[H]e was a pretty good preacher," Flora would remember. "[H]e did a lot of that at home, you know."

It would become embedded in Disney family lore that when Flora had a baby boy in the upper bedroom of their Tripp house on December 5, 1901, the child's name was part of a pastoral bargain. As the story went, Flora and the wife of the new young minister, Walter Parr, were pregnant

*In 1909 the address was changed to 2156 North Tripp Avenue in a citywide renumbering.

at the same time. Elias and Parr agreed that if their wives both had sons, Elias would name his after the minister and the minister would name his after Elias. This was supposedly how Elias and Flora's new baby came to be named Walter Elias Disney. The story, however, was only partly true. The Disneys' second son, Ray, may have originally been named Walter—that was the name on his birth registration—before the family reconsidered, which suggests that the Disneys had thought of the name previously. (The confusion would spur rumors later on about whether Walt was actually the Disneys' natural-born child, especially since Walt had no birth certificate, only a baptismal certificate.*) In addition, though Mrs. Parr and Flora had indeed been pregnant at the same time, with Flora late in her pregnancy and Mrs. Parr early in hers, the Parrs' baby boy, born the following July, was named not Elias but Charles Alexander. Not until the birth of another son two and a half years later, in May 1904, did the Parrs seem to keep their part of the bargain, if there was one, naming the child Walter Elias Parr.

Young Walter Elias Disney, fine-featured and golden-haired and favoring the soft Calls more than the flinty Disneys, would not remember much about Chicago. He was scarcely four years old in 1906 when Elias decided yet again to move, though the motive this time was less financial or even temperamental than moral. Two neighbor boys the same ages as Herbert and Ray and from an equally devout St. Paul's family had attempted to rob a car barn and had killed a policeman during a shootout. Terrified that his own boys might be led astray, especially since the neighborhood was growing rougher, Elias began searching for a more salubrious environment, even making a few brief scouting expeditions, before settling on a remote Missouri town where his brother Robert had recently purchased some farmland as an investment. In February Elias sold their house for $1,800 and another property a month later. He, Herbert, Ray, and two draft horses they had bought in Chicago then went on to Missouri in a boxcar to ready the farm while Flora, Roy, Walt, and their new baby sister, Ruth, followed on the Santa Fe train. "That was a big moment when we were going to go away," Walt recalled years later. "[I]t sounded wonderful to all of us," Roy would confirm, "going on a farm."

*One stubborn fabrication, traced to a Spanish magazine, *Primer Plano*, reported that Walt had actually been born in Mojacar, Spain, and that his parents had emigrated to the United States and gone to work for Elias, who adopted the boy. See Edmundo Lassalle to Walt, Jul. 12, 1945; Walt to Lassalle, May 3, 1945, L Folder, Walt Disney Corr., 1945–1946, L-P, A1535. Walt: "I assure you it was with utter amazement that I learned that I was born in Spain, which is certainly stretching the point by 5,000 miles."

II

Walt Disney would remember Marceline, Missouri. He would remember it more vividly than anything else in his childhood, perhaps more vividly than any place in his entire lifetime. "Marceline was the most important part of Walt's life," his wife would say. "He didn't live there very long. He lived in Chicago and Kansas City much longer. But there was something about the farm that was very important to him." He would remember the family's arrival—"clearly remember every detail of it," he later said. He remembered getting off the train and crossing to a grain elevator, where a neighbor named Coffman waited for them, and he remembered clambering onto Coffman's wagon and driving out to the farm about a mile from the town's center, north of Julep Road and of the railroad track that sliced diagonally through the heart of Marceline. And he remembered his first impression of the site—its dazzling wide front yard carpeted green and crowded with weeping willows.

It was a small farm. Uncle Robert's property, a mile west, was nearly five hundred acres, while Elias had purchased only forty acres on March 5, 1906, from the children of a Civil War veteran named Crane who had died recently, and then bought just over five acres more the next month from Crane's widow. Elias's property cost $3,000, money he did not have just then, but he had made an arrangement to pay in installments as he received the proceeds from the sale of his properties in Chicago. Despite its modest size, Walt would always recall the farm through the prism of a child's wonder and always think of it as a paradise. Game abounded; there were foxes, rabbits, squirrels, opossums, and raccoons. And there were birds. During migration teal and sprig would settle on the pasture pond. Of the forty-five acres, five were planted with orchards, apple, peach, and plum trees with grapevines and berry plants. "We had every kind of apple you ever heard of," Walt recalled, "including one called a Wolf River apple. Wolf River apples were tremendous in size. People came from miles to see ours." And there were a hog pen, chickens, a few milk cows, and four to six horses. "[I]t was just heaven for city kids," said Roy, which is exactly what Elias intended it to be.

And because it was in the country everything *seemed* heavenly, even when it wasn't. The wooden one-story farmhouse in which the Disneys lived was crudely constructed with whitewashed siding and green trim and so cramped that the back parlor had to be converted into a bedroom for Herbert and Ray. But surrounded by the willows, mock orange trees, silver maples, cedars, lilacs, and dogwoods, it was, in the words of Elias's aunt, "a very hansome [*sic*] place" with a front yard "like a park." She was so smitten that she debated whether she could ever return to Ellis.

Walt Disney had the same dreamy vision of the farm as his great-aunt. "Everything connected with Marceline was a thrill to us," he once reminisced. Coming from what he described as "crowded, smoky" Chicago, he was especially fascinated by the livestock and claimed that his time on the farm imbued him with a special feeling toward animals that he would never lose. He often told about herding the pigs by climbing on their backs, riding them into the pond to root, and sometimes getting shrugged off into the mud—a sight so comical that Elias invited guests to watch. Other times he and a few other children would get up on an old horse named Charley who, Walt said, had "his own sense of humor." Charley headed toward the orchard, forcing the children to jump off his back to avoid being hit by the limbs. Everywhere Walt went he was trailed by a little Maltese terrier he had been given, his first pet, that would snap at his heels and tear his socks. He counted it a "big tragedy" when the dog followed Roy into town one day and never returned.

Walt Disney would always speak of these as his halcyon days. He did not start school until he was nearly seven because, he said, there was no one to take him and because his parents decided he could wait another year and accompany his sister, Ruth, when she started school. "It was the most embarrassing thing [that] could happen to a fellow," he would later complain, "that I had to practically start in school with my little sister who was two years younger." But school did not seem to have much appeal anyway except as a stage on which he could perform, and his one memory from his Marceline education was a Tom Sawyerish escapade in which his teacher asked the children to bring in switches to use on misbehaving students and Walt surreptitiously laid a thick barrel stave on her desk. When she queried who had brought it, Walt, knowing he would get a laugh from his classmates, confessed, only to find himself being struck with the stave by the teacher.

When he was not in school or on the farm, he often spent languid afternoons fishing with the neighbor boys for catfish and bowheads in Yellow Creek and skinny-dipping afterward. In the winter they would go sledding or skating on the frozen creek, building a bonfire on the shore to keep warm. Sometimes Walt would tag after Erastus Taylor, a Civil War veteran, who would relive his battle exploits. ("I don't think he ever was in a battle in the Civil War," Walt later said, "but he was in all of them.") Even Sundays were no longer committed exclusively to church and Sunday school since there was no Congregational church in Marceline. Instead, the Disneys often spent the day going to the Taylor house just down the road, where Elias would take out his fiddle and play with his neighbors.

. . .

The town was no less enchanting than the farm. In seeking to escape the encroachments and dangers of the city, Elias Disney could hardly have found a better place than Marceline. Though it qualified as frontier, Marceline was sedate, even refined. Located east of the Locust River off State Highway 5, Marceline, like Ellis, Kansas, was a product of the railroad boom, specifically of the desire of the Atchison, Topeka, and Santa Fe Railroad to establish a "Chicago Extension," connecting that city to the west via Kansas City, which lay about 125 miles southwest of the town. The plan necessitated what were called "terminal" or "division" points roughly every one hundred miles along the route, where trains could be serviced and workers housed. Marceline, which became one of these division points, was incorporated on March 6, 1888, and named, depending on who told the story, after the wife or the daughter of one of the railroad's directors, or the daughter of the town's first resident civil engineer, or a French immigrant who was an early resident. Within six months 2,500 people had settled there, primarily to service the railroad. Within a year a prospector named U. C. Wheelock discovered coal there, eventually leading to the digging of five mines, which would employ five hundred more men. When the Santa Fe was reorganized in 1903 and was divided into an eastern and a western division, Marceline became the seat of the latter.

Young Walt Disney was impressed by the town's appearance—that it looked exactly the way a small town should look. From what the local newspaper described as a "motley array of tents and shacks" at its founding, Marceline had, by the time the Disneys moved there, become a "dignified and sturdy" town of roughly 4,500 residents, with two hundred houses built in the preceding two years alone. "A stranger coming here is amazed at the number of lovely lawns and elegant homes," a civic booster beamed a few years after the Disneys settled there. "In this feature she is excelled by no city of equal population on the continent." Down the main thoroughfare, Kansas Avenue, still unpaved at the time of the Disneys' arrival, were the Simpson & Miller Dry Goods Store; Hayden & Anderson's meat market; the Meriden Creamery; the three-story New York Racket Store, where, an advertisement boasted, a bride could order her complete trousseau and then select the furnishings for her new home; Hott's Tavern, run by Judge Hott, where "you are sure of getting a good bed—provided the house is not full"; R. J. Dall & Sons ice company; the Brown Hardware Company; Sutton's Tonsorial Parlor; the Allen Implement Company for farm machinery; Zircher's Jewelry Store with its freestanding clock on the corner; J. E. Eillis Big Department Store; and the two-story gray granite Allen Hotel. Just off Kansas Avenue at the center of town was another quintessential image of quaint small-town life—Ripley

Square, a wooded park with a band gazebo, a long pond, and a cannon sitting atop a four-sided plaster base with a mound of cannonballs nearby.

But however much it may have looked the archetype of hidebound agrarian America, Marceline was not especially conservative—with its large workforce, it was a hotbed of support for the Democratic populist William Jennings Bryan—and it prided itself on its progressivism, which allowed young Walt to receive his cultural education there and led him to comment once that "more things of importance happened to me in Marceline than have happened since—or are likely to in the future." In Marceline Walt saw his first circus and attended his first Chautauqua, a traveling tent show that prominently featured the leading orators of the day. In Marceline he broke his piggy bank to get money to watch Maude Adams play Peter Pan in a touring company, inspiring him to reprise the role in a school production. "No actor ever identified himself with the part he was playing more than I," he said, recalling how the hoist and tackle that brother Roy used to enable Walt to fly gave way and sent Walt "right into the faces of the surprised audience." In Marceline he was awaiting the parade for Buffalo Bill's visiting Wild West Show when Buffalo Bill himself stopped his buggy and invited Walt to join him. "I was mighty impressed," Walt later wrote. And in Marceline, after school one day, Walt coaxed his sister Ruth to see their first motion picture—a life of Christ, as Ruth remembered it. She also remembered her parents' scolding when the children returned home after dark, "in spite of Walt's telling me it was all right to go."

But it was not just the homely appearance of Marceline or the cultural rites of passage he experienced there that Walt Disney loved and remembered and would burnish for the rest of his life; it was also the spirit of the community. In Marceline people cared for one another and were tolerant of one another; even a black man who had gotten into a scuffle with some white roughs was exonerated by a local judge. "[E]verything was done in a community help," Walt recalled. "One farmer would help the other, they'd go and help repair fences. They would do different things." He especially enjoyed the camaraderie of threshing season, when the wagons would be hitched behind a big steam engine and rumble through the fields, and the neighbors would gather to help, sleeping in the Disneys' front yard, and their wives would arrive too, all joining forces to cook for their men in a scene that Walt would always think back on fondly.

Nor was it only the community of neighbors he recalled. Living in Marceline would be the first and last time in Walt's life that the extended Disney family would be a presence, and he clearly basked in the attention. His uncle Mike Martin, who was an engineer on the train running between Marceline and Ft. Madison, Iowa, and who was, Walt said, "one of the prides of my life," would arrive, walking or hitchhiking the mile from the station in town, and come up to the farm carrying a striped bag of candy for the children. Grandma Disney, a mischievous woman who in her old age seemed to relish bedeviling her dour, straitlaced son, would also come from Ellis and stay. During one of their frequent walks she had Walt crawl under a neighbor's fence to pick some turnips for her. (Elias was mortified by the transgression, but Walt admitted that he enjoyed these subversive adventures, no doubt because they did rile his father.)

The boy was even more enthused over visits from his uncle Edmund Disney, Elias's younger brother. Edmund was retarded; he was incapable even of signing his name. But he was an amiable man and free spirit who frequently left his sisters, Lizzie and Ethel, with whom he lived in Kansas, and went roaming. Marceline was one of his regular stops, and he would show up unexpectedly at the Disney door announcing, "It's me!" Walt said Edmund made a wonderful playmate for an eight-year-old boy since that was about Ed's mental age. Ed had no inhibitions. "Uncle Ed did everything he wanted to do," Walt observed. "He wanted to go to town, he would walk over to the railroad track and the train would be comin' up. And he'd flag it. The train would stop. He'd say, 'I want a ride.' He'd get up and go on to town." The two would also venture into the woods, where Ed knew the names of the plants and birds and could identify the latter's calls. And then, after what was typically a short visit, he would declare that he was going to see another relative and would leave. Walt admired this sense of juvenile freedom—Ed was a real-life Peter Pan—but he also loved his uncle's joy, and he considered Ed a role model. "To me he represented fun in its simplest and purest form."

If Edmund's visits were breezy reminders of the Disney wanderlust, Uncle Robert's frequent visits to view his property were reminders of their pretensions. Wearing a linen duster and sporting a Vandyke, he would step off the train as if he were a sovereign, which is exactly how he acted toward his older brother. Robert kept a buggy at Elias's farm, and Elias was expected to surrender it. Whether or not Elias was resentful, at least some of his neighbors were, and they referred to Robert disparagingly as "Gold Bug," both for his airs and for the gold stock in which he traded. Still, Walt enjoyed these visits because Robert's wife, Aunt Margaret—the only aunt, Walt said, whom he called "auntie"—would usually bring a gift, a Big Chief drawing tablet and pencils.

For most children these gifts might have seemed perfunctory. For Walt they came to represent something else of importance he took from Marceline: a nascent self-awareness and the first acknowledgment of his talent. Walt enjoyed art and claimed to have become interested in drawing "almost as soon as I could hold a pencil." But it was not until Aunt Maggie's visits that he received encouragement. "She used to make me think I was really a boy wonder!" he said, admitting that she had a "flattering tongue in her head." And Aunt Maggie's praise was reinforced by another mentor, an elderly neighbor named Doc Sherwood. By the time Walt met him, the doctor had retired from practicing medicine, so he had time on his hands, and he and his wife were childless, so he spent a good deal of that time with Walt, who became a kind of adopted son. Doc Sherwood was an imperious man; he wore a Prince Albert coat and drove a surrey in the summer and a cutter in the winter pulled by a prize stallion named Rupert. Walt often accompanied him, even into the drugstore, where the doctor conducted a "gabfest." Usually on their trips Walt peppered him with questions, and years later he marveled at the doctor's knowledge and patience. "Don't be afraid to admit your ignorance," Doc Sherwood told him, a philosophy that Walt, who was always inquisitive, said "lasted me a lifetime." But what Walt remembered most about Doc Sherwood—what he would recount throughout the rest of his life—was the time the doctor asked him to fetch his crayons and tablet and sketch Rupert. The horse was skittish that day. Doc Sherwood had to hold the reins, and Walt had difficulty capturing him. "The result was pretty terrible," he recalled, "but both the doctor and his wife praised the drawing highly, to my great delight." In one version of the story Doc Sherwood gave Walt a nickel for the drawing, which one neighbor called highly uncharacteristic of the tight-fisted Sherwood, and in another version the drawing was framed and hung in the doctor's house. Whatever was true, the drawing became, in his brother Roy's hyperbolic words, "the highlight of Walt's life."

Years later the Disneys would also frequently recall another episode in Walt's budding artistic career that they believed testified to his obsession. One summer's day Flora and Elias had gone to town, leaving Walt and Ruth at the farm. As Ruth told it, they began investigating the rain barrels around the house and discovered the barrels' tar lining. Walt announced that the soft tar could be used as paint, and when Ruth out of caution asked whether it would come off, he assured her that it could. So the two found big sticks, dipped them into the tar, and began drawing designs on the side of the Disneys' whitewashed house. "And I can remember an awful feeling," Ruth would say, "when I realized just a little bit later that it wouldn't budge—the tar." Their parents were not amused. ("He was old enough to know better," Flora snipped thirty years later.) The tar still adorned the side of the house when the Disneys moved away—the first memorial to Walt Disney's art.

. . .

The bliss of Marceline was undermined by only one thing: Elias Disney had absolutely no aptitude for farming. He told one neighbor that he did not believe in fertilizing his fields because doing so was like "giving whiskey to a man—he felt better for a little while, but then he was worse off than before." The crops suffered until Elias finally relented. Another neighbor remembered Elias ordering his sons to water the horses in midmorning and then questioning why no one else seemed to be watering their horses then, not realizing that what was required was to water them in the morning, at noon, and at night. Despite his shortcomings, he persevered and experimented. One year he planted an acre of popping corn. Another year, when the market was depressed, he had each member of the family go door to door with a basket selling their apples rather than take them to a wholesaler. And yet another time he collected apples from his neighbors and eliminated the middleman by taking them to the market in Kansas himself and splitting the proceeds. One fall after the harvest, when times were very hard, he resorted to carpentry again and remodeled a neighbor's house. Still, money was always tight and Elias always frugal. The Disney children recalled that Flora had to butter the bottom of their bread so that their father would not see her depleting one of the family's sources of income.

If it was money that battered Elias, it was money too that sundered the Disney family. In 1907 Herbert and Ray had arranged with Uncle Robert to grow some wheat on his land, which they then had neighbors harvest that fall. When Elias asked his sons what they intended to do with their money, and one of them said he was going to buy himself a pocket watch, Elias erupted at the indulgence. He insisted that *he* would take the money and help pay off the farm. "That was the straw that broke the camel's back," one neighbor said. That same day Herbert and Ray withdrew their money from the bank, and that night they crawled out a window of the house and hopped a train for Chicago. The wound of their departure was so deep that nearly one hundred years later, family members were still reluctant to discuss the incident. By the spring they had moved to Kansas City, where Uncle Robert got them jobs as bank clerks, and in the summer of 1909 Herbert became a mail carrier for the postal service. They would occasionally visit their parents in Marceline, but the rift never healed entirely. When Herbert and Ray would send back their old clothes for Flora to alter for Roy and Walt, they sometimes stuck a plug of tobacco in a pocket, knowing it would provoke their moralistic father.

Without Herbert and Ray's assistance, the farm became even more burdensome. Elias, who was nothing if not hardworking, blamed his travails on the system that forced farmers to market their crops through middlemen and trusts, taking the profits he believed the farmers themselves deserved. Within a month after his sons' departure, Elias and M. A. Coffman, the neighbor who had picked up the family upon their arrival in Marceline, formed a chapter of the American Society of Equity, which they described as a farmer's union. The society, headquartered in Dayton, Ohio, hoped eventually to provide granaries, elevators, warehouses, and cold storage throughout the country so that farmers could control their own crops, regulate their own supply, and set their own prices. Farmers were receptive—there were twenty-nine members at the chapter's inception—but even in pro-labor and progressive Marceline, Elias's involvement soon branded him as a "radical," according to a neighbor. He would not have disapproved of the label. "He had high ideals about living," his daughter said. "That was when he became interested in the philosophy of Socialism—which seemed to him then to be a fair way for people to live." He even called himself a Socialist, claimed to have voted for the Socialist candidate for president, Eugene V. Debs, and subscribed to the *Appeal to Reason*, an ardently Socialist journal for which Debs was an associate editor.

But Elias's radicalism was an excuse, not a remedy. Like his orange grove in Florida, the farm ultimately defeated him. Falling crop prices across the country squeezed him, exacerbated locally by a five-month-long coal strike in the summer of 1910. Moreover, earlier that year he had fallen ill with either typhoid or diphtheria, which left him weak and unable to work. Flora was convinced that his illness was the result of worry and insisted he sell the farm. By the fall he had done so. That November—a cold morning, as Roy remembered it—Elias conducted an auction to sell their stock and implements. Roy and Walt tacked the signs up throughout the area. Later that afternoon, in town, Roy and Walt saw a six-month-old colt that they had tamed and broken, now hitched to the rig of the farmer who had bought her. She whinnied in recognition at the sight of them, and they went to hug her and cried over their loss. Thus the idyll ended.

The Disneys moved into town to a small four-room house at 508 Kansas Avenue so that the children could finish the school term while Elias recovered. But the Marceline in which they now lived was a much different place from the one where they had arrived five years earlier, confirming what one Disney scholar wrote of Walt's attachment to the town: "Disney's small-town America, the source of his golden memories, was in fact beginning to vanish even as he experienced it." The population had swelled—nearly 50 percent since 1900, according to the census—and that did not account for striking miners who were gone at the time the census was taken. No longer a town whose roads were unpaved, Marceline now boasted more than twenty automobiles. It had a new school, a new power plant, and a new waterworks as well as the six-hundred-seat New Cater Theater, which showed films and featured vaudeville. The month before the Disneys left for Kansas City in the summer of 1911, "one of the largest crowds ever assembled in the City Park," according to the *Marceline Mirror*, cheered the lighting of Marceline's first streetlamps with power generated from her very own electrical station.

This Marceline was not, however, the Marceline that Walt Disney would remember. His was a more rustic place that would become more rustic still in his memory. He idealized Marceline. He later claimed that he felt sorry "for people who live in cities all their lives and . . . they don't have a little hometown. I do." His wife said that when he would take a train across the country and pass through Marceline, he would even dragoon passengers in the middle of the night to point out where he grew up. Associates said that his recall of events and animals in the town was almost total.

Disney scholars would cite the effect of Marceline on Disneyland's Main Street, U.S.A., or on its Tom Sawyer Island, or on the live-action films like *So Dear to My Heart* and *Pollyanna* that were steeped in small-town life and extolled small-town virtues, or even on the early cartoons' preoccupation with farm life and animals, which Disney himself acknowledged. It was as if Marceline were a template for how life was supposed to be, and he were trying to re-create the town, no doubt attempting in the process to recapture its sense of well-being, freedom, and community, essentially recapturing what he would call the most blessed passage of his childhood. Marceline would always be a touchstone of the things and values he held dear; everything from his fascination with trains and animals to his love of drawing to his insistence on community harked back to the years he spent there. And Marceline was an oasis as well as a touchstone—Walt Disney's own escape, of the sort the Disneys had so long sought with so little success. Years later, rhapsodizing about country life during a meeting on the mood he wanted to achieve in the "Pastorale" section of *Fantasia*, Walt said, "That's what it is—a feeling of freedom with the animals and characters that live out there. That is what you experience when you go into the country. You escape the everyday world—the strife and struggle. You get out where everything is free and beautiful."

He would spend the rest of his life trying to recover that feeling.

III

For Elias Disney, moving to Kansas City was another admission of defeat. He had left Chicago to escape the baneful influences of urban life, the noise and bustle and crime, but Kansas City, galvanized by the civic boosterism of *Kansas City Star* editor William Rockhill Nelson, was burgeoning at the time they arrived. Largely as a result of Nelson's campaigning, the city had launched a $40 million boulevard system that created wide, tree-lined streets, had begun construction on a new downtown train depot, and had nearly doubled capital investment and the value of manufactured products in less than a decade. In the first two decades of the century the city's population doubled as well—from 163,000 to 324,000. Yet for all its expansiveness and the sense that it was in the process of remaking and renewing itself, it was a city nonetheless. "The city was not pretty," one observer noted, "but it was lively in the lusty Western tradition."

If Kansas City was a comedown from Marceline, the house there was a comedown too. Located at 2706 East Thirty-first Street in a working-class section, it was so small that when relatives visited, Roy and Walt had to move to what they called the "barn," a shed out back, and it was so close to the road that the family had to draw the curtains so no one could look inside. Compared to the Marceline farmhouse with its sprawling pastures, the Thirty-first Street house had only a tiny vegetable patch, and it had no indoor plumbing. For the children its sole grace, Ruth remembered, was its proximity to the Fairmount amusement park, which was "a fairyland that you couldn't get into." Debarred, she and Walt would stand outside its gates, staring raptly at the all-white structures.

And if the city and the house were comedowns, Elias's job was even more demeaning. He listed himself in the Kansas City directory as a "clerk." In truth, he had sold the Marceline farm for $5,175 to a local family and purchased a paper route in Kansas City at three dollars per customer, roughly 650 of them, but whether he was ashamed of delivering papers or there was some business advantage in doing so, he listed eighteen-year-old Roy as the owner of record. The route, in a twenty-square-block area bordering the Disneys' own neighborhood, was reasonably lucrative by the standards of paper delivery. The section, called Santa Fe, was affluent and the *Kansas City Star* itself so popular that, as Walt later said, "the route book would list the people who DIDN'T take the paper"—those being rabid Democrats who resented the paper's pro-Republican editorial position. Customers paid forty-five cents a week for thirteen editions of the morning *Times* and evening *Star*, of which Elias kept twenty-one cents—about thirty-one dollars a week. Roy received three dollars of this; Walt, in Roy's recollection, got "some little amount," but in Walt's recollection nothing.

The route was not just a means of earning a living—it became a way of life for the Disneys. Everything was subordinated to the delivery of newspapers. Even when the family moved, sometime in the summer or fall of 1914, to a modest two-story bungalow at 3028 Bellefontaine on a quiet, tree-lined street of similarly modest bungalows, they had only crossed Thirty-first Street, compelled, as they were, to stay close to the route. And as their location was defined by the route, so was their time. Unlike other dealers, Elias would not buy a horse and wagon. Instead he had pushcarts, shaped like Roman chariots, one customer said, with down-sloping sides, and each morning, sometimes as early as three-thirty, Elias, Walt, and Roy would take the carts to the distribution point, load them with papers, and head back to Santa Fe to deliver. On Sundays, because the papers were too thick for the carts to accommodate them all, the Disneys would have to deliver one load and then return for another. This effectively prevented any churchgoing in Kansas City for Walt and Roy, though Ruth insisted that she was marched off to Sunday school each week.

Only nine years old, Walt was nevertheless tethered to the route. On weekdays he would rise early, in the darkness, to get his allotment of fifty papers and deliver them—the first year by foot, the second by bicycle. He returned home at five-thirty or six, took a short nap, and then woke and ate his breakfast. Since he received virtually no compensation, for pocket money he delivered medicine for a pharmacy along his route and eventually talked his father into letting him take fifty additional papers to sell for himself at a trolley stop and, when other newsboys evicted him from his curb, on the trolley itself. After he finished on the trolley, he headed for school, though he never completed the school day. He had to leave a half-hour early to pick up the papers for the afternoon run. At three-thirty the next morning the routine would begin again. On Saturdays, in addition to delivering the papers, he collected the fees. And on Sundays he had the double load.

At first Walt was excited by the route. He said he enjoyed seeing the lamplighters turn the gas off every morning while he was delivering his papers and turn it on again during his afternoon circuit. But his enthusiasm quickly waned. The *Star* had given Elias the route reluctantly, fearing he might be too old, so he was anxious not to disappoint them. Because he insisted that the papers be placed under a brick, so that they would not blow away, or behind the storm doors in winter, rather than just be tossed on the porch, Walt had to go up each walkway. Sometimes a customer would not see the paper between the doors, and Elias would have to send Walt to redeliver it. It got worse after Roy graduated from high school and left the route to clerk in a bank and Walt assumed his brother's route as well. Elias hired several other boys, but they were often unreliable, and once again Walt was dispatched to deliver the papers to homes the boys had overlooked, which is how he talked his father into getting him the bicycle. Before that, Elias made him run to houses for missed deliveries.

It was worst, of course, in winter, when Walt had to trudge through the cold and snow, slipping on the icy steps, often crying at the knives of frost he said he endured. Some of the drifts into which he waded were so deep he sank to his neck. At times the cold and his tiredness would conspire, and Walt would fall asleep, curled inside his sack of papers or in the warm foyer of an apartment house to which he had delivered, and he would awaken to discover it was daylight and he had to race to finish the route. What added to this picture of Dickensian drudgery was that Elias took the money Walt had earned by selling his own papers on the trolley and invested it, so that in addition to delivering for the pharmacy the boy began working at a candy store during school recess to earn money to buy more papers he could sell without Elias knowing. "So the upshot of it was I was working all the time," he told an interviewer. "I mean, I never had any real play time." What playtime he had was stolen from the route; he said he played with toys he would see on the porches, then left them exactly as he found them. In six years on the route he missed only five weeks—two with a severe cold, a third on a visit to his aunt Josie in Hiawatha, Kansas, in 1913 ("It stands out in memory," he wrote his aunt, "because it was one of the few vacations that my Mother and Father ever had"), and two more in 1916, when he kicked a piece of ice with a new boot he had just gotten for Christmas and was stabbed by a nail hidden in the chunk. (He screamed for help but had to wait twenty minutes before a deliveryman stopped, chopped the ice loose, and took him to a doctor, who pulled out the nail with pliers and gave him a tetanus shot.) Even then he spent his recuperation helping Elias put an addition on the Bellefontaine house—a new kitchen, a bedroom, and a bathroom finally to replace the outhouse.

Decades later, in the mists of revisionism, Walt would say that the paper route helped forge his character, that he "developed an appreciation of what spare time I did have and used it to great advantage in my hobbies." But in other moments he talked of how the route and its demands—the unyielding routine, the snow, the fatigue, the lost papers—traumatized and haunted him. Forty years later he was still awakening in a sweat with nightmares about the route—that he had missed some customers and had to hurry back because Elias would be waiting at the corner and might discover Walt's dereliction. And he remembered how much of his life he surrendered to the route, how hard he had to work for so little reward, so that, his brother Roy said, he never even learned to catch a ball the way other boys did.

Adding to the oppression of the route was the humiliation that, in the beginning at least, it scarcely provided enough money, forcing the Disneys to supplement their income. On his route Walt would deliver theater bills and sell ice cream in summer, while Elias arranged for the McAllister Creamery in Marceline to ship him butter and eggs, which he then peddled to his newspaper customers. And when Elias was too ill to make the deliveries himself, he would keep Walt home from school so that Walt and Flora could make them. Even then the Disneys scrimped. At Christmas Flora took the cranberry decorations off the tree and made sauce out of them, and Walt said his most memorable Christmas gift was not any toy but that pair of new leather boots with metal toe caps to replace the old worn-out shoes that he wore on the route. He said finding them under the tree was "like a dream come true! Now I could swagger among my young friends with proper pride."

Ruth Disney claimed that her father was not as draconian as Walt made it seem and that the children never lacked for the "comforts and good things of life and some of the luxuries." But even within the family Elias was known for his almost pathological frugality. Walt said his father walked everywhere—"He was a very fast walker"—so he did not have to pay for the streetcar. By another account, some years later, when a nephew asked him to come to Glendale, California, to help him build a house there, Elias stayed for three months and spent only a dollar by taking advantage of realtors' offers of a free meal in exchange for looking at property. He always paid his bills in cash and never owed money to anyone, and he tried to enforce the same fiscal stringency on his children. Walt clearly resented having to hand over his money to his father—on one occasion when he found a twenty-dollar bill, he paid off a fellow newsboy who threatened to tell Elias—though Roy said Elias took the boys' earnings only because he "just didn't believe in letting his kids waste their money. 'I'll take care of it for you—I'll put it away and save it for you.' "

The frugality, the discipline, the taciturnity, and the reproachfulness had always been constituents of Elias Disney's personality. The man who eschewed recreations, who never drank or swore and always said grace at the table, even though he now attended church infrequently, prided himself on his stern morality, put the fear of God into his children, and never let anyone doubt that he was the head of the family, the one whom the

Disneys had to obey. Walt found him so unapproachable and obdurate that, he said, he scarcely talked to him. As one close childhood acquaintance of Walt's observed, "The whole Disney family seemed to me aloof and unbending."

But in Kansas City Elias had grown even more sullen and unresponsive—a hard man hardened. He had, in Walt's words, "become very conservative . . . There probably was a day when he was a driver, when he was ambitious, but then he reached an age and then they start down that little hill." Elias, at fifty-five, was heading rapidly down that hill. One could see it in his politics. The man who had once chased populist William Jennings Bryan's buggy in Chicago so he could shake his hand and the man who boasted of his Socialism in Marceline had become a Republican, though he had not surrendered his belief in class warfare. One could see it in his mood. He had even given up the fiddle, his one indulgence, when he cut his hand on a rope and was no longer able to finger the instrument.

But above all one could see it in his temper. It had always been volcanic. Even back in Chicago Elias would send Roy to his room for some infraction, then head for the apple tree in the backyard, cut off a branch for a switch, and lay into the boy. "You had to take your pants down and get a switching," Roy said. "That was Dad. He'd give us impulsive whacks." Walt called Elias's temper "violent" and said that you could not argue with him without braving his wrath. Even Ruth, who would always defend her father, acknowledged that "he did have a temper" but said "he made up for it in all other ways."

Yet however irascible Elias had been before Kansas City, he seemed to be angrier after the move, after another disappointment, and Walt, at least in his own view, became the main target of his father's ire—in part because he was so different from his father. Indeed, as he grew up, Walt Disney was the antithesis of Elias Disney, almost as if he had willed himself to be so as a form of rebellion, which he very well might have done. Where Elias was dour, Walt, despite his perceived hardships and complaints, was blithe. "He was full of clowning," Roy recalled. "He was very lighthearted all the time. Very full of fun and gaiety." He loved to pull pranks, especially on his father. Once he sent away for a rubber bladder that he placed under his father's dinner plate, then had Flora squeeze a concealed bulb. The other Disneys buckled in hysterics as the plate rose and fell, but Elias kept eating his soup, oblivious. (Walt did say that even though his father was "very slow to catch on to a gag," when he did, "he would laugh until he had tears in his eyes.") Walt also enjoyed masquerading, and a cousin remembered a visit to Kansas City when Walt's "chief delight was in dressing up in odd clothes in order to scare my sister and brother." On another occasion Flora answered the door to find a tall woman who asked her "a lot of foolish questions." It took a few moments for Flora to recognize that the "woman" was wearing one of Flora's own best dresses. Walt had even borrowed a wig and hat and put on makeup to complete the disguise.

It was not only Walt's puckishness that contrasted with his father's severity. Where Elias was plodding and subdued, Walt was wildly enthusiastic—"enthused about everything," said a friend. Even Elias conceded of Walt that "[w]hatever he wanted to do he did without ever thinking of the harm. He would always go ahead with any of his ideas whether he had the means or not." Most people found him charming. Walt realized his effect—he was extroverted and attractive—but he also worked at it. Roy said that he always focused on whomever he was speaking with, that he "gave the impression he took a deep personal interest," and that in the family he was the one who remembered everyone's birthday and always got a present. He knew too that the effect could be disarming. At least when Walt was younger and Herbert and Ray were still living at home, it was, in Roy's recollection, the older boys who really took the brunt of their father's anger. Walt, on the other hand, would position a chair between himself and Elias and "just argue the dickens out of Dad. Dad couldn't get ahold of him." Finally Elias would capitulate.

By the time they were living in Kansas City, though, the charm no longer worked on Elias. "It reached the point," Walt said, "that to tell the truth with my father got me a licking." Elias was impatient with Walt too. When they were building the Bellefontaine addition and Walt would make a mistake, Elias would try to hit him with the broad side of the saw or club him with the handle of the hammer. Usually Walt would run to his mother until Elias cooled down. But a reckoning, a big reckoning, came when Walt was fourteen and Elias upbraided him for being too insolent, then ordered him to the basement for a beating. Roy pulled Walt aside and told him to resist. Obedient to his father, Walt headed downstairs anyway. Elias followed, yelling and grabbing a hammer to strike him. But this time, impulsively rising to his brother's injunction, Walt stayed his father's hand and removed the hammer. "He raised his other arm and I held both of his hands," Walt later recalled. "And I just held them there. I was stronger than he was. I just held them. And he cried." He said his father never touched him after that. Broken by work, Elias was now defeated in the family too.

It was Flora who provided the ballast for the Disneys—Flora who managed the money for Elias, made most of the children's clothes and sewed their quilts, cooked their meals and encouraged their reading, connived with the children, and always exercised restraint and an even temper, and for all these things she would be beloved in their memories. And it was Flora alone who could tease her husband out of what his children called his "peevishness" and calm his raging storms, though she did so carefully, without confronting or countermanding him. Walt said he could not confide in her because "she couldn't keep it from Dad if I told her." Still, he thought her saintly.

But if Flora was the family's peacemaker, Roy O. Disney was its protector—or at least Walt's protector. Walt was never close to either Herbert or Ray, who had left years earlier, though they both lived in Kansas City, and he referred to them as "strangers to me all my life." Indeed, Herbert had married a local girl and had had a daughter of his own. Roy seemingly had no more in common with Walt than the older brothers did, other than the fact that he still lived at home. He was eight years Walt's senior and hardly a comrade in arms. Nor did he share Walt's temperament. Though nowhere near as doleful as his father, whom he closely resembled physically, he was not an enthusiast or prankster or extrovert like Walt either, and he had little of Walt's appeal. But Roy and Walt formed a very close relationship, so close that Walt seemed to regard him less as a brother than as a surrogate father, confiding in him as he could never have confided in Elias. They might argue, but when night fell, they would crawl into bed together and trade stories.

It was easy to see what Walt got from this alliance—support. But Roy willingly assumed the paternal role, feeling as close to Walt as Walt felt to him. He would buy Walt and Ruth toys out of his earnings from the bank where he clerked, or bring them candy, or announce that they were going to the movies. He would play horseshoes or pinochle with them. Roy never explained why he was so protective of his younger brother, other than to say that he felt Walt was too open, trusting, and naïve and needed someone to watch over him—in effect, that he had no common sense. Years later Roy would tell about the old television inventor Lee de Forest, who had been cheated out of what was due him and who was forced in his declining years to cadge money from a friend at the Disney studio. "I really believe," Roy said, "that Walt would have gotten mired down with crooks. . . . [H]e'd have been easy prey for somebody to twist him up and take him like they took Lee de Forest, and that's what I gave him"—a shield. But it was not all self-sacrifice. Roy gained too. Walt provided what Roy did not have and could not generate himself. Roy fed off of Walt's energy and buoyancy and even recklessness. Walt was the vicarious outlet for a measured and cautious young man. Walt was Roy's own escape.

. . .

Meanwhile Walt found his outlet for release outside his family, two doors up the street. The Pfeiffers were, Walt Pfeiffer would say, Walt's "real family," and their house was what Walt later called, after Uncle Remus, his "laughing place." "My own family were all pretty unfrivolous, hard-working people," Walt wrote a correspondent, expressing his constant longing for a more exuberant environment. "There was nothing *un*happy about them—they just weren't used to having fun. But this wasn't so with the Pfeiffers. Whatever they did, they had the best time doing it, and they were always together." Walt Pfeiffer was more direct: "[O]ld Elias didn't like anything that had anything to do with entertainment. He was kind of 'churchy' as we called it in those days. . . . He'd read the Bible."

In effect the Pfeiffers adopted Walt, and he escaped into them. Walt had met Walt Pfeiffer in fifth grade at the Benton School even before the Disneys had moved to the same block on Bellefontaine as the Pfeiffers. They had become casual friends then, but the relationship was cemented later, when Walt Pfeiffer came down with the mumps and Walt Disney, dismissing Mrs. Pfeiffer's warnings and saying he had already had the mumps himself, came over and kept the bedridden Pfeiffer company, teaching him how to draw. The two soon became inseparable, spending their time drawing together or playing with Pfeiffer's dog Brownie.

The deeper bond between them, however, was not proximity; it was exhibitionism. As his masquerading attested, Walt Disney loved to perform, and so did Walt Pfeiffer, a moon-faced boy as extroverted as his friend. In fact, the Pfeiffers were a whole family of performers. Mr. Pfeiffer was the treasurer of the local United Leather Workers Union, but his real love was show business, and his son called him a "ham." At the Disney house Elias, thinking that Walt might become a musician, insisted that Walt take violin lessons and would slap his elbow when he stuck it out incorrectly. (Walt claimed to have a "tin ear," and the lessons ended in "mutual disgust" after a few months.) But what was punitive at the Disney house was joyful at the Pfeiffers'. Walt Pfeiffer's sister Kitty would play the piano while the others sang, or she would accompany her brother and Walt while they performed comedy sketches. Walt Disney so enjoyed these sessions that at night he would sneak out the window—he was ordered to bed at nine o'clock so he could get up for the paper route—and head over to the Pfeiffers' for the fun, then sneak back. "I went to bed tired," he said, "but knowing the past hour and a half had been the nicest part of the day."

Already Walt had been performing at school. "I'd do anything to attract attention," he would say. In the fifth grade he fashioned a stovepipe hat out of cardboard and blackened it with shoe polish, dabbed a wart on his cheek, wrapped himself in a shawl, and came to class as Abraham

Lincoln. He had even memorized the Gettysburg Address to recite. Delighted, Walt's teacher said he was going to be an actor—"because I squinted my eyes on certain passages"—and called in the principal, who then paraded Walt into every classroom. Walt also staged plays with his classmates. "I always got something where I could bring in fifty kids because the kids would always laugh at other kids. I'd get laughs that way."

Soon the "Two Bad Walters," as Pfeiffer and Disney called themselves, were performing routines at school. With Mr. Pfeiffer instructing and rehearsing them, they began entering talent contests staged at the local Agnes Theater and, depending on how Walt told the story, either won quite a few of them or once split a twenty-five-cent fifth prize. (Pfeiffer said that Walt had to slip out of the bedroom window for these forays too so Elias would not know, "'cause we were kind of afraid of him.") Some of the time they did what they called a "Dutch" act, playing Hans and Mike. Walt Disney would dress in Elias's old deacon's coat from his church days, and Walt Pfeiffer would decorate his jacket with various badges and medals that his father had collected from conventions. They would sing songs and tell jokes: "My sister is a princess." "How do you know your sister is a princess?" "Because she wears a princess slip!" "My brother wears a union suit, but that doesn't make him belong to a union!" Later they became fascinated with the film comedian Charlie Chaplin, whose popularity was soaring at that time. The boys would see each of Chaplin's films, not once but several times, studying them carefully and then discussing his technique. That changed the act. Walt Disney now played Chaplin. He "could do it to perfection," a boyhood acquaintance remembered, even recalling Walt "kicking that cigarette behind" himself in one of Chaplin's signature moves. Walt Pfeiffer played the Count, Chaplin's nemesis. "[W]e always got a little more applause than someone else imitating Chaplin because we were younger and it was a team of us," Walt said.

But even if the act was amateurish and the applause as much for youthful effort as for talent, Walt Disney found himself hooked on performing—hooked on the acknowledgment of performing as he had been hooked in Marceline on the acknowledgment of his drawing. These performances, he said, "reacted on me like the taste of blood on a lion. In other words, I *liked* acting! Liked the applause, liked the cash prizes that were being handed to us, liked the weird smells and weirder sights behind the scenes." He even began to think of acting as a career. In entertainment Walt Disney had found another escape.

Even before he began considering a career in show business, school had become an afterthought. As in Marceline, he had been placed in the same class as his younger sister, and both, due to the vicissitudes of the Kansas City school system, had been forced to repeat the second grade, which meant he was well over a year older than most of his classmates. The paper route did not help. Walt often dozed in class, and teachers later described him as "courteous" but also "sleepy," "preoccupied," and "seldom more than lukewarm about the funny business of the three Rs." One teacher placed him in the "second dumbest" seat in the classroom. Walt, who was clearly quick-witted, attributed his inattentiveness to his being creative rather than uninterested and called himself a "dreamer." A classmate said he was always imagining things. Walt admitted, "I'd sit in class and I'd be way off."

He was also something of an iconoclast, even if it was only to attract attention. He once caught a field mouse, tied a string around it, and brought it to class. When one of his classmates screamed, the teacher rushed to his desk and slapped him on the cheek. Walt, though, was anything but resentful. "I loved you all the more for it," he wrote the teacher years later, suggesting just how attention-starved he really felt. And when every other boy in his seventh-grade class took manual arts, Walt opted instead for domestic science, essentially homemaking, with the girls, carrying a little blue bag with his supplies. Even Walt Pfeiffer found this unusual. "[T]he kids used to make fun of him carrying this bag around," Pfeiffer remembered. "[T]hat kind of shows you that he was a little out of the ordinary." But Ruth said that rather than feeling chastened, Walt loved being the only boy in his class. "He used to come home and tell all about the fun he had there."

It may have been a sign of just how much Walt desired a sense of community, of belonging, especially after losing the support he felt in Marceline, that he would look back on his days at the Benton School fondly and often—not for the education he received there but for the warmth he felt. He recalled the principal, James Cottingham, who thought nothing of wandering into a classroom and interrupting the lesson with a story, and he recalled the teachers—especially Miss Daisy Beck, the one who slapped him for having brought the mouse—who demonstrated their concern even though Walt was, by his own description, a "laggard." (He would continue to correspond with several of them until their deaths.) Of Daisy Beck particularly, he cited the "great patience, understanding, and incredible faith" she lavished upon him. The paper route prevented Walt from participating in after-school activities, but he frequently recounted how Beck, who coached the school's championship track team with Cottingham, urged him one recess to try out. Walt wound up winning a medal on the sixty-pound relay team, and probably because he was never much of an athlete, he always cherished the memory and Beck's role in it, never failing to cite it whenever he discussed his days at Benton.

Most of the time, though, young Walt Disney was secluded in his own world—away from the route and Elias and school. The Pfeiffers and performing provided one escape from his vexations. Drawing continued to provide another, more powerful one. He had never stopped drawing. In school he propped up his books as a blind so he could draw. He spent hours decorating the margins of his textbooks with pictures and then entertaining his classmates by riffling them to make them move. One classmate recalled him going to the blackboard and drawing a perfect likeness of Teddy Roosevelt in chalk, while one teacher remembered him drawing flowers during an art assignment and animating them. Always encouraging, Daisy Beck had him draw the posters for school events, and Walt Pfeiffer said that he began drawing cartoon advertisements on glass slides for the Agnes Theater. After school, after the route, while most of the boys were playing basketball in the schoolyard, he, Walt Pfeiffer, and one or two other boys interested in art would sit on a stone wall and draw. When a group of neighborhood boys built a clubhouse, Walt decorated it with his drawings. At home he took his father's *Appeal to Reason* and practiced redrawing the front-page cartoons of capital and labor until "I had them all down pat."

This was what his Benton classmates remembered: Walt Disney drawing. He drew constantly. He drew even though it was not always socially acceptable to draw. "It was kind of sissy for a guy to draw," Walt Pfeiffer admitted, but that did not deter Walt Disney. He drew and drew well for a boy his age. He drew until it became the primary source of his identification at Benton: Walt Disney, the artist. "Even in our old 7th grade in Miss Beck's room," a classmate recalled, "we all knew you'd really be an artist + genius of some kind . . . & when I heard once that you couldn't draw I sure set *them* straight. Because even in the 7th grade that's all you did."

And it was not only at the Benton School that Walt Disney was gaining attention for his art. He hung around a barbershop at Thirty-first Street on his paper route, just around the corner from his house, idly drawing cartoons. Impressed, the proprietor, Bert Hudson, offered Walt a free haircut in exchange for the drawings and later, when Walt did not need a cut, ten or fifteen cents. More important for Walt, Hudson hung the pictures in the window in a special frame just as Doc Sherwood had hung the picture of Rupert. "It was a great stimulant to me to know my efforts were appreciated," Walt would write Hudson more than thirty years later, "and boy, how I looked forward to the showing of that weekly—or was it monthly [—] cartoon in your shop." One acquaintance remembered the shop being "plastered with drawings," and a neighbor said he often watched Walt sitting outside the shop drawing cartoons on a blackboard. Even Elias admitted that the drawings became an attraction: "The neighbors would go down to the shop 'to see what young Disney had this week.' "

Obsessed with drawing and encouraged by the attention he was getting, Walt would accompany his father to the *Kansas City Star* office when Elias picked up papers or conducted business there and head up to the art department or engraving room to watch the cartoonists, occasionally even receiving instruction from the art director, Mr. Wood. Once he was even emboldened enough to ask for a job, but he was told the paper was downsizing at the time and no position was available. "It was a sad day, believe me," Walt recalled. During this same period Walt, for the first time, sought formal instruction. Though Elias had no understanding of Walt's passion and no affinity for art whatsoever, when Walt turned fourteen he did permit him to attend Saturday classes at the Kansas City Art Institute in the YMCA Building downtown, where the boy not only drew but learned the rudiments of sculpture and casting.

Just as he had contemplated a career as a performer when he was receiving accolades for his act, he began to think of becoming a newspaper cartoonist now that he was receiving accolades for his drawings. He admitted that by the time he graduated from the Benton School—the school went only to the seventh grade—he had lost interest in anything but drawing and performing and that "[g]etting through the seventh grade was one of the toughest trials of my whole limited span of schooling." As Walt received his diploma in June 1917, Cottingham, who made a brief quip about each graduate, said of Walt, "He will draw you if you like," underscoring just how much art had become Walt's identity. (Walt even drew two pictures of girls in broad-brimmed hats in the style of the famous illustrator Charles Dana Gibson in his sister's graduation book.) Along with the diploma, Cottingham also awarded him a seven-dollar prize for a comic character Walt had drawn. "I am still prouder of that money than any I have earned since," Walt told the *Kansas City Journal-Post* nearly twenty years later. "I really think that is what started me as an artist."

Then Elias Disney escaped again. For several years he had been investing his money—and Walt's earnings too—in a jelly and fruit juice company in Chicago named O-Zell. In March he sold the paper route—by one account he made $16,000 on the sale—and bought additional shares of O-Zell with the intention of moving back to Chicago to head up construction and maintenance at the company's factory, obviously feeling that this time he might finally find the success that had so long evaded him. At fifty-seven this was almost certainly the last opportunity he would have to rival his brother. When Elias and Flora left, Walt stayed behind to assist the man who had bought the route, and lived with his brother Herbert, who had moved into the Bellefontaine house with his wife and year-old daughter. Once the transfer had been completed, Walt, at either Roy's or Herbert's suggestion, signed up with the Van Noyes Interstate News Company and spent the rest of the summer as a "butcher" selling papers, candy, soda, and tobacco to passengers on the Santa Fe train route between Kansas City and Spiro, Oklahoma. Roy, who provided the fifteen-dollar bond for his brother and who had been a butcher himself one summer, thought it would be "educational" for him.

As it turned out, it was. Though Walt just liked the idea of being on a train—sometimes he would bribe the engineer with a plug of tobacco so that he could ride in the coal car; other times he would sit in the yard staring at the engines and dreaming of firing them up—he got to see Colorado and Oklahoma and, filling in for other butchers, ventured as far east as Mississippi. He was especially struck by the Pullman sleeper cars and years later, according to one screenwriter who worked for him, would reminisce about the "elegance of this plush and velvet world he glimpsed for the first time." He got a brief education in the rough-and tumble business world too. One time a group of soldiers to whom he had sold soda refused to give him back the bottles on which he made his profit. (Walt had to get the conductor to force them to pay.) Another time Walt was replenishing his basket during a stop at Lee's Summit, Missouri, only to return and find that the cars had been detached from the engine at the station and his bottles had gone with them. He also claimed that there was "finagling" and that he was given rotten fruit in his hamper, but Roy chalked the losses up to Walt's own carelessness. "He'd go up and down the train, leave his locker unlocked and when he'd come back find . . . a lot of empty Coke bottles and some of the candy gone." Walt admitted he ate up his profits. After two months he resigned.

By that time Roy was gone. With America having entered World War I that spring, he had joined the navy just fourteen days after Walt's graduation. By summer's end Walt was gone too, reunited with his parents in Chicago. He would always say that even though he was a Chicagoan by birth, he was a Missourian by temperament and usually pointed to his childhood in Marceline as the foundation of his life, but his six years in Kansas City were no less formative. If Marceline had been where Walt Disney forged his fantasy, Kansas City was where he forged his personal mythology—what one Disney scholar would call the "opening chapters of an American success story where good triumphed over evil and progress overcame adversity." Though Ruth in particular would contradict her brother's somber vision of the Disney family, and though Roy himself, who confirmed Walt's depiction of their father's distance and temper, would nevertheless call the Disney family's home life "wonderful" and dismiss contentions that Walt was abused or neglected, Walt, a blatant self-dramatist, would fasten on the deprivations of his youth in Kansas City—on the hardships of the paper route, on the obduracy of his father, on the need to find release on the stage or the drawing pad. True or not, he conceptualized his early life in Dickensian terms, with the kindnesses of the Pfeiffers or Daisy Beck or Bert Hudson relieving the gloom. For Walt Disney, Marceline had to be recaptured, but Kansas City, the grit against which his life would rub, had to be remembered to show from what he had risen. In Kansas City, Walt Disney not only began to channel his escape; he began to create the idea of Walt Disney—the idea of someone who beat poverty, hardship, and neglect.

IV

For all his children's professions of his thrift, Elias Disney did not salt all his money away. Instead, most likely under the supervision of his brother Robert, he kept investing and speculating in hopes that he could still make his fortune, even at his advanced age. How he came to put money in the O-Zell Company is uncertain, though the firm, which was incorporated in Arizona and headquartered in Chicago, did have an office in Kansas City and a warehouse there housing equipment. But regardless of how it came to his attention, he began investing shortly after he arrived in Kansas City—and investing heavily. Flora got one hundred shares of stock in April 1912, and Elias bought two thousand more shares a few weeks later. In May 1915 he purchased 1,054 more shares and another 3,700 that September. The next year he bought fifty shares out of Walt's savings and 275 more shares for himself—all at a dollar a share. By December 1916, with O-Zell's officers complaining of "difficulties" in the business, a freight embargo, and "lack of capital," Elias agreed to invest an additional $3,000 and move to Chicago to work at the plant, with the stipulation that Walt would be put on the payroll "a little later."

When Walt arrived in Chicago at summer's end, passing through Marceline on the way, he enrolled as a freshman at William McKinley High School on Chicago's West Side, not far from the Disneys' house on Ogden Avenue. But McKinley, like Benton, held little interest for him.

Drawing did, and he fell into it with the same alacrity as he had in Kansas City. He had been at McKinley scarcely a month when the school magazine, *The McKinley Voice*, pronounced: "Walter Disney, one of the newcomers, has displayed unusual artistic talent, and has become *Voice* cartoonist." The magazine's circulation manager said he was always having to write passes so that Walt could be excused from class to draw. "[A]lready," the manager later wrote him, "it was THE PASSION of your life!" Walt seemed to spend most of his time that school year drawing cartoons for *The Voice*, many of them with a political bent, commenting on the war: a parody of Mark Antony's eulogy for Julius Caesar was illustrated with a group of flashily dressed burghers standing over the kaiser's body; another cartoon attacked slackers with two men, one in a straw boater, the other in a derby, quizzing a wounded doughboy with the caption, "Your summer vacation. WORK OF FIGHT. Will you be doing either?" One classmate remembered him scribbling cartoons "even when the teacher thought we all ought to be doing mundane things like schoolwork," while another remembered his desk cluttered with pictures of pretty dancing girls. His sister claimed that during school socials held every Thursday afternoon he would get up and draw, and another student recalled Walt entertaining classmates by sketching a man's head on a large sheet of paper, then turning it upside down to reveal a different face. Walt so excelled at illustration that when his art teacher gave a homework assignment of drawing the human body and Walt submitted a perfect rendering, she thought he had copied it and made him draw another in front of the class. Describing students with one- or two-word epithets, *The Voice* simply called Walt "Artist."

And when he wasn't drawing, he was thinking about it. Occasionally he played hooky, going to the Art Institute or hanging around the newspaper offices "with my mouth wide open, watching (to me, at least) the fascinating things that went on and hoping that some day I, too, would be on the staff of a big newspaper." He revered a *Chicago Tribune* cartoonist named Carey Orr who drew a feature called "The Tiny *Trib*" that summarized the news of the day through barbed illustrations, and Walt began drawing a takeoff of his own called "The Tiny *Voice*." By the winter, encouraged by one of the *Voice* editors, he was attending evening classes three times a week downtown at the Chicago Academy of Fine Arts in the Willoughby Building, where Orr taught, getting his father to foot the bill by convincing him it had educational value. It was the first time that Walt worked with live models, and he was so entranced by the process he would not even take a bathroom break. But despite these classes, Walt realized he would never be a fine artist and that his talent lay in caricature. His real excitement at the academy was taking a class in cartooning from LeRoy Gossett, who worked for the *Chicago Herald*. In the end he attended the academy for only a short time—probably until the spring of 1918—but he later called his time there "no doubt the turning point in my whole career."

Still, realizing perhaps how long the odds were of landing a newspaper job, he hadn't completely abandoned the idea of show business. While he drew at every opportunity, he also sent away for books on magic with the idea of doing tricks onstage. At the same time he and a fellow McKinley freshman named Russell Maas (his *McKinley Voice* epithet was "Small," which was intended as ironical since Walt described him as big and tall) formed a Dutch comedian act like the one Walt had done with Pfeiffer, but when they attended a tryout at a seedy theater one Saturday night, they promptly got the hook. Walt admitted he was devastated. He even began pondering photography as an alternative career path.

In truth, as a newcomer in Chicago without friends or footing, he had lost some of his Kansas City extroversion, which may have accounted for his failure on the stage. Whereas a Kansas City acquaintance called him a " 'smart alecky kid,' inclined to have slight snobbish actions," the editor of the *Voice* described him as "extremely shy and reserved," possibly, she suspected, because he was older than his classmates, and said that when Walt submitted his drawings, he "literally fled from the scene." With girls he was usually diffident, and though his sister Ruth described him as "something of a ladies' man," saying she once sighted him with a girl on each arm, this was more likely a function of how attracted they were to him—he was a handsome teenager—than of how comfortable he was with them. A girlfriend of one of the *Voice* editors had a crush on him, but she was unable to loosen him up. When he did find himself with a girlfriend, another classmate named Beatrice Conover, the relationship seemed social rather than romantic, with the two of them sharing ghost stories or romping through Humboldt Park. She thought of him as "happy-go-lucky Wally," though she also described his habit of gnashing his teeth, which suggested that he was not so carefree anymore.

Conover was convinced that Walt would be famous one day and told him so, but when school ended for the summer, he pursued neither drawing nor show business. Instead he took a job at the O-Zell factory constructing boxes, crushing apples for pectin (an ingredient in the jellies), and running a jar capper and washer. Occasionally he even filled in as the night watchman. It was uninspiring work, dull work, but Sarah Scrogin, the young wife of O-Zell's president, saw his drawings and encouraged him, even buying some. She also assigned Walt the job of drawing the poster for the annual picnic and gave him time during work to do it. Years later she would remember sitting with Flora and discussing Walt's potential as an artist.

Even so, in July he left O-Zell for a job in the post office as a substitute mail carrier. (He loved to tell how he was initially denied the appointment because he looked too young for the responsibility, then went home, changed his clothes, drew a mustache on himself, exchanged his cap for a hat, and returned to the same man and got the job.) He would arrive at the downtown post office at seven in the morning, sort the mail and deliver it, and return by three or four o'clock in the afternoon. Though he could have gone home then, frequently he would make the special delivery run or take a horse and buggy or the white Ford truck and pick up the mail from the boxes. On Sundays he would grab a large mailbag and take the subway to the Grand Avenue Pier to collect postcards. He made forty cents an hour, which he described as a "gold rush to me." On days when he finished his route and there was no additional work, he would take the elevated train to the Thirty-fifth Street terminus, pull on a uniform, and serve as gateman, loading the cars and closing the doors—typically working twelve to thirteen hours in all. "It was thrilling to ride on that thing," he later said.

But, amid the thrills, one brush that summer almost cost him his life. On September 3 Walt had just finished his mail run and was walking through the post office in the Chicago Federal Building when he heard what he described as a "WHOOOM!!!!"—a deafening blast that shook the ground. In the lobby, dust billowed everywhere. Police immediately locked down the building. It turned out that someone had planted a bomb, injuring thirty and killing four, including a man who had worked two desks from Walt's. Authorities debated whether the perpetrators were radicals hoping to free the head of the left-wing Industrial Workers of the World labor union, William Haywood, who was in custody in the eighth-floor jailhouse, or anarchists or German spies trying to cast suspicion on the IWW.*

The Germans were on every American's mind that summer of 1918, with the country at war with Germany and American troops in Europe. Walt had been thinking about Germany too. As the summer drew to an end, he had no plans to return to school, later writing Principal Cottingham that he had been "disgusted" by his year at McKinley, though he had

*Months later a woman fingered her estranged husband, a member of the Black Hand organized-crime gang, for having arranged to have his brother send the bomb through the mail. *New York Times*, Dec. 24, 1918.

no plans to do anything else either. Walking along the beach with Bea Conover one day, Walt had asked her whether he should buy a movie camera or a canoe with his post office savings, and when she said a canoe, he was "disappointed" and made a down payment on the camera anyway. He began having himself filmed in the alley behind his parents' house as Chaplin, with his friend Russell Maas presumably turning the crank, and then hatched a plan for making children's films. But before he could realize the project, the camera was repossessed.

Yet even as he dabbled in entertainment, he had gotten the war bug. Two of his brothers were already in the service; Ray had been drafted into the army, and Roy, an enlistee, was at the Great Lakes Naval Station outside Chicago. Walt later said he had felt the full flush of patriotism when he was seeing Roy off at the train depot in Chicago during a visit early that summer, and the officer, mistaking Walt for one of the troops, ordered him to fall in. The feeling only intensified when he read Roy's letters. "They were blowing bugles and it was more of what you call patriotism," he would recall. "I just had to get in there." Though he was underage, only sixteen, Walt admitted a sense of shame in his staying home as others marched off to war; he told Ruth that he never wanted his grandchildren to ask him why he did not go to fight. And one could not underestimate the unmistakable appeal of the uniform itself. Walt, who had been a cadet at McKinley as well as a postman, a gateman, and a train butcher in a suit with brass buttons, loved to dress in costumes. As he said of Roy, "He looked swell in that sailor's uniform."

Even before he went to work at the post office, Walt had attempted to join the navy with Maas, but they were rejected for being too young. Next they tried to join the Canadian forces, but Maas, who wore glasses, was rejected for his poor eyesight, and Walt did not want to go into the service without him. Dejected, they had both applied to the post office, where they found themselves dunned every noon by a fife-and-drum corps outside in the street urging men to enlist. It was Maas who got the idea to join the Red Cross Ambulance Corps, since the Red Cross was not as particular as the armed forces and the age of qualification was seventeen, not eighteen as in the regular services. (Walt said that the Red Cross attracted those who were too young, too old, or too incapacitated for the military.) Since they were still sixteen, they applied under false names as the St. John brothers, but the ruse did not work. They still needed their parents' signatures to certify their ages, and in any case Maas's mother had found his grip with a pair of socks in it, suspected something was happening, and alerted Flora. After Walt confessed, Elias refused to sign the papers. "If I did," he said, "I might be signing your death warrant." Flora was no more eager to send her youngest son to war than was her husband, but Walt begged her and she finally relented, signing for both herself and Elias and saying that if she did not, Walt would probably run off anyway. Flora evidently did not know that Walt, at sixteen, was still too young for the Ambulance Corps, so after his mother had the certificate notarized, he converted the last digit in 1901, his birth year, to a zero, and on September 16 he enlisted.

He thought of it not as war but as an adventure. He was assigned to Camp Scott, the Red Cross's new training facility on Chicago's South Side near the University of Chicago, on the grounds of what was once an amusement park and roller rink. The training called for a week of driving ambulances and trucks, another week in repair shops learning how to dismantle and assemble a car, and two more weeks of military drills before shipping out to France. Walt had no sooner arrived at the camp than he was writing Beatrice's friend Virginia Baker that he was having "a good time out here" and had met "lots of old friend [*sic*] and made new ones all ready." But within days he contracted influenza in an epidemic that would soon be sweeping the globe and would eventually result in at least twenty million deaths. Since hospitals were considered unsafe, Walt was taken by ambulance to his home to recuperate. By the time he recovered three weeks later, his company had already sailed to France. Walt returned to Camp Scott on November 4, only to be sent by train to Camp King in South Beach, Connecticut, to await transport to France as part of Company A of the Automotive and Mechanical Section. While he was at Camp King, bivouacked in an empty summer resort, Ye Olde Greenwich Inn, he received what for him was terribly disappointing news: an armistice had been signed ending the war. "I've never seen a sicker looking bunch than we were," he later recalled. "Everybody else was celebrating the end of the war, but all we knew was that we'd missed out on something big." Walt just assumed that he would now be sent home, but the company was roused at three one morning and told that fifty of them would be going to France after all to aid in the occupation. Walt always claimed that his was the last of the fifty names called and that he had gone back to sleep in despair at not being able to leave for Europe, when his compatriots awakened him with the announcement.

The next morning the fifty were heading for France on a converted cattle boat, the *Vaubin*, loaded with ammunition. The enlistees were so exhilarated that they joked about the possibility of being blown up. They arrived in Cherbourg on November 30, found the harbor clogged by a sunken boat, and steamed to Le Havre, where they disembarked and were herded onto a train for Paris, transferring to trucks there for the trip to a Red Cross outpost in St. Cyr, near Versailles. It was not an auspicious introduction to France. The food was execrable. The nights were cold, and the châteaux in which they billeted were unheated. Walt had to wrap himself in newspapers before pulling the blanket around him. St. Cyr was also dangerous: a group of discharged Algerian soldiers had been organized into a labor gang nearby, and there were occasional knifings. But amid it all Walt, small, baby-faced, and looking younger, celebrated his seventeenth birthday shortly after his arrival, toasting it with a round of grenadine for the younger enlistees and cognac for the older ones, for which he was forced to pawn a pair of shoes, and the next week the outfit was trucked to Paris to cheer President Woodrow Wilson's appearance at the peace conference. Walt shimmied up a tree to get a glimpse of him.

Though France was recovering from devastation and death, Walt, who before his enlistment had never been farther west than Colorado or farther east than Mississippi, seemed to regard his Red Cross duty as another escape. After indoctrination in St. Cyr, he was transferred to the Hotel Regina near the Louvre in Paris and then to Evacuation Hospital No. 5 on the Longchamps racecourse at Auteuil, where the infield was laid out with huts holding wounded men undergoing triage that would send them back to America, to England, or to base hospitals on the French coast. He was there only a short time when he was sent back to the motor pool in Paris, where he played poker and chauffeured Red Cross and army officials. This duty allowed him to see the city. Then he was transferred to Neuilly, just outside Paris, and by early February he had been transferred yet again, this time to Hospital No. 102 in Neufchâteau, situated in rolling country roughly 150 miles east of Paris, a classically Gallic village with narrow stone streets, quaint shuttered shops, clustered buildings, and a church whose spire dominated the skyline.

Though the Red Cross operated the hospital there, seventy to eighty beds used primarily to sequester contagious patients who might infect American troops, Walt had little contact with the ill. Mostly he ran errands for the canteen that served troop replacements passing through Neufchâteau by train on the way to Germany, or drove the canteen car, transporting the girls who worked there between the canteen and their quarters or to the commissary for provisions or to surrounding farms for eggs or even occasionally to picnics, especially when dignitaries visited. (He became such an accomplished tour guide that he was soon in demand.) The proprietress of the canteen and Walt's nominal superior was a portly, bespectacled middle-aged nurse from Nebraska named Alice Howell, whose primary responsibility was making six hundred doughnuts each day for the troops moving through there and then dispensing them on two long sticks, one in each hand. Walt loved Howell. She became his surrogate mother in France and the source of his fondest memory there. Howell happened to be a close friend of General John J. Pershing, the head of the American Expeditionary Force. Pershing, who had grown up near Marceline, was Walt's hero. Because of his family's relationship to Howell, the general, headquartered in nearby Chaumont, sent his ten-year-old son to her canteen one afternoon for a picnic. Though the boy had arrived in a limousine, he insisted on riding in Walt's old Ford to Domrémy, the birthplace of Joan of Arc, where they ate fried chicken on the lawn in front of her shrine. Walt always cherished that day with Pershing's son and cherished Howell for making it possible. As he did with his teachers at the Benton School, he would continue to correspond with Alice Howell until her death, and she in turn would send him the flag that had flown over the canteen.

Writing to Howell years later, Walt would recall these months in Neufchâteau as "mingled with joy and sorrow," but the sorrows seemed rare. He found the French cordial until the peace conference began turning against them and they grew increasingly hostile toward the Americans; once a French girl grabbed his hat and threw it off, and another time he got himself in a scuffle. As for the Germans, his only contact with them came when he was heading up a garbage detail of prisoners of war; they found themselves under attack from French children throwing stones. Otherwise, he joked in a postcard home, he was "doing something I very seldom do—'work.' "

His most eventful assignment was driving a truckload of sugar and beans to Soissons. During the trip it snowed, and the truck burned out a bearing. He sent an associate to get help, then spent the next two days at a railroad watchman's shack awaiting assistance. When the associate failed to return, Walt hiked into town for a meal, fell asleep, and hiked back, only to find the truck missing. The associate had gone to Paris, where he had passed out, drunk, before reporting the incident. By the time a rescue crew finally arrived, Walt had gone for his meal, and the crew had taken the truck. Walt faced a board of inquiry but, thanks to an understanding sergeant, was let off with a reprimand for leaving his post.

When he was not driving or running errands, he did what he had always done. He drew—sketches for the canteen menu featuring a doughboy character he had devised, posters advertising hot chocolate and baths to the troops, designs on the canvas flaps over the sides of the ambulances, caricatures for his fellow enlistees to send to their girls and families for which Walt charged a fee, editorial cartoons to *The McKinley Voice* and to friends back home with crude sentiments like an AEF soldier kicking the German kaiser off a cliff and saying, "Get off and stay off," and even comic strips. He drew on an easel that he set up in his barracks under the window, and he drew in his truck. "I found out that the inside and outside of an ambulance is as good a place to draw as any," he would remember. Soliciting ideas from his fellow troops, he began sending cartoons to *Life* and *Judge*, the most popular humor magazines then, but he received only yellow rejection slips. He had better luck when a discharged French soldier was assigned to maintain their barracks and Walt copied the soldier's Croix de Guerre on his own leather windbreaker as a joke. Impressed by the gag, many of his barracks mates wanted a Croix de Guerre painted on their jackets, and Walt earned ten or fifteen francs apiece for his work. He earned more when one of the mates, a boy from Georgia who was nicknamed the Cracker, realized that the troop replacements coming through Neufchâteau were willing to pay for souvenirs; he arranged with Walt to paint camouflage on German helmets the Cracker had rescued from the dumps outside town. Then the Cracker scuffed them in the dirt, shot a hole in them and sold them as authentic war booty, giving Walt a share of the money.

But for all the fun he seemed to be having in France, Walt was nevertheless feeling increasingly homesick. "France is an interesting place," he wrote *The McKinley Voice*, "but just the same I want to—" and he inserted in the letter a cartoon of a man shouting, "OH! I want to go home to my Mama." He signed it "your old artist." By this time, Ray and Roy had already left the service and returned to Kansas City. Walt, though, despite his homesickness, was considering re-upping with the Red Cross and transferring to Albania, where the salary was $150 a month—nearly three times what he was earning in France. In July he was reassigned to Paris, and years later he would say that while watching Pershing moving out his troops early that September, he was suddenly seized by loneliness and promptly put in a request to be discharged. But that was another bit of Disney drama. Even before Pershing left, Walt had already applied for a discharge, on August 7, "to be sent home as soon as possible."

While he waited in Paris, he was reunited with Russell Maas, who had also been assigned there. The two teenagers decided that when they returned home, they would pool their money to buy a scow and float down the Mississippi River like Huckleberry Finn. Meanwhile they each bought a German shepherd puppy. Walt kept his in his musette bag and carried him everywhere. The very afternoon that Pershing was pulling out, September 3, 1919, Walt was leaving Paris for Marseilles and the voyage back to the States. (Maas had already left with the puppies.) It was not an easy passage. A dock strike prevented him from sailing as scheduled. He spent the next twenty-three days waiting out the strike by going to Nice, where the accommodations were cheaper and the workers friendlier, and killed time by taking the streetcar each morning to Monte Carlo. He finally sailed on the SS *Canada* with a group of nurses, doctors, and correspondents returning from the peace conference. Progress was slow. Due to the strike the *Canada* had no cargo and little fuel, and not until the ship reached the Azores was it able to take on coal. The ship was not long back out at sea when it was hit by a savage storm. The *Canada* finally limped into New York Harbor on October 9. Walt was discharged the next day and was back in Chicago the day after that.

After nearly a year away he returned in high spirits, but they were quickly crushed. He hunted down Maas to retrieve his dog, only to find that the puppy had died of worms or distemper during the crossing. As for their trip down the Mississippi, Maas had met a girl, gotten a job, and abandoned his plans for adventure. Walt was even more disappointed by Beatrice. She had written him faithfully while he was in France; he had kept the letters. As he prepared to leave Paris, he had bought perfume and blouses for her. But when he arrived in Chicago, he later said, he was shocked to hear that she had gotten married. (In fact, though Walt would always insist that his girl had betrayed him, Beatrice was not married yet. She would not marry until April.) Devastated by the news, he never even bothered to see her but instead saved the presents for his sister-in-law in Kansas City and declared himself "through with women."

Added to all these disappointments was another. Walt had saved nearly six hundred dollars from his earnings in France, including three hundred in winnings from a crap game in Neufchâteau, and he had sent most of it home to be put in the bank until his return. Now he considered taking the money and staking himself while he tried to land a job as an artist. Elias was aghast at his son's impracticality. "He never understood me," Walt later said. "He thought I was a black sheep. This nonsense of drawing pictures! He said, 'Walter, you're going to make a career of that, are you?' " Elias had other plans for his son. He had secured a job for Walt at O-Zell for twenty-five dollars a week, and he could not possibly see why Walt would sacrifice the certainty of the jelly factory for the uncertainty of art.

But Walt Disney had returned from France a man transformed. He had been transformed physically. He had left Chicago five feet eight inches tall and spindly. He had returned weighing 165 pounds, strengthened by extensive manual labor, with broad shoulders and big hands. He had even begun smoking while in France, a habit that was anathema to his father. More, he had changed emotionally, having had in France, he said, "a lifetime of experience in one package." Though he still pulled childish pranks—upon his return he would carry a box with a hole in the bottom through which he stuck his own "bloody" thumb—he had matured, become more self-reliant and independent. "I was settled" was how he later put it. "I . . . was able to kind of line right up on an objective. And I went for it."

He knew that he was not going to work in the jelly factory. He had long harbored two alternative ambitions—to be an actor or an artist. "It seemed easier to get a job as an artist," he decided. So seventeen-year-old Walt Disney, newly armed with confidence and determined to avoid his father's fate, the joylessness and the constant disappointment, would do what the Disneys had always done. He would pursue his opportunity. He would escape.

Two

GO-GETTER

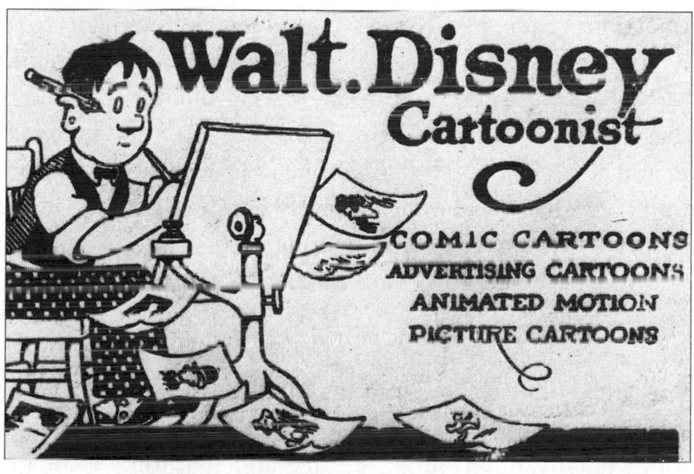

Now Walt Disney needed a job, and he threw himself into the pursuit. He had returned from France flush with his own youthful exuberance but also charged with the exuberance of the times. Though the war had devastated Europe, leaving what Willa Cather had called a "broken world," it had unleashed an optimism bordering on hubris in America, where the economy boomed and American global power was now unrivaled. As one historian put it of the country's good fortune, "America at the close of the Great War was a Cinderella magically clothed in the most stunning dress at the ball, a ball to which Cinderella had not even been invited; immense gains with no visible price tag seemed to be the American destiny." This was not only a mood. It translated into a new national ethos of hopefulness and heedlessness that gave rise, in turn, to a new national type who seemed to embody postwar hopeful heedlessness: the go-getter. The go-getter, perhaps best epitomized and caricatured by the 1920s film comedian Harold Lloyd with his round spectacles, straw boater, and brash can-do obliviousness, was young, boyish, enthusiastic, unflappable, indefatigable, lighthearted, high-spirited, and above all, determined. Like his country, he never doubted the power of his will to realize his dreams nor the essential righteousness of the quest. "Guts and goodness in tandem," the critic Walter Kerr would write of Lloyd.

"Guts and goodness" also described the intrepid, innocent young Walt Disney who landed in Kansas City during the fall of 1919 determined to be successful. Almost all of his acquaintances then remarked on his resolve and absolute faith in himself, manifested not so much in brow-furrowed grit as in a sunny ebullience. From the attention he had received at Benton and at McKinley High School and in France, he brimmed with a self-confidence that was neither entirely justified nor particularly well directed, since he had arrived without a plan. He was a go-getter who did not know where he was getting to, only that he would get somewhere.

Almost immediately upon arriving back in Kansas City, he spotted a want ad in the *Star* for an office boy at the newspaper, which was where he had long dreamed of working. Donning his Red Cross uniform because he thought it made him look more responsible, he went to the *Star* building to apply, but having filled out in France and matured, Walt no longer looked like an office boy, and despite his insistence that he was only seventeen, he was rejected for being too old. The manager suggested he apply to the transportation department instead, since he had been driving an ambulance. He did, but there was no opening. Discouraged and seeking consolation, he headed where he always headed in times of distress—to Roy, who was working as a teller at the First National Bank. One of Roy's colleagues mentioned that two friends of his ran a commercial art shop and were looking for an apprentice. Walt quickly returned home, grabbed samples of his drawings from France, and applied for the job that same afternoon. He was hired on the spot, with the stipulation that his salary would be determined after a one-week trial.

The custodians of the shop were two young commercial artists, Louis Pesmen and William Rubin, who were headquartered in the two-story brick Gray Advertising Building in downtown Kansas City. Walt was so anxious that first week that, as during his art classes, he never left his drawing board, not even taking a break to relieve himself until lunch. On Friday, with the trial at an end, Rubin approached him, mused for a moment, and offered him fifty dollars a month. Walt, later admitting he would have worked for much less, was so grateful, he said, "I could have kissed him!" His first impulse was to tell his aunt Margaret, who now lived with Uncle Robert in a nearby hotel and who, Walt still believed, had launched his artistic career by bringing him those tablets and pencils in Marceline. "Auntie, look, they're paying me to draw pictures. They're paying me to draw pictures," he gushed. It was a disappointment, a "kind of a heartbreak," Walt called it, when Aunt Margaret, now aged, frail, and crippled, showed so little enthusiasm for his achievement.

But Walt himself could barely contain his joy. He was, at seventeen, a professional artist and felt he was "making a great success," as he later put it. The work was illustrating advertisements and catalogs, and he admitted it was not terribly creative, especially since he only did "roughs," the raw outlines for the ads, after his bosses had laid them out. In fact, most of his drawings were redrawn by Rubin or Pesmen, so much so that Walt himself did not always recognize them when they appeared in print. Still, it was valuable experience. From his brief training in art school, Walt aimed for fineness in his drawing. At Pesmen-Rubin he learned about expediency—about cutting, pasting over, scratching out with razor blades, using a pantograph to copy drawings, and anything else that would get the job finished quickly. He worked doggedly. Pesmen remembered assigning Walt the front-cover advertisement for a doughnut shop in the Newman Theater magazine. When he approached Walt at the end of the day, the boy was grinning. Walt had done both the front *and* back cover ads and had even added some details that Pesmen had not included in his original layout.

His joy was short-lived. In late November or early December the Christmas advertising rush was over, and Walt was amicably terminated. He hooked on as a holiday employee at the post office, where his brother Herbert worked, and delivered mail until the end of the year. Then, jobless again, he stayed with Herbert's family and Roy in the Bellefontaine house and drew in his bedroom, still nursing the hope that he might land himself a comic strip or a job as a political cartoonist. (One cartoon of his drawn that month had a baby wearing a sash declaring "New Year of 1920" and standing outside a door labeled "The World," which was bursting under pressure as the words "IWW," "Mob Lynching," "Peace Treaty," "Strikes," "Turmoil," "Sugar Shortage," and "Reds" squeezed out through the jambs.) He drew several installments of a strip he titled "Mr.

George's Wife," about a husband browbeaten by his shrewish mate, and worked on several others he called "As Luck Would Have It" and "It's a Question for the Senate." When the federal census-taker came to the house that month, Walt first declared himself a "commercial artist," then, in an apparent change of mind, had the taker reclassify him as a "cartoonist," which fit his ambition.

For someone virtually without training or experience, for someone who had just lost his job, he was cocky—"I felt well-qualified," he would say after just six weeks at Pesmen-Rubin—already thinking of opening his own art shop while he awaited a strip or newspaper position. It seemed ridiculous, but the plan got an unexpected nudge early in January when he received a visit from one of his former coworkers at Pesmen-Rubin, a "hillbilly" Walt called him, with the improbable name of Ubbe Iwwerks. Usually taciturn and unemotional, Iwwerks was visibly distraught. He too had been laid off. He complained that he had no money or prospects and that he had to support his mother, which made him especially desperate. As Iwwerks sat moping and agonizing in Walt's room, Walt suddenly, impulsively, sprang the idea that they go into business together. Iwwerks, who was more of a plodder than a go-getter, was baffled and uncertain, but Walt told him to collect samples of his work so that Walt could begin soliciting clients for their shop.

Other than the fact that they were both high school dropouts and both putative artists without jobs, the two prospective partners could not have been more dissimilar. Walt, with Disney grandiosity, had big dreams and outsize aspirations. Iwwerks thought only of the immediate future. Walt was gregarious and outgoing, his manner dramatic, his hair carelessly swept back on his head but always with long strands falling incorrigibly over his forehead. Iwwerks was painfully shy, even withdrawn, doleful and forlorn; he seldom spoke, and his hair was carefully molded high on his head in almost comic effect. They differed in their approach to art too. For Walt, drawing was both an escape from his father's hard pragmatism and an appeal for attention. For Iwwerks, who specialized in lettering rather than cartooning, art was almost a way to avoid social contact by focusing on his drawing board. At Pesmen-Rubin, where Iwwerks had arrived about a month after Walt, they had been acquaintances rather than friends, and Iwwerks even seemed to resent Walt's self-absorption. He once remarked that while he and the other artists played poker during breaks, Walt would sit at his board practicing various renditions of his signature.

But if Iwwerks seemed to flinch from the world while Walt embraced it, his diffidence was understandable. "He just didn't have a childhood that was anything that he was happy about," one of his sons would say. He had been born in Kansas City on March 24, 1901, to a local girl and a fifty-seven-year-old Dutch immigrant who earned his living as a barber. It was his father's third marriage, and Ubbe was his fourth child. He had abandoned the others, and Evert Iwwerks was to leave Ubbe's mother too when the boy was in high school, forcing Ubbe to end his education and take a job at the Union Bank Note Co. making lithographs to support her. (Iwwerks never spoke of his father and rebuffed any talk about him; when Evert Iwwerks died and Ubbe was asked how he wanted to dispose of the body, he reportedly said, "Throw it in a ditch.") He left Kansas City briefly to do farmwork in Arkansas, then returned late in 1919 and took the job at Pesmen-Rubin, but he had been so remote and his life so sheltered that his mother once scolded Louis Pesmen for introducing her son to Coca-Cola.

Iwwerks's remoteness and social awkwardness, however, made him a perfect complement for Walt Disney, which is no doubt why Iwwerks sought him out. While Iwwerks, who was diligent, meticulous, and extremely facile with the brush, stayed at his drawing board, Walt could talk up customers and hustle business. In one version of the story Walt told, he went right out to printers and quickly landed jobs designing letterheads and theater ads. In another version he first made an arrangement with *The Restaurant News*, a giveaway published by the Kansas City branch of the National Restaurant Association that had evolved out of an effort by local restaurateurs to combat strikes by joining forces. Even here, however, the deal was not entirely the result of Walt's persuasiveness or charm, effective as these were; Clem Carder, the brother of the president of the association, Al Carder, was a neighbor of the Disneys on Bellefontaine. With this entree Walt approached Al for work, and when Carder complained that he could not afford an art department, Walt made him a proposition: let Iwwerks-Disney, as the two had named their partnership (Walt said he gave Iwwerks first billing because otherwise it might have sounded like an optometric practice), do illustrations and lettering for the magazine's advertisers; in exchange they would get free desk space in the *News*'s office, which was located at Thirteenth and Oak Streets, and ten dollars a page, which was what Carder was paying his printers to recycle the same old artwork each issue. Carder agreed.

Now Walt had office space, but he needed basic equipment—desks, drawing boards, an airbrush, and a compressor to run it. The money he had earned in France was still deposited in Chicago, and he asked his parents to withdraw the funds and send them so he could make the purchases. But once again Walt ran aground on his father's frugality. Before agreeing to release the funds, his parents wanted to know exactly what he would use the money for. He answered with indignation, saying that it was his money and he could do whatever he wanted to with it. There followed a flurry of letters, back and forth, after which Elias and Flora finally consented to send Walt half his savings—a concession that further loosened his bonds to parental authority.

With the equipment issue resolved and the partners ensconced in the *Restaurant News* office, Walt went out selling again. When he had arrived in Kansas City the previous fall, he had reconnected with Walt Pfeiffer. Pfeiffer now convinced his father to let Iwwerks-Disney do the letterheads for the *United Leather Workers Journal.* They wound up doing the cover for the February issue as well with an etching of saddles, harnesses, and gladstone bags. Meanwhile Walt continued to visit printers, offering to become a kind of ad hoc commercial art department for them. Some agreed. (He especially remembered one assignment calling for an oil well gushing dollars. Walt, fired with enthusiasm, said he drew so many dollars that they filled the page.) By month's end he and Iwwerks were successful enough to move into their own office in the Railway Exchange Building. Walt said they made between $125 and $135 that first month—more than their combined earnings at Pesmen-Rubin.

But despite its promising start, neither partner seemed to think of Iwwerks-Disney as a long-term proposition. Walt was still restless and Iwwerks still nervous about the uncertainty of running his own business. For his part, Walt had not given up his dream of drawing his own comic strip. Hoping to impress some prospective employer, he would bring strips he had drawn to the printers and have "cuts" made of them in the empty spaces of his client's plates, then print the strips on newspaper stock and surround them with news stories to make it look as if they had been published. It was a sign of the partners' wavering commitment that when Iwwerks spotted a want ad in the *Star* late in January seeking an artist for the Kansas City Slide Co., he recommended that Walt pursue the job. Walt thought the Slide Co., which produced promotional slides shown in movie theaters before the feature, might hire Iwwerks-Disney as a subcontractor, but when he brought his samples and made the suggestion, he was told that they wanted a full-time employee. Ubbe then advised Walt to take the position, which paid thirty-five dollars a week, since the ad called for a cartoonist. They agreed that Ubbe would continue to run their shop.

The Kansas City Slide Co., which Walt joined early that February, was located at 1015 Central Street, practically around the corner from his Railway Exchange office, in a narrow two-and-a-half-story vanilla-brick building with tall, hinged windows along the side to provide light for the artists. There were fewer than twenty employees at the time Walt started, but the company was already the largest mail-order slide firm in the country and was expanding rapidly. Walt said it did a million dollars' worth of business a year. The president of the operation and the interviewer who had hired Walt was Arthur Verne Cauger, though most people called him simply "A.V." Cauger referred to himself as "one of the pioneers of the Moving Picture business," and in a small way he was. He had been born in Indiana in 1878 and studied engineering, but his interest in mechanics apparently lured him to the movies. He opened a theater in Granite City, Illinois, in 1907, and when a competitor drove him out by offering a longer show for the same admission, he set up another theater in Carlyle, Illinois, and then another in Neosho, Missouri. Because Neosho would not permit Cauger's theater to draw electricity from its publicly owned power plant in the afternoons, he began making slides in his spare time. Eventually he sold the theater, moved to Kansas City, and entered the slide business full-time, shooting the pictures himself and then traversing the Midwest selling them to exhibitors. When competitors started making filmed ads, Cauger entered that business too, in time shifting almost exclusively to film.

It was the film ads that Walt was now drawing, and they fascinated him. Many of them were live action, but the ones for which he was hired were animated pictures. By any standard the animation at the Slide Co. was crude, intended less for artistry than for economy. Basically the artists would draw a picture, cut out the movable parts, tack them with pins to a board, move the parts slightly and photograph the image, move them slightly again and photograph again, repeating the process over and over so that when the film was run and the incremental movements were strung together, they would give the impression of continuous action. The fact that it was a primitive technique, though, made no difference to Walt, who just wanted to gain experience. "I got a fine job here in K.C.," he wrote one of his old Red Cross compatriots proudly a few months after joining the Slide Co., "and I'm going to stick with it. I draw cartoons for the moving pictures—advertiser films— . . . and the work is interesting."

Though Walt had intended to continue Iwwerks-Disney to supplement his income and provide some flexibility for his career, the company did not long survive his leaving it. Iwwerks simply did not have the temperament to run a business without him. As Walt later explained, "[T]he few customers I had would call him—he would just sit there [because] he couldn't give the old sales pitch." Unable to drum up business and seeking the safety of regular employment, Iwwerks asked Walt if there might be an opening at the Slide Co. So the partners closed the shop less than two months after it had opened, and that March Iwwerks went to work for Cauger too, sitting alongside Walt and the other artists at their long tables and drawing slides and cartoons.

Walt, who was sanguine about most things, did not seem terribly distressed by the demise of his small firm. Though he had already printed his own stationery featuring a caricature of himself at his drawing board, pages flying off, and declaring himself available for "Cartoons, Illustrations, Designs and Window Cards, Art Work for All Advertising Purposes," he had, in his short time at the Slide Co., begun redirecting his attention from commercial art and even from the dream of newspaper cartooning. Indeed by one account that spring he had finally received the offer he had so long coveted—to be a cartoonist at the *Star* or *Journal-Post*—only to reject it to stay at the Slide Co. That was because Walt Disney, a young man who always seemed to be in the grip of some passion, had found a new one: he had become as intoxicated with animation as he had originally been with drawing back at the Benton School. "The trick of making things move on film is what got me," he would tell an interviewer years later.

Walt clearly loved the combination of drawing and technology. He had always liked to tinker, and in his last spring in Kansas City before leaving for Chicago he had even bought the parts to construct a car chassis with the intention of putting Roy's old motorcycle engine under the hood, until Roy inadvertently scuttled the plan by selling the cycle when he joined the navy. But to the go-getter in Walt, and to the Disney in him, animation had another appeal. It was a way to make his mark since, unlike newspaper cartooning, animation was something that Walt thought he might do better than anyone else because so few people at the time were doing it and so few people had any expertise in it, and the idea of being the best, the most noted, clearly appealed to him.

Walt Disney seldom dabbled. Everyone who knew him remarked on his intensity; when something intrigued him, he focused himself entirely as if it were the only thing that mattered. Now animation mattered. That spring he began an intensive self-education in the medium, using the Slide Co. as his school. It might not have seemed a likely place to matriculate. Tall, burly, and lantern-jawed, A.V. Cauger was physically imposing, and he had a gruff voice and brusque manner that further intimidated; one employee recalled that A.V. would issue instructions or orders while simultaneously spitting in the drinking fountain. But to those who got to know him, his manner was less terrorizing than informal, and he ran his shop more or less democratically, which meant that Walt had extraordinary latitude for an eighteen-year-old. He had been there only a relatively short time when he convinced Cauger, as an economy measure, to let him write and shoot his own ads rather than rely on the copy department. (Already Walt had a facility with quips. For an ad promoting a company that refurbished canvas car tops, he had a man address the owner of a reconditioned car: "Hi, old top, new car?" "No, new top, old car.") And it was not long after that that Walt prodded Cauger into letting him borrow an old mahogany camera he had found in the office sitting on a shelf, overcoming Cauger's objections that the company might need the camera for some emergency by promising that he would return it immediately should that situation arise.

But if the Slide Co. was his school, he still needed a studio in which to practice making cartoons. He found one in his own backyard. That same spring Elias and Flora returned to the Bellefontaine house from Chicago, once again having failed. O-Zell had gone bankrupt—by one account due to the financial chicanery of its officers, which sent them to Joliet Federal Penitentiary, though this seems unlikely since the Disneys maintained cordial relations with the family of O-Zell's president, Earl Scrogin, for years afterward. Walt, obviously wanting to impress his family and always enamored of the grand gesture, greeted his parents and sister at Union Station in a rented touring car. His parents had no automobile of their own, but not long after his arrival Elias decided to build a garage in the yard behind the Bellefontaine house with the intention of making some additional money by renting it out. He had barely begun construction when Walt told him that he would rent it himself and offered his father five dollars a month, which, Roy would say, Walt never paid.

The garage, roughly fifteen feet square and dominating the small yard, became Walt's first studio. Inside he and Roy rigged Cauger's camera into an overhead camera stand with incandescent lights. Already during his short time at Pesmen-Rubin, Walt had, according to Louis Pesmen, borrowed a glass negative camera that he had found in the studio and begun experimenting in Pesmen's sister's garage with photographic images, possibly, Pesmen speculated, making slides of his own. (His sister was less than enthusiastic, Pesmen said, about the mess Walt left.) Focused now on animation virtually to the exclusion of everything else—"Walt was a focused man from childhood," his niece, Dorothy, who lived at the Bellefontaine house at the time, would say—he would repair to the garage after work each day, emerge for dinner, then return to his camera stand. "When he'd come home and long after everybody else was [in] bed," Roy remembered, "Walt was out there still, puttering away, working away, experimenting, trying this and that, drawing, and so on." "He was just busy every second," said Dorothy, though no one in the family paid much attention to him. "We didn't think it was any big deal."

But for Walt the nights tinkering out back *were* a big deal, and they signified a sea change in his ambitions. What his family did not seem to notice was that Walt Disney, who for years had been determined to become a newspaper cartoonist, was now suddenly just as determined to become something that to most outsiders was even more impractical, something for which he had had no real training and something for which a job did not even seem to exist. He wanted to become an animator.

II

He did not have a lot of catching up to do. In 1920, when he began puttering in his garage, animation was scarcely two decades old, and it had not evolved much in that time, in part because the idea of moving drawings was still so novel that it required very little besides movement to entertain audiences. The earliest animators, like the Frenchman Émile Cohl and the Englishman Stuart Blackton, borrowed from the stage tradition of "lightning sketchers"—performers who stood at an easel and, while lecturing, drew very rapidly, constantly transforming their drawings as they spoke. Taking advantage of the inherent nature of motion pictures to make continuous action out of a string of static images, animation pioneers did lightning sketching one better. Their films often self-reflexively showed the cartoonist's hand sketching the image before magically setting it in motion, calling attention to the technological gimmick and in doing so turning animation into a form of trickery. In effect, these first animations were about nothing more than the thrill of animation itself.

Not until 1910, when Winsor McCay originated a vaudeville act in which he (on stage) interacted with his animations (on screen), did the quality of the drawing dramatically improve and the integrity of the drawing as a separate reality rather than a trick become established. McCay had been an illustrator and cartoonist for the *Cincinnati Commercial Tribune* and then the *Enquirer* before defecting to the *New York Herald and Evening Telegram*, where he created several comic strips, most famously "Little Nemo in Slumberland," which brought him national fame and a vaudeville contract. Inspired by a "flip book" that his son brought home, in which riffling the pages set figures in motion, he converted "Nemo" into a short animation to be shown during his act. By the time he made his second film, *How a Mosquito Operates*, in 1912, he was declaring animation a "new school of art that will revolutionize the entire field," and when he drew "Gertie the Dinosaur" two years later, also for his vaudeville act, he accelerated that revolution by laying, in the words of one animation historian, the "foundations of *character animation*, the art of delineating a character's personality through a unique style of movement."

Where McCay led, many illustrators and cartoonists followed, until animation gradually emerged as a new film genre emphasizing characters rather than magic. Late in 1914 or early 1915 a French-Canadian illustrator named Raoul Barré and a longtime magazine and newspaper artist named John Randolph Bray opened the first animation studios in New York, and within a few years they had at least a dozen rivals there hoping to reap the profits of this novelty. For these pioneers the primary challenge was not artistic; it was technical. McCay, making only two-minute films, drew each of the roughly four thousand pictures his animations required on a separate sheet of paper with both character and background included and then had each one of them photographed. (His sole efficiency was in tracing the backgrounds.) But this was hopelessly time-consuming if one intended to produce animations of any length and in any quantity. As a matter of economizing, the goal was to separate the moving characters in the foreground, which had to be continuously redrawn, from the background, which did not move and thus could be drawn just once. Bray devised an alternative system to McCay's in which he printed multiple copies of the background and then removed those parts that would be obscured by the action, either by scratching them off or blanking them out. Barré, realizing that the background and action did not have to be put on the same sheet since the camera could combine them in a single frame, invented what came to be called the "slash and tear" method of animation because he would place the background on one sheet and then tear holes in it to reveal the action on a second sheet laid beneath the first. But it was another old newspaper cartoonist-turned-animator, Earl Hurd, who most successfully solved the problem by drawing the moving characters on sheets of translucent paper, later transparent celluloid, and placing them over a second sheet on which the background was painted, eliminating the need for tearing holes.* This gave rise to the term *cel* to refer to the individual celluloid sheets with their animation drawings. It was so efficient a system that it would remain the basic animation technique for more than eighty years, or until the rise of computer-generated images in the late twentieth century.

*Hurd patented his invention in June 1915. When he went to work for Bray that same year, Hurd wound up pooling his patents with Bray's. The two then launched a war against their competitors that lasted for years as courts attempted to determine whether Hurd and Bray had a monopoly on cel animation.

But if cel animation made animating much easier, it did not, it turned out, make it any more artistic. Drawings and movement were rudimentary, in part because animators had to feel their way along a trail that had yet to be blazed. Most of them were eager young print cartoonists like Walt who had no training in animating figures; at best they studied books—there were a handful of them in the postwar period—that purported to explain how to make pictures move. "Animators were scarce," Grim Natwick, an early cartoonist, recalled. "There was no one to tell them how to do it. They sharpened a fist full of pencils, sat down at a drawing board and started animating."

And what was true of the drawing was equally true of the stories the drawings told. Based primarily on familiar comic strips, early animations had no more narrative refinement than a day's installment of those strips—no real attempt to tell a story, much less create an arc. Usually when the animators began drawing, they did not even have any narrative master plan to follow. "The scenario would probably be on a single sheet of paper," Dick Huemer, an animator who had worked at Barré's studio back in 1916, said, "without any models, sketches, or anything; you made it up as you went along." Some twenty years after the introduction of animation, it was still largely its novelty that held the appeal, though that appeal was waning. "We got very few laughs," Huemer added. "I can remember taking my family to see some bit of animation I was particularly proud of, and just as it went on, somebody behind me said, 'Oh, I hate these things.' "

But if very little visual or narrative craft was involved, animation nevertheless had a powerful subtext that would slowly emerge and at least subliminally resonate with the public, a subtext of which the first animators themselves may not even have been aware. Most had come to animation as a lark—typically a way to take advantage of the movie boom for financial gain. Their "distinctive features," as one eminent animation historian described this pioneering group, were a "background in journalism, a compulsion to sketch, 'workaholic' tendencies, and a well developed but idiosyncratic sense of humor." Except for the journalism experience, for which he had once so achingly yearned, Walt Disney certainly fit this characterization. But Walt's growing attachment to animation seemed to be impelled by something beyond the inertia from print to film that ostensibly motivated so many other animators, or the prospect of money, or the technological appeal of the medium, or the possibility of success, or even the attention it might get him—all of which may have been the initial lures. Walt Disney also had a psychological connection to animation, a connection forged by his childhood experiences.

The process of animation was a process of giving life, of literally taking the inanimate and making it animate. It was, at base, a hubristic process in which the animator assumed and exercised godlike control over his materials, which was why it also offered a feeling of empowerment to its viewers who sensed the control. In Walt Disney's case the surge of empowerment was so great one might even have concluded that animation took the place of religion for him, since in his adulthood he showed little or no interest in formal religion and never attended church. Indeed, the animator created his own world—an alternative reality of his imagination in which the laws of physics and logic could be suspended. Though Walt Disney could never fully articulate why he was attracted to animation, falling back instead on vague generalities, it always had these two great and unmistakable blandishments. For a young man who had chafed within the stern, moralistic, anhedonic world of his father, animation provided escape, and for someone who had always been subjugated by that father, it provided absolute control. In animation Walt Disney had a world of his own. In animation Walt Disney could be the power.

By late spring, still determined to master animation, he had immersed himself completely. He had taken out a book from the Kansas City Library—"there was only this one book in the library [on animation]"—and devoured it. The book, *Animated Cartoons: How They Are Made, Their Origin and Development*, by Edwin G. Lutz, had just been published, but it immediately became, in one animation historian's words, the "vulgate of modern industrial animation." Lutz essentially brought the latest animation techniques of New York to the hinterlands like Kansas City. He described how one could draw backgrounds on a single sheet of celluloid and then place them over the animated action, and he suggested that one draw the static portions of a figure on the celluloid as well and animate the parts that moved on a paper beneath. He also explained how a putative animator, using a lightbox with two pegs at the top to hold the paper in place—if successive papers were unaligned, the image would shimmy—could sketch the extremes of an action and then have what he called a "tracer" fill in the pictures in between (what animators would call "working to extremes"), as most of the New York professionals did. Lutz even delineated the kind of person most likely to succeed in animation: someone with a "notion of form," someone who was "an untiring and courageous worker," and someone who possessed "skill as a manager."

Even though Walt would later dismiss the Lutz book as "not very profound" and "just something the guy had put together to make a buck," his associates said they all pored over it, and its effect on him too was nearly a revelation. At the Slide Co. he had been deploying the rudimentary cutout system of animation with moving limbs. Now he began experimenting with cel animation—*real* animation. He also began picking the brain of a former Slide Co. animator named "Scarfoot" McCory who had left to run an animation school in New York but who returned occasionally to Kansas City, and he may have taken a correspondence course offered by a prominent New York animator named Bill Nolan. To improve the quality of his work, Walt studied motion as well as technique. Iwwerks had taken out from the library a copy of Eadweard Muybridge's photographs of animal movements so that he could trace a greyhound's gait from the photos for an ad he was assigned, and Walt wound up making a photostat of the book for his own collection. Of the greyhound ad, Iwwerks later said it was "the best animation scene I ever did, before and since." And Walt began attending night classes again at the Kansas City Art Institute with Iwwerks and other colleagues from the Slide Co.

Still, the hours drawing at the Slide Co., and the hours more drawing and shooting with the camera afterward in the backyard garage, and the time studying Lutz, Muybridge, and Nolan, and the nights at the Art Institute, were not enough for him. He was besotted with animation. He needed more. By the summer the Slide Co. had moved to a new, more spacious building at 2449 Charlotte Street, a little over a mile southwest of the old headquarters, in what was called the hospital district, and had changed its name to the Kansas City Film Ad Co. to reflect the shift in business from slides to movies. With the passion of a convert, Walt attempted to wheedle Cauger into trying cel animation, but Cauger was a traditionalist. Rebuffed, Walt decided to pursue it on his own, and late that summer or early in the fall he recruited Fred Harman, the older brother of Hugh Harman, one of Walt's Film Ad Co. coworkers, to team with him on drawing an animation they called "The Little Artist" in which an artist and his easel came to life.

This was just a little learning exercise, but if Walt was obsessed, he was also ambitious. In his book Lutz suggested that would-be animators think topically: "For news picture reels it has been found judicious for variety's sake, as well as for business reasons, to combine with them cartoons satirizing topics of the hour." Walt and Harman had already made one live-action film they titled *Kansas City Journal Screen Review*, apparently hoping to interest the newspaper in a film adjunct. Though that did not pay off, Walt, no doubt inspired by Lutz's suggestion, decided to try making a short editorial cartoon and see if he could sell it to the three-theater Newman chain, for which he had illustrated programs at Pesmen-Rubin. Whose idea it was to go to Newman is impossible to say. Louis

Pesmen later remembered that Walt invited him to see the cartoons, which commented humorously on Kansas City's slow streetcar service. One showed a daisy growing on a woman's hosiery as she waited for her trolley, only to have her engulfed in flowers by the time it arrived; another had a young man growing a beard by the time his trolley arrived. Pesmen said he laughed "long and hard," then suggested Walt show them to their old client, Frank L. Newman.

Newman was the "big showman in Kansas City at that time," according to Elias Disney, and he looked the part. He was a big, beefy man with dark hair brilliantined back on his head, a prominent nose, and a square jaw. And if Newman looked like the king of Kansas City show business, his Newman Theater, which he had opened the previous year on Main Street, certainly looked like his palace. Seating one thousand and ranging over one hundred feet from the stage to the entrance and with seventy-five-foot ceilings, the Newman was done in Italian Renaissance style with "every square foot of floor space . . . of either terrazzo or white marble," according to the *Newman Theater Magazine*. Abandoning its motif, the theater even featured a Louis XV restroom, which, it boasted, was "unquestionably the most beautiful room of its kind ever constructed."

Walt Disney came to this ornate edifice early in 1921 carrying his one-minute reel of cartoons that he had preemptively labeled "Newman Laugh-O-grams." As he so often did, Walt would later tell two versions of what happened next—a prosaic version that was probably close to the truth and a heightened one that was more compelling. In the less dramatic one, he showed the reel to Milton Feld, Newman's manager, who would later become a Hollywood producer and circus promoter, and Feld promptly placed an order. (Years later Walt would write Newman: "Of course all of my contacts at that time were through Milton Feld and I did not see much of you.") In the more dramatic telling, he said he sat behind Newman himself in the theater, "nervous as a cat," while the reel was projected. When it concluded, Newman quickly spun around, said he liked what he had seen, and asked whether they would be expensive to produce. Walt blurted out that he could make them for thirty cents a foot, and Newman closed the deal on the spot, saying he would take as many Laugh-O-grams as Walt could draw. Walt said he left "walking on air." It was not until an hour later that he realized that the price he had quoted Newman was his cost with no profit.

Now, after his relatively short apprenticeship, he was an animator. His sample reel premiered at the Newman Theater on March 20, 1921. But producing the Laugh-O-grams was time-consuming, especially with Walt fully employed at the Film Ad Co., and they appeared irregularly over the next few months. He realized he would need coworkers and apprentices, and he placed a newspaper want ad for aspiring cartoonists offering not remuneration, since he had no money to give them, but experience. A high school student named Rudy Ising—"I was intrigued with the idea of animation," Ising would say—answered the ad and began assisting Walt in the Bellefontaine garage. For the Laugh-O-grams Walt was working in the "lightning sketches" tradition. Following another Lutz suggestion, he would draw an image in light blue pencil, which would not register on the orthochromatic film he used. Then Ising would ink in the lines, inserting a photograph of Walt's hand (the real hand would have been too thick to place between the camera and the drawing) after each increment, constantly stopping and shooting, so that when the film was run continuously the image appeared to be drawn by the hand with preternatural rapidity.

As one might have expected from a nineteen-year-old novice, the Laugh-O-grams were raw and unsophisticated, though competently drawn. They commented not only on streetcar service but also on potholes, new fashions, and a police scandal, which Walt ham-handedly satirized by showing cartoon officers filing into the precinct house and then filing out in prison uniforms. But Milt Feld was more than satisfied. He commissioned Walt to provide special titles for coming attractions and anniversary shows, and animations to be shown before the program advising proper theater protocol. In one a cartoon professor admonished moviegoers not to read the titles aloud, at the risk of being hit on the head with a large mallet.

For all their obviousness and crudeness, the Laugh-O-grams, playing as they did at Kansas City's largest and most opulent theater, got noticed, and though Walt did not make any profit on them, he gained something he seemed to relish more than money. He got attention. "I got to be a little celebrity in the thing," he said. As in the days when he became known for his drawings adorning Bert Hudson's barbershop, old Benton classmates now approached him as the man who drew the Laugh-O-grams. Even at the Film Ad Co., A. V. Cauger would now introduce him to clients as the Laugh-O-gram artist and would borrow Walt's reel to show them what the Film Ad Co. could do. Cauger even gave him a raise to sixty dollars a week.

Beyond recognition, he got encouragement to do more. Later that spring, despite his infatuation with animation, he and Harman began experimenting with live action, no doubt because it was easier and cheaper to produce than animation. Their efforts were mostly juvenilia and nonsense—a scene of Walt entering a door on which "Cartoonist Wanted" is posted, followed by a group of other young men who then run out when a gentleman emerges and tosses the sign away; a woman and her little girl playing patty-cake and then the woman and girl walking dolls in a buggy; Walt's niece Dorothy breaking a milk bottle, which Walt then ran backward so that the bottle seemed to reassemble; more footage of Walt and a group of friends mugging for the camera in Kansas City's Swope Park; an image of a girl unrolling her stocking and dipping her foot into water. In many of these films Walt starred, usually dressed in a costume; and in many the actors appeared and then instantly disappeared, as Walt played with the trick effects of the camera. Harman and Disney even had a name for their little enterprise: Kay Cee Studios.

Though the idea of his own studio was wishful thinking, it was not entirely frivolous, any more than the idea of his own commercial art studio had been. With the popularity of the Laugh-O-grams, which were only a minute or two in duration, he began to think of animating longer cartoons of six or seven minutes. At first he hoped to interest Cauger in the project, intending to make the cartoons under the auspices of the Film Ad Co., but Cauger, still uncomfortable with cel animation and making considerable profits with his ads, declined. A. V. Cauger did, however, order one hundred sheets of celluloid—discards, Walt would say—for Walt's experiments and let him rent a small studio in a vacant house on a dirt hillock, eighteen steps up as Cauger remembered it, next to the Film Ad Co. Here Walt would now retire, after work each day and in his spare time, to draw.

But he was not just drawing. Still as much an opportunist as an artist, he was beginning to think of branching out into business for himself, using his Film Ad job to subsidize his scheme. In the fall, with three hundred dollars in savings, he purchased a Universal camera and a tripod and began advertising again for prospective animators whom he would pay, as he paid Ising, in experience, promising that if the project were a success, he would give them jobs in his new studio. Several began stopping by the house at night and joining in the drawing. Meanwhile, to make additional money, Walt and Fred Harman, who now worked with his brother Hugh and Walt at the Film Ad Co., bought a secondhand Model T and trolled for jobs shooting news footage with the Universal camera. "Our sights," Harman said, "were set for long-range money and fame." They got an assignment from Pathé filming the American Legion convention late that October and early November—the father of a friend of Walt's had an office across the street from which Walt could film—and then, on a sudden inspiration, rented a plane to photograph the convention from above, but Walt underexposed the film and it came back black. "Our hopes for fast riches were wiped out," Harman lamented.

Walt was not deterred. These efforts were, whatever his dreams of financial glory, just extracurricular activities to help support his real project that fall, one more grandiose than the short animations and newsreels. Influenced by New York animator Paul Terry's spoofs of Aesop's fables called Terry's Fables, which had premiered in June, Walt decided that his animations would spoof fairy tales by displacing them into a modern context and giving them a contemporary slant. He proposed doing "Red Riding Hood," though it is unclear whether he animated this one first or a send-up of "The Musicians of Brementown," a fairy tale by the Brothers Grimm.* At the same time he practiced with a reel of jokes and commentaries similar to the Laugh-O-grams that he called Lafflets, possibly as a way to break in his staff. Since he could work only in his off-hours and since his recruits were young and inexperienced, it took him six months, into the spring of 1922, to complete the fairy tale. Walt immediately tried to sell it—a friend at a local film distributor collared producers for him—but in the meantime he drove the Model T to outlying theaters in Missouri and Kansas, offering exhibitors his services to make ads like Cauger's that could keep his anticipated studio running. "[T]hat was Walt all the time," Roy Disney recollected, "driving himself frantic, day and night."

Roy believed that Cauger began to suspect Walt might become a competitor, and Walt seemed to be angling to do so, but Fred Harman, who accompanied Walt on these selling expeditions, said that "we just couldn't swing it," and eventually their Ford was repossessed. Even so, Walt was far from defeated. On the contrary, he seemed strangely elated, certain that his fairy tales would find a distributor and that he would soon be running his own studio full-time, and he began seriously considering leaving the Film Ad Co., even though he had no concrete prospects, just more of his wishful thinking. His father, who had suffered so many economic setbacks of his own, advised him not to go into business, warning that he could go broke. Walt got more encouragement from Roy, but he had been inclined to leave anyway. Cheerful, self-confident, and even a little affected—at the Film Ad Co. he took to wearing an eyeshade and smoking a pipe—he was too independent-minded even at twenty to think of himself as someone else's employee for long. Taking the name Laugh-

*Though Walt Disney later claimed that *Red Riding Hood* was the first in the series of fairy tales, and though animation historians Russell Merritt and J. B. Kaufman also assert that it was his first production, it is likely that *The Four Musicians of Bremen,* a spoof of "The Musicians of Brementown," was actually the inaugural offering since that film and not *Red Riding Hood* is listed among Walt's assets in May 1922. See Articles of Association, Laugh-O-Gram Films, Inc., May 18, 1922.

O-Gram Films, Inc., from his Newman shorts, Walt had articles of association drawn up on May 18, and a certificate of incorporation was issued by the Missouri secretary of state five days later, with Walt listed as company president, even though he was still a minor and legally too young to be a corporate officer. The purpose of the association, as described in the articles, was to "own, make, produce, buy, lease, rent, sell, release, distribute and deal in screen, industrial and commercial advertising and motion pictures of every kind and character" and, for good measure, to rent out equipment and operate a photo lab too. Walt Disney, after scarcely more than two years in the business, was now the head of his very own animation studio. The go-getter seemed to have arrived.

Walt Disney had another motivation for starting a studio besides the tenacious pursuit of animation and the fame and profit he was sure would accrue from it. All this time, from his short stint at Pesmen-Rubin through his first year and a half at the Film Ad Co., Walt had lived on the quiet tree-lined street in his old two-level childhood house at 3028 Bellefontaine with his brothers Roy and Herbert, Herbert's wife, Louise, and their daughter, Dorothy, and later with Flora, Elias, and Ruth. It was comforting, but it wasn't to last. Since his return from the navy Roy had been beset with nagging illnesses. His doctor suggested he have his tonsils removed, and Herb recommended a doctor who offered to perform the operation while Roy was on his lunch break so he wouldn't have to miss work. The doctor, however, turned out to be a charlatan. Roy began hemorrhaging on the street and was rushed home by a coworker and then to the hospital. At the hospital an X-ray revealed a spot on his lung, which was judged to be tuberculosis. Since it was determined that he could have contracted the disease only while in the service, the Veterans Administration sent him in October 1920 to a sanatorium in Santa Fe, New Mexico, and, when he found the weather there too cold, to another facility in Tucson, Arizona. Thinking that he had little time left, he decided to leave Arizona too and go to California to spend his remaining days.

After his supporter, protector, and confidant went west, Walt lost the rest of his family too. Herbert applied to the post office for a medical transfer to Portland, Oregon, where he said the family physician recommended he move for the "milder climate." (Elias's sister Josephine had already moved there with her family, which is probably why Herbert chose that destination.) He, Louise, and Dorothy left Kansas City in July 1921. By the fall Elias, Flora, and Ruth, once again tired of the Kansas City winters, decided to join them. They moved on Sunday, November 6. Walt saw them off at the station. "I never knew Walt's emotions much,"

Ruth said, "but he suddenly couldn't keep his face straight. He turned and left. He was clearly very upset. He knew he was going to be alone."

For someone as social as Walt Disney, someone who loved sodality, loneliness was a curse, and he would have done anything to avoid it. He moved out of the Bellefontaine house—it was sold when Elias and Flora moved—and bounced around various boardinghouses that were occupied by other rootless young men like him. For a while he shared a furnished attic in a rooming house with Cauger's nephew Marion, who had come to work for his uncle at the Film Ad Co., but that did not meet Walt's need for companionship or fill the void left by his family's departure. In May 1920, even before Roy left, Walt had joined the Order of DeMolay. DeMolay, named after the last of the Knights Templar, was a fraternity for young men that had been founded in Kansas City the previous year by a twenty-eight-year-old restaurateur and Mason grandee named Frank Land. (His charges called him "Dad.") Walt would describe joining DeMolay as "one of the most important events of my youth, and one of the happiest, too," and would later write Land that DeMolay ingrained in him "belief in a Supreme Being, in the fellowship of man, and in the sanctity of home." All of this may very well have been true. But he also found an outlet for his drawing as the art editor of the DeMolay magazine, he undoubtedly enjoyed the opera bouffe uniforms that the DeMolay members wore, and, above all, he received camaraderie.

He seized another source of security after his family's departure as well: the family of Roy's girlfriend, Edna Francis. Roy had met Edna when her brother, Mitch, a coworker of Roy's at the First National Bank—Mitch was the one who took Roy home after his botched tonsil operation—suggested he take her to a dance. Edna, a plain, unprepossessing woman, was four years older than Roy (she was probably twenty-nine when they met) and something of a beaten soul. Her father, a railroad worker, was a wanderer who had moved his family of six children from Pittsburgh to Kansas to Kansas City before finally abandoning them. Her mother was almost totally deaf. For Roy, who seemed to enjoy the role of guardian and bulwark and who was just as modest and unaffected as she was, Edna Francis was the ideal companion, and their romance survived Roy's years in military service and then in the tuberculosis sanatoriums. Before he left for New Mexico, they had decided to marry should he survive. "It was a matter of my getting well and having enough money," Roy said.

While he was gone, the Francises would invite Walt to dinner. Sometimes he would accept, then get so involved in his work that he would not remember until ten or eleven o'clock that night. Other times he would arrive and, according to Edna, "*talk* and *talk* till almost midnight. He was having a kind of struggle and when he'd get hungry, he'd come over and we'd feed him a good meal and he'd just talk. I was always a good listener."

But the real cure for his loneliness, his real community, was not in the Francis family or in DeMolay. It was in work, and if Walt had formed his studio to pursue his passion for animation and make his name, he also formed it when he did to allay how bereft he felt with his family gone. Like DeMolay, Laugh-O-Gram would become a kind of fraternity—in this case one where footloose young men eager to learn animation could collaborate. It would be a place for work but also for fun, a place in which the sense of community would be almost as important as the animations, and a place in which the demands of adulthood could be kept at bay. And Walt Disney, who since his youth in Marceline had exulted in the bonds of community, would be the creator and the proprietor of this small, exuberant utopia where one need never grow up. Laugh-O-Gram would be his first Neverland. It would not be his last.

III

It was not much of a studio. Its primary assets were the Lafflets reel and *The Four Musicians*, a fairy-tale animation that Walt valued at $3,000, and equipment that he valued at less than $1,500. He had intended to finance the operation with his own money and whatever loans he could cadge from his trainees—Ising pitched in $1,000—but he realized that he could raise more funds by incorporating, and he wound up giving Ising shares of the company rather than repaying him. Laugh-O-Gram was capitalized at $15,000, about half of which was cash and equipment, divided into three hundred shares valued at $50 each. Walt took seventy and parceled out smaller numbers of shares to a few friends and to his young associates. Still, he had to secure the rest of the money, several thousand dollars after the broker's substantial cut, to rent an office and studio, pay the staff, and buy supplies.

The challenge was for someone so young and with only the Laugh-O-grams to his credit to attract investors. Walt Disney was certainly persuasive—"quite a salesman," Rudy Ising said. He was boyish, enthusiastic, and garrulous and had a way of filling one with enthusiasm too as he described his plans, which he loved to do, as his nights with the Francises attested. He had to be persuasive since the probable success of the enterprise for which he was soliciting funds, run by a young man with no managerial experience who employed younger men with even less experience, was by any measure a long shot. Roy contributed some money—and kept contributing thirty dollars here and there from his disability checks—but Walt Disney's real angel at Laugh-O-Gram was a well-connected Kansas City doctor named John V. Cowles.

Walt had probably met Cowles through another flamboyant speculator, Walt's uncle Robert, with whom Cowles was very likely associated in an oil refinery scheme for which the doctor himself was seeking investors at the time. Tall and heavyset, with a thick shock of hair that turned snow white as he aged and with a pronounced limp that was the result of a riding accident, possibly incurred during a brief stint at West Point, Cowles was both an ostentatious figure in Kansas City and a prominent one. He had been born there and had attended the University of Missouri and then the university's medical school. He returned home to build a lucrative practice as a surgeon/general practitioner; Thomas Pendergast, the head of the city's notorious Democratic political machine, and Harry Truman, later U.S. senator and president, were among his patients and friends. His success was evident in his large office downtown above the Main Street Bank and in his palatial home on Thirty-fourth Street.

But it was not as a medical practitioner that John Cowles was primarily known in Kansas City. It was as a fixer. From his association with Pendergast he knew people, and people knew he was politically connected, which is why they sought his help. He was also regarded highly for his financial acumen and even advised the First National Bank on investments. He was usually on the lookout for new investment schemes, which is no doubt how he hooked up with Robert Disney. Walt never said how he convinced Cowles to invest, though Uncle Robert's intercession probably helped, and Cowles's son claimed that his father could be very generous with supplicants: "Dad was always helping people out." Those first months the doctor provided $2,500 under his wife's signature.

Realizing he did not have enough money to procrastinate, Walt moved quickly. He rented two small, spartan rooms on the top floor of the two-story McConahy Building on Thirty-first Street just a few blocks from his old house on Bellefontaine. Within weeks he had the *Motion Picture News*, a prominent film trade paper, announce his company's launch: "They will produce Laugh-O-Gram animated cartoon comedies which will be cartooned by Walter E. Disney," though the ad also claimed that he had been making films for the Newman Theater for two years and that he had already completed six films—neither of which was true. That same month he bought a new tripod, and in July he took out his first advertisement, in the *News*, promising a series of twelve films, presumably the fairy tales.

At the same time he was hiring. Hugh Harman, Fred's brother, joined Walt as an animator, as did Walt's old trainee, Rudy Ising, and two others: Carmen Maxwell, a junior college student who was hired when he saw the Laugh-O-Gram sign in the office window and applied for a job, and a young man named Lorey Tague. William "Red" Lyon, who had run the camera at the Film Ad Co., became the camera operator at Laugh-O-Gram. An animator, Otto Walliman, joined them later. Walt also secured the services of a business manager, Adolph Kloepper, and a salesman, Leslie Mace. A few months later his old friend Walt Pfeiffer, who had continued his art training after high school at the Art Institute in Chicago before returning to Kansas City, became Laugh-O-Gram's scenario editor, which, he admitted, meant he subscribed to newspapers and scoured them for jokes.

Disney had a staff, but he did not have a contract for his animations, of which there was only one at the time he placed his *Motion Picture News* ad. Though certain of success as he always was, Walt seemed unaware of the generally weak market for cartoons at the time. No one went to the movies to see animations, and distributors did not feel the need to pay premium prices for them. As the seating capacity of theaters grew during the theater-building boom of the late 1910s and early 1920s and admission prices rose, cartoons were essentially add-ons meant to fill out a two-hour program that typically included a feature film, a one- or two-reel live comedy, a newsreel, and a serial, and less frequently a travelogue, a dramatic short, or even a live vaudeville performance. According to one 1922 survey, 73 percent of theaters used a two-reel live comedy, 59 percent a newsreel, and 35 percent a serial, but only 23 percent featured a cartoon, which meant that Walt was not entering the most lucrative of fields.

He soon discovered that for himself. After his *Motion Picture News* ad elicited only tepid responses, Walt sent Mace, who had been a local sales representative for Paramount Pictures, to New York in mid-August to hunt for a distributor. Mace was accompanied by Dr. Cowles, who had gone there to press his oil scheme. But Mace had no more success in person than he had had with the ad. As Adolph Kloepper, the business manager, later told it, Mace was staying at the McAlpine Hotel, and the "bills were amounting to more than the amount of money that we had in the bank." Walt had already ordered Mace home in defeat when, apparently at the very last moment, the sales manager concluded a deal with William R. Kelley, a representative of the Tennessee branch of Pictorial Clubs, Inc., which distributed films primarily to church and school groups.

It was not exactly a rescue. The Tennessee branch of Pictorial Clubs was every bit as inconsequential as it sounded, and the deal Mace made with them was as inconsequential as Pictorial itself. It was also one-sided. Though the contract called for $11,100 for six animations to be delivered by January 1, 1924, it also stipulated that Pictorial need put down only $100 on signing and that the remaining $11,000 was not due until that delivery date, almost eighteen months away. This meant, in effect, that the company would be working for nothing with only the prospect of a payout. (Mace, perhaps recognizing the corner into which he had painted the company, left Laugh-O-Gram almost immediately upon his return to Kansas City.) Walt had to parlay that promise into the repayment of old debts and the generation of new funds. Upon the signing on September 16 he immediately assigned the contract to Fred Schmeltz, the owner of a local hardware store who had advanced Walt money and equipment, to repay him and, in Schmeltz's capacity as trustee, to repay the $2,500 that Laugh-O-Gram already owed Mrs. Cowles as well as smaller sums the company owed as back pay to its employees.

Early that September, even before the Pictorial deal had been finalized, Walt had taken out ads in the *Kansas City Journal* and the *Post* seeking another scenario writer (he advertised in both the men's and women's sections) and girls "with artistic ability for mounting pictures, cartooning." Now that he had a contract in hand, that November he also convinced Iwwerks to leave the Film Ad Co. and join him to do the lettering for the titles and some animation. In a sign of confidence, he grandly offered Iwwerks fifty dollars a week.

This was more of Walt's dizzy unreality. For all of his studying and experimenting, no one at Laugh-O-Gram really knew very much about animation, at least not enough for them to function as a studio. "[O]ur only study was the Lutz book," said Hugh Harman, "that plus Paul Terry's films. . . . We used to get them at the exchange, through a girl who worked there . . . and then take scissors and clip out maybe fifty or seventy-five feet [to scrutinize]. . . . We learned a lot from Terry." Similarly, Walt Pfeiffer said he would get a new Krazy Kat cartoon, bring it to the studio, and run it so that the animators could determine how the New York professionals did it. And it was not only animation technique they lacked but basic drawing skills as well. At one point Walt even held an art class because, according to Rudy Ising, "Walt had the idea that maybe we should learn to draw a little better."

They were groping, learning as they went, improvising even their equipment. The camera stand was made of four-by-fours with a plank laid on them and Walt's Universal camera mounted above. A chain led from the camera to a crank; one turn of the crank meant one frame exposed in the camera. Characters were traced from model sheets to ensure consistency, but the sheets, which corresponded to full shot, medium shot, and close-up, also restricted flexibility. And though Walt used cels, it was not until the third cartoon that Ising suggested they draw directly on the cel rather than paste drawings onto it. Yet the groping sometimes resulted in improvements. At the New York studios the pegs that held the paper in place were at the top of the drawing board, away from the animators' hands. Walt put them at the bottom of the board so that animators could more easily flip the pages and see the action.

There was one area, however, in which Walt Disney did not improvise. Realizing that if he could not yet challenge the New York animators in their drawing prowess, he could at least challenge them in their narrative deficiencies, he did what the New York animators almost never did: he wrote out his scenarios in scrupulous detail as if they were live-action scripts. His story for *Cinderella* began: "FLASH TO CLOSEUP OF ONE FAT LADY IN HAMMOCK reading 'Eat and Grow Thin'—another girl very skinny sitting in chair—they are eating out of it—slim girl puts down book—she is cross-eyed—she begins talking to fat girl—fat girl answers back." In the margins, in blue pencil, were the initials of the animators for each scene: D for Walt himself, H for Harman, R for Ising, and U for Iwwerks.

The pressure to finish quickly was intense—they had no money—but Walt did not allow the financial strains to subvert his other purpose: to forge a community to replace the family he had lost. Only one of the employees, Lorey Tague, was married. The others, who had neither responsibilities nor romantic entanglements, formed an infantile gang of pranksters and hams. A friend who visited Walt's office at the time asked Walt if he was making any money. "You smiled and said, No, but you was having fun. Again I thought, Will he ever grow up?" Walt Pfeiffer said that the group arrived at the office at nine each morning and stayed until midnight. "It was more fun than pay," he recalled. "You didn't look at it as work." Adolph Kloepper spoke of the "happy spirit that existed that we could still laugh and appreciate a good gag. I well remember too that we all had many belly laughs when discussing a story or material and Walt would explode some wild gag to incorporate in the story." Sometimes they would head to the roof of the building and pose for the camera or they would go to nearby Troost Lake and shoot footage of themselves. On weekends the staff took out the Universal camera and prowled the streets, looking for accidents. If they failed to find one, they would often stage one to shoot. On one occasion, thinking that the Universal camera was not impressive-looking enough, they rigged two large cans to a box and then cruised, pretending to film. "[P]eople would come up and pose and say, 'Where are you from?' " Rudy Ising said. "And we'd say, 'New York.' "

The fun was a compensation for and a release from the constant duress of scratching for money. The studio was a wonderful club, but Walt was a poor manager and, by his own admission, incautious with money. (Of his father's frugality, Walt said, "I didn't inherit any of that thrift.") "It will take another five thousand to put the place over," Red Lyon, the cameraman, wrote his mother that October, "an additional fifty or hundred thousand to put in a real production plant next spring. We originally capitalized only enough to get out four pictures of our series. Our fifth is nearly done." But despite the pressure and the lack of funds, he said, "I am going to sit tight. I have the greatest opportunity I have ever had and I'm in for everything but my false teeth." The next month Cowles loaned Walt another $2,500, but it only tided them over. "Walt's checks kept bouncing," Ising recalled. "All of us eventually worked for nothing." Already a process server was visiting the office, asking for "Mr. Dinsey." Several times Walt fended him off by insisting that "Mr. Dinsey" was not there, until Walt Pfeiffer called Walt's name when the server happened to be in the office and Walt confessed: "Yeah, I'm Walt Disney. But my name is Disney, not Dinsey!" Within two weeks of his writing his mother that he was "in for everything," Lyon now wrote her that the company was "worse than broke," $2,000 in debt and losing $4,000 more each week, and that he was "going to try and sell my stock—loan the money to the company and possibly quit and get me something more sure." Still, he said, they had been "turning out some real pictures." These were the skewed fairy tales—a *Puss in Boots* where a cat convinces a young suitor that he can win a princess's hand by emulating "Rudolf Vaselino," a send-up of silent-film heartthrob Rudolph Valentino, and winning a bullfight; or *Red Riding Hood*, where Red is chased by a young man in a flivver while her granny is off at the movies.

Though the financial situation was never less than dire almost from the company's inception, Walt maintained his peculiar confidence and persistence. "He had the drive and ambition of ten million men," claimed a secretary who was dating a photographer across the hall and did some of Walt's clerical work at the time. It was an indication of both his desperation and his ingenuity that by the end of October he had taken out yet another newspaper ad, this one declaring that Laugh-O-Gram had added the "feature of photographing youngsters to its regular business of making animated cartoons" and offering customers a projection service to show the films. In effect, Walt was angling to shoot baby pictures to keep Laugh-O-Gram afloat.

As the company continued to sink, there was more scrambling. A month later, probably through the intercession of Dr. Cowles, Walt was approached by a dentist named Thomas B. McCrum of the Deaner Dental Institute in Kansas City. McCrum would receive grants of $500 from local merchants to finance educational films on dental hygiene, and he asked if Laugh-O-Gram might be interested in producing one, *Tommy Tucker's Tooth*, about two boys—Jimmie Jones, who did not take proper care of his teeth and was thus denied a job, and Tommy Tucker, who did exercise dental hygiene and won the job. Walt quickly agreed, but when McCrum asked Walt to come to the institute to finalize the deal, Walt had to demur. He had left his only pair of shoes at the shoemaker's and did not have the $1.50 he needed to retrieve them. McCrum, who lived just down the street from Walt, offered to pay the shoemaker and then pick Walt up to close the deal.

Walt recruited the cast from local schools, including Benton, and shot during school hours once or twice weekly that December. (The film included a brief animated section showing bacteria with pickaxes hacking away at teeth.) "Walt Disney at each filming knew exactly what he wanted us to do and how we were to do it," remembered John Records, who played Jimmie Jones. "We all liked him immediately." Records told another interviewer that it was obvious Walt liked kids and knew how to handle them. At the end of the shooting he brought them into the office, where the animators were bent over their desks working on the fairy tales, and rewarded the children with five- or ten-dollar bills.

But the fifty or sixty dollars Walt said he finally cleared from the film hardly provided a respite, especially when the Tennessee branch of Pictorial Clubs declared bankruptcy just months after concluding its deal with Laugh-O-Gram. The New York parent of Pictorial assumed the assets of its Tennessee outlet but none of that company's debts, triggering a long process of Laugh-O-Gram trying to enforce a contract for which it had already done significant work and toward which it had a substantial obligation. By early January 1923, with the economic pressure intensifying, Walt was being dunned by his landlord for failure to pay the office rent, and it was only through the largesse of Dr. Cowles again that the company eventually covered that debt, the light and telephone bills, and the salary still owed the departed Leslie Mace. Still, even with the loans from Cowles and from hardware store impresario Fred Schmeltz, the firm had nothing to spare. Kloepper recalled leaving Cowles's office with Walt after picking up the payroll one Friday and seeing a dollar bill in the gutter. "I think we both made a grab for it," Kloepper said, "but I got the dollar bill. And I held it up and I said, 'Walt, we're going to have lunch.' And we did, on the dollar bill."

But Walt, the go-getter, *still* had not surrendered hopes for success. With no money in the offing from Pictorial or any other source, he presented a new scheme that February. He announced a series of shorts that would combine "animated cartoons and spicy jokes." In truth, he had already done so with the Lafflets, and he simply hired a woman to detach them from the beginning of the fairy tales and re-edit them for distribution. That month he began contacting New York distributors, among them Universal Pictures, even writing another prospective buyer, in an obvious attempt at brinkmanship, that Universal was considering the Lafflets. This campaign also proved fruitless. "We have looked at your product and think the animation is extremely good," H. A. Boushey, Universal's general manager, wrote Kloepper on April 4, "but we do not see how we can place it on our release program at the present time." Another distributor responded that "we do not believe we would have any trouble whatsoever placing your 'Laughlets' with one of the better distributors on a percentage basis," but like all the nibbles this one came to naught.

With the Lafflets gambit having failed, Walt now hatched yet another plan of aesthetic bravado. For several months—inspired, he said, by a series created by New York animators Max and Dave Fleischer entitled Out of the Inkwell, in which cartoon figures entered a real world—he had been thinking about a live action–animation combination, though he wrote one putative animator that doing so was "very trying and expensive" and had "not proven profitable, as yet." In March, once again running out of money and alternatives, he decided to ignore those impediments and attempt another series that he thought might, in his words, "crack the market" and save the company. "We have just discovered something new and clever in animated cartoons!" he gushingly wrote a number of distributors, describing his innovation as a variation on Out of the Inkwell, "but of an entirely different nature, using a cast of live child actors who carry on their action on cartoon scenes with cartoon characters." He anticipated one-reelers, roughly seven minutes in duration, to be released every two weeks or once a month.

Specifically, the series would feature a little girl named Alice, like Alice in Wonderland, who entered a cartoon world and interacted with cartoon characters. For the lead role he chose a precocious blond four-year-old named Virginia Davis, a child actress whom he had seen in an advertisement made by the Film Ad Co. for Warneker's Bread. (Davis later said that she ate a piece of bread slathered with jam, smiled broadly, and smacked her lips.) He offered no salary—he did not have any to give—but promised her parents five percent of any money he received for the film, which he had titled *Alice's Wonderland.* The deal evidently included the use of the Davises' home as the set.

Though in May Walt had assured distributors that *Alice's Wonderland* would be finished "very soon," this was more wishful thinking. In addition to having to scrape for financing, the month they began shooting they were evicted from the McConahy Building and moved into new quarters above the Isis Theater on the second floor of the Wirthman Building just up the street. Already in June Walt was writing one distributor that he had not completed the film as planned due to "numerous delays and backsets [setbacks]" but that he fully expected to take a print with him to New York in July. By this time many of the staff, including Iwwerks, who had been paid only fitfully, had departed the company, and Pfeiffer had returned to Chicago.

In the end there would not be money enough for a New York trip. There would not be money enough for anything, save finishing *Alice's Wonderland*, and Walt wound up doing virtually all of the animation himself. "We twice had to move during the night because we couldn't pay the rent," Rudy Ising said. There was not even enough money for food. "We didn't ever have three square meals a day," Carmen Maxwell recalled. "My mom used to mail us a cake once in a while and that was really something." Walt and the others would take meals at the Forest Inn Café on the first floor of the McConahy Building where the owners, Jerry Raggos and Louis Katsis, extended them credit, and when the credit ran out, Nadine Simpson, the secretary who was dating the photographer Baron Missakian across the hall from Laugh-O-Gram, typed menus in exchange for their meals. Walt paid his own bill by taking pictures of Raggos's baby. "When my credit ran out I was tempted to go and eat, order my meal and tell them I couldn't pay," Walt remembered. "But I didn't have the nerve. I was so damn hungry." Instead, he lived on leftovers from Missakian's photo shoots until Raggos caught him scavenging and decided to extend him credit once again.

And if there was no money for food, there was no money to live either. At the time he made *Alice*, he was rooming in a two-story wooden frame house at 3415 Charlotte Street owned by Mrs. Gertrude McBride, who generously let Walt stay even after he had fallen twenty-five dollars behind in the rent—he would repay her a decade later—but eventually he left and slept on rolls of canvas and cushions in the office. He "slept there for quite some time in order to save money," Kloepper remembered, and subsisted on cold beans he ate from a can. (Walt had gotten so thin that Mrs. McBride was sure he had tuberculosis, like his brother.) He took his baths once a week at Union Station, where he paid a dime for the privilege.

Without a staff or finances, Laugh-O-Gram was now a shell. It did not even own its one asset, *Alice's Wonderland*, because Fred Schmeltz, in advancing his periodic loans, including the rent at the Wirthman Building that July, had secured them with a chattel mortgage on virtually all Laugh-O-Gram's equipment and products, among which was the new cartoon. Though in March the stockholders had decided to recapitalize at $50,000 and though the plan had been approved by the state in July, this was financial bluster. Nothing was left of Laugh-O-Gram, and it had no hope of producing more cartoons. Walt tried one last desperate scheme to save the company, trying to interest the *Kansas City Post* in a weekly newsreel, but that failed too. "That seemed to wash up all prospects in Kansas City," he said.

It was over. Uncle Robert advised him that his only recourse now was to leave Kansas City, and Roy told him he should "get out of there. I don't think you can do any more for it." Though Walt said he could have technically avoided responsibility by claiming that he was a minor at the time of the company's incorporation, he chose instead to declare bankruptcy. In any case, no one seemed to blame Walt for Laugh-O-Gram's demise. "[A]t no time did anybody enter a claim," said Nadine Simpson, not entirely accurately, "as we all knew it was the fault of no one person, especially Walt's." Roy attributed the problem to Walt's associates. Thinking either of Pictorial or of Schmeltz, he said that Walt had "gotten mired down with crooks." Rudy Ising saw problems elsewhere. He attributed the company's failure to location: "Our ideas were great, but we were in the wrong area. Kansas City wasn't the place for this kind of work."

But with his grand scheme for an animation studio dashed, Walt once again seemed surprisingly blithe. Throughout the failures—the fairy tales, Lafflets, and *Alice's Wonderland*—throughout the days without meals and nights with restless sleep, throughout the constant begging for funds from Cowles and Schmeltz and even Roy, throughout it all Walt Disney seemed never to lose faith. "I never once heard Walt say anything that would sound like defeat," Kloepper remembered. "He was always optimistic . . . about his ability and about the value of his ideas and about the possibilities of cartoons in the entertainment field. Never once did I hear him express anything except determination to go ahead." Phineas Rosenberg, the attorney who handled the bankruptcy, concurred. "Most people filing for bankruptcy are disturbed or bitter," he said. "Walt wasn't."

He seemed confident beyond any logical reason for him to be so. It appeared that nothing could discourage him. In later years he would say that he was constitutionally imperturbable, free of doubt, and happy—always happy. "I have no recollection of ever being unhappy in my life," he once said. "I was happy all the time. I was excited. I was doing things." But this was also for show. Though Walt normally did possess a kind of intrepid faith, a child's faith that things would turn out right, which explains his doggedness and his myopia, at the time of the Laugh-O-Gram bankruptcy, at the age of twenty-one, he was less unaffected than he may have seemed or wanted others to think. He was, he later admitted, "crushed and heartbroken"—crushed at having failed and heartbroken at having disappointed so many who had trusted in him and had lost money for their trust: "That first big setback got me right down and out." He swore he would make good and pay the creditors back. At the same time he said that the Laugh-O-Gram bankruptcy had left him tougher, more determined, and inured to failure.

Now he thought only of leaving Kansas City, leaving the failure. He considered going to either New York or Hollywood, then settled on the latter, where Roy was now recuperating and where Uncle Robert had relocated. He needed to leave. He would visit Union Station and "stand there with tears in my eyes and look at the trains going out . . . I was all alone. I was very lonesome." He still had no money—he lived now at Iwerks's house or with the Cowles family—but he did have a contact: Carl Stalling, the organist at the Isis Theater, in the same building to which Laugh-O-Gram had moved before its collapse. Through Stalling Walt managed to get a contract from the Jenkins Music Co. to make what he called a "Song-O-Reel," a live-action film with lyrics posted on the title cards, allowing the audience to sing along with the musical accompaniment. With his production of *Martha: Just a Plain Old-Fashioned Name*, based on a song by Joe L. Sanders, Walt earned just enough money to buy a used motion picture camera on trial. (He developed the negatives himself to cut costs.) He spent the next two weeks, as he had in the early days of Laugh-O-Gram, going door to door in a well-to-do residential section of Kansas City looking for parents who might want films of their children. Again he developed the negatives and printed the film himself, making ten to fifteen dollars per job, which allowed him to pay off the camera and save enough for a train ticket to Los Angeles. When a movie fan decided he wanted to make his own films, Walt sold him the camera for twice what he had paid, thus giving him a little extra for his trip.*

*Years later Mrs. Kathleen Viley would claim that she and her husband, Dr. Leland Viley, had helped bankroll Walt at Laugh-O-Gram with $6,000 and then, after he photographed their six-month-old daughter that July, gave him another $3,000 to go to California. Walt acknowledged photographing the Vileys' baby and earning enough to go to California, but there is no evidence whatsoever that the Vileys staked Walt in any other way. W.J. Viley to Walt, Sept. 8, 1958, V file, Walt Disney Corr., 1958, Q–Z, A1572, WDA; Kathleen Viley Cayot to Walt (Oct. 1962), C file, Walt Disney Corr., 1962, A-Christmas, A1590.

It was a bittersweet departure. Before he left, he visited the people to whom he owed money, telling them he had resolved to go west and offering small partial payments. He gave most of his personal belongings to the Harman brothers with the directive that they be sold and the proceeds distributed to his creditors, including Jerry Raggos. Of Laugh-O-Gram's remaining assets, Hugh Harman, Rudy Ising, and Carmen Maxwell got a note for $302 from Schmeltz allowing them to purchase most of the animation equipment, after which they set up their own short-lived animation studio, Arabian Knights Cartoons: A Thousand and One Laughs. The other creditors, according to Walt, wished him well, told him he would need a grubstake for California, and graciously said he could send the money when he succeeded.*

He spent his last night in Kansas City having dinner with Edna Francis and complaining about his business misfortunes. The next day the mother of Louise Rast, his brother Herbert's wife, prepared three bags of meals for him to eat on the train trip west and loaned Walt a suit of her son's clothes. He did not have a suit of his own, only a pair of loud threadbare black-and-white-checked trousers, a checkered jacket, a gabardine raincoat, and an old brown cardigan. His suitcase was frayed cardboard, half of which was packed not with clothes but with animation equipment, and his only extravagance was a five-dollar pair of Walkover shoes he had bought with the money from the sale of the camera. He was driven to Union Station by a friend of Louise's brother—a man whose main boast in life, according to William Rast, would later be, "I took Walt Disney to the station when he went to Hollywood." There was, Walt said, no one to see him off, though Rudy Ising later recalled that he and some of the other Laugh-O-Gram veterans were on the platform filming his departure.

Of Kansas City, where Walt had lived for ten of his nearly twenty-two years, he said he learned there "what it meant to shift for myself, to take advantage of opportunity, and the thing which every American kid must learn—to take the hard knocks with the good breaks." Kansas City had provided a tough lesson for an essentially carefree young man. But he was leaving with his hope intact. "It was a big day, the day I got on that Santa

*Even so Walt left behind a mess and left the hapless Iwwerks, who, probably at Walt's behest, filed the bankruptcy petition, and others to sort it out. The petition was granted in October, but it would be years before all the claims would be resolved—years during which Pictorial was finally successfully pressured for the remaining $11,000 on its contract plus an additional $1,000, years during which Schmeltz's priority from his chattel mortgage would be challenged, and years during which the court would approve a settlement of roughly forty-five cents on the dollar.

Fe, California Limited," he remembered. He was "free and happy." And he remembered another feeling too, a more powerful feeling, "as if he were lit up inside by incandescent lights." Bruised by disappointment in Kansas City, Walt Disney was now heading toward what he was certain, even now, would be success. The go-getter was heading to Hollywood.

Three

WONDERLAND

Though in later years he frequently invoked his midwestern roots and called himself a Missourian, Walt Disney was made for Hollywood. He loved dress-up and make-believe, was boisterous, outgoing, self-aggrandizing, and histrionic, and craved attention. Hollywood was his spiritual destination. Even for the general public, roughly forty million of whom, or one-third of the country's population, attended the movies each week in the early 1920s, Hollywood was more than a provider of entertainment. It was the capital of the imagination, the symbolic center of release and recklessness, the "most flourishing factory of popular mythology since the Greeks," as British observer Alistair Cooke would later put it. Hollywood was where one went to realize one's dreams, which was why Walt's grandfathers had both headed to California before being side-tracked and why Walt himself had now gone there. Just as his youthful energy converged with and was intensified by the postwar national spirit, in Hollywood the dynastic Disney dreams of escape—and Walt's own longing for transport that had been nursed on the farm in Marceline and then expressed in drawing and in animation—converged with a national vicariousness. In Hollywood he was home.

But if Walt Disney was made for Hollywood, he himself questioned whether Hollywood was made for him. He hardly looked like a movie swell. He arrived early in August 1923 in his borrowed suit with nothing but pluck and his peculiar self-confidence. (Despite his penury, as his wife would later tell it, he had traveled first-class because he "always wanted the best way.") His own clothes made him seem shabby and downscale, as did the months of near-starvation in Kansas City that had melted off the pounds he had gained in France and made him cadaverous. "He looked like the devil," Roy recalled. "I remember he had a hacking cough, and I used to tell him, 'For Christ's sake, don't *you* get TB!' "

Despite his outward confidence, he was worried about how he would make his way in Hollywood. Though he had brought his reel of *Alice's Wonderland* and his drawing implements with him, he was not hopeful about his prospects in animation. He now felt he had gotten into the business too late, that it was too insular, that he would not really be able to break into the big time of animation, which was, in any case, centered in New York. "I had put my drawing board away," he told an interviewer years later. "What I wanted to do was get a job in a studio—any studio, doing anything," though in truth his aspirations were larger and more fanciful. He now hoped to get a job as a live-action director somewhere.

He loved motion picture studios—the very source of fantasy. Early one morning that first week he took a bus out to Universal City in the San Fernando Valley and by flashing his old Universal News press card, which he had kept from the time he worked as a stringer shooting newsreels, he managed to wangle a pass. He wandered the lot, walking through the sets, not leaving until late that night. He called it "one of the big thrills I had." Soon afterward he toured the Vitagraph studio with his cousin Alice Allen, who was visiting from the Midwest. He also got onto the Paramount lot, where he ran into an old Kansas City acquaintance who was picking up work as an extra and who encouraged Walt to apply for a job on a Western riding a horse; he got the role, but the shoot was rained out, and Walt was replaced when it was rescheduled. He spent time exploring Metro too.

Roy, who had been working as a door-to-door vacuum cleaner salesman before suffering a relapse of his tuberculosis and landing back in the Veterans Hospital in Sawtelle in what would later become the Westwood section of Los Angeles, thought Walt was lazy and typically overconfident (an "infection," Roy called it) about his employment prospects, only pretending to apply for jobs so that he could linger at the studios. "Tomorrow was always going to be the answer to all his problems," Roy said. "He was hanging around this town and I kept saying to him, 'Why don't you get a job?' And he could have got a job, I'm sure, but he didn't want a job." But contrary to Roy's impression, Walt was not just wandering dreamily through studios. He spent his first two months on those expeditions trying to convince someone to hire him and even had the temerity to approach producers for advice. At the same time he unsuccessfully trudged around Los Angeles with his print of *Alice's Wonderland* hoping to find a distributor. Some suggested he take the print to New York, where the distributors might be more receptive. Since Walt did not have the money to go east himself to lobby, he sent the print to a well-connected intermediary named Jack Alicoate, who represented Lloyd's Film Storage Corp., where the film had been held during the Laugh-O-Gram dust-up with Pictorial, and Alicoate, a generous man, circulated it. Grabbing at anything while it made the rounds and he awaited the distributors' verdict, Walt revived his comic strip, "Mr. George's Wife," and pitched that too, without any more success than he was having with his film. He even had new stationery printed: "Walt Disney Cartoonist."

By September, already despairing of getting a job as a director and having no prospects on *Alice*, he reverted to an old plan. One of the first things he had done when he reached Los Angeles was to buy a Pathé camera at Peterson's Camera Exchange—"Cameras affected him the way alcohol affects dipsomaniacs," his daughter Diane would write—and rig it up with a secondhand motor. Now he visited the theater impresario Alexander Pantages, a prominent vaudeville promoter who also owned several of the larger motion picture houses in Los Angeles. Walt did not get to see Pantages himself. He met instead with a factotum outside Pantages's office, to whom he suggested a "special little joke reel" just like the Newman Laugh-O-grams, only with "the name of Pantages splashed all over it, to add prestige and keep the name Pantages before his theatre patrons." The man dismissed Walt, saying that they were not interested, but Pantages happened to have overheard the conversation, emerged from his inner sanctum, and said he would like to see a reel. Walt headed back to Uncle Robert's house, where he was staying, and began to animate a sample.

And there was another glimmer of hope. Even before leaving Kansas City, Walt had been sending dozens of letters soliciting distributors for

Alice with his promise of having "just discovered something new and clever in animated cartoons!" and receiving polite rejections when he received anything at all. But among those to whom he had written while he was still in Kansas City trying to stave off bankruptcy was an unusual distributor named Margaret Winkler—unusual because she was the first and only female film distributor in the country. An immigrant from Budapest, Hungary, Winkler was a petite, round-faced, plain, and pleasant-looking young woman—she was twenty-eight—but her appearance belied what her son would call a feral energy, a quick mind, and a short temper. She had been the secretary to Harry Warner of the Warner Bros. film company, who was stationed in New York, though she was ambitious enough to use her position to travel to film conventions on the West Coast and make connections. By one account, Pat Sullivan, the creator of Felix the Cat, had approached Harry Warner in 1921 to distribute his Felix cartoon series, which had recently been dropped by Paramount. Warner demurred, but he encouraged his secretary to explore the offer. She and Sullivan signed a contract in December. "I think the industry is full of wonderful possibilities for an ambitious woman," she told *Exhibitor's Herald*, shortly after the signing, "and there is no reason why she shouldn't be able to conduct business as well as the men."

Margaret Winkler did. By the time Walt contacted her in May 1923, she was also representing the Out of the Inkwell series devised by Max and Dave Fleischer, in which Koko the Clown escapes his inkwell into a real, which is to say photographic, world; between Felix and Inkwell she had become one of the leading animation distributors in America. But at the time Walt Disney wrote her, trouble was brewing for Winkler. The Fleischers were threatening to leave, and she and Pat Sullivan, who was so difficult and addled by alcohol that he once allegedly urinated on the desk of Paramount Pictures head Adolph Zukor to force a concession, were locked in a bitter dispute over the renewal of the Felix option. Walt's timing, then, could not have been better, which is no doubt why Winkler wrote back to this unknown novice almost immediately upon receiving his first letter, saying that she would be "very pleased" to have him send a print and that "if it is what you say, I shall be interested in contracting for a series of them." But however encouraged Walt may have been, he did not have the print to send while he was in Kansas City because Fred Schmeltz, the Laugh-O-Gram creditor, had it. He continued to correspond with Winkler, apologizing over the delays while refusing to admit that he did not own the print or that he would have to remonstrate with Schmeltz to show it; by the time he reached Los Angeles, Winkler was getting impatient over his foot-dragging. Corresponding, she wrote him drily early in September, was "about all it [their communication] has amounted to." But in a sign of her own desperation over the Felix and Inkwell threats and not realizing that Walt had no more than one Alice, she asked him "[i]f you can spare a couple of them long enough to send to me so that I can screen them and see just what they are, please do so at once."

Most likely the first week of October via Alicoate, Winkler finally screened *Alice's Wonderland* in New York and pounced. "BELIEVE SERIES CAN BE PUT OVER," she wired Walt on October 15, while emphasizing that the photography of Alice had to be more finely focused and the camera held steadier. She also cautioned, by way of limiting Walt's financial expectations, "THIS BEING NEW PRODUCT MUST SPEND LARGE AMOUNT ON EXPLOITATION AND ADVERTISING THEREFORE NEED YOUR COOPERATION." She offered $1,500 for each negative of the first six films and $1,800 for each of the second six. To show her "good faith," she said she would pay the full $1,500 immediately upon delivery of each of the first six rather than wait until she had gotten bookings or money for them. Walt, clearly with no room to negotiate and ecstatic at having any offer, promptly wrote back accepting. At the same time he abandoned the Pantages project.

The very next day Winkler sent the contracts, incorporating her financial terms and calling for the delivery of the first Alice no later than January 2, 1924. She also included an option for two series of twelve more films each in 1925 and 1926 and a clause that awarded her full rights to all of the films Walt produced during the contract term. That same day, obviously wanting to move quickly, she asked Walt for any photographs of the actress playing Alice and of Walt, and for biographies of each. Most likely in an attempt to impress him, she telegraphed Walt again the same day suggesting that he write Harry Warner, who would attest to her competence. Walt did contact Warner, who wrote back that Winkler "has done very well" and that "she is responsible for anything she may undertake," but by that time Walt, as anxious to proceed as Winkler, had signed the contract, with Uncle Robert serving as his witness. Returning the documents, he wrote Winkler that the first film, *Alice's Day at the Sea*, was already in production and would be delivered as early as December 15. She responded a week later, a bit extravagantly: "I see no reason why these should not be the biggest thing brought out for years."

But despite the months he had waited for just this news and despite his promise to deliver a new film quickly, Walt was ill prepared to launch another animation studio. The day he received Winkler's initial telegram on October 15, he headed to the Veterans Hospital, where Roy was convalescing from his tuberculosis. As he later told it, again dramatizing for effect, he arrived late, around midnight, crept onto the screened porch where the patients slept, and shook Roy awake to show him the offer and celebrate. But his enthusiasm quickly elided to panic. "What do I do now?" he asked Roy, and pleaded with him to leave the hospital and help him get started. Roy agreed to meet Walt the next morning at Uncle Robert's house for a strategy session. Roy left the hospital the following day—he claimed that an examination had shown that he was healed—and never returned.

Meanwhile Walt had a pressing issue to resolve. Winkler's contract had been predicated on having Virginia Davis play Alice, but Virginia was back in Kansas City. The day he received the contract from Winkler, the day he was meeting with Roy at Uncle Robert's, he wrote Virginia's mother urgently telling her that he had finally gotten a distributor, that he had been screening *Alice's Wonderland* in Hollywood, that "every one seemed to think that Virginia was real cute and thought she had wonderful possibilities," and that if Virginia came out to star in the series, "it would be a big opportunity for her and would introduce her to the profession in a manner that few children could receive." He pressed Mrs. Davis to make a decision as soon as possible since he was hoping to start production in fifteen to twenty days, and he ended rather grandiosely, not unlike Winkler in her letter to him, saying that "it will be but a short time till the series will be covering the world."

In point of fact, Mrs. Davis had brought Virginia out earlier that summer for a movie tryout but found that so many other mothers were attempting the same thing that the studios refused to see them. She had returned to Kansas City and was planning another assault on Hollywood in November when she received Walt's message. Four days after his first letter Walt wrote again, this time offering terms: $100 a month for the first two months, rising in $25 increments every two months to $200 for months nine through twelve, with an option of $250 a month for the next series. He justified what he admitted was a "low salary at start" by pointing to, as Winkler had pointed out to him, the initial advertising and publicity costs.

Though Walt could not have known it, the Davises did not need much encouragement. Virginia's father was a traveling furniture salesman who was on the road most of the time. Her mother was a stagestruck housewife who had enrolled Virginia in dancing school when the girl was two and a half years old, and she seemed determined to get her daughter into the movies. In addition, Virginia suffered from double pneumonia, and doctors told the Davises that the dry California climate would be beneficial for her health. Mrs. Davis convinced her husband that he could sell furniture from California as easily as from the Midwest and that Virginia would have a career, but even Roy was struck by a man giving up thirty years in Kansas City for the promise of only $100 a month. Mrs. Davis wired her acceptance to Walt on October 28.

Now he had his contract and his star, but he had neither a company nor a staff nor, most important, any money to jump-start the operation. So when Walt met Roy on October 16 at Uncle Robert's house on Kingswell Avenue in a quiet residential section of Hollywood, part of the plan was to ask their well-heeled uncle for a loan. Since Robert had encouraged Walt to come to Los Angeles, the brothers assumed that getting the money would be something of a formality. But their uncle balked. Walt's beloved Aunt Margaret, his advocate, had died of pneumonia, and Robert had married a much younger woman—Ruth Disney said that he had dated both the woman and her mother, and there was a "toss-up" over which would get him—who was pregnant at the time Walt requested the loan, which seemed to put Uncle Robert in a less-than-generous mood. Moreover, Walt and his uncle, who was as stubborn and disputatious as Elias, had gotten into a silly argument over whether Walt's train west had passed through Topeka, as Uncle Robert insisted it had, or had not, as Walt insisted. Even after Robert's new wife, Charlotte, called the railroad and proved Walt right, Robert bristled. "He demanded a lot of respect and didn't think I gave it to him," Walt remarked.

Finally, there was the matter of a sixty-dollar loan Walt had received from his brother Ray. Walt still owed him the money when, the previous Christmas, Roy wrote from California suggesting the brothers pitch in to buy their mother a vacuum cleaner and agreeing to kick in Walt's share since Walt was broke at the time, if Walt would collect Ray's share. Ray refused to contribute, saying that Walt should cover the cost out of what he owed. By the time Walt reached Los Angeles, Uncle Robert had heard that Walt had welshed on his debt and did not think his nephew was a good credit risk. But Walt, who was not about to lose his opportunity with Winkler over petty family squabbles and who did not want to be considered a failure like his father, was persistent and nothing if not ingratiating. By November Uncle Robert had softened and loaned Walt $200 in mid-month, another $150 ten days later, another $75 early in December, and yet another $75 on December 14, for a total of $500, albeit at 8 percent interest, all of which Walt repaid the very day he received his second payment from Winkler early in January. The Disney brothers were also begging money from their friends and other relatives. Even before receiving the offer from Winkler, Walt had gotten a $75 loan from Carl Stalling, the organist at the Isis Theater in Kansas City, and received $200 more from him after signing the contract; $50 from Robert Irion, who was married to Walt's aunt; $25 from Roy's girlfriend Edna Francis and even $200 from Virginia Davis's mother.

Though Roy had helped solicit these funds—all except the money from Edna, which Walt had requested without his knowledge—it had never been Roy's intention to join the enterprise, and in any case he had no experience whatsoever in entertainment. "I was just helping him, like you'd help a kid brother," he later said. But Roy could never resist his younger brother. He claimed that Walt, who was so enthusiastic and innocent-seeming, "would win your heart, and you wanted to help him, really," and he admitted that he was afraid that without his protection, his "fervent protection," Walt would have been taken advantage of. To prevent that, Roy, professing a "love of Walt," agreed to become Walt's manager and guardian angel in business as he had been in Walt's life. In late November, when Walt moved out of Uncle Robert's house to a room in the Olive Hill Apartments, Roy joined him there and moved with him again in December when Walt found another, cheaper room, for fifteen dollars a month, at 4409 Kingswell in an apartment building almost directly across the street from his uncle's house. The two even saved money by eating at a cafeteria where they could split the meat and vegetable courses.

The room was just two blocks from a cream-colored, one-story brick storefront at 4651 Kingswell with a large display window. Early that October, either in anticipation of the Winkler deal or as a work space for the Pantages reel, Walt had rented a cramped office at the rear of the building behind the Holly-Vermont Realty Company, which occupied the front. (The rent was only ten dollars a month, which was raised to fifteen dollars in December.) By December, with the contract signed, the brothers were also renting a lot nearby on Hollywood Avenue for outdoor shooting and had bought a new camera, lumber and tools, a curtain to separate them from the realtors, and a box of cigars as a thank-you present for Uncle Robert. They had a name for the studio too: Disney Bros.

So they began. Usually Walt would take Virginia to the vacant lot, drape a white tarpaulin over a billboard there for a backdrop, and shout instructions to her: "Look frightened!" or "Sit down and pretend you're mad." That was, Virginia said, his favorite instruction: *Let's pretend.* There were no real rehearsals and no more than a single take since Walt did not have enough film to reshoot. "It was very informal," Virginia Davis recalled. "During the silent days we would have a lot of the curious children and the neighbors come around to watch what was going on." More often than not, it was catch-as-catch-can, filming whenever he could, wherever he could. Once Walt was shooting in Griffith Park when he was stopped by a policeman who asked to see a permit. Walt didn't have one, so he packed up his equipment, only to sneak back through another entrance. Every time he spotted a policeman that afternoon, he would stop shooting, pack up again, and move.

While he shot the film of Alice, Walt had a hood over the camera and would mentally trace the position of the cartoon characters with whom the girl would be interacting. Then back in the Kingswell office he would run the film frame by frame so that he could animate the figures in what would be the white spaces around Alice—white because of the white tarpaulin. Using his camera stand, he would shoot the animations. Finally, he would combine the film of Alice and the animations in the development process so that they appeared to be in the same place—the real girl and her cartoon playmates.

Though he animated it alone—he animated the first six Alices virtually by himself—he nevertheless delivered *Alice's Day at the Sea* on December 26, ahead of the contractual schedule, and received his first $1,500 check. He knew the film wasn't especially good, and Winkler, who had been so lavish in her predictions of success, did not disagree. She called it only "satisfactory" and thought there was room for improvement, though she tempered her criticism by telling Walt that "the progress I have made in the film industry has been due to the fact that I know just what my people want," and she said her requests were made in that spirit. Two weeks later she sent another letter enjoining Walt to "inject as much humor as you possibly can" into the next cartoon, adding that "[h]umor is the first requisite of short subjects such as 'FELIX', 'OUT OF THE INKWELL' and 'ALICE.' " When he shipped his second Alice, *Alice Hunting in Africa*, late in January, he averred that he had "made a good deal of improvement" and assured Winkler somewhat abjectly that "I will make it a point to inject as many funny gags and comical situations into future productions as possible." She wrote back saying that she found the comedy still wanting and warned that "future productions must be of a much higher standard than those we have already seen." Ultimately she rejected the film as unreleasable and demanded that Walt redo it.

If this demoralized Walt, he certainly did not show it, any more than he had displayed defeat in Kansas City. He seemed impervious, continuing to forge ahead. By early February he had moved his studio next door to a nearly identical building, this time occupying the entire floor. Now anyone approaching saw the name "Disney Bros." in gold leaf on the large front window. Behind the window was Roy's office, just a nook really, with his desk at the front right and a utility table in the center, where he and Walt punched holes in the cels to keep them immobile on the camera stand. To the left was a row of tables for inkers and painters—the people who traced Walt's drawings onto the cels in ink and then painted them black, gray, or white before sending them to be photographed. At the rear, through a long entranceway, was the camera room where the cartoons were shot and film stock was stored, and to the right of the camera room at the back behind the front office was the animation room, where desks were lined up against the far right wall.

As yet Walt had no one to sit at those desks. It was essentially a two-man operation. Walt conceived the stories, directed the live action, drew the animations, and timed the exposures so that the movements were smooth. Roy did the books, occasionally manned the camera, and even washed the cels so they could be reused, though he still tired easily and often spent his afternoons back at the apartment resting. (They had asked Ray and Herb to join them, but the brothers declined.) In January they hired three women, to ink the outlines of the drawings on the cels and paint them, and two men, who probably helped operate the animation camera and generally assisted. The next month they hired their first animator, Rollin "Ham" Hamilton.

But Walt, who had very little executive talent or inclination, was never as interested in building an operation or running a business as he was in improving the product, not only as a way of satisfying Winkler, though obviously this was a consideration, but also as a matter of personal pride and psychological need. He sincerely wanted to make good animations, sincerely wanted to be counted among the best at his craft. As it was, Winkler seemed mollified by the next Alice, *Alice's Spooky Adventure*, calling it the "best you have turned out" and telling Walt that on the strength of it she was able to make deals for the series from southern New Jersey to the District of Columbia. But Walt, continuing to apologize for the quality of his cartoons, insisted he could make them better, saying that he had invited professional critics to his previews and that he was trying to be a "little different from the usual run of slap stick and hold them [the films] more to a dignified line of comedy." On receipt of his fourth film, *Alice's Wild West Show*, Winkler wired: "if none of the future ones are any worse we will have the leading single reel of the film market."

She was so well satisfied that early in June, when Winkler made her first visit from New York to Disney Bros., she discussed expediting the schedule to two films a month. Already by this time Walt had been hectoring Ubbe Iwwerks to leave the Film Ad Co., where he still made only forty-five dollars a week and complained of run-ins with Cauger's relatives, and come help him in Hollywood; but the invitations gained a certain urgency with the new impending workload, since Walt still had only Hamilton helping him with the animation. At just about the time Winkler arrived in California, Iwwerks finally agreed to Walt's proposition. "Boy, you will never regret it," Walt wrote him eagerly, using California as an enticement. "[T]his is the place for you—a real country to work and play in." Accompanied by his mother, Iwwerks made the trip from Kansas City to Los Angeles in seven days—Walt had arranged for him to drive Virginia Davis's father's big roadster, which Mr. Davis had left back home—and arrived just before July 1, when he was put on the payroll at forty dollars a week—a cut he was willing to take to get away from Cauger.

Little had changed about Iwwerks since Walt had first met him five years earlier, except his name; he had anglicized it from "Ubbe Iwwerks" to "Ub Iwerks," though no one but Iwerks would have regarded the change as significant. He was still meek, withdrawn, inexpressive, and monosyllabic. "Where two words would barely suffice, he used one," a colleague once remarked of him. But there was one change, and it was important. From his training in Kansas City he had become a deft and rapid animator, and over the following months that summer he assumed an increasing amount of the workload from Walt, who had begun to doubt his own artistic skills. "I never made a drawing that I liked," he would tell a reporter years later.

The change in Iwerks led to a change in the cartoons. Partly as a result of Iwerks's hiring, the emphasis in the series shifted from Alice to her cartoon compatriots, and by late summer Winkler was even suggesting that Walt do away with the live opening and closing entirely, even though this would make the films more difficult and expensive to produce. At the same time, Walt and Iwerks began experimenting with ways of improving the live action–animation combination, using what was called a "matte," a cutout that could be placed over the camera lens to block off areas where the animated figures would be, rather than photographing Alice against the white tarpaulin. By August Walt was already assuring Winkler that they were working to make the "girl stand out plain and distinct when she is acting with the cartoons," and that the photography would be "good, if not perfect," in future productions. He added that they would endeavor to "make nothing but sure-fire laugh-getters."

But for all Walt's continuing assurances of improvement, and for all his genuine desire to make outstanding films, the Alice movies, even with Iwerks's contributions, were only slightly better than routine. "Walt's concept of the photography of live action was about on a par with the average box camera enthusiast," one animator recalled, "and Iwerks's animation was no match for the sophisticated drawings of Dick Huemer's [the Fleischers' main animator] Koko." It wasn't just the comparative crudity of the photography and drawings that marked these films. They were also imitative and unimaginative. How much this may have been the result of Walt's inexperience or own lack of imagination is difficult to say. Winkler continuously stressed broad gags at the expense of story or personality and continuously pressed him to watch other animations, even though Walt was inclined, as he had written Winkler in February, to try something different from, and more refined than, the run-of-the-mill head-banging. Since Disney Bros. could not afford a projection room, the entire crew, including Roy, would jump into their cars and head down to the Hill Street Theater every time the program changed just to see the latest of Paul Terry's Aesop's Fables so they could borrow from it. "I was ambitious and wanted to make better pictures," Walt would say, "but the length of my foresight is measured by this admission: Even as late as 1930, my ambition was to be able to make cartoons as good as the Aesop's Fables series." Turning out a film every two weeks, he had no time to be terribly creative—to work, as he put it, "for a twenty dollar joke rather than a one dollar joke," adding that "[a]s fast as we thought of a gag, we animated it." The scenarios, though still written out as they had been in Kansas City, consisted largely of an enumerated list of "Gags and Situations" like "Cat does crazy roping in first scene" or "Cat makes toboggan out of horse to get down steep hill."

As for the Cat who performed these gags, the sudden appearance of a plump black feline with sharply pointed ears, goggle eyes, and a thick tail in *Alice's Spooky Adventure* was probably instigated by Winkler, no doubt as a way of copying the more successful Felix series and perhaps, some animation historians have speculated, even as a way of irritating Pat Sullivan, with whom she was constantly bickering. Walt had more or less specialized in cats when he was making his Laugh-O-Gram fairy tales; there was a cat in *The Four Musicians of Bremen* and obviously a prominent cat in *Puss in Boots*. But the emergence of the cat in the Alice series, whom he later named Julius, was Walt's first venture with a continuing cartoon character, and it was not long before he, no less than Margaret Winkler, was opting for the cat over the little girl, whose screen time kept diminishing as Julius's increased. Though Alice continued to receive top billing, it was Julius, cunning, brave, and self-possessed, who now initiated the action—Julius who pulled on a bull's skin so that Alice could best him in a bullfight and win $10,000 (*Alice the Toreador*), Julius who made a unicycle out of his tail to rescue Alice from a pack of vicious Chinese rats (*Alice Chops the*

Suey), Julius who grabbed a smoke ring to rise over a prison wall and then turned his tail into a ladder to fetch Alice (*Alice the Jail Bird*), and Julius who attached the "idea" balloon that billowed above his head to one end of a dachshund and the dachshund's own "idea" balloon to the other end to make the dog into a dirigible (*Alice's Balloon Race*). Many of these gags—particularly Julius's ingenuity with his detachable tail, his worried pacing back and forth, and the big question mark that sprouted over his head when he ruminated—were directly cribbed from Felix at the distributor's insistence, essentially turning the Alice comedies into not-so-thinly veiled Felix cartoons. At one point the likeness between Julius and Felix was so close that Walt warned his staff they were flirting with copyright infringement.

Yet for all their derivativeness and for all the concessions that Walt made to Winkler, subjugating his creative instincts to hers, the Alice comedies did express a fundamental vision of Walt Disney. Unlike Out of the Inkwell, where Koko cavorts in a photographic reality that is obdurate and unyielding, in the Alices a real girl enters a fantasy of her own devising—a pliable world that, whatever the girl's misadventures there, always finally conforms to her desires and Julius's machinations and in which chaos ultimately yields to control. And in creating this situation, Walt was also creating through his cartoons a metaphor of liberation and power. If the Fleischers suggested the implacability of the physical world, Walt suggested the malleability of one's own psychological world into which one could escape as Alice does. In Walt's world one was always eluding capture, always trying to keep the intrusions of reality at bay. But as beleaguered as they often were, the denizens of Walt's world were nevertheless free and omnipotent—so long as they stayed there, so long as the world remained intact, so long as they kept themselves separate from the real world.

And yet, sadly and eventually disastrously for Walt, reality did intrude on the Disney Bros. and kept intruding in the form of a man named Charles Mintz. Mintz, thirty-four years old at the time he and Walt Disney met, was something of a mystery even to those who claimed to know him. He was born in York, Pennsylvania, of German parents and was graduated from Brooklyn Law School, but accounts diverge from there. By one, he entered the jewelry business. By another, he entered the film business as a producer. What all agreed upon was that he could be cold, stern, and ruthless—in the words of one employee, "a grim-faced man, with a pair of cold eyes glittering behind the pince nez" who "never talked to the staff. He looked us over like an admiral surveying a row of stanchions." A chain-smoking tyrant with a swagger, he loved the trappings of authority too. His most prized possession was a large collection of police badges.

None of this would have mattered to Walt Disney except that just a month after he signed his contract with Margaret Winkler, she married Mintz, and Mintz moved into her company, effectively taking control when she became pregnant. Winkler had been forbearing, issuing gentle critiques but also offering encouragement. Mintz instead pressed constantly and curtly for improvements in the cartoons—they were too "jumpy," too unevenly exposed—and even temporarily dispatched his brother-in-law, Margaret's brother George, to Hollywood to supervise production. But by the summer of 1924 Walt was complaining that as much as he wanted to make better cartoons per Mintz's dictates, he simply did not have the resources to do so. The cartoons cost nearly as much to make as he received in compensation, he wrote Mintz that August, and the studio found itself in a "very tight place." If Mintz could not send him an advance of $900 due on their next picture—Walt offered to pay a forty-dollar premium—they would not even be able to get their last picture out of the laboratory where the film was being developed. That same month he was forced to give the Davises a promissory note for Virginia's services. "We need money," Walt wrote again, clearly desperate, two weeks later. "I am perfectly willing to sacrifice a profit on this series, in order to put out something good, but I expect you to show your appreciation by helping us out." Walt wanted the full $1,800 owed on the next film, minus what he called a "fair discount," but Mintz did not have the money either and instead advised Walt to be patient.

Patience did not come easily. Throughout 1924 the Disney brothers had been forced to continue borrowing from Uncle Robert to meet their payroll, loans of $100 or $150 or $175, which must have been especially difficult for Walt after Uncle Robert's initial reluctance. They had little money personally either. Walt and Roy took funds from the company as they needed them, five dollars here or ten dollars there, so as not to drain the treasury. For would-be film moguls they lived modestly; the rent on their apartment was only thirty dollars a month, though Walt, who always had his eye on the showier things, did splurge on a secondhand dark-gray Moon roadster that became a special source of pride. Not until December 1924, more than a year after forming the studio, did the brothers begin drawing a salary, fifty dollars each per week, and even then they drew it irregularly.

Yet as hard as it was, the patience seemed to be paying off. George Winkler left New York for Los Angeles on December 8 with a new contract and the prognosis that "while things are not 100% rosy, still there is a whole lot that looks favorable." The contract called for another twenty-six Alices at $1,500 per film, with $900 payable on delivery of the negative and $600 payable within ninety days after that—terms that were actually worse than those of the first contract, which had paid Disney Bros. $1,800 for the last six pictures. The only advantage was that Disney now shared in the receipts after the first $4,000, with the studio receiving the next $350 and splitting the proceeds equally after that, though it seemed unlikely at the time that the films would actually return enough of a profit for the Disneys to share.

There was one other revision in the contract, and this would bring another dose of reality. With the increase in the number of films to be produced from twelve to twenty-six, beginning March 1, 1925, the Disneys were now asked to deliver a new cartoon every three weeks for the first thirteen installments and every two weeks for the second thirteen. Even under the current schedule of one film every four weeks, Walt was having trouble delivering the pictures, not to mention profiting from them. What made matters worse was how seriously he took both Winkler's and Mintz's injunctions to make the cartoons better—injunctions he really didn't need. He was constantly crowing to Mintz over improvements—adding more gags to the cartoons, getting a new motor drive for the camera that sharpened the cartoon photography and a new "rock steady" tripod that kept Alice from jiggling on the screen—and seemed to relish telling Mintz how well he thought the films were being received.

Improvement was his mantra—the only way to succeed, the only way to get the recognition he so badly wanted, the only way to create a full fantasy world for himself. Walt admitted now that he had been a little too cocksure when he began the studio and that he had had a lot to learn about making films, even hiring a cameraman from Century Studios, apparently at George Winkler's behest, because he conceded he did not know enough about running the camera himself. In attempting that February to recruit two of his old Laugh-O-Gram colleagues, Hugh Harman and Rudy Ising, now that he needed to enlarge the staff to meet the new expedited schedule, his main selling point was how much California could offer since "You have'nt [*sic*] much chance for big stuff where you are," and how much they needed to learn if they hoped to succeed in animation—"things that can only be learned by actual experience with experienced people." As he had in Kansas City, Walt would provide the training. He added: "After you see Los Angeles, Hollywood and the surrounding country, you will feel ashamed of yourself for not coming sooner."

By the end of April, after much dickering over salary, both Harman and Ising decided to join Disney Bros., swelling the staff to nine, exclusive of Walt and Roy. By one account, their arrival that summer had an immediate effect, if not on the look of the animations then on the look of the animators, all of whom, including Walt, made a friendly compact to grow mustaches. "Walt wanted to shave it off," his wife would later recall, "but we didn't let him." But in point of fact Walt and Iwerks had actually grown their mustaches *before* Harman and Ising arrived, at least as early as April. And apparently Walt, with his love of disguise, had been thinking about growing a mustache for years, quipping to a friend in a photo inscription from France: "Well here I am but no mustache." Roy said the mustache was not the result of a lark but a corrective to Walt's youthful appearance; he needed it to look older than his twenty-three years so that he could better bargain with business associates and with his staff, many of whom were older than he. "[H]e did have a complex for a while of trying to make himself look older," Roy said, "because he was so young."

The small toothbrush mustache would become a permanent fixture on his face (and on Iwerks's too), and the physical feature most closely identified with Walt Disney once his image became familiar to the public. But there was another change in Walt's life that spring that would be just as permanent and far more significant to him. Walt Disney had fallen in love.

II

He had heretofore shown surprisingly little interest in women. Though his mother had thought of him as a high school lothario and though he could be sensitive and even tender—he routinely closed letters from France to his McKinley classmate and Bea Conover's friend, Virginia Baker, with "love"—he did not chase women or have especially close relationships with them. He seemed to prefer to pal around with the guys. "[H]e was a little different," Walt Pfeiffer remembered. "I mean he didn't have an eye for the girls then. And even when he enlisted and went over to France after the war . . . when he came back he didn't think too much of girls. In fact, I don't think that he ever had one that I know of." "I was normal," Walt explained years later, "but girls bored me." They didn't share his interests, he said.

Part of this feeling may have been disillusionment after Bea Conover jilted him. Part of it may have been a youthful desire to avoid complications and anything that he could not control. In Kansas City, even as a young man on his own, he concentrated on animation and on Laugh-O-Gram rather than on romance, though he occasionally dated Dorothy

Wendt, the young sister-in-law of his patron Dr. Cowles, taking her to the Alamo Theatre or the dance pavilion at the Electric Park, and he continued to write her after he left for California. And there was another girl named Peterson whom he saw infrequently and with whom he also maintained a correspondence. Still, he viewed marriage as a trap and said he had resolved—while watching his coworkers glumly clock in at the Film Ad Co., chained to their jobs—that he would not get married until he was at least twenty-five years old and had saved $10,000.

Nor was it only Walt who seemed to disdain romance. Roy, now thirty-one years old, had put his nuptials to Edna Francis on hold while he convalesced from his tuberculosis and saved money, but the delay had dragged on for years—dragged on, in fact, until one evening that spring of 1925. As Roy told it, most afternoons he would retire to the apartment the brothers shared for a nap to regain his strength, then return to the studio, work a few hours, and leave again to prepare dinner. On the fateful night Walt, dissatisfied with his brother's efforts, stormed out on the meal. Roy said he was so piqued by this little tantrum that he decided at long last to send for Edna. Though they had been betrothed since at least 1920, he formally proposed in a telegram. Edna, now thirty-five and the last of the six Francis children to marry, arrived in Los Angeles with her mother on April 7—"It was getting to be that time, you know," she later told an interviewer—and she and Roy were wed four days later in Uncle Robert's house on Kingswell Avenue. Walt was the best man, and a girl named Lillian Bounds was the maid of honor. In home movies of the wedding Walt can be seen bear-hugging her and kissing her passionately.

Bounds was an inker at the studio and one of its first employees. She had come to Los Angeles late in 1923 from Idaho to visit her sister Hazel Sewell, who was living with her husband and seven-year-old daughter on Vermont Avenue in Hollywood, not far from the Disneys' studio. A friend of Lillian's sister had taken a job at Disney Bros. painting cels, and when the Disneys asked the girl if she knew someone else who might be interested in working there, the young woman told Lillian that she would recommend her on the condition, Lillian later said, that "you won't vamp the boss." "I had no idea of vamping him," Lillian remembered, not seeming terribly impressed by Walt. The first time she saw him he was wearing his old brown cardigan and a raincoat and was complaining that he did not own a car. (He wouldn't purchase his Moon roadster until later that year.) She only took the job, she said, because it was within walking distance of her sister's house and didn't require her to spend bus fare. She went on the studio rolls on January 19, 1924, at a salary of fifteen dollars a week.

Just shy of her twenty-sixth birthday, nearly four years older than

Walt, Lillian was the very picture of a contemporary urban woman, short, slender, and pretty, with a broad smile and dark hair fashionably bobbed, but like Walt and Roy, she was actually the scion of pioneers and was steady rather than effervescent. Her paternal grandfather, James L. Bounds, was one of the first settlers in the Northwest Territory that became Oregon and then had made a small fortune in the California gold rush before retiring to Idaho. James's son and Lillian's father, Willard Bounds, was variously an Indian scout, a blacksmith, and the United States deputy marshal who drove the "hack" wagon in 1895 from Lewiston, Idaho, to Spalding carrying $626,000 in twenty-dollar gold pieces that the government paid the Nez Percé Indians to acquire their lands. Lillian, who was born three years later, grew up among the Indians in the outpost of Lapwai, which was settled in a narrow valley in Nez Percé country in the northern handle of Idaho, where the Indian Agency and the Indian school were both located and through which ranchers drove their cattle over the fenceless fields to the stockyards at North Lapwai. It was isolated country—though Lewiston was only twelve miles away, it was inaccessible except by ferry across the Clearwater River—and it made for rugged individuals. If the Disney forebears had looked like hardscrabble farmers, lean and ascetic, the Boundses looked redoubtable—Willard broad and bulky with an oversize mustache, and his wife, Jeanette, or Nettie, as she was called, short and stout at more than two hundred pounds. These were solid people.

But like the Disneys, they were no match finally for their environment. Willard and Nettie had ten children, of whom Lillian was the youngest, and the family struggled constantly. Whatever wealth the Boundses had acquired from the gold rush was long gone. Moreover, for years Willard, who had become the government blacksmith, was debilitated by intestinal problems that would eventually lead to his death in 1916. "They never knew if there was going to be enough to eat," Lillian's daughter said. "Mother never even had shoes that fit properly." After Willard's demise, Lillian and her mother relocated to Lewiston, where Lillian attended business school and where she was living when she decided to visit Los Angeles.

When she met Walt Disney that January, there was no attraction, much less romance. At most, even though she lived within walking distance of the studio, Walt would drive her and a coworker home. Yet Lillian observed that he always dropped off the other girl first and then stopped near but never in front of Lillian's sister's house—because, Lillian thought, he was probably embarrassed by his somewhat ragged appearance. Despite his threadbare clothes, Lillian admitted that it was during these rides home that "I began to look at him like he was a somebody." Walt had begun taking notice of her too. One night as he was letting her out, he asked whether he could see her socially if he got a new suit. Lillian assented, so he and Roy went to Foreman & Clark's, a downtown haberdashery, and bought themselves each a two-pant suit, which was a significant expense for them. (Roy had set a thirty-five dollar limit, but Walt exceeded it.) When Walt arrived to pick her up for their date—he had gotten tickets for *No, No, Nanette*—he stood up, proudly displayed his new gray-green double-breasted suit, and with no self-consciousness whatsoever asked her sister, brother-in-law, and niece how they liked his wardrobe. His naïveté, Lillian said, charmed them. Yet for all his winsomeness and attractiveness, Lillian made it seem as if they were dating by default. "I didn't have any other dates," she said, "and neither did he."

Even after they began dating regularly, it often seemed less a love match than a matter of companionship. Walt visited Lillian frequently—"All of a sudden Walt was at our house an awful lot," recalled Lillian's niece, Marjorie—yet even the Sewells could not figure out whether Walt was there because of Lilly or because Hazel was an excellent cook. Walt would go there in the evenings, roust Marjorie from the sofa where she slept, and send her off to Lillian's room so that he and Lillian could have privacy. Then, before he left, he would carry Marjorie back to the sofa and gently tuck her in. After he bought his Moon roadster with its light on the radiator—he had previously borrowed Virginia Davis's father's Ford for the rides home—he and Lillian would go for long drives through the orange groves east to Pomona and Riverside and even north to Santa Barbara. Other times they would go to Hollywood tearooms for dinner. Frequently they would go to the movies. On these drives and on these dates, Walt would be talking, incessantly talking, but he would talk not so much about their future as about his—about his work and plans and what he hoped to accomplish in animation. "He never thought of anything, I think," Edna Francis Disney recalled, more expansively than Lillian herself ever did, "except his work and Lilly. . . . [H]e just thought about her and his work."

After a courtship that lasted at least a year, the decision to get married, like the decision to date, also seemed to come by default—fulfilling an obligation. Even decades later Walt was less than sentimental about the betrothal. "How do you know it's not just a need for companionship?" he would ask his daughter about marriage. Roy suspected that Walt appreciated Lillian's compliant nature. "Walt was a dominating person. And she was the kind that just went along with him and what he did," he would later say. "She worshiped him, and anything he wanted to do was all right with her." Walt himself agreed that Lillian was a "good listener. I'd talk to her about what I'd hope to do, and she'd listen." By the time he began thinking about proposing, Lillian had advanced from inking cels to helping Roy manage the studio's business office, and even she later joked that she made so many mistakes while she was taking dictation that Walt said he had to marry her to relieve the studio of her, though at another time she said that Walt had decided to marry her because he was in debt to her for the paychecks he had asked her not to cash when the studio's coffers were empty. As Walt told it, he proposed indirectly—by asking Lillian to choose between their pitching in to buy a new car or a ring, as he had once asked Bea Conover whether he should buy a canoe or a camera. Lillian said the ring, so Roy and Walt found a wholesale diamond dealer who for seventy-five dollars sold them a ¾ carat diamond mounted on a thin platinum band and surrounded by blue sapphires. "It looked like a locomotive headlight to me," Walt said.

The couple's plan was to wait, but after Roy had married and left Walt the apartment, Lillian said they moved up the schedule because "Walt didn't like to be alone." Early that July they took a steamer to Seattle, then the train to Lewiston—in preparation Walt had taken $150 in cash from the studio and unilaterally increased his salary to $75 a week, $25 more than Roy's—where they were married at Lillian's brother's house in a small ceremony on July 13, 1925, with Lillian, in a lavender gown, giggling nervously throughout. They spent their honeymoon at Mount Rainier National Park and then in Seattle and its environs before stopping in Portland on their way home so that they could visit Elias and Flora, who had not been able to attend the wedding. But as Walt remembered it, even his wedding night, in keeping with his courtship, was less than romantic, possibly because he was just too timorous to make it so. He said he had a toothache so painful that he could not sleep and spent the evening helping the porter shine shoes until morning, when he found a dentist and had his tooth pulled.

III

When Walt returned to the studio in August, he was riding a wave. The trade reviews of the Alice comedies that summer and fall were positive, occasionally bordering on enthusiastic: "Here is a clever cartoon novelty . . . and should lend an acceptable variety to your program" (*Film Daily*); "Capital entertainment is furnished by the first of the new series of the 'Alice comedies' " which show "plenty of invention by their creator"

(*Motion Picture News*); "Each one of these Walt Disney cartoons . . . appears to be more imaginative and clever than the preceding [one]" (*Motion Picture World*). It was a measure of the Alices' success that Virginia Davis had begun making personal appearances, and George Winkler informed Walt that he was talking to publishers about a book tie-in for Christmas. In fact, the Disneys themselves were feeling confident enough about the future that a week before Walt and Lillian's nuptials the brothers placed a $400 deposit on a plot of land with an office building on Hyperion Avenue near Griffith Park, in the Silver Lake district just east of Los Angeles and close to Kingswell—Walt had let Roy make the choice between that plot and one in Westwood—where they intended to erect a larger studio than the Kingswell storefront.

But if Walt began to feel as if he were finally secure that summer, the feeling didn't last, and by the fall there were renewed tensions with Mintz. Ostensibly the main problem again was money. With the new contract in January, Mintz had accelerated the schedule, but Walt was so desirous of getting the money from Mintz even more quickly, especially now that he was married and contemplating the new studio, that he was delivering the films faster than the contract stipulated, one every sixteen days instead of every three weeks, and Mintz, just as desirous of holding on to his money, ordered Walt to desist. Walt answered that so long as he did not deliver pictures at intervals any *greater* than three weeks, he could ship them as frequently as he liked and threatened to seek another distributor if Mintz failed to remit the money due. The threat, almost certainly a bluff, prompted Mintz to send a long and angry letter that October decrying Walt's ingratitude ("had any of the first seven pictures that you made, [*sic*] been given to any other Distributor in the whole world . . . they would have thrown them out bodily"), his ineptitude ("the only reason you are making pictures today is because we sent our George Winkler out and, at our expense, taught you what it was necessary to know to produce the kind of pictures you are now making"), and his greed ("we have not made one single dollar on any picture that we have ever gotten from you").

Technically, Walt was right. He could deliver when he pleased. But as a twenty-three-year-old animation tyro, he did not have the clout to take on his distributor, and in any case the dispute was complicated by the fact that even as he and Mintz were trading charges, Mintz was also negotiating a deal with a big national distributor, the Film Booking Office, to pick up his entire product—the Krazy Kats, which he was now producing instead of Felix, and the Alices. Mintz had been distributing the films on what was called a "states' rights" basis, meaning that he sold them state by state to local theater circuits, but independent distribution was rapidly giving way to larger organizations selling to larger territories. Obviously knowing that Walt was ambitious and hoping that he would regard national distribution as a new opportunity to advance his career, Mintz suggested they put their differences aside and agree on a new contract on the same terms as the old contract—$1,500 per film, with $900 payable on delivery of the negative and $600 within ninety days after that, with a fifty-fifty split of all receipts above $3,000—and that Walt come to New York as soon as possible to conclude the deal. "I intend to make your product the leading subject of its kind in the entire world," Mintz wrote in obvious conciliation, echoing his wife's early promises.

As always, Walt needed money to maintain his operation, and he was barely breaking even despite what he believed was the growing popularity of the series. But once again money was not his only or perhaps even greatest consideration. Walt harbored two impulses that often warred: the go-getting impulse to succeed, which could be certified by money and recognition, and the deeper psychological impulse to control, which could be satisfied only by making his films exactly as he wanted to make them without interference. While finally prodding Mintz into sweetening the contract terms slightly—in addition to the $1,500, Walt was now to receive $350 for each film of gross receipts over $4,000 and a fifty-fifty split after that, just as the current contract had stipulated—he added a new clause of his own that indicated just how much he had been chafing at Mintz's aesthetic demands and criticisms and just how much the flare-up with Mintz may have been about power all along: that "all matters regarding making of comedies are to be left to me." Walt may have been bluffing over the money, trying to force Mintz's hand, but was not bluffing about control. There was little sense in creating an alternative world to escape to if one did not shape and command that world. When Mintz derisively rejected this demand, Walt broke off their negotiations and expressed his regrets that their partnership would soon end.

Meanwhile Walt found himself in another quarrel—this one with the Davises. To cut costs that summer, Walt had proposed that he pay Virginia only for the time that she was actually used—at a rate of twenty-five dollars per day. Since she had worked only roughly eighteen days the previous year, this would have amounted to a tremendous saving for the Disneys and a tremendous loss for the Davises. Understandably the Davises erupted at the suggestion, ripping Walt and accusing George Winkler of having angled to get rid of Virginia all along so that he could sign the daughter of a friend. Walt did not want to jettison Virginia now that she was so closely identified with the series, but the focus was increasingly on the animation, not on Alice, and financial pressures and pressures from Mintz forced him to sign another girl, Dawn O'Day, who appeared in only one film, and then four-year-old Margie Gay, both at the twenty-five-dollar-a-day rate. Gay, who had a short dark pageboy where Virginia had long golden curls, and a round baby face where Virginia's face was preternaturally mature, brought a different quality to the series. "Virginia Davis had had something of a post-Victorian image—her appeal was that of a juvenile Lillian Gish," wrote one animation historian, "—whereas Margie Gay was more of the flapper type." But Virginia Davis had a different interpretation of what distinguished her from Gay. She later sniped, "Margie was cute in her little Clara Bow haircut, but all she really had to do was clap her hands, put her hands on her hips and jump up and down," which, whether Davis knew it or not, was an implicit acknowledgment that Alice had become incidental to her own films.

In the midst of the Sturm und Drang with Mintz and the Davises, Walt had one respite: the Disneys moved the studio that February from the two rooms on Kingswell to their new quarters on Hyperion Avenue. It was not a particularly prepossessing place, situated among wild oats and abutting a pipe organ factory and a gas station. One employee described it as about the size of a grocery store—just a single sixteen-hundred-square-foot stucco bungalow into which the Disneys had poured about $3,000 for renovations. Walt later described it as a "little green and white structure with a red tile roof, and a nice little plot of grass in front of us." Still, it represented not only the company's growth and aspirations but also Walt's self-aggrandizement and even pomposity in the face of his modest success. This was *his* studio now. "One evening when Walt and I were discussing our move," Roy once told an associate, "Walt said to me, 'Roy, when we move to Hyperion, I'm going to have a large neon sign erected, reading "Walt Disney Studios." . . . He looked at me as if expecting an argument. I said, 'If that's the way you want it.' And Walt said, 'That's the way I want it and that's the way it will be!' And that's the way it was." The Disney Bros. studio had become the Walt Disney studio.

This was considerable bravado for someone who had reached an impasse with his distributor and was facing the end of his contract. But Walt wasn't going to succumb to Mintz without a fight. He was scheming. Just before moving to Hyperion, in an apparent attempt to break the stalemate, he had written Film Booking Office chief Joseph Schnitzer directly, complaining about Mintz. Schnitzer had notified Mintz, who fired off a letter to Walt saying he was "extremely disappointed" in him. When Schnitzer offered to mediate, Mintz refused, saying that he owned the rights to Alice and did not need Walt. Now Walt blinked, wiring Mintz on February 8 with yet another set of terms: a $500 payment after the first $4,000 gross, then $500 to Mintz and then a fifty-fifty split. Walt also asked to retain the rights to the films. Though Mintz agreed in principle, he continued to haggle, even coming out to Los Angeles to discuss the contract. When it was finally concluded, Walt realized the diminished advance would likely compromise the films. "I want you to understand that it is almost a physical impossibility to make each picture a knockout," Walt wrote Mintz during the final negotiations in what must have been a difficult concession for someone who wanted so badly to excel, "and I only hope that you will be fair enough to let me know when I have a good picture, as well as to tell me about the poor ones." As for the rights, Mintz retained them.

Thus Walt resolved the crisis with Mintz, but he had not resolved the deeper financial crisis or the crisis of status. Even with the new contract he was still scrambling for money and looking for ways to supplement what little he was making on the Alice films. Throughout his time in California he had been soliciting work from Dr. McCrum, the dentist for whom he had made *Tommy Tucker's Tooth* in Kansas City, though he knew any profits would be negligible. He had also offered to produce song films for Carl Stalling, for whom he had made *Martha.* In the meantime he had subcontracted with another company to draw the titles for a serial. By summer 1926 he had finally gotten Dr. McCrum to commit to a new dental hygiene film, *Clara Cleans Her Teeth*, in which Walt starred Lillian's niece, Marjorie Sewell, as a ragamuffin who is ostracized by other children because her teeth have gone rotten.

After his showdown with Mintz, it was clearly humbling to have to make a film on dental hygiene, especially as Walt was trying so manfully to maintain the fiction of his success, even to his own staff. "Walt's office looks like a bank president's loafing room," one of his employees wrote his family of Hyperion. But throughout 1926 the man with the large office was making no more than $300 profit per picture on the Alices, sliding to $100 as he neared the end of the year and of the contract, and plummeting further to a loss of $61.25 on the last of the series. When Mintz asked him to contribute to a fund to fight John Randolph Bray, who was accusing animators of copyright infringement, Walt begged off, saying he could not afford it: "I have borrowed to my capacity and have to squeeze very hard to make things come out right."

And if it was difficult to play the young mogul at the studio, it was impossible to do so at home. He and Lillian had returned from their honeymoon to a tiny apartment on Melbourne Avenue near the Kingswell studio that faced out on an alley. "I remember I was so unhappy because I had never lived in an apartment before," Lillian said. "I was used to homes in Idaho where you could step out of your front door and be in the open." Though Walt received a monthly allowance from the company for his car, it was not until the next year, when the couple moved several blocks south to an apartment on Commonwealth Avenue off Sunset Boulevard, that they were able to buy furniture of their own.

If the humiliations and scrimping weren't enough, yet another new tension arose—one that in its way was even more significant than the problems with Mintz, though it flowed directly from them. While Walt struggled with his finances and with Mintz, he was also, for the first time, beginning to struggle with his staff, which throughout 1926 still numbered fewer than ten, including the janitor. Walt had always been fun-loving, collaborative, and informal—a big kid. According to one employee, the crew would gather in the office or in Walt's apartment and bruit about gags. "Walt would have an idea," he recalled, "—well, let's let Alice be a fireman in this one, or let's let Alice go fishing, or whatever it was. And then we'd work up whatever the type of thing was, fire gags or fishing gags. And then Walt would put them all together to tell the story. He'd try to come up with an idea of continuity." When animating, they would sit in one room, side by side, a group of comrades, with Walt supervising and timing the scenes. Off the job, the group frequently socialized together, spending New Year's 1926 driving down to Tijuana in Walt's Moon roadster and Roy's Oakland.

But that winter the atmosphere at the studio suddenly sobered and soured. The pressures from Mintz, the financial stranglehold, and Walt's own obsession with improving the animations had changed him from a reckless young man to a martinet, pushing, prodding, provoking. Having always to appease Mintz, he now made the staff appease him. Everyone seemed to notice the change in temperament—the change from jovial to tense and snappish. Several cited a "clash of personalities." "I made mistakes," remembered Isadore "Friz" Freleng, a veteran of the Film Ad Co. who joined the studio early in 1927 at Walt's urging, "and Walt—even though he expressed patience in his letters prior to my joining him—didn't show any. He became abusive and harassed me." (Freleng had replaced Ham Hamilton, who had left, Freleng said, because he "couldn't bear the abuse that Walt heaped upon him.") Walt would "make insulting remarks to me," Freleng said, and Freleng would then fire back. "Walt could make you feel real bad when he wanted to," said another early employee. "He was that way," Hugh Harman concurred. "Unless you were 100% for Walt, unless you were doing for him, working for him, he thought you were double-crossing him."

Which, in fact, Harman was. Tired of the harangues and insults, he and Ising had conspired to lure other animators, including Iwerks, to abandon Walt and join them in starting their own rival studio. They had already held discussions with producer Jesse Lasky. "This will leave Walt in a mellavahess," Ising gleefully wrote Carmen Maxwell, an old Laugh-O-Gram colleague, in August 1926, "but business is business."* But before they could actualize the plan, Walt fired Ising for falling asleep at the animation camera with his hand on the button. He fired Freleng too after spotting him riding a double-decker bus when he was supposed to be at work. Freleng said he arrived at the studio the next day to find his desk cleared. Before he left, Ising described the studio as a "den of strife and vexation." Iwerks, who suffered Walt's new abuse with his typical equanimity and counseled others to do the same, described the studio as "Koo-Koo Hatchery" and "Knut Mansion." But the resentments would linger; they would linger long, and they would linger hard. They would linger until they wrecked the studio.

IV

Now there was a sense of crisis. The previous June, Walt had put his staff on a two-and-a-half-week-per-film schedule and had even awarded bonuses to speed the films' delivery to one every two weeks, but between personnel changes triggered by Walt's abusiveness and other bumps like Iwerks's marriage and honeymoon that January, it was becoming increasingly difficult to meet the timetable. Though Walt kept pressuring the staff to improve the animations and though the Alice films did show greater visual sophistication, even Walt realized that the series was losing steam. "I have felt we have sort of been in a rut in regard to the stule [*sic*] and general construction of our plots and gags," he wrote Mintz in February 1927. "I tried every way possible to find out just what was lacking and now I believe I have found 'IT.' " Though Walt didn't say what "it" was, he asked Mintz to take special notice of the new films and tell Walt what he thought. Still, it was a measure of how thin the novelty was wearing that the live action continued to shrink, even as Mintz, for economy's sake, was now urging Walt to increase the cheaper, live-action sections after years of insisting that he shorten them. By early 1927 George Winkler had replaced Margie Gay with yet another girl, Lois Hardwick, who Walt

*In one interview Harman said that he had nursed resentments against Walt since Walt had promised him and Ising a stake in the studio to get them to come out, then reneged. Will Friedwald, "Hugh Harman, 1903–1982," *Graffiti* (Spring 1984).

enthused was "full of life and expression" and the "best yet." Mintz, before reluctantly giving the go-ahead to use her, sniffed that "her legs seemed kind of heavy."

They needed to do something. At the time Mintz, apparently concluding himself that the Alices were in their death throes, was already conducting negotiations with Universal to provide a new cartoon character for another series, and he had asked Walt to provide drawings. "[T]hey seem to think there are too many cats on the market," Mintz instructed. "As long as they are doing the buying, naturally, we must try to sell them what they want." Walt sent him sketches of rabbit characters. Six weeks later, on March 4, 1927, Mintz signed an agreement with Universal, which was reentering the animation field after a ten-year absence, to provide twenty-six shorts featuring Oswald the Lucky Rabbit. Mintz headed to California that same week, presumably to meet with Walt, though *Motion Picture World* reported ominously that George Winkler was also heading out to "establish a specially constructed studio for the purpose of turning out these Oswald comedies." Walt finished the last of his fifty-six Alices that month.

Now suddenly there was an entirely new challenge—not only the new character but the need to produce the films quickly to prove Walt's efficiency to Universal. With Mintz urging him to "shoot the first picture as soon as possible," Walt immediately, even before George Winkler's arrival, began producing the Oswalds and finished the first one, *Poor Papa*, early that April in a little over two weeks. Walt surely recognized what a tremendous opportunity was being afforded him—making a major cartoon series for a major distributor—and how much a success would advance his career. But neither Mintz nor Universal was satisfied with the cartoon, and the latter took the drastic step of refusing to release it. Mintz thought there were too many competing characters in the cartoon and that Oswald needed to be "young and snappy looking with a monocle," not elongated with a heavy round torso, gangly arms, short legs and oversized feet, which is how Walt had had Iwerks draw him. In addition, Universal apparently complained that there was no real story, just a string of gags.

Walt answered that he was disappointed himself and had already begun reconceptualizing the character—"forget the monocle"—and making him lighter and less bottom-heavy, but he also defended his approach. He did not want Oswald to be just a "rabbit character animated and shown in the same light as the commonly known cat characters," he said, meaning that he did not want Oswald to be simply a peg for gags—the direction in which Mintz had always pushed him and which Universal had now rejected. Rather, he wanted to forge Oswald into a distinctive personality, "to make Oswald peculiarly and typically OSWALD." At the same time he fended off criticism that there was insufficient narrative by saying that "[o]ur poorest pictures have been the ones where we went into story detail" and asserting that cartoons cannot really be "built like a feature picture" without losing the constant stream of laughs.

What he was arguing for was something new: gags that weren't impasted on Oswald, as gags were in most cartoons, but instead arose organically from him—from who he was. Even during the Alices, creating personality had been a crusade of Walt's. When Freleng animated a kitten clinging to the edge of a washtub while being scrubbed, Walt beamed that Freleng had made the kitten act like a child. "That's what I want to see in the pictures," he told the staff. "I want the characters to *be* somebody. I don't want them just to be a drawing." One could debate whether Walt really incorporated personality into his revivification of Oswald, but already by the second one and the first to be released, *Trolley Troubles*, which featured Oswald as a harried streetcar conductor who must cope with everything from a recalcitrant cow blocking the tracks to an ornery goat who butts the car and sends it careering off the path, the reception had improved. "I am the LUCKY rabbit," Universal announced brightly in its promotional materials. "I'm the animule Universal discovered after two years' experimentation and preparation seeking the Krazy Kartoon Knockout that would set the industry on its rabbit ears." Though it was puffery—Walt had worked on Oswald for roughly two weeks, not two years—it was not much of an exaggeration, given the initial enthusiasm for the series in the trade press. "Oswald looks like a real contender," *Film Daily* gushed. "Funny how cartoon artists never hit on a rabbit before. Oswald with his long ears has a chance for a lot of new comedy gags, and makes the most of them." "This series is destined to win much popular favor," *Motion Picture News* concurred. "They are clearly drawn, well-executed, brimful of action and fairly abounding in humorous situations." *Motion Picture World* cited Walt by name for making his creations "simulate the gestures and expressions of human beings." Of the third in the series, *Oh, Teacher*, the same publication said, "It contains some of the best gags we have ever seen in cartoons."

To a large degree, this praise was less a reflection of Walt's creativity than of the rather low state of animation in the mid-1920s, when even crude gags and broadly drawn characters could seem inventive against the shapeless gags and barely drawn characters of most cartoons. Yet some animation historians do credit Oswald as an advance over his contemporaries in more substantial respects. One compared the rabbit to silent-film comedian Buster Keaton in his ability to "transform the absurd mechanical environment of the modern world into something useful and humane," and also cited numerous instances of phallic imagery—Oswald's straightening and collapsing ears, for example—that testified to his libidinous nature, something that had not been explored previously in cartoons. Two other historians distinguished Oswald from his predecessor, Julius the Cat, by noting both that Oswald was far more conscious of his body than Julius, more capable of enjoying pleasure and suffering pain, and that his body was far more plastic than Julius's, more stretchable, squeezable, and twistable, leading to more imaginative situations. Even in the 1920s some rival animators regarded the Oswalds as the industry standard. Dick Huemer, who worked for the Fleischer brothers at the time and who had been a standard himself, said that he and his colleagues there would seek them out since, "bad as they look today" (Huemer was writing in 1969), "they were tremendously superior to our things."

Once again Walt seemed to have ridden out a crisis, both aesthetic and financial, and the studio was suddenly thriving again. In preparation for the Oswalds Walt had added staff through the previous winter and spring of 1927, among them a soda jerk named Les Clark from a confectionery around the corner from the old Kingswell studio, who would rapidly become one of his most trusted employees, and Walt's own sister-in-law, Hazel Sewell, who was put in charge of an expanded ink-and-paint department. By the end of the year the staff had grown to twenty-two—a tribute to Oswald's success. Walt had also, no doubt under competitive pressure now that Iwerks's work was gaining recognition, hiked the laconic animator's salary from $70 a week, when he first began drawing the Oswalds, to $120 two months later. He was, Walt wrote Mintz, "a man of experience whom I am willing to put alongside any man in the business today."

Walt himself was only drawing $100 a week at the time and Roy only $65, but they were now clearing roughly $500 on each Oswald and splitting the year-end profits sixty-forty between them—$5,361 to Walt in 1927, $3,574 to Roy. Never one to hold on to his money, Walt bought ten acres of desert land in October and November, possibly at Uncle Robert's behest, since the Disney brothers were also investing in stock for Uncle Robert's and John Cowles's oil drilling venture. More important, in June Walt and Roy had each put a $200 deposit on adjacent lots on Lyric Avenue, in the Silver Lake district at the foot of the Los Feliz hills, not far from the new studio, and they began constructing homes that August.

The homes were not large compared to the mansions of the Hollywood moguls whose ranks they hoped to join; they were only eleven hundred square feet each, with two bedrooms, a dining room, a living room that, at thirteen by twenty feet, was the biggest space in the house, and a kitchen—all in a style that might be described as mock English Tudor. They were Ready-Cuts, meaning they were prefabricated, and, observed one reporter, among the "commonest type of middle-class construction in Hollywood." The total cost, according to Roy, was only $16,000 for both, not an inconsiderable sum at the time but not extravagant either, and even that estimate may have been high. Still, these were the Disneys' first homes of their own. Walt's niece, Marjorie, said his was the finest house she had ever seen.

The problem for Lillian was that Walt, always working and not terribly domestic to begin with, was seldom home to enjoy it. Possibly to keep Lillian company, Walt had her mother move in with them shortly after they took possession in December. "Walt was so good to my grandmother," Marjorie Sewell recalled. "He treated her like she was a queen." (Walt always said that he loved to hear the Bounds's tales of pioneer life on the Idaho frontier.) Walt was sympathetic to Lillian's loneliness. After becoming so preoccupied with a cartoon one night that he stayed at the studio while Lillian waited nervously at home for him, he was so goaded by guilt that he decided to get her another companion that first Christmas on Lyric Avenue. Lillian disliked dogs, though Walt pressed her one day to say what kind of dog she would want if she absolutely had to make a choice. Lillian said she had read somewhere that chows had little odor, so that would be her choice. So Walt went to a kennel, picked out a puppy, fetched it on Christmas Eve, and kept it next door at Roy's house until Christmas morning, when he put it inside a hatbox with a ribbon on top and then asked Marjorie to get it—a scene that would be incorporated into *Lady and the Tramp*. When she received the box, Lillian was upset that Walt would select a hat for her without her approval, but when she opened it and saw the puppy inside, she immediately melted. "I've never seen anybody so crazy over an animal," Walt would say, though he was every bit as smitten. They named her Sunnee. Lillian would not let the dog out of her sight. It slept in their room. When Walt would take Lillian and her mother and little Marjorie for Sunday drives, he always stopped on the way home for ice cream, and he made a point of buying an ice cream for the dog, standing on the curb and feeding it to her. One night when they could not find her, Walt canvassed the entire neighborhood in a rainstorm without success. It was two o'clock in the morning before he could coax Lillian to go to bed. "I've never seen anybody so upset." He found the dog the next morning in Roy's garage, where she apparently had gotten locked in when Roy returned home from work. Thus was calm restored.

V

Then, early in 1928, just as everything seemed to be going so well, came one of the most devastating episodes in Walt Disney's life, an episode that would haunt him throughout his career. With Oswald's success, Mintz had tired of Walt's financial haggling and his angling for control, especially since Walt did not even draw anything himself now and, as Mintz saw it, seemed superfluous. So Mintz instructed George Winkler, who had arrived, as promised, the previous July, to approach Hugh Harman about taking over the studio and relieving Walt of his duties. "I was interested right away," Harman said, "because I was very disappointed in Walt and wanted to get away from him." Walt was completely oblivious to these machinations until January, when Iwerks told him that Winkler, in anticipation of a renewal of the Oswald contract with Universal, had already surreptitiously signed up several of the animators and had asked Iwerks to join them—an offer Iwerks refused. Unaware of how much Mintz had come to doubt his importance or of how much his employees had come to dislike him, Walt couldn't believe that Winkler would try to double-cross him or that his staff would actually conspire against him, and he dismissed the idea out of hand, inadvertently wounding Iwerks by seeming to attack his credibility.

Meanwhile, on February 2, 1928, Mintz as expected signed a new three-year agreement with Universal to provide Oswalds. The Oswalds had been, *Film Daily* wrote in reporting the signing, "one of the best sellers of the 'U' short subject program," adding that "Charley Mintz's organization has been delivering and how." Still refusing to believe Mintz's treachery and brimming with confidence, Walt was in fact preparing to leave for New York to negotiate *his* new contract with Mintz and had planned to ask for an increase from $2,250 per film, which was what he had been receiving, to $2,500. He was so certain of a favorable outcome, if not with Mintz then with another distributor if Mintz proved intractable, that he had Lillian accompany him on what they regarded as a "second honeymoon."

They arrived the third week in February to a bitterly cold and blustery city and found their reception there just as chilly. With two Oswald prints under one arm and a book of clippings under the other, Walt had gone to see Fred Quimby at Metro-Goldwyn-Mayer with the hope, at the very least, of getting a competing bid to put pressure on Mintz, but Quimby told him that "cartoons [were] on the wane" and said he was not interested. (Walt, putting the best spin on the conversation, told Roy that Quimby was just playing hardball and said he would follow up in a few days.) Temporarily rebuffed, Walt headed directly from MGM to Mintz's office to continue negotiations, but Mintz was also playing hardball. Not only did he not offer to increase the advance, he was now offering only the negative costs, which he pegged at roughly $1,400 a film, a fifty-fifty split of profits, and "substantial salaries," which suggested that Walt was not a studio owner in his own right but a subcontractor for Mintz. Walt, aggrieved by the terms, which he no doubt feared would force him to compromise on quality again and cede more control, immediately contacted his old mentor Jack Alicoate, a "reserved and dignified" gentleman, in Walt's words, who had helped broker the original deal with Margaret Winkler for the Alices and who now edited the trade paper *Film Daily*. Alicoate advised Walt to continue dealing with Mintz, but as a hedge he set up meetings for Walt with Metro again and Fox.

"BREAK WITH CHARLIE LOOMING," Walt wired Roy later that day. Before any rupture could be announced, though, and resorting to a bit of chicanery of his own to thwart Mintz, he asked Roy to have an attorney draw up "ironclad" year-long contracts for the staff with two option years. "ALL CONTRACTS WITH ME PERSONALLY THEREFORE MY SIGNATURE NECESSARY BEFORE CONTRACT IS COMPLETE ASSURING US PROTECTION WITHOUT RESPONSIBILITY." Walt warned that the contracts should be "held in readiness" until he gave Roy the word. And he closed reassuringly: "DON'T BE ALARMED EVERYTHING OK."

But of course everything was not okay. Walt and Lillian had lunch at the Hotel Astor as guests of Mintz and Margaret Winkler the next day, Friday, March 2, where Mintz refused to discuss business, but "from what remarks were dropped," Walt wrote Roy, "I could see that he had something up his sleeve." After Mintz suggested they meet in his office the next morning, Walt wired Roy frantically to get the contracts with the staff signed immediately lest Mintz or George Winkler get wind of the plan and proffer contracts of their own. "MAKE THEM SIGN OR KNOW REASON BEFORE ALLOWING THEM TO LEAVE," Walt telegraphed Roy with the new imperiousness that had alienated the staff. When Roy wired back that the staff had refused to sign the contracts, Iwerks's warning to Walt was finally confirmed: since jobs for animators were scarce and the men should have jumped at Walt's offer, he realized that Mintz and George Winkler had indeed contracted with the staff behind his back. In fact, Walt was told that Mintz had been talking to an animator—referring no doubt to the conversation with Harman—to take over the operation under George Winkler's supervision. Walt had suffered two heavy blows. He had become expendable at his own company, and his own employees had betrayed him.

Walt pretended to be sanguine. "CAN GET PLENTY OF GOOD MEN," he wired Roy confidently later that morning after visiting the Krazy Kat studio, where the staff "treated me royal." But he spent the rest of a very long and frenetic day meeting with Bill Nolan, who had been one of the leading animators on Krazy Kat for Mintz and whom Walt had been seeing in New York in an attempt to lure him to California; with Metro, which told him yet again that it had decided not to release any cartoons that year; with Fox, which said it would not handle any cartoons that it did not produce itself; and with his advisor Alicoate, who told him discouragingly that the entire industry was now "topsy turvy" and that it would be another year before things settled. Finally he met again with Mintz, bluffing that he had already received two unsolicited offers but that he preferred working out a deal with his old partner. Mintz, however, was having none of it, raising his offer only slightly to $1,750 per cartoon plus 50 percent of the profits. Walt was so frightened and desperate that he said he would take the offer if Mintz would produce the contract immediately. Mintz said he could not do so and cagily told Walt that he should take one of the better deals he had mentioned, even offering to help advise him. As Walt was leaving, Mintz barked, "Go on home to your wife and come back and see me tomorrow and let's get down to business."

But Walt did not go back to his hotel. Instead, he turned once again to Alicoate with a new plan: he would approach Universal and promise to make the Oswalds himself without the middleman. It just so happened that Alicoate had recently attended a boxing match with Manny Goldstein, a Universal executive, who told Alicoate that Mintz was receiving $3,000 per picture and that he would be interested in meeting with Walt. That same day Walt met with Goldstein in "some big bug's office," as Walt described it to Roy. Universal had to deal with Mintz for the rest of the year because of the newly signed contract, Goldstein told him. But he said they would be happy to deal directly with Walt the following year since they "want good pictures" and "they won't stand for Mr. Mintz cutting down costs in any way that might lower the standard." In the meantime, if Walt could not find a rapprochement with Mintz, Goldstein offered to intervene for him. He asked Walt, however, not to tell Mintz about their meeting. Walt wired Roy late that night that he felt sure "WE WILL COME OUT ALL RIGHT EVEN IF IT IS A BIT DISSILLUSIONING [*sic*] WE WERE SHOOTING TOO HIGH." He added with a certain satisfaction that Hugh Harman and Ham Hamilton,* two of the traitors, would probably

*Hamilton, after leaving the studio in December 1926 in a dispute with Walt, had returned in May 1927.

find themselves "in the cold" because Universal was unlikely to take cartoons from an entirely new staff.

But Walt had underestimated Mintz and overestimated Universal. In concluding his deal with the distributor, Mintz had granted Walt no rights to the character that Walt had created, thus leaving Walt no recourse. That Saturday at his office Mintz made Walt a final offer. He would give Walt $1,800 per picture, up from $1,750, plus 50 percent of the profits from Universal, but he presented a new and startling stipulation: Mintz would take over the Disney organization, paying Walt and Roy each an additional $200 a week as his employees. Angered and distraught, Walt refused, went directly to Universal again, who offered to talk to Mintz, and hurriedly fired off a telegram to Roy asking him to find out the intentions of the rest of the staff and to send a check for $100 for additional expenses. He returned to his hotel, Lillian later recalled, fuming that he was out of a job but at the same time said he was glad of it because he would never work for anyone again.

"Well, we are still hanging around this Hell Hole waiting for something to happen," Walt wrote Roy ruefully on March 7, three days after his meeting with Mintz. "I can't rush things any faster—just have to do the best I can. BUT I WILL FIGHT IT OUT ON THIS LINE IF IT TAKES ALL SUMMER and all our jack." (The trip had, in fact, cost over $1,000.) As it turned out, it would only take another week, most of which he spent continuing to cajole Nolan, who was known for his speed and facility, about joining the studio, and continuing to chase prospects. But Nolan eventually joined the new team drawing Oswald, and no prospects were forthcoming. Walt could do nothing but wait out the year and hope that Universal would fulfill its vague promise to cast off Mintz. When Walt left the city for Los Angeles on March 13, he had nothing—no Nolan, no character, no contract except the one for the Oswalds that he was obligated to animate under the terms of his deal with Mintz, no staff save for the few who remained loyal like Iwerks, no plan, and perhaps most important of all, no cartoonland to provide a haven from the real world.

He would, in later years, talk often of this episode as a betrayal, saying he had warned Mintz that those who had turned on Walt would also turn on him someday, which in time they did. "He told it just like the plot of one of his stories where good will win and the villain will be defeated," recalled one of his longtime animators. "He loved telling that story because it was so poetically just." He would say that you had to be careful whom you trusted; that he had learned that you had to control what you had or it would be taken from you; that he had seen how duplicitous the business world could be. He said he had learned all these lessons and would never forget them. But as he and Lillian headed back to Los Angeles on the New York Central Cannonball with nothing but these lessons and the sunny bromides he was writing home to buck up Roy's spirits, the eternally optimistic Walt Disney, who had ridden out crisis after crisis, had one terrifying thought: he would have to begin all over again.

Four

THE MOUSE

If the story is to be believed—and it would be repeated endlessly over the years until few doubted it—this was to be one of the most momentous journeys in the annals of popular culture. At the outset Walt was furious. "He was like a raging lion on the train coming home," Lillian would recall. "All he could say, over and over, was that he'd never work for anyone again as long as he lived; he'd be his own boss." Lillian admitted that she had another response—not rage but fear. She was in a "state of shock, scared to death," since they had no source of income now and no idea of what the future held for them. Even before leaving New York, Walt said he had tried to devise a new character to replace Oswald, without success. When he was not venting about Mintz and his own treasonous crew, he spent most of his time on the trip sketching on the train stationery. Somewhere between Chicago and Los Angeles, he later said, he wrote the scenario for a cartoon he called *Plane Crazy*, about a mouse who, inspired by Charles Lindbergh's 1927 solo flight over the Atlantic Ocean, builds himself a plane to impress a lady mouse. Walt read the story to Lillian, but she said she couldn't focus because she was upset by the name Walt had bestowed upon his character: Mortimer. "The only thing that got through to me," she told an interviewer, "was that horrible name, Mortimer. . . . I'm afraid I made quite a scene about it." "Too sissy," she said. When she calmed down, Walt asked her what she thought of the name Mickey, an Irish name, an outsider's name. "I said it sounded better than Mortimer, and that's how Mickey was born."

As the legend would have it, Walt had been inspired in his choice of a mouse for a character by experiences in Kansas City. He had, variously, been sitting on a park bench when a mouse scampered by; or, while working for the Film Ad Co., he had caught mice in his wastebasket, where they were feasting on scraps from lunches the office girls had thrown away, then built a box for them and kept them as pets, naming one of them Mortimer; or, while bunking at the Laugh-O-Gram office, he had heard a mouse running about; or, at some undefined time, he had found a mouse scratching at his windowsill trying to escape and put him in a coffee tin—the first of many mice he supposedly captured. In these accounts, he sometimes trained the mice, tapping one of them on his nose as he ran across the top of Walt's drawing board and causing him to change direction. Or he would feed them from his fingers and then draw them in different poses. "I'll never forget the scream one girl gave when she came into the office one day and found a little mouse perched on my drawing board while I sketched him," he recalled. In one story he told, when he left Kansas City for Los Angeles, he took his pet mouse (just one here) and turned him loose in a field. "When I looked back he was still sitting there in the field watching me with a sad, disappointed look in his eyes."

Such was the legend, but the truth was likely much more banal. Years later Lillian would comment that when they returned to Los Angeles, Roy met them at the station, despondent that Walt had been unable to make any connection and seemingly uninterested in or unimpressed by what Walt called a "wonderful idea," presumably Mickey. Ub Iwerks told it somewhat differently. He said that Walt himself was deflated, hardly the frame of mind for someone who had just created a new character in which he was bursting with confidence. Iwerks called it "one of the absolute low points in Walt's life. Usually Walt was very enthusiastic and bubbly and bouncy, no matter what happened. But he had met a stone wall in the East." In fact, in Iwerks's version of events, as opposed to what he later derided as "highly exaggerated publicity material," he, Walt, and Roy began meeting daily as soon as Walt returned, flipping through magazines and batting around ideas, trying to come up with a new character. As for the inspiration, Lillian herself admitted that the Kansas City stories about Walt befriending mice were apocryphal. "We simply thought the mouse would make a cute character to animate," she said. The Aesop's Fables that Walt professed to admire so much frequently featured mice. Mice also figured prominently in several Alice comedies—in *Alice Rattled by Rats* Julius the Cat is beleaguered by an entire houseful of mice; in *Alice Solves the Puzzle* mice play in her washtub; in *Alice the Whaler* a mouse performs comic business in the galley; and in *Alice's Tin Pony* a band of rats attempt to rob a train. The rodents figured so prominently that when Walt moved into the Hyperion studio and wanted a new publicity poster, he had Hugh Harman draw cartoon characters, including mice, around a photograph of him in front of the bungalow. ("A couple of the mice looked like Mickey," Iwerks observed. "The only difference was the shape of the nose.") Later, when Walt was producing the Oswalds, theater posters were routinely adorned with a pesky, long-eared mouse who tried to steal the scene by committing acts of mischief like cutting the rope attached to a girder on which Oswald and his girlfriend sat (*Sky Scrappers*) or parachuting from a plane (*The Ocean Hop*) or holding the billboard on which the title was emblazoned (*Great Guns!*).

The real inspiration for centralizing the mouse in the cartoons and the model for his rough design, according to several of Walt's associates, including Iwerks, were the drawings of Clifton Meek, whose work ran regularly in the popular humor magazines *Life* and *Judge*, which Walt, Roy, and Iwerks were riffling through at the time. "I grew up with those drawings," Walt told an interviewer. "They were different from ours—but they had cute ears." It was Iwerks's rendering, essentially Oswald with shorter ears, that became the standard—as Iwerks later described him, "Pear-shaped body, ball on top, couple of thin legs. You gave it long ears and it was a rabbit. Short ears, it was a cat. Ears hanging down a dog . . . With an elongated nose, it became a mouse." As one animation historian put it, "He was designed for maximum ease of animation," since "circular forms were simpler to animate effectively." "Walt designed a mouse," animator Otto Messmer said, "but it wasn't any good. He was long and skinny." Iwerks redesigned him.

As Iwerks told it, having settled on the mouse, he, Walt, and Roy then hit upon the Lindbergh scenario by kicking around ideas at the studio. As for the name, though at one time Iwerks credited Lillian with having come up with Mickey, he later retracted. For his part Walt, in an autobiographical sketch that he dictated in the mid-1930s, recalled, "After trying various names out on my friends, I decided to call him Mickey Mouse," thus scanting Lillian's contribution. Longtime Disney archivist David Smith said that Lillian herself waffled on her claim to have named the character and on Walt's ever having called him Mortimer, and a profile of Disney in *McCall's* in 1932, just four years after Mickey's creation, stated that the name Mortimer was junked in favor of Mickey because the latter was shorter, not because Lillian objected. The nocturnal mice scurrying over Walt's drawing board, the training sessions in which Walt domesticated them and his sad parting in Kansas City, even the sudden burst of inspiration on the Santa Fe across the plains headed for California, and Lillian's indignation, were likely all embellishments. Rather, Mickey Mouse was the product of desperation and calculation—the desperation born of Walt Disney's need to re-create an animation sanctuary and the calculation of what the market would accept.

Now they had to animate the cartoon, even though they had no contract for it and even though they were still obligated to produce the three remaining Oswalds under their contract with Mintz. The strain was doubly heavy because the perfidious animators were still working in the studio to fulfill the Mintz commitment. Among his top staff only Iwerks, Les Clark, the soda jerk from the Kingswell neighborhood, and an animator named Johnny Cannon had remained faithful to Walt. Within a few weeks Walt had hired another young artist named Wilfred Jackson—he preferred to be known as "Jaxon"—who had little experience but had pestered Walt into giving him a one-week trial that kept being extended. Walt assigned him to help the janitor wash cels and then to the ink-and-paint department, where he was the lone man in a roomful of women.

Jackson may have been only twenty-two and a newcomer, but he sensed that something was amiss at the studio. At the end of his first week that April, he noticed that the animators not only collected their hats and coats at closing time but also their pens, their pencils, and even their seat cushions. Jackson also noted the frigid atmosphere that was the result of distrust between Walt's loyalists and the defectors. The distrust was intensified by the fact that while the defectors were animating Oswald, Iwerks was animating Mickey surreptitiously—surreptitiously because he and Walt did not want anyone to know their plan and possibly steal their idea. Iwerks called himself an "outcast," saying he worked on *Plane Crazy* in a locked room at the Hyperion studio and kept other cartoons on his table so that he could quickly cover the Mickey drawings should anyone enter the room. Frequently he worked at night after the others had left for the day. Hugh Harman recalled that the loyal animators worked behind a high black curtain or scrim to prevent him and the others from seeing "the great secret that was going on."

And they worked outside the studio too, where the defectors could not observe them. "The first Mickey Mouse was made by twelve people after hours in a garage," Walt would write—his garage on Lyric Avenue. Of the twelve, however, only one animated: Iwerks. Iwerks had heard that Bill Nolan, whom Walt had tried to recruit on his trip, could pen as many as six hundred drawings a day, so Iwerks admitted that as a point of personal pride he "really extended" himself, doing seven hundred drawings a day. When Iwerks had finished, Walt put benches in his garage, and Lillian, Edna, and his sister-in-law Hazel Sewell inked and painted the cels while longtime employee Mike Marcus cranked the animation camera—at night so that the other animators would not suspect that he was diverting time to Walt's secret project.

Given the pressure of trying to turn out *Plane Crazy* as quickly as possible so that Walt could find a distributor and keep his company afloat, it was grueling work. (The first charges on the company ledger against the film were listed on April 30, a week before the defectors were to finish their last Oswald and leave the Disney studio, and the film was completed by May 15 at a cost of $1,772.) And since Walt was working on speculation without a contract, there was no remuneration. "We worked night and day," Lillian recalled. "We ate stews and pot roasts, which luckily were cheap in those days. We were down so low that we had a major budget crisis when I tripped on the garage stairs and ruined my last pair of silk stockings."

Though Les Clark would later date the real advance of animation to the inception of Mickey Mouse, the first completed cartoon, which was intended to be the studio's salvation, provided no evidence of it; Walt's own children, seeing *Plane Crazy* years later, would be astonished by how primitive it looked. Mickey was crudely drawn with lines for legs and arms sticking out of his circular torso, and the scenario, equally crude, was lightly adapted from Oswald cartoons like *Trolley Troubles*, only here it is an airplane, jerry-built from a flivver, that careers out of control. As for Mickey's personality, his main characteristics are a raw ingenuity and a sadistic determination; he yanks the tail feathers off a turkey for his plane's rear strut and later grabs a cow's udder attempting to hoist himself back into the cockpit. In slightly lesser measure, he also proves to be aggressive, lecherous, and chauvinistic, tugging at his lady mouse, Minnie—she was named, Walt is said to have admitted, after Minnie Cowles, Dr. Cowles's wife—for a kiss and forcing her to leap from the plane to avoid his advances, after which the plane corkscrews and crashes. Unchastened when he sees her float to the ground using her bloomers as a parachute, Mickey laughs at the predicament and gets his comeuppance when he heaves a horseshoe she has given him, and it boomerangs to hit him on the head.

But as uninspired as it was, Walt moved rapidly to sell it because he had to. Virtually as soon as it was finished, he set up appointments in Los Angeles with Felix Feist and Howard Dietz of Metro Pictures, though he was also lugging it around town to distributors and theaters hoping to generate a buzz. One Glendale exhibitor recalled Walt personally taking the can of film down to the theater and convincing him to show the cartoon, which he did, asking the audience to applaud if they liked it. (As the exhibitor remembered it over twenty-five years later, "It was applauded more than the feature film.") According to Iwerks, Walt also previewed the cartoon at a Hollywood theater, coaching the organist to provide the proper accompaniment. At the same time he made an arrangement on May 21 with a New York agent named Denison to represent *Plane Crazy* with distributors in the East. When Feist and Dietz screened it, they told Walt they liked it enough to show it to Nicholas Schenck, Metro's president, and Robert Rubin, its vice-president. Elated and already anticipating a deal, Walt asked for a negative advance of $3,000 per film, adding in a wire to Denison that he intended to "make the name of 'Mickey Mouse' as well known as any cartoon in the market." But a week later Walt's hopes were dashed yet again. Metro decided against taking Mickey Mouse.

Since he had no alternative plan, Walt had little choice but to keep forging ahead, making new Mickeys and depleting his treasury. But the same week he received the rejection from Metro, he got another brainstorm that in its own way was just as monumental as the invention of Mickey himself. Lillian recalled that it happened during a conversation between Roy and Walt, when Roy was again dejected over Mickey's faltering future. Walt suddenly blurted, "We'll make them over with sound." Roy had a different version. He said that they had screened a cartoon after *The Jazz Singer*, the Al Jolson film that is credited with being the first motion picture to synchronize the spoken word and the image. "That's it. That's it," Walt allegedly said. "It looks realistic, it'll be realistic. That's what we've got to do. Stop all these silent pictures." As Wilfred Jackson remembered it, Walt first broached the possibility to his staff at a gag meeting for the second Mickey Mouse, which most likely was held on

May 29, 1928, at Walt's house. Everyone was immediately energized, which may have been part of Walt's calculation to keep his crew's spirits from flagging. Jackson said he was so excited by the idea of a sound cartoon that he could not sleep that night.

Walt, however, was not the only animator thinking of sound. *The Jazz Singer*, after all, which was acclaimed as having ushered in the sound era, had premiered the previous October, and the Fleischers had already worked with a sound system called DeForest Phonofilm, while Paul Terry had a synchronized sound film in production with the RCA Photophone sound process. Even Mintz and Winkler were planning a sound project. But deploying sound was not just a matter of slapping a sound track onto a silent cartoon, even though that was precisely what Walt would later do with *Plane Crazy*. In the first place, there were psychological hurdles to overcome in the very notion of talking animations. Though audiences expected to hear *people* talk or sing, they were not initially accustomed to hearing voices from drawings. "Drawings are not vocal," Wilfred Jackson said. "Why should a *voice* come out of a cartoon character?" Animators were concerned that it would seem unnatural, peculiar, and off-putting, which was one reason why Walt insisted that his sound had to be realistic—in Jackson's words, "as if the noise was coming right from what the character was doing."

In the second place, there was the daunting technical matter of how one synchronized the drawings with the sound—an area in which no one, Walt Disney included, had any expertise. "Damn it, I know how fast film goes," Jackson overheard Walt griping one day, "but how fast does music go?" Jackson was still among the lowest in the Disney hierarchy, but he popped his head in the door, said his mother was a piano teacher, and suggested that Walt use a metronome to determine the number of frames of animation per beats of music. In short order Jackson devised a "dope sheet," later called a "bar sheet," that indicated the number of measures in each piece of musical accompaniment and then related the cartoon actions to the music. "We could break down the sound effects so that every eight frames we'd have an accent, or every sixteen frames, or every twelve frames," Les Clark said. "And on that twelfth drawing, say, we'd accent whatever was happening—a hit on the head or a footstep or whatever it would be, to synchronize the sound effect to the music."

It was the prospect of sound now that motivated the staff—the prospect of doing something no one had done. They finished animating the second Mickey, *The Gallopin' Gaucho*, a silent that was already in production when Walt hatched his plan, then eagerly moved on to the third cartoon—the sound cartoon. Just as Walt had spoofed Lindbergh in *Plane*

Crazy and swashbuckler Douglas Fairbanks in *The Gaucho*, he decided to spoof comedian Buster Keaton's *Steamboat Bill, Jr.* for *Steamboat Willie.* Eager to test the proposition of sound, once again the staff worked quickly. Iwerks said that they resolved the story in a single night, and within weeks he had animated a musical test sequence of Mickey/Willie at the steamboat's wheel, tooting the pipes and whistling. Eager to see whether sound would augment the cartoon as he had anticipated, Walt had the scene inked, painted, and filmed even before the rest of the animation was completed, then recruited Jackson, who was the only member of the staff with any musical talent, to play "Turkey in the Straw," one of Jackson's favorite tunes, and "Steamboat Bill," Walt's choice, on the harmonica.

One night, probably in late June, at about eight o'clock, Walt had a projector set up in the yard behind the studio bungalow so that the whirring of the machine would not contend with the accompaniment.* The image was thrown through a window and onto a bedsheet hung in a large room off of Walt's office where the backgrounds were drawn. He stationed Jackson with his harmonica, animator Johnny Cannon, who could make sound effects with his mouth, and several other staff members behind his office door, which had a window in it that allowed them to see the back of the bedsheet. When Roy started the projector, Jackson played his music, Cannon made his sounds, and the others banged pencils against spittoons that served as gongs—all synchronized to Mickey's actions. They performed repeatedly so that each of the participants could witness the effect for himself. And with an appreciation for the magnitude of the event—the fate of the studio rested on the outcome—they had an audience. Walt had invited Lillian, Edna, Iwerks's wife Mildred, Hazel Sewell, and Jackson's girlfriend, later wife, Jane Ames, to watch what he hoped would be a historic occasion.

"I never saw such a reaction in an audience in my life," the usually taciturn Iwerks would recall, citing encore after encore. "The scheme worked perfectly. The sound itself gave the illusion of something emanating directly from the screen." Walt was exultant. He kept saying, "This is it, this is it! We've got it!" By the time the show finally ended, it was two in the morning, and the guests, hearing Jackson play his two tunes and hearing the staff hit the spittoons again and again, had gotten bored and drifted into the hallway, which only antagonized Walt. "You're out here

*It is difficult to determine exactly when this showing was held. Iwerks placed it at the beginning of June, but an entry in the *General Expense Account* designates an unspecified "preview" on July 29, which may very well have been the first *Willie* showing.

talking about babies and we're in here making history," he reportedly groused. Iwerks said he had never been so exhilarated, claiming years later that "nothing since has ever equaled it." It was "real intoxication," and like Walt, he said he knew they had been vindicated. "It was terrible, but it was wonderful!" Walt would say, criticizing the quality of the cartoon but appreciating the significance of the showing. "And it was something new!" which was, of course, the main point for the struggling studio. The staff were so jubilant that they reassembled at the studio at six in the morning, just a few hours after they had left, to finish the cartoon.

It would take another four weeks, during which Walt and Roy refinanced their Hyperion mortgage to raise money. On July 14 Walt requisitioned sheet music, and by month's end they held a second preview like the first, only this time of the entire cartoon. In the meantime Walt had become practically messianic about sound. He had his business cards reprinted. "Sound cartoons," they now read. As for *Steamboat Willie*, the eminent animation historian John Canemaker called it the "*Jazz Singer* of animation" for the effect it would have. After the loss of Oswald and most of his staff, Walt had, in a few short months, reinvented his studio and, he thought, the cartoon itself. Now all he had to do was find a way to get the sound and music on the film itself so that he could get a distributor to release the cartoons before his money was exhausted.

II

The race began. Even as he was making *Willie*, Walt was desperately soliciting distributors for his two silent Mickey cartoons, just as he had back in the days of Laugh-O-Gram for his fairy tales and just as he had when he arrived in Los Angeles with *Alice's Wonderland.* But he was having no success. The problem in landing a new distributor, he wrote one prospective company, was, oddly enough, the sound that he himself was so vigorously pursuing. "They are all afraid to tie up with silent product until they find out how far the sound idea is going," he complained, but they were equally wary about sound. He felt that sound was a "wonderful thing" so long as it was used judiciously, which it frequently was not, but he concluded that "things will shortly be back to normal, and they [distributors] will be considering the quality in a silent product instead of going crazy over a lot of useless and irritating noises." Of course Walt was hedging out of self-protection since he had yet to complete his own sound film, though he was among those who were going crazy over noises, and he was scheduled to go to New York after Labor Day for the express purpose of meeting with sound companies to determine how best to put a sound track on *Willie*.

He arrived on September 4 and immediately contacted his erstwhile mentor and matchmaker, Jack Alicoate of *Film Daily*, who arranged meetings for Walt with various sound companies—meetings that wound up only confusing him with the variety of rates and the differences in technologies. After his rounds and after rejecting the idea of synchronized recording disks, Walt all but decided to throw in his lot with Pat A. Powers, who was licensing a sound-on-film system called Cinephone that generated sound through optical impulses printed on the margin of the film, which were then read by a sound head in the projector. But Walt was clearly in uncharted territory and knew it. "I hope I have not stumbled," he wrote Roy and Iwerks uncertainly, before ending with his typical morale-booster: "All of you just hold your shirts on and believe me when I tell you that I think we have got something good."

Still in many ways a naïf, Walt had placed his faith and his fate in the hands of Powers, whose bonhomie had proven irresistible to more hardened men than the young animator. Powers was the very image of an Irish cop, which was what he had once been many years before. At fifty-nine he was tall and broad-shouldered with a square cleft chin, a wide nose, dancing eyes, thick brows, a bush of hair, a glad hand, and a welcoming smile. Walt called him a "[b]ig lovable friendly Irishman" and said, "You couldn't help but like him." To Roy and Iwerks he wrote that Powers was a "good natured cuss" who was "always in a good mood." But this bonhomie was deceptive. For all his outward affability, Powers was also one of the most notoriously belligerent figures in the entire history of the motion picture industry. Born in Buffalo, New York, he worked as a policeman, a foundryman, and a union organizer before contracting to sell phonographs in suburban New York City and eventually forming a small studio to produce motion pictures when films were just beginning to boom early in the twentieth century. When Universal Pictures was formed, Powers became a partner, quickly schemed to force out two other partners, and then had a falling out with Universal head Carl Laemmle, even hiring goons to cart off the props from one of Laemmle's Universal films while it was in production. "When in doubt," wrote one contemporary film historian, "Powers attacks." During the company's annual meeting at Universal's headquarters at 1600 Broadway in New York, Powers, in an incident that would become legendary in early movie lore, grabbed the books and tossed them out the window to an accomplice below.

By the time Walt met him, the dust of Powers's pitched battles had long settled, but the old movie veteran had lost little of his rapacity, and he knew a mark when he saw one. Twenty-six-year-old Walt Disney, who always seemed to be searching for a paternal figure from whom he could win approval and to whom he could attach his fortunes, was trusting and easily conned, and he had clearly fallen for Powers. After spending most of the day with "the good-natured cuss" shortly after arriving in New York, he wrote Roy that Powers regaled him with an account of his various travails at Universal with Erich von Stroheim, a director and actor known for his perfectionism and extravagance, and then introduced him to the general manager of Tiffany-Stahl Productions, who happened to stop by, which clearly impressed Walt. A few days later when Walt revisited Powers, the actor George Walsh was in the office, chatting up Walt about polo, as was the orchestra leader from the lavish Capitol Theater, Carl Edouarde, who, Walt said, was "very enthused over the possibilities of the picture." "Has oodles of Jack," Walt wrote Roy of Powers glowingly.

By this point Walt was just about snared. He visited RCA, which tried to stall him on making a decision on a sound system, and let him see a sample film, the Aesop's Fable. Walt found it appalling. "A lot of racket and nothing else," he wrote Roy. "We have nothing to worry about from these quarters." The demonstration apparently convinced him. That same afternoon he returned to Powers's office and closed the deal to use Cinephone for *Willie*. Powers was charging only fifty dollars for his technical expertise behind the microphone, while Walt would be responsible for the musicians and sound effects men, though even here Powers offered to recruit a small orchestra at a cut rate and expected the entire recording session to take no more than three to four hours. Walt estimated the cost at $1,000, including a royalty of one cent per foot on all prints. "My idea is to get the thing scored and preview it in a Broadway house and get the critics [*sic*] opinions and then get busy on a deal for a good release," he wrote Roy after closing his agreement with Powers.

Four days later, when Walt gave Powers a $500 check as a deposit—"Be sure and have enough money in the account to meet the check," Walt warned Roy, evidence of their precarious financial situation—the terms had abruptly shifted from Powers's flat fifty-dollar fee to a royalty of one dollar per foot of film, but even with this increase Walt was still convinced that "*our best bet is Powers*," and he prepared nervously for the grand recording session scheduled to begin early on the morning of September 15. Powers had arranged for Edouarde, the ruddy-faced, white-maned conductor whom Walt had met at Powers's office, to lead the orchestra, which consisted of seventeen musicians abetted by, as Walt effused, three of the "best Trap Drummers and Effects men in Town" at a rate of ten dollars an hour per man, all crammed into a tiny recording studio.

In its implications for the studio, September 15 was a day almost to rival the *Willie* experiment earlier that summer. Right from the outset, however, the signs were not encouraging. The first musician to arrive was a bass player with a bottle of whiskey in his case who blew a vacuum tube in the sound recording equipment every time he played, forcing the engineers to move him out of the room. Then Walt began fighting with Edouarde over incorporating "too many Symphonic effects," since the maestro seemed to believe that comedy music was beneath him. But there was worse to come—much worse. To assist Edouarde, Walt had provided a blank film with markings on it in India ink for the beat, but as the strip was projected, the conductor could never manage to get the orchestra to hit the marks and finally prevailed upon Walt to let him try it his own way. Yet as the time ran on and the costs mounted, Edouarde could still not get the orchestra in synchronicity with the film. By the end of the session Walt himself had blown a take when he coughed into the mike while providing the voice for a parrot, and the music and sounds still did not gibe with the cartoon. Walt had spent over $1,000 that the studio could scarcely afford and had nothing to show for it.

Walt recognized the magnitude of the calamity. Even before the session he had been anxious and distraught. He hated New York; hated being away from home; hated having to talk up people he barely knew, after years of having enjoyed doing so; hated not having anyone to provide counsel; hated the lonely nights; even hated *Steamboat Willie*, which he was now sick of watching and whose print he thought was "lousy." He was so busy that he often forgot to eat and had lost ten pounds, and he was so restless that he could not get to sleep before two or three in the morning. To make matters worse, he had been walking the city so much in a new pair of shoes that he had developed a painful abscess on his big toe, for which the doctor prescribed a wet dressing every hour. All of this was on top of the disastrous recording session. "If you knew the entire situation as I do," he wrote Roy and Ub with uncharacteristic gloom, "I feel sure you wouldn't be able to Sleep or Eat. . . . I can't."

Now they needed another session. Powers, obviously looking to the long-term rewards of having Walt sell his cartoon series and use the Cinephone process, had agreed to foot the bill for the technical expenses, and Edouarde, presumably embarrassed, had offered to try again, but Walt still had to pay for the musicians. Unfortunately he had virtually exhausted the studio's money, which forced him to hector Roy to do something the studio had heretofore refrained from doing: apply for a bank loan. "GET AS LARGE A LOAN AS POSSIBLE," Walt wired Roy a week after the botched session. "DON'T THINK THIRTY FIVE HUNDRED ENOUGH TRY FOR MORE OUR

FUTURE DEPENDS ON FIRST PICTURE THEREFORE AM NOT SPARING EXPENSE TO MAKE IT GOOD." Two days later, again both cheerleading and dunning, he wrote Roy that this is "Old Man Opportunity rapping at our door" and urged him to "slap as big a mortgage on everything we got and let's go after this thing in the right manner."

The group assembled for the second session at ten o'clock on the morning of September 30. This time, however, Walt had devised a new system to crack the problem of synchronization, which had been vexing not only the Disneys but all the animation producers. He had a ball printed on both the sound track and the film that rose and fell to the accent of the beat, creating a visual signal and a soft audio clack. All Edouarde had to do was watch the ball on the screen and change the tempo of the orchestra when the tempo of the ball changed. "It worked like clock works," Walt wrote the studio staff ecstatically later that day. "It saved this picture." With the ball system the entire recording session took only three hours and everything synchronized beautifully. "It proves one thing to me," he added. " 'It can be done perfectly' and this is one thing that they have all been stumped on." The next day he closed another letter to the studio, "All together now—'Are we downhearted'? HELL NO."

Once again Walt seemed to have averted disaster. But as thrilled as he was with the results of the new *Willie*, there was still one enormous hurdle to leap, the same old hurdle, before he could parlay the film into the revenue the studio so badly needed: he had to find a distributor. Reinvigorated from his doldrums, he felt that all they had invested in *Willie*, all they had scraped together, was money well spent because, he insisted, they now had an animation of superior quality, and he firmly believed, as he had with the Alices, that "[w]e can lick them all with Quality." Even before completing *Willie*, he had an intermediary approach Universal, which he knew admired his previous work, and he had continued investigating a relationship with Metro, despite being continually spurned there. When those efforts failed to pan out, he accepted an offer of help from another eager Samaritan: Pat Powers. Walt's admiration for Powers had if anything grown, even after the recording debacle. "What better salesman could we want than PAT POWERS," he wrote Roy and Ub. Powers, Walt thought, had the clout to get the "Big Boys" to see the film—the very top executives. "I am going to stick as close to him as I can without getting in his clutches," he said, apparently beginning to recognize how insidious Powers could be.

But Walt was already in Powers's clutches. By mid-October Powers had arranged to have Walt show *Willie* to Universal president Robert Cochrane and other Universal executives, and the reception was enthusiastic. "This is the original OSWALD," one kept repeating, while others remarked on its cleverness and perfect synchronization. "I have never seen an audience of hard-boiled Film Executives laugh so much," Walt wrote Lilly that night. Walt was invited to visit the Universal office the first thing in the morning to discuss a deal. He immediately hurried to Powers's office to tell him the news, and in the heat of the moment, without consulting Roy, he did something that he would come to regret deeply: he wound up signing an agreement with Powers that afternoon empowering the mogul to serve as the studio's sales agent for two years in return for 10 percent of all the monies Walt received.

Walt arrived at the Universal office the next day, obviously beaming and ready to bargain. By sheer coincidence he found Charlie Mintz sitting patiently in the waiting room, a reminder of what Walt was about to vanquish. Though Mintz was understandably sheepish, Walt made a point of smiling and greeting him cordially—a gesture of magnanimity he could now afford. Knowing how quickly word spread in the animation community, he was sure that Mintz had heard about the impending Universal deal. But when Walt met with a Universal executive named Metzger, it turned out that Universal did not want to distribute Mickey Mouse, at least not just yet. Instead, without paying any compensation to Walt, they wanted to put *Willie* on the bill with a Universal picture, *Melody of Love*, playing at the lavish Colony Theater, and see how the audience and the reviewers reacted. Then, assuming a positive response, they would contract for twenty-six Mickeys in 1928 and fifty-two the next year. Walt may have been disappointed, but he was receptive, and Universal prepared an option agreement. "I guess that means Charlie is out," he wrote Lillian with more than a tinge of vengeful gloating, noting that Mintz was still cooling his heels in the waiting room when Walt left.

The next day, however, Walt had second thoughts. What if Universal showed *Willie* and didn't make a deal with him? Wouldn't that undermine his bargaining position with other distributors? When Walt expressed his sudden change of heart to Universal, Metzger was enraged, though Walt just grabbed his hat and exited the office as Metzger boiled. But while Walt was waiting for the treasurer to return his option, Metzger reappeared and attempted to mollify him. Walt left Universal without signing a contract but leaving the impression that he had reconsidered. The next morning he headed to Powers's office for advice. Powers told Walt that Universal was trying to "pull a fast one" and counseled him to pretend he was negotiating with another distributor, hoping that this would force Universal's hand. Obviously parroting Powers, Walt wrote Lillian that "if I got down on my knees to them it would be far worse for us on this deal," and he was not going to let Universal "bulldose" [*sic*] him.

"They are all just a bunch of schemers," Walt concluded, "and just full of tricks that would fool a greenhorn," which is what he realized he was. He was just lucky, he said, to have a friend and adviser like Powers.

The sparring continued over the next week. Universal said that it needed to make more calculations before it could make an offer, while Walt said he could not wait, though privately he was certain Universal would eventually capitulate, and he was meeting daily with Powers to map strategy. "In this game the guy with the most patience seems to win out," Walt wrote Roy. Meanwhile Walt showed the film to Paramount executives who were "amased" [*sic*] and to executives of the Film Booking Office who "became very enthused." By the end of October, though, neither Paramount nor FBO had made an offer, and Universal finally decided that their contract with Mintz precluded them from distributing any other cartoons. Walt was crushed—his high spirits once again flattened.

Because he was so short on money, all this time Walt had been goading Iwerks to finish the fourth Mickey, called *The Barn Dance*, so that he could have that one scored and recorded along with musical tracks for *Plane Crazy* and *The Gallopin' Gaucho* before returning home. "If you ever worked like HELL in your life, do it now," he wrote him. The music for all the cartoons but *The Barn Dance* had already been written by Walt's old musical colleague Carl Stalling. On the train out to New York, Walt had stopped in Kansas City and proselytized Stalling on the future of sound movies, then left *Plane Crazy* and *The Gallopin' Gaucho* for him to score while Walt continued on to arrange to have *Willie* recorded. Stalling arrived in New York the morning of the day before the Universal verdict and holed up with Walt in his hotel room past midnight talking and working. Three days later a print of *The Barn Dance* had arrived, and they prepared to record the scores. Powers agreed to foot the bill for the recording so long as Walt paid the other costs. Walt saw this as a lifesaver. "I didn't tell him how bad we needed his help," he wrote Lilly.

Again, he was in dire financial straits. Between the musicians' fees and Stalling's salary, Walt estimated that he would need another $1,200 to $1,500 for the recording session, on top of the nearly $6,000 he had already spent on the trip. Several weeks earlier the brothers had taken out a second mortgage on their Lyric Avenue homes, which pumped another $4,000 into the company, but most of that was now depleted. Walt urged Lillian to have Roy take out an additional loan against their property and "dig up all the spare cash he can." It was a sign of just how the financial noose had tightened that Walt finally instructed Roy to sell the beloved Moon roadster with its red and green running lights and its folding top—the car in which Walt had courted Lillian.

But after nearly two months in New York, two months away from the studio and his home and Lillian, and after all the financial maneuvering, and after even the efforts of Pat Powers, Walt had four Mickey Mouse sound cartoons and *still* had no company to distribute them. He was running out of money. He was running out of time. He was running out of patience. He was even beginning to run out of confidence.

Then came Harry Reichenbach. Reichenbach, forty-four and prematurely silver-haired at the time he met Walt, looked like a diplomat, which belied the fact that he was actually a self-professed ballyhoo artist and proud of it. Born in Frostburg, Maryland, in the foothills of the Allegheny Mountains, where he was raised on "nickel thrillers" and dreams of the larger world, Reichenbach ran off with a carnival as a boy and became a performer there, then worked as a magician's assistant before leaving the stage and entering the nascent profession of press agentry. Brazenly duplicitous, he was soon a legend. As he once boasted of his exploits, "I took a young man who could wear plaited pants and in three weeks made him America's matinee idol. I changed the name of Michigan Avenue to Dream Street by popular vote, organized a cannibal tribe at Tarrytown, New York, to advertise a picture, turned a failure into a national success by having a lion stop at a first class hotel and even got Rudolph Valentino's heart to lie in state in a California museum."

When Walt met him in New York, Reichenbach, after years of representing a variety of film companies in promotional stunts, had become manager of the Colony Theater on Broadway, the very place where Universal had hoped to screen *Willie* before negotiations broke down. Ever since the recording session, Walt had been taking his print of *Willie* from distributor to distributor, sitting in the projection room while the cartoon was run and looking through the portholes to see the executives' reaction, only to be told they would be in touch if they were interested. Reichenbach happened to attend one of these screenings and was impressed enough to approach Walt about the possibility of showing *Willie* for two weeks at his theater. When Walt fretted to Reichenbach, as he had to Universal, that the showing might harm his chances to land a distributor, Reichenbach told him that distributors never knew if a film was good until they heard the public and press response, and he assured Walt that "they'll like it." Reichenbach offered him $500 for the run. Somewhat bravely by his own admission, Walt countered with $1,000—"the highest price that anybody's ever paid up to that time, for a cartoon on Broadway"—and Reichenbach, who obviously saw potential in *Willie*, agreed.

Willie debuted at the Colony on November 18, 1928, before the feature film *Gang War* starring Olive Borden, Eddie Gribbon, and Jack Pickford.* With the studio's future now riding on the audience's reaction, Walt and Stalling sat nervously near the rear of the theater and, as Stalling recalled, "heard laughs and snickers all around us." (Walt would attend every performance those two weeks.) In fact, the reception was astonishing. Even before the engagement ended, Walt was receiving accolades from the trade press and calls from some of the same distributors who had brushed him off. "Not the first animated cartoon to be synchronized with sound effects," raved *Variety*, "but the first to attract favorable attention. This one represents a high order of cartoon ingenuity, cleverly combined with sound effects. The union brought laughs galore. Giggles came so fast at the Colony they were stumbling over each other." The reviewer for *Exhibitor's Herald* said it "knocked me out of my seat." And even *The New York Times* took note, calling *Willie* "an ingenious piece of work with a good deal of fun. It growls, whines, squeaks and makes various other sounds that add to its mirthful quality."

Steamboat Willie seemed a slight film for such enthusiasm, much less for a cinematic milestone, which is what it would become. Scarcely six minutes in length, it had little narrative—essentially Mickey, in the throes of musical passion, carouses on a steamboat and turns everything he sees into an instrument: a goat into a hurdy-gurdy, a trash can into a drum, a set of pans into chimes, and a cow's teeth into a xylophone. With a bit of casual sadism, he also yanks a cat's tail to elicit yowls, uses a hapless goose as a trombone, and presses the teats of a sow to turn her into a kind of piano bleating notes. The only plot elements are a hulking cat of a captain who terrorizes Mickey—the intrusion of reality—and whose severity he escapes through his music, and Minnie Mouse, who joins his recital when Mickey swings her aboard with a loading hook. But what made it different from its animation forebears and competitors was the extent to which Walt had imagined it fully as a sound cartoon in which the music and effects were inextricable from the action—truly a musical cartoon rather than a cartoon with music. As Wilfred Jackson later analyzed the Disney musical technique, "I do not believe there was much thought given to the music as one thing and the animation as another. I believe we conceived of them as elements which we were trying to fuse into a whole new thing that would be more than simply movement plus sound." Even Mickey's walk

*As significant a date as this would be in the studio's history, Walt seemed to have difficulty remembering it. He variously cited the premiere as July 19, which may have been the date of the studio experiment (*Autobiography*, 1939, 4th installment, p. 9), September 19 (*Autobiography*, 1934), and September 28 ("Mickey Mouse is Eight Years Old," *Literary Digest*, Oct. 3, 1936, p. 18).

was conceptualized musically, according to two veteran Disney animators. It had a bounce to it from the beat.

Just as *The Jazz Singer* had sent shock waves through the film industry a year earlier, rival animation studios immediately recognized that *Willie* had wrought a revolution in their art. "It became the rage," wrote one producer. "Everybody was talking about it and raving about the funny action this mouse character did." Other studios raced to catch up, but Disney had both a head start now and his special synchronizing system, and it would be a year before competitors were making musical cartoons of their own with anything like the fusion of *Willie*. Some never could catch up. Felix the Cat animator Hal Walker lamented that "Disney put us out of business with his sound."

Now Walt, or more accurately Powers, was fielding offers, but what should have been triumph led again to disappointment. The problem was that the distributors, all of them, wanted to buy Walt's studio, not just his cartoons. After his experience with Mintz, he was adamant about not selling, not surrendering control, no matter how badly he needed revenue, because he didn't want to be just another animation producer. He wanted to be the king of animation. "I knew that I would be restrained as to what I could spend on pictures," he would write a few years later, "and held down to what their idea of cartoon costs should be." Walt, as fervent as ever that quality was his only real advantage, was determined to spend as much on his cartoons as producers were spending on their live one-reel comedies. As a consequence, instead of selling the studio, Walt, clearly emboldened by *Willie*'s reception, told distributors that he insisted on a negative advance of $5,000 against a sixty-forty split of profits in his favor after the distributor had recovered the advance and expenses. Every distributor declined. With Walt seemingly defeated, Powers offered to step into the breach. Already Walt's sales agent, he would also distribute the film on a states' rights basis, essentially franchising the picture to state and regional distributors in exchange for 10 percent of the gross he collected from them. Walt had been saved again by Pat Powers. Or at least he thought he had.

And so now in mid-December, more than three full months after he had arrived, three lonely and agonizing months, Walt could finally return to California with at least the promise of distribution—a promise that luckily began to be fulfilled a few weeks later. Just before Christmas Charles Giegerich, Powers's right-hand man, closed an agreement with the entire chain of Stanley-Fabian-Warner Theatres, a chain that included the prominent Strand Theatre in New York, for $3,000 per subject. "With this is [*sic*] the bag," Giegerich wrote Walt, "everything should go airplaning from now on." By the end of the month Giegerich had finalized several states' rights agreements, including upstate New York for $4,200. A few weeks later he sold the foreign rights to the Mickey Mouse series, and a month after that he sold western Pennsylvania, Michigan, Wisconsin, and Cleveland and was about to sign contracts for Minnesota and Illinois. By May Powers's California representative had signed up the entire West Coast. "We give them the stuff, and we won't have to worry much," Walt would write confidently to his partners, oblivious to the fact that he was in Powers's hands and that Powers, given his track record, was not to be trusted. "[A]ll we want to worry about is the pictures."

III

He wasn't home long. Since Powers had no recording capability in California, by the end of January Walt was on his way back to New York to score two more Mickeys and to promote other projects. Having had Oswald wrested from him, Walt was already worried that he would be too dependent on Mickey and that if he didn't diversify, he would be putting himself and the studio at risk. Before returning to New York he had begun considering a series of one-reel live-action talking comedies and had written his old investor John Cowles asking if he might be interested in financing it. (He even stopped off in Kansas City to consult with Cowles on his way to New York.) At the same time, he was also working on another cartoon series, one without a single central character, that he hoped would be sufficiently different from the Mickeys that it could be run in theaters that competed with those showing the Mickeys, providing him with another stream of revenue.

The idea for the new series had originated with Carl Stalling the previous September when Walt visited him on the way to New York, and Walt had apparently floated it to distributors during his stay. What Stalling had proposed was a "musical novelty"—a cartoon that *began* with the music and had the action animated to it. And he had a subject for the first installment as well. As a child Stalling had seen an ad in *The American Boy* magazine for a dancing skeleton and had badgered his father to give him a quarter to send for it. The image had stuck with him, and he suggested that Walt animate a group of skeletons dancing to one of Stalling's own compositions that incorporated passages from Edvard Grieg's "March of the Dwarfs." The image stuck with Walt too. As early as September he wrote Roy that "Carl's idea of the 'Skeleton Dance' for a Musical Novelty has been growing on me," and he cited what he called "dandy possibilities" that he evidently conveyed to Powers, who expressed interest. On January 1 the studio began animating the film, and two weeks later, just before he arrived in New York again, Walt wrote Giegerich that he had something "quite out of the ordinary," though Ub hadn't finished enough for Walt to show anything yet.

Meanwhile Walt was in New York recording the sound tracks for the new Mickeys and enthusing over the reception of the Mickeys already in release. Seeing *The Barn Dance* at the Strand, he wrote Lillian proudly that there was a large cardboard cutout of Mickey in the lobby, and he enclosed the theater's program as evidence of Mickey's growing popularity. "[H]e is what is known as a 'HIT,' " he declared with more than a little hyperbole. The distributors, he crowed, "give me lots of praise for their cleverness," and he admitted that he hoped to prove that the quality of the first Mickeys "is not an accident but a consistent standard." He added that one selling point was Ub Iwerks—not only his animation, to which, Walt said, "New York animators took off their hats," but also his name, which made people "look twice when they see it."

But while Walt was recording the Mickeys and soaking up praise, he had another, bigger mission in New York—a personal mission. During his first New York trip, when he was pushing Mickey and facing rejection, one distributor picked up a package of Life Saver candies. "The public knows Life Savers," he told Walt. "They don't know you. They don't know your mouse." That made an impression on Walt. As he recalled it years later, he said to himself, "From now on they're going to know, if they liked the picture—they're going to know what his [the producer's] name is." So on this trip he had decided to stage a full-scale assault on the animation industry and establish "Walt Disney" as its undisputed leader—the Life Savers of animation. The timing was propitious. During his stay he learned that Charles Mintz had lost his Universal contract, a fact that obviously had Walt reveling, and that the Fleischers had lost their contract too, narrowing the competition considerably and leaving him with an irresistible opportunity. "Now is our chance to get a hold on the industry," he urged Roy and Ub. "So let's take advantage of the situation."

Part of his strategy was to gain a foothold in sound recording. Having been rescued by sound himself, Walt now decided to open a recording studio in California for other independent producers on which, Walt had written his partners, "We should be able to clean up a nice sum." This also meant that Walt would no longer have to spend so much time in the East, where he had lived for five of the last six months—all without Lillian. As early as October, during his last trip, he was arranging to have Jimmy

Lowerre, who was running the camera at the studio, come to New York, learn sound recording, and become the studio's resident sound engineer.

In this endeavor Walt was strongly encouraged by Pat Powers, and for good reason. Powers would be furnishing the recording equipment and was even negotiating to lease the Marshall Neilan studio on Glendale Avenue, where Walt was planning not only to set up the recording studio but to relocate his entire organization for the bargain rental of $100 a month. Powers was also arranging to lend Walt his own sound specialist, William Garity, for six months at a salary of $150 a week. Walt was so enthused—or Powers had gotten him enthused—that he was even talking of optioning at least two more sound outfits from Powers, another on the West Coast and one in the Midwest. But none of this came cheaply from a sharpie like Powers. In addition to the 10 percent distribution fee he was to receive for the Mickeys, Powers demanded a royalty of twenty-five cents per foot of finished negative, plus—and this was the kicker—$13,000, a very substantial sum in 1928, each year for a term of ten years, whether Walt used Cinephone or not, whether any other producers used Cinephone, and whether Cinephone later proved obsolete or not. He also demanded $5,000 upon signing—$5,000 that Walt did not have. In short, Powers was essentially pulling in the line on which he had Walt Disney hooked.

The terms were onerous, but Walt, ever the go-getter and an enthusiast rather than a pragmatist, was not about to let money stop him from what he was now confident was an extraordinary opportunity to become a sound expert. He wrote Roy desperately asking him to badger Cowles or Cauger or Stalling, even Stalling's father-in-law, for funds, using a second mortgage on the studio as security. "But we must raise the Dough," he insisted. Stalling, in fact, did loan them $2,000. For the remainder Walt did something that must have been terribly difficult for him: he asked Elias, who, resettled in Portland, Oregon, with Flora, owned several small apartment buildings. Elias likely took a second mortgage on one of them to furnish Walt with a $2,500 loan that February—a loan Walt justified by telling his father that the recording studio is "no gamble but an opportunity." The very day he received the loan, February 14, he signed the contract with Powers, though he had done so, again, without consulting Roy, who was livid. "Did you read this?" he shouted when Walt returned to California later that month. "Of course I didn't," Walt responded. "What the hell! I wanted the equipment!" It was shipped out from New York that week.

Walt Disney, who had always eschewed the business side of his studio and depended upon Roy to raise the funds he needed, was now not only an animation producer but a sound recording entrepreneur as well. The month after he returned to California, he and Roy rented the Tec Art Studios on Melrose Avenue in Hollywood for the sound operation, though the animation operation remained at Hyperion. (Powers's deal for the Neilan studio had fallen through at the last minute.) In the meantime Jimmy Lowerre went to New York to learn how to use the system, and in April William Garity, Powers's sound man, arrived at the studio to supervise the use of the equipment. "When completed," Roy wrote one prospective customer, "this stage will be equal to any sound stages so far constructed." Intending to provide full sound services, the Disneys began outfitting two old trucks with recording equipment for location shooting, though what they were also doing was further indebting themselves to Powers.

While Walt was arranging this salient of his assault to make himself animation's indispensable man, he was having less success with his Stalling-inspired new series, which he called Silly Symphonies. He had had Ub rush the animation of *The Skeleton Dance* so that he could begin recording Stalling's track and show the film to prospective distributors, and Powers was already talking about a twelve-cartoon package, but Walt admitted that he was disappointed in what he saw. He sent it back to New York in early March after it had been completed, and had Powers screen it, but distributors found the dancing spooks odd and even gruesome, and Powers couldn't get a sale. Walt tried to get an exhibitor to show it in Los Angeles and met the same reaction. Yet he maintained an unwavering, instinctive confidence in the Symphonies. "It's hard to explain just what we have in mind for this series," Walt confessed to Giegerich, "but I feel, myself, that it will be something unusual and should have a wide appeal." Several months later, hoping that he might get Fred Miller, who managed the prestigious Carthay Circle Theater in Los Angeles, to watch it as he had gotten Harry Reichenbach to watch *Willie*, Walt buttonholed a friend who knew a film salesman who knew Miller. Walt found the salesman in a pool hall. He agreed to take a look, liked it, and got it to Miller, who also liked it and agreed to run it at the Carthay on a temporary basis, where it became the first cartoon ever programmed there. The audience responded positively, but Walt, who attended the screening with Iwerks, wasn't certain. "Are they laughing at us or with us?" he asked.

Giegerich was less than pleased with Walt's efforts, thinking that the showing at Carthay would undermine his efforts to sell the Silly Symphonies nationally, but Walt countered that the cartoon was "making a big hit" and "attracting an unusual amount of attention," including a favorable notice in the *Los Angeles Times*, that could only help their prospects.

When Fred Miller asked to book the cartoon for an extended run, Walt wrote Powers that "Fox officials will be sold 100 percent when they hear the audience reaction opening nite." Walt was right. Where exhibitors had hesitated over the cartoon's macabre escapades, audiences and critics seemed to swoon. "Here is one of the most novel cartoon subjects ever shown on a screen," gushed *Film Daily.* Samuel "Roxy" Rothapfel, the impresario at the grand Roxy Theater in New York, booked it and then wrote Walt that it was "without exception one of the cleverest things I have seen, and as you know, the audience enjoyed every moment of it." One young aspiring animator named Joseph Barbera sat in the Roxy's third balcony watching *The Skeleton Dance* "about seventy miles from the screen" but said the "impact on me was tremendous nevertheless. I saw these skeletons dancing in a row and in unison, and I asked myself: How do you *do* that? How do you make that happen?"

As another prong of his assault, all the time that Walt was manically promoting his new sound operation and the Silly Symphonies, he was also replenishing his staff with top-rated animators in expectation of having to produce both the Mickeys and the new series—as many as thirty-six new cartoons that year. While he had been in New York in February, Walt, again with the encouragement of Powers, who seemed to want the Mickeys as quickly as possible, had interviewed potential recruits and wound up hiring Burt Gillett, an animation veteran who was working at Pat Sullivan's studio drawing Felix the Cat ("which he says are not so hot") and whom Walt described as a "damn clever fellow." Gillett recommended Ben Sharpsteen, who had worked under him years earlier animating the Mutt and Jeff series. When Walt returned from New York, he wrote Sharpsteen, then freelancing in San Francisco, and invited him out to the studio. Before meeting with Walt, Sharpsteen had dinner with Bill Nolan and Walter Lantz, another animator, both of whom advised him not to join Disney because sound cartoons were too limited to succeed. But when Sharpsteen met Walt—he walked a mile from the streetcar stop to Hyperion—Walt was so excited about sound that he grabbed several Mickeys and drove Sharpsteen to a downtown theater to show them. (The studio still did not have its own screening room.) Sharpsteen was impressed by the quality and joined the studio late in March at $125 a week, more than twice as much as Walt himself was earning in salary at the time.

Over the next several months Walt added Jack King, a highly regarded animator from New York, and Norman Ferguson, another New Yorker, who had animated the Aesop's Fables that Walt had so admired. Walt also attempted to recruit the primary animators for Felix the Cat—

Al Eugster and Otto Messmer. "It was pressure!" Messmer remembered. "He begged and pleaded." But Messmer was settled in New York, and in any case he felt that Felix would continue forever. Later that summer of 1929 Roy went to New York and continued the recruiting drive, even attempting to pry loose veteran animator Dick Huemer for a possible Mickey Mouse comic strip, without success. Even so, by August Walt was employing eight animators on a staff of twenty—eight of the top animators in the business.

The studio to which the newcomers came, set in the hinterland of the Silver Lake district of Los Angeles, which one visitor described as "one of those endless suburban settings of Barcelona bungalows, pink roses and red filling stations," was still, after three years, physically underwhelming. It consisted of the one stucco building, the original bungalow, with offices for Roy and Walt and a large room that was divided by a partition down the center—ink and paint on one side, animation on the other. Next to this main building was a small shed where canisters of film and old drawings were stored, and behind that was the stage on which Walt had shot the later Alices. By the spring of 1929 Walt had begun making small additions as the need arose. There was what Sharpsteen called a "nubbin" for a camera room to shield the animators from the disturbance of the camera's noise, though a chimes factory next door once tested a doorbell all day, nearly driving the artists crazy. There was also another addition, about fourteen feet square, that Walt called the "music room" because he kept a piano there for Stalling to use, and shortly afterward a larger addition for more offices. All told, these later constructions tripled the original space.

But if the effect was slapdash and haphazard, the operation inside was anything but—at least compared to the low standards of the rest of the animation industry. When Sharpsteen had met Walt that afternoon at Hyperion, Walt had passionately expressed his longstanding conviction that "his salvation was in making a product that so excelled that the public would recognize it and enjoy it as the best entertainment and that they would more or less demand to see Disney pictures." From his own experience in animation, where everything seemed to be done on the fly, Sharpsteen thought that Walt was being overly ambitious, but he soon realized that the Disney studio was a "complete reversal" of what he had found in New York. At Disney the atmosphere may have been casual, but when it came to work, everything was carefully planned. Every cartoon had an exposure sheet precisely outlining each scene, each movement, and each individual drawing. At first Walt had all of the animators spend a portion of their time doing the layout work—laying out the backgrounds and the precise positions of the characters on those backgrounds—but he soon instituted one of his early divisions of labor by hiring a separate layout artist, Carlos Manríquez, for this task. As the staff grew, Iwerks too no longer provided all the basic animation but instead provided key sketches that other animators would then execute. At night he presided over animation classes. By the end of the year Iwerks was concentrating on preparing bar sheets and exposure sheets and heading up the Silly Symphonies unit, while Burt Gillett headed up the Mickey Mouses.

The biggest difference, however, between the Disney studio and the animation studios in New York was not in preparation or specialization; it was in expectation. Walt Disney had to be the best. As he had with the Alices and the Oswalds, though with indifferent results, Walt insisted upon excellence, and Sharpsteen admitted that he soon had some misgivings about joining the studio when he came to realize how high Walt's standards were. Assigned what he believed was a run-of-the-mill scene in one of the early Mickeys, he saw that Walt did not regard it or any scene that way. "In Walt's estimation, everything that was done had to be executed with a great deal of thought toward finesse in order to make it better." It could be a struggle convincing men who had spent their careers thinking of animation as a throwaway that they could and must accomplish something better. "I have encountered plenty of trouble getting my new men adjusted to our method of working," Walt complained to Giegerich that April, "but things are clearing up now and it looks like we are going to be able to sail along smoothly from now on."

Part of Walt's secret was that in insisting on quality from individuals of whom it had never been required, he inspired commitment. "We'd hate to go home at night," Iwerks recalled, "and we couldn't wait to get to the office in the morning. We had lots of vitality, and we had to work it off." Though only a short time earlier the atmosphere at the studio had been dismal, the success of the Mickeys lifted spirits. The animators would now play pranks on one another—pouring water on a chair as someone was about to sit in it or putting cheese on the light under a colleague's animation board or Art Gum eraser shavings in his pipe tobacco. "But all the horseplay and jokes," Iwerks said, "never got in the way of the work. We all loved what we were doing and the enthusiasm got onto the screen." Indeed, when a reporter glowingly described the carefree atmosphere at Hyperion, Walt actually took offense, griping to Giegerich that "one would gather we are nothing but a happy-go-lucky bunch of fellows without any system or organization about us, and that all I do is sit on my fanny and pass out the checks to the fellows."

There was something else too that gave the Disney studio an esprit and sense of fraternity: Walt's own informality. Freed from the constant demands and financial tensions of the Mintz era, he was a different man. He prided himself on being one of the guys, even cultivated it. "We haven't any president or any other officers," he told a visiting reporter proudly. "In fact, we are not even incorporated. I guess you couldn't call us a company. We voice our opinions and sometimes we have good old-fashioned scraps, but in the end things get ironed out and we have something we're all proud of." Most of the employees even had a key to the studio's front door. Walt could still be demanding and caustic, especially with longtime associates like Iwerks, but having learned from his experience with the mutineers who detested him, Walt drew closer to his animators, stopping by their desks to talk not just about their work but about their interests and making suggestions to them without seeming overbearing. "The men loved it," Iwerks said, "and they all responded."

But as smoothly as Walt had the new operation running, his pursuit of excellence eventually ran up against an intractable reality that always seemed to bedevil him: money. Quality was expensive, and there never seemed to be enough money to support it. The early Mickeys cost between $4,180 (*Mickey's Follies*) and $5,357 (*The Karnival Kid*) to produce, which didn't include the royalties to Powers for the Cinephone system, or the onerous yearly $13,000, or the debt to record *Steamboat Willie*, which the Disneys were still paying off nearly a year later. By May, Walt had received nearly $40,000 in fees and rentals from Powers, but he had to pay distribution costs and expenses, and had to retire loans, leaving him virtually nothing, especially since he had expanded his staff and was paying the new animators well. "The money has been coming in at a pretty fair rate," Roy determined later that summer, saying that *Willie* alone had grossed $15,000 and might eventually gross $25,000, "the question is what are the expenses—and they are enough you can bet." At the same time Walt was carrying the expenses of the recording studio, which despite his sunny predictions had yet to turn a profit and was draining money. He had, in fact, tried to borrow $2,500 from Powers to help keep it afloat.

To extricate himself from his financial predicament, Walt thought of trying an old remedy—turning out the Mickeys faster, one every two weeks, and making a Silly Symphony every month, adding up to thirty-eight or thirty-nine cartoons annually in all—but he would have needed another infusion of $10,000 to do so, and Powers refused, sticking to the original twenty-six shorts. Trying another tack, he had a friend make newsreels to sell to Powers, but Giegerich and another of Powers's associates, Ed Smith, "queered it." That June he even shot a sound short of film stars—Al Jolson, Douglas Fairbanks, Jr., and Joan Crawford among them—attending a movie premiere, and Will Rogers delivering an informal dinner speech, for a series he called Hollywood Screen Star News, and dangled it before Columbia Pictures, but they too demurred.

Increasingly desperate, Walt began hiking to studios again with his animations, hoping to interest one of them in securing the rights from Powers. The writer Frances Marion claimed that two editors at Metro-Goldwyn-Mayer had seen Disney's cartoons and recommended them to Marion and Metro directors George Hill and Victor Fleming. Standing in the projection room, Walt was, as Marion remembered, a "tall, shy youth who wore a shabby suit and whose apprehensive glance at us told very clearly of many past disappointments." He even apologized for the crudeness of the animations. But the group was enthralled by Mickey; Fleming, his "long arms flailing the air," exclaimed, "Man, you've got it! Damnedest best cartoon I've ever seen!" Marion said that Walt had also brought along a second cartoon, a Silly Symphony, which in her description sounded like *Springtime*, though this is unlikely since the cartoon had yet to be drawn, and that the group was just as enthusiastic about it—so much so that Marion immediately headed to the office of Metro head Louis B. Mayer to drag him down to the projection room.

Mayer, however, was not impressed. Watching the Symphony, he pushed a button to stop the projector, pronounced the cartoon "ridiculous," and groused that while men and women dance together, and boys and girls dance together, *flowers* do not dance together. When Mayer rose to leave, Fleming eased him back into his chair and advised he see the Mickey Mouse. No sooner did the film start, however, than Mayer let out a bellow and demanded that the cartoon be stopped. Driving his fist into the pit of his stomach, he declared that pregnant women go to see MGM films and that women are terrified of mice, especially a mouse ten feet tall on the motion picture screen. Mayer stormed out of the room, slamming the door behind him, while Walt stood there in embarrassment.

It was Columbia that provided him with a reprieve. Frank Capra, a Sicilian immigrant who had worked his way from writing gags for silent comedy producer Mack Sennett to becoming Columbia's leading director, had been prevailed upon by the studio's lab technician to watch a cartoon one night after Capra screened the rushes of his own film. Capra was tired and unenthusiastic about the prospect, and he was even less enthused when the lab technician introduced him to Walt—a "scrawny, nondescript, hungry-looking young man, wearing two days' growth of beard and a slouch cap." But when the cartoon hit the screen, Capra was entranced and insisted that Columbia head Harry Cohn see it. Cohn, who also grumbled about having to see a cartoon, turned out to be equally impressed. Columbia, not a major studio but an aspiring one, was willing to take on the cartoons.

Powers was amenable since he would be getting the bulk of the receipts. That August, after the successful showings of *The Skeleton Dance* at the Carthay Circle and the Roxy, Giegerich was able to conclude a distribution agreement with Columbia—one Symphony each month for a $5,000 advance. (It was a testament to just how successful *The Skeleton Dance* was and to the Disneys' growing reputation that Columbia made the offer without seeing another Symphony because there was no other Symphony to show.) Since Powers had already sold the foreign rights for $3,500, the Disneys would be receiving $8,500 for each cartoon, less the 10 percent commission to Powers and less other expenses like negatives, advertising, and the sound royalty. The deal also called for a sixty-five–thirty-five split of profits favoring Powers until all costs were repaid and a fifty-fifty split thereafter. Roy calculated that the actual studio receipts after all the deductions were roughly $6,000 per cartoon, which he admitted wasn't exceptional, but it was regular, and "even $6,000 net—for certain every few weeks for a year will be a big help towards establishing ourselves firmly."

But survival wasn't what young Walt Disney had in mind. After his problems at Laugh-O-Gram and with Mintz, he wanted domination—domination that would make his position unassailable. That fall, with the Columbia deal signed and a steady cash flow assured, and with most of his rivals reeling, he concentrated on a new objective in his larger quest to become the animation overlord: he was determined that Mickey Mouse would supplant Felix the Cat. Felix, a thick black cat with oval eyes, pointy ears, and an expressive tail, had long been the reigning cartoon star, not only in America but around the world. There was a Felix song, a Felix comic strip, Felix books, dolls, pencils, and figurines, even Felix cigars. When RCA demonstrated its new television system in the summer of 1928, a twelve-inch papier-mâché Felix figure was the first image transmitted. The best tribute to his popularity, however, may have been the fact that over the years he had given rise to at least a half-dozen imitations, including Mintz's Krazy Kat and Walt's own Julius.

But Felix's creator, the unpredictable Pat Sullivan, had none of Walt Disney's drive or foresight. When his distributor pressed him to convert Felix to sound after Mickey's triumph, Sullivan dallied, finally losing his

Flora and Elias Disney, circa 1913 in Kansas City. They had the weather-beaten faces of pioneers, which is what they were: the faces of American Gothic.

Uncle Robert Disney, the family dandy who provided an impossible standard for his brother, Elias, to meet even as he assisted him. He also provided a grubstake for his nephews Walt and Roy.

Marceline, Missouri: Walt Disney's Eden and his archetype for small-town America. He spent a lifetime trying to recover its sense of comfort and security. Main Street, shown here, wasn't paved at the time the Disneys arrived.

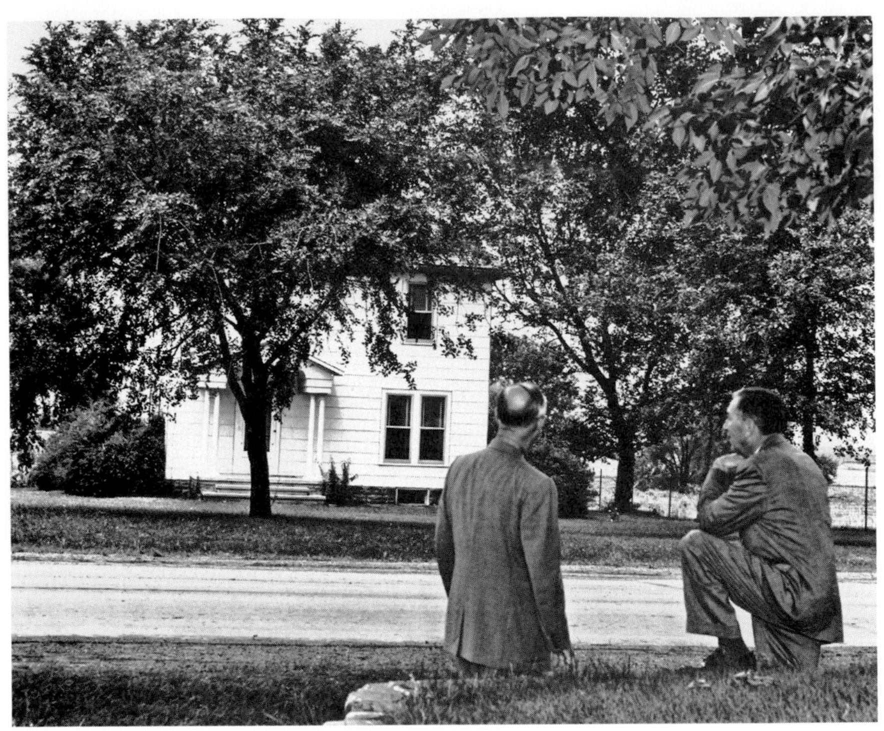

Walt *(right)* and Roy surveying their old Marceline farmhouse on a visit in 1956.

The two Walts: Disney *(right)* and Pfeiffer. Walt Disney called the Pfeiffer home, just down the street from his own, his "laughing place" where he could escape his father's discipline.

The Bellefontaine house in Kansas City where Walt spent most of his adolescence. It was located just off the paper route to which the Disney family was tethered. In front of the house is Walt's niece, Dorothy.

Walt in France in front of his truck on his Red Cross mission just after World War I: "doing something I very seldom do— 'work.'" He added: "every once and a while I make trips with this truck." When he wasn't chauffeuring visitors, he drew.

Walt, second from left in an eyeshade with a pipe, at the Kansas City Film Ad Co. where he first became interested in animation. Fred Harman, who joined Walt's effort to start his own company, is at his table on the far left. Ub Iwerks, Walt's onetime partner, is at the second table in the second seat.

On the roof of the McConahy Building where Laugh-O-Gram was headquatered: Walt (*left*) strangles a colleague while Ub Iwerks directs from his chair and business manager Adolph Kloepper runs the camera.

California: Walt *(right)*, who came to Hollywood to make his name in motion pictures, and Roy, who came to California to convalesce from tuberculosis, in an orange grove.

Walt (*left*) and Ub Iwerks, the painfully shy "inside" man to Walt's "outside" man and the cocreator of Mickey Mouse. Iwerks had one of the fastest pencils in the animation business.

Right: Margaret Winkler, the tough-minded businesswoman who distributed the Alice comedies that Walt Disney produced. Winkler's offer launched his career.

Bottom: Walt (*second from left*) a few blocks from the Kingswell office on the lot in Hollywood where the Alice comedies were filmed. Virginia Davis is at the center, her father at the far left, and Roy at the right, manning the camera.

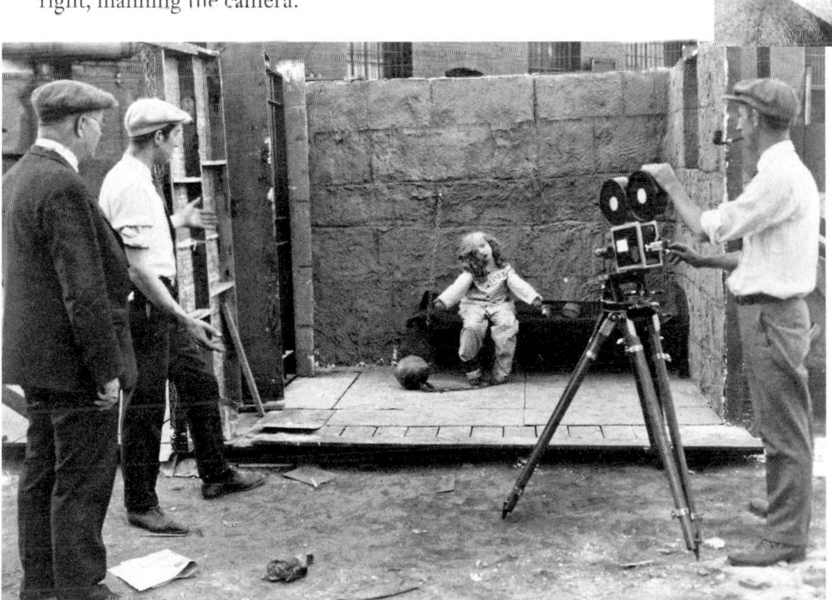

Walt and the Disney Bros. staff in front of the storefront on Kingswell Avenue in 1924. Left to right: Iwerks, Ham Hamilton, Walt, Thurston Harper, and Roy.

Edna Francis *(left)*, Roy's fiancée, and Lillian Bounds, the Idaho girl who would become Mrs. Walt Disney.

The wedding party of Walt and Lillian on July 13, 1925 at Lillian's brother's home in Lewiston, Idaho. Lillian's sister is at the left, her mother to Lillian's left and her brother Sidney, the local fire chief, at the far right. Lillian giggled nervously throughout the ceremony.

The house on Lyric Avenue in the Silver Lake section of Los Angeles. It was small and prefabricated and Roy had an identical one next door, but owning it was a sign of the Disneys' rising status in animation.

Charles Mintz *(middle)* with Oswald the Lucky Rabbit after signing the contract with Universal Pictures vice president Robert H. Cochrane. Mintz would become Walt's nemesis, and his betrayal would never cease to haunt Walt.

Pat A. Powers, one of the most legendarily belligerent figures in film history and the man in whom Walt naïvely placed his confidence. Powers would prove to be as nettlesome to Walt Disney as he had to his other partners.

contract. By the time he decided that he had to add sound to his cartoons, that was precisely what he did—*add* it to previously animated cartoons rather than conceive of them, as Walt did, in terms of sound. "By 1930 Felix was doomed," said one of his animators, "because he was a silent pantomime character. We tried sound but it was a flop."

Felix's sudden demise provided Walt Disney with his opening. At the beginning no effort to catapult Mickey into stardom was too small. Walt would even have friends call theaters asking what time the Mickey Mouse cartoon would show, and if they were told that there was no Mickey, he instructed them to ask why. More aggressively, Walt arranged with one downtown theater to make a cartoon of Mickey leading the theater's live orchestra and then being pelted by the musicians. In exchange the theater booked another Mickey cartoon and put the title on the marquee, where Walt could have it photographed for publicity. By August he was taking out full-page ads in the motion picture trade papers declaring Mickey Mouse "Amazingly Clever—Screamingly Funny—Perfectly Synchronized Sound Cartoons."

But the biggest boost to Mickey Mouse, aside from sound itself, occurred not through Walt's promotions, which were scattershot, but through those of Harry Woodin, the young manager of the Fox Dome Theater in Ocean Park, a Los Angeles suburb. On his own initiative late that summer, Woodin had organized a Mickey Mouse Club, filling his theater on Saturday afternoons with children who took a Mickey Mouse pledge, performed in an impromptu Mickey Mouse band, and then watched Mickey Mouse cartoons. Woodin had invited Walt to one of the matinees, and Walt said he got "quite a kick to see about one thousand kids cheering for MICKEY MOUSE." But Woodin himself, not unlike Walt Disney, had larger aspirations. He convinced Walt that what he was doing locally he could also do nationally. Walt was encouraging. "I feel positive that a stunt like this, combined with a Comic Strip and various toys and novelties that might be made around MICKEY," Walt wrote Giegerich eagerly, "would help us in making this series one of the biggest things that has ever come out."

By January, under studio auspices, Woodin had launched a Mickey Mouse Club campaign. Theaters would buy a charter from the studio for twenty-five dollars, which entitled them to run special Mickey Mouse matinees and stage various activities, from pie-eating contests to marble tournaments to the ever-present Mickey Mouse band. The studio then funneled that money to salesmen who hawked buttons, banners, and other Mickey paraphernalia to the theaters; the purchase of this, Walt advised, could be subsidized by local merchants. Woodin had even devised a

Mickey Mouse creed—"Mickey Mice do not swear, smoke, cheat or lie"—that was recited at every meeting, and a Mickey Mouse song, composed by Stalling, titled "Minnie's Yoo Hoo," that was sung before each adjournment:

I'm the guy they call little Mickey Mouse
Got a sweetie down at the chicken house,
Neither fat nor skinny
She's the horse's whinny
She's my little Minnie Mouse

It featured a chorus of animal sounds, concluding, "With all the cows and the chickens, they all sound like the dickens / When I hear my little Minnie's yoo hoo."

How much the clubs were responsible for propelling Mickey and how much Mickey was responsible for propelling the clubs is difficult to determine, but the promotion took off immediately and kept growing, giving theaters revenue from Saturday matinees, parents a three-hour respite from their children, the film industry a beacon of wholesomeness to which they could point to deflect critics, and Walt Disney a powerful means of promoting his creation and himself. The Biltmore Theater in Miami signed up 1,200 members; the Fox Eckel Theater in Syracuse, New York, 1,300; the Fox MacDonald Theater in Eugene, Oregon, 1,500, and it regularly turned away hundreds of others who arrived for the shows. At one theater children began gathering on the sidewalk at nine o'clock in the morning for an eleven o'clock matinee. In Milwaukee three thousand Mickey Mouse Club members staged a parade as a highlight of a Mickey Mouse Club convention. At their peak, Roy estimated, there were over eight hundred chapters in the country with, by another estimate, more than one million members—more, according to the *Motion Picture Herald*, than the combined membership of the Girl Scouts and Boy Scouts of America. The Mickey Mouse Clubs had become a movement.

Walt was looking to newspapers, too, in his campaign to establish Mickey as a national figure, just as Pat Sullivan had used a comic strip to establish Felix. At least since June 1929, when Iwerks received a letter from J. V. Connelly of the King Features newspaper syndicate lauding the Mickey Mouse cartoons and suggesting the possibility of a Mickey Mouse comic strip, Walt had been aggressively pushing the idea with Powers and Giegerich, not so much to exploit Mickey as to promote him further. By early August, King Features had made a firm offer—this was when Roy was attempting to enlist Dick Huemer to draw the strip—and on January

13, 1930, it made its first appearance. Walt contributed the stories while Iwerks drew the strip and another artist named Win Smith inked the drawings. When Smith suddenly quit four months later, Walt shifted a young animator named Floyd Gottfredson into the job on a temporary assignment. In the end Walt was too distracted by other obligations to find a replacement, and Gottfredson would continue drawing the Mickey Mouse strip until his retirement in 1975.

Like the Mickey Mouse Clubs, the comic strip was an instant success and another enormous boon to Mickey's popularity—perhaps as powerful an engine in disseminating his image as the cartoons themselves. By the summer the strip was being syndicated in as many as forty newspapers and in twenty-two countries and was earning the Disneys $1,500 a month, out of which they paid $800 in salaries and other costs. It was evidence of the strip's appeal that when, as a promotion for it, a dozen papers offered readers a Mickey Mouse photo, they received twenty thousand requests.

Throughout the months that he was pressing to launch the Mickey Mouse Clubs and the comic strip, Walt was also prodding Giegerich to make a deal to manufacture Mickey Mouse merchandise, offering him 10 percent of the profits—an offer that Giegerich ultimately rejected. In this Walt was almost certainly thinking of the tie-in between Pat Sullivan and George Borgfeldt & Co., which manufactured Felix toys, including a popular Felix the Cat doll that reportedly earned Sullivan substantial royalties; but he was also no doubt considering that there was already bootleg Mickey merchandise on the market from which he was not profiting—yet another sign of Mickey's popularity. As Walt later told it, he was in New York with Lillian early in 1930 when a man approached him at his hotel and waved $300 at him, which the man was offering for the right to put Mickey Mouse on cheap paper tablets for schoolchildren. Walt said he needed the money, so he took it, making this his first license for a Mickey Mouse product.

But this was more an accident than a premeditated effort. Walt had been urging Giegerich to contact Borgfeldt for months, and when Giegerich failed to act, Walt apparently contacted Borgfeldt himself during the same New York trip and made his own deal on January 29 for toys and novelties. By early April, the studio machine shop was making Mickey Mouse doll models to send to Borgfeldt, though Walt, as particular with his merchandise as with his animations, was displeased with them and asked that they be held off the market. At the same time Roy was soliciting publishers for a book of animal stories featuring Mickey, was discussing a Mickey comic book with one firm, and was attempting to interest various confectioneries, including the large Curtiss and Mars companies, in a Mickey Mouse candy bar.

"Things are happening fast for us now," Roy wrote his parents that January, with the clubs, the comic strip, and the merchandise all rapidly coming to fruition, "so much so they have our heads swimming." He added that, amid the success of Walt's Mickey campaign, they were looking for a new distributor as well—"trying to decide which is the best place, as we have had overtures from every outlet in the business, including Fox, Paramount and Warner Bros. How does that sound?" Of course, they were still obligated to Pat Powers for the Mickeys for some time to come, but that hadn't prevented them from quietly approaching other distributors and fielding offers without Powers's knowledge; nor had it prevented Charles Giegerich, Powers's right-hand man, from approaching *them* with an offer to serve as their distributor and freeze out Powers. Nat Levine, the president of Mascot Pictures, which specialized in serials, and a longtime adviser to the Disneys, offered them $50,000 up front to bind an agreement. At the same time Walt was in discussions with Metro-Goldwyn-Mayer and expected them to deliver a draft contract, and the old Van Beuren animation studio offered to buy them outright. "If they [the cartoons] weren't good, and good paying propositions," Roy assured Walt, who had gone to New York in January to listen to offers, "they [distributors] would not be fighting hard to take them away from us. We never were in as good a position before to fight them as we are now."

There was a reason the Disneys were conducting secret negotiations, and the reason was the chicanery of Walt's onetime savior, the genial Pat Powers. As early as the previous fall, tensions had begun to surface between Walt and Powers over the remittance of royalties from the cartoons. Jack Cohn of Columbia, believing that the dispute might explain what he saw as the inferior quality of the second Silly Symphony, had even ordered Walt to his office to discuss it. Walt insisted that relations were good and any hint to the contrary was "absurd," though he later complained about Columbia's own seeming lassitude when it came to promoting the Symphonies. That in turn prompted Powers to write him darkly, just as Mintz once had, that Walt had put him in an "embarrassing position" and shown ingratitude "after every distributor in the business had refused to handle the product under any kind of basis which would enable us to get even the cost of it back." In fact, Powers said, he knew of no instance "where they were even receptive or seriously considered handling the product."

If these insults weren't enough, tensions heightened considerably when Powers repeatedly refused to give the Disneys a full accounting of the money due them. Roy knew there was a lot of money at stake, but when he went to New York to remonstrate and Powers still refused, he returned to the studio and told Walt that Powers was a "crook."* Walt was suspicious but not entirely convinced ("You know, my greatest weakness is that I'm a lousy judge of people," he once said) and called Roy a "trouble-maker." Meanwhile Powers, sensing that the Disneys might be attempting to circumvent him with a new distributor, wired Walt testily that they had obviously decided to terminate the agreement, and he wanted the courtesy of a notification so that he could make arrangements with another animator. Wary of making any move until he received his money, Roy suggested that Walt go to New York himself and confront Powers. Walt left with Lillian on January 17, 1930.

By the time Walt arrived in New York, the skirmish had escalated into all-out war, eerily reminiscent of the showdown with Charles Mintz just two years earlier, right down to the betrayal by one of Walt's closest associates. The morning of January 21 Ub Iwerks had gone to Roy's office, abruptly announced that he wanted to leave the studio as soon as possible, and asked to be released from his contract and from the partnership he had formed with the Disneys. Roy was stunned and hurt, though he offered Iwerks $5,000 for his 20 percent share of the company. What Roy did not know at the time and only heard later that day in a wire from Walt—who had learned it when Powers gleefully sprang it on him during a meeting in Powers's office—was that Iwerks had been lured away by Powers himself. Though Iwerks had initially denied having a contract with Powers, he sheepishly admitted in a long talk with Roy as he was preparing to leave the studio that Giegerich had contacted him as early as September—the same time that Giegerich had contacted the Disneys with the plan to double-cross Powers—about forming a studio of his own.

Iwerks wasn't terribly ambitious and he had never shown any inclination or talent to run a studio, but he entertained the offer, he confessed, because he had long seethed silently under Walt's command. He bristled when Walt would visit his animation table at night and rearrange the drawings on the exposure sheets, even though Iwerks had already timed them. And he bristled when, after he had roughed out a scene for *The Skeleton Dance*, Walt insisted that he give it to an "in-betweener," or novice animator, to complete, believing that Iwerks's time was too valuable to have him fully animate everything. Indeed, animating to

*An account more sympathetic to Powers absolved him because he discovered that larger distributors had frozen him out of the market in certain territories, forcing him to sublet the cartoons to Columbia. More, by this version Powers refused to give the Disneys an accounting because he wanted a legal contract rather than the letters of agreement under which he and the Disneys had been operating. Arthur Mann, "Mickey Mouse's Financial Career," *Harper's* 168 (May 1934), p. 716.

"extremes," as it was called, was the way most animators now worked—providing the key or extreme poses and letting an assistant fill in the rest of the action. Iwerks, however, believed that he animated best when he animated straight ahead, and he had no desire to change.

Finally, and perhaps most important, Iwerks had come to feel that he had been living in Walt's shadow, and he resented not receiving the credit he felt he deserved for the cartoons, whose title card read, "A Walt Disney Comic by Ub Iwerks." Iwerks's wife recalled attending a party where a boy approached Walt with a pen and paper and asked him if he would draw Mickey. Walt promptly handed the paper to Iwerks, ordered him to do the drawing, and said that he would sign it. Iwerks, usually imperturbable, snapped, "Draw your own Mickey," and left. Indeed, Iwerks was so resentful of the credit denied him that, obviously under Powers's encouragement, after he left he threatened to sue the Disneys for Mickey Mouse on copyright grounds. "If Ub's action reaches crew," Walt wrote Roy from New York, "advise you ridicule it as foolish as he is being used as a cat's paw by Powers and may never make any pictures."

When Iwerks visited Roy's office three days after his resignation to explain himself, he insisted that he hadn't known that Giegerich was actually representing Powers until he'd received the contract just days earlier.* This mollified Roy slightly—"We know how gullible and easily led Ub is, and we have a good dose of how two-faced Charlie Giegerich and P.A. are," he wrote Walt—but he still expressed how "deeply shocked and hurt" he was at Iwerks's betrayal, and he rescinded his $5,000 offer. Now that Powers was involved, he would give Iwerks only $2,920, payable in one year, which Iwerks accepted as settlement for all his claims. The alternative, Roy warned, was to dissolve their partnership, which would force Powers to open his books and would undoubtedly ignite his anger at Iwerks. As Iwerks left Roy's office, he expressed his regrets and said he intended to write Walt because, he told Roy, he did not want Walt "to feel hard against him—that he would never have gone into this had he any idea it would turn out as it has." For Walt's part, though he and Iwerks had never been personally close, he nevertheless, according to one acquaintance, "obviously loved that guy," and when a young animator joined the studio the week of Iwerks's departure and met Walt, Walt was still wounded and angered by Iwerks's disloyalty and talked about little else.

*In fact, it was difficult to tell exactly for whom Giegerich was dealing. Though he worked for Powers, he had contacted the Van Beuren studio offering them the contracts of Iwerks and Carl Stalling, who hadn't even signed with him, and telling Van Beuren that "most publicity on Mickey Mouse and Silly Symphonies . . . was on the name of Ubbe Iwwerks [*sic*], with very little, if any, mention of Walt Disney." Roy to Walt, Feb. 1, 1930, Walt & Roy Disney Corr., 1929–1930, Walt Disney Early Corr., WDA.

Losing Iwerks would have been a blow in any case, but he was not the only defector that week. Unsettled by Iwerks's departure and increasingly upset himself at what he saw as Walt's high-handedness, Carl Stalling, who had known Walt since the Kansas City days, ambushed Roy the very morning Iwerks resigned and began complaining about his liability in the recording studio and the royalties he expected from "Minnie's Yoo Hoo," if it were published. (Stalling had a point. Walt's attorney had advised that the song be copyrighted in Walt's name because, Roy wrote Walt, "it would not be a good idea for us to have him [Stalling] having too many strings on things—at least until he takes a one hundred percent cooperation attitude.") Roy offered to buy Stalling's share in the recording studio, which seemed to appease him, but he was back at Roy the next morning saying that he was unhappy, that he couldn't get along with Walt, and that he felt, like Iwerks, that he should leave immediately. Roy thought Stalling had gotten "nasty," and when the composer demanded his back pay and brandished legal notices that he had written himself, Roy had the accounting office cut him a check and sent him off.

The disloyalty of Stalling and Iwerks, two men who had been with Walt since virtually the beginning, hurt Walt; so too did the fact of Iwerks's even being wooed. It was unclear whether Powers had signed Iwerks as a way to pressure Walt into renewing the Mickey contract, as Powers himself told Walt he had, or whether, like Mintz, Powers believed that Walt was superfluous and that Iwerks was the real talent behind Mickey. Whichever it was, Walt seemed to be stung by the idea that Iwerks would be more highly regarded than he was. To him, the studio *was* Walt Disney. Roy made a point of telling him that while the studio staff expressed shock at Iwerks's and Stalling's leaving, they had closed ranks behind Walt. Ben Sharpsteen told Roy that "US fellows who have been in this business so long, know who is the 'guts' of this organization. . . . [W]e know the difference of these cartoons over the average run, is nothing more or less than Walt's personality. . . . [N]obody could kid themselves that it was otherwise." Roy himself assured Walt that "the year to come will show them all who is really responsible for Mickey Mouse."

While the warfare with Powers continued—the Disneys had still not cut their ties or signed with a new distributor—and Powers geared up for his own studio by raiding Universal for Ham Hamilton, poaching Hugh Harman from Mintz, and attempting to pry sound engineer William Garity from Walt, Walt and Roy wasted no time bringing in reinforcements of their own. The very day Stalling resigned, Roy met with Ollie Wallace, a former organist at the Million Dollar Theater in downtown Los Angeles, who had been recommended by Mickey Mouse Club impresario Harry Woodin as a possible replacement. Wallace laughed derisively when Roy told him the salary, $150, but Roy said that if Wallace's contributions paid off, he would be amply rewarded. At Walt's insistence, Roy had also tendered a contract to Tom Palmer, who had been working for producer Walter Lantz at Universal, and promoted Bill Cottrell, who had joined the studio a year earlier in ink and paint, to animation. That same week Roy hired animator Dave Hand, who had been trained at the Chicago Academy of Fine Arts, where Walt had once studied, and then worked at the Bray studio. Nearly all the recruits earned more than Walt, whose salary fluctuated between $125 and $150 a week, depending on how much money was in the studio's till at the time.

Meanwhile Walt was girding for the final showdown. He and Roy had decided that they would try to enlist Columbia on their side by complaining that by luring Iwerks away, Powers had disrupted their organization, delayed their production schedule, and generally wreaked havoc, which was costing not only the Disneys but Columbia as well. Roy even suggested that Walt use Powers as an excuse to discontinue the Symphonies or deliberately produce a few inferior ones to support their case. (In fact, Walt advised Roy to suspend temporarily production on the Mickey Mouses, which Powers still distributed, and concentrate on the Symphonies, which Columbia distributed.) To press their claim, the brothers hired a young California attorney named Gunther Lessing, who headed to New York to help Walt cope with Powers. "ATTORNEYS POSITIVE CONTRACT CAN EASILY BE ABANDONED IF NOT SATISFACTORILY ADJUSTED," Walt wired Roy, adding that he and Lessing were trying to work out a settlement with Powers. Indeed, despite all the bad blood between them, Powers hadn't given up trying to keep Walt. Undercutting Iwerks, he told Lessing that he was willing to give Walt a salary of $2,000 a week, a staggering sum in 1930, if Walt would fulfill the current contract and sign another allowing Powers to distribute the Mickeys the following year.

Remarkable as it may seem, Walt still hadn't entirely closed the door on Powers—Roy was terrified that Powers would somehow sweet-talk Walt into signing another contract—but he had become too disillusioned by Powers's unwillingness to make an accounting of profits and by his stealing Iwerks to see him as anything but a last resort, and he was counting on a new distributor taking him on now that Mickey Mouse was so successful. "Powers is crooked," Lillian wrote Roy and Edna, no doubt echoing Walt, "so I don't know how it will all turn out." At the same time Walt had received an offer from Warner Bros. to buy the studio outright, had once again approached Felix Feist, the sales manager for MGM, about picking up the Mickeys, and was talking to Columbia itself about a similar deal.

The difference between this confrontation and his confrontation with

Mintz was that Walt now seemed to have the upper hand—the Mickeys, after all, were popular—but Powers was as shrewd and incorrigible as Mintz was bullying. Though MGM was ready to conclude a deal, Powers scared them off by threatening a lawsuit, and Walt worried that Powers and Columbia might collude somehow to force the Disneys to re-sign with him. Roy also worried that if they broke with Powers, Powers would set up another Cinephone operation to compete with theirs and they would never be able to meet their royalty guarantee. As if Powers's threats weren't enough, that same week John Randolph Bray, the animation pioneer, demanded a meeting with Walt during which Bray told him that he was going to enforce his patents and limit the number of cartoons allowed on the market. "Boy, they are gunning for him from all sides," Lillian wrote Roy and Edna, "and he is dying to get back and make pictures, is getting pretty nervous."

Indeed, Walt, usually imperturbable, was getting frantic, certain that Powers would intimidate other suitors as he had intimidated MGM, and concerned that Powers might file a breach-of-contract suit against him that would keep them tangled in court proceedings. He was constantly on the move, looking for a solution. Racing from meetings with lawyers to meetings with distributors to meetings with Powers, he had been in New York nearly two weeks before he could meet Lillian for lunch or see a Broadway show with her. At lunch with animator Dick Huemer, whom Walt was still trying to enlist for the studio, Walt was uncharacteristically distracted, sullen, and monosyllabic. "[A]ll through the meal," Huemer recalled, "I don't think Walt addressed five words to me," prompting Huemer to muse what a "strange guy" Walt Disney was, especially for someone who was recruiting.

After a week of fraying nerves and jousting with Powers, who still adamantly refused to open his books, Walt finally broke with him, instructing Roy to stop producing the Mickeys. Then he braced for the inevitable lawsuit, which, when it came, set off a farcical game of hide-and-seek. Lessing phoned Walt at the Algonquin Hotel that Powers was about to serve him with papers. Walt and Lillian hastily threw their clothes into a trunk, called a bellboy, paid the bill, and hailed a cab, telling the driver to go anywhere. They eventually found a small hotel, the Piccadilly, and registered under the names Mr. and Mrs. Walter E. Call, Flora Disney's maiden name. After another week they left New York for California.

All the time he was in the city, Walt had been sending basically cheery messages back to Roy, reassuring him again and again that everything would turn out satisfactorily. "[W]hen he really got kicked in the teeth and got out completely," Roy later remembered of the split with Powers, "on his way home he tells me, 'Everything's fine. When I get back we're going to make a big start.' . . . But he really didn't have anything. And then on the train he sweated out some plans. That was typical of him." It was, Roy might have added, Charlie Mintz all over again. Even with Mickey Mouse, they seemed right back at the beginning—back having to fight to make their cartoons.

But the situation that February was not as dire as Roy and even Walt seemed to think. For one thing, the recording studio had begun to generate profits, so much so that the company occasionally borrowed from it to meet its payroll and so much so that in that year's federal census, while Walt identified himself as a "producer," Roy identified himself as a "sound recorder." For another, and more important, Columbia Pictures, having grossed nearly $400,000 on the first thirteen Symphonies and obviously recognizing just how much profit it could earn if it distributed the Mickeys too, had surprisingly decided to step into the breach and take on Powers. Within weeks of Walt's returning to California, his attorneys had worked out an agreement with Columbia and then successfully arranged a settlement with Powers, though one attorney confessed that the settlement papers were "complicated," which was an understatement. Roy estimated that Powers had made $100,000 in his two years of distributing the Mickeys, but the old rascal was not about to let Walt go cheaply. He demanded $50,000, which Columbia had conceded to pay in ten monthly installments secured by the Disneys' overages from any source, and retention of everything he had collected on the Mickeys to date. Roy later bargained this down to 40 percent of Powers's collections from exhibitors to whom he had already rented cartoons and 25 percent from franchisees who had already bought the rights to the cartoons, but this was minus expenses of roughly $150,000 for negatives and sound equipment. In addition, Powers was to receive Walt's share of the net profits from Cinephone up to $62,000. Columbia would retire its note from percentages on the first fifteen Mickeys, which it was now authorized to redistribute, and the first six Silly Symphonies, while the Disneys would receive 80 percent of the profits on the remaining Powers bookings from which he had yet to collect rentals. The settlement was not particularly favorable for the Disneys; legal fees alone had cost them $50,000. But Powers had left them without an alternative. "While sacrifice burns me up," Gunther Lessing wired Roy, "I believe in straightening entire mess imperative and less costly in the long run."

Even then it wasn't over. Though Walt, Columbia, and Powers had all agreed to the terms, the deal wasn't concluded until Roy went to New

York early that April to iron out the final wrinkles, which, as was typical with Powers, proved stubborn. After eight hours of negotiations on April 22 Roy, Powers, the Columbia executives, and all the attorneys—"a regular army," Roy said—had to reconvene at eleven in the morning the next day for another eight hours. "[I]f someone didn't raise an objection to every single thing," Roy wrote Walt later that day, "some[one] else did." Throughout, Powers was jovial and kept referring to Mickey Mouse as Mickey Louse. At the end of the day, with the exception of the Cinephone agreement—which Roy later negotiated down from $13,000 a year to $8,500—the Disneys were rid of Pat Powers once and for all.

Now it was Roy providing the optimistic missives. "I HONESTLY FEEL ELATED OVER EVERYTHING," he wired Walt as he was finally leaving New York after three weeks of bargaining. "SETTLEMENT GOING TO WORK OUT GOOD AND FUTURE VERY BRIGHT." Having wriggled out of Powers's control, Walt was ecstatic. George Morris, who had recently joined the Disneys' business office, said that the deal had lifted "a weight of worry off Walt's shoulders" and enabled him to return to moviemaking again after the months of distraction.

Under the new Columbia contract Walt would be receiving a $7,000 advance per cartoon in addition to a percentage of profits. But having once again been betrayed in business—and Walt having once again been reminded of the treacherous reality that lay outside his cartoon world—the Disneys hardly regarded Columbia as a deliverance from deviousness. As he was negotiating with both Powers and Columbia, Roy learned that Columbia had secretly approached their nemesis with an offer of $60,000 for all his rights in the Mickeys or, alternatively, $30,000 and 20 percent of the profits they would make from them, telling Powers that they would, in Roy's words, "fight it out with us" themselves. Roy immediately corralled Columbia executives Joe Brandt and Jack Cohn, who backed down, but Roy was still distrustful of his new partners and insisted on the contractual right to examine Columbia's books periodically, fully expecting that he would have a showdown with them someday too.

But until then Walt could retreat back into the Mickeys and the Silly Symphonies. Until then he was free.

IV

The reason Columbia was willing to spend $50,000 to extricate Walt from Pat Powers, and the reason larger and more established distributors had avidly pursued Walt before Powers discouraged them, was that Mickey

Mouse was becoming a phenomenon. When Columbia took out a full-page advertisement in *Film Daily* that December proclaiming Mickey "The Most Popular Character in Screendom," they may not have been far off. Even before the Columbia deal one reviewer noted that " 'Mickey Mouse' is one of the very few 'cartoon stars' to have his name featured by theaters on an almost equal basis with the feature screen attraction." A cartoon in *The Saturday Evening Post* that fall showed a wealthy man with a pince-nez and cane at a theater box office window digging into his pockets for the admission and asking the ticket seller, "Am I too late for Mickey Mouse?" An article in *Literary Digest*, comparing Mickey Mouse to Charlie Chaplin, jazz bandleader Paul Whiteman, and detective stories, claimed that he had also been discovered by the intelligentsia as these other exemplars of popular culture had. Chaplin reportedly demanded that a Mickey Mouse cartoon be played with his new film *City Lights*, and Madame Tussaud requested permission to immortalize Mickey in wax. In one three-week stretch Mickey Mouse received thirty thousand fan letters, and by one estimate one million separate audiences saw Mickey Mouse cartoons each year in the early 1930s.

Nor was his popularity confined to America. *Photoplay* called Mickey the "most popular motion picture star in all European countries" and noted that English exhibitors often featured his name in lights "four times as large as well-known stars." The German biographer Rene Fulop-Miller called Mickey the "preeminent personality of the screen today, and the only 'artist' who exemplified in his work and technique the pure form of talking films." French critics from one end of the aesthetic spectrum to the other praised him, and an Austrian critic complained that he was now more popular than Mozart.

Perhaps most telling of all about Mickey's popularity was how many of Walt's competitors were already imitating the mouse just as they had once imitated Felix. The Disneys brought suit against both Pathé and Van Beuren for Mickey look-alikes and warned Mintz about a character who looked suspiciously like Mickey. At the same time Harman and Ising created a new character named Bosko who resembled Mickey. Dick Huemer told Walt that the animators at Paramount and those drawing Krazy Kat for Mintz got each Disney cartoon and ran them again and again so they could copy the work, at which Walt crowed, "Our pictures are the center of attention back here—all the New York artists are trying to compete with them."

By the early 1930s a raft of analysis dissected what exactly made a round, chirpy little mouse so enormously appealing. When Walt was pressed to explain, his early assessments were surprisingly routine and superficial. He cited the constant motion in Mickey cartoons, the sharpness and brevity of the gags, and the exaggeration of emotions that were grounded in human experience and familiar to everyone. He told another interviewer that Mickey's size elicited sympathy and that when he triumphed, the small over the big, the audience rejoiced with him. On another occasion, celebrating Mickey's twenty-fifth anniversary, he attributed his creation's appeal to simplicity: "Mickey is so simple and uncomplicated, so easy to understand, that you can't help liking him." And on still another occasion, when Aldous Huxley asked Walt what theory he employed behind Mickey, Walt threw up his hands and said, "We just make a Mickey, and then the profs come along and tell us what we got."

The profs couldn't agree either, though, on the source of Mickey's appeal. Some thought he drew his appeal from the cultural currents of the 1930s. Animation historian John Culhane would say that in his very circular design, signaling a kind of impregnability, Mickey was the "perfect expression of what he symbolizes—survival," which, at the time he rose to prominence in the early days of the Great Depression, was a powerful attraction to a nation that was itself trying and hoping to survive. More pointedly, writer and producer William de Mille saw in Mickey an idealistic altruist in the mold of Franklin Roosevelt whose whole life suggested the "beloved Don Quixote, with Minnie Mouse as the fair Dulcinea and good old Pluto [Mickey's dog] fulfilling the duties of Sancho Panza." Still another scholar saw him as a representative of a new jittery machine age in which "the jerky rhythm of his movements, the constant collisions, explosions, and projections, are symbolic of nervous modern man living in a whirl of mechanical forces that multiply every physical action by ten to a thousand." Naturally, anyone subject to the same forces—and everyone was—empathized with Mickey. Still others, looking at the rise of totalitarianism in Europe at the time, believed Mickey to be a counterweight and antidote to an "age of dictators and tyrants . . . who stride the world like a colossus"—in effect, meaning Mickey Mouse displaced reality for everyone the way he displaced reality for his own creator.

He was so much a part of his time that, writing nearly forty years after Mickey's first appearance, cultural historian Warren Susman claimed that while political historians were likely to call the 1930s the age of Franklin D. Roosevelt, cultural historians would consider it the age of Mickey Mouse, both for the way the mouse seemed to confront the period's dislocations and agonies and for the way he seemed to suggest a remedy to them. "The Disney world is a world out of order: all traditional forms seem not to function," Susman observed. "And yet the result is not a nightmare world of pity and terror, a tragic world, but a world of fun and fantasy with ultimate wish-fulfillment, ultimate reinforcement of traditional ways and traditional values." "No matter how disordered the world appears," he wrote, "Disney and his Mickey Mouse—any of his heroes or heroines—can find their way back to happy achievement by following the announced rules of the game."

Meanwhile some psychological approaches regarded Mickey as striking deep psychic lodes. These analysts found Mickey's visual iconography to be reassuring ("[C]ircles never cause anybody any trouble," observed longtime Disney associate John Hench, comparing Mickey's shape to breasts, babies, and bottoms, while people have "bad experiences with sharp points."); or suggestive of the human, since Mickey's face was flat like the human face; or as Iwerks once explained with a nod to Jung, expressive of wholeness since his face, a "trinity of wafers and the circular symbol," unites the irreconcilable. Paleontologist Stephen Jay Gould applied to Mickey anthropologist Konrad Lorenz's argument that certain features of juvenility—"a relatively large head, predominance of the brain capsule, large and low lying eyes, bulging cheek region, short and thick extremities, a springy elastic consistency, and clumsy movements"—trigger innate responses of affection, so that Mickey Mouse, who had all these characteristics, was virtually constructed to elicit love.

Children's author Maurice Sendak located Mickey's appeal in his plasticity. Sendak found in the early Mickey cartoons, which featured "kicking the ass, pulling the ears, tweaking noses, twisting necks," a "passionate investigation of the body." "Eminently gropable" in Sendak's view, and like a baby, Mickey finally gave the viewer the "license to touch." *New York Times* film reviewer and later screenwriter Frank Nugent took a different slant on the theme of plasticity. He believed that Mickey Mouse "stole" screen slapstick from its live practitioners and then extended it because his elasticity exceeded theirs, and that it was slapstick that made the cartoons appealing.

Other observers traced Mickey's appeal to the way he summoned memories of childhood in the viewer himself: "the spirit of the child in man [which] would delight in caricaturing all those heroes whom ordinarily we should regard with awe and reverence," as Harvard professor Robert D. Feild wrote. A Dr. A. A. Brill, writing in 1934, thought Mickey Mouse "narcotized" his adult audience by taking them back to childhood, when "everything could still be attained through fantasy," as Mickey attains things. Another doctor, drawing on Freud, called Mickey an "ego ideal" who appeals to that part of childhood that is happy.

One of the most popular veins of analysis was the idea of Mickey as a representation of freedom, which was inherent in the animation medium itself. "He can break all natural laws (he never breaks moral laws) and always win," observed *Time* in 1933. "He lives in the moment, has few inhibitions." It was not too great a stretch from this freedom to incorrigibility—Mickey as "quick and cocky and cruel, at best a fresh and bratty kid, at worst a diminutive and sadistic monster," in Richard Schickel's words, or possessing a "scandalous element in him which I find most restful," in E. M. Forster's. Indeed, some found Mickey too suggestive. A board of Ohio censors rejected one Mickey cartoon in which a cow was reading Elinor Glyn's scandalous novel *Three Weeks*, while the midwestern Balaban & Katz theater chain objected to Mickey milking a cow in *The Karnival Kid*, to which Walt protested that it has "never been our intention to insert anything of a smutty nature," but wrote, "I still cannot see where anyone could take offense at any of the 'stuff' contained in our pictures." Even so, Maurice Sendak found an "anarchy" and "greediness" in Mickey's grin, the "gleeful beam [of] a sexual freedom," and said that when he designed his own Wild Things for the book *Where the Wild Things Are*, he based his drawings on this lascivious Mickey.

That lasciviousness tied Mickey Mouse to another motion picture icon: Charlie Chaplin. Nearly every analysis of the early Mickey invoked Chaplin and cited the correspondences between the two—their leering aggressiveness, their impertinence, their sense of abandon, and especially what film historian Terry Ramsaye at the time called "the cosmic victory of the underdog, the might of the meek" that they shared. Walt himself was certainly aware of the similarities because he had consciously used Chaplin, whom he once called "the greatest of them all," as a model. In devising Mickey Mouse, he said, "We wanted something appealing, and we thought of a tiny bit of a mouse that would have something of the wistfulness of Chaplin—a little fellow trying to do the best he could." Ben Sharpsteen said that Walt was constantly screening Chaplin films trying to pinpoint Chaplin's basic appeal, and another animator, Ward Kimball, recalled that Walt was "always showing us how Chaplin did a certain thing." "He just couldn't get him out of his system," Dick Huemer said of Walt's obsession with Chaplin. "Walt kept the feeling of this little droll kind of pathetic little character who was always being picked on. But cleverly coming out on top anyway." When Edward Steichen photographed Walt for *Vanity Fair*, Walt sent him a sketch of Mickey impersonating Chaplin.

But if Walt Disney had thought of Mickey Mouse as an animated surrogate for Charlie Chaplin, Mickey's other father, Ub Iwerks, had thought of him in very different terms—as Douglas Fairbanks. "He was the superhero of his day," Iwerks said of Fairbanks, "always winning, gallant and swashbuckling." As for Mickey, "He was never intended to be a sissy. He was always an adventurous character. . . . I had him do naturally the sort of thing Doug Fairbanks would do." Thus Mickey Mouse was born between two conceptions—between Chaplin and Fairbanks, between the scamp and the adventurer, between sympathy and vicariousness, between self-pity that translated into power through ingenuity and the bold assertion of power itself. From the first he was an unstable creation, often veering from one pole to another, in one cartoon to the next, *Plane Crazy* to *Steamboat Willie*, which meant that he could satisfy a wide spectrum of demands but that he would always be on the verge of self-destructing. That is why the early Mickey seems so random and rootless, less a character than a visual icon. He does not know who he is.

In the end, though he was patterned after both Chaplin and Fairbanks, he would find his identity elsewhere. He would find it as a projection of Walt himself. Walt identified intensely, almost passionately, with his creation, as if Mickey were not just his brainchild but an extension of him. "Walt and Mickey were so *simpatico*," Lillian said, "they almost seemed like they had the same identity." Playwright, film critic, and later presidential speechwriter Robert Sherwood, meeting Walt in 1931, wrote, "Whenever he mentions Mickey Mouse a note of reverent awe is evident in his voice. He loves that weird little animal as any mother would love her favorite child." Animator Les Clark said that "Walt was Mickey and Mickey was Walt," observing that even Mickey's gestures were copied from Walt's when he performed Mickey at story meetings, and one of Walt's most frequent story criticisms was, "I don't think Mickey would act that way." Years later Walt insisted, in an expression of just how bound to Mickey he was, that "as long as there is a Disney studio, there'll be Mickey Mouse cartoons" because "I can't live without him!"

In some sense, twenty-eight-year-old Walt Disney, whose previous cartoons had purveyed a discrete world but not an attitude, found his voice in Mickey Mouse. Mickey's intrepid optimism, his pluck, his naïveté that often got him into trouble, and his determination that usually got him out of it, even his self-regard, branded him as Walt's alter ego—the fullest expression of Walt Disney. This was true of the themes of Mickey's films as well as his characteristics. When Mickey engaged in fantasy only to have it punctured by reality, as so often happened in his cartoons, he was acting out the central tension of Walt Disney's life. And if Walt found his voice in Mickey, Mickey Mouse literally found his voice in Walt Disney. The ninth Mickey, *The Karnival Kid*, released in July 1929, was the first in which Mickey spoke—his first words were "Hot dog, hot dog"—though henceforth, Walt told his distributor, the cartoons would regularly include singing and talking. But Walt was not satisfied with Mickey's voice, which was low, flat, and uninflected (it may have been Carl Stalling's), and he promised to find someone whose voice would better fit Mickey's personality, even postponing the synchronization of the next Mickey while he spent a week testing candidates. By one account, a woman named Helen Lind temporarily performed Mickey. But while Walt continued to search, he demonstrated one day how he thought Mickey *should* sound, assuming a falsetto. One of the staff asked him why he didn't just do the voice himself, and Walt agreed, joking, "I knew I'd always be on the payroll, so I did it." Walt was often embarrassed at performing Mickey, and he later admitted that there were others who could do it, but he said his was the best voice because "[t]here is more pathos in it."

While Mickey served as an expression of Walt's personal mythology of trial and triumph, he also provided a self-reflexive commentary on his creator's own imagination, and this, as much as the cultural resonances or the invocations of childhood or the sexual suggestiveness, may have accounted for Mickey's deep and abiding popularity. Whatever else he is—and he is indistinctly many things—Mickey Mouse is in thrall to his own abilities of imaginative transformation. Whether he is turning an auto into an airplane or a cow into a xylophone, Mickey, like Chaplin and like Walt Disney himself, is always in the process of reimagining reality, and this is his primal, vicarious connection to the audience—the source of his power. He sees and hears things others don't. He makes the world his.

It was no accident that Mickey arrived with sound and music because music became the metaphor for his inner muse and the sine qua non of his existence. In his early cartoons, some of which are musical revues, he is wholly a musical creature—as much Fred Astaire as Charlie Chaplin. Hearing notes, Mickey cannot help but dance, sing, and make music himself, turning everything he spots into an instrument and converting reality into happiness. Even his relationship with Minnie Mouse is musically inspired; they literally make beautiful music together and bring joy and harmony, even fluidity, out of what is often threat and chaos. And this is also why the cartoons typically end with Mickey beaming or laughing, a chipper spirit, no matter what has befallen him. For all the subliminal attractions of his shape or his size or his sexuality, Mickey's secret, the appeal of which is obvious and not limited to Depression America, is that he can always make things right in his head—just as Walt Disney, the escape artist, could. In the end Mickey Mouse was the eternal promise of cheerful solipsism.

V

With Mickey's surging popularity and with the new, potentially lucrative Columbia contract, Walt Disney's sanctuary on Hyperion Avenue was undergoing its own transformation. Once again, as he had previously done when things were going well, Walt was hiring—cherry-picking the best talent. That winter of 1930 he brought aboard Ted Sears, an animator and gagman at the Fleischer studio who was said to be responsible for some of the Fleischers' funniest material. Sears had made a "semi-promise" to the Fleischers that he would stay, but Walt, in a signal of the studio's increasing specialization, enticed him as the studio's first storyman and held out the possibility of his helping Walt produce live-action comedies—an idea to which Walt kept returning. Another animator, Harry Reeves, who had been working for Pat Sullivan on the Felixes, also signed on, his abandonment of Felix for Mickey a sign of just how the animation tables had turned. He was so eager to join the Disneys that he even offered to pay his own traveling expenses. At roughly the same time Walt approached Grim Natwick, another Fleischer veteran and the designer of the Fleischers' Betty Boop character, about coming west to the Disneys despite a competing offer from Walter Lantz at Universal. Natwick decided to stay in New York, but he had been tempted because, Sears told Roy, he "thinks a lot about the 'art' of it, and wants to be associated with only the best." (Several years later he did join the studio.)

The physical studio was also undergoing yet another series of makeshift additions and alterations to accommodate the new staff. Early in 1930, shortly after the Columbia deal, Walt had the office wall moved six feet to the sidewalk to provide more space, though the operation was still squeezed into the one snug bungalow and several even smaller cottages. A visitor in January 1931 found a

> quiet little building, one story high, a spot you would hardly notice as you drive along Hyperion Avenue. Inside smallish rooms, an over-full office, a council chamber with a big table and a piano, then narrow hall-like rooms in each of which sit rows of men and women with not much more than elbow room between them, each bending over a desk which sometimes has a panel of light in its center—about fifty people in all. Everything is quiet. Everything suggests definite and ordered work.

Already the previous summer Roy and Walt had purchased an adjoining lot, the old chimes factory, and made plans to erect a two-story stucco neo-Spanish combination business/animation building, fifty by eighty feet; a two-story concrete recording studio into which the recording operation would move from Tec Art; and a one-story music scoring room—all of which were completed early in the summer of 1931 at a cost of roughly $45,000, not including new equipment. Atop the new animation building, declaring his new status, Walt had placed a twelve-foot-square sign with the name "Walt Disney" in two-foot-high blue neon letters, "Mickey Mouse" and "Silly Symphony" in red neon, and a five-foot-high figure of Mickey in blue, red, and gold tubing. The once-nondescript studio was nondescript no more.

Yet inside, despite the growing staff and growing plant, the old spirit of camaraderie prevailed. Many in Hollywood in the 1930s sought solace in political community. The Disney employees found their community in the artistic enclave of Hyperion. One animator, obviously proud of the new Disney cachet as the best animation studio, said that working there made them all feel "as if we were members of the same class at West Point." Others recalled the fraternal atmosphere—the story sessions that frequently lasted into the night with Walt acting out Mickey or some character in the Silly Symphonies, the practical jokes, the weekend picnics and games in the park. "My, how the day flew!" said one gagman, fondly. And presiding over it all was Walt—as Wilfred Jackson said, "all day, every day, to talk with us about whatever we were doing, each step of the way."

At twenty-nine, with his sharp youthful features made even sharper by his thinness and his still-unruly mop of brown hair, he didn't look like the head of a studio or the king of animation. He didn't dress like one either. No more fashion-conscious in Los Angeles than he had been in Kansas City, he usually wore knickers and long wool socks, "very gay and colorful things," said his secretary at the time, "with lots of design in them." And he almost always wore a sweater rather than a jacket. When Roy Williams, who would become an animator and gagman, first applied for a job at the studio, he waited in Walt's office—"nothing but a pile of junk in those days"—and chatted with someone he thought was a messenger boy. When Williams finally said that he would come back another day since Mr. Disney was obviously too busy to meet with him, he discovered that the messenger boy *was* Walt Disney. Still, for all his youthfulness and informality, he radiated a sense of authority and certitude. "Walt struck me as being absolutely sure of himself," said Ben Sharpsteen. "[H]e was positive about what he was going to do. He impressed me as being 'young'—[but] the very fact that he was several years younger than I and had been in the business several years less, and yet had the ability to diagnose those requisites for better pictures, impressed me very much." And with his confidence came an ethos that permeated the studio and governed it: that, in Grim Natwick's words, "whatever we did had to be better than anybody else could do it, even if you had to animate it nine times, as I once did."

Achieving that quality was still extremely difficult, even with his new, more experienced staff. As early as November 1930 Walt was having a hard time meeting the Columbia release schedule and was trying to find a way to speed up production without sacrificing the values that had won him plaudits, but he also realized that making good pictures more quickly would cost more, eating up the Columbia advances. By March the production delays had become so severe that Columbia vice-president Joe Brandt came to the studio for what Roy described as a "showdown," which was averted only because Walt suddenly instituted a new system, dividing his staff into three crews, which would be working simultaneously on three different cartoons. This, Roy hoped, would cut the production time for each cartoon from three weeks or more down to two weeks or less.

But if the new system sped delivery, it did little to help the Disneys' bottom line. Their contract with Columbia was what was called a "60/40, 40/60," meaning that they received their advances against 40 percent of the grosses to Columbia as a distribution fee with the remaining 60 percent dedicated to repaying the advance plus the cost of prints and advertising. Once these costs were recovered, the Disneys received 60 percent of the profits and Columbia 40 percent. In effect, Columbia was secured with the first dollars it received while the Disneys were at the mercy of both the market and of Columbia, which not only raked in the money but also did the accounting. "It worked," Roy griped, "into a very unfair situation."

From the beginning of their association, after his experiences with Mintz and Powers and the aborted collusion between the latter and Columbia itself, Walt had been deeply suspicious of his distributor. He shared Roy's assessment, made the week of their agreement, that one had to be vigilant with Columbia because "they aren't overburdened with 'good intentions.' " Within months Walt felt that Columbia, seemingly content with the profits it was making on the Mickeys and the Sillies and with a fairly large collection of other shorts to distribute, was already sloughing off on its efforts to promote the Disney cartoons, not to mention shortchanging the Disneys on what it did collect. But this time Walt was determined not to be gulled or cheated. Instead, he began plotting a preemptive strike.

That fall Sol Lesser, an acquaintance of Walt's who was a longtime exhibitor and distributor, introduced Walt to Joseph Schenck, a leading figure in the industry who was himself a former producer and now the president of United Artists. Walt admitted that he was awed. Columbia was a small studio located on what was called "Poverty Row" in Hollywood. United Artists was the creation of four of the brightest luminaries in motion pictures: director D. W. Griffith, Douglas Fairbanks, Fairbanks's wife Mary Pickford, and Walt's idol, Charlie Chaplin. Walt's object in wangling the introduction to Schenck was simple: he wanted United Artists to distribute his cartoons when his Columbia contract expired in April. Walt and Gunther Lessing had gone to the United Artists lot in mid-November to discuss the possibility, only to be left waiting the entire day. To salve his ego, Walt made the excuse that the executives must have had an important meeting. When he and Lessing returned later that week, United Artists, working through Lesser, offered Disney what he said amounted to a $50,000 guarantee per picture for two years—a deal that, according to George Morris, the studio's new business manager under Roy, would "more than double your present income."* After a three-hour meeting at UA, Walt concurred that "if we can't do that good or better with our present outlet, . . . a change might be better." So the man who had so abhorred Mintz's secret deal with the Disneys' mutinous animators secretly concluded an agreement of his own that December. Young Walt Disney was now affiliated with the august United Artists.

The Disneys could not let Columbia know about the agreement lest the distributor begin to stint further on its efforts for the Mickeys and Sillies, especially since, between Columbia's assumption of the Powers contract and its own contract for the Sillies, there were still twenty-five cartoons to be released before UA took over. In fact, Roy continued negotiating with them as if a new Columbia contract were still a possibility, and to maintain the ruse he even met with Universal president Carl Laemmle, who had been pressing Roy to distribute the cartoons, as if there were still a competition. When, early in April 1931, Columbia executives finally learned of the UA agreement, they were incensed. Columbia vice-president Abe Schneider said he had been a "sucker" in negotiating with Roy, and the president, Jack Cohn, warned Roy ominously, "You are going to lose plenty as a result of this deal," meaning presumably that Columbia would not promote the Disney cartoons that remained on its schedule as

*The final agreement called for UA to receive a 40 percent distribution fee from the first dollar with an additional $1,000 to UA at $60,000 gross and another $2,500 at $75,000 and a sixty-forty split in Disney's favor for the gross over $60,000. As Roy explained it, "Our thought in the matter was to get our money out of the lower brackets, and the sooner and quicker money." Roy to Irving Lesser, Apr. 15, 1931, Irving Lesser File, Roy O. Disney Corr., G-Lo (1930–1941), A2996, WDA.

aggressively as it had, or account for them as accurately. Still, the Disneys seemed unrepentant, unbowed, and thrilled with their new association—payback for what they felt they had suffered. "We have been approached frequently on the matter of distributing short subjects," Joe Schenck declared after the official announcement of the Disney contract on April 13, "but we have heretofore held to the theory that United Artists is an organization only for the biggest stars. Mickey Mouse, however, is different. Disney has created a character whose type has never been equaled in motion picture history."

It should have been a moment of triumph, and in many ways it was, but even with the success of the cartoons and even with the prospect of more revenue under the new contract, the joy was tempered by the Disneys' endemic problem: they were still having trouble making ends meet while they continued to deliver what they owed to Columbia and while they waited the year for the new contract to take effect. "Very frankly, our business has been growing so fast and expanding in two or three directions, that we are still about as close run for money as ever," Roy wrote his parents shortly after the UA announcement, citing the skyrocketing cost of the cartoons—Walt put the budget per cartoon now at $13,500—and the expenditures on the studio expansion. Already in May, Roy was seeking—and received—a $25,000 loan from the Bank of America to be paid off by the Columbia overages, hoping both to infuse new money into the cash-strapped studio and to force Columbia, which was also financed by the Bank of America, to be "very careful on their trickery" since "[Joe] Brandt will hesitate before trying to get funny if the Bank of America is there to call Columbia to time." Roy agreed not to tell Walt "too much" about the loan for fear of his brother's burning through the new funds.

The sense of relief did not last long. By the end of June the Columbia remittances had declined, as Cohn predicted they would, leaving the studio in jeopardy of failing to meet its payroll, even though Schenck himself was pressing the distributor to treat the Disneys fairly. Roy tried to finesse the issue by simply shipping cartoons earlier than Columbia wanted them to, just as the Disneys had done with Mintz and Powers, and thus ending their commitment sooner, but Columbia refused to take delivery. By June the studio was paying out $27,000 in salaries each month, which was more than the $14,000 in advances they were receiving for two cartoons each month and the $9,000 in overages each month that Columbia was now remitting to the studio and that the studio was sending to the Bank of America to retire their loan. "[U]nless something very drastic in the way of a cut in our salary commitments is not made immediately," George Morris memoed Walt, "we are going to find ourselves in a situation that is fraught with complications so serious that they will effect [*sic*] the whole structure of our organization . . . if we are going to survive."

Morris wasn't crying wolf. Roy was already negotiating with Joe Schenck for a personal loan of $25,000, but the money wouldn't be available until August, and in any case $14,000 would be dedicated to paying off previous commitments. So desperate was the situation that Morris and Lessing had even proposed the unthinkable: selling off an interest in the studio. "The business has become too big for Walt to cling to his faith that 'Roy will raise the money some way,' " Lessing wrote Roy. "It is a beautiful idea to build up an ideal organization like Walt desires and make a product par excellence for future distribution hopes; but there is such a thing as running it into the ground. . . . It is absolutely essential that you cheapen your product for the present."

But if Lessing expected Walt to acquiesce in cheapening his product, he had little understanding of what Walt Disney wanted or why Walt Disney was in the animation business to begin with. In Walt's eyes, his studio was not to be subject to the pressures of the world; it was his refuge from them—a sacred place. And his animations could not be compromised; they had to be better than anyone else's or he would not survive in the business; nor would he want to survive. Excellence was not only Walt's business strategy, it was the reason he ran the studio and the force that kept his personal world intact. "If you want to know the real secret of Walt's success," longtime animator Ward Kimball would say, "it's that he never tried to make money. He was always trying to make something that he could have fun with or be proud of." Predictably, Walt called Morris to his office and insisted that he could not take on outside investors or ask his employees to take pay cuts or accelerate production or cut the staff since "that would mean cutting the quality of the pictures and a subsequent falling off of interest by the public in the Disney product." Instead, Walt suggested—unrealistically, Morris felt—that they take a loan from UA against future profits, while Morris thought of trying to tap Schenck for another personal loan. In the end Walt, after exploding at Lessing and Morris and sputtering that everyone on the business side was "pretty rotten," said he would attempt to produce five cartoons every two months rather than four, and the studio muddled through to the fall.

The constant strain focused Walt, but even without the financial pressures he would have been a man obsessed. He had always lived for his studio. Bill Cottrell, who often worked at night at the studio on the camera, said that Walt never left at five or five-thirty when most of the rest of the staff did. He stayed until six or seven and then returned, often with Lillian. Walt himself admitted that he liked to wander the studio at night, visiting the animation tables or looking at the layout of scenes and adding or subtracting drawings. Even when he wasn't at the studio, his mind wasn't far from it. Ben Sharpsteen remembered when Walt, on his way to work, received a traffic ticket. Disney was less than amused when he told his staff about it that morning, but as he reenacted his exchange with the policeman—and Walt always acted out his stories—he began to see the humor in it, and, Sharpsteen said, Walt's "attitude changed." The episode quickly became the basis for *Traffic Troubles.* Another time Sharpsteen ran into Walt as Walt and Lillian were entering a diner and Sharpsteen was exiting. Walt immediately blocked the door, oblivious to other patrons attempting to enter or leave, and began telling a story he had just concocted for a new cartoon about a barnyard revue with an audience of cats. Lillian was growing impatient at having to wait, and when Walt reached his denouement—the cats jumping onto a privy roof, which then collapses—she sneered that she wouldn't want to see that cartoon, but Walt didn't seem to hear or care. "For the moment, Walt didn't realize where he was or anything; all he knew was that he wanted to tell his story." "His hobby is his work," George Morris told a reporter profiling Walt, "as every moment of his time is given over to it."

But the obsessiveness took a far greater toll on Lillian than just having to wait for her husband or listen to his stories. She was lonely. To a *Time* reporter, she called herself a "mouse widow" and joked that she found her husband's conversation "fascinating" because "it is entirely given to Mickey Mouse." There was little time for anything else. The Disneys socialized only occasionally, usually at Roy's house for a Sunday barbecue and a game of croquet, and they had few close friends. His best pal, Walt said, was Lillian, with his dog, Sunnee, "running a close second." Most of his free time he spent with Lillian, her mother, and Sunnee, driving from theater to theater to watch cartoons—"He knew what time they would be playing," Lillian said—while his entourage waited in the car. When he wasn't on cartoon patrol, he and Lillian would be out for a ride and invariably Walt would say that he remembered something he wanted to do at the studio. "There wasn't a night we didn't end up at the studio," Lillian recalled. So she would curl up on the davenport in his office and sleep while Walt worked, waking up at intervals to ask how late it was, to which, regardless of the time, Walt would answer, "Oh, it's not late." Walt admitted years later that he would turn back his office clock while Lillian slept so that she never knew how late he had worked. Even in bed, Lillian said, he would usually toss and turn, thinking of studio problems, then rise early and declare, "I think I've got it licked."

Already stressed by Walt's obsession and the financial shortfall, the couple suffered another, more personal tragedy that summer. A child himself, Walt had always hoped for children of his own. "I want to have ten kids," he once told his sister Ruth, "and let them do whatever they want," in obvious compensation for the tribulations he endured during his own childhood. Despite her maternal feelings for Sunnee, Lillian, the youngest of ten, was more guarded about having children, saying that she had been discouraged at seeing how hard her mother and sisters had had to work. While Walt and Lillian pondered parenting, Roy and Edna had been attempting to have a child—even, by one account, agreeing to have intercourse in their doctor's office so he could monitor them. Finally, on January 10, 1930, just before the confrontation with Powers and the departures of Iwerks and Stalling, Edna gave birth to Roy Edward Disney. "Walt and Lilly are both crazy about him," Roy wrote his mother later that summer. "He seems somewhat afraid of Walt, but goes crazy over Lilly. Walt just doesn't know how to play with him yet."

Lillian's time with Roy Edward may have defused her reluctance to have a child of her own, while Walt got further encouragement that same year when Lillian's sister Hazel filed for divorce and she and her thirteen-year-old daughter Marjorie moved into the Disneys' Lyric Avenue home. Walt embraced the role of surrogate father and doted on Marjorie. "He used to wait up for me to come home," she recalled. "He'd be at the top of the stairs when I came in at night, especially if I was very late." When she went off to boarding school and came home only on weekends, Walt would get annoyed if she made plans, asking her, "Why'd you bother to come home? Why'd you bother if you're not going to be here?"

In the spring of 1931, a little over a year after Roy Edward's birth and after a year of Walt's oversight of Marjorie, Lillian was pregnant. Walt was overjoyed. He immediately began searching for a new homesite—one to three acres, he told realtors grandly. But on June 10 Lillian suffered a miscarriage. The couple were devastated. "It was very sad," Marjorie remembered. Walt wrote his cousin Lena mordantly, "I am married and so far all I can boast of is a cute little wife and a dandy Chow dog." Though studio business was obviously pressing and the financial situation desperate, Roy suggested Walt and Lillian take a trip for a few weeks, possibly to Honolulu.

If the birth of Roy Edward had lightened the burden during the battle with Powers in 1930, Lillian's miscarriage cast a pall during their struggle to survive that summer. Walt did not leave immediately on a vacation as Roy advised. He stayed, immersing himself—if possible, even more single-mindedly—in his work and becoming increasingly tense and irritable. Never content with the quality of what the studio produced—"No matter how good a picture we turn out, I can always see ways to improve it when I see the finished product," he would later say—he was now even less satisfied than usual. He became distracted and forgetful. Even his health began to deteriorate, and late that June, just two weeks after the miscarriage, he was rushed to the hospital to have inflamed tonsils removed. "Frankly, I am worried about Walt," Roy wrote Lessing and Morris. "He needs a good vacation and rest. We have both been hitting the ball too hard for a long time." He also endorsed the idea of bringing in a new investor and business associate, apparently Schenck, to relieve them. "Of course, in no event, would we relinquish control, but there would be a devided [*sic*] responsibility in place of it being on just us two. If for no other reason than to protect Walt's health, strength and enthusiasm, and talent, I am strongly in favor of the idea."

Though Walt would have never agreed to share responsibility, he realized that his enthusiasm was waning even as his intensity increased, and that something was terribly wrong with him. "I guess I was working too hard and worrying too much," he said later. "I was expecting more from my artists than they were giving me, and all I did all day long was pound, pound, pound. Costs were going up; each new picture we finished cost more to make than we had figured it would earn." While he drove his staff mercilessly and became snappish again, as he had been in the bad Mintz days, he was emotionally fragile. When he talked on the phone, he would suddenly and unaccountably find himself weeping. At night he couldn't sleep. At the studio he became physically ill looking at his latest cartoon and, unable to see anything but its flaws, claimed that he was sick of it—so sick of it that he never wanted to see it again. He became so concerned with his condition that he finally visited a doctor, who told him that he had to get away, ironically from the place that had provided refuge. As Walt himself described it, "I was in an emotional flap."

But it was more than an emotional flap. The years of fighting and losing and then having to fight back, the years of having to maintain a brave front like Mickey Mouse in the face of loss and betrayal, and the years of feeling compelled to produce cartoons so good that the Disneys would be unassailable in the industry, while struggling against oppressive, unrelenting financial constraints that barely allowed them to survive and that even now had not loosened, and then the setback in starting his own family for which he had longed—these had all accumulated until Walt, usually so willfully blithe and self-confident, cracked. Once again he could not keep the real world at bay or protect his imaginative world from it. Walt Disney, the new king of animation and the father of Mickey Mouse, had suffered a breakdown.

Five

THE CULT

Walt Disney had been largely unaffected by the economic depression that slowly descended after the stock market crash in October 1929 and then squeezed the nation—a depression that put a quarter of the workforce on the street and caused untold pain. Though one might have thought of movie theaters as refuges from the suffering, the film industry was hardly immune to the downturn. The Disneys, however, were. While other studios saw their revenues dip precipitously—not so much because audiences declined, though they did, as because the studios had overextended themselves in a wild theater-buying spree in the 1920s, and the value of the property collapsed—the Disneys, without theaters or personal investments beyond the shares they owned in one of Uncle Robert's get-rich-quick oil schemes and some plots of real estate, sailed along unscathed by the national trauma. Though they suffered financial wounds, most of them were self-inflicted, the result of Walt's unwillingness to compromise the quality of his films. Rather than cutting costs, he kept increasing them. Even usually reserved Roy felt that he and Walt had somehow cheated the Depression by constantly reinvesting in their own studio rather than investing in the stock market. "Anything that we had saved up was all put into our business," he wrote his parents in 1932. "We have been doing our own gambling. This past three years will be a very good lesson to the people at large," meaning apparently that others would have to learn to invest in themselves as well.

But if the Depression did not affect Walt economically, it was in many ways replicated in his own emotional depression. Just as the nation could not escape the economic buffets, Walt could not secure his fantasy world against the assaults of the real world, could not, in fact, make it perfect enough or impregnable enough, which led to his breakdown. His first plan, when his doctor told him he had to leave the studio, was to take an ocean trip to Seattle and then visit his parents in Portland and Lillian's relatives in Idaho. His second plan was to sail to Hawaii, and he booked passage for himself and Lillian on a cruise ship. In the event, though, he and Lillian acted impulsively, canceling the Hawaii trip and booking passage on a boat from Havana through the Panama Canal, then picking up traveler's checks and hopping a train to St. Louis, where they hoped to catch a riverboat down the Mississippi River, just as Walt and his old friend Russell Maas had intended to do when Walt returned from France in 1919. From their disembarkation point they planned to get to Key West and rendezvous with the boat to Cuba. As it turned out, there were no longer riverboats on the Mississippi, only barges, so the couple improvised again, taking a train to Washington, D.C., staying three days at the Mayflower Hotel, visiting the monuments and strolling aimlessly through the parks, or just sitting on the benches feeding the pigeons. Then they trained to Key West and caught their tug to Havana, where they spent the next week lounging at the Hotel Nacional and taking excursions to the countryside before heading home via the canal, as planned. Their two New York visits having ended in disaster, it was their first real vacation in six years of marriage. Walt said that he and Lillian had the "time of our life" because he had reached the point where "I didn't give a darn." He felt he had been liberated from the burden of his own perfectionism.

He returned to the studio looking, according to George Morris, "very much rested," but he was, he told Morris, "still nervous and sure would like to get away for a couple of weeks more." Instead, he dove into a new regimen—outside the studio. The breakdown, he said, "woke me up to the fact that life is sweet and work is not everything." So he took up sports, for which he had never had time even as a child—ice skating, swimming, horseback riding, and boxing. He even joined the Hollywood Athletic Club and wrestled there two or three times a week, though he admitted he didn't like having to "get down there in somebody's crotch and sweaty old sweatshirt." For a while he took up golf, rising at four each morning so he could be on the course by five-thirty without intruding on studio time, playing five holes, then eating a hearty breakfast and heading for the studio, as he put it, "full of pep." Lillian accompanied him in many of these pursuits, swimming at the club, horseback riding in Griffith Park, and even rising to join him for his early golf sessions, which were usually truncated. "Walt would fly into such a rage when he missed a stroke," Lillian said, "that I got helplessly hysterical watching him." Walt claimed all this activity relaxed him now, made him better able to focus and cope.

But despite his tributes to his new exercise regimen and his professions that he had returned to the studio a "new man," he was still restless and discontented. He had been back at the studio only a few weeks when he and Lillian left again, this time for a trip to Kansas City, where Walt received an award from DeMolay and addressed their convention, and on to New York for the first time as a tourist rather than as a petitioner. "Walt is feeling much better than he was before his vacation," Roy wrote Elias and Flora shortly after Walt's return, "but is not back to his old self. Confidentially, I am a little worried about Walt's health, feeling there must be something basically wrong." Walt was still tired and mopey. He continued visiting doctors in hopes of discovering what ailed him, and one found what he thought was an intestinal parasite that seemed to be sapping the patient's strength. Roy was consoled by the fact that Walt was finally tending to himself after years of tending only to the studio, where, Roy now thought, things were going well enough that "it is much less of a nerve wracking job for him than before."

Roy was correct that some of the financial pressure had abated. In January 1932 he concluded a revised agreement with United Artists, adding five new Silly Symphonies to the contract at an advance of $15,000 each and a 30 percent distribution fee. More important, Roy negotiated a loan of $195,000 to be used as Walt saw fit. Roy called it "our first good contract." The only hitch was that the studio had fallen behind in its delivery of Mickey Mouse cartoons, and in order to catch up it had to divert the animators from the Symphonies for six months.

All of this should have made Walt happy, but if he was no longer besieged by financial difficulties, he was still in the grip of his own obsession with excellence, which made him compulsively dissatisfied, and he now had a new burden—the burden of expectations. Everyone seemed to recognize that Disney not only consistently produced the best animations but had begun to reinvent animation. He was transforming it from a crude, juvenile novelty to something that approached a naïve art. Indeed, this was the new Disney enterprise, a revolution really: to do whatever it took to elevate animation to an art form. "Practically every tool we use today was originated at the Disney studio," Chuck Jones, a celebrated Warner Bros. animator and producer, would later observe, and he compared Disney to the great live-action director D. W. Griffith, who was similarly extolled for having brought art to the silent film. Disney's own animators appreciated that they were pioneers. Les Clark claimed that animation developed "because of Walt's insistence and supervision," and animators Frank Thomas and Ollie Johnston wrote that "The exhilaration of breaking through barriers to new frontiers was more than any of us could resist."

But the most striking difference between the animations of Walt Disney and those of his forebears and competitors was, as always, less a matter of innovation than aspiration—the old Disney demand that one strive for the very best. "Walt would not—repeat would not—OK any animation that did not meet with this very high standard of acceptance," one Disney employee wrote. In practice, this meant that everything one did had to be analyzed, endlessly analyzed, to make sure it worked, to make sure that it was up to standard, to make sure it could not be improved upon. As animator Dick Huemer put it, everyone at the studio found themselves "analyzing and reanalyzing . . . reanalyzing, discarding and starting all over again," which was so contrary to the routine at rival animation studios, where, as another animator put it, "You were paid to bat out thirty or thirty-five feet a week, some good, some bad, but the only important thing was that the footage got done."

The emphasis on analysis necessarily led to the development of new techniques that would facilitate it and that would soon become standard operating procedure in animation. Early on, animators at the Disney studio would make what they called "pencil tests" for their own use—shooting their rough drawings on inexpensive negative film so that they could see the outcome before finalizing the animation. By one account Tom Palmer, probably early in 1931, had shot a short pencil test and was feeding the film through the Moviola, a device with a small screen that enabled one to view the footage, when Walt happened by and asked what Palmer was doing. Impressed by the value of previewing the rough animation, he instituted it as a policy in the studio.

In short order, Walt installed a Moviola in a cramped, stifling, windowless closet that was soon dubbed the "sweatbox." Hunched over the tiny screen, no more than four inches by four inches, Walt and the animator would view and analyze the action by the hour, over and over and over again, trying to determine what would make it right, make it funnier. "I think it is astounding that we were the first group of animators, so far as I can learn, who ever had the chance to study their own work and correct its errors before it reached the screen," Walt would say a few years later. "In our little studio on Hyperion Street [*sic*], every foot of rough animation was projected on the screen for analysis, and every foot was drawn and redrawn until we could say, 'This is the best that we can do.' " Eventually Wilfred Jackson began stringing the pencil tests together, along with still drawings for the scenes not yet animated, into longer sequences that he called "Leica reels," after the Leica camera that was used to shoot them, so that the animators could see scenes in relation to one another. Walt encouraged them to add sound as well. In effect, then, Walt and the four or five animators who could squeeze into the "sweatbox" with him could preview the entire cartoon before the drawings were cleaned up and inked and painted on cels. This strengthening of his control seemed to energize Walt; he loved to pore over the Leica reels. But even then the process wasn't foolproof. After a cartoon was finished and previewed, Walt often ordered the staff back into the sweatbox for improvements.

The effect of the pencil tests and Leica reels was not only to upgrade the quality of Disney cartoons; they altered the very nature of animation. Before the inauguration of pencil tests animators focused on making clean drawings and tight "in betweens" that would require little revision. The result, however, was a certain inflexibility and rigidity. "Old animation was done from pose to pose without much thought," said Dick Huemer. "It was almost like it was a flat design. Without any weight." In those cartoons a character "would come to a complete stop and there he'd freeze. And his eyes would blink. Or his hair would stand up, or whatever. Or if his head did turn, the rest of him would be stuck there stiffly." As Walt said of this sort of animation, "Your character goes dead and it looks like a drawing."

Ub Iwerks had had a basic command of animation techniques and he could draw actions, but he could never give his characters a sense of mass or fluidity of movement. Still, Iwerks had been the exemplar at the studio, and Walt himself admitted, "The hardest job was to get the guys to quit fooling around with these individual drawings and to think of the group of drawings in an action." With Iwerks no longer the guiding light and with the pencil tests to aid them, the animators were liberated to experiment, and they did. When Norm Ferguson animated *Frolicking Fish* in 1930, Walt commanded the other animators to study it because Ferguson had made certain that there was a constant flow of action. "Soon everybody started drawing looser," another animator recalled. "This opened up more freedom of movement." Already by 1931 characters in Disney cartoons no longer shunted from pose to pose. They moved smoothly between them, creating what came to be called "overlapping action," in which action flowed. "Overlapping action was an invention of Disney's," Dick Huemer said. "That's why Disney's animation looked so different."

Disney's animations were narratively different too. All cartoons were predicated on the gag—a visual joke or brief comic situation. The gag was holy and inviolate, the reason for the cartoon's existence, and most animation studios simply linked gags willy-nilly. Walt would send an outline to the staff and then ask them to "gag" it: "So let's all hop to it and have some good belly laughs ready by Tuesday night," went a typical request. Walt would then award prizes for the gags he used—one or two dollars, occasionally as much as $3.50 in the early thirties, though the rate was soon standardized at $2.50. At Disney too the gag was the fundamental narrative component. It was the basis on which cartoons succeeded or failed. "You must sharpen your ability to get right at the basis of the gag, without mistaking the trimming for the meat of the action," Walt once instructed Dick Huemer, while warning another employee that he seemed to lack an "understanding of the proper portrayal of gags."

At other studios, where animators would either select or be assigned a basic situation and then animate as they desired, whether one animator's gag really connected to another's or not was irrelevant. Good gags were everything. Disney's gags may not have been any better than those of his rivals, but, as animators Frank Thomas and Ollie Johnston put it, "they were staged better, with more care taken to establish the situation. There was more concern for detail, for building comedy, for making the gag pay off." "Our mistake was that we weren't establishing anything first," Dick Huemer observed of his pre-Disney days animating gags. "We were giving the payoff without the buildup.... Disney always very carefully planned things, so that everything was understandable, and one thing happened after another logically." One animation historian cited the difference between the very early Disney cartoons and the cartoons of 1931 as a matter of "density." In the later cartoons, each individual gag was more complicated, and the gags accumulated, each gag building on the one that preceded it.

Yet even while he was analyzing and then refining the gag, Walt was also changing the basic narrative unit of his cartoons. He had begun to think not just in terms of gags but in terms of a story to which the gags would be subordinated, which may have been as revolutionary an advance in animation as his overlapping action. (Indeed, story was the very thing Walt himself had disdained while working for Mintz.) When he hired Ted Sears in 1930—the old Fleischer animator who, one colleague said, wore a high collar, plastered his hair on his head, spoke out of the side of his mouth, and looked like a "defrocked priest"—Walt had appointed him head of a new story department, something unheard of at any other animation studio. It consisted of Bill Cottrell, the ink-and-paint-man-turned-camera-operator-turned-animator, Webb Smith, a former newspaperman, and Pinto Colvig, who would later become the voice of the character Goofy. These men were initially charged with helping devise better gags without the responsibility of having to animate them. Walt would toss them a situation—say, Mickey's pet dog Pluto getting stuck on flypaper—and then let them develop it. "I came back in two days," Walt recalled of having given Webb Smith that instruction, "and there was a whole wall full of things that would happen to that dog if he got mixed up with flypaper, see? So then the process would be of sitting down with that, taking some of those ideas, copying them if we could, putting them into some kind of routine and continuity."

It was the continuity on which the storymen, with Walt's blessing, now began to concentrate. Walt wanted the story and gags to be as polished as the animation itself. To elevate the status of the story, Walt, rather than have the gagmen move from animator to animator with their ideas, installed them in their own room, where the entire staff would congregate at a cartoon's launch to discuss the storyline and gags, and where directors would later repair to flesh out the stories and convert them to visuals. Meanwhile one of the storymen—some sources credit Webb Smith, others Ted Sears— came up with the idea of laying out the entire cartoon scene by scene in a series of rough sketches, the plot equivalent of the pencil tests, and pinning them on a large four-by-eight-foot corkboard—a "storyboard," it was called—that permitted the storymen, the animators, and Walt to get an overview of the narrative flow of the film.* Now Walt could study the cartoon even before it had been put into pencil tests. As one animator said, "You get the feeling that every last frame of that thing has been worked over until it's perfect!"

Whenever one element changed, it set off a chain reaction. The new regard for story demanded a new approach to the animated figures. So

*According to animator Shamus Culhane, Sears had actually devised the storyboard in May 1930 for the Fleischers, just before leaving, as an expedient to help young animators get a better sense of sequence since most of the Fleischers' better animators had decamped to the West Coast and Disney. Culhane, *Talking Animals*, p. 36

long as cartoons simply linked slapstick gags, characters were little more than foils. Even the early Mickey Mouse was a device that accommodated the comic situation—leering when the circumstances demanded leering, fearful when they demanded fear, swashbuckling when they demanded courage, merry when they required merriment. But the more elaborated stories that Sears's department began turning out at Walt's behest required more elaborated characters as well—actors rather than *en*actors. "The big reason nobody remembers what happened in the early days was that there was no real story and no personality," one animator observed. "That's why everybody thinks that Walt Disney invented the cartoon."

A character like Felix the Cat, Walt once told Frank Thomas, had "little bits of personality here and there," and Walt himself had attempted to forge a personality for Oswald the Rabbit and later Mickey Mouse, but he felt that these bits were not sufficient. Walt, who was always trying to nudge animation closer to the live-action films of Chaplin or Keaton, understood that the audience needed involvement. They needed to care about the characters on the screen, not just to laugh at them, and he began stressing to his animators the importance of creating characters who could elicit *emotional* reactions from the viewers. "It was the uppermost thing," Wilfred Jackson remembered of this period, "and it all came about because Walt wanted to make the cartoon characters believable to the audience. Right from the start he didn't want them to be just something moving around on the screen and doing funny things." "[Y]our characters had to be the kind of characters that people could relate to," Eric Larson concurred. As Walt himself later put it in a succinct formulation of his aesthetic, "The most important aim of any of the fine arts is to get a purely emotional response from the beholder."

The only way to elicit that response, Walt believed, was through personality—a set of characteristics that were unique to the character and that coalesced to define him. At the Disney studio the edict came down from Walt that animated figures were no longer to be simply functional for the gag. They had to be full-bodied or, as one animator described it, "believable in motion and emotion." Aside from the general aspiration to excellence, of all the numerous contributions and innovations that Walt Disney bequeathed to animation, this may very well have been the single most important because it was the one that changed animation most radically, not just in its physical appearance or in its narrative amplitude but in its fundamental relationship to the viewer, and it was the one that most distinguished Disney animation from its forebears: all characters had to be treated as if they were not merely animated but living—an approach that came to be called "personality animation." "Everything in his cartoons had to have a personality," animator Ward Kimball said. "He insisted that if a tree was bashful, it had to act like it was bashful. If it was a villainous tree, it had to behave like a villain. He always demanded complete character delineation from his animators." At one story session Walt asked, "How would a piano feel if Mickey bangs on it too hard?"

For Walt, personality was not a function of physical behavior or even of the emotional responses that one could slap upon a character. The magic of animation, the magic of *Disney* animation, was that personality seemed to emerge from the drawings as if it had been internalized. "You have to portray not only [that] this thing is moving," Walt once said, "but it is actually alive and thinks." The idea of a thinking, feeling cartoon character, a character with psychology and emotional range, was a revelation even at the Disney studio, where just a few years before there was concern over whether an audience would accept a voice emanating from a drawing. When Norm Ferguson animated Webb Smith's sequence of Pluto struggling with the flypaper in *Playful Pluto* in 1934, the effect on the studio was electric—the "one big one," Wilfred Jackson called it. "It was a blockbuster because you could see the wheels going around in the character's head," Ward Kimball recalled. "And we were just more or less pulling out of that bouncing, dancing, musical age of Disney shorts, where all of our characters with big smiles on their faces kept time to the music or played an instrument. Here comes a character that gets stuck with a situation and keeps building, almost like a Buster Keaton, or Harold Lloyd, or a Chaplin sequence." Ferguson, whose animation had already won Walt's admiration for its fluidity, now won further admiration for its psychology and depth. "Fergy, you're a great actor," Walt announced in front of the staff one day, and when Ferguson simpered and shrank in embarrassment, Walt insisted, "Yes, you are. That's why your animation is so good, because you feel. You feel what these characters feel."

Walt Disney would be credited—and often criticized as well—for bringing greater realism to animation; and he almost single-handedly broke the long-standing tradition, to which he himself had once subscribed, of self-reflexive cartoons in which one saw the animator's hand, in favor of a new aesthetic in which the cartoon world was presented as self-contained. But the visual realism he encouraged was actually a product of the psychological and emotional realism he demanded, not a source. Walt wanted a credible visual field for his more credible animated characters in order to forge that emotional bond with the audience—an animated universe he called the "plausible impossible" that stretched natural laws without breaking them entirely.

As a result of this new imperative and of the analysis of scenes through pencil tests, Disney animators began to abandon the prevailing, tried-and-true style of animation disparagingly named "rubber hose," which forsook realism and its difficulties for ease of drawing. In "rubber hose" animation, when the shape of a figure or an object changed, so would its volume, as if it were made of rubber. There was no consideration of gravity or weight. This bothered Walt. He felt that the lack of realism compromised the psychological and emotional reality of the characters and snapped the emotional bond to the viewer. "As Walt began to bear down a little bit on making his characters believable," Jackson said, "all this [rubber hose] had to go." Now gravity entered the cartoon world for the first time, and so did "secondary actions," or the response of things like hair and clothes and leaves to gravity. Prior to Disney, Dick Huemer recalled, "[n]o one thought of clothing following through, sweeping out, and dropping a few frames later, which is what it does naturally." At the Disney studio, everyone began to think of these things, and the force of gravity became an obsession. Among the many signs that hung on the animators' walls was one that read: "Does your drawing have weight, depth and balance?"

Sometimes, however, the animators simply were not good enough. To meet the new standards for realism, they knew they had to improve their skills. "I definitely feel that we cannot do the fantastic things based on the real unless we first know the real," Walt had advised. They needed training. As early as 1929 Walt would drive several of his animators to downtown Los Angeles to attend Friday night classes at the Chouinard Art Institute, then go to the studio to work, and then return to pick them up. Sometime in 1931 he contracted with Chouinard to train a dozen or so of his artists one night a week. One of them, Art Babbitt, decided that it would be more efficient for the artists to gather at his house near the Hollywood Bowl for informal drawing sessions with live models, and in the late summer or early fall of 1932 he began hosting these get-togethers. The first week he invited eight artists, and fourteen arrived. The next week he invited the fourteen, and twenty-two appeared. Several weeks later Walt called Babbitt to his office. "Suppose it got in the newspapers that a bunch of Disney artists were drawing naked women in a private home," he said. "It wouldn't sit very well." Instead, obviously hoping to attract even more of the staff, he offered them the studio soundstage and free materials. After Walt's proposal another young animator who had been attending the sessions at Babbitt's house, Hardie Gramatky, suggested they formalize the instruction by inviting the man who had conducted the Chouinard classes, Donald Graham, to serve as the teacher. Babbitt contacted Graham, and on November 15 the "great Disney Art School," as Graham called it, held its first class.

At first the group met on the soundstage just two evenings a week, with twenty to thirty men in attendance. Within a month the numbers had swelled, compelling Graham to call in another instructor, Phil Dike, and divide the class in two. Over the next two years weekly attendance averaged better than fifty per session, and Graham occasionally had to enlist a third instructor to accommodate the group. Soon they were meeting five nights a week, and though attendance initially was not mandatory, as Babbitt put it, "you'd better go!"

Canadian-born and trained at Stanford as an engineer before taking instruction himself at Chouinard and committing to art, Graham was only twenty-nine when he took the helm—a handsome, compact man with dark wavy hair, a square jaw, deepset eyes, ropy arms, and the long fingers of an artist. He stood at the front of the cavernous room holding a lit cigarette that he kept passing from hand to hand as he talked, riveting the class as the ash edged closer to those fingers. The task that he set for himself was, in one student's words, "necessarily impossible." He had no training in animation himself, but it wasn't animation that Walt wanted him to teach. Rather, he taught a group of crusty New York animators, former newspaper cartoonists, sometime art students, and talented dabblers the art of figurative drawing without, said one animator, imposing a single style on them. He was laying a foundation, teaching them how to draw, really draw, which meant, as one animator came to realize, that "he was single-handedly attacking the traditional concept of animation as simply moving comic strips" and trading it for realism. It was Graham who now painstakingly showed them the effect of gravity on mass, and how flesh and muscle move, and the role of secondary effects. Art Babbitt said that Graham was the one who taught him "to analyze" and taught him as well that "only the slightest little offbeat element in a person's movement makes him a distinctly different character." Another animator, Shamus Culhane, went so far as to say that after Walt Disney himself, Don Graham had the "greatest impact on the philosophy of the medium [by trying to] create a group of sophisticated filmmakers educated in the theories of the Old Masters, modern art, acting, and the scientific principles of movement."

At a studio dedicated to excellence, Graham became a kind of hero for prodding the animators toward fine art. As the students drew and Graham wandered among them, gazing over their shoulders at their pads, he had only two assessments. Either he asked, "Having problems?" or he said, "Looks like you're having fun." The second, according to one animator, was the "supreme apothegm, the supreme tribute, the ne plus ultra, because having fun meant that something was sinking in; the lessons were bearing fruit. I would rather hear Don Graham say, 'Having fun?' " the animator said, "than win an Academy Award."

In due course Graham would be added to the studio payroll full-time, teaching three days and two nights each week, while the studio school expanded to five nights a week with 150 students at a cost, it was estimated, of $100,000 a year. Meanwhile Walt complemented Graham's instruction by commissioning slow-motion photographic studies, he said, of "glass breaking, bubbles forming and popping, water drops falling into a tub," even smoke swirling, for the animators to analyze; by instituting a studio library that eventually grew to two thousand volumes where a staff of three provided drawings and photographs for the animators; by having photostats of human movement sized to fit the animation board so that the animators could draw over the photos and discover for themselves the basis of action; even by having certain animators attend acting classes. Animators at other studios would grouse that had they been given the time Disney animators had, they could have produced work just as good, but the mentality was the difference, not the time. William Tytla, who had worked for Paul Terry in New York before joining the Disney studio, said that when he suggested Terry hire a model to help them improve their technique, he was told to get one himself and that Terry dismissed the idea of hiring an instructor like Graham. Finally Tytla abandoned the effort, complaining, "[T]hey said anyone who goes to art school is a 'homo Bolshevik.' " Shamus Culhane had a similar experience at the Fleischer studio. "They could never accept the fact that time wasn't the factor; it was education," he wrote. "Fleischer people were operating from instinct and a scornful rejection of the idea that principles of writing and animation even existed."

Now that realism was the basis of the rapidly evolving Disney animation, providing a connection for the audience that more rudimentary cartoons could not provide and permitting them to recognize themselves in Disney characters as they recognized themselves in live-action stars or the characters in literature, Walt Disney was in the business of creating life. "Most people think the word 'animation' means movement," Ken Peterson, a Disney animator, once explained, "but it doesn't. It comes from 'animus' which means 'life' or 'to live.' Making it move is not animation, but just the mechanics of it." "We invest them with life," Walt told a reporter of his animated creations.

Disney animations were of life, but they were larger than life too. What Walt sought was not an imitation of life as it was, which live-action films could do better than animation, but life as one could exaggerate it—a "caricature of life," as Walt called it, rooted in realism but expanding upon it. Walt's animated reality would not only be more outsized than real life, it would be simpler, clearer, sharper, and finally better. "Our actors must be more interesting and more unusual than you and [me]," Ham Luske, one of the studio's top animators in the 1930s, advised in a dictum to the staff. "Their thought process must be quicker than ours, and their uninteresting progressions from one situation to another must be skipped." And in this may have been the nub for Walt Disney. For all the prospective commercial benefits of animated realism, it had this deeply personal benefit for a man who had spent his young life creating an alternative reality as a compensation for the hurts he felt he had suffered: realism further allowed him to simplify and perfect his world and intensify his control over it. Realism allowed him to create a wonderful world of the plausibly impossible.

And what was realism without color? Even before he had begun exploring sound, Walt Disney had been captivated by the idea of color animations. He was so eager to improve the visual image of his animations that in January 1930 the studio began using the more sensitive positive film stock rather than negative even though it cost them $1,000 more per cartoon. Shortly thereafter Walt assigned Bill Cottrell, then in the camera department, to conduct an experiment for an atmospheric Silly Symphony titled *Night.* At Walt's instruction, Cottrell put silver nitrate on the film to see what effect he could achieve, then printed the cartoon on blue stock to imbue it with an inky tonality that approximated the color of the night sky. A fire sequence was printed on red stock, and an underwater scene on green. "I guess he was hoping that something would come up that we could do something [with] that would create a color picture," Cottrell later said.

Walt desperately wanted to press on, though the technology was lagging. "I am convinced that good color, not too hard on the eyes, would be of value to a cartoon subject," Walt wrote one prospective color laboratory, "however, all samples of color prints that I have seen to date would detract rather than add anything to a cartoon." Still, Walt kept searching, and when Technicolor, a company dedicated to color film, announced a three-color process early in 1932 that promised to reproduce tones more faithfully, Walt was said to have declaimed, "At last! We can show a rainbow on the screen."

Whether *he* could show it, however, was a point of contention with Roy. Walt admitted that color animations were prohibitively expensive—three times as much as black-and-white in lab costs and about a fourth more in production costs—with little chance of recovering those expenses in the short run, especially since the United Artists contract didn't call for color or for any adjustment should Walt decide to deliver his cartoons in color. Roy was adamantly opposed and asked others to dissuade Walt, but Walt was not to be dissuaded, arguing that color cartoons would have a longer life than black-and-whites. "I found out the people who live with figures as a rule, it's postmortem, it's never ahead, it's always what happened," Walt would say dismissively of Roy's objections. "Well, in my particular end I was always ahead." Walter Lantz at Universal had already made a Technicolor sequence for *The King of Jazz* starring Paul Whiteman. Now Walt felt it was his turn.

For its part, Technicolor was eager to assist, since it had had difficulty convincing live-action studios to bear the tremendous expense of color; in 1932 the company lost $235,000. Walt had already begun the next Silly Symphony in black-and-white, a story about two trees who fall in love, only to find their romance threatened by a jealous gnarly tree. Now, with Technicolor's cooperation, he decided midway to convert it to color. So he had the ink and paint department wash off the reverse side of the black and white cels, the side with the white and gray shades, leaving only the black outlines on the other side. Then he had the cels repainted in color on the reverse side. Walt was so excited by the outcome that he invited Rob Wagner, a friend, writer, and well-connected Hollywood bon vivant, to view scenes from the film. Wagner, in turn, recommended that the film be shown to Sid Grauman, Los Angeles's leading theater impresario and the chief of Grauman's Chinese Theater. Grauman was as floored as Walt and Wagner and booked it that July at the Chinese with MGM's *Strange Interlude*, a major release that ensured *Flowers and Trees* would receive wide attention. "Everybody is of the opinion that it will create quite a sensation," George Morris wrote Roy after a studio screening, correctly as it turned out. Grauman called it a "creation of genius that marks a new milestone in cinematic development." Walt later claimed that the showing at Grauman's brought "an avalanche of orders and bookings." *Flowers and Trees* would also win the Academy Award for animated short subject.

Now Walt was hooked, just as he had been hooked on sound with *Willie*. Black-and-white cartoons suddenly seemed antiquated and stylized, more drawing than life. "A black and white print looked as drab alongside *Flowers and Trees* as a gray day alongside a rainbow," he later wrote. "We could do other things with color! We could do many things with color that no other medium could do." The wheels, however, turned slowly. Nearly a year later Walt was still lobbying within the company to convert the entire program to color, whether UA would change the contract to compensate or not, whether the studio would have to stand the entire expense or not. "Walt is very hot on color," Gunther Lessing wrote Roy, who was in New York at the time. "He wants it." What Lessing couldn't convey was how badly Walt wanted it. He was so intent that even without the prospect of any additional compensation from UA he began negotiating with Technicolor for an exclusive right to use their process; he hoped to seal a deal when Technicolor head Herbert Kalmus met with his board of directors and feared that if he didn't close a deal soon, some rival animation studio would. Roy thought Walt was needlessly nervous, since everyone knew the Disneys weren't getting any larger advances for color cartoons than for black-and-white, but Roy, bowing once again to Walt's wishes, nevertheless met with Kalmus to discuss terms.

Roy was right that no other studio seemed to be beating down Technicolor's door and that Technicolor was even more eager than Walt to conclude an agreement, since Disney's cartoons were a way for them to showcase their process. In fact, Technicolor offered to loan the studio money to help offset the additional costs—complete conversion to color would have required an extra $195,000—and at one point proposed to foot the entire bill for the conversion in exchange for a 50 percent interest in the studio, which Walt politely declined. (Lessing was less polite.) Instead, Walt agreed to make thirteen Silly Symphony cartoons in color in exchange for the exclusive use of the three-color Technicolor process in animation for two years, enough to give him a significant head start over rivals, but he rejected any financial assistance from the company.

Roy was already edgy at the prospect of the new expenses and even convened a meeting of the staff on the soundstage, admonishing, "We've got to quit spending money on these films or we are going to go broke." Writing at the same time to his parents, he complained that Walt "continually (without letup in the least) always strives for something that has not been done before. That sort of policy, of course, is always costly." As always, Roy was charged with coming up with the money to finance Walt's ambitions. With UA reluctant to pay more for color, Roy, clearly scrambling to appease Walt, approached a New York investment banker named Rosenbaum to whom he had been introduced by a mutual friend, but the terms for the loan were usurious and the bank was said to be unscrupulous, and Roy broke off negotiations. There was even a press report, which the Disneys vehemently denied, that Roy would be forced to take the company public.

What complicated Roy's task was that at the very moment he was trying to secure financing for color, the remainder of the $195,000 loan that UA had advanced the studio under its revised contract was, according to a provision of that contract, coming due if UA decided to call it in. Roy and Walt both wanted to renegotiate with UA, hoping that they might be granted a two-year extension that would give them the resources to convert to color, and Roy went to New York that May to discuss terms. But UA—"depression-minded," Roy said—was not inclined to grant an extension, in part because it doubted that Walt could continue to deliver cartoons of such high quality. "They seem to think there must be a slipping point," Roy wrote Walt, "or that you will go stale, or go Hollywood, or some place else, but [not] to continue making good pictures." Since Roy, having taken up his brother's cause, believed that they had never "missed in the past by taking our gamble on ourselves and our product," he suggested that they forget an extension with UA and look elsewhere for funds. He left New York with another small loan from UA—$12,000 per film on those delivered between May 10 and June 27, when the balloon payment was due—and the determination to find another benefactor to support Walt's new obsession.*

As it turned out, the benefactor found them. Attilio Giannini, the son of Italian immigrants, was nicknamed "Doc" because he had earned a medical degree before entering his older brother Amadeo's California-based banking firm, the Bank of America. In Los Angeles, Doc Giannini had become legendary over the years for making loans on character rather than collateral, and he was especially esteemed in the motion picture industry, where he was among the first to provide capital for budding studios when no one else would. The Disneys had already secured small loans from the Bank of America, and while Roy was in New York, George Morris was holding discussions with the bank, seeking financial advice. (Hearing that UA was balking at an extension, Giannini told Morris that UA needed Disney more than Disney needed UA and that Morris should "[t]ell those sons of b's to go to Hell!") In late May, during one of these sessions at the Bank of America with an officer named Normanly, Dr. Giannini appeared, shook Morris's hand, and abruptly asked him "if United Artists would be sore if we pulled away from them," intimating that the bank might be willing to pay off UA's loan. When Morris said that he thought they would actually be relieved to have the loan—$112,000 of which was outstanding—repaid, Normanly and Giannini left for the latter's office to consult. When Normanly returned, he told Morris that the bank now wanted to assume the entire UA debt. Morris wrote Roy excitedly that this "absolutely severs any hold that United Artists may have on us," but, contrary to what he had told Giannini, he couldn't see why UA

*Hearing rumors of the financial troubles, Pat Powers, incorrigible as ever, wrote Walt—"This letter will, no doubt, surprise you. However, don't have heart failure"—to offer his assistance. Powers to Walt, April 3, 1933, Powers Cinephone Equipment Corp., Corr., 1930–1936, WDA.

would possibly agree. UA, however, did agree. Not only did the Bank of America assume the loan, to be liquidated within six months, it also agreed to loan the studio $12,000 per cartoon on the rest of the contract. A week later Roy met with Dr. Giannini to negotiate a general loan credit, irrespective of the delivery of films, that would allow the studio for the first time to borrow as it wished.

Now the Disneys finally had the resources they needed to make color cartoons or anything else they wanted to make. Under the deal with UA, which was still distributing the studio's films though no longer financing them, the Mickey cartoons were to remain in black-and-white for the foreseeable future—Roy saw no benefit in tampering with success—but the Silly Symphony series would henceforth be in color. In the end, then, despite Roy's misgivings, Walt Disney had gotten what he wanted, as he usually did.

II

By the time Walt was granted his exclusive from Technicolor, the Silly Symphony series had already begun to rival Mickey Mouse, if not yet in popularity, then at least in critical reception. Critic Gilbert Seldes, writing in *The New Republic* in June 1932, declared the Symphony series the "perfection of the movies," going on to say that the cartoons had "reached the point toward which the photographed and dramatic moving picture should be tending, in which, as in the silent pictures, everything possible is expressed in movement and the sound is used for support and clarification for contrast." The line between these critical hosannas and popular ones was crossed decisively the very week Walt closed the deal with Technicolor, with the release in May 1933 of one of the most extraordinary cartoons the studio would ever produce.

The project, about three fraternal pigs terrorized by a voracious wolf, apparently originated from a story in Andrew Lang's *Green Fairy Book* that had circulated through the studio the previous December with an outline and a long critique attached, probably from Walt, noting that "[t]hese little pig characters look as if they would work up very cute" and adding, apropos of the studio's new focus, that "we should be able to develop quite a bit of personality in them." When *Three Little Pigs* was storyboarded—by one account, it was the first of the animations to be given this treatment fully—Walt took special interest. Ben Sharpsteen recalled that "Walt practically lived in the music room while the director [Burt Gillett] was working on it. . . . He visualized the entire picture, and he spent more of his time on it than he had on any other picture up to that time." It was even animated somewhat differently than previous films with a small crew consisting primarily of Norm Ferguson and Dick Lundy, assisted by Art Babbitt and Freddie Moore, instead of the typically larger group in which each individual contributed a scene or gag.

Of the four, Moore, the youngest, would most distinguish himself. Moore, who had joined the studio in August 1930 just before his nineteenth birthday, was short, frumpy, and bulbous-nosed—in fact, he looked like a cartoon character himself. But his appearance notwithstanding, he was a graceful man and a natural athlete who picked up polo as soon as he grabbed a mallet, and he was just as much a natural when it came to drawing. "Animation came too easily to him," said Les Clark, whom Moore originally assisted. "He didn't have to exert any real effort." Moore's easy facility with the pencil made him especially adept at the new looser style at Disney introduced by Ferguson, and one eminent animation historian gave him the largest share of credit in displacing the old "rubber hose" animation at the studio with the more sophisticated "squash and stretch."

Moore's real forte, however, wasn't realism. It was charm. He had a knack for creating appealing characters who were soft, round, and cherubic and who seemed to exude the personality Walt so desperately wanted. While Ferguson drew the wolf in *Three Little Pigs*, Lundy most of the dance steps, and Babbitt the two action sequences, it was Moore's design and animation of the pigs that provided the film's core and that would prove so striking, indelible, and for the studio, iconic. Moore's pigs were a benchmark of personality animation just as Ferguson's Pluto had been a benchmark of psychology. Animator Ollie Johnston said of Moore that "[u]nder his influence the style of Disney drawing changed markedly for the better." Another animator, Marc Davis, went further. "The drawing that people think of when they think of Disney," he observed, "was inspired by Fred Moore," which is to say that his style, as evidenced in *Pigs*, quickly became the studio style. After *Pigs* Moore became such a dominant influence at the studio that even Walt would drop by Moore's animation table just to watch him.

Yet for all the obvious appeal of Moore's pigs, another element contributed just as mightily to the cartoon's success. During one storyboarding session Walt had perused the continuity and suggested that a little song should be inserted. Frank Churchill, who was now the studio composer, immediately began pounding out a tune on the piano. Ted Sears provided a couplet, and when he ran out of lyrics, Pinto Colvig, the storyman and voice artist, improvised a whistle to complete the musical line. Later two freelance singers were hired for a one-day recording session at ten dollars apiece, and "Who's Afraid of the Big Bad Wolf?" began its march on musical history.

Walt, always notoriously dissatisfied with anything the studio produced, pronounced himself happy with *Pigs*. "At last we have achieved true personality in a whole picture!" he was said to have written Roy after seeing it. Roy, who was at the time in New York meeting with UA on the contract extension, relayed Walt's enthusiasm to the distributor's salesmen. But when they screened the film themselves, they complained that it was a "cheater," meaning the studio had cheated them because *Pigs* had fewer characters than the previous Silly Symphony, *Father Noah's Ark*. It took UA publicist Hal Horne to defend the film as "the greatest thing Walt's ever done."

Audiences seemed to agree with Horne's assessment. Even at the very first preview, Dick Lundy recalled, moviegoers left whistling "Who's Afraid of the Big Bad Wolf?" The film had been open only a short time when the song began sweeping the nation—not just a musical phenomenon but a cultural one that played incessantly. "[Y]ou cannot escape," *New York Herald Tribune* film critic Richard Watts, Jr., complained.

> It bursts out at you in almost every film theater; the radio hurls it in your direction; try to escape from it by adjourning to a speakeasy and some unfortunate alcoholic will begin to sing it at you; you pick up a paper for relief and you will find it shrieking out at you in a cartoon on the editorial page. At teas, otherwise harmless men and women will suddenly burst, either coyly or determinedly, into its unceasing strains or its coy lyrics. Go to the theater and you will find it played by the orchestra in the intermission, while the handsomely clad men and women about town in the audience join merrily in humming it, just to show you that they are dashing sophisticates.

J. P. McEvoy, writing for the *New York Daily Mirror*, agreed. "Personally, I would like to get you into a corner and ask you if you have seen the 'Three Little Pigs,' and I would like to go on asking you about one hundred and fifty times," he grumbled. "This would give you some idea of what I have been going through for the last month [listening to 'Who's Afraid of the Big Bad Wolf?']."

United Artists, caught short by the demand for the cartoon, had too few prints and in some neighborhoods was forced to shuttle them between theaters by bicycle messenger. They even began running French and Spanish versions—anything they could get their hands on. One New York theater showed it for weeks, finally putting whiskers on a poster of the pigs outside the theater and lengthening the whiskers as the run continued. That fall, newspaper magnate William Randolph Hearst personally suggested that there be a *Three Little Pigs* comic strip, an idea Walt said he would entertain only if he got a full page in the comic section. The film industry took note as well. Walt was already a minor folk hero in Hollywood for Mickey Mouse, but shortly after *Pigs* he was feted by the Writers Club, where Chaplin, who rarely performed in public, climbed onto a small stage and did a pantomime in Walt's honor and where toastmaster Rupert Hughes announced that he would read a poem to Walt, took a stack of papers from his pocket, sipped from a glass of water, cleared his throat, and then said simply, " 'Walt Disney . . . Well, isn't he?' " as if there were nothing left to say. The next year *Pigs* won Walt another Academy Award.

Oddly enough, between the cost of the film, which George Morris put at $15,568, and the cost of the prints, which came to nearly $14,000, Morris worried that the studio might not break even on the picture, and when UA, taking advantage of the demand, began charging as much for *Pigs* as for some of its feature films, Walt felt compelled to issue an apology to the exhibitors in *The Hollywood Reporter*, saying that he had thus far failed to cover his costs and needed the money.* But whether it turned a profit or not, *Pigs*, like *Willie* before it, was widely regarded as a signal achievement in animation. "I realized something was happening there that hadn't happened before," animator Chuck Jones said of the effect of *Pigs*. It demonstrated that "it wasn't how a character looked but how he moved that determined his personality. All we animators were dealing with after 'Three Pigs' was acting." Jones even believed that personality animation really *began* with *Pigs*.

Walt, too, believed that *Pigs* had broken barriers. "It brought us honors and recognition all over the world and turned the attention of young artists and distinguished older artists to our medium as a worthwhile outlet for their talents," he wrote, and many of them trekked to Hyperion to join the cause. More, it had a financial ripple effect on the entire studio; the following year, thanks largely to the attention given to *Pigs*, the studio's net profit was estimated by *Fortune* at $600,000. But the cartoon's real effect was on the status of animation generally and on the status of the Disney studio specifically. As Walt put it years later, "[T]he main thing about the 'Three Little Pigs' was a certain recognition from the industry

*In the end Walt claimed to have made $4,000 on the film on gross rentals of $125,000. *New York Herald Tribune*, March 12, 1934; Disney, "Growing Pains," p. 139.

and the public that these things could be more than just a mouse hopping around or something." They could be art.

The difference between *Three Little Pigs* and most of the earlier Disney milestones was that it was not only an achievement in animation but also, like the song, a cultural achievement, which was certainly a source of its astounding popularity. Critics immediately acknowledged that it bored into the national consciousness, both reflecting and somehow ameliorating anxiety over the Depression. Walt, as usual, pleaded ignorance, saying that neither he nor his crew had had any message in mind when they made the film. In fact, after nearly four years of national economic turmoil, Walt was still amazingly cavalier about it, once even remarking to his staff that if it hadn't been for the Depression, he wouldn't have had any of his top animators. Even so, the Disneys were not entirely unafflicted. Flora and Elias in Portland were suffering; their tenants were unable to pay the rent, which was, in any case, half of what it had been before the crash; and when Roy suggested that his father "trade" the rent with a tenant for paint and brushes to refurbish the buildings they owned, Elias said that he had $100 in back rent due him. "Of course that ain't much to any one having a 'Mickey Mouse' Studio or something similar," he wrote his son Raymond snidely. "To us it means considerable." Their hope, they said, rested with the election of the new president.

When Franklin Roosevelt was inaugurated in March 1933 and declared a bank holiday that same week to help stem a possible run on financial institutions, Roy was shaken, frantic over how the studio would pay its staff with its assets frozen. He had gone down to the bank to remonstrate and was given a ten-dollar gold piece for each employee as a token on the account, but before the week was out gold had been declared illegal tender. Now Roy began "stewing," to use his own word. Walt, who had no interest in politics and whose primary interest in money was in reinvesting it in his cartoons, was unsympathetic. "Quit worrying," he shrugged. "People aren't going to stop living just because the banks are closed. What the hell, we'll use anything—make potatoes the medium of exchange—we'll pay everybody in potatoes."

As it happened, *Pigs* was released on May 27, a little more than two months after the inauguration and the bank holiday, and the timing couldn't have been more fortunate. Wrung out by the Depression and bolstered by the new president, the nation seemed to convert the cartoon of two carefree but shortsighted pigs and their hard-working, far-sighted brother into a parable of suffering (the wolf as economic adversity) and triumph (the industrious little pig as the embodiment of President Roosevelt's New Deal that promised the country relief), which was exactly how numerous political cartoons at the time framed it. Film historian Lewis Jacobs said that the film became "by force of circumstance and the time . . . a heartening call to the people of a troubled country." A few observers even credited it not just with reflecting the Depression but with helping vanquish it. "No one will ever know to what extent it may be held responsible for pulling us out of the depression," Harvard professor Robert D. Feild wrote a few years after its release, "but certainly the lyrical jeer at the Big Bad Wolf contributed not a little to the raising of people's spirits and to their defiance of circumstance." In his annual report Will Hays, the president of the Motion Picture Producers and Distributors of America, said that "historians of the future will not ignore the interesting and significant fact that the movies literally laughed the big bad wolf of depression out of the public mind through the protagonism of *Three Little Pigs*." Whatever the cartoon's impact on sagging morale, "Who's Afraid of the Big Bad Wolf?" indisputably became the nation's new anthem, its cheerful whoop hurled in the face of hard times.

Among the many effects on the Disneys of the success of *Three Little Pigs* was the further expansion of the studio, the staff of which by late 1933 numbered nearly two hundred. Walt said, not disapprovingly, that Hyperion was coming to resemble a "Ford factory," with the difference that "our moving parts were more complex than cogs—human beings, each with his own temperament and values who must be weighted and fitted into his proper place." Walt had always been as concerned with the process of making cartoons as with the cartoons themselves, and in comparing his studio to a factory production line, he was acknowledging the new pressure on him to streamline that process. For one thing, he was constantly being nagged by Roy, and now by George Morris as well, to find a way to economize so that the studio could turn a profit. For another, he was always seeking ways to optimize the talents of his staff, in the service not just of productivity but of quality. It was precisely because he didn't want to sacrifice his status as the best cartoon maker that he was driven to find a better way to make cartoons, effectively trying to mass-produce excellence.

Thus began another revolution. Just as he had been reinventing animation and attempting to perfect it through new techniques, Walt now began reinventing and attempting to perfect the system under which animations were produced. This put him in the unusual position of trying to reenchant a modern world that had been disenchanted partly through excessive rationalism by devising a system of production that would itself be more rational. Even if Walt had wanted it to, the studio clearly could no longer operate as a kind of giant fraternity where roles were ill defined and everyone pitched in on everything. Already before *Pigs* Walt had instituted his story department with Sears and Smith, which by late 1932 was segregated from the animators, and throughout 1932 and 1933 he had further divided the animators themselves into key animators, who drew the major poses or extremes, in-betweeners, who drew the action in between the extremes, and assistants, who cleaned up all the animation drawings and readied them to be inked and painted on the cels—a division that had the added bonus of allowing younger animators to learn from more experienced ones. Now new roles emerged, as well as even greater specialization, to make production less haphazard.

The process always began with the story. In the early days the stories usually originated with Walt, who would relate them to his animators to help him "gag" them during brainstorming sessions. When in the late 1920s Walt began assigning cartoons to directors to execute—either Iwerks or Jackson, and after Iwerks left, Burt Gillett—he would have them draw up rough sketches of the continuity, which Walt examined and approved or improved. "[T]he picture Walt was after was in his head, not on pieces of paper," Wilfred Jackson said. Though the hatching of the story remained the least formalized stage of the cartoon, that informality gradually changed thanks to the activities of the new story department. Walt might still present a situation to his crew on which they were to ruminate, or after the studio expanded, he might distribute a mimeographed outline of a new animation to solicit gags from the entire staff, which would then be bandied about at large gag meetings on the soundstage.* (By 1934 he was requesting that these gags be drawn rather than written: "This would be an ideal way to present your story because it then shows the visualized possibilities, rather than a lot of words, explaining things that . . . turn out to be impossible to put over in action.") But in the early 1930s Walt also created a new position, that of the sketch artist, who worked with the storymen and produced the storyboards. After a gag meeting the storyman and sketch artist would meet with a director to develop the continuity. When the storyman and sketch artist felt ready, they would drag the giant storyboards to one of the music rooms for a presentation to Walt. That part never changed, no matter how much the studio expanded: Walt was always the final authority, the one whom everyone had to please.

*As Walt later described the process, "What we do is this . . . all of the fellows, that is, the directors, the story men and all those concerned with story select the material to be made into short subjects and then I approve of their selections." Memo, Walt to Chuck Clark, Apr. 4, 1944, C Folder, Walt Disney Corr., Inter-Office, 1938–1944, C, A1626, WDA.

Standing in front of the boards, with an audience of the director, possibly the animators assigned to the short, and Walt, who invariably sat in the middle, the storyman would narrate the events and read the dialogue under the drawings. This was not just an informational session. The storyman had to "sell" his project to Walt. Being a good storyman meant not only devising a plot and gags but convincing Walt of their value. "The best story guys could act up a storm, laugh uproariously at their favorite gags, and outshout everyone, while using a wooden pointer to emphasize the main elements," recalled director Jack Kinney. One storyman, Roy Williams, would get so carried away with his pointer that he would smash it right through the board.

During these sessions Walt usually sat impassively, unless he saw something that inspired him, and then he would leap to his feet and be off in a creative convulsion, spinning new ideas, one after another, sometimes even shooting down his own contribution and adducing another and then another and another. When he wasn't inspired, one attendee remembered, "one eyebrow would go up and he would start to cough or thump his hand on the arm of his chair"—the raised eyebrow, the cough, and the drumming fingers, especially loud since Walt's fingertips were calcified from his chain-smoking, three telltale gestures that could strike fear into the heart of any storyman. At the end of the presentation Walt, "like a Roman Emperor at the gladiator combat arena," as one staff member described him, would typically sit in silence, and after this dramatic pause, during which the storyman and sketch artist would be quaking, begin his analysis, leading to a revision, to an abandonment, or to the coveted go-ahead. Even then, however, the story process was not quite finished. By the mid-1930s Walt was subjecting the storyboards to questionnaires in which studio staff were asked what they liked and didn't like and inviting suggestions, for which Walt offered prizes as he did for gags.

At first the storymen were basically interchangeable, but they soon began to develop specialties. One might be good at story structure, another at character development, a third at recycling old gags, and a fourth at finding visual possibilities, and Walt would "cast" them, like actors, depending on what a particular animation seemed to need most. By now Walt had added another specialization to the story process, the gagman, whose job was to take the continuity and further "gag it up." Sometimes this would take place in gag sessions with the storyman and director. Other times Walt would roam the studio with several gagmen in tow, visiting music rooms to add gags under his supervision. But even the gags were being routinized. At roughly the same time the gagman appeared, the studio was negotiating with UA publicist Hal Horne for his extensive gag file, and by decade's end the studio had a row of filing cabinets with 1.5 million jokes grouped under 124 classifications.

In the very early days, once the story had been developed and gagged, Walt would then supervise the animation, functioning essentially as both producer and director. By the late 1920s, under the pressure of two full programs of animations—the Mickey Mouse cartoons and the Silly Symphonies—he had surrendered the director's role. The director was a coordinator, synthesizing the story with the animation, the background layout, and the sound track. It was the director who finalized the "grays," the gray sheets of paper on which were listed all the dialogue and sounds, then drew up the bar sheets that listed the sounds and the images frame by frame and side by side. He also was responsible for recording the sound, assigning scenes to animators, preparing the pencil tests to be reviewed by Walt, overseeing the inking and painting of his film, editing it and assembling it, and perhaps most of all, conveying Walt's instructions to everyone on the project so that Walt's vision was realized—an unenviable task, since Walt was often inexact in expressing what he wanted and then usually berated a director for not being able to read his mind. As Ben Sharpsteen put it, "Walt was the antagonist. He would take no excuses for a poor picture and he was prone to blame the director for a picture's weaknesses." Iwerks and Jaxon (Wilfred Jackson) were the first directors after Walt relinquished those reins. Later, when Walt was forced to divide the work into units to speed production, he assigned Jaxon, Gillett, and Sharpsteen to head them, and when Gillett was lured away by Van Beuren after the success of *Pigs*, an animator named Dave Hand, who had joined the studio two days after Iwerks left, assumed control of a unit.

Now Walt interpolated two more positions into the process, which again seemed to contribute to quality at the expense of efficiency. He hired artist Albert Hurter, who had worked at the Barré studio in New York and whose style inclined to European illustration, to provide what were called "inspirational drawings"—drawings that were intended to create an atmosphere or suggest a look that would both guide and inspire the men entrusted with actually animating the cartoon. It was a luxury that other animation studios obviously could not afford. "Albert Hurter had a big room and a big desk and did exactly what he pleased," Grim Natwick remembered. "Walt would say, 'Well, we're going to make an animal picture, it'll be located so and so. See if you can think of funny little positions.' And Albert would play around with it."

At roughly the same time Walt also broadened the responsibilities of the background artists, who were themselves early specialists, into laying out the entire cartoon visually prior to its being animated. Hence the name *layout artist.* As animation historian John Culhane put it, "[T]he director 'saw' the story in time and the layout artist saw it in space." The latter worked closely with the director to devise not only the backgrounds, as in the past, but the characters and the staging of the scenes, even indicating camera angles and edits, so that the animators, who had previously worked primarily from the sketch artist's drawings, now had a clear directive to follow.

After the director and the layout artist had settled on their approach, the director would assign the animation, a procedure called the "handout," and the key animators would then draw the main poses. Walt's division of labor into head animators, in-betweeners, and assistants may have been partly a concession to economy, and it did conserve the key animators' time for the important things while relegating less important tasks to the less experienced animators, especially since each cartoon required anywhere from six thousand to seven thousand drawings, with the bonus that having assistants clean up the animation imposed a consistency between the work of one key animator and another. But another, less mercenary motive also lay behind Walt's thinking, one that meshed with the animation techniques he was encouraging. Walt believed that by confining the chief animators to drawing extremes, he could get looser, more active, more powerful animation than if they had to concern themselves with drawing more cleanly for ink and paint. By the early 1930s Walt was insisting that his best animators draw roughly and that the assistants in cleaning up a drawing then actually "[m]ake it stronger than it has been drawn," in Eric Larson's words, so that the process produced bold, striking work. (Thomas and Johnston said that this redrawing helped account for the beauty of the animation at the time.) Some had a difficult time adjusting. One animator, Jack King, so resisted Walt's injunction that he had his assistants rough up his clean drawings until Walt caught him and exploded.

Once the key animators got their handouts, they proceeded to draw poses. (Eventually they began making "pose tests" in which the poses were photographed so that the animators could see how the poses registered on the screen.) The rough animation led to the pencil tests, after which animators would revise their drawings, and then to the sweatbox sessions with Walt, which were the animators' equivalent of the storyboard sessions and just as grueling. "A sweatbox session could determine a man's fate in the organization; a good session could lead to fame and fortune, a bad one to the other side of the main gate," wrote Jack Kinney, who would work as both an animator and a director. "Consequently, as the session progressed, the air became hot, then steamy, and even gamy as a result of all the perspiration, carbon monoxide, and shattered hopes floating about in the gloom." That didn't change even when the sweatbox was relocated from its alcove under the stairwell to an air-conditioned projection room. After these sessions changes were made, a Leica reel was shot, and finally a rough reel was assembled of the cartoon not yet cleaned up or inked and painted.

Now came yet another quality control. Walt would screen the rough tests for each animation at noon on the soundstage for the staff and pass out questionnaires for comments, just as he had during the storyboard review. He would also record the audience reaction on acetate disks so he could hear precisely what worked and what didn't. Only then, after changes had been made in accordance with the response, would the animation be cleaned up, inked, painted, and photographed by a camera in which compressed air held the cels while the operator pressed a button to activate the shutter. And then, after the film had been processed, the cartoon would be previewed at a nearby theater, usually on an evening when there was a full house. Animators were expected to attend and engage in a postmortem with Walt either in the lobby or on the sidewalk outside the theater—yet another terrifying ordeal if the audience hadn't been enthusiastic. One embarrassed director slunk out to avoid Walt and raced to the parking lot, only to find him there fuming. "Even though he was blocking traffic in the parking lot," Sharpsteen recalled, "Walt stood there and let him know how unhappy he was with the picture!"

The entire process, from a cartoon's inception to its preview, could take as little as three months, which was in fact the typical interval, or as long as two years, but time never mattered to Walt except as an annoyance. The only thing that mattered to him was that he had done everything in his power to make the cartoon as excellent as it could be.

III

It was a burden. The demands not only in producing the animations but in reeducating the animators and reinventing the entire process would have been enormous even if Walt hadn't been the workaholic he was. To stave off another breakdown, he tried to maintain his new exercise schedule, continuing to ride on horseback with Lillian, occasionally returning early from the studio to do so, and to swim and ice skate. At one point he even took dancing lessons with Lillian ("in spite of all your work, I'm still a lousy dancer," he wrote his instructor self-deprecatingly years later) and at another point boxing lessons. Yet these were concessions, wrung grudgingly from him. Once gregarious and outgoing, he now channeled his enthusiasm into the studio and was virtually withdrawn outside it. He socialized even less than before, claiming that it "took too much of one's energy" and saying that he preferred to get a "good night's sleep as it leaves me in better condition in the morning to carry on the work." Sometimes he would invite a few of the animators—Fred Moore, Ham Luske, Norm Ferguson—to the house on Lyric Avenue for a backyard game of badminton, but these occasions were rare and gradually petered out, one attendee said, because Walt became too important to mingle socially with his staff; Walt claimed it was because Lillian preferred privacy and the "house belongs to the woman." Walt even stopped attending studio parties because, Lillian said, the animators' wives would sometimes get tipsy and reproach him for some imagined slight to their husbands. "That's a part of them I don't want to see," Walt said. Though he made another business trip to New York in July 1933 and stopped in Chicago on the way back to see the Century of Progress Fair there, taking his first plane ride on the final leg from Salt Lake City to Los Angeles, he seldom traveled either and admitted that he would rather spend a vacation at home.

But he did have one new recreational passion, one activity outside the studio that seemed to excite him: polo. Polo, oddly enough, had become something of a fad in Hollywood in the 1930s, where it was regarded as a way for those who had been previously marginalized, many of them Jewish immigrants, to raise their status by aping the manners of the wellborn. "From Poland to polo," went the quip about Hollywood moguls. As Walt told it, he was becoming frustrated with his morning golf games when sometime in the spring of 1932 humorist Will Rogers and film executive Darryl F. Zanuck, both of whom were polo enthusiasts, suggested that he take up polo instead. After watching a few matches at their invitation, Walt decided that "it was golf on horseback" and bought a few ponies. Of course it was not in Walt Disney's nature to do anything casually. He immediately began recruiting staff from the studio, including Roy, and hired a polo champion named Gil Proctor to lecture them in the studio conference room on the fine points of the game. At six every morning throughout the spring and summer eight players would gather at the DuBrock Riding Academy in the San Fernando Valley, where they would break into teams and practice. Walt eventually installed a polo cage at the studio so players could swat balls during their lunch break, and he put a dummy horse in his backyard and spent mornings even before heading to DuBrock sitting there knocking balls. On Sunday mornings the crew would often congregate at Will Rogers's ranch for impromptu matches. During the games Rogers would gibe Walt, calling him "Mickey" or "Mickey Mouse."

By the spring of 1933, dressed in a tweed jacket, jodhpurs, and high boots, Walt was ready to play matches at the more rigorous Riviera Country Club in posh Brentwood, where the movie stars and studio executives like Zanuck played—an indication of how Walt's status if not his polo skills had risen. Calling themselves the Mickey Mouse team, Walt joined with Roy and other studio personnel like Norm Ferguson, Dick Lundy, and Gunther Lessing, but he also played with, among others, Will Rogers, producer Walter Wanger, and actors Johnny Mack Brown, James Gleason, Leslie Howard, and Spencer Tracy, who became one of the "very few people outside the immediate family ever invited into the Disney home," according to fellow polo player Bill Cottrell, who was courting Lillian's divorced sister Hazel at the time and thus was almost part of the Disney family himself. Cottrell believed that Tracy was "for a while [the man] whom Walt considered his best friend," though he was basically a polo friend, which testified to how few real attachments Walt had.

Most Sundays now Walt and Lillian would drive out to Riviera, stopping to buy a big bag of popcorn on the way, which Lillian would munch while she watched the matches. By the end of the year, even though he was only a middling player—his best handicap was a one-goal rating out of a possible ten—he was recruiting ringers to play with him and had begun venturing throughout California and even Mexico for matches. At the time he had six ponies of his own and would soon buy a stable of four ponies for Roy, eventually supplying horses for those who could not afford them. "[I]t's my only sin," he wrote his mother that December. "I don't gamble or go out and spend my money on other people's wives or anything like that, so I guess it's okay. Anyway, the wife approves of it."

Walt's sudden exuberance over polo, and his athletic regimen generally, had not only been a way to keep his mood buoyant and his health sound. The doctors had advised both Walt and Lillian that they would have a better chance of conceiving a child if they exercised more vigorously, and this was a powerful incentive. Happily, it seemed to have its desired effect. In the summer of 1932 Lillian got pregnant again, setting off another wave of euphoria. Walt immediately bought one and a half acres on Woking Way, a narrow, quiet street near the studio in the Los Feliz section of Los Angeles that snaked up into the Hollywood hills, and began constructing a $50,000, twelve-room French Norman–style home there. "We had been living in a little place where I couldn't turn around," Walt told an interviewer, "so I made the architect add three or four yards to every room in the house." Walt admitted it was a rush job, roughly two months from start to finish—obviously racing against the baby's birth.

And then Lillian suffered another miscarriage. When, late in the spring of 1933, with the Disneys in their new and spacious home, they learned that Lillian was pregnant yet again, their mood was cautious. Only gradually as summer wore on did they allow themselves some elation. "Lilly has been feeling fine and having no trouble at all," Walt wrote his mother that September. "In fact she is so healthy that she has been worried about it." Lillian wanted a girl, Walt said, because "she seems to feel that she could get more pleasure out of dressing a little girl than boy. Personally, I don't care, just as long as we do not get disappointed again." As the expected December birth date approached, Walt prepared. He had fixed up a large nursery with a bassinet and pink and blue decorations, "tinies" he called them, bought a horse for the child in anticipation, and now just awaited the arrival. "Really, it's quite a strange atmosphere for me," he wrote Flora again. "I can't conceive of anything belonging to us. It seems all right for somebody else to have those things around, but not for us. I presume I'll get used to it, and I suppose I'll be as bad a parent as anybody else. I've made a lot of vows that my kid won't be spoiled, but I doubt it—it may turn out to be the most spoiled brat in the country."

After the kidnapping and murder of aviator Charles Lindbergh's infant son the year before, Walt hoped to keep the birth as quiet as possible. It didn't work out that way. He was in the act of receiving an award from *Parents* magazine for Mickey Mouse at a luncheon at the studio on December 18 before seventy-five members of the press, when someone interrupted and whispered to him. "Thank you," he told the magazine's representative. "This is the biggest moment of my life. You'll pardon, I hope, if I hurry away and show this beautiful award to my wife and . . ." Before finishing, Walt grabbed his coat and bolted, leaving the toastmaster, Dr. Rufus von KleinSmid, president of the University of Southern California, to explain to the befuddled guests, "I'm afraid I'll have to accept the award for Mr. Disney myself. His wife is going to present him with another kind of award. He is on his way to become a parent and thus become a fully qualified reader of the magazine which is honoring him today." Walt arrived at the hospital just before the delivery. Lillian said she knew he had arrived when she heard his distinctive hacking cough. "AM PROUD FATHER OF BABY GIRL LILLIE AND BABY DOING FINE," he wired Roy, who was on a train bound for home after fighting a copyright infringement suit in New York. The Disneys now had a new eight-pound-two-ounce daughter: Diane Marie Disney.

As for Walt's animated offspring, Mickey Mouse, he was still thriving, even as Walt's attention had been diverted to the Silly Symphony cartoons. The three little pigs, Walt admitted, had overshadowed Mickey, and Walt told one reporter that he was disappointed, but added, "I'll think of something that will bring Mickey back bigger than ever." In fact, though the pigs had swept the nation, Mickey continued over the following two years to enjoy a popularity that rivaled that of Chaplin in his heyday. The Mickey Mouse Clubs thrived, and Walt boasted, with a heavy dose of hyperbole, that the membership had swelled to fifty million by the fall of 1933. Less hyperbolically, *Literary Digest* reported that Mickey played before nearly 500 million paid admissions in 1935. He also continued to receive accolades from nearly every quarter. Gilbert Seldes, writing in *Esquire*, gushed of Mickey's first color cartoon, *The Band Concert*, that none of "dozens of works produced in America at the same time in all the other arts can stand comparison with this one," and *The Nation* extolled Mickey as the "supreme artistic achievement of the moving picture." Even First Lady Eleanor Roosevelt once commented that her husband "loved Mickey Mouse, and he always had to have that cartoon in the White House," though perhaps the highest compliment paid to Mickey was by a patient in a New York City convalescent home who was so overcome during a Mickey Mouse screening that he forgot his crutches and walked out of the theater unassisted.

Mickey was no less popular or lauded overseas. *Fortune* noted that he was an "international hero, better known than Roosevelt or Hitler, a part of the folklore of the world." By one account Queen Mary of England once arrived late for a tea rather than miss the end of a charity screening of *Mickey's Nightmare*. Orchestra conductor Arturo Toscanini saw *The Band Concert*, in which Mickey leads a band with disastrous results, six times and was so smitten by it that he extended an invitation to Walt to visit him in Italy. When a program of Disney cartoons featuring Mickey as well as the Symphonies was shown in Moscow, *The New York Times* reported that "[n]ot since the days of the food shortage have the streets of Moscow witnessed such queues as those waiting to buy tickets for the American movies." Russian director Sergei Eisenstein requested permission to publish several of the scenarios in a book.

By this time Mickey's burgeoning cottage industries had begun to eclipse his screen success. Late in 1930 the Disneys had renewed their contract with George Borgfeldt to license Mickey Mouse products, though they decided to restrict his representation to toys. At the same time a seamstress named Charlotte Clark had sewn a Mickey Mouse doll, which Roy raced to have ready for Christmas. Even though the company's strained financial situation limited the production and even though each was hand-made, the studio sold more than twenty-five gross in just five weeks. Within months Roy, who had been lobbying publishers for a

Mickey Mouse book just a year earlier, was now besieged by offers and, taking a page from Walt, was insisting on a "real high-class book." That spring, with Borgfeldt boasting to Roy that "we are building up a big Mickey Mouse business with many of the leading distributors," the studio opened a New York office to handle the merchandise that Borgfeldt did not represent.

But Walt and Roy, who were trying to raise money for the color conversion at the time, were impatient and dissatisfied. Roy said that the Borgfeldt royalty statement for 1930 arrived in "longhand like some bunch of farmers" and that the return amounted to only $63, while the Charlotte Clark dolls alone, which Roy handled himself, netted the studio $350. "They are great hands to do lots of talking," he groused about Borgfeldt. Moreover, the quality control was terrible—Disney products were often shoddy, which angered both Walt and Roy—and the interval from the conception of a product to its marketing was often interminably long. Despairing that the Borgfeldt company insufficiently exploited the character but yet being locked into the contract, the Disneys had even enlisted Harry Woodin of the Mickey Mouse Clubs and Irving Lesser, the brother of producer Sol Lesser, to troll for marketing opportunities that Borgfeldt seemed disinclined to find.

And then into this morass strode Herman Kamen, known to everyone—and Kamen did seem to know everyone—as "Kay." Kamen was, one acquaintance said, "one of the homeliest men I had ever seen." He was a large, shapeless, ungainly man with a spatulate nose and thick pop-bottle-bottomed glasses, and he parted his black hair unfashionably down the middle of his scalp, only adding to the impression of his gaucheness. Yet this look was partly by design. One associate said that Kamen was proud of his homeliness and used it to ingratiate himself with customers in his chosen profession, at which he was a master. Kay Kamen was born to sell.

He had come from a Jewish family in Baltimore, quit school to become a hat salesman, and after years on the road, where he became an expert pinochle player, joined a department store promotional firm in Kansas City. He and a colleague there, an advertising man named Streeter Blair, left to form their own company, Kamen-Blair, also headquartered in Kansas City, which, like the one they had departed, specialized in creating displays and campaigns for department stores. One of those displays, for a store in Los Angeles, apparently caught Walt Disney's eye early in 1932, when he was burning over Borgfeldt's dereliction, and he wired Kamen to gauge his interest in promoting Mickey Mouse. Kamen, then in New York on business, left for California that very day.

When he arrived at the studio, as Roy remembered it, Kamen walked into Roy's office and said, "I don't know how much business you're doing, but I'll guarantee you that much business and give you fifty percent of everything I do over." It was a sign both of his salesmanship and of the rather offhanded way the company conducted business that they signed a contract with him that July, after the Borgfeldt agreement had expired. Under its terms the studio was to receive 60 percent of the first $100,000 in royalties, with the fifty-fifty split thereafter, and Kamen was to foot all expenses including his staff, the New York office, and a showroom and hotel suite in Chicago.

Now Kamen set out to do for Walt Disney Enterprises, the new merchandise arm of the studio, what Walt had been doing for Walt Disney Productions, its filmmaking arm. He was going to reinvent it—transform it into a sleek, quality-controlled, revenue-producing operation that would in time have the added effect of making Mickey Mouse even more popular as a brand than he was as a movie star. Believing that Disney should be affiliated with only the finest manufacturers, Kamen quickly canceled contracts with less prestigious and aggressive companies and signed up with bigger and better ones—National Dairy Products, Ingersoll watches, General Foods (which would shortly pay a million dollars for the right to put Mickey Mouse and his friends on Post Toasties cereal boxes), and even Cartier jewelers, which was soon marketing a diamond Mickey Mouse bracelet. (However, his greatest achievement, Kamen said, was "Getting the Three Little Pigs up in lights in New York's strictly kosher Ghetto, and making them like it.") Kamen was a whirlwind. Within a year there were forty licensees for Mickey Mouse products. A year after that, in 1934, Kamen, with a staff numbering fifteen in New York alone, had helped orchestrate $35 million of sales in Disney merchandise in the United States and an equal amount overseas, and he had opened branches across Europe and even in Australia.

Thanks largely to Kamen's efforts, the image of Mickey Mouse was ubiquitous and unavoidable. "Shoppers carry Mickey Mouse satchels and briefcases," reported *The New York Times* in tribute to the marketing phenomenon, "bursting with Mickey Mouse soap, candy, playing cards, bridge favors, hairbrushes, chinaware, alarm clocks and hot water bottles wrapped in Mickey Mouse paper tied with Mickey Mouse ribbon and paid for out of Mickey Mouse purses with savings hoarded in Mickey Mouse banks." Children, it continued, lived in a new Mickey Mouse world:

> They wear Mickey Mouse caps, waists, socks, shoes, slippers, garters, mittens, aprons, bibs and underthings, and beneath Mickey Mouse rain capes and umbrellas. They go to school where Mickey Mouse desk outfits turn lessons into pleasure.
>
> They play with Mickey Mouse velocipedes, footballs, base-

balls, bounce balls, bats, catching gloves, boxing gloves, doll houses, doll dishes, tops, blocks, drums, puzzles, games.

Paint sets, sewing sets, drawing sets, stamping sets, jack sets, bubble sets, pull toys, push toys, animated toys, tents, camp stools, sand pails, masks, blackboards and balloons.

And even that list did not begin to exhaust the number of Mickey Mouse products.

Just as Mickey on film had come to be regarded as a tonic antidote to the Depression, so did Mickey's image on merchandise. Round, colorful, appealing Mickey Mouse had become the graphic representation of indomitable happiness even in the face of national despair. "Wherever he scampers, here or overseas," the *Times* observed, "the sun of prosperity breaks through the clouds." When Ingersoll issued a Mickey Mouse watch, it proved so popular that the company had to cancel its advertising campaign because it had already sold out its factory's capacity for months to come. (Even Roy bought a dozen for his personal use.) The Lionel Corporation, manufacturers of toy electric trains, had been in receivership in 1934 when it licensed a Mickey and Minnie handcar. The company sold 253,000 units at Christmas, making it profitable once again and allowing it to discharge its equity receivers. "There is no case that I remember where more success was met with than in this case," the bankruptcy judge commented.

The mouse as merchandiser had roughly the same effect on his own studio. In his first four years Kamen had increased the licensing 10,000 percent to just under $200,000 in royalties a year, and as early as 1934 Walt was claiming that he made more money from the ancillary rights to Mickey than from Mickey's cartoons. Thus Disney became the first studio to recognize what would become a standard business practice in Hollywood forty years later—that one could harvest enormous profits from film-related toys, games, clothing, and other products. Indeed, as *Literary Digest* reported, "[I]t is no exaggeration to state that Walt Disney Enterprises has become the tail that wags the mouse."

There was another reason, beyond Mickey's visual appeal, that the merchandise was seemingly becoming more popular than the cartoons: onscreen Mickey had faltered, if not in audience appeal, then with critics and even within the studio. He was scarcely five years old when, given his split personality between Chaplin and Fairbanks, he began to suffer the inevitable identity crisis. Recognizing the problem, Jack Hannah, an animator at the time, recalled, "We began to have an awful hard time defining stories for Mickey. . . . [He] began as a mischief maker, but he developed right off the bat into a little hero type, and you couldn't knock him around too much." Animation historian Michael Barrier believed that there had been different conceptions of Mickey in different media but that the cartoon Mickey, who had arrived with a gleefully puckish, anarchic streak, increasingly came to resemble the comic strip Mickey, who was thrust into situations in which he was required to act heroically—essentially sacrificing his Chaplin half to his Fairbanks half. Mickey now was always rescuing Minnie from the clutches of the sadistic Peg Leg Pete.

While these halves of Mickey were warring, he was plagued by yet another, almost metaphysical question: what exactly *was* Mickey Mouse? Was he a mouse with mouselike attributes that led him to bedevil his antagonists, or was he a human in the form of a mouse? More to the point, was he a little boy in the form of a mouse? This question had troubled Walt and the animators too and had even prompted some critics to speculate whether, as *Theatre Arts Monthly* put it, Mickey would be "abandoned gradually in favor of the symphonies" or whether his creators would "divorce him from the animal world and marry him into the human." Back in 1928 he seemed to have been conceptualized as a mouse with human affectations, but by 1932 he had come to resemble a happy and sometimes hapless child, which may have made Mickey Mouse the first casualty of the studio's growing obsession with realism.

The early and impudent Mickey Mouse seemed to belong in a universe not unlike the one cartoonist George Herriman created for his Krazy Kat—an arid abstract plane where rubber hose was more appropriate than squash and stretch. "In the beginning of the thirties," animator Eric Larson acknowledged, "Mickey could do almost anything: stretch his arms, use his body. Later in the thirties he was not able to do that." What had happened between these two Mickeys was realism. The early Mickey wasn't real in the sense that the little pigs were real, which is to say fully realized; in fact, he was barely a character. As he had rubber hose actions, he had broad rubber hose emotions too, which adapted to any situation, rather than a core personality that, as in squash and stretch, could change but retained its basic identity. But when Walt introduced realism as a means of developing personality and thus eliciting a stronger audience reaction, Mickey was bereft. Walt "realized the minute we got into believable stories that held up with motivations and character and personality," animator Ward Kimball said, "you open up a limitless world, whereas the mouse was limited."

Since Walt couldn't countenance dispatching his alter ego to oblivion, he tried to conform him to the new landscape. Throughout 1932 and

1933 Mickey gradually became rounder, shorter, thicker, less sinewy—his mouselike features shrinking and softening as his human features—his hands, his head, and his feet—grew, and his mouselike characteristics yielding to gentler, more human ones. By 1936 Les Clark was describing Mickey to a group of would-be animators as having a "feeling of cuteness and boyishness," and he said, "He is generally considered and handled as a little boy." Where he had been light-footed and snappy in the early days, his feet were heavy now—"His feet should be at least half the volume of his body," Clark advised—which literally gave him a gravity he had not had. More, he was not always dressed in his trademark shorts anymore. As early as 1932 he was wearing other clothes, lived in a house, and had his pet dog Pluto. Walt even insisted once that Mickey and Minnie were married in real life, though they played boyfriend and girlfriend on screen.

But the reconceptualization and domestication that were intended to "humanize" Mickey actually wound up neutralizing him by blunting what few sharp edges he had. Losing his angularity, he also lost his impertinence and cheek, so that where Walt had once compared him to the incorrigible Chaplin, he now compared him to eager-to-please Harold Lloyd. Mickey even lost the self-centered obliviousness that had made him so apt a figure for the Depression. "To me there was something perfect about the way Mickey looked in the '30s," children's book author Jan Wahl once remarked. "When they gave him that zoot suit and made him part of California suburbia, I stopped paying attention to him. It was when he fell into our ordinary world—that's when I think he lost his luster."

But if Mickey Mouse was a victim of pacification, he was a victim of his own popularity as well: the tragedy of success. He had won that popularity through an impish subversiveness; he could only maintain it, Walt felt, by becoming inoffensive. The rodent who had begun life by bucking Minnie out of an airplane and maliciously pressing a pig's teats to make music was now on his best behavior. "If our gang ever put Mickey in a situation less wholesome than sunshine," Walt wrote in 1933, "Mickey would take Minnie by the hand and move to some other studio." Indeed, Walt continued, "He is never mean or ugly. He never lies or cheats or steals. He is a clean, happy, little fellow who loves life and folk. He never takes advantage of the weak and we see to it that nothing ever happens that will cure his faith in the transcendent destiny of one Mickey Mouse or his conviction that the world is just a big apple pie. . . . He is Youth, the Great Unlicked and Uncontaminated." To which *The Nation* grumbled that Mickey had turned into "an international bore."

With Mickey beginning to fade as an aesthetic force, the studio needed a new star, a character who had been conceived with and internalized the insolence that Mickey had lost—a character who could generate gags as Mickey now could not and a character who was immune to the expectations of civility that burdened Mickey. The new character that evolved, in fact, would become a foil to Mickey—the unbridled id to his anodyne ego. For a studio that was already becoming exasperated with its star, he was the anti-Mickey, or rather all the things that Mickey had been and more.

But it was a long gestation. Mickey had begun life visually and then found a voice, so that he was a design before he was a character, which had been part of his problem. His foil began life as a voice and then had to find a physical form, which was part of his success. The voice belonged to a tiny, apple-cheeked twenty-nine-year-old Oklahoma-born milkman named Clarence Nash. In school in rural Missouri, where his family moved when he was nine, he found an early talent for making animal noises, which he later parlayed into an act playing the mandolin and performing bird calls on the Redpath Lyceum and Chautauqua circuit. When he got married, he promised his eighteen-year-old bride that he would quit show business for a more secure position, and the Nashes moved to California, where he got a job with the Adohr Dairy, visiting schools in a milk wagon pulled by miniature horses and making his animal noises to entertain the children. He also performed periodically on a local radio program. During one of these broadcasts late in 1933 Walt, who was listening for voices he could use in the cartoons, said he heard Nash and subsequently invited him to the studio. Nash had a different version. He said that he visited the studio on his own initiative, got an interview with Jaxon, and did a rendition of "Mary Had a Little Lamb" in a voice that he modeled after a bleating goat. While Nash recited, Jaxon secretly switched on the intercom to Walt's office, and Walt burst in, shouting, "That's our talking duck!" Walt didn't know exactly what to do with Nash yet but signed him to a retainer anyway.

It would be another year—during which Nash went back to work for the dairy—before Walt summoned him (Nash once said it was because he had told Walt that the Iwerks studio wanted to use his voice for a duck) and cast him in 1934 as an irascible, selfish, bottom-heavy, long-beaked, and long-necked duck in *The Wise Little Hen*, who begs off helping the hen plant and harvest her corn by feigning a bellyache every time she approaches. It wasn't instant stardom, though the studio did copyright the character shortly thereafter, dressing him in a blue sailor suit with a sailor's cap because, Walt later said, "Being a duck, he likes water. Sailors and water go together." When the studio decided to pair him with Mickey Mouse in *Orphan's Benefit*, the anti-Mickey and the Mickey together, Ward Kimball, who helped animate the cartoon, called it a "turning point" both for the studio and for the further development of personality animation. In the cartoon, Mickey, acting as master of ceremonies at a benefit for orphaned mice, introduces Donald, who recites "Mary Had a Little Lamb" and then erupts when the audience razzes him as he begins "Little Boy Blue." By cartoon's end the young mice are tormenting him with a bombardment of bricks and boxing gloves, and Donald is apoplectic. "Well, the reaction that came pouring into the studio from the country was tremendous," Kimball recalled. "The kids in the theater loved or hated or booed Donald Duck."

By early 1935, when Donald was harassing Mickey in *The Band Concert*, considered by many the best of the Mickey Mouse cartoons, the duck had already begun overtaking the cartoon's nominal star. "There have been signs that the impudence and cockiness of the Mouse were dwindling, that Mickey was going polite," Gilbert Seldes observed in *The New York Journal*. "In 'The Band Concert' the duck takes over. It is a bad, wicked duck, a malicious and mischievous duck, a duck corresponding to all the maddening attractiveness of bad little boys and girls—a superb character."

In some respects Donald Duck seemed to offer audiences both a vicarious liberation from the conventional behavior and morality to which they had to subscribe in their own lives and which the Duck clearly transgressed and, since he usually got his comeuppance, a vicarious revenge against the pretentious, unattractive, and ornery at a time when the entire world seemed to be roiling in anger and violence. Whereas Mickey had turned into a smiling cipher, the lumpy Duck was hot-tempered, vain, pompous, boastful, rude, suspicious, self-satisfied, and self-indulgent—a taxonomy of misconduct and offensiveness. Audiences quickly identified him with President Roosevelt's outspoken and irritable secretary of the interior, Harold Ickes, who was known generally as the "Great Curmudgeon." "Sometimes it was hard for an audience to tell whether Ickes was imitating the Duck or the Duck was imitating Ickes," Walt said.

Whether or not the curmudgeonly Donald liberated audiences, he certainly liberated the storymen and animators at the studio from the shackles of Mickey. "Every time we put him into a trick, a temper, a joke," said one writer of the mouse, "thousands of people would belabor us with nasty letters. That's what made Donald Duck so easy. He was our outlet. . . . Everyone knew he was bad and didn't give a damn. So we can whip out three Donald Duck stories in the time it takes us to work out one for the Mouse." Walt himself agreed, saying that Mickey was funny only when the situation was funny, while intemperate Donald was inherently funny. "The duck can blow his top and commit mayhem," Walt once told an interviewer. Mickey couldn't.

Nash, whose quacking voice had inspired the character, credited Walt with extending Donald's range and turning him into a personality by suggesting that Nash try being angry in the duck voice or laughing in it. Jack Hannah, who would later direct many of the Donald Duck cartoons, said that "Donald could be anything. He had every emotion a human being had. He could be cute, mischievous, go from warm to cool at any moment. You could half kill him and he'd come right back. He instigated trouble. Not mean, but he always saw a chance to have fun at other people's expense." In short, Donald was the prime example of Walt's caricatured reality and the first Disney star to be born full-blown from that aesthetic.

Now that he was beginning to move from featured player into leading man, the gangly duck that Art Babbitt and Dick Huemer had designed for *The Wise Little Hen* was shortened, softened, and rounded by animator Fred Spencer, just as Mickey had been, to make him visually cuter and more expressive. By 1935 he was being featured in his own series of books, and by the fall of that year, though Donald had yet to star in his own cartoon, Walt was already fretting that Nash, who had been offered a three-year contract extension at $55 a week, might try to strong-arm them. "If we start using the duck character a lot," Walt memoed Roy, "we don't want Clarence to get any inflated ideas of his importance here." Then he attempted to tamp his own worries by saying that if Nash were to leave the studio and voice a duck elsewhere, the Disneys could probably sue. In the end, Nash signed the contract, and Donald finally got a starring role, in *Donald and Pluto*, the following year, and then a full series of his own; but even before that *Variety* observed of Donald's appearance in another Mickey cartoon, "Again it's manifest how fast growing is the vogue of Donald Duck, the volubly irate gander who bids fair to par Mickey as Disney's favorite creation." To most Americans, Donald already had.

IV

Donald Duck was not the only character at the studio to achieve stardom in the mid-1930s. Awards and recognition had tumbled in for Walt himself. The Art Institute of Chicago exhibited one hundred Disney drawings, which the institute's director said "constitute art in nearly every sense." The Writers Club of Los Angeles had feted him at the dinner with Will Rogers and Chaplin in attendance, the American Art Dealers Association awarded him one of its four gold medals, and the Art Workers Guild of England, whose ranks included George Bernard Shaw, bestowed an honorary membership on Walt—the first ever in recognition of a filmmaker. The United States Junior Chamber of Commerce named him the outstanding man of the year over New York district attorney Thomas E. Dewey, who would soon be his state's governor and later the Republican presidential candidate. The French Legion of Honor awarded him its red ribbon, and he received a gold medal at the Venice Film Festival. Critics now regularly labeled him a genius.

Famous visitors clamored to tour the studio and meet him—among them Douglas Fairbanks and Mary Pickford, H. G. Wells and Chaplin, actress Madeleine Carroll, director Ernst Lubitsch, humorist Robert Benchley, critic Alexander Woollcott, and Russian director Sergei Eisenstein, who wrote that he was sometimes frightened watching Disney's films—"frightened because of some absolute perfection in what he does" and because Disney seemed to know "all the most secret strands of human thought, images, ideas, feelings." Later, among other notables, architect Frank Lloyd Wright, novelist Aldous Huxley, and composer Igor Stravinsky would also visit. "Everybody in the world beat a path to Walt's door," remembered Dick Huemer. And there was the media coverage—a 1933 profile in *Time*, a 1934 article in *The New York Times Magazine*, a full-page photo portrait of Walt by Edward Steichen in *Vanity Fair* with Mickey and Minnie behind him, and scores of newspaper interviews. His narrow, mustachioed face was familiar enough now to qualify him, while not yet thirty-five, as a celebrity. "I sometimes feel that I should pinch myself to make sure that I am not dreaming," he blushed to a reporter from a Kansas City newspaper.

If he had fame, he also had an image. He loved to recount the hardships of his youth and the adversity he had overcome, and these elements of his personal mythology now became part of his public story. Reporters referred to him as the "Horatio Alger of the cinema" for his long, hard grind to prominence, while generally ignoring the rambunctiousness that had got him there. They also found him humble, down-to-earth, and anything but a Hollywood glamour boy. Asked what it was like to be a celebrity, Walt demurred, saying that it helped him get better seats at football games and was a nuisance when he had to contend with autograph seekers. But, he added, "As far as I can remember, being a celebrity has never helped me make a good picture, or a good shot in a polo game, or command the obedience of my daughter, or impress my wife. It doesn't even keep the fleas off our dogs."

Playwright Robert Sherwood, meeting Disney for the first time, expected to find him overbearing and boorish and instead reported that he seemed "almost painfully shy and diffident." He was also self-deprecating, quipping when one admirer told him he had personality that "[i]t's the mouse that has the personality." Nearly everyone commented on his informality—on the casual clothes he wore and on the studio edict that his employees call him "Walt." His office was modest and austere with a plain dark-stained desk and a few framed awards on the walls. He was unaffected by praise. Once the wind of fulsomeness passes, wrote critic Otis Ferguson in *The New Republic*, the "air clears and he becomes what he was in the first place: common and everyday, not inaccessible, not in a foreign language, not suppressed or sponsored or anything. Just Disney," which made him the very paradigm of the homespun, unpretentious, hardworking American artist. Walt played up this idea, saying he seldom read and had little truck with art, leading one reporter to write, "Disney is as free as Al Smith [the raspy-voiced former New York governor] from the taint of book-learning; no man could be clearer of the curse of sophistication."

To complete the portrait, Walt was always portrayed as indifferent to everything but his work. Hundreds upon hundreds of desperate individuals petitioned him during the Depression, asking if he might have a job for them or could spare some money from his wealth. He almost invariably refused, even turning down Dr. Cowles, his old benefactor, now in financial straits, claiming that he had no money since he plowed everything he earned back into the company to maintain quality. He was not, an early profile suggested, much of a businessman, and he cared nothing for money except as a means to an end. Article after article promoted the idea that Walt's only ambition was to make great cartoons, not a great fortune.

All of these things were more or less true. Walt did believe he had overcome childhood hardships. He was informal and eschewed the Hollywood scene and celebrity, his polo fetish notwithstanding. He was not an intellectual and never pretended to be one. He did reinvest most of his money in the company. And he was driven to produce great cartoons both as a business proposition and as a psychological one. Still, Walt was also deeply aware of the value of disseminating and displaying these things publicly, even if it was only during his own personal appearances. In the studio he could often be brusque. In public he was typically accessible and generous, whether it was to a fan complimenting him on a cartoon or to a waiter serving him. Jack Kinney believed that Walt had studied Will Rogers and imitated his down-home mannerisms, belying the fact, Kinney said, that "he could swear like a trooper, and he had a terrific ego." Ward Kimball concurred that there was a certain deliberation in the construction of Walt's image. Walt, he said, "played the role of a bashful tycoon who was embarrassed in public," but "he knew exactly what he was doing at all times." In effect, Walt Disney was beginning to assume the role of himself. It was a role he would play with variations for the rest of his life.

But while Walt Disney had become an international figure, the father of Mickey and now Donald, confusion reigned over exactly what he did at his own studio. To many if not most outside the studio, he was thought to do the actual drawing—an impression he did little to discourage. In truth, Walt did no drawing whatsoever anymore, though he took credit for the productions and demanded it, no doubt in part because he was still wounded by the discourtesy shown him by Charlie Mintz and Pat Powers, who had seemed to dismiss him as nothing more than a glorified supervisor. "There's just one thing we're selling here," he told Ken Anderson, when the young animator joined the studio, "and that's the name 'Walt Disney.' If you can buy that and be happy to work for it, you're my man. But if you've got any ideas of selling the name 'Ken Anderson,' it's best for you to leave right now." It was expected for Disney employees to share credit. When Pinto Colvig was introduced as the lyricist of "Who's Afraid of the Big Bad Wolf?" at a dinner honoring Walt, he immediately stood up and credited others. "Well he knew," Colvig wrote a colleague, speaking of himself, "that such a breach in the code of 'Disney Ethics' would forever be a nasty stain upon his otherwise faultless character."

If Walt no longer drew the animations, it had also been a long while since he had written the scenarios or directed the cartoons or done any of the tasks now assigned to his extensive staff. In 1933, when Burt Gillett defected after *Pigs* to the Van Beuren studio, Walt was so incensed that he decided he was going to direct the next cartoon himself, apparently to show just how expendable Gillett was. The film was a Silly Symphony titled *The Golden Touch* depicting the story of King Midas. "This was a very hush hush operation with just two animators [Norm Ferguson and Freddie Moore], who were sworn to secrecy," recalled Jack Kinney. When, a year after its inception, the cartoon was previewed at the Alexander Theater in Glendale, the reception was unenthusiastic. Walt had failed, and word of the failure quickly spread through the studio, becoming a needle whenever an aggrieved employee felt the need to deflate the boss. During one argument with Jaxon where *The Golden Touch* was tossed in Walt's face, Walt stormed off, then returned, warning, "Never, never mention that picture again."

And yet even though Walt could neither animate, nor write, nor direct, he was the undisputed power at the studio, not only in the sense that he was the boss but also in the more important sense that his sensibility governed everything the studio produced. At first blush he was an unlikely dictator. He was young, though many of his employees now were even younger. He was unprepossessing. "He looked like just a nice, young American man, good looking, but in a healthy rather than a handsome way," said one animator, while another described him as exceptionally thin—he was five feet ten inches tall and weighed 150 pounds—and "rodent-faced." He didn't naturally exude power or charisma and didn't seem to mind. Unlike othe [illegible] he never arrogated power to himself for the sake of se[illegible]nd he sometimes vividly recalled a haunting childhoo[illegible]rceline where he caught an owl and, when it resisted [illegible]hrew it to the ground, killing it—an incident, he said, [illegible]tmares and seemed to indicate ambivalent feelings abo[illegible]trolling impulses.

Still, the studio bent to his w[illegible] and his alone. His moods, which were more changeable since the breakdown and under the increasing pressure, determined the mood of Hyperion, and some employees joked that Walt would stop in the basement each morning to change into his "mood costume" for the day, while others advised that one had to call the security guard at the gate to see which Walt had arrived. If Walt was in his "bear suit," as employees described his foulest mood, he could be cruel—"apt to rip a storyboard apart for no apparent reason," Frank Thomas and Ollie Johnston wrote. Similarly, the entire studio had to be attuned to his ideas and desires, making it the primary objective of every person in his employ to determine what it was Walt wanted.

The problem was that, for all the rationalization of the animation process, Walt operated almost entirely by instinct—a problem compounded by the fact that he had a difficult time conveying what his instinct told him, especially since he no longer drew well enough to show the animators, and because he was so instinctive he changed his mind as often as he changed his moods. "The big part of my career was to decide when Walt meant it and when he didn't mean it," Jaxon said. "Usually I tried to inform Walt what I had in mind by sending him a memo. In the note I'd tell him how I intended to spend his money. I'd send the memo up in the afternoon, and he usually read it at night at home. If the phone was ringing when I walked in, I knew it was a good thing I checked." Others said that sussing out Walt Disney was a matter of osmosis. You watched him in the story meetings and the sweatbox sessions and at the previews and tried to guess what he was thinking.

Despite the occasional griping and resentment that Walt was overbearing, mercurial, ungrateful, and impossible to please, all of which he was, no one at the studio doubted the overriding importance of his contribution, though everyone seemed to have a different opinion of what that contribution was. One thing on which everyone did agree was that he was a superb storyteller, and Walt himself seemed to think it was his primary attribute. "Of all the things I've ever done," he once told an interviewer, "I'd like to be remembered as a storyteller." From the earliest days he had a knack for constructing gags. Dick Huemer believed Walt had the "best gag mind I ever ran across." But as the stories became more elaborate, linking the gags organically and situating them in the idiosyncrasies of character, Walt really shone. Veteran director Ken Annakin, who worked with Walt years later, said, "Of all the studio chiefs I have ever worked with I have never known anyone who operated at [story] conferences so magnificently as Walt. You would go into a story session with him, full of great ideas, and he would scratch his nose and say, 'This is just from the top of my head, but I think we should do this and this. . . .' And it would usually be like listening to a new fairy tale, and we would break up the session happy and amazed that the solution to your story problems should be so simple and different."

Though the stories no longer originated with Walt, every story still ultimately had to meet with his approval before it was put into production. The storymen "would do a rough outline and send the idea up to Walt . . . and he'd either say, 'Go ahead with it' or 'No, you guys get over on that other thing. I think it has more possibilities,' " recalled Ward Kimball. But even after he granted his initial approval and the storymen provided a rough storyboard for him to critique and they incorporated his criticisms into a final storyboard, Walt would always return to the plot and gags at what were, typically, lengthy story sessions, looking for ways to improve them. "And he would be the leader in all those story meetings," Kimball attested. Indeed, some even said that Walt was the one who really wrote all the dialogue.

Of course, first there was that dreaded silence when Walt would listen and stare fixedly and inscrutably. "Walt was always very preoccupied in story meetings, thinking up new ideas for stories and characters," Ollie Johnston remembered. "One eyebrow would be raised, and he'd have that intent expression. Sometimes his gaze would settle on you, and you'd think he was preparing to pounce on you for something you'd said. Actually it was his tremendous powers of concentration at work, and I doubt that he knew who he was looking at most of the time." Eric Larson claimed that Walt wasn't really even listening—that as the storyman began running through the boards, he was already looking at the final sketches, which Larson interpreted to mean that Walt had visited the studio the night before and gone over the boards himself so that he would be fully prepared. (Some storymen swore they found Walt's Chesterfield cigarette butts in their ashtrays.) Then would come his analysis, which wasn't a suggestion but a directive. "He could be brutal," animator and later director Jack Hannah said. "[H]e'd start the idea for a sequence of gags and we'd say, 'That's great, Walt!' and suddenly his whole mood would change and he'd reply, 'Nah, we aren't going to do that.' " On one occasion a demonstrative storyman named Homer Brightman presented the boards for a Donald Duck cartoon and got the entire room laughing with his performance. When Brightman finished, Walt turned curtly to his stenographer and asked her if she had been laughing at Brightman or at the story. "At Homer," she said, after which Walt launched into his critique.

But it wasn't Walt's analysis that imprinted itself on the cartoons as much as his uncanny ability to inhabit the character and enter the situation. Walt *thought* like Mickey or Donald or Pluto. "If Walt said to me, 'Mickey wouldn't think this way,' " said storyman Leo Salkin, "who knows how Mickey would think? But in Walt's mind, this is what Mickey would think or feel, and it was valid." Layout artist John Hench said that Walt would go into a "kind of trance" when he listened to a presentation. "In his mind he could see the whole story so well and bend forward unconsciously and become like an old owl—hunched up, and his bill would clack a little bit. When he'd come out of it, he'd say, 'You know what we ought to do is . . .' and then he'd leap up and begin acting out the scene with all new dialogue and business."

Everyone at the studio marveled at his acting—how Walt, who was usually fairly reserved now, would get up at the story meetings, enter his trance, and suddenly transform himself uninhibitedly into Mickey or Donald or an owl or an old hunting dog. "Y'know this old guy would come snufin' along like a vacuum cleaner, his muzzle spread all over the ground," Walt would say as he recalled a dog from his childhood in Marceline and turned himself into that dog. "And as Walt acted it out, it became funnier and funnier," Frank Thomas and Ollie Johnston wrote. Then, as his audience began to respond, Walt would dive deeper into the character, finding more comic possibilities. "He would imitate the expressions of the dog, and look from one side to the other, and raise first one [eye]brow and then the other as he tried to figure things out." And by doing that he demonstrated to the storymen and the animators in the room, in Thomas and Johnston's words, "what was funny about the character itself," inspiring the animators to draw what Walt had performed for them. This became his chief means of communicating his ideas and the foundation for the studio's cartoons. "You'd have the feeling of the whole thing," Dick Huemer noted. "You'd know exactly what he wanted."

After the agreement on Walt's contributions as a storyteller, opinions diverged over how one would prioritize his other most important talents. Ward Kimball thought Walt was a "supersalesman" who believed so devoutly in his studio and its cartoons that he could convince anyone, even the stodgiest banker, of their value. Eric Larson credited him with having a unique sensitivity to knowing what the public wanted. Art Babbitt cited his unparalleled judgment: "He oftentimes didn't know what he was going after, but he could spot something that was wrong in a piece of work." His instincts were so keen that at one point Walt set up a table in the middle of the animators' room, had the animators bring him their drawings and then summarily told them what worked and what didn't. Sharpsteen believed that Walt's "forte was the supervision of his business—every bit of it—and in the feeling that everything that was done, every drawing that was made, was the result of his guidance." Others, not always with appreciation, adduced Walt's utter devotion to the studio with setting a tone of obsessiveness that affected everyone who worked there. "A lot of the guys I worked with at Disney couldn't stand him because of that," said writer Maurice Rapf. "He stuck his nose into everything."

Still others were awed by Walt's grasp of detail. He noticed "little things that would make a big difference," Jaxon said. Earl Colgrove, a cameraman, remembered Walt summoning him to a sweatbox session for a Silly Symphony titled *The Country Mouse* to view some scenes, including one in which the mouse sees his reflection in a plate of Jell-O. Walt asked if Colgrove noticed anything different about the scene, and when Colgrove answered that it "looked pretty good," Walt had the scene run again and stopped on a single blurred frame where the animation cel had apparently been placed under the camera backward. "After a brief silence Walt turned the lights up and said: 'Around here we try to be proud of *every bit* of work we do.' " Another time he noticed that Mickey's tail was missing in the comic strip and ordered it reinstated. "People don't realize the importance he had—down to deciding whether a character should look left or right or roll his eyes," Ward Kimball said. "Walt was the final editor of every damned scene."

Others cited Walt as an inspiration, setting standards, expecting perfection, drumming up enthusiasm, buoying spirits. "I think the outstanding thing about Walt," Jaxon said, "was his ability to make people feel that what he wanted done was a terribly important thing to get done." Another called Walt's "greatest gift" his knack for "making you come up with things you didn't know were in you and that you'd have sworn you couldn't possibly do." Walt was also a great cheerleader, exhorting his employees to think boldly. "I don't want just another picture," he would tell them. "It's got to be a new experience, a new theatrical experience." When he was enthused, as he usually was, he got others enthused too. "He was very excited about everything he was doing," John Hench observed, citing a quality Walt had had even as a boy. "And he lived and breathed it and finally it rubbed off on you."

Finally, and perhaps most important, there was Walt's ability not just to supervise but to coordinate the entire studio apparatus. Walt himself compared the cartoons to a symphony, with him as the conductor who took all the employees—the storymen, the animators, the composers and musicians, the voice artists, the ink and paint girls—and got them to "produce one whole thing which is beautiful." To another interviewer he dashed purposefully about a hotel room and imitated a bee as a way of demonstrating what he did at the studio. "I've got to know whether an idea goes here," he said, dumping "pollen" on a chair, "or here," racing to the interviewer and dumping the invisible pollen on the man's knees. Almost everyone at the studio admired how Walt, in either conducting them or flitting among them, forged them into a unit. "We all had egos," Eric Larson admitted, "but Walt had a way of taking those egos and making them work together as a team." "He could disarm people by using the word 'we' instead of 'I,' " Ben Sharpsteen said. "Obviously everything was based on what Walt Disney did, what he wanted to do and what he expected to do, but he would invariably say 'we.' " Bob Broughton, who worked in the camera department at the time, said, "That was what Walt's main talent was, I think. . . . He made you feel part of a family." Walt seemed to agree. Though he had said that he wanted to be remembered as a storyteller, he told his daughter Diane: "Of all the things I've done, the most vital is coordinating those who work for us and aiming their efforts at a certain goal."*

Among his employees, the sum total of all these attributes evoked unbounded adulation for the young man who possessed them. Many, including Walt, had previously observed the similarity between the animator and God. At the Disney studio this similarity was manifest in the attitude of the employees toward their leader, who was spoken of in quasi-religious terms. "When he'd come into a room, the hair would stand up on the back of your neck figuratively," Dick Huemer remembered. "He'd have that effect on you. You'd feel the presence. It was spooky." Director Jack Hannah claimed that Walt elicited "awe." "You just felt it if he was in the same wing of the building you were in. I know it sounds weird but you never got over that awe of him." "He had an overwhelming power over people and the voice of a prophet," said animator Joe Grant. "You always had the feeling he knew what you were going to say and he seemed to know things before they happened. That sort of omnipotence held a men-

*Maurice Rapf, who later worked as a writer at the studio, thought that Walt, by dividing responsibilities among employees as he did while retaining the coordinating authority himself, was able to maintain his power without having to worry about disgruntled or ambitious underlings. Patrick McGilligan and Paul Buhle, *Tender Comrades: A Backstory of the Hollywood Blacklist* (New York: St. Martin's Press, 1997), p. 296.

tal control over you." "You talk as if he were God," gagman Roy Williams's sister-in-law, who was married to a minister, scolded him when Williams spoke reverently of Walt. To which Williams snapped, "He is."

If it had been a deliberate tactic to rally his staff, it couldn't have been more successful. Just about everyone was desperate to please Walt Disney. "I couldn't understand it," a discontented writer at the studio confessed. "But you'd do anything to get his approval. You'd work like a dog, like a little kid saying, 'Hey, look at me. I'm doing something pretty terrific.' You'd do anything for a smile, even though the next day you might be fired." Some admitted that the tension of having to please him, needing to please him, was almost unbearable. The effect was that the Disney studio did not operate like any other studio in Hollywood with a tyrannical boss lording over a group of disaffected employees who complained of being thwarted. In fact, it didn't operate like a commercial institution at all, where talk of products and profits predominate. By the mid-1930s the Disney studio operated like a cult, with a messianic figure inspiring a group of devoted, sometimes frenzied acolytes. At Hyperion the employees were not just making cartoons to divert or entertain the public. They were disciples on a mission.

And that mission was about to change.

Six

FOLLY

Even when he was consumed by his work—and he was *always* consumed by his work—Walt Disney was restless, mindful perhaps, after the betrayals he had suffered at the hands of Charlie Mintz and Pat Powers, that the slightest complacency might lead to a setback. Sometime in mid-1933, at the very time he was enjoying the enormous success of *Three Little Pigs*, he decided that he needed to chart a new course for the studio—something big and dramatic. For years he had suffered from the vagaries of the business of producing shorts and from the relatively meager profits they delivered—which became more meager as his expectations and consequently his expenses grew. Though the Silly Symphonies fetched rentals that were 50 percent higher than those of competitors' cartoons, they also cost appreciably more to make, as much as $30,000 by the mid-1930s, which meant that with overhead and expenses they had to gross around $100,000 to turn a profit. Under the best of circumstances this wasn't easy, but it became especially difficult when theater owners, attempting to attract financially strapped viewers during the Depression, instituted double bills of two feature films, reducing both the time they had to show shorts and the money they had to rent them.

As far as the Disneys were concerned, between their rentals and their royalties from merchandise, the studio had made roughly $600,000 in 1934, which certainly wasn't bad during a depression. "The first decade was crawling—just bacon and eggs without the bacon," Roy would later say of the studio's early years. "Then the second decade when the country was in the doldrums—we were relatively prosperous, and while we were in small time . . . small money, we could pay all our bills, pay all our salaries. Up to that time we never drew a regular salary." But Walt recognized that if he hoped to continue to grow the studio, shorts had little future. "The short subject was just a filler on any program," he would recall dismissively. "And so I just felt I had to diversify my business and get into these other things, and it would give me a better chance." The "other things" he was then considering daunted even his own colleagues. He had decided to make a full-length feature cartoon.

While it was true that shorts couldn't generate enough profits, economic considerations were, as always for Walt Disney, only part of the reason he was changing course. He also wanted the aesthetic challenge—to stay ahead of the pack and remain better than everyone else, which was now a source of enormous pride. Even more personally, the deeper into his fantasy world he drew, the more fully realized he knew it had to be. Like his old Alice character, he needed to construct a better imaginative world in which to escape.

"I think that Walt was impatient with the restrictions of the cartoon," Ken Anderson, an art director at the time, said. "He strived for more and more realism, more naturalism in the features." Anderson remembered keeping a notebook of camera angles from live-action movies he had seen, and Walt being so impressed that he ordered others to keep similar notes. "He was always aiming at exceeding the limitations of the medium." Walt admitted as much himself. "[W]e sensed we had gone about as far as we could in the short subject field without getting ourselves into a rut," he wrote in 1941. "We needed this new adventure, this 'kick in the pants,' to jar loose some new enthusiasm and inspiration." In effect, Walt wanted to rattle the studio with an earthquake.

The idea of producing a feature, he once said, first occurred to him when he was in Europe and saw audiences sitting through a program of five or six Mickey Mouse cartoons in a row. The problem with this recollection is that three full years before he would visit Europe, he was already laying the groundwork for a feature, even dropping hints to the press. As early as June 1932 Roy was inquiring about the availability of the rights to *Alice in Wonderland*, which, he learned, was in the public domain. While the *Alice* project slowly advanced, M. Lincoln Schuster of the Simon & Schuster publishing house was prodding Walt to make a film of a Felix Salten novel, first published in Europe in 1923 and issued in the United States in 1928, titled *Bambi: A Life in the Woods*, about the life cycle of a deer. Though Sidney Franklin, one of the most highly regarded directors at Metro-Goldwyn-Mayer, acquired the rights to the novel while Walt dithered, Joseph Schenck of United Artists leaped in, offering to broker an alliance between Disney and Franklin. "Schenck talked like they would finance it for distribution and a share of the profits," Roy wrote Walt eagerly from New York. "Would sure like to see you attempt a feature, and I believe it is highly desirable for that feature to be handled by the same source handling our other product." Roy urged Walt to contact Franklin, who was apparently willing to cooperate, and get the ball rolling for a fall 1934 release. Walt evidently did talk to Franklin, though the project stalled, most likely because Walt feared the studio did not yet have the artistic capability to animate so realistic a story.

Meanwhile, Walt was being inundated with suggestions for feature projects he could tackle. The old silent film director and actor Hobart Bosworth wrote Walt, "You can't carry the animal and bird, and animated trees, flowers, etc. much farther," and thought he should try "all of the elfin, goblin, faery, fay [*sic*] sprite stories of all the folk lore of all lands, in your medium!" Cartoonist James Thurber recommended that Walt animate Homer's *Iliad* or *Odyssey*. Douglas Fairbanks had discussed the possibility of their collaborating on *Gulliver's Travels*. And as early as April 1933 Fairbanks's wife, actress Mary Pickford, was pressing Walt to do a combined live-action/animation of *Alice in Wonderland*. Pickford even offered to guarantee an advance equal to seven of his cartoons and underwrite the production costs, but Walt vacillated, fearing "great disappointment," he wrote, "should the deal fall through." When Paramount decided to put a live-action *Alice* film into production, Walt abandoned his plans with Pickford, prompting her to lament that "your apparent lack of enthusiasm on our last meeting, together with the many obstacles you seemed to anticipate was the crushing blow to my cherished hope."

In reality, that same week in May 1933 when he was exchanging letters with Pickford, which also happened to be the week that *Pigs* opened, Walt had already settled on his feature and had apparently instructed Al Lichtman of United Artists to register the title: *Snow White*. Walt would later say he had chosen the material on the grounds of its aesthetic potential. "[I]t was well-known and I knew I could do something with seven 'screwy' dwarfs," he said. Another time, enumerating the elements of the story, he said, "I had sympathetic dwarfs, you see? I had the heavy, I had the prince. And the girl. The romance." But the story also offered the lure of memory. Walt said he could remember seeing a *Snow White* play when he was a boy, though he was probably recalling a film version of the play starring Marguerite Clark that screened on January 27 and January 28, 1917, in the cavernous twelve-thousand-seat Kansas City Convention Hall when he was fifteen. The *Kansas City Star* had sponsored five screenings to reward its newsboys, and 67,000 of them showed up. To accommodate the crowds, the film was projected simultaneously on four screens arranged at right angles to one another in a kind of box. Because the projectors were hand-cranked and because the projectionists couldn't maintain perfect synchronization, Walt, seated high in the gallery, said that he could see on one screen what was going to happen on the adjacent one, which made the show seem somehow even more magical. Writing to Frank Newman, for whom Walt had made the Laugh-O-grams in Kansas City, he said, "My impression of the picture has stayed with me through the years and I know it played a big part in selecting SNOW WHITE for my first feature production."

But if he cited the aesthetic elements of the material and its appeal from his childhood as the reasons for choosing *Snow White*, he may also have had deep-seated psychological reasons. *Snow White* had nearly all the narrative features—the tyrannical parent, the sentence of drudgery, the promise of a childhood utopia—and incorporated nearly all the major themes of his young life, primarily the need to conquer the previous generation to stake one's claim on maturity, the rewards of hard work, the dangers of trust, and perhaps above all, the escape into fantasy as a remedy for inhospitable reality. (In discussing fairy tale conventions, psychologist Bruno Bettelheim cited "stories that tell about an aging parent who decides that the time has come to let the new generation take over. But before this can happen, the successor must prove himself capable and worthy"—a scenario that more or less fit both *Snow White* and the life of Walt Disney, with the exception that in each case the parent was reluctant to yield.) Though some analysts would apply a Freudian interpretation—one saw Snow White as possessing "remnants of an anal obsessive personality" that she had to overcome to achieve sexual maturity, and characterized the dwarfs as desexualized children—and others imposed a cultural interpretation in which the film promoted Depression values of hard work and community, the cartoon would ultimately become a parable of Walt Disney's own young life. *He* was Snow White, threatened by parental jealousy and capricious power and forced into his own world, the world of animation, where he would ultimately find nurturance, love, independence, and authority. *Snow White* was the story of Walt Disney's personal growth, the story of what he had had to surmount and what he had achieved.

Now he needed a version that would be adaptable for the screen. The original, as retold by the Brothers Grimm, was too rudimentary; the dwarfs weren't even identified by name. The Marguerite Clark film may have had more vivid elements—the film had been lost by the time Walt decided to make his feature and he was relying on memory—and Walt did consult the Winthrop Ames play from which the film had been adapted, even eventually acquiring the rights for fear that he might be sued. Still, the similarities were slight. He had also examined another *Snow White* play, this one from 1913 by a woman named Jessie Braham White, and though he used very little from it, he did borrow a few small touches: Snow White kissing the dwarfs good-bye as they head off to work, and the Queen, who wants to kill Snow White to certify her own place as the kingdom's reigning beauty, disguising herself as a peddler to gain access to the innocent girl.

But whatever sources Walt Disney drew upon, by the spring of 1933 he was already synthesizing them in his mind and forging something entirely new—something he was beginning to internalize by reciting the story at every opportunity. "We had a business meeting today for no good reason," one colleague that May wrote Roy, who was in New York at the time. "However, it was very interesting because among other things Walt told us his idea of developing the story, 'Snow White,' and honestly, the way that boy can tell a story is nobody's business. I was practically in tears during some of it, and I've read the story many times, as a child, without being particularly moved. If it should turn out one tenth as good as the way he tells it, it should be a wow." Animator Dick Huemer claimed that when he first went to work for Disney that same year, the two of them were sitting in Walt's office and Walt began to expatiate upon *Snow White*. "Walt was such a wonderful actor that my throat started to get tight, and my eyes began to moisten," Huemer recalled, "it was wonderful, the way he was telling it." During a visit to his old friend Walt Pfeiffer, who was living in Chicago at the time and working at an advertising agency, Walt began performing *Snow White* as they toured the Field Museum of Natural History. When he reached the point where the vultures swoop down on the peddler woman as she escapes, Walt was so demonstrative that a security guard thought Pfeiffer was being attacked, and the two Walts had to slink away.

It may have been as early as the winter of 1934* that Walt felt ready to make his first public presentation. As Ken Anderson remembered it, Walt approached a group of employees late one afternoon, gave each of them fifty cents, told them to grab dinner across the street and then return to the soundstage that evening. None had any idea of what Walt had in mind. When they arrived, about fifty of them, at roughly seven-thirty, and took their seats on wooden tiers at the back of the room, Walt was standing at the front lit by a single spotlight in the otherwise dark space. Announcing that he was going to launch an animated feature, he told the story of Snow White, not just telling it but acting it out, assuming the characters' mannerisms, putting on their voices, letting his audience visualize exactly what they would be seeing on the screen. He *became* Snow White and the wicked queen and the prince and each of the dwarfs. Anderson said the performance took over three hours. "He was a spellbinder," recalled animator Joe Grant. When it was over, the group was both enthralled and enthused. "[W]e were just carried away," Anderson said. "We had no concept that we were ever going to do anything else or ever want to do anything else. We wanted to do what he had just told us!" "That one performance lasted us three years," one animator claimed. "Whenever we'd get stuck, we'd remember how Walt did it on that night."

But if Walt had inspired his crew with the idea of a new mission, there were nevertheless doubts and trepidations. "We saw it at first as Walt's folly," said Joe Grant. Even Walt sometimes wondered whether anyone would want to sit through a feature-length cartoon, though at the same time he was telling the story of *Snow White*, he and Roy were also discouraging exhibitors from showing full programs of Disney cartoons for fear, as Roy wrote one of them, that they "may take the edge off this feature idea and give people the impression that a cartoon feature is merely a

*In *Walt Disney's* Snow White and the Seven Dwarfs, authors Martin Krause and Linda Witkowski dispute the date because animators Marc Davis and Ollie Johnston claimed to have been at this meeting, and they didn't join the studio until later (pp. 25–26). But Walt retold the story so many times and in so many situations that it is likely Anderson is right, and in any case the time frame is plausible.

hodgepodge of several connected subjects." There was also the issue of whether audiences, who, Walt had worried just a few years before, might not even accept a voice emanating from a drawing would have any emotional investment in drawings—an investment he felt was necessary to sustain a feature. And within the studio itself there was concern whether Walt, who had so many responsibilities, could focus on a single feature for what he said would be the year to eighteen months needed to complete it, while others debated whether his managerial style of constantly sparking new ideas and constantly changing his mind was compatible with the steadiness and certainty that a feature required. Despite his enthusiasm, Walt commented to a reporter in 1934, well after he had committed to *Snow White*, that he had to be certain the studio was up to it; otherwise "we will destroy it."

Finally, there was a more practical consideration: how would they finance the film? The Disneys had virtually no money of their own, reinvesting whatever they did have in the studio. For its part, United Artists, their distributor for the shorts, wasn't obligated to finance or distribute a feature, though, contrary to later accounts, it was not opposed to a feature either, and one UA executive told Gunther Lessing that "foreign countries were yelling for a feature and that we would easily gross, without trouble, $1,750,000.00 world[wide]," which would have been an extraordinary return at the time. Still, given the uncertainty about how long it would take to make the film and exactly how much it would cost, UA didn't seem eager to provide a substantial advance. Already by November 1933 Roy was meeting with Jock Whitney, the head of Pioneer Pictures and one of the nation's wealthiest men, about financing the feature, and he was also talking with Darryl Zanuck, the head of production at Twentieth Century Pictures, and Joseph Schenck, their old ally, about putting up the money. Roy thought they all wanted too large a share of the profits, but he wrote Walt that "they seemed sold to [*sic*] the idea that the first feature cartoon, at least, would be a big success." Even as the estimated budget kept rising, from $250,000 to $400,000, Schenck, who was one of the few executives the Disneys trusted, yielded and decided to underwrite the entire amount in exchange for a third of the profits, but when he suffered a sudden financial setback and had to pull out, the Disneys were forced to scrape together whatever they could for the time being and postpone getting the rest of the financing until they started actual production. When naysayers said that Roy was buying himself a sweepstakes ticket by investing so much of the studio's profits in *Snow White*, he said, "We've bought the whole damned sweepstakes."

Meanwhile, by the spring of 1934, Walt had launched the first phase of the project: honing the story and writing the screenplay. At live-action studios, executives typically assigned a story to a writer, who then produced a draft. Walt had a different process. He set up a small unit next to his office staffed by several of his cartoon storymen—Dick Creedon, Larry Morey, Harry Bailey—and then began funneling them various versions of the fairy tale with numerous variations, among them the Prince being imprisoned by the Queen, the Queen making three attempts on Snow White's life, and the Queen dying by dancing herself to death in red-hot shoes. By the time the group began producing outlines that summer, however, Walt's own recitation seems to have prevailed, and if anyone, amid the flurry of treatments and notes, can be said to be the author of the script, it is Walt Disney himself. When the group first met with Walt in October to review the treatments, Walt was already reprocessing and refining the material and making detailed suggestions: "Birds disturb dwarfs at work—'The Queen!' Wham! Over rocks—thru' the trees—swing on vines—'Tarzan' to the rescue—slip off log over stream—down cliffs—sand banks—see Queen beating it." Or after Snow White has taken a bite from the poisoned apple that the peddler/Queen has tricked her into eating: "Dwarfs back at house—'Too late.' Pull hats off—one leads in prayer—Sobbing pierces hush—all weep and sob." Though they seemed to have sprung directly from Walt's imagination, these scenes turned out to be very close to the ones in the finished film.

Mickey Mouse and Donald Duck were now afterthoughts, as Walt delegated as much responsibility for the shorts as possible so that he could focus on *Snow White*. Once the first outlines had been presented, he began meeting with the writers several times each week throughout October and November at what were often marathon sessions. His first order of business, after he and the staff had established the basic lineaments of the story, was naming the dwarfs. The initial lists included Scrappy, Cranky, Dirty, Awful, Blabby, Silly, Daffy, Flabby, Jaunty, Biggo Ego, Chesty, Jumpy, Baldy, Hickey ("always hiccoughing at wrong moment"), Gabby, Shorty, Nifty, Wheezy, Sniffy, Burpy, Lazy, Puffy, Dizzy, Stuffy, and Tubby, along with Grumpy, Happy, Doc, Bashful, and Dopey, which would eventually make the final cut, though not without considerably more scrutiny. While they pondered these names—and they would be pondering them for months—Walt decided to break down the story into narrative blocks the way he broke down animation into scenes, beginning with the introduction of the dwarfs to Snow White. "Rather than spend too much of our energy at the present time working out the first and less important sequences," went a studio instruction at the end of October, "Walt prefers to start actual work at the point where Snow White finds the cottage of the Seven Dwarfs. FROM THIS POINT ON, our basic plot development is fairly definitely established. What happens UP TO THAT TIME is still rather hazy." The first dialogue, most likely transcribed by Dick Creedon from Walt's recitation, was dated October 19, and Creedon delivered a full draft of the scene three days later.

The next week, in a sign of how furiously Walt was mobilizing the studio and drafting everyone into the project, he held a three-hour meeting on the soundstage to hash out more plot details and assign characters to the animators so that they could experiment with their own interpretations. (Among other things, Walt had yet to decide whether the Queen should be a "fat, cartoon type" with a comic element or a "high collar—stately beautiful type.") At the same time that the story department was writing scenes and dialogue, Walt charged the music department with composing songs for the film and circulated yet another outline, this one by story department head Ted Sears, to inspire gags from everyone in the studio. "Try to give at least one good gag on each individual section of the whole sequence," he urged on the introduction scene. "There are good gag possibilities throughout the sequence." He made similar requests every few days after each scene was submitted. In return he received boxes full of suggestions for gags, another sign of just how enthusiastic the employees were about the new project.

Though Walt had been edging away from gags for years in favor of larger narrative blocks that would elicit more complex responses from the audience, he was resorting to them for the feature as a form of security. Gags were what the studio knew best. "At the start [of *Snow White*] everything was gags, gags, gags," recalled animator Frank Thomas. But through the fall and winter of 1934, as the script was being developed, Walt, in Thomas's words, "was seeing something new and more things that he could do with animation, and the layout men would give him new drawings, and everybody was coming up with new ideas and so Walt was going, 'What have I got here?' He was like an organist playing all the stops." Essentially, Walt's vision was expanding as he conceptualized the film.

Throughout the winter he continued to meet endlessly with the story crew, not only during the day but occasionally at night as well, reviewing and revising each line, each gag, each story point in the introduction scene, not once or twice but a dozen times in session after session, before reluctantly moving on to the scenes in which the Queen questions her Magic Mirror over who is the fairest in the land, the Queen induces Snow White to eat the apple, and the Queen dispatches her huntsman into the woods with Snow White with the intention of killing her. But for all the attention lavished on the story and for all the talent commandeered to execute it, Walt was moving so incrementally, scene by scene, line by line, even word by word, that by the spring of 1935 he had yet to name all the dwarfs or characterize them, much less finalize the script. If there was any possibility to a scene, he seemed determined not to overlook it. *Snow White* would not be rushed, even if that meant disregarding the original schedule. It would percolate for as long as it took the film to brew.

There was another drag on the process that winter and spring besides Walt's perfectionism: Walt wasn't well. Feeling out of sorts, he had been taking injections for what his doctors had diagnosed as a "defective thyroid," but Roy found that the treatment seemed to make Walt more jittery. He was also spent. He had been working indefatigably on *Snow White* for months—his last vacation had been a three-week cruise to Honolulu the previous summer—while also having to oversee the entire production of shorts. Obviously cognizant of how dependent the entire studio was on Walt's well-being, Roy suggested that they take their wives on an extended tour of Europe to celebrate their tenth wedding anniversaries—the first time Walt would have visited the Continent since the war. Walt, who hated to leave the studio, reluctantly or not left for New York on June 2, 1935, and boarded the *Normandie* on its maiden voyage to Plymouth, England, on June 7, arriving five days later. Mindful of how much needed to be done, he instructed the staff not to let "matters accumulate until my return that will hold up production in any way," and he put Ted Sears in charge.

Even as Walt was weighed down with concerns, the cruise was giddy. "Everyone aboard is a 'somebody' or a reporter," Roy wrote his staff in Los Angeles. "[M]y god what a collection of snooty folk." Edna Disney recalled, "We weren't used to the celebrities so we were having a big time. We were just like farmers." One evening at dinner they sat next to one of the Rothschilds, who asked Walt to draw Mickey on the menu for the president of France. But if the Disneys felt like bumpkins among the wealthy and elite, they had underestimated their own fame. When they arrived at Paddington Station in London on the boat train, the crowds waiting for them were so large that the police had to protect the Disneys, and when they settled in Grosvenor House, according to one account, a "hundred pressmen followed Disney from room to room," even tailing him into the bathroom. From that point on, throughout the trip, Lillian kept chiding Walt, calling him "Big Shot."

Over the next six weeks the Disneys toured Europe, driving north to Scotland and the Lake Country, which Walt loved, then going to Paris, where they were feted by the League of Nations. Appreciating the formality of the occasion, Walt and Roy had morning coats made for them, "only to find," Walt would later recall, "that everyone there had wanted the boys from Hollywood to feel at home so they came in casual clothes!" Walt never wore the morning coat again. For two weeks they drove aimlessly through the French countryside, visiting the places where Walt had bivouacked during the war; then they drove into Germany, stopping at Baden-Baden and Munich, crossed the Alps to Switzerland, and took the train from Venice to Rome, where Walt was again greeted at the station by an appreciative mob and where he had audiences with Pope Pius XI and Benito Mussolini, who bragged to Walt that the Italian trains were now safe from brigands.

The trip seemed to have the intended restorative effect. When the Disneys returned home, after sailing on the Italian luxury liner *Rex* from Genoa on July 25, they said they were "tired but happy." Certainly they had been buoyed by the reception they received. Walt and Lillian "got such a welcome as Europe has given few Americans in recent years," reported the *Los Angeles Times*, citing a cartoon in the British magazine *Punch* in which John Bull greeted Walt as "Public Benefactor No. 1." Roy happily concurred. "Walt has been royally received everywhere," he wrote their parents. "You have good reason to be proud of Walt. He has conducted himself in a marvelous manner. Aside from the question of whether he deserves all the honors that have been conferred on him, he keeps his head and is still the same boy you knew." As for his physical condition, Walt felt rejuvenated. When his doctor's receptionist called and advised him to come to the office to resume his thyroid injections, Walt snarled, "You tell Doc I never felt better in my life. He can shoot those things in his own ass from now on."

He came back, he said, having learned some lessons about the world at large and about his animations within it. Asked what he thought of political tensions in Europe with the rise of Adolf Hitler in Germany, Walt said that he wasn't alarmed. "When a dispatch from Chicago says '150 stricken by heat' it sounds as if the whole Middle West were burning," he told a reporter, "but when you find that one prostration was in Columbus, one in Omaha, and so on, and millions of people are going about their business as usual, it doesn't seem so bad, though the reports are quite truthful." For his own business, Walt said he now believed that dialogue should be reduced to a minimum. "I found that all over the world people want to laugh," he told columnist Louella Parsons upon his return, "but you cannot translate American slang and American humor into any other language, so I will try to keep my comedy, so far as possible, in pantomime."

He also returned to his obsession with *Snow White.* He had decided that rather than divide his attention each day between the feature and the shorts, which was obviously driving him to distraction, he would instead spend alternate weeks on each. But before long he was violating his own rule. *Snow White* was the only thing that mattered. Writing to Roy that December, Walt called the feature "our one chance for real recognition, and with this thought in mind, I am going to concentrate on this feature, even at the expense of the shorts so I can have it out definitely one year from now." All that fall and winter he was meeting again with his writers on *Snow White,* meeting in long sessions during the day, meeting sometimes at night with animators to solicit gags, meeting even on Saturday mornings for hours where he again performed the scenes repeatedly (still concentrating on Snow White cleaning up the cottage and then meeting the dwarfs) and dictated the continuity. And all these months, while fighting off a nasty cold that he couldn't seem to shake, he was continually running the story through his head, picking up on the tiniest filigrees—"Snow White catches squirrels sweeping stuff under the rug—corrects them" or "Have some birds up in the rafters getting cobwebs around their tails"—and even writing out the dialogue in his own loopy scrawl on the back of the continuity, where most of his dialogue had already been typed, cutting just a word here or there, making Snow White a little more ingratiating and seemingly absorbing the story through his hand as he had through his performances. And all these months he was thinking and rethinking: Should there be more gags or more emphasis on personality? Should they aim for the cute or for the more deeply felt? By early December, after well over a year of intense concentration, he felt he had mastered at least the basic outline and tone if not all the details. "I've had continuity all wrapped around my neck like a bunch of spaghetti," he wrote Sidney Franklin that December, explaining why he hadn't been able to make further progress on *Bambi.* "While my story is not yet completely worked out, I believe we have something that is going to be good." He now hoped to have the story licked by spring, he told Franklin, and the entire film finished in a year, at which time they could proceed to animate *Bambi.* In the meantime Walt was eager to perform *Snow White* for Franklin and hear his criticisms.

But though Walt was already asking his top animators to begin conceptualizing scenes visually—he had even sent the continuity to animator Bill Tytla, who was in the hospital recovering from a polo accident—he had underestimated his own perfectionism and badly miscalculated the schedule. *Snow White* was still a long, long way from completion—and a long, long way from being everything he wanted it and needed it to be.

II

He required more staff. Even before he began to gear up for *Snow White*, the obligation to produce two full slates of cartoons—the Mickeys and the Symphonies—and the ever-increasing sophistication with which they had to be made now that he was *the* Walt Disney, required him to hire more animators. Walt was always hunting for talent, always seeking to add animators to his crew if they could improve the product. Some of his new recruits were veterans who wanted to work at the preeminent animation studio. Carmen Maxwell, one of Walt's old cronies from Kansas City who was then toiling for Harman-Ising, wrote Walt that "I can't be satisfied any more there, because they lack certain fundamental grown up ideas *without which* they are *never* going to be able to make really first class pictures." He added, "Believe it or not, I'd prefer to work harder and make less money, if I knew my efforts were going into pictures that were carefully planned and properly made."

Harboring the same sentiment, several animators throughout 1932, 1933, and 1934 decamped for the Disney studio, and Walt, with *Snow White* obviously in mind, welcomed them. One of eight children growing up in Nebraska and Iowa to an impoverished father, Art Babbitt had headed for New York as a teenager with the intention of working his way through Columbia University and becoming a psychiatrist, but after six weeks of sleeping under a church stairwell and scavenging food from garbage pails, he landed a job at an advertising agency, became a freelance artist, and eventually wound up at the Paul Terry animation studio. When he saw *The Skeleton Dance*, he had a revelation: "I knew that was the place I wanted to work." He quit Terry, left for California, and went directly to the Disney studio. When he couldn't get an appointment with Walt, he painted him a giant letter—twenty by twenty-four feet—in which he requested an interview and had it sent special delivery. Walt capitulated, granted him an audience, and then hired him a few days later.

This kind of quest to work at the Disney studio would become a familiar story among dissatisfied animators, prompting a kind of hegira to Hyperion. Dick Huemer, who had quit high school to go to the Art Students League and then quit the Art Students League to join the Raoul Barré studio in animation's early days, was working for Charlie Mintz when Mintz instituted a pay cut. Huemer immediately headed for California and joined Disney in 1933, though he would be earning roughly half of what he made from Mintz. Grim Natwick had been courted by Roy and Walt after Walt saw a scene that Natwick had drawn for the Fleischers of Betty Boop climbing aboard a moving train. Natwick declined the invitation and eventually went to work for Ub Iwerks's new studio in 1931 "because the rumor in the East was that the genius of the [Disney studio] was Iwerks." Three years later, like so many animators, he was making overtures to Disney, though it was said that Walt would never hire anyone who had previously rejected him. Nevertheless Ted Sears, a friend of Natwick's, intervened, and Natwick, after a two-hour tour of the studio conducted personally by Walt, was tendered a contract.

Perhaps the most important addition among the veterans was a large bear of a man who had been born in Yonkers, New York, of a Ukrainian father and a Polish mother. With his bushy mustache, thick brows, and unruly hair, Vladimir "Bill" Tytla looked like the Russian dictator Stalin, and at parties he would pound his chest with one hand, hoist a vodka in the other, and exclaim, "I'm a Cossack!" It wasn't just a pose—it was also an attitude of work. Grim Natwick said that Tytla "hovered over his drawing board like a giant vulture protecting a nest filled with golden eggs. He was an intense worker—eager, nervous, absorbed." Sometimes he drew with such focus and passion that his pencil tore holes in the paper. What made Tytla special was that he transferred his ferocity to the screen. His work at the Paul Terry studio was so distinctive that Walt could identify which scenes Tytla drew, and when Roy visited New York in May 1933, he took Tytla to dinner in hopes of luring him west. "He expresses a keen desire to have the opportunity to do 'better work,' " Roy wrote Walt, but he wouldn't leave Terry without a "lucrative offer."

While Tytla played hard to get, the Disneys played their own hardball. Ben Sharpsteen, who was in charge of recruiting and training, wrote Tytla in December that the studio had had difficulty indoctrinating animators from other studios in the Disney style and that "to bring a stranger in without rating his ability with the others, would be an injustice to members of our own animating staff." He offered $100 a week, which, for an animator of Tytla's stature, was clearly unacceptable. Still, as *Snow White* inched closer to realization, Roy kept wooing him over the next year, taking Tytla to dinner whenever Roy visited New York. Tytla described it as an "on-again off-again romance," until Walt and Roy convinced him to fly out to California and see their facilities. It was in November 1934, after an eighteen-hour flight and a studio tour, that he finally surrendered to the Disney onslaught. His arrival created what Don Graham, the studio's resident art instructor, labeled a new school of animation, Forces and Forms, predicated on the fact that Tytla conveyed power through the thrust of moving parts. He was so admired that after he left the studio for the day young animators would race to his office to pluck his discarded drawings from the wastebasket.

At the same time that he was signing veterans, Walt, with his urgent manpower needs, was also collecting a group of malleable young guns who had either been recommended to him or had worn him down through persistence; they would in time become both the main proponents of the Disney style and the bulwarks of the studio. As animator Ham Luske put it, Walt had imported these New York animators and "the idea was like a chain letter—every animator needed ten assistants and dozens of in-betweeners." So they came. Born in Germany, Wolfgang Reitherman, known as "Woolie," was the last of seven children of a bottled-water plant owner who brought his family to Kansas City to escape what he called "political unrest" and then to Sierra Madre, California, for the climate when one of his daughters contracted tuberculosis. After attending junior college and dabbling in art, Reitherman was working at the Douglas Aircraft Company—tall, lanky, and handsome in the Lindbergh mold, he dreamed of being an airman—when he lost hope and suddenly decided to go to art school at Chouinard instead. One of his instructors there was Phil Dike, who assisted Don Graham at the studio. Dike suggested that Reitherman, then twenty-four, apply for a job at Disney, where he began work in June 1933, gaining a reputation, Walt would say, as the "kind of guy you give him a tough assignment and he smiles . . . He's [got] an ability to take masses—big, bulky things."

Eric Larson was the son of Danish immigrants who had settled in Utah. Larson attended the University of Utah majoring in journalism until a prank—some fellow students broke into his office at the college humor magazine and one of them fell through a skylight and died—led him to find a job in Los Angeles at a firm that designed yearbooks. He stayed for six years, the last few as art director. When he got married in 1933 and needed to increase his income, he decided to write a radio script for station KHJ, which steered him to one of its former employees, Dick Creedon, for some tips on how to improve his radio play. Creedon, who was now working for Disney, suggested that Larson apply for work there since Walt was about to expand his staff for *Snow White*. Larson, then twenty-eight, reluctantly tried out as an animator and after two days was hired as an assistant.

Ward Kimball, another in this group of recruits, had just turned twenty when he went to work at the Disney studio in April 1934. Where Reitherman and Larson were easygoing and agreeable, Kimball was an edgy iconoclast and looked the part with a round, manic putty-face, a high forehead, full cheeks, and an oversize grin. Kimball's father had been an itinerant salesman who shuttled the family from one town to another—Kimball said that he attended twenty-two schools—before finally settling in California when Ward was a teenager. As a child he had been sent by his parents to live with his widowed grandmother in Minneapolis, where he first began drawing, and when the family relocated out west, he took art correspondence courses and attended the Santa Barbara School of the Arts. It was while he was working his way through school by playing in the Mickey Mouse Club band at the local theater that he saw *Three Little Pigs*, which "just knocked me out!" An instructor encouraged him to apply for a job at the studio, and Ward's mother offered to drive him down from Santa Barbara for an interview. As Kimball told it, he arrived with his portfolio, which apparently no one else had ever done, and when he was asked to leave it, he said, truthfully, that he couldn't afford the gas to drive back to pick it up. The receptionist slipped it to Walt, and Kimball started work the next week. By the time he ascended from assistant to animator, Kimball was known for breaking the rules. "He never did what was expected," wrote fellow animators Frank Thomas and Ollie Johnston, which is why, according to Sharpsteen, Walt eventually "looked for an opportunity to use Kimball on something where he could be an individual and not have to conform to others."

The month after Kimball started work, Milt Kahl, then twenty-five and living in northern California, headed to the studio at the suggestion of Ham Luske, an old friend who was already one of Walt's top animators. Kahl had had a rough childhood. After his father, a German immigrant, abandoned the family and his mother remarried, Kahl had disputes with his stepfather and was forced to quit school to earn money. Like Walt, he found an escape in art. At sixteen he began what would be a string of jobs working in the art departments of various newspapers in the San Francisco Bay Area—it was at one of these that he met Luske—before drawing ads for a West Coast theater chain and then freelancing until Luske made his suggestion. Kahl was hired.

Frank Thomas had taken up drawing as a child because he was lonely and friendless, and he pursued it through high school in Fresno, California, and later college, first at Fresno State College, where his father was president, and then at Stanford. Upon graduation Thomas, who was bespectacled and professorial, left for Los Angeles and enrolled at Chouinard. A Stanford friend and fellow artist named Jim Algar, who had also gone to Los Angeles, had come to Disney's attention, and he suggested Thomas apply as well. Thomas passed a one-week tryout and began work in September 1934. Meanwhile another Stanford friend of Thomas's named Ollie Johnston was serving as manager of the Stanford football team and visiting Los Angeles for the Rose Bowl when he decided to enroll at Chouinard himself. He was rooming with Thomas when Donald Graham invited him to try out at the studio. Three weeks later he was hired. A little more than a year later he replaced Thomas as Fred Moore's assistant.

Another of these prize recruits, John Lounsbery, discovered drawing at the age of thirteen when his father died, then attended art school in Denver after working briefly on the railroad. He continued his studies at the Art Center in Los Angeles, where one of his instructors referred him to the Disney studio in the summer of 1935. He was joined there by the last of what would eventually become the band of master animators, Marc Davis. Davis was the son of a first-generation Jew of Russian extraction who traveled the country with a mindreading act before landing finally in Klamath Falls, Oregon. Like Ward Kimball, Davis attended nearly two dozen schools, which provided him with the kind of lonely, peripatetic childhood that seemed practically obligatory for animators who amused themselves with drawing. Moving to northern California, Davis drew theater posters and newspaper ads. It was a theater owner in Yuba City who suggested he work for Disney, and when his father died, Davis and his mother relocated to Los Angeles. He visited the Disney studio and was hired that December as an assistant. "Attended classes day and night," he described his indoctrination into the Disney method, "and we worked a lot of overtime and we got meal tickets and we were delighted to be there."

Though they may have arrived at the studio haphazardly, many of them had been hired during a recruiting drive that Walt had launched in June 1934 to attract young animators for *Snow White*, despite the fact they had no idea the studio was embarking on such a project. "The qualification," went a recruiting letter drafted by Ben Sharpsteen that was sent to art schools throughout the country, "is an ability to draw well, creatively, plus a certain amount of imagination that would be helpful in the study of dramatics, which animators must acquire." Once the call went out, thousands responded—thirteen hundred from Chouinard alone by one account, and thirty thousand overall by the end of the decade.

As popular as the studio had become, it wasn't just the lure of Disney that beckoned them; it was the lure of any job at all. Years later Marc Davis would say, as Walt himself had, that "the Depression was the greatest thing that could ever have happened to Walt," since there was no way he could have gotten this talent otherwise. Davis was probably right. "It looked like a real utopia in the height of the Depression," John Lounsbery concurred. Of the thousands who responded to the ads or art school fliers by submitting samples or portfolios, roughly fifteen hundred were selected from an initial screening, and of these roughly seventy-five were given a one-week tryout at the studio. Of these, roughly twenty advanced to the next stage of training.

Now began the real test. Walt was not hiring these men to animate—

not yet—and certainly not to shoulder the main load. Indeed, according to one animator, it would take nearly ten years of apprenticeship for a trainee to move from in-between work to a classification as a master animator. He was hiring them to train for the herculean task that lay ahead of in-betweening and assisting on *Snow White*. Walt still griped that when he hired veteran animators, he had to put up with their "goddamn poor working habits from doing cheap pictures." It was easier, he believed, to start from scratch with young art students and inculcate in them the Disney system. In effect, Walt was sending these men to a kind of artistic boot camp.

It was intensive, but then Walt wanted *Snow White* to be perfect. The trainees spent all morning and then, after a lunch break, the rest of the afternoon in life classes taught by Don Graham—eight hours each day in all. After several weeks they were assigned to animators as in-betweeners at eighteen dollars per week. Even then, however, they would be excused to attend classes for a third or half a day, and beginning in February 1935, they were expected to attend an evening class every Wednesday night on the studio soundstage. Graham described his course as "[i]ntensive lectures on character construction, animation, layout, background, mechanics and direction [that] extended studio knowledge to the youngest neophyte."

But it wasn't only the trainees who were now attending classes. By the fall, with the *Snow White* script being fine-tuned and the film nearing the animation stage, Walt reinstituted mandatory classes for the entire studio art staff on Tuesday nights after having suspended them in the face of the heavy workload. Sessions alternated between action analysis and screenings of recent live-action films that, Walt announced, were "tied up in some way with the current stuff we are working on . . . with the thought in mind to prepare ourselves now for the future," meaning *Snow White*. In addition, Frank Thomas and Ollie Johnston said, animators attended classes two or three times a week, where Graham would analyze small pieces of film, running them forward and backward repeatedly; his lectures were recorded, transcribed, mimeographed, and then distributed throughout the studio. When he wasn't analyzing live action, Graham was analyzing the movements of Mickey Mouse and Donald Duck, not only to improve the animation of these characters but also to sharpen the animators' skills for *Snow White*. "Put in simple terms," Graham said, "it amounted to this: a drawing principle is a drawing principle. If it works in a Rubens, it must work in Donald Duck. If it works in the Duck it must work in SNOW WHITE."

As they edged closer to beginning the animation for *Snow White*—and given Walt's reluctance to begin without being fully prepared, they were always edging—he intensified the training. Besides the night classes, the screenings, and the action-analysis sessions headed by Graham and Phil Dike, Walt enlisted the older animators to give instruction to the younger ones—"to discuss with them Timing [and] means of obtaining certain effects . . . [I]n this way I hope to stir up in this group of men an enthusiasm and a knowledge of how to achieve results that will advance them rapidly." (Walt later wrote Graham; "Immediately following these talks, I have noticed a great change in animation.") He asked Joe Grant, a young artist who had specialized in caricature, to teach a "Caricature Class" where animators wouldn't just take instruction but would share ideas. He expanded courses to include other artists: Jean Charlot on composition, Rico Lebrun on drawing animals, and Faber Birren on theories of color. He invited guest lecturers to the studio, including notables like the architect Frank Lloyd Wright. He expanded his visual library so that animators wanting to see various animals or objects in motion could have films of them run in a sweatbox. He even had Graham take the animators on a monthly excursion to the zoo to observe the animals. "I am convinced that there is a scientific approach to this business," Walt wrote Graham in a long memo that December, "and I think we shouldn't give up until we have found out all we can about how to teach these young fellows the business." "A creative structure was being built," remembered I. Klein, who worked at the studio then, "an analytical, educational and artistically functional 'belt line' for producing animated cartoon films to compete with live action films and to go beyond the limitations of human actors." Animator John Hubley put it more succinctly: The studio was "like a marvelous big Renaissance craft hall."

Nor was the instruction restricted to visuals. Walt believed that he could give the same scientific treatment to the narrative side, so in May 1935 he recruited Dr. Boris Morkovin, the chairman of the department of cinematography at the University of Southern California, to conduct classes anatomizing the gag and subjecting it to the sort of scrutiny to which Graham was subjecting action. As Morkovin put it, "Walt's idea is that he has to prepare his young artists just as the U.S.C. football team is prepared." Morkovin claimed to have classified over two hundred gags into thirty-one basic types, though all were united by one basic idea: "Shock is the soul of the gag. . . . We can see that when two unexpected things are brought into contrast they give a jolt to the spectators' nerves and stimulate great hilarity." As a result, he advised his charges, "You must train your imagination and get into your blood the ability to bring about unrelated and contrasted gags." Taking his science one step further, he charted certain cartoons to examine the duration of their gags and to determine whether the gags were "properly proportioned," whatever that meant.

Walt, in his obsession with systematization, was so enamored of Morkovin that he even had him analyze story outlines as he was now having Graham review rough animation in the sweatbox, and Walt got his idea for distributing questionnaires at the studio after screenings when Morkovin began issuing bulletins critiquing animations, which, Walt felt, was "an ideal way to promote discussion among everyone." But Walt's enthusiasm for the professor was not widely shared. Most employees found Morkovin, gray hair lacquered back on his head and bespectacled, every bit as pompous as his name and thought his lectures bordered on the comical—a kind of parody of academic pretension. "[A]n hour a week under Ted Sears would have done more good than the four days' juggling with constantly changing, half-developed, confusing classifications," complained one employee after taking Morkovin's course. For years, long after he had left the studio, Morkovin remained a joke—one of Walt's few failed attempts at bringing rigor and enlightenment to his staff.

The intention, however, was not just education; it was infatuation. As always, Walt wanted the studio employees to be besotted, as he was, with the notion of excellence. He wanted obsession, and with the encouragement of Graham's classes, he got it. Following Walt, Graham had said that the "thinking animation character becomes a personality," so Ward Kimball and another animator, Larry Clemmons, would go out to Ocean Park on hot summer Friday nights, munch Cracker Jacks and popcorn, and muse about passersby, "analyzing people: what made them tick, and going into the psychology of the persons," as a way for Kimball and Clemmons to hone their animation talents. Frank Thomas, who was an accomplished piano player, said he would study the audience as he performed. "[Y]ou watch these [people] and you know that you've got a character for a picture."

And they studied not only people and movement but the behavior of inanimate objects. "It came to a [point] where bricks would be thrown through a plate glass window," recalled Eric Larson, "to see what the action looks like. And we would shoot it in slow motion." To understand ripples, the animators would drop rocks into water, but Josh Meador in the effects department wasn't satisfied, so he experimented with different-sized rocks and different liquids to appreciate better the effect of density. They even slammed doors to observe the reaction when the wood hit the jambs. Ham Luske would take off his tie while sailing to Catalina Island and dangle it just to see how the wind took it, or he would imitate a golfing partner's putt to demonstrate "anticipation." "Ham was studying animation all the time," said Eric Larson, "it was his whole life." But it was *everyone's* life at Disney to absorb for the greater good of animation. "We saw every ballet, we saw every film," remembered Marc Davis. "If a film was good we would go and see it five times. . . . Anything that might produce growth, that might be stimulating—the cutting of scenes, the staging, how a group of scenes was put together. Everybody was studying constantly." And calling it a "perfect time of many things coming together in one orbit," he added, "Walt was that lodestone."

Now they seemed to be ready. By late November 1935, two and a half years after Walt had first performed *Snow White*, he had set a schedule, basically starting with the comic scenes, moving to the frightening scenes, and ending with the sad scenes, apparently hoping that his staff's sophistication would grow as the project proceeded, and he began to assign the animation. Ham Luske would be the "first to start" and was clearly singled out as the primary animator. In mid-December, Walt instructed Luske to begin with Snow White's discovery of the dwarfs' cottage, then move progressively on to the dwarfs' discovery of Snow White asleep in their bedroom, the washing and soup-eating sequences, Snow White sending the dwarfs off to the mine, Snow White encountering the peddler woman and eating the apple, and finally Snow White in the woods meeting the birds. "It is possible that with the experience Ham will gain by the work he is now doing, plus his native ingenuity and ability," Walt wrote Paul Hopkins of the studio personnel department, "he will be enabled to handle all of the Snow White action, with the exception of the sequence when the dwarfs entertain her at night, which I intend Les Clark to handle."

As Joe Grant saw it, Walt was "casting" the animators the way a casting director for a live-action feature would have selected actors. "If he gave Grumpy to Tytla—Tytla *was* a grumpy character; whoever did Happy *was* a happy character. Walt figured it all out for himself." Bumptious-looking Fred Moore, who had drawn the little pigs and was working at the time on the pigs in a sequel called *Three Little Wolves*, was to join Luske animating the dwarfs' discovery of Snow White through the soup-eating sequence and in addition drawing the dwarfs starting out for the mine, meeting in the woods, and beginning work on a bed, a gift for Snow White. Effervescent Dick Lundy was to draw the dwarfs entertaining Snow White. Stern Bill Tytla, still in the hospital at the time recovering from his polo injury, was to draw the dwarfs in the mine, the dwarfs marching home, the dwarfs discovering a light in their house, and the dwarfs exploring the house. Johnny Roberts was to draw the dwarfs making the bed through the scene where the Queen leaps to her death. Master psychologist Norm Ferguson, the Pluto expert, was to draw the Queen's transformation into the peddler woman, the making of the poisoned apple, the Queen's visit to the Prince in the dungeon where she has imprisoned him (a scene that Walt would soon excise), and the Queen starting off for the dwarfs' cottage. He was also to draw most of the Queen's scenes up to her death. Les Clark would draw Snow White herself during the entertainment sequence. And Art Babbitt, who was charged with designing the Queen, would draw all the objects, liegemen, and animals with which the Queen came into contact, including her Magic Mirror, her huntsman, and her raven, feeling her out until he was able to finalize her look. Similarly, even after the animation had started, Grim Natwick, the old Betty Boop specialist, was to continue working with Luske and Clark on finding the right design for Snow White. (Natwick later said that he was allowed "two months of experimental animation before they ever asked me to animate one scene in the picture.") At the same time Walt assigned Frank Churchill, his in-house composer, to write the music, and he divided the story department into six units, each with a separate scene or set of scenes that they were to continue to revise and refine in conjunction with the animators.

By the time he began making assignments, Walt had settled on four supervising animators—Luske, Moore, Tytla, and Ferguson—who would be responsible for scenes and to whom the other animators would report. He still needed a supervising director to coordinate the supervising animators and make certain that the film was of a piece and not a collection of scenes with distinctive styles. Initially, he appointed an old animator-turned-storyman, Harry Bailey, because, Dick Huemer surmised, Bailey was tall and handsome and Walt was impressed by good looks. When Bailey faltered, Walt approached Bill Cottrell, his longtime employee and at the time the suitor of Lilly's sister, Hazel. Cottrell admitted that Dave Hand, who was directing shorts and who was a tough political infighter, wanted the assignment, so Walt turned to him. (Disappointed, Cottrell said that if Walt had really wanted him to direct, he would have said no to Hand.) Hand said that "all the key animators were thought of as ice cream sundaes, and I was described as another one, except with the cherry on top," but he modestly emphasized that "I was honestly never conscious of existing jealousy between any of the other co-workers and me—only full cooperation always." As a consolation and because there was far too much for one man to direct, Walt divided the scenes, thirty-two of them including the titles, among Cottrell, Ben Sharpsteen, Jaxon, a sententious, pipe-smoking storyman improbably named Perce Pearce, and Luske, who now doubled as animator and sequence director.

The Hyperion studio in spring 1931. It had mushroomed from the single building at the right off the sidewalk to an active production facility, though it was located in the largely barren hinterlands of Glendale. The neon sign proclaimed it the home of Mickey Mouse and Silly Symphony sound cartoons.

The Disney crew in front of the studio, circa 1929: *(rear from left)* Les Clark, Jack King, Ben Sharpsteen, Jack Cutting, Burt Gillett, Ub Iwerks, Win Smith, Wilfred Jackson, Bill Cottrell, and Floyd Gottfredson; front—Dick Lundy, Charlie Byrne, Carlos Manríquez, Norm Ferguson, Merle Gilson, Chuck Couch, Carl Stalling, Johnny Cannon, and Walt in one of his trademark floppy hats.

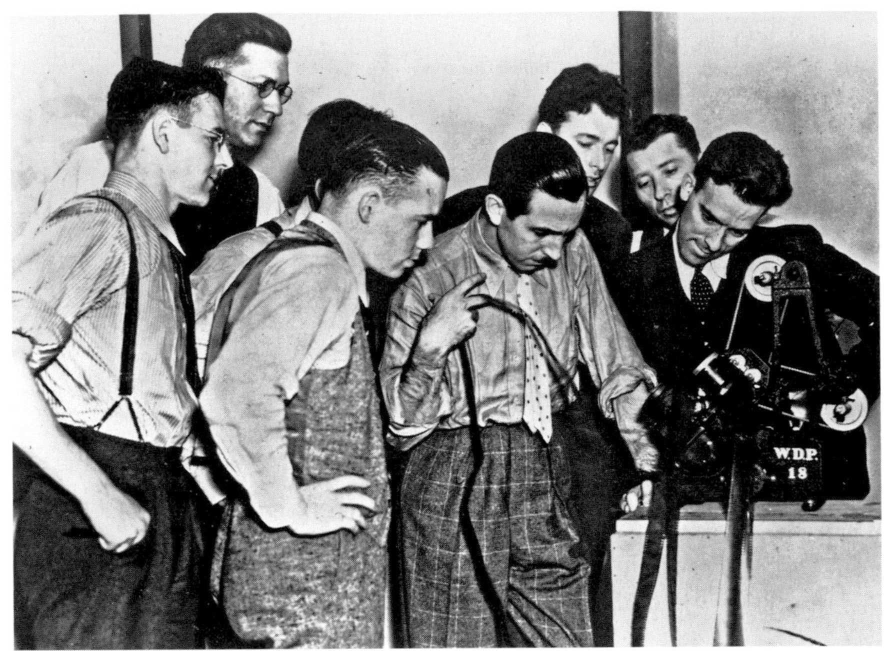

The "sweatbox," aptly named closet at Hyperion where Walt examined the animation roughs on the Movieola. This was a grueling experience for those awaiting Walt's verdict, which was the only verdict at the studio that mattered.

The Mickey Mouse Club in front of the Grand Theater at Yoakum, Texas. The brainchild of a young California theater manager named Harry Woodin, the clubs attracted hundreds of thousands of members (Roy would say millions) for Saturday matinees and helped establish Mickey Mouse as the leading animation character in the 1930s before the idea petered out in the mid-1930s.

Walt with Herman "Kay" Kamen, the homely merchandising genius who took over the licensing of Disney products and parlayed them into a fortune for himself and the Disney brothers.

Walt with Mickey Mouse merchandise. Already by the early 1930s, Mickey had become a cottage industry.

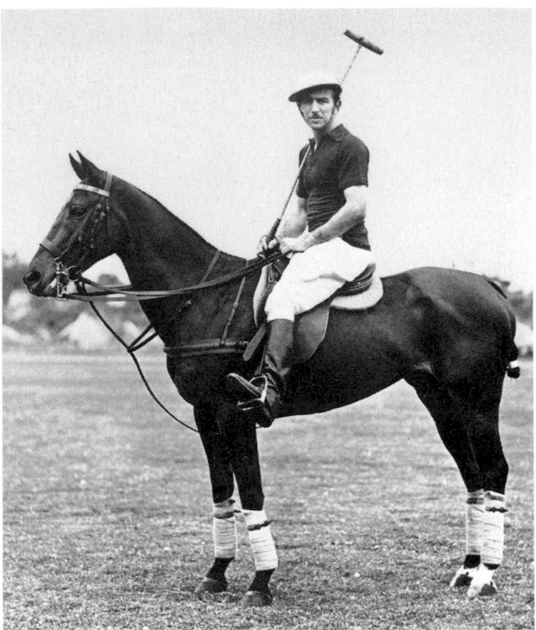

left: Walt surveying the view from his home on Woking Way in the Los Feliz hills above Los Angeles. He had built the home hurriedly in preparation for a new baby, but Lillian miscarried.

right: Walt in polo gear. He took up the sport for relaxation after his breakdown, buying ponies, instituting a studio team, and practicing each morning; he disengaged when an opponent died from injuries sustained during a match.

Walt watching two men dance, no doubt animators preparing a scene. Though Walt demanded perfection, there was a camaraderie and playfulness at the studio that made it the envy of the animation world. Ben Sharpsteen is at the rear to Walt's right, and Norm Ferguson is looking in a mirror.

Walt and his multiplane camera, designed in the service of realism to bring a sense of three-dimensionality to animation. First used in the short *The Old Mill*, it became a valuable if expensive tool in *Snow White*, *Pinocchio*, and *Fantasia*.

Norm Ferguson studying himself for an animation. Ferguson was regarded as the pioneer of psychological animation in which one felt that the animated character was actually thinking.

top right: Fred Moore, the incorrigible young animator who was as responsible as anyone for the soft, cute Disney style. Moore designed the pigs for *Three Little Pigs*.

bottom right: Bill Tytla, who looked like Stalin and who brought a highly dramatic, emotional element to Disney animation. Here he is with a model of the devil from "Night on Bald Mountain" in *Fantasia*.

Walt with Lillian at the *Snow White* premiere on December 21, 1937, at the Carthay Circle Theater in Hollywood, where he had managed to get *The Skeleton Dance* shown eight years earlier. He had scaled the heights.

Walt looking out at the water tower on the construction site of the Burbank studio, one of the fruits of *Snow White*'s success. Walt found the site and essentially designed the art moderne studio himself: a state-of-the-art animation facility.

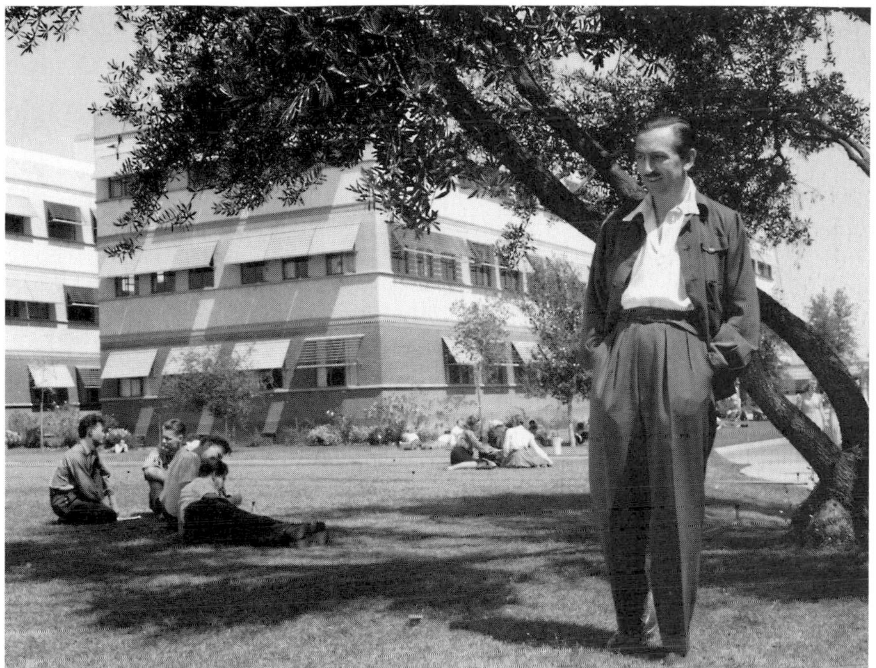

Walt standing in front of the Animation Building, where he and Roy both had their offices and which was the hub of Disney production. The new studio resembled a college campus. Note the slatted awnings that were designed to regulate light for the animators.

Walt acting out for his staff what he wanted. Though he was often personally reserved, at story sessions he was animated and transformed himself into the characters, so that his performances became the basis for the Disney oeuvre.

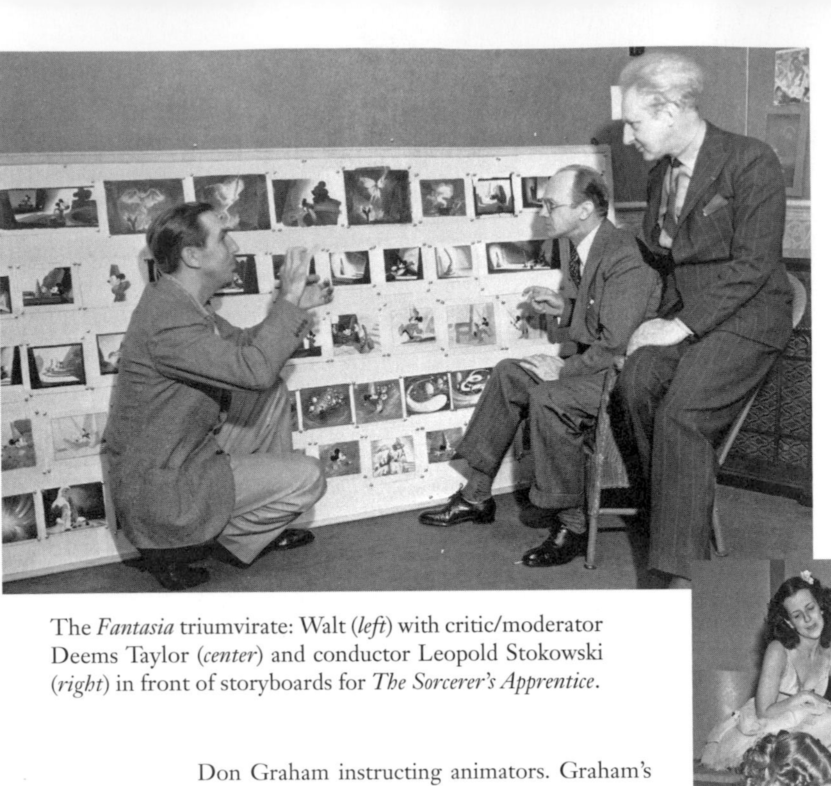

The *Fantasia* triumvirate: Walt (*left*) with critic/moderator Deems Taylor (*center*) and conductor Leopold Stokowski (*right*) in front of storyboards for *The Sorcerer's Apprentice*.

Don Graham instructing animators. Graham's studio school improved the quality of animation and symbolized Walt's commitment to animation as an art.

Disney animators preparing for *Bambi* under the instruction of artist Rico Lebrun. During the golden age of Disney in the late 1930s and early 1940s, animation was not only a profession at the studio; it was a way of life.

But even with all the talent now in place, one giant logistical obstacle remained. In making the shorts, the animators had never felt any confusion between drawing a scene and drawing the characters within it, because the scenes generally contained so few characters that one man could do most of the work. In making his assignments on *Snow White*, Walt married certain animators to certain characters (for example, Moore to the dwarfs, Babbitt to the Queen, Natwick to Snow White), but he also delegated animators to draw certain scenes. Since characters obviously appeared in more than one scene, the two approaches conflicted. You could have different animators drawing the same characters in different scenes and hope for continuity, or you could have the same animators drawing the same characters in each scene and hope that the scene itself would maintain its integrity and that the individual drawings would relate to one another. Oddly enough, as important a question as this was, Walt never satisfactorily resolved it, creating a good deal more confusion and chaos than the hierarchy would have suggested, since some animators sought to follow their character from scene to scene while others worked on entire scenes.

And to this chaos was added one more crisis just as they embarked on animation early in 1936. For all the recruiting and all the training, the studio simply did not have enough animators to do the grunt work of in betweening and cleaning up, much less the secondary animation. They needed animators, and they needed them very quickly. By one account, Walt called in Don Graham and said, "I need 300 artists—get them." By this time Sharpsteen, with his obligations on *Snow White*, had been relieved of overseeing the training program. (He later made a point of saying that Walt never thanked him for what he had done.) In his place was a screaming hatchet-faced martinet named George Drake whom Sharpsteen had originally brought into the studio as an in-betweener and whom he then assigned to supervise in-betweeners-in-training while Sharpsteen himself broke in the greenhorns. (Drake was widely believed to be Sharpsteen's brother-in-law, which was a source of his authority, though he was only a distant relative and no real friend.)

With their seemingly impossible assignment, Drake and Graham left for New York that March and set themselves up in a seven-room suite in the RKO Building that M. H. Aylesworth, RKO's chairman, had secured for them at the last minute. By placing ads in New York papers, they attracted would-be animators for what amounted to a trial course, though Drake and Graham were so discriminating that out of the seven hundred initial applicants they chose only thirty-two, thus underenrolling their courses. Walt wrote back suggesting not that they compromise their standards—Walt would never have advised that—but that they stay longer, which they did. When the mission ended, on July 1, it had cost the studio $15,000 and had provided many fewer than the hundreds Walt had wanted, while incurring some resentment at the studio among the young animators already there. Though it was difficult to determine the yield, especially since Walt was asking that promising candidates immediately be sent to the studio, the final group that Drake and Graham dispatched to California consisted of only twenty-two—out of more than two thousand hopefuls.

Even then the recruits weren't secure. The earlier group of prospects—among them Reitherman, Larson, Kimball, Kahl, Thomas, Johnston, Lounsbery, and Davis—had been indoctrinated by Graham and then mentored by Walt's first generation of master animators: Ham Luske, Fred Moore, Norm Ferguson, and Grim Natwick. But the current novitiates were entrusted to George Drake, once called the most hated man at Disney, who kept them under his whip hand during what amounted to a one-month trial that consisted largely of animating test assignments. "George had huge ears, great and red and wiggly," recalled Ken Anderson, one of his trainees, "and they lit up as he jumped up and down while screaming." Drake terrorized them, but he was the one they had to please, even though his own work was less than stellar. "During that one month period Drake kept us on edge by continually pacing the hall and popping in on us at odd moments," wrote Bill Peet, another trainee. "Every few days one or two of the group were let go, and as it came down to the last week we wondered if Drake would fire all of us."

It was agonizing, but those who survived moved on to Graham's classes and the other benefits that the studio showered upon its employees. Those who survived entered the very privileged precincts at the very apex of animation.

III

To be one of the roughly five hundred employees at the Walt Disney Studio in the mid-1930s as it began *Snow White* was to be swept up in a frenzy of exhilaration. One observer said that it was "so far in advance of the times that it became a place of pilgrimage, not only for Mickey devotees but for anyone interested in the growth of a contemporary experiment in art and entertainment." Grim Natwick called it a "mythical sun around which the other studios orbited." "Each new picture contained breathtaking improvements," Thomas and Johnston would write, "the effects were better, the animation had more life, and the whole studio had an upward momentum. It was like being a player on a winning team! To us, all this was pure magic." Another compared the animators to the disciples of Michelangelo: "We were part of a thing that was maybe going to last." There was very little griping and virtually no competition among the employees, only camaraderie. Work was joy. "It wasn't that you had to do these things," Marc Davis said. "You *wanted* to do them. You were so proud. Every write-up the studio got, everybody went out and got it. Very few people have ever, as a group, experienced that type of excitement."

The spirit was so immense that it could barely be contained within the studio, almost as if it were pushing Hyperion's physical boundaries, which in some sense it was. With the anticipation of *Snow White*, said background artist Maurice Noble, "the whole studio grew like Topsy." After erecting a two-story animation building in 1931, with the neon sign on top, the Disneys had bought lots along Hyperion Avenue and purchased other tracts on Griffith Park Boulevard, which angled down from the north to Hyperion. The adjoining organ chimes factory at the intersection of Griffith Park and Hyperion that had driven the animators to distraction for so long was either razed or renovated for Roy's new office, a dining and conference room, and the accounting department. When the staff outgrew the first animation building, another two-story building with 11,200 square feet of space, the centerpiece of the entire studio, was constructed directly behind it in the spring and summer of 1934, shortly after production on *Snow White* commenced. The animators were stationed on the first floor, and the projection rooms, replacing the sweatboxes though still called by that term, were located on the second. An ink and paint building was erected in the spring of 1935, beyond the soundstage, followed that fall by an apprentice animators' building, known variously as the annex or the incubator—because its roof reminded Walt of the chicken coops in Marceline—across the street. This was the place where George Drake held forth and where the in-betweeners—who had been toiling in the sweltering basement of the animation building, nicknamed the "bullpen"—now slaved. To accommodate the growing staff, two low-slung temporary wooden structures called "boxcars" were erected at the back of the lot on Griffith Park Boulevard. Still, there was not enough room for the *Snow White* army, and the studio spilled down the street and through the neighborhood into apartment buildings, offices, and bungalows—"any structure that was near and could house artists and storymen," as Thomas and Johnston put it. The story department was relocated across the parking lot to an old two-story stucco apartment house along Griffith Park Boulevard where the writers, according to one, "occupied all of the living rooms, bedrooms, dining rooms, and kitchenettes." By the time the expansion was finished, the studio had twelve buildings on five acres with a total replacement value of $187,000.

Yet for all its apparent clutter and jumble, most visitors found it, as Bill Tytla enthused, "a beautiful plant," with its little grass courtyard off Hyperion, a Ping Pong table on one side and a small garage with miniature cars for Mickey and Minnie on the other, and its flagstone walkway leading to the new animation building. One observer said it looked like a "small municipal kindergarten with green grass for the children to keep off of and, on the roof, a gigantic glorious figure of Mickey to show them the best way." Another visitor called it a "quaint, cozy look appropriate for a company dealing with fun and fantasy."

The interiors were no less fanciful, at least after the construction of the new animation building. "In the first place, everything was painted in bright tints of raspberry, light blue, and gleaming white, no institutional greens or bilious browns like the other studios," recalled Shamus Culhane, a young animator then. Where furniture at the New York studios looked as if it "had been stolen from the Salvation Army," at Disney "[e]ach animation team had its own room with three beautifully designed desks, upholstered chairs, cupboards for storing work in progress, and most amazing of all . . . each room had a moviola." "The desk furniture was something!" Ward Kimball concurred. "They decided to use a Spanish motif because the first building that was built on Hyperion had the Spanish roof tile, so this tile prevailed throughout the studio." In keeping with the style, the animation desks were painted white with sienna red trim. "Then they sprayed a kind of dirty umber mixture inside the shelves and in the corners to give an aged or antique effect. Early Hyperion Spanish!"

When most recalled the studio, however, it was not as a kindergarten or hacienda but as a college campus—"maybe an Ivy League campus," said one employee, "as there was a feeling of exclusivity." For all the intense pressures to get the work done and do it well, hard backbreaking work that required one to sit hunched over a hot drawing board hour after hour—in fact *because* of the pressures—the old spirit of collegiate jocularity and informality prevailed, intensified, no doubt, by the relative youth of the staff; by one report, the average age of the employees in the mid-1930s was twenty-five. Walt's secretary, Carolyn Schaefer, issued a mimeographed newsletter each month called *The Mickey Mouse Melodeon* that spread studio gossip. With Walt's blessing Pinto Colvig, a storyman and voice artist, started a twenty-five-piece studio band. At lunchtime the staff might head across the street to the annex, where Walt had set up a volleyball court for a match, or they might hurry to the vacant lot next to the soundstage or, when that was built upon, to the lot on Hyperion for a game of baseball, with the married men usually playing the single ones. Walt often played too, invariably getting on base thanks to his employees' largesse, even though he was still a clumsy athlete. "If he was called out, he was furious," remembered one player.

As the vise tightened with *Snow White*, the sophomoric pranks only became more frequent and elaborate. Fred Moore, who had mastered the art of throwing the pushpins that held drawings to the storyboards, would take two in each hand and fling them at the ceiling so that the ceiling tiles were eventually dotted with pushpins. Or Ward Kimball and fellow animator Walt Kelly would play football in the hallways. Or Kimball would arrive at work dressed in a gorilla outfit. Or Milt Kahl would back up to the vent leading from the lavatory to the in-betweeners' bullpen and pass gas. Or some pranksters would put a goldfish in Art Babbitt's water cooler. One storyman who kept a small pet turtle at the studio couldn't understand why the turtle grew so rapidly nor why it then just as rapidly shrank. The fellow's colleagues had substituted a series of other turtles for the pet. A visiting reporter described the studio as a "psychiatrist's heaven" and a "madhouse," and one new artist wrote friends, "If this is not a crazy house, then I don't know what is." Walt didn't intervene, though he did complain about the pushpins in the ceiling, and he was forced to issue an edict against "too much visiting from one room to another . . . I don't mean by this that in order to be conscientious you have to stick to your drawing board every minute of the day; but if you want to get up and relax, don't do it at someone else's expense." More commonly, after some prank he would say, "Why don't you get some of that in the pictures?"

Animators and storymen found two more consolations from the pressures—drink and sex. Typically animators drank heavily, both to relieve their tension and to loosen their inhibitions; alcoholism was practically an occupational hazard, though it may also have had something to do with the fact that the kind of men who were attracted to animation were likely to be emotionally stunted and loners, lost in their own heads. Every afternoon at four o'clock a traffic boy delivered beer to the animators, and they often retired afterward to Leslie's Bar near the studio. "Maybe more ideas were quenched than born in our frequent forays to favorite bars for liquid inspiration," recalled Jack Kinney. "But somehow the next day we'd pour out new ideas like the bartender had poured drinks the night before." As they were boozy, they were also randy. Occasionally someone would bring a stag film to the studio, and the animators would sit enthralled. Other times, to relieve the stress, they would spend hours drawing pornographic cartoons featuring the Disney characters. Though an informal policy forbade mingling between male and female employees (a large group of young women worked nearby in ink and paint), the animators never lacked female companionship—what Jack Kinney called "dipping your pen in company ink." (According to Kinney, animators who took their girls to hotels often signed the register "Ben Sharpsteen," using the name of their erstwhile supervisor, who was their antagonist.) One employee said he knew of at least thirty-five couples at the studio where "Cupid's arrows struck hard and often." Many of them wound up marrying, though casual sex was the more likely outcome. Answering a questionnaire, Milt Kahl listed his hobby as "sexual intercourse," and Art Babbitt gained a certain prestige among his colleagues for his reputation as a playboy.

Yet for all the daily hilarity and fun, the ease and informality at the Disney studio had never been accidental or incidental. It was essential to Walt Disney—even more essential now that they were making *Snow White.* If the film, through the character of Snow White, traced Walt's own maturation, it also limned his own sense of insecurity within his family and his ongoing search for a community or surrogate family to which he could belong and from which he could draw emotional sustenance—the family that Snow White finds in the dwarfs. Walt Disney, then, was not just producing a cartoon. In the very organization of the studio and in the means of production, he was creating an environment, the establishment of which was in its way every bit as important a mission for him as the cartoon feature itself. Put simply, the studio would replicate the cartoon.

From the Red Cross to DeMolay to Laugh-O-Gram to his first studio in Los Angeles on Kingswell Avenue, Walt had always loved social organizations, always loved to forge people into a happy unit—"Walt's big happy family," one reporter described the Hyperion studio. Some regarded it as paternalism, and certainly his management style contained an element of that. "Dad wanted to take care of everybody," his daughter Diane said. "He wanted to know if an employee was sick or needed something. He knew about everybody's personal lives." From this same impulse he made sure that working conditions at the studio were exemplary. As the rather haphazard arrangement for *Snow White* indicated, the studio had no formal organization chart, just Walt's hunches. It had no time clock to punch either, because Walt had resented having to punch one at the Kansas City Film Ad Co. Employees could take three sick days in any given week with full pay before anyone investigated, and if the excuse was legitimate, they would continue to be paid while they convalesced. Before *Snow White* Walt typically closed the studio in mid-August, giving his employees a long vacation, and select employees were granted even longer breaks. "I want you to take advantage of this vacation period to the fullest extent," he wrote Bill Garity, the onetime sound engineer who became Walt's production manager early in the summer of 1934. "Get out and go some place—the World's Fair is still on—then there's Hawaii, Cuba, New York, Alaska and many, many other places of interest—anyway do something that you will enjoy and come back to the Studio feeling great and rarin' to work." Even as they were gearing up for *Snow White*, anyone who had been with the studio a full year as of July 1, 1935, was granted a two-week vacation.

And it wasn't just perks Walt doled out. The studio paid well too. Animators generally made between $100 and $125 a week, a veritable fortune during the Depression, and the very top animators, like Art Babbitt, brought down as much as $15,000 a year, enough for him to afford three cars and two servants. Despite Roy's repeated warnings to monitor money closely, Walt refused to skimp. He was constantly on the lookout for any employee who he felt might be underpaid, and he would then instruct the payroll office to make a salary adjustment. "His ambition," wrote a reporter, "is to pay his employes [*sic*] well enough for them to save for old age and still enjoy living as they go along."

But if this was paternalism, it was paternalism in service of a higher principle—not just efficiency or happiness or public relations or even Walt's revered quality but a new kind of business organization that promised a new kind of social relationship that harked back to Elias Disney's old American Society for Equity: Walt Disney wanted to create a haven on earth as he had in his cartoons. He wanted an organization in which everyone would be selfless and happy. Joe Grant remembered working at his desk one Sunday when Walt approached. " 'You know, Joe,' he said, with a sense of pride at the way things were going, 'this whole place runs on a kind of Jesus Christ communism,' " doubtless without realizing that he was the Christ. Still, Walt was right that the Disney studio operated differently from any other studio, and from any other business generally for that matter, in its employees' sense of commitment, and he was not the only one who recognized it. Left-wing observers particularly lauded him for his collective approach to art. *New Republic* film critic Otis Ferguson, calling Disney a "pioneer in more things than his conception of and tireless experiment with the animation cartoon," cited Disney's "conference method" in which artists selflessly pooled their individual talents to make a film. Another critic praised "The Communalistic Art of Walt Disney," while a third, writing in the leftist *New Theatre*, extolled the "marvelous creative values engendered by collective collaboration" in Disney's films. Although in truth the studio was still a cult and individual contributions were always subsumed under Walt Disney's vision and usually under his name as well, Walt had come to view it as a community of artists united toward one goal. For a man who had long searched for escape into his art, the studio itself now had become an alternative world—a near-perfect world.

Even so, the organization came no easier than the animations. The tension between creativity and commerce, between doing the work well and making sure it was done profitably, was constant. Although resources had been shifted to *Snow White*, the studio was nevertheless obligated with the Mickeys and Symphonies to produce a cartoon every two weeks, which meant it had to turn out roughly seventy-five feet of film every day. To meet the schedule, in-betweeners began working nights but now found themselves, as personnel chief Paul Hopkins wrote Walt, "physically unable to produce the work" during the day, since they were now "tired and worn out with the night sessions." Even with the staff as committed and fulfilled as they were, and even as Walt tried to relieve the pressures of time as best he could, the situation was stressful given the demands of footage and of quality and of the self-imposed desire to do great work. Thomas and Johnston said that the animators felt they were only as good as their last scene and that they always fretted about slipping. Artist Rico Lebrun, who conducted art classes at the studio, claimed, "I have never found a more thoroughly self-critical bunch in my life." One frazzled animator, asking for a leave to go to another studio, thanked Walt for the release, saying, "I believe it will help me recuperate to some extent."

As a utopian, Walt did not like being the taskmaster; he preferred being the muse. When the staff's self-discipline didn't suffice to keep them on schedule, he appointed Ben Sharpsteen to enforce some semblance of discipline. Sharpsteen's own wife said of him, "Ben realizes he is not talented, that he can't compete. He was fired off of every job he had until Disney." Bald and bulb-headed with a tiny mustache, Sharpsteen—who had moved on from animation to become head of the training program and then the main director of the shorts and effectively their supervising producer while Walt was focused on *Snow White*—appeared to be a milquetoast, but he would tyrannize the other directors, who would in turn tyrannize the animators. Next to George Drake, he may have been the least liked person at the studio. Bill Peet said, "He's OK. He just doesn't mean well." Another, less diplomatic underling called him a "son of a bitch," adding, "and I'm one of his best friends." Ward Kimball thought Sharpsteen was abusive, especially to younger animators, because he was sensitive about his own inability to draw well, but he also thought that Sharpsteen's sadism was a payback for the tongue-lashings he suffered from Walt. "The verbal beatings and the sleepless nights I know he had (because I talked to his wife) were a hell of a price to pay for getting his name up there on the screen," Kimball recalled. Sharpsteen himself said as much: "I was constantly called upon to make decisions in behalf of him. Good decisions rarely received commendation. Errors were dealt with, often rudely."

As for balancing creativity and cost, Walt's constant bane, Walt and Roy hit on a bold new plan in light of the need to speed *Snow White*. They would take the 20 percent stake in the company that they had bought from Iwerks when he left the studio and hold it in a kind of trust for the employees, doling out bonuses to the best and most efficient of them, though even before the plan was fully implemented, Roy suggested it be revised so that bonuses earned remained with the company to help finance *Snow White* and then were "to be repaid to the bonus participants if and when the feature is finished and pays its way out." In short, the staff would be well rewarded if the film was well received.

Beginning in 1934, Walt had handed out bonuses, $32,000 that year, at his own discretion. "I was always trying to find ways that I could compensate my employees, if possible, that I was building the organization for them as well as myself," he would later testify, not entirely self-servingly. But as the studio grew and as the need to expedite production intensified early in 1936, Walt felt he was no longer capable of determining who deserved compensation. Decisions on incentives had to be made objectively, even scientifically. Under the new bonus system, each animator's salary was to be charged to an account. The animator and the director would settle on how much he was to draw. Once the cartoon—or in the case of *Snow White*, the scene—was finished, his work was to be rated on its quality by a panel of supervisors; a price per foot had been established for each grade on a sliding scale from eight dollars a foot for grade A animation to four dollars for grade C. To determine the animator's bonus, if any, the grade would be multiplied by the footage he contributed. Anything that exceeded his salary would be paid to him, and anyone who consistently exceeded his salary would be awarded a permanent adjustment the following year.

Not everyone appreciated the new system. "Nobody liked it really," said Sharpsteen with some hyperbole, "except for a few smart chiselers who somehow had a way of making it look good for them." Slower animators were obviously disadvantaged, which was the whole point, and some complained that better animators were forced to redo the work of poorer ones with no compensation. Moreover, those animators who worked on features felt that they were more difficult to rate since the work itself was more difficult than the work on shorts. Nor was the scale as objective as it was purported to be. Walt still closely examined each film and dabbled in making ad hoc adjustments, believing that the animators had to be amply rewarded if they were to do their best work. As Ward Kimball remembered it, "Some sort of magic light would shine over the studio . . . and all of a sudden you might get a raise." Though the bonus system would later have some devastating repercussions, in the near term, for all its flaws, it had its intended effect. It seemed to expedite production, particularly on the shorts, without necessarily sacrificing quality. It seemed to rein in costs. It seemed to give the animators a greater financial stake in the studio. Above all, it seemed to create an even deeper sense of loyalty and dedication. As one employee expressed it to Walt after receiving his bonus, "I definitely intend to do all I possibly can to uphold my responsibility to you and the firm."

Walt would need it.

IV

And so finally in February 1936—after nearly three years of incessant tinkering, after the training sessions, the ongoing recruitments, the expansion of the studio, and the establishment of the bonus system—the animation of *Snow White* began. But even as the staff drew its roughs and continued to experiment, Walt's passion did not abate. He was still fiddling, still agonizing, still reviewing the script with his staff scene by scene for three or more hours at a time several times each week and on weekends too—scenes that he had already been laboring over and picking at for years. It was as if he couldn't let go, possibly because he knew that since he couldn't draw it himself, he would be yielding his absolute control over the film once it was being animated. Frank Thomas said that Walt was involved with *Snow White* "night and day, night and day. Walt lived every sprocket hole of this film." Milt Kahl agreed: "It was the love of his life at that time."

Every week that winter right through the fall revised continuities would arrive from the story department, continuities that Walt had largely dictated, and every week Walt would pore over them again, making suggestions. "Open with dancing—Happy playing organ and different instruments by the various dwarfs," he advised at one typical story session on the sequence in which the dwarfs stage an entertainment for Snow White, "—finish it—folk dancing idea—concentrate on the stuff that would fit that—then a specialty, each dwarf wrote himself—then get gadget stuff—then Snow White wants to hear something else—then the Lady in the Moon [a song]—when they finish—they want her to do something and she tells them a love story—'Once upon a time'—very dramatic—we haven't touched the possibilities." Within a three-week period a single scene could be subjected to as many as five lengthy meetings.

And always, as he had been doing for years now, he would recite the story to anyone who would listen and to many who had already listened, anything from a short version to the full three-hour performance. Even as late as December 1936, after much of the rough animation had been completed and some had been okayed for cleanup, Walt was still telling the story in its entirety at a meeting—every cut, every fade-out, every line of dialogue. "[H]e was telling it all the time," Eric Larson remembered. "He would sit down and just talk to any of us about it, and he would tell the whole story maybe in five minutes. He was so enthused about it." Joe Grant said he drove the staff crazy. "Every time he'd come into a room where the storyboards were, he'd tell the whole story of the film over again, from the beginning to the end, to make sure nobody got anything wrong." Grant said he must have heard these performances three or four dozen times, but each was slightly different. Each time Walt would incorporate something new from the continuities, some small bit of business that one of the writers or animators might have added, so that he was constantly revising and refining verbally. As Sharpsteen described it, "Whether he used the idea in total or greatly modified, the idea had to become part of him."

Some of his contributions were conceptual. It was Walt who decided that the woods into which Snow White escapes should be alive and foreboding: "It would be good for her [Snow White] to be caught in the bushes showing these grotesque hands, then the wind and all the things that frighten her. Have it lead to things that make her think things are alive, but at the same time the audience should have a feeling that it is all in her mind. . . . Like the thorns changing back from hands to thorns." Some were dramatic. Of the scene in which the Queen's huntsman is about to kill Snow White before her innocence shames and converts him, Walt suggested that Snow White bend over to tend to a sick baby bird. "[S]he is stooped over which gives you a swell position for the knife in the back," he suggested. "Let the menace come in there where she kissed the bird and the bird perked up and flew away—it has a connection for the Huntsman to soften." Others were psychological. He was always thinking not only of what would work on the screen but how the characters would feel. It must be Grumpy, Walt decided, who cries when he finds Snow

White comatose from eating the poisoned apple while the others' eyes just mist up: "Let him break right down. Hard exterior, soft inside." Still other contributions were minute details, some of which were debated endlessly. In the scene in which the dwarfs return to their cottage and realize that someone may be lurking inside, should a pair of empty shoes into which frogs had leaped chase Dopey, run past him, or keep in step with him? (In the final version, it was none of these.) Even so, Walt proclaimed, "I like good comedy stuff, but I think we will have to tie the shoes in differently . . . our continuity as a whole is more important than one gag." And once done, nothing was too small for correction. Watching a sweatbox of an early scene animated by Eric Larson, Walt noted of a dwarf, "his fanny in the last half of scene is too high," and "Have hummingbird make four pick-ups instead of six." Even his offhand remarks could find their way into the film, as when Walt suggested during the scene of the dwarfs in the mine that "Dopey could come in and see two stones and clown. Put them in his eyes." He was visualizing the entire movie, shot by shot, gag by gag, detail by detail, as if there were a projector in his head.

And that is why, for all the talk of collaboration, no one at the studio doubted that the job was less to exhibit his own talent than to realize on screen what Walt was visualizing in his head. Indeed, there was a stenographer at each story session so that Walt's suggestions could be distributed and interpreted like holy writ. When Walt was describing, this was easy. But when he was brainstorming, tossing out ideas one after another, it could cause problems. One of the most frequent complaints at the studio had always been that one often couldn't know what Walt wanted because Walt couldn't always articulate it unless he acted it out. On *Snow White* this was especially harrowing for the staff. "It was often difficult to know precisely what Walt saw in a piece of business," Thomas and Johnston wrote, "and after each meeting there would be some disagreement over what he had said, and even more confusion over what he had meant." It was Ham Luske who usually clarified. "Someone would say that Walt said he wants it like this. Ham would say, 'No, that's not what he means. This is what he means.' " What Walt meant was the guide.

"What we are trying to do with Walt is build the picture as he sees it," Dave Hand, *Snow White*'s supervising director, told the staff. "We have got to trust in one man's judgment or we won't have a good picture." In later years the animator Joseph Barbera, a Disney rival, would joke of the old Disney animators he encountered that "everyone who had ever been associated with Walt Disney either created 'The Three Little Pigs' or *Snow White*." But despite this arrogation Wilfred Jackson believed that the animators were really irrelevant and that Walt was the only one who really mattered. "It is my opinion," he told Thomas and Johnston, "that if Walt had started in some different place at the same time with a different bunch of guys, the result would have been more or less along the same lines." *Snow White* belonged to Walt Disney, just as Walt Disney belonged to *Snow White*.

After months of preliminary animation, roughing out the action, and pencil testing, the artists began the final animation that summer of 1936* with almost as much trepidation as Walt was displaying in giving final approval to the story. Bill Tytla said that the animators were "all walking on tiptoes on that one. We didn't know what to expect. We were full of all kinds of emotions." Everyone realized that they were embarking on something new and important. "There is a lot of stuff you can get by with in shorts that you cannot get by with here," Tytla told an action analysis class that December, "and Walt won't let the poor stuff get by. . . . He has mentioned that certain business in sweatbox would be damned good for the shorts, but it would not do for the feature." Drawings for shorts were predicated, he said, on the simple shape of the ball, which, when inked, yielded a "hard, incisive line." For the feature there was a need for texture—"texture of the flesh, the jowls of the dwarfs, the drawing into the eyes, the mouth, the texture of the hair and of old cloth." Tytla suggested that they even try to get personality in the texture of the dwarf's hands. And he added menacingly, "[T]hey are strict with me in getting what they want—and that will go all the way down the line." Ted Sears wrote a memo expressing similar concerns on the story side. The feature required subtlety, but there was always the danger of being too subtle: "I think they're afraid that this subtleness cannot be fully brought out in a cartoon character." At the same time Ham Luske warned putative in-betweeners and assistants that if they approached the feature with too much reverence and reservation, it would suffer. "The one thing I don't want you to do is figure that this is a feature—and—consequently that we must make very careful individual drawings that are more carefully drawn than those on the shorts," Luske advised. "We want good work, but not hair line stuff that will tighten animation up."

As the animation began in this state of tension and anxiety, rivalries gradually surfaced in a studio that only a few months before had prided

*It is difficult to say exactly when animation on *Snow White* began. Walt had handed out assignments by late 1935 and was sweatboxing roughs and experimenting with action at least as early as February 1936, but the final model sheets for the characters weren't finished until September 28, 1936, which could be regarded as the date of the real or final animation.

itself on its collegiality—rivalries less for Walt's favor than over who was better at realizing his ideas. Some storymen objected that the animators were not maximizing the material, and the story department posted a sign: "It was funny when it left here!" Among the animators themselves factions now emerged, which led to sniping. Sharpsteen said that the new recruits regarded themselves and were regarded by others as "arty," while the old-timers, especially lower-rated animators and assistants, were "dedicated to getting laughs." The first group thought that the second wasn't up to the emotional demands of *Snow White*, while the second thought that the first didn't understand entertainment. "I don't know what they're looking for around here anymore," Burt Gillett, who had returned to the studio, complained. "Experience doesn't seem to matter for anything. They've got a bunch of smart kids around here you're not supposed to touch." Animator Bill Roberts called the art school graduates a "bunch of Cinderellas."

And while the animators were dividing into camps over the general approach to the feature, another division opened over Snow White herself. Everyone at the studio recognized that the greatest visual challenge in making the feature was drawing the humans. The studio had attempted human characterizations in *The Pied Piper* in 1933, but Walt was disappointed. When I. Klein submitted a storyboard with human characters that fall, Ted Sears wrote him that "we have come to the conclusion that our best screen values are in small cute animal characters, we haven't advanced far enough to handle humans properly and make them perform well enough to compete with real actors." The next year, obviously with *Snow White* in mind, the studio attempted *The Goddess of Spring*, which featured Persephone being captured by the devil. Again the animation was unsatisfactory, the humans too stiff, and Les Clark felt obligated to apologize to Walt, who simply said, "I guess we could do better the next time."

Not too much later Walt entrusted Ham Luske with the critical job of designing Snow White. By that time he had also hired Grim Natwick, who early in 1935 tested his own prowess in drawing more humanlike figures by animating the scene of the Cookie Girl being transformed into the Cookie Queen in a Silly Symphony titled *The Cookie Carnival*, and who, despite complaints that he was slow and disorganized and technically deficient, was assigned the task of animating scenes of Snow White, presumably from Luske's model sheets. From the first it was an unhappy partnership. Luske saw Snow White as young and innocent, essentially a child, and he had drawn her with slightly cartoonish proportions and soft, round, oversize features to convey those qualities. Natwick conceived of her very differently. Befitting the man who had made his reputation animating the sex siren Betty Boop, he saw her as mature and womanly, and he dismissed Luske's models, griping that they displayed no sense of anatomy—no spine, as he put it.

That these two conceptions competed for months, with animators lining up behind one or the other, was yet another example of how the studio was groping its way on the feature, learning as it went. Was Snow White to be a fanciful, traditional cartoon character or an edgier, more realistic one? Walt again was loath to make a decision, though he finally sided with Luske, in part because Walt had always spoken of her as a girl himself, in part because Luske's Snow White was easier to draw. But even after siding with Luske, he discarded most of Luske's trial animation and had Natwick, and later Luske's assistant Jack Campbell, redraw Snow White to make her leaner, sharper, less cartoonish, and more realistic. Natwick complied, later claiming, in a complete reversal, that "Snow White was a sweet and graceful little girl and we just tried not to clown her up." Even so Natwick was so uncertain about what Walt really wanted that by his own estimate he animated twenty-six scenes before showing any of them to Walt.

But for all the head-butting between Luske and Natwick, Snow White had become, in some ways, the least of Walt's problems. A much bigger concern was the dwarfs. It had taken nearly two years to winnow the list of possibilities, and as late as November 1935, when he was already assigning animation for models and roughs, Walt had still not finalized the names of the dwarfs or their personalities. It was late that month that Walt seemed to decide that Dopey would be mute (Doc: "That's Dopey! He don't talk!"), and it wasn't until sometime in January 1936 that a dwarf named Deafy, described as a "happy sort of fellow" who nevertheless takes umbrage at what he misconstrues, due to his deafness, as criticisms and who had often been used interchangeably with Dopey, was jettisoned for Sneezy.

With the deadline rapidly approaching, Walt knew he needed help in establishing the dwarfs, some handle for the animators to grasp. As early as the summer of 1935 he had asked the gravel-voiced character actor James Gleason, one of Walt's polo compatriots, if he would recommend comedians who could be used to help shape the dwarfs by serving as models. In January 1936, apparently at Ward Kimball's suggestion, a short burlesque comedian named Eddie Collins came to the studio to perform pantomimes as Dopey in the hopes of inspiring the animators. "[H]e did all these inspirational movements with his tongue," Kimball remembered, "which was great for the soup sequence." Walt sent other animators to see Joe Jackson and His Bicycle for ideas on how the dwarfs might move. That same month actors were being auditioned for the dwarfs' voices. In

February Fred Moore and Bill Tytla produced a model sheet, which was a kind of template for the animators. (Walt always took a malicious joy in pairing opposites, as he did with the fiery Tytla and the phlegmatic Moore, hoping that there might be sparks.) But it wasn't until November, little more than a year before the feature was now scheduled to open, that Walt, realizing that time was running out and that he had still not conquered the problem, assembled his staff to discuss the dwarfs yet again.

There was clearly a sense of urgency. Throughout November and December a group of storymen and animators met regularly for hours at night in Projection Room No. 4 down the hall from Walt's office, frequently with Walt in attendance, with the express purpose, as Dave Hand told them, of working up the "characteristics of the dwarfs." "There are seven of them," he warned, "and it is indeed difficult to get a hold of each." As always Walt would act out the dwarfs at these sessions, often becoming so involved that, Thomas and Johnston said, "he forgot we were there." But despite Walt's performances and despite his repeated descriptions, the animators still wrestled with how to make each dwarf emotionally and psychologically unique while making them all look basically alike. "[T]he animators themselves don't know yet how to draw them after working all this time," Tytla admitted to a class at the time, and Tytla had *designed* the dwarfs with Moore.

Increasingly desperate, the animators tried impasting quirks onto the dwarfs to individualize them—"[W]e have got to have characteristics for each dwarf so that we can get a hold of them, and every time we have that fellow, we will pull that characteristic," said Dave Hand at one meeting—and after weeks of fruitless debate, they hired a real-life dwarf named Major George and two midgets named Erny and Tom to perform on film to suggest some poses, but Walt was unimpressed. "To me, Erny, Tom and Major George are not very cute," Walt wrote his stymied staff. "I can't help but feel sorry for them. I believe, of course, that certain characteristics should be taken from these guys, but restricted, so that their actions are not caused by deformities." Of his own dwarfs, he said, "I can't help but feel that these guys are imaginary. They are creatures of the imagination." As the animators struggled to find signature behaviors, Art Babbitt recommended they eschew the "superficial mannerism." "You have to go deeper than that," he said, sounding very much like Walt. "You have to go inside, how he feels." Walt agreed. What he really wanted was what he always wanted: personality-driven animation. "I think you have to know these fellows definitely before you can draw them," he now advised the animators.

But it was no simpler to find a personality than it was to invent little habits or tics. Trying to work from the inside out, the animators began imagining real-life analogues who seemed to capture the dwarfs: actor Roy Atwell for Doc, whom the studio had already selected to "voice" that character in the film ("He is, like Doc, a windbag type," Walt wrote. "He loves to talk of the good old days when . . ."), Otis Harlan for Happy ("Harlan has a characteristic of listening with eagerness and anticipation. His face seems to become suddenly very blank when spoken to. . . . This is contrasted by a lighting up in his face as soon as he registers what has been said."), black comic actor Stepin Fetchit for Sneezy, Will Rogers for Bashful, and at Walt's suggestion the baby-faced silent film comedian Harry Langdon for Dopey. To break the logjam, at one meeting that December Fred Moore got up and, working from notes that Perce Pearce had transcribed in conversations with Walt, began drawing poses for each of the dwarfs that he thought would express their core selves and subtly distinguish them from one another based largely on the way they carried their weight. Doc: "He is a pompous guy. Even though he is big, he has to maintain a shape." Happy: "Happy is fatter and lets his weight slip and fall down, while Doc is holding his weight up." Grumpy: "Grumpy is a chesty little guy with his chest out and a pert fanny—bow-legged. He is a very aggressive type." Bashful: "Bashful, as Walt likes him, has short legs and is plump. He is the one that always carries his head down and looks out of the corner of his eyes with chin on his chest." Sleepy: "Sleepy has a long body, leaning forward almost as though he was off balance. . . . His head seemed to be tilted up when looking, but when in a kind of slump position, his head would fall down." Sneezy: "Sneezy's head should be drawn in sort of an oblong shape with more or less pretty good-sized nose stuck up in the air with a long upper lip." And Dopey: "His sleeves hang down covering his hands. . . . He has a kid personality with small nose and eyes fairly large with a little outward slant to make them elfish."

However difficult the other dwarfs were, Dopey was the most challenging because, as Walt put it, he was the one "we are depending upon to carry most of the belly laughs." There were even some qualms about the name itself. Some objected to its being too slangy and modern or possibly suggesting a "hop-head," as Walt put it, though Walt deflected those criticisms by saying that Shakespeare had used the word and that he couldn't take seriously the connotations of drug use because "[t]hat's not the way my mind works." As for delineating the character, everyone continued to search for a peg. "Dopey has some Harpo [Marx] in him," Perce Pearce declared at one meeting, picking up on what Walt himself had said back in April, "and Walt says he is made up of Harry Langdon, a little bit of Buster Keaton, and a little trace of Chaplin in the fellow. What I am getting to is that Dopey has a little bit of everything in him." The problem with this characterization was that there was only a thin line between being a little bit of everything and being nothing at all.

"The boys couldn't seem to get him at all," Walt would say years later. "They tried to make him too much of an imbecile, which was not what we had in mind," though Walt himself had contributed to this notion. "He is slow at figuring things out, the way [Stan] Laurel does," Walt said at an extended discussion of Dopey that December. "Dopey can't even get the spoon right. He has a hold of it in such a manner that when he dips the spoon down in the soup, he brought it up in such a way that it would be upside down with no soup in it." And he invoked Harry Langdon once again, recalling a scene where the comedian is invited to tag along with a group of coworkers at a factory, and he is so pleased to be with them that he keeps running ahead of them and looking back, beaming. But if Walt described Dopey as eager and addled, like Walt's old uncle Ed, he also insisted that he be cute. "I think the thing that expresses Dopey best is that he hasn't grown up—sort of childish," he told one meeting, which didn't seem to help the animators much. In a sign of their floundering, Dave Hand, again grasping at straws, suggested they invite Eddie Collins back to the studio to act out Dopey's part in the hope that he might stimulate them.

As Walt described it, the breakthrough came when they decided to think of Dopey not as an elf or as an innocent or as a child but as a "human with dog mannerisms and intellect," thus reverting to an idea in a note he had sent his staff a year earlier describing Dopey as "in a way like Pluto." "You know the way a dog will be so intent on sniffing a trail that he doesn't see the rabbit right in front of him," Walt said, "—and when the rabbit scurries away the dog does a delayed take? That's the way Dopey was. We made him able to move one ear independently of the other, the way a dog can shake off a fly. And when Dopey had a dream, he pawed with his hand the way a dog does while sleeping." With that decision, the dwarfs were finally solved, albeit provisionally, since everything on *Snow White* was provisional, and on January 8, 1937, Walt was able to issue a memo that had been a long time coming: "Details that Are to Be on Dwarfs, OK'd by Walt." Now the real work of bringing the vision to the screen could begin.

V

All the months during which Walt and the staff had been fine-tuning the script and ruminating about the dwarfs, they had had other, equally urgent tasks to complete if the feature was to be ready for its scheduled premiere in December 1937. For one thing, the animators drew to the voice track, so before they could animate any of the scenes in which characters spoke, voices had to be cast and the dialogue recorded. Early in 1936, several of the dwarfs had been cast with the actors who had inspired them—Atwell for Doc and Harlan for Happy—though storyman Pinto Colvig, who had done a live reel of Grumpy for Tytla, did two voices, Grumpy and Sleepy, veteran movie comedian Billy Gilbert who had a trademark sneeze voiced Sneezy, and longtime movie bit player Scotty Mattraw performed Bashful.

The studio auditioned dozens of actresses for the Queen, most of whom, according to Bill Cottrell, had been fatally affected by a cackling witch on a popular radio program. When Lucille La Verne, who had played La Vengeance in David Selznick's *A Tale of Two Cities*, auditioned, Cottrell offered her the storyboards to peruse, but she declined. "She read the lines," Cottrell recalled. "You could have recorded it and used the first reading she gave, she was so good. And when she came to the transition [to the peddler], she concluded with a blood-chilling, maniacal laugh that rang all through the sound stage." (According to Joe Grant, La Verne assumed the peddler woman's voice by removing her false teeth.) She was hired immediately.

As for Snow White, by one account 150 girls were tested for the part, allegedly among them Deanna Durbin, who would later become an acclaimed child star at Universal but whom Walt rejected because he thought she sounded like a thirty-year-old woman. Virginia Davis, who had played Alice in the Alice comedies a decade earlier, said that she had done some preliminary live action for the character and was set to do the voice when she rejected the contract as unacceptable. The successful aspirant, eighteen-year-old Adriana Caselotti, would always tell the story of how her father, a voice teacher, was talking on the phone to a talent scout at the Disney studio when she overheard the conversation on the extension and recommended herself for the job. As Walt told it, his talent scout would bring candidates to the studio and have Walt paged when the man thought he had a possibility. Walt would then head to his office next to the soundstage and listen in on a speaker so that the candidate's appearance wouldn't affect his judgment. When he heard Caselotti, he remarked, "She sounds to me like a fourteen-year-old girl," which was exactly what he had been looking for. She was signed for a nominal fee and recorded her first tracks on January 20, 1936.

At roughly the same time he was casting the voices, Walt was also working on the music, though like everything else on the project, the process dragged on for well over a year. Walt had always thought of *Snow*

White in musical terms, even describing the dialogue poetically, "not rhymed or definite beat rhythm," he told one story session, "but [it should] have meter, and at the right time, tie in with the music, so the whole thing has musical pattern . . . phrasing and fitting the mood to get away from straight dialogue." The immediate question—and one that was another source of continuous debate—was what kind of music would best suit the film. Walt was suspicious of modern popular music. "I don't like the Cab Calloway idea or too much OH DE OH DO," he explained during a discussion of the sequence in which the dwarfs entertain Snow White. "Audiences hear a lot of hot stuff. If we can keep this quaint, it will appeal more than the hot stuff."

As the staff worked to balance the quaint with the "peppy," per Walt's instructions, they also struggled with instrumentation. During one session where storyman and lyricist Larry Morey sang "You're Never Too Old to Be Young," which was later excised from the film, a long discussion ensued over how the dwarfs would present the song—Walt actually performed a Swiss dance, slapping his fanny to demonstrate what he imagined—and over what instruments they would play. To record an experimental track for the entertainment sequence, as Frank Thomas and Ollie Johnston remembered it, about thirty employees gathered and were "blowing on bottles and jugs and strange homemade instruments." Listening, Walt was pleased. "Yeah! That's a happy song . . . a happy group!" he said, and added that the only thing missing was someone yodeling. Sound effects man Jim Macdonald did, creating what would become a memorable moment in the film.

The staff began recording the songs in January 1936 and continued into 1937, but Walt, who attended many of these sessions, was no more satisfied with the music than he had been with the animation. As late as spring 1937, he was still instructing his staff how he wanted the dwarfs to sing ("Bashful could half talk and half sing. You can bring their personalities in there"), still complaining that one track lacked rhythm, and still working on new verses for "The Silly Song," even though the film was then less than six months from its completion date. In fact, he had sample verses played for the staff one afternoon and asked them to vote for their six favorites. (Walt even dragooned Lillian into voting.) But for all his refining and procrastinating in hopes of breaking new ground, he continued to be disappointed that the songs were not fully integrated into the film. "It's still that influence from the musicals they have been doing for years," Walt grumbled after reviewing a sequence. "Really we should set a new pattern. I hope we can do it in Bambi . . . a new way to use music; weave it into the story so somebody doesn't just bust [*sic*] into song."

This was always the injunction. It had to be different, better in all respects, and while Walt was seeking a way to make *Snow White* musically distinctive, he was also pressing to make it visually distinctive, not only in the style of its animation but in its palette too. Walt had worked for years to improve the colors on his cartoons. Though after much trial and error he used water opaque paints manufactured by the F. R. Miller Paint Company, inkers and painters complained of mildew, streaking, tackiness, lack of intensity, lumpiness, limited range, and staining. Walt sought to devise a solution. Eventually the studio developed its own binder, which held the paint together, with a gum arabic base that was even rewettable so that painters could correct mistakes. The studio also ground all of its own paint with a set of disk mills that had once been used to grind food, and it installed a spectraphotometer, one of only twenty in the world at the time, to measure colors exactly. By one count the Disney painting department had twelve hundred distinct pigments. Knowing that Technicolor couldn't reproduce them exactly, Walt had a large chart on the wall, some six or seven feet high, showing how the colors would register on the screen.

Ever since *Flowers and Trees*, color had been a preoccupation of Walt's, and some critics would credit him with being the first film artist to use color expressively rather than realistically, which usually meant that he deployed bright pop colors that one couldn't find in nature. That may have been perfectly acceptable for shorts, but for *Snow White* he had something else in mind. Speaking of a Harman-Ising cartoon he had seen recently, Walt told his layout men that he was striving for a more artistic effect. "They got colors everywhere," he said, "and it looks cheap. There is nothing subtle about it at all. It's just poster-like. A lot of people think that's what a cartoon should have. I think we are trying to achieve something different here. We are not going after the comic supplement coloring. We have to strive for a certain depth and realism." The color of the shorts, he instructed, would "begin to wear you out," were they to be used in a feature. Rather he needed a more muted palette, more earth tones, and some darker sequences where one could rest one's eyes. He even thought the application of the color had to be different in *Snow White* than in the shorts; where the colors in the shorts were typically bold and unsculptured, requiring that the paint girls simply fill in the outlines, *Snow White* had a soft, modeled, chiaroscuro effect that broke sharply with animation tradition and required more care. It was painterly.

To achieve the "depth and realism" he wanted, Walt also relied on his layout men to provide rich, detailed backgrounds: "For *Snow White*, . . . they had draftsmen working with the different storymen, and each gag man had his draftsman who did a beautiful, detailed drawing of the simplest gag," artist Carl Barks told an interviewer. "If it was nothing more than Dopey wriggling his nose, there was a $2,000 painting." The man chiefly responsible for conceptualizing these paintings, if not actually putting the brush to the canvas, was the longtime studio sketch artist Albert Hurter, who had drawn the initial sketches of the little pigs that Fred Moore rounded into the final characters. Even among the eccentrics at Hyperion, the Swiss-born Hurter, one of the oldest employees at just over fifty, was known for his peculiarities. "He'd just sit all day and scribble," recalled Eric Larson. "He didn't want to be involved in detailed layouts or the detailed this or that, but he wanted to be an inspiration." By one account, Hurter produced fifty to one hundred sketches each day—everything from Snow White herself to the dwarfs' cottage to the furniture inside the cottage to the forest. Obsessed with his drawings and lashed to his board, he arrived at the studio punctually at eight o'clock each morning, drew frantically and chain-smoked cigars, stayed until exactly five o'clock each afternoon, and never socialized with the staff or apparently had much of a life beyond his work, though some believed it was because he suffered from severe heart disease and felt he had to conserve his energy. On weekend excursions Larson and his wife occasionally ran into Hurter driving furiously across the desert, seemingly headed nowhere.

But Walt valued him and early on entrusted him with designing virtually everything in the film, even having him provide preliminary sketches of the characters. "I remember quite clearly [Walt] looking at some old things [Hurter had drawn]," Eric Larson said, "and he'd just go hog wild and give Albert a lot more things for Albert to work out." That made Hurter the closest thing to a visual mastermind on *Snow White*—the one who devised the overall Germanic look of the film by incorporating European illustration and painting techniques into the animation. In effect, he served as set designer, set decorator and costumer, and though Dave Hand as supervising director gave the head of the layout department, Sam Armstrong, nominal authority on "all prop coloring, background, figures, etc.," Hurter had specific authority to approve the style and the characters from scene to scene and make sure they were consistent. As Hand put it when Walt objected to some rocks in a background that Hurter had not okayed, "Albert knows the character of the picture better than anyone."

But if Hurter was the mastermind, he was nevertheless part of a team that was dedicated to Walt's vision of a more sophisticated visual field. Another European-born artist, Hungarian Ferdinand Horvath, provided preliminary drawings, and by the time animation was under way in 1936, Hurter and Horvath had been joined by the highly regarded Swedish-born illustrator Gustaf Tenggren, who helped conceptualize Snow White's flight in the forest and the dwarfs' pursuit of the peddler woman. Because these artists' renderings were so much more detailed than the backgrounds of the shorts, the studio had to introduce a new size of animation paper—from 9½ by 12 inches to 12½ by 12 inches—to accommodate them, and because they were so much more painterly the studio created a new texture by wetting the paper, squeezing off the excess moisture, and then applying watercolor with washes.

Yet however much the muted palette and detailed layouts contributed to realism and however much they suggested depth, when Walt spoke of the latter he was not only being figurative. He meant "depth" literally as well—another means of shaping a more fully realized environment, for a man who was always seeking to shape his environment to his own specifications. He was also thinking of the audience, which was accustomed to depth from live-action films.* "He was afraid eighty minutes of flat, one-dimensional animation would prove too hard for the public to take," his daughter Diane would write, reiterating Walt's argument about the need for subtler colors. Audiences needed more visual variety in a feature than they got in animated shorts.

The problem with traditional animation was that it was virtually impossible to replicate the changing perspectives of real life without constantly changing the size of the backgrounds in relation to the animated figures—a task that was prohibitively expensive. Ken Anderson remembered Walt, in discussions on *Snow White* as early as 1935, pushing for better ways to create the illusion of depth, and that year he had Anderson draw both the figures and the backgrounds in a scene for a Silly Symphony titled *Three Orphan Kittens*, apparently just so Walt could see what a more realistic, ever-changing perspective would look like. Wanting to push further for *Snow White*, Walt assigned Anderson to work with special effects animator Cy Young, lighting expert Hal Halvenston, and engineer Bill Garity to create actual layers of action for a test of the peddler woman in the forest—layers that would convey actual depth and perspective that a single cel set onto a background could not convey. As Anderson recalled it, they modeled trees from clay in the foreground and then drew three planes of animated trees receding into the frame, which they placed on large glass plates. The trees, the plates, and the camera were then

*Here Disney was anticipating the deep-focus photography that director Orson Welles would use so famously in *Citizen Kane* to create a psychological effect from spatial relationships. Though Walt was obviously looking for a greater sense of physical realism, he was also, if only subliminally, looking for a greater sense of psychological realism, which was what deep focus provided.

mounted on sawhorses as the crew experimented with distances. Walt was pleased with the result and ordered another test—this time of the dwarfs' cottage and Snow White. The real showcase, however, came when Walt, in a ruling reminiscent of the switch of *Flowers and Trees* from black-and-white to color, decided early in 1937 to transform a Silly Symphony then in production called *The Old Mill* from a traditional two-dimensional, cel-on-background short into one deploying planes of action like the tests.

It was difficult enough to photograph a cel on a background with a static camera. Photographing several planes of cels—from foreground to middle ground to background—while a camera seemed to move through them may have been the most imposing feat of animation to date. Also seeking to simulate three-dimensionality, Ub Iwerks had already built a "multiplane" camera at his own studio out of old Chevrolet parts, but it was so technically daunting to use that he deployed it infrequently. Walt was not so easily dissuaded. For *The Old Mill*, which was essentially a tone poem about animals nesting in an abandoned mill as a storm approaches, he had his machine shop construct its own multiplane camera. It was a huge, heavy, vertical box-shaped contraption, standing nearly twelve feet tall on four metal stanchions with one level at the top for the camera and four levels or shelves below for four layers of animation, and it required at least four men to operate it—though depending on the difficulty of the shot, there could be as many as eight men clambering around on it, each cranking his level one-hundredth of an inch forward to simulate a dolly or left and right to simulate a pan. Because each level had to be separately lit—by eight five-hundred-watt bulbs—and because the multiplane was necessarily situated in a closed dark room, the heat was unbearable. Moreover, since the staff had no experience with the camera, shooting on *The Old Mill* was painfully slow—more painful to Walt because he wanted to see results as soon as possible so that he could use the camera for *Snow White*, which was already deep into animation.

Still, Walt revered his multiplane, regarding it as the ultimate toy—both a key to his much-desired realism and a monument to his own success. "It was always my ambition to own a swell camera," he joked to *Time* the week *Snow White* opened, "and now, goddammit, I got one. I get a kick just watching the boys operate it, and remembering how I used to have to make 'em out of baling wire." Of course, it was what the multiplane did that made it so impressive. As the camera seemed to move through the layers or panned across them, animation gained for the first time a sense of real perspective and a three-dimensionality so astonishing that Thomas and Johnston said of the basically plotless *The Old Mill* that it demonstrated that "an audience could be swept up by sheer subtlety and become deeply involved in an animated film." Eric Larson gushed over the cartoon—the way the multiplane combined with the effects "to give you the beauty of the wind," or the way the raindrops "had not the hard outline feeling to them, but the real feeling of the rain," or the way the clouds were "soft and moving and . . . in their density went from real heavy clouds to light clouds to blue sky in such a subtle way." One observer fretted that the multiplane might prove too powerful, too much an end in itself. "Even in the eyes of the Studio," he wrote, "it is considered an instrument so loaded with artistic dynamite that, if not properly handled, it may blast the animated sound picture completely off its course."

But that was not Walt Disney's concern. For him, the multiplane was blasting *Snow White* further along its course, beyond animation to where it could challenge and even surpass live-action films. For him, the multiplane brought *Snow White* closer to realism and closer to his own fully realized world.

VI

It had become an incessant refrain: *time was running out.* In the late winter of 1936 Walt and Roy had closed a new distribution deal with RKO, a much larger operation than United Artists and one with more clout in the marketplace, which was what the Disneys needed. "[T]he big studios that have their own cartoons practically give away their cartoons with their feature pictures," Roy wrote his parents shortly after signing with RKO. "We, all of the time, have to stand on our own feet without any tie-in with any other product." Walt had been dissatisfied with UA for some time, complaining that the distributor was taking too big a share of the foreign receipts and insisting that while "competitive cartoons are falling by the wayside fast," Disney cartoons were "steadily increasing in audience value." When Roy importuned Walt to give UA a chance, Walt wrote back disgustedly, "If you would resign from U.A. and come over and work for Disney for a while, we might be able to make some headway. . . . In repentance, I suggest that you give them the plant, our trademarks, patents and copyrights, and work for them on a salary—or if perhaps they are not satisfied with this, I can go and get a job with Mintz and you can sell vacuum cleaners, again." In the end, with the blessings of the united artists themselves—Chaplin wrote Lessing that "I don't want to make any money on Walt, and anything I can ever do for him I will gladly perform"—the Disneys departed. One of the stated reasons for severing ties with UA was that it had wanted to retain television rights, and Walt, who had taken an early and avid interest in television, refused to grant them. A more likely reason, though, was that Walt and finally Roy too wanted the power of RKO behind *Snow White*, and RKO's chairman, M. H. Aylesworth, in announcing the compact with Disney, said, "[P]ersonally I have seen enough of his first feature length cartoon, 'Snow White,' to realize that it will rate as one of the most unusual features ever turned out in the field of animated cartoons."

Of course Aylesworth couldn't have seen much of *Snow White* at that point because there was very little to show. But Walt was eager to please his new distributor, which was apparently one of the reasons he embarked on *The Old Mill*—to make a big splash. In contracting to provide six Silly Symphonies and twelve Mickey Mouses (these included Donald Duck cartoons as well) for the coming year, after he had fulfilled his UA obligations, Walt intended "to make at least half of the Symphonies of the very beautiful, charming type, with musical, fantasy stuff," and urged RKO to sell them as a block, which "enables us to put in subjects about which we may feel inspired" rather than just slapstick comedies. But if Walt was determined to impress RKO, RKO was determined to get *Snow White*, and Walt had committed himself to presenting a print in November 1937 for a Christmas release. Now he was under tremendous pressure to deliver.

After what had amounted to years of deliberation and procrastination, he had reached the winter of 1937 with virtually the entire film left to animate and less than ten months to do so. Indeed, though the animation had begun in 1936, the first cels weren't sent to ink and paint until January 4, 1937, and didn't reach the camera department until March 13. "Many felt that to have the finished picture ready for showing by Christmas 1937 was impossible," Dave Hand later confessed, "but we responsible ones never wavered." Walt spent the spring either sweatboxing roughs for hours on end, usually whenever an animator had finished enough to show him, even if the entire scene was not complete, or meeting for long stretches with the storymen to refine sequences that had not yet gone to animation, once again line by line, inflection by inflection. The scene in which the dwarfs enter their cottage thinking it is inhabited by ghosts, one of the first discussed and one that had already been subjected to dozens of meetings, was the subject of another twenty meetings from early January to the end of September, many of them at night, and those were only the sessions with Walt in attendance. By July, Walt was in the sweatbox all day long, day after day, examining roughs. There was no detail, not a nod, a wink, an emphasis, or a posture, that wasn't still being analyzed.

The animators felt "tremendous pressure," Ollie Johnston said, and tempers began to flare. Dave Hand, the supervising director, reached the point where he couldn't talk to an animator without screaming. When Les Clark had trouble with a scene and tried to explain his problems, Hand exploded, knocking the drawing board into the air and bellowing, "We gotta get the picture out!" Aware that he was becoming a target of the animators' wrath, Hand protested, "My criticism is all impersonal and I don't hesitate to criticize anybody in the Studio excepting Walt." But tensions ran so high that Hand *did* criticize Walt. Hand had objected that one prospective scene played too long, and when Walt offered to perform it to prove that it wasn't too long, Hand secretly started a stopwatch in his pocket, then pulled it out to show by how much Walt had exceeded the allotted time. By Hand's own admission, Walt was "boiling mad" and stalked out of the room.

Trying to avoid these confrontations, Hal Adelquist, who had been named the head assistant director early in February, advised his staff not to take issues to Hand or Walt unless they absolutely had to. "We must avoid taking up the time of men who are making more money and whose time is therefore worth more," he said. But this created another problem. Employees doubted whether the orders they received had really come from Walt, prompting one department head to ask Walt to give his staff a pep talk. Walt responded by offering to throw them a dinner as a way both of asserting his authority and of lessening tensions, since a dinner "might put them in a more receptive mood and make the evening more beneficial to them." It wasn't the only time Walt had to boost flagging spirits. Many of the animators were now despairing of ever completing the project satisfactorily, and Walt complained that once scenes were finished and ready for cleanup, the animators seemed to lose the initiative in assuring that everything was ready for the camera. "This picture is a tremendous thing," Adelquist told the assistant directors, delivering instructions from Walt. "You think you will never be finished. There seems to be twice as much work on your desk at night when you leave, but if you will just keep plugging and checking I am sure you will find that things will work out all right."

Once again, needing more in-betweeners to rush the animation through, the studio was calling for trainees, taking out ads in magazines or recruiting at art schools—George Drake went to Chouinard himself to enlist artists—and running the prospects through an expedited program, all the while reinforcing how important their mission was in getting out *Snow White*. But with all the emphasis on speed, there was always the contradictory message of quality. At one class that June, Bill Tytla, indoctrinating the students in the Disney method, told them, "The work now being planned and the work they will continue to do here will call for men who can draw to beat hell, not just in the conventional sense, but men who have absolute control over what they are trying to do. The men who are surviving realize this." And he continued, "Today we are really on the verge of something that is new. It will take a lot of real drawing, not clever, slick, superficial fine-looking stuff but real solid, fine drawing to achieve these results."

As the summer approached and the deadline loomed, Hand took drastic action. For over a year the animators had been viewing live-action films, not only of the dwarfs but of the witch, who was played variously by a stage actor named Nestor Pavia and by the man who would voice the Magic Mirror, Moroni Olsen, dressed in drag, and of Snow White, who was played by Marjorie Belcher, the teenage daughter of a local dance instructor. (She would later marry dancer and choreographer Gower Champion and form a popular dance team with him in the 1950s.) Walt had even attempted to combine live footage of Belcher with a model of the dwarfs' cottage as designed by Albert Hurter. These films were intended to provide inspiration or suggest movement and behavior. "I think you can use this live action to get personalities, etc. that you are bound to absorb ideas that creep into your work," Fred Moore said at one meeting, while Art Babbitt, saying that the animators had been focusing too narrowly on mechanics, claimed that "we are getting something now that would take us years and years to acquire." By February all the important action of the dwarfs was being shot live first, and the animators were actually going to the soundstage and directing the live-action scenes themselves—with Pinto Colvig putting on a big nose and playing Grumpy or Sneezy or Eddie Collins playing Dopey or Dave Hand or Perce Pearce playing the other dwarfs to an audio playback of the dialogue. The animator then watched the developed film through a viewfinder and chose poses he liked. Walt feared that the animators would wind up copying the live action—"Stress the point over and over again that when drawing models, get the feeling behind the models instead of copying them," Babbitt told one meeting in expressing Walt's view—and explicitly ordered, as Sharpsteen recalled, that "he did not want any animators tracing that character and putting it on the screen as a tracing; they had to use it only as a guide."

But under the increasing pressure, Walt's order was breached. The staff had to trace live action—what was called "rotoscoping"—to finish the film on time. "Live action is what is going to lick the picture," Hand announced at one luncheon meeting in mid-February. Though Ham Luske was recommending that they bring in child actors to play the dwarfs in scale, this was especially true of Snow White and the Queen—the human characters that were still proving so difficult to animate well.

Already by March, Perce Pearce was suggesting that they do more rotoscoping of Snow White—"There is a lot of Snow White that has to be worked out in rotoscope"—and by June, photostats of the Queen coming down the stairs were being given to the in-betweeners to trace. There were certainly misgivings about having to do this, a sense almost of cheating, though the live action often betrayed how far the animators still had to go to capture reality. "[Y]ou look at some of that live action," Eric Larson admitted years later, "and it was actually more animated than we finally got on the screen in some, some instances." Still, Walt was adamant that the rotoscoping be concealed from the public. In preparing the publicity campaign, he dictated that no live action be shown. "I want this definitely left out as people will get the wrong impression of it," he wrote publicity chief Roy Scott. "The only thing we might say is that we use live models for the purposes of studying action, etc., but we do not photograph live action and blow up our drawings from same"—although, in fact, that was exactly what they did.

There was so little time and now more measures were needed to meet the deadline and tighten the film itself. Scenes had to be "snapped up," Walt said, "retaining all the good business, but snapping it up and taking out the excess dialogue." And the snapping-up even extended to cutting scenes altogether. As early as November 1936, storyman Dick Creedon had suggested the possibility of lopping two scenes—one in which the dwarfs meet to discuss whether they should let Snow White stay or, fearing repercussions from the Queen, make her leave, and another in which the dwarfs, having resolved to let her stay, decide to build her a bed so that she will not want to leave. "I don't think it has any purpose in the story now and will divert us at a point where we should start building our suspense tempo," Creedon asserted. Unconvinced, Walt proceeded to have the scenes animated anyway, as well as another in which the dwarfs are eating soup under the reproachful eye of Snow White, who is trying to teach them manners, though he warned of the bed-building: "Take out all the superfluous stuff." The scenes were still in the picture as late as June 1937—they hadn't even been finalized until April—but Walt, like Creedon, finally decided they had to go because they disrupted the flow of the narrative. Ward Kimball, who had animated the bulk of the soup-eating sequence, was crushed. He had spent nearly a year and a half on the section.

As Walt cut and rushed and pressed, the animators began to buckle under the pressure. As they fell behind schedule, one rumor had it that the Bank of America would soon take over the company—a prospect, wrote animator Shamus Culhane, that "created a feeling of tension in the studio that almost made the air crackle." Yet even as they were urged to speed up, they felt dread in producing anything that might disappoint Walt and dread in letting anyone else clean up and possibly sap their drawings' energy, so they withheld their footage from final cleanup even after it had been approved, resulting in a massive slowdown just when things should have been accelerating. "You fellows are all trying to get your work as good as possible," Dave Hand told them ruefully after learning that they were spending an average of two hours on each drawing. "We are in sympathy with that, but we are not in sympathy with the fact that you are so carefully watching every detail that you are not allowing it to move through"—an odd admonition at a studio where everyone knew Walt himself carefully watched every detail. It was a sign of the growing desperation that by July animators were being asked not to have their scenes cleaned up but rather to "finish the details in the rough state as this will be complete enough for the Inking of this fast action." By this point some of the animators were so benumbed that they found release by doing sketches of a nude Snow White surrounded by tumescent dwarfs—a way, opined Ward Kimball, to challenge the suffocating perfection of Walt Disney's world.

As they headed into the fall, the staff was working twenty-four hours a day in eight-hour shifts, and many of them worked on Saturdays and Sundays as well, for which, as further proof of their commitment to the cult, they received no overtime pay. The animation lightboards would grow so hot that the artists could burn their arms and hands. So many cels remained to be photographed that the camera department worked in two twelve-hour shifts—from eight o'clock to eight o'clock. Effects specialist Cy Young needed surgery but postponed it because he was working on the "ideal achievement," and when one animator asked for a leave because he was having to support his two brothers and their families and because he felt he was in a "rut," Walt snapped, "I suggest you get down to business and forget all about the situation and make the best of the opportunities you have here." To help out in ink and paint, Walt borrowed girls from the Harman-Ising studio, headed by two of his old Kansas City colleagues who had recently lost a contract to produce cartoons for MGM. As for the shorts, Roy prepared to farm some out to Harman-Ising while the entire studio shifted to *Snow White*, opining that RKO should have no cause of action since Walt would remain the nominal supervisor. "With all this additional help," Roy wrote Gunther Lessing, "it should increase our chances considerably of getting 'Snow White' out by Christmas." In the event, the studio discontinued the shorts entirely until the feature was finished.

But whatever pressures his staff suffered, the greatest pressures were on Walt Disney himself. Though he took a two-week business trip to New York in mid-May, in part to plan the publicity for *Snow White* with RKO, he was effectively holed up at the studio. "UNEXPECTED BUSINESS HAS COME UP THAT REQUIRES MY BEING AT STUDIO ALL DAY SATURDAY," he wired one acquaintance that July, begging off a social engagement. "WORKING LIKE HELL TRYING TO GET FEATURE FINISHED." Excusing himself from another social obligation, he wired film producer Hal Roach, "THE SUPER COLOSSAL SNOW WHITE HAS ME HOGTIED AND OUR ENTIRE STUDIO IS WORKING NIGHTS TO GET THE PICTURE OUT FOR CHRISTMAS." And Walt was not working only on *Snow White*. That August he was already meeting with storymen to set the structure for the first part of *Bambi*, and in November he was devoting many of his mornings to a short adapted from Munro Leaf's book *Ferdinand* about a shy, effete bull who didn't want to fight in the ring.

Added to all these demands was another, terribly familiar one: money. When, at the outset, Walt had told Roy that *Snow White* was likely to cost around $250,000, he was wildly miscalculating, as he later confessed, since by the late 1930s they were spending roughly that much on every three Silly Symphonies. Still, when Roy approached the Bank of America for a loan in August 1935, realizing that the entire financing would have to come from outside the studio, he asked for that amount. "Our only difficulty in securing the money," he wrote Walt confidently, "I believe, will be because of the length of time involved in making the feature, and not the condition of our business."

But as the length of time in production dragged on, the budget was ballooning. They had been forced to take another loan from the Bank of America for $630,000 in May 1936, and yet another for an additional $650,000 in March 1937, to be secured by the residual value of the short subjects. (This was what Walt meant when he told a reporter that "I had to mortgage everything I owned, including Mickey Mouse and Donald Duck and everybody else," to make *Snow White*.) Now tensions with Roy surfaced. "Roy was very brave and manly until the costs passed over a million," Walt said a few years later. "He wasn't used to figures over a hundred thousand at that time. The extra cipher threw him. When costs passed the one and one-half million mark, Roy didn't even bat an eye. He couldn't; he was paralyzed." In fact, Roy did everything he could to press Walt to reduce the budget, even inviting their Bank of America liaison, Joe Rosenberg, to the studio to have a talk with him, which was the ultimate ploy since Walt never dealt with the money men.

The Yale-educated Rosenberg was new to Hollywood, though he was hardly a tenderfoot. As a young man, he had ridden a horse 320 miles from Nevada to Arizona and forded the Colorado River to claim a job a friend had promised, and he had worked as a surveyor for a Mexican railroad and as a mining engineer before changing course and entering banking. When Bank of America head Doc Giannini assigned him to the Disney account and to *Snow White*, Rosenberg began making calls to Hollywood notables. Some warned him off the project, but producer Walter Wanger, one of Walt's polo cronies, told him, "Joe, if Disney does this thing as well as I know he's going to do it, millions of people will love it." Rosenberg later said that was all he needed to hear. But now Walt was chafing under the financial strain. As Rosenberg later remembered it, when he came to the studio early in 1937 to plead with Walt, Walt groused that bankers were all "a bunch of SOB's." Walt denied he said it, insisting he just called them "goddamn bankers."

Unfortunately, as *Snow White* inched forward, with Walt spending $20,000 a week, he needed the "goddamn bankers." Though Roy had written Walt after the March loan that "we are confident it is sufficient for our purposes; at least, until way late in the year," by September the studio was in need of another infusion of cash. That month, after the Disneys had asked for yet another loan, this one for $327,000, Rosenberg came to the studio one tense Saturday afternoon to watch a rough cut of *Snow White*, grudgingly hosted by Walt. Rosenberg sat through the screening silently while Walt nervously explained how certain scenes that were now just in pencil sketch would later be inked and colored. Even after the screening, as they headed to the parking lot, Rosenberg avoided talking about the film, only heightening the tension. When Rosenberg reached his car, he slid inside, said good-bye, and deadpanned, "That thing is going to make you a hatful of money." Then he drove off.

Or at least that was how Walt would tell it years later, as another example of his fortitude and the rightness of his vision. In fact, for all his professed reluctance to let anyone see *Snow White* before its completion, he had screened the color rushes of the film on the soundstage early one evening in September for the studio staff. (According to Frank Thomas, Walt was still so "innocent and unsophisticated" that he hurried Lillian from home for fear that they wouldn't have a seat.) It was a triumphant evening. As Walt wrote RKO head Ned Depinet, "[D]espite the fact that most of the audience have been pretty close to the development of SNOW WHITE for the past two and a half years—their reaction was all that could be hoped for from any audience." Walt had passed out a questionnaire—since Morkovin had worked at the studio, Walt routinely passed out questionnaires at the studio screenings—asking whether any sections seemed too long or whether any business was objectionable or whether any character's personality seemed inconsistent over the course of the picture and also for a scene-by-scene analysis. Of the 359 respondents, only one said he didn't enjoy the film. "Stick to shorts!"* the dissident apparently wrote on his card, words Walt would thereafter employ as a way of cutting anyone who displayed faulty judgment. "If you were trying to sell an idea that did not jell or go over in a meeting," Thomas and Johnston remembered, "suddenly there would be this loud, '*Ah haaa!*' and Walt's finger would come shooting out toward you; in a triumphant voice he would explain, '*You* must be the guy who said "Stick to Shorts!" ' And for that day you *were* the guy, and everyone else would keep looking at you and wondering."

For *Snow White*, however, the dissenters were few. Diane Disney, who wasn't quite four years old at the time, watched the film at a screening on the soundstage while peeking through her fingers and began to bawl when the Queen turned into the crone. The child was promptly escorted from the room. "Obviously, my reaction didn't deter my father from making the movie he envisioned," she would later say. Nearly everyone else seemed elated by what they saw—even cautious Roy. "I am so glad you are so enthusiastic about the way Snow White looks," Kay Kamen, the head of the studio's merchandising arm, wrote him. "I am just thrilled—it's really big time stuff."

When Walt screened one thousand feet of the film for Joe Rosenberg, Depinet, and several other RKO executives on that Saturday afternoon, September 14, they seemed equally enthusiastic. Depinet congratulated Walt on the picture and on his courage in making it and said it would make "plenty of money," then fired off a telegram to RKO chairman M. H. Aylesworth raving about the film. "Ned says your investment will be returned many times over," Aylesworth wrote Walt. In fact, according to Gunther Lessing, who also attended the screening, the only one who didn't seem especially effusive was Rosenberg. He followed Lessing to his office, declared himself "satisfied" with the film, and then met with Walt to warn him not to spend any money on *Bambi* until *Snow White* was completed. He also expressed his own concern that the film wouldn't be finished by Christmas. If he thought it would make a "hatful of money," he didn't appear to have told Lessing or Walt, despite Walt's recollection.

The fact that money was just instrumental for Walt, a way for him to make his films, explains why he was so often at loggerheads with Roy, who

*Longtime employee John Hench would later say that Roy was the culprit, though this seems unlikely since Roy was supportive of the project from the inception. Watts, *Magic Kingdom*, p. 426.

was charged with providing that money. "He keeps on hollering that I am spending too much money on Snow White," Walt complained to his staff one day. "I can't be strapped down by a limited budget." At any other studio, where the moneymen typically held the upper hand, Walt would have been curbed long before. It was only because he owned the studio himself and because it was his brother who held the key to the treasury that he hadn't been reined in and was allowed to spend. Among other things, Walt continued to insist that the staff be well compensated, despite the economic stringencies, both to get better work from them during the stretch run on *Snow White* and to fulfill his fantasy of a guild of happy artists. In February he tore up Sharpsteen's contract and awarded him a new one at $200 a week for three years. By April he was already handing out salary adjustments on *Snow White:* $2,500 to Fred Moore, $3,900 to Dave Hand and Sharpsteen, and $5,200 to Ham Luske. Most of these were paid out as additional increments in salary, though Walt would also give an animator a cash sum, as he did for Bill Tytla that April, if he thought the employee was being underpaid, or an advance if a man needed it.

Yet his generosity seemed to do little to energize the process, and the animators still seemed to be limping to the finish line. Though the average footage approved for cleanup should have been fifty feet a week if they were to make their Christmas deadline, the animators were averaging only half that as late as August. In a studio breakdown of how much footage each animator was producing each day, the results were startlingly low—among them, Tytla 1'10", Babbitt 2'2", Ferguson 4'7", Moore 2'1", Thomas 3'1". (Having worked on the picture the longest, Tytla and Moore would have the most final footage in the film—944 feet and 974 feet respectively.) Moreover, the cumbersome multiplane slowed progress even further. As late as September, many of the staff were conceding that the film probably wouldn't be ready by Christmas, and the animators were drawing right through October and into early November trying to make the schedule. The final animation wasn't completed until November 11, the last cels weren't painted until November 27, and the final photography wasn't done until December 1, just six days before the first scheduled sneak preview and just barely in time to make the general release. "It had gotten around to the theaters that there were no prints," animator Bill Peet recalled, "and we were all scared to death."

The final scenes—Snow White on her bier after taking a bite from the poison apple, the dwarfs placing flowers around her, her being awakened and riding off with the Prince—had been saved for last largely because Walt understood that they were the most difficult in the film. They were the scenes in which the audience would be invited to cry along with the dwarfs, an emotional province that animations had not previously entered, and they would constitute the major test of the film's effectiveness, though by this time Walt had little doubt they would succeed. "There is going to be a lot of sympathy for these little fellows," he said at a story conference that July. "We can tear their [the audience's] hearts out if we want to by putting in a little crying." Frank Thomas, Fred Moore's onetime assistant, was given the assignment of animating the dwarfs' grief from Albert Hurter's drawings, and he animated it with as little movement as possible—basically held poses with tears crawling down the dwarfs' cheeks and, as Walt had instructed at a story meeting, "concentrating on Grumpy when he breaks down and starts to cry," cracking his stoic facade. As with every scene, Walt tinkered with this one before cleanup—"The movement on the dwarfs is too abrupt." "As it is now there are two sort of hold positions on Grumpy that seem out of character, then suddenly he breaks." "Stagger the blinks on the animals instead of having them all blink at once."—and then he was finished. Whether he liked it or not, he had to be finished in order to deliver the film on schedule.

But he didn't like doing it. When the animators were being rushed in late spring, Dave Hand said that Walt "is actually tearing out his heart okaying some of the stuff which you know he would like to see better," and then excused him saying, "He is trying to move the picture as best he can." At one sweatbox session Walt lamented that the dwarfs acted as if they were following directions on an exposure sheet and not "as if they knew in their minds what they were going to do." At another he bemoaned that the Magic Mirror seemed to be working too hard to say his words. And at another he criticized the Queen for looking as if "she was carrying a big load of laundry," for moving suddenly without anticipation, and for having eyebrows that were too extreme. He was especially rough on Fred Moore, who had animated the dwarfs, sitting with him in the sweatbox and repeatedly reviewing his scenes, fixating again and again on the size of one of Grumpy's fingers, which Moore, intentionally or not, had refused to correct, until Walt ordered him to do so. He even grumbled that he found Adriana Caselotti's singing voice too strident. "When anybody sings, it should be good or he shouldn't sing at all," Walt told the staff. And all along he was aware of the real danger that he himself posed to his beloved project even as he was shepherding it: that it would lose spontaneity from the constant revisions. "Watch to keep it from sounding like it had been well-rehearsed," he warned at the end of one story conference. "We want spontaneous feeling in it."

In the end, even after all the final touches had been applied, Walt, ever the perfectionist, was disappointed. "We've worked hard and spent a lot of money, and by this time we're a little tired of it," he confessed to one journalist shortly after its completion. "I've seen so much of *Snow White* that I am conscious only of the places where it could be improved. You see, we've learned such a lot since we started this thing! I wish I could yank it back and do it all over again." Even more than a decade later Walt was sighing over the film's flaws. "There were some things in 'Snow White' that make me crawl when I see them now," he said. "The bridge on her nose floats all over her face. And the Prince jitters like he's got palsy." He was especially perturbed by the latter, so perturbed that Roy even suggested they reanimate the scene to eliminate the shimmying. Walt leaped at the offer, saying it would cost another $250,000 to $300,000. As Roy related it, "I said forget it." *Snow White* would be released with the shimmy.

If they had been flying blind in making the feature, they were also flying blind in promoting and distributing it. They had had experience in publicizing shorts; they had no experience in publicizing a feature film. Nevertheless, after the film's reception at the studio screenings, Walt was confident—almost too confident. He was fond of telling how, before *Snow White*'s release, many in the industry and the press had disparaged the project and called it "Disney's Folly, which one paper actually did," but this was most likely just more self-dramatization of Walt overcoming another purported hurdle, since there seemed, if anything, to be tremendous anticipation of the film almost from its inception. Indeed, at Walt's May meeting in New York with the RKO publicity staff he encouraged them not to think that the picture would sell itself just because it was a novelty. "I want everybody to be sold on it so they won't be underestimating or over-estimating the power of the picture to draw on its own," he apprised Roy of his plan. "I think we will have to do a lot of indirect selling to the press," by which he meant placing feature stories in papers and magazines.

Whatever small doubts they might have harbored over RKO's prospective publicity efforts, however, the Disneys had a much greater issue with their new distributor—one they almost seemed afraid to broach. As naïve as it may have sounded after their nearly fifteen years in the film business, they had no idea what to charge exhibitors for the film and no idea what RKO's return to them might be, which they fully realized made them vulnerable to RKO's machinations. The larger studios typically sold their films in blocks, so their advice wouldn't have been particularly helpful to a studio with only one feature to sell. What the Disneys needed was an independent producer to guide them, of which there were very few in Hollywood at the time. As it turned out, the knight who rode to their rescue was Walt's old idol, Charlie Chaplin. Chaplin offered to give the Disneys all his "records and experience," most importantly his ledgers from *Modern Times*, which permitted Roy to press RKO to "go out and ask Chaplin prices" and to get the same terms in foreign markets as Chaplin had gotten. Thanking Chaplin after *Snow White*'s release, Walt called it an "invaluable service" and wrote, "Your records have been our Bible—without them, we would have been as sheep in a den of wolves."

With the finances resolved, the day to which the entire studio had been pointing for years, December 21, 1937, was finally upon them. The last week of November Walt was filmed for a *Snow White* trailer, and the next week the studio headed en masse to Pomona, an hour's car ride east of Los Angeles, for the film's first sneak preview—its first exposure to a non-studio, nonindustry audience. As Ben Sharpsteen remembered it, most of the studio's employees were not informed, and those who were, the top personnel, arrived at the theater unceremoniously in a bus. The audience was taken totally by surprise, but only a few walked out, which apparently was a rarity for a sneak preview, and the employees left the theater feeling a sense of elation, vindication, and anticipation. With the premiere impending, the animators were so enthusiastic that they picked up posters at the studio and tacked them up all over Los Angeles.

The site of the premiere was the Carthay Circle Theater, a fifteen-hundred-seat Mission Revival–style house on San Vicente Boulevard near the Hancock Park section of Los Angeles, and the place where Walt had first shown *The Skeleton Dance* back in 1929. The Carthay was an ornate palace where searchlights roamed the skies at openings, and the *Snow White* premiere was a gala event, with grandstands packed with fans and dozens of Hollywood luminaries in attendance—a testament both to the expectations of the film and to Walt Disney's status, at only thirty-six, as an American icon. In thinking back on that evening, Walt would recall an incident that had occurred on the back platform of the train when he first headed west to Los Angeles. He was making conversation with a man there who asked what Walt did. When Walt said he was in the motion picture business, the man said he knew people in the movies and inquired what end Walt was in. "I make animated cartoons," Walt told him, which was met with a steely disdain that Walt never forgot and that led him to resolve that someday his cartoons would be afforded the same respect as live features. Now one was.

"AM CONVINCED ALL OUR FONDEST HOPES WILL BE REALIZED TONIGHT," Chaplin wired Walt that day, but despite the positive screenings, the encouraging feedback, and Walt's own brimming confidence, he still felt an inescapable anxiety, especially over how the audience would react to the dwarfs at Snow White's bier—the old anxiety over whether people could and would be moved by animated characters. Walt entered the theater both euphoric and edgy. "Well, it's been a lot of fun making it," Walt told interviewer Buddy Twist to a national radio audience, less than honestly. "And we're very happy that it's being given this big premiere here tonight and all these people are turning out to take a good look at it. And I hope they're not disappointed." Asked if he was going to be watching the film himself, he quipped, "Yes, and have my wife hold my hand."

But the nervousness that had slowly accreted from the years of imagining, scrutinizing, retelling, fiddling, mobilizing, and pushing, and from the huge debt of over a million dollars that the studio had incurred in the process, quickly dissipated. "I believe everyone in that first *Snow White* audience could have predicted the enormous success of the film," wrote the normally dyspeptic animator Bill Peet. "They were carried away by the picture from the very beginning, and as it went along everyone was bubbling over with enthusiasm and frequently bursting into spontaneous applause." Ken O'Connor, an art director on the film, said of the audience, "They even applauded the background and layouts when no animation was on the screen." O'Connor was sitting near the actor John Barrymore, who began "bouncing up and down in his seat he was so excited" when the shot of the Queen's castle came on screen with the Queen poling her boat through the fog.

But the "highlight," as Ward Kimball put it, was the bier scene. "Clark Gable and Carole Lombard were sitting close, and when Snow White was poisoned, stretched out on that slab, they started blowing their noses. I could hear it—crying—that was the big surprise. We worried about the serious stuff and whether they would feel for this girl, and when they did, I knew it was in the bag." Everyone in the theater seemed to be crying and dabbing at his or her eyes. And at the end the audience exploded into what one attendee called a "thunderous ovation." Even the animators seemed to be in awe of the achievement. "I don't know how we did it," Grim Natwick told an interviewer years later. "I don't think anyone really does."

"I have made a wager that the picture will set up grosses nearing the record mark and I expect to buy an Argentine pony with the money I shall win," producer Hunt Stromberg wrote Walt after the premiere. Expressing their "profound admiration," Harman and Ising wired Walt, "OUR PRIDE IN THE PRODUCTION IS SCARCELY LESS THAN YOURS MUST BE AND WE ARE GRATEFUL TO YOU FOR FULFILLING AN AMBITION WHICH MANY OF

US HAVE LONG HELD FOR OUR INDUSTRY." Producer Nat Levine compared it to the first sound film and said that in attending the premiere, "I could not help but feel that I was in the midst of motion picture history." Director Cecil B. DeMille sent a telegram saying, "I WISH I COULD MAKE PICTURES LIKE SNOW WHITE." And even Joe Rosenberg, who had seemed so grudging at the September screening, wrote Walt, "It's probably too soon to talk 'Box office' but regardless of the latter I shall always say it's a truly great job which you and your gang have done—and a lot of people will be happier for it."

The reviewers were no less ecstatic. Writing in *The New York Times* after *Snow White* debuted at the Radio City Music Hall, New York's premiere movie theater, Frank Nugent gushed, "Let your fears be quieted at once: Mr. Disney and his amazing technical crew have outdone themselves. The picture more than matches expectations. It is a classic, as important cinematically as 'The Birth of a Nation' or the birth of Mickey Mouse." *Time*, which featured Walt in a color cover photo playing with models of the dwarfs at his desk, immediately declared it "an authentic masterpiece, to be shown in theaters and beloved by new generations long after the current crop of Hollywood stars, writers and directors are sleeping where no Prince's kiss can wake them." Otis Ferguson in *The New Republic* went even further, anointing it "among the genuine artistic achievements of this country," and columnist Westbrook Pegler would call it the "happiest event since Armistice." Critic Gilbert Seldes, long a Disney admirer and advocate, was given a private screening and left saying "he thought Metro Goldwyn might just as well close their studios as long as you produce feature pictures." Even the Communist *Daily Worker* praised the film, seeing the dwarfs as a "miniature communist society" and the vultures that attack the Queen as "Trotskyites."

These critical verdicts would be enthusiastically endorsed by audience reaction, and *Snow White* would become firmly entrenched as one of the most popular films ever made. Observers differed, however, as to why people loved the film. At the time of its release, many critics attributed its appeal to escapism from the turmoil of the world, just as they had done with Mickey Mouse. Frank Nugent, revisiting the film in *The New York Times* in January 1938, wrote, "Wars are being fought as the picture unreels; crimes are being committed; hatreds are being whetted; riots are being brewed. But the world fades away when Mr. Disney begins weaving his spell and enchantment takes hold." Others cited the awesome power of the sheer technical achievement: the collaboration of the nearly six hundred employees who drew, inked, and painted the quarter-million drawings in what totaled two hundred years' worth of man-hours. While no animated cartoon had ever looked like *Snow White*, and certainly none had packed its emotional wallop, it was also true that in none would the investment of time, energy, and devotion be so palpable. In some respects it was the cinematic equivalent of a Gothic cathedral—only in this case all the man-hours were expended in service to one man's vision rather than God's glory.

Beyond both the political traumas of the 1930s and the novelty of the film's technical achievement, *Snow White* also had more subliminal but no less powerful appeals. The jealousy of the Queen toward Snow White's youth and nubile attractiveness provided a sexual subtext—the battle between one generation's fading sexuality and the succeeding generation's sexual awakening, the latter of which is literally rendered when Snow White receives her resurrecting kiss from the Prince. Seen this way, Snow White and the dwarfs enact a kind of pubescent ritual of unacknowledged yearnings, a practice round of maturity, until the Prince arrives to consummate her passion and bring her to adulthood. Though most viewers and especially younger ones obviously wouldn't have recognized these elements overtly, the sexuality was also a metaphor for something they most likely would have understood. As the child psychologist Bruno Bettelheim described the fundamental theme of all fairy tales, *Snow White* is about assuming one's place in the natural order, essentially about growing up, accepting responsibility, as Snow White does for the dwarfs and the dwarfs do for Snow White, and taking over.* The story is not only Walt Disney's expression of his own assumption of power, with the dwarfs representing his shorts and the Prince representing the larger ambitions of the feature cartoon itself, but an expression of the assumption of power for everyone who has grown up or intends to, and it would become the matrix for all of Disney's great animations in which a child overcomes the hurdles and treacheries of the adult world and then finds his authority within it.

In this idea of gaining control, the theme of the film and its technical virtuosity merged. Whatever else *Snow White* does, this most deliberated-upon movie in the history of film conveys a sense of control, a sense of a fully fabricated world. For Depression audiences specifically as well as for the audiences who would see the film in succeeding decades, *Snow White*'s effect, then, was not so much in its escapism, as critics at the time of its

*Bettelheim says of the power of fairy tales to help in working through complex problems for children: "They speak about his [the child's] severe inner pressures in a way that the child unconsciously understands, and—without belittling the most serious inner struggles, which growing up entails—offer examples of both temporary and permanent solutions to pressing difficulties." *The Uses of Enchantment: The Meaning and Importance of Fairy Tales* (New York: Alfred A. Knopf, 1976), p. 6.

release reported, as in its suggestion of vicarious power—for children over their own lives and for adults over the real world that often seemed beyond their control. As much as viewers may have resonated with the personal story encoded within *Snow White*—the story of Walt Disney's assumption of power, which translated into the assumption of power for everyone—they also resonated with its wondrous sense of absolute discipline. In creating a world of his own from scratch, Walt Disney demonstrated, more fully and forcefully than ever before in his work, man's potential mastery, which had always been the inherent metaphor of animation. This was real strength.

And at least as far as animation was concerned, it ushered in a new era. After *Snow White*, one could not really go back to Mickey Mouse and Donald Duck. One had to move forward. As Walt told a visitor who had come to the studio not long after the feature's release, "We became aware that the days of the animated cartoon, as we had known it, were over." Now everything would be different.

Seven

PARNASSUS

The nine months after *Snow White* debuted may have been the best months of Walt Disney's adult life. The picture was an astounding success. In its first week at the Carthay Circle, it grossed $19,000, in its second $20,000, and by the time it finished its ten-week run, it had grossed just under $180,000. At the Radio City Music Hall in New York, where the lines often stretched down the block, it grossed just over $500,000. After it went into general release in February, and after Walt had reanimated his shimmying Prince, it grossed $3.5 million in the

United States and Canada alone and returned over $1 million to the studio. By May 1939, with $6.7 million in receipts, it would become the highest-grossing American film to that point, eventually surpassing the previous record-holder, *The Singing Fool* with Al Jolson, by nearly $2 million. Because of the low ticket prices at the time and because children, who were a significant segment of the film's audience, paid even less, Walt always maintained that *Snow White* had been seen by more people in this country than any other motion picture.

Europe was equally rapturous. The film played for twenty-eight weeks in London, grossing over $500,000 at one theater alone, and when it was released to the seaside towns that summer, the theaters were forced to take reservations three weeks in advance, eventually instituting special morning performances to satisfy the demand. "They came in their hundreds," reported *The New York Times*, "little girls with spades and pails, little boys in bathing trunks, mothers with the family shopping, young sophisticates with wind-blown sets and the newest shade in sun tan." It grossed $155,000 at one first-run theater in Paris and over $1 million when it had completed its second run in the city. In twenty-one weeks at one Sydney, Australia, theater, it took in $132,000. When censors in Holland forbade children under fourteen from seeing it because they thought it too gruesome, the youngsters staged an impromptu nationwide boycott of a Dutch Snow White chocolate bar, and the censors relented. By the time it finished its runs in 1939, it had played in forty-nine countries and had been dubbed into ten languages.

But the phenomenon didn't stop at the theater door. There were, by one account, 2,183 different *Snow White* products, and 16.5 million drinking glasses alone were sold. Walt launched a *Snow White* comic strip and commissioned a play based on the movie, though it was finally decided that theater owners might object to the competition, and the play was scotched. Prompted in part by the success of *Snow White*, the studio inaugurated a national radio program in January that was quickly canceled because, Walt said, "if I listen in and the thing isn't right I'm all upset and worried." Walt even collected $15,000 by selling original cels from the film at the Courvoisier Art Gallery in San Francisco. When Kay Kamen reported as early as May 1938 that $2 million worth of *Snow White* toys had been sold and another $2 million worth of *Snow White* handkerchiefs, *The New York Times* merrily editorialized that animation might be a way out of the Depression.

Then there were the accolades. Already in January, Walt was investigating whether *Snow White* might qualify for an Academy Award and was told that "it is quite within the bounds of probability that the Award Committee might consider it for special honors." It had already been named one of the outstanding pictures of the year by the National Board of Review and had won a special citation from the New York Film Critics. When the Oscars were awarded in February 1939, Walt did receive a special acknowledgment for his achievement: one large Oscar statuette and seven smaller ones. "Isn't it bright and shiny?" ten-year-old actress Shirley Temple chirped as she presented the award. "Oh, it's beautiful," Walt said. "Aren't you proud of it?" she asked. "I'm so proud of it I think I'll bust," Walt beamed. To which Temple rejoined, "Oh, don't do that, Mr. Disney!" The exchange, one guest said, "brought down the house."

The sense of jubilation swept through the entire Disney family. Just two weeks after the Los Angeles premiere of *Snow White*, the Disneys—all but Ruth, who remained in Portland—gathered at the Ivar House restaurant in Hollywood to celebrate Elias and Flora's fiftieth wedding anniversary and to put an end to what had been a difficult decade for the couple, even as Roy and Walt's status had been steadily rising. The Depression was not a particularly good time to be landlords, which was how Elias and Flora earned their living. "Conditions for us have not improved," Elias wrote Walt in a typical letter late in 1933, "in fact, they are harder, as prices are harder. We have not rented and very few people are looking for apartments." With Roy and Walt plowing their profits back into the studio, they were unable to contribute much to alleviate their parents' plight, mainly giving them magazine subscriptions, periodic vacations to Los Angeles to visit, a new Sears Coldspot refrigerator, and in 1934 a trip to Florida via Kansas City and Chicago to see friends and relatives. Though it may have seemed niggardly considering that the Disney brothers were now national figures, Elias didn't think so. He wrote Ray that "Roy is very generous and I sometimes think too much so, but he don't seem to loose [*sic*] anything by it." Elias made no such claim about Walt's generosity. When Walt was asked to endorse a DeSoto automobile in exchange for a car, Walt objected, saying he didn't drive a DeSoto and wasn't going to say he did, but when Flora suggested that he give the car to them, he relented, posed for the ad, and presented them with the DeSoto.

In addition to their economic hardships, there were health problems. Flora suffered a succession of small strokes, and the doctor ordered her to rest every afternoon for ninety minutes to lower her high blood pressure. Elias's health had been failing too, and by 1937 he was nearly blind. His doctor proposed that Roy and Walt provide their father a loan of $2,000 to pay his medical bills, but Roy declined. "We have a tremendous load to carry at the studio and we need the strength of all our resources," he wrote, citing an episode in which he had cosigned a note for a friend six months earlier and the friend defaulted.

Flora and Elias were also lonely. They heard infrequently from Roy, and Walt wrote them only once a year. Herbert, his wife Louise, and their daughter Dorothy, whom Elias and Flora had followed to Portland, visited them every Sunday for dinner, but in July 1930 Herbert requested and was granted another transfer by the postal service, this time to Los Angeles, where he felt the climate would be better for Dorothy's persistent bronchitis. When Ruth married a local contractor named Ted Beecher and moved into Herbert's old house, Elias and Flora were left by themselves. Their house was adorned with Disney paraphernalia—a picture of Mickey Mouse stood beside a photo of Walt on the piano and Flora kept a scrapbook of Walt's exploits—but it only reminded them of how much they missed their boys. "We wish we could sell out here and move to L.A. so we could all be together," Flora wrote one of her nieces as early as 1931. "This depression will have to clear away before there is any chance of that."

Now, thanks to *Snow White*, the Depression had cleared away for the Disneys. For an anniversary present the brothers chipped in to buy their parents a house of their own choosing in California. "I think it's a great day in my life," Elias wrote his cousin Peter Cantelon. "I don't expect to have another like it."

Snow White had had a salutary effect on Walt's immediate family too. His years of obsession with the film, the days and nights and weekends spent at the studio, had taken their toll on his relationship with Lillian, who had never been especially interested in Walt's work to begin with and who once called herself her husband's "Severest Critic" because "I always look on the dark side." (She was one of the few in Walt's inner circle who failed to appreciate the prospects of *Snow White*, saying, "I can't stand the sight of dwarfs," and "I predict nobody'll ever pay a dime to see a dwarf picture.") When Walt was at the studio, which was most of the time, the two seldom communicated, though Lillian did say she made certain to be home by five o'clock or five-thirty every afternoon, Walt's dinnertime, to serve him. "He demanded a lot of everyone around him," she said as a way of explaining her schedule. "He always kept everybody in turmoil." It was turmoil that Lillian didn't always appreciate. By one account, around the time of *Snow White* the couple had even discussed divorce.

One problem was that as surely as Walt was focused on the studio, Lillian was focused on her family. "He was very close to Lilly until Diane was born," his secretary Dolores Voght told an interviewer years later. "[A]fter Diane came along, Lilly grew more interested in her, so she pulled away from studio affairs and concentrated on the home." It was, no doubt, her way to find herself while Walt was fixated on *Snow White*. Lillian certainly seemed to resent her husband's preoccupation with work and the avalanche of attention he received, but she was no silent, long-suffering helpmate. Lillian would erupt. Diane remembered coming down for breakfast one morning and seeing a large brown stain on the wall. She later learned that her mother had hurled a cup of coffee at Walt. "Mother was a well contained, poised person who never lost her temper with us children," Diane would say, "but also she would not let herself be put upon. She stood up for her rights."

Though Walt's deepest devotion seemed reserved for his daughter, his studio, and his pets—his chow, Sunnee, and a black cat, Manxie, who later disappeared when he went to sleep in the gardener's car and then leaped out in traffic—things seemed to improve with Lillian after she suffered her third miscarriage and the couple, at Walt's instigation, decided to adopt. On December 31, 1936, just as *Snow White* was reaching its most manic stage, Walt and Lillian received their new six-week-old daughter, Sharon Mae, though a bout of pneumonia sent her back to the hospital for a month's recuperation. Both parents were devoted to her. They made no distinction between her and Diane, and Walt would always bristle at any mention of her being adopted. Indeed, Walt and Lillian were so secretive about the adoption that he had his gardener, Diane's nurse, and Marjorie Sewell pick Sharon up from the hospital lest someone recognize the Disneys. When the fact of the adoption was cited nearly twenty years later in a profile of Walt for *Look* magazine, he wrote the editor fuming, "I do not care what you say about me, but deeply resent your reference to my daughter Sharon's adoption." (*Look* stopped the presses and deleted the line.) In any case, their mutual love of Sharon seemed to begin a rapprochement between Walt and Lilly, and shortly after *Snow White*'s release they may have been investigating a second adoption, which, for whatever reason, never came to fruition.

His family became more important to him as his social activities continued to diminish. Throughout *Snow White*'s long production Walt had been tense and frequently ill, even after the trip to Europe that had temporarily reinvigorated him. Various doctors visited him at the studio several times each week, sometimes daily, to provide everything from hair loss treatments (despite his abundant and wild shock) to chiropractic sessions for a polo injury that would bother him for the rest of his life, forcing him to hunch over to relieve the pain when he sat and stabbing him awake at night. Though during the production he continued to play polo, which had also diverted time from Lillian, his interest had waned after an accident at the Riviera Country Club on October 28, 1935. During a match there between MGM and the Disney studio, the horse of a thirty-one-year-old contract player at MGM named Gordon Westcott apparently collided with Walt's, and Westcott fell; by one account, Walt's horse then toppled onto the young man. He died three days later without ever having regained consciousness. A month later Roy informed Walt that he had decided to quit polo and was disposing of his ponies. Walt reduced his playing time until in May 1938 he wrote Riviera that the "studio demands so much of my time that I am going to have to give up polo entirely." He requested that the club field offers for ten of his twelve ponies—two he was having brought to Griffith Park so he and Lillian could ride there—and, failing a sale, he said he would turn them out to pasture. From this point on, his primary athletic activity would be badminton.

Less time for polo meant more time for Lillian, and a month after notifying Riviera that he was divesting himself of his ponies, he and Lillian left for a vacation in New York. But the end of polo also meant the end of his polo relationships, which were among the few friendships he maintained. He had never enjoyed much of a social life—he had never had time for one—and what little he had had been largely ruined by *Snow White*. In the studio's early days, when Walt fraternized primarily with his employees, his work life and his social life usually converged. But by the time he began producing *Snow White*, he had withdrawn from them socially. As animator Marc Davis put it, "[W]hen the Studio began to become really something, a few of these men weren't growing to the same degree that he was. So pretty soon his associations were mostly with people away from the Studio and his private life became divorced from the Studio. Many of these men could never understand that Walt had outgrown them—he had changed."

Yet even as he disengaged socially from his employees, Walt did not plunge into the Hollywood scene. Though he and Lillian socialized throughout the 1930s with the Spencer Tracys, inviting them to the new house on Woking Way for an afternoon of swimming and badminton, these invitations were occasional and were tendered via a telegram or a letter rather than by phone. Similarly, even after he managed to lure his childhood friend Walt Pfeiffer to the studio to work in the story department, the two were surprisingly distant and formal—employer and employee rather than pals. Most of his associates felt that he was close to no one. "Walt was a hard guy to get close to," animator Ward Kimball said. "He was a workaholic. His career was his whole life. I think I was as good a friend as he ever had." Another employee described Walt as "friendly, but a man who didn't appear to accept close friendships." Lillian agreed. Asked by an interviewer to name Walt's closest friends, she said,

"[H]e really didn't have time to make friends. . . . Walt had too much to do. He had to have a clear mind for work the next day." No one, not even Lillian, could crack him. He was so self-absorbed, so fully within his own mind and ideas, that he emerged only to share them and to have them executed.

Walt seemed to realize that he was hopelessly addicted to work at the expense of family and friends. For years he and Lillian had been shopping for a ranch where he could get away, only to conclude, as he wrote one prospective seller, that his duties at the studio left him "little time for actual recreation." Beginning in May 1938, one of his few extracurricular activities was an annual one-week horseback ride in the California outback near Santa Barbara with a club of business professionals who called themselves the Rancheros Visitadores, though another member, Disney producer Dave Hand, observed that the Visitadores "might just as well have brought along tables and chairs," since "Walt would talk more and more about his new ideas, always ending with directions for me to see that certain new or different operations were effected or workers transferred or revisions of schedule upon our return to 'civilization.' " "He didn't know anything else," Hand said, "he couldn't talk anything else but that studio."

While the studio remained Walt's priority, in the months after *Snow White*, during a brief lull in his workload, he had begun refocusing on his family, in part because it was only with his family that he didn't have to be "Walt Disney," an even more onerous obligation after his feature film's success. Walt enjoyed the limelight, but he hated the public persona he was forced to assume, and from his unpretentious midwestern upbringing, he hated the sense of inflated importance bestowed upon celebrities, of which he was now certainly one. If he was not a man without ego, he thought of himself as a man without airs, and so he was. Though the two-story house at 4053 Woking Way was attractive and considerably more spacious than the prefabricated bandbox on Lyric Avenue, with three bedrooms, a combination library–projection room–paneled bar, a swimming pool with its own pavilion, and a broad lawn sweeping down the hill, it was hardly the capacious mansion one might have imagined for Walt Disney. He lived modestly in other ways too. Until he got his first Cadillac in the early 1940s, he drove Plymouths and Packards, and he bought his clothes off the rack. He liked plain food; his favorite meal was canned beans. Nor did he surround himself with the trappings of his celebrity. He told one interviewer that he deliberately kept Disney products out of his house because "I've lived with it too much and I just didn't want to live with it at home."

But as preoccupied as he was, when it came to Diane and Sharon, he was a doting father who sheltered them from his own fame. He enjoyed telling how six-year-old Diane had asked him if he was Walt Disney. "You know I am," he answered. "*The* Walt Disney?" she questioned. When he chortled that he was, she asked for his autograph. He would chase the girls around the house, cackling like the witch from *Snow White*, or he would twirl them endlessly by their heels, "for hours and hours," Diane would say, or he would stand in the swimming pool and let them climb to his shoulders. "I thought that my father was the strongest man in the world and the most fun," Diane recalled. At night he read to them. And on the weekends, after he picked them up from church, he would take them either to Griffith Park to ride the merry-go-round or to the studio, where they would follow him as he snooped about, or pedal their bikes around the empty grounds while he worked. "They used to love to go with me in those days," Walt would reminisce. "And that [*sic*] was some of the happiest days of my life. They were in love with their dad."

In the wake of *Snow White* even the usually dolorous Roy was excited. That April, with the film raking in $200,000 a week, he had gone to Europe to work on foreign distribution deals and to conduct an acquisition spree of properties for future features. The Disneys had already secured rights to A. A. Milne's classic *Winnie the Pooh* (Diane always hugged a ragged Winnie the Pooh doll when she went to bed) and Kenneth Grahame's *The Wind in the Willows*, and they were negotiating for the rights to Don Marquis's *Archy and Mehitabel*, about a precocious cockroach and a cat. While in England, Roy struck a deal for rights to Sir John Tenniel's drawings for *Alice in Wonderland*, and he had hashed out an odd agreement for *Peter Pan* with the Great Ormond Street Hospital, the institution to which Sir James Barrie had willed the rights to his play when he died in 1937; the hospital had granted the Disneys the opportunity to make an arrangement with Paramount Pictures, which had acquired the live-action screen rights for *Peter Pan*, and failing that, it was willing to sell them the cartoon rights, thus keeping them from the Fleischers, who were embarking on their own program of cartoon features. Even so, upon Roy's return from this European foray, a reporter commented that he "still wears the look of a man who isn't quite sure yet whether the time has come to stop worrying."

It had. Though *Snow White* had cost a staggering sum of money (over $100,000 for the story development alone, nearly $300,000 for the animation, and well over $1 million overall) and though the studio had gone seriously into debt to finance it (the Disneys had borrowed a total of $2.3 million from the Bank of America between May 1936 and May 1938), the film's success had more than rewarded them. On May 20, 1938, just five months after *Snow White*'s premiere, they retired the entire obligation, vindicating Walt's belief in the project. "Roy brought Mr. Giannini for a meeting with me to hurry me along to finish *Snow White*," Walt gloated to a group of his animators over lunch after the conference. "[I]nstead I got Mr. Giannini so interested and excited about our next project, *Pinocchio*, that he advanced us another bundle of money. . . . I beat Roy in this one." Moreover, the studio for the first time was actually running ahead of schedule on the shorts, and RKO, the distributor, had offered to set up a revolving fund of over $1 million upon which Disney could draw for its next two features should they renew the contract. Reporting to Roy that RKO was willing to give them anything they asked for, Gunther Lessing joked, "We already took the last drop of blood, so it may not be equitable to extract liver, heart and stomach. However, no matter what we do Walt will raise hell and want a better deal." He ended: "There is no doubt in my mind that everybody connected with RKO considers Disney as the most important and prominent element in RKO. We are absolutely essential to them."

While Walt was waxing expansive over *Snow White*'s success, he wanted to deliver on his promise that everyone at the studio would benefit from it. That May he had stormed into George Morris's office and demanded that the bonuses on *Snow White* now be paid. (They initially amounted to $115,000, though in June he declared that each employee would receive three months' salary, which finally cost the studio roughly $750,000.) "They deserve it," Walt told columnist Ed Sullivan. "They made the picture possible, didn't they?" After years of working on Saturdays until noon, he also decided to put the studio on a five-day week that summer. Finally, in a gesture of gratitude, he announced that he would be hosting a weekend retreat for his employees and their families beginning June 4 at the Lake Narconian Hotel and Club near Palm Springs.

As it turned out, the retreat was a debacle. All the years of pent-up energy on *Snow White* gushed forth. Alcohol flowed freely. Men and women openly paired off for romantic liaisons. One of the studio watchmen threw his wife into the swimming pool, then ran to the roof of the hotel and made a high dive to rescue her. Another employee rode a horse into the hotel lobby. Drunken Fred Moore fell out of a second-story window but landed on a bush and walked away unhurt. Walt was embarrassed and disappointed.

The horseplay didn't square with the effusive encomia that Walt was now receiving. In addition to the praise he was garnering as one of the nation's greatest artists, that June he received an honorary degree from the University of Southern California, his first such award, but he had already been notified in February that Yale University would be awarding him a degree at its June commencement, and Harvard quickly followed suit—the first honorary degree it had ever awarded to a person in film. The Yale and Harvard degrees, in fact, were bestowed on successive days, June 22 and 23, and Walt received "prolonged applause" at the Harvard ceremony. These honors prompted Walt and Lillian's trip east, where he was also feted by a host of notables at the Music Hall in New York City, including Radio Corporation of America chief David Sarnoff and publisher Ogden Reid. When he returned to his office at Hyperion, he installed trophy cases to house the numerous awards he had received—as *New York Times* critic Frank Nugent enumerated them after a visit, "a crystal and silver goblet from Russia, loving cups from most of the junior Chambers of Commerce, medals and plaques from France and Brazil and countries in between, honorary scrolls from the Academy of Motion Picture Arts and Sciences," and of course his honorary degrees.

Inevitably, despite the shenanigans at Lake Narconian, a new sense of dignity began to pervade the studio—and a new pressure. *Snow White* had proven the power of the animated cartoon, and it had provided the studio with a financial cushion. But it had also raised the stakes once again, especially since Disney's rivals, the Fleischers and Walter Lantz, were also preparing features now. After the flush of *Snow White*, Walt was beginning to worry. "We have to prove to the public that SNOW WHITE and feature cartoons are not just a passing novelty," he wrote that May to one of his chief supporters, Gus Van Schmus, the general manager of Radio City Music Hall, "but that they have a very definite place in the entertainment world and are here to stay." He admitted to one reporter that after *Snow White* "he was afraid he could not equal it in other endeavors"—an attitude, the reporter observed, "quite in reverse of the Hollywood philosophy of coasting as long as possible on one successful film." And at a sweatbox session that July he was already lamenting that his directors were not thinking creatively but rather were "taking literally everything that is put in there . . . and just carrying it out mechanically—just by formula, instead of inventing all the time and improving." He exhorted them to start "raising their values."

Given the sudden emphasis on feature animations, it was natural to think of *Snow White* as the beginning of a new era in the studio, a golden age of cartoons in which the values were raised and the studio really was transformed into the communal guild of which Walt had dreamed. The truth as it turned out was something else. *Snow White* may have been less a beginning than an end—of old ways of crafting cartoons and running the studio. For one thing, with the feature's success had come a vast expansion in the workforce, as Walt braced for the new films to come. Nearly eight hundred employees were added to the payroll in the two years following *Snow White*, but because Walt had been slow to advance feature production as he awaited the results of that picture, he wound up creating a glut. Many of the new employees simply sat doing nothing through most of 1938. Sharpsteen didn't want to work with them because they weren't experienced enough. Ham Luske tried to find them assignments, but he remembered it as a "horrible deal."

Because there were so many new employees and because the studio was being converted virtually overnight from one that was dedicated to producing six- and seven-minute cartoons to one that was dedicated to producing seventy- and eighty-minute features, chaos began to descend. *Snow White* had been a long, deliberate labor of trial and error, but it was sui generis; it provided little guidance in making features on a regular schedule, which was what the studio needed to do now. By Walt's own admission, the two years after *Snow White* were "years of confusion, swift expansion, reorganization." And he described the training of the new recruits as being "fitted into a machine for the manufacture of entertainment which had become bewilderingly complex"—a far cry from the heady, messy, lurching collaboration on *Snow White*. As he would later tell his employees, "The only way to have a [commanding] position in the field is to have an organization so that there will be no weak sisters coming from the plant." But for all Walt's earlier fitful attempts to routinize the process of animation and for all the increasing specialization, the studio had never really been a machine. Now he had to try to make it one.

The transformation was reflected in a proposed change in the company's name that year. Roy had decided to consolidate the various Disney entities—the studio, the merchandise division, and a real estate investment arm that the brothers had formed in the early 1930s called Liled Realty after their wives, Lillian and Edna—under the banner "Walt Disney Enterprises." While the new name may have sounded more formal and majestic than Walt Disney Productions, it also ignited a firestorm of protest within the company. Critics charged, in Roy's words, that Walt Disney Productions "sounds less like a billion dollar project—world-wide enterprise with a lot of money and power," than the proposed name did, and that Walt Disney Enterprises might give the public the wrong impression, perhaps that the Disney studio had gone corporate. In the end Roy capitulated, but the incident nevertheless indicated a new tone and direction at the studio.

. . .

That May the studio saw a more direct and dramatic example of its own swelling status and corporatization. Embarking on an ambitious feature program with his newly enlarged staff, Walt realized that he needed new facilities. At first he decided to erect a new building for the shorts unit on Hyperion, across the street from the main studio, but as he mulled the idea one weekend and went over the plans with his chief engineer Bill Garity and a contractor named Frank Crowhurst, he suddenly changed his mind. Now, with virtually no deliberation, he decided that he was going to build an entirely new studio instead and promptly asked George Morris in the business office to lay out a financing scheme. When Morris protested that he needed to know what the cost of the new studio would be, Walt, with his customary disdain for money, shrugged. "Well, go ahead and figure on $500,000 and we will talk about the rest of it later."

In short order Walt whipped himself into a frenzy over the new studio. Even with Roy in Europe, he began scouting properties, and Morris helplessly memoed the absent brother: "It looks as though we're going ahead with the new studio." Indeed, Walt was now so enthusiastic about the prospect and so eager to proceed that Gunther Lessing also contacted Roy and urged him to return before matters got out of hand. Though the *Los Angeles Times* reported in June that Walt was considering sites in the Westwood section of Los Angeles and in the barren suburb of Burbank, north of Los Angeles, within three weeks of his decision to build the studio he had already settled on an isolated fifty-one-acre tract in the latter community, which had served as the polo field for the Black Fox Military Academy, and he had begun negotiations with the Department of Water and Power, which owned the property. The asking price was $100,000.

"You know how I got this studio, don't you?" Walt once asked a meeting of his employees. "They thought they would be very happy if *Snow White* grossed three million, so when it went over that I said: Let me have this—I want to build a new studio . . . and that is how we got the new studio." In fact it wasn't quite so simple. The lion's share of *Snow White*'s profits had gone to retire the debt, so Walt dispatched Morris and Garity to consult Joe Rosenberg at the Bank of America about a loan. Rosenberg was amenable, but after sending out an appraiser to look at the Burbank site, he thought it overpriced, said he would advance the Disneys only $30,000, and advised that Walt look at other properties. Undeterred, Walt quickly closed the deal with the Department of Water and Power and that July announced that construction would begin within weeks. As always, Roy would get him the money.

Having secured his sprawling tract set against the Hollywood Hills,

Walt was no more inclined to erect another slapdash studio like Hyperion than he was inclined to produce slapdash animation. Planned from scratch, the new studio was going to be perfect, the physical realization of his long-held dream for an animation utopia. To design it, he hired not a conventional architect but a lugubrious-looking German-born industrial designer named Kem Weber whose primary experience in architecture had been drawing sets and occasionally planning buildings for Paramount. Having undergone an artistic conversion during a trip back to Europe in the mid-1920s, Weber had become an exponent of the Moderne style, which sought to express the zeitgeist of technology in architectural form—clean, sleek, and streamlined like an airplane, with no ornate flourishes. It seemed the appropriate style for an industry that combined art with technology, not to mention for a studio chief who always regarded himself as forward-looking, and it was a style Walt clearly hoped would have a positive psychological impact on the employees as well since, as Weber would later write of Walt's instructions, the "comfort of mind and the happiness in the place of your work depends not only upon pure, practical, and functional solutions but also on their appearance."

Weber, for whom the Disney project was by far his largest commission to date, was described as the studio's "supervising designer," but Walt was not about to let anyone's vision supersede his own. No less than *Snow White*, this was *his* dream. "Walt planned out very carefully," recalled Ben Sharpsteen. "He planned out the buildings, he made mock-ups of the units on the ground with the old studio and called anybody in that wanted to contribute with ideas. . . . He went to as much work on that as he did in the creative side of his pictures." Because he wanted it to be a workers' paradise, he not only solicited suggestions from his employees but actively brought them into the process. Frank Thomas remembered Walt calling back the staff for night meetings at Hyperion, where he had a layout of the new studio and models of the buildings. "He'd say, 'How about if we put the theater here, the animation building there, the restaurant here, the sound stage there, the orchestra stage, the camera department, ink and paint, cutting, process lab, all those things.' We would move all those models around, then someone would say, 'What do you do in rainy weather?' " And then Walt would calculate how many rainy days there were likely to be and begin brainstorming about digging underground tunnels between the animation building and the ink and paint building. "He really thought it through and involved us in it all the way."

As always, he became obsessive. One employee remembered coming into Walt's office and finding him disassembling a chair to determine how he could manufacture one that was more comfortable for the animators.

Another recalled Walt entrusting Frank Thomas to design a prototype for a new animation table, which Weber then had fabricated. The new desks would have rotating disks, fluorescent lights, and larger animation paper—30 percent larger to make it easier to draw. On the Animation Building there would be slotted awnings designed specifically to let in light without letting in glare. Instead of cramped sweatboxes there would be two spacious projection rooms, one of them next to Walt's office. (The name "sweatbox," however, was still retained, as it had been for the projection rooms at Hyperion.) And after the stifling heat of the in-betweeners' bullpen and the animation rooms at Hyperion, there would be humidity controls, temperature regulation, and an air-conditioner pumping 250,000 cubic feet of cool air. Walt was overlooking nothing for his dream world.

II

By the fall of 1938, when Walt was planning the new studio, the desultory, blissful post–*Snow White* respite had ended, and he was back at Hyperion piloting *Snow White*'s follow-up, *Bambi*. He had been working on the project in fits and starts since early 1935, when he met with producer-director Sidney Franklin, who held the rights and was eager to get the film into production. Preoccupied with *Snow White*, Walt had kept stalling and Franklin had kept pressing, even notifying the Disneys that he was considering an offer for the material from MGM, the studio to which Franklin was under contract, though Roy thought he was bluffing just to get the project moving. By the spring of 1937 it had gotten moving, and Bianca Majolie, who had been a classmate of Walt's at McKinley High School in Chicago before petitioning him for a job and landing one in the story department, submitted a synopsis, which she continued to refine throughout the summer. In August, with *Snow White* sprinting to its finish, Walt met with Larry Morey and Dorothy Ann Blank, who were attempting to shape Majolie's synopsis into a script, and by month's end he had begun to organize the staff, though he was still loath to pull anyone off *Snow White* until it was completed.

When Walt convened the first formal story conference for *Bambi* on September 4, and Dave Hand announced the schedule—animation to begin on December 1, with the release set for a year later—it was immediately clear that things were going to be very different from how they had been on *Snow White*, where the story had undergone not months but years of intense scrutiny. Walt was different too. "The staff looked hopefully to Walt," Frank Thomas and Ollie Johnston would later write, "but he was not giving his usual strong leadership this time. The storymen reported that he seemed troubled by the whole idea of the picture and was not sure which way to go." Part of the problem was that Walt knew Franklin had been trying to lick the script for years without success; what Walt admitted that he liked in Felix Salten's novel, a series of incidents rather than a narrative, were the "possibilities with animals" and "not with doing the book the way it was." And part of the problem was that Walt was in a hurry to take advantage of the momentum created by *Snow White.* When Larry Morey suggested that they first work out the scene of Bambi and his mother walking through the woods, the sort of thing they did with the scene in which the dwarfs discover Snow White when they started *Snow White,* Walt countered that they should begin casting voices at the same time. "Let us start moving on this thing and not drag it out too long," he advised. He didn't want to waste time by designing the characters now. He said they should settle on the characters, write "business" for them, and construct the first half of the movie, then record the dialogue and music and make sketches afterward. "If we had on a track the music, the action, the dialogue, and the songs for your first 4000 feet," he told the staff, "you should be able to visualize it without the sketches." He even recommended that Luske use the voices they recorded for inspiration to draw model sheets of the characters, but he warned, "It is wisest to build through a few characters." In short, he was working almost entirely from the aural to the visual, and he was trying to do it quickly.

And the staff did work fast. Within two weeks of the story conference Perce Pearce, who was acting as the producer, constructed a rough continuity for the first section of the film, from Bambi's birth to his first walk in the woods; scenes had been parceled out to various members of the story department; and voices had been recorded. A month after that the story crew was meeting with Franklin and picking his brain. Franklin had latched onto the idea of a comical hare who throughout the film tries to tell Bambi a story but keeps getting harassed by a fox before he can finish. Finally, he is shot by a hunter, and as he attempts one last time to finish his story before expiring, he gasps, "It wasn't a very funny story anyway. There was no point to it." The scene never made it into the final script, but it did have an effect. According to Johnston and Thomas, "[I]t showed us a new dimension that was possible for animation: real drama with the communication of an idea that would move the audience." From his live-action experience Franklin was showing them how to move beyond *Snow White* into even more poignant and dramatic realms.

Franklin seemed to spark Walt too. When they met for an extended story session on December 15, a week before the *Snow White* premiere,

Walt was suddenly engaged with the material again, describing an opening montage of winter turning to spring virtually shot by shot just as he had done on *Snow White* and doing the same on a scene after a devastating forest fire. Franklin was impressed by Walt's sensitivity to the treatment. "You have hit the story with this," he told Walt. "This is *Bambi.* There is no gag that stands out above Bambi himself. He is part of everything." But in some ways Franklin's enthusiasm simply underscored Walt's problems with *Bambi.* It required *too* much sensitivity, *too* delicate a hand. It wasn't ready, and the studio wasn't ready for it. The very day of his meeting with Franklin, Walt announced to the press that he would be postponing the film and slotting *Pinocchio* in its place.

Pinocchio was supposed to be easier, and in any case, at the same time he was wrestling with *Bambi,* and partly because of his wariness about that project, Walt had been hurtling forward with it that fall. Animator Norm Ferguson claimed that he was the one who had given Walt a translation of Italian Carlo Collodi's famous novel about the adventures of an impertinent puppet that turns into a real boy, and that after reading it Walt was "just busting his guts with enthusiasm." Presumably thinking of it for his third feature, he instructed Lessing to secure the rights that September. By fall he had made the deal and assigned Majolie to synopsize the book, though Walt thought her outline was too faithful to the original text. "I think the thing to do is take the situations in the book and try to build the story around the ones that we can do something with and not feel bound to the book," Walt advised a story meeting, before sending off the staff to work on individual sequences. At the time the storymen assumed they would have months to work things through. They didn't. One day Walt walked into the music room, announced that *Bambi* was being postponed, and assigned Sharpsteen to be the supervising producer and Jack Kinney the animation director of its replacement: *Pinocchio.* Now speed was suddenly of the essence. As Kinney told it, " 'Crank it out' was the word, so we did."

That winter, in hopes of releasing *Pinocchio* the following December, Walt was meeting with the story crew for hours at a stretch, often sounding like the Walt Disney of the *Snow White* story sessions, visualizing scenes, defining characters, performing business, and "plussing" gags. Usually the group gathered in Projection Room No. 4, then Kinney or Webb Smith or another storyman, Otto Englander, or Walt himself would begin reading the continuity, triggering an almost Talmudic disquisition on each story point, each line, each gag—just as they had done on *Snow White.* And as on *Snow White,* as they did so Walt would keep revisiting scenes, repeating lines or bits of business again and again and again, internalizing the film since he was the only one at the studio, as F. Scott Fitzgerald said in *The Last Tycoon* of the rare Hollywood executive, who was "able to keep the whole equation of pictures" in his head. Roy E. Disney, Roy's young son, even remembered being bedridden with the chicken pox when Walt and Lillian visited his parents; Walt came in to see him, then sat on the edge of the bed and told the story of *Pinocchio* as he used to tell the story of *Snow White*.

But as much as it may have seemed like *Snow White*, the schedule made it different. Walt needed to get the story going; there was no time for the months and months of refinements, no time to agonize over every frame. Even before a scene was fully conceptualized, he wanted it sent to the gag men, and as soon as an individual sequence seemed ready for animation, he wanted it sent to the animators, whether the rest of the film had been worked out or not. And even as they pored over the script, given the new time pressures the process was far more catch-as-catch-can than on *Snow White*: scenes were rapidly worked out and then just as rapidly discarded. Sketch artist Bill Peet remembered the staff being summoned to a *Pinocchio* meeting and the animators carrying what he estimated to be at least seventy storyboards as they huddled around Walt's armchair in Projection Room No. 4. Walt's mood, which had been lighthearted as the morning session began, gradually darkened. "There's too much stuff here," he barked, and every so often he would, as Peet recalled it, get up and rip a whole row of sketches off the board, summarily shortening the film. The only calm in the storm was when they came to the character of Honest John Foulfellow, a conniving fox who waylays Pinocchio, and Walt transformed himself into the villain to act out the scene. By the time the two-day session ended, Walt had eliminated half the boards, though as he left, "he turned to us with a satisfied smile and said, 'That was a hell of a good session.' " To which Peet would write, "It left me wondering what a bad one would be like."

The bad sessions were to come. From January through June, while the animators worked simultaneously on sequences, Walt continued to meet with the story crew and sketch artists, working through the script more or less chronologically rather than conquering the key scenes first, as he had done on *Snow White*: puppetmaker Geppetto carving Pinocchio and then realizing his new marionette can move (but avoiding the sentimentality of the scene, because Walt felt there had been too much sentimentality in *Snow White*); Pinocchio getting waylaid by Honest John; Pinocchio getting sent to Boobyland (later changed to Pleasure Island), where he is allowed to indulge his desires and is turned into a donkey as a result; his escape from Boobyland; and his attempt to rescue Geppetto, who has been swallowed by Monstro the Whale. Occasionally Walt would recite scenes in minute detail, cut by cut. Other times he would establish the general motive and the meaning of the scene and leave the storymen to write the lines, then return to fine-tune them. As always his focus was less on the narrative than on the emotion and psychology of the scene. "I want to feel it before we start work on it," he said of Pinocchio's search for Geppetto.

As they worked, there was the presumption that this was a story Walt *did* feel. After his impasse on *Bambi*, he had decided to forge ahead on *Pinocchio* because, as one storyman put it, "*Pinocchio* was a picture Walt knew how to make, while *Bambi* still baffled him." The staff felt the same way. Emboldened by the success of *Snow White*, despite the expectations it imposed, they proceeded on *Pinocchio* with assurance. "[W]e were pretty cocky coming off of *Snow White*," Ward Kimball later admitted. "We thought we could just sit down and do another feature. And we plunged into it." In fact, Walt confidently predicted that the studio would be turning out a new feature every six months. But even as Walt tried to expedite the production of *Pinocchio*, he began encountering problems. Some were minor—having to recast the voices of Pinocchio and Geppetto or streamline scenes that moved too slowly in Walt's estimation. Others, however, proved as intractable as those on *Bambi*. Ken Anderson felt there was a problem from the outset—a problem of spirit. Ben Sharpsteen had been the one encouraging Walt to push *Pinocchio* when *Bambi* was delayed, and because Sharpsteen rather than Walt assumed the role of point man to many of the staff, Anderson felt "it became more of a technical achievement than . . . [one of] the heart," as *Snow White* so obviously was. Sharpsteen had his own analysis of why *Pinocchio* didn't run smoothly: there were too many directors working simultaneously without the strong coordinating hand of Walt that had impelled *Snow White*. Instead, Sharpsteen was responsible for supervising the units, and Walt was now beckoned only if there was a serious problem or if the units needed a boost. The result was a kind of chaos.

Walt had another perspective. He complained that in trying to keep his ever-growing staff engaged once *Bambi* had been postponed, he rushed *Pinocchio* into production without adequate planning, lest the animators sit idle. "We've tried to take care of the whole plant in *Pinocchio* and there's where we got into trouble," he told a meeting of the *Bambi* crew some months later. "Not having a thing prepared. Trying to build a story before we ever knew it." Another time he complained, "We went through *Pinocchio* and didn't plan any music to speak of at all. We didn't plan our music and dialogue in between."

The major drawback to the lack of preparation was the failure to tackle fully the character of Pinocchio. As Walt put it bluntly at the outset, "One difficulty in 'Pinocchio' is that people know the story, but they don't like the character," who, in the book, is often cruel. It was a sign of his dissatisfaction with the character that Walt suggested they enlarge the role of the Blue Fairy and have her appear in different guises, including that of a blue cricket, to help guide Pinocchio and keep him on a righteous path. But that was only an expedient. Walt clearly had no handle on Pinocchio, describing him at one point as "fresh," like ventriloquist Edgar Bergen's wise-cracking dummy Charlie McCarthy, or lusty, like Harpo Marx, grabbing for the fairy whenever she appears. He wasn't even sure whether Pinocchio should act like a puppet or a small boy and whether he should appear wooden or flexible. When Frank Thomas, Milt Kahl, and Ollie Johnston took the former tack and animated 150 feet of the puppet early that February, Walt was displeased.

As the story goes, including the official studio record, shortly after seeing Thomas's animation, Walt decided to put *Pinocchio* on hiatus from February through September while the staff reworked the script. In fact, Walt kept working on, revising, and even sweatboxing scenes right through July, but he knew he had hit a wall. Ham Luske claimed that after looking at the storyboards of a scene in which Pinocchio terrorizes Geppetto's cat, Figaro, he suggested to Walt that the audience would lose sympathy for Pinocchio unless the puppet had some way to discern right from wrong. That comment, Luske said, was the one that triggered Walt to begin thinking about reconceptualizing the film. As Ward Kimball told it, "[A]fter six or eight months, Walt looked at it and he says, 'It's not working right.' So he threw it out and everybody had to start all over again." This time he fastened on a character who had had only a minor role in Collodi's novel—a cricket whom Pinocchio stomps to death. In a revised synopsis that June, a "little CRICKET, who is singing on the hearth," makes his first appearance. This time, however, the Fairy appoints him as Pinocchio's conscience. Now the storymen had to rewrite the entire script to incorporate the cricket. As Walt later explained it, "We said, 'Here's a guy we've got to take all the way through this thing,' so we worked him back into all the sections."

Perhaps the real problem with *Pinocchio*, and with *Bambi* for that matter, and the primary reason that Walt wasn't able to find solutions to the dilemmas they posed as he had on *Snow White*, was that he was overextended, which was why he had to delegate authority to Hand and Sharpsteen. Not only was he revising the scripts of *Bambi* and *Pinocchio*, he was sweatboxing scenes, designing the new studio, supervising the shorts production, and launching yet another film, his most ambitious yet, tentatively titled *The Concert Feature*, which, in Walt's original plan, was to have been released after *Bambi* and *Pinocchio*. Indeed, in a single typical day in February, Walt was discussing a scene in which Pinocchio learns to pray, listening to recordings for *The Concert Feature*, watching live action that had been shot for *Pinocchio*, and attending a story meeting on the shorts. Added to all these chores was Walt's rededication to his family, though the family was always sacrificed when the studio called.

Even before *Bambi* and *Pinocchio* had been temporarily shelved, *The Concert Feature* had loomed large in Walt's consciousness. In a way, it was a fulfillment. Since *The Skeleton Dance*, Walt had harbored the dream of making Silly Symphonies in which, as he told an interviewer, "sheer fantasy unfolds to a musical pattern" without being restricted by the "illusion of reality"—in short, abstract films. With his obligations on *Snow White*, he hadn't had the time to implement this idea until sometime probably in the summer of 1937, when he was dining alone at Chasen's restaurant in Los Angeles, spotted the leonine Polish-born symphony conductor Leopold Stokowski, who was also dining alone, and invited him to his table. Walt already knew Stokowski, one of the most recognizable figures of high culture, with his long, wild hair and his tabloid romances; he had visited the Disney studio in 1934 and maintained an occasional correspondence with Walt. As Stokowski later told it, over dinner that night Walt discussed a project he was considering: a musical short of Paul Dukas's symphonic scherzo "L'Apprenti Sorcier" or "The Sorcerer's Apprentice," about a powerful wizard in whose absence a curious pupil uses the wizard's magical hat and scepter with unfortunate results. By one account, Stokowski offered to conduct the score for nothing. In another, he began expatiating on a dream of *his* own: to make an animated feature set to classical music. Either way, a collaboration began.

With *Snow White* winding down at the time, *The Sorcerer's Apprentice* seemed to strike a nerve with Walt. If the former was the story of Walt's youth, the latter was the story of his new power and his vexed relationship to it. Bill Tytla would draw the sorcerer with Walt's own famously cocked eyebrow and had named him Yen Sid, "Disney" backward, to make the connection between the sorcerer's magic omnipotence and Walt's. In the animation universe Walt Disney did control the elements as Yen Sid did in the cartoon. He was the master, the only one with the "whole equation" in his head, while his minions were the apprentices, helpless without him. But another possible interpretation may have been in Walt's own mind as he awaited the reception to *Snow White*: that he was not the sorcerer but was himself the hapless apprentice who dons the sorcerer's hat and summons the elements only to discover that they overwhelm him. As a continuity for *The Sorcerer's Apprentice* described it, "It is the picture of the typical little man and what he would like to do once given complete control of the earth and its elements." This turned *The Sorcerer's Apprentice* into a portent for the studio. (With war brewing in Europe and Asia, it may have also turned it into a portent for the world generally.) Once *Snow White* was completed, Walt must have sensed that the studio no longer served Walt Disney; rather, Walt Disney increasingly served the studio, unable to manage the forces that he had unleashed. In effect, the cartoon, which was itself a form of hubris, might be seen as Walt's own nightmare in which he is defeated by his own hubris.

But if Walt was using *The Sorcerer's Apprentice* to express his own concerns, he had another, more prosaic incentive for making the short: his dedication to one of his most stalwart supporters. Actress Helen Hayes recalled visiting the studio in 1937 and Walt showing her a new Mickey Mouse cartoon. "Of course you know Donald is the big thing now," Walt told her, "but it won't last. Mickey is forever. He'll have his moments in the shade, but he'll always come out in the bright lights again." In truth, if anything the shade had grown even darker for Mickey Mouse. The early Mickey Mouse had been, as John Updike described him, "America as it feels to itself—plucky, put-upon, inventive, resilient, good-natured, game." But as he had become increasingly domesticated, he had also become increasingly a cipher. "Our dilemma became one of trying to find new, logical material for Mickey, more sophisticated material, if you will," Ward Kimball reflected. "As we got more personality and character into the other cartoons, it became more and more difficult to cope with Mickey. . . . Mickey was really an abstraction. He wasn't based on anything that was remotely real." Animator Friz Freleng agreed: "Mickey Mouse was a nothing, really. After the novelty of animation was over, there was nothing left but a black-and-white drawing moving around. You really don't associate yourself with that character at all." Directors and animators began referring to him as a "Boy Scout" in reference to his lack of spikiness—his blandness.

Walt was not willing to surrender Mickey so easily. He asked Jack Kinney to develop Mickey narratively into something more than a supporting player to Donald Duck, and he charged Fred Moore and Ward Kimball (by one account Moore acted on his own initiative) with redesigning Mickey to make him look more appealing, which was Moore's stock in trade. As Thomas and Johnston reported it, Walt watched footage of Moore's newly redesigned Mickey in the sweatbox, demanding that it be run repeatedly until he finally paused, turned to Moore, and said,

"Now that's the way I want Mickey to be drawn from now on!" Moore had made Mickey softer. Where the mouse had previously been constructed as a series of circles, which made him easy to draw, Moore now suggested that the "body is to be drawn as somewhat pear shape, fairly short and plump" so that Mickey had more curve and less rigidity.* He also further enlarged the head and shrank the body. "Mickey is cuter when drawn with small shoulders with a suggestion of stomach and fanny and I like him pigeon-toed," he told an action analysis class.

Mickey gained mass and weight—"counter movements, counter thrusts," in Kimball's words. His cheeks began to move with his mouth, and Kimball himself converted Mickey's eyes from large, inexpressive black pupils to ovals surrounding pupils. All of these changes made Mickey even more childlike and less rodentlike, which had always been the direction of his evolution anyway. Though children's heads obviously become smaller in relation to their bodies as they grow, evolutionary biologist Stephen Jay Gould observed that Mickey had "traveled this ontogenetic pathway in reverse": the animators infantilized his appearance by enlarging his head, lowering his pants line, and covering his legs to shorten them, thickening his snout and moving his ears back on his head to make the forehead larger and more rounded.

This new Mickey was indisputably cuter, as Moore had said, than the old Mickey, and cute seemed to be the order of the day. "I think people think of Mickey as a cute character," Walt would tell a story meeting after the redesign. "[H]e is a cute character—and he should be more likable in everything he does." But in making him cuter and more of a child, the animators had removed the last remnants of his rude energy—"his vitality, his alertness, his bug-eyed cartoon readiness for adventure," in Updike's words. The old Chaplinesque devilry was completely expunged. (In truth, Chaplin had lost most of his devilry too.) If he became more expressive, he had less to be expressive about. As Updike wrote, referring specifically to Mickey's new eyes but equally applicable to the entire redesign, "It made him less abstract, less iconic, more merely cute and dwarfish."

Though he had approved the redesign, Walt understood that it had not solved the Mickey problem. (Years later he would say of Mickey's demise, "We got tired & we had new characters to play with.") Mickey needed something more to survive. He needed a vehicle. Ben Sharpsteen denied that Walt had decided to make *The Sorcerer's Apprentice* because he

*Though Ub Iwerks had described the original Mickey as "pear-shaped," he was not entirely accurate. Mickey was circular—in part, because a circular construction made him easy to draw. Sometimes the artists would simply take quarters and trace them for the basic components.

thought it was a way to rehabilitate Mickey, saying that Dopey had been considered initially. Still, apparently very early in the process, storyman Chester S. Cobb had been assigned to investigate possibilities for the film and concluded, "It would be difficult to invent an interesting apprentice—a kid wouldn't be comic enough." But, Cobb went on, "Mickey or the Goof [referring to a subsidiary character] in a good imaginative atmosphere would have a lot more audience value as the apprentice than any symphony-type character we might invent." Stokowski wasn't persuaded. "What would you think of creating an entirely new personality for this film instead of Mickey?" he wrote Walt in November 1937. "A personality which could represent You and Me—in other words, someone that would represent in the mind and heart of everyone seeing the film their own personality, so that they would enter into all the drama and emotional changes of the film in a most intense manner." It was one of the few times Walt disregarded a Stokowski suggestion. Walt did think of Mickey Mouse as "you and me," and in a last-ditch rescue mission, he had decided that the sorcerer's apprentice would be his alter ego.

Whatever appeal *The Sorcerer's Apprentice* held for him, Walt, usually so painstakingly deliberate, moved with uncharacteristic haste, most likely because he needed *something* to advance. In July 1937 he had secured the rights to the music, and by late August storyman Otto Englander had submitted an outline, with Walt insisting that "we should try to follow out the idea of the music as much as possible and not change it any more than necessary." Once Stokowski had entered the picture, Walt was especially energized—"all steamed up," as he put it in a letter to Gregory Dickson, an RKO publicity executive who had happened to meet Stokowski on a train and discussed the project with him. "We would all like, very much, to have the opportunity of working with him on this picture and, if possible, to get started on it immediately," Walt continued, offering to put "the finest men in the plant, from color men down to animators, on THE SORCERER." He closed, "I am greatly enthused over the idea and believe that the union of Stokowski and his music, together with the best of our medium, would be the means of a great success and should lead to a new style of motion picture presentation." He asked Dickson again to see if he could convince Stokowski to begin work on the film as soon as possible. The next week Stokowski wrote Walt, equally excited—"you have no more enthusiastic admirer in the world than I am"—and saying he would be making a preliminary recording of the score in a few days.

While Stokowski made his recordings in Philadelphia, where he led the Philadelphia Orchestra, Walt hurried the story crew through a treatment and began soliciting suggestions from the staff, though he advised them to "avoid slapstick gags." "I have never been more enthused over anything in my life," Walt wrote Stokowski in mid-November, informing him that "while anxiously awaiting your arrival[,] to get the wheels of production turning we are preparing a story which we hope will meet with your approval." Stokowski arrived in Los Angeles on January 2, 1938, with great fanfare—Walt was not above suggesting that Dickson exploit Stokowski's recent divorce and reputed romance with actress Greta Garbo for publicity—to approve the story and record the final score. The Hyperion soundstage was too small for the eighty-five musicians whom Stokowski had personally selected, so Walt rented the Selznick studio, and at midnight on Sunday, January 9, Stokowski conducted Dukas's score. (He chose nighttime, he said, because the musicians had to drink coffee to stay awake, which he felt made them more alert.) The conductor was so galvanic that the entire session—recorded, at Stokowski's insistence, on six separate tracks—lasted only three hours. As one observer recalled, when it was over, Stokowski stepped down from the podium drenched in perspiration. It took two bath towels to dry him.

But the collaboration only began there. Stokowski had arrived in Los Angeles armed with what one associate would later call a "sizable portion of his repertory," and he was apparently lobbying Walt to go beyond *Apprentice*. Within weeks of the recording session, no doubt as a result of discussions that Walt and Stokowski held through the end of January, Walt came to a decision: *The Sorcerer's Apprentice* would now be just one segment of a feature that would set animation to classical music, just as Stokowski had allegedly described his vision to Walt at Chasen's. Again Walt moved quickly, perhaps fearing that Stokowski's passion might ebb. By February the studio had canceled Stokowski's *Apprentice* contract, which called for 10 percent of the gross, and drafted a new contract paying him $125,000 to conduct the score for and appear in the new *Concert Feature*.

Exactly why Walt had moved so rapidly on a new feature when he already had *Bambi* and *Pinocchio* in production and was doing preliminary work on *Peter Pan* and *Alice in Wonderland* may not have been readily apparent to those at the studio. Sharpsteen would say that it was a matter of economic expediency. *The Sorcerer's Apprentice* was simply too long and too expensive to be either theatrically or financially viable as a short, and Stokowski's compilation feature gave him a way out. Sharpsteen may have been right that economics were a consideration—Walt said that he needed to make another challenging feature or his animators might get bored and restless and decide to leave—but it hardly seemed the major one. Walt had always wanted to do more poetic, musically inclined shorts, and throughout 1935, 1936, and 1937 he kept returning to an idea for a Silly Symphony he called *Flower Ballet*, for which he explicitly argued against a tight story in favor of something tonal. Even with *Snow White* in high gear, Walt couldn't seem to let it go.

His growing animus toward conventional narrative and his predilection for this kind of animation was another example of Walt's ongoing need for a challenge, his need to make sure that he wasn't stagnating and was still the very best, his need to enlarge his creative world and fend off incursions from pretenders to his throne. "I can't get into a rut or let my boys get into ruts," he would tell a reporter. "If we quit growing mentally and artistically we will begin to die." During the preparation for *The Concert Feature* Walt would sound this idea again and again, just as he had throughout his career: *They need to grow. They need to outdo themselves. They need to keep "plussing."* Asked by one storyman if Walt felt they were taking full advantage of the cartoon medium, he riposted, "This is not the cartoon medium. It should not be limited to cartoons. We have worlds to conquer here. . . . We've got more in this medium than making people laugh." The gags that had been so integral to his shorts, the gags around which the entire studio had once seemed to orbit, now infuriated him. "[I]t's a continual fight around this place to get away from slapping somebody on the fanny or having somebody swallow something," he complained to his staff. "It's going to take time to get ourselves up to the point where we can really get some humor in our stuff, rather than just belly laughs; and get beauty in it, rather than just a flashy postcard." Another time, speaking of *The Concert Feature*, he exhorted, "[W]e're not making an ordinary cartoon and I feel that we've got the wrong slant on this stuff," then bluntly added what would have been heresy even a few years earlier: "I don't believe in this gag stuff."

He was aspiring to something much higher than gags—much higher even than the sentimental fantasy of *Snow White* and *Pinocchio* or the realism of *Bambi*. In extending his hand to Walt, Stokowski, who carefully cultivated the romantic image of a long-haired artiste for popular consumption, was trying to forge a union between the classical and the mass as a way of popularizing not only classical music but also, and not incidentally, himself. Walt was working for the same union, only from the other side. This time he was explicitly bidding to join forces with high art and pry the cartoon from its origins in popular culture, where he felt it was doomed to be crude and juvenile. Walt would have never called himself an artist—he was too skeptical of culture and too plainspoken for that—but he did want to make art, if only because that was the natural evolution for him, and *The Concert Feature* was, he thought, certifiably art. "[T]hey're worried about the high-brow angle," Walt groused at a story meeting after having lunch with RKO counsel Neil Spitz. "The only thing I'm worried about is that it might be a little too low-brow. . . . If you put Dopey in it they would say swell."

Like Stokowski, Walt seemed to take pride in serving as the conduit between the classical composers and his unaffected American audience. Classical music, he thought, had been made to seem rarefied and inaccessible. In *The Concert Feature* he and Stokowski would demystify the music by visualizing it. "I wouldn't worry a damn bit about the stiff shirts that are supposed to be the ones that this music is created for," Walt told his storymen at one session, recalling a recent visit to the opera. "There's a great mass of people who would appreciate this music if they didn't have to sit through stuff like that—like the opera. They want excitement." At another meeting, discussing his reasons for doing *The Concert Feature*, he cited Bach's "Toccata and Fugue in D Minor," one of the pieces he was considering. "There are things in that music that the general public will not understand until they see the things on the screen representing that music," he said, taking the view that the music had a visual analogue. "Then they will feel the depth in the music. Our object is to reach the very people who have walked out on this 'Toccata and Fugue' because they didn't understand it. I am one of those people; but when I understand it, I like it."

For Walt it was, once again, a mission much more than a commercial venture, and he would not allow it to be compromised by commercial considerations. When Roy asked during a discussion of possible scores why they couldn't select some music that "just the ordinary guy like me can like," Walt flashed him an icy stare and ordered him out of the room, telling him, "Go back down and keep the books." The importance of the piece was educating the audience and expanding the medium. "Even if the thing's a flop," he told his staff, "we'll have gained a thorough appreciation of what can be done with music."

But as enthused as he was over *The Concert Feature*—and it seemed to reenergize him after the enervating difficulties on *Bambi* and *Pinocchio*—he was proceeding cautiously again once *The Sorcerer's Apprentice* was recorded and Stokowski had left the studio to resume his duties with the orchestra. "I am up to my neck in PINOCCHIO," Walt wrote the music critic Deems Taylor, whom he was consulting on the new project, "and with BAMBI just getting started and the new studio under way, I do not believe I am going to have much time to devote to the musical feature that I discussed with you while in New York."

Indeed, no sooner had Walt returned from his trip east to receive his honorary degrees than he plunged back into the stalled features, though if he remained the governing spirit, reviewing the scripts and approving the roughs, he was no longer the presiding spirit. That October, with Hyperion unable to accommodate physically all the production staffs working simultaneously, the *Bambi* crew had been shuffled first across the street and then to a rented warren of tiny rooms in a building on Seward Street in Hollywood where Harman-Ising had had their offices. (It was, Marc Davis remembered, enjoying the incongruity, across the street from a pornographic film studio.) According to Thomas and Johnston, the staff was initially resentful at being furloughed; it removed them from the excitement of the studio. But in time they realized they had an advantage in not being at Hyperion: no one would be bothering them. Marc Davis guessed Walt appeared there maybe only three, four, or five times. Instead, pipe-sucking Perce Pearce conducted the story sessions and guided the production, very much in the spirit of Walt, acting out scenes and elaborating the continuity with his story crew. Significantly, Walt did not attend any of these sessions.

For a studio now in desperate need of a new feature, progress was agonizingly incremental. Frank Churchill, who had written the music for *Snow White*, had been signed to compose the score for *Bambi*, though he was a melancholic and unreliable alcoholic, and storyman Larry Morey was, as Gunther Lessing put it, "riding herd on him." The studio was also importing animals for the animators to study, while sending other animators to reserves to observe deer. At the same time a young Chinese-born artist named Ty Wong, who had been hired as an in-betweener on *Pinocchio*, had on his own initiative submitted drawings for *Bambi* that, with Walt's approval, soon became the basis for the style of the film, just as Albert Hurter's inspirational drawings had set the style for *Snow White*. Suggestive rather than highly realistic, Wong's design provided a visual breakthrough for the artists.

But even as they moved forward, they were slogging—trapped between the tight, compressed narrative of *Snow White* and the loose poeticism of *The Concert Feature*, between the cartoon exaggerations that they had already mastered and the more painterly abstract effects of Wong that were far more difficult to achieve. Still disappointed, Walt at one point reassigned Ham Luske to work on shorts while the *Bambi* script was revised. Meanwhile the rest of the staff, though happy to be out from under Walt's gaze, was growing discontented. Thomas and Johnston said that they were never confident they would succeed in capturing the story's emotional power, and they eventually began to wonder whether the film would ever be made at all—a dread intensified by the fact that, as they put it, "Walt never came."

Now, as the studio was laboring on *Bambi*, *Pinocchio*, and *The Concert Feature*, a labor that had ended Walt's respite, there came an event that would end the ebullient times for Walt Disney altogether. Ever since they had received the fiftieth-anniversary promise of a new home, Elias and Flora Disney had been living in a rented apartment on Commonwealth Street while they and Roy hunted for a suitable residence. They finally found one that September—a brand-new home at 4605 Placedia in the Hidden Village section of North Hollywood on a 75-by-125-foot lot whose owner had suddenly died, leaving his widow to dispose of it for $8,300. It had three bedrooms, two baths, a living room, and a double garage, but, Roy wrote Walt, "more important it has a good heating system"—a central gas heater with forced circulation. The brothers put down $2,300 and spent between $2,500 and $3,000 to furnish the house, and their parents moved in shortly thereafter.

But as soon as Elias and Flora moved in, the much vaunted heating system began to malfunction. "We better get this furnace fixed or else some morning we'll wake up and find ourselves dead," Flora was said to have told her housekeeper, Alma Smith. Roy and Walt dispatched a workman from the studio to repair it. On the morning of November 26, 1938, Flora went to the bathroom adjoining her bedroom. When she didn't return, Elias got up to investigate and found her collapsed on the bathroom floor. Feeling overcome himself, he staggered out into the hallway and fainted. Downstairs in the courtyard Alma Smith was emptying a dustpan of oatmeal that she had spilled when she felt herself getting woozy and realized that something was amiss. She rushed back into the house and raced up the stairs, found Elias on the floor, called a neighbor, and then phoned Roy. Meanwhile she tried to open the window, but it was stuck. Then she and the neighbor dragged Flora and Elias down the stairs and outside, and the neighbor administered artificial respiration. Elias revived. Flora did not. She died of carbon monoxide poisoning from the defective heater; a lid on the air intake had slipped, recirculating the exhaust into the house.

It may have been the most shattering moment of Walt Disney's life. Though he seldom exhibited emotion outside the studio, he was inconsolable—a misery deepened no doubt by the fact that she had died in the new home Walt had given her, and by the culpability of his own workmen. (A report on the furnace ordered by Roy determined that the "installation of the furnace showed either a complete lack of knowledge of the requirements of the furnace or a flagrant disregard of these conditions if they were known.") When his parents had arrived in Los Angeles, they had only wanted to see the vast Forest Lawn Cemetery, so Walt had let them off at the gate in the morning and returned later in the day to pick them up. Now Walt and Roy decided to bury their mother there. "You should have seen those two brothers," recalled the Reverend Glenn Puder, the husband of Herbert's daughter Dorothy and the man who officiated at the funeral. In the following months they regularly visited their mother's gravesite, but Walt never spoke of her death to anyone thereafter. When, years later, Sharon asked him where her grandparents were buried, Walt snapped, "I don't want to talk about it."

III

He didn't have time to be immobilized by grief. With the *Bambi* crew crawling ahead at Seward Street, that fall Walt began to refocus on *Pinocchio*—once again analyzing scenes, assigning animation, recording voices, reviewing Leica reels, and most of all, constructing a new story arc. To solve the problem of Pinocchio's moral aimlessness, the emphasis and identification had shifted to the cricket—"Jiminy," as he was now named—as a moral agent and conscience. During the hiatus that spring and summer Jiminy's role had been substantially expanded, and the singer-comedian Cliff Edwards had been hired to voice him.* Unlike for *Bambi*, Walt generally attended the story meetings and made suggestions—everything from the kind of music best suited for the undersea sequence ("vibra harps, soft temple blocks"), to Pinocchio's reaction to his transformation into a donkey ("His little laugh goes into a hee-haw as he tests it. He swallows. It's him!") to the seriousness with which Jiminy Cricket should accept his assignment as Pinocchio's conscience. By December, Walt declared himself pleased. "[T]he general outline seems pretty good to me now," he told the story staff. "In other words, I think we

*Walt was taking a somewhat different attitude to casting voices now after the triumph of *Snow White*. He wanted to get a popular child actor named Frankie Darro to play Pinocchio's dissolute companion Lampwick and confidently predicted he would. "When you get people like Burgess Meredith who want to do the voice,—certain actors who want to do voices for our characters, they look at it differently than they used to." He now suggested they give screen credit to the actors "so it attaches some importance to it, and a certain prestige. Because we need those good actors, you know." Story Meeting, *Pinocchio*—Boobyland and Escape, Dec. 8, 1938, Story Meetings 1938–1939, *Pinocchio*, Story Material, A2961, WDA.

can safely go ahead. We have tried it every way and I feel that it's safe." In reality, given the schedule and the need for a feature, he had no choice but to approve the material.

Walt made, however, one last fix. That January he met with Bill Cottrell, and Jaxon, and Ted Sears, Dorothy Blank, and Dick Creedon of the story department, to discuss the possibility of Jiminy Cricket becoming not only the moral center of the film but also its narrator. "I kind of like that where he starts to tell a story in this little prologue affair some way," Walt said, then proceeded to describe Jiminy's new entrance as the camera tracks through the village and into Geppetto's window while Jiminy sings "When You Wish Upon a Star," stopping to tell his story. This tracking scene would, in the final film, be one of the most striking uses of the multiplane camera, and it wound up costing nearly $50,000.

Centralizing Jiminy Cricket in this way and unifying the film around him seemed to have solved the film's major problem, but it created another. While the cricket had now been thoroughly conceptualized in narrative terms, no one seemed to know how he ought to look. Ham Luske suggested that Walt talk to Ward Kimball. Kimball had been stewing ever since Walt had cut his scenes from *Snow White*, and he had decided to quit. He was in Walt's office to tender his resignation when Walt began his sales pitch, talking about Jiminy and how he reminded him of his own beloved addled uncle Ed. Then he asked Kimball if he would take control of him. "God, he did such a wonderful job," Kimball remembered, "that I walked out very happily and said: What a wonderful place this is!" Kimball set about designing a "sort of halfway thing" with bulging eyes, a top hat, teeth, feelers, arms, and an elongated body with thick legs. Walt was unimpressed. "We can't have a character like that. He's gotta be cute," he said, issuing the same injunction he had used for the new Mickey Mouse. "That's too gross." So Kimball went back to his drawing board and converted him into a little man with an oversize head. Though Jiminy now bore no resemblance to a cricket, Walt was pleased. As Kimball put it, "[H]e was a cricket because we called him a cricket."

That still left Pinocchio and the ongoing debate about whether he was more a wooden puppet or a little boy. The wooden concept made sense—he *was* a puppet who later *became* a boy—but Walt had seen the footage that Fred Moore had animated and, as Ollie Johnston remembered, "felt the character needed to be more appealing," just like Jiminy. Milt Kahl had been critical of the character, thinking that he didn't move well, so Luske, who had recommended Kimball for Jiminy, recommended that Kahl take a crack at Pinocchio himself and make him essentially a boy with wooden joints. Kahl accepted the challenge, animated the scene of

Pinocchio undersea knocking on an oyster shell, and then showed it to Walt, who, Johnston said, "flipped." Even Fred Moore was impressed, though the redesign knocked him from his perch as the most favored animator in the studio. From that point on, Kahl was in charge of animating Pinocchio, assisted by Frank Thomas and Ollie Johnston, while Moore animated Lampwick, Pinocchio's dissolute guide on Pleasure Island, a character with more than a passing resemblance to Moore himself.

But even having resolved the narrative problems and having settled on Jiminy and a more boylike Pinocchio, Walt was concerned. He knew that *Pinocchio* was more conventional than *Bambi* or *The Concert Feature*; that was precisely why he felt he could hasten it into production. But he didn't want it to be just another cartoon—a *Snow White* knockoff. It was imperative that it be bigger, grander, and more realistically animated. Otherwise there was no aesthetic reason to make it. Indeed, one of the reasons Walt was so intent on an underwater sequence was that, as he wrote Otto Englander, "[i]t all gives us a chance for something very fantastic." Though virtually the entire film was already being shot in live action for rotoscoping, Walt had asked artist Joe Grant, who was an excellent caricaturist, how they might improve their technique. Grant suggested a model department where they could fashion little statues of the characters so that the animators could study them from different angles. (He had, in fact, fashioned just such a statue for the crone in *Snow White*.) Walt agreed and then put Grant in charge. Eventually they built models not only of the characters but of inanimate objects, like the cage into which Pinocchio is thrown, then filmed it swinging so they could trace the photostats. Walt also wanted even more dimensionality to the backgrounds and characters than he had had in *Snow White*, so he devised yet another system of application of paint called a "blend" that combined dry brushing and airbrushing to create roundness, especially on cheeks. It was an extremely expensive process—by one account there were twenty women in the airbrush department alone—and Walt advised they use it sparingly ("We must keep from going broke on this picture"), but he nevertheless insisted upon it as a way of bettering the look of *Snow White*. Jiminy Cricket alone had twenty-seven parts and twenty-seven different colors. As Frank Thomas later told an interviewer, "[T]his was an era when he wanted things to be real. He wanted it to be round, solid, reaching for perfection."

But *Pinocchio* had become a chore, an obligation. Walt's real obsession now was *The Concert Feature*. He would tell the animators that, as Ollie Johnston put it, it would "change the history of motion pictures." *The Concert Feature* would be entirely different from anything he had done. "I don't think it will be common," he told his staff. "We've always wanted to do this sort of thing, but couldn't risk it—between a newsreel and a feature." Now, because *Snow White* had given him the aesthetic capital to do so, they could. All that summer, even as he was hard at work on *Pinocchio,* he was edgy waiting for Stokowski to return from Europe, where the conductor was visiting composers' relatives—among them Debussy's widow and Ravel's brother—to secure releases for possible musical selections, even writing to Walt in code for fear that he would be found out and coopted. When Stokowski arrived back in Los Angeles in September 1938, along with the critic Deems Taylor, Walt couldn't wait to start listening to and selecting music. The three of them spent virtually the entire month in Room 232 listening to records of classical pieces, dozens of them, and pondering possible visualizations: Paganini's "Moto Perpetuo" or Mosolov's "Iron Foundry" ("We could do something good with machinery," Walt said); Stravinsky's *The Firebird,* "Renard," or *Petrouchka;* Prokofiev's *Love for Three Oranges*; Gounod's "Funeral March of a Marionette;" Mussorgsky's "Song of a Flea" (with opera star Lawrence Tibbett scratching himself during the performance); Berlioz's *Roman Carnival*; a work of Debussy's that Walt called "Fate"; Wagner's *Ring of the Nibelungen* (which, one staff member suggested, might be used for a new children's story called *The Hobbit* by J. R. R. Tolkien); and even a symphonic rendering of "Pop Goes the Weasel." They debated whether to introduce a single pianist for a piece (Walt wanted Rachmaninoff and thought of having a Russian scene with snow falling, and the snow turning into crystal formations) and whether to include American pieces. (Walt decided that "Americans wouldn't feel insulted if you left the American music out," while Stokowski declared, "Disney is a genius who is going into new things. To go back to Swanee River and that sentimental stuff—it isn't for this picture I don't think.") For all the deliberate, intense scrutiny of each score, Walt could barely contain his enthusiasm. After dragging along on *Bambi* and *Pinocchio,* hitting roadblock after roadblock, he told Stokowski that he was going to assign a number of units to *The Concert Feature* and thought he could rough out a story in two to three weeks—once they settled on the compositions. That way, when Stokowski returned to the studio in January, they could actually begin the orchestrations and record the music by the spring.

They made an odd pair—the epitome of the classical artist and the epitome of the commercial artist—which may have been part of the personal attraction, just as it was part of the artistic partnership. Stokowski seemed to love the free-spiritedness of the Disney studio. Walt seemed to love the highbrow legitimization that Stokowski bestowed. At times they could sit together, usually with Deems Taylor, and listen to music for hours. At other times, as one animator described it, Stokowski would be "swooping through the halls followed by Disney and a retinue of writers and story sketch men, all struggling to keep pace." At meetings Walt was deferential to his partner. As informal as he was, he always called his associate "Mr. Stokowski," never "Leopold" or "Stoki," which was his nickname, and he always privileged Stokowski's opinions, rarely contradicting him.

But for all the comity and real friendship between them, sometimes the cultures clashed. At one session Walt kept turning up the volume when the music was soft and turning it down when the music was loud, prompting Stokowski to explode, "What is loud should be loud and what is soft should be soft!" And if Stokowski could reprimand Walt, Walt wasn't above poking fun at his esteemed partner. At a recording session he remarked to a colleague that Stokowski with his long hair looked like the comedian Harpo Marx. Still, despite their different places in the cultural constellation, the two did share a sense of entertainment and bombast. Discussing one especially loud section of music, Walt compared it to "blowing the top off the mountain," adding, "Stokowski loves to do it. He would blow the top off the speakers on this." Of course, so would Walt.

After two months of labor Walt, Stokowski, and Taylor had winnowed the compositions to roughly a dozen, and on the evening of September 29, 1938, Walt convened fifty to sixty of his artists on the soundstage for a two-and-a-half-hour piano concert while he provided a running commentary on what the audience would be seeing in the feature. He also showed them a rough of *The Sorcerer's Apprentice*, which, according to one attendee, had them cheering and applauding "until all hands were red." As this observer saw it, "It seemed indeed as if Walt and his boys had crossed a threshold into a truly new art form." Clearly inspired, Walt, Stokowski, and Taylor, in a postmortem the next morning, promptly lopped off an overture, the piano solo, "Moto Perpetuo," and, with startling confidence, selected the final compositions: Bach's "Toccata and Fugue in D Minor," Pierné's *Cydalise and the Goat-Foot*, Tchaikovsky's "The Nutcracker Suite," Mussorgsky's "Night on Bald Mountain," Schubert's "Ave Maria," Ponchielli's "Dance of the Hours," Debussy's "Clair de Lune," Stravinsky's *The Rite of Spring*, and of course Dukas's "The Sorcerer's Apprentice," for a total running time of just over two hours. "I don't know what more the audience would want for their money, do you?" Walt beamed to his collaborators. He was already setting crews to work on each sequence, ending what may have been the most productive month of his life.

Walt was happy, and the story meetings on *The Concert Feature* that fall were smaller and much more playful and freewheeling than the meetings on *Bambi* or *Pinocchio*. In part, it was because this time Walt wasn't carrying the entire burden; since he clearly didn't know as much about music as his collaborators, he was sharing the burden with Stokowski and Taylor. Another reason was that Walt didn't feel he had to have the entire movie in his head; since this was not a densely plotted film, he could brainstorm and experiment. "We're searching here, trying to get away from the cut-and-dried handling of things all the way through everything," he told his story crew with what seemed a sense of relief, "and the only way to do it is to leave things open until we have completely explored every bit of it." In fact, his concerns were less aesthetic than cultural. Though he would later be accused of bowdlerizing the compositions, Walt was nearly reverential toward the scores, fearing to make any cuts and worrying what the reaction would be if he departed from the composer's stated idea for a piece of program music. It was Stokowski who assured him that cutting a score was perfectly acceptable ("It is like pruning a tree. It sometimes grows stronger from pruning"), and that providing one's own visual interpretation of the music was fine "if the spirit of the music is with us."

But the main reason Walt was so enthusiastic about *The Concert Feature* was that he felt he was blazing trails again. The effect was liberating. Having already expressed his antagonism toward gags, he was now expressing antagonism toward the idea of narrative itself. Not everything had to connect, he instructed his storymen. Not everything had to be worked out in story terms. "I know everybody has the tendency to have story," he told a meeting on *The Concert Feature*, "but I keep telling myself that this is different—we're presenting music," which meant that the score wouldn't just embellish the visuals but would be absolutely coequal to them. "I would like to have this thing kind of weave itself together and complete itself, but not have a plot." At another meeting, describing admiringly a recent package of eight unrelated shorts that the studio was releasing that September as a kind of test run for *The Concert Feature*, he told his story crew that the "story annoys you."

But Walt wasn't thinking only in terms of new narrative departures. He was thinking of *The Concert Feature* as an entirely new kind of theatrical experience. Watching a Pete Smith short called *Audioscopiks*, for which he donned special glasses to see a three-dimensional effect, Walt got the idea of using a similar effect for a sequence in his film and attaching glasses to the top of the program, and he set one of his special effects men to work on it. He also discussed with Stokowski the possibility of wafting perfume into the theater during the scenes with flowers. "I'm serious about this whole perfume idea," he told Stokowski. "You could space the perfume to come in only at certain times." Most of all, he latched onto the idea of devising a new sound reproduction system for the movie, one with a speaker at the front and center of the theater and other speakers to the left and right and down the sides to convey a sense of a full orchestra. "It would be quite a sensation if you get that dimensional thing on the screen and have the horns working with it," Walt said. "The sound and pictures will be around you." He called it Fantasound.

That fall, as he was concocting new ways of presenting his film, he began working through the visuals with the same determination and enthusiasm that he had lavished on the music. For "Toccata and Fugue" he had decided to put the oscillations of the optical sound track on the screen and dispense with any representational depictions, but he warned special effects man Cy Young, "We don't want to follow what anyone else has done in the abstract." For "Night on Bald Mountain," Walt had the idea of having the devil playing either a violin or an organ and rising from the depths of a volcano—"a sort of mad musician, gloating over the effect his music has on the spirits." Later—in fact, at a three-and-a-half-hour-long meeting on the afternoon of the studio concert—he had elaborated the idea into the devil as a "huge Gulliver in the village with his cloak blowing and all these spirits around these houses," which would be accompanied by the sound of a wind sweeping across the theater, thanks to the new sound system. For "Cydalise," Walt thought of centaurs and fauns frolicking on an Elysian Field where an old faun is holding class at a mythological music school and keeps having to scold a smart-alecky young faun; then he decided to add a scene with centaurettes and a finale in which the fauns chase the centaurettes. But he had doubts about the fauns—"If you treat them as being cute, you can't be too cruel to them"—thinking that centaurs might serve just as well, and he began to doubt whether the music itself fit the images he had in mind. When Dick Huemer suggested that they hire Stravinsky to write something, Walt countered, "Those guys don't work that way," though he was so confident of his efforts that he told Huemer he could foresee the time when composers would write for animation as they wrote for the stage.

For "Dance of the Hours" Walt, citing the illustrations of Heinrich Kley, imagined a ballet of animals, with each group representing a different time of day—ostriches (dawn), hippopotamuses (day), elephants (evening), and alligators (night)—but he objected to any "obvious slapstick type of stuff" to which the animals might lend themselves. "I think the main thing we must keep in mind is that the animals are serious," Walt told his story crew. "They are not clowning." He wanted real personality. "It could be some big fat person up there trying to do a ballet. That's what we are going to drive for, and we will have animators who can give us that." By November Walt was having young Marjorie Belcher, who had served as the live model for Snow White, perform on film to give the animators suggestions, though Walt himself seemed inspired too, tossing off ideas with the same excitement and detail as he had on *Snow White*. Visualizing a dance between a hippo and the alligator, he said, "I think there at the end the guy finally just lets her drop, boom, and it bounces everything in the background. . . . You see the expression on her face—blank and immediately she goes into one of those poses."

"The Nutcracker Suite" was harder, in part because it had several sections. At first, Walt had the idea of fading in from Stokowski leading his orchestra to his leading an orchestra of bugs in a kind of overture. That would lead into a March Processional, the Dance of the Sugar Plum Fairy with dewdrops, and a Russian Dance with turtles that would segue into the Chinese Dance featuring "lizards with flowers on their heads like Chinese hats," who perform before a mandarin frog, and the Arab Dance using "little animals." The finale would be a Flower Ballet following the blossoms through the seasons. As Walt described it, a "ballerina comes out—a graceful, beautiful girl—and she puts a little sex into the damn thing. . . . When she whirls up, you see the panties and her little butt—it will be swell! The audience will rave if you can make them feel Sex in a flower." At the end leaves would fall over the dancers as the flowers exhaust themselves. As the leaves continued to fall, the film would return to the orchestra, now in shadow.

But on *The Concert Feature* nothing was set in stone. By November, Walt had reconsidered, then reincorporated, and finally dropped the overture entirely ("You mean it's okay?" Walt asked his staff incredulously as he would never have asked on *Snow White*. "I expected a battle"), replaced the turtles of the Russian Dance with thistles, and eliminated the little animals of the Arab Dance for what he called "an underwater extravaganza embodying all types of marine plant life and beautiful fish." The one section that still troubled him was the Chinese Dance. He felt that they hadn't quite found the exact visual correlative. But he did fasten on one element he liked. "[T]here's something very valuable in these little mushrooms that look like Chinese characters," Walt said at the story meeting. "Take the little mushrooms—there's something there that will be very cute, and people will remember it—every time they look at a mushroom after that they'll try to see those Chinese." By January 1939, the March Processional had gone the way of the overture, the lizards and the frog mandarin were gone, and the mushrooms had become the stars of the segment.

The sequence that really fired Walt's imagination, however, was Stravinsky's *The Rite of Spring*. Walt had already contacted Stravinsky in April 1938 about the possibility of using *The Firebird* in *The Concert Feature*, though that plan was ultimately scrapped. But Stravinsky's name arose again in September, when Walt, Taylor, and Stokowski were poring over scores and Walt suddenly asked if there was a piece of music to which they could stage "something of a prehistoric theme—with prehistoric animals." Taylor immediately answered, *Le Sacre du Printemps*,* and Walt, without pausing, began to visualize: "There would be something terrific in dinosaurs, flying lizards and prehistoric monsters." When Stokowski had the piece played, Walt was ecstatic. "This is marvelous!" he said, and once again described prehistoric animals and cavemen. "This prehistoric thing would be something entirely different from anything we have done. It would be grotesque and exaggerated."

Now Walt was soaring. If *The Concert Feature* provided a new direction from his previous work, *The Rite of Spring* provided a new direction from anything else in *The Concert Feature*. When some who had attended the studio concert griped that the piece was too long and downbeat, Walt dismissed their complaints—"The happy ending again!"—and rhapsodized, "I feel there is an awful lot that we have wanted to do for a long time and have never had the opportunity or excuse, but when you take pieces of music like this, you really have reason to do what we want to do." What Walt wanted to do was trace the history of the earth beginning with the creation and ending with man triumphing over his environment by using his intellect—not only animation as an act of creation but animation as Creation itself. It should look, he told one animator, "as though the studio had sent an expedition back to the earth 6 million years ago," and at Joe Grant's suggestion, he decided to ask the esteemed science fiction writer H. G. Wells to vouch for the film's scientific accuracy. Though Walt later gave up the idea of man's evolution and triumph—one associate said he didn't want to antagonize Christian fundamentalists—he never surrendered the basic idea of a cosmic cataclysm that would test the bounds of animation. "That's what I see in the last half," he said. "Continual volcanoes—the sea was lashed into a fury. Get the volcanoes and the lava and the sea and everything—the animals trying to escape. End that with the big blowup somewhere. Something blows up big to finish the

*Dick Huemer would suggest that Walt was so ignorant of classical music that when he heard the word "sacre," he asked, "The sock?" But the transcript of this session indicates that Walt did no such thing. In fact, he hardly paused. Dick Huemer, "Thumbnail Sketches," *Funnyworld*, Fall 1979, p. 41.

fourth side [of the record] there." In effect, Walt was playing the sorcerer's apprentice, orchestrating the forces of nature.

Of course, this was Walt's personal interpretation of the music. Stravinsky had written *The Rite of Spring* not as a musical rendition of creation or evolution but as a celebration of American Indian rituals, and some on Walt's own staff felt that reimagining the score this way did an injustice to the music, though Walt tried to justify himself by saying that Stravinsky had once admitted he was striking primitive themes. Others objected that no one would take the dinosaurs seriously and that the segment would be derided. Walt pondered this charge and for a while he considered making the whole sequence comic. "It will be safer and we will have more fun making it, and I think we will make something good," he told his story department in an abrupt about-face, and then began imitating how dinosaurs walked, hobbling around the room with bent knees and sticking out his rump. Within a week, though, Walt had regained his bearings and was back uninhibitedly free-associating to the music: "Something like that last WHAHUMMPH I feel is a volcano—yet it's on land. I get that UGHHH WAHUMMPH! on land, but we can look out on the water before this and see water spouts." At the end, he said, "there's a sort of stop. . . . pulsating like an old steam engine. . . . Chuh! CHUH! . . . CHSSSSSH." He got himself so worked up as he listened that he blurted, "Stravinsky will say: 'Jesus, I didn't know I wrote that music.' "

By this time Walt's mother had died and Stokowski had left the studio to fulfill other obligations, though he told Walt that he could always be there within a few hours should Walt need him, and the film was in a temporary limbo. When Stokowski returned in January 1939, Walt was ready. Together over the next two months they reviewed the scores, reexamined the continuities, looked at Leica reels, and organized the sequences so that there would be a rhythm to the film. They even decided to remove "Cydalise" and replace it with a segment from Beethoven's Sixth Symphony, the "Pastorale," for the faun and centaur section. "If you had selected any other Beethoven Symphony," Deems Taylor wrote Stuart Buchanan, who was in charge of the musical rights at the studio, "I would say nix; too dangerous. You can't monkey with the Master." But the "Pastorale," he felt, was lighthearted enough for one to take some liberties with it, besides which, "Beethoven was a good deal of a pagan himself, and would have liked nothing better than to meet up with a gang of fauns and centaurettes."

By March, Stokowski had departed once again, this time to return to Philadelphia to record the sound track. Walt joined him a few weeks later for the sessions at the Academy of Music, and though the maestro chafed at some of the restrictions—he had to station different sections of the orchestra between partitions for better sound reproduction and had to listen to a "click track" as he conducted to keep the tempo for the animation—Stuart Buchanan wrote Walt that "Mr. Stokowski is a little difficult at times, but I think we are managing him alright." In fact, by at least one account, Stokowski was happier with the recordings than were Bill Garity, the studio's engineer, and Leigh Harline, its musical director. In any case, at the end of April Walt was heading back to the studio with the recordings finished. Now all they had to do was animate the film.

But he also had *Pinocchio* to contend with, and he needed to get it finished before too much time had elapsed and the studio lost its momentum. In just over six months he had managed to work out *The Concert Feature*. *Pinocchio* had always been a much more stubborn proposition, and even before the key animation had started, the film was already well over budget. He spent much of the summer and early fall sweatboxing scenes and presented a rough assemblage to his employees on the studio soundstage that September. The response was less than enthusiastic, though Walt dismissed most of the criticism. "There's certain guys that write you these long letters . . . and they'll criticize everything up and down," Walt sniped, even though his was the most critical voice at the studio, "and I have known certain ones that go for art, and they don't even know what the hell art is themselves." In any case, he left a few days later with Lillian for a three-week vacation to Hawaii. He would be less dismissive when he returned from his holiday and showed the rough to Joe Rosenberg of the Bank of America and Ned Depinet and George Schaefer of RKO on October 26. "These people had come to examine the picture under special and very unusual circumstances," publicist William Levy wrote Walt later that week, clearly trying to rally him from what had apparently been a less-than-satisfying preview, and closed, "I consider it can and should outgross 'Snow White' in every normal market by a considerable margin."

But Walt himself wasn't so sure. He bragged to the *Bambi* crew that the enforced extra time on *Pinocchio*, when they had had to reconceptualize the film, had actually paid dividends because the animators, with the benefit of live action and dialogue tracks, now had a firmer grasp on the characters—firmer even than they had had on the characters in *Snow White*. Rather than operate within the kind of loose arrangement that had prevailed on *Snow White*, where animators were often shuttled where they were needed, the directors of *Pinocchio* were working with the animators in small units on single characters and even doing their own sweatboxing so that there was never a need to call in, say, Fred Moore to explain the characters as Walt had had to do on *Snow White*. Walt was so satisfied with the way the directors and animators had internalized the characters that he thought every feature should be organized this way from now on: a director and a chief animator responsible for each character working with his own crew of checkers, in-betweeners, and cleanup men.

Yet Walt knew the system sounded better and more efficient than it really was. He admitted that because some animators could only draw Pinocchio and others only the cricket, certain scenes didn't "jell so well." Worse, because directors and animators were working exclusively on their own sequences without much coordination among them, they were blindered to the rest of the film, especially since Walt, who had provided this coordination on *Snow White*, was preoccupied at the time with *The Concert Feature*. "The whole damn thing was a mixed-up operation," animator Milt Kahl later said. "They had multiple directors. . . . Either four units or five directorial units. And then each guy was inclined to . . . I don't know, his sequence became the most important in the picture. . . . If you were left with all the sequences [at] the length the directors wanted them, the picture would have run six hours." Art director Ken O'Connor agreed that the film was something of a muddle: "You had people trying to outdo each other. . . . I always found it remarkable that the features hung together as well as they did."

With *Pinocchio*'s release targeted for Christmas 1939, the studio found itself once again racing toward completion. "We worked every night all through the preceding months, and we were all just absolutely exhausted," remembered painter Jane Patterson. Though the release was rescheduled to February, the staff still had to work on Christmas Eve. But that night at about nine-thirty the doors of the ink and paint department opened and in came Walt, a porkpie hat on his head, silently pushing a laundry cart. In the cart were Christmas presents for the girls—compacts and cigarette cases, each "beautifully wrapped." "Walt didn't wish anyone a merry Christmas," Jane Patterson recalled. "He didn't chat. . . . He just passed the presents out to all the girls and left," though in doing so, she said, he had lifted their morale considerably. In the end, despite the round-the-clock labor, the studio missed the original Christmas target by over a month. Walt was both weary and discouraged. As he lamented to Gus Van Schmus of Radio City Music Hall, "It's the toughest job the animators have ever had, and I hope I never have to live through another one like it."

While *Pinocchio* was barreling to its finish, Walt was focused on his true passion of the moment: *The Concert Feature*. Now, in Stokowski's absence, the studio faced an urgent task. It needed a title for the film. Since its inception, it had been called *The Concert Feature* or *Musical Feature*, but as it proceeded, RKO publicist Hal Horne was pushing for something more euphonious—something, he hoped, that they might copyright to preclude any other animation studio from using it. His own suggestion was *Filmharmonic Concert*, but Stuart Buchanan decided to conduct a contest at the studio for other possibilities. Two hundred and fifty-nine employees submitted nearly eighteen hundred titles, including *Bach to Stravinsky and Bach* and *Highbrowski by Stokowski.* Still, the favorite among those supervising the film remained a very early working title, *Fantasia.* By the time of the contest, even Horne had warmed to it. "It isn't the word alone but the meaning we read into it," he wrote Buchanan that May. Writing at the bottom of the same letter, Roy gave his approval: " 'Fantasia' has grown on us until it seems appropriate, has a nice sound & is intriguing." Only Stokowski seemed unconvinced. That October he suggested he and Walt bat around titles themselves "by trying to find what we want to say to the public through this picture and its name." Whether or not they did so, the title remained. The film was thenceforth known as *Fantasia.*

By this time the animation on the film was well under way, and Walt was deeply involved despite periodic detours for *Pinocchio* and *Bambi.* He was aiming for greatness. For "Toccata and Fugue" he had enlisted a German animator named Oskar Fischinger, who was well known in animation circles for his abstractions. Though Walt liked Fischinger's work, he wasn't impressed by Fischinger personally—he was a large, pompous man who dressed entirely in black—and Fischinger returned the compliment, complaining that there were "no artists" at the studio, "only cartoonists." Jules Engel, another fine artist who had gotten work on *Fantasia,* said he had been warned never to use the word *abstract* at the studio because, he was told, "you're going to have people look at you like you're a strange character." In point of fact, while Walt advised the animators to eschew what he called "wild abstraction," he was even more wary of figurative animation for the section. "You bring figures in and it gets common," he told a story meeting that August. "We're going to sell this thing for five million dollars and not cheapen it and sell it for peanuts." Despite Fischinger's and Engel's complaints that Walt wouldn't let go of representation, the opposite was in fact true. In "Toccata and Fugue" Walt was not trying to actualize his conscious vision, as he had done with *Snow White* and *Pinocchio*; he wanted to plumb his psyche. "This is more or less picturing subconscious things for you," he told his staff after describing how the music seemed to come to him "through the skin." "It's a flash of color going through a scene, or movement of a lot of indefinite things. It's the nearest I can come to giving a reason for abstract things."

He took the same approach to "The Nutcracker Suite." He was looking for something that felt as if it had been dreamed. "It's like something you see with your eyes half-closed," he told his staff, waxing poetic. "You almost imagine them. The leaves begin to look like they're dancing, and the blossoms floating on the water begin to look like ballet girls in skirts." Sometimes at the story meetings he would play the music and just have the staff listen so they could discover what impressions it evoked in them. He always wanted more imagination. His fear was never that the animation would be too artful or esoteric for his audience. His fear was that he was determined to do so much in *Fantasia* he would overwhelm them. "[T]here's a theory I go on that an audience is always thrilled with something new," he said at a story meeting, "but fire too many new things at them and they become restless." At another meeting he advised that "things must be big, impressive but simple. Not too much stuff in there."

Because Walt could do whatever he pleased without having to worry about a narrative or realistically representative drawings, *Fantasia* seemed to sail along that spring and summer of 1939 without any of the hurdles that he had encountered on *Bambi* and *Pinocchio*—except for one section. When Walt had jettisoned "Cydalise" for Beethoven's "Pastorale," he was fitting a preconception to the music. He had envisioned a section inspired by Greek mythology featuring the gods on Mount Olympus and the mythological creatures at the foot of the mountain—those centaurs and fauns. "We don't get too serious because I don't feel anything really serious," he told his storymen that August as they were beginning to flesh out the segment; but he warned that "we're not going to be slapstick; there is a certain refinement in the whole thing." Walt was so eager to proceed that he promised to put the entire studio to work on the sequence.

Up to this point Stokowski, who attended many of the story meetings early that spring and late that summer, had been generally supportive of Walt's ideas, even encouraging him to ignore the anticipated criticisms by classical music aficionados. But when it came to the "Pastorale," Stokowski drew a line. "I don't want to come out of my own field—I'm only a musician," Stokowski said disingenuously at a story meeting that July, "but I think what you have there, the idea of great [*sic*] mythology, is not quite my idea of what this symphony is about. This is a nature symphony—it's called Pastoral [*sic*]." He repeated his objection a few weeks later when it was suggested that the nature forms be eliminated altogether. "If you are going to leave out the trees and nature forms," he said, "you're going to leave out what it is." When Walt seemed to brush aside his complaints, Stokowski, saying that he wanted to be "loyal to you and the picture," nevertheless forcefully explained that Beethoven was "worshipped" and that if they strayed too far from his intent, they would be asking for trouble from offended music enthusiasts.

On this point Walt held his ground with Stokowski. He didn't want to put nature up on the screen, he rebutted, because he thought it would be too conventional to have bucolic scenes. "I defy anybody to go out and shoot centaurs or gods making a storm," he said. "That's our medium, and that's how I feel about this." He thereby expressed, intentionally or not, that the real theme of the film was power—*his* power. And he insisted that in any case the liberties he was taking were slight. Instead of being about the woods outside Vienna, as Beethoven had intended, the sequence would be about the Elysian Fields, and instead of country dancing it would have Bacchus. "He brings all the centaurs and centaurettes to his gay party, and they are having a gay time." And he made a pronouncement that critics would later use to lacerate him for his alleged philistinism and sense of cultural imperialism: "I think this thing will make Beethoven."

Even as Walt was finalizing *Fantasia*, he still had *Bambi* to resolve. That spring he had begun pressing the crew to accelerate production. He expected them to have the death of Bambi's mother animated in rough by May, and the entire film finished by August. The problem was that the crew on Seward Street, largely left to their own devices while Walt worked on *Pinocchio* and *Fantasia*, had yet to determine how they were going to proceed. After nearly a year and a half of Walt's telling them to ruminate on the characters before animating them, he was now directing them to begin animating sections as soon as possible, review them in the Leica reels, and then revise them. Only then would they bring on the key animators, the "best animal animators we have in the studio," as Perce Pearce put it, to set the characters in motion. As Pearce described the process at a story meeting that April, the Leica reels gave them an opportunity to experiment and discard what didn't work. "There is no formula for any of it," he said, essentially admitting that they hadn't licked the project. "It's only trial and error."

By late August, Walt, who said he didn't want to sit in on long story meetings, had reviewed the first four Leica reels, and he wasn't happy. Some of the action was too slow, there was too little tension in a scene when Man enters the forest, and the voices were inadequate. Still, he instructed the crew to begin animating in the hope that the characters would thereby be solidified. "[W]e've found that out in *Pinocchio*," he told the staff, in a reversal of the method on *Snow White* and of what he had been telling the *Bambi* crew, "that you don't find your character until you begin to do a little animation on them." But the question of *how* to animate lingered. Did you assign an animator to a character throughout the film, as they had done on *Pinocchio*, or did you assign him to a single scene in which he would draw all the characters? Did you divide the film into sequences with their own story crews and animation crews, or did you have a single story crew and animation crew working on the whole film?

The answers came during a daylong meeting in the sweatbox on September 1, 1939, the day Germany invaded Poland—an event that seemed to have no effect on the studio. Walt, acting on a suggestion from Milt Kahl, who protested that he had grown stale animating only Pinocchio, decided to break the logjam by assigning Kahl, Fred Moore, and Frank Thomas to the project as a team because "they have a very analytical mind," even though Kahl and Thomas were still preoccupied with *Pinocchio* and wouldn't be available for another two months. A week later Larson had replaced Moore, but the idea still held that instead of parceling out the animation to individuals, as Walt had done on *Snow White* and *Pinocchio* and as he was doing on *Fantasia*, these three animators, acting together, would control the entire animation of the film—conceptualizing the characters, blocking the action, and then supervising the additional animators needed to finish the project. Again reversing course, he advised that they begin as they had on *Snow White* by concentrating on a single scene, the scene in which Bambi learns to walk, then master it as a guide for the animators to come.

It was a longer process—just letting the animators draw and animate until they got the feel of the characters—but Walt had already conceded that *Bambi* wasn't going to be ready anytime soon and that *Fantasia* would be released after *Pinocchio* and that he would then release what he called "feature shorts," which would be three long cartoons packaged as a feature, and then another feature, and *then*, "maybe," he said, *Bambi*. "There would be a disaster here if we started rushing everybody on this picture," he told the staff. When Kahl asked Walt when he anticipated that actual production would start, Walt replied that it would start whenever Kahl and his team felt they were ready to start. He was through pushing them. "It's wise to move easy," he said, citing his experience on *Pinocchio*, "and everybody get a chance to feel what they're doing."

The animators used some of the time to study deer. In *Snow White*, Eric Larson commented, the deer had been "sacks of wheat" because the staff hadn't yet acquired the technique to draw them properly. For *Bambi* the animators spent three or four months just concentrating on drawing deer. Walt had collected thousands of feet of film of deer, borrowing some from other studios and hiring a photographer of his own, Maurice Day, to go to Maine to shoot studies, including one of a fawn being born—"quite an assortment of deer stuff," as Walt put it. To provide even more guidance, Day eventually sent two does to the studio, where they were kept in a pen outside the animation building, which led to adventures when a rutting buck descended and had to be lassoed by an assistant director, and then when the deer themselves escaped into the hills and the animators were sent to recover them. Meanwhile artist Rico Lebrun conducted classes in the late afternoon to analyze deer anatomy. He had gotten a fresh carcass from a forest ranger, and at each session he would remove another layer of the skin or muscle until he finally reached the bone—by which time Eric Larson was the only one of the staff who could tolerate the stench, so Larson made drawings and distributed them. "[H]e just drilled us and drilled us to understand what the anatomy was, what the bone structure was . . . what happened when a leg lifted, what happened when the body weight went on that leg," Larson said of Lebrun's classes.

For most of this time Walt paid scant attention to *Bambi.* But Perce Pearce, the nominal supervisor, obviously taking his cues from Walt, moved so slowly and fixated on such small details that he was beginning to frustrate the staff, and Walt assigned Dave Hand, who had coordinated *Snow White*, to oversee Pearce. Hand was correct when he later said that some major decisions were made without Walt's input. It was Ham Luske, for example, who suggested at a meeting that September that they centralize one of the bunnies to act as a kind of guide, just as Jiminy Cricket had done in *Pinocchio.* That gave Bambi's friend Thumper a much enlarged role and changed Bambi's introduction to the forest. As Thomas and Johnston later described it, "[N]ow the first part of the picture began to be about wonderful children who happened to be animals, innocent and unaware of the realities of their futures."

But contrary to Hand, Walt did spend a considerable amount of time that November and December reviewing continuities, and if he did not participate as actively as he had on *Snow White* or *Pinocchio*, he was nevertheless the primary sensibility who could devise an entire sequence in a sudden burst of inspiration. In the middle of one meeting Walt abruptly interjected what he called "just the flash that came to my mind here" and started describing a new opening for the film: "Say we open up with morning in the forest. Everything is getting up. And then you come to the old Owl and he's going to sleep. And then we introduce the Squirrel and the Chipmunk. We introduce all the characters we want to in that morning." And then "this noise breaks loose that it's here—it's happened—where they begin flying around, and the whole damned woods begins to fuss and swarm" with the birth of Bambi. The final version was very much as Walt described it at the meeting. A few weeks later, musing on the winter sequence, he came up with the idea of Bambi on the ice pond. "He has never been on ice before. It is like putting Pluto on ice with skates on him. He just can't stand up. He is having a hell of a time." This scene too wound up in the final film.

IV

That December as he was tinkering with *Bambi*, Walt Disney had yet one more imposing task before him: he was supervising the move from Hyperion to the new studio in Burbank. All the time that he was working on *Pinocchio*, *Fantasia*, and *Bambi*, through the dozens upon dozens of meetings and sweatbox sessions, he had also been engaged in the planning and construction at Burbank, typically consulting with the engineers and architects three times a week and advancing the project in a trial-and-error manner not unlike that on *Bambi*. "All was nebulous then," Frank Crowhurst, the general contractor, said of the various ideas they considered. "We *hoped* it would work." They had broken ground on the Animation Building in late February 1939, with the intention of finishing everything but the Administration Building by October. Once again time was of the essence. With so many films in production, the studio couldn't afford a protracted transition. "It is going to save the studio a lot of money if we can get all these buildings built and ready for occupancy as soon as possible and close to the same time, and causing as little loss of time or confusion as possible in the move over," Roy wrote Crowhurst and Bill Garity, who was taking care of the technical details, with the idea that if they kept most of the work in house, they could expedite construction.

If time was of the essence, so was money. Even before the groundbreaking, Roy was debating whether, to cut costs, they could put the administrative offices in the Animation Building or whether to eliminate a wing of the Animation Building or whether they really needed a large soundstage and theater.* They also discussed whether they should keep the training program at Seward Street, where it had been temporarily installed, because space at the new studio would be at a premium and they wouldn't have the resources to build anything new for years. In the end they cut surprisingly few corners, despite the fact that, with the production delays, money was no longer flowing into the studio as it had after *Snow White*. Instead Roy, at the urging of Joe Rosenberg and with the

*In the event, they eliminate the Administration Building and housed the business offices in the Animation Building.

intervention of the Bank of America's Doc Giannini, applied to the government for a Reconstruction Finance Loan in June 1939 and traveled to Washington later that month to press his case personally. "Any questions and discussions all seemed to be pointing to their trying to find reasons and excuses for presentation to the board of a recommendation that the loan be made," Roy wrote George Morris after his meeting.

While Roy raised the money, Walt seemed to be relishing the construction as much as he had relished the planning. He visited the site often, sometimes taking Diane and Sharon, who loved to stand in the cavernous empty rooms and yell. (Walt cited his admonishments to them to a *Bambi* story crew to suggest behavior for the Owl.) He also brought his father there, hoping to jar him out of the depression into which he had sunk since Flora's death. "I thought he would be excited by this big thing," Walt later said, perhaps tipping his hand that the new studio was another demonstration of his success and power to a father who had so often denied him. But Elias was unimpressed. "What else is it good for?" he asked, prompting Walt to tell him that the entire facility could be converted into a hospital if the studio failed.

When it opened in December, three months late, it was as much a fulfillment as *Fantasia* promised to be. Now Walt had his physical utopia. Saying that he eschewed aesthetic niceties, he claimed he had designed it primarily for function. "Give me the plans, functions, intelligently laid out," he had ordered Crowhurst, "then I don't care what you do after that so long as you do not destroy those functions." But for Walt function was generously defined, which meant that aesthetics were very much taken into consideration. He wanted there to be a sense of comfort, even exhilaration, so that the employees would work from joy rather than obligation. To avoid monotony and provide a change of pace, he directed that the wings and floors be painted different colors, bright bold colors, which was something that designer Kem Weber had never done previously. To alleviate any sense of a somber industrial plant, he approved different shades of brick, incorporating a California palette with desert beige offsetting the red. Hyperion had often been described by reporters as having the ambience of a college campus; Walt determined that the new studio should have the appearance of a campus as well. Nothing soared at the Burbank studio. Everything was built low and horizontal, embracing rather than imposing. The pathways were broad, the lawns green and planted with oaks, the air still and quiet and filled with the fragrance of freshly mown grass. There were even quail, doves, rabbits, and the occasional deer, and one could often see Walt underneath one of the trees watching them. It was Walt's very own Marceline.

Yet it was imposing in its own way. "[I]t wasn't until you got to the new Studio on 50 acres of land that you realized what a big plant it was," Bill Cottrell would say. The estimated cost was just under $2 million, with nearly half of that slotted for the Animation Building, which was, at 152,000 square feet, over three times as large as the Animation Building at Hyperion. Ink and Paint was also three times as large as the sheds at Hyperion, and the soundstage nearly five times as large as those at the old studio. All told, Burbank was four times larger than Hyperion.

But it wasn't just a matter of size. Where Hyperion had been attractive but ramshackle, Burbank was clean and efficient, just as the new production process was intended to be. The Animation Building had three floors and eight long wings jutting from a corridor to form two side-by-side H-shapes. The idea was that production would flow smoothly downward from the third floor, where Walt had his office in wing H next to the story department and where the films were initiated; to the second floor, where the directors and layout men divided the feature stories into sequences, devised the staging of the scenes, and eventually screened the roughs in the sweatboxes located there; to the first floor, where some two to three hundred animators were separated into groups under head animators in each wing to do the actual drawings; to the basement, where the test camera was housed and the roughs were shot. Each wing contained a unit—three devoted to features and one to shorts.

Amid the purported new efficiency Walt had not stinted on the amenities. There was not only an elaborate commissary, where Roy and Walt democratically took their own meals, but also a snack bar on the first floor of the Animation Building and a buffet in the penthouse. Anyone who wanted a sandwich or a milk shake could simply order one, and it would be delivered by a traffic boy to the office. There was a barbershop for anyone needing a haircut. Walt also provided a gymnasium on the top floor, where a Swedish exercise trainer named Carl Johnson led workouts and a roof deck where animators could and did sunbathe nude. Every noon in the studio's theater there would be a thirty-minute show of animations, newsreels, and scenes from other features. In fact, though the studio had been modeled after a college campus and was still frequently described as one, it had so many frills that Walt himself compared it now to a "swank hotel." The only thing missing, he felt, was housing on the lot for the employees so that they would never have to leave the studio, and he was contemplating how to do it. That was the last element of his old communitarian dream.

Some felt that Walt had transplanted the feeling of camaraderie and fellowship from Hyperion. "The whole atmosphere is conducive to the light-heartedness and gayety that you find in Disney's pictures," gossip columnist Hedda Hopper chirped shortly after the move. "After lunch you'll find executives playing everything from softball to ping pong with their employees." She cited the oft-repeated fact that everyone called the boss "Walt." A *New York Times* reporter visiting the studio later that year wrote in a similar vein that a "walk across the lawns at noon was like a walk through Central Park on Sunday. Employees sat or reclined leisurely on the grass; they called, 'Hello, Walt . . . Hi, Walt . . . Walt . . . Walt.' And Disney waved and halloed back"—an effect that was underscored by the fact that the studio's streets were named after Disney characters: Dopey Drive and Mickey Avenue. Others described the same old practical jokes, the same collegiality, the same devotion, the same sense of purpose as at Hyperion. "[Y]ou can't help feeling that you're going to grab that goddam Holy Grail," one employee told a writer doing a story on the new studio for *The Atlantic Monthly*. A dancer who had performed some live action for "Dance of the Hours" wrote Walt thankfully, saying, "Everyone seemed happy and contented" and attributing it to Walt's "good humor, kindness and courteousness."

But something had changed—something ineffable but important that undermined the sense of happiness and contentment. After the initial flush of appreciation, some employees began to feel as if the studio were *too* good, *too* perfect. The "collegiate atmosphere became almost oppressive," one employee complained. Another recalled, "Everything looked so nice I almost felt like wearing a tie." Before the studio moved to Burbank, Joe Rosenberg, the banker, had warned Walt vaguely that the new plant would be so nice "*you will cause discontent!*" He was right. Some charged it to a new sense of impersonality now that the studio was bigger and more routinized. Ollie Johnston said that if you wanted to talk to a fellow animator, you now had to walk past secretaries or up and down floors. Even Walt now had two adjoining offices—one he called a formal office, the other a working office—down a long corridor and guarded by two secretaries who effectively cut him off from the rest of the studio. Another Disney employee believed that the attempts at greater efficiency, ineffective as they usually were, had nevertheless taken hold, sapping the new studio of the old Hyperion informality and spirit. Instead of what this employee called an "impromptu art form," Disney animation had become an "efficient business." At least one animator attributed the change to a change in Walt himself now that he was even more insulated from his employees and spread even thinner than before. "When Disney began to get the idea for this Burbank studio," the animator said, "he became a different man. From a man who worked closely and collectively with his workers he got to be boss." He even described Walt at Burbank as a despot.

Whatever it was that had happened, many employees would, in time, come to think of the move to Burbank as, in the words of one, a "line of demarcation in the era of good feeling" and the "beginning of a loss of morale." Just how thick the line of demarcation was, Walt would discover a year later.

Walt himself noticed that something was changing. A year earlier, amid the production delays, he had been concerned about flagging morale and pushed Roy to rent a theater so that Walt could address the employees and announce a new wave of bonuses to be paid over time. "[I]t was his thought," George Morris told Roy, "that he wanted to keep the spirit of the organization up so that he would get the full benefit of the announcement and later payment when he most needed that cooperative effort from those who participate in it." That didn't happen, but on January 30, 1940, after the move to Burbank and with *Pinocchio* finally about to be released, Walt convened selected employees in room 3C12 of the Animation Building. As he addressed them over the next two hours and forty-five minutes, in what may have been the single most exuberant and soul-baring performance of his life, he was bursting with confidence. The studio was now large enough, he said, that they could do whatever they wanted to do—whatever *he* wanted to do—and he described how they would henceforth have three units working simultaneously on three features. "This plant, this studio—it's more than an ordinary thing," he said with emotion. "There is a certain spirit that prevails here. I can see it in the guys. They have a feeling that it isn't a racket." But what he wanted, what he hoped for, what he may have begun to sense he was losing with the new divisions in the Animation Building and the rivalries that seemed to arise among the crews working on different features, was a spirit of collaboration. "I haven't felt that *Bambi* was one of our productions," Walt confessed. He wanted to change that. "I want a group of guys who will get together and will discuss their problems and we will take care of their recommendations," he announced. "We want to find out what they think . . . and I want it first-hand from them." He called for a "certain informality" in discussing ideas. And he went on: "I want the story groups to get together. I want them to talk over their work. . . . I want to get the directors together and layout and the background men. . . . We must find the most effective way to unify this plant. I want to unify it in such a way that everybody will be working together." He wanted the fun to return.

But this wasn't just a pep talk to rouse the troops or a summons to regain what they had had at Hyperion during the making of *Snow White*. Walt wanted, he said, to create a financial community as well as an artistic one. He told the group that under the animation rating system he expected a salary adjustment of $150,000 on *Pinocchio*, and he wanted to pay it out to them in bonuses just as he had on *Snow White*. But even that was not the point. Walt said he had been working for some time on a larger scheme in which each employee would be rated by his value to the company, his tenure there, and his cooperation and ambition, then allotted a commensurate share of the profits. It was, Walt told his employees, the only way to ensure that the organization would remain strong and would continue to make quality films. It was, he even said, the only way to ensure that the company would survive him "in case I got bumped off." "We've got to fix this thing so the business won't collapse. . . . I'm afraid that this business will be thrown into the regular Hollywood groove and that they will start throwing these cartoons at the public," he said. "Maybe I've had too many bad experiences. I know guys, though, who are like that. All they think of is how much money they can get out of a thing." At Disney it would be different. Everyone would have a stake in the company's ongoing success. Everyone would have a stake in maintaining quality, which Walt had always felt was the key to success. He wasn't sure how he would distribute the money—whether he would issue preferred stock, which he hesitated to do, or set up an employees' fund, which he also disliked, or some other mechanism—but he was sure he would do it. If this was Walt Disney's utopia, then everyone at the studio would be part of it.

What had made this sort of discussion possible was Walt's anticipation of some return—he was uncertain of how much—on *Pinocchio* after its seemingly endless problems and delays. A week after the meeting on February 7, 1940, *Pinocchio* premiered in New York, eighteen months after its original scheduled release date. (Walt, citing the recent move to the new studio, had begged off attending the gala.) But the delay hadn't muted the critical reception. If in the critics' eyes *Pinocchio* hadn't quite the heart of *Snow White* or that film's tight narrative, they recognized that it did have more breadth and was far better animated, sometimes breathtakingly so. " 'Pinocchio' tops any animated cartoon I ever saw," *Los Angeles Times* critic Arthur Miller wrote. Frank Nugent in *The New York Times* called it the "happiest event since the war" and "superior to 'Snow White' in every respect but one: its score." Still, he concluded, it was the "best cartoon ever made." Otis Ferguson, writing in *The New Republic*, found it episodic but thought it "brings the cartoon to a level of perfection that the word cartoon will not cover. We get around the problem of no old word for a new thing by saying, it's a Disney." Howard Barnes in the *New York Herald Tribune* went even further. He called Disney "infallible." Congratulating Walt after the opening, Stuart Buchanan, the studio's casting director as well as its musical director, said that if Walt had been there, "any worries you may have had about the success of Pinocchio would have ended. The reviews speak for themselves but I have never seen a more appreciative audience." He pronounced himself "proud to be part of the Disney organization." Even Roy, wiring Walt on his way to New York to discuss the issue of stock to employees, seemed pleased: "Everything from my viewpoint is going ahead OK in every way."

But Walt did worry—and rightfully so, it turned out. Despite the effusive reviews, attendance was well below that for *Snow White*, and by April, George Morris was already warning that the estimated revenue from *Pinocchio* would have to be cut by a million dollars, which meant, among other things, that Walt's proposed bonuses would have to be eliminated. Morris now predicted a "severe loss" on the film. Something had gone wrong. Ben Sharpsteen attributed the disappointing audience reception to the fact that *Pinocchio* appealed only to children, whereas *Snow White* had greater adult appeal. "[T]he expression was at the Music Hall that the matinees were terrific at reduced children's price," Sharpsteen told an interviewer years later. "But, my God, you could shoot a cannon up the aisle at night!" Others would feel just the opposite: that *Pinocchio* was too dark and disturbing a film for children and presented, as one Disney scholar would put it, the "bleakest vision of any Disney feature." Indeed, far more than *Snow White*, *Pinocchio* soberly limned the central Disney theme of the responsibilities of maturity and what one had to sacrifice to grow up, so that where *Snow White* provided relief for a Depression-weary world, *Pinocchio* seemed to serve as a reminder of the travails of the Depression and the war in Europe. Walt himself, though bristling at any suggestion that *Pinocchio* had not done well, had a simpler explanation. He blamed the competition from *Gone with the Wind*, the movie blockbuster that had been released just a few weeks earlier, and the war itself, which significantly cut profits. Because of the war, the film was translated into only two languages, Spanish and Portuguese, and received only 45 percent of its gross from outside the United States and Canada, significantly less than *Snow White*. In England alone, where *Snow White* had grossed $2 million, *Pinocchio* grossed only $200,000. When all was said and done, it took in roughly $2 million, out of which the studio received $1.2 million on a total investment of $2.7 million. Even so, many would regard *Pinocchio* as Walt Disney's masterpiece, the pinnacle of animation art. Walt reluctantly disagreed. "Pinocchio lacked an intangible something," he finally confessed to a reporter.

Now, with the fresh defeat of *Pinocchio* having temporarily dashed Walt's confidence, it was back to *Bambi*, which he had been dragging like a millstone for over two years. The *Bambi* story crew had been among the first to relocate at Burbank, in wing 3B of the Animation Building. With the move and with the completion of *Pinocchio*, Walt's involvement intensified. By one account, whenever Walt approached the room, Perce Pearce would shout, "Man is in the forest!"—the line from *Bambi* that announces the threat of hunters. After all the fits and starts, and after Walt's long absences from Seward Street, he was now promoting the idea that the staff was to work closely with him and, apparently realizing they might have been intimidated by him, that they were not to be afraid to speak up during meetings, at which point Pearce made a remarkable admission given the years they had been working on the script: "We would like to pull you in to the extent that we don't feel we have to have the thing entirely making sense."

Obviously Walt understood that *Bambi* was difficult. He knew it had less a riveting story than a cycle and that it required subtlety. The characters couldn't be too broadly drawn or the film would miss the poetic tone it needed to be great, and greatness was the goal, especially now that *Pinocchio* seemed to have fallen short of expectations. Though Walt vacillated between letting the story crew take even more time to shore up the continuity and urging them to pick up their pace, he always came down on the side of allotting more time, even suggesting that they think of making the film longer and presenting it as a "roadshow" picture with limited performances and reserved seating at theaters specially outfitted with his Fantasound multispeaker system and perhaps a special wide-screen projection. "These pictures represent a lot of work and a lot of thought," he told the *Bambi* staff. "They're not just an ordinary run-of-the-mill type of production that's been coming from Hollywood . . . they stand out." Striving to get it right, needing to get it right, he spent most of February in meetings analyzing and reanalyzing scene after scene, just as he had done on *Snow White*, and by the end of the month had concluded that the film would take at least another fifteen months—two and a half months for the special effects alone.

He felt it had to be big. From working on *Fantasia*, Walt had become fascinated with the idea of presentation. It wasn't enough for a film to be great. It had to be mounted in such a way that the exhibition of the movie was also great. "I wanted a special show" was how he later put it. That was part of the reason he had latched on to the notion of a customized sound system for *Fantasia*. In May 1939, a month after the recordings in Philadelphia, Walt had contacted David Sarnoff, the head of the Radio Corporation of America, proposing that RCA manufacture the new system, which, Walt wrote, would "create the illusion that the actual Symphony Orchestra is playing in the theater." Sarnoff balked at the idea, saying that while it was technically feasible, it was commercially problematic, but Walt and Roy were persistent. Each visited RCA in New York that spring, and by July, Roy had reached an agreement by which RCA would make the equipment so long as they could hold down the costs, estimated by RCA's engineer at $200,000. Walt had his six-track Fantasound.

Given that it could be used only in a few selected theaters, Fantasound was a very expensive proposition. But then so was the new studio and *Fantasia* itself, as well as *Bambi* and the prospective *Peter Pan* and *Alice in Wonderland*—all of which began to tighten like a noose around Walt, especially with the reduced receipts from overseas and with the diminished prospects for *Pinocchio*. Walt didn't discuss the new economic contingencies with his employees; it had always been a point of honor with him that he could resist financial pressures, that he could shelter his employees and protect his films, and in any case he always expressed nothing but disdain for money. Dave Hand recalled a meeting where Roy complained, as he often did, that the pictures were costing too much. "There was complete silence," Hand related. "Then Walt's loose eyebrow shot up at an unusually sharp angle, and turning to Roy in an uncompromising matter-of-fact straight-from-the-shoulder answer, said quite simply, 'Roy, *we'll* make the pictures, *you* get the money.' That was that."

Even before the success of *Snow White*, Walt himself made a generous salary—among the highest in the film industry. After *Snow White* his base salary was listed as $108,298, not including another $25,605 from the studio's foreign corporations, and on March 11, 1940, he signed a seven-year contract with the studio at $2,000 a week, which again didn't include compensation from the stock that he held. By comparison, Roy made $72,000, and Gunther Lessing under $15,000. Still, as much as he actively cultivated his image as an artist or at least an artisan rather than an entrepreneur, Walt was being honest when he said the money was a happy by-product of the work, not the motive for it. "I could buy a big place in Florida and fill it with expensive paintings and other junk," he told a reporter who asked what he would do with his riches. "But what for? That's for people who are bored or want to impress the neighbors."

He was also being honest when he said that he continued to reinvest most of the profits back in the studio. Money wasn't for personal indulgence. Money was for quality, and money was for independence. "I belong to this studio, this 'thing' that has grown up here," he once said. "This is where my money goes." When the company had been formed back in 1923, it was a partnership between Walt and Roy, and later among Walt, Roy, and Ub Iwerks when he joined them in California. In 1929, after

Iwerks had departed, Walt Disney Productions was incorporated and issued 10,000 shares of stock—3,000 each to Walt and Lillian and 4,000 to Roy. When the company was reorganized in 1938 and its real estate, merchandise, and production branches were consolidated, the new entity issued 150,000 shares of stock with Walt and Lillian each receiving 45,000 and Roy and Edna each receiving 30,000. No one but a Disney held any stake in the company, and with the exception of his employees to whom he was willing to grant stock, that was exactly how Walt wanted it. As early as 1928, when he let promoter Harry Reichenbach exhibit *Steamboat Willie* at the Colony Theater, Walt said he understood that one should never sell the rights to a film. After his experiences with Charlie Mintz and Pat Powers, he had the same philosophy toward the entire company. "We don't have to answer to anyone," Walt boasted after *Snow White*, conveniently ignoring the fact that he did have to answer to the Bank of America. "We don't have to make profits for any stockholders. New York investors can't tell us what kind of picture they want us to make or hold back."

But that could be true only so long as the studio continued to make profits, and in the wake of *Pinocchio* suddenly a new financial crisis emerged. While the studio had awaited the results of *Snow White*, it had hesitated to put any new feature into full production; that may have been sensible, but it meant that when *Snow White* proved to be successful, the studio was in no position to take immediate advantage of that success—a situation worsened by the unexpected problems and postponements on *Pinocchio* and *Bambi*. It worsened even more with the effects of the war in Europe and *Pinocchio*'s disappointing returns. At the same time the Burbank studio, when all was said and done, had cost nearly $3 million, a million more than the projections, and *Fantasia* was costing well over $2 million—all of which meant that the studio had nearly $8 million in outstanding investments. From having reaped a profit of $1.25 million in fiscal year 1939, the studio was reporting a loss of $260,000 in fiscal year 1940. In addition, after paying off its loans with the profits from *Snow White*, the company had gone back into debt and owed the Bank of America $4.5 million. With so little money coming in, Roy was summoned to the bank's San Francisco headquarters for a discussion of the situation, and described the atmosphere as "real cool," until Doc Giannini once again came to the Disneys' defense, asking his staff how many Disney pictures they had seen. When they collectively stammered, he said he had seen nearly a hundred, then declared, "I suggest that we give these boys a chance. This war won't last forever."

But it wasn't that easy. On top of the money hemorrhaging from the features, it also was draining from the shorts, which the studio was still contractually obligated to produce. Though Walt had delegated much of the responsibility for the shorts to his staff, he still met with the story crews, approved the scripts, and examined the storyboards. They did bring in over a million dollars in rental income, but the rentals didn't keep pace with the costs—Walt estimated that he spent $45,000 on a typical short without factoring in the expenses for prints, marketing, distribution, or what Roy called "administrative overhead"—and the net income scarcely exceeded that from merchandise, comics, and licenses. Moreover, Walt had grown increasingly resentful of having to make them, not only because they gave so little return on the investment but because he felt he had outgrown them. Though many of the animators were idle while *Bambi* was being readied for production and *Peter Pan* and *Alice in Wonderland* were being written, Walt complained to George Morris that he would not reassign animators from the features to the shorts because, he told Morris, "[Y]ou spend a hell of a lot of money and what have you got?"

Once again the Disneys needed money. As early as February 1939 Roy had gone to New York to investigate the possibility of issuing long-term debentures, which were loan certificates backed by general credit rather than by specific assets. This way, Roy obviously felt, the studio would not have to assign the future profits on the features, as it had had to do to secure the financing from the Bank of America. By February 1940 rumors were circulating that the company was considering doing something that Walt had always insisted it would not do, issue stock to the public, and Roy had gone to New York again to consult with the investment banking firm Kidder, Peabody. It was a tough negotiation, but the Disneys had little leverage. In the end the studio arranged to issue 155,000 shares of preferred stock worth $3.875 million at 6 percent interest, convertible into common stock when the price of a share of the preferred stock reached 30.4 percent of the value of a share of common stock.* (Since the Disneys owned all of the common stock and didn't want to dilute their holdings, Roy thought the percentage was too low, but Kidder wouldn't budge.) Kidder also insisted on placing one of its own executives, Jonathan B. Lovelace, on the Disney board. And it asked the studio to buy a $1.5 million insurance policy on Walt's life payable in trust to the stockholders should he die before April 1, 1944, four years from the day of the issue, and to the studio should he die after that date. In effect, Kidder was pro-

*Honoring his commitment to his employees, Walt reserved five thousand shares of the preferred stock for the top members of his staff, including his top-rated thirty-five animators. *In the Matter of Walt Disney Productions and Arthur Babbitt*, Decisions of National Labor Relations Board, Case No. C 2415, Mar. 31, 1943, p. 899.

tecting the stockholders against the loss of the studio's greatest asset: Walt Disney himself.

"It will seem a little odd to run one's finger down the columns on the financial page some day and see Mickey, Inc. (or Walt Disney Productions, if one insists on being formal) going up and down like a thermometer," *The New York Times* commented in an editorial shortly after the offering. It *was* incongruous, but less because of Mickey Mouse than because Walt had never operated by standard business procedures and had always considered Wall Street anathema. Business was what got in the way of creativity. When Fred Moore, not the animator but a Kidder executive, visited Walt vacationing at Palm Springs the week before the offering, he found him much more interested in talking about skiing at the Sugar Bowl resort than about the stock deal. He was trying not to think about the issue. Walt clearly had misgivings about giving over his studio to the vagaries of Wall Street and the tyranny of profits. Three days after the issue he impulsively decided to go to New York to hear a demonstration of a stereophonic sound reproduction system at Carnegie Hall, wheedling Lillian and Ben Sharpsteen and Sharpsteen's wife into joining him. On the way back the group stopped at Dearborn, Michigan, where Walt visited the Ford automobile factory and Greenfield Village, a historical park erected by Henry Ford. At the conclusion of a lunch in Walt's honor, Ford himself, one of Walt's heroes, made a surprise appearance. During small talk Walt happened to mention the recent stock issue. Ford was blunt. "If you sell any of it, you should sell all of it," he warned. Walt admitted that "kind of left me thinking and wondering for a while," wondering if he had crossed a bridge and could never go back, wondering if he had surrendered ultimate control.

V

If they had needed an infusion of money, they also desperately needed to rush a new feature into production after *Fantasia* to generate profits. Though Walt was already hurrying a version of *Jack and the Beanstalk* starring Mickey Mouse as Jack for release at Easter 1941 and though he optimistically thought *Bambi* might be ready by the fall of that year, he had, in the meantime, pounced on another project. He had read a slim new children's book titled *Dumbo*, about a young circus elephant who gets ridiculed for his oversize ears, only to discover that those flapping ears can serve as wings. What Walt loved about the idea—after wrestling with *Bambi*, *Pinocchio*, and even his beloved *Fantasia*—was that it was so simple.

"It's there," he pronounced to one *Bambi* story meeting. "I mean I can see personalities right away." Conveniently Norm Ferguson's crew was just finishing animating the hippopotamuses and elephants in the "Dance of the Hours" sequence for *Fantasia* so they could be shifted to *Dumbo* without months of having to learn how to draw the characters, and the studio had other animators as well, Walt believed, who might not be well suited to the realism and subtlety demanded by *Bambi* but could do the broader figures of *Dumbo*. Even better from Walt's perspective, *Dumbo* required none of the special effects that had slowed the production and added to the budgets of *Pinocchio, Bambi, and Fantasia*. "Dumbo is an obvious straight cartoon," Walt proclaimed. "I'll deliberately make it that way. It's the type to do that with. It's caricature all the way through."

The object was to avoid the agonizing over the story that had plagued the other features and led to months and months of revisions and higher and higher costs. "He let me know very emphatically that this picture had to be made for $350,000," said Ben Sharpsteen, who was assigned to produce the film, realizing that Walt couldn't possibly hold him to that budget but that Walt was serious this time about things being done economically albeit without producing shoddy work. Walt had assigned the task of adapting the book to Joe Grant, who headed the model department, and Dick Huemer, and they submitted a 102 page treatment that January. "The reason we brought it in for a low price," Joe Grant would say, "was that it was done quickly and with a minimum amount of mistakes. The story was clear and air-tight to everyone involved in the project. We didn't do a lot of stuff over due to the story-point goofs. There were no sequences started and then shelved, like in *Pinocchio*. Walt was sure of what he wanted and this confidence was shared by the entire crew. *Dumbo*, from the very opening drawing, went straight through to the finish with very few things changed or altered." Ward Kimball remembered being waylaid by Walt in the parking lot one day and being told he was going to start on a circus picture, animating a scene in which crows sing a song about seeing an elephant fly. Walt then recited the entire story in five minutes. "And listening to him tell that story," Kimball said, clearly recognizing that Walt had told the story in what for him was record time, "I could tell that the picture was going to work. Because everything sounded right. It had a great plot."

And there was another reason they were able to make *Dumbo* so quickly: Walt for the first time had removed the burden of expectation for perfect animation, meaning that the animators were not to agonize any more than the story crew had. In fact, he assigned many of the newcomers to the picture. "I was one of the 'poor boys,' " animator Bill Peet recalled.

"They put all the rich boys, the top animators making the big salaries, working on *Bambi*. They wanted to make it a gem." This wasn't entirely true. Bill Tytla, who was certainly one of the top animators and who had done the devil for the "Bald Mountain" sequence in *Fantasia*, animated the baby Dumbo, but even he admitted that "[i]t was in the nature of the film to go very fast and get it out in a hurry." To expedite the animation, Walt used photostats of story sketches instead of the full layouts as on the other features, and he recruited some of his better animators to oversee younger, less experienced ones who had been put on the picture. One animator said he didn't even draw key poses but animated "straight-ahead," just as in the old days.

But as rapidly as it sped forward, *Dumbo* still wouldn't be ready in time to generate the income the studio needed then. Walt had to find another contingency, something he could get ready even faster. Earlier that year he had invited the humorist Robert Benchley to the studio to discuss Benchley's possible narration of a cartoon titled *How to Ride a Horse*, starring a tall, flop-eared, dim-witted dog named Goofy who had previously been featured in Mickey Mouse shorts. After that meeting Walt hatched the idea of having Benchley appear in a combination live-action/animated featurette in which he tours the new studio, and by early May, Walt was fielding ideas on exactly what the content would be—"to figure something out," as he put it. To his staff he was frank about the situation, espousing something he would have derided just a few months before but his endorsement of which now conveyed the gravity of their current condition: he would not just be rushing production, as he was doing with *Dumbo;* he would be making a film solely for profit as a way, he felt, of protecting the quality of the better features. "The answer [to the financial crisis] I thought was to get out a couple of things that we call 'quickies' and on low budgets, but which would be damn good entertainment." The Benchley film was one of those quickies.

Though Walt and the story crew batted around various ideas, he finally settled on what he called the simplest and most direct plot: Benchley has come to the studio to pitch a cartoon called *The Reluctant Dragon*, and in the process of trying to find Walt, he finds himself bouncing from one department to another, just missing the boss each time but essentially letting the audience see the entire studio and observe the process of animation. At the end, when he finally encounters Walt, he discovers that *The Reluctant Dragon* has already been made by the studio.

The advantages, as Walt saw it, were not just that the film allowed them to cut corners, since it was much easier and faster to make a live-action film with a bit of animation than to make an animated feature. He also regarded it as a kind of advertisement for the Disney studio and recommended including references to *Bambi* and *Dumbo* as "teasers." When one of the staff suggested that the movie might be better as a "how to" film about animation, Walt adamantly disagreed. "I don't think you should have *any* cartoon studio," he snapped. "I think it should be this studio. This studio is known all over the world. . . . There is audience value in showing this plant in operation if you properly present it." In making the film, he had one other motive as well. At the very time when morale was beginning to sink and there were rumbles of discontent, Walt, ever the social engineer, wanted to show the world just how blissful a community he had created. "The thing we should play up throughout the entire picture," he memoed Al Perkins, who was writing up the story, "is that the gang generally have a good time."

Though it obviously wasn't the first time that Walt had tried to pick up the pace of production, halfhearted as his efforts often were, it was the first time it worked—in part because he wasn't intimately involved enough to nitpick and slow things down. He did attend the main story sessions and made substantial points, but the live-action director Alfred Werker, who was borrowed from Twentieth Century–Fox, said, "Walt gave me a completely free hand in making the picture," even though the live action, like the animation, was completely storyboarded. Production moved so quickly that Benchley arrived at the studio in mid-October to shoot his scenes, and by the end of the month Walt was watching a rough cut. He even thought it possible that the film could be released in time for Christmas.

But not everyone at the studio was enamored of the idea. Some felt that in the haste of making it and in the shortcuts they had taken with the animation, they had made a film about the new Disney studio that was distinctly un-Disneylike. Ward Kimball, who worked on the film's animated sequences, called it a "very revolutionary type of Disney cartoon" because it was minimalist rather than maximalist, some of it really only sketches with a sound track, making no pretense at realism, and he said that some of the "great brains" at the studio warned him that Walt would be incensed when he finally saw it. They were wrong. According to Kimball, "The first night we ran that at the Studio, it killed everybody. It was a milestone. . . . You can't imagine the contrast it had to what we were doing when it came out." In fact, Kimball remembered, "Walt thought it was great and made other people go in and look at it."

The urgency of *The Reluctant Dragon* that summer of 1940 was reinforced by the continued foot-dragging on *Bambi*, though Walt and the staff were meeting throughout June and had at long last finalized the continuity. "All remaining sequences of BAMBI are now in active story shaping," Perce Pearce reported to Walt early in the month, "including the final sequence of the picture." The last narrative sticking points had been the issue of the portrayal of Man and the staging of the death of Bambi's mother at the hands of hunters. Walt felt they had to play up the threat of Man, "the dread of Man that they have," and play down the natural hardships they faced. It was Man who was the real enemy. He was also keenly aware of the impact that Bambi's mother's death would have on the audience and kept returning to it at the story meetings. Do you see her getting hit? Does she get hit while she is protecting Bambi? Does Bambi see her fallen body? Walt finally decided that she would be shot while leaping a log but that the audience would not see her getting hit and would not see her body afterward. It was, he decided, more than an audience could bear—"sticking a knife in their hearts," he said. Instead he opted for understatement. "He's hunting for his mother, and he never finds her," Walt described the scene at one session, "and the Stag just tells him. . . . He just sort of wanders around. The last you see of them is just some faint silhouette forms back of this blizzard and pretty soon they have disappeared and there is nothing but snow falling." Yet again, in amplifying upon what his storymen had done, he provided one of the most famous and powerful scenes in the history of motion pictures.

But if, after nearly three years, they had finally licked the narrative problem of shaping a plot out of a life cycle, one major problem remained, the one they had continually encountered in trying to find a style of animation that would fit the mood of the piece. It was what had made *Bambi* so intractable from the first. Ollie Johnston and Frank Thomas wrote that "Walt was demanding eloquence from images that he hadn't even imagined before. He was no longer pushing for extra characters, comic situations, and funny attitudes as much as feelings and sensations we each carry away from visiting the deep woods." Some animators, Johnston and Thomas reported, had become so frustrated that they begged off the project. The objective was to strike a balance. Walt wanted realism—it was the way he would advance animation—but he needed caricature too for appealing personalities. (The characters that had received the most favorable response at a showing of the Leica reels back in September had been the Skunk, designed by Marc Davis, and the Owl, both of which were broadly drawn.) "I'd like to see us find things, you know, that keep us away from just the naturalistic stuff—that has a certain amount of fantasy to it," he told a meeting as late as February 1940, reversing direction slightly. Too much realism, he had finally come to realize, would be stultifying.

Still trying to find a style that would combine realism and caricature and taking their cue from Davis's drawings, Milt Kahl and Frank Thomas had each animated one hundred feet of the movie, and on March 1, 1940, they showed their footage to Walt in room 3C13. It was, Johnston and Thomas would write, "possibly the most important day in the history of the film." Walt watched the footage, then turned to them, they said, with tears in his eyes—a highly uncharacteristic gesture from a man who, save for outbursts of temper, rarely showed emotion. "That's great stuff—no kidding," he told them. And Johnston and Thomas said he added warmly, "It's your picture. You guys have a feeling for this picture. You belong to this picture," which was no doubt how he had felt about *Snow White*, *Pinocchio*, and *Fantasia*. He left the meeting saying that he trusted the animators to do their own sweatboxing and even set their own schedule. He was so satisfied he said he could now take a trip.

As it turned out, March 1 was a historic day not only for *Bambi* but for the entire studio: the beginning of a changing of the guard. What Walt had come to realize through *Bambi*, *Dumbo*, *Fantasia*, and even *The Reluctant Dragon* was that there could no longer be *a* Disney style since no single style could fit all the various projects that Walt had in mind. For years Walt had trained his artists in a method of drawing that kept inching closer to realism, and he had tried to impose that technique and goal on everyone; accepting these standards had become a condition of working at the studio. He had always felt that animation had to evolve, and in *Bambi* Walt clearly felt he had finally found something different, something exciting, even if he couldn't quite put his finger on it. "This is opening up something here," he enthused to the *Bambi* animators. "This is a new style," one to which he said he would assign his very best animators like Davis, Thomas, Kahl, and Larson. "I think this is going to be one hell of a big step forward," he told them.

At the same time he had come to understand that a film like *Dumbo* and certainly the shorts didn't require the subtlety of *Bambi*; demanding it would have been not only expensive but counterproductive. The less experienced animators and the animators who didn't evolve and whose technique wasn't as refined could be assigned to these pictures. By introducing the idea of different styles rather than a studio style, Walt had also created a pecking order not just between the supervising animators and the rest of the staff but between the first tier of supervising animators and a second tier. Bright young animators would now be in the studio vanguard. Some of the old-timers, including Norm Ferguson and Fred Moore, who had been the stars of Walt Disney Productions just a few years earlier, when the studio first embarked on realism, were relegated to a secondary role because they couldn't master the *Bambi* style. As Walt now said of Ferguson, the man who had practically invented psychology in the animated cartoon, "He needs broader things."

With the story crew having conquered the narrative and the animators the style, Walt was confident enough to show a reel of *Bambi* to Bank of America executives late that June, and on Saturday, July 6, Joe Rosenberg came to the studio to view the footage. Roy and Walt were courting Rosenberg again because they had decided to hit the Bank of America for another loan. (The stock issue had helped pay off the debts, but it was not a fund on which they could continually draw.) "They have absolute confidence in us," Roy wrote Walt the day before Rosenberg's visit. "They rely on everything we tell them to the nth degree, but they are so pessimistic with regard to the outside world that they do not believe they are justified in loaning any money based on expectations involving foreign countries, no matter where they are." The bank was willing to loan the studio another $2 million with a $250,000 cushion, but Roy warned Walt that the bank had already been told Walt was going to economize, cutting staff and reducing salaries. "I believe strongly," Roy closed, "that the thing for us to do is not to cross them or even argue with them too much, but to go along with them."

VI

If the studio's desperation for more money never changed, another thing at the studio never changed either—the frenzied rushes to meet a release date. After much scheduling and rescheduling, the studio had decided to release *Fantasia* in November 1940 rather than rush *Bambi* or *Dumbo*, which was already moving at a breakneck pace. Deems Taylor arrived at the studio in mid-August to shoot narration while Stokowski headed off for a tour of South America with Walt's assurance that "we are using our best judgment in making the picture and music blend together as it [*sic*] should." As with *Snow White* and *Pinocchio*, the staff worked long shifts that summer and into the fall. One cameraman said he spent twelve hours each day for an entire year working on *Fantasia* because the special effects were so extravagant; a scene that might last only three seconds on screen might require twelve exposures. (Walt was especially keen on effects to evoke awe.) Unlike *Bambi* and *Dumbo*, Walt supervised everything. He would watch the dailies, the film that had been shot the previous day, every afternoon at three o'clock in room 3E down the hall from his office. Meanwhile the animators were working just as furiously. Years later, when college students would smoke marijuana while watching *Fantasia* for its wild hallucinatory effects, Art Babbitt would be asked whether he had animated under the influence of any drugs. "Yes, it is true," he answered. "I myself was addicted to Ex-Lax and Feen-a-Mint," two laxatives.

Once again Walt had saved the most difficult scene for last. He had decided that the "Ave Maria" sequence should follow "Bald Mountain," partly as an antidote: "We are portraying good and evil." As Walt conceptualized it, the church bells in "Ave Maria" would sweep from the speakers at the back of the theater forward, chasing the demons of "Bald Mountain" offscreen. It would provide, he thought, exactly the sort of slow, somber note needed to end the film—the sort of grace note he lamented he didn't have at the end of *Snow White*, where he thought he had raced too quickly from her sleep to her awakening. He also thought the scene would be commercial. "There's still a lot of Christians in the world, in spite of Russia and some of the others," he had said at a story meeting, "and it would be a hell of an appealing thing from that angle." If it was being shown in a non-Christian country, Walt advised, they could simply snip it off.

He had set himself and the staff a difficult task. Just as he hoped to create the feeling of being in the woods in *Bambi*, the effect Walt was looking for in "Ave Maria" was the "feeling that you are inside a cathedral without showing anything that is actually recognizable as a cathedral." And it had to be a big climax: "It must be like a spectacle on the stage," Walt ordered, something practically hypnotic in the spell it would cast. But Walt wasn't just issuing general ideas to be implemented. He gave the director, Wilfred Jackson, detailed instructions on what he wanted, right down to the dissolves.

If that weren't enough, Walt had come up with one more idea for the sequence, an idea he thought would supply the necessary awe, even as the deadline was hard upon them. He decided he wanted a 220-foot tracking shot into the Gothic cathedral. To get it, he shut down one entire soundstage because he needed a space that large to move the camera through the panes of glass that constituted the planes into the church. By one account, it took six days with the crew working twenty-four hours each day in twelve-hour shifts to finish the shot. At one point the entire crew worked forty-eight hours straight without relief. When Walt heard that production was going to shut down briefly because one of the camera operators was going to be married, he offered to get Stokowski and the Philadelphia Orchestra to play at the man's ceremony if he and his bride would take their vows on the soundstage and keep the film in production. And yet after all that, when Walt saw the developed film, he decided it couldn't be used because there was a jitter. "It's a lousy job," he told them, and ordered that it be done again. During the reshoot there was a small earthquake, and once again the scene was ruined and had to be reshot. By the time they got it right, it was the day before the New York premiere. Herb Taylor, who later became head of the sound department, remembered that a motorcycle was idling at the door to take the film to the airport so that it could be flown to New York and spliced into the last reel. Taylor didn't leave the studio until eight o'clock the next morning. Writing Walt two days after the premiere, Stokowski lauded the film as "something that will arrest the attention of all classes of men and women in every part of the world," but he felt that "Ave Maria" needed to be redubbed "to give it more appeal." Walt declined. He had tampered enough.

Now the film was in the hands of the public. Walt had long recognized that while *Fantasia* was going to be an aesthetic milestone and a completely new departure in animation, it was also going to be a "slow money maker, but a big money maker in the long run." This was not exactly the kind of talk that endeared him to his distributor, RKO. With little prospect of an immediate return, they seemed to have little interest in the film, especially since, to enhance its prestige, Walt had always insisted that it be exhibited as a roadshow attraction with reserved seating in a limited number of theaters outfitted with his expensive Fantasound system. It was Roy who proposed as early as February that the studio find its own backers and then release the film themselves. He suggested that someone like Nelson Rockefeller, an heir to the Rockefeller oil fortune and a strong proponent of the fine arts, might want to become part of a joint venture. The Rockefeller name, he thought, would also help legitimize the film. In the end there would be no Rockefeller. The Disneys financed the film through their usual loans, but they hired a young film salesman named Irving Ludwig to arrange the distribution of the first-run exhibition in eleven cities.

The problems with RKO, however, were a harbinger of things to come. At the very time they were quarreling with RKO about releasing *Fantasia*, Roy and Walt were also in negotiations with the company for a new contract. The previous December, RKO executive M. H. Aylesworth had written Walt a letter promising a "bang-up financing program" and joking that as long as Walt continued to work, "Roy and Gunnie [Lessing] have a living but if you lay off God knows what any of us will do." By the summer, however, the sides were still trading terms, and United Artists, Warner Bros., Paramount, and Metro-Goldwyn-Mayer were all wooing the Disneys. Despite RKO's misgivings about *Fantasia*—as late as July, RKO publicist Hal Horne was having second thoughts about the title as too upscale—they wanted to keep the Disneys and offered terms that allowed RKO to recoup the cost of prints, advertising, and promotion from the first proceeds but prevented them from collecting their distribution fee, 22.5 percent in the United States and Great Britain and 27.5 percent in the rest of the world, until the Disneys had recouped the negative costs of making the films, thus giving RKO a further incentive to promote the picture. Roy reluctantly agreed, saying that while he didn't trust any distributor, he trusted RKO more than the others. But even as he closed the deal, he had already begun contemplating distributing their films themselves, just as they were doing on the first run of *Fantasia*.

For *Fantasia* the Disneys had secured a year's lease on the two-thousand-seat Broadway Theater at Fifty-third Street in New York, the same theater, then named the Colony, where Mickey Mouse had premiered twelve years earlier, and they had William Garity, the studio engineer, refurbish the theater for the Fantasound system. (The equipment weighed more than seven thousand pounds and, true to Disney form, took over a week of crews working round the clock to install.) After being hospitalized for two days with a severe cold, Walt himself left for the New York premiere on November 1 with Lillian, Ham Luske, and Bill Cottrell, taking a roundabout route via New Orleans and Atlanta, where he said he was soaking up atmosphere for a possible feature based on the stories of southern fabulist Joel Chandler Harris, also known as Uncle Remus. His New York schedule included an address to a women's club, which, he joked, "only goes to show what FANTASIA has already done to me!" He spent much of the time in the city, however, at the Broadway, conducting runthroughs and talking to the press. "I don't know how much money this picture is going to make or lose," he told one reporter, hedging his bets. "But the boys and I have gained some incalculable experience." He admitted he was taking a huge risk without a foreign market, but he felt he was "expanding, opening up new fields," which was the aesthetic equivalent, he said, of plowing profits back into the company. To another reporter he was less grandiose and more edgy. With his leg thrown over one of the theater chairs and his hand nervously running through his hair, he declared, "We're selling entertainment and that's the thing I'm hoping *Fantasia* does—entertain. I'm hoping, hoping, hoping."

Rain fell hard the entire day of the premiere, November 13. Oddly, a man who had spent the last year completely immersed in his own work and scarcely acknowledging the tumult of the outside world, with the war raging in Europe, and whose work served as a kind of refuge from that tumult, would hold the premiere as a benefit for British War Relief. The patronesses of the event included Mrs. Henry F. DuPont, wife of the chemical company mogul; Mrs. Henry Luce, wife of the magazine publisher; Mrs. William Randolph Hearst, wife of the newspaper titan; Mrs. David Sarnoff, wife of the RCA head; Mrs. William K. Vanderbilt, wife of the philanthropist; Mrs. Paul Felix Warburg, wife of the investment banker; and Mrs. Kermit Roosevelt, wife of the former president's son—which only further signified how far Walt and the animated cartoon itself had come since the early days of Mickey Mouse. Even Walt was impressed by the turnout, writing his old teacher Daisy Beck like a starstruck fan about the "gala premiere" and the "socialites" who attended.

By any measure it was a triumphant evening. The audience thrilled to the film, and they thrilled to the experience; thanks to Fantasound, the seats actually vibrated when the music blasted. Bosley Crowther of *The New York Times*, who attended, could barely contain himself in his review the next morning. He wrote that "motion picture history was made at the Broadway Theatre last night" and called *Fantasia* as "terrific as anything that has ever happened on screen." He ended his notice with a nod to the war: "It's a tremendous blessing these days." The *Times* editorial page also praised the film for its "fusion of music, drama and graphic art" and, like Crowther, said that Walt Disney had made history by bringing them together.

But if the evening and the early returns were triumphant, many of the later returns cast a pall.* While film critics were largely enchanted, some music critics complained that the film did a disservice to the classics. (As Stokowski had predicted, many of them were offended by Walt's interpretation of the "Pastorale.") Olin Downes of *The New York Times* lavishly praised the sound reproduction but found the film itself a mess, trying to do too much. "It is clear," he wrote accurately a few days after the premiere in a Sunday consideration, "that in many cases Mr. Disney's noble and highly provocative experiment separated certain lovers of the respective arts rather than united them." Others thought that Disney hadn't despoiled art but had finally capitulated to it. Otis Ferguson of *The New Republic*, who had been one of Walt's most ardent admirers, called *Fantasia* "his first mistake" because it had pretensions. "First Chaplin learns about class struggle," Ferguson wrote, referring to Chaplin's *Modern Times*, "now Disney meets the Performing Pole," meaning Stokowski.

*In a breakdown of reviews from both film and music critics, Paul Anderson, a Disney scholar, found 33 percent were very positive, 22 percent positive, 22 percent both positive and negative, and 16 percent negative, meaning that the general response was still overwhelmingly favorable. Paul F. Anderson, "The Disney Statistic," *POV* 1, no. 2 (Winter 1992), p. 6.

The harshest criticisms, however, were political. Harry Raymond in the *Daily Worker* grumbled that even left-wing critics were so beguiled by *Fantasia*'s technical achievements that they failed to recognize how reactionary the film really was, especially at a time of international crisis. "The forces of evil are not shown as the exploiters and war makers," he said, "but as a mythical devil on a mountain top against whom human powers are helpless." In short, Walt had abdicated personal and social responsibility for what Raymond, obviously thinking of "Bald Mountain" and "Ave Maria," called "theology." Far more stinging was nationally syndicated columnist Dorothy Thompson, who seethed that she had left the theater "in a condition bordering on a nervous breakdown" and felt as if she had been subjected to an "assault"—a "brutalization of sensibility in this remarkable nightmare." Thompson's complaint was that Disney and Stokowski seemed to extol the savagery of nature at the expense of man. (What Thompson missed was that Walt was extolling not so much nature as his own power to re-create the savagery of nature on screen.) In Thompson's eyes, Disney's nature was so overwhelming that man had no choice but to succumb, and like Raymond, she saw this as an abdication of responsibility that she obliquely connected to the Nazi terror in Europe. Along with Disney's other recent work, the film was, she concluded, "cruel," "brutal and brutalizing," and a "caricature of the Decline of the West."

Walt professed to be amused by the controversy. Two weeks after the premiere he wrote a friend that the fray "couldn't have been sweeter" because it generated so much publicity for the film. "The public responded by lining up at the box office with the result that our advance sale has been simply terrific. We've had practically a full house every day with Saturdays and Sundays being sold out for at least a month in advance." He said he left New York "walking on air." As he headed to Los Angeles aboard the *Twentieth Century* for the West Coast premiere, he wrote Stokowski airily brushing off the criticisms of "Ave Maria" and announcing that he intended to concentrate on adding some new segments to the film.

If anything, the audience at the Los Angeles opening at the Carthay Circle on January 29, 1941—it had been delayed by contractual problems in securing the theater—was even more enthusiastic than the one in New York, even though fewer celebrities attended. "The premiere audience was unquestionably enraptured by the production as a whole," Edwin Schallert, a film reporter for the *Los Angeles Times*, wrote in an article titled "Fantasia Acclaimed as Cinema Masterpiece." "The applause was enthusiastic during the majority of the interludes and even broke in from time to time on the action." The film was, he said, "courageous beyond belief." Arthur Miller, also writing for the *Times*, called it "an earthquake in motion picture history." Director Cecil B. DeMille, who had been so enchanted by *Snow White*, said, "There is nothing in our earthly imaginings which can equal, let alone surpass, what Disney has accomplished."

Walt himself still seemed ebullient. Before its release he had called *Fantasia* the "big experience" of his life. After its release he claimed it was the apex of animation and doubted that it could ever be duplicated since the loss of the foreign markets would make any attempt to make a film as costly and ambitious as *Fantasia* "suicidal." Yet as proud as he said he was of the film, he was deeply hurt by the criticism and began to harbor doubts about it himself. Roy would later say that *Fantasia* was a "disappointment" to Walt. "[I]t was that he saw more in it—the possibilities—than he got out of it," Roy said, because Walt "didn't really have the artists." According to Joe Grant, for all Walt's outward expressions of confidence, even on the way back from the New York premiere he was depressed. "He said something to the effect of 'All that work and all that fanfare,'" Grant recalled. "He realized that he had gone over the public's head with *Fantasia*, and that he had also disappointed them, because the film wasn't what they expected from Disney." Years later Walt himself would say, "Every time I've made a mistake is when I went in a direction where I didn't feel the thing actually. And I did try to be a little smarty pants."

Perhaps the criticism that stung the most was that of Igor Stravinsky, who may simply have been trying to distance himself from the film after so many music critics found fault with it. Walt recalled Stravinsky visiting the studio with the choreographer George Balanchine back in December 1939 when he showed them *The Sorcerer's Apprentice* and the storyboards for *The Rite of Spring*. It was, by Walt's account, a pleasant if uneventful meeting. Stravinsky would remember it differently. He said that he had received a request from the studio for permission to use *Le Sacre* "accompanied by a gentle warning that if permission were withheld the music would be used anyway," since the piece had not been copyrighted in the United States. Walt proposed $5,000 for foreign rights, which, Stravinsky claimed, was reduced during negotiations. As he remembered it, during his visit he was offered a score, and when he said he had his own, he was told that the music had been changed. "It was indeed," Stravinsky would write scornfully. The instrumentation was different, the order of the pieces rearranged, the difficult passages eliminated. As for the visuals, Stravinsky said, "I do not wish to criticize an unresisting imbecility."

Yet for all his alleged objections at the time, Stravinsky returned to the studio on October 12, 1940, to see the final cut, after which, he said, he stormed out. The studio's version, once again, was different. When Walt suggested that Stravinsky visit the animators, Woolie Reitherman remembered them laughing and joking while the track of *The Rite of Spring* played backward on the Movieola. "Doesn't sound bad backwards either," Stravinsky quipped. Stravinsky returned to the studio yet again on October 23 to discuss the possibility of having the studio animate "Renard," an old piece of his, and wound up selling the rights to that, *Fireworks*, and *The Firebird*. "Doesn't sound as if he's very sore, does it?" Walt remarked wryly to the *Los Angeles Times*.*

Despite the carping about its pretensions, its naïve misunderstanding of the music, and its fascistic brutality, Roy was more than satisfied with *Fantasia*'s initial returns. "WILL FINISH THIS WEEK WITH TWENTY SEVEN THOUSAND [DOLLARS]," he wired Walt from New York after the second week. "ALL NIGHTS HAVE BEEN SELLOUTS AND MONDAY TUESDAY WEDNESDAY MATINEES ABOUT EIGHTY PERCENT." With expenses at $11,000 a week, Roy thought the prospects were "VERY SOLID AND ENCOURAGING." In its first sixteen weeks at the Broadway, where the demand was so great the theater had to add eight telephone operators to handle the calls and rent an adjoining store for the walk-up advance sales, it grossed more than $300,000. It netted more than $20,000 each of its first ten weeks both at the Majestic Theater in Boston and at the Carthay Circle, and it had netted nearly as much after only five weeks at the Geary Theater in San Francisco. Meanwhile Roy was pressing RCA to deliver Fantasound systems to the other first-run theaters so they could broaden the release. "I see no reason why we should not be able to get our full negative cost back by the end of 1941," he wrote Walt gleefully. "We may do better than that."

Even before he knew the outcome, Walt had been planning a sequel, and as early as May 1940 he met with Stokowski to discuss it. At the time both were nearly giddy with enthusiasm, mulling over Richard Strauss's *Till Eulenspiegel*, Brahms's First Symphony, Respighi's *The Pines of Rome*, Holst's *The Planets*, and even Gershwin's jazz symphony *Rhapsody in Blue*. When Stokowski suggested using Dvorak's *New World Symphony* but cutting it, Walt countered that he didn't think it should be cut and that some of the pieces in *Fantasia*, he felt, had been cut too much. "[W]e were

*Also contradicting Stravinsky's supposed outrage was the fact that he cordially welcomed Disney executive Don Niles to his home in September 1942 when Walt had dispatched Niles to discuss renewing the option on Stravinsky's music. Niles reported that Stravinsky was "happy to negotiate a new option," though he thought the war obviated the necessity for doing so, and that Stravinsky "stated that he would be only too willing to make his services available to us" at an appropriate fee once the war was over. Memo, Don Niles to Walt, Re: Stravinsky Option, Oct. 1, 1942, N folder, Walt Disney Corr., Inter-Office, 1938–1944, N-Q, A1630, WDA.

frightened," he admitted. And when Stokowski brought up Debussy's *La Mer*, saying it was difficult to understand, Walt waved off the objection. "You said the RITE OF SPRING was difficult to understand, remember?" he told Stokowski. "Maybe we ought to open up on these things instead of playing down to our medium or our public. That's the very thing we like to have, a challenge."

While he contemplated a sequel, Walt also thought of adding individual sequences to the original film, which had the advantages of being easier to do and of providing ongoing work for the animators when they needed it, always one of Walt's major considerations. It also had the advantage of allowing Walt, who always hated to surrender a film, the opportunity to keep "plussing" it—making it better. By the time the film was released, Walt was talking about it as if it were analogous to an opera or ballet company with its own repertory. "The prospective patron will consult a program in advance, and determine his time of attendance at *Fantasia* on the basis of his preference in musical numbers and motion picture characters," he told the *Hollywood Citizen News*. He even said that the film might vary from theater to theater, from week to week, day to day. At another point he said he was thinking of remaking the film each year. Stokowski, who was still attending performances and checking the sound levels at theaters more than a month after the premiere, heartily agreed that *Fantasia* should be an organic mechanism. "From all the talk I hear in and around New York about *Fantasia* I think if we put in one new number, almost everybody would go to hear the whole picture again," he wrote Walt.

When Walt returned to the studio after the *Fantasia* gala in New York, he immediately plunged into developing the new sequences. Whatever hadn't been done right in the original *Fantasia* could now be made right in the additions. He was especially eager to do Wagner's "Ride of the Valkyries" because, he told his story staff, it would "stir up musical circles." He was also excited about the prospect of animating Sergei Prokofiev's "Peter and the Wolf." As Walt would later relate it, some years earlier Prokofiev had visited the studio, played the piece for Walt while a translator narrated, and told him that he had written it expressly for the purpose of having Disney animate it. Now Walt intended to.

But already that January, with his early fervor perhaps dampened by some of the critical brickbats hurled at *Fantasia*, Walt was raising the issue of costs. As much as he wanted to make "Valkyries," he told his staff that it depended on whether they could make it within budget. "If we can't do it for a set figure," he said, "then we better forget it." Similarly, discussing Sibelius's *The Swan of Tuonela*, Walt suggested that they photograph a model of a swan and animate the ripples in the water. "[W]e don't have to be making every drawing of that swan—which costs," he told the crew, sounding very unlike himself. Discussing a sequence of Tchaikovsky's "Humoresque," featuring the mushrooms from the "Nutcracker" segment, he advised that the animators repeat cycles of action to save money and that of six mushrooms three replicate the actions of the other three so the animators would only have to trace the actions for one set rather than animate all six from scratch.

By this time the heady excitement over the *Fantasia* returns had begun to deflate too. The Fantasound system, upon which Walt insisted, was proving prohibitively expensive, forcing the studio to exceed its loan limit from the Bank of America and preventing the film from being exhibited more widely and taking in more receipts. "It is my opinion that it is positively not in the cards for us to continue using Fantasound," Roy wrote Walt that April, in what he must have realized would be a crushing blow. "I don't think there is another spot in the country that will warrant the costs." Meanwhile, in a defeat of his own, Roy was meeting with RKO head George Schaefer to discuss RKO's taking over the film's general release, though insisting that it continue to be exhibited on a roadshow basis with reserved seating, "down to the smallest town that can possibly stand such a show."

RKO did continue to distribute *Fantasia* that spring as a roadshow attraction, and RCA engineers even devised a modified sound system that was less costly than Fantasound and thus could be installed in more theaters. But the handwriting was on the wall. To put it into even wider release on a nonroadshow basis, RKO now insisted that the film be cut. Roy asked Walt to tell Stokowski, whom the studio was contractually obligated to notify of any changes, though it was Ed Plumb, the musical arranger, and not Walt, who passed on the news: "For most people," Plumb wrote Stokowski, "the experience of Fantasia is more than they can take without fatigue." Stokowski wouldn't be mollified, but Walt, who was equally distressed, felt helpless. "I frankly don't know what to do about it," Walt wrote Roy, saying that Roy might want to talk to Stokowski himself.

If he didn't want to talk to Stokowski, Walt would have nothing to do with the editing either. Ed Plumb and Ben Sharpsteen did the cutting without any input from Walt, trimming the film from its original two-hour-and-five-minute running time to an hour and forty minutes and then to an hour and twenty-four minutes, largely by scaling back Deems Taylor's introductions. Walt was despondent. "We must remember there are a lot of people who have seen it," he warned Roy, "and who will now come back to FANTASIA again, and we do not want to spoil it for those who appreciate the finer things to sell a few highschool [*sic*] tickets." But they did, though even after doing so, Roy fretted: "I'm fearful for what it will do in general release." At roughly the same time Stokowski pronounced himself ready to return to the studio to prepare recordings for the additional sequences. But the idea for a sequel had long since been dropped—"[T]he segments would now be thought of as 'individual Specials,' " studio production control manager Herb Lamb informed the studio, and even the "Specials" were in jeopardy. If the film proved successful in its general release, Walt abjectly wrote Stokowski, "I am sure I will be permitted to proceed with the numbers that we had in work last Spring. Until that time, I shall have to hold everything in abeyance." Speaking to *The New Yorker*, he was, if possible, even less optimistic. "That damn thing cost two-hundred thousand dollars," he growled about "The Nutcracker Suite" and the difficulties in animating it. "We're getting back to straight line stuff, like 'Donald Duck' and the 'Pigs.' " It was a sad retreat for a man who had boasted for years about the new horizons that *Fantasia* would open.

Barricaded in his studio while the world was roiling around him, Walt hoped, as always, to insulate himself from reality. Once, as he was arranging blocks representing the new studio's buildings, he was asked how the war would affect things. Walt supposedly snapped, "What war?" This was the power of his wish fulfillment and one of the chief appeals of his work: contrary to Dorothy Thompson's interpretation, Walt Disney's animations continued to demonstrate man's ability to construct his own reality. It was why audiences were still awestruck by what they saw. But if Walt had become more serious and less fanciful in *Pinocchio* and *Fantasia* than he had been in the Mickey Mouse cartoons or *Snow White*, it was also true that the social and political terms had shifted around him. As with the notion of responsibility, it was one thing to convey power to a nation hoping to vanquish the Depression and another to speak to a nation hoping to avoid getting ensnared in a war in Europe, which may have been another reason why audiences were cooler to *Pinocchio* and *Fantasia* than to *Snow White*. In effect, though the films were often regarded as relief for a troubled nation, Walt couldn't protect them from social considerations. He couldn't protect his studio either. Indeed, early in 1941 the world would invade even the Elysian Fields of Burbank, and when it did, everything in which Walt Disney had believed would be destroyed, all his illusions shattered.

Eight

TWO WARS

The storm clouds had been gathering at least since the move to Burbank and possibly even before, as the studio plowed ahead on its features in anticipation of profits it would not receive. During *Fantasia*, Roy had ordered a belt-tightening, forbidding any new hiring, requisitioning of any new materials, or starting any new film without the approval of the business office—thus directly infringing on Walt's power for the first time. Shortly after *Fantasia*'s release Walt pleaded with Roy to restore some merit raises to boost sagging morale yet again, but Roy, who had always capitulated in the past, was in no mood to humor his brother this time. Instead Walt, apparently without Roy's knowledge, advised Herb Lamb, the production control department manager, to increase salaries gradually over an extended period to escape notice.

In having to reward his employees surreptitiously, Walt's concern was that the Bank of America would find out and "raise hell with us." Though the studio had reported a pretax profit of $140,000 in the first four months of the 1941–42 fiscal year and though it had actually distributed $149,000 in bonuses to the staff, most of it in preferred stock, the bank was concerned again about the company's financial prospects, especially with the war continuing to erode foreign receipts. Thanks to the stock issue in April 1940, the company had managed to retire all of its real property loans for the new studio and most of its production loans. But by August, with the losses from *Pinocchio*, the studio had been forced to increase its credit line and seek more funds, which it optimistically thought it would retire with the profits from *Fantasia*. With *Fantasia* a disappointment too and the debt edging toward $3 million, the Bank of America summoned Walt to its San Francisco headquarters on February 24 to institute some cost-cutting measures. It was not a pleasant encounter. When a business associate asked him if he'd won the battle, Walt snapped, "You never win with bankers." The next month Joe Rosenberg visited the studio to continue his lecture on fiscal responsibility, and he and Walt had an argument in front of a reporter in which Rosenberg insisted that the company must toe the bottom line and Walt insisted that the business community had to expand its horizons rather than concentrate narrowly on immediate returns. As the reporter put it, "Between the two was a gulf as profound as the human mind."

"I know the bank is nervous now about our indebtedness," Roy wrote in a memo to Walt early in March, "and are [*sic*] going ahead to a higher figure reluctantly because they are on the spot and can't do much otherwise," but Roy realized that the studio was on "very thin ice." He recommended a 20 percent reduction in expenditures, in part by dropping every project save the shorts and the feature films due to be released over the next year—*Bambi* and *Dumbo*. He also advised that they close their film-processing lab and Walt's cherished art school and that they run down the list of employees and terminate anyone who "can possibly be released without affecting the immediate work in process." Unaware of Walt's raises, he demanded that every employee take a salary cut. Roy acknowledged that these measures would no doubt undermine everything Walt had done to build his studio as a workers' paradise, but he said the only alternatives were selling their films through a franchise at derisory terms or being forced into receivership or bankruptcy. The situation was so bad that when a film editor requisitioned a splicer, Walt felt he had to deny the request.

Even before the new financial pressures, strains had begun to emerge between Walt and the staff. Part of it was a function of size. In just five years the studio had swelled from three hundred employees to twelve hundred, and where Walt had once known the name of everyone in his employ and had interacted with many of them as well, it was impossible for him to do so now. Indeed, at Burbank he was not only physically separated—on one wing of the third floor, unit 3H—from the animators on the first floor, but anyone wanting to reach his office had to go up two flights of stairs, down a corridor, and past two offices, a reception room, and a secretary's cubicle. (Walt was aware of the isolation. The night before he moved to Burbank he told Joe Grant that he had had a dream that he was wandering through empty halls.) Part of it too was the competing claims on his attention and the necessity to delegate. "Walt began to become disengaged with the animations after *Pinocchio,*" Wilfred Jackson recalled, obviously forgetting *Fantasia.* "Up until *Pinocchio*, absolutely nothing happened without his being in on it. All the color models he saw before they got okayed. All the rough animation. We ran it for him before anything moved into clean-up, and ink and paint." But "in later years there was a gradual withdrawal on Walt's part of the intimate close working on all the details of every department, and he began to leave more and more to the judgment of the animators, to the judgment of the directors, and of the story department. He controlled things along a broader base."

But if Walt was, to the consternation of many of his staff, less visible and less personally engaged, it was in fact as much by choice as by necessity. Though he had loved the sense of community at Marceline and then at Kansas City and later Hyperion, he had no time now for japery or charm, and in any case he was more distrustful of associations once he had become "Walt Disney"—more distrustful of what people wanted from him. One production manager said that Walt "seemed to have trouble fully relating to his employees. He kept his guard up, his employees at arm's length, and was more touchy." Dick Huemer, the animator and storyman, recalled that Walt seldom engaged in small talk now and that it was tense being around him. Animator Milt Kahl said that no one at Burbank would ever have barged in on Walt or palled around with him, though that was exactly what the animators had once done. Surprisingly, it was draconian Roy who was much more accessible and likely to fraternize. "You could put your arm around Roy's shoulder, too, and did," Frank Thomas said. "Not with Walt." For all his bonhomie and his insistence on being called "Walt," he was now distant—if not exactly a despot, as the one employee had called him, then at least the "boss."

Only to those who had known him before his celebrity—his family and boyhood friends and even his earliest employees—was he gracious and loyal, apparently feeling that they had been loyal to him when they hadn't needed to be.* That was no doubt one of the reasons he lured Walt Pfeiffer to the studio and then kept giving him new assignments even as he failed at the old ones, and one of the reasons he hired his old McKinley High School classmate Bianca Majolie in the story department. Walt took one guard with him from Hyperion to Burbank to patrol the front gate even though the man was often inebriated, because, one employee speculated, "[h]e'd stuck with Disney during some hard times and Walt would never fire him."

Perhaps the most dramatic demonstration of his regard for the ghosts of his past was his treatment of the man who had committed what was, in Walt's mind, one of the worst betrayals: his old partner, Ub Iwerks. After leaving the studio abruptly in 1930, lured by the blandishments of Pat Powers, Iwerks had fallen on hard times. His own studio had failed, forcing him to subcontract with Warner Bros. and then Columbia, but these arrangements were ultimately terminated too. "He was one of the first—if not *the* first—to give his characters depth and roundness," animator Chuck Jones explained. "But he didn't have any story capacity, and I don't think he knew very much about humor; he wasn't a funny man at all." In 1940 he was teaching animation at a local vocational school and had gotten up the nerve to write Walt that July about the possibility of opening a school of his own, presumably to help train Disney animators. Walt referred the letter to Vern Caldwell in personnel, who dismissed the suggestion. Meanwhile Ben Sharpsteen, hearing about Iwerks's plight, phoned him, said that starting a school would be "belittling," and offered him a job checking animation, which Iwerks gratefully accepted. Sharpsteen was obviously trying to broker a rapprochement between Iwerks and Walt, and when he told Walt that he had asked Iwerks back, Walt said it

*Though Walt was besieged with requests for money, some from perfect strangers, others from friends and acquaintances, and though he usually pleaded that he had nothing to spare, he did occasionally reward past service. He gave $200 to the sister of an old Kansas City friend so she could clear her mortgage and $200 more to a Kansas City pal who needed to make payments as he looked for another job; money to a Red Cross buddy; loans to Carl Stalling, the composer who had stalked out of the studio early in 1930; and over a thousand dollars to Jerry Raggos, the proprietor of the café in Kansas City who had given him meals when he was down on his luck, so that Raggos could open a restaurant in Phoenix. He even wrote a letter of reference for George Winkler, who had helped engineer his ouster from the Mintz operation.

was Sharpsteen's prerogative to hire whomever he liked. But on August 9 Walt and Iwerks had lunch at the studio, over which, as Iwerks later told it, Walt asked him what he really wanted to do there. Iwerks, always more interested in technology than animation, said he answered, "Prowl around." Overlooking their past dispute, Walt assigned him to help develop a new optical camera for special effects, illustrating both Walt's commitment to anything that would help his studio regardless of his personal feelings and his attachment to his old colleagues now that he presided over an increasingly impersonal bureaucracy.

But he displayed no hint of sentiment when it came to newer employees, especially as his dream of utopia faded under the glare of economic realities. Walt saw them purely in instrumental terms: what could they contribute to realizing his vision? Even a long-timer like Ben Sharpsteen would say, "I always knew that he was only intimate with me up to a purpose where he thought it could be worthwhile." Walt thought nothing of firing someone who he felt had outlived his usefulness, calling it "weeding out marginal people" or getting rid of "deadwood." No one was safe, not even members of his own family. When his sister-in-law Hazel Sewell suffered a nervous breakdown and he docked her pay, Sewell—who had been at the studio for eleven years, eventually heading up the ink and paint department—tendered her resignation, arguing that her economies had saved the studio tens of thousands of dollars. Walt was brusque: "Personally, I am greatly shocked by your unwarranted attitude. However, if I were in your place and felt the way you do about the organization where I worked, I would probably do the same thing." Another longtime employee complained that he was never promoted. "The reason that you have not been put at the Head of your Department," Walt wrote him coldly, "is that we do not feel that you are capable of giving us the standard of work that we must have. . . . If you will consider the quality of your work, I believe you will understand why you have not advanced further." When Clarence Nash, Donald Duck's voice, requested a raise, Walt talked to him "like a Dutch uncle in order to whittle him down to his proper size," and when Pinto Colvig, who did the voices for Goofy and two of the dwarfs, complained that he was being underpaid, Walt ordered him dismissed. "He is just a clown and not at all the type of fellow we need to keep production moving," Walt wrote Roy. "He's been crying to me ever since he's been here." One storyman was even fired when, during a conference, he announced that it was noon and they should break for lunch.

Despite his distance and icy dismissiveness, many of the employees still revered Walt, who, though only thirty-nine in 1941, was nevertheless significantly older than his animators, whose average age was now twenty-seven, and who was one of America's most famous cultural icons. But after years of slavishly obeying his commands and after years of gladly subscribing to his cult, some had begun to resent him too, and director Jack Kinney observed a growing division in the staff between those who continued to worship him and those who didn't.

Many of the apostates had begun to question what they saw as Walt's paternalism, which they thought was expressed by his habitually calling his staff "my boys" whenever he spoke of them. Some saw paternalism too in Walt's bonuses, which disgruntled animators viewed as arbitrarily dispensed. They felt they were being manipulated, not only by the bonuses but also by Walt's general approach to them. (Walt proudly admitted that he had read a psychology book and tried applying its precepts to his relations with his staff.) Others had begun to chafe at the fact that for all the talk of collaboration, Walt was an autocrat whose word was the only word. "Usually each of us felt, 'Why didn't I think of that?' " Frank Thomas and Ollie Johnston wrote of the respect for Walt's ideas while acknowledging a new rebelliousness, "but every so often we secretly would feel, 'My way is better!' " They all knew that Walt entertained only those ideas that comported with his own. "God help you if you took his idea and ran it in the wrong direction," a writer at the studio commented. "If you did, one eyebrow would rise and the other would descend, and he'd say, 'You don't seem to get it at all.' " When Bill Cottrell suggested a scene in *Pinocchio* and Walt vetoed it, Cottrell protested, "But if we don't try it my way, we'll never know whether or not it would have worked." To which Walt replied, "No, we won't." Ward Kimball noted, "You learned early on never to argue with him or to cross him." Indeed, during sweatbox sessions everyone would sit silently and nervously while Walt watched, pondered, and issued his verdict. Only then would the others express their opinions—always parroting Walt's. As one employee put it, "Everybody with any sense waited on Walt."

Along with the distance and the autocracy, the staff now began to voice another raw grievance: Walt never gave them credit. "No one person can take credit for the success of a motion picture," he had once said. "It's strictly a team effort." Nevertheless Walt had always made certain that *his* name was the most prominent, even if he claimed that this was essentially a marketing decision. It was, according to Dave Hand, an edict at the studio: "don't mention anybody but that one person, Walt." On the shorts the storymen and animators seldom cared. But the features, on which many of them had labored for years, were a different matter. Not getting credit hurt and generated deep hostility. "Being left off the credits made me realize I was still just another sketch man, just one of the mob, and I was depressed for weeks afterward," Bill Peet remarked when he attended a preview of *Pinocchio* and didn't see his name on the screen. When one animator approached Walt with the idea of giving awards for the best animation, Walt told him, "If there's going to be any awards made, I'm going to get them." Indeed, it was Walt who often expressed resentment at his animators for what he saw as their haughtiness and self-regard, calling them "touch-me-nots" and "holy cows." In return, where they had once celebrated Walt for orchestrating the team, one of them would later gripe, "He's a genius at using someone else's genius."

And the rift wasn't only between Walt and the staff but among members of the staff themselves now that Walt wasn't there to deflect the discontent and now that the sense of mission was being compromised by economic woes. In-betweeners and cleanup men, most of whom made less than $20 a week, began to resent the animators, who made anywhere from $75 a week (Don Lusk and John Lounsbery) to $300 a week (Norm Ferguson and Freddie Moore). Since many of these underpaid employees worked on a trial basis for months and even then didn't advance up the studio ranks, they became, in Ben Sharpsteen's word, "soreheads," and since Walt seldom fired these underlings, their resentments festered. But even among the key animators there was dissension. West Coast animators resented the artists Walt had hired from the East, often at higher salaries, especially since the West Coasters felt they had to train the Easterners, and Walt's vaunted bonus system created tensions not only between Walt and the animators but between animators who felt they were doing essentially the same work but getting paid lower salaries and those who were receiving the higher salaries. "If I gave one person a bonus then they could never figure out why someone else didn't get a bonus, and they hadn't earned it, but they couldn't understand that," Walt later observed. The system was so complicated no one ever fully understood it.

Over and above the bonuses, some employees burned over what they believed was the favorable treatment given to other employees. To help foster a sense of community, Walt permitted Ward Kimball to organize a jazz band that Kimball called the "Huggajeedy 8," but it had the opposite effect. "Their practicing could be heard all over the studio during business hours and their sounds weren't always pleasurable to the ears," one animator later commented. "Such goings-on spread discontent among those who didn't believe in such and those who were just plain jealous." Others blamed the new studio for underscoring class distinctions. At the Penthouse Club, for example, membership was restricted to employees making two hundred dollars a week or more, cleaving the best-paid staff members from everyone else. "I don't think any of us knew about unions," Ken

Peterson, an in-betweener at the time, said. "But we were all feeling sort of left out."

Left out and angry—a condition that made them ripe for an incipient rebellion. For years, as part of a general mobilization within the film industry, organizers had been attempting to unionize animation studios and the animation departments of major studios. At the old Iwerks studio, several animators decided to unionize after one of their colleagues died of a heart attack, but the studio called for overtime to prevent the employees from attending a membership meeting, and the effort expired. Animators made more headway at the Fleischer studio in New York, which was struck in May 1937, shortly after the Fleischers fired fifteen employees who had joined the union to protest working conditions. The strike lasted six months—picketers carried signs declaring "I'm Popeye the Union Man" after the Fleischers' most popular character—until an election was finally held and the union was certified. (Max Fleischer countered by moving the studio to Florida and dissolving the union.) Next Herbert Sorrell, the head of the Conference of Studio Unions into which the Screen Cartoonists Guild was incorporated, targeted the cartoon department at Metro-Goldwyn-Mayer, largely because it was so small he knew the studio wouldn't risk a strike for it; then he aimed at Warner Bros., where, under animation head Leon Schlesinger, the animators were earning 50 percent less than the animators had at MGM. Schlesinger scoffed at Sorrell's threats, insisting that his animators loved him and that whenever they needed money, he loaned it to them. A strike ensued, during which Schlesinger posted a sign on his door saying he was off on his yacht. Within a short time he called Sorrell to make a deal, then asked him, "Now, what about Disney?"

That was the question ringing in animation circles. In fact, after the Fleischers settled in 1937, an assistant animator named Dave Hilberman told key animator Art Babbitt that the International Alliance of Theatrical Stage Employees (IATSE), a rival union to Sorrell's, was launching a new campaign to unionize the film industry, apparently including the Disney studio. IATSE was headed by two notorious thugs, George Browne and Willie Bioff, who had been associated with the Al Capone crime family in Chicago, and Babbitt was frightened. That same day he ran into Bill Garity, then head of production control, and when Babbitt mentioned his concerns, Garity told him that IATSE had already sent a delegation to the studio, and if Babbitt didn't like it, he should act. Babbitt met with Roy Disney, who shunted him off to attorney Gunther Lessing. Lessing, eager to head off IATSE, advised Babbitt to form what Lessing called "some sort of an organization, preferably a social organization," and offered his help. Early in December 1937 Babbitt, forty employees, and Lessing met in sweatbox 1 at the Hyperion studio to create a federation to represent the studio's employees in its relations with management. The group held a general membership meeting at the American Legion Hall in Hollywood on January 25, 1938, at which Babbitt was elected president, and the organization, now called the Cartoonists Federation, applied for certification from the National Labor Relations Board (NLRB), which granted it in July 1939. By this time IATSE had been rebuffed, forestalling any interest in a union. But with the certification the leaders of the federation were inspired to draw up a list of contract demands. Roy was astonished, saying he had "no use for any unions" and wouldn't negotiate. It indicated how thoroughly Walt had won their allegiance, despite their grievances, that the board decided to disband the federation rather than fight.

But in October 1940, after Sorrell had negotiated his truce with MGM, Dave Hilberman, the animation assistant who had originally warned Babbitt about IATSE, decided to begin organizing the Disney studio on behalf of Sorrell's Screen Cartoonists Guild (SCG). On December 5 the SCG informed the company that it had collected cards from a majority of Disney's employees and would ask for recognition. Walt was frantic. The very next morning he called Babbitt to a meeting in his office, showed Babbitt a letter from the SCG's attorney announcing its claim, and ordered Babbitt to reconvene the federation so "we can stop this thing." When Babbitt declined, saying he would be ridiculed after the company had refused to bargain with him, Walt cracked, "Well, where would I be if I couldn't stand a little ridicule?" Walt insisted he would never bargain with unions. "You know how I am, boys," he told them, "if I can't have my own way . . . if somebody tries to tell me to do something, I will do just the opposite, and if necessary I will close down this studio." Walt's idea was to sign a closed-shop agreement with the federation to freeze out any other union. The next day the studio sent out application slips to employees through the department supervisors.

Most of those who reflected on the union fracas would lay the federation plan at the feet of Gunther Lessing, the Disneys' legal counsel. As a young attorney in El Paso, Texas, Lessing had gotten entangled in defending a number of Mexican revolutionaries and had ridden into Mexico City with Francisco Madero when Madero took over the government. After Madero's assassination, Lessing would go on to represent the bandit-revolutionary Pancho Villa. Lessing called himself an "idealist." By the time he joined the Disneys in the early 1930s, however, his idealism had given way to a truculent conservatism that made him a pariah among most of the studio's employees, including those who shared his politics. Even Roy said that after *Snow White* everyone took to calling the bald-pated Lessing "Dopey."

Whatever Lessing's influence, the Disneys themselves had never looked kindly on unions. For all his alleged socialism, Elias Disney had told his children a story about being attacked by union organizers when he was working on a construction site; and Walt certainly hated the idea of anyone trying to intimidate him, especially his own employees. But whatever antagonism the Disneys may have felt was further fueled by Lessing, whom they had appointed to advise Babbitt back in 1937 on the formation of the federation. "A more unwise choice could not have been made," animator Shamus Culhane would write. "During the preliminary seminars about unionism, Lessing's approach was too slick, too facile, and too arrogant. When some employee had the temerity to get up and ask a question, Lessing, while listening, would roll his eyes up toward heaven, in the age-old gesture of weary patience with blatant stupidity." As Culhane saw it, Lessing only fomented hostility to the very company union he was charged with organizing.

Over the next month Babbitt defected and joined Hilberman in helping organize the animators under the Cartoonists Guild. (He said he was moved to do so when one of the inkers at the studio fainted because she couldn't afford to buy lunch.) At an organizing meeting at the Roosevelt Hotel, Sorrell delivered an impassioned speech, promising to "[s]queeze Disney's balls 'til he screams." Meanwhile the old federation, with Walt and Lessing's blessings, held an open meeting on January 28, 1941, at the Abraham Lincoln School, three blocks north of the studio, to discuss a plan under which it would serve as the bargaining agent for the workers, using an impartial chairman with an advisory board composed of two representatives each from labor and management to settle disputes. (Exactly how the chairman was to be selected wasn't specified.) A few days later the SCG charged the studio with sponsoring a company union. Walt retaliated by posting a bulletin on February 6 forbidding employees to engage in union activity on company time or on company property.

But Herbert Sorrell was not a man to be easily deterred. He was coarse-looking, compact, with round sloping shoulders, a high forehead and square chin, and a nose flattened perhaps by too many punches from his days as a prizefighter. He was also, at forty-four, every bit as tough as he looked. The son of a peripatetic drunkard, Sorrell went to work at the age of twelve in a sewer pipe plant in Oakland, where he was beaten mercilessly by his fellow workers until he whacked one with a shovel and sent him to the hospital. He later sold pipe, worked as a riveter, was drafted into the service during World War I, and returned to become a professional prizefighter, then moved to Los Angeles to work as a painter at the studios. The seminal moment in his life, he said, was when a supervisor at Universal asked him whether he was a union member and, when he answered that he was, summarily fired him. That radicalized him. It was during a strike at Paramount in 1937, however, that Sorrell became a power to be reckoned with. He called sixteen "scab" laborers, said they were needed immediately at the studio, and offered to pick them up. "We came and got them," he later reminisced drily, "and Monday there were sixteen broken right arms." In forming the Conference of Studio Unions (CSU), a bloc of ten motion picture unions, and assuming its presidency, Sorrell became the most powerful organizer in Hollywood—one to be taken seriously. Now, as Walt later told it, Sorrell threatened to turn the Disney studio into a "dust bowl" if the Disneys didn't recognize the SCG.

Bracing for a showdown between these two larger-than-life figures, the studio was tense. Walt knew that he had to seize the initiative and act quickly, and he did what he had always done when faced with crisis: he appealed to the missionary zeal of his employees and their belief that they were not merely industrial workers toiling for a wage but were engaged in a great enterprise. In two shifts, at five o'clock on February 10, 1941, and then again the next day, Walt addressed his staff in the studio theater. Announcing that he had been advised to read his speech and have it recorded, lest there be any legal consequences for what he said, he began soberly by saying that the studio was in a financial crisis, a crisis that he admitted was partly of his own making. He had simply had too much faith in animation. "I have had a stubborn, blind confidence in the cartoon medium," he told them, "a determination to show the skeptics that the animated cartoon was deserving of a better place; that it was more than a mere 'filler' on a program; that it was more than a novelty; that it could be one of the greatest mediums of fantasy and entertainment yet developed." That conviction had guided his life and often driven him into poverty. Yet he persisted, refusing to cut salaries when every other studio had done so and even distributing the bonuses so that he could keep his staff intact and contented. He took virtually nothing for himself, even voluntarily taking a 75 percent cut in his own salary when the foreign markets dried up. There were, he said, three options now: cut salaries drastically, cut production and lay off workers, or sell the company to someone who was interested only in profits. He was resisting all of these, preferring instead to economize through smaller salary cuts and budget reductions. Would they agree?

Addressing the personal grievances, Walt denied that a class system existed at the studio. Creative staff got certain advantages over the business staff because, he said, they contributed more, but the Penthouse Club was now open to everyone. To those who complained of a new police presence on the lot, presumably to stop union organizing, Walt insisted it was necessitated by insurance. Of the rumor that he was training low-priced girls to take over cleanup animation, he said the studio needed flexibility, particularly with the prospect of war. And of the complaints that he was no longer available and that he delegated too much authority, he said, "It's my nature to be democratic," but he came to realize that "it was very dangerous and unfair to the organization as a whole for me to get too close to everybody" because it rewarded the "apple-polishers" at the expense of the hardworking men. Moreover, he said that he didn't want the studio to be a one-man operation. It had to survive him so that the animated cartoon would survive. And he closed by invoking once again the studio's sense of mission: "Believe me when I say that if we should go out of business tomorrow, the animated cartoon would drop to a low commercial level." Quality was still the primary goal, and the best animators would still be the ones best rewarded. "Don't forget this—it's the law of the universe that the strong shall survive and the weak must fall by the way, and I don't give a damn what idealistic plan is cooked up, nothing can change that." Each of the two speeches lasted nearly three hours, and Walt said nothing about unions in either one.

Though his intention had obviously been to defuse the situation by rallying the troops, Walt instead exacerbated it by seeming to underscore the very faults his employees had discovered in him. Many of them found his speech a "sob story," in Ward Kimball's words, and were unpersuaded by Walt's invocation of crisis. One said he had treated them as if he were the "benevolent and understanding father" and they were "wayward sons" and claimed that some in the audience even booed him. As the left-wing magazine *The Nation* later put it, "This speech recruited more members for the Screen Cartoonists Guild than a year of campaigning."

If so, Walt seemed oblivious, thinking he had tamped down his employees' dissatisfaction. The very next day he met with the production control manager Herb Lamb to discuss how they might contain expenses by breaking down the cost of every department in the studio and setting strict budget controls so that everyone would know exactly what targets he had to hit to stay profitable. Those who did hit the targets would get bonuses. "When the fellows see that this economy is bringing them increases in salaries, it will go over the whole plant and then you will see something happen," Walt told Lamb. And he recommended that they post a huge sign in front of the studio theater—Walt offered to pay for it personally—listing each department and the footage it delivered per day so everyone would know which was falling behind. But even Walt now realized that he was foundering. "I became all confused," he later confessed of his desperation. "I didn't know where I was. I had a big staff. I hated to lay off anybody. I tried to hold on to 'em. I tried to think of different ways. The war was not here yet. But they were still drafting. Some of my boys had to go. It was a terrible period."

It became more terrible as the employees began to revolt over the cracks in the utopia Walt had tried so hard to maintain. "We were disappointed in him," said one animator, "in the promise of the big happy studio where everyone would be taken care of—that was simply not working out in reality." Writing just days after his speech, the Communist paper the *Daily Worker* called Walt "almost a pathetic character" and said his labor relations were a fairy tale based on Walt's image as an ordinary fellow, though the employees were being ground down by a system that sped up work. One union leader observed of the influx of younger employees into the studio that, unlike the longtime animators, they didn't have "stars in their eyes about Walt . . . They had knocked about during the Depression, and they had some kind of social consciousness," while the older animators were likely to say, "If it weren't for Walt, I wouldn't be where I am."

Now the discontents began to boil. Five days after Walt's speech many of the disillusioned employees gathered at a meeting of the SCG at the Hollywood Hotel where Art Babbitt, the former president of the federation, told his colleagues over a loudspeaker that the federation was toothless. Shortly thereafter, Babbitt began to get fewer assignments, and when he protested to Hal Adelquist, the head of studio personnel, he was told it was a result of his union activities. Still, three weeks later, seemingly despairing of winning the battle, Gunther Lessing agreed to let the SCG cross-check the Disney payroll against the union's applications for membership to support the union's claim that it represented a majority of the studio's employees. Then, just as suddenly, Lessing insisted that the National Labor Relations Board conduct the cross-check, knowing full well that the NLRB was proscribed from doing so while it judged the legality of the federation. Four days later the federation called a meeting at the studio and announced that Anthony O'Rourke, a former NLRB official and an attorney the studio had hired to advise it on union matters, had been named the "impartial chairman" of the studio's proposed labor board.

Walt, seeming to think that he could douse the union by asserting his control, instead kept fanning the flames. On March 22, with union activity intensifying, he announced a new austerity plan, cutting salaries 5 percent for those earning between $50 and $100 a week, 10 percent for those earning between $100 and $200, and 15 percent for those earning over $200 and instituting a five-day, forty-hour workweek, thus reducing overtime. The studio was also eliminating food service to the rooms and shutting the coffee shop except during the noon hour. "Let us now be assured that we can once more get to work with a mental attitude tuned to producing the amount of work which we feel certain you are all thoroughly capable of doing," Walt declared with the same peremptory attitude that had already so riled the employees.

Of course the employees didn't meekly get to work as Walt instructed. But it was still unclear how much stomach he had for a union battle and how willing he was to let his beloved studio be torn asunder. In mid-April he seemed ready to concede and recognize the SCG, but O'Rourke, the "impartial" chairman, wrote him calling such a gesture a "Munich," in reference to the 1938 agreement between England and Nazi Germany meant to appease the latter, saying it amounted to an "eventual alliance with the 'Soviet,' " and declaring his intention to quit if Walt did so. In any case Walt soon quashed the rumors and cheerily urged his employees to forget the tensions and just "get out the much-needed production which, after all, is the most vital thing now or any other time."

Meanwhile, even as the NLRB was conducting hearings on the SCG charge that the federation was a company union, the federation was negotiating with the studio over recognition and a new contract and even held a vote for new officers. In early May the NLRB ruled against the federation—the examiner said responsibility for the "union" must be "laid at the door of Gunther Lessing"—and ordered it to disband. Reluctantly the studio, with a new labor adviser named Walter Spreckels, began negotiating with the SCG, which now demanded immediate recognition, and after the months of jockeying, Walt, writing to Eleanor Roosevelt—who had visited the studio that same week and expressed concerns about the labor situation there—dismissed all the strife as nothing more than a jurisdictional dispute. "In our entire history we have never had the least bit of labor trouble," he told the First Lady.

But even after the demise of the company union, the so-called jurisdictional dispute just wouldn't end. Though the studio had signed a consent decree agreeing not to discourage union organizing, Walt, clearly unwilling to cede any authority, refused to give the SCG recognition and insisted on a secret ballot, not a cross-check of payroll lists, to determine if it represented the majority of studio employees. As that stalemate dragged on, the federation held a meeting at the Hotel Knickerbocker at which it officially dissolved as ordered, only to reappear that same weekend under a new name, the American Society of Screen Cartoonists, with essentially the same officers as the federation and even the same mailing address. Like the federation, it also wanted recognition. Clearly, even under government order, Lessing wouldn't relent.

Walt wouldn't either. All this time he had been stewing over the attempts to challenge his power. Just after the NLRB ruling he left for his annual ride with the Rancheros Visitadores, but before he did so he encountered Art Babbitt in the hallway one morning and ordered him to desist organizing. "I don't care if you keep your goddamn nose glued to the board all day or how much work you turn out or what kind of work it is," Walt snarled, "if you don't stop organizing my employees, I am going to throw you right the hell out of the front gate." It was a threat Walt would have been only too happy to execute.

That was because, however much Walt Disney detested the idea of a union, he also detested its organizer: Arthur Babbitt. Babbitt had come to work at the studio in July 1932 and had steadily risen through the ranks, becoming one of the top animators. Among other things, he had animated the witch in *Snow White*, the mushrooms in *Fantasia*, and the stork sequence in *Dumbo*. But almost from the first he experienced a tension with Walt—Babbitt called it an "electricity between us." Harry Tytle, a studio executive, observed that Babbitt was the "one person who seems to push all the wrong buttons" for Walt. Babbitt was loud and obstreperous and by his own admission indiscreet. He disdained office politics and wouldn't play them. He was also a notorious womanizer: "My attitude was if it moves, screw it!" Walt was especially irritated when Babbitt began an affair with young Marjorie Belcher, the model for *Snow White*, and Walt was about to fire him when Babbitt decided to marry her.

Naturally the hatred intensified when Babbitt defected from the federation and not only joined the SCG and was elected its in-house representative but also called for a boycott of Disney films unless the studio recognized the union. Lessing had warned Babbitt that if he accepted the position as union head, "I was letting myself in for a lot of trouble," but Babbitt seemed to welcome the threat. "He was a fighter," Ward Kimball said. "He liked to have a cause. He was a showman. He liked to be onstage." Already that March, Walt had begun complaining about Babbitt's work, calling it "stiff, old-fashioned stuff" and told Jaxon to pressure him to do better. "He's a very stubborn punk," Walt said, "but we've got to get him out of the groove he's in." As further harassment, someone at the studio, probably Lessing, arranged to have Babbitt arrested and jailed, allegedly for possession of a concealed weapon, on the day he was to testify before the NLRB on the federation—"so concealed," Babbitt would say years later of the weapon, "that to this day they have not found it." But

Babbitt also goaded back. In mid-April he had called Walt to ask for a raise for his assistant, who was earning only eighteen dollars a week. Walt erupted, telling him to "mind your own goddamn business" and calling him a "Bolshevik." He continued to electioneer at the studio and distributed copies of *Variety* with the story on the NLRB decision. "It is Babbitt," Lessing wrote Walt, "who is keeping this plant in a turmoil."

By this time Walt had reached the end of his patience. On May 20, apparently hoping to quash the revolt once and for all, he began releasing animators, twenty of them, all SCG members. Protesting what it called a "blitzkrieg," the union wired Walt requesting a summit to discuss the dismissals or face a strike vote. Walt refused. On May 27 Walt called another studio meeting in the theater at which he read a brief statement claiming he would not agree to any settlement that would force his employees to join the union and he would bargain only with a union chosen by a majority vote on a secret ballot. The SCG, insisting that its cards already proved it had a majority, believed a vote was unnecessary and a union-busting tactic. After the speech Anthony O'Rourke, the labor attorney who was still advising Walt, phoned Lessing and told him that the statement "went over with a bang and that it had a wonderful effect." The union, he averred, was already suffering a backlash, and he predicted that within five days the "backbone of the strike will be broken." The union responded by granting Walt a thirty-six-hour extension to explain the dismissals and then took a strike vote.

Walt had now gone too far to give in. He could restore paradise only by expelling the traitors. The next afternoon Babbitt was exiting the commissary after lunch when the chief of the studio police took his arm and handed him a letter, telling him it was "bad news." The letter, from Lessing, advised Babbitt that he was being terminated for union activities and had to leave the studio immediately. Babbitt asked the chief if he could drive his car up to the Animation Building entrance so he could load his effects. By the time he arrived, a small group had collected there and helped him take his belongings to the car. By the time they finished, an hour later, several hundred employees had gathered, shouting that they would see him on the picket line the next morning.

II

"Strike—6:00 AM—today" read the first entry in Walt Disney's desk diary on May 28, though with the extension the strike actually began the next day. The atmosphere that morning was both festive and festering. Sorrell had the picketers crowding the gate while loudspeakers blasted music and messages at the employees driving through. Ward Kimball, who kept a diary, wrote, "Cars stopped all the way along Buena Vista Street," which fronted the studio. "The guys were pouring their individual speeches into the ears of those on the fence." Kimball was struck by the "magnitude of it all." As one might have expected from animators, the picket signs were colorful. One striker sat on a knoll in a smock and beret and painted the scene. Others sang and yelled. As Kimball entered the gate, Babbitt collared him and told him that the SCG had placed supervising animators like Kimball under its jurisdiction. In entering the studio, he was defying the union.

As Walt himself entered the gates that morning, easing his way through the throng in his Packard and genially waving to the strikers, Babbitt grabbed a megaphone from actor John Garfield, who was on the picket line to support the strike, and yelled, "Walt Disney, you should be ashamed of yourself!" Then, as Babbitt told it, he turned to the crowd and shouted, "*There he is, the man who believes in brotherhood for everybody but himself!*" When the crowd cheered, Walt bolted from the car and took off after Babbitt until he was restrained. Walt was much more sanguine behind the studio's gates. Kimball was taking lunch in the women's cafeteria and saw Walt there, beaming. Later that afternoon he called several of the nonstriking animators and storymen to his office. Blow-ups of photographs of the strikers were already arranged around the room, and as Walt passed them, he commented, "Damn, I didn't think *he'd* go against me," or "We can get along without him." As Jack Kinney recalled, "We got the uneasy feeling that he was filing his feelings away in his prodigious memory for some future revenge." Meanwhile Lessing appeared and said that he thought the strike would last only twenty-four hours. Walt broke out a bottle of Harvey's Bristol Cream for a toast.

Exactly how many people were striking depended on which side was doing the counting. Babbitt claimed that of the 500 employees in positions over which the guild had jurisdiction, 472 signed with the union and 410 of those had gone on strike. James Bodero, who headed the rival American Society of Screen Cartoonists, said that 735 workers fell under guild jurisdiction and 435 of those were still working. Lessing told *The New York Times* that only 293 employees were on strike. The guild itself estimated that 700 employees were on strike. Most of them were the lower-paid workers—in-betweeners, assistants, inkers. Only two of the supervising animators—Babbitt and his close friend Bill Tytla—struck. The others, said one animator, were "indoctrinated by Disney . . . They grew up there." Walt, insisting that the unrest was no fault of his own, branded the strikers "malcontents"—"the unsatisfactory ones who knew that their days were numbered and who had everything to gain by a strike."

Writing Walt shortly after the strike began, a former employee, commiserating with his old boss, wistfully recalled the "good old days when we had a big happy family all packed into a small building . . . In those days every man in the organization had the good old 'do or die for Disney' spirit." Then, when the company grew, he said, a "feeling of working for personal gain started creeping in. The present condition seemed inevitable." Success necessarily destroyed comity. But Walt, for whom the shattered peace now meant shattered dreams, did not think it had been inevitable. As he analyzed it, his utopia had been despoiled not by the ineluctable forces of corporatism but by a few rotten apples manipulated by a few determined ideologues. He may not have believed, as did Leon Schlesinger at Warner Bros., that his employees loved him, but he did believe that they were dedicated to the greater good of animation and to the artistic community he had created. "It hurt him," Ward Kimball said of the strike, "because guys he had trusted were letting him down." Walt saw himself as benevolent, and he thought that after he had kept nearly everyone on the payroll, even during the Depression, the angry workers were ingrates for calling a strike just because he demanded a secret ballot. It made no sense to him that they were chafing over a few relatively minor grievances. The only explanation that made sense was that they—Hilberman, Sorrell, Babbitt, and others—were Communists or Communist sympathizers bent on destroying Walt Disney. "Commie sons-of-bitches" was how Walt put it.

This would always be the Disney version of the strike. The studio had had no labor troubles until, as Walt later put it, the "Commies moved in." Roy concurred. "[M]oney was never the basic problem in this thing," he said, "as much as Communism." In this view Walt, who was politically naïve, was no doubt fed by Gunther Lessing. But he was also influenced by right-wing government agencies that had a political stake in blaming Communists for labor unrest. Walt said he showed his photographs of the strikers to the FBI and to representatives of the House Committee on Un-American Activities, which investigated Communism, and was told that the strikers were professional instigators. Anthony O'Rourke drafted a letter for Walt's signature inviting California state senator Jack Tenney, who chaired a fact-finding committee on un-American activities in that state, to investigate the affiliations of the strike leaders, and the FBI had a dossier on Herbert Sorrell listing him as a registered member of the Communist Party despite his claims to the contrary. "I had a lot of people just hoping that it was the end, you know?" Walt would say, meaning Communists wanting to take Walt Disney down.

Though it was a typical antilabor tactic at the time to brand unions as Communist to delegitimize them, Walt's belief that the SCG was Communist-inspired was undoubtedly sincere. It also may not have been entirely wrong. Arthur Babbitt certainly wasn't a Communist, nor were any of the other animators, but Dave Hilberman, the assistant who had begun organizing the studio, had by his own admission been a member of the Communist Party and had even traveled to Russia when he was a young man. Moreover an FBI report called William Pomerance, soon to be the union's business manager, "one of the leading Communists in the movie industry" and claimed that at least since July 1941, a month after the strike began, the union had followed the Communist Party line. Citing an internal source close to the labor situation, the report concluded that the Disney strike proved "conclusively" that the SCG was Communist-dominated and said that the Communists "threw the entire strength of the Communist machine in Hollywood" into the dispute. True or not, all of this provided Walt with a convenient excuse for holding the line against the SCG. It also excused him from having to deal with the very real dissatisfactions that had been building at the studio.

Now, despite Lessing and Walt's optimism, both sides hunkered down for a long siege. Sorrell had set up strike headquarters across the street from the studio on a little swell in a grove of eucalyptus trees, where a kitchen with camp stoves was erected by Warner Bros. carpenters and manned by striking Disney cafeteria workers. One striker compared the line of cars crawling up the hill to "something out of *The Grapes of Wrath*." It made for a picturesque scene, but then this seemed to be a picturesque strike. Pickets held signs reading "Michelangelo, Raphael, Titian, Rubens, Da Vinci and Rembrandt all belonged to guilds!" or "No wise quacks [with a picture of Donald Duck] We want our guilds!" or "Snow White and the 700 Dwarfs" or "1 Genius Against 1,200 Guinea Pigs." Another sign, featuring Pinocchio, said, "No strings on me." And one with Mickey Mouse declared: "Are we men or mice?" The left-wing newspaper *PM* called it the "most unique picket line in labor's history." Film stars walked the line to show support. Leon Schlesinger let his animators out early to picket and harass Disney, and one day Schlesinger himself drove up to the line, prompting a union spokesman at the loudspeaker to announce, "Herb Sorrell is now speaking to Leon Schlesinger, who has signed a very nice agreement with the Cartoonists Guild."

Driving through the crowd each morning, Walt seemed, in Babbitt's words, "very jaunty." One day, according to Ollie Johnston, he even stood near the entrance, with his coat over his arm and his hat tilted back on his head, smiling at the strikers and making quips. But if the strike began with a certain gaiety, it soon turned ugly and violent as both sides realized that, O'Rourke's prediction notwithstanding, no settlement was imminent. Strikers would yell at the workers entering the gate—"mighty uncomplimentary things," Dick Huemer remembered, "like how one guy was an alcoholic or something." Jack Kinney recalled strikers letting air out of tires or scratching cars with screwdrivers as nonstrikers drove onto the lot. Occasionally there were fistfights, and Kinney said that some shots were fired. Walt asked the Burbank Police Department for fifty officers, but the chief declined, saying that he couldn't post that many men without the union's cooperation for fear of a confrontation. Instead Walt hired fifty former Los Angeles policemen to try to push away the pickets, until the Burbank chief ordered them inside the studio gates. At a mass rally and parade in front of the studio early that June, Gunther Lessing was hung in effigy, while the American Federation of Labor (AFL) formed a "flying squadron" to picket theaters showing Disney films.

With the negotiations continuing fitfully, the union increased the pressure. The AFL put all Disney films and products on its "unfair" list, soundmen refused to cross the picket line, and perhaps worst of all, the lab technicians at Technicolor refused to process Disney film until the studio recognized the guild. A scheduled preview of *The Reluctant Dragon*, Walt's testament to studio harmony, had to be canceled because the American Newspaper Guild, which represented reporters, asked them not to attend, and when Walt did release the film late that June, picket lines were thrown up at the RKO and Pantages Theaters in Los Angeles while a parade of guild sympathizers in New York marched down Broadway to the Palace Theater where the film was playing and set up another picket line.

Still, Walt remained intransigent. He continued to insist that he would recognize the SCG only if it were elected by secret ballot, a call that the union again rejected, this time not only because a majority of the workers were on strike—prima facie evidence that the SCG already represented the workers—but because there was no impartial agency to conduct the election and count the votes and because it clearly distrusted Walt to do so fairly. At the same time, during daily negotiations late that June, Walt agreed to reinstate the workers he had dismissed in May—except Art Babbitt—while warning that there were more layoffs to come. This was also rejected unanimously by the union board. Despite the impasse Walt still seemed oddly jovial, writing a journalist that "we feel very much like the young couple having their first baby!" and ridiculously telling another reporter that the studio had actually *increased* its output during the strike because it had gotten rid of "deadwood," "doubtful talent," and "green hands."

But Walt never despaired of finding a way around the union. At one point Dave Hand, Ben Sharpsteen, Wilfred Jackson, and others met—one of them would say with Walt's knowledge—to discuss disbanding the studio altogether and forming another one headed by Roy and Walt but without any union involvement. At another point Bill Tytla, who had gone out on strike but nevertheless felt a deep allegiance to Walt, happened to see Walt at a local diner and approached him, saying he thought the whole thing was "foolish and unnecessary." Brightening, Walt suggested that Tytla come back to the office, where they might hammer out a solution the way Walt might solve a problem on a film. Tytla agreed but wanted first to go home, shower, and change. By the time Tytla arrived at his house, Walt had phoned Tytla's wife and told her the meeting was off. Tytla believed someone had gotten to Walt, presumably Lessing.

At roughly the same time, after the union had rejected Walt's proposals, quite possibly the most notorious figure in Hollywood arrived on the scene. IATSE head Willie Bioff was a moon-faced, jowly little man with hexagonal wire-rim glasses and an ever-present cigarette dangling from his lips. It was Bioff whom Babbitt had so feared two years earlier that he had met with Lessing about forming the federation. Since that time Bioff had been indicted on federal racketeering charges, but that seemed to have had little effect on his power. Bioff's IATSE was the rival of Sorrell's CSU. Whether Walt contacted Bioff to help broker a settlement (Bioff was famously tight with the studios) or whether Bioff volunteered as a way to undercut Sorrell is unclear.* However it happened, on June 30 Bioff reached a quick settlement with Disney, then had one of his lieutenants approach the strike leaders at the union's hall on the corner of Sunset and Highland and request a meeting at the Roosevelt Hotel. All of them piled into a car and set off for the conclave, only realizing once they were on the road that they were being taken not to the Roosevelt Hotel but rather to Bioff's ranch in the San Fernando Valley. (Hilberman, fearing what Bioff might do in the privacy of his home, demanded that the driver stop the car and then jumped out.) When the rest arrived, Roy, Lessing, and Bill Garity were waiting for them along with Bioff, who announced that if they signed with the IATSE they could go back to work in the morning. Babbitt said he was even offered a fifty-dollar raise and time off whenever he wanted it.

But like Walt's March speech, the meeting had exactly the opposite

*Walt later claimed that Bioff got involved when Sorrell asked the IATSE leader to call out projectionists, whom Bioff represented, all over the country wherever Disney films were playing. That was when Bioff offered his services to resolve the strike. *Los Angeles Daily News*, Jul. 10, 1941.

effect to resolving the strike. The strikers were incensed that Walt had involved the racketeer Bioff and rejected the offer, after which the studio announced that it was breaking off all negotiations with SCG. "[H]e honestly tried to settle it," Walt would say of Bioff. But when Sorrell rebuffed him, it "proved to me that Sorrell is dirty, sneaky and as foul as they come and there is no doubt but he is a tool of the Communist group." A week after the Bioff fiasco the federal government offered to step in, and Stanley White, an officer from the Conciliation Service of the Department of Labor, flew into Los Angeles to confer with the parties and see if he could mediate an agreement. He recommended binding arbitration by a three-man panel, during which the strikers would return to work. The SCG at a mass meeting unanimously accepted the offer. Lessing, however, rejected it, saying that yet another reformed company union, the Animated Cartoon Associates, really represented the workers and fuming that the NLRB had meddled in the company's affairs, even contacting its bankers to press for a settlement, and that the NLRB's actions warranted a congressional investigation, and he once again accused the union of being Communist.

Then, suddenly and unexpectedly, on July 23 Lessing reversed himself and wired the Conciliation Service accepting its mediation offer. The Disneys clearly had not softened; they still vehemently believed that the SCG was a Trojan horse to take over the studio. But they now had another force to reckon with, a force even more resolute than Sorrell. As Sorrell later told it, Stanley White, the federal conciliator, had called him, hoping to break the stalemate, and recommended they contact the Bank of America, which was what Lessing had accused the NLRB of doing. Sorrell, who happened to know A. P. Giannini from the time Sorrell had lived in Oakland, phoned him and was referred to Doc Giannini, A.P.'s brother. White then arranged to meet with Doc Giannini. "Sorrell wouldn't strike for anything that he couldn't win at arbitration," Giannini said, and suggested that it would soon be resolved. When White asked if Disney, after weeks of obstinacy, would agree, Giannini answered, "I guarantee he'll arbitrate or he won't have any studio." The strikers returned to work as the arbitration began, and a tentative settlement was reached on July 30. The strike was over.

Or so it seemed. The sides had agreed to wage increases—10 percent for artists earning less than $50 a week—one hundred hours of back pay for the strikers, reinstatement of the fired workers, including Babbitt, and of course, recognition of the SCG as the bargaining agent for most of the studio's employees. Future layoffs were to be decided by a joint committee to be agreed upon, but Babbitt was expressly excluded from termination. Some workers were stunned. "I went from $32.50 a week to $65 a week for the same job," recalled camera operator Bob Broughton. "My pay just doubled overnight." Walt, however, was not happy. Writing columnist Westbrook Pegler, who had asked for Walt's version of events, he called the strike a "catastrophe" that had destroyed the spirit of the studio. Without mentioning the Bank of America, he groused that he had had to settle, but insisted, "I'm not licked. . . . I'm incensed." His eyes were now open to "what is happening to our government today," presumably Communist infiltration. And with so many workers now and so little work, he said he might have to close the studio for a time to survive.

But Walt wouldn't be there for the pain of layoffs. Instead, he left.

III

While the thorniest issues of the settlement were being hammered out—the inevitable layoffs—Walt headed for South America. He called the trip a "godsend," even though he admitted, "I am not so hot for it but it gives me a chance to get away from this God awful nightmare and to bring back some extra work into the plant." He said he had a "case of the D.D.'s—disillusionment and discouragement." The studio desperately needed films now both to bring in revenue and to keep the staff working. One potential source that had suddenly availed itself that summer was the Office of the Coordinator of Inter-American Affairs, established in August 1940 to promote relations between the United States and Latin America. The office had been the brainchild of multimillionaire oil heir Nelson Rockefeller. Rockefeller had long been interested in South America, first through his art collecting, then through investments in the Standard Oil subsidiary in Venezuela, and later through a hotel-building campaign in Caracas that he had launched at the behest of the Venezuelan president, Eleazar López Contreras. On his frequent trips Rockefeller had been moved by the poverty there, and in the spring of 1940 he managed to deliver a memo to President Roosevelt on ways to improve inter-American relations. The memo led to his appointment as coordinator in a new government bureau.

One of Rockefeller's methods of bringing the two Americas together was sharing culture. He sent to South America scores of celebrities, including Douglas Fairbanks, Jr., and actress Dorothy Lamour, even the Yale Glee Club. He also recruited his friend and fellow millionaire John Hay Whitney, known as "Jock," to head up a motion picture division to provide films for South American theaters that might otherwise be showing movies from the Axis powers. Somehow, possibly through Walt's intervention, Gunther Lessing was appointed the chairman of the short subjects committee of Whitney's Motion Picture Section. In autumn 1940 Walt was meeting with Whitney about the possibility of making films for the Coordinator's Office. The following May, Walt met with Whitney and with Whitney's assistant, Frances Alstock, at the studio, and by June, Roy and Lessing were meeting with Whitney to discuss a $150,000 contract for several films on South American themes. "Lets [*sic*] try to bring the show down [*sic*] with Jock Whitney, this question of S.A. films," Roy wrote Walt from New York. "The way he talked to me they are waiting *on us* to give them some definite plan."

Within a month Rockefeller and Whitney upped the ante. They asked Walt to take a goodwill trip to South America, where he was obviously well known and well liked. It is unclear whether the trip was originally intended as anything other than a kind of ambassadorial mission, but by the time Walt agreed, it had become a filmmaking venture as well. The Coordinator's Office would underwrite the entire cost of the trip for Walt and a group of his artists and pay for the films that Walt would ultimately make. Walt called it a "combined 'business and pleasure' trip" and, despite the work, said he hoped to "get in a good rest at odd times." Of course, the films and the rest were a bonus. Mainly Walt just wanted to forget the studio. "We don't know whether we'll have jobs there when we get back there!" he joked sourly.

The group (Walt, Lillian, and seventeen associates including Norm Ferguson, Bill Cottrell, Ted Sears, and Webb Smith) left Los Angeles on a DC-3 on August 11 and hopscotched across the country, stopping in Fort Worth, Nashville, and Jacksonville before arriving in Miami, where they took a Sikorsky flying boat across the Caribbean to San Juan, Puerto Rico. The next morning they left aboard a Boeing Strato Clipper for Belém, Brazil, a remote outpost at the mouth of the Amazon River. "We landed for refueling in some little place cut out of the jungle in Brazil," Cottrell remembered. "And there were hundreds and hundreds of school children there to greet Walt. They knew who Walt Disney was. They might not have known who the president of their own country was, but they all knew Walt Disney." From Belém they flew to Rio de Janeiro, where they stayed ten days. The stated idea was to soak up atmosphere for the films the studio intended to produce on South American customs and folklore. But the real business seemed to be displaying Walt Disney to adoring fans and South American aristocrats, including heads of state. As Frank Thomas said, "Mainly we were wined and dined all over the place, where it was real hard to do any work."

From Rio the group descended upon Buenos Aires, Argentina, where they hunkered down for the next month in a large room on the top floor of the Palace Hotel to begin plotting out the films. Here they drew up storyboards, entertained locals with ideas for the movies, and listened to South American music for inspiration. And as in Rio, Walt was feted—"dances and feasting and drinking," Cottrell recalled. (Lillian observed that he was much more recognized and fussed over in South America than in his own country.) Walt, who cared more for work than for public acclaim, was patient, visiting zoos and ranches, but at the end of the month he announced to his staff that he was leaving for Chile because he was "goddamned tired of being dressed up like a gaucho and put on a horse."

As Walt departed in a DC-3 for Santiago, taking the mail flight route that he would depict in one of his South American shorts about a little mail plane named Pedro, the remainder of the group divided, one contingent heading to northern Argentina for more research, the other heading to La Paz, Bolivia, and the Lake Titicaca region. After a week in Chile Walt and his crew went north, taking a boat for a desultory trip along the coast to Peru, Ecuador, and Colombia, where they grabbed a launch and went thirty miles upriver into the jungle. Though the staff commandeered a section of the boat to work on the films, Walt later confessed to a friend that he was "so worn out by the time we reached Chile that the boat trip home was the only way I could get any rest." They took the liner *Santa Clara* from Colombia up through the Panama Canal—where a local film exhibitor ordered them off the boat so that Walt could attend the Panama City premiere of *Fantasia*—and then up the Eastern Seaboard to New York for the premiere there of *Dumbo*, then back to Los Angeles by plane. "In all we were gone twelve weeks," Walt wrote his old teacher Daisy Beck, "and could have stayed much longer but we were homesick for the kids . . . and of course they were tickled to see us come home, all of which made us very happy."

The one thing they did not discuss during the trip was the strike. On August 12, the day after Walt left, the studio, under pressure from the Bank of America, had submitted its list of layoffs to the union, which objected that the layoffs discriminated against the strikers. (There were 207 guild members and 49 nonguild members on the list.) Both sides asked the federal conciliator, James F. Dewey, to review the matter, but Dewey was hospitalized in Detroit at the time. Rumors and ill will were now swirling through the studio, so Roy decided to fly to Washington the next day to discuss the matter directly with the head of the Conciliation Service, Dr. John Steelman. But before Roy left he instructed the board of directors to close down the entire studio on August 18, save for a skeleton crew finishing *Dumbo* and another doing the Mickey Mouse comic strip, pending Dewey's arrival in Los Angeles. As it turned out, Dewey, either too ill or too exasperated, never did arrive, and the guild refused a request from the Conciliation Service to accept the layoffs until the list could be revised. Over the next two weeks, as the studio remained closed, Roy made two more trips to Washington attempting to resolve the issue—"hat in hand and on bended knee," according to Dave Hand, who accompanied him—and on September 10 the Conciliation Service finally issued a ruling, setting a ratio in each department of strikers to nonstrikers and ordering that the layoffs maintain that ratio.

And so on September 16, after three and a half months, work finally resumed at the Burbank studio with 694 employees on the payroll—down from nearly 1,200 at the beginning of the strike. Despite the cutbacks, Roy and Walt felt they had been sandbagged by the Conciliation Service, which, they thought, had favored the union.* Of his forays to Washington, Roy wrote Walt, "We are definitely in a period of social revolution and changes and if we're going to continue to conduct our business, we're going to have to find out how to work with the present social problems and the Washington administration attitude." In short, the government, as Lessing had implied earlier, was now as much of a problem as the union.

While Walt was in South America, something else had happened. Ever since Flora Disney's death Elias Disney had been, in his daughter Ruth's words, "completely lost and heartbroken." Though his doctor found him in "remarkable physical condition for a man of his age," at eighty-two Elias nevertheless suffered memory lapses, as one might have expected, and occasionally seemed to think that his wife was still alive. Ruth thought he was still discombobulated by the gas. Walt would take Diane and Sharon to visit him every Sunday at the house in Toluca Lake to which Elias had returned after Flora's death, but he was, in Walt's description, "really a lost person." Walt said he had never felt so sorry for anyone in his whole life. The hard man who had once tyrannized his sons and driven Walt to seek a better imaginative world was no longer.

*As with the Communist influence in the union, Roy may not have been wrong about a government fix. Years later Sorrell boasted that when Roy was in Washington pleading his case, Sorrell contacted Senator Sheridan Downey, who phoned the Conciliation Service and told them to do right by the union. Then Downey took Sorrell to see Senator Hiram Johnson, who called the office with the same request. The final contract included retroactive pay and strike pay, which Sorrell had been demanding. Sorrell, pp. 73–75. "I feel to this day that he [Sorrell] just had the 'in' in Washington," Walt complained years later. Walt Disney int., Pete Martin, Reel 6 & 7, Reel 7, p. 40.

On September 6, with Walt in South America, Roy left for one of his trips to Washington to discuss the strike settlement. The afternoon before he left, a Friday, he got an urgent call from Alma Smith, Elias Disney's housekeeper. Elias had started vomiting. Late on the afternoon of his departure Roy spent the last hour before takeoff with his father, who was still in bed and heaving periodically, though, Roy wrote Walt, "between his vomiting he was very rational and said he felt very well except that he had a bloated abdomen and some distrubance [*sic*] in his bowels." He and Roy talked primarily about Walt's trip. As Roy was leaving, Elias bade him a "casual farewell." Elias slept through the night, but when he awoke the next morning, he began vomiting again, and the doctor ordered an ambulance to take him to Hollywood Hospital. On Monday he took a turn for the worse. The doctors suspected a bowel obstruction and debated whether to operate. Uncle Robert, who had gone to the hospital to be at his brother's bedside, accused the doctors of trying to make money, but Roy phoned from Washington with the decision to proceed. Elias was on the operating table for two hours. He came out of the surgery well, and Roy flew home that Friday to visit him. Already there was a gurgle in his lungs, suggesting the onset of pneumonia. When Roy and brother Ray arrived the next morning, September 13, Elias was running a temperature of 105, and the doctors pronounced his condition "hopeless." The brothers left at nine to get breakfast and went home while Elias rested. At noon they received a frantic call from the attending nurse summoning them to their father's bedside. As Roy was picking up Edna to return to the hospital, he learned that Elias's doctor had called: Elias Disney was dead.

Funeral services were held at the Wee Kirk o' the Heather at the Forest Lawn Cemetery, and Elias was interred in a crypt there in the Sanctuary of Truth next to his wife. When Roy had first heard of his father's condition, he had written a cable to Walt from Washington, then decided not to send it because he didn't want to alarm Walt unnecessarily. When Elias expired, Walt received a telegram, but he chose not to return for the funeral—perhaps one last act of rebellion against the man he felt had so tormented him. Instead the South American crew sent a three-and-a-half-foot cross of lilies for the chapel. "I believe that by the time you get home, we'll have it settled down and some sense of the whole thing," Roy wrote Walt after the funeral, speaking again of the strike. "Don't be surprised at anything you find when you come home. We have been up against a tough proposition and have done the best we could."

Walt returned to the studio in mid-October to find that nearly everything had changed, though as a result less of the negotiations between management and the union than of the negotiations between the studio and its primary benefactor. Now that the strike was settled, the Bank of America was making new demands. Roy had written Joe Rosenberg that he expected *Dumbo* to gross $2 million, *Fantasia* the same, and the impending *Bambi* $3 million, which would allow the company to reduce its debt to less than $1 million. But Rosenberg was not mollified. Concerned about what he saw as Walt's profligacy, he ordered Roy and George Morris to the bank's San Francisco headquarters on October 9 and issued an ultimatum. The bank would permit an absolute loan limit of $3.5 million. In return, he ordered the studio to restrict itself to the production of shorts. It would be allowed to finish the features already in production—*Dumbo*, *Bambi*, and *Wind in the Willows*—but no other feature was to be started until these had been released and earned back their costs. Though Roy remonstrated that concentrating exclusively on shorts would cost the studio in terms of manpower losses, depleted inventory, and overhead, not to mention the difficulty of remobilizing should they decide to resume making features, Rosenberg was unmoved, and Roy wound up abjectly telling him that the "entire organization now has an entirely new mental attitude and approach" designed to cut costs and that he would talk to Walt about accepting the changes, which he knew would devastate him.

But there was more. The bank was so fearful that Roy could not control Walt that Rosenberg insisted on the creation of an "executive committee," including a bank representative, that would, as Roy later explained it to Walt, "function as the governing body of the Studio, where all matters of general policy will be discussed and agreed on before any action is taken." Roy added that while the bank didn't lack confidence in them, "they do have qualms about your 'enthusiasm and possible plans for future production' "—though it had been that enthusiasm that had built and sustained the studio. Hal Adelquist, the head of personnel, and Vern Caldwell, who worked under him, had even drawn up a new organization chart. In effect, the studio was no longer Walt Disney's fiefdom. He was now under the control of the businessmen.

What was especially galling in this new arrangement was the moratorium on feature film production. Feature films had become the reason for the studio's existence. Just the year before, Walt had claimed that he had put the studio on a footing to release as many as nine features in two years. Now he was having to shelve everything: the Mickey Mouse feature; *Alice in Wonderland*; a film based on the stories of Uncle Remus; another called *Lady*, about the romance between a pedigreed dog and a street cur; and a film of the Sinclair Lewis story "Bongo." They continued to proceed slowly on *Wind in the Willows*, one of the films permitted because it was already in production, though after mulling it over during Thanksgiving,

Walt informed Roy that he was going to make *Peter Pan* instead because he thought the two films would cost the same amount and the latter would have more box office appeal. In the end, the studio soon stopped work on that film too.

But the effects of the Bank of America weren't felt only on the production schedule. The economies it demanded resulted in the shuttering of all the studio restaurants save the commissary, the return of the IBM machines they had rented, and the installation of a time clock—the clock that Walt had so dreaded in Kansas City. "It was like being in another world!" Dave Hand would later write. "I think that that one decision [of the time clock] ended my closeness to Walt" because Walt insisted that Hand, a supervisor and Walt's right-hand man, punch the clock with the other employees. At the same time all the bonuses and incentive plans were discontinued. Even Walt's beloved art classes were disbanded. "My wife used to accuse me of running a Communistic outfit," Dick Huemer recalled Walt remarking grimly. "Well, all that is over now."

"From all the reports I get and my own observations, I feel there is a new life, understanding and appreciation on the part of the present Studio personnel," Roy wrote Walt that October. "I really think a lot of good will has come out of all our past trouble and that we are now on a good firm basis on which to go ahead." But this was wishful thinking. Nothing good had come of it, unless one regarded the necessary belt-tightening as a blessing. With another round of layoffs that November, the number of employees at the studio was more than halved. Making the best of it, Walt later claimed that this move was a necessary purgative and that he had rid the studio of a bad element. "Sometimes you've got to kind of build yourself up and explode," he would say. "And then you kind of begin to pick up the pieces and kind of take stock, you know?"

But this was a rationalization. Between the downsizing and the recriminations following the strike, he would lose some of his best animators, including Bill Tytla, who had animated the washing sequence in *Snow White*, the devil in the "Bald Mountain" sequence in *Fantasia*, and Stromboli, the cruel puppetmaster, in *Pinocchio*. "He was aloof; he just stayed by himself," Bob Carlson, his onetime assistant, observed of Tytla after the strike. "He just came to work and stayed in his room and went home." Though he persevered as long as he could, eventually, feeling discriminated against by Walt for having struck, he left for the Paul Terry studio in the East. Others left too, among them some of the most innovative young animators in the studio, like Walt Kelly, who later created the popular *Pogo* comic strip, and John Hubley, who became a highly regarded experimental animator in his own right. Some, like Hubley, joined former Disney animator Frank Tashlin at the Screen Gems studio, where, in Hubley's words, "We were doing a lot of crazy things that were anti the classic Disney approach."

Walt's relationship with those who remained also suffered. Already increasingly distant before the strike, Walt became churlish and suspicious. "It hurt him deeply," Joe Grant said of the strike. "He felt betrayed, felt that everyone who had formerly been behind him had now left him." Ham Luske believed that it "almost broke Walt's heart" and that his "attitude changed radically from the strike on." He was bitter. He sincerely believed that he had created a perfect world for his employees and that they hadn't appreciated it. He even turned on Gunther Lessing, who he thought had failed him during the strike. Lessing kept his position and his office but, according to Ward Kimball, "only out of pure sympathy." He was, said Kimball, a "broken man."

The place where everyone had once caroused was now a "very hard-nosed place," said Jack Kinney, just like the other studios. The joy was gone. Walt may have been inspiring, but he had never been a very effusive leader, and now he was worse. He had always doled out compliments parsimoniously, once telling an employee that "praise accomplishes nothing but a feeling to a small extent of self-confidence" and warning that it is "just as likely to be a dangerous factor." When he did issue a compliment, it was seldom directly to one's face. Typically an animator would hear that Walt had praised him to a colleague. By the same token Walt was contrarian when it came to anyone else's praise. "[W]e always said if you wanted to get even with somebody—praise them in front of Walt," Ward Kimball observed, "or if you wanted to do someone a favor, run them down in front of Walt and he would stick up for them."

But the new atmosphere after the strike wasn't just a matter of Walt's curtness or contrariness. There was a fear of Walt now, a fear that had always been latent in the sweaty palms and nervous silence at the story sessions, a fear of displeasing him, but that now surfaced as a fear of arousing his wrath. Even Bianca Majolie, who had known Walt since high school, would vomit after she made a presentation to him. Everyone in the studio was terrorized by the swift distinctive clack of his heels on the hard gray tile floor and his hacking smoker's cough as he approached a room, and the animators would jump into their seats when he entered. "Don't be afraid of me," Walt would growl. "I don't want to see you jumping into your seat like that." But they *were* afraid. "He had a way of giving you the evil eye, with his finger pointed at your chest, that was very intimidating," Jack Kinney would write. "He'd punctuate his words with 'y'know, y'know, y'know,' until you were answering 'yeah, yeah, yeah'—whether you knew what he was talking about or not."

The fear was so thick that anyone who was thought to be out of favor with Walt became a pariah with everyone else at the studio. On one occasion layout artist Ken Anderson inadvertently singed Walt's mustache while lighting a cigarette with a new lighter during a storyboard session, and Walt jumped out of his chair, howled at Anderson, "What the God damn hell are you trying to do, burn me up?" and ran out of the room. Anderson threw away the lighter and never smoked again. Meanwhile no one at the studio would talk to him. Anderson admitted he cried and thought he would be fired, though this time Walt called him, asked him to lunch, and demonstrated to the staff that Anderson was back in his good graces. It was a rare instance of benevolence.

Beyond the fear he inspired, Walt now displayed a vindictiveness, occasionally even bordering on cruelty, that hadn't been there since his days with Mintz—a cruelty that only his most ardent supporters could excuse as pushing for improvement. He could be scathing to an errant employee, embarrassing him in front of the entire staff. "You'd go to a meeting and try to be as invisible as possible because you wanted to avoid this," Ward Kimball said. On one occasion a story sketch artist visibly grimaced as Walt was about to pluck one of the man's sketches from the storyboard, so Walt "carefully and deliberately," according to Frank Thomas and Ollie Johnston, "pulled down that sketch and the next three clear off the board, tearing the corners where the pushpins had held them captive; then he released the paper to let it flutter helplessly to the floor." Another time he screened some old footage that Ben Sharpsteen had animated, then ridiculed it before the staff. "[H]is whole approach to everybody," Kimball said, "was to put somebody down."

But he reserved his greatest wrath for the man he believed was most responsible for ruining his paradise. Art Babbitt had returned to the studio when it reopened on September 17 after the strike settlement. He was pleasantly surprised to find that nonstrikers like Jack Kinney and Dick Lundy seemed to accept him and were willing to work with him again, but he also discovered that his old office had been assigned to a nonstriker and that his new office didn't have a Movieola. He received assignments to reanimate two scenes that had been unacceptably animated during the strike, one for a Goofy cartoon and another for a Donald Duck short, and completed them by November 1. He asked for additional work and received none, then was in his office on November 24 when a traffic boy delivered a notice that he was being terminated in the latest retrenchment, effective in forty-five minutes. Walt claimed, disingenuously, that Babbitt was no longer a "progressive" animator and that ever since *Snow White* he had relied too heavily on rotoscoping so that his work had gotten stiff. Asked once why he paid Babbitt so well if his work was inferior, Walt said it was because he needed to "throw confidence" to him. Walt was only slightly more honest a few months later when Lessing was coaching him for a deposition. Ignoring the union organizing as the cause for dismissal, he said that Babbitt was a "difficult person to work with."

Walt may have thought he was finally rid of his nemesis. That January Babbitt sailed for South America to work for an Argentine animation company. He returned four months later and that summer took a job with Leon Schlesinger at Warner Bros., then resigned and enlisted in the Marines in November. But before he did so, Babbitt had filed an unfair labor practice charge with the NLRB against the Disney studio for his termination. Walt must have known that the studio had little chance of winning, especially after several prominent animators testified that Babbitt was among the best in the business. In November the trial examiner ruled against the studio, declaring that Walt's stated reasons for laying off Babbitt were "false and without merit" and ordering Walt to reinstate him within forty days of his discharge from the service with back pay.

But even with Babbitt temporarily gone and the strike presumably settled, the studio roiled. Longtime friends became lifelong enemies. "It used to be, 'Hello, how are you?,' pat you on the back," one employee recalled of the prestrike days. After the strike the tone of voice and demeanor changed. On the union side, one group of guild members would walk five abreast down the hallways not letting any of the nonstrikers pass. On the other side, recalled animator Bill Melendez, who had struck, the nonstrikers "never forgave us for destroying the spirit of the studio." Shamus Culhane believed that both sides harbored a sense of guilt—the nonstrikers over whether they had sided with Walt out of cowardice, the strikers over whether they should have rent the studio as they did. In the end, wrote Culhane, the "esprit de corps that made possible all the brilliant films of the 1930s was dead as a dodo." In the end Walt Disney's dream of a perfect haven was dashed.

IV

One war was over, but another was about to begin. All the time Walt was in South America, the supervising animators who had remained at the studio during the strike were working to finish *Dumbo* so that the studio would have something that might generate revenue. When the film was released in October, it received extravagant reviews, even though it had cost considerably less than its three feature predecessors and even though the animation was less painterly and realistic than on the previous features. Bosley Crowther in *The New York Times* called it the "most genial, the most endearing, the most completely precious cartoon feature film ever to emerge from the magical brushes of Walt Disney's wonder-working artists!" Otis Ferguson in *The New Republic* rhapsodized over a scene in which Dumbo, having inadvertently drunk some liquor, hallucinates pink elephants. "I have never seen anything to approach it and neither have you," Ferguson wrote, "because there hasn't been anything." Some saw it as a return to Disney's unpretentious pre-*Fantasia* form. Saying that Disney had recently been sold a "bill of very inferior goods" by the "long-word intellectuals," columnist Westbrook Pegler cheered that Disney had now made "another great work which manages to ignore the evil all about and lift his fellow men." The curmudgeonly critic Alexander Woollcott, who admitted that he had been less than enthusiastic about *Snow White*, *Pinocchio*, and *Fantasia*, wrote Walt, praising *Dumbo* as the "highest achievement yet reached in the Seven Arts since the first white man landed on this continent" and the "divine event towards which your whole creation has moved." To which Walt responded: "It was just one of those little things that we knocked out between epics!"

Walt wasn't being entirely self-effacing. It *was* a little thing they knocked out, and though it once again traced the Disney theme of embracing maturity and responsibility and taking control of one's own destiny, even at the risk of being exiled from one's safe and satisfying childhood oasis, Walt didn't really have very much to do with it. When *Time* ran a piece giving the main credit to his staff, Walt grumbled to Dick Huemer and Joe Grant, who had written the film, that the article made it seem that he was irrelevant. The *Time* article had been originally scheduled to run as a cover story on December 8, 1941, but it got bumped by another more newsworthy event, and a *Time* editor apologized to Walt that he had tried to reschedule it for the Christmas cover but was overruled by coeditors who feared that readers would think the magazine was trying to be "facetious" in light of what the country now faced.

What the country faced—what had bumped *Dumbo* from the cover—was its entrance into World War II, triggered by the Japanese bombardment of the American naval base at Pearl Harbor in Hawaii on December 7. Since it was a Sunday, Walt heard the news of the attack on the radio and then received a call from the studio manager, who had been advised by the police that five hundred army troops were already moving onto the Burbank lot and bivouacking on the soundstage, where their job was to provide an antiaircraft installation to protect the nearby Lockheed factory, which made airplanes for the armed forces. In short order army trucks pulled onto the lot, camouflage was draped across buildings, parking garages and storage sheds were converted into ammunition depots, and a mess kitchen was established. Essentially the army had commandeered the studio.

The day of the attack Kay Kamen, the head of the company's product division, was in Washington, D.C., seeking potential clients for commercial and industrial films and sounding out agencies about the possibility of the studio doing films for the government—the government that Walt had so recently characterized as Communistic. Though Kamen mourned the loss of lives at Pearl Harbor and wrote Walt about the necessity of winning the war, he also saw new business possibilities in America's involvement and thought Walt's relationship with the coordinator of inter-American affairs could serve as an entrée to other branches of government that would now need films for training and public relations. "[Y]ou should be a part of this, Walt," Kamen wrote, urging his boss to visit the capital, "and they need you and want you and I think the trip is very important."

In truth, though Walt had always disdained anything that was contrary to the studio's "essential purpose," which was to entertain, he had begun soliciting government work long before the strike as one way out of the studio's financial doldrums. In October 1940 he had met with a service representative about training films, and the next month he offered his assistance to the defense committee, which had been formed by the Association of Motion Picture Producers to cooperate in making movies for the government. By March he had placed storyman Robert Carr in charge of a Walt Disney Training Films Unit to solicit industrial and government work, and that month Carr sent a memo to the educational directors of the aircraft industries offering the studio's assistance. As the memo put it: "An engineer or other representative of the client merely sits down at a conference table in the Disney studio and tells his story to a group of highly-trained mechanical draftsmen and artists." The studio would do the rest.

But Walt was leaving nothing to chance. On April 3, 1941, he hosted a luncheon and conference at the studio for government officials and representatives of the defense industries—thirty people in all. "[W]e have the plant, the equipment, and the personnel," he told them, "and we're willing to do anything we can to help in any way." He followed up with a letter stating that he was motivated "solely by a desire to help as best I can in the present emergency" and that he would make the films for cost and without profit. The studio was organized in such a way, he lied, that he could make the films without hampering his own feature production, not mentioning that the feature production was already imperiled by economics. While he waited for a response, he hired a Lockheed engineer, George

Papen, to help him make an animated instructional film titled straightforwardly *Four Methods of Flush Riveting*, which he showed to John Grierson, a documentary filmmaker who was attending the conference in his capacity as film commissioner of Canada. Shortly afterward Walt landed his first contract, from Grierson, for a film on the fundamentals of flush riveting, an instructional film on an antitank rifle, and four shorts promoting the sale of Canadian war bonds. The riveting film was budgeted at between $4,000 and $5,000, a far cry from what the studio had been paying for its own shorts, but then the animation was a far cry from what the studio had been producing. Walt was relying on recycled scenes from old cartoons and on using more limited animation—that is, animation with less movement than that in his features and shorts.

In May 1941, with the strike looming, he felt a new urgency in getting government work, and the studio stepped up its efforts. Walt dispatched Vern Caldwell of the training department to Washington with the *Flush Riveting* film and had him take it from government office to government office, including the offices of General George Marshall and the general army staff. Walt continued to insist that the company was just doing its patriotic duty, but the fact was that the studio needed the contracts, if only to keep the animators working and to offset the overhead. Throughout the summer and into the fall, Walt kept trolling for business with the lure of the Canadian riveting film, which, according to Bob Carr, the Canadians had extolled as "Miraculous! Best we ever saw!" In November, after he had returned from South America, Walt was meeting with members of the defense committee and had talked with an advertising man and adviser to the Lend Lease Food Division of the Department of Agriculture named Henry Sell about making movies promoting the program and possibly making other promotional films for several of Sell's commercial clients, something Walt had previously refrained from doing because he thought it demeaning.

When Pearl Harbor was attacked, then, Walt Disney was already deep into government work and was about to get in much deeper. Early the very next evening, December 8, he received a call from a navy official offering the studio a contract for twenty films on aircraft and warship identification at a total cost of $90,000, and shortly thereafter the Navy Department Bureau of Aeronautics sent an officer to Burbank to supervise the project.* (The animators drew wings on the Animation Building, where the navy was now headquartered.) Meanwhile Walt had completed

*As one studio employee told the story, the navy officer bludgeoned Walt into accepting a minimal budget then told him that the conversation had been recorded to certify the deal. Erwin Verity, interview by Dave Smith and Rick Shale, Jan. 19, 1976, p. 2 WDA.

and shipped the films for which Grierson had contracted promoting the purchase of Canadian war bonds, and he was still dickering with Henry Sell on films for Lend Lease.

Yet the biggest measure of just how dramatically things were about to change at the studio came that very same week in early December, when Walt received a call from John L. Sullivan, the assistant secretary of the treasury. Even before the Pearl Harbor attack, the Treasury Department had been considering producing films that might encourage Americans to pay their taxes, something that became suddenly more urgent with the country at war. Acting on a suggestion of Undersecretary George Buffington, Sullivan had told Treasury secretary Henry Morgenthau that "what John Barrymore can't do, maybe Mickey Mouse could," and advised they meet with Walt Disney. Walt had no desire to go to Washington, especially since it was Diane's birthday, but the Treasury Department insisted that the issue was pressing, so Walt flew out on December 12, met with Morgenthau, had dinner at Sullivan's house that evening, where they roughed out a scenario over martinis, and then phoned Diane to wish her a happy birthday. He signed a letter of agreement the very next day, promising to produce the film for not more than $40,000, which was less than the cost of a typical Disney short.

It wasn't the budget, meager as it was, that presented a problem—Walt was getting accustomed to cutting corners when he had to. It was the schedule. The Treasury Department wanted the film on or before February 15, which effectively gave the staff a month to write and then polish the scenario, compose the music, and animate. Ben Sharpsteen, who was producing, and Hal Adelquist of personnel told Walt that they would need twenty men for the film, which was now titled *The New Spirit*, and that given the deadline, the entire short would have to be animated in a week. Never, not even during the final days of *Snow White* and *Pinocchio* when they were racing to make the premieres, had the studio been under such a crunch.

What added to the tension was that they were no longer their own masters. They had to please Morgenthau. After working tirelessly on the storyboards, including sessions late on New Year's Eve, Walt flew back to Washington with Roy and storymen Dick Huemer and Joe Grant on January 4 to get Morgenthau's approval. The secretary delayed the meeting one day when there were no days to spare—he had a migraine headache. He finally padded out to greet them in his bedroom slippers with his Great Dane at his side. An aide objected to Walt's intention to use Donald Duck—to which Walt riposted that for the Disney studio to give the Treasury Department Donald Duck was like MGM giving them Clark Gable—

but Morgenthau signed off, and Walt rushed back to Burbank to finish the project.

"We slept on the job," Walt later recalled. "We got beds in there. We stayed right there. We worked eighteen hours a day." There was no rough animation. Instead the original drawings went directly to cleanup and ink and paint. It was completed and sent to the lab for processing on January 20; a title song was recorded the next day; Technicolor got it by the end of that week and struck a print three days later, and three days after that it delivered 250 prints. "This is the fastest time ever made on any cartoon production," Walt wired Undersecretary Buffington.

But it came at a psychological cost. As Wilfred Jackson remembered it, when Walt, still the perfectionist, saw the finished film, he was unhappy that some of the animation was not smooth, and he sat there pondering uneasily, not wanting to sign off on the film. "Finally, he turned around and said, 'Jack, ah . . .' " Jackson said. "He rubbed his head. 'You know . . . Well, Jack . . .' He shifted in his seat. He got up and said with finality, 'Yeah.' And he walked out. He had all sorts of ideas and he couldn't fix it up. He didn't have time." Walt Disney had had to make a concession that his animation would not be the best.

The Treasury Department had no such qualms. Buffington and Morgenthau both pronounced themselves pleased with the picture and, as George Morris wired Roy, "greatly excited over ideas for other films." Morgenthau invited Walt and Lillian to Washington for the premiere on February 2 and a celebratory dinner. As it turned out, *The New Spirit* was a tremendous success. By one estimate over 32 million Americans eventually saw the film at nearly twelve thousand theaters, and of these viewers, according to a Gallup poll, 37 percent said that the film had had an effect on their willingness to pay taxes, and 86 percent felt that Disney should make shorts for the government on other subjects.

Still, the poll contained one unsettling number that would soon bedevil Walt: only 46 percent of Americans believed that the government should foot the bill for the film. Just days after the premiere the House debated the Treasury Department appropriations and voted 259 to 112 to eliminate $80,000 that the department had requested to pay for *The New Spirit.* (The amount included costs for prints, distribution, and promotion.) "They have hired him to make a moving picture that is going to cost $80,000 to persuade people to pay their income taxes," declaimed Republican congressman John Taber of New York on the House floor. "My God! Can you think of anything that would come nearer to making people hate to pay their income tax than the knowledge that $80,000, that should go for a bomber, is to be spent for a moving picture to entertain people?"

"Billions for defense," Taber orated, "but not one buck for Donald Duck." Representative Carl Curtis of Nebraska called the appropriation the "most outrageous and scandalous piece of money-wasting I know of." Other Republicans opposing the Roosevelt administration lumped Walt with an apparent boondoggle—a dancer who had been appointed to a civil defense post but whose major qualification, said the Republicans, was an apparent friendship with Eleanor Roosevelt. In the upper chamber, though several senators came to Disney's defense, the expenditure for *The New Spirit* was not restored to the appropriations bill.

The irony was that Walt had actually lost money making *The New Spirit*, roughly $6,000 on the production itself and another $50,000 in forfeited bookings of commercial shorts that were replaced by the government short. In his business naïveté he had also signed an unfavorable agreement with the Treasury Department, saying that he would make the film for "out of pocket costs" up to $40,000, not realizing (as Roy later chastised him) that this didn't include the "indirect costs of supervision, lighting, heat, taxes, depreciation and many other such things" and that the government's General Accounting Office would hold him to the letter of the contract. In effect, then, Walt learned two awful but valuable lessons that would dominate his business conduct throughout the war: first, that government films operated by a different schedule and under different standards from commercial pictures, and second, that the studio was now always accountable to the government, which would prove an even sterner taskmaster than the Bank of America.

If Walt had any relief from the work, the criticism, the disappointment, and the financial crush, it came when he and Lillian headed back to Los Angeles after the *New Spirit* premiere. Walt had never been a nostalgist. He was more likely to dramatize the worst moments of his life than to burnish the best. Yet what he had always cherished about his upbringing in Kansas City amid the traumas of the paper route was the Benton School. All these years he had kept in touch with his sixth-grade teacher, Daisy Beck, writing her faithfully, and he corresponded with other teachers as well, so when he was invited back to the school on his way from Washington to celebrate the installation of two murals he had donated, he accepted, even though he now routinely declined invitations to speak or be honored. He always said he was too busy and too poor a speaker.

The one-day return to Benton was triumphant. Accompanied by a Works Progress Administration orchestra, eight hundred students, parents, and teachers serenaded him at an assembly where he showed the *New Spirit* and another cartoon and then had Clarence Nash perform as Donald Duck. He was also awarded the silver loving cup that the school's seventy-pound relay team had won in 1917 when Daisy Beck had convinced Walt to compete. At a luncheon in his honor at a cafeteria on Troost Street near his old Laugh-O-Gram studio, Walt introduced Arthur Verne Cauger, his boss at the Film Ad Co., and the woman whose baby films had financed his trip to California back in 1923. Afterward he visited Bert Hudson's barbershop, where his drawings had first been displayed. He ended the stopover having dinner with Daisy Beck at a local home—which, like the other events of the day, showed where he had come from and just how far he had traveled since.

The studio needed work. In the short term, while Walt waited for his government solicitations to bear more fruit, the South American films were his lifeline. Even late in the afternoon on the day of the Pearl Harbor attack, a Sunday, he was at the studio discussing how to enliven these cartoons. His intention, he told *The New Yorker*, was not to repeat the mistakes of his more imposing and financially unsuccessful features, which he now apparently felt had been *too* carefully tended. "I'm going to make these South American pictures simple and not arty," he said in a complete reversal of his usual working arrangements. "The best way is to work off-the-cuff. Don't have any script but just go along and nobody knows what's going to happen until it's happened."

The original plan had been to make a series of South American–themed shorts, twelve in all, that would nevertheless be released on the world market with, Roy told their distributor RKO, "just as broad appeal as our present subjects." RKO was unconvinced. Already in January the producer David O. Selznick, who had also gotten involved with the Coordinator's Office through an organization called the Motion Picture Society for the Americas, was lobbying Walt and Jock Whitney to package the shorts as features, which he thought would give them both greater visibility and greater salability, and Walt began to warm to the idea as a way of stretching his staff artistically and fulfilling their Silly Symphony commitments. "If the 12 South American Shorts can be put into Packages of 4 each, making 3 in all, to be released during this year," he wrote Roy, "I think we could enlarge our Shorts Program which would give us a chance to include some Silly Symphony ideas that are now in various stages of production in the plant." To tie these disparate shorts together under the larger rubric of South America, however, Walt had to use 16mm film footage that he had personally shot during his trip, apologizing to Selznick for "my bad photography and nervous hand."

Now came the deluge. On his trip to Washington the previous December, Walt had been encouraged by Jock Whitney to see if he could help convince government officials there to centralize all film production in Hollywood, with a special unit to be established at the Disney studio. "Maybe the development above will be the answer to our problem," Walt wrote Kay Kamen hopefully. As it turned out, the officials guarded their power too jealously to cede any authority to a central organization, but with Kay Kamen aggressively soliciting government agencies and defense contractors for films, the Disney studio found itself at the vortex of government activity. Within weeks after Pearl Harbor the films for the navy on warship identification were in production; the Department of Agriculture had contracted for a film promoting the Lend Lease program; the Council of National Defense had commissioned a series of posters for a campaign cautioning Americans not to divulge sensitive information; and the director Frank Capra, who had been appointed a major in the Army Signal Corps for the purpose of expediting production, met with Walt to convince him to join the Signal Corps. Walt declined, saying that if Capra needed him, he had only to make a request for the studio's services. Capra did, and Walt provided animation for Capra's Why We Fight series that explained why America had gone to war. At the same time that Walt was wading through these offers, the coordinator's office was pressing the studio to produce a new series of educational films on health and agriculture and yet another series that would, as Whitney put it, "deal directly with the Axis menace to freedom in Latin America." Moreover the studio was inundated by requests from military squadrons for insignia, which it did its best to satisfy by setting up a five-man crew, even though there was no remuneration for the service.

Nor did it stop there. Walt had personally lobbied with Lieutenant J. C. Hutchinson, who headed the naval film program, and wound up with contracts for films that spring on aerology, meteorological conditions, aircraft carrier landing signals, carrier approaches and qualifications, aviation forming methods, fixed gunnery, and finally one called *Rules of the Nautical Road.* Meanwhile, under pressure to diversify from the Bank of America and Kidder, Peabody, which had issued the Disney stock, Walt was meeting with executives from the aircraft manufacturers Curtiss-Wright, Lockheed, Beech, and Aeronca about the possibility of making training films for them. "There is nothing at the moment more important than getting a start in this industrial field," Fred Moore of Kidder, Peabody wrote Walt, adding a vague threat that "so long as you do not reach outside for broadening your field, your future outlook is not what we had hoped." The best part, Roy enthused to Walt after meeting with Curtiss-Wright representatives, was that these companies, unlike the government, could afford to pay more than cost. The studio could actually make the profit it so desperately needed.

Of course, if the best part to this work was the potential profits, the worst part was that the Disney studio was no longer the Disney studio. It was now an educational and industrial film facility, an arm of the government, with Walt and Roy virtually commuting from Los Angeles to Washington. And though Walt clearly recognized how imperative it was to do business with the government if the studio was to survive, he, who had lived only to produce great films, was frustrated. For one thing he was frustrated by the nickel-and-diming of the government bureaucrats. The navy, for one, had vetoed the idea of the studio adding a fixed percentage to its contracts for overhead and profit. An official suggested instead that the studio set a fixed price. If the actual production costs were lower than the budget, the navy would demand an adjustment; if the costs exceeded the budget, the studio would have to absorb the loss. He was also frustrated by minor bureaucrats reviewing storyboards and issuing warnings and orders where he had been the ultimate power just a few months before. When the navy's J. C. Hutchinson threatened Walt that he would either deliver the film on approach and landing promptly or bear the criticism "which can be heard in the halls re Disney," Walt wrote back indignantly that he was disturbed by the comment. But in truth he could do nothing about it because he needed to maintain good relations with the department. "Walt more or less lost control," recalled Joe Grant, "because we had so many of the army brass there at the studio, and all of them considered themselves producers."

Finally, he was frustrated over the *kinds* of films he was now forced to make. He had bristled at the idea of having to produce largely unimaginative training and educational films with primitive animation, but he understood the economic and patriotic necessity of doing so. He was less amenable when he was approached by both the Treasury Department and the Coordinator's Office to produce overt propaganda, films that were designed to influence opinion rather than educate. "Disney is fearful of being labeled as a propagandist in the public mind, with consequent damage to his reputation as a whimsical, non-political artist," Wallace Deuel, the coordinator for information, told a Treasury Department official before Walt was to visit the department that March to discuss another set of films. "He is bothered by a few abusive letters he has had about the New Spirit, charging him with various political, racial and other affiliations," and Walt apparently recalled a question that Lowell Mellett, the head of the Office of War Information, had asked him over dinner at Secretary Morgenthau's house during Walt's earlier visit: "Aren't you afraid that you will hurt your reputation by this sort of thing?"

The propaganda films that Morgenthau and Jock Whitney were both pressing him to make, with the lure of their providing joint financing, were a series that would directly attack the Nazis and their way of life. That February *Reader's Digest* had published a story titled "Education for Death" that described and lamented the Nazi indoctrination of children. The next month, after his trip to Washington, Walt had gone to Pleasantville, New York, the headquarters of the *Digest*, to discuss a film series that might be sponsored by the magazine, and the editors quickly pushed the idea of a film based on "Education for Death." Jock Whitney took up the cause, and Morgenthau did too, though there was disagreement on whether the government should underwrite the films (in which case Walt felt that exhibitors would refuse to show them) or whether *Reader's Digest* should underwrite them (in which case exhibitors would be more likely to show them but the coordinator and the Treasury Department would lose control over the content). The rights to "Education for Death" had already been sold to Paramount, but Whitney was certain he could retrieve them.

Reluctantly Walt Disney crossed the line into propaganda. With financing from the coordinator "in the background," as Roy put it, the studio put *Education for Death* into production that June. Later that summer, at the recommendation of producer Walter Wanger, who headed up the Motion Picture Society for the Americas, Walt began preparing to animate a short entitled *Reason and Emotion* from a book called *War Politics and Emotion* that showed how the latter had overwhelmed rationality in Nazi Germany. Still later he put into production a short called *Donald in Nutzi Land* that used Donald Duck to ridicule German leader Adolf Hitler. Both films were apparently made with financing from *Reader's Digest* and the Coordinator's Office. Walt commissioned studio composer Oliver Wallace to write a song for the latter, which Wallace said he banged out in an hour, incorporating a "razz" at Hitler in the chorus. When Spike Jones (then a trombonist in John Scott Trotter's orchestra and the leader of his own comical band called the City Slickers) selected the song, "Der Fuehrer's Face," complete with the razz, as the B-side of a new record, it became an instant hit, prompting the studio to change the film's title to the song's title. Jones's version sold 1.5 million copies and provided an anthem for the war just as "Who's Afraid of the Big Bad Wolf?" had provided an anthem for the Depression. Finally, again at the urging of the coordinator, Walt prepared a Nazi-themed version of *Chicken Little* in which Foxey Loxey gains access to the chicken coop by deploying Nazi tactics.

But these were small propagandistic forays, buttressing the popular mood by attacking Nazism and the Nazi leader. They didn't change public opinion; they reinforced it. Now Walt aimed higher. If he was going to make propaganda, he wanted to lead a crusade, not follow one. He wanted to help change the course of the war, and, perhaps more important after the hiatus on the features, he wanted to make a film that actually mattered to him. Still angling to make a compact with the Disneys, *Reader's Digest* had excerpted and then sent Walt the galleys of a new book by a former Russian air commander with the imperious name of Major Alexander P. de Seversky, who had lost his right leg at the age of twenty-two in an airplane crash during World War I but was so good a pilot that he had received special dispensation to return to his post and then shot down thirteen more planes before coming to the United States as an assistant naval attaché to the Russian embassy and, after the Russian Revolution, a consultant to the U.S. Air Service. In America, where he became a citizen, he developed the first automated bombsight and the first turbo-charged, air-cooled engine for fighter planes.

It was not only his name that was imperious. So was the man. Seversky was the son of an opera singer who was the first Russian to own and operate his own private plane. At forty-eight, the major made a dramatic impression himself with heavy-lidded, deep-set green eyes, an aquiline nose, full lips, and dark hair tinged with gray that swept back from a thick widow's peak. He had an office on the thirty-fourth floor of Rockefeller Center, where the only signed photograph among the memorabilia was one of General Billy Mitchell, the champion of American air power. He also owned a townhouse on Central Park and a beachhouse in Northport, Long Island. Supremely confident, Seversky, like his friend Billy Mitchell, didn't hesitate to take on the military establishment, which was exactly what he was doing now. His book, titled *Victory Through Air Power*, propounded the thesis that, as he put it, "[o]nly air power can carry an offensive war to the enemy, and only the offensive can win the war." In essence both the army infantry and the navy battleships were irrelevant. He further proposed that air power now made it possible "to reduce an enemy nation to helplessness without the time-honored preliminaries of invasion and mile-by-mile conquest." And he maintained that the best way to achieve this objective was with long-range bombers with heavy payloads attacking our enemies' nerve centers rather than through small aircraft flying from carriers.

When the book was published in late April 1942, it became an immediate best seller—it would wind up the fifth best-selling book of the year—but it also stirred controversy and rebuttals. The *Philadelphia Record* thought Seversky discounted the cooperation between the services that was needed for victory. The *Washington Post* said he relegated "all other weapons to a class with the javelin and crossbow." The New York *Daily News* complained that it would take until 1945 to have enough long-range bombers to fulfill Seversky's mission, and *The New York Times* opined that if Seversky could guarantee where the theater of war would be in two years and what kind of aircraft would be needed, the "military and naval authorities will receive the information with delight."

But if the critics—and most of the military—were skeptical, Walt Disney was enchanted. Walt loved technology generally, and he believed fervently in the airplane specifically. "The thing that I felt just went right along with our century, you see," Walt would later tell an interviewer. "I just felt, well, gee, if they're going to go out and try to use battleships and all those other things, I just didn't believe it would ever work." In May, even before he had read the book, he had sent out feelers to Seversky about the possibility of adapting it for the screen, though he warned his contact to "definitely eliminate my name from all inquiries made." By July, Walt had closed the deal.

He knew that making the film wouldn't be easy. The navy, which gave him much of his government business, feared that long-range land-based bombers would obviate the need for aircraft carriers, was adamantly opposed to Seversky's theory, and even called Walt into a staff meeting during one of his frequent Washington visits to dissuade him from making the film. "The whole point with Seversky, Walt, is not that anybody quarrels with him upon the value of air power," one navy official wrote him tactfully, "but that he believes in the application of air power by long-range, land-based bombers which, to carry out his ideas, would have to carry impossible bomb loads and go impossible distances." (Later the navy went so far as to promise the studio enough business that it wouldn't be able to produce any other films.) Others, like Commander John S. Thatch, a decorated flier who had served as the technical adviser on the fixed gunnery and fighter tactics series, told Walt that Seversky's ideas were unrealistic and that short-range missions were preferable; he even challenged Seversky to an aerial dogfight—Seversky in his big, long-range bomber, Thatch in his fighter plane.

But Walt could not be dissuaded. Excited by the prospect of a *Victory* film that could use animation to *show* how long-range bombers could win the war, he felt his old passion rising again. He began to feel engaged. He had discovered something that could occupy him throughout the summer, something important, while the rest of the studio churned out its routine training and educational films. Animator Marc Davis said that Walt was "sold completely. Dedicated to it." And once he had committed, Walt boasted that the studio "became a sort of Mecca for visiting airmen" who agreed with Seversky and delivered the latest intelligence to him, so that Walt was now part of a small movement. Seversky himself may have had a reputation for being arrogant, tough-minded, and cantankerous, but Roy had met him that July and was impressed, calling him "refreshing and interesting," and—what was important to Roy—not out to squeeze the studio for additional money. For Seversky as for Walt, this was all about patriotism, all about promoting a new way to win the war—what Seversky felt was the only way to win the war.

Now, pressed to convince the public of the theory as soon as possible so that he could make a difference, Walt began yet another push. (He felt another pressure too: a preliminary survey conducted for the studio showed that the public was tiring of war films, so that, as the pollster put it, "the sooner VICTORY THROUGH AIR POWER can be released, the better.") Walt met Seversky for the first time on July 28 at the studio, already armed with storyboards and surrounded by his staff, including Dave Hand, Bill Cottrell, and Perce Pearce. As he had been with Leopold Stokowski, Walt was deferential, recognizing that this was Seversky's project and that Walt was really just the facilitator. Layout artist Ken Anderson remembered one rainy weekend that August when he and fellow artist Herb Ryman were essentially locked into the studio and forced to come up with a final storyboard. "Seversky would come in and encourage us," Anderson said, "and Walt would give us threatening looks like, 'You guys better do a good job because I'm counting on you,' " by which Anderson thought he meant that the *country* was counting on them.

Walt was focused again, maybe for the first time since *Fantasia*. That August and September, as Seversky shuttled between the studio and various speaking engagements, sometimes snatching just a few hours before having to leave again, the staff raced to complete both the script and the storyboards. Walt kept emphasizing plausibility. "We have got to build it up so that the people are convinced—they are right with us on this," he said at a story meeting. "If we get too fantastic, it is going to cause people to discount the whole thing." In fact, it was Seversky, not Walt, who was more likely to insist on the entertainment value of the film rather than on its propaganda value, and when Walt objected to one point, Seversky snapped, "If we're going to get stuck in the mud of today we may just as well wipe out the whole picture."

Still, Walt saw aesthetic possibilities too. Though he called it a "bastard picture," like *The Reluctant Dragon*, since it combined live scenes of Seversky lecturing with animation illustrating his points just as *Dragon* had combined Robert Benchley and animation, and since, as in *Dragon*, the animation itself was less refined than in the features, he spoke glowingly of how the animators could present the future. "[W]e can show torpedoes striking ships," he said. "We can show huge cargo and bombing planes such as Seversky foresees." He was especially excited by a projected final sequence that showed the enemy as an octopus and America as an eagle. "You bomb the heart of the octopus and we show the big thing as we hit it," he gushed, "hammer on the vitals of the things, it knocks out the supplies and weakens every tentacle . . . while we're hammering away at the tentacles, we're still driving at the heart with our American air power." As Walt saw it, this wasn't going to be ordinary propaganda, any more than the features were ordinary cartoons. This was going to be great, earth-shaking propaganda. "The basic idea is big," he wrote Perce Pearce, Dave Hand, and the film's screenwriter, R. C. Sherriff, after hearing that audience interest was high. "It is the first time that Gallup has been able to report this on any picture he has surveyed," and Walt urged that they try to rush the film out no later than December to take advantage of public anticipation.

Walt began shooting Seversky's scenes in early October 1942. The filming had to take place at night because of the roar of planes taking off and landing nearby at the Lockheed plant during the day. Given the schedule, it was hectic. "I've scarcely been in my office for the last ten days," Walt wrote producer Walter Wanger at the end of the month, "what with shooting live action on the de Seversky [film] along with everything else, I haven't had a minute at my desk." He was haggard-looking and worn too, often unshaven and bedraggled in his loose pants and open-collar shirts. But for all the time he devoted to his oversight of *Victory*, Walt was, as usual, not entirely satisfied. Watching the rushes, he complained that Seversky kept saying the same thing over and over again and that he was skipping information that the public needed to appreciate his theory. He also felt that they might be relying too heavily on what he called visual "stunts" and suggested that they turn "our thinking from tricks to guts." And Walt worried that time was running out. As he told two visiting United Artists executives who had agreed to release the film when RKO declined, "There is a little too much optimism now," with Americans thinking that the war might end in a year, when Seversky believed that it was likely to continue for another five.

If Walt felt he was saving the country from Nazism with *Victory Through Air Power*, he was also helping to save South America with his other films. All that spring and into the summer of 1942 the studio had been completing the package of shorts, now called *Saludos*, inspired by the South American trip of the previous year. "We had better whip it into shape now or else forget it," Walt conceded after watching a reel of the film that May, though forgetting it was really not an option. He spent much of May and June polishing the film, then shipped it out in July so that Nelson Rockefeller and President Roosevelt could screen it. "Everybody in our office is most enthusiastic about SALUDOS," Fran Alstock, now the director of the coordinator's Motion Picture Division, wrote Walt after a July 29 preview. "It was shown last night to a number of the most important people in the Government," and "its success far surpassed any of the pictures we have shown." Rockefeller himself wrote Walt that the film "quite exceeds our highest expectations." Already the studio was considering a sequel, featuring other South American countries.

Meanwhile, as he was attempting to save South America from the Nazis, Walt was also charged with saving that continent from disease, pollution, and malnutrition. Late that May, even before completing *Saludos*, he and seven of his artists had gone to Washington to discuss a series of health and educational films—with uninspiring titles including *The Winged Scourge* (about mosquitoes), *Water: Friend or Enemy*, and *The Grain That Built a Hemisphere*—as well as the four propaganda pictures, with the Coordinator's Office, and to meet with Vice President Henry Wallace. Walt certainly understood the importance of these films both for South America and for the studio, but they were basically makework, used to keep the animators drawing and the studio running. In effect the studio, which had once existed to make films, now made films so that it could continue to exist. To Walt, who understood exactly what was happening, it was dispiriting.

While *Victory* seemed to satisfy his need for a major project commensurate with his ambitions, he was also looking for a property for an animated war film that might have commercial possibilities, since he was stymied from making his own entertainment features. He thought he might have found one that July when he received a story from a young Royal Air Force lieutenant named Roald Dahl. Dahl's story concerned "gremlins," fictional creatures who were blamed for the various little malfunctions that seemed to bedevil war pilots. Walt clearly liked the idea, especially after a brief national gremlin craze that fall, and he managed to deter other studios from making gremlin films of their own by saying that he was putting one into production. Walt eagerly commissioned a script, and Dahl visited the studio that November, but the project seemed as vexing as the gremlins themselves. Even before signing the contract, Roy complained that Dahl failed to give a logical reason or motive for the gremlins' behavior. Perce Pearce thought that the only feasible approach would combine live action with animation, but that no matter what they tried, the gremlins were "very very heavy villains" for mucking up the planes and threatening the pilots. Ward Kimball said that one problem was that no one seemed to know what a gremlin should look like.

Dahl returned to the studio in April 1943 to develop the film, and Walt continued trying to hammer the story into shape, but his interest had begun to wane as he confronted the material's problems. One artist accompanied Walt to a meeting of RAF fliers to discuss their encounters with the "gremlins," but the fliers preferred to tell stories instead, and Walt left at midnight, frustrated, declaring that he wasn't going to make the film. "Definitely, the GREMLINS will not be made as a feature because of the feeling on the Distributor's part that the public has become tired of so many war films," Walt wrote Dahl in December 1943, after what was now a year and a half of attempting to crack the story. He said he had tried to interest his crews in making it into a short but had had little success there either. "[I]f we ever hit upon an angle that seems right for production, we'll get in touch with you." He never did.

V

Even as the studio was almost totally devoted to war output, one commercial feature was still slowly making its way through production, a relic of a time that now seemed so long ago: *Bambi*. All through the strike and after America's entrance into the war, thirty-five to forty employees continued to toil away, though even with another small infusion of $150,000 from the Bank of America, Walt had had to economize on the picture. Some scenes were cut, others were changed to place characters in silhouette where they wouldn't have to be fully animated, camera movements were simplified, final cleanup tests were being sent directly for inking, and the inking was less precise. When Walt advised Frank Thomas that there wouldn't be any picture if they didn't drastically cut costs and Thomas began tearing up, Walt bent over him and said, "Frank, I know it hurts you, but dammit, it's got to go, that's all there is to it." To another director who lamented after Walt ordered cuts that they would be "losing something," Walt said, "You're telling me what you'd be losing. Here I am, sitting here, losing my shirt, and you're telling me what *you'd* be losing." In the end Walt had no choice but to cut scenes wholesale, slashing the film from 8,500 feet to 6,259 feet. "There was not much excitement or the usual thrill of completion during the last days of *Bambi*," Frank Thomas and Ollie Johnston would later confess, "but finally it was finished."

Bambi, which had cost over $1.7 million even after the cuts, would need to return $2.5 million to break even, but the early signs were not encouraging. The studio had missed its target preview date in December 1941 because Walt decided to add lyrics to some of the songs, and when the film was finally previewed in Pomona the following February, a teenager shouted after Bambi's mother's death and Bambi's calling out for her, "Here I am, Bambi!," breaking the film's spell. "The ride back to Burbank was even quieter than the ride out had been," Thomas and Johnston wrote. It seemed a harbinger. The postponements had hurt the publicity campaign, and Walt's plans to release the film as a roadshow attraction with Fantasound had to be dropped. A Gallup survey commissioned by the studio found that "ready-made viewership is low" and the "want-to-see" was the lowest of all the films on the survey's index. Respondents said they "don't like full-length cartoons," that they considered them "childish" and that they expected it to be a "jungle picture." The only hope, reported Gallup, was to sell the film as "tomorrow's classic" and get testimonials from famous individuals. Meanwhile Roy wrote Walt that "BAMBI deals are coming in slowly," in part because the market was crowded with pictures, in part because the recent Disney films had been disappointing, and in part because the Disneys' distributor, RKO, had seemed to lose faith in them, though Roy still believed that the film would return its negative cost and might even turn a profit.

The whole project now seemed shrouded in gloom. That May, Frank Churchill, the frail, doleful, alcoholic composer who had written the scores for *Snow White* and *Bambi*, committed suicide with a shotgun. Always sorrowful and sensitive, he had no doubt been further depressed by Walt's ongoing dissatisfaction with his work on *Bambi*. (Churchill had written a great score for the "musical circle of Hollywood," Walt griped, but one that was monotonous and did not provide the excitement the movie needed.) Churchill's last request was that "Love Is a Song," which he had written for *Bambi*, be dedicated to his wife, Carolyn, who had been Walt's personal secretary from June 1930 to January 1934, when she married Churchill. But even that was denied since the song had already gone to the publisher.

When it was finally released in August 1942, critics received *Bambi* almost as if it were an afterthought, which is what it had become, and the realism that Walt had striven so hard over so many years to achieve, the realism that had caused him so much grief, was seen not as an advance of the animation art but as a decline. "In his search for perfection, Mr. Disney has come perilously close to tossing away his whole world of cartoon fantasy," *The New York Times* observed in what would become an increasingly common complaint against Disney. Critic Manny Farber, calling *Bambi* "entirely unpleasant," agreed that by attempting to "ape the trumped up realism of flesh and blood movies, he [Disney] has given up fantasy, which was pretty much the magic element. Mickey Mouse and

Donald Duck lived in a beautiful escape land, where they flew through the air, swam under water, died a thousand deaths, and lived to see the end of each picture." In *Bambi* the animals "behave just as Hollywood thinks we do," which makes the film "old stuff and boring." In short, critics found that in attempting to perfect the world on screen, Walt had tamed the rough, subversive energy of the earlier cartoons and forsaken the very reason to have animations in the first place—because they challenged the laws of reality—though what these critics seemed to miss was that Walt's animated realism was every bit as much an exercise of control as his wilder and more "imaginative" animations, and that control was the objective.

The larger problem with *Bambi* may have been a cultural dissonance between the film and its audience. On the one hand, while citizens around the world professed to want escape from the gravity of war, they seemed to think that animation was now juvenile and inappropriate, which clearly accounted for some of the antipathy in the Gallup survey. Cartoons had boosted morale and provided diversion during the Depression, when spirits needed to be raised and when animations seemed a correlative for a plucky nation under duress and trying to fight back. War provided an altogether different and far more difficult trial—one for which the buoyancy of animation seemed insufficient. On the other hand, the realism and seriousness of *Bambi* were not the sort of qualities that audiences seemed to desire at a time when everyone lived within harsh reality and seriousness. Young Diane herself complained to her father that Bambi's mother needn't have died, and when Walt answered that he was only following the book, Diane protested that he had taken other liberties and that in any case he was *Walt Disney* and he could do anything he wanted. But Walt hadn't wanted to lighten the drama. "Life is composed of lights and shadows," he would later say, "and we would be untruthful, insincere, and saccharine if we tried to pretend there were no shadows." In taking that position in wartime, however, Walt Disney, who had once strummed the psychic chords of the entire world, was now out of tune.

With the lukewarm critical reception to *Bambi*, the only source of effective publicity for the film was an attack from another quarter. Raymond J. Brown, the editor of *Outdoor Life*, had seen the film in preview and lauded it to Walt as an "artistic triumph and your greatest achievement." But Brown had quibbles too. Certain sequences, he thought, might be offensive to sportsmen and conservationists, and he suggested that Walt add a prologue stating that the film was a fantasy and not a depiction of reality. Whether Walt smelled a publicity coup or was actually offended himself, he responded the same day that it was too late to add a prologue and that in any case (obviously speaking disingenuously) he never saw the film as reflecting negatively on hunters: "[A]ll I ever saw in it was an entertainment that would appeal to everyone."

Brown, taking the bait and intensifying his criticism, wrote an editorial condemning the movie as the "worst insult ever offered to American sportsmen and conservationists," and Walt, at the behest of Howard Kemp, a sports columnist for the *Rochester Democrat and Chronicle*, countered that his audience would think he rated them "morons" if he had added a prologue advising them the film was fantasy when it was clearly not real. The exchange then triggered a heated debate in newspapers across the country about whether *Bambi* had unfairly tarnished hunters. Roy thought it inadvisable to get Walt embroiled in this sort of controversy, but publicist Vern Caldwell wrote Walt that the attacks were "getting results." "The problem is to keep this thing alive & at the same time not allow Disney to be placed in a compromising position," Caldwell said, and he recruited newsmen Bob Considine, Grantland Rice, and Paul Gallico to defend Walt as "being falsely accused by either a fanatic . . . or a shrewd exploitation man."

Whatever burst the picture might have received from the publicity, however, was short-lived. Roy fought to have the Radio City Music Hall, where *Snow White* had played for weeks, keep *Bambi* for merely a third week, but he admitted to George Morris that "our friends in the Music Hall seem determined to slide us out at the end of two weeks." By the end of its run Morris calculated that the studio had lost roughly $200,000 on it. Desperate as Walt was to see a profit so that he could put another feature into production, he didn't seem surprised. "Living with BAMBI, as we did, for five years, we lost all sense of perspective," he wrote columnist Jimmy Starr, who had praised the film, "but your wire and editorial comment raises our hopes that we have achieved what we aimed for when we first decided to make it." Then he added remorsefully, "One thing we learned from this experience[,] and that is we'll never again spend so much time on another subject."

It was a painful admission. Walt Disney had *lived* to spend time on his features, *lived* to create a fully realized universe that testified to his power and provided his escape. But *Bambi* was a reminder of how much everything had changed since the strike and the advent of war. The war had imposed a kind of grimness on Burbank. At Roy's urging the studio had been classified as a strategic defense industry, and every employee was now fingerprinted and given a bright orange identification badge. At the same time, even though Walt personally visited draft boards to insist that his animation was a vital service for the war effort (he even dug out his old Veterans of Foreign Wars badge to show up a "billboard patriot" on one board who expressed skepticism about the value of the studio's work), 173 employees, including Woolie Reitherman and Frank Thomas, had left the studio for the armed forces—almost 28 percent of the staff. Soldiers patrolled the lot, protecting a top-secret bombsight that was stationed there, and one naval officer who supervised the production of *The Rules of the Nautical Road* commandeered the bedroom off Walt's office to live in, washing his clothes there in a bucket. Animators even fired small rockets off the Animation Building roof to see the patterns of the explosions so that they could better draw them. Adding to the military presence was the fact that Lockheed was renting space on the lot. And then there was the wartime economizing. Employees carpooled to save gasoline, as did Walt. Upset with the new militarization of the studio, Carl Barks, an animator who would later become the main force behind the Donald Duck comic books, left. "You were just going to be locked in there for the duration," he said, "and I just didn't think I wanted to be locked into that place for the duration."

The bigger change was philosophical—what Carl Nater, whom Walt had put in charge of the government films, called a necessary reprogramming of the employees' "mental equipment." The studio that had emphasized quality no longer put any premium on quality. Efficiency and economy were paramount. Early on, Hal Adelquist, the head of personnel, wrote Walt that the economies on *The New Spirit*—rushing animation through without sweatboxing, showing directors drawings instead of tests, having cleanup men touch up roughs as they were delivered—were to be standard operating procedure now. "We must throw out entirely the trial and error methods, the redo systems," Adelquist advised Walt. "We must restrict Animators to one test. We must abolish layout cleanups and all animation must be restricted to 2's [meaning two exposures] on a single cel. Complicated pans, difficult scene mechanics and multiplane planning, must, by necessity from the standpoint of cost and speed, go by the boards." Simply put, the Disney studio, which had prided itself on its excellence, was now to be like every other animation studio, priding itself on its expedience. Or, as Roy proudly told *Fortune*, "I really believe that Walt is beginning to know what a dollar is."

The irony, the terrible irony for Walt Disney, was that for all the shortcuts and economizing it had imposed, the war was the one thing that was saving him. Had he been dependent on his features and shorts, the studio almost certainly would have been driven into bankruptcy and forced to close. It wasn't that Walt was making much on the government work; he charged the government an average of $12 a foot and sometimes as little as $4, where his commercial animations had cost roughly $65 a foot and sometimes as much as $250. (He wasn't making as much income personally either, having voluntarily taken a cut from $2,000 a week to $850.) Though the Disneys added overhead charges, the studio, partly out of patriotism and partly out of naïveté, was still asking the government only for costs, which enraged Joe Rosenberg. At a meeting in January 1942, where George Morris and Gunther Lessing were discussing the Bank of America loans, Rosenberg snapped that he was "passing on loans every day to concerns doing government work and in not one instance was there any question of the contractor making a fair profit." When Morris countered that the government films provided a "show case" for the studio, Rosenberg warned that he expected a profit anyway, and he would be watching them closely, with the threat of freezing the loan.

And there was one more irony. Though he had been failing as a commercial filmmaker, by the end of 1942 Walt Disney had become the leader of government movie production. "This past year has been not only one of the most exciting," he wrote his uncle Robert at Christmastime, "but one of the most exhausting I have ever experienced. Since last January, when we made the Income Tax picture for the Treasury Department, we have plunged into a type of work I never expected to touch." The plunge included nearly 300,000 feet of film produced that year, up from a prewar total of 30,000, which was why the shortcuts were so necessary. Over 75 percent of the studio's output was now targeted for the government. With the training films demonstrating the educational potential of motion pictures, Walt was also increasingly recognized as, in *Fortune*'s words, "one of the great teachers of all time." But even as Walt put a gloss on this renown and called it a great opportunity to "show what our medium can do," it was a far, far cry from the great things *he* had always wanted the medium to do. "At times it seemed we had slipped over a parallel but slightly altered universe" was how studio executive Harry Tytle put it, "where the usual rules were changed or no longer applied." Tytle was right. They had changed.

VI

Walt was busy. He ended 1942 with a two-week trip to Mexico accompanied by Lillian and twelve members of his staff to research a sequel to *Saludos*. He began the new year with another trip, this one east to attend the premiere of *Saludos* (which had been retitled *Saludos Amigos*), to discuss the other films to be produced for the coordinator, and to meet with a Harvard anthropology professor named Earnest A. Hooten who had written a book on Nazi racial theories that Walt was thinking of turning into one of his propaganda films for the coordinator. Though it was a compilation of animated shorts mortised together with those home movies that Walt had taken of South America, and though its intended effect was as much goodwill as entertainment, *Saludos* was nevertheless as close to a commercial feature as the studio was likely to produce now that *Bambi* was finished. It was also one of the few reasons for optimism. The critic Gilbert Seldes, long Walt's champion, saw it that January and wrote him: "I hope it has all the success it deserves—and escapes all the troubles that you are afraid of."

It didn't. Bosley Crowther in *The New York Times* saluted the film as recording "one of the happiest missions ever dispatched from these shores," and called its effect "one of ascending enthusiasm," but his was a minority opinion. Critics who had carped at Walt's pretentiousness in *Fantasia* and at his subdued realism in *Bambi* now decried his strained and strident joyfulness. James Agee, writing in *The Nation*, said the film "depresses me." "Self-interested, belated ingratiation embarrasses me, and Disney's famous cuteness, however richly it may mirror national infantilism, is hard on my stomach," he said. John T. McManus in the left-wing *PM* agreed and admitted to a "mingled pride and sadness over the growing up of a beloved something we all foolishly hoped could stay young forever." In other words, the famous Disney touch had become cloying.

But the film hadn't been made for the critics, and Walt's only comfort was that his patrons in the Coordinator's Office had liked the film enormously and that the vice president had told Rockefeller it was the "outstanding achievement in the development of hemispheric solidarity." More important, the South Americans had liked it too. Some theaters discontinued their double-feature policy so that they could show *Saludos* more frequently, and by one account, at least one audience had threatened to tear down the theater if the projectionist didn't show *Saludos* again. One embassy official in Bolivia wrote Walt that Disney was "completely adored in South America since *Saludos*" and that his name "electrifies" the Bolivian employees at the embassy. In fact, the only problem with *Saludos* was that the countries that had not been represented in the film were complaining to the coordinator about the neglect, prompting one of his representatives to suggest leaking a report that Disney was at work on a sequel in which those countries would be shown, as indeed he was.

But *Saludos* and its sequel had never interested Walt much. They were essentially jobs to maintain cash flow. He was much more enthusiastic about *Victory Through Air Power*, to which he returned early in 1943. More than ever Walt was convinced that the war could not be won with land forces and naval attacks, and that in any case the country could not afford a fully equipped army, navy, and air force simultaneously. And he still believed that *Victory* could change not only the course of the war but also the course of the world. "It's important," he told *The New York Times* that February. "People need to know about it. A lot of them are still bound by traditional ways of thinking and a movie like this can break through a lot of misconceptions."

The stumbling block was entertainment value. *Victory* was not another subsidized government film. It was being financed by the studio, and it had to return a profit. When he was shown finished reels and storyboards late in February, theater chain executive Spyros Skouras emphasized that the film had to be entertaining and not a "scientific exhibit." Walt, who had always emphasized entertainment value himself until *Fantasia*, wasn't so sure. This time there was something more valuable than entertainment. "Don't you think that if the public after seeing this picture feel they have learned something—for once it's clear in their minds," Walt countered, "—isn't that important?" And as Skouras kept hammering away about entertainment, Walt kept insisting that he was making the film not because it could provide escapism but because "we believe in the thing so badly. I felt HERE'S A MESSAGE THAT IS GREATER THAN A LOT OF THE STUFF WE'VE BEEN DOING HERE ON PROPAGANDA. I thought here was a message that might do some real good."

Walt forged ahead, fending off the navy's continuing objections and threats and working around Seversky's increasingly heavy speaking schedule. That winter, after rethinking the film, he had decided to scrap the live scenes of Seversky he had shot in October and rewrite the script to reduce the major's dialogue and simplify and strengthen his argument. Corralling Seversky for two months beginning in April 1943, Walt hired director H. C. Potter, fresh from *Hellzapoppin'*, and cinematographer Ray Rennahan, fresh off an Academy Award for *Blood and Sand*, to shoot the new scenes. Potter's main tasks were to "smooth out" Seversky's thick Russian accent and to make sure that the major hit his marks as he delivered his dialogue. When Seversky complained that it was too difficult to speak and hit the marks at the same time, Potter reminded him of how much Seversky had had to do simultaneously when he flew and told him, imitating Seversky's accent, to "diwide the attention," which the crew began to shout whenever filming began.

Working at breakneck speed—Seversky's scenes were shot in six days—Walt managed to finish the picture by the end of May and then hosted a celebratory combination screening and bon voyage party for the major at the studio that June. Even before the completion, though, the publicity campaign had started. Roy was in New York that May flogging the picture and writing Walt delightedly that "I am sure we are going to raise a furor with it from coast to coast!" Perce Pearce had accompanied Seversky east to ghostwrite articles promoting the film, and by late June the studio was screening the movie in New York and Washington for assorted notables, among them the former advertising executive Albert Lasker, who was so enamored of the film and its theory that he organized a separate publicity campaign of his own for it. Lasker and his wife, Mary, called the film the "most powerful and vital document yet put before the American public" and predicted that its impact would be "dynamic."

Lasker was right. Walt had wanted to change the world, and he got his opportunity. Even before the formal premiere in New York on July 17, 1943, Walt was receiving private accolades. Newspaper magnate William Randolph Hearst wired Walt after a screening that the film was a "truly great production" that had "rendered a valuable service to the community," and Nelson Rockefeller said it was not only a contribution to the war effort but a demonstration of the limitless possibilities of motion pictures. At a gala preview hosted by Lasker and Washington social queen Elsa Maxwell, the audience applauded spontaneously throughout the showing and gave a sustained ovation at the end. Reviewers were equally enthusiastic, calling it "exhilarating," "stimulating," "ingenious," and so simple that "even a youngster of 11 or so would have no difficulty in understanding what it's all about." The only dissents came from Agee again, who worried that he was being "sold something under pretty high pressure," and the Communist *Daily Worker*, which objected that Seversky's theories were fantastic and militated against a second front to aid America's Russian ally.

But the most important reactions were those from the military, which would have to accept and then implement Seversky's new policy. Vern Caldwell had screened the film for the navy, which had been so averse to the project, and wired Walt: "Response enthusiastic." (Walt was at great pains in the film to reassure the navy that its missions were still necessary.) At the same time Henry "Hap" Arnold, the commanding general of the army air force and long one of the country's leading advocates of air power, saw the film but didn't convey his reaction—in Caldwell's view, because Arnold, like Seversky, was lobbying for a separate air force and believed that his approval of the film might have been seen as a "tip-off." Still, Arnold's aide asked for a second screening the next day for a half-dozen other air force generals who, Caldwell said, applauded the film despite the fact that they didn't hold Seversky in very high personal regard. Roy and Caldwell spent the evening with them until three A.M.

By some accounts, the most important official to see the film that summer was the commander in chief himself. Apparently Albert Lasker had managed to get a copy to British prime minister Winston Churchill, who was so impressed by what he saw he asked that a print to be shipped overnight to the Quebec Conference that August, where he was meeting with Roosevelt and where Roosevelt not only watched it but asked that it be screened for the Joint Chiefs of Staff as well. "I was assured," Seversky wrote Elsa Maxwell proudly, "that this strengthened greatly the views of those who contended that invasion could not be undertaken until control of the air was achieved."

Walt had made *Victory* for influence and for his own sense of usefulness, "Whether it makes money or not," he wrote radio commentator Upton Close, "I shall be happy so long as it helps stir up the country and starts people thinking about the importance of real air power," though just how much it really affected policy was a matter of debate since the government didn't actually deploy the long-range bombing strategy during the war and since, as Woolie Reitherman, who had left the studio to join the air corps, said, "There wasn't any doubt that we were going to have air power." Still, for all the officials who praised it and for all the controversy it generated, the film did not find an audience. It had cost just under $800,000—only $5,000 of which went to Seversky. George Morris reported to the board of directors that fall that the film could wind up costing the studio between $400,000 and $500,000 in losses. In the end, years later, after its runs were completed, when Walt was carving it into pieces for other uses, it barely broke even—yet another failure in what was becoming a long string of failures for Walt Disney.

Now, without films to interest him but with a studio to maintain, he had become less a filmmaker than a salesman and a goodwill ambassador, attracting government work to the studio because he was Walt Disney, one of America's favorite celebrities. His chief client remained the Coordinator's Office, and Walt undertook yet another trip to Mexico that March to record music for the *Saludos Amigos* sequel and to gather material in preparation for a conference that the coordinator was hosting at the studio in May for the purpose of determining how best to eradicate illiteracy in South America—a project that promised as much as $500,000 to the studio in the first year alone. At the same time Walt dispatched Bill Cottrell and Jack Cutting to Central America and another delegation to Cuba to lay the groundwork for the pictures; and later that summer, in part to prepare for a $200,000 film on literacy financed by the coordinator and in part to receive an award from the Mexican government for his efforts, he, Clarence "Ducky" Nash, and studio public relations head Joe Reddy flew to Mexico City. In October, Walt and Lillian joined his staff in Mexico again for another "field trip," as they called it, and had a scare when their return flight was grounded by a hurricane that wound up leveling the city of Mazatlán.

If Walt seemed to be commuting to Mexico, he was also still shuttling between Los Angeles and Washington, still trying to drum up more government business, still trying to keep the studio solvent, though at one point so much work was already pouring in that Roy and Walt had to issue an edict forbidding any contract that was not personally approved by one of them. In a way, the studio had become addicted to the government work, gorging itself on it both because it needed it and because it could do nothing else. Indeed, the studio had strayed so far from its original mission that Walt now began to entertain another idea he had long been urged to consider, and had considered, but had always finally rebuffed: commercials and industrial films for public relations rather than training purposes. The studio had produced a Mickey Mouse short for the Nabisco pavilion at the 1939 New York World's Fair, but Walt had gently rejected other suitors. Now he hired a liaison named John Sheehan, whose job was to field offers. Among the companies wanting the Disney touch were Westinghouse, Firestone Tire, General Motors and the Ford Motor Company, Owens Glass, Standard Oil of Indiana, and National Dairy Products, most of whom wanted to deal with Walt personally. Walt even closed a deal to make a film for Coca-Cola, then solicited a series for its rival, Pepsi-Cola.

Roy, looking for a way to streamline the process and to protect the studio "against making bad boners in presenting ourselves and our propositions to big accounts," eventually suggested that the studio tie in with its advertising firm, Foote, Cone & Belding. But Walt—seeing no residual value in commercials and feeling vaguely humiliated about making them after years of bold pronouncements about greatness—vacillated, even as he instructed his staff to keep pursuing them. He told clients that they could find someone else to do the films more cheaply, or he told them that he could see himself making commercials for television someday, just not now; on the other hand, he also mused that commercials might help absorb manpower at the studio. In any case, making commercials was not what he wanted to do, and for all the work the studio discussed, little was actually contracted for and even less was delivered.

But, then, in 1943 the studio had only slipped further into the war morass, had only become more of a defense factory and less of a movie studio. Ninety-four percent of the output now went to the government, and in June 1943 alone the studio produced just 2,300 feet less film than it had produced in all of 1941. "If every American could visit the [Disney] studio," Walter Wanger wrote glowingly that September in *The Saturday Review of Literature*, "he would have a new admiration for his country. There is nothing comparable to it in the world. More experts, scientists, and technicians operate under Disney's roofs than in any other one organization in the universe." Patriotic as he was, Walt nevertheless complained to A. V. Cauger's wife, when she wrote asking whether Walt might have a job for his old Kansas City Film Ad boss, "We all have to adjust ourselves to the War capital conditions and await the time when the world once more returns to a state of normalcy." Until then he just had to keep going.

But as he waited, he was distracted and disconsolate. Ollie Johnston, who was classified 4-F due to an ulcer, remembered meeting Walt in the hallways and he would begin to converse, then stop suddenly and lean against the wall for several minutes without saying a word. "And I didn't want to walk away," Johnston said, "because I knew he wanted somebody there. He was down because there just wasn't anything he really could get involved in." Though the shorts—the Donald Ducks, the Goofys, and the Plutos—continued to move through the studio to fulfill the contractual obligations to RKO, the market was oversaturated, and in any case Walt had long since ceased to care. After *Victory* he tried to interest Roy in the possibility of combining *The Wind in the Willows*, which was still slowly snaking its way through production, and the Mickey Mouse featurette on Jack and the Beanstalk into a single film, or even combining *Willows* with *Gremlins*, but Roy wasn't encouraging. If they were to get any return, the budget couldn't exceed $450,000—even *Dumbo* had cost $200,000 more than that—and the best Walt could do, after cutting and slashing, was $523,000. Even at that, Roy said single-subject features were still more promising, despite the fact that the studio couldn't currently produce them, and if it did, the business office had set a maximum budget for new productions far below that of *Snow White*, *Pinocchio*, or *Fantasia*. Walt's only option was to keep going to Washington to toady to the officials there in hopes of keeping the government pump primed.

He had no harbor. If the studio's mission suffered during the war years, so did Walt Disney's family. Even before the war had placed such heavy demands on him, Lillian and the girls had always been subordinated to the studio. Walt made attempts to mollify them. Lillian often accompanied him on his trips east and even to Mexico, and he was as attentive a parent as he could possibly be under the circumstances, still taking the girls to the studio on weekends, where they followed him from room to room, or to the airport to see the planes take off and land, or to the train station where he would put his ear to the track and listen for the train the way he had when he was a boy in Marceline. And he bought them a cocker spaniel puppy, Taffy, that he admitted he and Lillian seemed to appreciate more than the girls. When he was feeling self-important, it was the girls, he said, especially serious ten-year-old Diane, who could give him a look that "brings me off my high horse." But despite his very real devotion, the press of business and the need to decompress from it made it difficult now for him to be as engaged a father as he would have liked. "Last Sunday was the first time in months I didn't listen to the radio," he wrote Deems Taylor early in 1944. "For a change I took my oldest daughter horseback riding and later on played a hot game of tag with the both of them in the yard."

The best times now were the vacations at the Sugar Bowl ski area or at the Lake Arrowhead resort ninety miles east of Los Angeles—or better still at the Smoke Tree resort in Palm Springs, where even before the war he would spend several weeks with the family each spring, usually shuttling back and forth to the studio every few days, and where he typically spent Thanksgiving with Lillian and the girls during the war. Lillian said he loved the "openness" of Palm Springs, but it clearly wasn't only the physical openness of the hot, flat expanse of desert with the purple mountains in the distance that he appreciated. It was, no doubt, the absence of feeling suffocated by the studio and the overwhelming government work there. It was the freedom from having to tend to a thousand details about which he didn't really care but for which he knew he would be held responsible.

By 1944 the workload hadn't lifted, but Walt's sense of commitment had. He had become so cavalier that when Dave Hand, who had been Walt's primary production associate for years, tendered his resignation, Walt, rather than urge Hand to stay, coolly called Roy and told him to cancel Hand's contract—an admission that the resumption of feature animation was not imminent. Walt spent much of the year traveling, back and forth between Los Angeles and Washington, or to New York—he took a month-long trip there with Lillian late that May—and then went on another long trip that August that was scheduled to take them to Mexico, Cuba, Williamsburg, Virginia, and then New York again, though the Cuban leg was later canceled. (It was Walt's first visit to the colonial recreation at Williamsburg, and it left a deep impression.) The main order of business, besides just keeping the studio running, was the sequel to *Saludos Amigos*, which had been titled *The Three Caballeros* after its three cartoon protagonists—Donald Duck, a parrot named José Carioca, and a gun-toting rooster named Panchito. As early as March, Roy had shown Nelson Rockefeller storyboards and played him recordings, but the studio missed its June deadline, and in mid-July, Walt wired Vern Caldwell that he couldn't give any definite date when the film would be completed. A large part of the delay could be attributed to the studio experimenting with new techniques to combine a live actor with an animated character in the same frame—just as Walt had done with far less sophistication in the old Alice comedies.

The film wasn't completed until November, though when it was, Walt seemed pleased by the technological advances of the combined live-action/animation and by the film's manic modernist energy, telegraphing Rockefeller that "IT MOVES WITH THE TEMPO OF AN EXPRESS TRAIN." Ward Kimball, who had animated a song in the film in which, as he recalled it, Donald Duck races frantically all over the screen and sometimes right past the edges, later called it the "one bit of animation that I'm proud of." Director Gerry Geronomi disagreed. He didn't even want to show the sequence to Walt, because, Kimball said, Donald would run off the frame on one side, only to reemerge through the top of the frame—a violation of the old Disney principle of realism.* Kimball told him to "[s]tuff it up your ass," because the film was already overdue and because Walt now demanded to see all the footage. As Kimball related it, Walt saw the scene and "howled." "He just thought it was so great. He said, 'Jesus, this is it.' " Ollie Johnston and Frank Thomas believed that the scene, along with another that Kimball later animated for the short *Pecos Bill*, initiated a "whole wave of preposterous actions and brittle timing throughout the industry," which meant that the Disney studio, which had spearheaded realism, was now spearheading the self-reflexive movement away from it.

But not everyone was enamored of this new direction. James Agee detected a "streak of cruelty" in *Caballeros*, a streak he thought had been gathering force for years in Disney's films, perhaps as Walt's retribution for the tribulations he felt he had suffered. Barbara Deming, writing in *Partisan Review*, also believed that Disney had "wrought something monstrous," but she thought that in doing so he had made a telling commentary on the times. As Deming saw it, Disney's "gift" was "to be able to accept wholeheartedly the outlook of the hour, and to improvise with it, whatever it might be," which was how Mickey Mouse could express the aggressive rebelliousness of the Depression and *Pinocchio* the new moral commitment required by the coming war. In *Caballeros*, by making the

*Kimball may have been confusing scenes here. While there are several scenes of a frantic Donald, it is the aracuan bird who leaves the frame on one side and then reappears on the other.

entire film into a phantasmagoria in which characters and shapes keep morphing into other characters and shapes, in which the object of one's desire seems to be attained only to disappear, and in which both the characters and the audience keep losing their bearings, Walt Disney had managed to find the perfect metaphor for a world spinning in the vortex of war. "Nothing holds its shape," Deming observed, concluding that Donald Duck in *Caballeros* "could be likened in his adventures here, his confusions and translations, to most major characters now passing across our screens" and presumably to Americans generally: lost.

None of these reactions made its commercial prospects any more favorable, and Kay Kamen had overheard an RKO representative grumbling that he was going to have a hard time selling the film. As it turned out, the chaos of *Caballeros* was more appealing than either the tender solemnity of *Bambi* or the tendentiousness of *Victory Through Air Power.* It accrued $900,000 in billings in just 11 weeks, compared to 31 weeks for *Bambi* and 48 for *Dumbo*. In South America it was wildly popular. The Mexican magazine *Tiempo* lauded Walt as "one of the greatest creators in the motion picture world" and said he had brought a "world of friendship and understanding to the people of all countries." A Brazilian newspaper, *A Noite*, went even further, calling it the "best thing Disney has made so far."

Financially if not artistically speaking, it was shaping up to be a good year. Thanks to the quantity of product generated by the war and by the release of $141,000 in funds that had been impounded in Britain as well as the suspension of dividends after April 1941 on the stock it had issued, the studio had managed to reduce its debt to the Bank of America to just under $1 million and had working capital of $3 million. Now that the company was beginning to post profits again, however, the Bank of America warned Walt and Roy that stockholders were unlikely to be as patient as they had been and suggested that the company convert its preferred stock into debentures and common stock, which would give the Disneys even more working capital and eliminate a large "sinking fund" they had had to maintain as a hedge for the preferred stockholders.

This wasn't just a matter of economics—it was a matter of control. "Do we want to maintain 100% control and operation of a company burdened with debt and confronted with big possibilities, hoping for a windfall, such as a big grossing picture or television, to let us keep going?" Roy asked Walt. "Or, shall we reconstruct our whole stock set-up in some way that is more secure and more sure, and have a lesser interest—but nevertheless a controlling interest—of a company that is sound and, therefore more safe and more able to meet the future properly?" Roy left no doubt where he stood, especially since, as he warned Walt, should any of the Disneys die, they would have to sell some of their stock to pay the inheritance tax anyway, and as for letting their employees hold the stock, he adduced Carl Stalling and Ub Iwerks as examples of ordinary stockholders who had lacked the foresight to understand the value of what they had actually been granted. After the strike Walt may have given up his grandiose idea of the studio as a workers' community—he complained that his employees had sold their stock when the value plummeted because they "lost faith in me"—and he had already surrendered power to the executive committee instituted by the Bank of America, but he had always wanted to retain as much control as he could; it was a part of his redoubt against the world. Now, with the studio foundering aimlessly, he conceded to Roy. He chose stability over authority, the money over the risk.

Yet the studio gained another source of income that year in addition to the refinancing, and it reminded Walt of what the studio had been before the war. While coming back on the train from one of his Washington trips early in 1942, he had met Nate Blumberg, the head of Universal Pictures, who told Walt how Universal had mined its old film library for pictures they could reissue and advised that the Disney studio do the same. Walt had prodded Roy on the matter, asking him to consider re-releasing *Snow White* and possibly some of the other features in time for Christmas in 1943. Roy finally agreed on *Snow White,* though the company missed the holiday season and opened it instead in February 1944. It was the first time in years that RKO seemed energized by the prospect of selling a Disney film, even if it was an old one, and Vern Caldwell wrote Walt that they expected an "exceptional gross." In fact, its success had become so important to the studio that Roy, citing "your production problems," urged Walt to attend the Cincinnati premiere, which he did. When it opened in New York early in April, Walt bragged that in all of its return engagements to that point *Snow White* had equaled the gross of the average A feature and exceeded the grosses of the most recent Disney films.* Even Roy crowed to Walt that "SNOW WHITE really seems hot."

Meanwhile, as American troops invaded the Normandy beaches in France that June—at Allied headquarters the code name for the operation was "Mickey Mouse"—and the war began its long slog to a conclusion, Walt was supervising the training films and South American pictures for the coordinator. When the European phase of the war ended in May 1945 and the Japanese phase four months later, the studio closed for three days

*In October 1944 the studio business office calculated that *Pinocchio, Fantasia, The Reluctant Dragon, Bambi,* and *Victory Through Air Power* had lost a total of $2,396,500. Memo, Paul L. Pease to Board of Directors, Oct. 24, 1944, Paul Pease Folder, Walt Disney Corr., Inter-Office, 1938–1944, N-Q, A1630, WDA.

in celebration. Though he had shown surprisingly little interest in the war itself outside of *Victory*, Walt Disney had made significant contributions to the American success. Among the smaller contributions, he had provided twelve-hundred designs for military insignia, and the Treasury Department credited him with helping to sell more than $50 million worth of savings bonds. Among the larger ones were the government movies—by one estimate (inexact because the records were inexact), he had made between 150 and 300 hours of them in just over four years, though Walt couldn't have been more ecstatic now that the production of them was over. "For Christ's sake, Marc," he told animator Marc Davis shortly after the war, "I never want to do another training film as long as I live!"

As important as the training films were, Walt may have left an even greater mark with the films he had produced for the coordinator. The movies on health and literacy had had a deep effect on people's lives, and Jack Cutting, who headed the studio's foreign department, wrote Walt early in 1945 that *The Winged Scourge*, the film on mosquito control, "created a greater sensation than 'Gone With the Wind' " in a small Cuban village where mosquito infestation was rampant. Writing a year after the war's end, Nelson Rockefeller called Walt's South American trip and his films that flowed from it the "most effective work in inter-American relations" and said "they did more than anything else to bring the people of the Americas closer together."

Now that work was over. And Walt Disney could look forward once again to doing what he had always wanted to do: make great films that would entertain audiences and demonstrate his own power to create life. At least, that was what he thought he would do.

Nine

ADRIFT

For nearly four years Walt Disney had waited—waited to reclaim command of the studio from the soldiers and bankers who had taken over, waited to put his beloved features back into production so that he could be a filmmaker again, waited to restore his imaginative world, waited to blaze new trails. "I am now hoping that we can get out two or three features a year now," he wrote his sister Ruth that December, "and are preparing stories for nearly five years ahead." He already had in the hopper not only *The Wind in the Willows* but *Alice in Wonderland*; *Peter*

Pan; the Mickey Mouse feature; a new set of Mickey Mouse shorts based on the stories of Horatio Alger; the Sinclair Lewis story "Bongo"; a biography of Hans Christian Andersen with animated sequences that he had been discussing as a joint production with producer Samuel Goldwyn throughout the war; Andersen's story "The Emperor and the Nightingale"; a package of musical shorts; an Irish fairy story titled "The Little People"; Sterling North's best-selling children's novel *Midnight and Jeremiah*; an adaptation of *Don Quixote*; a series on American folk heroes; the Uncle Remus film that he had been preparing since 1940; and at least a half-dozen other projects he had acquired before the war in the glow of *Snow White*'s success. At the same time he told columnist Hedda Hopper that he planned to increase shorts production and, with his war experience, move into educational and industrial films, if only, he admitted, to keep his staff active. He was even investigating a Disney radio program again.

The war had boosted audiences and generated profits for the film business generally, if not for Walt, and though Walt believed that once the war was over the "motion picture business was gonna be really hit in the jaw," he was nevertheless practically manic at the prospect of making real movies again.* "I think we have a great future ahead of us," he wrote Lee Blair, who had worked at the studio with his wife, Mary, before Blair joined the service, "and we have some marvelous plans with some good stuff in work that will be out during the coming year. . . . [T]here's no doubt in my mind that when better cartoons are made, you know where they'll be made!" To another correspondent he said that he was devoting his facilities "100% toward building up our inventory so we can get the company on a profit basis," adding, "with the old profits rolling in, you're in a position to experiment and do the thing you want."

After the four years just past, doing what he had been doing before the war wasn't enough. If only to demonstrate that he was not passé, Walt wanted, *needed*, to do something new, something different, something unusual. Sometime early in 1944, he had seen a book of surrealist paintings by the Spanish-born artist Salvador Dali lying on animator Marc Davis's desk, and he asked Davis if he could take it home. That February Walt wrote Dali requesting an autograph on a copy of his own and sug-

*After a record year in 1946 the motion picture industry would be hit on the jaw by the final disposition of an antitrust suit that the government had brought against the major studios. A consent decree agreed to in 1946 would result in the divorcement of exhibition from production and distribution and the eventual dismantling of the old studio system. Disney, which owned no theaters and no distribution arm, was not directly affected, but the entire industry suffered.

gesting a collaboration. It was an incongruous combination—the plain-spoken, down-to-earth midwesterner and the eccentric Dali—and Walt's brush mustache versus Dali's thin, lacquered, loopy one was a visual representation of that incongruity. But Dali, who happened to be in southern California at the time of Walt's note, responded enthusiastically, calling a possible joint venture "unique, of 'the never seen'!" They didn't meet until June, when Dali visited the studio and lunched with Walt, and they didn't close a deal until November, but by this time they had been meeting and corresponding frequently. Dali said he was finishing a synopsis of a short based on a Mexican folksong that Walt had had scored called "Destino," about how destiny shapes the lives of two lovers and expressing "NEW FRESH POSSIBILITIES OF VISUALIZATION." "We await with great hope the new world that will be born from our collaboration," Dali wired Walt that December.

So did Walt Disney. The criticisms of *Bambi* had especially hurt. Though he had sought realism from the first as the best means of creating an alternative universe, he knew that even if he could continue the march toward realism (which he couldn't), he was now increasingly regarded by intellectuals as an aesthetic troglodyte and that he had lost the cachet he had once enjoyed as a folk artist. "The thing I resent most is people who try to keep me in well-worn grooves," he said to a reporter after embarking on his partnership with Dali. "We have to keep breaking new trails," citing *Fantasia* as an example of a pathbreaking film that was "panned" at its release but that had continued to build an audience. And he said that he kept a slogan pasted inside his porkpie hat from the time he had been urged to make a sequel to *Three Little Pigs*: "You can't top pigs with pigs!"

Aesthetically speaking, he saw himself as a new Walt Disney—a rehabilitated Walt Disney. Always remarkably attuned, as critic Barbara Deming had said, to shifts in the public temper, even when the public didn't respond, he was now less interested in simply replicating an external reality than in plumbing an internal, psychological reality, as Dali had and as some American artists, in a postwar soul-searching, were doing, and he was interested in incorporating more fine art and fewer commercial elements of design into the animations. (As for his interest in fine art, in 1943 Walt had been named a trustee of the Museum of Modern Art in New York.) It wasn't only Dali whom he was enlisting in trying to stretch the bounds of animation by bringing a new, more subjective sensibility to the medium; he had recruited the executive director of the Los Angeles County Museum of Art to search the country for fine artists who might also want to collaborate with the Disney studio, and he had already met with the painter Thomas Hart Benton about a project.

Dali settled into the studio that winter, and he and Walt spent much of the early months of 1946 working on *Destino* before Dali departed for Del Monte, where he continued to meet with one of Walt's layout artists, John Hench. The Disney-Dali collaboration, like the Disney-Stokowski teaming, was a happy one. "The night of our meeting I spent almost entirely without sleep," Dali wrote Walt after one session, referencing the ideas churning in his head. Walt, in turn, said that where animation ideas usually came slowly and grudgingly, they seemed to pour out of Dali—"in fact, they spilled over into all directions such as machines, furniture, jewelry . . . even an extraordinary device to indicate when a painting was finished." After Dali and Hench had devised Daliesque storyboards in which the god Jupiter morphed into a sundial and a sundial into a hand covered by ants and the ants into bicycle riders, while the heroine appeared as the shadow of a bell, which morphed into a real girl and then into a dandelion puff, and the whole thing concluded with a baseball game transforming itself into a ballet, Dali's wife Gala gushed, "[I]t will become one of the most brilliant moments of his artistic career." But Walt, who just months before had been constantly pushing for speed and economy, advised Dali not to rush: "We are not going to let the pressure of time stop us from getting something that will be worthy of Dali's talents."

This fresh approach was typical of Walt's new orientation in the months after the war. Now that the troops had departed and the gloom seemed to be lifting, the restraints were off, and he thought he could undo what the war had done. He could be great again. But there were problems and they surfaced quickly. For one thing, Roy wasn't inclined to let Walt pursue his ambitious plans. Despite the economies that the studio had adopted as a result of the war and despite the infusion of cash from the debentures, despite even the fact that the largest of the outside stockholders, industrialist Floyd B. Odlum, the president of the Atlas Corporation, was encouraging the studio to resume feature production, Roy didn't feel the studio had sufficient resources to return to its old production schedule now that the government work had dried up. It wasn't that he wanted to assert power over Walt or to avenge Walt's peremptory treatment of him; he always saw his role as one of compliance and facilitation. It was rather that he felt he had to save Walt from Walt's own excesses. As he later explained it, "After the war was over, we were like a bear coming out of hibernation. We were skinny and gaunt and we had no fat on our bones at all, and I remember the years '47, '48 and '49 were lost years for us." Walt Disney, however, didn't have time for any more lost years. In his estimation, he had already lost four years.

Of course, despite his personal warmth, Roy had usually been the doomsayer and disciplinarian—in one animator's words, "the typical, tightfisted, Machiavellian businessman." He would even occasionally visit the animators when Walt was away and urge them to hold down costs. And Walt had always been resistant to these incursions, literally ordering Roy back to his office whenever he trespassed on the creative side. But this was not one of their ordinary disagreements. Walt called the argument "quite a screamer" and "one of my big upsets." Roy was confused, Walt later concluded, and exhausted. Among other things, he'd been debilitated by arthritis and, feeling generally out of sorts, had checked into the hospital to have his appendix removed. He lacked energy and focus. "It seemed like quite a chore to get the ball rolling," Walt observed, but he insisted to his brother that the studio couldn't coast. "If you do," Walt yelled, "you go backwards. I said it's just a slow way of liquidating," and he demanded that they do anything to, in his words, "get some action."

But Roy's concerns were legitimate—and not the least of them was his brother. One of the chief reasons he resisted Walt's pleas and emphasized fiscal accountability was Walt's own management style, which was capricious, idiosyncratic, extravagant, and hopelessly inefficient but that Walt had justified on the basis that creativity, not efficiency, was what counted. Employees had always complained that Walt seldom provided clear guidelines and had no real chain of command. "Walt had a way of telling one person to go ahead and get what was needed, to do whatever was necessary to complete the job without telling any of the other people who would be involved in such a project," animators Frank Thomas and Ollie Johnston would write. That led to supervisors "trying to solve new, unheard-of problems, run their departments efficiently, and still give Walt what he wanted." Others said it was always difficult to distinguish between the times when Walt was, in Wilfred Jackson's term, "just talking" to test ideas and the times when he "really meant what he was saying," though Walt expected one to know the difference and act upon it. One executive said that he could "suddenly shift course without notifying the appropriate able-bodied seamen, then lash them to the mast when they pursued the original plan as charted." Marc Davis believed that however much Walt talked about the studio as a family, he "did not like people being too close together," and he was constantly breaking up teams of animators or storymen in the belief, Davis surmised, that "if two guys liked one another too much they just sat there and got fat," though it also had the effect of disrupting continuity. Dick Huemer accused Walt of being an awful judge of people—a charge that Walt had once leveled against himself—and said he had a "habit of taking any given individual and putting him into an arbitrary job, giving him a title and expecting him to do the job," which frequently he could not do.

But the biggest complaint against Walt was that he had an aversion to organization—organization that was absolutely necessary now that the studio had grown and bureaucratic discipline had to be imposed. No matter how many times he asked one of his subordinates to devise an organizational chart, no matter how many times he attempted to delegate authority—usually preceded by his announcing, "We are all disorganized here. We don't know what we're doing"—he wound up either absenting himself entirely and letting issues be resolved by default only to return at the end of the process and overrule what others had decided, or more likely, micromanaging every detail to the point where, according to one soundman, Walt even knew the entire inventory of studio equipment, including the number of lightbulbs in stock. As executive Harry Tytle put it, "The most prevalent complaint I recorded about Walt by his producers, writers, directors, and management is that he would not delegate creative authority." In Walt's own words, "A studio cannot be run by a committee. Somebody has to make the final decision," though in another sign of his irresolution he also wrote an employee after describing a new studio routine, "I am convinced that there is a greater feeling of security in such an organization rather than allow one person to make all the decisions."

As much as Walt hated bureaucracy and corporate boxes and as much as he saw them as jeopardizing his power, he permitted the studio to hire Edward DeBord, an efficiency expert, to provide a reorganization plan in 1941, after the strike. Like all the others, this plan was never implemented, but with overhead as a percentage of studio costs having risen from 18 percent in 1942 to 30 percent in 1944, DeBord, presumably at Roy's and the bankers' behest, returned to the studio in the waning months of the war to suggest how the Disneys could control costs and increase productivity. Most of DeBord's recommendations were efficiency boilerplate: determine a practical cost for every foot of film in the studio, then set strict budgets for the shorts and features and stick to them; offer incentive bonuses to employees whose films come in under budget; and streamline the personnel department and install a central casting department to coordinate assignments of talent and prevent downtime. But one recommendation was far more problematic for Walt: DeBord suggested the appointment of a general manager to coordinate the studio's operations.

Walt agreed, albeit reluctantly—he had never wanted anyone at the studio to do anything but execute his orders. He knew how much the studio depended upon him, and he realized how much the burdens on him were about to increase with a revitalized operation. He also recognized how badly the studio needed a new jolt of energy after the numbing routine of the war. Walt and his staff spent the better part of 1945 reviewing candidates before settling on a forty-two-year-old Dartmouth-educated New York advertising executive named Jack Reeder, who had come recommended by Vern Caldwell. Reeder joined the studio that August as the new vice president and general manager, the first the company had ever had, at a salary of $30,000. He was followed the next month by a new production and studio manager named Fred Leahy, who had worked at Paramount for fifteen years before rising to production control manager and then moving to MGM.

Other things changed as well. That December, Walt Disney, who had always ignored any kind of organization plan, announced a new one for the studio on the basis that he was so busy now, he was forced to delegate authority. Henceforth a management committee with Reeder as chairman would make business decisions. On the creative side there was to be a tight chain of command leading from Harry Tytle (who was to supervise shorts production), Walt Pfahler (who was to manage production services), Jack Lavin (who was to negotiate talent contracts), and Chuck Wolcott (who was to serve as musical director), up to Fred Leahy and from Leahy to Walt himself. Meanwhile Walt said he would be resigning as the president of Walt Disney Productions, his nominal title, to become chairman of the board, while Roy assumed the presidency and Reeder assumed Roy's duties. Walt even announced that a new organizational chart was being drawn up for distribution throughout the company.

This announcement sparked what amounted to a reorganization fever over the next eighteen months, which Walt seemed to have legitimized because he believed that the studio was beginning to rev up again. In addition to establishing the management committee and reassigning the staff, he installed Ub Iwerks as head of a department called Special Processes and Camera to develop new effects, and he later created a new Animation Board, composed of top animators personally selected by Walt, that was entrusted with helping advise Walt on other animators and devise policy on the forthcoming animations. (Of course, for those not selected, this board was yet another source of resentment and another blow to morale.) It had nine members: Les Clark, Marc Davis, Ollie Johnston, Milt Kahl, Ward Kimball, Eric Larson, John Lounsbery, Woolie Reitherman, and Frank Thomas, the latter two of whom had recently returned to the studio from military service. In a joking aside Walt once dubbed the members of the Animation Board his "nine old men," after President Franklin Roosevelt's reference to the nine members of the Supreme Court. The group would be known as the "Nine Old Men" thereafter.

But having set up what seemed to be a formalized bureaucratic structure, Walt was clearly ambivalent about it. He didn't want to surrender his own prerogatives. Harry Tytle claimed that neither Walt nor Roy had done the paperwork for Reeder's appointment, even as their new general manager was about to report to the studio, and that Walt initially wasn't going to issue a memo announcing Leahy's hiring, preferring to wait until Leahy had arrived and Walt had discussed his duties with him before telling anyone. And even as he held those discussions, Walt openly fretted that Leahy, while at Paramount and MGM, had been "just another rubber stamp," signing off on whatever producers had wanted, and he began to doubt as well whether Jack Reeder could adjust from the culture of an advertising firm to the very different culture of a motion picture studio, especially the Disney studio. As for the new management committee, Walt never attended a single meeting, believing that its role was to handle routine matters only, not general policy, which was his and Roy's domain. In fact, Roy stopped attending meetings too.*

The lines of communication and command, always so tangled, were no straighter under the reorganization plan. Walt had first told executives Harry Tytle and Hal Adelquist that the hiring of Leahy would have no effect on them; then that they were to report to Leahy on management matters but to Walt on all creative matters; then that they were to report to Leahy exclusively. But no sooner had Reeder and Leahy tried to exercise their authority than strains developed between Walt and his new management team. When Walt demanded that some of the secondary management sit in on deliberations about salaries, because he wanted to resist pressures to limit salaries or institute waiting periods for raises, they quarreled, and when the committee declared itself too busy to discuss individual merit raises, they also quarreled. They quarreled again in April when the committee, enforcing the new push for increased productivity, tried laying out terms of production. Walt exploded at what he considered an arrogation of power. He said that *he* was in charge of production and no one else—even though Reeder and Leahy had been hired to help shepherd production—and according to one attendee, he stated and restated this "not once but six or seven times." He also insisted that he and Roy were running the company, "the Board of Directors notwithstanding," and that if he wasn't permitted to control production, he was going to quit. "Life is too short," he told them.

*Walt seldom attended board of directors meetings either, despite Roy's prodding. Outside directors, Roy wrote Walt in January 1946, "have shown evidence of being disinterested and of feeling they were not being treated right when you, as chief spark plug and production head, did not attend." Memo, Roy to Walt, Re: Confidential, Jan. 31, 1946, Walt Disney 1941–1954 Folder, Roy O. Disney, Inter-Office Corr., Disney, Roy O.—trips to Disneyland (1954–1961), A3002, WDA.

But Reeder and Leahy still didn't seem to get the message that this was Walt Disney's studio, not theirs. That August, Reeder prepared a report for Walt on the state of the studio. (In the past Walt wouldn't have needed a report; he would have known.) Reeder, citing the urgent need to cut costs and boost productivity yet again and facing a new negotiation with the Screen Cartoonists Guild, suggested another round of layoffs and submitted another reorganization plan, apparently at Walt's recommendation. Under the new plan, Leahy would be promoted to Reeder's position and placed on the board of directors. They would need a "top administrative post to be filled by a man in whom both you and Roy have complete confidence"; the appointee was to have responsibility for all departments in the studio. "He must be welcomed *everywhere* in the Studio," Reeder wrote, "not as a front office man or as a production man or as a selling man but as the co-ordinator who is doing his best to make the organization click as a whole." Reeder didn't have to say that he saw himself in this role. There was only one problem. At the Walt Disney Studio, Walt Disney was the one who coordinated all the departments and made sure the organization clicked. That had always been his primary responsibility.

Walt didn't fire his new managers, but they were soon dangling, just as all of Walt's managers had dangled, not knowing exactly where their authority left off and Walt's began. Tytle thought that Walt realized he needed someone in Reeder's position to do the logistical work while Walt did the creative work—"in the mechanical, though not the spiritual," as Tytle put it—but "it was almost impossible to let someone else call the shots, no matter how mundane," which was why Walt kept undermining them. At the same time, with the new team constantly promoting new measures for greater productivity and barking at underlings—Reeder even closed the friendly poker games at the Penthouse Club—the reorganization resulted less in streamlining and energizing the studio, as Walt had intended, than in further enervating it. As one employee remembered, "The new people were interposed between Walt and Roy and the staff, and as the spring and summer wore on, the atmosphere became even grimmer."

If the studio atmosphere was grimmer, the high spirits upon which Walt had briefly soared at war's end had been dampened too, as he began to realize how difficult it would be for the studio to return to its former glory. He was ready once again to dispense with the ever-imperiled shorts when the studio finished those it was contractually obligated to provide over the next two years, until the new management team imposed draconian efficiencies that brought down the price, but even then Walt said that the studio couldn't maintain quality, and he lost interest. (*Destino* would be among the casualties.) The studio produced fewer Mickey Mouse cartoons, only two during the war, now that Mickey had been practically sanitized out of existence, and Walt absolutely hated the Goofy cartoons, threatening constantly to terminate them before relenting, largely to provide work for his animators—yet another example of Walt's vacillation under the new financial exigencies. The only surviving star was the sputtering, hot-tempered Donald Duck, and even he needed to be revitalized, as he was when he was given two new foils, a pair of pesky chipmunks named Chip and Dale, who had first appeared in a 1943 Pluto cartoon.

The decline in the quality of the shorts, however, was only symptomatic of a general decline in the quality of animation at the studio after the war had enforced its limits. With no features on which to apply the old animation techniques, the animators' skills had withered. "[G]radually people forgot how things had been done," Frank Thomas and Ollie Johnston would later write. Even Walt's precious, once-innovative equipment, they said, "was all rusting on the back lot, and newcomers walking around the lot at noon wondered why anyone would keep junk like that around." Eventually, it was scrapped in favor of newer machinery.

What was worse, the old *animators* had withered too. Between June 1945 and July 1946 fifty-three of them left the company for various reasons, and the studio continued the process, as one memo put it, "of weeding out marginal talent" and even a "higher standard of people should production reasons require this decision." Several of the casualties had once been stars of the studio. Fred Moore had been the "Chopin" of animators, according to his onetime assistant, Frank Thomas. He could pour his "pure emotions" onto the paper, and everyone admired the appealing style of his drawings, which had been the standard for the Disney style. In the right mood he would cheerfully draw picture after picture, humming while he worked at his board. But Thomas also noted that Moore was wracked by "dissatisfaction" and "torment." Ward Kimball said the boyish Moore, who was only thirty-four at war's end, felt that his star was falling, and he would grouse endlessly about how the studio was "giving him a bad deal." Always a heavy drinker, his growing discontent led to even longer binges, so much so that Kimball, his assistant, frequently had to finish his drawings.

If Moore thought he was losing favor, he wasn't wrong. The new, more modern minimalist and seemingly more artistic aesthetic that Walt was pursuing with Dali and that he was encouraging as a way of keeping pace with a change in visual tastes and of regaining his own favor with critics was a long distance from Moore's aesthetic. The younger, more academically trained animators like Frank Thomas (whom Walt personally welcomed at the studio gate when he returned from service on April 1, 1946), and Woolie Reitherman (whom Walt cornered for hours and convinced to return when Reitherman visited the studio after his service to pick up some belongings) were now the fair-haired boys because they wielded their pencils more nimbly and they were more au courant. Within this new aesthetic where line and technique mattered more than emotion, Moore's work began, Kimball said, "to look crude." Whatever it possessed in charm, it lacked in subtlety—or at least that was what the self-proclaimed progressive animators, who had a stake in Moore's demise, seemed to think. Moore and Norm Ferguson, who had been a star even before Moore, "had not followed what the studio had progressed in," Eric Larson recalled—a situation that Larson described as "tragic." Ben Sharpsteen concurred, saying that they "lacked the ability to analyze animation and to grasp the finesse it required," and Sharpsteen believed that Moore and Ferguson realized that they were falling behind, which was why they were both miserable. Though Ferguson hung on, despite Walt's increasing dissatisfaction with his work, Moore, hopelessly lost in drink, was fired in August 1946. He had become, in Walt's term, deadwood.

Moore wasn't the only one who was losing his way in the postwar period. So was Walt Disney. As his plans met resistance that spring and as the studio faced yet another financial crisis, he had become "psychologically fragile," in Frank Thomas's estimation. He had begun to lose his footing and his confidence, and with Roy pressuring him to slash budgets and even to begin another round of layoffs, he had come to a terrible, almost crippling realization, one that seemed to sear him: even if he were to move ahead with his features, they would never be as good as the films he had made before the war—never as beautifully animated, never as deliberately plotted, never as painstakingly fussed over, never as fully the product of a near-religious commitment to greatness. The studio simply did not have the financial resources, the time, the talent, or perhaps most important of all, the sense of spiritual mission that it had previously had. The cult was over. It was even questionable whether the new, leaner, less realistic aesthetic lent itself to the sort of full-bodied dramatic greatness of the early features. And if the films could never be as good as they had been, was there really any point in making them—other than to keep the studio intact and running, just as Walt had been compelled to do during the war? He understood that where he had been an unpretentious artist before the war, then a salesman and goodwill ambassador during it, he was becoming an employer after it, which was why he began to talk now about selling the studio or leaving it. "We're through with caviar," he reluctantly conceded. "From now on it's mashed potatoes and gravy."

It was bleak. Nineteen hundred and forty-six may have been the unhappiest of a skein of unhappy years at the studio, especially because the motion picture industry, thanks to returning troops and peacetime, was enjoying its best year ever. "Walt was a bear in those worrisome times," animator and storyman Bill Peet would write, "always in a growling mood and hard to deal with." And when he wasn't growling, he was sighing—"prodigious" sighs, according to one employee. He was so uncertain that he increasingly surrendered his own judgment to the judgment of the Audience Research Institute (ARI), which now conducted audience surveys not only of completed movies or their rough animations, as Walt had done under his own auspices to test his own instincts in the mid-1930s, but of the story sessions themselves, so that even before a film proceeded to animation, it had to score with two focus groups—one made up of people recruited off the streets, the other of the creative personnel at the studio. (Walt made it a point never to preview with children because he always insisted that his films were not made for children.) Walt attended nearly all of these sessions, mostly held in the projection room down the hall from his office, and some films were subjected to as many as twenty separate evaluations. Walt, whose taste had once been the only gauge that mattered at the studio, invariably bowed to the audience. Indeed, as far as the shorts were concerned, he had decided that the ARI would be the sole determinant of quality.

While he waited on the features, hoping to advance them, he compromised once again. During the war, when Walt had despaired of making another feature, he had begun planning a series of musical shorts—mainly remnants from the proposed *Fantasia* sequel—that he was hoping to package in a forty-minute featurette, just to keep his animators limber and just to keep his own hand in real animation. "I had a strong conviction," Walt would say, "that we needed to change our direction. The cartoon field was flexible enough. It forced me to make either a cartoon short seven or eight minutes long or a feature cartoon seventy to eighty minutes long. And I had a lot of ideas I thought would be good if I could fit them in between those two extremes." But this was another of Walt's rationalizations. The truth was that the shorts weren't profitable, and he couldn't make a feature. The best he could do was sew together these remainders, now ten of them, swelling the film to feature length. The segments included "Blue Bayou," which was a reworking of the animation for "Clair de Lune" that he had cut from *Fantasia*; "Peter and the Wolf," which Sergei Prokofiev had composed for Disney years earlier; "All the Cats Join In," with jazz clarinetist Benny Goodman, which Walt had had in preparation since 1940; "Casey at the Bat," narrated by comedian Jerry Colonna; and "The

Whale Who Wanted to Sing at the Met" featuring the voice of opera star Nelson Eddy. The total cost was set at a modest $395,000, though even then one executive wrote Walt that he should meet with the creative team to set the direction "in order to complete the PACKAGE as economically as possible."

Walt didn't fool himself about the quality of the film, which at Perce Pearce's suggestion had been retitled *Make Mine Music* after being called *Swing Street.* The characters were far more stylized than the typical Disney figures, and Marc Davis felt that Walt "didn't feel warmly towards those." In addition, the lovely but prohibitively expensive blending that had provided a chiaroscuro effect in the early features was gone, and so was the round, soft tactile quality that had made those earlier images seem so warm and cute. In their place were a sharper line and a brighter, harder surface. And if Walt didn't care for these new compilation packages, the animators didn't care much for them either. "[W]e at the studio there kind of laughingly joked about them as Walt's remnant sale!" Ben Sharpsteen recalled. The critics were no kinder. Even Bosley Crowther of *The New York Times* felt disappointment, calling the film an "experience in precipitate ups and downs" and scolding Disney for "adjusting his art to what he considers the lower taste of the mass audience" by using bathetic popular music in the film rather than the classical pieces of *Fantasia.* Writing in *The Nation,* James Agee, no fan of Disney now, thought it "tacky" and said the film "sickens" him, though probably not as much as it must have sickened Walt.

Nevertheless, given its cost, *Make Mine Music* did reasonably well at the box office, which encouraged the studio to produce more compilation films, though Walt's sudden enthusiasm for bundling new shorts and repackaging old ones was also an indication of the studio's creative bankruptcy. Another "remnant sale," *Fun and Fancy Free* was already in production at the time when *Make Mine Music* was released in the early spring of 1946. It incorporated two stories, one about Bongo, a circus bear who finds himself back in the wild where he has to use his wiles, introduced by Jiminy Cricket, and *Mickey and the Beanstalk,* narrated by ventriloquist Edgar Bergen, one of the very few people with whom Walt socialized. Both stories had been kicking around the studio for years—*Mickey and the Beanstalk* since at least 1940, when Walt was vainly searching for ways to revive his mouse by starring him in a series of fairy tales. At the time Bill Cottrell and another storyman with the improbable name of T. Hee (actually Thornton Hee) had presented the story to Walt and, as Hee later told it, Walt "burst out laughing, tears running down the side of his face," and called in others to hear the presentation. But when Cottrell and Hee asked how soon it would be put into production, Walt said it wouldn't. As much as he liked it, Walt told them that "you murdered my characters" and "destroyed what I've been working years to build up." The audience had certain expectations of Mickey Mouse, and this wasn't what they expected.

The film had, in any case, been suspended by the strike and the war, but even before the war the studio was in such desperate need of cheap and simple material—Walt wanted the film to be made with the shorts crews and with the efficiencies of the shorts—that he had overcome his misgivings about Mickey as Jack. It was yet another example of how much Mickey had ceased to *be* Mickey—of how much he had been deracinated over the years until he was essentially just another actor. Another example of Mickey's demise was Walt himself. Almost from the beginning Walt had been Mickey's voice, even through a throat operation and a tonsillectomy back in the early 1930s—a sign of his devotion to his creation. But during the production of *Mickey and the Beanstalk* a sound effects man named Jimmy Macdonald, who had worked at the studio since 1935, got a call to come to Walt's office. As Macdonald told it, Walt said that the animators were pressuring him for Mickey's dialogue, and he just didn't have the time. (Macdonald also suspected that Walt was getting too hoarse to voice the falsetto Mickey, possibly from his chain-smoking filterless Camels.) He asked if Macdonald might give it a try. Macdonald, a beefy, blunt-featured man for whom Mickey's high-pitched voice was incongruous, recorded a track, Walt another for comparison. Walt listened and approved, and as Macdonald later recounted, "right then we switched over to using my voice for Mickey, right in the middle of *Mickey and the Beanstalk*." Macdonald would provide Mickey's voice for the next thirty-eight years, but the casualness with which the transition was effected was telling. It testified to Walt's growing estrangement from Mickey and perhaps from the animations generally.

With these movies, Walt's artistic reputation among critics and intellectuals, long sinking, reached its nadir. Most found the films coarse, overly commercial, and utterly charmless. (One exception was Sergei Eisenstein, who thought *Make Mine Music* "absolutely ingenious" and was especially struck by the "Willie the Whale" section, which he compared to *Moby Dick* and Edgar Allan Poe's *The Pit and the Pendulum*.) The deeply felt if occasionally overwrought emotion of the early features had given way to what many critics regarded as cheap sentimentality and kitsch in *Make Mine Music* and *Fun and Fancy Free*, as if the films had been created by committee for money, which they were. The critic Richard Schickel believed that it was when Disney began disavowing claims to art and emphasizing his common man persona after the war that the intellectuals

The Disney family at the fiftieth wedding anniversary of his parents, Elias and Flora, in January 1938. At the rear, left to right, Ray and Roy, in front Herbert, Flora, Elias, and Walt. As a present the brothers bought their parents a home in the Silver Lake section of Los Angeles, not far from the studio.

Walt and his beloved mother. Her death shattered him, no doubt because he felt partly responsible.

Gunther Lessing, the studio's longtime legal counsel and the individual who encouraged Walt and Roy to hold the line against the strikers—a decision that destroyed the studio's spirit. The strikers burned Lessing in effigy.

The man Walt held chiefly responsible for the end of his workers' utopia: animator Art Babbitt *(center)*, flanked by Fred Moore (*left*) and assistant Tom Codrick (*right*).

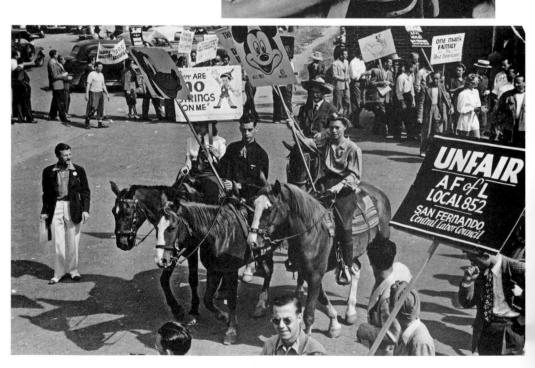

Paradise lost: strikers outside the Disney studio gates in 1941. Walt refused to recognize the Screen Cartoonists Guild as his employees' representative. Art Babbitt is in the white slacks at the left.

Abandoning the chaos: Walt in Argentina during his South American goodwill tour in 1941 financed by the coordinator for inter-American affairs, Nelson Rockefeller. Walt entertained his hosts, even standing on his head. He returned to make two features on Latin America, *Saludos Amigos* and *The Three Cabelleros*.

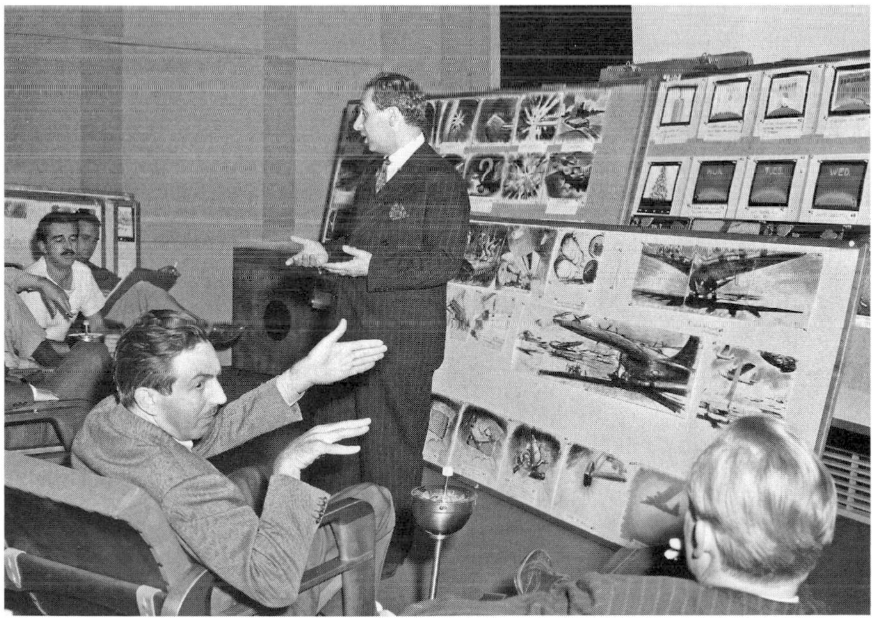

Walt with Major Alexander de Seversky *(standing)*, the gadfly Russian-born air corps officer whose best-selling 1942 book, *Victory Through Air Power*, promoted the idea of long-range bombers to win the war. Walt was determined to change the course of the war himself by making a film of the book and thus popularizing the idea.

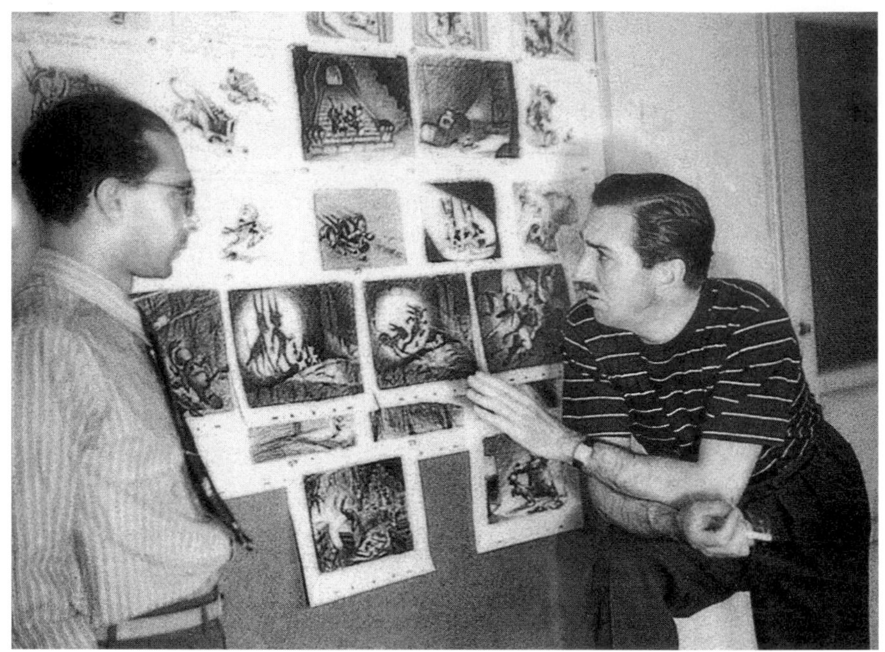

The Walt of old, reviewing *Pinocchio* storyboards with storyman Otto Englander. The war and financial problems would sap his enthusiasm.

Joining the red-baiters: Walt testifies as a "friendly" witness before the House Un-American Activities Committee on October 24, 1947 and describes how the Communists tried to strongarm him during the strike. He also carelessly implicates the League of Women Voters as a group sympathetic to Communists and later has to recant.

Walt in the late 1940s reading to his daughters, Diane *(left)* and Sharon *(right)*, whom he loved deeply and to whom he was a devoted father.

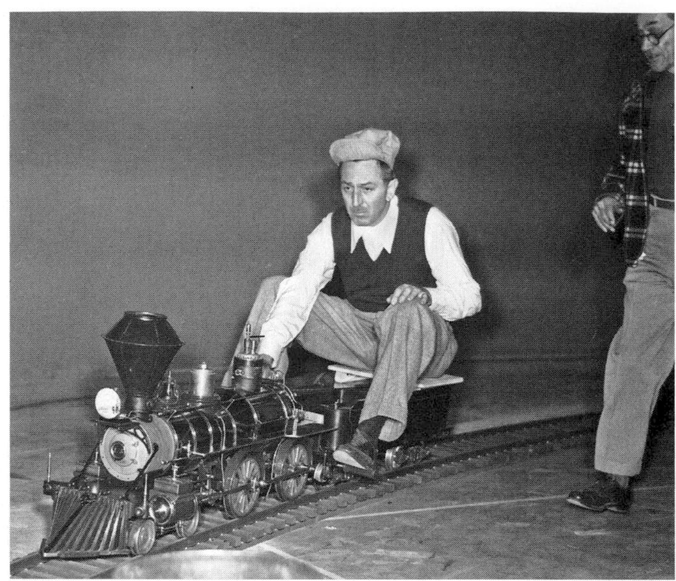

Adrift: The animations having lost their appeal, Walt turned to model trains. Here he tests his train, which he had helped manufacture, on the studio soundstage.

Walt riding the train with the locomotive Lilly Belle at his new home on Carolwood Drive in the tony section of Holmby Hills, where he moved in 1950. One of the chief attractions of the property was that it had room for his train.

Looking for new worlds to conquer: Walt directs dancer Buddy Ebsen in a dancing scene he will use to construct a small mechanical dancing man.

Walt studying a tiny ship in a bottle in front of Granny Kincaid's cabin, which he had designed for an exhibit he called Disneylandia. He intended to build a series of miniature tableaus of Americana and have them tour the country. Much of the work in crafting the small objects he did himself.

Walt with ABC Television president Robert Kintner *(far left)*, ABC executive Robert O'Brien, and Roy in 1954 at Walt's office signing the contract for the *Disneyland* television show, which would help finance the Disneyland theme park.

Walt and Disneyland supervisor C. V. Wood examining plans for the park. Wood, a fast-talking Oklahoman, would be fired when Walt thought the young man had begun to usurp Walt's authority.

began disavowing him, but the process had in fact started with *Fantasia*, when Walt's artistic aspirations had been highest. For those who thought that *Fantasia* had exposed Walt's cultural obtuseness, the compilation films only confirmed it. "Suppose you visit a friend," wrote one former admirer in the left-wing *Theatre Arts* in June 1946. "You know that he has a warm heart and is kind to animals, that his sense of humor is infectious, his professional skill beyond compare. But when you enter his house you find to your dismay that his walls are festooned with second-rate art" and "his furniture is carelessly assembled with little regard for harmony or any other concern except to fill space." This wouldn't cause you to hate the man, the critic said; it would only cause you to "admit with regret that his taste was deplorable." Walt Disney was now that man.

II

He was no longer the king of animation, only one among a group of pretenders to the throne. The intellectuals and critics who had fawned over him in the 1930s and anointed him one of America's greatest artists now preferred his competitors. For years everyone else, remarked one animator at a rival studio, was in a "pack of greyhounds chasing a mechanical rabbit." Everyone had imitated him. Mickey Mouse had spawned a host of other mice, dogs, cats, pigs, a frog, even a black boy named Bosko who resembled Mickey—all trying to claim Mickey's crown. The Silly Symphonies had spawned Warner Bros. Merrie Melodies, Harman-Ising's Happy Harmonies, Iwerks's Comicolor Classics, the Fleischers' Color Classics, and Charles Mintz's Color Rhapsodies. And even *Snow White* had spawned the Fleischer brothers' feature-length animations *Gulliver's Travels* and *Mr. Bug Goes to Town* as well as Walter Lantz's prospective *Ali Baba*, which was scotched almost as soon as it was announced because Universal did not have the money for it. For years rival animation studios had poached Disney artists, as Van Beuren had lured Burt Gillett and Pat Powers had lured Ub Iwerks, hoping to capture the Disney magic. But the result was always the same. One might imitate Disney, but one couldn't match him. As Paul Terry admitted: "Disney is the Tiffany of this business, and we're the Woolworth's."

One reason for this success was money. Disney was spending roughly $40,000 per short while Warner Bros., MGM, and Paramount were spending half that. Another reason was Disney's initial monopoly on the three-color Technicolor process that made his cartoons look so much better than anyone else's. But a much greater reason was the old disparity between the talent at the Disney studio and the talent everywhere else and, what had helped draw that talent, between the commitment at the Disney studio and the commitment everywhere else. If animation was a sacred obligation to Walt Disney, a way to reimagine the world, for the others it had always been just a product. "Making cartoons is like delivering milk" was how one of Paul Terry's animators described Terry's philosophy. "People expect the bottles at the door every morning. If you miss a morning, people get upset. I see to it that we don't miss a morning and nobody gets upset." Similarly Dick Huemer said of Charles Mintz, "He didn't care. He wasn't really interested much in the pictures. He was just a promoter, he bankrolled it." Mintz once gathered his staff, showed them a Fleischer cartoon about two romancing swans, and then ordered his animators to make a cartoon like it with no more than two characters. At all the studios save Disney the cartoons were still thrown into production. Walter Lantz at Universal didn't even have a story department, just a bulletin board on which a story idea would be pinned. Indeed, the only studio that harbored dreams of matching Disney, that of Max and Dave Fleischer, was hopelessly out of its depth when it tried, and by the early 1940s it had been forced to sell its operation to Paramount after having decamped to Florida and having borrowed heavily from that company to make its features.

But after all the Disney studio's years of unchallenged preeminence, the war created opportunities for its competitors, not only because Disney's own animation was stagnating under the press of government business but because many of the rival animators, some of them refugees from Disney, felt increasingly emboldened to attack the Disney style. As director Frank Tashlin, who left Disney for Screen Gems just before the strike, would later put it, "We showed those Disney guys that animated cartoons don't have to look like a fucking kid's book."

At MGM the head of the shorts department, Fred Quimby—a man known for his impeccably tailored double-breasted suits, his Brahmin accent, and the whiff of talc—spent his day reading the Hollywood trade papers, getting a shave at the studio barbershop, taking lunch, returning to the office for a nap, and then driving home at three o'clock—a routine that one of his animators called "as inevitable as death and taxes." But while Quimby idled, his directors used their comparative freedom to cut loose. Two of them, Joseph Barbera and William Hanna, teamed to create a warring cat and mouse who in early 1940 were named Tom and Jerry and at the end of the war were starring in a series of cartoons that veered wildly between sentimentality and ever-increasing violence of a sort that Disney wouldn't have tolerated for fear of offending his audience. (Usurping Disney, who had had a virtual lock on the Oscar in the 1930s, Hanna and Barbera won four consecutive Academy Awards for Best Animated Short, from 1943 through 1946.) Another director, Tex Avery, who had defected to MGM in 1942 after years at Warner Bros. and a brief tenure at Paramount, specialized in self-referential cartoons with a zany, unrestrained energy, the most famous of which—starting with a contemporary 1943 version of "Little Red Riding Hood" titled *Red Hot Riding Hood*—featured an oversexed wolf of the sort, again, that would have been far too suggestive for Walt Disney.

While MGM was firing its raucous fusillades, Warner Bros., an even bigger rival, took dead aim on the Disney aesthetic, not only by outgunning it but by outsmarting it. The difference between the animation departments at Disney and Warner Bros. couldn't have been greater. Where the Disney studio in Burbank was sylvan and pristine, the Warner Bros. unit on Sunset Boulevard in Hollywood was housed in an old building the animators called Termite Terrace that, according to one of its denizens, "looked and stank like the hold of a slave ship." Its unpainted pine floors were cured with motor oil, the odor of which clung to the animators, and the planks were pocked with holes that the animators had drilled to see the floor below. The flimsy walls were made of composition board, which the animators would punch their fists through and which one of them once tried to light just to see if it would burn. Even Leon Schlesinger, the head of the department, who visited weekly to deliver checks, would comment, "Pew, let me outta here! This looks like a shit house."

Befitting its office, the animations produced at Warner Bros. were equally unprepossessing. As Friz Freleng, who had worked for Disney on the Alice comedies, put it, "Walt spent more on the storyboards than we did on the films." Where Walt's extensive crews included as many as a half-dozen writers and gagmen on a short, at Warner Bros. a cartoon started with a single director, a single writer, and a single layout man. The director was assigned four animators, each of whom was assigned an assistant. There were four units in all. Animators were expected to turn out twenty-five to thirty feet of animation per week or twenty seconds of screen time, much more than at Disney, which may have added to the already antic sense.

The studio chiefs were also a study in contrasts. Schlesinger was a small, round, pompous man who, said one animator, "always smelled of Parma Violet" and "dressed like a vaudeville hoofer who had suddenly come into money." Though he tried to maintain his dignity, he spoke with a thick lisp that was later immortalized in the voice of Warner Bros. character Daffy Duck. Schlesinger never recognized the affinity, leaping to his feet and saying, "Jeethus Christh, that's a funny voice! Where'd you get that voithe?" after he saw the first Daffy short. And if his demeanor was the antithesis of Walt Disney's unaffected midwestern style, so was his attitude toward his animations. "[H]is wallet spoke" was how Frank Tashlin put it.

Even with Schlesinger's eye fixed securely on the bottom line, Warners was at first as much a Disney imitator as the other studios and just as unsuccessful at it. Then Tex Avery joined the department in 1936. As Avery later remembered it, Schlesinger told him that he had some boys—"they're not renegades but they just don't get on with the other two crews"—and he suggested that Avery work with them. Among these unsociables were two young animators named Bob Clampett and Chuck Jones. The teaming of Avery with Clampett and Jones was a signal moment in animation history. Working every night, pushing one another beyond the far reaches of acceptable Disney animation, beyond what one called the "cute stuff," they created a loose, madcap, smart-alecky style that broke the plane of realism and intentionally defied Disney's illusion of life. Looney Tunes, the rubric under which many of the Warner cartoons were produced, was a fitting name.

"The Warner Bros. animators didn't have any delusions of grandeur that they were doing something special," one of them later said. At Warners it was about having fun—about the staff making themselves laugh. "We were laughing ten, twelve, fourteen hours a day," recalled Chuck Jones. "It never occurred to us that Warners and Walt were in the same business." At Disney, even back in the days when the animators participated in juvenilia of their own, everything on the animations was carefully planned and endlessly deliberated upon in pursuit of perfection. At Warner Bros., Jones said, "directors, animators, and writers were indeed a laboratory for creative inconsistency, for unanticipated mutations, for happy accidents—a primal soup to discover the delight of the undiscovered." "We did our thing and nobody seemed to say, 'Don't do this' or 'Don't do that,' " Friz Freleng recalled. It would never even have occurred to the Warners crew to make a feature like *Snow White*, and Jones imagined that Schlesinger, if asked whether he had any feature aspirations, likely would have responded, "I need a feature cartoon like I need two assholes."

But out of this unpretentiousness and chaos came something wonderful. The Warners artists embraced the contrary and the irreverent. If they had neither the resources nor the artistic talent to make *Snow White*, they could spoof it with Bob Clampett's *Coal Black and de Sebben Dwarfs*, and if they had neither the resources nor the artistic talent to make *Fantasia*, they could puncture its pretensions with Clampett's *A Corny Concerto*, in which a bulb-headed dunce by the name of Elmer Fudd played the role of Deems Taylor while a rabbit named Bugs pranced about as a ballerina. Meanwhile Tex Avery torpedoed Disney's sentimentality in *The Peachy Cobbler*, and Frank Tashlin attacked Disney's realism with self-reflexive shorts in which the characters kept addressing the audience and acknowledged that they were in a cartoon. These were clever, snappily paced animations full of cruelty, violence, and antisocial behavior, animations in which characters were dim-witted like Fudd, who took the obliviousness of Goofy to another level, or unmanageably wacky like Daffy Duck, who was a manic version of Donald Duck, or so overwhelmingly ineffectual like Porky Pig that he parodied the anodyne Mickey Mouse, or wickedly smart like Bugs Bunny with his trademark "What's up, Doc?" who had been designed by Disney expatriate Charles Thorson after a rabbit in *The Tortoise and the Hare* but who had a mean streak and a quick mind that no Disney character had ever had.* And while Disney's animations by design seemed to be the product of some invisible force, which was, after all, the point of realism, in the Warner Bros. cartoons the directors' sensibility was nakedly evident, manipulating the action and spinning the gags. In effect, it was the return of the old animator's hand that Walt Disney had banished long ago, only now it was the animator's mind one saw at work.

Watching these cartoons with their wordplay and puns, their wisecracking or tongue-tied characters, their adult acceptance of lust, their occasional Pirandellian twists, their satirical digs, their vicious wit, and their lunatic frenzy, the Disney animators were the envious ones. Speaking of their competitors, Jack Kinney admitted that "many of us wished we had the freedom they had" and applauded their "funny pictures—uninhibited, fresh, not worked over too much, as happened sometimes at Disney's at that time." Dick Huemer cracked, "It was like admiring the kind of dame that you couldn't introduce to your mother." Disney storyman Leo Salkin was more precise, saying how he and fellow staff member Milt Schaffer were "jealous of how funny the Warner Brothers cartoons were just before the war. We thought: 'All this personality stuff isn't really funny. It's cute and people kind of chuckle at it, but Warners cartoons get *laughs*.' " In a reversal of the typical artistic flow, Disney did try appropri-

*This was an evolution. Bugs began life in 1940 as a rather dumpy madcap who frolicked wildly around the screen and evolved into a sleeker, brainier character—or, as animation historian Charles Solomon described the transformation, "Bugs started out in a sort of Harpo Marx mode, then moved through Groucho Marx." Solomon, *Enchanted Drawings*, p. 155.

ating some of the Warners spirit in cartoons like *Saludos Amigos* and *The Three Caballeros,* where Donald Duck sometimes seemed to have been possessed by Daffy, and in doing so Disney did advance the cause of surrealistic animation, but it meant trying to deconstruct what the studio had spent more than a decade carefully constructing, and they hadn't the skill or the heart for it. Disney cartoons had many virtues. *Saludos Amigos* and *The Three Caballeros* notwithstanding, riotous energy was not one of them.

But it was riotous energy, not control, that most audiences as well as most critics now appreciated and applauded—riotous energy that captured the liberating force of a war that had, in the words of historian David M. Kennedy, "shaken the American people loose and shaken them up," and it was riotous energy that made the more sedate Disney animations seem dull and anachronistic.

III

Walt Disney would not rest on the animations because he *could* not rest on them anymore. He needed something less costly, something new to restore the studio as well as his sense of self. Cartoons had become, Woolie Reitherman said, a "pain in the ass to Walt: the personnel problems, waiting around for animation to come in, changes, and all those things. I don't know of any features that sailed through." Reitherman might have added that the real reason for Walt's dismay was that cartoons had become too expensive to do as well as Walt Disney had done them. But there was a way around these obstacles, and Walt had already been considering it long before the war, during the first economic pinch. He could reduce the amount of animation needed in a feature by combining the animation with live action, which was much cheaper and much faster to produce. He had thought of *Alice in Wonderland* as a prime possibility, with Alice as a real girl and Wonderland in animation—like the old Alice comedies he had made in the 1920s. But as the studio struggled with an *Alice* script, Walt seized on a new candidate: the Uncle Remus stories of Joel Chandler Harris. Walt would animate the tales themselves, but to accommodate the live action he would frame them in a melodrama about a bullied and neglected white boy who seeks solace in the wise Uncle Remus. Thus Walt would literally create two distinct worlds—a "real" one and a fanciful one. It was for Walt Disney, said animator Marc Davis, "a way to get into live action, and have his cartoon too."

At least since 1939, when he first began negotiating with the Harris family for the rights, Walt had been considering these stories, told in black dialect by a retainer in the Reconstruction era, for an animated feature, and by late summer of that year he had already had one of his storymen synopsize the more promising tales and draw up four boards' worth of story sketches. A year later, in November, while on his way to the *Fantasia* premiere in New York, Walt had stopped in Atlanta to visit the Harris home, to meet the Harris family, and as he told *Variety*, "to get an authentic feeling of Uncle Remus country so we can do as faithful a job as possible to these stories." Roy had misgivings about the project, doubting that it was "big enough in caliber and natural draft" to warrant a budget over $1 million and more than twenty-five minutes of animation, but in June 1944, even before the war ended, Walt hired a southern-born writer named Dalton Reymond to write the screenplay, and he met frequently that summer with Reymond, his own staff, and director King Vidor, whom he was trying to interest in making the live-action sequences. It may have been the only time during the war after he had finished *Victory Through Air Power* that Walt seemed thoroughly engaged. Writer Maurice Rapf, whom Walt had hired to assist Reymond, called Walt "insatiable." "He ended every conference by saying, 'Well, I think we've really licked it now,' " Rapf would recall. "Then he'd call you the next morning and say, 'I've got a new idea.' And he'd have one. Sometimes the ideas were good, sometimes they were terrible, but you could never really satisfy him." Rapf didn't know it, but this was the Walt Disney of old.

As Reymond and Rapf finished the screenplay late that summer and the studio announced the project, a problem arose: members of the black community protested that any film version of the Uncle Remus stories was bound to portray black Americans in a servile and negative way. A "vicious piece of hocus pocus," one group called it. Walt Disney was no racist. He never, either publicly or privately, made disparaging remarks about blacks or asserted white superiority. Like most white Americans of his generation, however, he was racially insensitive. At a story meeting he had referred to the dwarfs piling on top of one another in *Snow White* as a "nigger pile," and in casting *Song of the South* he noted a "swell little picaninny [*sic*]" he had found. Like most Hollywood producers, he had also engaged in racial stereotyping, from a blackbird in the short *Who Killed Cock Robin?* who speaks in a thick drawl and blanches white when frightened, to the hipster crows in *Dumbo*, though the case has been made that the crows were sympathetic to Dumbo precisely because they understood what it was like to be ostracized themselves. Worse, in the "Pastorale" sequence of *Fantasia*, Walt enthused over the idea of a little black centaurette with a watermelon who is terrified when Pegasus gallops after her. "She sees him and Jesus! She goes like hell," Walt said at a story meeting. "There would be a lot of laughs and it would give a definite lift to the whole thing."

But if Walt had been racially insensitive, he now appreciated the minefield through which he was tiptoeing with the Uncle Remus film. "The negro situation is a dangerous one," Disney publicist Vern Caldwell wrote producer Perce Pearce as the script was getting under way. "Between the negro haters and the negro lovers there are many chances to run afoul of situations that could run the gamut all the way from the nasty to the controversial." Roy apparently had asked RKO, the Disneys' distributor, to investigate "negro picture experiences" and said he foresaw interference from at least one organization, the League for the Advancement of the Negro; and Walt had instructed one of his publicists to meet with Bill Kupper, the sales manager of Twentieth Century–Fox, to hear their experiences in distributing *Stormy Weather*, which featured a black cast. Kupper said that in the South the film had to be booked into two theaters, one for whites and one for blacks; that the studio got grief from both whites and blacks; and that the film had to be made in such a way that scenes featuring blacks could be cut or southern exhibitors wouldn't show them.

One of the reasons Walt had hired Rapf to work with Reymond was to temper what he feared would be Reymond's white southern slant. Rapf was a minority, a Jew, and an outspoken left-winger, and he himself feared that the film would inevitably be Uncle Tomish. "That's exactly why I want you to work on it," Walt told him, "because I know that you don't think I should make the movie. You're against Uncle Tomism, and you're a radical." Rapf made small changes in Reymond's script, omitting references to "negro boy" and "negro girl" as if the children were generic and cutting a line that a boy ran "like a black streak," and he claimed to have made larger ones too—plunging the white family into poverty so that it would be clear the film was set during Reconstruction and Uncle Remus and the other blacks were not slaves scraping and bowing to white power, though in the final film the whites were so well-dressed and genteel that one couldn't help but think of them as masters on a plantation.

In addition to hiring the radical Rapf—at a time when Walt was still steaming over what he had perceived to be Communist influence during the strike—Walt did something else that was uncharacteristic: he sent out the script for comment both within the studio (Gunther Lessing wrote Walt, "I can't find a damn thing to criticize or suggest," and fondly recalled his own black nanny) and outside the studio, to producers Sol Lesser and Walter Wanger, financier Jonathan Bell Lovelace, who sat on the Disney board, and Ward Greene, the head of King Features Syndicate. Most of all, he solicited comment from black Americans, among them the actress Hattie McDaniel, who had won an Academy Award for her supporting role in *Gone with the Wind* and who praised the script after taking a role in the film. He even invited Walter White, the secretary of the National Association for the Advancement of Colored People, to come to the studio and personally work with Walt on revisions, though White begged off, saying that the NAACP had no West Coast representative and that he wouldn't be coming out to California until November, and then as a war correspondent.

Meanwhile Joseph Breen, who was charged with approving scripts under the Production Code of the Motion Picture Producers and Distributors Association, had sent the Remus script to a Mississippi-born colleague for comment, and Walter Wanger had passed it along to Dr. Alain Locke, a prominent black scholar and philosopher at Howard University, asking that he write Disney directly with his criticisms. Breen's colleague suggested a few changes—eliminating the word "darkey"—but he also warned that scenes of blacks singing happily could be resented by contemporary blacks. Dr. Locke wrote Walt that the film could do "wonders in transforming public opinion about the Negro" but only if he shunned stereotypes, and he advised that Walt consult other black representatives. But to Wanger, Dr. Locke confided that Walt had shown "bad judgment" in not having contacted black leaders *before* having the script written. Now, he said, there would be a controversy that could have been avoided.

The controversy was gaining momentum. One correspondent wrote Breen that the black press was already prepared to launch an attack on the film and that the film might "cause serious trouble for the industry." With this hint of trouble Walt reverted to form. He asked an associate to determine if the black newspapers leading the protest were Communist-controlled, and he apparently enlisted the FBI to find out why the black community was harassing him, once again suspecting that Communists were targeting him. The FBI responded that Leon Hartwick, the theatrical editor of the black paper *Los Angeles Sentinel*, had launched his own investigation into the Uncle Remus film and learned that the black actor Clarence Muse had been asked by the studio to "render an expert opinion on the contemplated picture." Muse said he told the studio that the black characters were insufficiently dignified, an objection that he said Disney dismissed. Muse then appealed to black newspapers to protest the film. This was all Walt needed to know. In Walt's version, Muse had come to him and said he wanted to play Remus. Walt refused, and now Muse had launched a personal vendetta with, no doubt, Communist assistance.

Ironically, Walt had had someone else in mind for Remus: the athlete, singer, actor, and political activist Paul Robeson, whose politics were well to the left of Muse's. Walt had contacted Robeson as early as February 1941 after seeing him on the stage in George Gershwin's *Porgy and Bess*, and Robeson had agreed to review the general outline of the script and offer suggestions or criticisms. Though the film was in hiatus after the war began, Walt nevertheless kept open his lines of communication with Robeson, apologizing when he was unable to attend a reception in Robeson's honor and saying how much he was looking forward to working with him on *Remus*. Somehow, possibly because of politics, Robeson was no longer under consideration when Walt revived the film in 1944. Instead he tested a number of other black actors—"practically every colored actor," he once said—before finding, virtually by accident, forty-year-old James Baskett, who had appeared on the *Amos and Andy* radio program but had no film experience.

The fact was that Walt himself had had very little experience in live-action films either—only the Alice comedies, *The Reluctant Dragon*, and Seversky's scenes in *Victory Through Air Power*. Though Stokowski's scenes in *Fantasia* and Seversky's in *Victory* had been shot on soundstage 1, it was not fully equipped for live action, and the estimated cost of refitting it for that purpose was just under $200,000, or about a third the entire cost of *Dumbo*. In fact, Jonathan Bell Lovelace was as worried about the Disneys' inexperience as about the objections from the black community; he suggested that they partner with one of the major studios. Instead Walt contracted with Samuel Goldwyn, with whom he had collaborated for years on the aborted Hans Christian Andersen project and to whom he had as close a relationship as he had with any producer in Hollywood with the possible exception of Walter Wanger. Goldwyn also lent the studio his cinematographer, Gregg Toland, who had shot Orson Welles's legendary *Citizen Kane*. The total cost of Goldwyn's services would be $390,000—steep but necessary under the circumstances.

The filming began in December 1944 in Phoenix, where the studio had constructed a plantation and cotton fields for outdoor scenes, and Walt left for the location to oversee what he called "atmospheric shots," missing Diane's birthday and just barely making it home in time for Christmas. So eager was he to make a real movie amid the government work that he was back again in February and then again in March. Even as the live action was shot, the bulk of the animation was going to have to wait; with its war contracts, the studio could spare only a few animators, and the ones who did work on the film proceeded slowly. Wilfred Jackson and Perce Pearce, who directed in tandem—Jackson the animation and Pearce the actors—took the same deliberate approach to the live action, and Walt, obviously tense and hoping to save money, wasn't pleased, scolding Jackson that they were spending too much time on these scenes. Yet for all their care Walt had to come to the rescue on the final day of shooting when Jackson discovered that the scene in which Uncle Remus sang the film's signature song, "Zip-A-Dee-Doo-Dah," hadn't been properly blocked. "We all sat there in a circle with the dollars running out, and nobody came up with anything," Jackson would recall. Then Walt suggested that they shoot Baskett in close-up, cover the lights with cardboard save for a sliver of blue sky behind his head, and then remove the cardboard from the lights when he began singing so that he would seem to be entering a bright new world of animation. Like Walt's idea for Bambi on ice, it made for one of the most memorable scenes in the film.

But all of that seemed to have taken place a long time ago when Walt returned to the project after the war to complete the animation. In June 1946 the film, now called *Song of the South* (to the consternation of the Harris family, who preferred the original *Uncle Remus*), was finally completed—the first nonwar-themed Disney feature in nearly four years. Walt was pleased. Though it contained less than a half-hour of animation, that limit allowed the animation to be done as painstakingly as in the old days. Marc Davis, alluding perhaps to how enervating the war work was, said that "almost all of the animators that worked on it would have to say that they never did anything that was more fun than that," in part because they had such great voices with which to work. Milt Kahl went further. He called it "kind of a high in animation." They weren't the only ones who thought it might be a return to form. "SAW WALT DISNEY'S SONG OF THE SOUTH THIS MORNING AND IT IS IN MY OPINION THE MOST DELIGHTFUL CREATION THAT WALT HAS THUS FAR BROUGHT TO THE SCREEN," RKO executive Ned Depinet beamed in a telegram he sent to Gus Eyssell, the manager of the Radio City Music Hall, "AND HAS SAME WIDE AUDIENCE APPEAL AS SNOW WHITE," though Vern Caldwell wrote Walt skeptically that while this might be Depinet's "real feeling," it was at least "the way he is talking it up."

Walt heard the same kind of enthusiasm from other quarters but also a more sobering prediction. The Audience Research Institute had determined that the "highest potential" of the film was $2.4 million—less than half what the studio had expected. Disney publicist William Levy said the figure "surprised and shocked" him, until he realized that the studio had been "feeling the pulse of the Trade" while ARI had been "feeling the pulse of the Public." Now, Levy wrote Roy, they could only hope that word-of-mouth might save the picture. Meanwhile Walt left the studio on November 6 for the film's premiere at Loew's Theatre in Atlanta.

The dim financial prospects notwithstanding, if Walt Disney had hoped to regain his artistic standing with the critics, he did not. Bosley Crowther in *The New York Times* complained, "More and more, Walt Disney's craftsmen have been loading their feature films with so-called 'live action' in place of their animated whimsies of the past, and by just those proportions has the magic of these Disney films decreased." Citing the ratio of live action to animation at two to one, he concluded that is "approximately the ratio of its mediocrity to its charm." Still, the film wound up grossing $3.3 million, better than the ARI estimate and more than the $2.2 million gross of *Make Mine Music.*

The most scathing criticisms, however, weren't aesthetic; they were political. The release of the film had revived all the protests in the black community that had lain dormant while the film itself had lain dormant. Many found abhorrent the idea of Uncle Remus happily serving a wealthy white family while he lived in a shanty. Walter White of the NAACP complained that the film perpetuated the impression of an "idyllic master-slave relationship which is a distortion of the facts." Congressman Adam Clayton Powell called it an "insult to minorities." The Theatre Chapter of the National Negro Congress threw a picket line around the Palace Theatre in New York, where the film was playing, and had its protesters carry placards reading, "We fought for Uncle Sam, not Uncle Tom." Producer and columnist Billy Rose accused Walt of having caved to corporate interests and warned, "You stopped being Walt Disney, and became Walt Disney, Inc." And he added, "You know, chum, you're not just another movie producer. You're the guy we brag about." Even Maurice Rapf, who cowrote the film, said he agreed with the attackers. But the worst criticism, certainly the most telling, may have been a remark in the *B'nai B'rith Messenger,* the publication of the Jewish social and charitable organization, that *Song of the South* "tallies with the reputation that Disney is making for himself as an arch-reactionary."

Walt might have been mystified if he hadn't had the Communists to blame. He liked the film, and he especially liked James Baskett, who he told his sister Ruth was "the best actor, I believe, to be discovered in years." Long after the film's release Walt stayed in contact with Baskett, even picking up a record of the singer Bert Williams for him when Walt was in New York because Walt knew Baskett was a fan of Williams. More, when Baskett was in ill health, Walt began a campaign to get him an honorary Academy Award for his performance, saying that he had worked "almost wholly without direction" and had devised the characterization of Remus himself. Thanks to Walt's efforts, Baskett did get his honorary Oscar at the 1948 ceremonies, then died a few months later, after which his widow wrote Walt thankfully that Walt had been a "friend in deed and [we] certainly have been in need."

Even with *Song of the South* under his belt, Walt Disney was restless. "Let's do *anything* to get some action," he said he told Roy during this period. Restlessness was his congenital condition, expressing his fear that if he wasn't moving forward, he was moving backward. His early features—from *Snow White* through *Bambi*—spoke to maturity and the assumption of responsibility; they didn't address what happened after maturity was attained. For a man who usually had to be pried away from his beloved studio and traveled only because the war work had compelled him to do so, he was frequently on the road after the war, as if to burn off energy that he could no longer burn off on his films—heading to his retreat at Smoke Tree in the desert or to the Sugar Bowl for skiing or to confer with the Dalis at Del Monte. As *Song of the South* was being completed, he even took a brief trip to St. Louis, stopping in Kansas City along the way and driving dreamily through his old neighborhood, lamenting how dilapidated it now looked. And in November 1946, after the Atlanta premiere of *Song of the South*, he flew to New York, then boarded the *Queen Elizabeth* with Lillian, Perce Pearce, screenwriter John Tucker Battle, and their wives for the crossing to England and on to Ireland to gather material for a film on leprechauns. It was his first European trip since the triumphant tour in 1935.

If he was restless, he was spinning in a dozen different directions, none of which seemed to excite him the way the old animations or even *Song of the South* had. He returned to Los Angeles on December 17, the day before Diane's birthday, which he had missed so often, and began the new year juggling the compilation film about American heroes, another combination live action–animation called *So Dear to My Heart*, an animated version of Washington Irving's *The Legend of Sleepy Hollow*, and an animated Edgar Allan Poe story that had been suggested to him by the British actor James Mason. "It would, of course, be a new departure for us and something the public would never expect," Walt wrote Mason, clearly searching for ways to change his image and reinvigorate the studio. He was even thinking of asking Alfred Hitchcock to direct.

But with the economic gloom still not having lifted as he had hoped and the cartoons still not finding favor, Walt was beleaguered and despondent, and though he always claimed that he functioned better in adversity and that a "kick in the teeth may be the best thing in the world for you," he had been kicked in the teeth for years now, and the kicks were not abating. "When he came back to animation after the war," Frank Thomas observed, "Walt never had the same enthusiasm. . . . It was never like it was on the early pictures, where he knew every frame of the film." Moreover, the layoffs in 1946 and attrition had shrunk the workforce; despite Walt's promises to stockholders that the studio was on the rebound, only an emergency loan of $1 million from RKO late in 1946 rescued the company from insolvency. When Woolie Reitherman returned to Burbank in 1947, he recalled that "there was quite a lot of down feeling at the studio." He would see Walt eating at the Penthouse Club, and Walt "always seemed to be a little worried." One animator remembered a story conference where Walt was clearly distracted. The man who had been pitching the story was forlorn at Walt's lack of interest. "Walt looked at him and said, 'You haven't anything to worry about. It's me. I'm the one that has to worry. Goddamn, I've got to stay up all night thinking about things for you guys to do.' "

He was always thinking about ways to save the studio, always worrying. One night after work Walt sauntered down to Roy's office on the second floor of the Animation Building, and the two brothers sat there until roughly eight o'clock pondering their predicament. "Look," Roy said he told his brother angrily, breaking the silence, "you're letting this place drive you nuts. That's one place I'm not going with you." And Roy stormed out. He didn't sleep that night. Neither, he said, did Walt. The next morning Roy was sitting at his desk still fretting when he heard Walt's footsteps in the hallway and his hacking cough. "He came in and he was filled up," Roy said, "he could hardly talk." And Walt said, "Isn't it amazing what a horse's ass a fella can be sometimes?"

Though he was only forty-four, in addition to the mental strain he wasn't feeling well physically either, which made it even more difficult to cope. Always slight and fragile, save for his time in France when his frame filled out, he suffered from a painful flare-up of an old polo injury, for which he received daily diathermy treatments in his office and which got so bad that he had to be hospitalized early in 1947; his cholesterol rating was just under 250 milligrams, where 180 milligrams was normal; his teeth bothered him; he would soon need reading glasses; and he couldn't seem to shake colds, possibly because of his chain-smoking. Between the tensions at the studio and the nagging problems with his health, one of the most famous and celebrated men in America wrote his robust postman brother, Herbert, about how much he envied Herbert's life. Of his brother's new trailer and the freedom it provided, Walt wrote, "I'd give a lot for a little of it, and believe me, I mean it."

But it wasn't just the sense of corporate crisis or middle-age infirmities that were afflicting Walt Disney. In the same way that the strike had stiffened and soured him, he had undergone another personal transformation during the war, one that paralleled his country's transformation. America had entered the war powerful but naïve. It emerged from the war as the dominant nation in the world; in President Truman's words, spoken on V-J Day when Japan surrendered, it held the "greatest strength and the greatest power which man has ever reached." Within the next two years the United States would enjoy unprecedented prosperity and abundance. In 1947 it produced nearly half the world's manufactures, which led to a sinking unemployment rate, rising wages (roughly a 45 percent rise in just four years), and a skyrocketing birthrate (nearly one million more births per year than during the Depression). After two decades of isolationism, not unlike Walt's own isolation in his studio, the country had also been forced to assume a new international responsibility—what publisher Henry Luce had called for in his famous 1941 *Life* essay, "The American Century." In Luce's view, the nation had to change its sense of itself as it shouldered new global obligations. It had to become the custodian to the world.

Walt Disney, who represented America to much of the world, had entered the war as one of the nation's most popular entertainers, "the guy we brag about," as Billy Rose had said, not only for the quality of his work but also for the seemingly naïve and unpretentious way he produced it—that appealing American primitivism of Walt's. Despite the studio's ongoing problems, Walt had emerged from the war as something else: a corporate burgher and the embodiment of the new imposing, powerful America, helping to transmit its values around the globe or, as historian Jackson Lears would later put it, a "central figure in the corporate reclamation of the national mythology, the redefinition of the American Way of Life from a vague populism to an equally murky notion of free enterprise."

As Lears indicated, it was difficult to put one's finger on exactly what constituted the change, but like the country, Walt Disney now seemed somehow hegemonic, which was another reason he lost favor with intellectuals and critics. Even his employees saw it. "If no one [else] was in the room, if you were one-on-one with Walt," Ward Kimball recalled, "things were a lot more agreeable. He didn't feel he had to demonstrate his position, and you could talk to him. . . . But when you got into a room full of people, he was a different man." In a room full of people he was no longer a folksy outsider charged with making people laugh or cry. He wore his responsibility heavily. The war and the war films had moved him inside the Establishment.

He even looked different. The boyish young Walt Disney had dressed casually and flamboyantly, often with a scarf or a handkerchief around his neck rather than a tie and with a sweater rather than a suit or sports jacket and often with a floppy fedora. One reporter writing in 1939 described a Tyrolean jacket to which Walt had become "addicted"—purple on the outside, red satin on the inside, with silver buttons the size of half-dollars. "It's the sort of thing that would overwhelm a lesser man," the reporter observed, "but he wears it gracefully," proud of "the sensation it creates." Another reporter called Walt's outfits a "pied ensemble" and said he was wearing moccasins at the time of their encounter. But now, though he still favored those crushed hats that, according to Lillian, he thought made him look dashing, and though he still often wore sports shirts and sweaters, he was also going to Bullock's Department Store for fittings two or three times each year, and his suits were more likely to be solid blue or gray and conservatively cut than wildly patterned and loose-fitting. Even his once-unkempt hair, which had added to the rakish effect, was increasingly tamed with pomade.

One reason for this transformation from a heedless entertainer to a cautious corporate leader who consulted ARI surveys rather than rely on his own instincts was the need to make films without also making mistakes. The studio couldn't afford the risk. Another reason was a growing conservatism in Walt that was itself a function of the studio's embattled status; of his government work and his role as American goodwill ambassador; of his suspicions of Communist intrigue after the strike; and even possibly of his age, now that he was in his mid-forties and no longer a reckless young visionary. Walt, who had never aspired to be a businessman or industrial kingpin, seemed to recognize the change and gamely struggled against it with his Dali and Poe projects and the more modernist animation style, but the dull, uninspired animations, the sluggishness in the studio now, and the racial obtuseness of *Song of the South* were unmistakably the products of an artist who was less dexterous and less contrarian than Walt Disney had been before he had a large studio apparatus to maintain. It was the Warners who now played the subversive role that Walt Disney had once played with the early Mickey Mouse cartoons. Walt's animations seemed to be aimed squarely at the middle so as not to offend, which made them a function not only of a different Walt Disney but of a different America. As art critic Robert Hughes would describe the change in Disney, "He turned himself from a cartoonist into the Old Master of masscult." What this meant in cultural terms, according to historian Steven Watts, was that Disney's "critiques of the social order gradually gave way to a powerful preservationist impulse."

If the evidence of Walt's transformation was his conservatism and the lead-footed animations devoid of energy or menace, the change also registered in his image in the press. The young Walt Disney whom reporters had loved to extol as democratic, informal, unselfconscious, self-effacing, and even childish (though in reality he had long ceased being so) had been supplanted by another Walt Disney who almost seemed to be carved in granite like Washington or Lincoln. This Walt Disney was a symbol of a different side of postwar America from the one the Warners purveyed—not so much plucky and emancipated as mature, decent, genial, solid, self-confident, successful, responsible, and a bit complacent. He was a man without vices, passions, or peccadilloes—the very personification of square midwestern probity. In effect, just as Mickey Mouse's success had converted Mickey from an imp to a logo of harmless happiness so that by the late 1940s he had traded his red shorts with their bright yellow buttons for a suburbanite's shirts and slacks, Walt Disney's seeming success had converted him from what he once jokingly called a "careless, temperamental artist" to the country's favorite businessman. As one studio veteran put it, "The late forties was the time when Walt Disney discovered Walt Disney." He had been subsumed by his studio. Now he was beginning to be subsumed by his new image.

Having succumbed to the change, it was almost as if he were searching for the Walt Disney within him, the old human Walt Disney, when he embarked in June 1947 on a visit to Goderich, Ontario, to which his grandfather had come from Ireland nearly a century earlier and in which his father had been born. Walt and Elias had often talked of making this trip together, but Walt had always been busy and Elias had died. Now Walt flew to New York with Lillian, Lillian's sister Hazel, and Hazel's husband, Bill Cottrell. In New York they picked up a car and drove unhurriedly through Connecticut, Massachusetts, Vermont, New Hampshire, and Maine before heading across the Canadian border to Montreal, Toronto, and then Goderich. With his father's first cousin, Peter Cantelon, he visited the cemetery in nearby Holmesville where Disneys and Richardsons, Walt's grandmother's family, were buried and drove to a farm near Goderich where the ruins of his great-grandfather Robert Richardson's log cabin survived. It was in that cabin, he was told, that Walt's grandfather and grandmother had been married. (Walt eagerly snapped photographs, only to discover later that it was not the actual house; Lillian, who had reluctantly accompanied him, never let him forget his mistake.) Then he drove out to Potter Farm, where the Disneys had once lived. He even visited his father's old schoolhouse. It was the sort of solemn, nostalgic pilgrimage that Walt Disney seldom made. But he needed the journey now. He was lost.

. . .

With the animations no longer holding his attention and the combination films only an expedient, Walt kept searching for something that might pique his interest and help spark the studio. During the war he had waxed enthusiastic over the educational potential of films and filmstrips. "It is not visionary or presumptuous for us to anticipate the use of our own medium in the curriculum of every schoolroom in the world," he had told a national radio audience in 1943. Indeed, educators were clamoring for Disney, and as early as 1944 William Benton of the *Encyclopaedia Britannica* had entered into negotiations with Walt to make a series of educational films—anywhere from six to twelve annually. "Probably the worst student you ever had has now become connected with education!" Walt joked in a letter to his old teacher, Daisy Beck. The following spring the president of Stanford University, Donald B. Tresidder, invited Walt and Lillian to the campus in Palo Alto for a weekend to discuss educational films and models. Meanwhile Walt assigned Carl Nater, who had worked on the war films, to head an educational film division at the studio.

But as with most of his contemplated projects in this period, he was soon disillusioned when he discovered that the quality of the films would be severely compromised by the minimal return he could hope to get, so that had he made them, he would have been back in the same position as when the studio was producing the training films. His real objection, though, may have been psychological rather than financial. In making educational films, he would have been conceding that he was edging away from entertainment—a concession he was not yet ready to make. "He would make entertainment," wrote Jimmy Johnson, who worked at the studio, "and if the educators discovered some educational value in his films, then that was fine with him." Ben Sharpsteen said that Walt was blunter. "We can't bore the public with these things," he recalled Walt saying repeatedly. "We can't be boring. We've got to be entertaining." Eventually Nater left the studio for academe, and the division closed.

But Walt had not given up entirely on finding a way to be both entertaining and educational, particularly if he could do so inexpensively. During the war the coordinator for inter-American affairs had suggested a documentary on the Amazon Basin, which was made as *The Amazon Awakens.* At the same time the studio was inundated with requests from naturalists about the possibilities of collaborating on nature documentaries, and one of them, apparently at Walt's request, had even laid out a program of shorts. Roy promptly quashed it, saying it would "certainly take a long time and a lot of film," but Walt was not deterred. From his days on the farm in Marceline he had loved animals and was fascinated by them and thought others would be fascinated too. (One visitor to the studio remembered Walt gently plucking a worm from a tree and saying, "This is one of God's creatures, and we don't harm them.") Late in 1944, even as the studio was deep into its war films, Carl Nater and Walt had visited with an official of the New York Zoological Society with a plan, as Nater described it, "to eventually make films on animals, bird life, fish life, and any other type of living creature around which there is a real story to tell."

While Walt was considering subjects for the series, Ben Sharpsteen approached him in the hall one day, observed that returning veterans were beginning to homestead in Alaska, and suggested that there might be a story in it. Walt told him to pursue it. Inspired by a book written by a former Stanford University president named David Star Jordan, who had helped negotiate a treaty between Russia and Japan on seal hunting (the book was told from the seals' point of view), Sharpsteen said he contacted a husband-and-wife photography team in Alaska, Alfred and Elma Milotte. In fact, Al Milotte had written Walt in 1940 offering pictures of animals on the Alaskan range, which Walt, who was in preproduction for *Bambi,* declined. But according to Milotte, it was Walt, not Sharpsteen, who contacted him sometime later about shooting film of Alaska—nothing specific, Milotte remembered, just Walt saying, "You know—mining, fishing, building roads, the development of Alaska."

So the Milottes shot. They shot for months. They shot, in Milotte's words, "everything that moved": people cutting timber, catching salmon, building railroads, climbing Mount McKinley, hunting game—more than 100,000 feet of film. The idea, inchoate as it was, was that the film would tell a story about America's last real frontier. Unfortunately, the footage was precisely what Walt said he had wanted to avoid: it was boring. "Too many mines. Too many roads. More animals. More Eskimos," Walt had wired Al Milotte. To which Milotte wired back: "How about seals?" Walt okayed the couple going to the Pribilof Islands, which were the mating grounds for thousands of fur seals. The couple stayed for a year—much of the time in darkness, due to the shortened days at the Arctic Circle—filming the battles between young unattached males and older bulls, the matings, the births of the pups, and the seals' winter migration to the Pacific Ocean. The only communication they said they received from Walt as they shipped back their footage was an occasional telegram with the same command: "More seals."

Roy had been right about the nature documentaries. They did take a long time and a lot of film to produce. Walt had conferred with the Milottes at the studio shortly after the end of the war, and they visited again a year later with Sharpsteen in December 1946, while Walt was in Ireland, though Sharpsteen said it wasn't until a few years later, as the project languished, that Walt decided to cut the Eskimos altogether and focus exclusively on the seals. Walt professed not to care what these cuts did to shorten the film's length. He told Sharpsteen, "[W]hatever it ran, it ran." In August 1947, Walt visited Alaska himself, "to see some of the things first hand and get a little idea of Alaska to help him in making the picture," Roy said, but also to spend some time with his eleven-year-old daughter Sharon, who accompanied him as he jumped around the territory. It would be yet another year before the Milottes' footage would be edited into what would be called *Seal Island.*

Now that the film was finally finished after all these years, RKO, the Disneys' distributor, was not interested. Without the Eskimos or the story of Alaskan homesteading, the film was only twenty-eight minutes long—too short for a second feature and too long for a short. RKO saw no way of distributing it. Then there was the subject matter. "They all say, 'Who wants to watch seals playing house on a bare rock?' " Roy told Walt after returning from a sales trip to New York. Though the film had been made cheaply—for just over $100,000—Walt was not about to let it disappear. As he had done so many years before with *The Skeleton Dance*, when he convinced an exhibitor to preview the cartoon, he arranged to have the film shown at the Crown Theater in Pasadena the last week of December 1948. The audience was spellbound. "It knocks the people right in their bloody hat," said Disney artist Harper Goff, who attended the first screening. But Walt wasn't interested only in demonstrating the film's audience appeal. By showing *Seal Island* for a week at the theater, Walt had qualified it for the Academy Award for Documentary Short Subject, which it won a few months later. Now it was salable. When Sharpsteen walked into Walt's office the morning after the ceremony carrying the Oscar he had picked up for the studio, Walt ordered his secretary to take it to Roy's office and "tell him to hit RKO over the head with it."

It was the first of what Walt would call his True-Life Adventures, nature documentaries that brought Walt's old narrative skills to natural events, and in its own way it would prove just as revolutionary as his first sound animation or *Snow White. Seal Island* would become the model not only for Disney documentaries but for nature documentaries generally: a strong plot, anthropomorphized animals with emotions imputed to them, and a musical track that Jim Algar, who directed *Seal Island*, compared to the music in the Disney animations, which made the documentaries into real-life cartoons. "[W]herever we saw a change we tried to take rhythmic natural action and edit in such a fashion that a musical score could accompany it," leading some people to marvel, Algar said, at how they got the animals to perform to the music. On the other hand, while audiences marveled, these devices prompted purists to complain that Disney had falsified nature in the service of his postwar kitsch—a complaint that would dog him for the rest of his life.* But Walt for once seemed undisturbed. He had found a way to combine entertainment with education. He had won a small battle in what was becoming a long losing war.

IV

Besieged and miserable, Walt Disney knew who was responsible for his studio's declining fortunes, knew that these people were "hoping it was the end" for him, as he later put it, and two months after he returned from Alaska, he headed to Washington to help vanquish them. The enemy wasn't just the economics of animations or the bankers with their constraints or changing aesthetics or a new postwar mood that Walt couldn't quite tap the way he had tapped the mood of the Depression. The enemy was Communism—Communism that had wracked the studio during the strike, Communism that had sneaked into Hollywood like a Trojan horse to promote values deleterious to democracy, Communism that was even now undermining the nation as it had undermined the motion picture industry. Walt Disney was going to fight Communism.

This was a rather unusual mission for him. Despite their father's radicalism—Elias and apparently Flora as well had voted for the socialist presidential candidates, Eugene V. Debs and then Norman Thomas—neither Walt nor Roy had ever shown much interest in politics. Politics was the outside world, the world that Walt had built his studio to protect himself from, and anyone hunting for a consistent political subtext to the cartoons would have been baffled by the oscillation between the impertinent Mickey Mouse cartoons of the early 1930s and the Silly Symphonies like *The Grasshopper and the Ants*, *The Tortoise and the Hare*, and *The Country*

*"The tone of a Disney nature film is nearly always patronizing," Richard Schickel would write in a typical criticism. "It is nearly always summoning us to see how very nicely the humble creatures do, considering that they lack our sophistication and know-how." *The Disney Version*, p. 290. The bigger problem was fabrication. "I wanted to take them [otter cubs] to Yellowstone Park . . . get off beaten track trail," wrote a naturalist who was working with the studio on a film. "Have them meet cub bears we had lured by feeding regularly near a lake. Then watch and photograph them meeting and playing. Would be a real natural comedy spot. Of course this will take time, but theatrical when we get it. Will be inimitable and always remain a Disney classic." Emil Liers to Ben Sharpsteen, n.d., V Folder, Walt Disney Corr., Inter-Office, 1945–1952, M-Z, A1636, WDA.

Cousin that promoted traditional values like hard work, thrift, and discipline. The oscillation reflected the Disneys' lack of political conviction. When writer Upton Sinclair won the Democratic gubernatorial primary in California in 1934 on a platform promising to end poverty with government programs and then was defeated in the general election by an influx of Hollywood money, Roy chided his parents for supporting Sinclair but admitted, "Many of the things he advocated are going to come around in some form or other. However, I don't believe you can upset society overnight," and he closed his letter, "I can hear Dad saying, 'Now, since the boys have joined the capitalist class and the employers' class, they sing a different tune.' Well, of course, it is true."

Walt would claim that he came to his political conservatism by another route. He told Maurice Rapf that when he was a boy in Kansas City, he had been attacked by a gang of Irish kids whose fathers worked for the Democratic political machine and who put hot tar on his scrotum because Elias was a socialist. Rapf never believed the story and Walt's old benefactor Dr. John Cowles had been a large cog in the Democratic machine, but Walt insisted the episode had turned him into a "dyed-in-the-wool Republican." More likely Walt's politics were the result of his rebelliousness against Elias, but the fact was that Walt hadn't really been a conservative or a Republican or much of anything else for the better part of his adult life. Rather, his politics had been marked by either confusion or neutrality. He had voted for Roosevelt in 1936, even as Roy had voted for Republican Alf Landon, and though he said he supported Republican presidential candidate Wendell Willkie in 1940—Willkie had visited the studio and discussed education with Walt—he declined a request from the Willkie campaign for an endorsement, writing, "[A] long time ago I found out that I knew nothing whatsoever about this game of politics and since then I've preferred to keep silent about the entire matter rather than see my name attached to any statement that was not my own." As for his conservatism, he told another correspondent who was lobbying him to make a reel of flags with patriotic music that "I don't go in for bill-board patriotism." "He was very apolitical, believe me," said Joe Grant, who accompanied Walt on several wartime visits to Washington.

Disney's detractors, after the fact, would say that he had been an admirer of German chancellor Adolf Hitler and Italian dictator Benito Mussolini, and Art Babbitt in later years claimed to have actually seen Walt and Gunther Lessing at Bund meetings of Nazi sympathizers that Babbitt himself had attended out of curiosity; that was highly unlikely, not only because Walt had little enough time for his family, much less political meetings, but because he had no real political leanings at the time. Others would find evidence of pro-Nazi sentiment in Walt's invitation to German filmmaker Leni Riefenstahl, who had directed the Nazi propaganda film *Triumph of the Will*, to tour the studio. Riefenstahl did visit the studio on December 8, 1938, through an invitation solicited from Walt by a close friend of Riefenstahl's and an acquaintance of Walt's, Jay Stowitts, who had been a ballet dancer with Anna Pavlova, a star of the Folies Bergère, a painter, and an actor. Stowitts wrote Walt that Riefenstahl had slipped into California quietly and had asked to meet him because she considered him "the greatest personage in American films." As Riefenstahl later described the meeting, she spent the entire day with Walt at the studio (Walt's desk diary shows a sweatbox session for the "Claire de Lune" sequence of *Fantasia* at two o'clock) then offered to have a print of her film *Olympia* messengered over when Walt expressed interest in seeing it. But Walt, she said, suddenly hesitated, saying, "If I see your film then all of Hollywood will find out by tomorrow," since his projectionists were unionized. He feared that he might be boycotted. Three months later, Riefenstahl wrote, Walt disavowed her trip, claiming that he hadn't known who she was when he issued the invitation.

Of course Walt had known who Riefenstahl was; to Stowitts's original letter, someone, presumably a studio publicist, had attached an ad from *Variety* placed by the Hollywood Anti-Nazi League declaring that Riefenstahl was in Hollywood and calling for the industry to ostracize her. Still Walt, who was something of a political naïf, may not have known exactly what she represented, and he certainly would not have wanted to get embroiled in any political controversy at the time. As Europe churned in the mid-1930s, Walt had expressly told one reporter that America should "let 'em fight their own wars" and that he had "learned my lesson" from the last one. Once the war started, even after the 1941 strike, left-wing groups frequently asked for his contributions and support, in everything from helping to underwrite a series of lectures by Owen Lattimore (a left-leaning China expert who would later be condemned by Communist-hunting Senator Joseph McCarthy) to serving as a patron for the Congress of American-Soviet Friendship, all of which suggested that Walt was not perceived as a hopeless reactionary. Walt sometimes agreed, sending his "heartfelt greetings to the gallant people of the Soviet Union" on that country's twenty-fifth anniversary, appearing as guest of honor at a "Night of the Americas" sponsored by a group designated by the attorney general as subversive, and signing an ad in *the Daily Worker* along with Paul Robeson, Langston Hughes, Communist leader Earl Browder, and others for "A Tribute to the Memory of Art Young," a left-wing cartoonist. (Though Walt would have a long association with the FBI, helping promote the bureau, his own file cited the "Night of the Americas" and the Young tribute as casting doubt on his patriotism.) At the same time, however, having been shaken by the strike, he was lauding *Reader's Digest* for an anti-Soviet article by Max Eastman that Walt thought would counteract pro-Soviet Hollywood propaganda like the film *Mission to Moscow*, and he had joined staunch conservatives like actors Ginger Rogers, Robert Montgomery, and George Murphy in forming a Hollywood Republican Committee to counteract the more liberal Progressive Citizens of America.

The biggest assault on the Hollywood left wing, however, was yet to come. In early October 1943 the University of California at Los Angeles, under the auspices of the League of American Writers, hosted a conference of writers from South America. Walt was among the attendees at the opening session, along with Theodore Dreiser and Thomas Mann. Either during or shortly after the conference James Kevin McGuinness, a reactionary screenwriter who had led attempts to undermine the Screen Writers Guild in the mid-1930s, hosted a dinner with like-minded friends where he and his guests stewed over the conference, which they evidently regarded as another sign of Communist perfidy, and decided to form an "investigating group" to combat what they saw as Communist influence in the film industry. Sometime in late October or early November thirty members of the industry met at Chasen's restaurant, a Hollywood hangout, to formalize the group, and again at the Beverly Wilshire Hotel on November 29 and December 9 to draw up an organization plan. Among the names floated for possible membership at the December meeting was Walt Disney.

Though Walt had never been a joiner, after the strike it probably didn't take much convincing to get him to participate. He called on Rupert Hughes, another notoriously reactionary screenwriter, on the way home from the studio on January 31, apparently to discuss the political situation, and on February 4 he attended a dinner at Hughes's home for an organization that was listed in his desk diary as the "Pro-American Committee of Hollywood" but that had actually been named the Motion Picture Alliance for the Preservation of American Ideals—the group that had been born at James McGuinness's dinner party. Later that night at a meeting at the Beverly Wilshire Hotel attended by some two hundred members of the film community, director Sam Wood was elected president of the new organization and set designer Cedric Gibbons, writer/director Norman Taurog, and Disney were elected vice presidents. In a declaration of principles, the MPA proclaimed: "We find ourselves in sharp revolt against a rising tide of Communism, Fascism and kindred beliefs" and vowed to do battle against anyone who tried to "divert the loyalty of the screen from the free America that gave it birth," though it was really Communism, not any of the other beliefs, that exercised them, including Walt Disney.

The next month the MPA escalated the battle. It wrote a letter to Senator Robert Reynolds of North Carolina accusing the film industry of harboring Communists and using as proof the fact that people like Walt Disney had felt the need to form an organization to combat the threat. Reynolds placed the letter in the *Congressional Record*, though the real purpose of the MPA was not to get Congress's attention so much as to spur Congress to investigate. There had even been rumors that Representative Martin Dies, the chairman of the House Committee on Un-American Activities, was retiring so that he could become the head of the MPA. Up to this point there had been a good deal of intramural squabbling between the Right and the Left in Hollywood. But with the Reynolds letter the MPA—and Walt Disney—had crossed a line. They weren't simply attacking Communists; they were attacking their own industry.

The Left, which had so often ridiculed Hollywood in the past even as it was taking its money, ironically leaped to the industry's defense. The Screen Writers Guild called a meeting at the Roosevelt Hotel on May 2 at which thirty-eight unions passed a resolution "reaffirming confidence in the achievements of the motion picture industry" and promising to protect it against "irresponsible and unwarranted attacks." (The FBI, which was monitoring the entire situation at the invitation of the MPA, called the movement Communist-inspired.) Others accused the MPA of protofascism. "[T]he public pronouncements of the more active members of the M.P.A. are modeled strictly along orthodox Red-baiting and witch-hunting lines," wrote screenwriter and playwright Elmer Rice, ". . . and one need not look far below the surface to discover that the organization and its leading spirits are deeply tinged with isolationism and anti-unionism and off-the-record, of course—with strong overtones of anti-Semitism and Jim Crowism." Meanwhile an informant had told the FBI that the executive secretary of the Los Angeles Communist Party had been discussing ways of sullying the MPA, but the secretary had exempted Walt Disney from the criticism because Disney had done such fine work for South America.

But if the Communist Party was sparing Walt Disney, his friend, producer Walter Wanger, was not. Wanger and Walt engaged in some frank talks about the MPA, and Wanger sent Walt a scathing letter that he had written to one of the MPA's officials in which he blasted the group for attracting "irresponsible people" and permitting them to speak for it and for picturing the leaders of the industry as "at best, inept, and as at worst, fools." And Wanger was worried about Walt, about where he was headed. Walt had sent him an article by the red-baiting columnist George Sokolsky lacerating Vice President Henry Wallace, for whom Walt had once attended a dinner, and urged Wanger to read it. Wanger wrote back regretfully, "The minute you become a producer of the Sokolsky theme in your films, I am afraid you will never make a SNOW WHITE, a DUMBO, a SALUDOS AMIGOS, a BAMBI OR a PINOCCHIO. These pictures are full of faith, decency, ideals and charm." And he closed: "You had better look in the mirror and not be impressed by rabble rousers."

But he *had* been impressed by the rabble rousers, and he *hadn't* made another *Snow White*, *Pinocchio*, or *Bambi*. Though he publicly professed to be nonpartisan—"As an independent voter I owe allegiance to no political party," he told a national radio audience before endorsing 1944 Republican presidential nominee New York governor Thomas Dewey—he donated heavily to the Republican Party, allowed a Dewey rally on the studio grounds, delivered a speech for Dewey at the Los Angeles Coliseum, and was selected as one of California's electors should Dewey win, even if he was stirred less by enthusiasm for Dewey, who was a comparative moderate, than by antipathy to the Roosevelt administration. To a Republican fund-raiser, he wrote, "I'm sorry I can only give money."

Yet by 1947 he could give more, and he did. The invitation that the MPA had tendered to Congress back in 1944 had finally been accepted. With Congress coming under Republican control after the 1946 midterm elections, the House Un-American Activities Committee (HUAC) announced that it was going to investigate Hollywood, and in September 1947 it issued subpoenas to nineteen so-called "unfriendly" witnesses (the term was actually the *Hollywood Reporter*'s) and twenty-six "friendlies."* Among those "friendlies" was Walt Disney, the quintessentially American face of Hollywood. Walt wasn't a passive recipient. He was firmly entrenched now with the professional red-baiters on the Hollywood right—McGuinness, Hughes, Wood and actors like Adolphe Menjou, Ward Bond, and Robert Taylor. Throughout the year he continued to attend MPA meetings and meet with fellow conservatives like George Murphy and with the staff of HUAC. He even had Gunther Lessing submit questions to the committee that he thought he should be asked. Then on October 18 he left for New York for a brief stay to celebrate the twentieth anniversary of Mickey Mouse at a dinner before heading to Wash-

*There is a discrepancy between the names of those subpoenaed, as listed in the *Hollywood Reporter*, and those who later testified. Twenty-four so-called "friendlies" finally testified.

ington for the hearings. The juxtaposition of the celebration with the testimony showed what a long twenty years it had been. He had gone from iconoclast to guardian of the social order.

He arrived at the less-than-packed House Caucus Room on Capitol Hill on the afternoon of October 24, 1947, in a sober gray flannel suit, albeit with a loud tie, his ordinarily wild hair plastered to his head, the first witness of that session on the second day of the hearings. (Actors Gary Cooper and Ronald Reagan, among others, had testified the first day, when the Caucus Room had been jammed.) After preliminary inquiries about Walt's background in the film industry and his producing propaganda during the war, committee co-counsel H. A. Smith asked the big question: were there any Communists or fascists at his studio? No, Walt asserted in his soft, flat, nasally midwestern voice, "I feel that everybody in my studio is 100 percent American." But *had* there been Communists at the studio in the past? Yes, Walt answered, and proceeded to tell the story of how union chief Herbert Sorrell strong-armed the studio into the strike, even though, he said, his employees, whom Sorrell claimed to be representing, actually protested against Sorrell's union. When Walt said that he wouldn't recognize the union, Sorrell, who, Walt told the committee, he believed was a Communist, sneered that he would "smear" Walt, and Sorrell had been true to his word. Walt couldn't remember all the groups that smeared and boycotted him—"one that is clear in my mind is the League of Women Voters"—but he did cite *People's World*, the *Daily Worker*, and *PM* as three publications that he knew had flayed him. He couldn't remember the Communist employees who had incited his studio either—only the union agitator David Hilberman. And as for whether the Communist Party deserved to be outlawed, Walt called the party an "un-American thing," though he said he wasn't qualified to determine whether it would violate rights to banish it. Chairman J. Parnell Thomas praised his films and his testimony, and Walt Disney's day was done.

Walt had played his part—the part of the aggrieved hero of the common man, the Horatio Alger industrialist, who had been besieged by left-wing ideologues—and H. A. Smith called his testimony "as effective as that of any witness." Save for one problem. In citing Communist organizations that had attacked him in the wake of the strike, Walt had indicted the nonpartisan civic group the League of Women Voters. The league, astonished, immediately ordered an investigation to determine if any of its members in the California chapter had taken part in the Disney labor dispute, and an officer wrote Walt asking for the names of the women involved. Walt answered the request with a tepid retraction to the committee, saying that in 1941 "several women [supporting the strikers] represented themselves as being from the League of Women Voters," but averred that he was not criticizing the current league. Meanwhile, Gunther Lessing was frantically conducting his own investigation and discovered four letters in his file, at least one of which Walt had seen, from the Hollywood League of Women *Shoppers* supporting the strikers, though Lessing also wrote Walt that he thought the local chapter of the League of Women Voters "appear[s] to have followed the party line about the time of the Disney strike," which was patently false. A few weeks later Lessing conceded and wrote the league to apologize for Walt's mistake, suggesting that Walt would "recommend your organization whenever the opportunity presents itself."

But with his appearance and his careless denunciation, Walt Disney had gotten himself ensnared in the politics of red-baiting. Shortly after his testimony he was invited to an American Legion rally at which the legion's commander, James F. O'Neil who had been spearheading a drive for an industry blacklist of Communists and Communist supporters, would be in attendance. Walt begged off, saying he would be at Smoke Tree at the time for a much-needed rest, but he added, "I would have no hesitancy in joining your group," and said, "I am sure the Hollywood people who were in Washington will all be glad to attend." When a number of studio heads met in November at the Waldorf Astoria Hotel in New York to discuss instituting their own blacklist, Walt sent his New York publicity chief, William Levy, who approved the plan for the studio. "Blacklisting me would have been embarrassing for him," Maurice Rapf observed, blaming Roy and Lessing for stoking Walt's anti-Communism. "He wouldn't have liked to fire me, but he would have fired me, of course," Rapf said, had Rapf not already left the studio. Rapf was right. Walt did enforce a blacklist, and he didn't do so reluctantly. He was among the first subscribers to *Alert*, which billed itself as the "weekly report on Communism in California," and he routinely cooperated with the FBI, even funneling names of prospective employees to the bureau for clearance.

Of course by this time it was no secret that Walt Disney was a fervent anti-Communist. Another question—one that would haunt him for the rest of his life and even haunt his reputation decades after he died—was whether he was also an anti-Semite. As with race, one could certainly point to some casual insensitivity. Shortly after the release of *Three Little Pigs* in 1933, Rabbi J. X. Cohen, the director of the American Jewish Congress, wrote Walt angrily that a scene in which the wolf was portrayed as a Jewish peddler was so "vile, revolting and unnecessary as to constitute a direct affront to the Jews," especially in light of what was then happening in Germany, and he asked that the offending scene be removed. Roy, speaking for Walt, responded that he felt the scene was neither vile nor revolting, that the studio had Jewish friends and business associates whom it would not dare to demean, and that the characterization was no different from that of Jewish comedians in vaudeville or on the screen. (Years later, when *Pigs* was re-released, the scene was reanimated.) Whether it came from this kind of insensitivity or from the fact that the Disney studio was one of the few in Hollywood at the time that was not run by Jews, a perception apparently arose that the company was anti-Semitic. Kay Kamen, the head of the company's merchandising arm and himself a Jew, seemed to acknowledge this when he sent Roy a clipping of a photo of Walt and Lillian from a Hebrew newspaper with a note, "This proves that we are not prejudiced."

How any of this translated into Walt's and Roy's personal feelings about Jews is difficult to determine. In 1933 Roy had called one business agent with whom he was dealing a "cheap kike," and A. V. Cauger's son said his father told him that Walt had groused about Jews when he returned from New York after his fateful showdown with Charlie Mintz in 1928, though this may very well have been Cauger's own interpretation of Walt's postmortem and not Walt's own remarks. In fact, Walt had been around Jews all his life. There were a number of Jews at the Benton School in Kansas City and an even larger contingent at McKinley High School in Chicago. And though he did make insensitive ethnic remarks and occasional slurs, talking about "coon voices" or referring to an Italian band in *Pinocchio* as a "bunch of garlic eaters," he was tolerant where it counted most and where it wasn't for public display—in his personal life. He had sent Diane to a Catholic school and wrote his sister Ruth that though some people, presumably Lillian, were worried about a conversion, he felt differently. "I think she is intelligent enough to know what she wants to do," he said, "and I feel that whatever her decision may be is her privilege. . . . I have explained to her that Catholics are people just like us and, basically, there is no difference." And he said that by giving her this exposure, he hoped to "create a spirit of tolerance within her."

There is some dispute whether the same spirit of tolerance prevailed at the studio, but of the Jews who worked there, it was hard to find any who thought Walt was an anti-Semite. Joe Grant, who had been an artist, the head of the model department, and the storyman responsible for *Dumbo* along with Dick Huemer, declared emphatically that Walt was not an anti-Semite. "Some of the most influential people at the studio were Jewish," Grant recalled, thinking no doubt of himself, production manager Harry Tytle, and Kay Kamen, who once quipped that Disney's New York office had more Jews than the Book of Leviticus. Maurice Rapf concurred that Walt was not anti-Semitic; he was just a "very conservative guy." Still, when Tytle—who had changed the spelling of his name from Teitel, shortened from Teitelbaum, to hide his ethnicity—joined the studio, he felt compelled to tell Walt that he was half-Jewish. To which Walt snapped that if he were *all* Jewish, he would be better.

Moreover Walt contributed frequently to Jewish charities: the Hebrew Orphan Asylum of the City of New York, Yeshiva College, the Jewish Home for the Aged, even after the war to the American League for a Free Palestine. At the very time that Walt was appearing before HUAC, Ned Depinet of RKO had passed along a folio from some friends trying to get Walt to make a Jewish-themed film, which certainly would have been unlikely had they thought of Walt as anti-Semitic. A decade later, in 1955, he would be named Man of the Year by the Beverly Hills Lodge of the B'nai B'rith, the organization that had branded him an "arch-reactionary" during the *Song of the South* dustup. The plaque read: "For exemplifying the best tenets of American citizenship and inter-group understanding, and interpreting into action the ideals of B'nai B'rith, Benevolence, Brotherly Love and Harmony, and for bringing laughter and happiness to all people."

So why then was Walt so often called anti-Semitic? For one thing, the idea was encouraged by disgruntled employees like Art Babbitt and David Hilberman. Hilberman told one Disney biographer that an animator named Zack Schwartz had been fired shortly after the presentation of the union cards. "He wasn't a troublemaker, he was a good artist and didn't give anybody a hard time. What he did have was the last name of Schwartz and a big nose." (In fact, Walt seldom involved himself in hiring or firing except at the very top tier.) Many years later an animator and director named David Swift, also a Jew, told another biographer that when he informed Walt he was leaving the studio for a job at Columbia, Walt called him into the office, feigned a Yiddish accent, and said, "Okay, Davy Boy, off you go to work with those Jews. It's where you belong, with those Jews." When Swift returned to the studio after the war, he claimed that Walt, still resentful, told him that the studio hadn't "come to any harm while you were away with those Jews." It is certainly possible that Walt made these remarks out of bitterness shortly after the strike, though it would have been uncharacteristic of him even under those circumstances. No one else, not even Art Babbitt, had ever accused Walt of making anti-Semitic slurs or taunts, and Babbitt hated Walt. In any case, for a man who had been insulted, Swift always treated Walt cordially, often effusively, and said he owed everything to him. Walt, in return, told Swift when Swift left the studio a second time that "there is still a candle burning in the window if you ever want to come back."

Another factor that may have contributed to the idea that Walt Disney was anti-Semitic was that he lived in a nimbus of rich, white, conservative Protestantism that had tinges of anti-Semitism. Walt intimated to Harry Tytle that Walt's own beloved Smoke Tree was a restricted community, and though he occasionally invited executives there for the weekend—he had had a guest house built outside the ranch grounds—he gently warned Tytle from accepting for fear of Tytle's being embarrassed. Josie Mankiewicz, a school friend of Sharon's and the daughter of screenwriter Herman Mankiewicz, did accept and would tell of how she was having lunch with the Disneys at Smoke Tree when a man came to the table and asked them to leave. She did not report Walt's reaction.

Yet another theory traces the perception of anti-Semitism not to Walt himself but to one of his most trusted employees, Ben Sharpsteen. The man who had suffered so much of Walt's abuse had heaped abuse of his own. An animator named Art Davis, who had interviewed at the studio but was not hired, said that Sharpsteen, despite having a name that might be mistaken for Jewish, was actually a vicious anti-Semite who did not knowingly hire Jews and who reviled the ones who had been hired, which was how the studio got its reputation for hostility to Jews. In this version Walt was guilty of anti-Semitism by association.

The most plausible explanation, however, is another case of guilt by association, only a much more serious one: Walt, in joining forces with the MPA and its band of professional reactionaries and red-baiters, also got tarred with their anti-Semitism. Though Morrie Ryskind, a Jew, was one of the MPA's most conservative and voluble members, it was widely thought both inside and outside the film industry that the group was toxic when it came to anti-Semitism and that Ryskind merely provided cover. Even the FBI was concerned. One FBI agent reported at the time of the MPA's formation, "There is every possibility that persons anti-Semitic will attempt to rally around the MPA, making that organization definitely an anti-Semitic group." Another report quoted John Howard Lawson, a Communist screenwriter and later one of the unfriendly HUAC witnesses, as accusing directors Victor Fleming and King Vidor, two MPA members, of each being a "notorious anti-Semite." Producer David Selznick held the same opinion of the MPA leadership. Outside an MPA meeting in March 1944 Selznick made the charge publicly to MPA president Sam Wood. Wood, obviously trying to disarm him, invited Selznick inside to air his complaints, but Selznick, unmollified, called James K. McGuinness, the MPA founder, the "biggest anti-Semite in Hollywood" and charged him with harboring a secret anti-Semitic group called the Hundred Haters at the Lakeside Golf Club, where McGuinness was president. The charges were credible enough that Selznick's father-in-law,

MGM head Louis B. Mayer, and Warners' production head, Jack Warner, both of whom were at the far right of the political spectrum, began to worry about the anti-Semitic element in the group.

Walt Disney certainly was aware of the MPA's purported anti-Semitism, but he chose to ignore it, possibly feeling that the accusation was Communist propaganda. The price he paid was that he would always be lumped not only with anti-Communists but also with anti-Semites. Regardless of whether he himself was one or not, he had willingly, even enthusiastically, embraced them and cast his fate with them. And having done so, regardless of the awards and charitable contributions, he would never be able to cleanse himself of the taint.

V

So many projects, so little progress. By late 1947 the studio had undergone yet another reorganization plan, this one putting Ben Sharpsteen in charge of all feature animation and Hal Adelquist, who had been head of personnel, in charge of the story department. But this was really just shuffling the chairs on the deck of a sinking ship. As Ben Sharpsteen later explained it, "We knew that it would never endure. Certain people would be put in charge of this or that, but there was very little likelihood that they would stay in that position for very long. Walt would probably give their job to someone else in a sudden move." Still, Sharpsteen said, Walt "persisted in complaining that we had no plan for management and that we had to organize ourselves." Fred Leahy, who was still nominally the head of production under Walt, had lost most of his authority when he suggested that the studio cut *Fantasia* into shorts. Jack Reeder, who was nominally the head of the entire studio operation, ran afoul of Walt by taking his own command seriously until Walt finally forced him out of the studio in May 1948. Two months after Reeder left, Walt reinstated gambling at the Penthouse Club as a kind of final kick at the bureaucrats.

But even after retaking the helm, he was still largely diddling, disengaged, and uninterested. He spent the early part of the year finalizing *The Wind in the Willows* and *Ichabod Crane*, which he intended to release as a single film since neither part was long enough or substantial enough to constitute a feature in itself. (Walt had once written to a fan who had suggested a film of *Willows*: "[W]e have never considered it particularly well suited for cartoon material.") While the studio lumbered ahead on various feature projects, Walt was also working on a live-action film set in rural Indiana about a young boy who adopts a black lamb, and a second True-

Life Adventure, this one on beavers. It was another sign of the studio's financial and imaginative stagnation, however, that its big release in 1948 was *Melody Time*, a compilation of seven shorts, and though it had originally been intended as an anthology of American folk heroism, the only heroes who survived were Johnny Appleseed and Pecos Bill; the rest of the film had sections as disparate as a musical interpretation of Joyce Kilmer's poem "Trees" and a Currier and Ives–style animation titled "Once Upon a Wintertime." The film cost a staggering $2 million and returned only $1.3 million—a loss Roy attributed to a polio scare that kept children out of theaters—forcing him to memo Walt: "It makes it all more necessary all the economies we can effect." More layoffs followed.

With the studio in the red, Walt had only one glimmer of hope that he might produce another feature film to win back his audience, silence the critics, and pump money back into the operation. But it was a small glimmer, because as the studio had bled animators, it had lost one of the primary resources that might have made a feature viable. And it was small because Walt, knowing that he no longer had the talent at the studio, was loath to commit himself to another feature—loath to permit himself to dream. In any case, Roy was insistent that they not gamble everything on a feature. When Woolie Reitherman returned to the studio after the war, he said that Walt was "very, very teetered," by which he meant indecisive over whether they should make a feature or just sell the studio. At the time Walt was pondering *Cinderella*, which he had been developing in fits and starts since 1938, with the obvious hope that it could recapture the magic of *Snow White*; and he was also looking at *Alice in Wonderland*, for which he had hired English writer Aldous Huxley to do a screenplay and for which he had floated the name of child actress Margaret O'Brien, not only because O'Brien might attract an audience but also because she was under contract at MGM and her involvement might entice MGM to distribute the film rather than RKO, with whom the Disneys were disillusioned.

The decision was clearly less a matter of passion than of expediency. By one account, Walt, unable to choose between the projects, called a meeting of his nonanimation employees, played them the songs composed for each film, showed them the storyboards, and then had them vote on which film they preferred. They chose *Cinderella*, though *Alice* was kept in production as well so that the animation crews on both films were effectively competing to see which might finish first. In the spring of 1946 Walt received a treatment on *Cinderella* from his veteran storymen Ted Sears, Homer Brightman, and Harry Reeves, and he ordered storyboards with the intention of having the film ready for a late 1949 release. Woolie Reitherman had seen the *Cinderella* storyboards and went directly to

Walt's office to tell him how much he liked the film and how much potential he thought it had. Years later, Reitherman said, Walt told him that "he was sure glad that I'd come to see him," as if he might not have proceeded otherwise, which only underscored just how uncertain the once-infallible Walt Disney had become.

At long last the studio seemed to regain some of its fire. "*Cinderella* really brought back the good feeling with a bang there," Ben Sharpsteen said. Milt Kahl cited a degree of euphoria now that the animators were back working on something "important." But it was soon clear that *Cinderella* was not *Snow White*, at least not in the way it was produced, and for a film that was meant to be the studio's salvation, it received little of the attention that the early features had had lavished upon them. Walt was so reluctant to take any chances (the sort of chances he had taken on *Snow White*, *Pinocchio*, *Fantasia*, and *Bambi*) that early in 1948 he had the entire film shot in live action on the soundstage with actors mouthing the dialogue track. The aim was not to provide film to rotoscope, as the studio had done in the past, but, Frank Thomas recalled, "to see whether the scenes were going to work. Would they be too long? Too short? Will it hold your interest?" This footage was then edited and sent to the animators on large photostat sheets to duplicate. The problem, said Thomas, was that the animators were not allowed to imagine anything that the live action did not present, since that kind of experimentation might necessitate changes and cost extra money—an approach that effectively defeated the purpose of animation and gave validity to the old criticisms that Walt Disney was too beholden to realism. The animators were even instructed to draw from a certain directorial perspective—head-on—to avoid difficult shots and angles. Thomas said he felt that "your feet were nailed to the floor."

Moreover, the style of the animation was different; it was in the new, sharper, flatter, more minimalist Disney mode. As Walt admitted to one prospective artist who recommended a florid approach, the drawings "have to be done with a great deal of simplicity." In fact, Walt was so determined that *Cinderella* not resemble *Snow White* visually that he asked his onetime artist Mary Blair to return to design the characters, which she did in a delicate, almost greeting-card fashion—against which, Ben Sharpsteen claimed, the animators rebelled. Whole scenes were reimagined too, to cut the detail and the cost of animating that detail. Harry Tytle suggested that during the ballroom scene the other dancers dissolve into the faces of Cinderella and the Prince so that the dancers wouldn't have to be animated, and he further suggested that the coach in which Cinderella rides to the ball seem to float in the air so that the animators could avoid drawing the turning wheels and the coach's filigrees. At the same time Walt was having individual scenes run for ARI audiences as soon as the animators finished them.

In November, Sharpsteen informed Walt that Bill Peet was working on the Dress Building sequence, in which Cinderella gets her gown; composer Ollie Wallace had recorded a track for "So This Is Love"; Ham Luske and Wilfred Jackson were continuing to shoot live-action scenes; and writers Winston Hibler and Ted Sears had moved from *Cinderella* to the *Ichabod Crane* story. There was nothing unusual about any of this. What *was* unusual was Sharpsteen having to tell Walt these things while the studio pressed on with its first fully animated feature in nearly eight years, the feature Walt had been desperate to make. In the past Walt would have known it all already. In the past Walt would have been there supervising every last detail. But then, in the past it would have mattered.

Nothing seemed to matter because Walt felt that everything now was hopelessly compromised. As always when he was disengaged, he traveled—this time to Smoke Tree, to Arrowhead Springs, to Alisal Ranch, and to Oak Creek Lodge in Arizona. In June 1948, after the release of *Melody Time*, he took a three-week cruise to Hawaii. It was a chance to spend time with his family and forget the studio. He was especially close to Sharon, whom one of Walt's secretaries once described as "sort of like a little puppy dog," willing to go with him on junkets like the one in Alaska or on a night train to San Francisco or on a transcontinental train trip to New York, where the two of them rode in the engine for a spell. He still routinely drove both girls to their respective schools on his way to the studio each day, and he was an involved parent, even scolding Sharon's principal for giving the children too much homework because it took away from family time. He was also a loving and supportive father, encouraging Diane when she began attending the Chouinard Art Institute ("He would collect all my drawings and make me think I was wonderful," Diane would recall) and attending Sharon's school plays and afterward telling her how good she had been. At one point Diane got interested in music and asked her father to buy her season tickets to the opera. "He'd go with me to every one of them," Diane said, "unless I could get three other girls to go. Then he would drive us down to the Shrine Auditorium and then come back and pick us up again." Diane admitted she thought he "hated" the opera. But he never made the slightest objection about going. At the dinner table he liked to tell the family what he was doing, but he always asked them what they were doing as well. "And he would listen," Diane said.

He seldom disciplined them or displayed the anger in their presence that his employees so often saw; though with the girls, as with his employees, he had only to arch his eyebrow to chasten them. Sharon said that the only time he spanked her was when she had made an inappropriate comment at dinner, was sent to her room, and then complained to her aunt Grace about the punishment. It was the complaining that irked him. And Diane remembered a time he erupted when she spent most of a Palm Springs vacation driving around in his Oldsmobile convertible and socializing with the daughters of Twentieth Century–Fox production chief Darryl F. Zanuck, who had a house nearby. "You're running a rat race," Diane said her father yelled at her when he finally caught her at home. "You're never here! Why am I here if you're never around?" as he had once chastised Marjorie Sewell. Then he left for the studio. A few days later Diane was driving the Oldsmobile when she got into a "fender bender." Walt drove right down to the scene of the accident and never said a word of reprimand. "That's the way he was," Diane said. "He only got mad when he felt hurt."

Lillian could be thoughtless with the girls. She and Walt had decided never to let Sharon know that she was adopted, but when Sharon was a teenager two of her classmates at the Westlake School who were themselves adoptees, told her that she was adopted too. When Sharon confronted her mother with the information, Lillian said matter-of-factly and without softening the blow, "Well, you are." Diane said, "That was Mother's attitude about a lot of things, maybe a little insensitive but not realizing it." Walt was different. Most of the time he was considerate, even tender, with his girls. When he took Sharon to Alaska, she called him the "picture of patience," saying that he braided her long hair every morning, washed out her clothes, and cleaned up the plane after she gorged herself on Hershey chocolate bars and got sick. When Diane experienced her first menstrual period and ran to her parents in shock and confusion, she said that it was her father, not her mother, who consoled her.

But as much as he cherished his girls and enjoyed spending time with them, there was something solitary about him when he wasn't at the studio—something self-absorbed and distant. With nothing to occupy him, he had impulsively decided that he was going to hack a path around the perimeter of his Woking Way property, and he spent most of his weekends the summer of 1947 blazing what the family jokingly referred to as his "Burma Trail" after the southeast Asian World War II supply line—shirtless in the hot sun, digging and lifting, perspiring profusely, alone in his own world except for Sharon, whom he paid to fetch him soft drinks. Lillian said that at Smoke Tree she once caught him out on the terrace acting out a scene on which he was working, laughing and talking to himself, so completely engrossed that he didn't notice anyone else. His beloved chow Sunnee had died—"no other dog could equal that dog," he would say—but he got a new dog, a brown standard poodle named Duchess, who followed him around the house and even accompanied him on his weekend forays to the studio, where employees who happened to be there got to know the *clip, clip, clip* of her nails on the tile floor. Paul Smith, a composer, said that when Duchess heard him playing the piano, she would bound down the hall to his room.

If his evenings and weekends with Duchess were a measure of Walt's loneliness now that the girls were growing up and he didn't feel the same sense of collaboration at the studio, so was his time with Hazel George. George was a stocky, plain-faced, tough-talking young woman who had grown up hardbitten in the Arizona border town of Bisbee, where she somehow became a ward of the juvenile court, received training as a psychiatric nurse, and was advised by a counselor to head out to California and see if she could get a job, of all places, at the Disney studio. She began working there as the company nurse during the strike. Walt's doctor warned her, "You're going to have a hell of a time with him."

In fact, she didn't. Walt needed a confidante, someone he could just talk to, and Hazel George became that person. Every day, usually after five o'clock, she would come to his office or he would go to hers, where she administered a diathermy treatment or gave him a massage for his polo injury, and then Walt would sip a scotch and unwind by unburdening himself to Hazel. They called the offices their "laughing place," after Uncle Remus's shack in *Song of the South*—the same description Walt had used for Walt Pfeiffer's home in Kansas City, where he had once shared gay times. There was nothing sexual about the relationship; in fact, Hazel was involved with the composer Paul Smith. For Walt, it was strictly a matter of companionship and confidence, of not having to be Walt Disney. In time it would be said that Hazel knew all Walt's secrets and that she was probably the most secure employee in the studio. But it was more than solace Walt found in Hazel. He trusted her, no doubt because he knew she was outspoken, honest, and unintimidatable at a time when he was afraid everyone else would tell him what they thought he wanted to hear. (Of course, the employees were engaged in self-preservation precisely because Walt *didn't* like to be contradicted.) He would show her storyboards, and she would render her judgments. She even claimed to have named *Seal Island* and *Beaver Valley*, the True-Life Adventure on beavers.

Hazel George, perhaps better than anyone else including Lillian, knew that Walt was anxious and aimless, without real animations to engage him. It was she who suggested he go to a railroad fair in Chicago, even though he had returned from Hawaii only a few weeks earlier. She said he still needed to relax. Picking up on the idea, Walt mused that Ward Kimball, a railroad enthusiast himself, always seemed relaxed, so he called Kimball and asked if he wanted to accompany him. They took the *Super Chief* from Pasadena. At one point the president of the Santa Fe Railroad invited Walt and Kimball to ride in the engine and pull the cord to blow the whistle. Kimball said that Walt pulled long and hard. When they returned to their car, Walt "just sat there, staring into space, smiling and smiling," Kimball recalled. "I had never seen him look so happy."

Walt received more of the same courtesy once they arrived at the fair, a general commemoration of the building of the railroads in America. The president of the Chicago Museum of Science and Industry, Lenox Lohr, who hosted the fair, let Walt and Kimball backstage at a pageant called *Wheels a Rolling*, presented on a 450-foot platform off Lake Michigan embedded with tracks for historic locomotives. Walt was even allowed to run several of the old engines and appeared briefly in the show. "We were like little kids, running famous locomotives like the Lafayette, the John Bull, and the Tom Thumb," Kimball remembered. In addition to the show, the fair featured exhibits—"lands," one observer called them: a replica of the New Orleans French quarter erected by the Illinois Central Railroad; a dude ranch; a generic national park with a geyser that erupted every fifteen minutes, sponsored by several of the western railroads; and an Indian village set up by the Santa Fe.

But for all the fun and diversion Walt enjoyed at the fair, it was, like the trip to Goderich the previous summer, a journey into the past as well—a journey to rediscover himself and to rekindle his passions. During the trip out Walt, obviously lonely, would rap on the door to Kimball's quarters, invite him into his sleeper, pour two whiskeys from a glass decanter, and talk. "He was very preoccupied with his own history," Kimball said, "and he spent two nights telling me his entire history from the time he was a boy, sold papers and the whole thing." As always Walt especially savored telling about Mintz's treachery and the creation of Mickey Mouse—savored it even more now that he was foundering. "You see, I was right," he would tell Kimball. "You see, I got back at them and they lost their ass." Once they were in Chicago, Kimball, a musician, wanted to visit some of the jazz clubs. Walt refused. Instead, one night Walt coaxed Kimball into riding the elevated train with him as Walt, looking out the window, described the scenes of his youth in the city. At one isolated, dirty station, Kimball said, Walt and he got off, and Walt explained that this was where he would transfer trains to get to his post office job in 1918. "Walt was reliving his youth," Kimball assessed.

But the fascination with trains was more than a way to relive his youth in Marceline, when his uncle Mike, the engineer, would come up the lane to the Disney farm with his bags of sweets, or the summer in Kansas City, when Walt rode as train butcher selling candy and soda, or the elevated train rides in Chicago before he left for war. Walt thought of the trains as a recreation and a way to decompress from the pressures of the studio. Lillian once claimed that after the war Walt had come close to another breakdown like the one he suffered in 1931, because he was working too hard, she said, though the better explanation was that he was depressed from his work showing so little result, even as he kept pressing ahead. "No matter what plans I made for the weekend," Lillian recalled, "we would always end up at the studio. He couldn't get it out of his mind." Walt was a little more candid when he called the trains "just a hobby to get my mind off my problems."

But as much as Walt Disney loved trains—he was always urging Lillian to put her foot on the rail so she could feel the vibrations—and as much as he needed a distraction, they were clearly becoming more than a hobby. The trains were turning into a replacement for animation, a new form of control in a world that was yielding less readily to him than it had in the golden days. Kimball said that he himself had planted the seed as early as 1945, when he finished a full-scale railroad on his two-acre plot in San Gabriel, complete with nine hundred feet of narrow-gauge track, an operating locomotive, and a passenger car. He called it the Grizzly Flats Railroad, after a sign he had once seen in an abandoned Sierra logging town. Walt attended the "steam up" party and got to play engineer as the locomotive crawled out of Kimball's engine house; he grinned broadly as he pulled the whistle and clanged the bell. Kimball could see that he was hooked on the power and the thrill. Once Walt even brought home a train piston and proudly displayed it on the dining room table.

Apparently wanting people to share his enthusiasm, Walt bought three of his grandnephews Lionel model train sets for Christmas 1947, then decided to get one for himself too, justifying it on the grounds that his doctor told him he needed a hobby. "I bought myself a birthday Christmas present," he wrote his sister Ruth, sounding almost exactly like a child, "—something I've wanted all my life—an electric train. Being a girl, you probably can't understand how much I wanted one when I was a kid, but I've got one now and what fun I'm having. I have it set up in one of the outer rooms adjoining my office so I can play with it in my spare moments. It's a freight train with a whistle and real smoke comes out of the stack—there are switches, semaphores, stations and everything. It's wonderful!" Walt was actually soft-pedaling his new train set. In actuality, with the help of a machinist in the studio shop, Roger Broggie, he had built an elaborate layout in the office. According to one visitor, it was large enough to fill half of a two-car garage, boasting two trains with tunnels, miniature towns, and lead counterweights to raise and lower bridges. He loved playing with it, but when it was finished, he asked Broggie, "This is an electric train. Now what's for real?"

In point of fact, Walt had seen what was for real when he saw Kimball's engine. When Kimball invited animator Ollie Johnston to Walt's office to look at Walt's electric train, Johnston told Walt about a one-twelfth-scale steam locomotive that he was having built for his yard in the Sierra Madre foothills, and Walt began visiting the machine shop in Santa Monica, where the parts for Johnston's railroad were being milled. Meanwhile Kimball introduced Walt to another train enthusiast, Dick Jackson, who had made a fortune in auto accessories before retiring and devoting himself to scale railroads. Walt, along with Lillian and Sharon, visited Jackson at his Beverly Hills home and got to run Jackson's steam engine. Walt had met yet another railroad buff that spring, William "Casey" Jones, who also had a scale railroad at his home in Los Gatos and who also let Walt work the throttle. "Personally, I envy you for having the courage to do what you want," Walt wrote Jones, clearly thinking of his own predicament.

Now Walt wanted a train of his own—not a model but a real train that was just large enough for him to sit on. He had Richard Jones, the head of the studio machine shop, begin making discreet inquiries of people who might be willing to sell miniature trains—discreet because he obviously did not want potential sellers to know that it was Walt Disney who wished to make the purchase. Jones also placed an ad in *Railroad Magazine* requesting information on where he might buy a live-steam eight-gauge or sixteen-gauge railway, and he wrote other enthusiasts for information on how to lay a mile of miniature track. Later that summer Walt and Sharon attended a fair of little engines in Lomita, California. When he returned to the studio, he had Dick Jones and Eddie Sargeant, a draftsman, draw up blueprints and then begin work on an inch-and-a-half scale model of the Central Pacific 173 engine, a prototype of which he had seen at the Golden Gate International Exposition on the same trip. As Roger Broggie told it, Walt had shown up in the shop at seven-fifteen the morning after returning from the exposition and told Broggie to get to work on the train. Meanwhile Walt entrusted William Jones with finding him a scale locomotive engine "if it can be had at a reasonable price."

But Walt's plan was not simply to purchase a train or even to have one made for him at the studio to his specifications. The train, like the animation, was to be all-consuming—his escape from the animations, as the animations had been intended as an escape from reality. In effect, the train would be his job. And so Walt was going to *make* the train himself alongside Dick Jones, Eddie Sargeant, and Roger Broggie. At night for three or four hours at a time and for long stretches on weekends, he began visiting the studio machine shop, located near the studio entrance in what were called "boxcars," where Broggie had set up a workbench for him and taught him how to use the jeweler's lathe, a miniature drill press, and a milling machine. He would go down there on Saturdays in his workclothes, often accompanied by Duchess or by Sharon, who would play in his office or ride her bicycle or drive her father's car slowly around the lot while he worked. (Walt had taught her to drive there.) Just as often he was the only one in the shop. Fabricating the train became his new passion.

And if he loved the model trains, he also loved this uncomplicated, democratic process of making them—a process in which he was just a "rookie machinist," as he called himself, and in which there were no expectations on him and no demands. "You know, it does me some good to come down here and find out I don't know everything," he told Roger Broggie. It was like the early days at the studio when it was still fun. Ollie Johnston would remember occasions working side by side with Walt on their trains and Walt saying, "Hey, I think I found out where they keep the hardwood," and off they would go to find scraps of lumber. And Walt enjoyed the craft—the sense of finally doing productive work again and doing it with perfection the way he had done the early features. Indeed, the detail work was such that it demanded perfection. He would carry his unfinished train wheels with him wherever he went that fall and winter. "If he took his family to Palm Springs the box of wheels went along," Diane recalled, "and he sat there filing in the sun." And sitting there filing, Walt Disney was as contented as he had been in years.

Just before Christmas 1948, a year after setting up his electric train set in his office, Walt finished the Central Pacific 173, laid a circle of three hundred feet of track on the soundstage, and fired up the engine. He arranged another test run shortly before New Year's. Eddie Sargeant was at the throttle and took a turn too quickly, falling off the tender and pulling the engine off the track, but Walt was ecstatic anyway. He had his train. He had the joy of collaboration again. He had an object on which to lavish his affection. He had the pleasure of doing work exactly as he wanted and an opportunity to exercise the control that he had lost.

But if he was ecstatic, others were bewildered. Visiting the studio during this period, *New York Times* film critic Bosley Crowther was struck by how uninterested Walt seemed in movies and how "wholly, almost weirdly, concerned with the building of a miniature railroad engine and a string of cars in the workshops of the studio. All of his zest for invention, for creating fantasies, seemed to be going into this plaything." Crowther said, "I came away feeling sad"—sad because Walt Disney, the man who had helped shape the American imagination, was now spending most of his time playing with trains.

VI

As distracted as he was and as much as he wanted to avoid them, the demands of the studio still made claims on his time and attention. While he was playing with his trains, his staff was finishing another live action–animation combination film, *So Dear to My Heart*, based on a popular novel by Sterling North titled *Midnight and Jeremiah*, about a boy and his pet lamb. It starred Bobby Driscoll and Luana Patten, two children whom Walt had put under contract after their appearances in *Song of the South*. Like most Disney features, it had been in production a long time; Walt had begun meeting with screenwriter Edwin Justus Mayer in 1945, and Perce Pearce had gone to Indiana, where the film was set, that summer to get a sense of atmosphere, just as Walt had gone to Atlanta to soak up atmosphere for *Song of the South*. The actual filming, on location in California's San Joaquin Valley where the Indiana town was re-created, began late in the spring of 1946. Walt was on the set for long stretches at the beginning and then on weekends, making suggestions over Sunday breakfast, though director Harold Schuster, whom Walt had recruited from Twentieth Century–Fox after seeing Schuster's horse movie, *My Friend Flicka*, said that Walt never pressed him. "He left the reins firmly in my hands," Schuster claimed.

In postproduction, however, Walt was forced to retake the reins. He wasn't particularly happy with the outcome of the film and had decided to rework at least one entire section, ordering Bill Anderson, who was responsible for the budget, out of the meeting at which he discussed the changes because Walt didn't want to be encumbered by financial considerations. But even as he reworked scenes, he was discouraged. While preoccupied with his trains, he nevertheless spent another year on the picture after the filming was concluded, finally deciding to add animated sequences as he had done in *Song of the South* and justifying them as "figments of a small boy's imagination." As publicist Card Walker put it, "He knew he had a problem." (It was to escape tensions on the film that he had gone to Hawaii and then to the railroad fair.) The addition of the animation prompted "Mr. Harper" in *Harper's* magazine to observe, only half in jest and while the film was still in production, "No good, certainly, can come of breaking down the barrier that still protects live, three-dimensional people from the inhabitants of Mr. Disney's two-dimensional world who have been so firmly protected from the mediocre and the phony"—a protection that had been the point all along. Now they no longer were.

But it wasn't only mediocrity from which Walt Disney himself needed protection. In fact, *So Dear to My Heart* was actually a warmer, more sincere, and, in most reviewers' assessments, better film than *Song of the South*. For Disney, the problem was that it was a concession, an exercise in excessive nostalgia no doubt influenced by his memories of Marceline. In celebrating small-town life and small-town values, he had ostensibly gone over to Norman Rockwell territory and reinforced his new postwar image not as a daring folk artist but as a conservative folksy artist. *So Dear to My Heart*—even the title was sentimentalized—was not a bad film. It was, however, on its face a kitschy, syrupy, unimaginative one—essentially a greeting card. Still, Walt needed a hit so desperately that he spent three weeks that January attending premieres in Indiana, Ohio, Kentucky, and Tennessee—this from a man who once couldn't spare the time to attend the American premiere for *Bambi*.

Yet in one respect, one important respect, the film was a departure and a hope. Walt had conceived it as a fully live-action feature, his first, even though it hadn't turned out that way, and as such it was a kind of fulfillment. Almost from the moment he had arrived in Los Angeles, making live-action films had been his ambition. Live action was easier than animation and cheaper, and at least when Walt had begun, it was much more prestigious than animation. Unable to break into live action, he had retreated to the one thing he knew, cartooning, but he had never quite surrendered the dream, and by the time the strike was approaching, Walt, presumably in anticipation of losing some of his animators, had drafted a treatment for a film titled *Hound of Florence*, which he sent to RKO's production head, George Schaefer, with the instruction that Schaefer keep in mind "this is not intended for combination cartoon–live action, but instead it is written entirely for live action, using all the tricks we know a dog can do and playing it for comic suspense throughout." He thought it could be made for under $400,000, which was considerably less than he was spending on his feature animations.

The film was not made, another casualty of belt-tightening, but Walt had edged closer to live action, largely as an economy measure, with *Song of the South* and then *So Dear to My Heart*, and the animators were concerned. "As soon as Walt rode on a camera crane," one animator quipped, acknowledging Walt's love of both control and technology, "we knew we were going to lose him." Ben Sharpsteen admitted that many animators were "very upset" and asking whether Walt was deserting them and abandoning animation altogether. When one of them, Milt Kahl, went to Walt's office to protest, Walt said, "Well, I'll tell you, Milt. I have to make a whore of myself to pay your salary. It's as simple as that."

But it wasn't quite that simple, because there was another consideration in deciding to make a live-action feature. The British government, in an attempt to revive its own film industry after the war, had imposed a 75 percent import tax on American films shown in Britain and ordered that 45 percent of the films shown in British theaters be made in England. (The American State Department had agreed to a similar quota with France, restricting the number of imported American films there to 110, to be supplied by the major production companies, which effectively froze out the Disneys, and Roy wrote Secretary of State General George Marshall to protest.) For a studio that had always relied heavily on foreign receipts and had been devastated by wartime restrictions, these were terrible blows. To make matters worse, the French and British governments had both impounded receipts earned by American studios in those countries, insisting that the currency be spent there. For the Disney studio, this amounted to more than $1 million. Obviously, Walt couldn't set up an animation studio in England or France, but he had another option. He could make a live-action film in England and finance it with the blocked funds. In effect, then, when Walt Disney finally crossed over into live action, it was because the British government had forced him to do so.

The project Walt selected for his British live-action feature, as he was winding down with *So Dear to My Heart*, was Robert Louis Stevenson's *Treasure Island*, about a young boy who joins up with a group of pirates, and he dispatched Perce Pearce and Fred Leahy to England to supervise the production. But Walt, who was still at loose ends, decided that he would take Lillian and the girls for a European vacation on the pretense that he had to supervise the film personally. (Later he was candid about it. "I did them in summer," he said of his English productions. "That gave me a chance to . . . get away.") It was clearly a relief to be free of the studio that he had once loved so deeply, and Disney representative William Levy wrote Roy that Walt had arrived that June "in excellent spirits and full of confidence and repeatedly remarked that with any luck the picture should be brought in at a reasonable budget."

The shooting began on July 4, 1949, in "fantastically wonderful sunshine," the Disneys' British agent, Cyril James, wrote Roy. The weather seemed to portend a relatively stress-free production. Walt, despite the professions of supervision, visited the set at the Denham Studios outside London only occasionally, and director Byron Haskin's agent wrote Jack Lavin, the studio talent coordinator, that Walt "seems pleased with everything." With the film sailing along calmly, Walt had provisions sent to the Dorchester Hotel in London (two cases of Johnnie Walker Black Label whiskey, six cans of bacon, four cans of corned beef hash, Spam, and franks, six cans of boiled ham, and twenty-four cans of his favorite dish, chili and beans) and played tourist with his family. When they tired of London, they visited Ireland for two days, then spent three weeks in France, where Walt revisited the sites of his Red Cross service, then crossed to Switzerland.

After five weeks in all, he and the family left for America, but in yet another sign of Walt's restlessness, he returned to England a month and a half later, this time without Lillian or the girls, as the production rolled to its climax. The only suspense had been whether the British government would issue a work permit to Bobby Driscoll, who was to star in the film, since a British law prohibited the employment of actors under thirteen years of age. Frantic upon learning this, Fred Leahy arranged to have the Educational Bureau agree to "look the other way" during the filming, while Driscoll was to say that he was only in England on a visit. But when Driscoll was forced to stay longer than had been expected, due largely to weather delays, the crew worried that the police might issue a summons, so Driscoll was shuttled between the first unit (doing the principal photography) and, when that unit was setting up, the third unit (usually assigned to do the scenes in which actors were not necessary). That way Driscoll's time was maximized, though it meant that all his scenes had to be shot first. In the end Driscoll's parents and the studio were both fined for violating the work permit law, but it was a small price to pay to complete the photography.

Now came the typical race to finish the film in time for its contracted release in the summer. Though Walt had left most of the production to Pearce and Leahy, he was unusually involved in the postproduction—at least compared to the offhanded way he had been treating recent films. He had asked Pearce and Leahy to air-mail him specific takes for editing, and after a test screening in early January, he ordered them to cut ten to twelve minutes and provide a more forceful musical score; he also advised them that a more detailed criticism would follow. Two days later he ordered the editor to fly from England to Los Angeles, apparently so that Walt could oversee the editing himself.

The finished film, Walt Disney's first all-live-action feature, was both a critical and a financial success—the first in a long, long time. *Treasure Island* grossed $4 million, returning to the studio a profit of between $2.2 and $2.4 million. Roy, looking to the future, crowed that if "we have a subject that seems to have a world-wide appeal—we have it in Technicolor and sell it as a Walt Disney picture," the studio could safely spend as much as $1.5 million in negative costs and still have a "reasonably safe investment." This euphoria led Disney fans to worry, as the animators had, that Disney animation was dead, but Walt wrote Douglas Fairbanks, Jr., one of those concerned, "We are not forsaking the cartoon field—it is purely a move of economy—again converting pounds into dollars to enable us to make more cartoons here." It was a strange turn. Walt Disney had to make live-action films now to save his animations.

As they were finishing the shooting, the Disneys suffered another blow. Through all the adversity, all the economic ups and downs, they had had one bedrock: the merchandise division headed by Kay Kamen. Though Walt often micromanaged his studio, he never interfered with Kamen, and Kamen had repaid the trust by following a policy as simple as Walt's own. "The prestige and dignity of the name Walt Disney had to be maintained," he wrote a merchandising representative. "The production of the Disney prestige was always more important than any royalties we would get." The policy worked. In 1947 Kamen claimed that the Disney label was selling roughly $100 million in goods each year, including toys, clothes, statuettes, snacks, and a full line of Donald Duck foods including field peas with snaps, peanut butter, catsup, chili sauce, macaroni, mayonnaise, and egg noodles. In 1948, when the Disneys renewed their agreement with Kamen for another seven years, the five-millionth Mickey Mouse watch was sold and more than two thousand Disney-related products were being manufactured. These sales brought in $1.25 million in profits, which the Disneys split with Kamen on a seventy-thirty basis, the bulk going to the Disneys, up from the fifty-fifty split the parties had had prior to the war. That didn't include a ten-year license extension on books and magazines that Roy himself had negotiated with the Whitman Publishing Company early in 1948 that also required Whitman to underwrite a bank loan to the studio for $1.06 million.

The Disneys not only trusted Kamen but liked him and enjoyed his company, and by happy coincidence Walt, Roy, and Kamen all happened to be in Europe that October—Walt overseeing *Treasure Island*, Roy conducting business, and Kamen vacationing with his wife. The night before the Kamens were to depart for the States, they had dinner with Walt and Roy in Paris. Walt recalled that they were "very happy." Earlier that day

Kamen had written the vice president of his company in New York raving over his vacation but expressing his fear of flying back. The Kamens died the next day, October 27, 1949, in an Air France crash over the Azores.

Thus ended seventeen years of one of Walt Disney's happiest and least tempestuous collaborations. At the time of Kamen's death the studio's profits from merchandise had reached a "new high in our history," Roy wrote Walt. Kamen was irreplaceable, the Disneys knew, and they didn't even try to find a new agent. Instead they decided to run the merchandising arm themselves, appointing O. B. Johnston, who had been a studio accountant, to head the division. (A few months earlier the Disneys had set up their own music-publishing division to retain the rights to Disney songs and to acquire rights to other songs that had a Disney flavor, like the hits "Mule Train" and "Shrimp Boats.") Roy admitted nine months later that in taking over merchandising from Kamen's estate, they had had "some ups and downs" but that "we are now finally beginning to get hold of it and make progress." Still, though it was one of the most profitable divisions of the company, it only added to the growing if mistaken impression of Walt Disney as a corporate magnate rather than an artist—someone who was now out to exploit rather than to create.

VII

Since the very beginning of Disney Bros., the studio had been Walt Disney's refuge and his real home. "[N]o matter what you were talking about, he'd get back to this goddamn Studio," Ward Kimball said, referring to the train ride to the Chicago Railroad Fair. "He wanted to talk about it. This was HIM. This was his SEX! This was EVERYTHING. . . . The orgasms were all here." Milt Kahl told one interviewer that "he lived here, really. God, his home life was nothing compared to his studio life." (There was, in fact, the room off his office with a bed and shower where the naval officer had stayed for a time during the war and where Walt would occasionally spend the night.) His secretary recalled how he frequently ignored the clock and at seven or eight in the evening would still be in his office, and she would phone Lillian to tell her that Walt wouldn't be home for dinner.

So it was yet another sign of Walt's discontent that as he was embarking on his train-building, he was also investigating building a new house for his family as what he called "sort of a wedding anniversary present—our twenty-fifth." The Disneys had lived in the home on the hill at 4053 Woking Way, from which they could see the Pacific Ocean and Los Angeles below, since before Diane's birth, and even then, despite its five bedrooms and five baths, its pool and playhouse and badminton court and screening room in the library where wood panels slid back to reveal the projector, it had been a modest structure for a film executive of Walt Disney's stature. The new house was partly a project, something to hold Walt's attention, partly a haven to replace the studio as the trains had replaced the animation, and partly a way to secure himself against the assaults of the world by retreating to his family. "All in all, I think it is going to be a very happy set-up," Walt wrote his aunt Jessie Perkins, "and I am looking forward to spending more time at home than I have in the past."

One of the major lures was Walt's train. In looking for a new home site, he was seeking a place where he could lay track for the railroad that consumed him. Diane and Lillian had found a site off Wilshire Boulevard, but Walt vetoed it because there was no place for the train. Meanwhile Lillian had phoned Harold Janss, a well-known developer, who suggested a heavily wooded two-and-a-half-acre property at Holmby Hills, a rich development in western Los Angeles that Janss's family had owned since the 1920s. Walt and Lillian drove out to view the plot one Sunday in May 1948, and as Lillian put it, "Walt took one look and said, 'That's it!' He could see that train here." Unlike Woking Way, which was close to Burbank, the site had the additional advantage, Walt would say, of being far enough from the studio so that he could use his drive there for precious time to meditate.

They closed the deal on June 4 for $33,250. (Walt applied for a $25,000 building loan from the Bank of America and listed his income as $104,000.)* The site gently sloped down from a bluff on which the home was to be built to a canyon that would separate the home from the road. Walt's neighborhood in Los Feliz had been something of a bohemian district; it spoke to the exclusivity of the new neighborhood that one adjacent home was owned by William Goetz, MGM head Louis B. Mayer's son-in-law and one of the top executives at Universal-International. The new house itself, designed by a highly regarded Russian-born architect and furniture maker named James Dolena, sometimes called the "architect to the stars," was a 5,669-square-foot split-level modern sheathed in white that flared out into two wings. The lawn behind the house led to a 22-by-44-foot swimming pool. Beyond the pool was a fifteen-hundred-square-foot recreation building that housed a screening room, a bar, a

*Two years earlier Walt had purchased a lot at Smoke Tree with the intention of building his own cottage there instead of renting one.

four-car garage, and Walt's own pièce de résistance—a fully operational soda fountain.

The Woking Way house had been completed in two months as the Disneys awaited the birth of the child Lillian would miscarry. The construction of the new house at 355 Carolwood Drive was much more languorously paced, though Walt, seeming to want the distraction, wasn't impatient. It took well over a year to finish, and even after the family moved in late in May 1950, Walt spent another six months laying the track for his railroad and building a small engine house and workshop that had been adapted from the design for the barn in *So Dear to My Heart*, which, Walt claimed, had itself been adapted from his father's barn in Marceline, making the Carolwood house yet another reminder of Walt's happiest memories. The Disneys even planted fruit trees as on the Marceline farm.

Though it had seventeen rooms, the house was hardly palatial. (Having reinvested his money in the studio, he "didn't make the kind of money those guys [film moguls] did," Diane recalled.) Walt said that it was scaled to the family's needs and designed to simplify Lillian's housekeeping, and it was, but it was also designed to allow Walt to withdraw not only from the world generally, as he had always desired to do, but into the kind of delayed childhood that he was now enjoying. He often spent his evenings in the workshop making tiny furniture for his railroad while Duchess, to whom he slipped bologna and hot dogs that he had stuffed in his pockets, slept on a blanket. Then exactly at midnight, he said, she would get off the blanket and begin nudging him to go to bed. "And she'd sit and look at me until I came," Walt would recall. "She wouldn't leave my side until I came." Other times he manned his soda fountain with its red leather barstools and its long bar with shelves of glasses behind it. Walt jokingly complained that he supplied sundaes to the entire neighborhood, but he relished playing the soda jerk. Ward Kimball said he had every kind of syrup and topping, and he would "fix these huge goopy things for his guests, ice cream sodas and the biggest banana splits you ever saw." Sharon remembered his mixing "weird concoctions," including on one occasion a champagne soda that even he admitted was barely potable. But he had another motive in installing the soda fountain besides indulging his childhood fantasies. He was hoping to freeze time. For the father of two teenage daughters, the soda fountain, the pool, and the other amenities were, he confessed, a "means of keeping them from going away from home to school, which will be all right with me," so that the sprawling wings of the house not only welcomed, they also held dear.

Of course the main attraction of the house, as far as Walt was concerned, was the railroad. He had intended for the train to run around the property—about a half-mile of track—but Lillian protested that the plan would ruin a flower garden that she had had designed. So Walt countered by having one of the studio's construction supervisors draw up a ninety-foot-long tunnel to run *under* Lillian's garden. And for good measure the supervisor threw in an S-curve to give riders a special thrill. To memorialize the compromise, Walt had Gunther Lessing draw up a mock contract in which Lillian granted the "Carolwood Pacific Railroad" a right-of-way on the property. By the time he was finished, he had his tunnel, a forty-six-foot trestle, and just over 2,500 feet of track girdling the property; and he had spent nearly $17,000, not including $10,000 in labor costs that he had transferred from his home account to his railroad account. "We spent the first half-year in the house with a bulldozer in the back yard fixing grades for the railroad," Lillian told an interviewer. "Bulldozers cost a lot to rent. They drive you crazy with their noise." Still, Walt was not going to sacrifice his railroad, no matter how much Lillian complained. "Father was sympathetic but firm," she said.

Just as he loved to play soda jerk, he loved to play engineer. He would don an engineer's cap and a plaid shirt, straddle the tender behind the engine, which he had named *Lilly Belle*, in Lillian's honor, and fire up. Guests to the Disney home were invariably invited to take a ride on the train, and Walt would issue passes to "vice presidents" of the Carolwood Pacific—a list that included Walter Wanger, gossip columnist Hedda Hopper, ventriloquist Edgar Bergen, singer Dinah Shore, actor Dick Powell, and even Salvador Dali, who thought the detail so perfect that he feared the train would have accidents that mimicked real train crashes "or even sabotage . . . like miniature train wreckers!" Dali told Walt, "Such perfection did not belong to models!" But that had been the whole point. With his train Walt Disney had regained perfection.

As Walt was preoccupied with his trains and his house, his animators—three crews headed by Gerry Geronomi, Wilfred Jackson, and Ham Luske—were barreling ahead to finish *Cinderella*. Walt supervised, as always, and his was the final word, but he was considerably less involved than on *Snow White* or even *Dumbo*, and some of the staff complained about it. "Walt is not an artist," one former employee told a reporter. "He doesn't have the instincts or the imagination of an artist. His little-known virtue is that of a great producer, who happens to recognize the importance of putting out a product technically better than anyone else's." Another employee described Walt's demeanor as more "businesslike" now, less excitable but also less exciting. Harry Tytle found him more unpredictable. Walt had ordered Tytle not to renew the contract of composer Oliver Wallace, who had written some of the score for *Cinderella*, because Walt wanted to divert the raise Wallace was due to in-betweeners; then a few months later he demanded to know why Wallace wasn't under contract.

Still, despite Walt's disengagement and unpredictability, everyone knew what was at stake on *Cinderella*. It was the first real animated feature since *Bambi*, and Walt had told his employees early in the production, "Boys, if *Cinderella* doesn't make it, we're through!" He certainly wouldn't have had the resources to begin another feature once *Alice in Wonderland*, already in production, was completed. When the film was finished late that fall of 1949, Walt was, typically, not entirely happy. "The finished picture is not everything that we wanted it to be," he told one magazine editor, "but, today, it is quite a problem what with costs, labor, etc., to do all the things you would like to," and he boasted that "we are now getting our organization in such shape that I think we are going to come out with a real post-war production—ALICE IN WONDERLAND—which is now in work. It looks unusually good." To another interviewer he said of *Cinderella*, "That was just a picture."

In fact, despite the shortcuts in the animation and the eventual lack of passion from the staff, most people saw *Cinderella* as a welcome return to form for Walt Disney after the years of disappointments. William Levy, now Walt's eastern press representative, had held four days of screenings that November and reported "unstinting praise from all," saying that many "rate Cinderella above Snow White." How much of this was wishful thinking or the desperation of Disney admirers to see him regain his art and popularity is difficult to say. But *Cinderella*—with an effervescent score and a tense subplot of helpful mice menaced by a wicked feline named Lucifer (Walt had asked Ward Kimball to model it on one of Kimball's own cats)—was a more fully realized and dramatic animation than any the studio had done since *Bambi*, and it received the best reception a Disney animation had gotten since *Dumbo*. In personal correspondence director Michael Curtiz hailed it as the "masterpiece of all pictures you have done." Producer Hal Wallis declared, "If this is not your best, it is very close to the top." Walter Wanger wrote him, "You are still the number one producer on my 'Hit Parade.' " When it opened in February 1950, most reviewers were equally effusive. *Cinderella* was an unqualified critical hit, and it would soon join the early Disney features as an acknowledged classic.

Far more important for the studio, *Cinderella* was a financial success as well. Sailing from New York to London, Roy wrote Walt, "I feel stronger than ever that we should do in the United States and Canada a minimum of $5,000,000. I wouldn't be surprised if we hit $6,000,000. It is the talk of the business." In the final analysis, Roy had actually underestimated the film's return. *Cinderella* had cost the studio $2.2 million. It would gross $7.9 million. And that didn't include what the film generated in sales of merchandise and music, especially since one of the film's songs, "Bibbidi-Bobbidi-Boo," became a popular hit and would receive an Academy Award nomination. The film, the failure of which would have sunk the Disney studio, wound up rescuing it from financial disaster and spiritual despair.

Yet Walt Disney didn't seem particularly elated. He saw the problems and the compromises and the shattered camaraderie, and even as he focused on his trains and his new house, he began looking elsewhere to recover what he felt had been stolen from him and to find what he hoped would save him. He was looking to create an even better fortress for himself, an even more perfect world than the world of animation had been.

Ten

CITY ON A HILL

It had always been about control, about crafting a better reality than the one outside the studio, and about demonstrating that one had the capacity to do so. That was what Walt Disney provided to America—not escape, as so many analysts would surmise, but control and the vicarious empowerment that accompanied it. And that was what America seemed to want from him. Though the immediate postwar period had been triumphant for the country, the mood quickly turned from euphoria to uncertainty—what historian William Leuchtenberg would describe as a "troubled feast" in his account of the time. The feast was the nation's unprecedented economic growth, fueled largely by military spending. In the ten years after the war wages rose and working hours decreased, home ownership jumped, higher education was made available to returning veterans, and general consumption soared. All of which led sociologist Seymour Martin Lipset to declare, "The fundamental problems of the industrial revolution have been solved."

But despite the hopefulness, a general sense of malaise wafted through the nation. In part it was a result of the Cold War between the capitalist and Communist blocs, colder still after the Soviet Union detonated an atomic bomb in August 1949. Americans understandably felt they were threatened from without by Russia. They would also come to feel that they were threatened from within by a cadre of Communists and Communist sympathizers who had wedged their way into the government—the alleged fifth columnists that Senator Joseph McCarthy would ride to headlines. But it wasn't just the Communist threat to government that led to anxiety. No less an authority than President Truman's attorney general, J. Howard McGrath, said Communists were everywhere—"in factories, offices, butcher stores, on street corners and in private business. And each carries in himself the death of society."

Dire as that sounded, probably more important was the feeling of dislocation that accompanied rapid change during the period. Along with the rise of wages and the growth of consumption, America was undergoing suburbanization, a revolution in mass communication with the introduction of television in the early 1950s, increased physical mobility with automobiles, a national highway construction program and a boom in commercial airlines, new technologies, bureaucratization, and even the development of a new personality type to negotiate the new society—a type that sociologist David Riesman would describe as "other-directed," or driven less by an internal compass than by a need to please others, and what William Whyte would call the "organization man," who was concerned as much with managing the bureaucracy as with acquiring skills. What all these phenomena—from McCarthyism to suburbanization to the organization man—had in common, historian William Chafe would write, was that all were related "to the existentialist dilemma of finding a way to create meaning in the face of forces over which one had no control."

Walt Disney, like General Dwight Eisenhower, who would be elected president in 1952 and hid an iron will behind a facade of affability, promised control. When America was enjoying its burst of self-confidence immediately after the war, critics generally disdained Disney's cartoons, in part because the films were shabbily made and the sense of control in them seemed to have diminished. But once the Cold War began, Americans seemed again to need reassurance, which may explain why *Cinderella*, an old-fashioned and familiar sort of Disney animation, a *controlled* animation, found favor. (Walt's own comment on the nuclear peril was, "If people would think more of fairies they would soon forget the atom bomb.") Disney, a tonic force during the Depression, was now a touchstone, providing comfort in a time of foreboding.

As was so often the case, what was true for the country was true for Walt Disney personally. If America found control and reassurance in his films, he had found both in his model trains, which was one reason he pursued them. But that was not the only reason. The trains were also the bridgehead of a much larger scheme that was organizing itself in Walt Disney's mind. At least as early as 1947 he had begun collecting miniatures—furniture, figurines, coaches, boats, farm machinery, even tiny liquor bottles and crates. Ostensibly these were adornments for the train layout and another pastime to take his mind off the studio when, as he wrote his sister, "problems become too hectic." But as Walt scoured miniature shops during his trip to Europe in 1949 and on his various forays to New York and even up into New England; as he attended miniature shows; as he enlisted friends to find miniatures for him; as he solicited miniatures through catalogs, midwestern newspapers, and hobbyist magazines (using the name of a studio secretary as he had used machinist Dick Jones to solicit model train information), he hit upon a plan. With his own two hands he would create an entire miniature American turn-of-the-century village, a sort of Lilliputian Marceline, and then display it in large cases across the country. True to Walt's new postwar persona, he said that the project would be a means to convey traditional values, though the underlying metaphor couldn't have been more transparent. Building the village was another way for Walt to assert his control at the very time he seemed to be losing it.

To realize the plan, Walt buttonholed layout artist Ken Anderson and offered to put him on his personal payroll: Anderson was to paint scenes of Americana that Walt would then bring to life with the miniatures. "You can paint some paintings like Norman Rockwell," Anderson recalled Walt saying, "and I'll build them." The work would be done secretly, not so much, it seemed, because Walt was afraid of the idea getting out as because he didn't want the project to be infected and corrupted by the studio's corporate mentality. This was his—not the company's. He installed Anderson in a room on the third floor of the Animation Building to which only he and Anderson had the keys. Here Anderson painted. Eventually the two of them would take little expeditions to downtown Los Angeles, hunting for materials. Sometimes Walt would disappear for a day or two, Anderson said, and then return with a "whole sack full" of various items from which to construct the scenes. Walt himself admitted to one vendor of materials, "I become so absorbed that the cares of the studio fade away . . . at least for a time." Indeed, as Anderson explained it, Walt was "having such fun making these things that he completely forgot to pay me," and when Walt happened to ask whether Anderson had been compensated and Anderson said he hadn't, "I got paid and paid and paid."

Over time Anderson drew nearly two dozen sketches of archetypal American scenes—among them a blacksmith reading a newspaper, a minister in the pulpit, a klatch of gossiping women, a general store, a granny in her rocker before a hearth. But even before he began constructing his tableaux, Walt came to two realizations. The first was that he couldn't fabricate the scenes completely by himself and that he would need more assistance. He recruited a sculptor named Christodoro to help make the figures and a sketch artist named Harper Goff, whom he had met in a London model train shop during his European trip to oversee *Treasure Island.* The second realization was that the scenes couldn't be static. They had to move, which required the additional recruitment of machinist Roger Broggie, who had helped Walt build his train, and an animator-cum-sculptor named Wathel Rogers.

Now Walt, inspired by wind-up toys that he had found and dissected in Europe, began an experiment. In February 1951 he hired the actor and dancer Buddy Ebsen to perform a short tap dance in front of a grid. (Walt directed it himself.) The performance was filmed on 35mm stock and then analyzed by Broggie and Rogers to determine how they might replicate the movements with a mechanical figure that Christodoro had made. Broggie later recalled that they examined the footage frame by frame, only to discover that Ebsen never exactly repeated his steps. Moreover, just as it had been difficult to animate clothing, Broggie and Rogers could never quite get the mechanical figure's pants to flop in the same way that Ebsen's did. Still, they made the man dance, using the same kind of cam system that the wind-up toys employed, and Walt entered a new territory that further extended the metaphor of control. As the historian Jackson Lears would observe of this departure, "The quintessential product of the [Disney] empire would not be fantasy, but simulated reality; not the cartoon character, but the 'audio-animatronic' robot," of which the "mechanical man" was the first. Walt Disney had crept closer still to creating and perfecting life.

Already in January, even before the Ebsen experiment, Walt was writing a specialist in display cases that "it always takes a lot of time to work the bugs out of mechanical contraptions and this one must be absolutely right before I can go ahead on the others," but that he expected to have a "pretty good show worked up by next Christmas." At the time he had the crew work on another tableau, this one of a barbershop quartet, while he personally worked on the scene of Granny in her rocker. By March, when he asked shorts production chief Harry Tytle to handle the logistics of the touring show, he had already spent nearly $24,000 on the miniatures and the train, and he demanded as much value for his money as he had on the animations. He was constantly having miniatures sent to him on approval, then returning them for shoddy craftsmanship or lack of detail. For a man of his stature, he was also surprisingly concerned about the value of his own craftsmanship. He had designed and fabricated by hand small pot-bellied stoves that he sent on consignment to a miniatures dealer in New York, but he was incensed when the dealer charged only fifteen dollars and asked that she "keep them on display for a while longer and see what you can really get for them." When the dealer boosted the price to twenty-five dollars and sold one, Walt glowed. "The thing that pleases me is that you sold a stove for $25.00!"

Meanwhile, Walt forged ahead on his exhibition, which was now called Disneylandia and which he described as a series of "visual juke boxes with the record playing mechanism being replaced by a miniature stage setting." He was considering exhibiting the show in department stores or in railroad cars, where schoolchildren could bring coins to "play" the scenes, though Walt hesitated at having children come to freight yards, and in any case he had been told emphatically that the exhibition couldn't possibly be profitable. In the end, he settled for unveiling the scene of "Granny Kincaid" at a Festival of California Living at the Pan-Pacific Auditorium in Los Angeles in November 1952. The vitrine, roughly eight feet long, contained tiny rugs, a plank floor, a stone fireplace, lace curtains, dishes, and even an outhouse with a potty, and it featured a narration by actress Beulah Bondi, who had played Granny Kincaid in *So Dear to My Heart.* Columnist Hedda Hopper, who had visited the festival, marveled at Walt's handiwork and asked, "Why does he do it?" To which Walt answered, "Damned if I know."

But he knew very well why he did it. Beyond the psychological benisons of control and the tactile exhilaration of his own craftsmanship, beyond the way it preoccupied him while the studio seemed to wobble, he did it because he harbored an even larger, more audacious plan—a plan for which Disneylandia was only a trial run and a plan that seemed to sustain him even as he was losing interest in the rest of his company.

It is impossible to say exactly when, but Walt Disney had decided to build an amusement park.

Rudy Ising, an old Kansas City friend and one of the Laugh-O-Gram employees, recalled his and Walt's visits to Electric Park, an amusement complex, and how on one of these excursions Walt had told him, "One of these days I'm going to build an amusement park—and it's going to be clean!" Diane Disney thought the inception took place during the Sunday afternoons when Walt picked the girls up from religious services—he never attended them himself—and took them to the Griffith Park merry-go-round, where they would spend hours. "He'd see families in the park," Diane would recall, "and say, 'There's nothing for the parents to do. . . . You've got to have a place where the whole family can have fun.' " Diane thought he used those afternoons and later ones with Sharon at a small amusement park at La Cienega and Beverly in Los Angeles as a "sort of research project." Roy thought that it had all begun with the model trains. Once Walt began building his locomotive, Roy told an interviewer, "he always wanted to build a big play train for the public," though it was unclear whether Walt built the model trains because he had the park in mind or whether he had the park in mind because he built the model trains. Wilfred Jackson said that Walt had first broached the idea for an amusement park during the *Snow White* premiere, where Walt had a dwarfs' cottage erected outside the theater as a display. As they walked past it, Walt told Jackson that he wanted to build a park scaled to children's size. Ben Sharpsteen said he first heard about a park in 1940 when he accompanied Walt to New York for a demonstration of Fantasound and Walt discussed his plans for setting up displays on a strip of land across the street from the studio between Riverside Drive and the Los Angeles River—"just something to show people who wanted to visit the Disney Studio," Walt said. Dick Irvine, an art director at the studio, remembered Walt coming into the office during the war and describing a public tour of the studio that Irvine felt later expanded into the amusement park. And John Hench, an animator and layout man, recalled Walt in the 1940s pacing out the parking lot and imagining the boundaries for an amusement park there.

As he was prowling shops and poring through catalogs for miniatures, and as he was milling parts for his own railroad, he was thinking and even talking in earnest about installing a scale-model passenger train to circumnavigate the studio and about landscaping its route with what he referred to as a "village." In the spring of 1948 Walt had mentioned to Harry Tytle the idea of constructing a train ride on the seven-acre Riverside Drive plot and in the summer of 1948 Ward Kimball was gushing to Walt about the railroad concession at an amusement park outside San Francisco that had reaped $50,000 the previous year—"enough to pay for all the other concessions in the park!" By the time Walt and Kimball left for the Chicago Railroad Fair that August, Walt was pressing Casey Jones, his fellow railroad enthusiast, to find him a locomotive for the "village" as an anchor and was half-apologizing for the scale of his project: "While I know the whole plan I have in mind sounds quite elaborate, yet I feel the success of it depends upon the project being very complete." On the way back from Chicago, Walt and Kimball made a two-day detour to Henry Ford's Greenfield Village in Michigan, Walt's second visit there, and Walt returned to California more inspired and expansive than ever about his park. Kimball said it was all Walt talked about on the trip.

He could visualize it just the way he had once visualized the animations. He could *see* not just the train ride but the park around which it would run, and by the end of August he had made extensive notes for a production designer named Dick Kelsey. He described a Main Village with a railroad station and a village green—obviously modeled after Marceline. "It will be a place for people to sit and rest; mothers and grandmothers can watch over small children at play," Walt wrote. "I want it to be very relaxing, cool and inviting." A small town would be built around the green, with the railroad station at one end and a town hall at the other and police and fire stations in between. A "variety of little stores" would ring the green, where Disney merchandise would be sold. There would be a three-hundred-seat combination opera house and movie theater. In the middle of the park he envisioned an ice cream–hot dog stand, but he also thought of a restaurant. And there would be other sections too: an old farm, a western village, an Indian compound (no doubt influenced by the Santa Fe compound at the railroad fair), and a carnival area with rides—"typical Midway stuff." A buckboard would carry passengers through the western village and the old farm. Already he was securing plans for a riverboat, and he had sent Jack Cutting, the head of the foreign operation, to scout merry-go-rounds in Europe.

By October, however, the plans had been temporarily sidelined. "To tell the truth, I have been so involved in production matters since I got back," he wrote a Santa Fe executive to whom he had been enthusing over his plans, after returning from the railroad fair and then two weeks in Arizona, "that I haven't given any further thought to my project." Instead, with neither the time nor the resources to devote to his village, he launched Disneylandia, most likely because it was an inexpensive and manageable way to dip his toe into the waters of amusement and to test concepts for the larger park while he supervised production. For a man who was always impatient—always drumming his fingers during presentations, or snapping at subordinates when they didn't grasp his ideas immediately, or dragging nervously on cigarettes—it was also a way to keep moving forward rather than wait. "I'm going to move on to something else because I'm wasting my time if I mess around with that any longer," he would often tell nurse Hazel George about various stalemated projects. "And instead of trying to solve what momentarily was an insoluble situation," George would say, "he would go on to something else. So he kept constantly in movement."

The production matters that now diverted him were the completion of *So Dear to My Heart*; the combination of *The Wind in the Willows* and *The Legend of Sleepy Hollow*, which were being packaged as a single film, *The Adventures of Ichabod and Mr. Toad*; and *Cinderella*—all of which were released in a period of just over a year between January 1949 and February 1950. While none of these films alone might have commanded his attention now that he was playing with his trains and contemplating his village, together they made incursions. He was also contending with *Alice in Wonderland*, Lewis Carroll's story of a girl who follows a rabbit down his hole and into a series of surrealistic adventures. No project had been at the studio longer—Walt had first discussed it with Mary Pickford in 1933 and bought the rights to the Lewis Carroll books with the Tenniel illustrations in 1938 shortly after *Snow White*—and none had proved more intractable. Over the years Walt had assigned various writers to the film, among them novelist Aldous Huxley, who, according to Dick Huemer, couldn't get in a word at story meetings without being outtalked by Walt. "Five meetings or so and we never saw him again," Huemer said of Huxley's brief 1945 tenure. Huxley wasn't the only one who had difficulties. "There is no story in the book," said Bob Carr, who had been the head of the story department during one early go at *Alice*. Moreover, he observed, "Alice has no character. She merely plays straight man to a cast of screw-ball comics. It is too bad for any leading character to be placed in this untenable position." Walt didn't disagree. "You could hear him with the animators at work," Diane recalled, "saying Alice was cold, you couldn't get any warmth into her." Ben Sharpsteen said that the animators were none too enthusiastic about the film either but that so many people over the years—"especially sophisticated people," in Sharpsteen's words—had urged Walt to make *Alice* that he had felt compelled to produce it whether he liked it or not.

His ambivalence was evident. As they plodded forward, Walt debated whether to make it a full animation or a combination live action–animation. He announced that actress-dancer Ginger Rogers would play the title role; then a year later that Luana Patten, the young girl slated for *Song of the South*, would play her; and then neither. He hired a Barnard professor to find the right "voice" for Alice, which ignited a controversy in Britain over whether the country's beloved character might wind up sounding American, then signed a ten-year-old English actress named Kathryn Beaumont to voice the role in what was now to be a full animation. He had even consulted a psychiatrist to take a new approach to the material and assigned storymen T. Hee and Bill Cottrell to have another crack at it, but they were stymied too. Roy hated it, and Walt admitted that he would have bumped it for *Peter Pan* had that film been ready, which it wasn't, but the studio had too much invested in *Alice* to shelve it. Instead, everyone soldiered on slowly and unhappily and with premonitions of disaster, despite Walt's rosy predictions at the time of *Cinderella*'s release.

In the end, the premonitions proved all too accurate. Ward Kimball thought the sequence directors had started trying to outdo one another, which had a "self-cancelling effect on the final product." Harry Tytle's analysis was that *Alice* had "too much sameness." Walt had always felt that it lacked heart and would later say, following Sharpsteen, that he got "trapped into making 'Alice in Wonderland' against my better judgment" and called it a "terrible disappointment." "It's terribly tough to transfer whimsy to the screen," he said. To another interviewer he admitted, "We just didn't feel a thing, but we were forcing ourselves to do it." The animation suffered because the staff had been further depleted by defections to the new medium of television. And just five days before its scheduled release, in July 1951, a rival producer rushed a puppet version of the story into theaters. Walt sought an injunction, arguing that the new film was trying to capitalize on his, but he lost. Even a promotional appearance by Walt for *Alice* on the radio turned sour when he suddenly went blank and had to fumble his way through the interview. The film received tepid praise—"Watching this picture is something like nibbling those wafers that Alice eats," wrote Bosley Crowther in the *New York Times*—and in its first release returned only $2 million on a $3 million investment.

But again Walt wasn't in Burbank to suffer the disappointment. At the time of *Alice*'s release he was in Europe with Lillian and the girls to supervise the second of the British live-action pictures, *The Adventures of Robin Hood and His Merrie Men*, financed by the blocked monies of RKO and Disney, though this visit, like the one for *Treasure Island*, seemed to be more an excuse for an extended vacation than a business trip. Before leaving, Walt had screened films at the studio, looking at prospective actors and directors and making what he himself called "merely suggestions," while he left the final decisions to Perce Pearce, who was producing. For his part, Pearce had laid out every shot in the movie in thumbnail sketches, just as the studio had done with the animations, and sent them on, along with photostats and the final script, to Walt for his approval, which Walt freely gave, though not without a veiled threat that Pearce had better make the film as quickly as possible. "[T]his is important not only to the organization but to you as the producer," he wrote. Meanwhile, as the film was shot, Walt, Lillian, and the girls wandered through Europe, visiting the Tivoli Gardens in Denmark, and did not return to the studio until August.

When he did return, he plunged back into Disneylandia and his park. At home, Lillian recalled, he would come in after running the *Lilly Belle* and then regale the family with his plans. He had first talked of the park being located on the seven acres across from the studio, with the train traversing the land separating the studio from nearby Griffith Park, but his plans kept growing larger until, Diane admitted, "his conversation about it at home became so sweeping that I didn't take it seriously anymore." Walt, however, was deadly serious. Late that summer or early in the fall he had Harper Goff draw overhead plans and sketches of the park, which now included a small lake and an island, and he talked about the park at every opportunity just as he had talked incessantly about *Snow White* when he was conceptualizing it in the mid-1930s. "[E]very time you had a meeting with Walt on something else," Milt Kahl said, "why, the Park would come up. Especially if you were up in his office, where he had all his drawings and stuff." One executive at ABC television remembered Walt coming to the office, even before his European trip and even before he had any of Goff's sketches, to discuss possible projects but said that Walt could talk only about the park: "Walt just carried on and on about it, and built a word picture." The executive left "with a great deal of enthusiasm," but he admitted that "our people seemed not to understand what he was talking about."

The ABC executives weren't the only ones who couldn't get their minds around the concept of an imaginative park. Lillian said she was "afraid" of the park, afraid it was too ambitious. Roy said he wasn't initially enthusiastic either, though he grudgingly justified the project on the grounds that the park could be used as a broadcast studio for television. None of this had the least effect in dissuading Walt, who was more energized than he had been in years. He asked John Cowles, a young architect who was the son of Walt's early Kansas City benefactor, Dr. J. V. Cowles, to expand upon Goff's sketches with architectural drawings, and he set him up in a bungalow on the Burbank lot. In March, using sketches made by animator Don DaGradi, Walt sent a presentation to the Burbank Parks and Recreation Board, whose approval he needed, announcing his plans for a park that would generate a small profit rather than one that would operate on a "full bore moneymaking scale," though it now included a canal boat, a spaceship mock-up, and a submarine ride. That same week Walt had one of his associates begin searching for a small coach and Shetland ponies to pull it; he had already installed a Shetland pony trainer named Owen Pope at the studio to put up stalls and build carriages. Pope, who lived with his wife Dolly in a trailer on the lot under the water tower, said that Walt would stop by every day to talk about the park.

The project hadn't a name yet—occasionally it was called "Mickey Mouse Village"—but a few months earlier Sharpsteen had written a memo to Walt referring to an anticipated 16mm nontheatrical release of the old *Snow White* promotional film for the RKO sales force as "A Trip Through Disneyland," and the miniature project had already been dubbed "Disneylandia." "I don't recall a specific occasion when anyone said it's going to be called Disneyland," said Bill Cottrell. "I do recall that the name was suddenly said by Walt, and it sounded good, and that was it." Thenceforth the park would be known as Disneyland, which was exactly what it would be: a land of Walt Disney's imagination, a land under his absolute power.

But studio business kept interfering, and the plans kept stalling. Though producer Perce Pearce and writer Lawrence Edward Watkin did most of the work on the next British live-action feature, a costume drama called *The Sword and the Rose*, as they had on the first two, Walt did comment on the script and examine the storyboards in his office to make sure the action never slackened, and he felt the need once again to spend the summer in Europe, ostensibly to keep an eye on the production.* But even if he was essentially relaxing, the pressures were mounting again. Shortly after his return to the studio he wrote Pearce that he had been "as busy as the proverbial 'ten cats on a tin roof.' " He was helping shepherd *Rob Roy, the Highland Rogue*, another British film, into production for the following year, and he was beginning preparations for the studio's first American-made live-action feature, Jules Verne's *20,000 Leagues Under the Sea.*

And even as he was planning these films and even as he was riveted on the park, he was finishing *Peter Pan*, Sir James Barrie's account of a boy who has never grown up and his encounters with the wicked Captain

*Though Walt delegated a good deal of authority on these films, he nevertheless took his approval of the storyboards seriously. When he noticed that one sequence wasn't shot exactly as agreed, he questioned the director Ken Annakin as to why. Annakin replied that he was going over budget and wanted to economize. "Have I ever queried the budget?" Walt asked. "Have I ever asked you to cut? Let's keep to what we agreed." Ken Annakin quoted in Katherine and Richard Greene, *Inside the Dream: The Personal Story of Walt Disney* (New York: Roundtable Press, 2001), pp. 87–88.

Hook, which had been in production nearly as long as *Alice in Wonderland.* He had acquired the rights in the post–*Snow White* buying spree, had completed a Leica reel as early as 1939, had spent $200,000 on developing the property by 1943 as opposed to only $15,000 on *Alice*, and, clearly feeling affinities for the material, had persistently pushed to get it into production before other films that were in the pipeline. (Aside from *The Wind in the Willows*, which was already in production at the time, it was the only feature that the Bank of America allowed to proceed during the war.) As it slowly made its way through the typical Disney process, Walt talked to actress Mary Martin, who was appearing in a stage production of the play, about voicing Peter (Roy thought her voice "too heavy, matured and sophisticated"), and the actress Jean Arthur had contacted Walt asking to be considered. Walt had also talked to Cary Grant about voicing Captain Hook, who said the "idea intrigued him." (Walt talked to Grant as well about starring in a live-action adaptation of *Don Quixote* with the Mexican star Cantinflas as Sancho Panza, another project that was eventually nixed.)

As with virtually all the features, while the preparation for *Peter Pan* dragged on, the studio encountered difficulties. At one point shortly after the war, impatient with the delays, Walt ordered director Jack Kinney to work on sequences consecutively rather than finish the entire script before it was sent to be storyboarded, so that a scene would be approved at a morning story meeting and then immediately be put into development. When Kinney asked Walt if he wanted to see what they were doing as they proceeded, Walt insisted that they keep going until the storyboards were finished. After what Kinney said were six months and thirty-nine storyboards bearing one hundred sketches each, he made his two-and-a-half-hour presentation to Walt. When he finished, Walt sat silently, drummed his fingers, then announced, "Y'know, I've been thinking of Cinderella."

Now, even after *Cinderella* had been completed and released, *Peter Pan* continued to inch forward. As with *Cinderella*, Walt had an entire live-action version shot on the soundstage. It starred Bobby Driscoll as Peter and Hans Conried as Captain Hook, both of whom would do the voices for those characters, and Conried said he would be called into the studio intermittently over a two-and-a-half-year period to do a few days' or a few weeks' work. But with the live action to work from, Walt complained that he thought the animators had let too much of Driscoll seep into the drawings. "Some of these Peter Pans look like hell," Walt told Milt Kahl. "They are too masculine, too old, There is something wrong down there." "You want to know what's wrong?" Kahl replied. "What is wrong is that they don't have any talent in the place."

Kahl was right that the talent and commitment at Burbank had continued to decline, but even the talent the studio did have struggled. Storyman Bill Peet thought it was another example of too many individuals contending against one another and said that the picture finally got moving when just a few of the staff huddled to finalize the material. Still, they were having to do it themselves without the guidance that Walt had always provided. In the golden days Walt had imposed his vision and settled disputes. Now Walt himself was uncertain. Frank Thomas, who was charged with animating Captain Hook, said Walt couldn't decide whether Hook should be a slightly comical dandy or a snarling villain and finally left the determination up to Thomas. When Walt saw Hook's first scenes, he told Thomas, "I think you're beginning to get him," and advised he keep going, which meant that Walt was conceding nearly everything to the animators and that the man who once ordained every frame of his features was now letting the film develop organically.

In the end, when *Peter Pan* was released in February 1953, Walt was much more pleased with the film than he had been with *Alice*, and so were critics and audiences. It was greeted with a special segment on the highly rated *Toast of the Town* television program, hosted by columnist Ed Sullivan, that recounted Walt's life, and with the cover of *Newsweek* lauding Walt's plans. Bosley Crowther in *The New York Times* called it "frankly and boldly created in the 'Disney Style' "—a turn that since *Cinderella* had regained its positive connotation. "I might say that Roy is wearing his 'Cinderella smile' again!" Walt bubbled to one correspondent after the receipts started coming in. He was so satisfied that he attended the London premiere that April with Lillian, and later in the year (after spending most of the summer in Europe again on the pretense of overseeing the British live-action production *Rob Roy*) he attended the Mexican premiere as well.

But even with the success of *Peter Pan* and the media acknowledgment that Walt Disney's worst days seemed to be behind him, Walt was still trying to find ways to improve the animation without raising the cost, and he had assigned Ken Peterson to come up with suggestions on how to do so. Peterson's advice was predictable and familiar, given the longtime problems at the studio: better preparation and integration of talent and assigning animators only after the script has been thoroughly worked out; but he also counseled slanting stories toward "broader cartoon action and cartoon characters" that would be easier for less talented animators to draw, and bringing in animators from outside the studio—something that Walt had strenuously avoided all these years, believing as he did in the superiority of the Disney method. Peterson also told Walt that despite the successes of *Cinderella* and *Peter Pan* and despite the desire to "produce better pictures at a lower cost," there was a "defeatist or negative attitude which asserts that nothing can be done about it."

II

But Walt Disney, who had been in despair for so many years, was not defeatist now, even if his studio was. He knew the studio was unwieldy. He knew the level of talent was not as high as in its heyday and that the spirit had never recovered from the strike, much less from the drudgery of the war. He knew that the heady days of collaboration were long since gone and that, as far as the animations were concerned, they would never return. He knew that, and he missed those days, missed them terribly, which may have been one reason why he drifted. For all the pressure he had had to endure, Walt had loved the days when he and his boys turned out the first Mickey Mouse cartoons or when they labored over *Snow White*, knowing that they might be making history. Now, finally, the park had restored that sense of doing something epoch-making. But it wasn't only the fact of the park that had reenergized him. He also cherished the idea of the process of planning the park, of returning once again to the old days, the days before the big studio and the strike and the relentless financial strains, when the employees were locked in brotherhood. Walt Disney, the utopian who had spent a lifetime trying to re-create the communal spirit of Marceline, wanted the park in part because he thought the planning of it would allow him to reestablish the creative community he had lost.

He knew that it couldn't be done within the bureaucratic studio structure. The process had to be fresh and distinct—new. Roy, always protecting the studio from his brother and his brother from the studio, gave Walt the opportunity. Back in the summer of 1951 Roy had tried to acquire the rights to the *Oz* books of the late L. Frank Baum, and had discovered that Baum's heirs didn't hold those rights. Roy, appalled, got to thinking that Walt Disney had to protect *his* rights for *his* family, and he suggested to Walt that September that Walt sell his name to the company on the condition that the payment be regarded as a capital gain for tax purposes. He also suggested that Walt offer the studio a ten-year personal services contract, since his last contract had expired in 1947 and they hadn't bothered to extend or renegotiate it. Some advisers told Roy that the Treasury Department wouldn't permit Walt to sell his name to a company that he effectively controlled. Roy thought otherwise. Still, he said he was also acting in the company's best interest since the company used Walt Disney's name "in ways that bring us a lot of revenue," and "I feel keenly that the company should have this right beyond any doubt in place of going along as we are now on the basis of indulgence on your part"—recognition that the name Walt Disney was now just as valuable as the man. What Walt needed, however, was a separate entity from the studio, one wholly owned by Walt and his family, to whom Walt would grant the rights to his name and with whom the studio could make an agreement both for tax purposes and to give the contract legitimacy.

It took over a year, until December 1952, for Walt to form what eventually was called WED Enterprises, after his initials, and another three months for the board of directors of Walt Disney Productions to agree to license Walt Disney's name for forty years and to give Walt a personal services contract—of seven, not ten, years as it was finally drafted. WED, in turn, received $3,000 a week and 5 to 10 percent of what the company collected from the use of Walt's name on anything outside of production. Walt was also permitted to make one live-action film per year outside the studio's auspices and could purchase up to a 25 percent ownership interest in any live-action film if he were to contribute a like percentage to the film's budget. In addition, Walt was granted an option to buy up to $50,000 of the $1.5 million life insurance policy that the company had taken out on him and was guaranteed a royalty of $50,000 annually for ten years. The terms were favorable to Walt—so favorable that one angry stockholder brought suit against the company that summer, and Walt personally appeared in court to make his own case.

But if Roy had encouraged WED to protect Walt Disney's interests and to maintain the company's claim on his name and services, Walt himself had something very different in mind for his new organization. WED would be the place where Disneyland could germinate and grow—an intimate place that was physically inside the studio but not really of the studio. He set it up either in an old bungalow at the edge of the lot that, appropriately enough, had been transported from Hyperion or in a temporary trailer. (Accounts differ.) And then he began to recruit a small staff to help him plan. Less than a week after the board and WED agreed to terms, Walt hired Lillian's brother-in-law Bill Cottrell as the new company's first employee to work both on nascent television projects and on the park. Art director Dick Irvine joined three weeks later, and Irvine's associate Marvin Davis, also an art director, came with him. Harper Goff, who had drawn the original Disneyland sketches, arrived too.

Walt was also cruising the studio for candidates. Layout artist John Hench, the man who had worked with Dali on *Destino*, remembered Walt stopping at his desk one day and telling him, "I want you to work on Disneyland, and you're going to like it." Hench said he had only the slightest idea of what Walt was talking about, but he joined the new crew anyway. Others would eventually follow: animators, machinists, additional layout artists. "When he actually got into Disneyland, he brought any number of people over to WED from the Studio," Bill Cottrell remembered. "Business was slowing down in the Studio, and instead of laying them off, he put them on his personal payroll, the WED payroll."

But these were all movie people, people who knew how to make animations and live-action pictures, not amusement parks. Walt had Goff's drawings, which were the equivalent of the thumbnail sketches for the features, but he needed an architect and engineer to execute them. In April 1952, nearly a year before the formation of WED and just weeks after the presentation to the Burbank officials, Walt invited architects William Pereira and Charles Luckman to the studio to discuss the park, and afterward Pereira conceded to Walt that he had fallen "hook, line and sinker" for the project. Of all the local architects, it was not surprising that Walt should have asked Pereira to a conference. Pereira was not only a notable Los Angeles architect—he had designed the Pan-Pacific Auditorium where Walt had shown Granny's cabin; the Robinsons Department Store in Beverly Hills; the Marineland of the Pacific aquatic park; and the Los Angeles International Airport—but he had also been an art director and production designer at Paramount who had then partnered with Luckman, a former president of Lever Brothers, to form an architectural and engineering firm of their own. In brief, Pereira had flair.

In January, Walt Disney Productions agreed to give Pereira and Luckman up to $3,000 to help design Disneyland, after which they were to return to Walt for further authorization. The plan was still to build the park in Burbank. In the spring Dick Irvine was assigned to serve as a liaison between the imaginative people in the bungalow at WED and the architectural firm, while Marvin Davis was assigned the task of taking Goff's sketches and turning them into elevations of the Main Village. But by the time Pereira and Luckman submitted their plan for the park, Walt was beginning to have doubts. By one account, Dr. Charles Straub, the president of the Santa Anita Turf Club and an acquaintance of Walt's, convinced him that he didn't need a big architectural firm, that the park was essentially a matter of entertainment rather than design, and that building the park, in the words of one art director, was "very much like doing a set for a motion picture." Walt may have also disliked the formality of using a large firm when he so enjoyed the informal excitement of WED. By the summer Pereira and Luckman had been terminated. WED was now on its own.

Now they mobilized as they hadn't mobilized since *Snow White.* Almost from the moment Walt first hatched the idea of a theme park, he and his cohorts fanned out into the field for ideas. As early as March 1951 Harper Goff went to Europe to take photographs of parks, and by the fall even Roy was investigating purchasing amusement rides in Europe. The following March, Goff was visiting New Orleans during Mardi Gras, then went on to Atlanta to examine available train stock for the park. He would make another extended reconnaissance trip a year later to New York museums, Old Sturbridge Village in Massachusetts, the old Erie Canal, Greenfield Village in Michigan, the Lincoln Museum in Chicago, the Smithsonian Institution in Washington, Colonial Williamsburg, Marineland in Florida, the Tallulah Falls Railroad in Georgia, and the Steamboat Museum in St. Louis, and he was part of a delegation that visited parks around Los Angeles to gather information on how to run a facility. There was so much activity at WED that at the same time Goff was making his tours, he was also working on the Dancing Man miniature, assembling a coach for the park, and drawing elevations for the submarine in *20,000 Leagues Under the Sea.*

Walt himself was also spinning in a whirlwind. Despite the distractions of the features, he was personally negotiating with a specialist in miniature horsedrawn carriages about the possibility of the man selling his work to Disneyland for a separate miniature section; he was consulting with the operators of other attractions (one advised him to charge a high admission price to the park and a parking fee "to keep out the loafers and undesirable characters"); and he was visiting other amusement venues, like Knott's Berry Farm south of Los Angeles, with Dick Irvine. These were hardly casual trips. "[W]e'd measure the width of the walkways, the traffic flow, and study how people moved about," Irvine recalled. "Even at that time, Walt had in the back of his mind how he wanted to move people."

Walt was expansive again, and after the years of working under restrictions, he wanted his crew to exercise their imaginations too, though when it came to the rest of the studio, WED operated in relative secrecy. "Walt said, 'Heavens! The dream's wide open. There's nothing cut or dried about it.' " "We would write our ideas out on squares of paper," Dick Irvine recalled, comparing the planning of the park to the planning of the features, "put them up on a board, and he'd come down in the afternoon and sit there and look at them and juggle them around." These sessions would last anywhere from four hours to six hours to the entire day. And though Lillian said that he would come home exhausted after the long days of planning, he had a drawing board at Carolwood where he could work on Disneyland at night too—"as a hobby," he said.

As in the old days, when he had been constantly "plussing" the animations, he was never satisfied. "The first scheme you had, Walt would completely tear apart," Marvin Davis said. "Eventually you would come up with something better. He wanted to see every idea that you could possibly have before he settled on something." Davis remembered a time when he had drawn a layout for an attraction and Walt had come in at night, just as he used to do with his animators, and taken it home with him. When Davis arrived at his desk the next morning, he found a sheet of tracing paper on which Walt had redrawn the entire attraction. "Here, quit fooling around and draw it the way it should be," he ordered Davis.

Yet for all the work and for all the long hours, Walt was happier than he had been in years. He visited the WED bungalow frequently as he had once visited the animators' rooms—overseeing, brainstorming, musing, enthusing, goading. And he reveled in WED the way he had once reveled in the old Hyperion studio. "Dammit, I love it here," he exulted to Marc Davis, who would move from animation to WED. "WED is just like the Hyperion studio used to be in the years when we were always working on something new." He had found not only a purpose again but also, as he had hoped, the small joyous community he so desperately wanted: a revivification of the cult. "I thought that was why he enjoyed himself so much at the beginning of WED," Bill Cottrell observed. "Because once again, he owned WED as he once owned the Studio, before it went public. . . . I think there was a feeling that Walt must have had, and certainly I had it, that at WED you no longer had any big departments to deal with. . . . It was just fun to get back into that small scale again." Walt called it his "sandbox."

Over the months, as the WED staff loosed their imaginations, the project underwent what one might call a philosophical transformation. From the first, Walt had never thought of Disneyland as a traditional amusement park; the whole idea had been to make something different, something better. But the conceptualization, in part limited by the relatively small site, had nevertheless been narrow too—a sort of combination of Knott's Berry Farm, with its rustic American setting, and a kiddieland with rides. By the time WED and Walt embarked on their constant plussing, Disneyland had evolved into something much more unusual and much more grandiose—not just a park that could provide fun and diversion but a kind of full imaginative universe that could provide a unified experience. It was truly a *land* rather than an amusement park. At least that was how the planners and Walt had come to think of it. Disneyland would be something for which there was no antecedent.

But if there was no antecedent, in its planning the park had been the beneficiary of a host of forces and influences—the Edenic European gardens, like Tivoli, that Walt had visited; the expositions and fairs, like the Century of Progress in Chicago in 1933, the New York World's Fair in 1939, and even the Chicago Railroad Fair; historical re-creations, like Knott's Berry Farm, Greenfield Village, and Colonial Williamsburg, all of which Walt had seen and enjoyed; and, what may have been the most important influence of all, California architecture itself. As Edmund Wilson had once described Los Angeles flamboyance: "Here you see mixturesque beauty," a "Pekinese pagoda made of fresh and cracky peanut brittle then a snow white marshmallow igloo—or a toothsome pink nougat in the Florentine manner, rich and delicious with embedded nuts." Los Angeles was a fantastic, eclectic, architecturally unruly city, affected as it was by Hollywood, which was also fantastic, eclectic, and unruly, as well as by a general sense of possibility. All of Los Angeles was a movie set or, as one commentator in the 1920s called it, the "child of Hollywood out of Kansas" and the "Middle Westerner's Nirvana," which almost perfectly described the city's relationship to Walt Disney. His Disneyland would in many ways be the apotheosis of Los Angeles architecture, an apotheosis of Hollywood, and in talking about the park he would even describe its layout as if it were a movie: "This is scene one, this is scene two, and this is scene three."

Having borrowed the idiom of motion pictures for his park, Walt Disney had also borrowed the movies' intent. Hollywood—the creation largely of Eastern European Jews who expunged their pasts by devising a better world of their imaginations—refined and idealized reality. So would Disneyland, the creation of a wounded man who expunged what he saw as the darker passages of his past by devising a better world of his imagination, though one that was obviously colored by the images of Hollywood. One of the sources of the power of Hollywood was that it created archetypes that, it was often said, managed to plumb some deep Jungian ocean of collective consciousness. Disneyland, essentially a giant movie set, would deploy the same archetypes and would plumb the same depths. As one Disney historian put it, "One could take every feature of the parks [Disneyland and later Walt Disney World] and explain its appeal in terms of some instinctive or emotional response common to almost all of us."

At Disneyland, Walt imagined a western town that was the movies' idea of the West, even, according to architectural historian Karal Ann Marling, instructing Harper Goff to model the saloon after one that Goff had designed for the recent film *Calamity Jane*. He imagined a jungle cruise ride that would be modeled after another recent film, *The African*

Queen, which Goff loved. He imagined a castle that was the Platonic castle of everyone's imagination. He imagined a Main Street with its quaint shops, its horse-drawn carriages, its train station, fire station, and police station, its town hall and town square that was so quintessentially turn-of-the-century American that even Walt's promotional material boasted, "We want everyone to feel that this is MAIN STREET, U.S.A. and that you are actually living this period."

As Walt drew on these archetypal American images, he also drew on the archetypal images that he himself had created and that had become embedded in the American consciousness. "We enter the land of Disney with the sense of having been there before because we return to an America unified by our common experience," wrote one visitor in *The New York Times*, including in that collective past the experience of *Snow White*, *Cinderella*, *Three Little Pigs*, *Peter Pan*, and Mickey and Minnie Mouse. It was a testament to how much Walt Disney had helped shape the American imagination. And to make absolutely certain that guests to Disneyland would stay within their imaginations, Walt planned a high berm, or embankment, to surround the park and blot out the surroundings, like the berm he had built at the studio and at Carolwood so that his neighbors wouldn't be disturbed by his train. The berm literally kept the world at bay as Walt had always wanted to do at his studio. "[W]hen you enter DISNEYLAND," the promotional brochure announced, "you will find yourself in the land of yesterday, tomorrow, and fantasy. Nothing of the present exists in DISNEYLAND."

As Disneyland was designed to block out the world, it was also designed to offer a particular kind of psychological experience that one didn't ordinarily find at an amusement park or carnival, much less in reality. Most amusement parks, in fact, were like the Warner Bros. cartoons of the late 1940s—noisy, chaotic, bombastic, subversive. One was made to feel that the social rules didn't apply there, that one was entirely free. Walt Disney, the purveyor of comfort, intended his park to provide just the opposite—not freedom but control and order. John Hench, one of its designers, said that the park had been drawn with the same kind of circles and loops as Mickey Mouse and with the same effect. Everything was harmonious, soft, and unthreatening, making Disneyland one of the most profound expressions of what Marling calls an "architecture of reassurance," in which one feels the palpable sense of "an order governing the disposition of things." When critics would later carp that Disneyland was too serene, too clean, too controlled, too perfect, they were right. It was what one might have called the "tragedy of perfection"—that in seeking perfection Walt seemed to drive out anything human and real. Yet perfection was the whole basis for Disneyland's existence and the foundation of its appeal. It was a modern variant on the City on a Hill of Puritan dreams. It was the consummate act of wish fulfillment.

As such, of course, it was a reflection of its creator and his own overweening sense of wish fulfillment. But it reflected him in a much more personal way as well. By formulating the park with a walk down Main Street at the park's entrance, which led to Sleeping Beauty Castle at the street's end (what Walt, borrowing an old carnival term, called a "wienie" because it enticed guests to it presumably the way a wienie entices a dog) and then to the various lands that radiated from the castle (Fantasyland, Adventureland, Frontierland, and Tomorrowland), Walt Disney re-created his own life's journey: "the road map of Walt Disney's life," as WED veteran Marty Sklar would describe it. One entered the gates of the park into what was essentially the Main Street of Walt's boyhood Marceline. (At "story sessions" for Disneyland he would reminisce about Marceline by the hour.) At the end of the street one was offered a variety of options—fantasy, adventure, the frontier, the future—so that a trip through the park became a metaphor for possibility. Like young Walt, visitors to the castle seemed to stand at the portal to their dreams with a child's sense of omnipotence. "The symbolism," Richard Schickel would write, "is almost too perfect—the strangers forced to recapitulate Disney's formative experiences before being allowed to visit his fancies and fantasies in other areas of the Magic Kingdom."

What was uncanny, as always, was how much Walt Disney's personal experience converged with the national experience. Early in the planning stages Walt had described the park as providing a lesson in American heritage, just as Disneylandia had been intended to do, and he wanted visitors to appreciate the kind of bedrock values of which he had become a representative after the war, values that were especially salient with the onset of the Cold War. "There's an American theme behind the whole park," he told columnist Hedda Hopper, which meant that Disneyland was intended to re-create not only Walt Disney's moment of possibility but also America's, when the country, like Walt, had been both innocent and ambitious.

Some regarded this nostalgia for a bygone era in a time of anxiety as yet another form of comfort and another source of the park's appeal. "So the Disney parks touch on two sources of the modern desire to return through time to an earlier state of mind: the childhood of the individual (Main Street; Fantasyland, based on children's literary classics; and the play orientation of the parks' activities)," wrote one analyst, referring both to Disneyland and to its sequel, Walt Disney World, "and the childhood of the nation (early twentieth century settings and back through the frontier and colonial periods)." Another analyst observed that visitors to Disneyland "found themselves completely submerged in a fantasized but nearly pitch-perfect representation of their deepest commitments and beliefs"—commitments and beliefs that, like so much else in his life, had now been idealized by Walt Disney. In the end, then, Disneyland was neither just a park nor even an experience. It was also a repository of values.

It had gotten too big. A year before the formation of WED, before Walt had launched his full-scale planning, and just two months after he had made his presentation to Burbank officials, he was already confiding to an RKO official that he had been "looking into the advisability of securing a plot of ground—something up to 200 acres—not that we would use this much for the project, but it would give us control of the surrounding area, which we feel is important." By the time WED was in operation, Burbank began to balk, fearing how a park might affect the calm of the community. "Burbank city did not want a kiddieland in Burbank," John Cowles, who had negotiated with the city, recalled. Meanwhile Walt scouted a police pistol range in the Chatsworth area of the San Fernando Valley; Palos Verdes south of Los Angeles; a 440-acre spread called Descanso Gardens (Walt concluded "it is in the wrong area"); Calabasas, where Roy bought a plot of forty acres fronting the parcel on margin, to protect the plot; and Sepulveda; and he sent Dick Irvine and another WED employee, Nat Winecoff, on a mission down the Santa Ana Freeway to survey possible sites there.

He wanted a big site now, but the decision was too complex and difficult and the stakes far too great to be left to Walt's band of happy amateurs. At a party that summer Charles Luckman introduced Walt to Harrison "Buzz" Price of the Stanford Research Institute (SRI), who had done surveys for Luckman on a stadium project in Hawaii, and suggested that Walt hire Price to examine sites for Disneyland. Walt and Price met in July 1953, and Walt explained that he had conceptualized the entrance down Main Street and the four lands radiating from it and that it would need roughly one hundred acres, but that he had no idea where the park should be located. Price agreed to have his office analyze potential areas, which were promptly narrowed down from ten (in a large square that was bounded by Chatsworth on the north, Tustin on the south, Pomona on the east, and the ocean on the west) to four along the Santa Ana Freeway corridor that Winecoff and Irvine had investigated. When Price issued his report late that August, he concluded that Los Angeles was becoming increasingly decentralized and that the highest rate of growth was likely to be in Orange County, just south of L.A., whose population had swelled by 65.4 percent from 1940 to 1950 and by another 30.4 percent in the three years from 1950 to 1953. Orange County also seemed to have the least rainfall, the least humidity, and the least extreme temperatures of the areas under consideration, and perhaps best of all, it was well situated for transportation. After eliminating more than forty sites in and around Orange County (for reasons ranging from sporting unsightly oil wells to housing a labor camp for Mexican nationals), SRI settled on a 160-acre parcel in Anaheim called the Ball Road subdivision, which was basically a large grove of orange trees, four thousand of them, in an area that was the country's largest provider of Valencia oranges. In addition to its location, it had the advantage of having only seventeen owners, most of whom had been thinking of turning the land into a housing development, and only fifteen homes scattered across the property; the price was relatively inexpensive—$4,800 per acre, save for one plot that had been leased to a trailer factory, which, after the studio agreed to buy the company's assets, settled for $6,200 per acre. Walt got the news of the purchase from an associate while walking in Piccadilly Square in London, though the purchase wouldn't be announced publicly until the following May.

Now all Walt Disney needed was the money to build his park.

III

All the time he had been planning Disneyland, Walt admitted that he hadn't paid particular attention to how he would finance it. The preliminary work from Pereira and Luckman and SRI had been authorized and underwritten by Walt Disney Productions. But even before the planning had accelerated, Walt had to dip into his own funds. He borrowed against his life insurance policy—"My wife kept complaining that if anything happened to me I would have spent all her money," he told a reporter only half facetiously—and, in part to offset the cost of the new house, had borrowed another $50,000 from the bank, which he called the "limit of my personal borrowing ability." He had no sooner completed a house at Smoke Tree, (which, he gushed to his aunt, was the "first time we have ever had a place away from town and we are all getting quite a kick out of having it,") than he had to sell it, arguing that he was just too busy to get away but actually because he needed the money. He even coaxed Hazel George to invest, and she formed a Disneyland Boosters and Backers Club of studio employees.

Walt claimed that Roy was less amenable, though this claim may have been more self-dramatization by someone who always liked to portray himself as having to battle the conventional wisdom. Whenever Walt broached the subject with his brother, Walt said, "he'd always suddenly get busy with some figures, so I mean I didn't dare bring it up. But I kept working on it and I worked on it with my own money." Roy told a reporter that he "wondered where the money was coming from, but I didn't ask; it was his baby, and he could have it." Then, Roy said, he got a call from a banker saying that Walt had come to see him to ask for a loan on the park. "We went over the plans," the banker told Roy. "You know, Roy, that park is a wonderful idea!" Roy said, "I nearly fell out of my chair." Walt got his seed money from the bank, and Roy was more favorably disposed.

But Roy, though hesitant, wasn't as unsympathetic as either he or Walt later portrayed him as being, any more than he had been when Walt had wanted to make *Snow White*. In fact, as early as March 1952 Roy had written Walt that he had been "thinking considerable" about the "Amusement Park matter" and recommended that Walt present the idea to Walt Disney Productions through a third party so that Walt would be insulated from charges that he was using the company for his personal ends. "I don't see it clearly yet," Roy admitted, "but I do think the idea should be considered and studied on its merits [—] the whole idea to me has great possibilities." It was also at this time that Roy first asked Walt to consider revising his personal relationship to the studio—a revision that would lead to WED. "In that way," he closed, "this Amus. Park idea could be the vehicle to straighten out your entire matters," which was exactly what happened.

But even as he was financing the park's planning largely out of his own pocket and hoping to get additional financing from the studio, Walt already had a plan: television. Television would save him.

Walt Disney had been fascinated by television at least since the mid-1930s, when he had gone to Camden, New Jersey, to see a demonstration of the new medium by RCA head David Sarnoff. When he decided to terminate his distribution agreement with United Artists at the same time and sign instead with RKO, one of the sticking points had been television rights. Walt demanded that the studio retain them. Over the years he had only seemed more prescient, and his interest had only intensified. Shortly after the war's end the studio applied to the Federal Communications Commission for a television station license and announced plans to build a television broadcasting center on the lot, though Roy decided to withdraw the application, fearing that the expense would be too great and that the studio would be better served waiting for color broadcasts that would better showcase the studio's animations. But the interest never wavered. In

1947 Roy ordered ten-inch television sets for all the executives, and the next year Walt spent a week in New York with the sole purpose of watching television "day and night" to get a handle on the medium. Hazel George said that when he returned to the studio, he had become messianic about television. "Television is the coming thing," he told her, and dismissed all those motion picture moguls who perceived it as a threat.

As Walt saw it—and he was largely alone among film executives in this respect—television was not the enemy of the motion picture; it was its ally. It might have the effect of killing off the B-movie, he told *The New York Times*, but it would help advertise movies, he believed, and he intended to "take full advantage of its potential to create a new motion picture audience and to encourage the fullest box office patronage of our forthcoming pictures." Roy was no less enthusiastic. Offering possibilities to recycle old films and make new films backed by corporate sponsors, television, he saw, was a way to underwrite the entire studio operation. "We wouldn't have the pressure of putting entertainment product into work unless you really felt good about it," he wrote Walt, "and that would give us a better batting average in the entertainment field and more safety—as well as more peace of mind. The sponsored films would change our business over to almost a new business with unlimited possibilities, in place of the ever pinching outlook in the strictly theatrical field."

Walt was eager to take the leap. As early as March 1950, he had suggested to Roy that the studio launch its own television program using old Disney shorts. Roy agreed, calling it a "grand formula," and told Walt to select a crew and draw up a budget. That idea foundered, no doubt a casualty of the other demands on Walt's time, but that summer Roy and Walt were talking with Coca-Cola about the company sponsoring an hour-long Christmas broadcast featuring Walt hosting several cartoons as well as a scene from the upcoming *Alice in Wonderland*, which Roy believed would not only give the film a "tremendous send-off" but allow them to "find out a lot about television that we don't know now." The program, set for NBC, would cost about $100,000, all of which would be paid by Coca-Cola, but Roy, sounding very much like the old Walt, advised that "you think in terms of pouring every dollar they give us into the show. . . . Give them a socko show that will be the talk of the industry—or even broader than that—the talk of the entertainment world." Whether it was the talk of the industry or not, Walt acquitted himself well. Jack Gould in *The New York Times* wrote, "Walt Disney can take over television any time he likes," and called the show "one of the most engaging and charming programs of the year." But what the special really did was prove that Walt's thesis about the value of television to the film industry was correct. A Gallup poll indicated that the program created new awareness of *Alice* and prompted Walt to talk about using TV "for point of sale."

What Walt wanted, though, was a regular series that would pump a regular stream of income into the studio. A few months after the special, he gathered a group in his office to discuss a half-hour program, and though Walt immediately began waffling, citing the difficulty of producing a weekly program and wondering who would be able to execute it, he charged the staff with developing three show ideas by the end of the year. Roy was also working the television front. That May he met with Jules Stein, the head of the Music Corporation of America. MCA was the most powerful talent agency in the country, and for years, even before television was a going proposition, Stein had been dogging the Disneys, trying to interest them in having him represent them in the medium and offering to seek sponsors for a Disney series. Roy found Stein "glib and offhand"—Walt called him the "octopus" because he seemed to have his tentacles in everything—and said that every time he talked with him, he got the "feeling of fearing to get in his clutches," à la Pat Powers. But Roy was nevertheless willing to agree because he feared that if the studio didn't act quickly, other film companies would move into the breach. His only stipulation was that the term of the agreement be short.

But even with MCA, television wasn't proving so easy. Discussions with Ford and Chrysler that summer to sponsor films for television that might be used in a series, and discussions with the American Broadcasting Company to air the series, all had fizzled, and Roy had backed away from doing a weekly hour-long program at least until the fall of 1952, though even as that time approached, Roy found himself without his program or the prospect of one. Talks with Lever Brothers had run aground on the Disneys' desire for a three-year commitment, and Roy was now recommending a fifteen-minute show to promote upcoming movies. The additional benefit, he wrote Walt, who was in Europe at the time, was that a show, *any* show, would "be a wonderful help in the building up of our financial and corporate program for the amusement company, as it would intrigue third parties into coming into it and having a part of it." In short, a television show might attract interest in Disneyland.

Whether Roy knew it or not at the time, and he probably did, Walt already saw this as the plan. As much as he appreciated television as a promotional tool for the features and as much as he valued the revenue that television could bring to the studio so that the company wouldn't constantly be in financial straits, Walt believed—Walt hoped—that in return for a Walt Disney television program, he could induce a network or a corporate sponsor to invest in Disneyland; that was the reason he had had

Roy insist on a three-year commitment. He was, in effect, trying to sell his old films and the value of his reputation to finance his park.

All the time that Roy was talking to MCA, to ABC, and to various corporate sponsors, Walt hadn't been idle. Through WED he had bought the television rights to a popular book titled *The Mark of Zorro* that had provided the basis for several film versions, including one starring Tyrone Power as the aristocrat in Mexican-governed California who dons a black mask and becomes the sword-wielding Zorro, a champion of the poor and oppressed. Walt's idea was to film the series in Mexico, and early in 1953 he assigned Bill Cottrell to produce, hired a movie veteran named Norman Foster to write and direct the shows, and appointed Dick Irvine to design the sets. Walt described the *Zorro* series as "my own private venture and not part of the studio's"—a further attempt to put distance between himself and the inferior product the studio was producing. Now Walt approached the networks. He went to the National Broadcasting Company, the Columbia Broadcasting System, and ABC. (This may have been the meeting at which he waxed so enthusiastic about Disneyland.) All three demanded that Walt shoot a pilot or sample episode. Walt was nonplussed and irritated. "Well, why should I make a pilot film with all the years that I've been in the film business?" Cottrell said he asked. Cottrell believed that Walt was so discouraged, he dropped the idea and decided to put all his efforts into designing Disneyland instead.

But however much he may have resented the networks' high-handedness, Walt Disney knew he needed television, needed it to provide the money for Disneyland. All through 1953, as the fraction of American families with television sets reached two-thirds, Roy continued meeting with advertising agencies and various corporate sponsors about a series, and he was even negotiating seriously with General Foods, though he told Walt that he thought it advisable not to mention anything yet about the financing of Disneyland. That, he said, could be a bargaining chip; he would concede some points in the television budget in return for the sponsor taking a position in the theme park. With a third party involved, either by buying debentures in the park or by taking common stock, he thought he might be able to lure what he called "other friendly associated interests, such as Western Printing," which published the Disney books and comics.

Meanwhile, as the plans for the park continued to jell, as the studio purchased the property, and as desperation began to set in, Roy sped to New York late in September to discuss yet again the possibility of a television series with ABC but also to discuss with them now, unavoidably, the idea of the network investing in Disneyland. Roy had already left for New

York when Bill Cottrell sent him an outline for four television possibilities, which apparently, after all the months of deliberation, had nevertheless been conceived in such haste that the main program, the proposed one-hour series, was only vaguely described as incorporating material from Disney movies, promotions for new Disney films, and an ongoing progress report on Disneyland. Cottrell also suggested a five-day-a-week, fifteen-minute program called *The Mickey Mouse Club* to air live from Disneyland, a weekly half-hour True-Life program taken from the studio's nature footage, and a thirty-minute *World of Tomorrow* series that would combine live action with animation to depict man's past and future.

Astonishingly, for all the time he had spent on the park and for all his emotional investment in it, Walt hadn't given much more thought to the presentation of Disneyland to ABC than he had to the programs, which testified to just how loosely and spontaneously he had been working on the park. The problem was that Roy needed something to show the ABC executives, something more up to date than Harper Goff's old sketches and more visually suggestive than Marvin Davis's elevations. After the months and months of brainstorming, it wasn't until September that Walt convened a meeting in his office with the Walt Disney Productions management team to describe the park finally and to discuss producing a brochure for prospective investors. "Walt was very 'hot' with his suggestions," Harry Tytle remembered, "and gave us all an insight into the terrific scope of Disneyland"—a scope that had previously been known only to the WED staff in the bungalow.

With Roy heading to New York, there was no time to lose, not even a day. Herb Ryman, an art director who had worked at the studio in the story department in the 1940s before leaving for Twentieth Century–Fox, was painting at his home on the morning of Saturday, September 23, when he received a call from an old colleague, Dick Irvine. Irvine told him that he was at the studio with Walt and that Walt wanted to have a word with him. As Ryman later related it, Walt got on the phone and asked him how long it would take for him to get to the studio. Ryman said fifteen minutes if he came as he was, a half-hour if he dressed. Walt told him to come as he was and that Walt would meet him at the studio gate.

After Ryman arrived and Walt escorted him to the WED bungalow—the Zorro Building, as it was now called—the artist wanted to know what the hurry was. "Well, I'm going to do an amusement park," Walt explained, and said that Roy was going to make a presentation on Monday to show the investors what the park would look like. Ryman said that he was curious himself and asked to see the drawing. "*You're* going to do it," Walt said. Ryman immediately objected. He was afraid he would embarrass himself with so little time. "Walt paced back and forth," Ryman recalled. "Then he went over into the corner and he turned his head around with his back to me and said coaxingly, 'Will you do it if I stay here with you?' " Ryman didn't see how that would necessarily help, but Walt was so plaintive—"like a little boy," he said in one interview, "with tears in his eyes," he said in another—that Ryman reluctantly agreed. Plied with tuna sandwiches and milkshakes and coached by Walt, who provided detailed descriptions and chain-smoked, Ryman worked straight through Saturday and Sunday, sleepless, forty-two hours in all by one account, finishing an overhead rendering of the park just in time for it to be hand-colored by Davis and Irvine and air-mailed to Roy in New York.

As ABC chairman Leonard Goldenson remembered the ensuing discussions, it was *his* idea to trade a stake in the park for a one-hour television series, and *his* idea to have Roy address the ABC board. If so, he had been premature. As it turned out, the board, worried that ABC wouldn't be able to secure financing itself for an investment in Disneyland, declined. But Goldenson knew he needed the Disneys as much as the Disneys needed him. ABC was the newest of the television networks and the weakest of them. It had only fourteen affiliates where NBC had sixty-three and CBS thirty, and its advertising rates were substantially lower than those of its rivals. United Paramount Theaters, which had been set up as an independent entity after being severed from Paramount by the government antitrust action against the major film studios, had acquired ABC earlier that year and had pumped $30 million into the network. To catch up to its rivals, ABC wanted to use the money to build relationships with the motion picture studios rather than pursue the much more time-consuming and laborious process of developing its own programming. Philosophizing that viewers wanted familiarity, ABC especially valued series and especially series that might appeal to the growing demographic of what one ABC executive called "youthful families." Goldenson thought that the Walt Disney company, with its appeal to those families, was the perfect match for ABC.

As the ABC board balked, time was running out for Walt Disney if he were to have any hope of opening the park in 1955, as he had planned. He not only needed a deal, he needed one quickly. NBC had already passed on the proposal, but as late as February 1954, while ABC stalled, Walt and Roy had scheduled an appointment with CBS chief William S. Paley. Paley stood them up, due, he said, "to the pressure of some vitally important negotiations we were conducting." Apparently insulted, the Disneys never rescheduled. Meanwhile Goldenson at ABC was just as desperate as Disney to forge an alliance, especially since the other film studios he was courting were proving reluctant to enter television. To keep the lines of communication open, ABC executives continued to meet with Disney representatives about various programs. "They see tremendous tie-in values between Disney and ABC," Nat Winecoff and Dick Irvine wrote Walt after conferring with Goldenson, ABC president Robert Kintner, and programming head Robert Weitman in New York. "Leonard Goldenson was most emphatic that we convey to you that they are 'most interested' and want to make a deal," and Goldenson suggested they stay in "close contact" with ABC's West Coast representative.

But Goldenson did more than convey professions of interest. He was so eager to close a deal before the new fall television season that, as he later told it, he sent two of his executives to Texas to meet with a man named Karl Hoblitzelle, who owned several theater circuits and with whom Goldenson had worked at United Paramount Theater before buying ABC. Goldenson knew that Hoblitzelle had struck oil and gone into banking, and now Goldenson asked if he might give ABC a loan to back Disney—money, Goldenson said, he couldn't get from the New York banks, which had doubts about the park. Hoblitzelle agreed to underwrite $5 million, and after several days of fierce negotiations between Roy and Kintner, the deal was concluded and approved by both boards on April 2, 1954. ABC would have its Disney program. Walt Disney would have his money for Disneyland. Or, as Walt would later joke, "ABC needed the television show so damned bad, they bought the amusement park."

The park didn't come cheap. Earlier in the year Walt had asked SRI for an estimate of its cost. Their figure was $5.25 million—$750,000* of which was for the property—in addition to the $150,000 that had already been expended for planning, much of that from Walt himself. SRI suggested that the company could cover some of the cost by issuing long-term leases to vendors at the park, which would allow the studio both to collect advances and to borrow against the leases, and it suggested the sale of securities. That left television, ABC, to cover most of the rest.

The deal was complex. ABC agreed to a three-year contract for twenty-six one-hour programs each year, for which it would pay Walt Disney Productions $50,000 per show the first year, $60,000 the second, and $70,000 the third, with $25,000 per repeat the first year, $30,000 the second, and $35,000 the third. Fifteen percent of those funds was then to be funneled from Walt Disney Productions to Disneyland, Inc., a new

*It actually came to $879,000 Memo, C. V. Wood, Jr., to Walt, Re: Disneyland Construction Progress Schedule, Sept. 9, 1954, C. V. Wood Folder, Walt Disney Corr., Inter-Office, 1953–1955, R-Z, A1640, WDA.

corporate entity, as a location fee, out of which the latter was to pay off its mortgage bonds. But since Disney estimated that each program would cost the studio roughly $65,000, the real force of the ABC deal was the network's investment in the park. ABC had committed to take $2 million of ten-year bonds, would guarantee loans up to $4.5 million (Hoblitzelle's crucial contribution to the package), and would put $500,000 directly into the park—in return for a 34.48 percent interest, the same share as that of Walt Disney Productions. Not incidentally, that investment enabled the studio to increase its credit line with the Bank of America to $8 million. As Roy had hoped, the ABC deal also prompted another of the "friendly interests," the Wisconsin-based Western Printing and Lithographing Company, to take $500,000 of ten-year bonds and engineer a $500,000 loan from a local bank secured by Western's Disney royalties, in return for a 13.8 percent stake. (Unfortunately, Western's head and one of Walt's longtime allies, E. H. Waldewitz, described by one colleague as a "rotund little man with a squeaky voice," would die suddenly before the park's opening.) Walt was to keep the remaining 16.55 percent as compensation for his contributions to the park.

With the financing in place, the studio made a public announcement on May 1: Walt Disney would be building an amusement park.

But the ramifications of the deal, as significant as they were, went beyond ABC and Disney. In agreeing to provide a program for ABC, the Disney studio had broken ranks with its motion picture brethren who had, much to ABC's consternation, held firm against television. Though Columbia and Republic Pictures had produced television programs, they did so through subsidiaries so as to keep the lines of demarcation between movies and television clear. Walt Disney, in putting his production company directly in the service of television without any subterfuges, had made what *The New York Times* called the "first move by a leading studio into the home entertainment field," and the *Times* predicted that "if it turns out to be successful, it may very well lead to more such working alliances among the major studios and the networks." The *Times* concluded: "The end result could, indeed, change the complexion of the entertainment business." That was exactly what would happen.

When ABC and Walt Disney Productions announced their agreement in a joint press release on April 2, 1954, they promised that Disney would provide the network with "an entirely new concept in television programming," one that would incorporate the "use of both live action and cartoon techniques in a series of programs based on variety, adventure, romance and comedy." At least, that was the stated intention. The problem was that Walt Disney, six months after Cottrell's memo on possible television formats, had yet to conceptualize the show for which he now had a three-year contract. While the negotiations were heating up that March, Walt had called on fourteen members of his staff, along with Roy, to discuss a format. Walt knew the program had to be synergistic; it had to promote both Disney films and Disneyland, and he suggested that they set up four production units—one for each "land" in the Disneyland park. As he put it bluntly, "The main idea of the program is to sell." A program on how the True-Life Adventures were shot would promote the latest True-Life Adventure on Africa and Adventureland while a program on American folk heroes would promote the Frontierland area of the park. And he was excited about the idea of sponsor tie-ins between the show and Disneyland. At the same time, Walt told his staff, he didn't want to stint on quality. They shouldn't recycle so many Disney cartoons and movies that the audience would "think of the show as a bunch of old Disney material." The programs had to be worthy of the Disney brand: "We are honestly trying to see how many [shows] we could give that we would be proud of and that would be good for Disney. We don't want to cheat on this." And he exhorted them to "establish a format and see what we can do with it," which only revealed that they hadn't yet fully devised a format.

Three days later, when Walt met with ABC president Robert Kintner and other ABC executives to describe the program he had in mind, he was clearly vamping. "Disneyland actually is the format of the Disneyland show," Walt said, no doubt relying on Bill Cottrell's old outline. "It becomes a real place springing out of what we present on the TV screen. The public is going to see it on TV and actually feel they are a part of it." But aside from Disneyland itself, he didn't say exactly what it was that the public would be seeing. He couldn't even commit to the twenty-six shows anticipated in the contract. "We have to get organized first," he told Kintner.

That was an understatement. With the program, *Disneyland*, scheduled to debut in October, so as to give Walt a full season to boost the park before its opening, the staff scrambled. Though Walt was nominally involved in signing off on ideas, his main role was playing "Walt Disney" and meeting with potential sponsors to convince them to advertise on the program. The real leaders of the effort were production manager Bill Anderson and a former press agent and current writer-producer at the studio named Bill Walsh, who had become Walt's television maven when Walt happened to meet him in the hall shortly before the Coca-Cola special and told him, "You—you be the producer of TV." Walsh protested that he knew nothing about television. To which Walt snapped, "Who does?" Together Walsh and Anderson raced to make a presentation to ABC that April, formatting a program that was essentially a potpourri of old cartoons and live-action clips, documentary footage of the construction of Disneyland, behind-the-scenes stories of the latest Disney productions, and made-for-TV cartoons and live-action films. Kintner pronounced himself "delighted," though this may have been a matter of trust in Walt Disney as much as anything else.

Jerry-built as the show was, when *Disneyland* premiered on October 27, 1954, it met with virtually unanimous acclaim, which was partly a function of the generally feckless fare on television at the time and partly a function of the residual power of the name "Walt Disney." The first program was a kind of sampler. It began with Walt describing his dream of Disneyland before segueing into a preview of future programs and then to a showing of the "laughing place" sequence from *Song of the South*, *Plane Crazy*, *Lonesome Ghosts*, and *The Sorcerer's Apprentice*, thereby doing precisely what Walt had warned against—simply recycling old material.

If the show sounded as if it were an extended commercial and looked as if it had been tossed together randomly, it didn't seem to matter. The program had just ended when Kintner, watching it in his New York office with George Romney, the president of American Motors, a sponsor of the show, and a group of Romney's friends, received a call from an advertising executive staking claim to the first sponsor vacancy. Critics were just as responsive as the advertisers. "[I]f the evening's promise is fulfilled in future weeks," Jack Gould wrote in *The New York Times* the next day, "the rest of the television industry may decide to suspend operations between 7:30 and 8:30 Wednesday nights." *Variety* proclaimed that Walt Disney "will prove a dominant figure in this season's television picture" and predicted that he would "unquestionably push ABC into the top 10 of all and sundry rating services for the first time in years."

Variety turned out to be right. Over the course of the season *Disneyland* consistently attracted over 50 percent of the audience in its time slot, and its audience kept growing, its ratings climbing, until even its repeats outdrew every program on television save the Lucille Ball situation comedy *I Love Lucy*. (Before *Disneyland*, ABC didn't have a single program in the top twenty-five.) All but one of those repeats that spring and summer posted a higher rating than when originally broadcast. As far as the network was concerned, *Disneyland* gave ABC an identity that the fledgling company had not had, and astonishingly it accounted for nearly half of the network's advertising billings. By April, with only twenty shows broadcast, *Newsweek* was already calling it "an American institution"—the "first big-budget television show consistently and successfully aimed at the whole family," which was critical. Walt Disney had not only conquered television as he had conquered the screen; he was being credited with using the new medium to bring America together. He was the country's great national uncle, "Uncle Walt," as some took to calling him.

Walt was now consciously fostering that image. Though he always claimed to be terrified about performing onscreen, no doubt sincerely, ABC wanted him on the programs as a host, apparently to provide them with an identity. That May, Walt reluctantly agreed to appear on not more than three programs each year and on commercials, subject to his "reasonable approval." At a meeting two weeks later, after he had already filmed the first introduction—he would introduce the program in a wood-paneled mock-up of his office—he conceded to appear more frequently. Walt was extremely self-deprecating about his performances. He said he didn't consider himself an actor, that he had a bad voice with a "nasal twang," and that he had gotten "stumped" in worrying "about being in too much of it," meaning the show. On the other hand, he said, he was always himself, which "will be the gimmick," and he realized, whether he liked it or not, that his participation was probably necessary to get the show off the ground before he and the production staff could establish other personalities. "Got to be an M.C. to get it going," he told his staff. "We've been selling the name and the personality."

Walt may have been "scared to death," as he later said, and he may have frequently fumbled the scripts, garbling words or tripping over them and requiring repeated takes, but for all his demurrals, he seemed rather to like the chance to create a television persona. At nearly 190 pounds on his five-foot, ten-inch frame, he was huskier now than he had ever been, fleshier, and at fifty-two he had finally lost the ferret-faced intensity of his youth and had physically grown into the imposing postwar corporate figure that was being depicted in the media. As his creations conveyed reassurance, so did the man. He was calm, modest, unprepossessing, homespun, curious, charming, and of course, avuncular—the perfect guest to have in one's living room each week.

With *Disneyland*'s popularity, Walt was now not only a kind of logo for the studio; he had himself become one of its stars, like Mickey Mouse and Donald Duck, with even a personal publicist to promote him—to promote "Walt Disney." That December, seventeen years to the day after his first *Time* cover, for *Snow White*, he was featured again on the cover of the magazine, which conveyed the new image of Disney as a homegrown cultural behemoth—a "genuine hand-hewn American original with the social adze-marks sticking out all over"—and claimed that "Disneyism has swept the world." Ward Kimball remembered that when he and Walt went to

Greenfield Village in 1948, no one had recognized him until word circulated that Disney was there. It had always been the name "Walt Disney" that created a stir, not the face of Walt Disney. Television changed that—"*the* change in his life," Kimball felt. After *Disneyland,* Walt Disney was perhaps the most widely recognized filmmaker in the world, and Kimball believed that Walt had to conform to the public persona, which made him the very personification of American wholesomeness and decency. He was not merely subsumed by the persona, as he had been in the postwar years; he felt he had to internalize it, live within it, becoming a prisoner of his image as he had been a prisoner of his studio. "I smoke and I drink and there's a whole lot of things I do that I don't want to be part of that image," he told an employee. Diane Disney agreed that he had changed. "You could see how he grew between the beginning of television and Disneyland," she said. "Television didn't change him as a person, but I do think it led to a more polished personality."

Even at social gatherings at his Carolwood home, Kimball remembered, Walt would appear in a straw hat, brand-new blue jeans with big cuffs, and an old plaid lumberjack shirt (Diane denied he ever wore the outfit except for publicity), and he would excuse himself to go work in his shop, emerging occasionally to mingle—"letting people know he was a common man," as Kimball said. And although, Kimball observed, Walt may have "played the role of a bashful tycoon who was embarrassed in public, he knew exactly what he was doing at all times." To his detractors, this duality vindicated their judgment that Disney had betrayed his early cultural subversion. Social historian Jackson Lears would see him as the "most flagrant example of that widespread phenomenon in American cultural history: the innovator presenting himself as a traditionalist, the mortal enemy of folk life declaring himself its chief defender, the capitalist tricked out as a populist." "In the last analysis, Walt Disney's greatest creation was Walt Disney," critic Richard Schickel would write. "In retrospect it is possible to see that this is precisely what he was working at for some forty years," even though, Schickel observed, none of his admirers seemed to notice that their "loved object was less a man than an illusion created by a vast machinery"—just like the animations and the theme park.

But the real testament to *Disneyland*'s popularity was neither Walt Disney's recognizability nor the ratings nor the advertisers nor the generational union it seemed to effect. The real testament was Davy Crockett. Since the mid-1940s Walt had flirted with the idea of doing an animation on Davy Crockett, probably as part of his prospective American heroes anthology, the Tennessee Indian fighter and frontiersman who later died defending the Alamo in Texas. He had even recruited the realist painter Thomas Hart Benton to participate, though Benton eventually begged off, writing Walt that "Walt Disney's stuff is good enough for my money as it is without a lot of damn painters getting in it" and that he, Benton, was "too 'set' in my ways to be very adaptable." By the time *Disneyland* was in its planning stages, Walt was urging the Frontierland unit to come up with stories on American heroes. As *Disneyland* producer Bill Walsh remembered it, the staff, under the press of time and with a meeting impending, decided to choose one hero and go with it. "And the first one we pulled out," he said, "by dumb luck, was Davy Crockett." Walt was suspicious—he was afraid, Walsh said, of "too much fighting Indians"—but the unit elaborated a long treatment with storyboards, and Walt signed off, albeit reluctantly. When the director Norman Foster retailed Crockett's adventures at length, Walt asked, "Yeah, but what does he *do*?" which Walsh described as "typical" of Walt. "He never let you sit down without pouring a little turpentine on your rear end."

If the studio's selection of Crockett first was a matter of luck, its selection of who would play Crockett was even more serendipitous. Walt had screened the horror film *Them!* to see whether the film's star, James Arness, might be a suitable Crockett, but he was struck by another player in the picture named Fess Parker, a tall, rangy actor with a drawl who then auditioned for Walt and won the part by strumming a song on his guitar. Parker had given himself thirty-six months after graduating from the University of Texas to make a living as an actor. The deadline was the very month he began shooting *Crockett*.

And there was more dumb luck still. When Bill Walsh returned from Tennessee, where the show had been shot—Walt had actually visited the location with Lillian that September—and then had it edited, he discovered that they had not shot enough footage for three full sixty-minute programs, which was the original plan. Walt suggested that Walsh think of using the storyboards themselves as a kind of introduction at the top of each show to fill out the hours, but when Walt reviewed the drawings, he thought they looked dull and offered another suggestion: that they find a song to accompany them. Walsh enlisted the studio composer, George Bruns, and the scenarist, Tom Blackburn, who together quickly wrote a ballad for the beginning of the program.

Then something happened that no one at the time could quite explain: *Davy Crockett* became an overnight national sensation. Within a few weeks of the feature's debut on *Disneyland* on December 5, 1954, "The Ballad of Davy Crockett," with its opening lyric, "Born on a mountaintop in Tennessee/Greenest state in the land of the free," had become as deeply entrenched in American popular culture as "Who's Afraid of the Big Bad Wolf?" or "Der Fuehrer's Face" had been in their day. (Bill Walsh, in fact, attributed the show's success to the song.) Children not only sang the song and bought the record—seven million copies in the first six months—they also bought Crockett T-shirts, Crockett toy rifles, Crockett knives, Crockett books, Crockett jackets, Crockett bandannas, and dozens of other Crockett paraphernalia in a buying mania that had been rivaled only by the consumption of Mickey Mouse merchandise in the 1930s. Above all, ten million Crockett coonskin caps were sold, becoming part of the essential uniform of every boy, and many girls, in the nation. At the same time *Crockett* pushed the *Disneyland* audience well over the forty million mark—one-quarter of the entire country. No one at the studio had anticipated the response; by the time the first program aired, Norman Foster had already filmed the third episode in which Crockett dies, thus precluding sequels. "ABC couldn't believe it. Parker couldn't believe it. Neither could Walt nor I," Bill Walsh recalled. Walt compared *Crockett* as a phenomenon to Mickey Mouse, *Three Little Pigs*, and *Snow White*. The country went so Crockett-crazy that even in political circles the historical frontiersman was now the subject of debates over whether he was the embodiment of conservative values, as *National Review* editor William Buckley asserted, or had really been a hard-drinking, mendacious rascal, as *Harper's* editor John Fisher asserted.

Parker went to Washington that spring, met with Speaker of the House Sam Rayburn and Senators Estes Kefauver and Lyndon Johnson, and then found himself mobbed by autograph seekers at a luncheon where the guests were so entranced by Parker they ignored the speakers. On a personal appearance tour through the Southwest and Southeast that June, unprecedented crowds of 18,000 to 20,000 people greeted him at the airport. "And wherever he goes, the reaction is tremendous," publicity chief Card Walker wrote Walt. "And it was an extremely emotional reaction," Parker later said. "I'm not kidding you. I had people handing their babies to me. I signed pictures for infants. It was very intense." Parker, who had been unknown just six months earlier, was awed. "No young man has ever had a greater share of good fortune!" he wrote Walt appreciatively, and even better fortune since Parker, by contractual agreement, received a ten percent royalty on all the Crockett merchandise, Crockett publications, and Crockett recordings. Still, a year after the tour Walt was forced to renegotiate Parker's seven-year personal services contract since, as Bill Anderson wrote Walt of their new star, "[s]ooner or later he will either get some kind of an adjustment or he will give us trouble."

In trying to analyze why *Davy Crockett* suddenly seized the national imagination, one could certainly point to the physical and narrative amplitude of the broadcasts and to their quality, which was vastly superior to that of most television programs and much closer to that of films. (One could call it the first television miniseries.) Children, to whom the program had largely been targeted, had never had anything on television so grand. The three installments had, in fact, cost nearly $750,000, and though MGM had loaned some old stock footage of Indians from *Northwest Passage*, Walt didn't stint.* When he had visited the location the previous September, and Foster had braced to be fired for falling behind schedule, Walt instead approached him and told him to reshoot a scene in which Crockett wrestled a bear because, Walt said, he could see a zipper on the bear costume.

Walt Disney had clearly struck a national nerve, even if accidentally, in reviving the idea of a plainspoken, fearless, idealistic, compassionate, but intrepid hero, at a time when Americans were harking back to values that they believed distinguished them from the conformity and coldbloodedness of their global antagonist, the Soviet Union, and that would demonstrate their superiority to Communism, Crockett's death at the Alamo notwithstanding. "Davy's Time," *Time* called it, seeing Crockett as an expression of growing national confidence, and boasting, "The people of the U.S. had never been so prosperous. Never before had the breadwinner taken home so much money. . . . Not since the first delirious mistaken weeks after V.J. day had there been so much expectancy—with caution this time—for peace." And one *Time* correspondent, reflecting on the meaning of Crockett's popularity for Americans, opined, "Davy Crockett is the epitome of a man who can lick any problem with his wits and his own two hands." Fess Parker himself thought it may have been a matter of what he called "hero-hunger," and at least one analyst would observe that the phenomenon may have had less to do with self-confidence than with self-doubt after the recent trauma of Senator Joseph McCarthy's red-baiting, and that Crockett was a palliative. Whether Crockett was symbolizing optimism or trying to reestablish it, Walt was engaged, as he had been since the war's end, in a national reclamation, and the country responded, presumably because it liked the image that Walt was fostering for it. As historian Steven Watts put it, "Walt Disney, with his instinctive feel for cultural pressure points, half-consciously shaped an ideal, reassuring representative of the American way as it faced a daunting challenge from without."

*The production values were so high that a Texas exhibitor named Bob O'Donnell recommended that Walt take the three shows and edit them into a single feature film for theatrical exhibition, which Walt did. The feature grossed $2.5 million.

Reclamation of the past was not all that Walt Disney promoted on his *Disneyland* television program. He also offered the appeal of Tomorrowland. While preparing the *Disneyland* show, he instructed Ward Kimball to hunt for subjects for the Tomorrowland episodes, and Kimball came upon a three-part series on space exploration, in *Collier's* magazine by three of the foremost experts on space, Wernher Von Braun, Willy Ley, and Heinz Haber. Walt read the series in one night and came to the studio the next day fired with enthusiasm. He told Kimball to get Von Braun, Ley, and Haber to the studio to prepare the programs. The result was another three-part miniseries, beginning with an animated documentary called *Man in Space*, that premiered on March 9, 1955. More than two years before the Soviet Union launched its Sputnik satellite and heated up the space race, *Man in Space* went a long way toward building a large constituency for space exploration, and President Eisenhower ordered that it be shown to his rocket experts. At the end of 1955 Walt met with nuclear scientists Glenn Seaborg, Edward Teller, and Ernest Lawrence about a program on atomic energy, to be titled *Our Friend the Atom*, that would have the same effect in creating a consensus behind that technology. As a result Walt Disney, who had become one of the chief purveyors of American values from the past, also became one of the chief popularizers of and cheerleaders for American science in the future.

Whether or not Disney had, as Watts believed, really shaped an American ideal—and he doubtless contributed to it—one could meaningfully speak in the 1950s of "Walt Disney's America." Evolving in the postwar decade, as the new Walt had, this America drew on democratic traditions of modesty, self-effacement, naïveté, and determination, which was what Crockett personified. Yet it also was forward-looking, evincing an almost childlike confidence in science and technology, the very sorts of things that seemed to threaten those old democratic traditions. On the one hand, it projected a quaint, white-picket-fence nostalgia of the sort Walt had celebrated in *So Dear to My Heart*; on the other, it projected a futuristic vision of the sort he expressed in *Man in Space*. Like Walt's own image, "Walt Disney's America" was a confection and an aesthetic—smoothly blended from Hollywood, Booth Tarkington, Horatio Alger, Norman Rockwell, Thomas Edison, and Buck Rogers—but in the same way that Walt had begun to internalize his image, America in the 1950s began to internalize hers. As *Time*'s chest-thumping suggested, "Walt Disney's America" was a reassuring artifice that was embraced as a reality—the spiritual equivalent of Disneyland. It was the face, or the carapace, that the country had assumed to show to itself and to the world.

. . .

While the success of *Disneyland* had many markers, including Walt's stardom, *Davy Crockett*, the interest in space, and the idealization of America itself, one thing the program did not do was turn a profit for the studio. When all was said and done, the studio figured to earn $73,000 per program from ABC, including repeats. But the budgets—which ranged from $14,500 for a program on *Alice in Wonderland* to the nearly $300,000 for each of the *Crockett* episodes and for the first *Man in Space*—averaged just over $100,000. As he had done with the features, Walt plowed every cent back into production and then some, though he also made commercials for several of the sponsors and contracted with several companies for them to underwrite programs that would serve essentially as hour-long promotions for the companies' agendas. (The Portland Cement Association, for example, gave the studio $200,000 to produce a film titled *Magic Highway U.S.A.*) The objective, however, had never been to make a profit. It was to promote Disneyland and publicize the new features, which made *Disneyland* itself a commercial.

That synergy became even more important with a decision made by Roy just before the first program aired. For years Roy had been dissatisfied with RKO's distribution, and though he renewed the contract in 1943, the very next year, unhappy with RKO's lax publicity, he recommended that the studio hire an ad agency to promote its films. Even with the contract, RKO had initially refused to distribute *Seal Island* and *Two Fabulous Characters*, which had been renamed *The Adventures of Ichabod and Mr. Toad*. "By and large, they are all nice fellows," Roy wrote Walt in September 1948, "and they all try to cooperate on the surface, but underneath you feel that resistance, and sometimes it flares into an open break." Roy thought RKO wasn't getting the studio half of what the pictures should be making, especially since, he felt, the major studios were colluding to protect their exhibition interests, which the government had ordered them to divest. To speed the divestiture, Roy joined other independent producers in a suit against the studios, but he was not sanguine. "Sometimes I get very blue," Roy wrote, "thinking about it all and I have a feeling that continuing down this road of high cost, quality pictures is just a road to bankruptcy." The only solution, he felt, was for the best independents to join forces in a distribution organization of their own.

Two years later Roy hadn't acted on his idea but contracted once again with RKO to release *Cinderella* and *Alice in Wonderland* and to continue releasing the studio's reissues for a 30 percent fee and to distribute the True-Life series, though RKO was still less than enthusiastic about the last. But RKO was soon in turmoil. The eccentric billionaire industrialist Howard Hughes had bought RKO in 1948, siphoned off the company's resources, and then put it back on the market four years later, but not before he offered the company to Walt. "They had a lot of liabilities," Card Walker, Disney publicity chief at the time, recalled, "and he offered them ten million dollars credit besides. But Walt said, 'What do I want that problem for? I've got my own little thing over here. I don't need another studio on my hands.' " (Ironically, Walt said he had also been asked to take over the studio back in 1948 to thwart Hughes.) Instead, Hughes sold his studio to a syndicate.

Almost immediately the Disneys had trouble with RKO's buyers. RKO had balked at distributing the shorts, claiming that it was no longer profitable for them. Within a few months Walt and Roy were talking with Jules Stein of MCA, with whom they had already been discussing television projects, about another scheme to split from RKO. As Walt explained it to Roy after a meeting with Stein, Stein wanted the company to undergo a "complete liquidation and reorganization . . . wherein we will be able to secure a certain amount of cash for ourselves and still retain control of the company." The "vital part," however, was that the Disneys make a distribution agreement with one of the major studios under which the major would finance Disney films in return for a percentage of the profits. Walt concurred. "I feel that we have to take care of ourselves personally," he wrote Roy, "and a new releasing deal is imperative." Even Roy, who had feared Stein, seems to have warmed to the idea, elaborating that they could put the studio land and buildings into a separate corporation, sell the corporation to their new distributor to raise money, and then lease them back.

That plan never reached fruition, and Roy chose to ride it out with RKO for the time being, telling Walt that, despite RKO's problems, the Disney studio was "so important to them that you might say we are getting added emphasis in the selling of our product." (Roy may also have had second thoughts about putting himself at the mercy of either Stein or another studio.) But with the studio's first American live-action feature, the big-budget *20,000 Leagues Under the Sea*, scheduled for release in December 1954, and with another feature animation, *Lady and the Tramp*, due out the following June, neither Walt nor Roy wanted to leave the company's fortunes in RKO's increasingly unsteady hands. In September 1954, Roy announced that the studio would end its eighteen-year alliance with RKO and distribute films itself through the Buena Vista arm it had created for *The Living Desert*, another True-Life Adventure, when RKO expressed reluctance to release it. (The company was named for the street on which the studio fronted.) Turning the tables on Roy, Walt called it "my big brother Roy's project, which I hope works out as he has planned it." Now for the first time in its history the studio would control the production, the publicity, and the distribution of every one of its films.

Occasionally, however, such synergies went awry. In December, the week before the first airing of *Davy Crockett*, *Disneyland* had featured a one-hour documentary, *Operation Undersea*, on the making of *20,000 Leagues* in conjunction with the film's release that month. (After the show remarkably won the Emmy for Best Individual Program, Walt admitted to its editor, "It was shot for TV, but did a swell job as a trailer on 20,000 LEAGUES.") A subsequent program, also promoting Disney films, contained a clip showing the film's star, Kirk Douglas, and his family riding Walt's train on a visit to Walt's home. Douglas objected that he hadn't agreed to have the footage made public. Furious after it was shown again on a repeat, he sued the studio for $415,000 for invasion of privacy. Walt parried, claiming that Douglas had come to the house voluntarily and given his permission orally. The case wasn't resolved until 1959, when Douglas finally dropped the suit. "It makes me a little sad—that such a thing should exist," he wrote Walt, "—because I have nothing but pleasant memories of our association together."

As far as ABC's Leonard Goldenson was concerned, *Disneyland* was the "turning point" for the network, the point at which it could finally begin to compete with NBC and CBS. It also, as *The New York Times* had prophesied when the ABC contract was signed, changed the relationship between Hollywood and television. The very next year, 1955, Warner Bros. and MGM contracted with ABC, and Twentieth Century–Fox with CBS. As one Warner executive testified, "I am not sure just where the initiative started, but as a result of the success Mr. Disney was having with a feature motion picture called *20,000 Leagues Under the Sea*, I personally felt that his ability to exploit pictures on television was of great value, and began to wonder why we couldn't do likewise."

ABC was so ecstatic with the results of the show that in December Robert Kintner wrote Walt to exercise the network's option on another of Cottrell's ideas, *The Mickey Mouse Club*, and recommended that they meet the next month to finalize a deal for a five-day-a-week one-hour telecast. As on *Disneyland*, Walt would be given "absolute creative control." And, Kintner rhapsodized, "I believe that in this kid strip, there is the potential for the highest-rated show in the daytime; for the greatest impact on children in the history of communications; and for the creation of a product that not only will have the enthusiastic support of parents, Parent Teacher Associations, etc., but will bring a new dimension to daytime programming."

As tempting as the offer was, the studio had a difficult enough time producing one hour of programming a week. To produce five hours, in addition to *Disneyland*, was an incredibly daunting task. By one account Roy, obviously concerned, had deflected Kintner's entreaties until Walt came into the meeting and asked Kintner if he really thought the studio could do it; when Kintner expressed confidence that Walt could, he waved off Roy's protests. Of course Walt wasn't the one who would have to do the work. Hal Adelquist, Bill Walsh, and Perce Pearce were the people actually charged with creating and then running the program while Walt issued approvals and made comments. Indeed, by February 1955, Adelquist and Walsh had prepared preliminary outlines for the first one hundred shows, which Walt had only to review.

The Mickey Mouse Club had been conceptualized with recurring segments—a children's newsreel, a talent show, serials on the Hardy Boys and Spin and Marty, and a daily cartoon from the Disney library—but the real innovation was the casting. Kintner had wanted a regular host to function as Walt had functioned on *Disneyland*. Most likely either Walsh or Adelquist decided instead to hire a group of young performers, though Walt warned Walsh not to choose "those kinds with tightly curled hairdos." He preferred children "who look like they're having fun," even if they didn't have professional skills. Then they could be taught to sing and dance. And Walt suggested that Walsh recruit by going to schoolyards, watching children at recess, and seeing which one drew his attention. When Walsh said that the child might not have any talent, Walt countered that the one Walsh found himself watching would have "star quality." "The talented kids on the Mickey Mouse Club will be called MOUSEKETEERS," Walt memoed Adelquist that April, "while the adults will be known as MOOSKETEERS [*sic*]."

The Musical Mooseketeer, who served as the master of ceremonies, was a thin, boyish, sandy-haired composer named Jimmie Dodd. Walsh had picked him, but knowing how proprietary Walt was, he told Dodd, "We've got to let Walt discover you." So he invited Dodd to a story session Walt was attending and had him perform a song he had written for a *Disneyland* segment. "Hey, Jim is the one who should be on 'The Mickey Mouse Club'!" Walt told Walsh. Dodd also wound up writing the program's theme song, "The Mickey Mouse Club March," with its signature spelling out of Mickey's name: "M-I-C-K-E-Y—Why? Because we like you—M-O-U-S-E." The Big Mooseketeer and Dodd's sidekick was Roy Williams, a lumpy bear of a man—"fat and funny lookin'," Walt called him—who had been a longtime gag writer at the studio before Walt tapped him for the show. It was Williams who, recalling a scene from an old Mickey Mouse cartoon in which Mickey tips his skull to Minnie, ears and all, as if it were a hat, came up with the idea of a black mouse-ears cap that all the performers on the show would wear.

Though Walt personally signed off on each cast member and though he approved segments and often visited the set, *The Mickey Mouse Club* was a Walt Disney production in name only. There was just too much to do, and for Walt too many other priorities, and the show was basically thrown together on the fly. "We would discuss an idea in the morning," Walsh recalled, "the songwriters would write songs that day, and we would shoot in the afternoon. It was probably the quickest draw on television." That didn't escape unnoticed. Jack Gould in *The New York Times* called the debut in October 1955 "disastrous" and found the Mouseketeers' production numbers "only irritatingly cute and contrived and bereft of any semblance of the justly famous Disney touch." He thought the whole show "keenly disheartening and disappointing."

Gould may have been right that *The Mickey Mouse Club* was cheap and cutesy, beneath Disney's talents, but it was clearly not a program intended for the critics. A group of 131 children previewed the show at the studio three days before its debut; all 131 said they liked it, and all said they would want to watch it every day. That proved to be a prediction. In its first season over ten million children watched the show each day and more than half as many adults. Dodd's theme song became an instant classic, still sung decades later, and two million mouse-ears were sold within the first three months of the program's debut. One of the Mouseketeers, dark-haired Annette Funicello, became the nation's prepubescent heartthrob. When Dodd visited New York in February 1955, socialite and fashion doyenne Babe Paley, the wife of CBS chief William S. Paley, asked if her children could meet him. Afterward Dodd told Walt that the kids knew all the show's songs and that *The Mickey Mouse Club* was the "only show Babe Paley lets her children watch."

Walt may have found this gratifying, but it didn't necessarily translate into profits, any more than *Disneyland*'s popularity had. As with *Disneyland*, the studio wound up spending more on the program, however economically it was made and however many repeats it broadcast, than it received from ABC—about $3 million the first season—which Roy chalked up to his own ignorance of the daytime television market. Nevertheless, as with *Disneyland*, the objective was neither quality nor profitability nor even popularity. *The Mickey Mouse Club* was another subsidy for the theme park, not only because Walt, in the words of the program's newsreel editor, had personally issued "damned serious and direct orders" for the show to feature at least one story on Disneyland every week, but

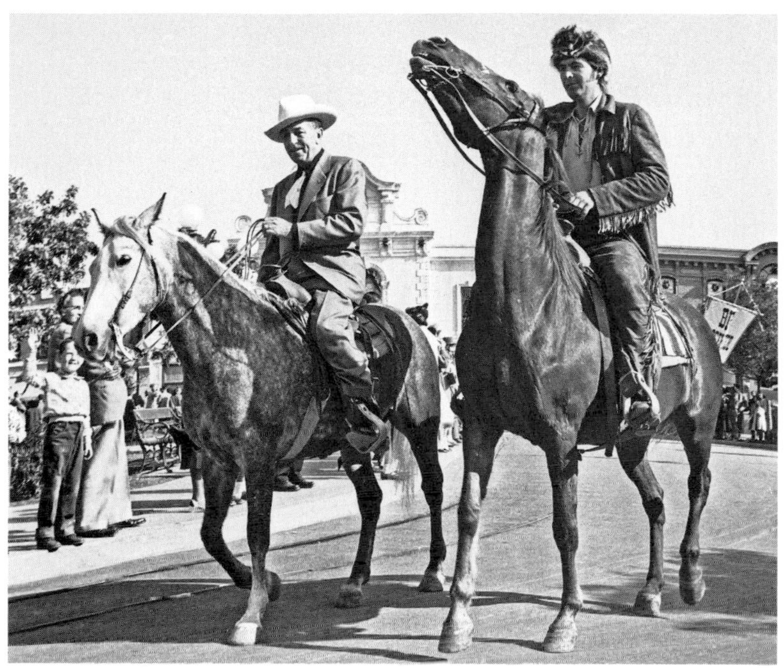

Walt and his Davy Crockett, Fess Parker, on July 17, 1955, at Disneyland's opening day parade. The opening was a debacle, but Walt had achieved his dream.

Walt with his first grandson, Christopher, reflecting the Davy Crockett mania that swept the nation in 1955.

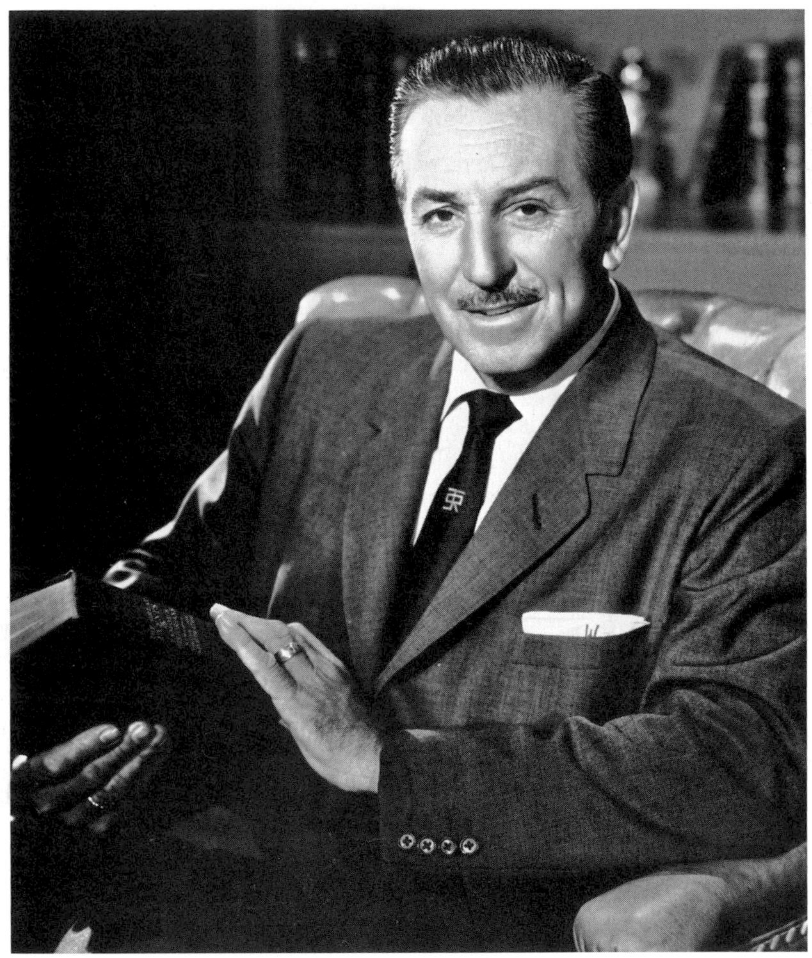

"Uncle Walt": the conservative image that had subsumed Walt Disney in the 1950s and transformed him into the personification of traditional values and square aesthetics. He is wearing his favorite cravat—a Smoke Tree Ranch tie.

Walt surrounded by his Mouseketeers of *The Mickey Mouse Club* on the fourth anniversary celebration of the program.

Walt on Main Street at Disneyland, which was his utopia and his retreat from the rigors of the studio. He often wandered the grounds and spent evenings at his apartment over the fire station.

Walt examining the Carousel of Progress, the General Electric exhibit for the New York World's Fair in 1964 and 1965. Disney designed three more exhibits: Ford's Magic Skyway, Pepsi and UNICEF's It's a Small World, and the Illinois pavilion, which featured an Audio-Animatronic robot of Abraham Lincoln.

At the Carolwood house with his family: *(left to right)* son-in-law Ron Miller, Sharon, Diane with baby Joanna, Lillian with Christopher, and Walt with Lady. Walt loved the train, he loved his workshop, and he loved the recreation room where he concocted sodas.

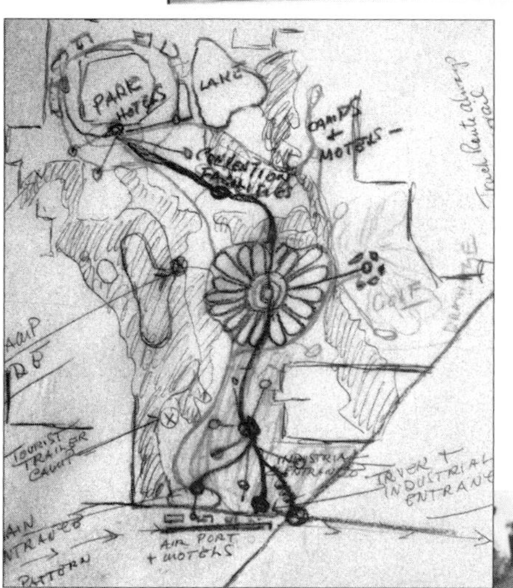

Above: The press conference in Florida on November 15, 1965, with Roy and Governor Haydon Burns, announcing the Walt Disney World complex. Walt had little interest in the amusement park, much more in an experimental city connected to it.

Left: Walt's own drawing of EPCOT. The Imagineers would fish Walt's scribbles from the wastebasket to see what he wanted.

Bottom: Walt visiting the Walt Disney World site the day after the news conference—with Joe Potter, the former New York World's Fair executive whom Walt hired to supervise the new park.

Walt at the premiere of *Mary Poppins* with the book's author, P. L. Travers. Travers had been an obstacle in the production, but she pronounced herself happy with the film, and it went on to win a Best Actress Oscar for its star, Julie Andrews.

Walt and Roy: brothers, antagonists, and comrades. Walt saw himself as the creative force. He saw Roy's job as getting him the resources he needed.

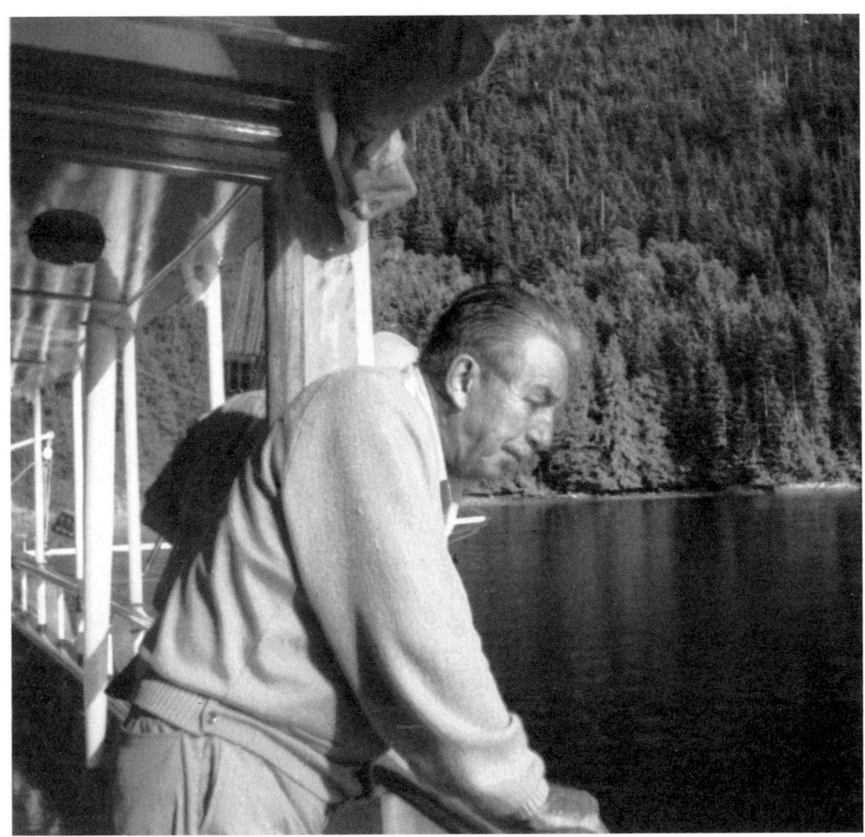

Walt during the Vancouver trip in July 1966. Diane described him as "serene," though with his health flagging he already seemed to be having intimations of the end.

because ABC, in order to land the program, had agreed to furnish $2.4 million more to the park. It was the park that Walt Disney cared about, the park that was his dream now. Television was just a means to that end.

IV

The park. All the time that Walt had been working on the *Disneyland* television show, all the time he had been negotiating, preparing, and approving, he had been thinking about the park. Everyone knew that he was only tangentially involved with the other projects, even as the studio was overwhelmed. "This avalanche of work hit the studio," said producer Winston Hibler when *Disneyland* began. "We augmented the staff by adding additional writers. We used our nature photographers to start moving out on projects. We had to get ourselves in high gear, from a program that included maybe three, four or five features a year to the prospect of twenty-six shows a year." But Walt was barely part of the ramp-up. "Those were the days when he didn't have any contact with the picture," Ward Kimball said of Walt's lack of participation in *Man in Space*. He simply attended the screening, laughed throughout, and then asked, "How in hell did you guys think up all that stuff?" Milt Kahl, who was working on feature animations at the time, had the same experience. He said that Walt would sit in on the story meetings but not as often as he once had. "[T]he difference was," Kahl believed, "that on weekends and evenings and sitting on the john and all that stuff, he wasn't thinking about our pictures. He was thinking about Disneyland."

He was *always* thinking about Disneyland. In September 1953, as soon as he had confirmed the deal on the Anaheim property, he asked Marvin Davis to draw up new plans for the much larger park, and Davis, working frantically, would turn in a new plan every two or three days. A visitor to WED the following year, as the plans were firming up, described wading "through a fascinating jumble of miniature worlds—the frontier and of the past, the rocket space world of the future, the never-never fantasyland where the fairy tale and the Disney characters all live together happily ever after. Maps covered the walls, tables overflowed with contour models and scale drawings, and the floors of the studios, shops and hallways were knee-deep in models of old-time locomotives, paddlewheel boats, Wild West saloons, Sleeping Beauty Castles and gleaming, jet-propelled spaceships to the moon which looked quite capable of making it. This was the chaotic chrysalis of 'Disneyland.' "

Walt was collecting still more ideas, more data, more suggestions. In

June 1954, after signing the ABC contract, he sent a four-man expedition headed by Bill Cottrell on another information-gathering junket to amusement parks, museums, even arcades and shooting galleries, across the country, and he sent another representative to the Playland Park in Rye, New York, just to count the patrons. He had also hired as advisers two longtime amusement park operators, George Whitney, who ran the Cliff House in San Francisco, and Ed Schott, who ran the Coney Island Park in Cincinnati. "While we were planning Disneyland, every amusement park operator we talked to said it would fail," John Hench recalled. "And Walt would come out of those meetings even happier than if they'd been optimistic."

He loved the fight now that he had something to fight for, loved the hurdles he had to leap, loved the idea that he had to prove himself right again, and he talked of waging the same old battles that he once had had to wage in making the animation features. With the exception of his advisers, he didn't want anyone on the staff who had amusement park experience because, he told them, Disneyland wouldn't be an amusement park and because he wanted young people who would be willing to learn and make mistakes. To be the general director of the project, he hired a tall, thirty-three-year-old Oklahoman named C. V. Wood, who had been both a champion lariat twirler and the director of industrial engineering at an aircraft company during the war before becoming the manager of the Los Angeles branch of the economic research division of Stanford Research Institute, which had done the feasibility studies for the park. Wood was charming and affable with a down-home manner and a thick southwestern drawl—"the most winning and likable personality that one could ever expect to find," said one acquaintance—and he had acquitted himself well while at SRI by using that charm to coax holdouts on the Ball subdivision to sell their land to Disney. Walt was charmed too. "Walt reacted to him the way the farmer reacts to the fast-talking city slicker," recalled Buzz Price. Wood, in turn, recruited a retired admiral named Joe Fowler, who had once headed the San Francisco Navy Yard, as a consultant, though Walt later "trapped" the admiral, as Walt put it, into assuming the role of construction supervisor. The officers set themselves up in two old ranch houses on the site, where, just as at the old writers' apartment at Hyperion, the staff commandeered the kitchen, dining rooms, even closets. Walt's office was in a bedroom. There was a single bathroom in the facility.

They broke ground on July 12, 1954, which meant that they had to finish within a year to meet Walt's self-imposed deadline. Everyone had to rush. A structural engineer, who had been hired to assist in designing the buildings and coordinating with the WED staff, had to lay out foundations and framing even before the architectural details were finished, which caused problems, especially on Main Street. And there were other problems. The soil in Anaheim was so sandy and porous that the Rivers of America kept seeping into the ground and clay soil had to be trucked to the site. Unions were aggrieved. A strike at the Orange County plant that was supplying asphalt necessitated hauling asphalt from San Diego. A plumbers' strike limited the number of water fountains that could be installed before the opening. One group of disgruntled machinists "forgot" to bring their tools, while another crew of laborers cut the wires on the Mr. Toad ride because they were angry at being driven so hard. On one occasion union painters at the park sandblasted the locomotive *Casey Jr.* and repainted it because it had been painted at the studio by members of a rival union. Even nature rebelled: the weather in the spring was the wettest the county had had in twenty years.

And then there was Walt Disney trudging over the site in a straw hat and loud sport shirt, as in the old days, ordering the workers about, alternately hurrying them up and slowing them down, willing the property to conform to his dream. "He walked over every inch of Disneyland," Ward Kimball said, "telling them to move a fence a little more to the left because you couldn't see the boat as it came 'round the corner. I'd be with him out there, and he'd say, 'The lake is too small. Maybe we should make it larger. Let's find out if we can move the train wreck over another fifty feet.' He thought of everything." Morgan "Bill" Evans, whose brother had landscaped the property at Carolwood and who had been hired to landscape the park, recalled, "Walt's approach was to say, 'I need a jungle,' or, 'I need a touch of Alpine flavor for the sky ride.' He didn't know which trees would work, but he knew what he wanted." He wanted perfection. He wanted the park as realized to match the park in his mind's eye. Evans remembered a Saturday morning when Walt complained that a Brazilian pepper tree had been planted too close to the walk at the entrance to Adventureland. Evans had to pack up the six-ton root ball and move the tree.

Having come to dread the studio, he cherished the park and the time he spent there; he would even sit in the catering tent eating hot dogs with the workers. Still, he was impatient with the pace of construction and nervous that guests might not *see* where the money and the effort had gone. He wanted the spending to show, and it bothered him that so much money was invested in infrastructure. Several months before the opening he grumbled to Harper Goff, "You know, I've spent 50% of the total budget already, and there isn't one thing you'd call terrific out there right now." Goff remembered that Walt was actually crying when he said it. Another time, watching the foundation being poured for the Main Street train station with Joe Fowler and Dick Irvine, he fumed, "By the time Joe gets through burying all our money underground, we won't have a thing left for the show!" He made a similar complaint when Fowler ordered a drydock dug for the *Mark Twain* Riverboat that would ply the Rivers of America. He called it "Joe's Ditch."

But construction was only one front. While Walt was tending to the building, wrangler Owen Pope was gathering livestock from across the country for Frontierland. (He and his wife Dolly would move to the park three days before its opening; Walt had given them a choice of their house and a ten-acre plot for the animals—about two hundred head at the time.) And while the Popes were gathering their menagerie, staff members at WED were manufacturing the rides for the park. Walt had personally visited the Arrow Development Company south of Palo Alto, which produced mechanisms for amusement park rides and which would provide the mechanisms for Disneyland's Snow White's Adventures, Mr. Toad's Wild Ride, and King Arthur Carousel, all of which the WED engineers would decorate on the soundstages. And while the staff was decorating the rides, George Whitney, Walt's amusement park consultant, was visiting parks and factories and acquiring a merry-go-round from Toronto, horses from a carousel at Coney Island, arcade games, "Music Machines," and a test track for "dark rides" (that is, rides, like the Snow White and Mr. Toad attractions, that took passengers through a dark environment), and Nat Winecoff was contracting for miniature cars from Germany for the Autopia speedway in Tomorrowland. And while George Whitney and Nat Winecoff were acquiring rides, Walt was pressuring Casey Jones to get him a locomotive; failing that, he pressured Ward Kimball to lease his locomotive to the park. "He'd call all hours of the day and night," Kimball said, with an offer that Kimball could engineer the train as much as he liked on Mondays, when the park would be closed. Kimball refused, so Walt built the trains and bought locomotives.

And while they were frantically engaged in all these activities, Walt and Roy were also engaged in one more essential task: trying to get additional money to finance them. Even before they had finalized the ABC deal, the brothers were courting executives of major companies, escorting them through the studio and making their Disneyland pitch for the companies to lease concessions or underwrite attractions; among the wooed were American Machine and Foundry, Coca-Cola, Pepsi-Cola, Ford Motors, B. F. Goodrich Tires, and the Kellogg cereal company. Contrary to Walt's accounts of resistance to the park, almost everyone swooned. An officer of the DuPont Chemical Company told Walt that "he would hate to be the one not to recommend anyone to come into Disneyland."

Winecoff and Irvine visited the General Electric headquarters in Cleveland and found them "greatly enthused." Even the usually reserved Joe Rosenberg, their longtime liaison at the Bank of America, was buttonholing prospective lessees, and a Standard Oil of California vice president had told him that "never in his life had he seen such wonderful imagination and complete detailed planning"; Rosenberg said that "they definitely wanted to be part of it" and that the vice president had even asked him to lobby with the Disneys for them.*

Many of these targets would surrender to the Disney vision and sign on: Walt collected $2.3 million in lease payments, including $50,000 from the Santa Fe Railroad to sponsor the railway, $45,000 from American Motors to sponsor a 360-degree movie attraction called Circarama, $45,000 from Richfield Oil to sponsor Autopia, the same amount from the Swift meatpacking company for its Main Street Red Wagon Inn, and another $43,000 for a grocery. Yet the estimated cost of the park kept spiraling upward, from the $5.25 million at the time of the ABC signing to nearly $17 million at the time of the opening. Walt and Roy had calculated a cushion; among other contingencies, they had purchased eleven and a half acres of land nearby worth $230,000 that they could sell if necessary. But despite the television contract, the loans, and the leases, despite even the cushion, they still fretted that there might be too little money, just as there seemed to be too little time.

This time Walt did not want to cut corners, did not want to compromise his vision. When an employee suggested that he use cut glass instead of stained glass in an attraction called Storybook Land, Walt objected. "Look, the thing that's going to make Disneyland unique and different," he insisted, "is the detail. If we lose the detail, we lose it all." But as the time of the opening approached, money was dwindling and the clock was racing, and just as the Prince in *Snow White* shimmied because Walt couldn't afford to correct it, he was forced to make concessions at Disneyland. He had wanted Fantasyland to resemble a Gustaf Tenggren watercolor. Instead, economies dictated that the rides be housed in prefabricated industrial sheds festooned with medieval pennants. The Canal Boats of the World, which were supposed to drift past miniature landmarks and then were later reconceptualized as transport through a Story-

*Among the petitioners who wanted to get into Disneyland was a fast-food franchiser named Ray Kroc. "I have recently taken over the national franchise of the McDonald's System," Kroc wrote Walt. "I would like to inquire if there may be an opportunity for a McDonald's in your Disneyland Development." Walt palmed him off on C. V. Wood. There was not to be a McDonald's at Disneyland. Ray Kroc to Walt, Oct. 20, 1954, K Folder, Walt Disney Corr., 1953–1954, G-K, A1552, WDA.

book Land of fairy-tale scenes, drifted past scrub and brush because Walt couldn't afford to finish the attraction. Bill Evans had landscaped the park largely with indigenous trees that had been uprooted by highway construction, but even then Walt didn't have enough money to finish the job and instructed Evans to put Latin names on the weeds, as if they were specimen plants. "Toward the opening," Evans said, "we did a lot of irrigating to get the weeds to grow on the barren areas, particularly on the high dirt berm that surrounded the Park." It was just another illusion.

The final illusion was the staff that was hired to man the park. Walt didn't want them to spoil his fantasy, so he instituted what he called the "Disney University" to train them. "[W]e don't hire for jobs here," the training program's head, Van Arsdale France, told a reporter, in keeping with the theme that this was not a park but a set, "so much as we cast for parts, especially the onstage roles—ticket takers, ride operators, tour guides." As a Disney training manual would say, "[Y]ou can't go on stage unless you are set to give a pleasant, happy performance." Walt demanded that the cast be both cheerful and presentable, and though dress at the studio had always been casual and Walt himself obviously had a mustache, Disneyland employees had to observe a strict dress code, and an edict that forbade facial hair. One employee, the first manager of Adventureland and Frontierland, felt that Walt didn't particularly like him because he was heavy. "Walt doesn't like fat guys," the man said.

There was also a question as to whether Walt liked minorities working at the park. The studio had never overtly discriminated. There were some Asians, like Ty Wong and Bob Kuwahara, in prominent positions, but very few African-Americans—the old strikers would say because Walt had an antipathy toward blacks. This may have just been another example of the strikers' antipathy toward Walt, who never expressed even a hint of racism. But he, or someone at the company, may have felt that African-American cast members would have spoiled the illusion at Disneyland, since as late as 1963, the Congress for Racial Equality, a civil rights group, was conferring with Disneyland officials about the hiring of blacks and was told that the Disneyland board of directors would only consider their requests, not necessarily act upon them.

Walt certainly hated dirt and mess. One of the spurs for creating the park, of course, was the filth that Walt had so detested on his Sunday amusement park excursions with the girls. Disneyland was going to be almost eerily clean—so much so that cleanliness would become not only a hallmark of the park but a kind of running joke about it. "It is calculated that a discarded cigarette butt will lie dormant for no longer than 25 seconds before it is pounced upon," one reporter later wrote of the famous Disneyland sanitation crew. Another called the park a "Simonized Coney

Island" that "glistens in innocence not only of discarded popcorn boxes and cigarette packs but also of any least film of pavement dust or fading paint or unpolished brightwork, and in which one feels guilty [for] dropping a cigarette butt, and relief at seeing it whisked instantly into a stylish little dustpan by a juvenile lead elegantly costumed as a period street cleaner." The park would never stay clean, a journalist predicted during a tour a week after its opening. To which Walt riposted that it would stay clean because "people are going to be embarrassed to throw anything on the ground." This was, after all, utopia.

Now, as the July 17, 1955, opening neared, national anticipation grew. For nine months Walt had been promoting the park on his television program, and ABC had taken out $40,000 worth of full-page newspaper advertisements to ballyhoo the ninety-minute live telecast of the event, for which the network had marshaled what it called the greatest ever concentration of television equipment and personnel—twenty-nine cameras stationed around the park. ABC had already sold out the advertising in March, and crews had been rehearsing every Sunday since May 22. The interest in the park was so intense that in April, the studio reported, the staff counted 9,500 people stopping for information at the site one weekend, Saturday noon to Sunday evening, even though there was no sign identifying the property as Disneyland.

If the country was waiting expectantly, so was Walt Disney. In spite of the park's shortcomings, he seemed rejuvenated, almost giddy. He was the first one to ride the attractions—"just like a little kid," Marvin Davis recalled. "He'd get off and giggle or if he didn't like it too well, his eyebrow would go up and he'd say, 'Fix this thing and let's get this show on the road.' " Ten-year-old Harrison Ellenshaw, whose father, Peter, was an artist at the studio, remembered visiting the site one Saturday while his father painted a map of the park. The boy was watching the workers lay track for the railroad when Walt approached him, spotted a board on a train carriage near the track, and offered to give him a ride. Harrison jumped on the board, and Walt pushed. Then, when it had reached speed, Walt jumped on himself. "He was acting just like a kid," Harrison Ellenshaw would say years later, echoing Davis, "on the same level as a ten-year-old kid!" In fact, Walt's own capacity to experience the park the way guests would, with the same childlike abandon, contributed to the appeal of the attractions. One acquaintance called the park the "world's biggest toy for the world's biggest boy."

Even with the opening hard upon him and even with the clear exhilaration he was feeling, Walt was still examining, still tinkering and plotting. An assistant landscaper remembered watching him five days before the dedication walking up and down Main Street and scrutinizing the facades. "[H]e would stop and face a building and look at it, step back, his head would kind of turn," the man said, "and then he would make some notes in his little flip notepad. He then would look up at something else and make another note, look down at the bottom of the sidewalk, check out everything, and a last-minute glance and he would go on to the next building." As a final test, Walt invited families of the members of the studio's Penthouse Club to a kind of sneak preview. "We had a tent set up, we had a barbecue and three barrels of beer and Walt would be running the train around," Walt Pfeiffer recollected. "Everybody was waving and the Mark Twain would go by with everybody singing—it was just a glorious day."

And Walt clearly wanted to prolong the joy he felt. The park's opening had been scheduled just four days after his and Lillian's thirtieth anniversary, so Walt decided to host a party on the evening of July 13 not only to celebrate his marriage but to show off his park to friends and notables. (He invited everyone from his aunt Charlotte and Joe Rosenberg to Spencer Tracy, Cary Grant, Gary Cooper, and Louis B. Mayer.) He waited cheerily at the gate to greet them; then, when most of them were delayed by a traffic snarl, he stood there smoking nervously and grumbling. It was no doubt a measure of how tense he had been over the months of construction and how relieved he now felt that as the party was drawing to a close at the Golden Horseshoe Saloon, he had drunk a little too much and was firing imaginary bullets at the stage from the balcony. Diane had to drive him home, during which time Walt was "tootling" through a rolled map of Disneyland as if it were a trumpet; then he sang a song and fell asleep holding the map.

Continuing the long festivities, the very next night he was feted at the Hollywood Bowl. Fess Parker and Buddy Ebsen, who had played Crockett's sidekick on the television show, flew in from location in Kentucky, where they were shooting a prequel to *Davy Crockett*; Sterling Holloway, who had voiced a number of Disney characters, narrated "Peter and the Wolf," as he had done for the film; Cliff Edwards, who had been the voice of Jiminy Cricket, sang songs from *Pinocchio*; producer Winston Hibler narrated suites from two True-Life Adventures; and Disney characters performed a ballet. At the conclusion California governor Goodwin Knight declared Walt the state's honorary governor and presented him a coonskin cap dipped in silver. According to the *Los Angeles Times*, as Walt was introduced, "[a]pplause rose like a hurricane in the great verdant Bowl and knocked against the stars." Children whistled. The celebration was repeated the following evening, two days before the opening.

Even after three thousand workers had cut twenty thousand feet of timber, poured five thousand cubic yards of concrete, and laid a million square feet of asphalt, Walt still wasn't finished. The night before the opening he suddenly seized upon the idea of taking the giant rubber squid from *20,000 Leagues Under the Sea* and exhibiting it at the park. The problem was that the squid's latex skin had deteriorated since the shooting, so it had to be restored and repainted. Ken Anderson, who had designed the Disneylandia miniatures, was assigned the task along with two other staff members, but then Walt appeared. "Walt put on a mask," Anderson would recall, and "helped us spray-paint the screen [for the exhibit] with fluorescent paint." The area was enclosed, and the paint, Anderson said, "filled the air and clogged our masks." It took all evening to finish the operation, and Walt stayed up too—"the whole night before the opening." Yet, for all the flurry of activity—Walt had had to go to the airport that day as well to greet lessees who had flown in for the dedication—he was preternaturally calm. "Just about everyone was worried except Walt," said Jack Sayers, the director of guest relations. "He seemed to love the excitement." That was because Walt Disney knew he was in his element again. And he knew he was back.*

The day bloomed bright and hot and less festive-seeming than restive. C. V. Wood had printed fifteen thousand invitations, which was the estimated capacity of the park at any given time, but he soon discovered that people had counterfeited tickets. One man even leaned a ladder against the fence and let people over for five dollars a head. The staff tried to regulate the crowd by opening the gates and then closing them at twenty-minute intervals, but even so the press of people overwhelmed the facility. Van Arsdale France, who trained the staff, thought as many as 28,000 people fought their way into the park. With the crush came problems. As the broadcast opened and the tide of guests began surging down Main Street, the women's high heels got stuck in the hot, soft asphalt. Many of the guests complained about the lack of drinking fountains. Others were mystified when the walkway in Tomorrowland ended abruptly at a field of dirt because Walt hadn't had the funds or the time to complete the area. Even

*The only pall on Walt's mood during this period was the sudden death from a heart attack on July 4 of Perce Pearce, the pompous, pipe-smoking, hardworking writer-producer who had been with him from *Snow White* through the English live-action features through *The Mickey Mouse Club*, for which Pearce was filming segments in Europe when he expired. June Pearce to Walt, July 11, 1955, Perce Pearce Folder, Walt Disney Corr., Inter-Office, 1953–1955, M-P, A1639, WDA. "WHILE I HAD MY LITTLE DISAGREEMENTS WITH PERCE THROUGH THE YEARS I REALLY LOVED AND RESPECTED HIM," Walt wired his widow. Ibid., Jul. 13, 1955.

Walt, rushing from one location to another for the show, found himself stopped by a guard who had been instructed not to let anyone through. "Either you let me through here," Walt boiled, "or I'm going to hit you right in the face and walk over your body."

The broadcast, which was viewed by an estimated seventy million Americans, or roughly half the population, was similarly plagued. It featured three hosts hopscotching around the park—TV personality Art Linkletter, who was a friend of Walt's and who had visited Tivoli Gardens with him when Walt was mulling the park; and actors Ronald Reagan and Robert Cummings—and continually shuttled among them. But cues were missed, signals were crossed, and mishaps and technical glitches were telecast. By one account, even before the broadcast the director was so frazzled he suffered a breakdown and wound up orchestrating from a local hospital. Walt was certainly aware of the chaos. He told Reverend Glenn Puder, his niece's husband, whom he had asked to deliver the invocation at the opening, that "things weren't going quite well." Yet through it all Walt remained remarkably composed and unruffled. Dressed in a dark suit and a light silk tie, his voice hoarse and his hair touched with gray, he read aloud the plaque that declared Disneyland "your land": "Here age relives memories of the past. And here youth may savor the challenge and promise of the future." Elsewhere he would call it the "happiest place on earth."

It was certainly that to its creator. Diane, observing her father that day, said, "I have never seen a happier man." Mouseketeer Sharon Baird said she was watching the festivities with Walt at his apartment above the Main Street Fire Station, and when she looked up at him, his hands were clasped behind his back, he was grinning widely, and there was a "tear streaming down his cheek." But he had never been a man to indulge his pride or rest on his laurels. At the end of the day—the longest and quite possibly the best of Walt Disney's life in spite of the numerous calamities—he and Linkletter had dinner on the patio of the apartment and watched the fireworks display over the park. Linkletter noticed that Walt kept taking notes during the show. A stickler for detail even amid the pandemonium, he was counting the rockets being shot off to confirm that he was getting the full number.

Though there were criticisms—one reporter said, "Walt's dream is a nightmare" and called the opening a "fiasco the like of which I cannot recall in thirty years of show life"—these were minority opinions. More generally the visitors understood that this had been not just the opening of another amusement park but a signal event in the culture, a threshold crossed. "I think that everyone here will one day be as proud to have been at this opening as the people who were there at the dedication of the Eiffel Tower," Cummings remarked on the broadcast. Most seemed to realize that Disneyland was an extension of Walt's animations, that it was the fantastic and imaginary now made corporeal, or as *McCall's* put it, "Walt Disney's cartoon world materializes bigger than life and twice as real." Others saw it as the physical expression of Walt Disney's America that had crept into the American psyche. "Mr. Disney has tastefully combined some of the pleasantest things of yesterday with the fantasy and dreams of tomorrow," *The New York Times* blandly editorialized. Whatever it was—a childhood regression, a magnificent act of will, or an aestheticized rendition of America—it immediately made its claim on the national imagination.

The claim was so compelling that as soon as the park opened, both its observers and its creators felt a need to analyze the experience, a need that would continue as long as the park existed. Almost from the moment Disney first imagined it, he had thought of Disneyland in cinematic terms—a "cute movie set is what it really is," Walt told his staff. As the planning proceeded, Ben Sharpsteen said that Walt had repeatedly explained that the "success of Disneyland was primarily based upon the skills of motion picture set building and special effects techniques." To achieve cinematic effects, he had manipulated the park's proportions. It would often be said that Walt had built the entire park in five eighths scale. In truth, the railroad was five-eighths scale, which allowed Walt to use narrow-gauge rails and refurbished narrow-gauge trains. Main Street was a function of clever foreshortening. The lower floors of the shops were nine-tenths scale, the second floors eight-tenths, and the third seven-tenths. As for the rest of the park, Walt wrote an old acquaintance that the "scale of objects varies according to what and where they are"—what he called a "matter of choosing the scale that would be practical and still look right." The *Mark Twain*, he said, was built on a three-quarters scale.

The reason, Walt averred, was psychological—a lesson learned, no doubt, from his miniatures at Disneylandia. For one thing, the altered size "made the street a toy," he felt, and provided the subliminal fun that toys did. For another, it underscored the sense of nostalgia because it associated the past and the fantastic with the small and quaint. "[P]eople like to think their world is somehow more grown up than Papa's was," he said. And finally, he thought, the scale made the park more inviting and accessible—a human monument. Ken Anderson recalled Walt saying, "You know, tyrants in the past built these huge buildings—look how big and powerful I am. And they towered over the people just to impress the people." At Disneyland the people would be made to feel that they towered over the buildings.

Even more sophisticated effects re-created the sense of watching a film. One analyst compared the park to a Disney animation, with each of the main attractions playing the same role as the "key frames" in the films: "conveying the extremes of the action." This effect made the images and experiences more indelible. John Hench, who helped design the park, claimed that Walt had devised a "kind of live action cross dissolve when passing from one area of Disneyland to another," referring to a film technique in which one scene gradually fades while the next gradually appears. "He would insist on changing the texture of the pavement at the threshold of each new land because he said, 'You can get information about a changing environment through the soles of your feet.' " But this also kept the experience fluid and organic—not just a disjointed series of rides but a complete sensory flow from one to the next.

The WED staff, or "Imagineers," as they would later be dubbed, to acknowledge the combination of engineering and imagination that went into the task of designing the park, had not only been inspired by movies in thinking of rides; Walt had coached them to think of the rides as movie experiences. One would pass through "scenes" physically just as one did while temporally watching a film. Indeed, during the planning stages Walt, while examining the storyboards for the attractions, would actually act out guests' reactions as he had always acted out the scenes of the animations. In effect, then, the park was designed not only to provide archetypal tableaux but to tell a story or series of stories in which the guest was put in the role of the protagonist: Snow White or Mr. Toad or Peter Pan or Alice. And the stories, one analyst believed, all resolved to an overriding theme, one that Disney had sounded repeatedly: "that Good triumphs over Evil, that the little fellow, through a combination of luck, courage, and cunning, can always overcome in the end the big bad person in his or her numerous guises, all of which signify Power and its abuse." Subliminally, the park empowered the guest.

Because the park had been imagined as a set or group of sets, it also necessarily addressed the transaction between the reality outside the park and the fantasy within it—moving from one to the other, usurping one with the other. Walt had always intended to transport his guests to a separate space, and he once scolded a publicist who had parked his car where it could be seen from the *Mark Twain* because passengers in 1860 could not possibly imagine an automobile from 1955. "I want them to feel they are in another world," he would tell his Imagineers, something he could just as easily have said about his animations. There was general agreement that he had largely succeeded. One reporter visiting Disneyland called it "less an amusement park than a state of mind, in the real meaning of the term," which would become a common sentiment when journalists tried to pin down Disneyland's appeal. More specifically, because it seemed so distinct from everyday reality, some would think of it as a place in which people weren't so much indulging themselves as being transformed. "Something in the Disney parks, if not Disneyism as such," critic Greil Marcus would write, "brings out not necessarily the best or the worst but so often the most in people—it strips them bare, reduces them to babble or prompts curses and slurs." John Hench saw Walt's intention as therapeutic. "When Walt built Disneyland, he was striving to make people feel better about themselves," Hench said. "I think he had discovered what people were looking for—the feeling of being alive and in love with life," which gave the park an almost religious aura.

The reason the visitors felt so good, Hench believed, was that Walt Disney had painstakingly conceived of his park as ordered and harmonious. Disneyland had no ambiguity, no contradictions, and no dissonance. The layout and the way guests were subtly directed to destinations, the cleanliness, the efficiency with which crowds were queued up to wait for attractions, the weather, even the sounds of the park—all contributed to a sense of absolute well-being. Publisher Walter Annenberg, after visiting the park, said that if he were forced to reduce it to a "single descriptive word I would say wholesomeness."

Wholesomeness was certainly part of it, part of the perfection that Disneyland seemed to convey and the cocoon of joy it provided. But in the final analysis, the deepest appeal of Disneyland may have been less the perfection itself than the construction of it, as it had been in the Disney animations where the theme of responsibility meshed with the act of creation. Whatever else Disneyland did, it gave its visitors not just the vicarious thrills of the characters whose personas they assumed on the rides or their sense of triumph; it gave them the vicarious power of the man who had created it all: Walt Disney. Everything in Walt Disney's life had pointed to this park. All his efforts, a *New Yorker* contributor observed, had reached their climax in Disneyland, "where, in this most elaborate of the Master's animated productions, his live public has been fitted into the cartoon frame to play an aesthetic as well as an economic role." At Disneyland the guests were part of the overall atmosphere of happiness, and they reveled in their own manipulation because it was so well executed, because it was so comfortable and reassuring, and perhaps most of all, because it was so empowering to know that someone could actually have achieved this. In the end, it was not the control of wonder that made Disneyland so overwhelming to its visitors; like so much else in Walt Disney's career, it was the wonder of control.

V

Walt Disney, who had been disappointed so many times in his life, was not disappointed by his park. When one of his animated features had been completed, however far short it may have fallen of his expectations, there was nothing he could do, which was why he had developed the ability to disengage from his projects as soon as they were finished. "You're always so absorbed in the next thing, in the thing to come, that when I finish a picture, I forget the damn thing," he once said. The park was different. The park was organic. If it fell short, he could keep plussing it, changing it, expanding it. He liked to say that it would never be finished.

He didn't want to disengage from Disneyland—Disneyland was his life now. "He knew everything that went into the park," Dick Irvine said as one might have once commented about Walt's knowledge of the studio. "He knew where every pipe was. He knew the height of every building." Lillian said he knew where every nail in the park was located. After its disastrous opening and during the sweltering one-hundred-degree heat wave that followed, he was spending virtually all his time at the park "ironing out some little problems," as he told one journalist. But even with the problems ironed out, he could not pull himself away, and as late as December he was still spending most of his time at the park, especially on the weekends. "You know, Joe," he told Joe Fowler, "I come down here to get a real rest from the humdrum of making pictures at the studio. This is my real amusement. This is where I relax."

Though he had an electric cart, he would usually prowl the park on foot, with that long, loping farmboy's stride of his, often being mobbed by guests who recognized him from television and asked for his autograph. (He would later institute a policy of asking them to send requests to the studio because he could scarcely make his way through the park with the interruptions.) He would swoop down on the rides. Sometimes, remembered one Jungle Cruise boat operator, he would just stand on the dock and watch. Other times he would jump in a boat by himself or with other passengers. When he got a four-minute ride instead of the seven-minute one, he complained to Adventureland manager Dick Nunis: "If the trip is seven minutes and you cut out three minutes, it's like going to a movie and having some important reels left out." When he wasn't supervising, he was enjoying the park like a child with a giant playset. An employee at the Sunkist Citrus House remembered him coming by on Sunday mornings to stuff oranges into the juicing machines. Sometimes he would suddenly appear at night—even at four o'clock in the morning. "He practically lived there," Lillian would say, as he had once lived at the studio, and just as he had living quarters off his office at Burbank, he had an apartment over the fire station at Disneyland; it was decorated in red velvet, lace, and brocades to resemble a late-nineteenth-century home. One employee said she would occasionally see him standing at the window of the apartment, as he had on opening day, crying, moved by the achievement.

After all the doubts that the networks, his staff, his brother, and even his wife had harbored about Disneyland, Walt had been vindicated. The opening-day fiasco notwithstanding, the park was an instant triumph. In its first week it tallied 161,657 visitors, and by the end of the month it was attracting well over twenty thousand attendees each day—over a half-million visitors in all after four weeks of operation. In August nearly half of all tourists to Southern California visited Disneyland, it was estimated, and the park welcomed its one-millionth guest by the end of September. In its first year it would attract 3.6 million visitors. By the end of its second year it would greet four million more guests, for a 13 percent increase—25,000 on the second anniversary alone. It would receive its ten-millionth visitor less than two and a half years after its opening, by which time it exceeded the Grand Canyon, Yellowstone Park, and Yosemite Park as a tourist attraction.

And for the first time in nearly seventeen years—since the wake of *Snow White*—Walt Disney Productions was flush. Each adult visitor to the park paid a one-dollar admission; each of the children, fifty cents. In addition, they paid anywhere from ten to twenty-five cents for individual attractions. Parking at the twelve-thousand-car lot cost an additional twenty-five cents. That October, because some guests objected to the dollar admission, and because larger attractions like the Jungle Cruise and the *Mark Twain* were drawing a disproportionate share of riders, publicist Ed Ettinger suggested offering along with the admission a booklet of eight tickets—differentiated by A, B, and C attractions, from the least to the most sophisticated—for a single price of $2.50 for adults and $1.50 for children. The original plan was to offer the booklets for a limited time, but the system proved so efficient and popular that they became a staple of the park. A D ticket was added in 1956, and an E ticket for the most popular rides in 1959. *E ticket* soon became slang to describe any experience that was especially exciting.

As these millions of dollars poured into the park—the company had a gross revenue of $24.5 million in 1955, against $11 million the previous year—Walt began brainstorming again. To attract patrons at Christmastime, when he feared attendance would slacken, he created a Mickey Mouse Club Circus to run from late November through New Year's. It had been a lifelong ambition of his to own a circus, he wrote a friend, but when attendance proved disappointing, he concluded that visitors to Disneyland did not want to spend their precious time watching a circus for two hours, and the venture wound up losing $125,000. Even before the circus ended its run, Walt had also come to another conclusion—that "it is not unique enough to be in the park."

Disneyland needed big attractions, thrilling attractions, attractions one could find nowhere else. Just months after the opening, he was meeting with representatives of a Swiss firm to install a $200,000 cable gondola, or what Walt called an Alpine Skyway, that would traverse the park. At the same time he was meeting with executives from the Monsanto chemical company to discuss a plastic House of Tomorrow for the deficient Tomorrowland. (Monsanto had engineers at the Massachusetts Institute of Technology design the house, and the company was looking for a venue.) "It is possible that we could handle the TV treatment of your House of Tomorrow in the same manner as we did the construction of DISNEYLAND PARK," Walt wrote Monsanto, explaining how they could document the phases of the house on *Disneyland.* By January, Monsanto and Disney had closed the deal. Meanwhile Walt had entrusted Bill Cottrell with making an overall reappraisal of the park—Cottrell would revisit Europe that fall for inspiration—and in May, Walt announced a $7.1 million expansion, including the completion of Tom Sawyer Island and Storybook Land, the Alpine Skyway, an Astro Jet ride, a Rainbow Caverns mine train pegged to a True-Life Adventure titled *The Living Desert*, and an Indian village—all made possible, Walt told the *Los Angeles Times*, because the park had proven so successful that banks were lending it money at rates of 3.75 percent, a significantly lower rate of interest than the one they were willing to grant for films. Still, even Walt Disney's power had limits. He had asked Joe Fowler to see if Fowler could provide snow for Main Street and freeze over the Rivers of America. Fowler politely told him it couldn't be done.

Now that Disneyland was successful, there came a reckoning. All the time that the park was being constructed, Walt had had to delegate authority, primarily to C. V. Wood, the personable young Oklahoman whom Walt had put in charge of logistics while Walt himself floated above most of the practical concerns. Once Disneyland was opened, Wood headed a three-man Operations Committee that effectively ran the park. But as he had with John Reeder and Fred Leahy at the studio, no sooner did Walt delegate power than he resented the individuals to whom he had granted it. Walt needed control, especially since he feared that Wood had begun building a cadre of employees who were loyal to him rather than to

Walt. By January, Wood was gone, and Walt announced that he would personally assume the duties of general manager, working directly with a new five-man, theoretically all-powerful Park Management and Operations Committee that he, as the president of Disneyland, had appointed. In effect, Walt replaced Wood with himself. When a Disneyland Policy and Planning Committee met the next month to determine the park's philosophy and set its agenda—questions like whether it should close during the off-season or whether it should be open only six days a week—there was no doubt who was now in charge. Walt Disney, the spiritual leader, had taken temporal command.*

If Walt was besotted by the park, he was still resentful at having to play corporate chief at a studio that was increasingly making films he didn't particularly care about, and as he assumed more control of Disneyland, he yielded more control of Walt Disney Productions. "I feel what's wrong there's been too much of me," Walt told an interviewer to justify his absence from the studio, and, recalling the words he had used to describe himself just before his 1931 breakdown, he said, "I have been the slave driver. . . . I just sometimes feel like a dirty heel the way I pound, pound, pound." He admitted that he was essentially a strategist now, the first and last resort, rather than a hands-on producer—"[W]e can talk something over and we arrive at something and they're off"—and that the studio staff was more autonomous than it had ever been. Potential screen material was now considered by a committee at a monthly "synopsis" meeting, which Walt never attended, and eventually he entrusted Bill Anderson, who had been the production manager at the studio and then the vice president of studio operations, with the job of supervising the films.

Technically, Anderson assumed authority only in Walt's absence, but Walt was usually absent now, at the park or abroad or sequestered in his office. As Ben Sharpsteen, who was producing True-Life Adventures, described the new process, "Walt says in effect, 'I'm gonna be gone for quite a while,' say six weeks, and he says, 'You know we've been accumu-

*This was not the last confrontation between Walt and C. V. Wood. Not long after leaving, Wood began luring away Disneyland employees for a new amusement park project called Magic Mountain in Golden, Colorado. When that failed to materialize, Wood, calling himself the "Designer-Builder of Disneyland," resurfaced at the head of another amusement park venture, this one in New York called Freedomland. Walt, furious at the presumptuousness, decided to sue him. Memo, Donn Tatum to Walt, Re: C. V. Wood Matter, June 3, 1960, C. V. Wood Folder, Walt Disney Corr., 1961, M-Z, A1589; Memo, Cottrell to Walt, April 14, 1960, Bill Cottrell Folder, Walt Disney Corr., Inter-Office, 1960-1964, A-Disney Aircraft, A1648, WDA.

lating a lot of footage about birds, you know, that stuff and this stuff, and down there,' and he says, 'By the way, I want you . . . to put that in some kind of order and draw a bead on it.' " This was a responsibility—one that Walt had previously assumed himself—but Sharpsteen felt it was also a threat: "I want to see that stuff in usable shape when I come back or else." That was the conundrum throughout the studio. Now that he was insulated by layers of management, Walt didn't want to be bothered, but he also expected things to be done precisely as he wanted.

If anything, with Walt distracted by the park and often absent, the tension at the studio, which had been steadily rising since before the strike more than ten years earlier, only intensified. The staff lived in fear—total abject fear. Richard Fleischer, a film director and the son of Walt's old rival Max Fleischer, came to the studio to make *20,000 Leagues* and was surprised at what he found: "There was a general feeling of nervousness and insecurity about the place, which was attributed to the frequent mass firings that seemed to take place capriciously," he would write. Fleischer said he dismissed the theory until Walt confirmed it. " 'You know,' he said to me, 'every once in a while I just fire everybody, then I hire them back in a couple of weeks. That way they don't get too complacent. It keeps them on their toes.' " Another employee said that Walt's staff greeted him "with the total respect peasants usually show to their king," and remarked how they "would fervently agree even if he said 2 plus 2 was 22." A young writer who was being considered for a biographical television special on Beethoven observed how cautious the staff was lest they make a decision that might upset Walt, even though some of them had been at the studio for decades. "Fear, in fact, seemed to be their normal state—one that I would soon learn was warranted," she wrote. "They had witnessed the summary firing of others who had disagreed just once with Disney. They liked their work; they valued their careers; they knew better than to cross their tyrannical boss." Ben Sharpsteen, who had been at the studio since 1929, often in the role of Walt's whipping boy, developed a nervous condition that required him to take frequent leaves from the studio. "These seem to be occurring oftener and for longer durations," he wrote Walt.

An associate described Walt as "steel springs inside a silk pillow," but the springs kept poking through. He was often cold and baleful now. "[A]ll the dead wood is going to be weeded out," he wrote Gunther Lessing after being reelected as chairman of the board just as Disneyland was ramping up, and he saw dead wood everywhere. After ordering Bill Anderson halfway through the first season to fire one member of the staff of *The Mickey Mouse Club*—"I feel he is still on our payroll, but I do not know why"—Walt added: "Also check on everybody in the Mouseketeer Group who has been carried over. I believe that outside of the 9 Mouseketeers, Jimmy [*sic*] Dodd and Roy Williams, we should start from scratch. . . . Let's make a thorough check on the setup of the Mouseketeers and see that we are not carrying people who are not needed"—this after the staff had practically broken themselves to rush the program to the air. Similarly A. G. Keener, who had been the paymaster at the studio for fifteen years, was dismissed and given a reference letter more appropriate to a short-term employee: "Because of world market conditions, our organization has been compelled to undergo a drastic reduction in personnel. And in line with this cut, Mr. Keener's Department has been absorbed by the general Accounting Department." Norm Ferguson, once the premier animator, was terminated because he had become "dead wood." Fred Moore had been reinstated, then terminated again—still dead wood. (He would die a short time later in an automobile accident; Walt did not attend the funeral.) Fred Leahy was finally fired (Walt insisted he had resigned), and Hal Adelquist, after two decades of performing some of the most thankless tasks at the studio, decided to leave too. When Adelquist obsequiously petitioned Walt to return not long thereafter—"I'm not particular about the kind of work involved"— Walt refused. Jack Kinney, who had been at the studio since 1931, first as an animator, then as a director of sequences in *Pinocchio* and *Dumbo*, and then as director of most of the Goofy cartoons, was laid off and later left the studio. The wife of another former Disney sketch artist sent Walt a silver Madonna in the hope that he might buy it to finance a cataract operation that the artist needed to save the sight in his only good eye. Walt offered to buy it for $100. "I do not believe we are justified, in view of the market, to make the price any higher," he wrote her.

The man who had once been so collaborative now brooked no dissent at the studio. When the young writer of the Beethoven film suggested an approach that differed from Walt's, he gave her a chilling look, then slammed his fist on the desk, sending books and papers to the floor. "In the ominous silence, Disney's face hardened," she later wrote. "He said coldly that the conference was over." Even a longtime employee like storyman Bill Peet felt Walt's lash—not because Peet was out of phase with Walt but, Ward Kimball thought, because he was too closely in phase with him. Peet would make a presentation, according to Kimball, and then Walt would "pick away at little details." So Peet would change the material, and two weeks later Walt would return to Peet's room to say, "I don't think it should be this way," and then "outline exactly word for word the way Bill had it originally." But, said Kimball, the "unwritten law was that you couldn't point this out to Walt. . . . That's like putting your head in the tiger's mouth. This went on all the time." Peet himself said he had been warned early on, "Once you get in Walt's doghouse, you may never get out," as Peet discovered when he refused to redo a sequence in the new *Sleeping Beauty* and Walt exiled him to animate a Peter Pan Peanut Butter commercial.

Walt's eruptions at the studio now were more frequent, his temper more easily lost. When Harper Goff forgot to make a medallion for the seal in *20,000 Leagues*, Walt, according to director Richard Fleischer, "blasted him up one side and down the other," and Goff ran off "like a scalded cat" to remedy the mistake. On the same film Walt had assigned the matte artist Peter Ellenshaw to work with a veteran special effects man. Ellenshaw asked to be reassigned. Walt insisted he stay. When Ellenshaw remonstrated, Walt barked, "I'm talking. You shut up." As Ellenshaw put it, "He cut me down as if he had had a scythe in his hand." "You have to have a humble attitude, don't argue," Harry Tytle wrote his wife from Europe after Walt had snapped at another longtime employee, Gerry Geronomi, over dinner there. And as always he was mercurial. "You were being patted on the head by this kindly old uncle who wanted you to be happy and have a nice warm lunch when you suddenly realized you were talking to Attila the Hun," said producer Bill Walsh.

Such behavior may have been caused by a still-simmering desire for revenge for the strike, or frustration at a studio that could no longer produce films of which Disney could be proud, or hostility at having to deal with the studio at all when Disneyland clearly claimed his attention. Bill Cottrell thought that after the initial emotional rush of the park, Walt was seized by a deeper sense of responsibility for the construction of Disneyland. "As time went on, Walt grew more serious," Cottrell said, adding, "I don't think Walt was having as much fun as he should have had." Animator Eric Larson noticed it too. Walt, who had always hated the thought of money, now began to talk about it and worry about it "because they brought in people from the outside who talked him into the value of money." But whatever it was, to those at the studio, Walt Disney, who had long been a distant and a terrifying presence, had become even more distant and even more terrifying.

VI

Walt's image was that of a "lovable genius," as columnist Louella Parsons called him. The image was that even if he had necessarily become more corporate as the company had grown, he had not become more "Hollywood." He and Lillian were, in Parsons's words, "two of the really happily married people in our town." Lillian herself seemed to endorse that view. Near the end of her life she told one interviewer that she wouldn't have traded a minute of "our wonderful life together" and said that she "adored him." In truth, however, their marriage had tensions—serious ones, persistent ones. Though Lillian loved being Mrs. Walt Disney and was willing to subordinate herself to her husband—when asked for an autograph, she would sign on the flourish of the *y* in Walt's "Disney"—and though she knew she had to share him with his public, she was not particularly happy about having to do either. Once, at the Calgary Stampede in Canada, where Walt was invited as a special guest, Lillian had to wait, sitting on a barrel, for two hours. "[S]he used to be provoked at being left alone like that," Roy said, and quoted her as remarking that Walt "thought more of the public and the press than he did of her." Even Diane admitted that her mother was "possessive" of Walt and "jealous of other people that were fond of him," while Lillian herself was aloof with the public, haughty to them.

She didn't share his enthusiasms or his childlike effusions—not his animations or his miniatures or his trains or even Disneyland. Ward Kimball claimed to have seen Lillian at the opening of the park—actually she did not attend—and to have asked what she thought of it. "Well, it keeps Walt from playing around with other women," she told him flatly, though Walt never played around with other women or even seemed to notice them. (His midlife crisis was his model trains.) On another occasion, at a July 4 company picnic, the artist T. Hee, who raised goats as a hobby, gave Walt and the girls a kid with a red ribbon and a bell as a pet. Walt packed the kid in the car to leave, but Lillian insisted that the goat was not going with them. Just as persistent, Walt said it was a gift and began driving off, but Lillian sobbed "furious tears," Diane said, so Walt let them out at home, turned around with the kid still in the car, and spent the night at the studio. "That situation all but caused a divorce in the Disney household," Walt wrote Hee.

To Lillian, Walt was capricious. She told one interviewer that being married to him was like being "attached to one of those flying saucers they talk about," and that she never knew "when Walt's imagination is going to take off into the wild blue yonder and everything will explode." That was exciting, she said, but she focused less on the excitement than on the uncertainty. "I've always been worried. I've never felt secure," she told another interviewer, "but it got beyond the point where I could do anything about it. I just thought, 'That's it. He's going to do it and that's all there is to it.' " (For his part, Walt once told an animator who asked for a raise after the man's wife had said they needed more money, "You listen to your wife, huh? I'd hate to tell you where I'd be if I had listened to my wife.") Still, Lillian had never been one to accept Walt's decisions meekly or his status unquestioningly, and she admitted that he was always telling people "how henpecked he is." "Heavens, Mother had quarrels with him!" Diane recalled. "Good healthy ones. Nothing was ever under the surface in our family. If there were any irritations felt, there was an explosion." And Lillian was usually the one to explode.

She was unimpressed by him. Speaking of a negative magazine profile of himself, Walt told Hedda Hopper that Lillian didn't care what reporters said about him. "In fact, she usually agrees with anybody who writes things like that," he continued. "I keep reporters away from her. She'd give them the lowdown." When Harry Tytle's wife mentioned to Lillian that Walt was a genius, she cracked, "But how would you like being married to one?" "She was sort of unconscious, oblivious," Diane said. "She moved in her own circle of beauty parlor appointments, reducing exercises, dressmaker appointments, and occasional shopping sprees. . . . Always had to redecorate the corner of some room. That was her life." Walt called her "Madam Queen."

Walt was proud of her, proud of the way she dressed and the way she managed the household with so little help, only a cook and, when the girls were younger, Grace Papineau, Lillian's sister, who lived with them and cared for the girls when Walt and Lillian were occupied or when the couple traveled, though Diane thought that having interlopers in the house, first Lillian's sister Hazel and Hazel's daughter Marjorie, and then Grace, contributed to family tensions. And he was physically affectionate with Lillian as he was with his daughters, whether she invited his attentions or not. He "always had his arm around her," Diane said. She thought of them as "romantic." He also tried to pacify her, if only to keep the domestic peace. He took rumba or mambo lessons so he could dance with her when they attended functions, and animator Frank Thomas remembered seeing him intently practicing steps behind a palm tree at one of them. And though he grumbled about Lillian's spending—as he seldom grumbled about expenses at the studio or at Disneyland—he indulged her, albeit without being particularly thoughtful about it. One year, Lillian said, he handed her a catalog of fur coats and said, "Here's your Christmas present." Similarly, when Lillian asked for a radio, Walt had a large box of radios delivered to the office. Another year he gave her a petrified log as a present, which was promptly relocated to Disneyland. And another year, for their anniversary, he presented her with a necklace hung with miniature gold replicas of all the Oscars he had won—a tribute not to the marriage but to Walt.

. . .

In the end, the new house that was intended to bring him closer to his family didn't, if only because in the first few years, with the construction of Disneyland, he wasn't at Carolwood any more than he had been at Woking Way. According to his secretary, he would usually arrive at the studio in the morning, then immediately go out for a meeting in one of the animation rooms or take a meeting in his office with the staff. If he was off roaming the studio or, more likely, looking in at WED, he often wouldn't return to the office until noon. Then he would read his mail, drink a V-8 vegetable cocktail, eat a light lunch either in the office or at the commissary—"he had a theory," his secretary said, "that too much food made you think confusedly"—and then conduct more meetings through the afternoon until closing time at five o'clock. Then he would return calls and sign letters and, of course, meet with nurse Hazel George for his end-of-the-day diathermy treatment, his wind-down, and his drink—a Scotch Mist with water. And then he would head home for dinner.

But at home he was usually either drafting plans for Disneyland or puttering about in his workshop or playing with his train—at least until he retired his beloved Carolwood Railroad after the opening of the park. On one of its runs the train derailed, breaking its whistle and emitting a hiss of steam. A curious young passenger hopped off to look and was slightly scalded. By one account, Walt took the train to the studio machine shop and lodged it under the drafting table of one of the Imagineers, Bob Gurr, where he would occasionally visit it. "He would always touch it in a special way," Gurr said, "making sure it was all right." Sharon had another version. Though he stopped running the train after that incident, she said, he kept it at the house and one Sunday afternoon decided to run it himself with a remote control from his work barn. But in a scene out of *The Sorcerer's Apprentice,* the train, as Sharon described it, "ran full tilt into the side of the garage. Daddy took a lot of pictures of it and stashed it for good in a cubby at Disneyland. He was through with toy trains." Walt told it differently. He said he got tired of seeing everyone else riding the train and enjoying themselves while "I was wearing myself out stoking coal all day."

In any case, even if Disneyland hadn't intervened, after Duchess died he was less inclined to spend time in the workshop tooling items for his train. She had had gallstones, and rather than operate on her, the veterinarian wanted to put her down. Walt refused and stayed with her. "I feel you take them and you owe it to them," he said. She actually seemed to be recovering and was being given a bath at the vet's office when she suddenly expired. Perhaps nothing spoke more forcefully of the nature of Walt and Lillian's relationship than the fact that Walt suspected Lillian had countermanded him and told the vet to have Duchess euthanized. "He was furious," Diane recalled, and demanded that an autopsy be performed. "That was the only way he could believe she hadn't done anything behind his back." Even after Duchess was gone, he kept her blanket undisturbed in his workshop.

If the house didn't provide a retreat from the studio and bring him closer to the family, it didn't keep the girls at home either, as he had hoped. In the fall of 1951 Diane, always a good student, entered the University of Southern California, located in central Los Angeles, from which she could come home on weekends. Walt welcomed the visits, even though he continued to complain that she was "always on the go" and "I don't get to see much of her these days." But he noticed a change in her since her years of attending private girls' schools. "Heretofore with the association of only girls and more girls," he wrote his aunt Jessie, "the matter of her appearance didn't seem to be too important, but it's an entirely different situation now with the boys on hand."

Diane had fallen in love with a tall, strapping, handsome end on the USC football team named Ron Miller, though it was her father who suggested she marry him because Miller was about to go into the armed forces, and Walt was worried Diane might marry "Mr. Wrong" while Miller was gone. (Inviting his brother Herbert to the wedding, Walt called Miller a "wonderful boy—a big six-foot athlete whom we all love.") They were married on May 9, 1954, in the ivy-clad All Saints by the Sea Episcopal Church in Montecito, California, up the coast from Los Angeles, in what was described as a "football" ceremony. The minister who officiated was a former football player and coach, and the five-tier cake was topped not with figurines of a bride and groom but with two football players—one male, one female.

They wasted little time in starting a family. Diane gave birth to Christopher Disney Miller on December 10, seven months and one day after the wedding. Except for the name, Walt was ecstatic. "Diane pulled a name out of the blue," he wrote an associate, obviously wounded. "She seemed determined no son of hers was going to be tagged with my name. She had a particular aversion to the 'Elias' part of it." Actually, Diane had thought of calling the child Walter, then decided that he was "a new person" and needed a new name. She said later that she regretted it. Still, Walt doted on him as he had doted on his daughters. He would introduce Diane now as the "custodian of his grandson."

By the time Ron completed his military obligations at Fort Ord in northern California, Diane had had a second child, Joanna, born in April 1956, and Walt was building the family a house in Encino, in the San Fernando Valley, one that he had personally designed after rejecting each of Ron and Diane's choices. While the house was being constructed, the Millers moved in with Walt and Lillian at Carolwood, and though Walt conceded that "it gets a bit hectic at times, Granddaddy and Grandma are having the time of their lives with little Chris and Joanna. Joanna is as cute a little pixie as ever drew a breath and Chris is still as wonderful as ever." Indeed, Lillian, who had never been particularly social, further contracted her life around her grandchildren. "[W]hat with our new granddaughter in the family, I am having quite a time these days in getting her to go anywhere," Walt wrote the head of a charity that was holding a function and had invited the Disneys to attend.

Though Walt cosigned the mortgage for the Millers' new house, he had another source of financing in mind for the young family. For years various authors and publishers had begged him to cooperate on a biography. Walt had always demurred, saying that he was still in his prime and that any biography would consequently be incomplete. Even when he did grudgingly agree to a series in *The Saturday Evening Post*, he was frank that his biography would only be a promotion for *Alice in Wonderland*, telling the writer that he recognized "in writing such a story or serial based on life stories, it is frequently necessary to change actual events and experiences and to dramatize and fictionalize them"—a veiled admission that he had been embellishing for years.

That series never came to pass, but shortly after the *Disneyland* television show hit the air, Walt was approached by another writer, Paul Hollister, who had written an earlier piece on Disney for *The Atlantic Monthly* and had been commissioned by the magazine to do a biographical series on him, which would then be released as a book. Hollister, who had been led by the *Atlantic* to believe it had Walt's authorization, completed the book, only to discover that Walt had not authorized it and, worse, that Roy, to whom Walt had passed the manuscript for approval, vehemently advised Walt not to let it be published because its style was "annoying" and its facts inaccurate. Incensed when he was offered a small payment to drop the book, Hollister accused Walt of having "old Fixer Roy" try to buy him off because Roy and Walt knew that Hollister needed money. Neither the series nor the book ever appeared.

But now Walt decided that if anyone were to capitalize on his story, it should be his daughters. Early in 1956 *The Saturday Evening Post* approached Walt once again about a biographical series, and Walt countered by proposing that Diane be at least the nominal writer. "I can't get any money to you kids," he told his daughters, apparently referring to tax implications, "and this is a way to do it!" Diane as the writer of her father's story was only a conceit. At most she prompted the conversation. The actual author was a veteran journalist named Pete Martin, who conducted extensive interviews with Walt at Carolwood that summer—more than thirteen hours' worth—and interviewed associates at the studio as well. The series appeared in the magazine that fall, and Diane received $75,000 from the *Post*—it is unclear whether she split the proceeds with Sharon—and another $11,000 from Henry Holt, which had contracted to publish a book version, *The Story of Walt Disney*. (Martin received a portion of the Holt money and a portion of the foreign serial rights.) Walt was so eager to see the girls benefit that he even offered to rearrange his schedule so that he could come east to promote the series.*

Life was more difficult for Sharon, whom Walt had classified as the family beauty while Diane was called the family brain. While Diane "just sails through her classes," as her father wrote his sister Ruth, Sharon had never been a good student. Walt himself conceded that "school has always been tough for her" and that "she'd rather ride horses than study." She was also much shyer than Diane. Walt told one educator that her "personality seemed to be hidden under a curtain of apprehensive timidity," until he found a special program for her from which she emerged "well-poised and completely confident of herself." After graduating from the Westlake School for Girls in the Westwood section of Los Angeles, she enrolled at the University of Arizona—Walt took her there himself—and though he told his sister that she "loves" it, she lasted only a year and a half before she quit. Back in Los Angeles she attended USC at night for a semester, then quit that too. "I really just didn't like it," she said years later.

What she did seem to like was modeling. She was tall—5'8½" in her stocking feet, to Diane's 5'4½" in heels—slender, and attractive, with reddish, light-brown hair and blue eyes. Walt had even put her in one of his films, a Revolutionary War drama titled *Johnny Tremain*, to see if she

*Walt was also thinking of his animation legacy now. At least since 1953 he had been soliciting writers for a book on the art of animation, only to reject every candidate because he didn't trust them. The project languished for several years until Walt finally settled on an Associated Press reporter named Bob Thomas. Walt suggested that Thomas work with Jaxon and Dick Huemer, and "since I am working with them on other projects, I could be close to it, too." The book was eventually published. Memo, Walt to Jimmy Johnson, Re: Bob Thomas, March 25, 1957, Jimmy Johnson Folder, Walt Disney Corr., Inter-Office, 1956–1957, Disneyland J, A1642, WDA.

might like acting, but, he wrote Ruth, "after this one stint, she has decided that modeling is still her first love and will stick to that." For two years she drifted, working various odd jobs at the studio from secretarial to assisting Lillian's niece, Phyllis, who was producing television commercials on the lot with her husband, the acclaimed Hollywood glamour photographer George Hurrell. For most of this time she dated a young Kansas City–born interior designer named Robert Brown, who had worked at Pereira-Luckman and then, when that partnership ended, for Charles Luckman Associates. Sharon introduced him to her father in March 1959, while Walt was in the hospital convalescing from a bout of kidney stones, and the couple were married two months later, on May 10, in a small ceremony at the First Presbyterian Church in Pacific Palisades. (It was so hastily arranged that Roy, having made other plans, couldn't attend.) Though he genuinely liked Brown, Walt seemed traumatized at "losing" his daughter. During the ceremony, Diane said, he "shook like a man with a fever," and when Sharon and her new husband were dancing at the reception, Walt cut in, snapping to his new son-in-law, "This isn't your dance yet. You get her the rest of your life." Sharon admitted that her father was "a little annoyed."

Now Walt and Lillian were alone, thrown back on themselves. The only other person in the house was their cook and housekeeper, Thelma Howard. Like Lillian, Howard had been born in Idaho, one of a large family, but hers had been dogged by tragedy. Thelma's mother had died in childbirth when Thelma was six, and a sister had died at the age of eight when she and Thelma were cooking dinner on a wood-burning stove and the girl's dress caught fire. At eighteen Thelma left for Los Angeles. By the time she came to work for the Disneys in 1951, at the age of thirty-eight, she had been annealed by life. She was a slight woman but feisty, with thick, short hair and a rugged face. She loved to smoke, as Walt did, and play gin rummy. Walt, finding in her the same brassy, iconoclastic spirit he had found in Hazel George, enjoyed her company—in part, no doubt, because Lillian often seemed so sharp and brittle by comparison. He could joke with Thelma, tease her, criticize her cooking, and tell her she ought to go to Biff's, a local watering hole, and find out how they prepared their food. She was fully a part of the Disney family.

As for Lillian, she knew Walt's priorities. "If it ever comes to a showdown between his studio and his wife, Heaven help me!" she half-joked to a reporter. She was right, but at least she knew her only co-respondent was the company or Disneyland. Walt was diffident around most women, and outside of the ink and paint department, which some used to refer to as the Nunnery, there were very few women on the lot.* Some of his associates thought Walt didn't particularly like women. "He didn't trust women or cats," Ward Kimball observed. "Almost all of his villains were either women or cats." Marc Davis agreed that Walt had a "great suspicion of women" and was happiest working on masculine films like *20,000 Leagues* and *The Great Locomotive Chase*. But Hazel George took just the opposite view, saying that Walt was "more at ease with women than he was with men" and that he felt "identification and camaraderie with women" though the difference may have been that he was comfortable with strong, no-nonsense women like George herself and Thelma and shy around the others.

In any case, however Walt felt about women, no one ever accused him of infidelity or even of showing much interest in the opposite sex. Back when he was absorbed by his animations, he told Ward Kimball, "I love Mickey Mouse more than any woman I've ever known." Now that Walt was obsessed with his park, Ken Anderson recalled having a chicken dinner with him at the Plantation restaurant at Disneyland about a week before the opening. It had gotten back to Walt that many of the men who had been working down at the site away from their families for long stretches were having what Anderson called a "wild time at nights." Walt was incredulous. " 'You know, Ken, I can't understand it. Some of these guys . . .' he was even looking at me, he said, '. . . are majoring in women down here.' He said, 'Boy, I just can't understand that, Ken,' he said. 'It's like women were their hobby.' You know. 'This is my hobby.' " And he swept his arms across the expanse of Disneyland.

With Disneyland opened and Walt increasingly disillusioned with his studio, he and Lillian settled into a routine. As he headed home from work each day, his secretary would phone to alert Thelma and Lillian so dinner would be ready. (Lillian never cooked; if Thelma was off, she and Walt

*Retta Scott on *Bambi* became the "first girl animator," in Walt's words, but there would not be many more. In an Associated Press interview in 1946, Walt attributed the dearth of women animators to the fact that women were not particularly good at cartooning and that they lacked a sense of humor—statements for which Walt received a great deal of criticism. When Joe Lee, the chief editorial writer of the *Topeka State Journal*, came to Walt's defense, Walt wrote him, "I suppose the first thing I should tell you is that I am sleeping inside again," then admitted, "I guess there isn't any sucker bigger than the one who sounds off about the fair sex, in a manner which they like to construe as detrimental to them, but I must plead either nolo contendere or non compos mentis." Still, he concluded unrepentantly, "[I]f you think they possess a real sense of humor I'd like to be around some night when you are explaining how come you stayed out at the poker game 'til two o'clock in the morning." Bob Thomas, AP, March 18, 1946; Walt to Joe Lee, Mar. 25, 1946, L Folder, Walt Disney Corr., 1945–1946, L-P, A1535, WDA.

would go to the Tam O'Shanter or the Brown Derby.) When he arrived, he and Lillian usually had a cocktail together before sitting down for dinner, invariably in front of the television set. While the girls were still home, he usually watched just the news. After they left he became less discriminating. "He looked at everything," Lillian would recall. "We'd get a lousy program and I'd say, 'Do you want me to change it?' 'No, no, I just want to study it,' he'd say. I'd get annoyed and go upstairs and let him keep watching it. He was the same with pictures. I'd say, 'That one had a bad review.' 'I don't care,' he'd say. 'I want to see what the director did.' " When it came to his own programs, he was especially riveted and demanded that Lillian be riveted too. "Every time I would take a mouthful of food," she remembered, "he would look over and say, 'You're not looking.' " He had also had a wide-screen Cinemascope projection system installed at the house to view movies, but he stopped bringing home the studio's films because, he told his secretary, Lillian and Thelma didn't laugh loudly enough.

Since the Disneys seldom socialized and since Walt was no longer racing back to the studio at night as he used to do, their evenings usually ended early. Walt was in bed by nine or ten o'clock. But just as he hummed with nervous energy during the day, he was often restless in bed, especially when he was working on a project. Lillian said that he would sometimes get up in the middle of the night and stand at his dressing table talking to himself or sketching or reading a script there, because his old polo injury had made it uncomfortable for him to sit without hunching over.

Given Lillian's snippiness, he still was often exiled, or exiled himself, to the studio or to his apartment at Disneyland. Sometimes it was a matter of work. An employee remembered seeing Walt at the studio one evening because, Walt said, Lillian "wouldn't get off his back," and he had a script to read before a meeting the next morning. Other times it was Lillian's temper that sent him away. Even before Disneyland opened, he earned Lillian's wrath when he dissuaded her from attending the 1954 Oscar ceremonies with him because he was sure he wouldn't win and then wound up with four statuettes. He decided to spend the night at the studio. On yet another occasion Lillian erupted when Walt rehired her niece, Phyllis Hurrell, despite the fact that Lillian's sister Hazel thought he had already given flighty Phyllis too many chances. Walt stayed at the studio for three nights. He did not phone Lillian once.

Mostly they traveled. Walt called these journeys "trips" rather than "vacations"—when Milt Kahl, upon Walt's return, once asked if he had had a good vacation, Walt snapped, "Goddamn it, I've been working"—but though he often visited film locations and toured sites that might inspire something for Disneyland, his excursions were not really for business. They were primarily a way to leave the studio behind, as they had always been. Lillian and Walt traveled constantly. They attended premieres across the country, they went to resorts, and they sailed on long Caribbean cruises; on one trip they drove up and down the Eastern Seaboard to revisit Williamsburg, meet with various government officials and associations, see dioramas at the Museum of the City of New York, and consult with a professor at MIT in Cambridge. Walt even returned to Marceline in the summer of 1956 to attend a dedication of a park in his name and revisit his childhood haunts with Roy.

On the old pretense that Walt had to supervise productions in Europe, he and Lillian now made a yearly visit there too and stayed there for weeks, sometimes months. For all his professions that he was conducting business, he set his own agenda. Often he and Lillian drove themselves—on several of the European trips they were accompanied by William Sprackling, the president of Anaconda Wire and Cable, and his wife, who became the couple's closest friends and who shipped their Cadillac overseas—and tried to avoid the glare. "I don't want any publicity at all," Walt wrote an associate, explaining that he had even taken to traveling under the name Jones. "I just want to be myself and do and see what I'd like to."

When their 1957 European trip ended, Walt wrote Ruth that "[w]e were more than glad to return home." They had seen "some wonderful places" while touring the backcountry of England, France, Germany, Italy, and Spain; Walt was especially cautious that his Spanish visit not be publicized because of the longstanding but erroneous rumor that he had been born there. But "Lilly just about had a fit having to be away from the grandchildren for so long," he said, "and I guess I'll have to admit to being homesick for them too." While they had been away, Walt had had another home built at Smoke Tree in Palm Springs, to replace the one he had sold to raise money for Disneyland. Now, when he and Lillian weren't traveling around the country or abroad, they would retreat to the desert, where, Walt wrote a friend, he made it an "inviolable rule not to do anything but rest and relax." To which one might have fairly asked, what did he need to rest and relax from, save the pressure of having to be Walt Disney?

VII

Animation, the base on which the empire had been founded, was now being sustained more out of tradition and habit than for profits—something Walt acknowledged as early as 1953, when he told Bill Anderson that while *he* didn't want to spend his time on animation, it nevertheless "has to go on." The shorts, having hung for years by a thread, finally fell, as movie audiences plummeted through the 1950s, defecting to television, and as theaters either closed or opted for double features. It had taken drastic budget reductions to keep the shorts profitable, and then only barely, and Ward Kimball said that the studio had increasingly used them as make-work—as "something to keep the animation and story departments afloat between features; if Walt was having a problem with a new feature, you'd mark time by picking up work on a short." By 1957 the shorts units had been dismissed one by one, and when the storymen importuned Walt to let them try their hand at live action, which was taking up a larger and larger portion of the studio's resources, Walt was unsympathetic, saying that he couldn't afford to train them and that if they wanted to write live action, they could do so at another studio.

He wasn't much more supportive of the animated features. Watching footage from *Snow White* one day with Wilfred Jackson to find excerpts for television, he said that "it didn't seem possible to make a better picture than *Snow White*," and he didn't seem inclined to try. All the animators knew that his passion had been redirected from animation to the theme park. "You had to ask Walt to come into meetings on 'Lady and the Tramp,' " Frank Thomas said, comparing it to the times when Walt would be "rummaging around in every room looking to see what people had done." As Thomas analyzed it, "I think he had really spent himself on what he wanted to do in animation." Now he would come into an animator's room when one asked for his input, look at the work, and say blandly, "You're not in any trouble." Thomas took that remark to mean that Walt was making his staff depend on themselves, "like a mother bear shoving her cubs up a tree," but others took it, probably more accurately, as a sign of Walt's lack of interest. Where once he had a dozen pictures in the pipeline and was frantic over which to do next, he now had so few that the animators had to prod him to put animations into production.

Ironically, as Walt lost interest, the studio was actually generating more animation than it had produced in years as a result of the *Disneyland* program and *The Mickey Mouse Club*, but it was simplified to make it easier to draw and thus less costly. In fact, by 1956 the quality of the animation within the studio—the studio that every animator had once tried to emulate—had so deteriorated that Harry Tytle advised Walt that the work could be "farmed-out" to outside animators, "not only greatly reducing cost," Tytle said, but also, in what would have been heresy even a few years earlier, "getting a better quality." Walt may have been disengaged, but he wasn't blind to these shortcomings. He knew that much of what the studio produced was junk. He was just willing to accept it now because, as he would tell Hazel George, "[w]hat the hell. It's going to help build Disneyland, kid."

Disney wasn't the only studio where animation was in decline. Animation of the sort that the Disney studio had inspired was endangered everywhere—a casualty of high costs, fewer trained animators, and more competition from television, where the animation necessarily had to be more primitive to meet tight deadlines and budgets. Paul Terry sold his studio to CBS in 1955 and retired. MGM closed its animation unit in 1957 because, according to Joseph Barbera, who was running it along with William Hanna at the time, the studio discovered that a reissue earned as much as 90 percent of what a new cartoon made. Even Warner Bros. temporarily shuttered its animation unit in 1953 because it had too many cartoons in its inventory. When it reopened, it never had quite the same energy or flair as it had had in the 1940s.

Beyond economics, the sort of full-bodied personality animation that Walt Disney had pioneered and that others had imitated faced another threat: a new animation aesthetic. Animator John Hubley, who had worked at the Disney studio before the strike, remembered a Russian cartoon that architect Frank Lloyd Wright had brought to Burbank during a visit. "It was very modern," Hubley said, "with flat backgrounds, highly stylized characters, modern music." When Hubley and other like-minded animators left the studio after the strike and scattered to various companies, the modernist aesthetic stuck with them—an early salient in what Hubley, who went to Screen Gems, admitted was a "revolution" against the "characteristic Disney round and opaque forms."

It wasn't until the war that the political and aesthetic revolutionaries found an instrument to advance their cause. As David Hilberman, the onetime Disney gadfly, told it, he, another former Disney animator named Zack Schwartz, and a third animator named Stephen Bosustow formed an informal partnership, Industrial Film and Poster Service, to make cartoons and posters for industry and government. Eventually they landed a contract for a film sponsored by the United Auto Workers to promote Franklin Roosevelt's reelection in 1944. By the end of the war—with encouragement from the business manager of the Cartoonists Guild, Bill Pomerance, the support of some former Disney strikers who had landed in positions of authority and could steer work to them, and several films underwritten by unions—the studio, renamed United Films and then United Productions of America (UPA), began to attract other former disaffected Disney animators.

It was a small shop, and it survived in its early days only because its employees were willing to forgo their salaries. But if it was hardscrabble, it was also infused with a vision every bit as powerful as the vision that had infused the old Disney studio. It was Zack Schwartz, according to animation historian Michael Barrier, who had the revelation that "our camera is closer to being a printing press, in the way we use it, than it is to being a motion picture camera." What Schwartz meant is that animation should be the handmaiden not of film, as it was at the Disney studio, or of comic strips, but of design, and that it should be a product not of popular culture but of high art. (Of course Disney had had the same revelation, but the necessity of making money kept him from doing much about it, save his aborted flirtation with Dali.) As Hilberman explained the evolution of UPA, "It was simply that you had designers who had art training who were beginning to push out and feel their oats. People who knew who Picasso was and could recognize a Matisse across the room. And here they were at Disney, Warners, working on this really corny, cute stuff. They were ready. UPA was the first studio that was run by design people, and we were talking to an adult audience, to our peers." "[O]ur approach was a painterly approach, or an artist's approach," said Jules Engel, another former Disney animator who had gone to UPA, "[the approach of someone] who was aware of the flat surface and knew what the hell that is all about."

As enemies of Disney, both politically and aesthetically, UPA animators consciously forswore all the hallmarks of Disney animation: the realism, the depth, the sense of gravity and secondary effects, the sentimentality and emotional affect, even the animals that Disney typically featured. "They thought they [Disney cartoons] were dead," animator Bill Melendez said of UPA's sense of superiority and sophistication. "We had a very low opinion of Disney." They disdained Warner Bros. cartoons too, dismissing slapstick, in the words of one former Warners writer who came to work for UPA, as "Warner Bros. humor." When it came to technique, UPA animators were interested less in movement or the development of personality than in graphics, in how shapes played on a flat surface; their inspirations were the Bauhaus, Klee, Kandinsky, Dufy, and Léger. When it came to subject matter, they were masters of what one animation critic called the "wry grimace: self-mockery per se"; their inspirations here were *New Yorker* cartoons and other sources of what they considered mature, understated humor.

For all its antagonism toward Disney—Art Babbitt had gone to work for UPA—and for all its artistic self-consciousness, UPA was also very much the product of its own stringent economies. "The big change," said

Faith Hubley, John's wife and an animator in her own right, speaking of the difference between UPA and Disney, "was that we figured out how to make films in a very small space. It's as simple as that—personal films—that required half a dozen people." UPA animations had less movement than Disney's, less detail, less refinement. "I am a bit of a slob," Hubley added, "and I like a free-flowing line and texture. . . . That was our contribution . . . to liberate animation from itself, and to go to watercolors and to paint pastels." Expediency became style. The result was a series of popular cartoons featuring a myopic old man named Mr. Magoo and then a breakthrough, *Gerald McBoing Boing*, based on a phonograph record by Theodore Geisel, known professionally as Dr. Seuss, about a young boy who can speak no words, only sound effects, and who suffers as a result until he is rescued by the manager of a radio station who can use Gerald's talents. *Time* predicted that Gerald's "boing!" "may prove as resounding as the first peep out of Mickey Mouse."

McBoing Boing did become a milestone. Not only did it win the Academy Award for Best Animated Short Subject of 1950, an award that Disney routinely won in the 1930s; it drew the sort of critical hosannas that had once been reserved for Disney animation. With *McBoing Boing* and Magoo, realism was officially passé. Minimalism was in. So was the arch attitude of the UPA cartoons. A critic, writing in 1953 and comparing Disney's *Peter Pan* to UPA's Mr. Magoo, noted that a "new cult is forming; a new word is perhaps already being minted, *Magooism*, describing benevolent nearsightedness." He concluded that Mickey Mouse and Donald Duck had lost their popularity because they were creations of the 1930s, a time when audiences enjoyed their anarchism, while Magoo had become popular in the postwar period, when people understood the awful results of irresponsibility. "Mr. Magoo represents for us the man who would be responsible and serious in a world that seems insane," the critic observed; "he is a creation of the 1950s, the age of anxiety; his situation reflects our own." Of course, there was a much simpler explanation for UPA's critical favor: its animations seemed more adult than Disney's, more highbrow.

Though Walt's own animation style had been changing—and been minimalized—since the great animations of the late 1930s and early 1940s, he wasn't fond of UPA. "There isn't enough money in the world to make me go back and try to make cartoons the way they're making them now," he told Pete Martin. But despite that disparagement, he did try. "We had a lot of product coming where we had to bring it in for a low budget," Ward Kimball recalled. "He realized we had to cut corners and he didn't expect the full animation quality that he was getting on the features." Kimball had been assigned a short describing the history of musical instruments titled *Toot Whistle Plunk and Boom* and began animating while Walt was on one of his European trips. He decided to use a more modernist style. "[E]verybody said you'll never get this by Walt—you guys are crazy . . . straight lines, things like that, unheard of—backgrounds that were tippled and things glued on—you'll never get away with it," Kimball said. His associates felt that Kimball was imitating UPA and that he had betrayed the studio. Kimball confessed that he had been emboldened only because Walt was gone, but when Walt returned, he said he liked it, and the short won an Academy Award. Still, for all Kimball's protestations that he had devised a new visual approach very different from UPA's, he had clearly been working under UPA's influence. "In style a clean steal from the Bosustow [UPA] cartoons," *Time* reported, but added approvingly, "Toot takes Disney in one jump from the nursery to the intellectual cocktail party."

The intellectual cocktail party, however, was not Walt Disney's métier, and he did not succumb without a fight. While UPA was producing Magoos, the studio put *Lady and the Tramp* the story of an effete female dog who finds herself in the company of mongrels, into production. The project had been in development since 1937, when Walt bought the story from his friend Ward Greene, the head of the King Features Syndicate, which distributed Walt's comic strips. It had gone through a series of scripts. Joe Grant and Dick Huemer introduced two calculating Siamese cats, Ted Sears introduced a dog pound, and Greene himself apparently introduced a romance—though Grant and Huemer objected to the idea of two dogs falling in love as "distasteful" and "utterly contrary to nature." (It was Walt who had scratched out the name "mutt" in the script and inserted "Tramp.") Like everything else at the time, the film was a casualty of the war—Walt confided to Greene that "I should confine my efforts to things that have more of a plus value"—but by 1952 Roy was encouraging Walt to put it back into production rather than make another anthology film, provided they could keep the cost down to not more than double the price per foot of a short and provided they released it in smaller first-run theaters where it could play for weeks. The film missed its original target date, in part because it was being animated in the widescreen Cinemascope process, which took so much more time than standard-format animations that it doubled the cost of the backgrounds. Animators had to work six-day weeks down the stretch, and the film's budget escalated to just under $3 million. But when it was released, it was another Disney success and a temporary rebuff to the UPA style.

There was another reason for the delay on *Lady*, besides the troubles with Cinemascope. Walt had decided to take the animators off the film for a hiatus because he felt that they were becoming too involved with the detail and had lost sight of the characters. He reassigned them to *Sleeping Beauty* for six months, then put them back on *Lady*, where, he said, they "tackled the project with new enthusiasm and whizzed right along to the finish." Even so, *Lady*, despite its long gestation and despite the fact that it turned out well, was essentially more make-work. *Sleeping Beauty* was something else. It was intended to be a magnum opus—"our most ambitious cartoon feature, to date," Walt wrote author Dodie Smith, whose book *101 Dalmatians* he had purchased for another animation. *Sleeping Beauty* was to be a grand last hurrah designed to demonstrate conclusively the superiority of the Disney style, and in so doing, it would also constitute a major assault on everything UPA represented.

As Walt would tell it, he gave his animators only one instruction for the film: "Make them [the characters] as real as possible, near flesh-and-blood." To achieve this, he said, the studio "used living models more carefully than ever before." In truth, however, Walt seemed to have little interest in the vaunted Disney realism or even, for that matter, in the vaunted Disney story sense. Though he had entrusted the project to Wilfred Jackson, and though Jackson and veteran storyman Ted Sears had reworked the entire script after Walt declared himself dissatisfied with their first attempt, Walt was much more focused on the visual design of the film than on its story. He had hired the painter Eyvind Earle in 1951 as a background artist (he did one hundred backgrounds for *Peter Pan*), and Earle had impressed Walt enough that Walt asked him to provide inspirational art for *Sleeping Beauty*.

"When I first saw his stuff, I almost fainted," sketch artist Vance Gerry said. Earle had filled every wall of his room from floor to ceiling with detailed paintings heavily influenced by Dürer, Van Eyck, and Brueghel, but with a modernist twist in that the images were more abstract and less realistic and three-dimensional than typical Disney work. The layout artists and animators were both impressed and depressed by Earle's paintings—impressed by the quality of the work, depressed that they would have to work within a style that many of them regarded as too cold, too flat, and too modernist for a fairy tale. "I had to fight myself to make myself draw that way," Ken Anderson said. But Walt was insistent, claiming that in the past the inspirational art he commissioned had always been homogenized by the animators. This time he wanted Earle's distinct vision on the screen. He told Eric Larson, whose unit was the first to work on the film, that the picture was to be a "moving illustration, the ultimate in animation." He added that he didn't care how long it took.

It took a long time—longer in terms of steady, uninterrupted work than any Disney animation since *Snow White*. It was started in 1951, was revised in 1953, and was finally ready for Walt to see at an "overall story board discussion" early in 1955. Milt Kahl blamed Walt for the delays. "He wouldn't have story meetings," Kahl said. "He wouldn't get the damn thing moving." Kahl finally surmised that Walt cared about everything but this picture. Meanwhile the release date slipped from Christmas 1955 to Christmas 1957 to Christmas 1958. In addition to Walt's inattention, one problem was that he just didn't have the staff to do this kind of animation anymore, especially since television was tying up three animation units. Even after promoting fifteen assistants to animators, the studio had to bring in a group of trainees for the first time since the 1930s. Another problem was that the process of working within Earle's style was slow and onerous—so slow that the cleanup staff was moving half as quickly as it had on *Lady and the Tramp*. By January 1957, after over five years of work, 2,500 feet had been animated with 3,775 feet yet to go.

This work had proceeded while Walt was focusing on Disneyland, and when he finally turned his attention to *Sleeping Beauty*, he was not pleased. The budget of the film had soared to the point, Harry Tytle said, where Walt was questioning whether the studio could afford to do any more features. To keep costs down, one animator recalled, a quota system was instituted. "[Y]ou had to do eight girls a day, thirty-two medium sized birds a day, twenty-two squirrels a day," he said. "That's how they got through it." But Walt's interest in making this *the* great animation was already flagging. After a screening of finished footage in August 1957, Tytle noted "a noticeable, marked difference" in Walt from the old days. "He seems to be tired, has so much on his mind; didn't give this the treatment he would have in years past, where he'd go in for a couple of days and fine tooth comb the whole picture." His comments were general rather than specific. Dick Huemer agreed that Walt couldn't seem to get engaged with the film and that he blamed the animators for concentrating on the visuals to the detriment of the story, Walt's traditional interest, apparently not realizing that this had been his injunction to them. Bill Peet compared him to a "ringmaster directing a twenty ring circus": "Walt the bear was the one who came to our story conferences, and he usually came with a scowl and left with a growl."

For their part, the animators worked as devoutly as they had worked on all the great animations. One animator said that they were so cautious in drawing Aurora, the sleeping beauty, that the staff was cleaning up only one drawing a day, which translated into one second of screen time per month. "They measured the width of the line, the density of the line, the taper of the line," he said. " 'Cause we thought we were making the Lord's Prayer for sure." Frank Thomas worked so hard and under such pressure that he developed a red blotch on his face and had to visit the doctor each week to have it attended to. Wilfred Jackson, the supervising director, suffered a heart attack during the production. He was replaced by Eric Larson, who called the assignment his "downfall." Larson was eventually replaced by Gerry Geronomi.

But for all the years of development, all the hard work, all the innovations, all the money spent (roughly $6 million, easily making it the most expensive animated feature to that time), all the hopes that had been placed upon it, and all the predictions of success for it ("Will be a bonanza at the box office," one respondent crowed at a screening of the rough cut), *Sleeping Beauty* was a failure when it was finally released late in January 1959, both aesthetically and financially. Earle's design had been visually stunning, but the wary animators had been right: it lacked warmth and charm. Then there were the story issues. Sharpsteen thought the problem was that the film concentrated too heavily on the three fairies who abet Sleeping Beauty. "[I]t got monotonous in the picture," he said. Dick Huemer said the problem was Walt's lack of involvement, but Walt had been no more involved on most of the recent features, and they had turned out better. In truth, the real problem may have been that the film sagged under the weight of its own ambitions—the ambitions Walt had imposed upon it. Walt seemed to know it. After screening the film shortly before its completion, he charged out of the projection room, approached Milt Kahl and Marc Davis on the steps of the Animation Building, and upbraided them for, Kahl said, "how heavy the animation was and how rotten the picture." In the end Buena Vista, Disney's distribution arm, lost $900,000 that year due largely to the film.

By this time the studio's aesthetic nemesis, UPA, which had been one of the targets of *Sleeping Beauty*, had begun to shatter. As early as April 1952 Columbia, which distributed UPA's cartoons, had demanded that the company secure loyalty oaths from its employees vowing that they were not members of the Communist Party. Most agreed. But the whole idea of taking oaths undermined the studio and its camaraderie. Eventually John Hubley, one of UPA's most imaginative animators, left. When its contract with Columbia expired in 1953, UPA renewed, but the distributor insisted that the studio make only Magoos. At the same time the company was being harassed by a union because, UPA animator Bill Melendez felt, Walt had negotiated a contract with the International Alliance of Theatrical Stage Employees and then sicced them on his rival. Bosustow eventually sold out, and UPA survived but only as a shell of itself—no longer the spearhead of modernist animation.

Yet even as it was expiring, its influence would be profound—as profound, in its own way, as Disney's had been. The inexpensive, stylized animation it pioneered quickly became the industry standard, especially as television became the primary market for cartoons. Animators "cheated" now. They used fewer drawings held for a longer time onscreen, they economized on detail and movement, and they often used sound to suggest an action without actually showing it. (One producer had a dictum that if the stack of drawings couldn't fit under his door, the scene was too long.) Joseph Barbera, who left MGM with William Hanna to form their own studio and who specialized in television animation, called this "limited" animation his "secret weapon." All the squash-and-stretch effects for which Disney had striven, the sense of dimensionality, mass, gravity, and nuance, were largely gone and with them any vestige of the dreams that Walt had held about the possibility of providing a new world onscreen, much less a new art. Those dreams had been transferred to Disneyland. Disneyland was the refuge now. Disneyland was the hope.

Eleven

SLOUCHING TOWARD UTOPIA

Now after the many years of struggle, doubt, insecurity, and unhappiness, Walt Disney had won. Thanks largely to the success of Disneyland, the earnings of Disney stock kept rising from 35 cents on revenues of $7.7 million in fiscal year 1952, before the park, to $2.44 on $35 million in revenue five years later. "Sales and net profits have enjoyed a growth trend matched by few corporations over the past five to seven years," an investment adviser reported in 1958. The formula, commented *The Wall Street Journal* in a front-page article that year raving over the new Disney success, was to "[w]ring every possible profitable squeal and squeak out of such assets as The Three Little Pigs and Mickey Mouse—first by diversifying into a wide variety of activities, then by dovetailing them so all work to exploit one another." The article quoted Roy Disney as saying that "we don't do anything in one line without giving a thought to its likely profitability in our other lines," adding, "Our product is practically eternal."

At the time the company, in diversifying, had reduced its income from films to 38 percent of its total revenue, while television accounted for 28 percent, Disneyland for 21 percent, and royalties on merchandise for 13 percent. In 1960 Roy recommended that Walt Disney Productions and Disneyland merge so that they could offset profits in one company against any potential losses in the other, and he asked Prudential, from whom WDP had recently been borrowing, to revamp their deal to include the $5.5 million that the company owed ABC for Disneyland, raising its total indebtedness to Prudential to $20.5 million—this at a studio that had once scrounged to borrow tens of thousands of dollars to complete *Snow White* and that had to suffer economic indignities from the war right up to the opening of Disneyland. Within the year the studio brought in $70 million, netted $4.5 million, and paid off its loans to the Bank of America, prompting Walt to joke to columnist Art Buchwald, "For the first time the banks owe me money."

Meanwhile early in 1957 the studio renewed its agreement with ABC to continue to produce *Disneyland* for two more years at a cost of $4.16 million and *The Mickey Mouse Club* for one more year at a cost of $3.2 million, though the show was cut back to a half-hour, and at long last Walt got ABC to finance and broadcast *Zorro* as well, the rights to which he had bought for WED long before opening Disneyland. Walt seemed especially excited by this last, most likely because he had personally initiated it, boasting to one potential sponsor that the studio was constructing sets "which will be unequaled in television film production history" and that the show would have a "quality and a flavor and character different from any other program on the air." When the songwriting brothers Robert and Richard Sherman were asked to compose the show's theme (Norman Foster and George Bruns wound up doing the actual writing), they were struck by "Walt's finely focused intensity and the complete dedication with which he discussed the story." They said he made it seem that "this was the most important project in his entire career." After John Hench suggested that the titles feature Zorro slashing a *Z* with his sword, Walt went from office to office with a yardstick challenging employees to a duel. Bill Walsh said he would hear Walt walking down the hall with his yardstick, cutting the air in a *Z* and laughing.

At the same time he was still aglow over Disneyland and still intent on expanding and improving it. He told one interviewer that Disneyland "will never be finished" and that it "will be a live breathing thing that will need changes." To another he called Disneyland "my baby" and said, "I would prostitute myself for it." He told yet another correspondent that "working, planning and developing it" afforded him "endless pleasure." He had entrusted WED with devising improvements, and he was always scouring Europe himself for new attractions and ideas. In late 1958 he decided to add a 150-foot-high Matterhorn bobsled ride, keyed to a recent feature, *Third Man on the Mountain*; a submarine ride that would provide the illusion of going undersea, inspired by *20,000 Leagues*; and a monorail that would circle the park. Jack Lindquist, the advertising manager at Disneyland, remembered Roy telling the staff that they were just "getting out of the hole" and that they would have to wait two or three years before realizing any further expansion. Then he left for Europe. "Two days after he left," as Lindquist told it, "Walt called WED and said, 'We're going to build the Matterhorn, Monorail and Submarines.' " When one of the staff said that Roy had ordered them to desist, Walt responded, "Well, we're going to build them. Roy can figure out how to pay for it when he gets back." (The three attractions, at a cost of $5.5 million, opened in June 1959 with another ninety-minute television spectacular, this one featuring Vice President Richard Nixon.) On another occasion Marc Davis was presenting the plans for a new Audio-Animatronic attraction called Nature's Wonderland to a studio group that included Walt. Davis opened by saying that there were two ways of executing the project—an inexpensive one and an expensive one. "And Walt got all the way up from his seat and walked around to the front of the room where I was," Davis remembered, "and put his hand on my shoulder and he said, 'Marc,' he said, 'you and I do not worry about whether anything is cheap or expensive. We only worry if it's good.' "

He had big ideas. Off of Main Street he had conceived of another street, Liberty Street, and another town square, Edison Square, which would feature buildings in nineteenth-century American architecture housing exhibits on science and technology, and which would be sponsored, Walt hoped, by America's leading technology, companies, most prominently General Electric. On the square Walt also envisioned a President's Hall that would house animatronic robots of American presidents. He had thought as well of a New Orleans quarter with a Haunted Mansion, and he had dispatched Herb Ryman and John Hench to the city to take photographs, which later became models for the attraction. In the summer of 1961 he introduced costumed characters to the park as a regular feature, and early the following year he announced a $7 million expansion that would add eight new attractions and improve and expand current attractions. The new construction brought the cumulative investment in the park to $44 million. That amount didn't include Walt's secretive efforts to buy additional parcels of land around the park, on which he planned to build hotels and motels, a bowling alley, a campground, and a swimming pool.

As he always had on past projects, Walt delegated the running of the park to subordinates while he remained the chief strategist, and as always he kept shuffling the positions whenever he detected that someone was arrogating too much power to himself. But while executives came and went, the park's press agent told a *New Yorker* reporter that Walt was clearly in command. "You never know when you'll bump into Walt prowling around the park in an old sweater, checking on whether a dead light bulb he reported earlier has been replaced," the agent said, "or timing the rides, or complaining that a 'Ride Not Operating Today' sign is inartistically lettered, or plotting what to tear down next and what to put up instead." And though Walt did appoint the Operations Committee to deal with the day-to-day operation of the park and the Management Committee, on which he himself sat, to make policy and set long-term goals, the agent stressed, "[t]he first thing you have to understand is that this whole place *is* Walt."

By the time Walt installed the Matterhorn, the monorail, and the submarine ride, the park was attracting over five million visitors a year and was considered one of the essential destinations in the country for foreign dignitaries. Prime Minister Jawaharlal Nehru of India told Los Angeles mayor Samuel Yorty that the main reason he was visiting the area was to see Disneyland, and Nehru's daughter said, "We looked forward to Disneyland as much as anything on our trip." Nehru spent three hours there. Secretary of State John Foster Dulles, in extending Indonesian president Sukarno's thanks to Walt after a visit, wrote, "I am told that in Indonesia there are two prominent Americans who are affectionately known by their first names—'Ike' and 'Walt.' " One African president continued his visit even after his public relations officer keeled over and died of a heart attack while dining at the park's Plantation restaurant.

The passion of foreign dignitaries to see what was now one of America's landmarks was so intense that once it even triggered an international incident. Russian premier Nikita Khrushchev was making a tour of America in September 1959. Khrushchev's wife Nina had seen a Disney film in 1942, found herself entranced, and requested that during the visit she and her family be allowed to see Disneyland. Walt and Lillian planned to welcome the party and escort them around the park. But when Khrushchev arrived in Los Angeles from New York, he was told that his security could not be assured and that the trip to Disneyland would have to be canceled. Khrushchev "exploded," as *The New York Times* described it. "I would very much like to go see Disneyland," he shouted. "But then, we cannot guarantee your security, they say. Then what must I do? Commit suicide?" Continuing to boil, Khrushchev asked the gathered journalists, "What is it? Is there an epidemic of cholera or something: Or have gangsters taken hold of the place that can destroy me?" He was still fuming at a star-studded luncheon in his honor at the Twentieth Century–Fox studio, Los Angeles police chief William Parker said, because Mrs. Khrushchev had passed her husband a note while he spoke reminding him of the insult. "We have come to this town where lives the cream of American art," he began as his voice shook with indignation. "And just imagine, I, a Premier, a Soviet representative, when I came here to this city, I was given a plan—a program of what I was to be shown and whom I was to meet. But just now I was told that I could not go to Disneyland." He closed: "I cannot find words to explain this to my people."

But Khrushchev went even further. Denied his visit, he told a Los Angeles audience that he could return to Russia even faster than he had arrived. "If you want to go on with the arms race, very well," he warned. "We accept that challenge. As for the output of rockets, well, they are on the assembly line. This is the most serious question. It is one of life or death, ladies and gentlemen. One of war and peace." And this serious question about the fate of civilization was raised all because Nikita Khrushchev had been, as he put it, "deprived of the pleasure of visiting the city of Fantasy."

He was king, if no longer of animation, then of American popular culture generally. With the success of Disneyland and his visibility on the television show, Walt Disney's personal status was higher than it had ever been—as high as anyone's in the country. The Screen Producers Guild unanimously awarded him its Lewis Milestone Award for his "historical contribution to the American motion picture." The United States Olympic Committee appointed him the chairman of its Pageantry Committee for the 1960 Winter Games, to be held at Squaw Valley, California, and Walt planned and oversaw the torch relay, the opening and closing ceremonies, and the awarding of the medals. President Eisenhower named him to the President's Committee on Education, which was charged with holding a conference on education beyond high school, though Walt later tendered his resignation, calling himself unqualified since he had never gone beyond the first year of high school. Eisenhower's successor, President John F. Kennedy, appointed Walt to a nine-member executive committee under Eisenhower's chairmanship to lead the People to People program, which was designed to promote cultural, scientific, and athletic contacts between countries. The students of Tullytown, Pennsylvania, voted to name their school in his honor, and Marceline named its new elementary school for him too. (His grammar school desk from Marceline's old Park School, carved with his initials, was placed in a glass case in the hallway.) Walt attended both dedications. Seventeen more universities offered him honorary degrees, though Walt refused all but one—from the University of California at Los Angeles. The Museum of Modern Art contacted him about the possibility of an exhibition: *The Work of Walt Disney.* And the actresses Lillian and Dorothy Gish visited Oslo to campaign for Walt to receive the Nobel Peace Prize. His had become such a charmed life that even nature seemed to favor him; in November 1961, when fires roared through Bel-Air and Brentwood and were threatening his Carolwood house, the flames suddenly stopped and veered away.

Despite his status—and despite the "magnetic field," as Ken Anderson put it, that he seemed to have around him at the studio—most outsiders still found him unprepossessing. Edith Efron reporting in *TV Guide* found him "shy." "His eyes are dull and preoccupied, his affability mechanical and heavy-handed," she wrote. "He gabs away slowly and randomly in inarticulate, midwestern speech that would be appropriate to a rural general store. His shirt is open, his tie crooked. One almost expects to see over-all straps on his shoulders and wisps of hay in his hair." Another reporter found an "unearthly quality" about his conversation and thought he "laughs in the wrong places."

Of course, this image of him as the common man was largely created by intention. Walt had cultivated it, even if he had long since outgrown it and even if he had become an American institution that in the postwar period seemed more an emperor than an uncle. But he was still, after all the years in the spotlight and after all the wealth he had accrued from Disneyland and WED, surprisingly and genuinely plebeian by temperament. By his own admission he seldom read anything other than a script. His sense of humor, while never prurient, did often run to the scatological, and he laughed with a deep, guttural chortle. Though he was more likely to wear conservative suits now, he usually preferred a western kerchief with the Smoke Tree emblem to a tie, unless the occasion demanded one, and when he wasn't in the public eye, he liked loose sweaters, either gray or blue, or gabardine jackets. He never wore jewelry, save for a DeMolay ring from his youth and a Cladagh ring that he had acquired in Ireland of two hands holding a heart. He wore the same 14-carat gold Hamilton watch for over twenty years until Lillian bought him a Rolex, and one of his few indulgences was a used Mercedes 230 SL that he bought late in life. The same barber cut his hair for nearly twenty-five years, and, preferring to drive his own car, he did not have a regular chauffeur. His gastronomical tastes still ran to meat and potatoes, chili and tapioca pudding. He still garbled words and still peppered his speech with colloquialisms. Things were "effective as hell" or "cute as hell," and when he was angry, he could, according to one employee at the time, "out-cuss a drunken pirate's parrot!"

Many of those who saw him now seemed to detect a lack of intensity, which one could recognize in his eyes. The young Walt Disney had had "burning dark eyes," as one reporter described them—eyes "so dark brown in color that they seemed black," wrote another. Even Roy had described how Walt's eyes would latch on to his listener's and wouldn't let go. But the older Walt Disney's eyes weren't so much dark and penetrating as "bright," according to Mary Costa, who voiced Sleeping Beauty, as if they were "plugged into sockets." Actress Julie Andrews said there was a "kind of cheerful merriment in his eyes," the sign of a contented man.

But while Walt Disney at long last may have seemed contented and at ease with himself, underneath he smoldered. One visiting journalist noticed that Walt "appeared to be under the lash of some private demon." He had never fully trusted success or tranquillity. "I function better when things are going badly than when they're smooth as whipped cream," he would say, underscoring the irony that the man whose life was dedicated to perfection was never entirely happy within it. Walt Disney always needed action, even friction. "I've got to have a project all the time," he had told Ollie Johnston, "something to work on." Otherwise he had no place to direct his nervous energy.

Among the projects to which he directed his attention as the new decade dawned was television. Even before Walt re-signed with ABC, the network had been complaining about the cost of producing *The Mickey Mouse Club* and about the fact that, as ABC president Robert Kintner put it, "there are only a certain number of sponsors that will sponsor a so-called 'kid' show, and they have only a certain amount in their budgets." Meanwhile Walt bristled over the paltry budget that ABC had dedicated to promoting *Zorro* and to the constant pressure he felt from ABC to produce Westerns, which the network obviously believed would be profitable. Walt aquiesced—he made *Texas John Slaughter* and *The Nine Lives of Elfego Baca*—but he was so unhappy about it that he largely ceased to care. Publicity chief Card Walker had to beg Walt for "approximately one hour of your time" to discuss the new schedule for the *Disneyland* show, which had been renamed *Walt Disney Presents.*

When the ABC-Disney contract came up for renewal early in 1959, the seething tensions erupted. Roy proposed a new three-year deal for *Walt Disney Presents, The Mickey Mouse Club*, and *Zorro*. When ABC resisted, he countered with a short-term proposal excluding *The Mickey Mouse Club*, in which the network had lost interest, or, in lieu of that, a long-term deal that would allow Disney to sell to other networks any program on which ABC had not exercised its option. This last provision was especially salient since ABC had concluded that *Zorro*, despite its high ratings, was not profitable enough either and that in any case it could produce that kind of programming on its own. Still, ABC rejected these initiatives too, prompting Roy to write Walt, "I think they are a bunch of stinkers."

But Roy did not settle for invective; he was also trying brinkmanship. Even as he flew to New York to meet with ABC chairman Leonard Goldenson, he advised Walt that he was going to file an antitrust suit against the network, asking for a declaratory injunction against ABC that would prevent it from enforcing the contract and would allow Disney to negotiate with other networks. "In all common sense and business reasoning," Roy wrote Walt on the verge of his meeting, "I can't believe they will let this go to a big court fight. . . . They have too many things they would rather have kept quiet and not brought out in court."

Walt and Roy had one more consideration beyond the television series, one that was more important than television: Disneyland. ABC had initially invested $500,000 in the park. Roy wanted to use the disagreement over the television contract to buy out ABC's stake, writing Goldenson that "it seems to us you are not as eager to continue a long-term association with Disney as you once were." Or, as Walt would later tell it at the tenth anniversary of Disneyland, "[M]y brother figured, 'If we don't buy 'em out now, we're gonna be payin' a lot more later.' " After Roy filed his suit, and as the dispute dragged on for nearly a year, he admitted that he had no idea what ABC's stake would now be worth and that he had plucked a figure, $7.5 million, more or less out of the air. Just an hour before closing the deal, in June 1960, he nervously phoned Walt one last time for his input, but Walt demurred. "[D]o what you think's necessary," he said. So Walt Disney Productions, with a loan from Prudential, bought ABC out of Disneyland. In the agreement Roy dropped his suit, ABC released the studio from its contract, and the Disneys promised to refrain for four months from pursuing another television outlet. As collateral damage, *Zorro* and *The Mickey Mouse Club* were canceled.

But even before the four-month moratorium was up, the company was negotiating for a new home for *Walt Disney Presents*. Robert Kintner, with whom Walt had made his original television deal, had left ABC for the presidency of NBC, and as early as August, Card Walker was meeting in New York with Kintner and Robert Sarnoff, the chairman of RCA, NBC's parent company, about relocating. Though NBC said it needed to evaluate the possibility of a long-term association with Disney, the network promised not to let the discussions "drift" as they had six years earlier when Walt had approached them. Walt, who was in London at the time, told Walker to "get this deal," emphasizing how important it was to him. "I'll stand on my head in Macy's window," he said, "if that will make the deal."

For both Walt and NBC, the urgency didn't come simply from the need to put a new television show on the air. The stakes were much higher. RCA was now manufacturing color television sets, and the company was looking for flagship programming that would promote the infant technology, which was why NBC was subjecting the proposed partnership to such extended deliberations. Walt Disney's colorful animations seemed a perfect vehicle. As far as the Disneys were concerned, Walt, who had pioneered color on the motion picture screen, had always wanted to produce color television programming. It was virtually inevitable, then, that the two sides would come to an agreement, which they did that October: three years at $5 million per year for twenty-five installments each year of *Walt Disney Presents*, which was to be renamed *Walt Disney's Wonderful World of Color*. *Variety* called the agreement the "most important and far-reaching in recent video annals."

Walt was excited. At ABC he had effected the truce between the film industry and the television industry. At NBC he would be leading the transformation from black-and-white to color television. Creatively speaking, after being forced to make those Westerns at ABC, NBC had given him carte blanche. "I shouldn't have listened," he told one reporter about his surrender to ABC. "I'm not listening now. I'm an absolute dictator about what goes into my show." "I never saw such an overnight change in a man," said a friend of Walt after the NBC contract. "Where he had been preparing the ABC programs almost automatically like a man in a dream, all of his old enthusiasms returned. . . . [O]ne new idea after another tumbled out of him. He kept saying over and over again, 'Oh boy! Color and no Westerns. I can do whatever I want. Do you hear me? I can do whatever I want.' "

"Newton Minow can relax," opined the *New York Herald Tribune* after *Wonderful World of Color*'s Sunday night premiere on September 24, 1961, referring to the Federal Communications Commission chairman who had recently called television a "vast wasteland." "Here, for a wonderful change, was something out of Hollywood that contributed to the enlightenment and thorough enjoyment of the entire family." Most reviewers agreed, with only a few dissenters carping that Walt had pushed color television a little too aggressively. But that, of course, had been the whole point. Shortly after the premiere Card Walker, who was now the head of advertising at the studio, wrote Walt that sales of color televisions were soaring—105 percent ahead of the previous September. NBC couldn't have been happier. When Walker and Donn Tatum, the head of television sales, met Kintner in New York that November, they reported that the "whole atmosphere is pleasing and on a high note" and that Kintner wanted to discuss other series. Within the month NBC renewed *Wonderful World* for an additional two years.

II

Walt was a changed man yet again. Despite his efforts to portray himself as ordinary—and despite the fact that in many ways he *was* ordinary, especially in his tastes and manner—he had come to have a much more expansive sense of who he was and what he could accomplish. With the success of Disneyland, he saw himself not just as an entertainer or even an amusement park operator but as a visionary planner who could impose his will on the environment as he had imposed it on the screen. Disneyland was just a prototype for what he felt he could do all over the country. Less than a month after visiting Marceline late in 1960 to dedicate the Walt Disney School, he was meeting with a local entrepreneur named Rush Johnson to explore turning his childhood homestead into a model farm. When Johnson asked how they would attract visitors, Walt said, "You know, Rush, when I introduce 'Disney's Wonderful World of Color' on Sunday night, I'd set the cheek of my ass up there on the table and I'd say, 'By the way, folks, when you're on vacation, go by my hometown.' What are you going to do with all the damn people?" He also wanted to buy the old Disney family farm in Ellis, Kansas, but Roy wouldn't let him.

One advertising executive proposed building a chain of Disney child care centers near large shopping areas. Walt was interested, but once again Roy and Card Walker dissuaded him. Another suggestion was a chain of Disney Kiddielands across the country, and Walt Disney Productions did buy a one-third interest in the Arrow Development Company, which had manufactured many of the rides for Disneyland, but the Kiddieland idea expired too. WED even hired a development consultant who was investigating relocating one of the Disneyland trains to Newport Beach, California, and building a convention center in Anaheim near the park. As early as 1958, Walt even regarded Smoke Tree as a potential development site for a new golf course, bowling alley, restaurant, and cocktail lounge, all surrounding a square with tourist shops and all to be financed by Smoke Tree under Walt's personal supervision. He was also weighing a motel and a twelve-hundred-car mobile home "ranch" there. But after years of vacillation—the Palm Springs city council first rejected the plan, then reversed itself—Walt lost interest.

If he had lost interest in developing Smoke Tree, he hadn't lost his fervor for creating some kind of bowling-recreation complex under the Disney aegis, and he invested in a sports center outside Denver that included not only eighty bowling lanes but a swimming pool and restaurant—a model for a new kind of Disney franchise. Once again, though, the project dragged on, and by the time Celebrity Lanes opened in September 1960, Walt had resigned from the board. Walt Disney Productions filled the breach, purchasing a $277,000 stock interest and floating a $650,000 loan within the year to take control of the center. Walt and Lillian attended the center's second anniversary, and the company kept it operating even as it drained money. Roy later admitted the entire project had been ill-conceived. "We wasted a million dollars there by putting in a deluxe dining room and a swimming pool," he told one interviewer. "We had 80 lanes, one of the biggest bowling alleys in the country. . . . But who wants to bowl in a wet bathing suit and what bowler wears the kind of clothes that are necessary for a deluxe dining room?"

But even as Celebrity Lanes was gasping for life, Walt had not lost his monumentalist impulses. Inspired by his experience with the Winter Olympics, he enlisted Harrison Price, the man who had found the site for Disneyland, to investigate possibilities for a family-oriented ski lodge–entertainment facility. Price discovered that southern California had one skier per hundred people. "The data pointed out a crying need for good skiing in the vast active, athletic, mobile southern California market," he later said. Price surveyed the Mammoth Mountain area, roughly forty miles northwest of Bishop, California, located in the Inyo National Forest, and he and Mickey Clark, a Disneyland executive whom Walt had charged with analyzing the prospects, determined that the "government looks favorably upon any development that tends to enhance the beauty of the park and give additional recreational facilities to the public." But Price thought he had found a better candidate in the Mineral King area, south of Mammoth inside the Sequoia National Forest, and he and Walt immediately began pressing state legislators to provide a highway to the location. While that project wended its way through the government bureaucracy, Walt was about to buy 2,200 acres outside Aspen, Colorado, when the deal suddenly fell through because the seller raised his asking price.

In the eyes of many developers, and in his own eyes as well, Walt Disney had become a magical force, and the company made dozens of forays—and was requested to do so by dozens of others—to seize an area and transform it the way he had transformed the Anaheim orange grove into Disneyland. Jules Stein suggested that Walt buy Ellis Island, the portal through which immigrants had passed into the country. "I am so excited about this, Walter, I just can't sleep," Stein wrote him. A developer in Monterey, California, asked if Walt would consider erecting a Vacation Village with an amusement park on an Early California theme. (Walt actually visited the area one weekend.) Joyce Hall, the head of Hallmark greeting cards and a fellow member of the People to People board, asked Walt to participate in the development of 110 acres in Kansas City, which would include a zoo, aviary, butterfly garden, and international village, and Walt met with Hall and city planner James Rouse before deciding to decline. Another group, including the Seagram's liquor company, was discussing Walt's involvement in the development of Niagara Falls.

But already Walt was thinking less of development than of something much more ambitious, something more commensurate with his status, something worth his time and energy, something so grand that it seemed almost outlandish: he wanted to design an entire city. At least as early as 1958 he was discussing with his WED staff what he variously called a City of the Arts or the Seven Arts City. As Walt envisioned it, the city would be a shopping and dining area centered on the idea of the arts. It would include a variety of art themed shops—music, books, glassware, pottery, photography—as well as a theater, a TV broadcast hub, a hall of design featuring the latest concepts, an avenue of model homes, and an international street. In the middle would be a mall and fountain. But what transformed it from another commercial project into an urban planning project was that Walt was also trying to entice the Chouinard Art Institute, with which his studio had been affiliated in the 1920s, to relocate from downtown Los Angeles to his planned city, along with the Pasadena Playhouse, the Los Angeles Conservatory, and the Buckley Schools. He even visited the Lincoln Center arts complex, then under construction in New York, to investigate the relationship between the performance halls there and the Juilliard School. And what transformed this urban planning project into a real city was that just as he had once imagined building housing on the studio lot for his employees, Walt intended to build, as one draft put it, "apartment houses, dormitories, duplexes and single-unit dwellings" within the immediate environs to accommodate the students, faculty, and employees of the schools. He was already scouting potential sites in the Los Angeles area when he heard that the architect William Pereira, who had briefly worked on Disneyland, was planning to develop the Mountain Park section. Walt suggested they merge their plans, offering to take "one entire village or valley area and develop it from start to finish," and adding that he hoped to "make this city into the internationally known tourist and entertainment attraction and educational center which it must be to be successful." By this time he was soliciting investors and sounding out foundations for grants to create what would be not a faux utopia, like Disneyland, but at long last a real one.

At the time there was one man who had dreams and an ego as large as Walt Disney's: Robert Moses. Yale- and Oxford-educated, Moses had been the *über*-bureaucrat of New York since the 1920s, when the young man gained the favor of Governor Alfred E. Smith. Using a series of political appointments at both the state and local levels, Moses, big and bull-headed, was chiefly responsible for the planning of New York City and its suburbs in the automobile age. He built Jones Beach on Long Island and other parks, plowed highways through neighborhoods, erected bridges and dug tunnels, hoisted edifices of public housing, and even cleared the land for Lincoln Center in the middle of Manhattan. Now Moses had been appointed to head the New York World's Fair, scheduled for 1964, and early in 1960 he sought Walt Disney's help. Moses had set aside eight acres on the fairgrounds for what he called a "children's village"—or, as *Variety* termed it, a sort of permanent eastern Disneyland. Who better to design the park than Walt?

It wasn't the first time that a world's fair had come calling. Walt had produced a four-minute Mickey Mouse cartoon for the Nabisco pavilions at the San Francisco and New York World's Fairs in 1939, and the coordinator of the United States pavilion at the 1958 World's Fair in Brussels had asked Walt to design an attraction there—"something that will impress the Europeans without offending them and without making us appear to be 'beating our chests,' " said the coordinator. Walt wound up contributing a nineteen-minute, 360-degree Circarama film, like the one he had installed at Disneyland, called *America the Beautiful*, which according to one official quickly became the "hit not only of the American Pavilion, but of the whole Expo." It was so popular that visitors found it even though there was no sign posted. When Walt had the exhibit transferred to a nylon geodesic dome at the Moscow Fair the following year, it was again one of the most popular attractions. The line of those waiting to see it typically wound one hundred yards around the exhibition grounds.

Walt declined the invitation to design the "children's village" for the 1964 New York World's Fair, thinking that New York State would not dedicate the funds to make the park permanent and seeing no way of making a profit otherwise. When Walt explained the problem to Moses over dinner at Jones Beach on August 3, 1960, Moses understood and immediately countered with another proposal: that Walt design pavilions for companies that would be exhibiting at the fair. Whether Moses knew it or not, WED had already been contacting various companies about the possibility of having Disney plan their exhibits; on the very trip during which Walt was meeting Moses, he was also meeting with executives of RCA, American Machine and Foundry, IBM, AT&T, the American Gas Association, General Dynamics, and General Electric. Meanwhile Jack Sayers, who had once headed Disneyland's lessee program, was touring the East, pressing executives to sign up with Disney, and by December he had closed development deals with the Ford Motor Company and IBM and had received a request from Owens-Corning Fiberglass to research an exhibit for them. At the same time, Ford officials visited Disneyland to see Walt's plans for Liberty Street and to discuss its feasibility as a world's fair attraction, and executives from GE spent a week at the studio to discuss an agreement.

Obviously Walt thought providing exhibits for major corporations could be lucrative for WED. The GE research and development deal alone called for $50,000, a figure that did not include any costs for the actual design and fabrication of the attraction. But no one at WED thought Walt was motivated primarily by money. Donn Tatum, a Disneyland executive who was involved in the world's fair planning, said that Walt had gathered the WED staff, told them about the world's fair, and charged them with devising attractions because, Walt said, "It will help us. We'll learn a lot and it will give us a chance to develop technology we're working on." Bill Cottrell, who also worked on the fair, thought that Walt saw it as a showcase for what WED could do as a kind of engineering firm and also as a commercial for Disneyland, especially since Walt was hoping to move some of the attractions to the park after the fair under the sponsorship of the corporations. Another WED employee, Marty Sklar, believed that Walt was using the fair as a "trial balloon" for future plans. "He wanted," Sklar said, "to see if his kind of entertainment would appeal to the more sophisticated eastern audience—'sophisticated' in that that's where the nation's leaders, the decision-makers were based." And there may have been one more consideration, this one psychological: the fair, like Disneyland before it, allowed Walt to hole up with his Imagineers in yet another small, creative enterprise where he could enjoy their camaraderie and actually see the uncompromised results of his own imagination now that even Disneyland had outgrown its origins.

At least that was what he may have expected. In actuality the planning would take years, nerves would be frayed, and Walt's own visions would be beset by corporate interference. The first to commit was Ford. Walt tried to get the company to sponsor his Hall of Presidents, but Ford rejected the idea. Instead, Walt and the Imagineers devised a twelve-minute trip through the history of invention using 160 Ford convertibles to "drive" through tableaux of Audio-Animatronic figures. (Ford had suggested the cars be chauffeur-driven; Walt, realizing the impossibility of such a system, recommended that the cars be automated, and according to head engineer Roger Broggie, he himself had the idea that the cars be pulled by a series of underground wheels, after he saw a hot ingot at the Ford factory in Dearborn, Michigan, being sent down a system of rollers.) Still, all was not entirely peaceful. When, after nearly a year of planning, Walt and a small delegation from WED accompanied a prototype of the attraction to Ford's Dearborn headquarters and demonstrated it to Henry Ford II, Ford got up, expressed his thanks, and said that he would let Walt know. Walt, who had assumed the meeting was a mere formality, was shocked, and only when the vice president for public relations chased after Ford, then returned to tell Walt that the project was indeed a go, did the tension dissipate.

The situation was even more nerve-wracking at GE. Walt had been courting the company for years to sponsor Edison Square at Disneyland. What he got instead was a version of Edison Square at the fair. Walt would settle on a six-part Audio-Animatronic show, loosely inspired by Thorton Wilder's *Our Town*, about progress through electricity featuring GE appliances—a "Carousel of Progress," as he called it, since the entire auditorium would literally rotate like a carousel from one tableau to the next. In addition, Walt agreed to provide several exhibits in the pavilion: a Corridor of Mirrors, a Skydome Spectacular slide show, a demonstration of controlled nuclear fission, and a model of a Medallion City of the future. The budget for all this was just under $10 million, $850,000 of which was to be paid as a retainer to WED. Walt suggested that GE also pay something for the use of his name, so Bill Cottrell, who was conducting the negotiations, asked for a million dollars for "Walt Disney." When GE reluctantly agreed, Walt, joking or not, told Cottrell, "Don't you think you might have asked for a little more?"

The initial agreement was signed in September 1961, and GE executives approved Walt's historical approach the following May. But by the time the executives came to the studio in late July to view the outlines, they had had a change of heart. Now the company decided it didn't want the history of electrical progress and offered to provide its own storyline. By one account, Walt exploded. "I spent my whole life telling stories with nostalgia," he supposedly chided the GE officers, "and this is the way you communicate with people!" Walt even asked the legal department if he could break the contract. Within a month another GE vice president smoothed the ruffled feathers, and the company agreed to support Walt's vision, but Walt was not entirely appeased. GE executives would occasionally visit the studio to view the progress on the pavilion. At one of these sessions, according to Jack Spiers, one of the writers for the show, Walt stood at the head of the table and announced: "All right, gentlemen, what I want you to do is go down to the Coral Room and have a good lunch. Then I want you to go back to Burbank Airport and get in your Grumman Gulfstream and fly back east where you came from and stay there until I've got something I want you to see. Then, I'll call *you*. Thank you, gentlemen." And he turned around and left the room.

The art director, Dick Irvine, would dismiss the Carousel of Progress as a "refrigerator show," since it essentially hawked GE products. But Walt took it very seriously, in part because the show, featuring a family enjoying the advances of electricity from the turn of the century through the 1960s, gave him a chance to experiment with Audio-Animatronic figures on an unprecedented scale, and in part because it was a huge and unique entertainment. Walt ordered a full-scale mock-up of the carousel to be built in Glendale, where WED had relocated, and sculptor Blaine Gibson, who helped fabricate the figures, said Walt would climb onto the stage and act out the actions the way he had once acted out the scenes from the animations. For one scene, in which a visiting cousin was taking a bath and wound up inventing air-conditioning by placing a block of ice in front of a fan, Walt jumped into the tub, mused about what a bather would be doing, then began wiggling his toes and extemporizing dialogue. "Walt had his foot in everything," Blaine Gibson recalled. "I would be working late at night at the studio on something for the Fair and I would leave around 2 a.m. There he would be, in his pajamas and bathrobe—he was there reviewing our work and working on something." As Joe Fowler put it, "There was more of Walt in the Carousel of Progress than in anything else we've done."

But as the fair grew closer, Walt was not content with just Ford and GE. Throughout 1962 and into 1963 he was still approaching companies to sponsor a Circarama film, to no avail, and he and Charles Luckman met with the Deparment of Commerce in Washington to sound them out about installing the Hall of Presidents in the United States pavilion. The department declined. He solicited Coca-Cola about sponsoring an Audio-Animatronic attraction of birds at Disneyland, and he commissioned Buzz Price to do a feasibility study for a monorail for the fair that he hoped would later become a permanent part of the New York transportation system, but Moses balked at the price. (Imagineer Bob Gurr suspected that Walt had also been victimized by standard manufacturers who "were always putting us down as 'For amusement parks only,' " which could only have riled Walt, whose own vistas had expanded into engineering.)

Even with the raft of rejections, Walt did not despair of convincing some corporation to sponsor his beloved Hall of Presidents and give him yet another opportunity to pursue Audio-Animatronics. He had been toying with the idea since the late 1950s, assigning Jim Algar, who wrote many of the True-Life Adventures, to read up on the presidents and write a script for a historical presentation. Walt produced a thirty-two-minute show with Algar's script, as well as scale models and paintings by studio artist Sam McKim, and he invited potential corporate backers to the studio to see it, but the project was expensive, and it foundered. In June 1961, with the prospect of the world's fair, Walt revived the presentation, retitled it *One Nation Under God*, and had it brought to New York to show Moses and corporate chiefs from, among others, Coca-Cola, Colgate-Palmolive, Union Carbide, and Hallmark, at the RCA Victor Theater on Forty-ninth Street. Moses was impressed, but he now felt the show shouldn't have corporate sponsorship; he thought it should be a major installation at the United States pavilion. Trying to get them to reverse their initial rejection, Moses lobbied Undersecretary of Commerce Franklin Roosevelt, Jr., to convince the deputy commissioner and the assistant commissioner for the federal pavilion to visit the studio and see the Hall of Presidents presentation themselves; when he was told the cost of the attraction was prohibitive, he circumvented Roosevelt and personally pressured the deputy commissioner to go to the studio. The commissioner finally did but concluded once again that the cost was too high for the government. Still undeterred, Moses and his deputy, Martin Stone, encouraged Disney to construct the hall under WED's own auspices, with Stone saying that it was "too important to the Fair and to Walt Disney to drop this without exhausting all possibilities."

For Walt, the appeal of the Hall of Presidents had always been less the appeal of history than the appeal of creating life. "I'd like to not be able to tell them from real people," he had told Sam McKim of his presidential robots. Ever since his experiment with the Dancing Man in the early

1950s, he had sought a way to make human robots, and though he had gotten distracted with Disneyland, in the late 1950s he asked WED to reinvestigate. Walt decided to create a Chinatown at Disneyland with two two-story buildings across an alleyway connected at the top floors by a pedestrian bridge. One of the buildings would house a Chinese restaurant, and Walt foresaw a robotic Confucius who would answer questions from loudspeakers scattered throughout the dining room that would make it sound as if diners were the ones doing the asking. (It was at this time, apparently, that Bill Cottrell coined the word *Animatronics*, to which Dick Irvine added the *Audio*.) Ub Iwerks actually erected the Confucius head and had it talking, but the rubber "skin" allegedly tore, and in any case the Chinatown idea was aborted.

The idea of human Audio-Animatronic robots, however, survived, if only, Walt said, because "you can't have human beings working three or four shifts; we can't afford to pay 'em, or they'll make mistakes, or somebody won't show up. We've got to figure out a way to have automated shows." He set some of his Imagineers to devise for Disneyland a show of mechanical birds that he called the Enchanted Tiki Room. (This was the exhibit in which he tried to interest Coca-Cola.) Another group went to work on the Hall of Presidents and on a specific idea of Walt's for the attraction that seemed as chimerical as his idea to construct an entire city: Walt had decided he wanted to create a life-size robot of Abraham Lincoln.

Walt had always admired Lincoln, and though he read very little beyond newspapers and scripts, he had devoured information on the sixteenth president—one American institution channeling another. He was certainly aware of the hubris of trying to bring Lincoln to life. When he showed Audio-Animatronic prototypes to a minister, the minister told him, "It was all right for you to bring fairy tales to life and for you to create a humanlike mouse, but to create a man—that's usurping the powers of a higher authority." Even some of Walt's own Imagineers had qualms about trying to make human robots. "It seemed that we were getting into areas that were competitive with acting, something that could be done much better by live performers," Blaine Gibson said. Walt rebutted that only a robotic Lincoln could look exactly like Lincoln. (He had actually had Gibson sculpt the face from a life-mask of Lincoln.) He may have been more honest, however, when he said, "We're making the legend of Pygmalion come true."

How much of the project was about Abraham Lincoln and how much about Walt Disney was difficult to say. Harriet Burns, who helped fabricate the robot, said that Walt visited WED "and cocked his eyebrow, and with his mouth he clenched and gritted his teeth. He pointed to his cheeks and said, 'We have to do this—the muscles in the body. There's no reason we can't do this.' " For the mechanics of the robot, Walt had WED adapt a tape system used on the navy's Polaris nuclear submarine, the patent for which he paid $17,000. Each tape had fourteen tracks capable of delivering sixteen electromagnetic impulses each. "All we have to do is set the time and we can put on the shows without even a coffee break," Walt told a *New York Times* reporter in describing the forthcoming Tiki Room, which was itself a test run for Lincoln. The movements were programmed onto the tape from a harness that one of the Imagineers wore, and the machinery was placed inside the figure, though when Lincoln began to drip oil during a test, Walt ordered Bob Gurr to fabricate the parts of lighter material so that, in Gurr's words, the robot would "weigh half as much and do twice as much."

Already by the summer of 1961, the Imagineers had made a Lincoln figure that could rise from its chair. Early the next year, to squelch a dispute between the machinists (who made the mechanical components) and the sound engineers (who made the electrical and control elements), Walt had his Lincoln moved to a small, secret room in the Animation Building where the WED staff continued to work on it. "Walt was always running people in and out [of the room]," remembered machinist Neil Gallagher. "We were always running it for a bunch of people. Sometimes we couldn't even run it. He would just talk them through it." Among those whom Walt ran into the room was Robert Moses. Moses had come to the studio that April to see the Ford and GE drawings, to review WED's other possibilities, and to encourage Walt's continued participation in the fair. Walt asked Moses if he would like to meet Abraham Lincoln and took him to the room, where he made the introduction. Lincoln extended his hand, and Moses was instantly captivated. He insisted that he had to have Lincoln at the fair. When Walt protested that the project was five years from completion, Moses waved him off. He was determined to have his Lincoln.

The obstacle, like the obstacle for the Hall of Presidents, was finding an institution that would sponsor what was sure to be an extremely expensive endeavor. But Moses wasn't going to be dissuaded. He hunted for months and finally found a prospect when the legislature of Illinois, Lincoln's home state, established a commission for the fair, and the commission decided that the theme of its exhibit would be "The Land of Lincoln." Moses immediately had Joe Potter, the fair's executive vice president, and Martin Stone, its head of the industrial sector, contact the commission's temporary chairman, advertising executive Fairfax Cone, urging him to see Disney's Lincoln. Cone visited the studio in April and pronounced himself "overwhelmed." Two weeks later Cone phoned Jack Sayers to confirm his interest and say that he and key Illinois leaders "look with great favor on the possibility of the Lincoln figure as the 'show' feature of their Fair exhibit." The commission convened that May to discuss the Lincoln figure, and Walt tentatively agreed to $400,000 for the first year and $200,000 for the second, but when the state legislature appropriated only $1 million for the entire pavilion, the commission's new permanent chairman, a Lincoln scholar named Ralph Newman, asked Walt to reconsider. Even Moses wired Walt urging him to lower his demand. Walt would not budge, calling his offer the "best business proposition we can consider" and claiming to be relieved that "we do not have to proceed with the Lincoln figure," though privately he admitted that he would be willing to settle for $250,000 the first year of the fair and $350,000 for the second once the attraction had proven itself.

Walt was playing hardball not only with the Illinois commission but with Moses who, Walt knew, was not about to lose his Lincoln over a few hundred thousand dollars. As negotiations stalled that summer, Moses made concessions to Illinois on security, rental fees, and utilities, then finally offered the state a secret $250,000 subsidy to pay Disney.* With that Illinois had its exhibit. On November 19, the centennial observance of Lincoln's Gettysburg Address, Walt, Moses, and Ralph Newman flew to Springfield, the Illinois state capital, to meet Governor Otto Kerner and announce the project. Not everyone in Illinois was pleased. One paper objected that the Lincoln robot was a "cheap carnival trick that would demean the memory of Abraham Lincoln and degrade the Illinois exhibit," while another called it "macabre." But speaking before an Elks Club luncheon in Springfield that day, Walt assured his listeners that his own reputation was on the line and that the exhibit would be anything but a trick. "Imagine you're in the presence of that great man," he suggested, then promised that Lincoln would seem genuinely alive—"Maybe more alive than I am." The criticism subsided. Pygmalion had charmed them all.

While Walt was negotiating with the state of Illinois, WED received an urgent call from the Pepsi-Cola Company. With the opening of the fair

*When, as the fair drew to a close, the subsidy was revealed, it became a subject of controversy. No other state received a similar loan or grant from the fair, and though the money was supposed to be repaid through concession income, the concessionaire later admitted that "[t]here isn't any chance of the fair getting much of that money back." In effect, Moses had misallocated the money. Robert Alden, "Illinois Received Loan from Fair," *NYT*, Sept. 3, 1965, p. 31.

little more than a year away, Pepsi, which was collaborating with the United Nations International Children's Fund (UNICEF), had been dithering over its own proposals and had finally contacted Disney to inquire whether it might plan an exhibit. The offer was daunting. Pepsi had a space of roughly 94,000 square feet at the fair and a budget of only $650,000. It was more daunting given the schedule. The old Disneyland supervisor, Joe Fowler, who had been the liaison between Disney and Pepsi, told Pepsi there simply wasn't enough time. That, Dick Irvine later recalled, infuriated Walt. "I'll make those decisions," he insisted, then instructed his staff to tell Pepsi that he would do it.

By any rational assessment, Fowler was right: there *wasn't* enough time. Walt did not even meet with Pepsi vice president Don Kendall until March 1963. But as WED sculptor Rolly Crump recalled, Walt rounded up his WED staff one day and announced that there was "one more piece of real estate that they've offered to us." Walt said he already had an idea for it. He described to them a "little boat ride that maybe we can do." Crump said the designers were shaken. "[W]e thought a *little boat ride*? I mean, God, we were working on Lincoln, the Carousel of Progress, both of which were using the highest technology and animatronic figures. And we were working on Ford, too. All of this, and Walt wants a little boat ride!"

What Walt really seemed to want was the challenge, the excitement, the race to the wire, to prove once again that he could succeed under the most difficult of circumstances—to prove that he couldn't fail. The basic idea of the attraction, appropriate to UNICEF, was a large boat that would float on a canal through a universe of small animated dolls representing all the countries of the world and demonstrating the fundamental unity of mankind—a platitude given the archetypal Disney treatment. Originally Walt had thought to have the dolls "sing" their national anthems, but the result was cacophony. Instead he asked the Sherman brothers, who had written songs for various films at the studio, to write a composition that could be sung by all the children. Harriet Burns, who worked on the exhibit, remembered Walt telling the Shermans offhandedly, "It's a small world after all," which became the title of their song and of the attraction.

With time so short, Walt mobilized just as he had with *Snow White* and the war training films and Disneyland. He had Claude Coats design the route through the lands. He had animator Marc Davis provide small comic flourishes and Davis's wife, Alice, the costumes. He had Rolly Crump draft a colorful 120-foot mobile sculpture to stand outside the pavilion. When he decided that the drawings of the dolls lacked a certain charm, he had them redesigned by Mary Blair, who had been a sketch artist at the studio in the 1940s, before moving east to draw greeting cards and illustrate children's books. Finally, he had a full-scale mock-up of the ride constructed at WED, just as he had done with the Carousel of Progress. According to Crump, "We would put Walt on a boat that was on wheels and that was elevated to the right sightline, and then push him through the ride" so that he could experience exactly what a visitor would experience and tinker with what he felt needed improvement. In the end, as with everything in which he was personally invested, he was determined not only to meet the deadline but to meet it spectacularly because, as he now imagined, nothing less than perfection was suitable for Walt Disney.

III

As Walt approached sixty, with his hair and mustache beginning to gray, he was thinking again about his legacy—about what would happen to the studio when he was gone. Storyman and sketch artist Bill Peet remembered sitting at the coffee table in Walt's office discussing a project with him when Walt, suddenly enveloped in sadness, rose, went to the window, and stared out silently. "You know, Bill," he finally said, "I want this Disney thing to go on long after I'm gone. And I'm counting on guys like you to keep it going." Sometimes he would say that he was delegating more responsibility to his subordinates and continually reorganizing them so he would be sure the company would survive him, then was quick to add that he was in perfect health and expected to outlive them all. Other times he seemed to despair of the company existing after he was gone. "They won't be able to handle it, anyway," he once told director Ken Annakin, speaking of his executives. "So just let it fritter away."

The studio, in any case, was very different from the one he had founded, different even from the one he had constructed at Burbank. It was different physically. Walt had added a third soundstage at a cost of $250,000 to house the 90-by-165-foot water tank for *20,000 Leagues*, and he built a fourth soundstage in 1958 both for television and for the film *Darby O'Gill and the Little People* as part of a $1.6 million studio expansion. Early the next year the studio purchased the 315-acre Golden Oak Ranch, about twenty-five miles from Burbank near Newhall, the site of California's first reported gold strike, which the company used as a backlot for its television and film productions and as a pasture for the studio's livestock. Walt kept buying adjacent parcels until early in 1964 the holding totaled 726.5 acres.

If the studio was different physically, the men who now populated it were different too. Wilfred Jackson and Ben Sharpsteen had both retired, or rather been retired—the last of the executive old guard who had worked on Mickey Mouse and *Snow White*. But then longevity had never mattered much to Walt, only usefulness. As Marc Davis told it, Walt had even fired Ward Kimball after giving him a chance to direct *Babes in Toyland* and then arguing with him over his approach. Kimball went to Walt "on bended knee" asking to be reinstated, and he was, but Walt relegated him to animating Ludwig Von Drake, a new character, for *Wonderful World of Color*, a clear humiliation.

As the old guard left, a new guard had moved in, headed by Bill Anderson, the production chief, and Card Walker, a longtime employee who had worked his way through the ranks from a traffic boy to a camera operator to a member of the story department to publicity chief to vice president of advertising and sales, though his purview seemed to incorporate much more. Within this operation Walt called himself the studio's "executive producer," having resigned all his official titles in 1963. "I'm the boss of everything that's produced here," he told a journalist, to explain his function. "I work on story ideas and gags; I work on every script, writing dialogue and planning scenes. When the story is set, I turn it over to the boys, and they make it."

Of course while Walt had been working on Disneyland, that description hadn't been entirely true. His involvement in production had been minimal then; he generally just reviewed the scripts, approved the casts, and fired off memos on small rectangles of distinctive dark blue paper or scribbled instructions in a bold red crayon, typically "NO" or "OK." "I'm not the perfectionist anymore," he told a reporter, not altogether accurately. "It's my staff. They're the ones always insisting on doing something better and better. I'm the guy trying to hurry them to finish before they spoil a job." But as Disneyland settled into a routine, Walt, evidently bored again, slowly disengaged from the park as he had from the studio, resigned all his titles there as well, and reasserted his control in Burbank. He became the paterfamilias again, not only reading the scripts but also painstakingly polishing them, not only approving the casts but also making sure the actors were comfortable at the studio, not only sending memos but also sitting in on endless production meetings to make certain the films were ready before they were put before the cameras. "It was run from the top down, but there were no middlemen," wrote one employee at the time. "At the top, alone, like Napoleon (and at times like Attila the Hun), was our leader and captain, *el Jafe* [*sic*], *Numero Uno*, the Man, the Boss—in short, Walter Elias Disney. All things started with Walt. And

Walt had the final word—always!" "Walt would never let any person get in and start building a big team, an empire," director Robert Stevenson said, echoing earlier criticisms of Walt. "The tradition here was that if anybody got so important that they put the name on the door, they would not be here in a couple of weeks," though Stevenson charitably believed this had less to do with Walt's ego, which everyone acknowledged was large, than with his fear of political cliques forming within the studio. Walt may have delegated power and appointed committees to do work that he had once done himself, but he reserved the right to be the ultimate and only authority.

If the studio and the staff were different from the ones over which Walt had presided before Disneyland, so now were the films they produced. For one thing, animation had practically disappeared; in the five years after *Sleeping Beauty* the studio produced only two animated features, *101 Dalmatians* and *The Sword in the Stone*. As for Mickey Mouse, he hadn't appeared in a short since 1953. The emphasis had shifted to live-action films. Of these, some were family-oriented historical costume dramas of the sort he had done in England, children's adventures, and even an occasional tearjerker like *Pollyanna*, based on the Eleanor H. Porter novel about an orphaned girl who comes to live with her aunt and changes people's lives through her goodness. But the studio had also begun to specialize in a new genre: family comedies like *The Absent Minded Professor*, about an inventor who discovers a substance that allows things to fly, and *The Shaggy Dog*, about a boy who turns into a sheepdog.

While other studios were discharging their stars and retrenching as audiences declined with the growth of television, Walt recruited a Disney repertory company—among them, former Mouseketeer Annette Funicello, now a teenager; a gap-toothed little boy named Kevin Corcoran, who appeared in *Mickey Mouse Club* serials, then advanced to features like *Old Yeller* ("I think he is a find," Walt wrote Bill Anderson. "We better get some kind of option on him."); Tim Considine, another young veteran of the *Mickey Mouse Club* serials; another serial actor, Tommy Kirk; longtime Hollywood star Fred MacMurray, who had migrated to television; and perhaps most important of all, a young blond British actress named Hayley Mills, the daughter of the actor John Mills. She had come to the attention of the studio when Walt, having searched fruitlessly for an actress to play Pollyanna, was about to shut down production on the film. Bill Anderson and his wife were in England at the time, and Mrs. Anderson had seen Hayley there in her debut film, *Tiger Bay*. At his wife's suggestion, Bill Anderson rushed out to see the film, liked it, then had a print sent to Walt in California. *Pollyanna*'s director, David Swift, wasn't impressed, but Walt overrode him. A natural, unaffected actress, Mills became one of the studio's biggest stars, not only headlining hits like *The Parent Trap* and *The Moon-Spinners* but also becoming a recording artist for the Disney label.

Since the days of Mickey Mouse, the name "Disney" had been a brand: the best in what seemed to be, oxymoronically, mass-produced folk art that appealed to everyone from sophisticates to innocents. Indeed, Walt had always pointedly insisted that his films were not made primarily for children or even primarily for profit, and few critics had treated them that way, at least until the postwar period when the art largely disappeared and there seemed no motive other than profit. Beginning with *Cinderella*, Walt received a new critical pass through most of the 1950s, but by the end of the decade the live-action films—broad, simple, and clearly child-oriented—had changed the brand and revoked the pass. Now the name "Walt Disney" was synonymous with wholesome family entertainment that no one could possibly mistake for art, folk or otherwise. As Dr. Max Rafferty, the superintendent of public instruction in California, put it in praising Disney, "His live movies have become lone sanctuaries of decency and health in the jungle of sex and sadism created by the Hollywood producers of pornography."

Walt understood the change and defended it, no doubt in part because his films proved so profitable. *The Absent Minded Professor* grossed $8.9 million domestically on a budget of $1 million, *The Shaggy Dog* $9.6 million, and *The Parent Trap* $9.3 million, while *101 Dalmatians* grossed only $6.2 million. By comparison, two of the most popular films of Hollywood's reigning star at the time, perky Doris Day, grossed $7.4 million *(Pillow Talk)* and $7.7 million *(Lover Come Back)*. (Walt had asked the studio for the comparison.) Walt, who was happily unsophisticated himself, sincerely enjoyed some of his studio's live-action films. He wrote the manager of Radio City Music Hall that he honestly felt *The Absent Minded Professor* was "one of the funniest comedies that ever came out of this town," and director David Swift said that Walt broke down in tears watching *Pollyanna* in the sweatbox. Swift, who made the film, said he personally "hated it," but when he told Walt that they would have to cut twenty minutes out of the picture because it was running long, Walt protested, "No, no, no, don't *touch* it!"

On the other hand, Walt did not delude himself about the meaning of the studio's new brand. "Our part in things is to build along the lines we are known for, with happy family stories and comedies," he told *Newsweek*, contradicting the long-standing Disney position. "I've never thought of this as art. It's part of show business." To an employee, he was more candid. "We're making corn, Peter," he would tell matte artist Peter Ellenshaw. "I know it's not your kind of corn, but it's got to be good corn. Let's make it the best we possibly can. We're trying to please people." As for the increasingly mature competition in Hollywood that was tackling serious issues, Walt turned philistine. "These avant garde artists are adolescents," he griped to a reporter. "It's only a little noisy element that's going that way, that's creating this sick art. I don't think the whole *world* is crazy!" Referring to a recent film about alcoholism, *Days of Wine and Roses*, he said, "I don't want to see that kind of thing. If I did, I'd go down to the county nut ward, or something."

As Richard Schickel saw it, Walt Disney's live-action films denied mankind its "infinite possibilities" by "reducing it to comic clichés, by imitating old imitations of life." And so," Schickel concluded, "he passed, at last, beyond—or beneath—criticism," while at the same time serving as a convenient bulwark against those who criticized the motion picture industry for excessive sex and violence. But it wasn't only the critics who felt Walt Disney's films had sanitized art out. Bill Roberts, who wrote the original screenplay for *The Absent Minded Professor*, demanded that his name be removed from the credits after reading Bill Walsh's revision. "I feel that wit has been replaced by cuteness," Roberts wrote Walt angrily. "Almost every character speaks alike, with a kind of vapid juvenility reminiscent of comedies of twenty years ago." Hayley Mills's parents chafed over the kind of saccharine scripts she was being given and decided not to renew their contract until, as Bill Anderson relayed their concerns to Walt, "they have had the opportunity to read the material involved and the role to be played." Walt, in turn, felt that the Millses didn't know what kind of pictures were right for their daughter, and he huffed to Anderson that "I do not want my name attached to the type of pictures Mary [Mills] apparently wants Hayley to do." Yet even Walt, for all his belligerence toward Hollywood's new frankness, seemed to have misgivings about being stuck making puerile movies. After watching *To Kill a Mockingbird* at a screening in his home, he lamented, "That's the kind of film I wish I could make." But he couldn't. He was Walt Disney, and Walt Disney was now committed to making films that were innocuous enough to be enjoyed by the entire family.

As he pondered the future of his empire, he thought of his own family's security too. While in England, he had seen an article about the demise of a company after its proprietor died, and, he wrote Roy, "it set me to thinking about our own situation here of having all our eggs in one basket," meaning having their assets tied up in Disney stock. Walt was concerned about what would happen if his family were forced to sell the stock to pay estate taxes. "When I'm up in heaven playing my harp, I really couldn't put my heart into it, if I thought I had left things in a mess down here!"

Roy, however, had another financial concern. Back in 1953 he had piloted both the deal between WED and WDP and the personal services contract between Walt and WDP through the board of directors over the objections of three members, who eventually resigned, and over the objections of the dissident stockholder who had brought suit against the company. Now Roy worried that the growth of WED over the years with Disneyland and the world's fair and the large sums of money that both it and Walt were drawing from WDP might bring renewed and unwelcome scrutiny from the Securities and Exchange Commission and even a possible stockholders' revolt over the sweetheart contract with Walt.

The problem was broaching the issue with his brother. As Roy's biographer, Bob Thomas, told it, Roy decided to confront Walt over what was expected to be a long weekend at Smoke Tree. What ensued instead was a one-day shouting match—"a lot of yelling and screaming and everything else," Ron Miller, who was there with Diane, told Thomas—after which Roy and Edna promptly returned to Los Angeles. Walt couldn't see why anyone would possibly object to his contract. "I tried to explain to Walt one time that even though everything was proper and aboveboard," studio attorney Neil McClure told Thomas, "he had to be like Caesar's wife—above suspicion. Walt blew. 'What do you mean? I haven't done a damn thing that's wrong.' "

Walt's relationship to WED was a sensitive issue. Walt loved WED and guarded its independence from WDP and from Roy, moving it in 1961 at the time of the Ford exhibit to a rented building in a Glendale industrial park that Imagineers called the Pancake House because it had a high peaked roof and was painted orange and blue like the International House of Pancakes franchises. As Disneyland expanded and as the world's fair contracts came in, WED had grown too, to three hundred employees, necessitating organizational charts and building plans; but Walt continued to regard it as his refuge from the studio and its bureaucracy. "Nobody had to ask anyone at the studio for permission," Bill Cottrell said. "If you wanted to start developing a thing like Audio-Animatronics, you'd do it as long as you had the money to do it. And by this time, Walt had the money."

The reason Walt had the money was WED's contract and his own contract with WDP. Walt not only received the royalty for the use of his name and the percentages from his personal investments in films; WED also received engineering and design fees from WDP and the grosses of the train and the monorail at Disneyland, both of which were owned by WED, presumably on the grounds that Walt had developed these attractions personally. In fiscal year 1960 those fees amounted to $156,000 paid to Walt himself and $188,835 paid to WED. (By this time he had sold his interest in Disneyland to WDP.) Now at the end of 1960, as the seven-year personal services contract approached its expiration—it had previously been extended for one year—Loyd Wright, Walt's attorney and one of the most prominent lawyers in Los Angeles, was asking Roy for a 5 percent share of the gross of all the films that Walt supervised and 10 percent of the gross of all the films that he personally produced. Roy, who had always been in the untenable position of having to navigate between his brother and his company, was adamantly opposed. He thought that no one, not even Walt, was entitled to a share of the gross, only a share of the profits.

Over the years the brothers had had their differences over money, over control, and over the direction in which to take the company. "You could hear them shouting at each other all the time, even through closed doors," Walt's longtime secretary Dolores Voght would say. "The language was terrible." Roy's son, Roy E. Disney, said that he always knew when his father and Walt had had a fight because he could hear the car door slam when his father came home. Walt was often disdainful of Roy, dismissing him as a businessman with little sensitivity to art. Once when Walt screened a film for Roy and Roy afterward asked how long the running time was, Walt snapped, "We work for years creating these pictures and all Roy can say is, 'How long does it run?' " After surviving so many prophecies of doom, he also thought that Roy was fainthearted. As John Hench explained the ongoing, unabating tension, "Roy's great ambition in life, I suppose, was to stay out of debt. And it was Walt's method in life to keep Roy constantly in debt."

These disputes were typical of Hollywood, the product of the fundamental clash between the creative and financial halves of the motion picture business. It may have been occasionally exacerbated at Burbank because, unlike the situation in other studios, where the filmmakers were in the West and the businessmen were in the East, the creative and financial arms shared not only the same coast but the same building. The tension, many felt, was also a source of the company's strength—Walt's adventurism balanced by Roy's pragmatism. By the same token, if Roy balanced Walt's recklessness, he also balanced his callousness. Harry Tytle saw their individual contributions in terms of family dynamics. Walt was the "striving father, heading the family" and Roy the "more relaxed grandfather," providing a dose of wisdom; Walt was the brusque one who drove everyone ruthlessly, while Roy was the calm and personable one who compensated for his brother's severity.

But now, as they bickered over Walt's new contract, the years of simmering animosity seemed to boil to the surface. Roy clearly resented Walt's imperious attitude and his willingness to wrest as much money as he could from the company—the company they had built together—as if it were just another corporate safe to be raided. Walt clearly resented Roy's attempts to fence him in as if he were just another employee and not the name in the company's title and the creative force who was chiefly responsible for its success. Once Roy assumed the financial helm at the studio, the brothers had never thereafter been particularly close. Since the 1930s, when their families would gather on Sundays at Walt's house and occasionally vacation together, they had seldom socialized, and they didn't even share a lunch table at the commissary. But as the 1961 negotiations continued, the brothers stopped speaking to each other altogether. Card Walker became the intermediary. "Walt would tell him, 'You go down to Roy and tell him what I said,' " Walt Pfeiffer recalled, "and Roy would tell Card what he said and [to] go back to Walt and tell him. I don't know how long that lasted."

In fact, it lasted for months—months of silence, anger, and recrimination in which Walt felt wounded and Roy protested that he was only trying to protect both Walt and the company from disgruntled stockholders. Some felt that the tension was further heightened by a rivalry between Roy E., who worked on the creative side at the studio, and Ron Miller, whom Walt had brought to the studio after Miller suffered an injury during a brief career in professional football playing for the Los Angeles Rams. Whether or not that was true, the situation certainly worsened considerably when, during negotiations, Loyd Wright threatened to hire Walt an agent who might shop him to another studio, which Roy saw as an act of perfidy. "That was the first time I had witnessed Roy explode in anger," Bill Cottrell said. It was also the final assault in the battle. When Cottrell reported Wright's warning to Walt, Walt, apparently tiring of the dispute and the ill will it had engendered, advised Cottrell to get the matter settled.

Roy was apparently of the same conciliatory mind. As Cottrell would tell it to Thomas, Roy walked in on his negotiators in the conference room next to his office during a particularly heated exchange and said, "None of us would be here in these offices if it hadn't been for Walt. All your jobs, all the benefits you have, all came from Walt and his contributions." When the negotiations were concluded that April, the studio had reluctantly agreed to a new seven-year personal services contract that would award Walt $3,500 a week, up $500 from his previous contract, and $1,666 a week in deferred payments—in addition to the percentages on the profits, but not the grosses, of the pictures in which he personally invested. Walt had gotten most of what he wanted. At the same time WDP also agreed to a new contract with WED at $1,500 a week for its design services and agreed to pay another 20 percent of the payroll costs of any personnel WED had at Disneyland, which was now wholly owned by WDP. Both of these contracts were subjected to stockholder approval.

In June, Roy's birthday, the ice finally began to melt. Walt sent Roy an Indian peace pipe with a card. "It is wonderful" it read, "to smoke the Pipe of Peace with you again—the clouds that rise are very beautiful.

"I think between us over the years, we have accomplished something—there was a time when we couldn't borrow a Thousand Dollars and now I understand we owe Twenty-four million!"

Roy put the pipe atop a large portrait of Walt that hung in his office. "We've made peace," he explained to a visitor.

As he pondered his legacy at the studio and his financial legacy to his family, Walt Disney also pondered something much larger: his legacy to the world. With his sense of himself having swelled, he knew that entertainment wasn't enough and that not even Disneyland constituted a lasting contribution. Walt Disney needed to do something that would improve society, not just distract it. Since the early 1930s he had been interested in the Chouinard Art Institute, and he never forgot Mrs. Chouinard's generosity in letting his animators study there when Walt couldn't afford to pay their tuition. When Mrs. Chouinard suffered a stroke in the early 1950s and became physically unable to administer the school, Walt not only supported it financially—with tens of thousands of dollars in donations—but also assigned Mickey Clark from Disneyland to audit the school's books and do a systems survey. Clark discovered that $12,000 of the school's funds had been embezzled and that years of accounts receivable had not been collected. Eventually, with Mrs. Chouinard's agreement, Walt sent executives from WED to run the school and set up a planning committee charged with answering, among other questions, "What would we like to have starting from scratch?"

One of those things, Walt decided, was a new site, and as early as 1957 he asked Harrison Price to find one. While Price searched, Walt's idea began to expand from a new site for Chouinard to his much more ambitious City of the Arts, of which Chouinard was now to be one element. For a long time Walt had been thinking of an academy of arts to be subsidized by the studio for the purpose of giving his artists the broadest possible creative education. "We could get the best instructors from all over the country," he had written one educator in 1939, "and it would be sort of a school for post-graduate work." Walt never expressed any regrets about his own lack of formal education; in fact, when a new secretary transcribed a letter exactly as he had dictated it, Walt, realizing his own deficiencies, told another secretary, "You have to do something about this girl. She's too literal!" But as Roy later told it, "Walt was obsessed with the idea that in life you just continually go to school. You never reach any plateau of perfection."

In the City of the Arts, Walt hoped to combine education with another of his passions: community. He envisioned the city as an American version of the German Bauhaus, where students could find practical applications for their work, and he had WED lay it out as a place where students would mingle not only with one another but with the public to whom they could sell their art. In the early 1960s he grudgingly gave up the idea of his city as too costly and impractical, but he was, if anything, even more devoted to the idea of his school. When Chouinard merged with the Los Angeles Conservatory of Music in 1962, he named his putative institution the California Institute of the Arts. "He wanted to build that school!" Harrison Price recalled. "It was the most pervasive objective in a man's mind that I've ever run into. He was very close to the evolution of CalArts, he was passionate all the way. He said, 'This is the thing I'm going to be remembered for.' "

Walt was messianic again. As he had once cornered employees to discourse on *Snow White* and then on Disneyland, now he would corner them to discourse on CalArts. "I want people to come there that are really able to do things," he told animator T. Hee in a long late-night phone call. "I don't want a lot of theorists. I want to have a school that turns out people that know all the facets of filmmaking. I want them to be capable of doing anything needed to make a film—photograph it, direct it, design it, animate it, record it." He told another associate that CalArts would be a place where "we had schools of music, of drama, or cinematography, or dance, and of the graphic and applied arts, all under one roof, as the students walk from one class to another, passing art exhibits or students and others, they're hearing music, and they're living in dormitories with people that are all in the arts." He told Alice Davis, Marc Davis's wife, that the school would have a closed-circuit television system "so the students who were studying fine arts or illustration could watch and draw the dance students as they performed," and he told Marc Davis that he was going to invite Picasso and Dali to teach. He even suggested that he might teach a course himself. "I don't mean teach *drawing*, for God's sake!" he said to Davis modestly. "But I'm a damn good storyman! I could teach *story*!"

Walt had always operated on the principle of renunciation when he felt that something had reached its potential and could not be improved, and the energy he had poured into Disneyland was now being diverted into CalArts. "He was losing interest in a lot of the things he'd done before," Marc Davis said, "because he was seeing the new world ahead." And while Walt was providing the vision, he was already strong-arming contributors, setting up a trailer on the lot with a model of CalArts that he showed to potential investors. "[I]f you see fit to set up a Joseph P. Kennedy Scholarship," Walt wrote the president's father in a typical solicitation, "I can assure you your grandchildren will receive originals from all of Walt Disney's cartoon features to come." Kennedy contributed.

IV

New York loomed. When 1964 arrived, the Imagineers at WED were still making final preparations for the world's fair that would open that April. Once Walt got over the problems with Henry Ford, the Ford attraction had proven surprisingly easy. He had ridden it shortly before the opening of the fair and pronounced himself pleased with the results. The GE Carousel of Progress had been a more difficult project, particularly since the pavilion had so many elements besides the central show. When the Imagineers finished it, Walt invited GE executives to the studio to take a look. They were satisfied with the result, but Walt, after all this time, had a hesitation of his own. "It doesn't have a wienie!" he told them. "Come back in a couple of weeks and I'll show you." As one of the GE officials later told it, he had no idea what Walt meant. But within a week, they received a call asking that they return to the studio. This time the show was virtually identical to the first one—except that Walt had added a comical Audio-Animatronic dog to each scene. It was the finishing touch on the exhibit.

The main problem with It's a Small World had been time. Walt didn't even see the prototype for the singing children until September. "We were living off of black coffee in the morning and martinis for lunch," Rolly Crump recalled. When it opened, in what was essentially a metal shed since the budget provided for nothing more, Roy complained about the expense but wrote Walt that "it is very gratifying to see that the show is getting such a good reception," and he predicted that "we will have a good chance of breaking even on it."

The major headache was Abraham Lincoln. It had taken a year just to design Lincoln's head and longer than that to program the robot. But the matter of Lincoln's voice was even more difficult. Several Lincoln scholars recommended Raymond Massey, who had played Lincoln in John Cromwell's 1940 film *Abe Lincoln in Illinois*, but Walt feared that Massey might sound too theatrical and not homespun enough. Instead, he invited to the studio Royal Dano, who had played Lincoln on an *Omnibus* television program, on the pretense that he would be filmed to help the programmers devise body movements. As Imagineer Bob Gurr remembered it, Walt had Dano deliver the speech, and when he finished, "Walt jumped up and said, 'No! No! No! You don't understand. Do it again.' " When Dano delivered it a second time, Walt leaped to his feet again, and again told Dano that his performance was all wrong. After the third try Walt rose and led the entire crew in "The Battle Hymn of the Republic." Gurr said that at the time it made no sense to him. Only later did he learn that Walt was looking for a weary, agonized Lincoln and that he had finally elicited what he wanted from Dano by provoking him.

But even after Lincoln was delivered to the fair and the public preview drew near, his problems weren't over. The Imagineers just couldn't get the robot to function properly. "Oh, yeah, [Walt] was upset," Marc Davis recalled, "but I must say I think he felt for us. He had to see the condition of the guys and what they were doing. And he would ask questions and say, 'Well, guys, I'll get with you in the morning again,' " to work out the bugs. At a special preview for Robert Moses and the borough presidents of New York City, the robot performed serviceably—"not as perfect as we had wanted, but he worked," said Davis. But it was soon malfunctioning again, and Walt even summoned Ub Iwerks to New York to see if he could fix it. "You never saw such a stack of electronics magazines," said one studio employee of Iwerks's cargo.

Walt was nervous. On April 20, the day Lincoln was scheduled to be shown to a preview audience including Illinois governor Otto Kerner, UN ambassador Adlai Stevenson (a former Illinois governor), and the press corps, he dallied outside the GE pavilion signing autographs before telling designer Chuck Myall, "Well, I guess we've prolonged this as long as we can." When he arrived at the Illinois pavilion, however, either Jack Gladish, who had helped design Lincoln's head, or Dick Nunis, a Disneyland executive, gave Walt a sobering report: the robot was not reliable enough to be shown. Walt reluctantly broke the news to the audience. "Ladies and gentlemen," he said, "there's an old saying in show business. If you're not ready, don't open the curtain." As he made his announcement, beneath the stage the Imagineers were weeping.

Later Walt would blame the problems on a delay in the installation of power at the pavilion and on traffic delays in New York that prevented parts from being delivered, and he warned, "This is not a toy." Other accounts attributed the difficulties variously to dust, a blown transformer, fluctuations in current, and even unions that failed to complete the wiring. Ralph Newman believed that Walt actually *wanted* to delay the opening so he wouldn't have to compete with other attractions. But Lincoln didn't start operating until April 30, ten days after the aborted preview, and he delivered only seven flawless performances before malfunctioning once again, prompting Marc Davis to pose another explanation: "Do you suppose God is mad at Walt for creating man in his own image?" Eventually, the Imagineers managed to repair the problems, and Lincoln began regular performances that erased the earlier embarrassments. As Sharon later remembered, "Dad cried every time he sat through it."

Yet for all the problems with Lincoln—Walt immediately checked himself into the hospital for an examination and a rest when he returned to California from his two harrowing weeks at the fair—Disney was triumphant. At the end of the first season (the fair would have a second season after a six-month hiatus) GE's Carousel of Progress was the third most popular attraction, behind only the General Motors exhibit, which had a capacity two and a half times as large as GE's, and the Vatican's, which featured Michelangelo's *Pietà*. Ford's exhibit ranked fourth. Lincoln didn't qualify because the pavilion's capacity was too small, but the robot had worked reliably enough that Walt, much to the consternation of Ralph Newman, was having another one made for Disneyland, which, Walt advised Newman, was "always its ultimate destination."

During the hiatus after the fair's first season, while Walt was being showered with accolades, something else happened: he enjoyed his greatest cinematic triumph since *Snow White*. As Walt told it to the Sherman brothers, years earlier, most likely in 1943, he had seen Diane and Sharon reading a book and "chuckling, really enjoying it." A few nights later he watched Lilly reading the same book and laughing, and she recommended that Walt read it. The book was *Mary Poppins* by P. L. Travers, which chronicled the adventures of the magically empowered nanny of the title. (Joe Grant had a different version: Walt first heard of the book when Grant mentioned it to him after Grant's wife had read it to their children.) Shortly thereafter Walt asked Roy to contact Travers directly rather than through an agent to see if the rights were available and, if they were, to raise the possibility of turning the book into a film. Though she was Australian-born and an English émigrée, during the war she was a single mother living with her adopted young son in a five-story walkup in New York, and she seemed to be angling for a way to go west, telling Roy that she was thinking of relocating in Santa Fe or Tucson. Roy was cagey—he wasn't about to make a commitment with the war raging—but he did tell Travers that Walt was "intrigued" with *Poppins* and suggested that she consider working with the studio on an adaptation of the book.

In fact, the studio was clearly more interested in *Mary Poppins* than it was willing to let on. Roy had been casual in his note to Travers, but then he met with her in New York, and Walt wrote her that he would fly to Arizona to see her if she made the trip, and he added that "these stories would be ideal material for a combination of flesh and blood characters with cartoon." Roy phoned her again in March, careful not to seem too eager, just to let her know that the studio was still considering working with her. Not until 1946, when the war was over, did the studio and Travers reach agreement on the rights for $10,000—or at least Roy thought they had reached agreement. The deal fell apart when Travers insisted on script approval, something Walt Disney was not about to grant anyone.

This was, however, only a harbinger of things to come. Thirteen years, and the creation of Disneyland, would pass before the studio again contacted Travers, now sixty years old, about securing the rights. This time her agent wanted $750,000. Two months later, at a meeting with Walt in London, Travers herself upped the ante. She was now demanding 5 percent of the profits, which would have amounted to considerably more than $750,000, with a guarantee of $100,000 and an additional £1,000 to do the treatment. Upon meeting her back in the 1940s, Roy had described Travers, a delicate-looking woman with a dainty chin, thin arching brows, and wide-set eyes, as an "Amelia Earhardt [*sic*] type," by which he presumably meant that, despite her appearance, she was, like the late aviator, tough-minded and not easily cowed. He had read her correctly. She was no fan of Walt Disney's work, and she wasn't about to let him intimidate her.

But if she was strong-willed, she was also more than a little dotty. At the same time that she was disparaging Disney's films, she had written her own *Poppins* treatment with a collaborator and submitted it to Walt, and she kept revising it, even though she refused to sign a contract with the studio. Walt attempted to appease her, inviting her to visit the studio so that, he said, she could get acquainted with his staff and so that they would have the "benefit of your reactions to our presentation." When, after reading the Disney script, Travers protested that Mary should not subvert the authority of the parents of her charges in asking them to slide *up* the banister with her, and that she should not encourage the little boy to jump in puddles after his mother has told him not to, Walt was more than obliging, wiring her that the "Mary Poppins project is so important in the overall [scheme] if the two points raised in your letter will make you happy I shall be pleased to go along with your suggestions." But even with this coddling, Travers kept the studio dangling; at one point she agreed to a contract that stipulated unconditional approval of the script, which Walt signed off on knowing full well he wouldn't honor it, then a full year later she said she still "wanted to give it some thought." Walt had been working on the film for nearly two years before Travers finally signed the contract.

Even then she wasn't happy. "When we sat down with Mrs. Travers to present our treatment," recalled the Sherman brothers, who were writing a musical score for the picture and had helped block out the story, "she hated everything we had done. Disliked it with a passion! For every chapter we developed, she had a definite feeling we had selected the worst one. She started naming the chapters she felt we should adapt—and they were the ones we thought were absolutely unusable." Even on the eve of production, after a full year of delays, Travers was writing extensive criticisms of the script, and Walt was writing to thank her and assure her that "we will make use of it whenever we can."

She was no more forgiving when it came to the casting of the film. In March 1961, just before Travers arrived in California, Walt and Lillian had seen Mary Martin in New York in the stage musical *The Sound of Music*, and Walt had wired to ask her to consider the role of Poppins. Walt also suggested that Travers see the play on her way out to the studio, and she did, even requesting a meeting with the actress. Travers, however, had decided that Julie Harris should play the role, even though the film was to be a musical and Harris had demonstrated no talent in that area. Harris, no doubt at Travers's urging, had written Walt to express her interest, forcing him to decline her services.

Meanwhile that August, Walt saw the musical *Camelot* in New York and came away so impressed by the twenty-seven-year-old English actress Julie Andrews, who played Queen Guinevere, that he promptly concluded *she*, not Mary Martin, should be Poppins. Though Andrews was relatively unknown at the time—she had starred in the original Broadway production of *My Fair Lady*—Walt assiduously courted her for nearly a year, inviting her to fly out to the studio. "We can play the songs, lay out the story line and I am sure after seeing this sort of presentation you will be able to make your decision," Walt wrote her. Accepting the offer to come to the studio, Andrews, now pregnant, and her husband, the costume-and-set designer Tony Walton, spent a weekend with Walt in June 1962, though even then Walt wasn't leaving anything to chance. He offered

Walton a job consulting on the film's design, and he later arranged to have a handicapped patient of Walton's father, a doctor, come to America for a special operation. Like Travers, Andrews was hesitant to commit herself to a Disney film, her first film, with all that the Disney name now connoted, but Walt was helped considerably by the fact that Warner Bros. head Jack Warner had recently bypassed her in favor of Audrey Hepburn for the role that Andrews had coveted—Eliza Doolittle in the screen version of *My Fair Lady*—because, Warner said, nobody had heard of her. Poppins was a consolation prize. (Travers, obtuse to the ways of Hollywood, suggested Audrey Hepburn as a possible backup for the Poppins role.) The negotiations for Andrews's services began that October.

As for the role of Mary Poppins's confederate, Bert the chimney sweep, Walt had Cary Grant in mind and decided to expand the part to make it equal to Mary's to lure Grant, who told Walt that he was receptive. Travers was not happy. She argued that while Grant would be fine as the father of the family to which Mary ministers, to build up the role of Bert for him would be "mutilating the story" and throwing it out of balance. Grant did not agree in any case, and Walt sounded out Laurence Harvey and Anthony Newley before settling on the loose-limbed television situation comedy star Dick Van Dyke. "Walt had rooms of storyboards that he showed me," Van Dyke later recalled, "and his enthusiasm for the film grew as he spoke. He was like a kid, getting so excited about it that by the time I left him I was excited about it too. He had me sold. I wanted to be a part of that movie so much."

As Van Dyke observed, Walt was energized. Despite the fact that the *Mary Poppins* screenplay was written by the old studio hands Bill Walsh (who had authored *The Absent Minded Professor* and *Son of Flubber*) and Don DaGradi (who had co-written *Lady and the Tramp* and collaborated with Walsh on *Son of Flubber*) and was directed by another old studio hand, Robert Stevenson (who was coming off *Son of Flubber*), the film had an aura, if only because it had been worked on for so long and if only because it was the most elaborate and expensive live-action feature at the studio since *20,000 Leagues.* "There wasn't a sad face around the entire studio," Walt said, and admitted he became concerned when, as the budget swelled, not even Roy attempted to interfere or request that he show the "dailies" to the bankers. It had been years since Walt was so personally invested in a film. On just about every picture now, no matter how much he might labor over the script or the casting, he would fix, approve, and then disappear. On *Mary Poppins,* which was shot entirely on the Burbank lot, he visited the set almost every day with the objective—in the words of Karen Dotrice, who played the little girl under Poppins's authority—of "making sure that everybody was happy. That was the thing—he wanted everybody to enjoy the experience." Later Dotrice, echoing Van Dyke, said he was "like a big kid."

Though he didn't—couldn't, given his other responsibilities at the time—work on the script line by line, he obviously connected with the film in ways that he had not connected with most of the studio's recent pictures. Despite their emphasis on childhood release, Disney's best movies had only secondarily been concerned with liberation; his chief concern had always been maturation and the power that accompanied it. Even Pinocchio's transformation from a puppet to a boy, and Dumbo's from a put-upon little elephant to a circus star, were effected by accepting responsibility, demonstrating empathy, testing courage, and, finally, expressing love—hallmarks of adulthood. *Mary Poppins* was a kind of reversion to childhood before responsibility or, rather, a reaction to it. In a household that encouraged them to suppress their antic spirits and behave like adults, Poppins taught the children joy—how to fight bureaucracy, convention, and complacency, which were the drawbacks of adulthood. If his earlier films had spoken to young Walt Disney's need for empowerment, *Poppins* spoke to the older Walt Disney's predicament as a corporate captain burdened with duties, and he could certainly identify both with Mr. Banks, the stodgy banker who has a child lurking within him, and with Mary Poppins, the magical nanny who manages to emancipate that child. The film embodied his new vicarious dream of shirking responsibilities he knew he really couldn't shirk, of being the child that reporters often said he was but that he couldn't really be.

Made with a kind of joyful abandon that the studio hadn't felt for years, *Poppins* concluded its principal photography uneventfully at the end of the summer of 1963, with Walt writing his sister Ruth, "I think it's going to be one of our best." But even with the photography completed, the picture was far from over. It had taken a long time to prepare the film—to choose the scenes from the book, to write the dialogue, to compose a score, to find the cast, to parry Travers. It would take a long time, another full year, to finish it. The problem was that even though Walt had always intended the film to be a combination of live action and animation and had authorized Ub Iwerks to spend $250,000 to purchase the rights to a special traveling matte process that would better combine the live actors with the cartoons—"chickenfeed," he called the money—the live footage had not always been planned to accommodate the animation.* One reason was that Walt would often spring new ideas on the

*Some accounts say that Walt invited the staff to a screening of *Song of the South*, after which he suddenly decided that *Mary Poppins* could use animation, which threw the crew into a tizzy. See Greene, *Man Behind the Magic*, pp. 152–53. But memos indicate that Walt had thought of *Poppins* as a live action–animation combination as early as the 1940s.

staff. For the song "Jolly Holiday," the Sherman brothers had decided that one of the choruses would be sung by waiters harmonizing as a barbershop quartet. Walt mused that waiters had always reminded him of penguins and suggested that the waiters should be animated penguins, which necessitated a wholesale revision. As Frank Thomas and Ollie Johnston wrote, "The animator would fuss and complain and call a few names, but in the end he would become more inventive and more entertaining than he would have been if everything had been made easy for him. No animator ever would back away from such a challenge," and, they said, "Walt knew that, too."

Moreover, everyone seemed to know that the film was special. Even at a rough screening at the studio for the sales force before the score or animation had been added, Walt reported to Bill Anderson that the reaction was "terrific," though Walt was still so afraid that he might be deluding himself that he asked a longtime exhibitor to see it. The exhibitor confirmed Walt's enthusiasm. At the premiere at Grauman's Chinese Theater in August 1964, a benefit for CalArts, the audience stood and cheered. "You have made a great many pictures, Walt, that have touched the hearts of the world," producer Sam Goldwyn, who had discussed a *Poppins* collaboration with Walt in the early 1950s, wrote him after seeing the film, "but you have never made one so wonderful, so magical, so joyous, so completely the fulfillment of everything a great motion picture should be as MARY POPPINS." Goldwyn's was the general sentiment: *Mary Poppins* ranked with Walt Disney's very best films. Even Pamela Travers, who had caused Walt so much grief, came to Los Angeles to see the film and pronounced herself happy. "The whole picture is a splendid spectacle," she wrote Walt, "and I admire you for perceiving in Julie Andrews an actress who could play the part," praising Andrews's "understated" performance. She closed, "Yours, with a bouquet of flowers." (Still, for years Travers would express her disappointment in the film, apparently to those who disliked Walt Disney.)

The public was no less enchanted. Though the film cost $5.2 million, more than Disney had ever spent on live action, it would gross nearly $50 million worldwide, $30 million in the United States alone, boosting the company's gross that year to better than $100 million where, ten years earlier, it had never exceeded $10 million. When it was shown in Moscow, the government had to convert the Sports Palace into a theater and welcomed eight thousand viewers at each of two screenings. The film was nominated for thirteen Oscars, including Best Picture, and it won five—for Best Special Visual Effects, Best Score, Best Song ("Chim Chim Cher-ee"), Best Editing, and Best Actress, which was a vindication for Julie Andrews since

Audrey Hepburn had not even been nominated for *My Fair Lady*. "That lovely statue—which I will find hard to believe in my possession—would not be there at all if it hadn't been for your help," Andrews wrote Walt after the ceremony. "I just wish with all my heart that we had bagged an Oscar for 'best film' too! It so deserved it." Walt, however, seemed resigned to the fact that, not being a member of the Hollywood establishment, he couldn't win that award. (*My Fair Lady* did.) "Knowing Hollywood, I never had any hope that the picture would get it," he replied to Andrews with a touch of self-pity. "As a matter of fact, Disney has never actually been part of Hollywood, you know. I think they refer to us as being in that cornfield in Burbank."

It had been a very good year, and Walt was having to deny rumors that he might finally sell the studio and the theme park to CBS and retire, telling columnist Hedda Hopper, "With the business 'Mary Poppins' is doing, Disney might make an offer to buy CBS." Still, Walt confessed to another journalist that, far from reducing the pressure on him, *Mary Poppins* had actually increased it. "I'm on the spot," he said, sounding very much the way he had after *Snow White*. "I have to keep trying to keep up to that same level. And the way to do it is *not* to worry, *not* to get tense, *not* to think, 'I got to beat *Mary Poppins*, I got to beat *Mary Poppins*.' . . . The way to do it is just to go off and get interested in some little thing, some little idea that interests me, some little idea that looks like fun"—which was exactly what he did.

When the second season of the world's fair started the following April, after the release of *Mary Poppins*, Walt, much more relaxed, was ferrying employees from California to the fair as a reward. When he arrived with Marc Davis near the fair's closing to see how his attractions had held up, he became something of an attraction himself. Everywhere he went he was mobbed by well-wishers—"He *touched* me!" one woman squealed—except at the Ford pavilion, where he decided to wait in line with the other visitors, all of whom respected his privacy and none of whom approached him. But, said Davis, "[w]hen we got in the car [that took guests through the exhibit] the whole crowd applauded. And they had left him alone all this time. It was an amazing experience. And he was very touched."

By the time the fair closed in October 1965, after two seasons, 51 million visitors had attended and nearly 47 million of them, or 91 percent, had seen one of Disney's four exhibits, making Walt Disney clearly one of the main successes there. But not everyone was enamored of Walt's contributions. Writing in *Life* shortly after the opening, the architect and architectural educator Vincent Scully wailed, "If This Is Architecture, God Help Us." Fastening on the idea that Disney was now creating facsimiles of experiences that paled in comparison to the real thing and yet substituted for the real thing, Scully accused him of being a man who "so vulgarizes everything he touches that facts lose all force, living things their stature, and the 'history of the world' its meaning. Disney caters to the kind of phony reality—most horribly exemplified by the moving and talking figure of Lincoln elsewhere in the Fair—that we all too readily accept in place of the true. Mr. Disney, I'm afraid, has our number." It was a charge that would increasingly be leveled at Walt Disney: he had not only taken the edge and danger out of his art; he had found a way to take them out of life generally.

But Walt seemed immune to the criticism. The fair hadn't been about pleasing intellectuals. It had been a rehearsal. The Carousel of Progress was shipped back to Disneyland, where it was installed without the Skydome Spectacular and the nuclear fission demonstration but with a diorama of a futuristic city. It's a Small World was also shipped back to California and opened at Disneyland under the sponsorship of the Bank of America. Even before the fair ended, the new and improved Abraham Lincoln debuted at Disneyland as part of the park's tenth-anniversary celebration. Only Ford, despite Walt's enticements, decided not to transfer its exhibit to Disneyland, though Walt did take the dinosaurs and later set them up at the park as part of Disneyland's Primeval World along the Santa Fe & Disneyland Railroad. Meanwhile, Walt was inundated with offers from around the world to do similar projects. Madame Tussaud's Wax Museum even asked him to do an Audio-Animatronic Winston Churchill. Though Walt declined these invitations, he had always intended to use the exhibits to lure other corporations to sponsor attractions at Disneyland, and as the fair was winding down, Jack Sayers was meeting with IBM, Johnson's Wax, Hertz, Clairol, and the House of Formica to gauge their interest.

But it wasn't only the exhibits that Walt was taking from the fair. At the end of the first season he had invited Major General William E. "Joe" Potter, the fair's executive vice president, to the studio to discuss the possibility of his joining the company in a special and highly secret capacity, and Potter had agreed to do so. Potter's role was to head a new project—Project Future, the Disneys initially labeled it—for which the fair had been what Card Walker called a "testing ground." Now, with Potter aboard, the test was over, and the next phase, the "little thing" that would keep him from obsessing over how to top *Mary Poppins,* was about to begin—except it wasn't little. It was large—large beyond belief.

V

Almost as soon as Disneyland opened, Walt had been peppered with questions about whether he would build another theme park. In fact, though Walt always disavowed plans to erect a new park, claiming that Disneyland was unique and that he couldn't imagine having a park that wasn't close enough for him to supervise, in 1958 he and NBC, apparently realizing that it had missed out on Disneyland, jointly commissioned SRI to do a feasibility study for a park off the New Jersey Turnpike in a marshland near Secaucus. The report concluded that it would require 76,000 hours of ride capacity, as compared to 46,000 at Disneyland at the time; that it could operate for only 120 days annually given the weather; that it would cost $46.4 million; and that it would yield a low return on the investment that "does not point to a profitable venture." Walt had his own doubts. He didn't feel that the New York area would support a theme park because, he told Harrison Price, "*that* audience is not responsive." Other offers came from the new Brazilian capital of Brasilia—"Walt is interested and might come to Brazil personally if the whole thing looks promising," a Disney executive told officials—Niagara Falls; Monterey, California; and Kansas City.

The most promising prospect was a plan for downtown St. Louis, which Walt apparently had encouraged when a commission planning the city's two-hundredth anniversary asked if the studio might produce a film for the occasion, and Walt countered with a suggestion for a development. Officials pounced on the idea. A delegation from St. Louis, including the city's mayor, met with Walt at the studio in March 1963, after which Walt called in Harrison Price to conduct yet another feasibility study. Two months later Walt visited St. Louis himself with Lillian, Sharon, and Sharon's husband, Robert Brown, to assess the redevelopment area, called the Riverfront Zone, and he made another visit in November, at which time he laid out his terms: the local Civic Center Redevelopment Corporation would provide a building to house the attractions, and Disney would provide the attractions themselves, which the Disney company would own and control. By the end of the month he was meeting with WED Imagineers to discuss potential exhibits: a Circarama film on St. Louis, an Audio-Animatronic exhibition, a New Orleans French district, a haunted house, an Audubon bird room, a Davy Crockett cave, and a pirate ship walk-through.

Walt continued to confer both with St. Louis officials and with his Imagineers through the spring, and in July *The New York Times* reported that Disney had finally committed to a second Disneyland, an indoor park, to be installed in a five-story building in the downtown St. Louis area. But Walt hadn't committed to anything yet, and despite the news story, he wrote one correspondent that the "St. Louis project is only in the talking stage." By the end of the year he had lost interest. Some claimed, falsely, that August Busch, Jr., the head of the Anheuser-Busch brewery located in St. Louis, had scolded Walt and called him "crazy" for declaring that liquor would not be sold on the premises; others claimed that Walt and the local officials couldn't agree on the finances, which were projected by Disney to be $40 million.

But the real reason may have been that Walt had by that time found another, better location. From the beginning, when he had first contemplated another theme park, one of the most logical sites was Florida, largely because of the weather, and as early as 1959 Walt candidly told a reporter for the *Miami Herald* that he had been driving through the state and had come to the conclusion that "Florida would be better than California in many ways." This wasn't just idle talk. At the time Walt was already in discussions with RCA and with multimillionaire John D. MacArthur, head of Banker's Life Insurance, about developing a "recreational enterprise" called the City of Tomorrow on five to six thousand acres north of Palm Beach that MacArthur owned. The plan was to place a new theme park within a planned community, just as Walt had hoped to place his schools within a City of the Arts. As always, Walt commissioned Harrison Price to do a feasibility study, and Price determined that the "area offers a theme park attendance potential which equals or exceeds that experienced by Disneyland in Southern California." Even Roy reconnoitered the property in MacArthur's limousine, specially equipped with a hydraulic system that lifted the car above the palmettos, then went to New York to lobby with RCA, hoping, he said, that WED's world's fair projects would "influence RCA's plans."

As it turned out, the plan faltered and was eventually abandoned. "It just wasn't working" was how Bill Cottrell put it. But enthusiasm for building a new park in Florida still ran high. In his studies Price had come upon one stubborn fact: "It was that Disneyland, in Anaheim—for all of its high penetration in the available Southern California tourism—had a low rate of penetration each year in the Eastern populations." By his calculations, it would take one hundred years at the present rate of attendance to saturate the population east of the Mississippi River, which then constituted two-thirds of the population of the country. The only way to reach those people, Price believed, was to build a park in the east, and the best place to build it was Florida. Price was already providing Walt with possible sites as early as spring 1961, while Donn Tatum, now the vice president of administration at the studio, went to Florida to survey available real estate in the central belt of the state. "We are more enthusiastic than ever about the potentials and await your guidance in carrying the ball further," Tatum wrote Walt upon his return.

That guidance wasn't immediately forthcoming, most likely because Walt was preoccupied with planning the world's fair exhibits and steering the studio again. But sometime early in 1963 he convened a small, highly select, and discreet group of executives—among them Tatum, Card Walker, and Joe Fowler, the vice president of Disneyland—and charged them with finding five to ten thousand acres in Florida for a new park. (The size was necessary because Walt had always regretted not having more property around Disneyland to keep the surroundings from seeming tawdry and spoiling Disneyland's effect.) He code-named the enterprise variously Project Future or Project X to maintain its secrecy. When Walt revealed his plans to Lilly, she later admitted she was aghast. "What do you want to do that for?" she asked. To which Walt, who was working at the time on the world's fair and CalArts as well as on the studio's production schedule, replied that "he would get stagnant if he didn't do new things."

From the first, it was a cloak-and-dagger operation. No one was to know that Walt Disney was trying to buy property, or prices would soar. As Card Walker laid out the scheme to Walt that September, "We would carefully select a third party (like Governor Arnell) who would be our front. He would actually be seeking the land for another carefully selected company or person. In turn, this third party would select a real estate man or lawyer knowledgeable in real estate who, on a pre-determined plan, would assemble the land. The real estate man would *never* know we are involved. We would have a 'team' to follow and call every move as it develops. The land, for example, might be a 'retirement village' for senior citizens, as it would be similar to our project."

Meanwhile the ongoing St. Louis negotiations and the discussions with Seagram's on developing Niagara Falls had become subterfuges. That November, Walt, Sharon, Bob Brown, and a handful of executives flew to St. Louis and then on to Niagara Falls and Washington, D.C., before detouring to Florida, where Walt drove from Tampa to Ocala, looking the land over. On the way back to California they flew low over the Florida coast to survey it, and as they headed westward, according to one account, Walt conclusively decided that the park would be set in central Florida near Orlando so that it wouldn't have to compete with the ocean or the gulf. That same day, November 22, during a refueling stop in New Orleans, Walt learned that President Kennedy had been assassinated.

Walt would revisit Florida several times over the next six months, though Robert Price Foster, the vice president of legal affairs for Disneyland whom Walt had entrusted with implementing Card Walker's plan to buy land, thought that Walt seemed less interested in the prospective park than in flying in his new Gulfstream jet, which the studio had bought that March. In April, while Walt was attending the opening of the world's fair, Foster headed to Miami to meet with a Florida attorney named Paul L. E. Helliwell, who had come recommended by Disney's New York counsels. Foster was so cautious that he waited hours to tell Helliwell, an old World War II OSS officer himself, that Walt Disney was the client, and when Helliwell recommended a realtor named Roy Hawkins to identify properties, Foster didn't immediately let him into his confidence either. In fact, Foster began using the name Bob Price, lest someone trace him back to the Disneys.

One by one that spring and summer Foster targeted properties and began purchasing them through a series of front corporations, nine in all, though Roy risked exposure when he decided to go to Jacksonville himself to negotiate the purchase of a particularly large and important plot. Still, the company operated in secrecy. Only in June 1965, according to Foster, did Walt assemble a group in his office, including not only the Project X committee but the board of directors, to announce that the new park would be built and to describe its contours—a meeting Foster called "our own constitutional convention."

Of course, all of this was kept within the company. Even internal memos on the park were numbered so that they could be tracked; when, during one Florida visit, a waitress recognized him, Walt first denied that he was indeed Walt Disney, then asked her to promise not to tell anyone else who he was. Publicly Walt continued to disavow any interest whatsoever in a Florida theme park. "There are so many things we haven't done yet at Disneyland," he told a reporter for the *Daytona News-Journal* that April. "Right now, we're getting ready to spend $50 million in the next five years to revamp our 'Tomorrowland.' " But by that time Disney had already purchased 27,400 acres at a price of just over $5 million—about one-tenth the cost per acre of what he had spent on Disneyland twelve years earlier—with all the money coming from the studio.

Even state officials were to be kept in the dark. As late as August 1965 Roy received a call from an old contact at Prudential who had retired and become chairman of the Florida Development Commission asking if he and the Florida governor on the way back from a trade visit to Hong Kong could meet with Walt and Roy at the studio to "sell you on the idea of your possibly building an entertainment plant in Florida." Roy cagily answered that neither he nor Walt would be available. "I fibbed a bit about us being away," he wrote Walt, because "I think it would be premature for us to expose our hand." Both Helliwell and Hawkins, who had finally been let in on the secret, advised that Roy and Walt meet with the governor only in the presence of county officials and leading citizens of Orlando so that the governor wouldn't be able to renege on any promises he might make.

But the company could conceal its plans only for so long. A reporter from the *Orlando Sentinel-Star* visited the studio with a press contingent early that fall of 1965 and asked why Walt had been touring the Orlando area, to which Walt, evidently surprised, gave a rambling answer. "He looked like I had thrown a bucket of water in his face," she said. A few weeks later Walt's secretary warned him that the reporter, Emily Bavar, was suspicious. In fact, that October, Bob Foster and Bob Jackson, the vice president of public relations for WED, were in Florida scouting locations for a press conference at which to announce plans for the park when they spotted the headline of the *Sentinel-Star* in the lobby of the Cherry Plaza Hotel. "WE SAY: 'MYSTERY' INDUSTRY IS DISNEY," ran the banner. The story by Bavar explained that Helliwell and Hawkins had been purchasing land for a new Disney theme park, and it even quoted the proprietor of a local grocery at the periphery of the Orlando property who claimed that strange men from California kept coming to get sodas from him. "The only thing I can tell you is that it is big and fat," Helliwell commented inscrutably.

Florida governor Haydon Burns confirmed the story that day, and Walt made his own formal announcement at the Cherry Plaza in Orlando on November 15, 1965, at a news conference—actually two conferences—attended by close to five hundred reporters. "We've still got a lot of work to do before we can even begin to think about starting construction," he told them. "You just can't go out and build a whole new world of entertainment without a lot of studies and before our people solve a lot of problems." He anticipated that the project would take eighteen months to plan and another eighteen months to implement, aiming for an opening in early 1969, and he said he would spend $100 million just to "get the show on the road." Then he presented a slide show illustrating the effect that Disneyland had had on Southern California—nearly $1 billion in revenues. Governor Burns, who called November 15 the "most significant day in the history of Florida," predicted a 50 percent rise in tourism and tax revenues. But Walt said that while they obviously expected to make money, "making money is the furthest thing from our thoughts in this new enterprise. I mean it. We want it to be a labor of love."

Walt also waxed philosophical, saying, "We want something educational, something to keep the family together—that would be a credit to the community, to the country as a whole," but he was vague as to specifics and told an associate afterward that he had done a "lousy" job in his presentation. In fact, he had not been specific because there were no specifics to mention other than the notion that there would be two "cities"—the City of Yesterday and the City of Tomorrow. Indeed, according to Robert Foster, Walt hadn't actually seen the exact property until the morning of the announcement, when he flew over it in his Gulfstream, and he didn't set foot on it until the morning after the announcement, when he tramped there with Roy, Donn Tatum, General Potter, and a local politician, motorboating across a lake on the site with what Foster called a "rare expression of approval."

The truth was that Walt wasn't especially interested in building another amusement park in Disney World, as the new complex was to be called, and when Roy formed a central committee to set general strategy for the park, Walt was not even a member. Walt had already built a park, and as Roy told one journalist, "Walt instinctively resists doing the same thing twice. He likes to try something fresh." What he had not done—what he had long hoped and dreamed of doing since at least the City of the Arts—was create an entire urban environment from scratch: a perfect city. Walt didn't particularly like cities—while riding in the train from the Chicago Railroad Fair in 1948, he commented to Ward Kimball that he couldn't understand why people lived in cities when they could live in open spaces—and he especially hated Los Angeles's urban sprawl. Imagineers said that when they were planning Tomorrowland, Walt would carry around books on city planning and mutter about traffic, noise, and neon signs, and he kept three volumes in his office to which he frequently referred: *Garden Cities of Tomorrow* by Sir Ebenezer Howard (originally published in 1902 and reissued in 1965), which promoted a vision of a more pastoral urban life; and *The Heart of Our Cities* and *Out of a Fair, a City*, both by an architect and mall designer named Victor Gruen, who urged the reconceptualization of the city as more ordered, rational, and humane. Walt's interest in city planning was so intense that the science fiction writer Ray Bradbury, who had met Walt in a department store during a Christmas shopping spree and become a friend, once approached him about running for mayor of Los Angeles. "Why should I run for mayor when I am already king?" Walt told him.

The appeal of Disney World to Walt—its only real appeal to him—was that he would finally have a chance to build a utopian city adjacent to the theme park as a place where employees of the park might live. For those who said Disney had no interest in addressing contemporary problems, only an interest in ignoring them, this was also his response to social ills, especially urban unrest. "Walt was intrigued with solving the problem of a central commercial area and a residential area co-existing and making the whole thing work for the moving of people and traffic in and out," said WED Imagineer Marvin Davis. Walt knew he couldn't solve all the problems himself no matter how extensive his planning, and he knew that he couldn't solve them all immediately. What he foresaw instead was an experimental community, one in which, Davis said, the "people living there could be a constant source of testing out materials and ideas and philosophies." He called it an Experimental Prototype Community of Tomorrow, or EPCOT, and as Marvin Davis said, "It was the real wienie" of Disney World.

Still, if it was an experiment, it was also to be a real community—a "living, breathing community," as Walt put it—with 20,000 residents by 1980, though at other times Walt pegged the population at 60,000 or even 100,000. "It will worry about pre-school education," he said, "home environment, employment." It would have a teen center in an effort to prevent delinquency, and a nearby facility for senior citizens. It would have recreational zones and areas for houses of worship. As for government, though Walt would never have surrendered his ultimate authority, he contemplated a bifurcated system in which the company controlled all the planning and building while other issues were determined by a democratic process. At another time he suggested that residents be rotated on "sabbaticals" so that no one would have permanent voting rights.* Indeed, so expansive and futuristic was his vision that in some ways it owed as much to his animations as to his park. "Walt expected things that people have been hoping for, twenty-five and thirty years in the future," Joe Fowler said. "He expected a house that would be completely self-sufficient, its own power plant, its own electricity, no garbage or trash collection, all

*This issue would prove to be sticky. Walt did not want to be subject to the whims of voters or local bureaucrats, and his attorneys had recommended that he get the Florida legislature to approve two or three municipalities in the Orlando area to create zoning, share in tax proceeds, adopt building codes, control liquor consumption, and regulate licenses. "The primary benefit derived by forming our own municipalities is control," attorney Richard Morrow wrote Walt bluntly. Walt didn't immediately warm to the idea, apparently because Universal head Jules Stein had warned him about the problems Stein had encountered with his own Universal City in California. But Walt finally agreed to—and the Florida legislature finally approved—a separate district for the park, which effectively removed the park from the control of Orlando voters and officials, but it left unresolved what would happen when EPCOT was inhabited. Memo, Richard T. Morrow to Walt, Re: Florida Municipalities, Nov. 24, 1965, M Folder, Walt Disney Corr., Inter-Office, 1965–1966, J-Reddy, A1654, WDA; Foster, pp. 160–61, 188–91.

automatically taken care of with pipes that belong to the place. . . . He expected transportation in all of its modern forms, without automobiles in the streets. He expected educational facilities that are twenty years ahead." Robert Moses, another monumentalist who appreciated the scale of Walt's ambition, called EPCOT "overwhelming" and predicted that it would be the "first accident free, noise free, pollution free city center in America."

Of course WED was not equipped to provide the technology by itself. Walt needed partners, just as he had needed them at Disneyland, but rather than look for corporate lessees who would help provide financing, as he had at Disneyland, for EPCOT he wanted intellectual capital. (This was no doubt one reason he had been so keen on forging corporate alliances for the world's fair.) Within months of the announcement he and his staff were visiting various companies again—GE, Westinghouse, RCA—to inquire about what they were working on and whether they might be interested in using EPCOT as their own laboratory to test new technologies, so that EPCOT would be a showcase for American knowhow as well as a showcase for Walt Disney's imagination.

Now with EPCOT he was back at WED, as he had been in the planning stages of Disneyland and before the world's fair. He asked his friend and neighbor, the distinguished architect Welton Becket, who was designing the Century City complex in Los Angeles at the time, to draw up a plan for EPCOT, but according to Marvin Davis, Walt was disappointed by Becket's presentation; Davis suspected Walt felt the buildings looked inhospitable to Walt, and so that was why, as he had done on Disneyland, Walt gave the assignment to his Imagineers. Davis said that Walt's original plans had been scribbled on the back of a paper breakfast napkin and that whenever Walt had a new idea, he would give Davis another napkin with a drawing. Sometimes the Imagineers, trying to divine Walt's intentions, would pluck the napkins from the garbage where Walt had tossed them.

As the plans took shape, Walt would visit the offices three or four times each week, usually rearranging the models on the layout, and when the EPCOT operation moved from its tiny warren at WED to a larger, high-ceilinged room that was dubbed the Florida Room, Walt would sit at the worktable, as one Imagineer remembered it, "sketching away with a big pencil while the rest of us were sitting around, ideas going back and forth, right and left." When they finished, they had devised a five-thousand-acre city arranged in a wheel three miles in diameter. (As with Mickey Mouse's body, the circle was the shape of comfort.) At the center was the fifty-acre downtown commercial hub; in some plans it was a fully enclosed air-conditioned complex with a thirty-story hotel, shops, markets, and theaters arranged into international zones. Radiating in concentric circles from the hub were a greenbelt park, high-density apartments, and low-density residential areas. Traffic and garbage collection were to be routed underground on an expressway, and public transportation, a monorail, was to run from the outlying circles to the inner ones, where residents would board "people movers" or small electric trains. An industrial park was to be situated nearby, connected by the monorail, and the entire city was to be serviced by a jet airport. And in the middle of it all, as Walt imagined it, would be Walt Disney himself. "I vividly remember sitting next to Walt on a plane when he pointed to the center of EPCOT, an oval-shaped area," Imagineer Bob Gurr later related. "Walt said, 'When this EPCOT gets up and running, and we have all the participants there, this spot with a little bench is where Lilly and I are going to sit and watch.' " But that restful moment would have to wait.

VI

If Hollywood used Walt Disney to defend itself against charges of depravity, so the protectors of American culture used him to defend the country against the charges of materialism, imperialism, racism, and hypocrisy that were now being leveled as civil rights protests escalated, military involvement in Southeast Asia intensified, and fissures in America's social fabric widened. Walt Disney was the living antidote to all of this turmoil, the embodiment for the country's cheerleaders of everything that was still right with the nation. He was a Horatio Alger hero whose life demonstrated social mobility. He was a naïve artist whose work demonstrated a Jamesian unpretentiousness and common sense. He was a visionary whose plans demonstrated the breadth of American imagination and the power of American will. And however he behaved privately at his studio, he was publicly a modest, affable, and decent man whose image demonstrated America's own decency and generosity of spirit.

Though he barely acknowledged the country's problems himself in public (save for periodic grumblings about Hollywood's moral decline), and though he had long since forsworn much interest in politics, even resigning his membership in the Motion Picture Alliance when, without consulting its members, it attacked the Writers Guild for rejecting a resolution barring writers who had not signed a loyalty oath, politicians still sought his support. Occasionally he gave it, actively soliciting donations for the Eisenhower campaign in 1956 and plastering a bumper sticker for the 1960 Republican presidential and vice-presidential candidates Richard Nixon and Henry Cabot Lodge on the little motorized cart he rode around the studio. (According to Ward Kimball, Walt tried to strong-arm employees into contributing to Nixon's campaign until Milt Kahl, himself an ardent Republican, objected.) He was involved in the presidential campaign of Barry Goldwater in 1964, meeting Goldwater at the Republican convention in San Francisco, donating over $16,000 to him, and offering him the use of the company planes. In thanking Diane for likewise supporting Goldwater, Walt compared it to "taking up the gun against the enemy."

As enthusiastically as he supported Goldwater, a self-professed conservative who opposed social security insurance, he was even more fervent about the candidacy of George Murphy, a former dancer and musical film star whom Walt had known for years. When Murphy first contemplated running for the U.S. Senate in 1964, he said he consulted Walt, who confidently predicted, "Talk to enough people and you'll win." After Murphy declared his candidacy, Walt not only donated generously, he loaned the Murphy campaign furniture for its headquarters, chaired a fund-raising dinner for him, took out full-page newspaper ads the last week of the campaign, and allowed his name to be used in a mass mailing. Even Lillian, a registered Democrat, joined a group called Democrats for George Murphy. Still, after Murphy won, Walt wasn't especially politicized. "I had my little fling at politics last year," he told a reporter late in 1965. "It's really not very interesting."

In effect, despite his Republicanism, Walt Disney belonged to everyone. When the Tournament of Roses was looking for a grand marshal for its January 1, 1966, parade, the first to be televised overseas, via the Telstar satellite, they asked Walt because, the organizers told studio executives, they felt he was "one person no country could find fault with." He was, *The New York Times* reported at the time, "revered and honored almost to the point of absurdity," though none of his honors may have been greater than the Presidential Medal of Freedom, the highest civilian award the nation can bestow. Walt received it from President Lyndon Johnson at the White House during the 1964 presidential campaign—Walt wore a Goldwater button under his lapel—and it was a measure of his status that among his fellow honorees that day were the poets T. S. Eliot and Carl Sandburg, the novelist John Steinbeck, the urban historian Lewis Mumford, the naval historian Samuel Eliot Morison, the artist Willem de Kooning, the composer Aaron Copland, the columnist Walter Lippmann, the journalist Edward R. Murrow, and Helen Keller. Walt Disney was in the pantheon.

But with the lionization came a backlash. Before the war Walt Disney had been considered a happy exception to the mass culture that many observers—including Dwight Macdonald, C. Wright Mills, and William Whyte—warned was threatening the nation's cultural health. Since the war some intellectuals had come to feel, as Vincent Scully did, that Walt had himself become a corporate vulgarian who coarsened the culture through commercialization and simplification. One authority on children's literature said she found "almost everything objectionable" in his rendition of fairy tales. He "takes a great masterpiece and telescopes it," she said, and "leaves nothing to the imagination of the child." After the success of Disneyland, however, a more profound critique emerged, in which Disneyland itself was the primary target. These detractors felt that Walt Disney had not perfected reality so much as glossed it; his synthetic world from which danger had been purged was a means of avoiding the issues now confronting the nation and of papering over its contradictions. Not only did Disneyland provide a fortress against reality, which, of course, had been Walt's intention; it also provided a model and even a sensibility for transforming reality that was becoming all-encompassing, meaning that Disney had impregnated himself into the American consciousness. As the French philosopher Jean Baudrillard would put it, "Disneyland is presented as imaginary in order to make us believe that the rest is real, when in fact all of Los Angeles and the America surrounding it are no longer real, but of the order of the hyperreal and of simulation." Disneyland had become a metaphor for America—an America that had increasingly opted for fantasy and, its critics believed, was paying a price for doing so. More than even the archetypal nation of the imagination that he had created in the 1950s, this was Walt Disney's America.

If Disneyland was a metaphor, so too was Walt Disney himself, his image no less synthetic than his theme park. Just as the postwar Walt Disney had become the personification of American corporate power, all the bonhomie, all the bromides, all the professions of anti-intellectualism and the hints of moralism, all the dramatic accounts of personal struggle, perseverance, and triumph, had converted Walt Disney into the very personification not just of sturdy American values but of something else: of a cultural and political conservatism that could countenance neither criticism nor change. Since the 1950s, America had seen what journalist Godfrey Hodgson called a "disappointment in expectations." Americans had enjoyed a postwar economic boom that raised wages and the standard of living, but these gains, Hodgson wrote, "seemed negated emotionally by a sense of loss and sense of threat," especially among the white middle class—Walt Disney's stock—"which had seen its relatively privileged status successively eroded by almost every social development of the past hundred years: by immigration, urbanization, the eclipse of Protestantism, inflation, depression and now by wartime boom and the high wages it brought to every other group." Put another way, the old nineteenth-century ideal of America was rapidly fading.

Walt Disney, as the representative of all that was good and decent about that old, endangered America, had long been a bulwark against the sense of loss and threat. But in the roiling America of the 1960s—politically unsettled by assassinations and urban riots, protest marches, and war, and aesthetically unsettled by the Beatles, graphic violence, and increasingly frank sexuality—the nation's favorite uncle turned into an anachronism: an emblem of conformity in a time of dissent. He knew it. Occasionally he even flashed resentment at it. During a photo shoot at his Disneyland apartment, Walt, according to the photographer, suddenly slouched in his chair, lifted a gin bottle, unzipped his pants fly, pulled out his shirttail, and said, "How's this for the cover of a gossip magazine?" But the photographer refused to take the picture, refused to compromise his subject. The image of Walt Disney was sacrosanct.

Yet the image of the stolid conformist was at variance with the content of the films—the *real* content. Though they were unmistakably conservative in their aesthetics—even juvenile, as critics claimed—when one bothered to examine them closely and did not just assume that as products of Uncle Walt Disney they were necessarily old-fashioned and empty, the movies were surprisingly modern in outlook and not quite as innocuous as even Walt had declared them to be. The rock-ribbed Republican who practically created the popular vision of nineteenth-century America, had, after all, also suspected authority and often questioned it, hated money and its acquisition, was wary of materialism, detested affectation, and came to believe fervently in internationalism; and all of these values had found their way into his movies and quite possibly into the mind-set of the generation who had been weaned on them. Moreover, ever the self-dramatist who drew on his own struggles, Walt had always identified closely with the outcasts and the marginalized rather than with the powerful, and this tendency found its way into his films too—*The Ugly Duckling*, *Ferdinand the Bull*, *Morris the Midget Moose*, *Lambert the Sheepish Lion*.

As one scholar reevaluated them forty years later, Disney's films actually often squarely contradicted the conservative values of the 1950s and 1960s. They promoted the ideas that life could be arduous and unhappy but that one had to soldier on nevertheless (as in *So Dear to My Heart* and *Old Yeller*) and that one often must painfully reconcile one's ideals with reality, even if Walt himself fought having to do so; that innocence is always in jeopardy in an increasingly materialistic world (as in *Peter Pan* and *Mary Poppins*); that while order is desirable, authority is often stifling and sometimes has to be disrespected (as in *Johnny Tremain*); that rebelliousness is a perfectly acceptable form of protest (as in *Robin Hood*, *Rob Roy*, and *Davy Crockett*, where the hero expressly disobeys orders); that class distinctions are not a natural product of Social Darwinism and that classes need to find common ground (as in *Cinderella*, *Lady and the Tramp*, and the Spin and Marty serial); that acceptance of others is a positive good (as in Davy Crockett's gospel of understanding the Indians); that public recognition is less important than personal fulfillment; and finally that individualism, as essential as it is, is best when it operates in the service of the community. Even *Pollyanna*, seemingly the most bathetic of Disney movies if one of the most moving, exposes not small-town virtues but small-town hypocrisy, attacks the forces of tradition and wealth, and makes a call for a progressive alliance to promote tolerance; and in a lesser-known film, *A Tiger Walks*, the Menckenian impulse is so strong that ordinary Americans are depicted as greedy and self-serving. In short, though Walt Disney was made to seem conservative—and made himself seem conservative because it fit the cultural ethos of the time—in his films, at least, he may have not been so very conservative after all, nor the barrier against the new America that he was often purported to be.

While Walt promoted community, quite possibly the most famous man in America may also have been among the loneliest. Age had made him no more social than he had been as a young man yoked to his studio. Dinner invitations to the studio almost always bore Walt's emphatic "NO!," in his red crayon, underlined, sometimes twice, and he was no more receptive to invitations to appear at public events, invariably begging off. Even with the girls gone he and Lillian seldom entertained, and old friends, like the Spracklings with whom they had traveled in the 1950s, faded from their lives. He had always found solace with his pets, and after Duchess died, he got himself another poodle named Lady, but Lady died too. At the studio, despite all the activity, he sometimes seemed bereft. Bill Peet recalled Walt slumping into his chair with a "mournful sigh" and announcing, "It gets lonely around here. I just want to talk to somebody," then beginning to relate the tale of his childhood travails and his father's cruelty. But when Peet began to talk about his own childhood miseries, Walt "jumped to his feet and said, 'Gotta get goin'!' " Marc Davis remembered seeing Walt sitting alone at the Tam O'Shanter restaurant one evening. Davis invited him to go to a movie with himself and his wife. "[A]nd he drew a curtain just like that and said, 'No, I'm going to stay at the studio.' " "He always had a certain reserve which he had for individuals," Davis said.

At the end of the day he would drink. Tommie Wilck, one of his two secretaries, would serve him his Scotch Mist with water—mainly water, she said. "He may have consumed a lot of liquid, but I don't think he really got much liquor." Still, studio veterans knew enough to schedule meetings with him in the morning or early afternoon. "[S]tarting at five o'clock every day, a lot of people would say, 'I've got to get to Walt before he uncorks the bottle because you really can't get the decision you want [afterward],' " Ward Kimball told an interviewer. Jack Kinney said that when he worked late at the studio, he would sometimes see Walt's car swerving out of the lot as he headed home. "That was quite a long way to go," Kinney would write, "but he always made it. He must have had someone watching over him." Of course when he got home, one of the first things he and Lillian did was have a cocktail, and at one point, when a doctor recommended that to lose weight Walt spend his Palm Springs weekends drinking rather than eating, he began drinking heavily.

If he didn't have many friends, he didn't have many recreations either. He enjoyed watching baseball, and for years he had had a season's box for the Hollywood Stars minor league team, eventually buying a share in the club. When a group of local notables organized to attempt to bring an American League team to Los Angeles, Walt joined the advisory board and even attended spring training games after the city was awarded the franchise, the Los Angeles Angels. But if he was a baseball fan, Walt also seemed to have an ulterior motive: he wanted to establish the team in Orange County near Disneyland, presumably as a way of helping his park.

His main diversion, now that he no longer had his train, was lawn bowling. He had joined the Beverly Hills Lawn Bowling Club and was a member of a small bowling club at Smoke Tree as well. He wasn't particularly good—Walt had never been good at sports—and when an eighty-year-old bowler beat him, Walt advised him not to let it "go to your head" since "[e]verybody beats me!" Still, Walt, who had a hand-tooled bowling bag, took the game seriously enough to arrange to send thirty bowlers from his Beverly Hills club to Smoke Tree for a tournament, and to fly with a group of friends to Buck Hill Falls in Pennsylvania to compete in the U.S. Doubles Tournament. He and Lillian, who, according to Diane, found the idea of bowling tournaments "silly," even discussed an Australian vacation with two fellow enthusiasts and their wives to coincide with the Australian Championship Lawn Bowling Tournament there. These lawn bowlers had become Walt Disney's closest friends.

To spend the restless energy that wasn't being exhausted by the studio, he still traveled, almost always accompanied by Lillian and always booking double beds—the annual summer trips to Europe, a cruise to Bora Bora, a Fourth of July spent in Sun Valley, a weekend in Baja for marlin fishing, a junket to Mexico City for People to People, a trip to Banff with Diane and the grandchildren. When the studio bought its planes—a Beechcraft Queen Air in January 1963 and the Gulfstream in March 1964—Walt began zipping around the country as he had zipped around Europe. As someone who had made a practice of detaching himself from reality and who had used even his trains less as a way of connecting places than of isolating himself from them, he liked the air. He had always wanted to learn to fly himself ("badly," Sharon said), but Roy discouraged it, apparently fearing that some tragedy might befall him. So instead he logged time in the jet—150 hours between August 1965 and August 1966 alone.

Many of those hours were spent being ferried from Burbank to Smoke Tree, where he had renovated his cottage and installed a swimming pool, largely to entertain his grandchildren, upon whom he lavished attention as he had once lavished attention upon his daughters. He was especially ecstatic when, in November 1961, Diane gave birth to a second son and named him after her father: Walter Elias Disney Miller. "I'm thrilled to have a male heir bearing my name," he wrote director Robert Stevenson, calling it the "BIG NEWS" and still complaining that she hadn't named her firstborn for him. Walt loved the children's company. He would have them out to Smoke Tree, or he would drive them to school and have them picked up afterward and taken to the studio where they played in his office, or he would drive them out to Disneyland to stay in his fire station apartment and have the run of the park. Usually they would spend one weekend a month at the Carolwood house. "We'd play on the lawn and around the great big pool," recalled Joanna Miller. "We'd stack up the patio furniture to make jets and rockets. And Grandpa would often be sitting there on the lawn, reading scripts, enjoying the glow of all the activity around him."

VII

It was almost as if Walt had a premonition. It wasn't only the talk of succession or the wistful reveries about what would happen to the company after he was gone. A sense of melancholy seemed to shroud him. He was reflective and increasingly pensive. On Fridays, at the end of the workweek, he would occasionally invite the Sherman brothers to his office and discourse about the future. Then inevitably he would wander to the window, stare into space, as he so often did now, and ask them to "play it!"—a command so familiar to the Shermans that they knew he meant "Feed the Birds" from *Mary Poppins*, about an old woman outside St. Paul's Cathedral who sells bags of crumbs to feed the birds there. Whether Walt related to the song because he related to the woman's loneliness, or whether in a life of grand gestures he appreciated her small one, or whether he recognized in her his own mortality, or whether the woman simply reminded him of his mother, he never said, and no one would ever know. But hearing the song, he would always cry.

Still, not so much sadness but busyness, a seeming need for constant activity, characterized him now. He was back in the tumult and glad of it. When Richard Schickel proposed to write a biography—"The guy just has a sincere desire to write the best book ever on Walt's contribution to the education, entertainment and the happiness of the world," one studio press representative told press head Joe Reddy after Schickel visited the studio—the studio and Walt both agreed; then, suddenly, Walt changed his mind and decided to table the project. "As far as I'm concerned I am just in the *middle* of my career," he wrote the editor who had suggested Schickel. "I have several years and several projects to go before my life story should be written. I don't want to be judged on just what I have accomplished up to now for I have many plans for tomorrow and I'm too involved with those future projects to take time to rehash the past." (Instead of the hagiography Schickel had promised, he wound up writing *The Disney Version*, a scathing attack on Disney.) To his niece's husband he said that he couldn't even leave the studio to accept an award out east, admitting, "I don't know how much time I have," and saying, "I need to stay here to do as much as I can to keep this enterprise twenty-five years ahead of the competition."

He was in a hurry, and he had so much to do. The studio produced five films a year—all of which Walt at least casually supervised and a few more than casually. He had actually outlined one, *Lt. Robin Crusoe, U.S.N.*, a comic updating of Daniel Defoe's novel about a man stranded on an island, on the back of an envelope or an air-sickness bag, then gave it to Bill Walsh and Don DaGradi to convert into a screenplay. When Walsh asked Walt if he wanted credit, Walt insisted he did. The original story was attributed to "Retlaw Yensid"—"Walter Disney" backward. He continued to host the television program, for which he would occasionally take trips to gather material, as he did on a visit to the U.S. Space and Rocket Center at Huntsville, Alabama, for another show on space travel. He worked on the Marceline Project, though Roy believed that not enough of the original Disney house remained there and that the town should set up a nonprofit corporation to which WDP would consider licensing Walt's name and providing the company's expertise. And he had the Mineral King ski resort project. Walt visited the site with Buzz Price, Card Walker, and Donn Tatum in August 1965, and that November he and a delegation flew to Washington and spoke to officials of the Agriculture Department for two and a half hours to try to convince them to issue a permit for a $35 million development in the Sequoia National Park. In December the U.S. Forest Service awarded him the permit, which granted the company three years to submit its plans to a review board for approval.

Though he had long since given up any supervisory control of Disneyland, Walt continued to visit the park once a month, usually when it was closed or when it was very crowded and he could race through the hordes to avoid autograph seekers. He still signed off on a new Monsanto-sponsored exhibit for Tomorrowland, approved a new Audio-Animatronic attraction called Pirates of the Caribbean, and oversaw the completion of a New Orleans Square that opened in July 1966 and of which the New Orleans mayor said, "It looks just like home." To which Walt riposted, "Well, I'd say it's a lot cleaner."

As for CalArts, Walt would regale his secretaries at the end of the workday with word paintings of what he intended to do there. But as with almost everything in Walt Disney's life, there was action behind the talk. In September 1965 WDP, at Walt's behest, gave the school thirty-eight acres of its backlot at Golden Oak for a new campus, and Roy was advising that the studio donate additional money for a detailed study and appraisal of the project, while the Disney Foundation, a charitable organization that Walt had formed, was to contribute another million dollars. "[W]ith that kind of a start we should be able to impress a lot of substantial people and get another five or seven-and-a-half million without too much difficulty," Roy wrote Walt. They did. The following April the federal government loaned the school $4 million. In the meantime Walt raised $2 million from private donors. It was a sign of how dedicated he was to CalArts that Walt, who could barely sit without wiggling, tapping, grimacing, and smoking, spent two hours listening to an opera by a friend of one of the major contributors.

Even as he was immersed in these projects, the animations remained an ever-vexing problem. He continued to feel that they drained resources that might better be devoted to other things, but he also felt obligated to produce them since they were so closely associated with the studio. Long before, he had streamlined the system, appointing one supervising director (Woolie Reitherman), one art director (Ken Anderson), four master animators (Frank Thomas, Ollie Johnston, Milt Kahl, and John Lounsbery), and one storyman (Bill Peet)—that is, one man who would write the screenplay, make the storyboards, and record the voices where, as Peet himself complained, more than forty men had once been assigned to these tasks. Walt also sought to streamline the physical process by putting the animators' drawings directly on the cel, without need of cleanup men or ink girls. Iwerks had been working fitfully on this concept, essentially Xerographing the pencil lines onto the cels, at least since *Fantasia*, and in the late 1950s he returned from a visit to the Xerox factory with a means of copying the lines onto a light-sensitive aluminum plate and from the plate to the cel.

The animators were generally ecstatic. For years they had had to see their lines thickened and smoothed by the inkers, who traced them. Now the drawings got onto the screen exactly as they had been on their animation boards. "It was the first time we ever saw our drawings on the screen, literally," Marc Davis said. "Before, they'd always been watered down." A film like *101 Dalmatians* could not have been made any other way; the inkers and painters would have had to draw each spot of each dog on each cel in which it appeared. But in eliminating the middleman and gaining speed and immediacy, something was also lost. Eric Larson thought the Xerography "spoils the beauty of the design of the character" because the consistency and the sinuousness of the lines were gone. Instead one got much sharper, rougher, more angular lines, like those drawn by a pencil rather than a paintbrush, and a more vivid sense of the animator's hand, which pointed the animation back toward the less realistic self-reflexiveness from which Walt Disney had turned it so many, many years before. The effect was to put the animators in charge—and to put their visions, not Walt's, on the screen.

To the extent that Walt cared, he was not impressed by the visual style, but he didn't care very much. After *Dalmatians*, as Marc Davis told it, the business side of the studio was so adamantly opposed to doing another animated feature that Walt once again was ready to yield and drop animation altogether. "Then he had second thoughts," Davis said. "He felt the guys knew how to make these films and that he owed it to them to continue." Still, after the *Sleeping Beauty* debacle, the studio had slashed the budgets, and after *Dalmatians* it slashed them yet again; *The Sword in the Stone* was budgeted at 40 percent less than *Dalmatians*, which, Ken Peterson wrote Walt, would "require drastic steps in our production procedure, in order to make it possible." Meanwhile Walt further retreated, leaving the animators to bicker among themselves, their old esprit almost entirely gone, and he intervened only when they begged him to do so to resolve some thorny issue. As Milt Kahl put it, "He was interested in a picture until he had all the problems solved and then he just lost interest."

As the staff worked that spring of 1966 on *The Jungle Book*, adapted from Rudyard Kipling's stories about a boy who grows up among animals in the wild, the problems kept mounting. Reitherman importuned Walt for a meeting—"It would take about ½ hour," he memoed Walt plaintively—and Walt complied but was not happy with what he saw. The stories were episodic rather than cumulative; they lacked a spine. He thought that the audience would not identify with the boy, Mowgli, and that the film's tone was too sober. He was afraid that the villain, a tiger named Shere Khan, would be a cliché. Yet despite his preoccupation with other projects and his lack of interest in this one, he quickly salvaged the production, as he had done so many times in the past, by suggesting that singer Phil Harris, known for his loose, boozy, throwaway style, voice a bear named Baloo who befriends Mowgli. "When Walt heard Phil's test track he loved it," Frank Thomas and Ollie Johnston would later write, "even to the point of starting to act out how the bear would first come dancing into Mowgli's scene." The bear, who had been intended as a minor figure, became the film's costar, converting the picture from a series of disconnected adventures into the story of a boy and his hedonistic mentor—a jungle Hal and Falstaff.

Finally, while he was engaged with the animation and television and Mineral King and CalArts, he also had EPCOT, the center around which all these other projects swirled, and now the overriding passion in his life. Walt spent the better part of the spring of 1966 on reconnaissance missions for his futuristic city, first visiting the Monsanto offices in St. Louis to discuss what that company might contribute to EPCOT and then boarding the Gulfstream for a long tour that took him to a Gruen-designed six-acre mall in Rochester, New York, which boasted three levels of underground parking; another shopping mall in Philadelphia; the new Nieman-Marcus department store in Dallas; a Westinghouse trash-disposal project in Tampa that recycled the garbage; and the model city of Reston, Virginia, a fully planned community. He also made a detour to the Disney World site. "I'm making this trip with some of my staff in order to do some checking on the latest developments in housing and shopping centers around the country," he wrote a friend. "We need to know what is good and what is bad about some of the so-called modern concepts so we can take advantage of that in our Florida project." It was a joyous spasm of activity, and he said to Harrison Price that between Mineral King and Disney World, he now had "enough work to keep my organization busy for forty years!" That seemed to be the point—to keep the company going.

But despite the surge in work and the pleasure it clearly gave him, he was not feeling well. For years he had suffered with various ailments, nagging ailments that chipped away at his health. He had kidney stones. His teeth ached, sending shafts of pain up his face so that his entire head throbbed and forcing him at night to apply hot compresses to relieve the agony. He had a sore elbow, for which he had received injections and X-ray therapy. He had a chronic sinus condition that required a weekly visit to the doctor. He always seemed to be fighting a cold and at least twice was diagnosed with walking pneumonia. And he waged a losing battle against weight gain, so that where once he had been lean and hatchet-faced, then fleshy, as he passed sixty he became paunchy. Embarking on one diet, he wrote Hayley Mills, "I am in the process of losing my big, fat stomach."

Most of all, he still ached from that old polo injury he had suffered in the 1930s, when he had taken a spill from his horse; the cracked vertebra in his neck had calcified over the years, pinching his nerves and causing him excruciating pain. On an overnight trip with him, Peter Ellenshaw recalled that Walt lay awake all night in pain, rising frequently to go to the washbasin to apply compresses to his neck. By early 1966 the calcification had advanced, and Walt had begun dragging his right leg and occasionally listing as he walked. Even his secretary admitted "it got so bad that there were times when you'd have sworn he had been drinking, but he never drank during the day," meaning the workday. "He constantly complained of this bad hip," Marc Davis said, calling himself "gimpy" and talking of being "pooped." He would ride his golf cart around the studio now, and at the end of the day he would retreat to Hazel George's office to receive his traction and infrared treatments while he sipped his scotch through a straw. Concerned by how much alcohol he seemed to be consuming, George told him that he was in danger of becoming a "lush" and asked him what Lillian thought of his coming home with liquor on his breath. Walt told her that he kept out of Lillian's breathing space, but he defended himself. "My nerves are all shot to hell," he told George, "and nowadays the fuckin' pain here is driving me nuts!" When George asked him if the treatments were not working, Walt confessed that he came for the liquor.

Ward Kimball thought that after all the years of constant pressure and constant activity, Walt had finally broken down. "Here is the same man who had just built the park, then been in on every phase, who was sitting in his office okaying and reading scripts far into the night, going to people's rooms and looking over their story work, making decisions on films, making decisions on [the] corporate level, laying out the new Florida complex, plus the decisions on the Lake Buena Vista EPCOT city of tomorrow, making personal appearances, greeting visitors, going down on sets, choosing," Kimball told an interviewer. "[H]e wouldn't admit that, physically and mentally, he couldn't handle this . . . his body just gave up." Another coworker, watching him late one night at the studio, observed how much Walt had been forced to surrender to age and infirmity, even as he fought them. "His proud head dropped forward on his chest," the man wrote. "His usually squared shoulders lowered until they became round. Thinking no one else was around, he dropped all pretense of youth. He seemed to age 20 years right before my eyes." Cameramen on *Wonderful World of Color* began using diffusion filters to hide Walt's wrinkles, though Walt objected that the filters made him look out of focus.

He had always been terrified of death, terrified of the very idea of mortality. "Whenever Father gets depressed, he discusses his impending demise," Diane wrote in her biography of him, asserting that "he never goes to a funeral if he can help it"—he didn't even attend his brother Herbert's—and that if he does go to one, "he plunges into a reverie which lasts for hours after he's home." When he attended the funeral of onetime studio artist Charlie Philipi, Herb Ryman recalled that Walt kept drumming his fingers and rubbing his hands nervously during the service and that when he got back to the studio, he was irritable, yelling at Marc Davis and Milt Kahl to "get the hell back to work." He hated even the mention of death. When Harrison Price joked about death statistics, Walt gave him a "fierce reaming out." "[D]eath is not an acceptable topic," Herb Ryman warned Price. Still, as he did with most aspects of reality, Walt used wish fulfillment to deny death. He had once boasted to his aunt Jessie that "[l]ongevity seems to run with the Disneys—on both sides of the family, I would say," and he seemed comforted by the fact that his father had lived into his eighties and his uncle Robert, who had died in 1953, well into his nineties, and that his mother's sisters had lived long lives as well.

With mortality increasingly on his mind, he seemed to receive a reprieve that winter when he went in for a checkup at UCLA and was pronounced "normal for my age," as he wrote Hayley Mills. "However after my annual check-up a couple of weeks ago I decided to leave tonight for an extended stay in the desert where I'm going to relax and read the trunkful of scripts which I should have read months ago and will finally have a chance to catch up on." His mood brightened, and he seemed not only relieved but rejuvenated. By the spring he was making his eastern swing for EPCOT. In June he visited Mineral King and attended the premiere of *Lt. Robin Crusoe* on the aircraft carrier USS *Kitty Hawk* anchored off San

Diego, where he was permitted to sit in the cockpit while a plane took off and landed on the deck. "Just about the most interesting and exciting two days in my whole life," he wrote the captain in charge. And in July he, Lillian, Diane, Sharon, and their families—Sharon had given birth to a girl six months earlier—flew to Vancouver for a two-week cruise on a 140-foot yacht with two sixteen-foot fishing boats and a crew of eight, ostensibly to celebrate Walt and Lillian's forty-first wedding anniversary but primarily to bring the family together. "It's something I've always wanted to do," Walt wrote one of the studio's bankers, "and it's the first time everything has worked out so that we could all go." "We are just going to cruise in and out of the inlets," he explained in another letter to a former secretary, "drop anchor and explore and fish." Diane admitted that the families were "at each other's throats sometimes" and that she and her mother had their quarrels, but her father served as "peacemaker." "He was becoming so much more serene," she would recall. He would often sit alone, quietly, on the top deck with his scripts or a book on city planning, wearing a captain's hat and an ascot, while the wind whipped around him.

The serenity didn't last. Several weeks after returning from Vancouver, Walt and Lillian flew to Reno on personal business and several weeks after that to Denver. In September, back at the studio, he suddenly began pressuring the staff to prepare a film that would explain EPCOT and attract corporate partners. He watched the "rushes" of *The Jungle Book*, arguing angrily with Milt Kahl over whether a tiger could climb a tree, and left the meeting, according to one account, remarking ruefully, "I don't know, fellows, I guess I'm getting too old for animation," even as he was charging Harry Tytle with finding how the studio might further lower its animation costs. That same month he held a press conference with California governor Edmund Brown to announce plans on Mineral King.

Yet, even as he was aggressively laying out his agenda for the company, he was also considering something new, something that seemed to belie his outward confidence and underscore just how exhausted he was. Under cover of attending a ceremony to receive an award from an exhibitors' group, he, Roy, and Donn Tatum flew to New York on October 3, 1966, for an all-day conference with General Electric to discuss what was vaguely called a "relationship" between the two companies, though what they really seemed to have in mind was a merger. "How would the relationship of GE and WDP work?" an internal white paper at the studio asked. "Structure: if other than subsidiary, why? Lines of authority. How will GE use WDP—continue in entertainment business? Future financing for WDP projects." It also contained an analysis of how a merger might affect EPCOT, though protecting EPCOT from the business side of his own studio, which was less than enthusiastic about it, may have been the reason that Walt approached GE in the first place. "ESSENTIAL THAT ALL DISCUSSIONS ARE TO BE KEPT CONFIDENTIAL" was emblazoned at the top of the agenda.

The discussions did not seem to lessen Walt's enthusiasm for his projects. He returned to the studio for more consultations on EPCOT and to shoot the EPCOT film, rehearsing his presentation before the actor Walter Pidgeon, Art Linkletter, and the architect Welton Becket. But if he had been hoping to fend off pain by continuing to push ahead, he failed. Though his hair had obviously been darkened, he looked old and weary, and during the filming he was so fatigued that he had to be administered oxygen. "You could just see him sag," said one member of the crew. Still, at the end of October, after the film was completed, he was flying back east yet again to visit Charleston, Newport News, and Williamsburg with Lillian, Sharon, and Sharon's husband to gather material for Disney World.

As much as Walt may have wanted to deny it, he was clearly ailing. Before the eastern trip his neck and his leg had been bothering him so much that, at the suggestion of his doctor, he finally and reluctantly agreed to see a specialist who, in turn, recommended an operation to relieve the pressure on the nerves. The procedure was scheduled for November 11 at the UCLA Medical Center and was considered routine. Roy headed off for a vacation, scheduling his return just before Walt's " 'D' date," as he called it, and writing him, "I will be thinking and praying that you get everything out of that operation that you hope for." The studio prepared a press release nearly two weeks in advance with the assurance that he would be released within ten to fourteen days.

Walt, while no hypochondriac, was nevertheless distrustful of doctors and was concerned. He had shortness of breath, and the excess weight, with which he had been struggling for years, suddenly began melting away, so that now he looked emaciated and ill. He must have known that his employees were commenting on his appearance—commenting on whether he was seriously ill. Writer Jack Spiers was standing uncomfortably with Walt in an elevator the week before Walt's hospitalization when their eyes locked. Walt was wearing a bright yellow cardigan, a reminder of wardrobes past. Spiers joked that he would like to wrestle Walt for the sweater, and the two made small talk before exiting. Then, just as Spiers stepped into his office, he heard Walt's voice booming from down the hall, calling him. "When I get out of the hospital," Walt said when Spiers reentered the hallway, "I *will* wrestle you for the sweater." At roughly the same time Peter Ellenshaw saw Walt and expressed alarm about the impending operation. "I'm not going over there to die," Walt told him evenly. "There's no problem."

But there *was* a problem, and Walt must have suspected it. In doing a diagnostic workup prior to the surgery, the doctors had discovered spots on Walt's left lung and immediately ordered him into St. Joseph's Hospital, directly across the street from the studio, for surgery. Lillian, who phoned Diane nearly every day, was at her kitchen door the next morning. "They took an x-ray of your father's lung," she told her daughter, "and they found a lump the size of a walnut." The official press release said that Walt was in the hospital to undergo tests and to be treated for the polo injury. The truth was that Walt almost certainly had lung cancer.

He had smoked for years, since his days with the Red Cross in France, chain-smoking, nervously smoking, his fingers stained from the nicotine, his voice raw and hoarse, and almost every conversation was punctuated frequently by his throat-clearing. "I just can't picture him without a cigarette," Diane would recall. His hacking cough was dreaded not only among his employees, who had long regarded it as a kind of klaxon of Walt's impending arrival, but among his own family. Sharon had once asked him not to attend a school play she was acting in because she said if she heard him cough, she would forget her lines. Lillian said that Walt had "burned more furniture and more rugs and more everything with his cigarettes than anybody I ever knew," and Diane claimed that one could always identify Walt's butts in an ashtray because he would smoke the cigarettes down to the last quarter-inch, until he could barely hold them. "He would forget to put them out," she said. "He would light them and get carried away with what he was thinking about and just hold them. Sometimes he would hold them in his mouth or in his hand and get an ash on it two inches long."

He was often encouraged to quit. At one point he switched to a pipe, which he had smoked as a young man; then when the pipe burned a hole in his pocket, he summarily decided that pipe smokers were, as Joe Grant remembered it, "too slow" and "laid back," and he abandoned the pipe. Early in 1957, when Gunther Lessing celebrated his first anniversary of not having had a cigarette, Lessing made a point of telling Walt, but Walt wasn't interested. When doctors came to the studio to lecture the staff on the hazards of smoking, Walt wouldn't attend. One Christmas, Diane bought him two cartons of filtered cigarettes, thinking they would at least be better for him than the filterless ones he smoked, and Walt promised her he would use them. He just broke off the filters. "I didn't tell her *how* I would use them," he joked to a confederate. During one of his last meetings with him, Ward Kimball remembered Walt breaking into a long coughing jag. "When I timidly asked why he didn't give up smoking," Kimball said, "Walt looked up at me, his face still red from the coughing, and rasped, 'Well, I gotta have a few vices, don't I?' " By this time Walt was smoking Gitanes imported from France.

Now, after nearly a half-century of smoking, he was undergoing surgery that just a few days earlier was thought to be relatively routine. Though Walt had typically been outwardly confident, even at times ebullient, he knew his condition was serious. The day before the operation, a Sunday, he drove the short distance from Diane's recently vacated house in Encino—where he and Lillian were staying while the Carolwood house was undergoing renovation—to Diane's new house in Encino for a visit. At the end he got into his car, drove down the driveway to the bottom of a swell, and stopped; he sat there for some time in the car, alone, watching his grandson Christopher play ball with Ron, then finally drove off. He knew. When the doctor emerged from surgery the next day, he told the family gathered there that it was as he had suspected and feared: Walt had a malignant tumor that had metastasized. The doctor gave him six months to two years to live. Lillian, Diane said, was in denial. Roy too was benumbed, exploding when he said that Walt had a carcinoma and his daughter-in-law "corrected" him and said he had "cancer."

Walt remained in the hospital for cobalt treatments and attempted to conduct business. He asked a writer named Spec McClure to do a complete review of the studio's story selection process and then report on "what the elements essential to a successful Disney film might be," as if the staff might be able to manufacture one by specifications should Walt no longer be there. Marty Sklar and Marc Davis completed a Preliminary Master Photoplan for EPCOT, and Bill Anderson was advising him on cuts for an upcoming live-action feature, *The Happiest Millionaire*, which was running nearly three hours long, while Card Walker prepared next year's release schedule. Harry Tytle said that he had come to the hospital to discuss several projects when the doctor appeared and notified Walt that they thought they had removed all of the cancerous lesion on his lung and that with a little rest he would be "good as new." But this, Tytle soon learned, was a ruse to keep Walt's spirits from dipping.

Walt never mentioned the cancer, though he carried with him a telegram from the actor John Wayne, another lung cancer victim, saying, "Welcome to the club." No one at the studio knew. "Several papers carry story of Walt falling off horse playing polo, in hospital with neck injury," wrote one anxious employee to another. "Would appreciate confirmation that it is not serious." Not even all the members of Walt's own family knew what had happened. Ruth and Ray both learned of the surgery through the newspapers, though one of Roy's secretaries assured them, "He's going to be okay." The official press release reported that a lesion had been found on his left lung, which had caused an abscess, and a portion of the lung was removed. It made no mention of a malignancy.

By this time, Walt, weak but restless, demanded that Tommie Wilck, who had been delivering his mail each day, check him out of the hospital and get him back to the studio. He arrived there on November 21, the very day he was discharged, for what everyone on the staff seemed to realize might be a valedictory, though Walt was having none of it. After everyone he met greeted him with big, plastered smiles, he bristled, "You'd think I was going to die or something." Ben Sharpsteen, who happened to be visiting the studio that day, met Walt in his office and was struck by how gaunt and ashen he looked, but when they reconvened later in the Coral Room for lunch, Walt expatiated about his plans, and Sharpsteen noted that "he was gaining strength and feeling like his old self again."

Imagineer John Hench noticed the same transformation when, after lunch, Walt asked to visit WED in Glendale and discuss the future. "[H]is voice took on enthusiasm and deepened," Hench remembered. Walt spent twenty minutes in Marc Davis's office viewing sketches for a bear band that Davis was designing for Mineral King, and he "laughed like hell," Davis said. Afterward Davis showed him a mock-up for a moon trip ride, and then Walt turned to Dick Irvine and asked to be driven back to the studio. As he was walking down the hallway, he turned to Davis and said, "Goodbye, Marc," which hit Davis like a blow. "He never said goodbye. It was always 'See ya later.' "

At Burbank, Walt ran into producer Winston Hibler, who, like everyone else, was struck by how pale and frail he looked but who also saw him gain vitality as he talked of his plans. "I had a scare, Hib," he said. "I'm okay, but I may be off my feet for a while. Now, I'm gonna be getting over this and I want to get into Florida. You guys gotta carry some of this load here. But if you get a real problem and you get stuck or something, why, I'm here." He spent most of the rest of the afternoon watching a rough cut of *The Happiest Millionaire* and wept throughout. Then, without returning to the office, he asked to be driven home. He had tried to reassure everyone that he would be coming back, that there was still so much more for him to do. But the sense of gloom was inescapable. Bill Walsh, whom Walt had seen that day on the set of *Blackbeard's Ghost*, knew Walt wouldn't be returning. "We decided he was doomed," Walsh said. Walt almost certainly knew it too. Visiting Hazel George, he sputtered, "There's something I want to tell you," but he couldn't find the words, and they wound up collapsing into each other's arms. Ward Kimball, seeing

Walt at a distance that day, observed, "He looked defeated for the first time."

Even so, the pretense of recovery continued. Roy and Edna, who were in England when Walt was discharged, wrote him and Lilly a chipper postcard: "Just heard that Walt was better and had lunch at the studio. Congratulations. Happy Day. News we like to hear." Two days after his studio visit Walt himself wrote a former secretary, "As far as my problem is concerned, it's all over with and taken care of. I've been released from the hospital and am well on the road to recovery," adding that "I've been given a clean bill of health and have even put in a few hours in the office just to be sure my girls here don't get rusty." He spent the next three days at Diane's home because his own house was still being renovated, and the family celebrated Thanksgiving there, watching movies Ron had taken of the Vancouver trip. The next day, Friday, November 25, he flew with Lillian to Palm Springs aboard the Gulfstream, planning to read scripts and recuperate at Smoke Tree. On Wednesday he was so wracked with pain that he had to be flown back to Burbank. He was driven directly from the airport to St. Joseph's Hospital.

Lillian still clung to the hope that Walt would recover. She believed that Walt did too, though whether he was trying to buck up her spirits or his own was impossible to determine. They had even planned a trip after he regained his strength. "I don't think he accepted it," Ward Kimball said, "knowing Walt, not until he closed his eyes for the last time was he ever convinced." As he lay in the hospital, he told Ron Miller that he felt Miller and the current executives could handle the studio in the future. Walt himself would still read the scripts and serve as the final authority, but when he recovered, he would be devoting most of his time to Disney World and especially EPCOT. And, no doubt thinking of EPCOT, he told Miller that if he could live for another fifteen years, he would surpass everything else he had done.

But even as he spoke confidently of the things he intended to do once he was released, he was also putting his affairs in order. With the announcement of Disney World, Walt had sold WED to Walt Disney Productions and formed a new company, Retlaw, to handle his personal business—primarily the rights to his name and the receipts from the trains at Disneyland. It was a measure of the value of these assets that the previous year Retlaw had received $3.75 million from WDP. Walt also held just under 26,000 shares of WDP himself and 250,000 jointly with Lillian, which, with Lillian's own 28,000 shares, amounted to 14 percent of the company, worth just under $20 million. (WDP's fiscal year had ended with a $12 million profit.) Walt had drafted a will that March leaving 45 percent of his estate to Lillian and the girls in a family trust, another 45 percent to the Disney Foundation in a charitable trust, of which 95 percent was dedicated to CalArts, and the last 10 percent to a trust to be divided among Walt's sister and his nieces and nephews. But he was concerned about what he saw as his daughters' profligacy, and while he was in the hospital he sold ten thousand shares to settle their debts. "The last thing he said to me was, 'Gee, I'm glad that deal went through,' " Roy told an interviewer. "That was worrying him. The children kept coming and coming, houses had to be bigger, expenses piled up. So Diane was always in debt. He got her out before he died."

He celebrated his sixty-fifth birthday on December 5 in the hospital. Roy wired him from New York about the grosses at Radio City Music Hall for *Follow Me, Boys!* and closed, "Hope this finds you feeling better. This is your day and Edna and I send our love not only for today but always." But he wasn't feeling better—he was flagging. On his instructions no one was allowed to visit him, save the family, who had taken a room next to his. When Peter Ellenshaw asked to see Walt and was refused, he painted him a desert scene with a smoke tree, which Walt hung in the hospital room, telling the nurses, "See that? One of my boys painted that for me."

Even as his condition continued to worsen, the family wouldn't accept that he would succumb. On December 14 Diane went Christmas shopping, buying him fleece slippers because he complained that his feet were always cold in the hospital. "Somehow that would make him *not* die," she later said. That evening Lillian phoned her to say that Walt had seemed improved that day. When he put his arms around her to kiss her goodbye, she said, she could feel his strength. "I know he's going to get better," she told Diane. Roy visited that night, and the two brothers talked for hours as Walt traced his EPCOT plans with his fingers, using the ceiling tiles as a grid. Sharon's husband, Bob Brown, had also visited and told Lillian that Walt did indeed look as if he had rallied.

The next morning Lillian and Diane got a call from Tommie Wilck that Walt had taken a turn for the worse. Diane drove to the old Encino house to pick up her mother, but Lillian was still dressing, putting on her earrings with great deliberation and staving off the hospital visit, and Diane recalled that everything seemed to be occurring now in slow motion, as if she might be able to arrest time and delay the inevitable. When they arrived at the hospital and got off the elevator, Diane saw her husband enter her father's room, then suddenly back out as if someone had shoved him. In fact he was recoiling from the shock of seeing his father-in-law's lifeless body. Inside, Walt's hands were folded on his chest. "Uncle Roy was standing at the foot of his bed, massaging one of Dad's feet,"

Diane later recalled. "Just kind of caressing it. And he was talking to him. It sounded something like, 'Well, kid, this is the end I guess.' " Sharon and Bob Brown arrived shortly afterward, and Brown asked Diane if she would accompany Sharon into the room. Diane took Sharon's hand and placed it on Walt's. "Now Daddy, now you won't hurt anymore," Sharon whispered. Walt had died at 9:35 a.m. on December 15 of "Cardiac arrest due to Bronchogenic ca[rcinoma]." "I took care of Walt in his final days," a nurse wrote the family, "and just want you to know that the poor man was so fearful."

Word trickled back to the studio across the street, even before the announcement was made to each department over the public address system. The studio was to close and everyone was to be sent home, but most, stunned, couldn't leave, preferring to stay and talk to one another for consolation. Many couldn't talk. Many wept. Many, in utter disbelief, went to Hazel George seeking confirmation or, more hopefully, refutation. "I knew that he was very sick," said Lucille Martin, one of his secretaries, "but I had such faith that they would fly in some super doctor and save him."

"The death of Walt Disney is a loss to all the people of the world," Roy said in a statement issued by the studio. "There is no way to replace Walt Disney. He was an extraordinary man. Perhaps there will never be another like him." But, Roy promised, "We will continue to operate Walt's company in the way that he had established and guided it. All of the plans for the future that Walt had begun will continue to move ahead." This was not entirely to happen. Just before entering the hospital for his operation, Walt, clearly feeling the press of time, had scolded General Potter and Marvin Davis for not expediting EPCOT. "Why are you dragging your feet?" he asked them. "Is it because of the money? Have you been talking to Roy? Roy thinks EPCOT is a loser, but don't take any notice of him. Disney World will make all the profits we need for this operation." He had come to fear that EPCOT would not be built if anything happened to him, and he had cried to Hazel George over what his legacy would be if it weren't. "Fancy being remembered around the world for the invention of a mouse!" he lamented. A few months after Walt's death Marvin Davis presented the Imagineers' EPCOT plans to Roy. "Marvin, Walt's dead," Roy said.* And so was EPCOT.

The nation mourned him. "All of it, everything Walt Disney put his hand to, conjures up a sense of innocent, skipping gaiety and childlike curiosity; his achievements epitomize what is called 'good, clean, Ameri-

*When EPCOT finally was erected at Walt Disney World Resort, it was a permanent international fair, not the city of tomorrow that Walt had visualized. Mineral King would expire too, in part because of environmentalists' objections but mainly because Walt wasn't there to guide it.

can fun' that need be neither dull nor dour," *The New York Times* editorialized. "That is what Walt Disney gave to us and the world, and it is all summed up in that friendly engaging mouse named Mickey. It was not a small bequest." The *Los Angeles Times* eulogized him as an "Aesop with a magic brush, [Hans Christian] Andersen with a color camera, Barrie, Carroll, Grahame, Prokofieff, Harris—with a genius touch that brought to life the creations they had invented." "One wonders how a greater legacy will ever be accumulated by one person," it closed. Citing the throngs still going through Disneyland and lining up outside the Radio City Music Hall to see *Follow Me, Boys!*, *Time* in a full-page obituary opined that "Disney was dead, but not his vision of innocence, not the dreams he made." In Los Angeles county supervisors ordered flags to be flown at half-staff.

He had changed the world. He had created a new art form and then produced several indisputable classics within it—films that, even when they had not found an audience or been profitable on first release, had, as Walt predicted, become profitable upon reissue. He had provided escape from the Depression, strength during war, and reassurance afterward, and he had shown generations of children how to accept responsibility while at the same time allowing them to vent vicariously their antagonisms toward the adult world they would soon enter. He had refined traditional values and sharpened American myths and archetypes, even if, as his detractors said, he may have also gutted them. And from another vantage point, he had reinforced American iconoclasm, communitarianism, and tolerance and helped mold a countercultural generation. He had advanced color films and then color television. He had reimagined the amusement park, and in doing so he had altered American consciousness, for better or worse, so that his countrymen would prefer wish fulfillment to reality, the faux to the authentic. He had encouraged and popularized conservation, space exploration, atomic energy, urban planning, and a deeper historical awareness. He had built one of the most powerful empires in the entertainment world—one that would, despite his fears, long survive him. And because his films were so popular overseas, he had helped establish American popular culture as the dominant culture in the world. He had founded a school of the arts, and nearly forty years after his death his name would adorn a concert hall in downtown Los Angeles financed largely with Disney family money. Yet all of these accumulated contributions paled before a larger one: he demonstrated how one could assert one's will on the world at the very time when everything seemed to be growing beyond control and beyond comprehension. In sum, Walt Disney had been not so much a master of fun or irreverence or innocence or even wholesomeness. He had been a master of order.

The master of order had been so terrified of death that he hadn't left instructions for his interment. He had told Lillian only that he wanted to be cremated and that he wanted the ceremony to be small and private because he desperately wanted to avoid the undignified public displays he had seen at other celebrity funerals. It was his sons-in-law who chose the Little Church of the Flowers at Forest Lawn in Glendale for the funeral service, which was held at five o'clock the day after his death. Only the family attended, and even then Ruth didn't appear for fear that she might be hounded by the media on her way from Portland to California. At Lillian's request the Episcopal minister from Diane's church in Encino officiated. Bob Brown had suggested that "Battle Hymn of the Republic," which Walt had loved, be played at the close of the service, and as the song concluded Lillian slowly made her way to the front of the church where the coffin was, placed her hands on it and keened, "I loved you so much. I loved you so much." No one spoke publicly about the funeral afterward.

For nearly a year after the cremation, Walt Disney's ashes remained at Forest Lawn uninterred, the family resisting making a decision on a final resting place. It was only after Bob Brown, Sharon's husband, was suddenly felled by cancer less than a year after Walt's death that Sharon, having decided her father and her husband should be interred together, moved to take action on burying her father's ashes. She and Diane chose an inconspicuous plot outside the Freedom Mausoleum at Forest Lawn, dedicated as a "sacred memorial to the freedom bequeathed to us through the courage, the wisdom and the faith of our forefathers," located at a remote corner of the three-hundred-acre cemetery where their father, resting with Bob Brown, would not be alone in death as he had so often been alone in life.

A plain, rectangular bronze plaque now adorns the white brick wall of the mausoleum that encloses a small garden to mark the burial place of his ashes. It bears only the name "Walter Elias Disney." It was here, guarded by a hedge of orange olivias and red azaleas, and hidden behind a holly tree and behind a white statue of Hans Christian Andersen's Little Mermaid gazing contemplatively at invisible water, that Walt Disney seemed to have fulfilled his family's destiny. He had escaped. And it was here that he fulfilled his own destiny, too, for which he had striven so mightily and restlessly all his life. He had passed beyond the afflictions of this world. Walt Disney had at last attained perfection.

APPENDIX

FEATURE-LENGTH PICTURES PRODUCED BY WALT DISNEY

A = ANIMATION
LA = LIVE ACTION
C = COMBINATION ANIMATION AND LIVE ACTION
TL = TRUE LIFE ADVENTURE
TLF = TRUE LIFE FANTASY (DOCUMENTARY FOOTAGE IN A FICTIONAL FRAMEWORK)

1. 1937 *Snow White and the Seven Dwarfs* (A)
2. 1940 *Pinocchio* (A)
3. 1940 *Fantasia* (A)
4. 1941 *The Reluctant Dragon* (C)
5. 1941 *Dumbo* (A)
6. 1942 *Bambi* (A)
7. 1943 *Saludos Amigos* (C)
8. 1943 *Victory Through Air Power* (C)
9. 1945 *The Three Caballeros* (C)
10. 1946 *Make Mine Music* (A)
11. 1946 *Song of the South* (C)
12. 1947 *Fun and Fancy Free* (A)
13. 1948 *Melody Time* (A)
14. 1949 *So Dear to My Heart* (C)
15. 1949 *The Adventures of Ichabod and Mr. Toad* (A)
16. 1950 *Cinderella* (A)
17. 1950 *Treasure Island* (LA)
18. 1951 *Alice in Wonderland* (A)
19. 1952 *The Story of Robin Hood and His Merrie Men* (LA)
20. 1953 *Peter Pan* (A)

21. 1953 *The Sword and the Rose* (LA)
22. 1953 *The Living Desert* (TL)
23. 1954 *Rob Roy—The Highland Rogue* (LA)
24. 1954 *The Vanishing Prairie* (TL)
25. 1954 *20,000 Leagues Under the Sea* (LA)
26. 1955 *Davy Crockett, King of the Wild Frontier* (LA)
27. 1955 *Lady and the Tramp* (A)
28. 1955 *The African Lion* (TL)
29. 1955 *The Littlest Outlaw* (LA)
30. 1956 *The Great Locomotive Chase* (LA)
31. 1956 *Davy Crockett and the River Pirates* (LA)
32. 1956 *Secrets of Life* (TL)
33. 1956 *Westward Ho the Wagons!* (LA)
34. 1957 *Johnny Tremain* (LA)
35. 1957 *Perri* (TLF)
36. 1957 *Old Yeller* (LA)
37. 1958 *The Light in the Forest* (LA)
38. 1958 *White Wilderness* (TL)
39. 1958 *Tonka* (LA)
40. 1959 *Sleeping Beauty* (A)
41. 1959 *The Shaggy Dog* (LA)
42. 1959 *Darby O'Gill and the Little People* (LA)
43. 1959 *Third Man on the Mountain* (LA)
44. 1960 *Toby Tyler, or Ten Weeks with a Circus* (LA)
45. 1960 *Kidnapped* (LA)
46. 1960 *Pollyanna* (LA)
47. 1960 *The Sign of Zorro* (LA)
48. 1960 *Ten Who Dared* (LA)
49. 1960 *Jungle Cat* (TL)
50. 1960 *Swiss Family Robinson* (LA)
51. 1961 *One Hundred and One Dalmatians* (A)
52. 1961 *The Absent-Minded Professor* (LA)
53. 1961 *The Parent Trap* (LA)
54. 1961 *Nikki, Wild Dog of the North* (TLF)
55. 1961 *Greyfriars Bobby* (LA)
56. 1961 *Babes in Toyland* (LA)
57. 1962 *Moon Pilot* (LA)
58. 1962 *Bon Voyage* (LA)
59. 1962 *Big Red* (LA)
60. 1962 *Almost Angels* (LA)
61. 1962 *The Legend of Lobo* (TLF)
62. 1962 *In Search of the Castaways* (LA)
63. 1963 *Son of Flubber* (LA)
64. 1963 *Miracle of the White Stallions* (LA)
65. 1963 *Savage Sam* (LA)
66. 1963 *Summer Magic* (LA)
67. 1963 *The Incredible Journey* (LA)
68. 1963 *The Sword in the Stone* (A)

69. 1963 *The Three Lives of Thomasina* (LA)
70. 1964 *The Misadventures of Merlin Jones* (LA)
71. 1964 *A Tiger Walks* (LA)
72. 1964 *The Moon-Spinners* (LA)
73. 1964 *Mary Poppins* (C)
74. 1964 *Emil and the Detectives* (LA)
75. 1965 *Those Calloways* (LA)
76. 1965 *The Monkey's Uncle* (LA)
77. 1965 *That Darn Cat* (LA)
78. 1966 *The Ugly Dachshund* (LA)
79. 1966 *Lt. Robin Crusoe U.S.N.* (LA)
80. 1966 *The Fighting Prince of Donegal* (LA)
81. 1966 *Follow Me, Boys!* (LA)
82. 1967 *Monkeys, Go Home* (LA) *
83. 1967 *The Adventures of Bullwhip Griffin* (LA) *
84. 1967 *The Happiest Millionaire* (LA) *
85. 1967 *The Gnome-Mobile* (LA) *
86. 1967 *The Jungle Book* (A) *
87. 1967 *Charlie, The Lonesome Cougar* (LA) *

*Released after Walt Disney's death

NOTES

INTRODUCTION

xi **Source of freezing story.** Bill Burnett, "Walt Disney Is Frozen: He'll Be Back in 1975," *National Spotlite*, n.d., Walt Disney Archive, Burbank, Calif. (hereinafter WDA).

xi ***Ici Paris.*** Pierre Grillet, "Disney In Deep Freeze Awaiting Resurrection," *National Tattler*, Jun. ?, 1969, WDA.

xi **"obsessed."** Frank Cusimano, "Walt Disney Is Being Kept Alive in Deep Freeze," *Midnight*, Oct. 4, 1971, WDA.

xi **A writer for *Mickey Mouse Club*.** Charles Shows, *Walt: Backstage Adventures with Walt Disney* (Huntington Beach, Calif.: Windsong Books International, 1979), p. 198.

xi **Ward Kimball . . . took some pride . . .** Jim Korkis, "Ward Kimball," in *Walt's People*, Didier Ghez, ed. (Xlibris, 2006) p. 297.

xi **Posthumous Disney film.** Jim Korkis, "The Final Days of Uncle Walt, "*Persistence of Vision* (hereinafter *POV*), Jul. 17, 1992, p. 52. Apparently animator Eric Larson testified to the screening.

xii **By one estimate . . .** Richard Schickel, *The Disney Version: The Life, Times, Art and Commerce of Walt Disney*, 3rd ed. (1968; reprint Chicago: Elephant Paperbacks, 1997), p. 19.

xii **By another estimate . . .** Richard G. Hubler, *Walt Disney*, unpub. ms., Richard Hubler Collection, Special Collections, Mugar Library, Boston University (hereinafter RHC), pp. 489–90.

xii **60 million visitors to Disneyland.** Martin A. Sklar, *Walt Disney's Disneyland* (New York: Disney Productions, 1964), n.p.

xii **"world's most celebrated entertainer . . ."** Jack Alexander, "The Amazing Story of Walt Disney," *Saturday Evening Post*, Oct. 31, 1953, p. 84.

xii **"probably the only man . . ."** *New York Times* (hereinafter *NYT*), Dec. 16, 1966.

xii **"[I]t happened . . ."** Robert Hughes, "Disney: Mousebrow to Highbrow," *Time*, Oct. 15, 1973, p. 91.

xiii **"greatest piece of urban design . . ."** Quoted in Randy Bright, *Disneyland: The Inside Story* (New York: Harry N. Abrams, 1987), p. 29.

xiii **"[I]t seems unlikely . . ."** Peter Blake, "The Lessons of the Parks," in Christopher Finch, *The Art of Walt Disney: From Mickey Mouse to the Magic Kingdom*, rev. ed. (New York: Harry N. Abrams, 1993).

xiii **"[H]is achievement became . . ."** Hughes, "Mousebrow."

xiv **"modern multimedia corporation."** Richard Schickel, "Ruler of the Magic Kingdom," *Time*, Dec. 7, 1998, p. 124.

xiv **"precise, clean, insipid, mechanical image."** Max Apple, "Uncle Walt," *Esquire*, Dec. 1983, p. 166.

xiv **Mickey Mouse's circular shape.** John Hench quoted in Steven Watts, *The Magic Kingdom: Walt Disney and the American Way of Life* (Boston: Houghton Mifflin, 1997), pp. 438–39.

xiv **"sentimental populism."** Ibid., pp. xvi–xvii.

xiv **"God has things well under control."** John Gardner, "Saint Walt: The Greatest Artist the World Has Ever Known, Except for Possibly, Apollonius of Rhodes," *New York*, Nov. 12, 1973, p. 68.

xv **middle-class, Protestant ideal of childhood.** Nicholas Sammond, *Babes in Tomorrowland: Walt Disney and the Making of the American Child* (Durham, N.C.: Duke University Press, 2005).

xv **"primary creator of the counterculture . . ."** Douglas Brode, *From Walt to Woodstock: How Disney Created the Counterculture* (Austin, Tex.: University of Texas Press, 2004), p. x.

xv **"makes dreams come true."** Adela Rogers St. John, "Walt Disney's Gambles," *American Weekly*, May 1, 1955, p. 18.

xvi **"[H]e emerged from the very heart . . ."** Robert D. Feild, *The Art of Walt Disney* (New York: Macmillan, 1942), p. 23.

xvii **"[o]f all the activists . . ."** John Bright, "Disney's Fantasy Empire," *Nation* Mar. 6, 1967.

xvii **"Walt Disney had the innate bad taste . . ."** Art Babbitt quoted in Leonard Mosley, *Disney's World: A Biography* (New York: Stein & Day, 1985), p. 204.

xviii **"rallying point for the subliterates . . ."** Schickel, *Disney Version*, p. 339.

xviii **"A few years ago when you mentioned Walt Disney . . ."** Gardner, "Saint Walt," p. 64.

xviii **"the illusion of life without any of the mess."** Apple, "Uncle Walt," p. 166.

xviii **"The borders of fantasy . . ."** Robert Sklar, "The Making of Cultural Myths—Walt Disney," in *The American Animated Cartoon: A Critical Anthology*, ed. Gerald Peary and Danny Peary (New York: E. P. Dutton, 1980), p. 65.

xviii **"to a sickening blend of cheap formulas . . ."** Julian Halevy, "Disneyland and Las Vegas," *Nation*, Jun. 7, 1958, p. 511.

xix **"an illusion created by a vast machinery"** Schickel, *Disney Version*, p. 44.

xix **"Disney was a callous man . . ."** Edmund Carpenter, "Very, Very Happy; Very Happy," *New York Times Book Review*, May 5, 1968.

xix ***Hollywood's Dark Prince.*** Marc Eliot, *Walt Disney: Hollywood's Dark Prince* (New York: Carol Publishing Group, 1993).

xix **selling the name "Walt Disney."** Ken Anderson quoted in Bob Thomas,

Walt Disney: An American Original (1976; reprint, New York: Hyperion, 1994), p. 192.

xix **"I'm not Walt Disney anymore."** Marty Sklar quoted in Bright, *Disneyland*, p. 189.

xix **"He was a difficult man to understand . . ."** Ben Sharpsteen, interview by Richard Hubler, Oct. 29, 1968, p. 1, WDA.

xx **"I do believe I knew Walt . . ."** Bill Peet, *Bill Peet: An Autobiography* (Boston: Houghton Mifflin, 1989), p. 171.

xx **"I've always said that if you get . . ."** Amy Boothe Green and Howard E. Green, *Remembering Walt: Favorite Memories of Walt Disney* (New York: Hyperion, 1999).

ONE || Escape

3 **"walking a straight and narrow path."** Roy Disney, interview by Richard Hubler, RHC, Box 14, Folder 51.

4 **Disney family.** Diane Disney Miller, as told to Pete Martin, *The Story of Walt Disney* (New York: Holt, 1956), p. 6

4 **"classed among the intellectual . . ."** Quoted in Richard G. Hubler, *Walt Disney*, unpub. ms., RHC, p. 45.

4 **Arundel Elias Disney.** Sherry Foresman, *The History of the Disney Family* (Des Moines, Ia.: Foresman, 1979), p. 192; District of New York—Port of New York Manifest, New Jersey, Oct. 3, 1834, Disney Family, Europe Canada Documents, Box 2560, WDA.

4 **Goderich.** James Scott, *Pioneer Times* [Huron County] quoted in David Smith, Disney-Call Family History, Sept. 1971, WDA.

4 **Mary Richardson.** *Goderich Township Families*, n.d., Goderich Public Library, p. 267.

4 **"as handsome a man . . ."** Peter Cantelon quoted in clipping, *Stratford* [Ontario] *Daily*, Jul. 15, 1938, Elias Disney Box, WDA.

5 **reluctantly resumed farming.** Victor Lauriston, "Walt Takes Snapshots of Huron Gravestones," *Chatham Daily News*, Feb. 18, 1953, *Rob Roy* file, Walt Disney Corr., 1953–1954, P-S, A1554, WDA.

5 **set out in 1877.** Bob Thomas, *Building a Company: Roy O. Disney and the Creation of an Entertainment Empire* (New York: Hyperion, 1998), p. 9; Leon Cantelon, "Village of Bluevale Became Thriving Industrial Center," no source, Jun. 25, 1960, Canada Photographs File, Disney Family, Europe-Canada Documents, A2560, WDA. Peter Cantelon says that the family traveled with Kepple. See "Disney Family Settled in Huron County in 1848," *Goderich Signal Star*, July 7, 1999.

5 **Purchased just over three hundred acres.** Warranty Deed Record, Kepple Disney, Jun. 14, 1887, Register of Deeds, Ellis County, Kansas.

5 **Indian massacres.** Maureen Winter, ed., *Indians to Industry* (Ellis County Star, 1967), p. 13.

5 **one Indian scare.** Will Disney quoted in Kittie Dale, "Disneyland, Ks., Had Its Historic, Exciting Moments," *Ellis Review*, 1972, Ellis, Kansas, Folder, Disney Family: Genealogy, etc., A2382, WDA.

5 **"Sodom of the Plains."** *At Home in Ellis County, Kansas, 1867–1992* (Hays, Kan.: History Book Committee, 1991), p. 1:115.

5 **scavenged for buffalo bones.** Ibid., p. 1:128.

5 **Winter of 1885–86.** Dale, "Historic, Exciting Moments."

5 **Visit to Florida.** Jessie Call Perkins, *The History of the Call Family*, unpub. ms., Dec. 1947, Perkins, Jessie, Folder, Walt Disney Corr., 1956, M-R, 1564, WDA.

5 **the Calls.** Ibid.

6 **Leaving Ohio.** David Smith, *Call Family History*, Sept. 1971, pp. 32–33, WDA.

6 **Flora and Albertha.** Ibid., p. 18.

6 **"howling wilderness."** David Smith to Irene Campbell, Feb. 23, 1972, Call Family Corr., Disney Family: Corr., A2379, WDA.

6 **"beautiful."** Perkins, *History of Call Family.*

6 **Pine Island.** Call Family—Jessie Perkins Folder, Disney Family: Genealogy, Etc., A2382, WDA.

6 **Seven families.** Call Genealogy, compiled by Erma Campbell Statler, 1971, Call Family—Erma Statler Folder, Disney Family: Genealogy, Etc., A2383, WDA.

6 **Teaching in Florida.** Ibid.

6 **Flora teaching in Paisley.** David Smith, Notes on Call Family—Notes, Drafts, Etc. Folder, Disney Family: Genealogy, Etc. A2383, WDA.

6 **Elias delivered mail.** Ernest Belligio to Dave Smith, Aug. 11, 1980, Call Family—Jessie Perkins Folder, Disney Family: Genealogy, etc., WDA.

7 **Bought an orange grove.** Gainesville, Fla., Land Office, no. 9666, Oct. 30, 1888.

7 **"Elias was very much . . ."** "Disney Family Settled in Huron County in 1848," *Goderich Signal Star*, Jul. 7, 1999.

7 **"real dandy . . ."** Walt to Clara McKenzie, May 7, 1958, Mc Folder, Walt Disney Corr., 1958, H-P, A1571, WDA.

7 **Gold mines.** Stock certificate, Dahlonega Gold Mine and Milling Co., Aug. 2, 1906, Disney Family Corr. Folder, Disney Family Corr., A2379, WDA.

7 **Robert's hotel.** Peter Cantelon quoted in "Disney Family Settled in Huron County in 1848."

7 **3515 South Vernon.** Commission on Chicago Historical and Architectural Landmarks, *Early Chicago Residences of the Elias Disney Family* (1991).

8 **Dollar a day.** Walt Disney, interview by Pete Martin, Reels 3 & 4, p. 14, A2361, WDA.

8 **cottage for his family.** Cook County Recorder of Deeds, Book 221A, p. 302, 1249 Tripp Ave., Oct. 31, 1891; Record of Building Permits for Permanent Structures, Cook County, 2156 Tripp (formerly 1249 Tripp), Nov. 23, 1892.

8 **two paved roads . . .** "Way Back When," clipping [no source], Sept. 13, 1950, Chicago Folder, Disney Family Genealogy, Etc., A2383, WDA.

8 **"hammer and saw planks . . ."** Walt quoted in Richard Schickel, *The Disney Version: The Life, Times, Art and Commerce of Walt Disney*, 3rd ed. (1968; reprint Chicago: Elephant Paperbacks, 1997), p. 47.

8 **Seven dollars a week.** Flora Disney in "Disney Biography, 50th Wedding Anniversary of Mr. & Mrs. Elias Disney," WDA.

8 **Two additional homes.** *Early Chicago Residences of the Elias Disney Family*, Cook County Recorder, Book 6760, p. 83, September 18, 1899.

8 **"[H]e was a pretty good preacher . . ."** "Disney Biography, 50th Wedding Anniversary of Mr. & Mrs. Elias Disney," WDA.

8 **the child's name.** Bob Thomas, *Walt Disney: An American Original* (1976; reprint New York: Hyperion; 1994), p. 24.

9 **Second son, Ray.** Register of Births, Illinois, Dec. 30, 1890, Regional Archives Depository, Ronald Williams Library, Northeastern Illinois University.

9 **Walter Elias Disney.** Baptisms, St. Paul's Congregational Church, Hammond Library, Chicago Theological Seminary.

9 **Car-barn robbery.** Roy Disney, interview by Richard Hubler, Nov. 17, 1967, RHC, Box 14, Folder 51.

9 **Elias sold their house.** *Early Chicago Residences of the Elias Disney Family.*

9 **"[I]t sounded wonderful . . ."** Roy Disney interview, RHC.

10 **"Marceline was the most important . . ."** Lillian Disney Truyens, interview by Bob Thomas, Apr. 19, 1973, Disney, Lillian, Folder, WDA.

10 **"clearly remember every detail of it."** Walt quoted in Hubler, p. 53.

10 **First impression of Marceline.** Walt Disney, "The Marceline I Knew," *Marceline News*, Sept. 2, 1938.

10 **It was a small farm.** Elias Disney deed, Linn County, Mo., Recorder of Deeds, book 160, p. 206.

10 **Installments.** Affidavit, Jean P. Taylor, Jan. 14, 1960, Marceline, Mo., Western Historical Manuscript Collection, University of Missouri.

10 **Teal and sprig.** Jack Jungmeyer, "The Marceline Farm Days in the Boyhood of Walt Disney," unpub. ms., Dec. 20, 1954, Disney Family, General Folder, Disney Family, Genealogy, Etc., A2383, WDA.

10 **"We had every kind of apple . . ."** Miller, *Story of Disney*, p. 11.

10 **"[I]t was just heaven . . ."** Roy Disney interview by Hubler.

10 **Mock orange trees . . .** Affidavit, Marie Mercy Taylor, Jan. 14, 1960, Marceline, Mo., Western Historical Manuscript Collection, University of Missouri.

10 **"a very hansome place . . ."** Mary Disney to granddaughter [unnamed], Jul. 2, 1907, Disney Family, General Folder, Disney Family, Genealogy, Etc., A2383, WDA.

11 **"Everything connected with Marceline . . ."** Disney, "The Marceline I Knew."

11 **"crowded, smoky."** Miller, *Story of Disney*, p. 12.

11 **Special feeling toward animals.** Ibid.

11 **Herding the pigs.** Walt Disney, speech at Marceline, 1956, WDA; Miller, *Story of Disney*, p. 12.

11 **Charley.** Hubler, *Disney*, p. 53.

11 **Maltese terrier.** Walt Disney interview by Martin, Reels 3 & 4, p. 20, WDA.

11 **"It was the most embarrassing thing . . ."** *Walt Disney: An Intimate History of the Man and his Magic*, CD-ROM, Pantheon Productions, 1998.

11 **Barrel stave.** Walt Disney, *Autobiography*, unpub. ms., 1939, 2nd installment, pp. 5–6, WDA.

11 **Fishing.** Clem Flickinger quoted in Katherine Greene and Richard Greene, *The Man Behind the Magic: The Story of Walt Disney* (New York: Viking, 1991),

p. 8; Frank Van Tiger to Walt, Jan. 26, 1947, V Folder, Walt Disney Corr., 1947–1948, T-Z, A1540, WDA.

11 **sledding or skating.** Ibid., p. 8; Disney, "The Marceline I Knew."

11 **"I don't think he was ever in a battle . . ."** *Walt Disney: An Intimate History*, CD-ROM.

11 **Sundays.** Don Taylor, Marceline, Mo., Aug. 6, 1971, WDA.

12 **Marceline.** *Marceline, Missouri: Past and Present, Progress and Prosperity* (1913; repr., Walsworth Publishing Co., 1975), p. 1.

12 **Name of town.** James Aucoin, *A History of Marceline, 1888–1988, Centennial Edition* (Marceline Mo., 1988), p. 68.

12 **Coal mines.** *Marceline Past and Present; Marceline Mirror*, Jul. 28, 1905.

12 **"motley array of tents and shacks"** *Marceline Mirror*, Jul. 28, 1905.

12 **"dignified and sturdy."** Ibid.

12 **"A stranger coming here . . ."** *Marceline Past and Present*, p. 3.

13 **"more things of importance . . ."** Disney, "The Marceline I Knew."

13 **Circus.** Dick Williams, "Disney Maps New Frontier," *Los Angeles Times* (hereinafter *LAT*), Dec. 10, 1961.

13 **Peter Pan.** Jim Korkis, "Disney's Pre-Production Peter Pan," *POV* 1, no. 2 (Winter 1992), p. 47.

13 **Buffalo Bill.** Walt to Martin L. Wolf (editor in chief, Library Publishers), Wi Folder, Walt Disney Corr., 1955, S-Z, A1560, WDA.

13 **First motion picture.** Ruth Flora Disney Beecher, "Recollections of Marceline"; Ruth Disney, interview by David Smith, Nov. 4, 1974, Beecher, Ruth Folder, WDA.

13 **"[E]verything was done . . ."** Walt Disney interview by Martin, Reels 3 & 4.

14 **"one of the prides of my life."** Disney, "The Marceline I Knew."

14 **Uncle Mike's arrival.** *Walt Disney: An Intimate History* CD-ROM.

14 **Grandma Disney's visits.** Walt to Mrs. George Miles, May 21, 1965, Walt Disney—Personal Folder, Walt Disney Corr., 1965, Committees—Disney School, A1607, WDA.

14 **"It's me!"** Ruth Disney interview by Smith.

14 **Wonderful playmate.** Lawrence Edward Watkin, *Walt Disney*, unpub. ms., WDA.

14 **"Uncle Ed did everything . . ."** Walt Disney interview by Martin, Reels 3 & 4.

14 **In the woods with Uncle Ed.** Miller, *Story of Disney*, p. 14.

14 **"To me he represented fun . . ."** Ibid.

14 **Uncle Robert's visits.** Jean P. Taylor affidavit; Interview with Don Taylor.

14 **"auntie."** Walt Disney interview by Martin, Disc 3, CD.

14 **Aunt Margaret's gifts.** Lowell Lawrance, "Mickey Mouse—Inspiration from Mouse in K.C. Studio," *Kansas City Journal-Post*, Sept. 8, 1935, untitled folder, Kansas City Box, A2364, WDA.

15 **"almost as soon as I could hold a pencil."** Walt to Jerome Tunney, Nov. 1, 1961, Mc Folder, Walt Disney Corr., 1961, M-Z, A1589, WDA.

15 **"boy wonder," "flattering tongue."** Walt Disney, *Autobiography*, unpub. ms., 1939, 2nd installment, WDA.

15 **Doc Sherwood.** Int with Don Taylor.

15 **"Don't be afraid . . ."** Walt Disney, "The Best Advice I Ever Had," unpub. ms., Walt Disney Folder, Walt Disney Corr., 1962, Committee–H (Misc.), A1591, WDA.

15 **"The result was pretty terrible . . ."** Phil Santora, "A Kid from Chicago," New York *Daily News*, Sept. 30, 1964.
15 **Nickel for the drawing.** Miller, *Story of Disney*, p. 17.
15 **Uncharacteristic.** Interview with Don Taylor.
15 **Framed and hung.** Walt Disney, *Autobiography*, p. 7.
15 **"the highlight of Walt's life."** Quoted in Amy Boothe Green and Howard E. Green, *Remembering Walt: Favorite Memories of Walt Disney* (New York: Hyperion, 1990), p. 5.
15 **"I can remember an awful feeling . . ."** Ruth Disney interview by Smith; *Walt Disney: An Intimate History*, CD-ROM; Roy O. Disney, interview by Richard Hubler, RHC, 14, Folder 51.
15 **"He was old enough . . ."** Richard H. Syring, "One of the Great Geniuses," *Silver Screen*, Nov. 1932.
16 **"giving whiskey to a man . . ."** Interview with Don Taylor.
16 **Watering the horses.** Jean P. Taylor affidavit.
16 **Popping corn.** Clem Fleckinger quoted in Bob Thomas, *Building a Company*, p. 22.
16 **Selling apples door to door.** Walt Disney interview by Martin, Reels 3 & 4, p. 23.
16 **Collected apples from neighbors.** Jean P. Taylor affidavit.
16 **Remodeled neighbor's house.** Ibid.
16 **Flora buttering bottom of bread.** Miller, *Story of Disney*, p. 15.
16 **Rift with Herbert and Ray.** Jean P. Taylor affidavit.
16 **Herbert and Ray in Kansas City.** Interview with Don Taylor; Postmaster, Portland, Ore., to Herbert Disney, Feb. 15, 1927, Herbert Disney File, National Personnel Records Center, Civilian Personnel Records, National Archives.
16 **Tobacco in pocket.** Miller, *Story of Disney*, p. 16.
17 **American Society of Equity.** *Marceline Mirror*, Nov. 8, 1907.
17 **"radical."** Jean P. Taylor affidavit.
17 **"He had high ideals . . ."** Ruth Disney interview by Smith.
17 **Socialism.** Miller, *Story of Disney*, p. 10.
17 **Elias's illness.** Ibid., pp. 14–15; Roy O. Disney interview by Hubler, Jan. 18, 1968, RHC.
17 **Auction.** Roy O. Disney interview by Hubler.
17 **"Disney's small-town America . . ."** Steven Watts, *The Magic Kingdom: Walt Disney and the American Way of Life* (Boston: Houghton Mifflin, 1997), p. 6.
18 **Population growth.** *Marceline Mirror*, Feb. 2, 1911.
18 **Changes in Marceline.** *Marceline Mirror*, Mar. 23, 1911 (autos), Sept. 20, 1907 (school), Jun. 11, 1909 (power plant), Oct. 23, 1908 (waterworks), May 25, 1911 (lighting streetlamps).
18 **"for people who live in cities . . ."** Disney speech at Marceline.
18 **Dragoon passengers.** Green and Green, *Remembering Walt*, p. 13.
18 **Recall of Marceline.** John Culhane, *Walt Disney's* Fantasia (New York: Harry N. Abrams, 1983), pp. 134–35.
18 **Preoccupation with farm life.** Rush Johnson, interview by author.
18 **"That's what it is . . ."** Meeting on Sound Stage—Beethoven's Symphony No. 6, Story Meetings 1939, *Fantasia*, Story Meetings, Etc., A1782, WDA.
19 **Kansas City.** *Kansas City Directory* (Kansas City: Gate City Directory Co., 1913); Workers of the Writers Program of the Work Projects Administration in

the State of Missouri, *Missouri: A Guide to the "Show-Me" State* (New York: Duell, Sloan & Pearce, 1941; rep. 1973), pp. 244–45.

19 **"The city was not pretty . . ."** Writers of the WPA, *Missouri Guide.*

19 **Size of house.** Memo, Roy to Walt, Feb. 27, 1962, Roy Disney Folder, Walt Disney Corr., Inter-Office, 1960–1964, A-Disney Aircraft, A1648; Greene and Greene, *Man Behind the Magic.* There is some dispute over the exact address. The city directory lists the address as 2704 Thirty-first Street, and school records as 2716.

19 **No indoor plumbing.** Brian Burnes, Robert W. Butler, and Dan Viets, *Walt Disney's Missouri: The Roots of Creative Genius*, ed. Donna Martin (Kansas City: Kansas City Star Books, 2002), p. 49.

19 **"a fairyland . . ."** Ruth Disney interview by Smith.

19 **Sold the Marceline farm.** Elias Disney Deed, Book 178, p. 374.

19 **Paper route.** Burnes, Butler and Viets, *Disney's Missouri*, p. 53.

19 **Owner of record.** Ibid.

19 **"the route book would list . . ."** Walt Disney interview by Martin, Reels 3 & 4, pp. 39–40.

19 **Economics of the route.** Paul Hollister, *Man or Mouse: The Story of Walt Disney, So Far*, unpub. ms., 1955, WDA, chap. 1, pp. 11–12.

20 **"some little amount."** Roy Disney, interview by Richard Hubler, Jun. 18, 1968, RHC.

20 **Roman chariots.** Lorena Butler (Coomber), interview by David Smith, Feb. 2, 1972, WDA.

20 **Sunday papers.** *Walt Disney: An Intimate History*, CD-ROM.

20 **Churchgoing.** Roy Disney interview by Hubler, Jun. 18, 1968.

20 **Ruth's Sunday school.** Ruth Disney interview by Smith.

20 **Routine.** Hollister, *Man or Mouse*, chap. 2, pp. 1–2; Disney, *Autobiography*, p. 10.

20 **Excited by the paper route.** Walt Disney, "Newspaperboys, Ah, How Well I Remember!" *Family Weekly*, Oct. 14, 1961.

20 **Seeing the lamplighters.** "Disney's No Comic Character: Burris Jenkins in Disneyland," *The E Ticket* Fall 2002, p. 36; in *Baltimore News-Post*, May 1959.

20 **Insisted that the papers be placed.** Miller, *Story of Disney*, p. 22.

21 **After Roy graduated.** Walt Disney interview by Martin, Rees 3 & 4, pp. 44–45.

21 **Falling asleep.** Ibid., Reel 11, p. 25.

21 **"So the upshot of it was . . ."** Ibid., Reels 3 & 4, pp. 45–46.

21 **Playing with toys.** Miller, *Story of Disney*, p. 21.

21 **"It stands out in memory . . ."** Walt to Aunt Josie [Barnes], Dec. 24, 1952, B Folder, Walt Disney Corr., 1953–1954, A–B, A1550, WDA.

21 **Nail in boot.** Walt Disney interview by Martin, reel 11, pp. 26–28.

21 **Putting on an addition.** Richard Hubler, *Walt Disney*, unpub. ms., RHC, p. 71.

21 **"developed an appreciation . . ."** Walt to Doris Kanter, Jun. 3, 1957, E Folder, Walt Disney Corr., 1957, E–O, A1567, WDA.

21 **Nightmares.** Walt Disney interview by Martin, Reel 11, p. 22.

22 **Catch a ball.** Roy quoted in Robert De Roos, "The Magic Worlds of Walt Disney," *National Geographic*, Aug. 1963.

22 **Delivering theater bills.** Paul H. Hefty to Walt (1938), He Folder, Walt Disney Corr., 1938–1939, De-I, A1516, WDA.

22 **McAllister Creamery.** Walt Disney interview by Martin, Reels 3 & 4, p. 55.

22 **Cranberry sauce.** "My Most Memorable Christmas Gift," draft, *McCall's*, [1957], Mc Folder, Walt Disney Corr., 1957, E–O, A1567, WDA.

22 **Leather boots.** Ibid.

22 **"comforts and good things . . ."** Ruth Disney Beecher to David Smith (Dec. 1976), Beecher, Ruth, Folder, Disney Family Corr., A2379, WDA.

22 **"He was a very fast walker."** Walt Disney interview by Martin, Reel 11, p. 19.

22 **Nephew in Glendale.** Thomas, *Building a Company*, pp. 123–24.

22 **Paid his bills in cash.** Ruth Disney Beecher to Smith.

22 **Finding a twenty-dollar bill.** Miller, *Story of Disney*, pp. 25–26.

22 **"just didn't believe . . ."** Roy Disney interview, June 18, 1968.

22 **Elias Disney's personality.** Hollister, *Man or Mouse*, chap. 1, p. 5; Roy Disney interview, June 18, 1968. Dorothy Puder, interview by author.

23 **"The whole Disney family . . ."** Walt Pfeiffer in Hubler, *Disney*, p. 120.

23 **"become very conservative . . ."** Walt Disney interview by Martin, Reel 1.

23 **Chasing Bryan's buggy.** Ibid., Reel 11, p. 10.

23 **Republican.** Hollister, *Man or Mouse*, chap. 7, p. 7.

23 **End of fiddle playing.** Walt Disney interview by Martin, Reels 3 & 4, p. 62.

23 **"get a switching."** Quoted in Thomas, *Building a Company*, pp. 14–15.

23 **"violent."** Walt Disney interview by Martin, Reels 3 & 4, p. 43.

23 **"he did have a temper."** Ruth Disney interview by Smith.

23 **"He was full of clowning . . ."** Roy O. Disney interview by Hubler, Nov. 17, 1967.

23 **Plate trick.** Miller, *Story of Disney*, pp. 28–29.

23 **"very slow to catch on . . ."** Walt Disney interview by Martin, Reels 3 & 4, p. 22.

23 **"chief delight . . ."** Marjorie Walters to Walt, Jan. 18, 1957, W Folder, Walt Disney Corr., 1957, P–Z, A1568, WDA.

24 **Dressing as a woman.** Syring, "Great Geniuses," pp. 47–48.

24 **"enthused about everything."** Walt Pfeiffer quoted in Greene and Greene, *Man Behind the Magic*, p. 16.

24 **"[w]hatever he wanted to do . . ."** Syring, "Great Geniuses," p. 46.

24 **"gave the impression . . ."** Quoted in Hollister, *Man or Mouse*, chap. 2, p. 9.

24 **"just argue the dickens . . ."** Roy Disney interview by Hubler, Jun. 18, 1968.

24 **Elias's impatience.** Walt Disney interview by Martin, Reels 3 & 4, pp. 57–58.

24 **"He raised his other arm . . ."** Ibid., pp. 59–60.

25 **"peevishness."** Roy Disney interview by Hubler, June 18, 1968.

25 **"she couldn't keep it from Dad . . ."** Walt Disney, Big Brothers of America speech, Mar. 14, 1957, WDA.

25 **"strangers to me . . ."** Walt Disney interview by Martin, Reels 3 & 4, p. 17.

25 **Crawl into bed.** Walt quoted in Thomas, *Building a Company*, p. 32.

25 **Roy as father figure.** Ruth Disney interview by Smith; *Walt Disney: An Intimate History* CD-ROM.

25 **"I really believe . . ."** Roy Disney interview by Hubler, Jun. 18, 1968.

26 **"real family."** Walt Pfeiffer quoted in Hubler, *Disney*, pp. 64–65.

26 **"My own family . . ."** Walt to Richard Gehman, Feb. 7, 1964, G Folder, Walt Disney Corr., 1964, Disney—Gifts, A1601, WDA.

26 **"[O]ld Elias didn't like anything . . ."** Walter Pfeiffer, interview by Bob Thomas, Apr. 26, 1973, WDA.

26 **Meeting Walt Pfeiffer.** Ibid.

26 **"ham."** Ibid.

26 **Violin lessons.** Ruth Disney Beecher to Smith; Miller, *Story of Disney*, pp. 30–31; Ruth Disney, interview by Smith.

26 **"I went to bed tired . . ."** Walt to Richard Gehman.

26 **"I'd do anything . . ."** Walt Disney interview by Martin, Disc 11 CD.

26 **Dressing as Lincoln.** KCKN Disney Transcription Spot, Mar. 29, 1945, Kansas City Broadcast (*Three Caballeros*), Walt Disney Corr., 1945–1946, L–P, A1535, WDA.

27 **"I always got something . . ."** Walt Disney interview by Martin, Reel 11, p. 12.

27 **"Two Bad Walters."** Ora Newsome (teacher) to Walt, Feb. 5, 1945, N Folder, Walt Disney Corr., 1944, F–N, A1531, WDA.

27 **Talent contests.** Walt Disney, *Autobiography*, pp. 12–13; KCKN Disney Transcription Spot.

27 **Walt had to slip out the window.** Pfeiffer interview by Thomas.

27 **Hans and Mike.** KCKN Disney Transcription Spot.

27 **Studied Chaplin.** Pfeiffer quoted in Hubler, *Disney*, p. 120.

27 **"could do it to perfection"** LeRoy "Lefty" Greene to Walt, Jan. 6, 1936, Jan. 22, 1936, Gr Folder, Walt Disney Corr., 1936, E–L, A1512, WDA.

27 **"[W]e always got a little more applause . . ."** *Walt Disney: An Intimate History* CD-ROM.

27 **"reacted on me like . . ."** Disney, *Autobiography*, pp. 12–13.

28 **repeat the second grade.** Benton School Annual Register, Room 14, District Year Ending Jun. 7, 1912, Registrar, Kansas City School District.

28 **"courteous . . ."** Margaret Hamilton, "Walt Disney: Back to School," *Kansas City Star*, Feb. 8, 1942.

28 **"second dumbest."** Greene and Greene, *Man Behind the Magic*, p. 14.

28 **Imagining things.** Bert A. Teeters to Walt, May 19, 1961, T Folder, Walt Disney Corr., 1961, M–Z, A1589.

28 **"dreamer" and "I'd sit in class . . ."** Edith Efron, "Still Attacking His Ancient Enemy—Conformity," *TV Guide*, Jun. 17, 1965, p. 11.

28 **Mouse in school.** Walt Disney, "A Roving Mouse Landed Me in a Hole!" *New York Enquirer*, May 5, 1957; Walt to Daisy Beck, Sept. 27, 1940, B Folder, Walt Disney Corr., A–B, A1520, WDA.

28 **"[T]he kids used to make fun . . ."** Pfeiffer interview by Thomas.

28 **"He used to come home . . ."** Ruth Disney interview by Smith.

28 **"laggard."** JWM, "Walt Disney, Showman and Educator, Remembers Daisy," *CTA Journal*, Dec. 1955, p. 5.

28 **"great patience . . ."** Ibid.

28 **Relay team.** Walt to Daisy Beck, Sept. 27, 1940; Margaret Hamilton, "Back to School."

29 **Drawing.** "Mickey Mouse a Local Boy," *Kansas City Star*, Feb. 13, 1942.

29 **Likeness of Teddy Roosevelt.** Mildred Pease Smalley to Walt, (received March 29, 1960), S Folder, Walt Disney Corr., 1963, O–Z, A1598, WDA.

29 **Animating flowers.** Hubler, *Disney*, p. 67.

29 **Miss Beck's posters.** Ibid.

29 **Glass advertisements.** Pfeiffer interview by Thomas.

29 **After school . . .** Katherine Rhels to Walt, March 23, 1940, R Folder, Walt Disney Corr., 1940–1941, N–R, A1524, WDA.

29 **Decorating the clubhouse.** Laura Francis Cottingham to Walt, Jul. 1, 1945, Co Folder, Walt Disney Corr., 1945–1946, A–K, A1534, WDA.

29 ***Appeal to Reason.*** Walt Disney interview by Martin, Reels 3 & 4, p. 7.

29 **"It was kind of sissy . . ."** Walt Pfeiffer, interview by Christopher Finch and Linda Rosenkrantz, Jul. 5, 1972, WDA.

29 **"Even in our old 7th grade . . ."** Smalley to Walt.

29 **"It was a great stimulant . . ."** Walt to Bert Hudson, Feb. 9, 1949, Walt Disney Corr., 1949–1950, H–Q, A1542, WDA.

30 **"plastered with drawings."** Joseph Becker to Walt, Feb. 18, 1953, B Folder, Walt Disney Corr., 1953–1954, A–B, A1550, WDA.

30 **Drawing outside on a blackboard.** John C. Harvey to Walt, Feb. 6, 1956, H Folder, Walt Disney Corr., 1956, G–L, A1563, WDA.

30 **"The neighbors would go down . . ."** Quoted in Syring, "Great Geniuses," p. 47.

30 **Receiving instruction.** Pfeiffer interview by Thomas.

30 **"It was a sad day . . ."** Roger Swanson, "Disney Holds Fond Memories of Years in Kansas City," *Kansas City Star*, n.d., Kansas City Box, A2364, WDA.

30 **Thinking of becoming a newspaper cartoonist.** JWM, "Disney, Showman and Educator."

30 **"[g]etting through seventh grade . . ."** Ibid.

30 **"He will draw you . . ."** *My Golden School Days,* comp. and arr. Janet Madison (Chicago: Reilly-Britton Co., 1911), Ruth Disney, WDA.

30 **"I am still prouder . . ."** Lowell Lawrance, "Mickey Mouse—Inspiration from Mouse in K.C. Studio," *Kansas City Journal-Post*, Sept. 8, 1935.

30 **Made $16,000.** Greene and Greene, *The Man Behind the Magic*, p. 20.

31 **"educational."** Walt Disney interview by Martin, Reels 3 & 4, p. 64.

31 **Bribing the engineer.** Phil Santora, "A Kid from Chicago," *New York Daily News*, Sept. 30, 1964.

31 **Butcher route.** Ibid.

31 **"elegance of this plush . . ."** Schickel, *Disney Version*, p. 61.

31 **Group of soldiers.** Walt Disney interview by Martin, Reels 3 & 4, pp. 64–68.

31 **Detaching cars.** Ibid.

31 **"finagling."** Ibid., Reel 4, p. 1.

31 **"He'd go up and down the train . . ."** Roy quoted in *Walt Disney: An Intimate History Magic* CD-ROM.

31 **"opening chapters of an American success story . . ."** Watts, *Magic Kingdom*, p. 14.

32 **Family home life "wonderful."** Roy Disney interview by Hubler, Jun. 18, 1968.

32 **O-Zell in KC.** Articles of Incorporation of O-Zell Co., Sept. 14, 1911, Arizona Corporation Commission.

32 **Buying O-Zell shares.** Inventory of Moore Collection, Beecher, Ruth, Folder, Disney Family Corr., A2379, WDA.

32 **"difficulties" in the business . . .** O-Zell to Elias, Dec. 2. and Dec. 21, 1916, ibid.

33 **"Walter Disney, one of the newcomers . . ."** *McKinley Voice*, Oct. 1917, Disney Drawings Folder, WDA.

33 **Excused from class.** Vilma Gloss to Walt, Apr. 17, 1954, G Folder, Walt Disney Corr., 1953–1954, G–K, A1552, WDA.

33 **"it was THE PASSION of your life!"** Ibid.

33 **"even when the teacher thought . . ."** Lena B. Stein to Walt, Aug. 3, 1955, S Folder, Walt Disney Corr., 1955, S–Z, A1560. See also A. Alvin Abrams to Walt, Mar. 22, 1940, A Folder, Walt Disney Corr., 1940–1941, A–B, A1520, WDA.

33 **Pretty dancing girls.** Birdie Cohan to Joel Cohen, Sept. 30, 1987, Chicago Folder, Disney Family: Genealogy, Etc., A2383, WDA.

33 **Drawing at school socials.** Ruth Disney interview by Smith.

33 **Sketching a man's head.** Minnie M. Dunwell to Walt, May 7, 1957, Do–Dz Folder, Walt Disney Corr., 1957, A–D, A1566, WDA.

33 **Drawing the human body.** Elias quoted in Syring, "Great Geniuses," p. 47.

33 **Playing hooky.** Roy Disney interview by Hubler, June 18, 1968.

33 **"with my mouth wide open . . ."** Walt to Carey Orr, *Chicago Tribune*, Mar. 16, 1949, O Folder, Walt Disney Corr., 1949–1950, H–Q, A1542, WDA.

33 **Chicago Academy of Fine Arts.** Miller, *Story of Disney*, p. 36.

33 **Live models.** Ibid.

33 **Never be a fine artist.** S. J. Woolf, "Walt Disney Tells Us What Makes Him Happy," *NYT Magazine*, Jul. 10, 1938.

34 **"no doubt the turning point in my whole career."** Walt to Ruth Van Sickle Ford (director of the Chicago Academy of Fine Arts) Jul. 12, 1957, C Folder, Walt Disney Corr., 1957, A–D, A1566, WDA.

34 **Magic books.** Untitled clipping. 8 MWEZ, n.c., 17, 901, New York Public Library for the Performing Arts.

34 **Dutch act with Maas.** Disney, *Autobiography*, 2nd installment, pp. 1–2.

34 **" 'smart alecky kid' . . ."** Harry F. Gilliam to Walt, Nov. 23, 1946, G Folder, Walt Disney Corr., 1945–1946, A–K, A1534, WDA.

34 **"extremely shy and reserved."** Rochelle Bregstone Livingston to Diane Disney Miller, Oct. 11, 1983, Chicago Folder, Disney Family: Genealogy, Etc., Box A2383, WDA.

34 **"something of a ladies' man."** Ruth to Walt, Dec. 5, 1950, Walt Disney Corr., 1949–1950, A–G, A1541, WDA.

34 **Crush on Walt.** Livingston to Miller.

34 **Beatrice Conover.** Mrs. Beatrice Conover Peterson to Walt, Jan. 17, 1933, Misc. File, WDA.

34 **Working at O-Zell.** Miller, *Story of Disney*, pp. 35–36.

34 **Sarah Scrogin's encouragement.** Walt to J. C. Parsons, (Wahl Co.), May 4, 1935, Misc. File, WDA.

35 **Picnic poster.** Walt to Sarah York Scrogin, Nov. 7, 1934, Misc. File, WDA.

35 **Walt's potential.** Sarah York Scrogin to Walt, Oct. 31, 1934, Misc. File, WDA.

35 **mail carrier.** Walter E. Disney, National Personnel Records Center, Civilian Personnel Records, National Archives and Records Administration.
35 **Getting mail job.** *New York Journal American,* Jan. 29, 1938, 8 MWEZ, n.c., 17, 901, New York Public Library for the Performing Arts.
35 **Mail routine.** Walt Disney interview by Martin, Reel 12, pp. 10, 13–16.
35 **"gold rush to me."** Ibid., p. 10.
35 **"It was thrilling . . ."** Ibid., Disc 13, CD.
35 **Bombing.** *NYT,* Sept. 6, 1918.
35 **"disgusted."** Walt to J. M. Cottingham, Feb. 10, 1931, Misc. File, WDA.
36 **Dressing as Chaplin.** Syring, "Great Geniuses," p. 48.
36 **Losing the camera.** Ibid.
36 **Seeing Roy off.** Walt Disney interview by Martin, Reels 3 & 4, p. 4.
36 **"They were blowing . . ."** Walt Disney interview, Marceline, audiotape, WDA.
36 **Shame.** Ruth Disney interview by Smith.
36 **"He looked swell . . ."** Walt Disney interview by Martin, Disc 4, CD.
36 **Joining the Canadian forces.** Walt to Barney Yanofsky, (editor of *Foreign Service*), Jul. 2, 1934, Misc. File, WDA.
36 **Fife-and-drum corps.** Walt Disney interview by Martin, Reels 3 & 4, p. 5.
36 **Too young, too old . . .** Ibid., Disc 4, CD.
36 **St. John brothers.** Miller, *Story of Disney,* pp. 37–38.
36 **Finding Maas's grip.** Ruth Disney interview by Smith.
36 **"If I did . . ."** Miller, *Story of Disney,* p. 39.
37 **Flora relenting.** Syring, "Great Geniuses," p. 48, Miller, *Story of Disney,* p. 39.
37 **Camp Scott routine.** Jack Lait, "The Short Cut to France and Other Fronts," *American Red Cross, Central Division Bulletin* 1, no. 42 (Oct. 19, 1918), Red Cross Photos Folder, WDA.
37 **"a good time out here . . ."** Walt to Virginia Baker, Sept. 6, 1918, Walt Disney Early Corr. Folder, Disney, Walt, Corr. 1918, A3381, WDA.
37 **"I've never seen a sicker . . ."** Miller, *Story of Disney,* p. 40.
37 **Selected for France.** Walt Disney interview by Martin, Reel 4, p. 9.
37 ***Vaubin.*** Ibid., p. 10.
38 **St. Cyr.** Ibid., p. 14; Miller, *Story of Disney,* p. 41.
38 **Longchamps.** Disney, *Autobiography,* pp. 8–9; Hollister, *Man or Mouse,* chap 3, p. 4.
38 **Duties in Neufchâteau.** Walt to Alice Howell, Dec. 29, 1931, Misc. File, WDA.
38 **Accomplished tour guide.** Walt Disney interview by Martin, Reel 4, pp. 32–33.
39 **Pershing picnic.** Walt to Alice Howell, Dec. 29, 1931, Misc File, WDA.
39 **Receiving flag.** Alice Howell to Walt, Dec. 1, 1939, Ho Folder, Walt Disney Corr., 1940–1941, G-M, A1523, WDA.
39 **"mingled with joy and sorrow."** Walt to Howell, Dec. 5, 1942, Ho Folder, Walt Disney Corr., 1942–1943, D-H, A1527, WDA.
39 **French hostility.** Walt Disney interview by Martin, Reel 5, pp. 28–29.
39 **German garbage detail.** Ibid., Reel 4, pp. 25–28.
39 **"doing something I very seldom do . . ."** *Walt Disney: An Intimate History* CD-ROM.

39 **Trip to Soissons.** Miller, *Story of Disney*, pp. 43–44.

40 **"I found out that the inside . . ."** *New York Journal American*, Jan. 29, 1938.

40 **Sending cartoons to *Life* and *Judge*.** Walt Disney interview by Martin, Reel 5, p. 32.

40 **Painting German helmets.** Walt Disney interview, Marceline, audiotape.

40 **"France is an interesting place . . ."** *McKinley Voice* annual, 1919, Disney, Disney Drawings Folder, WDA.

40 **Considering Albania.** Walt Disney interview by Martin, Reel 4, p. 36.

40 **Watching Pershing leave.** Ibid., p. 37.

40 **Discharge.** Captain F.A. Fellows (chief of personnel, Transportation Department) to Bureau of Personnel, Aug. 7, 1919, Hazel Brough Records Center, Red Cross, Falls Church, Va.

40 **Reuniting with Maas.** Miller, *Story of Disney*, p. 50; Walt Disney interview by Martin, Reel 5, pp. 39–40.

41 **Returning from France.** Walt to Mark [?], May 12, 1920, Disney, Walt, Corr., Walt Disney Early Corr., WDA; Walt to Edwin McQuade, Sept. 24, 1963, Red Cross Photos Folder, WDA.

41 **Maas in Chicago.** Walt Disney interview by Martin, Reel 5, p. 40.

41 **Beatrice.** Ibid., p. 31; Walt to Mrs. Beatrice Peterson, Aug. 18, 1933, Misc Folder, WDA.

41 **Saving money.** Walt Disney interview by Martin, Reel 5, p. 34.

41 **"He never understood me."** Walt Disney, speech at Big Brothers ceremony, Mar. 14, 1957, WDA.

41 **Smoking.** Diane Disney Miller, "A Plea to Eradicate a 'Pediatric' Disease," *LAT*, Aug. 9, 1995.

42 **"a lifetime of experience . . ."** Miller, *Story of Disney*, p. 48.

42 **"bloody" thumb.** Roy Disney interview by Hubler, June 18, 1968.

42 **"I was settled."** Walt Disney interview by Martin, Reel 4, p. 35.

42 **"It seemed easier . . ."** Quoted in Hubler, *Disney*, p. 93.

TWO || The Go-Getter

43 **"America at the close of the Great War . . ."** Ann Douglas, *Terrible Honesty: Mongrel Manhattan in the 1920s* (New York: Farrar, Straus & Giroux, 1995), p. 4.

44 **"Guts and goodness in tandem."** Walter Kerr, *The Silent Clowns* (New York: Alfred A. Knopf, 1975), pp. 190–91.

44 **Looking for a job.** Walt Disney interview by Martin, Reel 5, pp. 43–44, A2361, WDA. Louis Pesmen claimed that Walt returned with samples the next day. Louis Pesmen, [Notes], Aug. 11, 1971, Pesmen, Louis A., Folder, Kansas City, A3256, WDA.

45 **"I could have kissed him!"** Walt Disney interview by Martin, Reel 5, p. 45.

45 **Aunt Margaret.** Ibid.

45 **"making a great success."** Lowell Lawrance, "Mickey Mouse—Inspiration from Mouse in K.C. Studio," *Kansas City Journal-Post*, Sept. 8, 1935.

45 **Newman Theater magazine ads.** Pesmen [Notes].

45 **Delivering mail.** Walt Disney *Autobiography*, unpub. ms., 1939, 2nd installment, p. 12, WDA.

45 **Political cartoonist.** Disney Drawings Folder, WDA.

45 **Comic strips.** Inventory of Moore Collection, Beecher, Ruth, Folder, Disney Family Corr., A2379, WDA.

46 **"Cartoonist."** Federal Census, [Jan. 7,] 1920, Jackson County, Mo., ed. 166, sheet 5, line 37.

46 **"I felt well-qualified."** Walt Disney *Autobiography*, unpub. ms., 1934, WDA.

46 **"hillbilly."** Walt Disney interview by Martin, Reel 5, p. 48.

46 **Practicing his signature.** Leslie Iwerks and John Kenworthy, *The Hand Behind the Mouse* (New York: Disney Editions, 2001), p. 4.

46 **"He just didn't have a childhood . . ."** Donald Iwerks interview by author.

47 **Iwwerks's youth.** David R. Smith, "Ub Iwerks, 1901–1971," *Funnyworld*, no. 14 (Spring 1972), p. 33.

47 **"Throw it in a ditch."** Iwerks interview.

47 **Scolding Pesmen.** Hal Pesmen (son of Louis Pesman), interview by author.

47 **In one version . . .** Disney, *Autobiography*, 1934.

47 **Deal with Carder.** Ibid.

48 **Half his savings.** Walt Disney interview by Martin, Reel 5, p. 50.

48 ***United Leather Workers Journal.*** Walt Pfeiffer, interview by Bob Thomas, Apr. 26, 1973, WDA.

48 **Between $125 and $135 that first month.** Walt Disney interview by Martin, Reel 5, p. 50.

48 **Comic strip plates.** Ibid., p. 51.

48 **Ad for Kansas City Slide Co.** "The Mouse That Won a Nation," *Kansas City Times*, Nov. 11, 1978. Iwerks and Kenworthy, in *Hand Behind The Mouse*, give the date as Jan. 29, 1920.

48 **Joining Kansas City Slide Co.** Walt Disney interview by Martin, Reel 5, pp. 52–53.

49 **Million dollars' worth of business.** Ibid., Disc 5, CD, WDA.

49 **"one of the pioneers . . ."** A.V. Cauger to Walt, Sept. 11, 1942, C Folder, Walt Disney Corr., 1942–1943, A-C, A1526, WDA.

49 **A. V. Cauger.** "Kansas City's Own 'Daddy' of Ad Films Is Honored by his Hollywood Alumni," *Box Office*, Feb. 3, 1945.

49 **"I got a fine job here . . ."** Walt to Mack [?], May 12, 1920, Disney, Walt, Corr., 1920, Walt Disney Early Corr., A3381, WDA.

49 **"[T]he few customers I had would call . . ."** Walt Disney interview by Martin, Reel 5, p. 54.

50 **Offer of cartooning.** Brian Burnes, Robert W. Butler, and Dan Viets, *Walt Disney's Missouri: The Roots of Creative Genius*, ed. Donna Martin, (Kansas City: Kansas City Star Books, 2002), p. 79.

50 **"The trick of making things move . . ."** Don Alpert, "The Man of the Land Disney," *LAT*, Apr. 30, 1961.

50 **Gruff voice.** Theodore Cauger, interview by author.

50 **Spitting in the drinking fountain.** Phillip Fisher to Walt, Jan. 25, 1934, D.V.'s Letters, 1934, Walt Disney Corr., A1504, WDA.

51 **Developing his own ads.** Walt Disney interview by Martin, Reel 5, pp. 56–57.

51 **Car ad.** Diane Disney Miller, as told to Pete Martin, *The Story of Walt Disney* (New York: Holt, 1956), p. 64.

51 **Borrowing a camera.** Walt Disney interview by Martin, Reel 5, p. 64.
51 **Financial chicanery.** David Smith, *Call Family History*, Sept. 1971, p. 16, WDA.
51 **Rented touring car.** Ruth Disney Beecher quoted in Lawrence Edward Watkin, *Walt Disney*, unpub., ms., p. 118, WDA.
51 **Garage.** Roy Disney quoted in *Walt Disney: An Intimate History of the Man and His Magic*, CD-ROM, Pantheon Productions, 1998.
51 **Glass negative camera.** Louis Pesmen, untitled ms., Jul. 7, 1971, Pesmen, Louis A., Folder, Kansas City, A3256, WDA.
51 **"Walt was a focused man . . ."** Dorothy Puder, interview by author.
51 **"When he'd come home . . ."** Roy O. Disney quoted in *Walt Disney: An Intimate History* CD-ROM.
51 **"He was just busy . . ."** Puder interview.
52 **"lightning sketchers."** Donald Crafton, *Before Mickey: The Animated Film, 1898–1928* (Cambridge, Mass.: MIT Press, 1982), p. 48.
52 **Winsor McCay.** Charles Solomon, *Enchanted Drawings: The History of Animation* (New York: Alfred A. Knopf, 1989), pp. 14–17; see also John Canemaker, "Winsor McCay," in *The American Animated Cartoon: A Critical Anthology*, ed. Gerald and Danny Peary (New York: E. P. Dutton, 1980), pp. 13–15.
53 **Animation methods.** Crafton, *Before Mickey*. See also Michael Barrier, *Hollywood Cartoons: American Animation in Its Golden Age* (New York: Oxford University Press, 1999), pp. 9–16.
54 **"Animators were scarce."** "Snow White Animator," *Cartoonist Profiles* 1, no. 4 (Fall 1969), p. 14.
54 **"The scenario would probably be . . ."** Dick Huemer in Charles Solomon, *The Disney That Never Was: The Stories and Art from Five Decades of Unproduced Animation* (New York: Hyperion, 1995), p. 8.
54 **"We got very few laughs."** Joe Adamson, "A Talk with Dick Huemer," in Peary and Peary, *American Animated Cartoon*, p. 31.
54 **"distinctive features."** Crafton, *Before Mickey*, p. 60.
55 **"there was only this one book . . ."** Alpert, "Man of the Land."
55 **"vulgate of modern industrial animation."** Crafton, *Before Mickey*, p. 201.
55 **Lutz recommendations.** Edwin G. Lutz, *Animated Cartoons: How They Are Made, Their Origin and Development* (1920; repr., Bedford, Mass.: Applewood Books, 1998), pp. 62–66, 58–59.
55 **"not very profound."** Walt Disney interview by Martin, Disc 5, CD.
56 **"Scarfoot" McCory.** Richard G. Hubler, *Walt Disney*, unpub. ms., p. 105, RHC.
56 **Correspondence course.** Ben Sharpsteen, interview by Dave Smith, Oct. 21, 1974, p. 3, WDA.
56 **Photostat of Muybridge book.** Walt Disney interview by Martin, Reel 5, p. 56.
56 **"the best animation scene . . ."** Quoted in Hubler, *Disney*, p. 106.
56 **Kansas City Art Institute.** Iwerks in KCKN Disney Transcription Spot, Mar. 29, 1945, Kansas City Broadcast, Walt Disney Corr, 1945–1946, L-P, A1535, WDA.
56 **Cel system at Slide Co.** Disney, *Autobiography* 1934.
56 **"The Little Artist."** Barrier, *Hollywood Cartoons*, p. 36.

57 **Pesmen and Newman.** Louis Pesmen, untitled ms., July 7, 1971, Pesman, Louis A., Folder, Kansas City Box, A3256, WDA.

57 **"big showman in Kansas City . . ."** Quoted in Richard H. Syring, "One of the Great Geniuses," *Silver Screen*, Nov. 1932, p. 48.

57 **Description of Newman Theater.** *Newman Theater Magazine* 1, no. 1 (n.d.), WDA.

57 **Showing Milton Feld Laugh-O-grams.** Diane Disney Miller, as told to Pete Martin, *The Story of Walt Disney* (New York: Holt, 1956), pp. 61–62.

57 **"Of course all of my contacts . . ."** Walt to Frank Newman, Jun. 21, 1933, N, D.V.'s Letters, 1934, Walt Disney Corr., 1930–1934, J-O, A1504, WDA.

57 **Showing Newman Laugh-O-grams.** Don Eddy, "The Amazing Secret of Walt Disney," *American Magazine*, Aug. 1955, p. 113.

57 **Laugh-O-gram premiere.** Russell Merritt and J. B. Kaufman, *Walt in Wonderland: The Silent Films of Walt Disney* (Baltimore: Johns Hopkins University Press, 1993), p. 38.

58 **"I was intrigued . . ."** Quoted in "The Mouse that Won a Nation," *Kansas City Times*, Nov. 11, 1978.

58 **Laugh-O-gram method.** Merritt and Kaufman, *Walt in Wonderland*, p. 38.

58 **Cartoons on theater protocol.** Walt Disney interview by Martin, Reel 5, pp. 66–67.

58 **"I got to be a little celebrity . . ."** Ibid.; Miller, *Story of Disney*, p. 64.

58 **Live action.** I was shown these films in Marceline through the kindness of Kay Malins.

59 **Studio on dirt hill.** A. V. Cauger, interview, Mar. 29, 1915, Ted Cauger Collection.

59 **Setting up the studio.** Disney, *Autobiography*, 1934, WDA.

59 **"Our sights . . ."** Fred Harman, "New Tracks in Old Trails," *True West*, Oct. 1968, pp. 10–11.

59 **"Our hopes . . ."** Ibid.

60 **friend at a local film distributor.** Jim Foland to Walt, Jul. 30, 1931, F, D.V.'s Letters, 1931–33, Walt Disney Corr., 1930–1934, D-I, A1503, WDA.

60 **"[T]hat was Walt . . ."** Roy Disney, interview by Richard Hubler, Jun. 18, 1968, RHC, box 14, folder 52.

60 **"we just couldn't swing it."** Harman, "New Tracks," p. 11.

60 **his father's advice.** Walt Disney interview by Martin, Reel 1, p. 27.

61 **Laugh-O-Gram purpose.** Articles of Association, May 18, 1922, Missouri Secretary of State File, 39844. There is some dispute over whether the company's name was "Laugh-O-Gram" as in the legal documents, or "Laugh-O-gram" as on the posters. I have chosen to use the former for the company name and the latter for the name of the films.

61 **Roy's tuberculosis.** Hubler, *Disney*, pp. 96–97.

61 **Roy moving to California.** Gilbert Seldes, "Mickey Mouse Maker," *The New Yorker*, Dec. 19, 1931, p. 24.

61 **Herbert's transfer.** Herbert A. Disney to Bayles Steele, Postmaster Kansas City, May 12, 1921, Herbert Disney File, National Personnel Records Center, Civilian Personnel Records, National Archives.

61 **Elias's sister in Portland.** Lawrence Edward Watkin, *Walt Disney*, unpub. ms., p. 137, WDA.

61 **Tired of the Kansas City winters.** Puder interview.

61 **November 6, 1921.** Flora Disney to Raymond Disney, Nov. 4, 1932, Disney Family: Genealogy, Etc., A2383, WDA.

61 **"I never knew Walt's emotions . . ."** Quoted in Katherine Greene and Richard Greene, *The Man Behind the Magic: The Story of Walt Disney* (New York: Viking Press, 1991), p. 37.

62 **Boardinghouses.** Marion Cauger to David Smith, Nov. 11, 1970, Cauger, Marion, Folder, Kansas City Box, A325; Walt to Mel Cauger, Aug. 16, 1946, C Folder, Walt Disney Corr., 1945–46, A-K, A1534; Esther Hammond to Walt, Dec. 10, 1940, H Folder, Walt Disney Corr., 1942–1943, D-H, A1537, WDA.

62 **"one of the most important events . . ."** Walt to Mrs. R. B. Cowell, Apr. 26, 1965, D Folder, Walt Disney Corr., 1965, Committees—Disney School, A1607, WDA.

62 **"belief in a Supreme Being . . ."** Walt to Frank Land, May 25, 1951, Land, Frank S., Folder, Walt Disney Corr., 1951–1952, H-L, A1546, WDA.

62 **Art editor of DeMolay magazine.** C. B. Liter to Dr. Cecil Munsey, Aug. 22, 1977, Untitled Folder, Kansas City Box, A2364, WDA.

62 **Meeting Edna.** Roy quoted in Hubler, *Disney*, p. 200.

62 **Edna Francis.** Bob Thomas, *Building a Company: Roy O. Disney and the Creation of an Entertainment Empire* (New York: Hyperion, 1998), pp. 32–33.

62 **"It was a matter of . . ."** Quoted in Hubler, *Disney*, p. 200.

62 **Forgetting dinner invitation.** Mrs. Walt Disney as told to Isabella Taves, "I Live with a Genius," *McCall's*, Feb. 1953, p. 104.

63 **"*talk* and *talk* . . ."** Edna Disney quoted in Hubler, *Disney*, p. 100.

63 **Assets.** Ibid.

63 **Ising's loan.** Merritt and Kaufman, *Walt in Wonderland*, p. 40.

63 **"quite a salesman."** Ibid.

64 **Oil refinery scheme.** Transcription of tape, Jack Kloepper [Oct. 1970], Kansas City Box, A3256, WDA.

64 **Dr. John Cowles.** John Cowles, Jr., interview by author.

64 **Cowles's advice to First National Bank.** Nadine Missakian, interview by David Smith and Jim Stewart, Aug. 12, 1970, WDA.

64 **"Dad was always . . ."** Cowles interview.

64 **$2,500 those first months.** *In the Matter of Laugh-O-Gram Films, Inc.*, District Court of the U.S. Western Division of the Western District Of Missouri, File 4457, National Archives, Central Plains Region.

64 ***Motion Picture News* announcement.** *Motion Picture News*, Jun. 17, 1922.

65 **Hiring Carmen Maxwell.** Merritt and Kaufman, *Walt in Wonderland*, p. 44.

65 **Walt Pfeiffer as scenario editor.** Walt Pfeiffer, interview by Bob Thomas, Apr. 26, 1973, WDA.

65 **1922 theater survey.** L. C. Moen, "Statistics of the Motion Picture Industry," *Motion Picture News*, Dec. 2, 1922, p. 2772, cited in Richard Koszarski, *An Evening's Entertainment: The Age of the Silent Feature Picture, 1915–1928* (Berkeley, Calif.: University of California Press, 1990), p. 48.

65 **Mace in New York.** *Motion Picture News*, Aug. 26, 1922.

65 **"bills were amounting to . . ."** Kloepper, transcription of tape.

66 **Ads.** Cited in Alma Vaughn (Newspaper Library, State Historical Society of

Missouri) to David Smith, Mar. 17, 1977, Laugh-O-Gram Film Co., A2378, WDA.

66 **"[O]ur only study was . . ."** Quoted in Barrier, *Hollywood Cartoons*, p. 37.

66 **Krazy Kat cartoon.** Pfeiffer interview.

66 **"Walt had the idea . . ."** Quoted in Barrier, *Hollywood Cartoons*, p. 82.

66 **Setup.** Merritt and Kaufman, *Walt in Wonderland*, p. 44.

67 **Model sheets.** Ibid., p. 45.

67 **Draw directly on cel.** Ibid.

67 **Pegs at bottom.** Frank Thomas and Ollie Johnston, *The Illusion of Life: Disney Animation* (New York: Hyperion, 1981), pp. 31–32.

67 ***Cinderella* scenario.** *Cinderella* (Laugh-O-gram), original script, 1922, Laugh-O-Gram Film Co., A2378, WDA.

67 **"It was more fun than pay."** Pfeiffer interview.

67 **"happy spirit that existed . . ."** Jack Kloepper to David Smith, Oct. 27, 1970, Kloepper File, Kansas City Box, A3256, WDA.

67 **Looking for accidents.** Mrs. Rod Thurlow to Walt, Apr. 27, 1956, T Folder, Walt Disney Corr., 1956, S-Z, A1565, WDA. Thurlow was the daughter of Lorey Tague.

68 **"[P]eople would come up . . ."** Quoted in Merritt and Kaufman, *Walt in Wonderland*, p. 44.

68 **"I didn't inherit any of that thrift."** Walt Disney interview by Martin, Reel 11, p. 10.

68 **"It will take another five thousand . . ."** Mac [Red Lyon] to mother, Oct. 7, 1922, Laugh-O-Gram Film Co., A2378, WDA.

68 **"Walt's checks kept bouncing."** Quoted in "The Mouse that Won a Nation," *Kansas City Times*, Nov. 11, 1978.

68 **Walt Dinsey.** Merritt and Kaufman *Walt in Wonderland*, p. 40.

68 **"worse than broke."** Mac [Red Lyon] to mother, Oct. 16, 1922, Laugh-O-Gram Film Co., A2378, WDA.

68 **"He had the drive and ambition . . ."** Nadine Missakian, Notes, Missakian, Nadine, Corr. Folder, Kansas City Box, A2364, WDA.

68 **"feature of photographing youngsters . . ."** *Kansas City Star*, Oct. 29, 1922.

69 **Dr. Thomas B. McCrum and the shoes.** Miller, *Story of Disney*, p. 71.

69 **"Walt Disney at each filming . . ."** *Introduction to Film on Dental Hygiene*, "Tommy Tucker's Tooth," *Tommy Tucker's Tooth* File, Laugh-O-Gram Film Co., A2378. [Records is erroneously referred to here as "Reynolds."]

69 **Records told another interviewer . . .** Merritt and Kaufman, *Walt in Wonderland*, p. 47.

69 **Dr. Cowles covering debt.** *In the Matter of Laugh-O-Gram Films.*

69 **Spotting dollar bill.** Quoted in David R. Smith, "Up to Date in Kansas City," *Funnyworld*, no. 19 (Fall 1978), p. 26.

70 **"animated cartoons and spicy jokes."** Paul H. Cromelin to Laugh-O-Gram, Feb. 10, 1923, Walt Disney Corr., 1923, Walt Disney Early Corr., A3381, WDA.

70 **Reediting Lafflets.** Merritt and Kaufman, *Walt in Wonderland*, p. 46.

70 **Universal.** General manager, Laugh-O-Gram, to Paul H. Cromelin, Inter-Ocean, Mar. 28, 1923, Walt Disney Corr., 1923, Walt Disney Early Corr., A3381, WDA.

70 **"We have looked at your product . . ."** H. A. Boushey to Jack Kloepper, Apr. 4, 1923, ibid.

70 **"we do not believe . . ."** Commercial Traders Cinema Corp. to Laugh-O-Gram, May 12, 1923, ibid.

70 **"very trying and expensive."** Walt to Eunice Snyder, Nov. 13, 1922, ibid.

70 **"crack the market."** Walt Disney interview by Martin, Disc 5, CD.

70 **"We have just discovered . . ."** Walt to Paul H. Cromelin, May 16, 1923, Walt Disney Corr., 1923, Walt Disney Early Corr., A3381, WDA.

70 **Seeing Virginia Davis.** Davis quoted in Merritt and Kaufman, *Walt in Wonderland*, p. 49.

70 **Contract.** David Smith notes on letters, Walt to Mrs. Davis, Apr. 13, 1923, Alice Comedies, Oswald, A2357, WDA.

71 **Davis's home as set.** "The Virginia Davis Interview," *Hogan's Alley*, no. 2 (Summer 1995), p. 108.

71 **"very soon."** Walt to Frank Duffey (Pathé) May 9, 1923, Walt Disney Corr., 1923, Walt Disney Early Corr., A3381, WDA.

71 **"numerous delays and backsets."** Walt to Paul H. Cromelin, June 18, 1923, ibid.

71 **"We twice had to move . . ."** Quoted in Michael Harris, "Original Disney Cartoon Gang Remembers Laugh-O-Grams" [no source], May 25, 1978, Laugh-O-Gram Film Co., A2378, WDA.

71 **"We didn't ever have three square meals . . ."** Ibid.

71 **Forest Inn Café.** Nadine Missakian Note, Missakian; Walt Disney interview by Martin, Reels 6 & 7, p. 4.

71 **"When my credit ran out . . ."** Walt Disney interview by Martin, Disc 5, CD.

71 **Mrs. Gertrude McBride.** Gertrude McBride to Walt, Mar. 24, 1932, M, D.V.'s letters, 1930–1933 File, Walt Disney Corr., 1930–1934, J-O, A1504, WDA.

71 **Moving into the office.** Walt Disney interview by Martin, Disc 5, CD; Jack Kloepper, transcription of tape.

71 **Sure he had tuberculosis.** Walt Disney interview by Martin, Disc 6, CD.

72 ***Kansas City Post* newsreel.** Lowell Lawrance, "Mickey Mouse—Inspiration from Mouse in K.C. Studio."

72 **Uncle Robert's advice.** Walt Disney interview by Martin, Disc 6, CD.

72 **"get out of there."** Quoted in Thomas, *Building a Company*, p. 43.

72 **"[A]t no time did anybody enter a claim . . ."** Nadine Missakian, Notes.

72 **"gotten mired down with crooks."** Roy Disney interview by Hubler, June 18, 1968, RHC, Box 14, Folder 52.

72 **"Our ideas were great . . ."** Quoted in "The Mouse That Won a Nation," *Kansas City Times*, Nov. 11, 1978.

72 **"I never once heard Walt . . ."** Kloepper, transcription of tape.

72 **"Most people filing for bankruptcy . . ."** Quoted in "The Mouse That Won a Nation."

72 **"I have no recollection . . ."** Walt Disney interview by Martin, Reel 4, p. 34.

73 **"crushed and heartbroken."** Walt Disney, *Autobiography*, 1939, 3rd installment, p. 6.

73 **Inured to failure.** Walt Disney interview by Martin, Disc 6, CD.

73 **"stand there with tears . . ."** Ibid.

73 ***Martha*.** Ibid., Reels 6 & 7, p. 7.

73 **Baby pictures.** Walt Disney, *Autobiography*, 1934; Walt Disney interview by

Martin, Disc 6, CD; Garrett D. Byrnes, "Looking at Hollywood," *Evening Bulletin*, Dec. 27, 1935, Mickey #1, M-16, 3182, WDA.

74 **Gave belongings to Harmans.** Walt to Jerry Raggos, Mar. 4, 1935, Misc. File, WDA.

74 **Laugh-O-Gram equipment.** *In the Matter of Laugh-O-Gram Films.*

74 **The other creditors.** Miller, *Story of Disney*, p. 80.

74 **Dinner with Edna Francis.** Thomas, *Building a Company*, p. 43.

74 **Meals for the train and clothes.** William Rast to Donn Tatum, Sept. 18, 1979, William Rast Folder, Disney Family: Genealogy, Etc., A2382, WDA.

74 **Suitcase and shoes.** Walt Disney interview by Martin, Disc 6, CD.

74 **"I took Walt Disney . . ."** William Rast to Walt, Jan. 9, 1959, Awards Folder, Walt Disney Corr., 1959, A-Ca, A1573, WDA.

74 **Filming his departure.** J. B. Kaufman, "Rudy Ising," in *Walt's People*, ed. Didier Ghez (Xlibris, 2005), p. 1:59.

74 **"what it meant to shift for myself . . ."** Walt to Floyd C. Shoemaker (secretary of the State Historical Society of Missouri), May 4, 1945, S Folder, Walt Disney Corr., 1945–1946, R-Z, A1536, WDA.

74 **"It was a big day . . ."** Walt Disney interview by Martin, Reels 6 & 7, p. 8.

75 **"as if he were lit up inside . . ."** Miller, *Story of Disney*, p. 73.

THREE || Wonderland

76 **"most flourishing factory . . ."** Alistair Cooke, *Alistair Cooke's America* (New York: Alfred A. Knopf, 1973), p. 319.

77 **"always wanted the best way."** Lillian Disney quoted in Amy Boothe Green and Howard E. Green, *Remembering Walt: Favorite Memories of Walt Disney* (New York: Hyperion, 1999), p. 8.

77 **"He looked like the devil."** Roy Disney quoted in Richard Hubler, *Walt Disney*, unpub. ms., p. 127, RHC.

77 **He was not hopeful.** Walt Disney, interview by Tony Thomas, Jan. 1959 (excerpt), p. 1, WDA.

77 **"I had put my drawing board away."** Quoted in "The World of Walt Disney," *Newsweek*, Dec. 31, 1962, pp. 49–50.

77 **"one of the big thrills . . ."** Walt Disney, interview by Pete Martin, Reels 6 & 7, p. 17, A2361, WDA.

77 **Toured Vitagraph.** Alice Disney Allen, interview by David Smith, Oct. 5, 1972, Allen, Alice Disney, Folder, WDA.

77 **Visiting Paramount.** Walt Disney interview by Martin, Disc 6, CD.

78 **"Tomorrow was always going to be . . ."** Roy Disney, interview by Richard Hubler, Jun. 18, 1968, RHC, Box 14, Folder 51.

78 **Convince someone to hire him.** "The Ups and Downs of Walt Disney," *Film Daily*, Oct. 4, 1966.

78 **Approaching producers for advice.** Walt Disney, "The Best Advice I Ever Had," Walt Disney Folder, Walt Disney Corr., 1962, Committees–H (Misc.), A1591, WDA. Walt had talked to Bryan Foy of the Seven Little Foys, who told him "you're trying to be too original. Don't be afraid to try a gag just because it has been used before."

78 **Sending print to Alicoate.** Roy Disney, interview by Richard Hubler, Nov.

17, 1967, WDA, p. 62; Diane Disney Miller, as told to Pete Martin, "The Coming of the Mouse," *Saturday Evening Post*, Dec. 1, 1956, p. 67.

78 **"Mr. George's Wife."** Richard G. Hubler, *Walt Disney*, unpub. ms., RHC, p. 132.

78 **"Cameras affected him . . ."** Diane Disney Miller, as told to Pete Martin, *The Story of Walt Disney* (New York: Holt, 1956), pp. 72–73.

78 **Secondhand motor.** Walt Disney, "Growing Pains," *American Cinematographer*, Mar. 1941, p. 106.

78 **"special little joke reel . . ."** Walt Disney, *Autobiography*, 1934, WDA.

78 **Animating a sample for Pantages.** Garrett D. Byrnes, "Looking at Hollywood," *Evening Bulletin*, Dec. 27, 1935, Mickey #1, M-16, 3182, WDA.

79 **Margaret Winkler's temperament.** William Mintz, interview by author.

79 **Signing Felix the Cat.** John Canemaker, *Felix: The Twisted Tale of the World's Most Popular Cat* (1991; repr., New York: DaCapo Press, 1996), p. 60.

79 **"I think the industry is full . . ."** *Exhibitor's Herald*, Dec. 30, 1922.

79 **Dispute with Sullivan.** Canemaker, *Felix*, pp. 79, 81.

79 **"very pleased."** Margaret Winkler to Walt, May 16, 1923, Winkler Film Corp. Folder, Early Corporate Documents, WDA.

80 **"[i]f you can spare . . ."** Winkler to Walt, Sept. 7, 1923, ibid.

80 **"BELIEVE SERIES CAN BE PUT OVER"** Winkler to Walt, Oct. 15, 1923, ibid.

80 **Contracts.** Oct. 16, 1923, ibid.

80 **Photographs of Alice.** Winkler to Walt, Oct. 16, 1923, ibid.

80 **"has done very well."** Harry Warner to Walt, Oct. 23, 1923, ibid.

80 ***Alice's Day at the Sea.*** Walt to Winkler, Oct. 24, 1923, ibid.

80 **"I see no reason . . ."** Winkler to Walt, Oct. 30, 1923, ibid.

81 **Awakening Roy in Sawtelle.** Roy Disney, interview by Richard Hubler, Jun. 18, 1968, RHC.

81 **Letter to Virginia Davis's mother.** Walt to Mrs. T. J. Davis, Oct. 16, 1923, Alice Comedies, Oswald Box, A2357, WDA.

81 **Virginia's summer trip to Hollywood.** Mrs. T. J. Davis to Walt, Aug. 6, 1923, Davis, Virginia, Folder, Laugh-O-Gram Film Co., A2378, WDA.

81 **Virginia Davis terms.** Walt to Mrs. T. J. Davis, Oct. 20, 1923, ibid.

81 **The Davises deciding for California.** "The Virginia Davis Interview," *Hogan's Alley*, no. 2 (Summer 1995), p. 109.

82 **Roy was struck.** Hubler, *Disney*, p. 134.

82 **Uncle Robert's courtship.** Ruth Disney, interview by David Smith, Nov. 4, 1974, WDA.

82 **"He demanded a lot of respect . . ."** Miller, *Story of Disney*, p. 78.

82 **Debt to Ray.** Ibid., pp. 79–80.

82 **Uncle Robert's loans.** Studio Accounting Books, 1923–1930, A2384, WDA.

82 **Loans.** Ibid.

83 **"I was just helping him . . ."** Roy Disney interview by Hubler, Nov. 17, 1967, p. 22.

83 **Taken advantage of.** Roy Disney interview by Hubler, Jun. 18, 1968.

83 **"love of Walt."** Lawrence Edward Watkin, *Walt Disney*, unpub. ms., p. 144, WDA.

83 **Moving out of Uncle Robert's.** Louis Sobol, "Voice of Broadway," *New York Journal-American*, Feb. 5, 1938.

83 **Renting 4651 Kingswell.** Check Stub no. 1, Studio Accounting Books, 1923–1930, A2384, WDA.
83 **Single take.** Virginia Davis quoted in Katherine Greene and Richard Greene, *Inside the Dream: The Personal Story of Walt Disney* (New York: Roundtable Press, 2001), p. 30.
83 **"It was very informal."** "Virginia Davis Interview."
84 **Policeman in Griffith Park.** Walt Disney, speech at Milestone Awards Banquet, Producers Guild, Feb. 17, 1957, Screen Producers Guild Folder, Walt Disney Corr., 1959, P-Sm, A1578, WDA.
84 **Making Alices.** Luncheon Meeting on Production F-1, *Snow White*, Feb. 18, 1937, Story Meetings, Feb.–Mar. 1937 Folder, *Snow White and the Seven Dwarfs*, Story Meetings, Oct. 1934–1937, Box 1, A1731, WDA.
84 **Animating by himself.** Disney, *Autobiography*, 1934.
84 **"satisfactory."** Margaret Winker to Walt, Dec. 26, 1923, Winkler Film Corp. folder, Early Corporate Documents, WDA.
84 **"inject as much humor . . ."** Winkler to Walt, Jan. 9, 1924, ibid.
84 ***Alice Hunting in Africa.*** Walt to Winkler, Jan. 21, 1924; Winkler to Walt, Jan. 31, 1924, ibid.
85 **Hiring.** See Ledger, 1923–1924, Studio Accounting Books, 1923–1930, A2384, WDA. It is difficult to determine exactly how many employees Disney Bros. had in these early months because some were doing only daywork and were not fully employed.
85 **"best you have turned out."** Winkler to Walt, Mar. 4, 1924, Winkler Film Corp. Folder, Early Corporate Documents, WDA.
85 **"little different . . ."** Walt to Winkler, Feb. 26, 1924, ibid.
85 **"if none of the future ones . . ."** Tel. Winkler to Walt, Apr. 7, 1924, ibid.
85 **Winkler visiting Disney Bros.** Walt to Ubbe Iwwerks, Jun. 10, 1924, ibid.
86 **"Boy, you will never regret it . . ."** Walt to Iwwerks, Jun. 1, 1924, ibid.
86 **Iwwerks's trip.** Walt to Dr. Thomas B. McCrum, Aug. 4, 1924, ibid.
86 **"Where two words would barely suffice . . ."** Shamus Culhane, *Talking Animals and Other People* (New York: St. Martin's Press, 1986), pp. 71–72.
86 **"I never made a drawing . . ."** Clipping, *Mobile Press Register*, Me-Mz Folder, Walt Disney Corr., 1957, E-O, A1567, WDA.
86 **Emphasis on animation.** Walt to Winkler, Aug. 29, 1924, Winkler Film Corp. Folder, Early Corporate Documents, WDA; also Michael Barrier, *Hollywood Cartoons: American Animation in Its Golden Age* (New York: Oxford University Press, 1999), p. 40.
86 **"girl stand out . . ."** Walt to Winkler, Aug. 29, 1924, Winkler Film Corp. Folder, Early Corporate Documents, WDA.
86 **"Walt's concept of the photography . . ."** Culhane, *Talking Animals*, p. 8.
87 **Driving to Hill Street Theater.** Hubler, *Disney*, p. 235.
87 **"I was ambitious . . ."** Disney, "Growing Pains," p. 107.
87 **"for a twenty dollar joke . . ."** Walt quoted in Miller, *Story of Disney*, p. 123.
87 **"Gags and Situations."** *Alice in the Wooly West*, Alice Comedies Folder, Oswald Box, A2357, WDA.
87 **Irritating Sullivan.** Russell Merritt and J. B. Kaufman, *Walt in Wonderland: The Silent Films of Walt Disney* (Baltimore: Johns Hopkins University Press, 1993), p. 63.

88 **Copyright problems.** Canemaker, *Felix*, p. 90.
88 **Charles Mintz.** William Mintz, interview by author; Friz Freleng, *Reflections of Friz Freleng*, unpub. ms., 1969, Special Collections, Young Research Library, UCLA; *NYT*, Dec. 31, 1939.
88 **"a grim-faced man . . ."** Culhane, *Talking Animals*, p. 25.
89 **Police badges.** Mintz interview.
89 **"very tight place."** Walt to Mintz, Aug. 15, 1924, Winkler Film Corp. Folder, Early Corporate Documents, WDA.
89 **Promissory note.** Ledger 1924–1927, Studio Accounting Books, 1923–1930, A2384, WDA.
89 **"We need money."** Walt to Winkler, Aug. 29, 1924; Mintz to Walt, Oct. 6, 1924, Winkler Film Corp. Folder, Early Corporate Documents, WDA.
89 **Salary.** Ledger 1924–1927, Studio Accounting Books, 1923–1930, WDA.
89 **"while things are not 100% rosy . . ."** George Winkler to Walt, Dec. 8, 1924, Winkler Film Corp. Folder, Early Corporate Documents, WDA.
90 **Contract terms.** George Winkler to Walt, Jan. 8, 1925, ibid.
90 **Improvements.** Walt to Winkler, Sept. 29, 1924; Walt to Mintz, Dec. 2, 1924, ibid.
90 **"You have'nt . . ."** Walt to Hugh Harman, Feb. 27, 1925, Walt Disney Corr., 1925, Walt Disney Early Corr., A3381, WDA.
90 **"things that can only be learned . . ."** Walt to Rudy Ising, Mar. 30, 1925, ibid.
91 **"Walt wanted to shave it off . . ."** Lillian Disney, interview by Richard Hubler, Apr. 16, 1968, Disney, Lillian, Folder, WDA.
91 **Growing mustache.** Ising to Walt, Apr. 8, 1924, Walt Disney Corr., 1925, Walt Disney Early Corr., A3381, WDA.
91 **"Well here I am . . ."** Red Cross Photos, WDA.
91 **"[H]e did have a complex . . ."** Roy Disney interview by Hubler, Jun. 18, 1968.
91 **"[H]e was a little different . . ."** Walt Pfeiffer, interview by Bob Thomas, Apr. 26, 1973, WDA.
91 **"I was normal . . ."** Quoted in "Father Goose," *Time*, Dec. 27, 1954, p. 44.
91 **Dorothy Wendt.** John Cowles, Jr., interview by author.
92 **Peterson.** David Iwerks, interview by author.
92 **twenty-five years old and had saved $10,000.** Miller, *Story of Disney*, p. 73.
92 **Roy's proposal and wedding.** Roy Disney interview by Hubler, Feb. 20, 1968; Mrs. Edna Disney, interview by Richard Hubler, Aug. 20, 1968, RHC, Box 14, Folder 52.
92 **Lillian joining Disney Bros.** Lillian Disney Truyens, interview by Bob Thomas, Apr. 19, 1973, Disney, Lillian, Folder, WDA; Greene and Greene, *Inside the Dream*, p. 34.
92 **The first time she saw him . . .** Hubler, *Disney*, p. 758.
93 **Lillian's grandfather.** *An Illustrated History of North Idaho Embracing Nez Perce, Idaho, Latah, Kootenai and Shoshone Counties* (Western History Publishing, 1903), p. 142.
93 **Driving "hack" wagon.** Clipping, Disney Family General Folder, Disney Family: Genealogy, Etc., A2383, WDA.
93 **Lapwai.** Clara Glasby, "Old Spalding Class Has Just One Left," *Lewiston*

Morning Tribune, Aug. 18, 1972; Carol Wilson, "Lapwai Became Village 60 Years Ago Today," *Lewiston Morning Tribune*, Jan. 30, 1971.

93 **"They never knew if there was . . ."** Quoted in Hubler, *Disney*, p. 757.

93 **Driving home.** Lillian Disney, interviewed by Richard Hubler, RHC, Apr. 16, 1968.

94 **"I began to look at him . . ."** Quoted in Green and Green, *Remembering Walt*, p. 11.

94 **Asking Lillian for a date.** Lillian Disney interview by Hubler; Bob Thomas, *Building a Company: Roy O. Disney and the Creation of an Entertainment Empire* (New York: Hyperion, 1999), p. 11.

94 **"I didn't have any other dates . . ."** Hubler, *Disney*, p. 759.

94 **"All of a sudden . . ."** Quoted in Greene and Greene, *Inside the Dream*, p. 35.

94 **Tucking in Marjorie.** Katherine Greene and Richard Greene, *The Man Behind the Magic: The Story of Walt Disney* (New York: Viking, 1991), p. 46.

94 **Dates.** Lillian Disney Truyens interview by Thomas; Hubler, *Disney*, p. 760.

94 **"He never thought of anything . . ."** Edna Disney, interview by Richard Hubler, Aug. 20, 1968.

94 **"How do you know . . ."** Ibid., p. 88.

94 **"Walt was a dominating person."** Quoted in Thomas, *Building a Company*, pp. 51–52.

95 **"good listener . . ."** Miller, *Story of Disney*, pp. 87–88.

95 **Managing the business office.** Clipping [n.d.], Alice Comedies Folder, Oswald, A2357, WDA. The clipping reads: "Miss Lillian Bounds is manager of the business office."

95 **Taking dictation.** Thomas, *Building a Company*, p. 51.

95 **"It looked like a locomotive headlight . . ."** Miller, *Story of Disney*, p. 88.

95 **"Walt didn't like to be alone."** Lillian Disney interview by Hubler.

95 **Steamer to Seattle.** Walt to Carl Stalling, Sept. 16, 1925, Disney, Walt, Corr., 1925, Walt Disney Early Corr., A3381, WDA. Roy said that Walt had driven up in his Moon roadster, but this seems improbable. See Roy Disney interview by Hubler, Feb. 20, 1968, p. 4.

95 **Walt had taken $150.** Ledger, 1924–1927, Studio Accounting Books, 1923–1930, A2384. See Jul. 13, 1925.

95 **Lillian giggling.** Greene and Greene, *Man Behind the Magic*, p. 48.

95 **Honeymoon.** Walt to Carl Stalling, Sept. 16, 1925.

95 **Wedding night.** Miller, *Story of Disney*, p. 88.

95 **Trade paper reviews.** Promotional flyer, Alice Comedies, [1925], Alice Comedies Folder, Oswald, A2357, WDA.

96 **Virginia Davis appearances.** Merritt and Kaufman, *Walt in Wonderland*, p. 63.

96 **Book tie-in.** Walt to George Winkler, Aug. 17, 1925, Winkler Film Corp. Folder, Early Corporate Documents, WDA.

96 **Deposit on studio.** David R. Smith, "Disney Before Burbank: The Kingswell and Hyperion Studios," *Funnyworld*, no. 20 (Summer 1979), pp. 34–35.

96 **Disputes with Mintz.** Mintz to Walt, Sept. 26, 1925; Walt to Mintz, Oct. 2, 1925; Mintz to Walt, Oct. 6, 1925; Walt to Mintz, Oct. 15, 1925, Disney, Walt, Corr., 1925, Walt Disney Early Corr., A3381, WDA.

96 **Distribution terms.** Tel. Mintz to Walt, Nov. 11, 1925, Winkler Film Corp. Folder, Early Corporate Documents, WDA.

97 **"I intend to make your product . . ."** Mintz to Walt, Nov. 24, 1925, Disney, Walt, Corr., 1925, Walt Disney Early Corr.

97 **"all matters regarding making of comedies . . ."** Walt to George Winkler, Jan. 9, 1926, Winkler Film Corp. Folder, Early Corporate Documents.

97 **Mintz rejecting demand.** Mintz to George Winkler, Jan. 14, 1926; Tel.: Walt to Mintz, Jan. 17, 1926, ibid.

97 **Davises erupted.** Mintz to Mrs. Margaret J. Davis, Oct. 1, 1925, Christie's brochure, April 18, 1994, Alice Comedies Folder, Oswald, A2357, WDA. See also Jeff and Margaret Davis to Walt, Jan. 7, 1925, Davis, Virginia, Folder, Laugh-O-Gram Film Co., A2378, for an example of tensions between the Davises and Walt.

98 **"Virginia Davis had had something . . ."** Christopher Finch, *The Art of Walt Disney: From Mickey Mouse to the Magic Kingdoms* (1973; repr., New York: Harry N. Abrams, 1993), p. 44.

98 **"Margie was cute . . ."** "Virginia Davis Interview," p. 112.

98 **Size of a grocery store.** Ben Sharpsteen, interview by Don Peri, Feb. 6, 1974, p. 3, WDA.

98 **"little green and white structure . . ."** Disney, *Autobiography*, 1939, 3rd installment, p. 5.

98 **"One evening when Walt . . ."** Jack Kinney, *Walt Disney and Other Animated Characters: An Unauthorized Account of the Early Years at Disney's* (New York: Harmony Books, 1988), p. 198. The associate to whom Roy told the story was Jack Cutting. Others, however, including Dave Smith, say that Roy told them it was *his* idea to name the studio after Walt because the public could better identify with a single individual.

98 **"extremely disappointed."** Mintz to Walt, Jan. 28, 1926, Winkler Film Corp. Folder, Early Corporate Documents, WDA.

98 **Walt's new terms.** Tel. Walt to Mintz, Feb. 8, 1926, ibid.

99 **"I want you to understand . . ."** Walt to Mintz, Mar. 1, 1926, ibid.

99 **McCrum and Stalling.** Walt to McCrum, Aug. 20, 1924, Walt Disney Corr., 1924, Walt Disney Early Corr., A3381, WDA; Walt to Stalling, Sept. 16, 1925, Disney, Walt Corr., 1925, Walt Disney Early Corr., A3381, WDA.

99 **Subcontracted.** Merritt and Kaufman, *Walt in Wonderland*, p. 79.

99 **"Walt's office looks . . ."** Rudy Ising to family, Apr. 13, 1926, quoted in Michael Barrier, *Hollywood Cartoons*, p. 43.

99 **Profits from Alice.** General Expense Account, 1925, 1926, 1927, WDA.

99 **"I have borrowed . . ."** Walt to Mintz, Dec. 27, 1926, Winkler Film Corp. Folder, Early Corporate Documents, WDA.

99 **"I remember I was so unhappy . . ."** Lillian Disney Truyens interview by Thomas.

100 **"Walt would have an idea . . ."** Rudy Ising quoted in Merritt and Kaufman, *Walt in Wonderland*, p. 73.

100 **When animating . . .** Friz Freleng, *Reflections of Friz Freleng*, 1969, p. 5, Special Collections, Young Research Library, UCLA.

100 **New Year's 1926.** Rudy Ising to Nadine Missakian, Jan. 22, 1926, Untitled Folder, Kansas City Box, A2364, WDA.

100 **"clash of personalities."** Thurston Harper to David Smith, Oct. 26, 1973,

Alice Comedies Folder, Oswald, A2357, WDA; Freleng quoted in Brian Burnes, "Cartoon History Stars KC Artists," *Kansas City Star*, Feb. 22, 1990.

100 **"I made mistakes . . ."** Quoted in Barrier, *Hollywood Cartoons*, p. 46.

100 **"couldn't bear the abuse."** Ibid.

100 **"make insulting remarks to me."** Freleng, *Reflections*, p. 25.

100 **"Walt could make you feel real bad . . ."** Wilfred Jackson, quoted in Frank Thomas and Ollie Johnston, *The Illusion of Life: Disney Animation* (New York: Hyperion, 1981), p. 34.

100 **"He was that way."** Quoted on *Walt Disney: An Intimate History of the Man and His Magic*, CD-ROM, Pantheon Productions, 1998.

101 **"This will leave Walt . . ."** Harman and Ising to C. G. Maxwell, Aug. 1, 1926, Alice Comedies Folder, Oswald, A2357, WDA.

101 **Firing Ising.** Barrier, *Hollywood Cartoons*, p. 45.

101 **Firing Freleng.** Steven Watts, *The Magic Kingdom: Walt Disney and the American Way of Life* (Boston: Houghton Mifflin, 1997), p. 45.

101 **"den of strife and vexation."** Ising to Thurston Harper, 1927, quoted in Barrier, *Hollywood Cartoons*, p. 67.

101 **"Koo-Koo Hatchery."** Drawings by Iwerks and Les Clark reprinted in John Canemaker, *Walt Disney's Nine Old Men and the Art of Animation* (New York: Disney Editions, 2001), p. 12.

101 **Bonuses and schedule.** Ising to C. G. Maxwell, Jun. 10, 1926, Alice Comedies Folder, Oswald, A2357, WDA.

101 **"I have felt we have sort of been in a rut."** Walt to Mintz, Feb. 26, 1927, Winkler Film Corp. Folder, Early Corporate Documents, WDA.

102 **"full of life and expression."** Walt to Mintz, Jan. 26, 1927, ibid.

102 **"legs seemed kind of heavy."** Mintz to Walt, Jan. 31, 1927, ibid.

102 **"[T]hey seem to think . . ."** Mintz to Walt, Jan. 31, 1927, ibid.

102 **"establish a specially constructed studio . . ."** *Motion Picture World*, Mar. 12, 1927.

102 **"shoot the first picture . . ."** Mintz to Walt, Apr. 1, 1927, Winkler Film Corp. Folder, Early Corporate Documents, WDA.

102 **"young and snappy looking . . ."** Tel. Mintz to Walt, Apr. 15, 1927, ibid.

102 **"rabbit character . . ."** Walt to Mintz, Apr. 27, 1927, 1926–1927 Folder, Walt Disney Early Corr., WDA.

103 **"That's what I want to see . . ."** Freleng quoted in Merritt and Kaufman, *Walt in Wonderland*, p. 81.

103 **"I am the LUCKY rabbit."** *Universal Weekly*, May 28, 1927, Oswald Photos, Alice Comedies, Oswald, A2357, WDA.

103 **"Oswald looks like a real contender . . ."** *Film Daily*, Jun. 7, 1927, ibid.

103 **"This series is destined . . ."** *Motion Picture News*, Aug. 19, 1927.

103 **"simulate the gestures . . ."** *Moving Picture World*, Aug. 13, 1927.

103 **"It contains some of the best gags . . ."** *Motion Picture World*, Sept. 10, 1927.

104 **"transform the absurd . . ." and libidinous nature.** Donald Crafton, *Before Mickey: The Animated Film, 1898–1928* (Cambridge, Mass.: MIT Press, 1982), pp. 294–95.

104 **Two other historians . . .** Merritt and Kaufman, *Walt in Wonderland*, p. 32.

104 **"bad as they look today . . ."** Richard Huemer, *Recollections of Dick Huemer*, p. 30, Special Collections, Young Research Library, UCLA.

104 **Twenty-two on staff.** Disney, *Autobiography*, 1934. The account in the Ledger, Disney Bros. 1923–1924, Studio Accounting Books, 1923–1930, seems to indicate there were only sixteen employees at the end of 1927.

104 **Iwerks's raise.** David R. Smith, "Ub Iwerks, 1901–1971," *Funnyworld*, no. 14 (Spring 1972), p. 34.

104 **"a man of experience . . ."** Walt to Mintz, Apr. 27, 1927, 1926–1927 Folder, Walt Disney Early Corr., WDA.

104 **Splitting the profits.** General Expenses Account, 1925, 1926, 1927, WDA.

104 **Buying land.** Ibid.

105 **"commonest type of middle-class . . ."** Gilbert Seldes, "Mickey Mouse Maker," *The New Yorker*, Dec. 19, 1931.

105 **Cost of homes.** Roy Disney interview by Hubler, Jun. 18, 1968.

105 **Finest house she had ever seen.** Quoted by Diane Disney in Greene and Greene, *Inside the Dream*, p. 36.

105 **"Walt was so good to my grandmother."** Ibid., pp. 36–37.

106 **"I was interested . . ."** Quoted in Barrier, *Hollywood Cartoons*, p. 4.

106 **Signing away staff.** Ub Iwerks interview, ca. 1956, WDA.

106 **"one of the best sellers . . ."** *Film Daily*, Feb. 16, 1928.

106 **"second honeymoon."** Mrs. Walt Disney, as told to Isabella Taves, "I Live with a Genius," *McCall's*, Feb. 1953, p. 104.

106 **Meeting Quimby.** Walt to Roy, n.d. [Mar. 1928], RHC, Box 27, Folder 107.

107 **Meeting with Mintz.** Walt to Roy, n.d. [Mar. 1928], ibid.

107 **"reserved and dignified."** Walt to Roy, Feb. 28, 1928, ibid.

107 **"BREAK WITH CHARLIE LOOMING."** Tel. Walt to Roy, Mar. 1, 1928, ibid.

107 **"from what remarks were dropped . . ."** Walt to Roy, n.d. [Mar. 1928], ibid.

107 **"MAKE THEM SIGN . . ."** Tel. Walt to Roy, Mar. 2, 1928, Walt Disney 1928 Corr., Walt Disney Early Corr., WDA.

108 **"CAN GET PLENTY OF GOOD MEN."** Tel. Walt to Roy, Mar. 2, 1928, ibid.

108 **"Go on home . . ."** Walt to Roy, Mar. 2, 1928, 10:30 p.m., ibid.

108 **Meeting with Goldstein.** Ibid.

109 **Mintz's last offer.** Tel. Walt to Roy, Mar. 5, 1928, ibid.

109 **Returning to hotel.** Mrs. Walt Disney, "I Live With a Genius," p. 104.

109 **"Well, we are still hanging around . . ."** Walt to Roy, Mar. 7, 1928, Walt Disney, 1928 Corr., Walt Disney Early Corr., WDA.

109 **"He told it just like the plot . . ."** Ward Kimball quoted in Hubler, *Disney*, p. 778.

FOUR || The Mouse

111 **"He was like a raging lion . . ."** Don Eddy, "The Amazing Secret of Walt Disney," *American Magazine*, Aug. 1955, p. 113.

112 **New character.** Quoted in Richard Hubler, *Walt Disney*, unpub. ms., 1968, p. 144, RHC.

112 **Mickey Mouse story.** Eddy, "Amazing Secret," p. 113; Mrs. Walt Disney, as told to Isabella Taves, "I Live With a Genius," *McCall's*, Feb. 1953, p. 104; Jack Alexander, "The Amazing Story of Walt Disney," *Saturday Evening Post*, Oct. 31, 1953, p. 92; Disney, *Autobiography*, unpub. ms., 1934, WDA; Diane Disney

Miller, as told to Pete Martin, *The Story of Walt Disney*, (New York: Holt, 1956), p. 92.

112 **Mouse stories.** *LAT*, Nov. 15, 1931, sec. 2, p. 2; *New York Journal American*, Jan. 29, 1938; Nadine Missakian, interview by David Smith and Jim Stewart, Aug. 12, 1978, WDA; A. V. Cauger quoted in Walt Disney interview, Mar. 29, 1945, Ted Cauger Collection; Gerald Nachman, "Walt Disney: Portrait of the Artist," *New York Post*, Oct. 10, 1965; Walt Disney, "Mickey Mouse Is 5 Years Old," *Film Pictorial*, Sept. 30, 1933, p. 36; J. P. McEvoy, "Walt Disney Goes to War," *This Week*, Jul. 5, 1942.

112 **"wonderful idea."** Quoted in Bob Thomas, *Building a Company: Roy O. Disney and the Creation of an Entertainment Empire* (New York: Hyperion, 1998), p. 57.

113 **"one of the absolute low points . . ."** Quoted in Hubler, *Disney*, p. 150. Iwerks recalls this as Walt returning from New York after trying to sell *Plane Crazy*, but Walt did not attempt to sell *Plane Crazy* in New York until later that summer, returning in a different frame of mind.

113 **"highly exaggerated . . ."** Ibid., p. 147.

113 **"We simply thought the mouse . . ."** Mrs. Walt Disney, "Genius," p. 104.

113 **"A couple of the mice . . ."** Ub Iwerks, interview by George Sherman, Jul. 30, 1970, WDA.

113 **Clifton Meek.** Ben Sharpsteen, interview by Don Peri, Feb. 6, 1974, p. 5, WDA; Ub Iwerks interview, ca. 1956, WDA.

113 **"I grew up with those drawings . . ."** Mary Bragiotti, "Mickey Mouse's Dearest Friends," *New York Post*, Jun. 30, 1944, p. 17.

113 **"Pear-shaped body . . ."** Iwerks to John Culhane quoted in Robert W. Brockway, "The Masks of Mickey Mouse: Symbol of a Generation," *Journal of Popular Culture*, Spring 1989, pp. 27–28.

113 **"He was designed for maximum ease . . ."** Christopher Finch, *The Art of Walt Disney: From Mickey Mouse to the Magic Kingdoms* (New York: New American Library, 1975), p. 25.

113 **"Walt designed a mouse."** Quoted in John Culhane, "A Mouse for All Seasons," *Saturday Review of Literature*, Nov. 11, 1978, p. 50.

114 **"After trying various names . . ."** Disney, *Autobiography*, 1934, WDA.

114 **Mickey was shorter.** Henry F. Pringle, "Mickey Mouse's Father," *McCall's*, Aug. 1932, p. 28.

114 **Wilfred Jackson.** Wilfred Jackson, interview by David Smith, May 14, 1971, WDA.

114 **Jackson's first week.** Ibid.

114 **"outcast."** Iwerks interview, ca. 1956.

115 **"the great secret . . ."** Harman quoted in Michael Barrier, *Hollywood Cartoons: American Animation in Its Golden Age* (New York: Oxford University Press, 1999), p. 49.

115 **"The first *Mickey Mouse* . . ."** Walt Disney, "Growing Pains," *American Cinematographer*, Mar. 1941, p. 106.

115 **Seven hundred drawings a day.** Iwerks interview, ca. 1956.

115 **Cost of *Plane Crazy*.** General Expense Account, 1925, 1926, 1927, WDA.

115 **"We worked night and day."** Mrs. Walt Disney, "Genius," pp. 104, 106.

115 **Les Clark dated . . .** Frank Thomas and Ollie Johnston, *The Illusion of Life: Disney Animation* (New York: Hyperion, 1981), p. 39.

115 **Walt's own children . . .** Ibid., p. 103.

116 **Minnie's name.** John Cowles, Jr., interview by author.

116 **"It was applauded more . . ."** Tel. Charles McManus to Walt, Jul. 17, 1955, Disneyland Premiere Folder, Walt Disney Corr., 1955, C-D, A1557, WDA.

116 **"make the name of 'Mickey Mouse' . . ."** Iwerks interview, ca. 1956; E. J. Denison to Bob C. Baldridge, May 18, 1928; Walt to Denison, May 21, 1928, Walt Disney 1928 Corr., Walt Disney Early Corr., WDA.

116 **Metro's decision.** Tel. R. W. McGrath (MGM) to Walt, May 29, 1928, ibid.

116 **"We'll make them over with sound."** Mrs. Walt Disney, "Genius," p. 106.

116 **Roy's version.** Roy Disney, interview by Richard Hubler, Jun. 18, 1968, RHC, Box 14, Folder 51.

116 **Broaching sound.** Jackson interview by Smith.

117 **"Drawings are not vocal."** Wilfred Jackson, interview by Richard Hubler, Mar. 26, 1968, WDA.

117 **"as if the noise . . ."** Quoted in Barrier, *Hollywood Cartoons*, p. 51.

117 **"Damn it, I know how fast . . ."** Jackson interview by Smith.

117 **"We could break down . . ."** Quoted in Leslie Iwerks and John Kenworthy, *The Hand Behind the Mouse* (New York: Disney Editions, 2001), p. 62.

118 ***Steamboat Willie* showing.** Mike Barrier, " 'Building a Better Mouse': Fifty Years of Disney Animation," *Funnyworld*, no. 20 (Summer 1979), pp. 6, 8; Jackson interview by Smith; Iwerks interview, ca. 1956.

118 **"I never saw such a reaction . . ."** Quoted in Hubler, *Disney*, pp. 152–53.

118 **"You're out here talking about babies . . ."** Quoted in Iwerks and Kenworthy, *Hand Behind*, pp. 63–64.

119 **"nothing since has ever equaled it."** Iwerks interview, ca. 1956.

119 **"It was terrible . . ."** Disney, "Growing Pains," p. 107.

119 **Reassembled at six.** Hubler, *Disney*, p. 153.

119 **"*Jazz Singer* of animation."** John Canemaker, *Felix: The Twisted Tale of the World's Most Famous Cat* (New York: Da Capo Press, 1996), p. 6.

119 **"They are all afraid . . ."** Walt to Nat Levine, Aug. 21, 1928, Mascot Pictures Corp. Folder, Roy O. Disney Corr., Lu-Mi (1930–1939), A2997, WDA.

120 **"I hope I have not stumbled."** Roy to Walt and Ubbe, Sept. 4, 1928, Walt Disney 1928 Corr., Walt Disney Early Corr., WDA.

120 **"[b]ig lovable friendly Irishman."** Walt Disney interview by Martin, Reel 2, p. 17.

120 **"good natured cuss."** Walt to Roy and Ub, Sept. 14, 1928, Walt Disney 1928 Corr., Walt Disney Early Corr., WDA.

120 **"When in doubt, Powers attacks."** Terry Ramsaye, *A Million and One Nights* (New York: Simon & Schuster, 1926), p. 591. For more on Powers see pp. 497–504.

120 **Tossing books out window.** Ibid., p. 592.

121 **"very enthused . . ."** Walt to Roy, [Sept. 1928]; Walt to Roy and Ubbe, Sept. 7, 1928, Walt Disney 1928 Corr., Walt Disney Early Corr., WDA.

121 **"A lot of racket . . ."** Walt to Roy and Ubbe, Sept. 7, 1928, ibid.

121 **Costs of recording.** Walt to Roy and Ubbe, Sept. 4, 1928; Walt to Roy and Ubbe, Sept. 7, 1928, ibid.

121 **"My idea is to get the thing . . ."** Walt to Roy and Ubbe, Sept. 7, 1928, ibid.

121 **"Be sure and have enough money . . ."** Walt to Roy, Sept. 11, 1928, ibid.

121 ***"our best bet is Powers."*** Ibid.
122 **"too many Symphonic effects."** Walt to Roy and Ub, Sept. 20, 1928, ibid.
122 **First recording session.** Walt Disney interview by Martin, Reel 2, pp. 17–23; Diane Disney Miller, as told to Pete Martin, *The Story of Walt Disney* (New York: Holt, 1956), pp. 100–101.
122 **Hating New York.** Walt to Roy, Sept. 11, 1928; Walt to Ub and Roy, Sept. 23, 1928, Walt Disney 1928 Corr., Walt Disney Early Corr., WDA.
122 **Abscess.** Ibid.
122 **"If you knew the entire situation . . ."** Walt to Ub and Roy, Sept. 20, 1928, ibid.
122 **"GET AS LARGE A LOAN . . ."** Tel. Walt to Walt Disney Studio, Sept. 21, 1928, ibid.
123 **"Old Man Opportunity . . ."** Walt to Roy and Ub, Sept. 23, 1928, ibid.
123 **Ball system.** Walt to Roy, Sept. 25, 1928, ibid.
123 **"It worked like clock works."** Walt to "Gang," Sept. 30, 1928, ibid.
123 **"It proves one thing to me."** Ibid.
123 **"All together now"** Walt to Roy, Oct. 1, 1928, ibid.
123 **"[w]e can lick them all . . ."** Walt to Roy and Ub, Sept. 23, 1928, ibid.
123 **"What better salesman could we want . . ."** Walt to Roy and Ub, Sept. 14, 1928, ibid.
123 **"Big Boys."** Walt to Roy and Ub, Sept. 20, 1928, ibid.
123 **"I am going to stick as close . . ."** Walt to Roy, Oct. 1, 1928, ibid.
123 ***Willie* screening for Universal.** Walt to Lilly, Oct. 15, 1928, ibid.
124 **Agreement with Powers** Patrick A. Powers et al. with Walt Disney, Oct. 15, 1928, Powers Cinephone Folder, WDA.
124 **Universal deal.** Walt to Lilly, Oct. 19, 1928, Walt Disney 1928 Corr., Walt Disney Early Corr., WDA.
124 **Universal meeting and Powers office.** Walt to Lilly, Oct. 20, 1928, ibid.
125 **"In this game . . ."** Walt to [Roy], Oct. 22, 1928, ibid.
125 **"amased."** Walt to Lilly, Oct. 26, 1928, ibid.
125 **Universal's decision.** Walt to Lilly, Oct. 27, 1928, ibid.
125 **"If you ever worked like HELL . . ."** Walt to Roy and Ubbe, Oct. 6, 1928, ibid.
125 **Stalling's arrival.** Walt to Lilly, Oct. 26, 1928, ibid.
125 **"I didn't tell him . . ."** Walt to Lilly, Oct. 27, 1928, ibid.
125 **Finances.** General Expense Account, 1925–1926–1927; Walt to Lilly, Oct. 27, 1928, ibid.
126 **Harry Reichenbach.** Harry Reichenbach, as told to David Freedman, *Phantom Fame: The Anatomy of Ballyhoo* (New York: Simon & Schuster, 1931).
126 **Deal with Reichenbach.** Walt Disney interview by Martin, Reel 2, pp. 25–26; Miller, *Story of Disney*, p. 104. By another account, Walt received $250 a week for two weeks. See Hubler, *Disney*, p. 160.
127 **"heard laughs and snickers . . ."** Quoted in Brian Burnes, Robert W. Butler, and Dan Viets, *Walt Disney's Missouri: The Roots of Creative Genius*, ed. Donna Martin (Kansas City, Mo.: Kansas City Star Books, 2002), p. 132.
127 **"Not the first . . ."** *Variety*, Nov. 21, 1928.
127 **"knocked me out of my seat."** *Exhibitor's Herald*, Nov. 1928.
127 **"an ingenious piece of work . . ."** *NYT*, Nov. 21, 1928.

127 **"I do not believe . . ."** Quoted in Thomas and Johnston, *Illusion of Life*, p. 288.

127 **Mickey's walk.** Ibid., p. 346.

128 **"It became the rage."** David Dodd Hand, *Memoirs* (Cambria, Calif.: Lighthouse Litho, 1990), p. 66.

128 **"Disney put us out of business . . ."** Quoted in Canemaker, *Felix*, p. 7.

128 **"I knew that I would be restrained . . ."** Disney, *Autobiography*, 1934.

128 **Contract demands and terms.** Walt Disney interview by Martin, Reel 2, p. 27.

129 **"With this is [*sic*] the bag . . ."** Charles Giegerich to Walt, Dec. 19, 1928, Powers Cinephone Equipment Corp., Correspondence, 1928–29, WDA.

129 **Deals for *Mickey Mouse*.** Giegerich to Walt, Dec. 31, 1928; Giegerich to Walt, Mar. 24, 1929; Walt to Giegerich, May 3, 1929, ibid.

129 **"We give them the stuff . . ."** Walt to Roy and Ubbe, Feb. 9, 1929, RHC, Box 27, Folder 107.

129 **One-reel live-action talking comedies.** Walt to Dr. J. V. Cowles, Dec. 28, 1928, ibid.

129 **Originating with Stalling.** Walt to Roy and Ubbe, Sept. 7, 1928, Walt Disney 1928 Corr., Walt Disney Early Corr., WDA.

129 **Floating idea.** Walt to Roy, Sept. 11, 1928, ibid.

129 **Skeleton ad.** Iwerks and Kenworthy, *Hand Behind*, p. 75.

129 **"Carl's idea of the 'Skeleton Dance' . . ."** Walt to Roy, Sept. 25, 1928, Walt Disney 1928 Corr., Walt Disney Early Corr., WDA.

130 **"quite out of the ordinary."** Walt to Giegerich, Jan. 16, 1929, Powers Cinephone Equipment Corp., Corr., 1928–29, WDA.

130 **"He is . . . a 'HIT.' "** Walt to Lilly, Feb. 10, 1929, Walt Disney 1928 Corr., Walt Disney Early Corr., WDA.

130 **"The public knows Life Savers."** Walt Disney interview by Martin, Disc 9, CD.

130 **"Now is our chance . . ."** Walt to Roy and Ubbe, Feb. 9, 1929, Walt Disney 1928 Corr., Walt Disney Early Corr., WDA.

130 **"We should be able to clean up . . ."** Walt to [Roy], [Nov. 1928], ibid.

130 **Jimmy Lowerre.** Walt to Lilly, Oct. 27, 1928, ibid.

131 **Optioning sound outfits.** Walt to Roy and Ubbe, Feb. 9, 1928, ibid.

131 **"But we must raise the Dough."** Walt to Roy and Ubbe, Feb. 9, 1929, ibid.

131 **"no gamble . . ."** Walt to Elias [1929], ibid.

132 **"When completed . . ."** Roy to Nat Levine, Mar. 11, 1929, Mascot Pictures Corp. Folder, Roy O. Disney Corr., Lu-Mi (1930–1939), A2997, WDA.

132 **Sound operation.** See Disney Film Recording Studio Folder, WDA.

132 ***Skeleton Dance*.** Disney, *Autobiography*, 1934; Miller, *Story of Disney*, p. 107; Walt Disney interview by Martin, Reel 2, pp. 33–35.

132 **"It's hard to explain . . ."** Walt to Giegerich, Jun. 12, 1929, Powers Cinephone Equipment Corp., Corr., 1928–29, WDA.

132 **"Are they laughing . . ."** Iwerks interview, ca. 1956.

132 **"making a big hit."** Walt to Giegerich, Jun. 12, 1929, Powers Cinephone Equipment Corp., Corr., 1928–29, WDA.

133 **"Fox officials will be sold . . ."** Tel. Walt to Powers, [July 1929], ibid.

133 **"Here is one of the most novel . . ."** *Film Daily*, July 21, 1929.

133 **"without exception . . ."** Ad, *Film Daily*, July 22, 1929.

133 **Joseph Barbera.** Joseph Barbera, *My Life in 'toons: From Flatbush to Bedrock in Under a Century* (Atlanta: Turner Publishing, 1994), p. 37.

133 **Hiring Burt Gillett.** Walt to Roy and Ubbe, Feb. 9, 1929, Walt Disney 1928 Corr., Walt Disney Early Corr., WDA.

133 **Sharpsteen.** Ben Sharpsteen, interview by David Smith, May 19, 1971, WDA.

134 **"It was pressure!"** Quoted in Donald Crafton, *Before Mickey: The Animated Film, 1898–1928* (Cambridge, Mass.: MIT Press, 1982), p. 319.

134 **"one of those endless . . ."** Janet Flanner, *Harper's Bazaar*, Nov. 1, 1936, quoted in Finch, *Art of Disney*, p. 124.

134 **Description of Hyperion.** Sharpsteen interview by Smith; Jackson interview by Smith.

134 **"his salvation was in making . . ."** Sharpsteen interview by Peri, p. 3.

134 **"complete reversal."** Quoted in Barrier, *Hollywood Cartoons*, p. 60.

135 **"In Walt's estimation . . ."** Sharpsteen interview by Peri.

135 **"I have encountered plenty of trouble . . ."** Walt to Giegerich, Apr. 10, 1929, Powers Cinephone Equipment Corp., Corr., 1928–29, WDA.

135 **"We'd hate to go home . . ."** Ub Iwerks, interview by George Sherman, July 30, 1970, WDA.

135 **"one would gather . . ."** Walt to Giegerich, Dec. 14, 1929, Powers Cinephone Equipment Corp., 1928–29, WDA.

136 **"We haven't any president . . ."** Florabel Muir, "Animated Cartoons Going Over Big," *New York Sunday News*, Dec. 1, 1929.

136 **Key to front door.** Jack Cutting quoted in Finch, *Art of Disney*, p. 67.

136 **"The men loved it . . ."** Iwerks interview by Sherman.

136 **"The money has been coming in . . ."** Roy to Edna, Walt, Lilly, Aug. 10, 1929, Walt & Roy Disney Corr., 1929–1930, Walt Disney Early Corr., WDA

136 **Finances.** Statement of Account with Walter E. Disney, May 31, 1929; Walt to H. A. Post, May 31, 1929, Powers Cinephone Equipment Corp., Corr., 1928–29, WDA.

136 **Turning out the Mickeys.** Tel. Walt to Giegerich, Jun. 30, 1929, Powers Cinephone Equipment Corp., Corr., 1928–29, WDA.

137 **"queered it."** Roy to Edna, Walt, Lilly, Aug. 10, 1929, Walt and Roy Disney Corr., 1929–1930, Walt Disney Early Corr., WDA.

137 **Hollywood Screen Star News.** Walt to Giegerich, Jun. 3, 1929, Powers Cinephone Equipment Corp., Corr., 1928–29, WDA.

137 **Mayer and MGM.** Frances Marion, *Off With Their Heads! A Serio-Comic Tale of Hollywood*, excerpted in *The Grove Book of Hollywood*, ed. Christopher Silvester (New York: Grove Press, 1998), pp. 116–18.

137 **Frank Capra and Walt.** Frank Capra, *The Name Above the Title: An Autobiography* (New York: Macmillan 1971), p. 104.

138 **Columbia deal.** Roy to Walt [Aug. 9, 1929], Disney, Walt, Corr., 1929, Walt Disney Early Corr., WDA.

138 **Felix.** See Canemaker, *Felix*.

139 **"By 1930 Felix was doomed."** Hal Walker quoted in ibid., p. 130.

139 **Calling theaters.** Roy Disney interview by Hubler, Jun. 18, 1968.

139 **Cartoon of Mickey leading orchestra.** Roy Disney interview by Hubler, Feb. 20, 1968, WDA.

139 **Ads.** *Exhibitor's Herald World*, Aug. 31, 1929.

139 **Mickey Mouse Clubs.** Walt to Giegerich, July 30, 1929; Walt to Giegerich, Sept. 16, 1929, Powers Cinephone Equipment Corp., Corr., 1928–29, WDA.

140 **Mickey Mouse charter.** General Campaign, Mickey Mouse Club, 1930, Mickey Mouse Clubs, Alpha-M, General 1934–37 Folder, Roy O. Disney Corr., Lu-Mi (1930–1939), A2997, WDA.

140 **"Minnie's Yoo Hoo."** *Columbia Beacon*, Apr. 29, 1930.

140 **Mickey Mouse Club popularity.** Clipping, n.d., Mickey Mouse and General Stories, 1925–1931, M-17, Box 3182, WDA.

140 **Milwaukee parade.** Hank Peters to Roy, Jun. 8, 1931, P-D.V.'s letters, 1931–1933, Walt Disney Corr., 1930–1934, P-U, A1505. WDA.

140 **Membership.** Roy quoted in Hubler, *Disney*, p. 260; *Motion Picture Herald*, Oct. 1, 1932, cited in Lorraine Santoli, *The Official Mickey Mouse Club Book* (New York: Hyperion, 1995), pp. xiv–xix.

140 **King Features and comic strip.** J. V. Connelly to Iwerk [*sic*], Jul. 24, 1929; Iwerks to Connelly, Jul. 30, 1929; Walt to Giegerich, Jul. 30, 1929; Giegerich to Walt, Aug. 12, 1929, Powers Cinephone Equipment Corp., Corr, 1928–29, WDA; Walt to Roy, Aug. 3, 1929, Disney, Walt, Corr., 1929, Walt Disney Early Corr., WDA.

141 **Shifting Gottfredson.** George Morris to Roy, Apr. 19, 1930, Walt & Roy Disney Corr., 1929–1930, Walt Disney Early Corr., WDA.

141 **Syndicated in forty papers.** Roy to Flora Disney, Aug. 25, 1930, Roy O. Disney—1930 Folder, Roy O. Disney Corr., Disney, Roy O.—Personal & Trips (1930–33), A2994, WDA.

141 **twenty thousand requests.** Carolyn Kay Shafer (publicity director, Walt Disney Productions) to J. P. Murphy, *Boston Daily Record*, Jun. 8, 1931, B -D.V.'s Letters, 1931–1933, Walt Disney Corr., 1930–1934, A-C, A1502, WDA.

141 **Prodding Giegerich.** Walt to Giegerich, Oct. 4, 1929, Powers Cinephone Equipment Corp., Corr., 1928–29, WDA. See also Giegerich to Walt, Oct. 8, 1929, and Walt to Giegerich, Oct. 24, 1929.

141 **First license.** Miller, *Story of Disney*, p. 133.

141 **Deal with Borgfeldt.** Tel. Walt to Roy, Jan. 29, 1930, Walt & Roy Disney Corr., 1929–1930, Walt Disney Early Corr., WDA.

141 **Doll models.** George Morris to Roy, Apr. 7, 1930, ibid.

141 **Promoting books and candy bars.** Roy to Buzza Co., Mar. 20, 1930; Roy to Curtiss Candy Co., Mar. 21, 1930, Toys + Novelties, Misc. Folder, Roy O. Disney Corr., Mo-T (1928–1939), A2998, WDA; Roy to Walt, Apr. 26, 1930, Walt & Roy Disney Corr., 1929–1930, Walt Disney Early Corr., WDA.

142 **"Things are happening fast . . ."** Roy to Mr. and Mrs. E. Disney, Jan. 6, 1930, Roy O. Disney—1930 Folder, Roy O. Disney Corr., Disney, Roy O.—Personal & Trips (1930–33), A2994, WDA.

142 **Mascot offer.** Roy to Walt, Jan. 25, 1930, ibid.

142 **"If they [the cartoons] weren't good . . ."** Roy to Walt, Jan. 24, 1930, Walt & Roy Disney Corr., 1939–1930, Walt Disney Early Corr., WDA.

142 **Dispute with Powers over Columbia.** Walt to Giegerich, Oct. 21, 1929; Walt to Powers, Dec. 20, 1929; Powers to Walt, Dec. 26, 1929, Powers Cinephone Equipment Corp., Corr., 1928–29, WDA.

143 **"crook."** Roy Disney interview by Hubler, Jun. 18, 1968.

143 **"You know, my greatest weakness . . ."** Paul Smith and Hazel George, interview by David Tietyen, Aug. 29, 1978, p. 27, WDA.
143 **Powers sensing dissatisfaction.** Tel. Powers to Walt, Jan. 2, 1930, Disney, Walt—Corr., 1929, Walt Disney Early Corr., WDA.
143 **Iwerks's leaving.** Tel. Roy to Walt, Jan. 21, 1930; Roy to Walt, Jan. 24, 1930, Disney, Walt—Corr., 1929, Walt Disney Early Corr., WDA.
143 **Tensions with Walt.** Iwerks interview, ca. 1956.
144 **"Draw your own Mickey."** Iwerks and Kenworthy, *Hand Behind*, p. 83.
144 **"If Ub's action . . ."** Walt to Roy, Jan. 21, 1930, Walt and Roy Disney Corr., 1929–1930, Walt Disney Early Corr., WDA.
144 **Settlement and meeting.** Resignation, Jan. 22, 1930, Security First National Bank of L.A. Folder, Roy O. Disney Corr., Mo-T (1928–1939), A2998; Roy to Walt, Jan. 25, 1930, Roy O. Disney—1930 Folder, Roy O. Disney Corr., Disney, Roy O.—Personal & Trips (1930–33), A2994, WDA.
144 **"obviously loved that guy."** Leonard Mosley, *Disney's World: A Biography* (New York: Stein & Day, 1985), p. 201.
144 **Talking to young animator.** Dave Hand quoted in Barrier, *Hollywood Cartoons*, p. 66.
145 **"it would not be a good idea . . ."** Roy to Walt, Jan. 18, 1930, Roy O. Disney—1930 Folder, Roy O. Disney Corr., Disney, Roy O.—Personal & Trips (1930–33), A2994, WDA.
145 **Stalling's departure.** Roy to Walt, Jan. 24, 1930, Disney, Walt—Corr., 1929, Walt Disney Early Corr., WDA.
145 **"US fellows who have been . . ."** Roy to Walt, Jan. 24, 1930, Walt & Roy Disney Corr., 1929–1930, Walt Disney Early Corr., WDA.
145 **"the year to come will show them . . ."** Ibid.
145 **Ollie Wallace.** Roy to Walt, Jan. 25, 1930, Walt Disney—1928 Corr., Walt Disney Early Corr., WDA.
146 **Enlisting Columbia.** Roy to Walt, Jan. 25, 1930, ibid.
146 **Suspending production on Mickeys.** Walt to Roy, Feb. 1, 1930, Walt & Roy Disney Corr., 1929–1930, Walt Disney Early Corr., WDA.
146 **"ATTORNEYS POSITIVE . . ."** Tel. Walt to Roy, Jan. 29, 1930, ibid.
146 **Offering Walt $2,000.** Lilly to "Folks," Jan. 30, 1930, Walt & Roy Disney Corr., 1929–1930, Walt Disney Early Corr., WDA.
146 **"Powers is crooked . . ."** Lillian to Roy and Edna, Jan. 29, 1930, ibid.
147 **Powers's shrewdness.** Walt Disney interview by Martin, Reel 2, p. 39; Roy to Walt, Feb. 1, 1930; Roy to Walt, Jan. 29, 1930, Walt & Roy Disney Corr., 1929–1930, Walt Disney Early Corr., WDA.
147 **"Boy, they are gunning for him . . ."** Lillian to Roy and Edna, Jan. 29, 1930, Walt & Roy Disney Corr., 1929–1930, Walt Disney Early Corr., WDA.
147 **Two weeks before meeting Lillian . . .** Ibid.
147 **Lunch with Huemer.** Richard Huemer, *Recollections of Richard Huemer*, unpub. ms., Special Collections, Young Research Library, UCLA.
147 **Breaking with Powers.** Tel. Walt to Roy, Feb. 7, 1930, Walt & Roy Disney Corr., 1929–1930, Walt Disney Early Corr., WDA.
147 **Escaping the process server.** George Sherman, interview by Hubler, RHC, Box 17, Folder 65; Bill, Hotel Picadilly, Feb. 1930, Walt & Roy Disney Corr., 1929–1930, Walt Disney Early Corr., WDA.

148 **Borrowing from sound studio.** George Morris to Roy, May 3, 1930, Roy O. Disney—1930 Folder, Roy O. Disney Corr., Disney, Roy O.—Peronsal & Trips (1930–33), A2994, WDA.

148 **$400,000 gross.** Roy to Walt, Apr. 24, 1930, Walt & Roy Disney Corr., 1929–1930, Walt Disney Early Corr., WDA. Roy adds, "Not so bad is it?"

148 **"complicated."** Bert Nayfack (Newgass, Nayfack and Waldheim) to Walt, Mar. 10, 1930, Powers Cinephone Equipment Corp., Corr., 1930–36, WDA.

148 **Powers made $100,000.** Hubler, *Disney*, p. 166.

148 **Powers settlement.** Draft tel. Roy to Lessing, [Apr. 9, 1930], Roy O. Disney—1930 Folder, Roy O. Disney Corr., Disney, Roy O.—Personal & Trips (1930–33), A2994, WDA; Contract, Patrick A. Powers—et al. with Walt Disney, Apr. 22, 1930, Powers Cinephone Folder, WDA.

148 **"While sacrifice burns me up . . ."** Lessing to Roy, Apr. 9, 1930, Powers Cinephone Equipment Corp, Corr., 1930–36, WDA.

149 **Negotiation meetings.** Roy to Walt, Apr. 23, 1930, Walt & Roy Disney Corr., 1929–1930, Walt Disney Early Corr., WDA.

149 **"I HONESTLY FEEL ELATED . . ."** Tel. Roy to Walt, May 6, 1930, ibid.

149 **"a weight of worry . . ."** George Morris to Roy, Apr. 24, 1930, Roy O. Disney—1930 Folder, Roy O. Disney Corr., Disney, Roy O.—Personal & Trips (1930–33), A2994, WDA.

149 **Columbia terms.** Arthur Mann, "Mickey Mouse's Financial Career," *Harper's* 168 (May 1934), pp. 717–18.

149 **Columbia's offer to Powers.** Roy to Walt, Apr. 15, 1930, Walt Disney—1928 Corr., Walt Disney Early Corr., WDA.

150 **"The Most Popular Character."** *Film Daily*, Dec. 1, 1930.

150 **" 'Mickey Mouse' is one of the very few . . ."** Clipping [1929], Mickey Mouse and General Stories, 1925–1931, M-17, 3182, WDA.

150 **"Am I too late for Mickey Mouse?"** *Saturday Evening Post*, Oct. 4, 1930.

150 **Discovered by intelligentsia.** Creigthon Peet, "Mickey Mouse's Miraculous Monkey Shines," *Literary Digest* 106 (Aug. 9, 1930), p. 36.

150 **Chaplin's demand.** Karen Merritt and Russell Merritt, "Mythic Mouse," *Griffithiana*, no. 34 (Dec. 1988), p. 59.

150 **Madame Tussaud.** *Boston Herald*, Nov. 13, 1930.

150 **thirty thousand fan letters.** "Mickey Mouse Publicity Items," Oct. 29, 1931, Mo, D.V.'s letters, Walt Disney Corr., A1504, WDA.

150 **One million audiences.** Gilbert Seldes, "Mickey Mouse Maker," *The New Yorker*, Dec. 19, 1931, p. 23.

150 **"most popular motion picture star . . ."** *Photoplay*, Nov. 1930.

150 **"preeminent personality . . ."** Clipping, Iza Schallert, "German Author Looks Us Over," Aug. 17, 1930, Mickey Mouse and General Stories, 1925–1931, M-17, 3182, WDA.

150 **French critics.** "Europe's Highbrows Hail 'Mickey Mouse,' " *Literary Digest* 110 (Aug. 8, 1931), p. 19.

150 **More popular than Mozart.** "Mickey Mouse Publicity Items," Oct. 29, 1931.

150 **Filing suit and warning Mintz.** *NYT*, Apr. 1, 1931; Tel. George Morris to Roy, May 5, 1930, M, D.V.'s letters, 1930–33 Folder, Walt Disney Corr., 1930–1934, J-O, A1504, WDA.

150 **Paramount and Krazy Kat copying the work.** Lilly to "Folks," Jan. 30, 1930, Walt & Roy Disney Corr., 1929–1930, Walt Disney Early Corr., WDA.

150 **Walt's early assessments.** Fenn Sherie, "Meet Mickey's Master," *Pearson's* [April 1930], *Pearson's Mag*, Sherie, Fenn, Folder, Walt Disney Corr., 1930–1934, P-U, A1505, WDA.

151 **Mickey's size.** Shelly Fored, "He Wanted a 'Little Fellow,' " *Hollywood* [?], June 1930, Mickey Mouse and General Stories, 1925–1931, M-17, 3182, WDA.

151 **"Mickey is so simple . . ."** Barbara Berch Jamison, "Of Mouse and Man, or Mickey Reaches 25," *NYT Magazine*, Sept. 13, 1953, sec. 4, pp. 26–27.

151 **"We just make a Mickey . . ."** John T. McManus, "Speaking of Movies," *PM* [Aug. 1943], A Folder, Walt Disney Corr., 1942–1943, A-C, A1526, WDA.

151 **"perfect expression . . ."** John Culhane, "A Mouse for All Seasons," *Saturday Review of Literature*, Nov. 11, 1978, p. 50.

151 **"beloved Don Quixote . . ."** William DeMille, "Mickey Versus Popeye," in *The Animated American Cartoon: A Critical Anthology*, ed. Gerald Peary and Daniel Peary (New York: E.P. Dutton, 1980), pp. 241–44.

151 **"the jerky rhythm . . ."** "The Mechanical Mouse," *Saturday Review of Literature* 10 (Nov. 11, 1933), p. 252.

151 **"age of dictators . . ."** Edward G. Smith, "St. Francis of the Silver Screen," *Progress Today*, Jan.–Mar. 1935, quoted in Steven Watts, *The Magic Kingdom: Walt Disney and the American Way of Life* (Boston: Houghton Mifflin, 1997), p. 76.

151 **"The Disney world is a world . . ."** Warren I. Susman, *Culture as History: The Transformation of American Society in the Twentieth Century* (New York: Pantheon, 1984), p. 197.

152 **"[C]ircles never [illegible] . . ."** Quoted in Robert W. Brockway, "The Masks of Mickey Mouse: Symbol of a Generation," *Journal of Popular Culture*, Spring 1989, pp. 31–32.

152 **Mickey's flat face.** Calvin Trillin, "Disney World, Fla." *The New Yorker*, Nov. 6, 1971, pp. 173–80.

152 **Wholeness.** Quoted in Brockway, "Masks," p. 31.

152 **"a relatively large head . . ."** Stephen Jay Gould, "A Biological Homage to Mickey Mouse," in *The Panda's Thumb: More Reflections in Natural History* (New York: W. W. Norton, 1980), pp. 95–107.

152 **"passionate investigation of the body."** Merritt and Merritt, "Mythic Mouse," p. 61.

152 **"Stole" screen slapstick.** Frank S. Nugent, "The Slapstick Professor," *NYT*, May 5, 1935, sec. 9, p. 3.

152 **"the spirit of the child . . ."** Robert D. Feild, *The Art of Walt Disney* (New York: Macmillan, 1942), p. 34.

152 **"narcotized."** Dr. A. A. Brill, "Dr. Brill Analyzes Walt Disney's Masterpiece," *Photoplay* 45 (April 1934) p. 103.

152 **"ego ideal."** David I. Berland, M.D., "Disney and Freud: Walt Meets the Id," *Journal of Popular Culture* 15 (Spring 1982), p. 96.

153 **"He can break all natural laws."** "Profound Mouse," *Time*, May 15, 1933, p. 37.

153 **"quick and cocky and cruel . . ."** Richard Schickel, *The Disney Version: The Life, Times, Art and Commerce of Walt Disney*, 3rd ed. (1968; reprint Chicago: Elephant Paperbacks, 1997), p. 129.

153 **"scandalous element . . ."** E. M. Forster, "Mickey and Minnie," in Peary and Peary, *Animated Cartoon*, p. 239.

153 **Ohio censors.** Clipping, Feb. 4, 1931, MWEZ, n.c., 17,901, New York Public Library for the Performing Arts.

153 **"never been our intention . . ."** Walt to Giegerich, Dec. 23, 1929, Powers Cinephone Equipment Corp., Corr., 1928–29, WDA.

153 **"anarchy" and "greediness."** Merritt and Merritt, "Mythic Mouse," p. 61.

153 **"the cosmic victory of the underdog . . ."** *Motion Picture Herald*, Oct. 1, 1932.

153 **"the greatest of them all."** Disney, *Autobiography*, 1939, 2nd installment, p. 11.

153 **"We wanted something appealing . . ."** *Exhibitors Complete Campaign for Walt Disney's "Mickey"* [1931] Mouse, United Artists, Pamphlet #4, Margaret Herrick Library, Academy of Motion Picture Arts and Sciences.

153 **Screening Chaplin's films.** Sharpsteen interview by Peri, p. 5.

153 **"always showing us how Chaplin . . ."** Ward Kimball, interview by Christopher Finch and Linda Rosenkrantz, May 10, 1972, p. 113, WDA.

153 **"He just couldn't get him . . ."** Huemer, *Recollections*, p. 41.

153 **Sketch of Mickey Mouse impersonating Chaplin.** Walt to Steichen, Nov. 11, 1933, Si, D.V.'s letters, 1931–33 Folder, Walt Disney Corr., 1930–1934, P-U, A1505, WDA.

153 **"He was the superhero of his day."** Iwerks interview by Sherman.

154 **"Walt and Mickey were so *simpatico* . . ."** Quoted in Katherine Greene and Richard Greene, *The Man Behind the Magic: The Story of Walt Disney* (New York: Viking, 1991), p. 54.

154 **"Whenever he mentions Mickey Mouse . . ."** Clipping, Robert Sherwood, Aug. 29, 1931, [no title], MWEZ, n.c. 19,000, New York Public Library for the Performing Arts.

154 **"Walt was Mickey . . ."** Clark to Barrier, Aug. 19, 1976, quoted in John Canemaker, *Walt Disney's Nine Old Men and the Art of Animation* (New York: Disney Editions, 2001), p. 21.

154 **"I don't think Mickey . . ."** Henry F. Pringle, "Mickey Mouse's Father," *McCall's*, Aug. 1932, p. 7.

154 **"as long as there is a Disney studio . . ."** Barbara Berch Jamison, "Of Mouse and Man, or Mickey Reaches 25," *NYT Magazine*, Sept. 13, 1953, pp. 26–27.

155 **Dissatisfied with Mickey's voice.** Walt to Giegerich, July 26, 1929, Powers Cinephone Equipment Corp., Corr, 1928–29, WDA.

155 **Helen Lind.** *Variety*, Dec. 3, 1930.

155 **Doing MM's voice.** Walt Disney, interview by Tony Thomas, Jan. 1959 (excerpt), pp. 3–4, WDA.

155 **"[t]here is more pathos . . ."** Quoted in Hubler, *Disney*, p. 172.

156 **Ted Sears.** Tel. Walt to Roy, Nov. 21, 1930; Draft Tel. Roy to Walt, Dec. 7, 1930, Roy O. Disney—NY Trip—Nov. 1930 Folder, Roy O. Disney Corr., Disney, Roy O.—Personal & Trips (1930–33), A2994, WDA.

156 **Harry Reeves.** Walt to Roy, Nov. 15, 1930, ibid.

156 **Grim Natwick.** Roy to Walt, George Morris, Gunther Lessing, Nov. 21, 1930; Roy to Walt, Morris, Lessing, Nov. 16, 1930, ibid.

156 **"quiet little building . . ."** Alice Ames Winter, "Animated Cartoon Pictures," *Motion Picture Monthly*, Jan. 1931, p. 7.

156 **Expansion.** Superintendent's contract, Roy Disney and F. Scott Crowhurst,

Feb. 4, 1931; Roy to F. A. Munsie (secretary, Board of Building and Safety Commission), Jun. 2, 1930; George A. Conlon (sales department, QRS Neon) to Walt, Dec. 1, 1930, Building Bids Folder, Roy O. Disney Corr., A-C (1927–51), A2993, WDA. See also David R. Smith, "Disney Before Burbank: The Kingswell and Hyperion Studios," *Funnyworld*, no. 20 (Summer 1979), pp. 36–38; Thomas, *Building a Company*, p. 89.

157 **"as if we were members . . ."** Schickel, *Disney Version*, p. 184.

157 **Fraternal atmosphere.** Sharpsteen interview by Peri, p. 6; Bill Peet, *Bill Peet: An Autobiography* (Boston: Houghton Mifflin, 1989), p. 99.

157 **"My, how the day flew!"** Huemer, *Recollections*, p. 56.

157 **"all day, every day . . ."** Barrier, *Hollywood Cartoons*, p. 70.

157 **Roy Williams.** Amy Boothe Green and Howard E. Green, *Remembering Walt: Favorite Memories of Walt Disney* (New York: Hyperion, 1999), p. 10.

157 **"Walt struck me . . ."** Sharpsteen interview by Peri, p. 6.

158 **"whatever we did . . ."** John Canemaker, "Grim Natwick," *Film Comment*, Jan.–Feb. 1975, p. 60.

158 **Speeding production schedule.** George Morris to Roy, Nov. 11, 1930, Roy O. Disney—NY Trip—Nov. 1930 Folder, Roy O. Disney Corr., Disney, Roy O.—Personal & Trips (1930–33), A2994, WDA.

158 **"showdown."** Roy to Irving Lesser, Mar. 16, 1931, Irving Lesser Folder, Roy O. Disney Corr., G-Lo (1930–41), A2996, WDA.

158 **"It worked into a very unfair . . ."** Quoted in Hubler, *Disney*, p. 244.

158 **"they aren't overburdened . . ."** Roy to Walt, Apr. 26, 1930, Walt & Roy Disney Corr., 1929–1930, Walt Disney Early Corr., WDA.

159 **Awed.** Walt Disney interview by Martin, Reel 7, p. 9.

159 **United Artists negotiations.** George Morris to Roy, Nov. 17, 1930; Tel. Morris to Roy, Nov. 17, 1930; Morris to Roy, Nov. 20, 1930, Roy O. Disney—NY Trip—Nov. 1930 Folder, Roy O. Disney Corr., Disney, Roy O.—Personal & Trips (1930–33), A2994, WDA.

159 **Meeting with Laemmle.** Roy to Irving Lesser, Apr. 3, 1931, Irving Lessser Folder, Roy O. Disney Corr., G-Lo (1930–41), A2996, WDA.

159 **"sucker."** Irving Lesser to Roy, Apr. 10, 1931, ibid.

160 **"We have been approached . . ."** "Mickey Mouse Publicity Items," Oct. 29, 1931, Mo, D.V.'s letters, Walt Disney Corr., A1504, WDA.

160 **"Very frankly . . ."** Roy to Elias and Flora, May 8, 1931, quoted in Thomas, *Building a Company*, p. 89.

160 **Cost of cartoons.** Walt Disney, "Growing Pains," *American Cinematographer*, Mar. 1941, p. 107.

160 **$25,000 loan.** Roy to Irving Lesser, May 14, 1931, Irving Lesser Folder, Roy O. Disney Corr, G-Lo, (1930–41), A2996, WDA.

160 **"too much."** Tel. Lessing to Roy, Jun. 1, 1931, Roy O. Disney—1931 file, Roy O. Disney Corr., Disney, Roy O.—Personal & Trips (1930–33), A2994, WDA.

160 **Delivering more rapidly.** Roy to Walt, Jun. 5, 1931, D, D.V.'s letters, 1931–1933, Walt Disney Corr., 1930–1934, D-I, A1503, WDA.

160 **"[U]nless something very drastic . . ."** Memo, George [Morris] to Walt, Re: Studio Finance, Jun. 27, 1931, Mo, D.V.'s letters, 1934, Walt's Corr., A1504, WDA.

161 **"The business has become too big . . ."** Lessing to Roy, Jun. 27, 1931, Roy

O. Disney Folder, Roy O. Disney Corr., Disney, Roy O.—Personal & Trips (1930–33), A2994, WDA.

161 **"If you want to know the real secret . . ."** Ward Kimball, "The Wonderful World of Walt Disney," in *You Must Remember This*, ed. Walter Wagner (New York: G.P. Putnam's Sons, 1975), p. 267.

161 **Walt's meeting with Morris.** Morris to Roy, Jun. 29, 1931, Roy O. Disney Folder, Roy O. Disney Corr., Disney, Roy O.—Personal & Trips (1930–33), A2994, WDA.

161 **In the end . . .** Lessing to Roy, Jul. 6, 1931, ibid.

161 **Walt never left . . .** Bill Cottrell, interview by Jay Horan, Aug.–Oct. 1983, p. 66, WDA.

161 **Wandering the studio at night.** Walt Disney interview by Martin, Reel 2, p. 42.

162 ***Traffic Troubles.*** Sharpsteen interview by Peri, p. 17.

162 **Walt telling story to Sharpsteen.** Sharpsteen interview by Smith.

162 **"His hobby is his work . . ."** GM [George Morris] to Fenn Sherie, *Pearson's*, May 23, 1930, Sherie, Fenn, Folder, Walt Disney Corr., 1930–1934, P-U, A1505, WDA.

162 **"mouse widow."** "Profound Mouse," *Time*, May 15, 1933, p. 38.

162 **Socializing with Roy.** Greene and Greene, *Man Behind the Magic*, p. 86.

162 **Best pal.** GM [George Morris] to Fenn Sherie, May 23, 1930.

162 **Free time with Lillian.** Lillian quoted in Green and Green, *Remembering Walt*, p. 107.

162 **Turning back clock.** Jamison, "Of Mouse and Man," pp. 26–27.

162 **"I think I've got it licked."** Lillian Disney, interview by Pete Martin, Disc 16.

163 **"I want to have ten kids . . ."** Diane Disney Miller interview by author.

163 **Lillian's attitude to children.** Miller quoted in Greene and Greene, *Inside the Dream*, p. 54.

163 **Intercourse in doctor's office.** Thomas, *Building a Company*, p. 78.

163 **"Walt and Lilly are both crazy . . ."** Roy to Flora Disney, Aug. 15, 1930, Roy O. Disney—1930 Folder, Roy O. Disney Corr., Disney, Roy O.—Personal & Trips (1930–33), A2994, WDA.

163 **"He'd be at the top of the stairs . . ."** Quoted in Greene and Greene, *Inside the Dream*, p. 37.

163 **New homesite.** H. F. Elliot (sales manager: Frank Malins Co.) to Walt, Mar. 18, 1931, M, D.V.'s letters, 1930–33 Folder, Walt Disney Corr., 1930–1934, J-O, A1504; Leonard A. Hardie (sales manager, Santa Monica Land & Water Co. Ltd.) to Walt, Mar. 20, 1931, H, D.V.'s letters, 1931–33 Folder, Walt Disney Corr., 1930–1934, D-I, A1503, WDA.

163 **"It was very sad."** Quoted in Katherine Greene and Richard Greene, *Inside the Dream: The Personal Story of Walt Disney* (New York: Roundtable Press, 2001), p. 54.

163 **"I am married . . ."** Walt to Cousin Lena, Aug. 6, 1931, Misc. File, WDA.

163 **Roy suggested trip.** Roy to Walt, Jun. 18, 1931, Misc. File, WDA.

163 **"No matter how good a picture . . ."** Disney, *Autobiography*, 1934.

164 **Tonsils removed.** Roy to Walt, Jun. 30, 1931, Roy O. Disney—1931 Folder, Roy O. Disney Corr., Disney, Roy O.—Personal & Trips (1930–33), A2994, WDA.

164 **"Frankly, I am worried . . ."** Roy to Walt, Gunther [Lessing], and George [Morris], Jul. 2, 1931, ibid.
164 **"I guess I was working . . ."** Miller, *Story of Disney;* p. 111.
164 **Visiting doctor.** Walt Disney interview by Martin, Reel 2, p. 44.
164 **"I was in an emotional flap."** Miller, *Story of Disney*, p. 111.

FIVE || The Cult

166 **"Anything that we had saved . . ."** Roy to Flora and Elias, Jun. 15, 1932, quoted in Bob Thomas, *Building a Company: Roy O. Disney and the Creation of an Entertainment Empire* (New York: Hyperion, 1998), p. 93.
166 **Vacation plans.** Carolyn Kay Shafer to Archie B. Sharp, *Honolulu Advertiser*, Jun. 18, 1931, Misc. Folder, WDA; George Morris to Roy, Jun. 30, 1931, Roy O. Disney 1931 Folder, Roy O. Disney Corr., Disney, Roy O.—Personal & Trips (1930–33), A2994, WDA; Walt Disney, interview by Pete Martin, Reel 2, p. 45, A2361, WDA.
166 **Washington trip.** Walt Disney interview by Martin, Reel 2, p. 46.
166 **"very much rested."** George Morris to Roy, Sept. 9, 1931, Roy O. Disney 1931 Folder, Roy O. Disney Corr., Disney, Roy O.—Personal & Trips (1930–33), WDA.
167 **"woke me up . . ."** Walt Disney, *Autobiography*, unpub. ms., 1934, WDA.
167 **"get down there . . ."** Walt Disney interview by Martin, Reel 2, p. 47.
167 **"full of pep."** Ibid., p. 48.
167 **"Walt would fly into such a rage . . ."** Mrs. Walt Disney, as told to Isabella Taves, "I Live With a Genius," *McCall's*, Feb. 1953, p. 103.
167 **"new man."** Walt Disney, interview by Martin, Reel 2, p. 46.
167 **"Walt is feeling much better . . ."** Roy to Elias and Flora, Dec. 30, 1931, quoted in Thomas, *Building a Company*, pp. 71–72.
167 **United Artists revision.** Roy to George Morris, Jan. 22, 1932, Roy O. Disney 1932 Folder, Roy O. Disney Corr., Disney, Roy O.—Personal & Trips (1930–33), WDA.
167 **"our first good contract."** Quoted in Richard G. Hubler, *Walt Disney*, unpub. ms., 1968, p. 243, RHC.
167 **Diverting animators from Symphonies.** George Morris to Roy, Jan. 22, 1932, Roy O. Disney 1932 Folder, Roy O. Disney Corr., Disney, Roy O.—Personal & Trips (1930–33), WDA.
168 **"Practically every tool . . ."** Quoted in Mike Barrier, " 'Building a Better Mouse': Fifty Years of Disney Animation," *Funnyworld*, no. 20 (Summer 1979), p. 6; Greg Ford and Richard Thompson, "Chuck Jones," *Film Comment*, Jan.–Feb. 1975, p. 30.
168 **"because of Walt's insistence and supervision."** Quoted in Frank Thomas and Ollie Johnston, *The Illusion of Life: Disney Animation* (New York: Hyperion, 1981), p. 30.
168 **"The exhilaration of breaking through barriers . . ."** Ibid., p. 266.
168 **"Walt would not—repeat would not—OK . . ."** David Dodd Hand, *Memoirs* (Cambria, Calif.: Lighthouse Litho, 1990), p. 71.
168 **"analyzing and reanalyzing . . ."** Dick Huemer, "Thumbnail Sketches," *Funnyworld*, no. 21 (Fall 1979), p. 43.

168 **"You were paid to bat out . . ."** Shamus Culhane, *Talking Animals and Other People* (New York: St. Martin's Press, 1986), p. 131.

168 **Origins of pencil tests.** Dick Lundy cited in Michael Barrier, *Hollywood Cartoons: American Animation in Its Golden Age* (New York: Oxford University Press, 1999), p. 71.

169 **"I think it is astounding . . ."** Walt Disney, "Growing Pains," *American Cinematographer*, Mar. 1941, p. 107.

169 **"Leica reels."** Ben Sharpsteen, Answers to Questions Submitted by Dave Smith, Sept. 1964, p. 10, WDA.

169 **After a cartoon was finished . . .** George Morris to Roy, Oct. 19, 1933, Disney, Roy O.—1933 Folder, Roy O. Disney Corr., Disney, Roy O.—Personal & Trips (1934–41), A2995, WDA.

169 **"Old animation was done . . ."** Joe Adamson, "A Talk with Dick Huemer," in *The American Animated Cartoon: A Critical Anthology*, ed. Gerald Peary and Daniel Peary (New York: E. P. Dutton, 1981), pp. 33–34.

169 **"Your character goes dead . . ."** Thomas and Johnston, *Illusion of Life*, p. 99.

169 **"The hardest job . . ."** Walt Disney interview by Martin, Reel 10, p. 57.

169 ***Frolicking Fish.*** John Canemaker, *Walt Disney's Nine Old Men and the Art of Animation* (New York: Disney Editions, 2001), p. 245.

170 **"Soon everybody started drawing looser . . ."** Jack Kinney, *Walt Disney and Other Animated Characters: An-Unauthorized Account of the Early Years at Disney's* (New York: Harmony Books, 1988), p. 42–43.

170 **"Overlapping action was an invention . . ."** Adamson, "Talk with Huemer," p. 34.

170 **"So let's all hop to it . . ."** Cited in Richard Schickel, *The Disney Version: The Life, Times, Art and Commerce of Walt Disney*, 3rd ed. (1968; repr., Chicago: Elephant Paperbacks, 1997), p. 147.

170 **Gag prizes.** Gag Prizes Folder, Walt Disney Corr., 1930–1934, D-I, A1503, WDA.

170 **"You must sharpen . . ."** Memo, Walt to Dick Huemer, Jun. 1, 1935, Inter-Office Communications, Walt Disney Corr., 1935, He-R, A1509, WDA.

170 **"understanding of the proper portrayal . . ."** Walt to Bob Wickersham, Jun. 1, 1935, ibid.

170 **"they were staged better . . ."** Thomas and Johnston, *Illusion of Life*, p. 34.

170 **"Our mistake . . ."** Quoted in Charles Solomon, *Enchanted Drawings: The History of Animation* (New York: Alfred A. Knopf, 1989), p. 28.

170 **"density."** Barrier, *Hollywood Cartoons*, p. 91.

171 **"defrocked priest."** Bill Tytla, interview by George Sherman, in *Walt's People*, ed. Didier Ghez (Xlibris, 2005), p. 1:97.

171 **"I came back in two days . . ."** Walt Disney interview by Martin, Reel 11, p. 4.

171 **Story department room.** Barrier, *Hollywood Cartoons*, p. 94.

171 **Invention of "storyboard."** Schickel, *Disney Version*, p. 147; Richard Shale, *Donald Duck Joins Up: The Walt Disney Studio During World War II* (Ann Arbor, Mich.: UMI Research Press, 1982), p. 4. One employee dated the storyboard to *Babes in the Woods* in 1933: see Don Graham, *The Art of Animation*, unpub. ms., n.d., WDA.

171 **"You get the feeling . . ."** Thomas and Johnston, *Illusion of Life*, p. 195.

172 **"The big reason nobody remembers . . ."** Anonymous animator quoted in Hubler, *Disney*, p. 140.

172 **"little bits of personality."** Frank Thomas quoted in John Canemaker, *Felix: The Twisted Tale of the World's Most Famous Cat* (1991; reprint New York: Da Capo Press, 1996), p. 128.

172 **"It was the uppermost thing . . ."** Wilfred Jackson, interview by Steve Hulett, Jul. 25, 1978, WDA.

172 **"[Y]our characters . . ."** Eric Larson, interview by Mica Prods., n.d., p. 12, WDA.

172 **"The most important aim . . ."** Walt to John Culhane, Aug. 26, 1951, quoted in Canemaker, *Nine Old Men*, p. 7.

172 **"believable in motion . . ."** Mel Shaw quoted in Thomas and Johnston, *Illusion of Life*, p. 505.

172 **"Everything in his cartoons . . ."** Ward Kimball, "The Wonderful World of Walt Disney," in *You Must Remember This*, ed. Walter Wagner (New York: G. P. Putnam's Sons, 1975), p. 275.

173 **"How would a piano feel . . ."** Henry F. Pringle, "Mickey Mouse's Father," *McCall's*, Aug. 1932, p. 7.

173 **"You have to portray . . ."** *Official Report of the Proceedings Before the NLRB, In the Matter of Walt Disney and Arthur Babbitt*, Oct. 8, 1942, p. 49.

173 **"one big one."** Quoted in Barrier, *Hollywood Cartoons*, p. 115.

173 **"It was a blockbuster . . ."** Ward Kimball, interview by Rick Shale, Jan. 29, 1976, p. 10, WDA.

173 **"Fergy, you're a great actor . . ."** Dick Huemer, "Thumbnail Sketches," *Funnyworld*, no. 21 (Fall 1979), p. 38.

173 **"plausible impossible."** Graham, *Art of Animation*, p. 22.

174 **"As Walt began to bear down . . ."** Quoted in Barrier, *Hollywood Cartoons*, p. 74.

174 **"[n]o one thought . . ."** Adamson, "Talk with Dick Huemer," p. 33.

174 **"Does your drawing have . . ."** Thomas and Johnston, *Illusion of Life*, p. 67.

174 **"I definitely feel that we cannot . . ."** Quoted in Katherine Greene and Richard Greene, *The Man Behind the Magic: The Story of Walt Disney* (New York: Viking, 1991), p. 81.

174 **Chouinard classes.** Les Clark quoted in Barrier, *Hollywood Cartoons*, p. 82.

174 **Inception of classes.** Culhane, *Talking Animals*, p. 116; Christopher Finch, *The Art of Walt Disney: From Mickey Mouse to the Magic Kingdom* (New York: Harry Abrams, 1975), p. 57; Charles Solomon, *Enchanted Drawings: The History of Animation* (New York: Alfred A. Knopf, 1989), p. 52; John Canemaker, "Art Babbitt: The Animator as Firebrand," *Millimeter*, Sept. 1975, p. 12.

175 **Dividing the class.** Finch, *Art of Disney*, p. 57.

175 **"you'd better go!"** John Canemaker, "Disney Design: 1928–1979: How the Disney Studio Changed the Look of the Animated Cartoon," *Millimeter*, Feb. 1979, p. 102.

175 **Graham's cigarette.** Thomas and Johnston, *Illusion of Life*, p. 72.

175 **"necessarily impossible."** Chuck Jones, *Chuck Amuck: The Life and Times of an Animated Cartoonist* (New York: Avon Books, 1989), p. 53.

175 **"he was single-handedly . . ."** Culhane, *Talking Animals*, p. 136.

175 **"to analyze."** Quoted in Barrier, *Hollywood Cartoons*, p. 84.

175 **"greatest impact . . ."** Culhane, *Talking Animals*, p. 137.

175 **"Having problems?"** Jones, *Chuck Amuck*, p. 54.

176 **Graham joining staff.** Canemaker, "Disney Design," p. 106.

176 **"glass breaking . . ."** Diane Disney Miller, as told to Pete Martin, *The Story of Walt Disney* (New York: Holt, 1956), p. 121; Janet Martin, "Librarian to Walt Disney," *Wilson Library Bulletin*, Dec. 1939, pp. 292–93; Thomas and Johnston, *Illusion of Life*, pp. 321, 474.

176 **"[T[hey said anyone who goes to art school . . ."** John Canemaker, "Vlad Tytla: Animation's Michelangelo," in *The American Animated Cartoon: A Crtical Anthology*, ed. Gerald Peary and Danny Peary (New York: E. P. Dutton, 1980), p. 84.

176 **"They could never accept . . ."** Culhane, *Talking Animals*, pp. 226–27.

176 **"Most people think . . ."** Thomas and Johnston, *Illusion of Life*, p. 146.

176 **"We invest them with life."** Douglas W. Churchill, "Disney's Philosophy," *NYT Magazine*, Mar. 6, 1938, p. 23.

176 **"caricature of life."** Ibid.

176 **"Our actors must be . . ."** Ham Luske, "Character Handling," Oct. 6, 1938, quoted in Canemaker, *Nine Old Men*, p. 61.

177 **Positive film stock.** Tel. Roy to Walt, Jan. 29, 1930, Walt & Roy Disney Corr., 1929–1930, Walt Disney Early Corr., WDA.

177 **"I guess he was hoping . . ."** Bill Cottrell, interview by Jay Horan, Aug.–Oct. 1983, p. 25, WDA; Thomas and Johnston, *Illusion of Life*, p. 307.

177 **"I am convinced . . ."** Walt to L. P. Wright (Colorcraft Corp.), Sept. 18, 1931, C, D.V.'s letters, 1931–1933, Walt Disney Corr., 1930–1934, A-C, A1502, WDA.

177 **"At last! . . ."** John Culhane, *Walt Disney's* Fantasia (New York: Harry N. Abrams, 1983), p. 159.

177 **Costs of color.** Disney, *Autobiography*, 1934.

178 **"I found out the people . . ."** Walt Disney interview by Martin, Reel 10, p. 35.

178 **Lost $235,000.** Richard Neupert, "Painting a Plausible World: Disney's Color Prototypes," in *Disney Discourse: Producing the Magic Kingdom*, ed. Eric Smoodin (New York: Routledge, 1994), p. 106.

178 **Repainting the cels.** William Cottrell quoted in Barrier, *Hollywood Cartoons*, p. 80.

178 **"creation of genius . . ."** Grauman to Walt, July 27, 1932, RHC, Box 27, Folder 107.

178 **"an avalanche of orders . . ."** Walt Disney interview by Martin, Reel 10, p. 38.

178 **"A black and white print . . ."** Walt Disney, "Growing Pains," p. 139.

178 **Lobbying for color.** George Morris to Roy, May 9, 1933, Roy O. Disney—1933 Folder, Roy O. Disney Corr., Disney, Roy O.—Personal & Trips (1930–33), WDA.

178 **"Walt is very hot . . ."** Memorandum on United Artists Extension from G.R. Lessing, May 24, 1933, ibid.

179 **Feared that if he didn't close a deal . . .** Tel. George Morris to Roy, May 24, 1933, ibid.

179 **Roy met with Kalmus.** Roy to Walt, May 15, 1933, ibid.

179 **Technicolor loaning money.** Lessing to Roy, Jun. 5, 1933, ibid. In fact, had the studio gone entirely to color, it would have relied on a substantial loan from Technicolor to do so.

179 **"We've got to quit spending . . ."** Cottrell interview by Horan, p. 40.

179 **"continually (without letup in the least) . . ."** Roy to Flora and Elias, Apr. 14, 1933, quoted in Thomas, *Building a Company*, p. 96.

179 **Rosenbaum.** George Morris to Roy, May 6, 1933; Morris to Roy, May 8, 1933, Roy O. Disney—1933 Folder, Roy O. Disney Corr., Disney, Roy O.—Personal & Trips (1930–33), WDA; Roy to L. N. Rosenbaum, Jun. 8, 1933; Memo, L. N. Rosenbaum, May 11, 1933, Rosenbaum, L. N., Folder, Roy O. Disney Corr., Mo-T (1928–1939), A2998, WDA.

179 **Report of taking company public.** Untitled clipping, 8-MWEZ, n.c. 17,901, New York Public Library for the Performing Arts.

180 **"depression-minded."** Roy to Walt, May 15, 1933, Roy O. Disney—1933 Folder, Roy O. Disney Corr., Disney, Roy O.—Personal & Trips (1930–33), WDA.

180 **New loan from UA.** Roy to Walt, George [Morris], Gunther [Lessing], May 10, 1933, ibid.

180 **A. P. Giannini.** See Julian Dana, *A.P. Giannini: Giant in the West* (New York: Prentice Hall, 1947).

180 **"[t]ell those sons . . ."** Morris to Roy, May 8, 1933, Roy O. Disney—1933 Folder, Roy O. Disney Corr., Disney, Roy O.—Personal & Trips (1930–33), WDA.

180 **Bank of America loan assumption offer.** Morris to Roy, May 17, 1933, ibid.

181 **Bank of America terms.** Roy to Morris, May 29, 1933, ibid.

181 **Revolving credit.** Morris to Roy, Jun. 7, 1933, ibid.

181 **"perfection of the movies."** Gilbert Seldes, "Disney and Others," *New Republic*, Jun. 8, 1932, p. 101.

181 **"[t]hese little pig characters . . ."** From Ben Sharpsteen Papers quoted in Barrier, *Hollywood Cartoons*, pp. 99–100.

181 **"Walt practically lived . . ."** Ben Sharpsteen, interview by Don Peri, Apr. 24, 1974, p. 7, WDA.

182 **Natural athlete.** Ken Anderson, interview by Bob Thomas, May 15, 1973, p. 10, WDA.

182 **"Animation came too easily . . ."** Clark to Michael Barrier, Aug. 19, 1976, quoted in Canemaker, *Nine Old Men*, p. 16.

182 **Displacing the old "rubber hose."** Barrier, *Hollywood Cartoons*, p. 90.

182 **Apportionment of *Pigs*.** J. B. Kaufman, "Three Little Pigs—Big Little Picture," *American Cinematographer*, Nov. 1988, p. 39.

182 **"[u]nder his influence . . ."** Quoted in Solomon, *Enchanted Drawings*, p. 50.

182 **"The drawing that people think of . . ."** Quoted in ibid.

182 **Walt dropping by Moore's table.** Claude Smith to Barrier, in Barrier, *Hollywood Cartoons*, p. 90.

183 **"Who's Afraid of the Big Bad Wolf?"** Cottrell interview by Horan, p. 14; Walt Disney interview by Martin, Reels 6 & 7, pp. 36–37; Kaufman, "Three Little Pigs," p. 41.

183 **"At last we have achieved . . ."** Graham, *Art of Animation*, p. 1.

183 **UA reaction.** Walt Disney interview by Martin, Reels 6 & 7, pp. 32–33.

183 **Whistling "Who's Afraid . . ."** Kaufman, "Three Little Pigs," p. 41.

183 **"[Y]ou cannot escape."** Richard Watts, Jr., "Sight and Sound: What Disney Did," *New York Herald Tribune*, Oct. 15, 1933.

183 **"Personally, I would like to get you . . ."** J. P. McEvoy, "Letters I Would Love to Mail," *New York Daily Mirror*, [1933], Disney Clippings, Margaret Herrick Library, Academy of Motion Picture Arts and Sciences.

183 **Too few prints.** Dick Lundy quoted in Kaufman, "Three Little Pigs," p. 40.

184 **Lengthening whiskers.** Katherine Greene and Richard Greene, *Inside the Dream: The Personal Story of Walt Disney* (New York: Roundtable Press, 2001), p. 44.

184 **Comic strip.** Roy to Walt, Oct. 26, 1933, Disney, Roy O.—1933 Folder, Roy O. Disney Corr., Disney, Roy O.—Personal & Trips (1934–41), A2995, WDA.

184 **Writers Club dinner.** Owen Crump to Walt, Mar. 28, 1963, C Folder, Walt Disney Corr., 1963, C-Complaint, A1595, WDA.

184 **Not break even.** Morris to Roy, Oct. 18, 1933, Disney, Roy O.—1933 Folder, Roy O. Disney Corr., Disney, Roy O.—Personal & Trips (1934–41), WDA.

184 **Apology.** Kaufman, "Three Little Pigs," p. 41.

184 **"I realized something was happening . . ."** Quoted in Solomon, *Enchanted Drawings*, p. 52.

184 **Personality animation began . . .** Quoted in Stefan Kanfer, *Serious Business: The Art and Commerce of Animation in America from Betty Boop to Toy Story* (New York: Charles Scribner's Sons, 1997), p. 82.

184 **"It brought us honors . . ."** Disney, "Growing Pains," p. 139.

184 **"[T]he main thing about . . ."** Walt Disney interview by Martin, Reels 6 & 7, p. 31.

185 **Pleaded ignorance.** Harry Tytle, *"Walt's Boys": An Insider's Account of Disney's Golden Years* (Royal Oak, Mich.: Airtight Seals Allied Production, 1997), p. 147.

185 **If it hadn't been for the Depression . . .** Ken Anderson, interview by Bob Thomas, May 15, 1973, p. 8, WDA.

185 **Elias and Flora in Portland.** Flora to Raymond, Nov. 4, 1932, Disney Family: Genealogy, Etc., A2383, WDA; Elias to Raymond, Feb. 31, 1933 [?], Elias Disney Box, WDA.

185 **"Quit worrying."** Richard G. Hubler, *Walt Disney*, unpub. ms., 1968, pp. 189–90, RHC.

186 **"by force of circumstance . . ."** Lewis Jacobs, *The Rise of the American Film: A Critical History* (1939; repr., New York: Teachers College Press, 1968), p. 500.

186 **"No one will ever know . . ."** Robert D. Feild, *The Art of Walt Disney* (New York: Macmillan, 1942), p. 46.

186 **"historians of the future . . ."** Will Hays, *Annual Report to the Motion Picture Producers and Distributors of America* (New York, 1934).

186 **"Ford factory."** Disney, "Growing Pains," p. 140.

187 **"[T]he picture Walt was after . . ."** Quoted in Barrier, *Hollywood Cartoons*, p. 92.

187 **"This would be an ideal way . . ."** Ibid., p. 116.

188 **"The best story guys . . ."** Jack Kinney, *Disney and Animated Characters*, p. 62.

188 **"one eyebrow . . ."** Bill Justice, *Justice for Disney* (Dayton, Ohio: Tomart Publications, 1992), pp. 49–50.

188 **"like a Roman Emperor . . ."** I. Klein, *Cartoonist Profiles*, no. 39 (Sept. 1978), p. 95.

188 **Questionnaires.** See Story Meeting on *Sailormen All*, Apr. 4, 1938, Sea Scouts Folder, RM 26, WDA; Memo, Walt to All Concerned, Feb. 28, 1936, Inter-Office Communications, Walt Disney Corr., 1936–1937, E-L, A1512, WDA.

189 **Gag files.** Roy to Walt, Jun. 6, 1936, Drake, George, Folder, Walt Disney Corr., 1936–1937, A-D, A1511, WDA; Paul Hollister, "Genius at Work: Walt Disney," *Atlantic Monthly* 166, no. 6 (Dec. 1940), pp. 689–701.

189 **Director's responsibilities.** Justice, *Justice*, p. 56; Thomas and Johnston, *Illusion of Life*, p. 81.

189 **"Walt was the antagonist."** Ben Sharpsteen, Answers to Questions submitted by Dave Smith, Sept. 1974, p. 16, WDA.

189 **"Albert Hurter had a big room . . ."** Quoted in John Canemaker, "Grim Natwick," *Film Comment*, Jan.–Feb. 1975, p. 59.

190 **"[T]he director 'saw' the story . . ."** John Culhane, *Walt Disney's* Fantasia, p. 25.

190 **"[m]ake it stronger . . ."** Eric Larson, interview by Christopher Finch and Linda Rosenkrantz, Jul. 25, 1972, p. 9, WDA.

190 **Redrawing contributing to beauty.** Thomas and Johnston, *Illusion of Life*, p. 229.

190 **One animator so resisted . . .** Barrier, *Hollywood Cartoons*, p. 79.

190 **"A sweatbox session . . ."** Kinney, *Disney and Animated Characters*, p. 44.

191 **Previews.** Shamus Culhane, *Talking Animals*, pp. 148–49; Kinney, *Disney and Animated Characters*, p. 113.

191 **"Even though he was blocking . . ."** Sharpsteen interview by Peri, p. 10.

191 **"in spite of all your work . . ."** Walt to Eleanore Humiston, Jun. 13, 1962, H Folder, Walt Disney Corr., 1962, Committees-H (Misc.), A1591, WDA.

192 **"took too much . . ."** Disney, *Autobiography*, 1934, WDA.

192 **Badminton games.** Marc Davis, interview by Richard Hubler, May 21, 1968, pp. 1–2, WDA.

192 **"That's a part of them . . ."** Lillian Disney Truyens, interview by Bob Thomas, Apr. 19, 1973, Disney, Lillian, Folder, WDA.

192 **Travel.** Walt to Edith Hughes, Aug. 3, 1933; Walt to Flora, Sept. 8, 1933, Misc. File, WDA.

192 **Introduction to polo.** Hedda Hopper, "O'Connor's Grove Opening," *LAT*, Mar. 23, 1963.

192 **Polo instruction.** Cottrell interview by Horan, p. 65; Lucille Benedict to Roy, May 17, 1933, Roy O. Disney—1933 Folder, Roy O. Disney Corr., Disney, Roy O.—Personal & Trips (1930–33); Disney, *Autobiography*; Walt to Mrs. L. E. Francis, May 13, 1958, F Folder, Walt Disney Corr., 1958, D-G, A1570, WDA.

193 **Polo compatriots.** *Los Angeles Herald & Express*, Apr. 14, 1933; *Mercury*, Nov. 22, 1934; *New York Post*, May 14, 1934; *Daily Trojan*, Jan. 9, 1934.

193 **"very few people outside . . ."** Quoted in Marc Eliot, *Walt Disney: Hollywood's Dark Prince* (New York: HarperCollins, 1994), p. 82.

193 **Sunday drives.** Lillian Disney Truyens interview.

193 **"[I]t's my only sin."** Walt to Flora Disney, Dec. 5, 1933, Lawrence Edward Watkin, *Walt Disney*, unpub. ms., p. 279, WDA.

193 **Doctor's advice.** Diane Disney Miller, as told to Pete Martin, *The Story of Walt Disney* (New York: Holt, 1956), p. 113.

193 **Adding yards to new house.** Thomas Wood, [no title], 1944, Disney Clippings, Margaret Herrick Library, Academy of Motion Picture Arts and Sciences.

193 **Rush job.** *LAT*, Jun. 12, 1932.

194 **"Lilly has been feeling . . ."** Walt to Flora, Sept. 8, 1933, Misc. File, WDA.

194 **"Really, it's quite a strange . . ."** Walt to Flora, Dec. 5, 1933, ibid.

194 **Keeping birth quiet.** Walt to Rob Wagner, Jan. 13, 1934, Wagner's, Rob, Script Folder, Walt Disney Corr., 1930–1934, V-Z, 1935, A-B, A1506, WDA.

194 **Birth of Diane.** Miller, *Story of Disney*, p. 131; *NYT*, Dec. 19, 1933; *LAT*, Dec. 19, 1933.

194 **"AM PROUD FATHER . . ."** Tel. Walt to Roy, Dec. 18, 1933, Disney, Roy O.—1933 Folder, Roy O. Disney Corr., Disney, Roy O.—Personal & Trips (1934–41), A2995, WDA.

195 **"I'll think of something . . ."** Sidney Skolsky, "Mickey Mouse—Meet Your Maker," *Hearst's International Cosmopolitan*, Feb. 1934, p. 173.

195 **Mickey Mouse Club membership.** Walt Disney, "The Cartoon's Contribution to Children," *Overland Monthly and Outwest Magazine*, Oct. 1933, p. 138.

195 **500 million paid admissions.** "Mickey Mouse Is Eight Years Old," *Literary Digest*, Oct. 3, 1936, p. 18.

195 **"dozens of works produced . . ."** Gilbert Seldes, "No Art, Mr. Disney," *Esquire*, Sept. 1937.

195 **"supreme artistic achievement . . ."** "The Pie in the Art," *Nation*, Nov. 7, 1934.

195 **"loved Mickey Mouse . . ."** Quoted in John Culhane, "A Mouse for All Seasons," *Saturday Review of Literature*, Nov. 11, 1978, p. 50.

195 **Highest compliment.** "Miracle Mickey," *Film Daily*, Aug. 7, 1935.

195 **"international hero . . ."** "The Big Bad Wolf," *Fortune*, Nov. 1934, p. 89.

195 **Queen Mary.** Ibid., p. 146.

195 **Arturo Toscanini.** *LAT*, Feb. 2, 1936.

195 **"[n]ot since the days . . ."** *NYT*, Dec. 11, 1935.

195 **Sergei Eisenstein.** Eisenstein to Walt, Mar. 16, 1935, RHC, Box 27, Folder 107.

195 **Charlotte Clark.** George Morris to Roy, Nov. 8, 1930, Roy O. Disney—NY trip—Nov. 1930 Folder, Roy O. Disney Corr., Disney, Roy O.—Personal & Trips (1930–33); Roy to Irving Lesser, Mar. 4, 1931, Irving Lesser Folder, Roy O. Disney Corr., G-Lo (1930–41), A2996, WDA.

196 **"real high-class book."** Roy to Irving Lesser, Mar. 26, 1931, Irving Lesser Folder, Roy O. Disney Corr., G-Lo (1930–41), WDA.

196 **"we are building up . . ."** George Borgfeldt Co. to Roy, Apr. 27, 1931, Bi, D.V.'s letters, 1931–1933, Walt Disney Corr., 1930–1934, A-C, A1502, WDA.

196 **"longhand like some bunch of farmers."** Roy to Irving Lesser, Mar. 23, 1932, Irving Lesser Folder, Roy O. Disney Corr., G-Lo (1930–41), WDA.

196 **Quality control.** Tom Tumbusch, "Walt's Businessman," *POV*, Jul. 17, 1992, p. 47.

196 **"one of the homeliest men . . ."** Jimmy Johnson, *Inside the Whimsy Works: My Thirty-Seven Years with Walt Disney Productions*, unpub. ms., 1975, chap. 2, p. 17, WDA.

196 **Proud of his homeliness.** DeWitt Jones quoted in Leonard Mosley, *Disney's World: A Biography* (New York: Stein & Day, 1985), p. 151.

196 **Kamen background.** M. J. Hirsch, Jr., "Mouse Minter," *Advertising and Selling*, Jul. 18, 1935.

196 **"I don't know how much business . . ."** Roy Disney, interview by Richard Hubler, Feb. 20, 1968, p. 19, RHC.

197 **Kamen deals.** Tumbusch, "Businessman," p. 48; Hirsch, "Minter."

197 **"Getting the Three Little Pigs . . ."** Hirsch, "Minter."

197 **Forty licensees.** "Mickey Mouse Financier," *Literary Digest*, Oct. 21, 1933, p. 41.

197 **$35 million.** Hirsch, "Minter."

197 **"Shoppers carry . . ."** L. H. Robbins, "Mickey Mouse Emerges as Economist," *NYT Magazine*, Mar. 10, 1935, pp. 8, 22.

198 **"Wherever he scampers . . ."** Ibid., p. 8.

198 **Mickey Mouse watch.** Roy to Lucille [Benedict], May 29, 1933, Roy O. Disney—1933 Folder, Roy O. Disney Corr., Disney, Roy O.—Personal & Trips (1930–31), A2994, WDA.

198 **Lionel Corporation.** *NYT*, Jan. 22, 1935, p. 21.

198 **Kamen increasing licensing.** "Mickey Mouse Is Eight Years Old," *Literary Digest*, Oct. 3, 1936, p. 19; Summary of Income Statements from Dec. 31, 1934 to Oct. 2, 1943, Morris, George, Folder, Walt Disney Inter-Office Corr., 1938–1944, L-M, A1629, WDA.

198 **Ancillary rights.** *NYT*, Mar. 12, 1934, p. 20.

198 **"[I]t is no exaggeration . . ."** "Mickey Mouse Is Eight Years Old," p. 19.

198 **"We began to have an awful . . ."** Quoted in Marcia Blitz, *Donald Duck* (New York: Harmony Books, 1979), p. 13.

199 **Resembling comic strip Mickey.** Barrier, *Hollywood Cartoons*, p. 98.

199 **"abandoned gradually . . ."** "1933: A Trial Balance—Mickey Mouse," *Theatre Arts Monthly*, Feb. 1934, p. 87.

199 **"In the beginning of the thirties . . ."** Eric Larson, interview by Thorkil Rasmussen, Feb. 22, 1978, p. 10, WDA.

199 **"realized the minute we got . . ."** Ward Kimball, interview by Steve Hulett, p. 5, WDA.

200 **"feeling of cuteness . . ."** Les Clark, Training Course Lecture: Discussion of Mickey, Aug. 17, 1936, WDA.

200 **Mickey and Minnie were married.** Walt Disney, "Mickey Mouse is 5 Years Old," *Film Pictorial*, Sept. 30, 1933, p. 36.

200 **Comparing to Harold Lloyd.** Walt Disney, interview by Hooper Fowler, *Look*, Jan. 1964, p. 8, WDA.

200 **"To me there was something . . ."** Quoted in Karen Merritt and Russell Merritt, "Mythic Mouse," *Griffithiana*, Dec. 1988, p. 59.

200 **"If our gang . . ."** Disney, "Cartoon's Contribution," p. 138.

200 **"an international bore."** "Puppets—Two Styles," *Nation*, May 8, 1935.

201 **Clarence Nash.** Tony Hiss and David McClelland, "The Quack and Disney," *The New Yorker*, Dec. 19, 1975, p. 35; Miller, *Story of Disney*, pp. 123–24; Blitz, *Donald Duck*, p. 17.

201 **Nash and Iwerks.** Culhane, *Talking Animals*, p. 82.

201 **"Being a duck . . ."** Miller, *Story of Disney*, p. 124.

201 **"turning point."** Ward Kimball, "Wonderful World," pp. 275–76.

202 **"There have been signs . . ."** Gilbert Seldes, "True to Type," *New York Journal*, Apr. 8, 1935.

202 **"Sometimes it was hard for an audience . . ."** Miller, *Story of Disney*, p. 125.

202 **"Every time we put . . ."** Anonymous quoted in Irving Wallace, "Mickey Mouse and How He Grew," *Collier's*, Apr. 9, 1949, p. 21.

202 **"The duck can blow his top . . ."** Robert De Roos, "The Magic Worlds of Walt Disney," *National Geographic*, Aug. 1963.

202 **Walt extending Donald's range.** Hiss and McClelland, "Quack," p. 40.

203 **"Donald could be anything . . ."** Ibid., p. 33.

203 **"If we start using the duck . . ."** Memo, Walt to Roy, Oct. 9, 1935, Clarence Nash Folder, Inter-Office Communications, Walt Disney Corr., 1935, He-R, A1509, WDA.

203 **"Again it's manifest . . ."** *Variety*, Feb. 12, 1936.

203 **"constitute art . . ."** *NYT*, Dec. 15, 1933.

204 **"frightened . . ."** Sergei Eisenstein, *Eisenstein on Disney*, ed. Jay Leyda (London: Methuen, 1988), n.p.

204 **"Everybody in the world beat a path . . ."** Richard Huemer, *Recollections of Richard Huemer*, 1969, p. 119, Special Collections, Young Research Library, UCLA.

204 **Media coverage.** "Profound Mouse," *Time*, May 15, 1933; Douglas W. Churchill, "How Mickey Mouse Enters Art's Temple," *NYT Magazine*, Jun. 3, 1934; *Vanity Fair*, Oct. 1933, p. 26.

204 **"I sometimes feel . . ."** Lowell Lawrance, "Mickey Mouse—Inspiration from Mouse in K.C. Studio," *Kansas City Journal-Post*, Sept. 8, 1935.

204 **"Horatio Alger of the cinema."** Churchill, "Art's Temple."

204 **"As far as I can remember . . ."** "By the Way, Mr. Disney," *NYT*, Dec. 1, 1935, sec. 9, p. 9.

204 **"almost painfully shy . . ."** Clipping, Robert Sherwood, Aug. 29, 1931, MWEZ, n.c. 19,000, New York Public Library for the Performing Arts.

204 **"[i]t's the mouse . . ."** Brian Burnes, Robert W. Butler, and Dan Viets, *Walt Disney's Missouri: The Roots of Creative Genius*, ed. Donna Martin (Kansas City: Kansas City Star Books, 2002), p. 161.

204 **Informality.** "Big Bad Wolf," p. 93.

205 **"air clears . . ."** "Extra Added Attractions," (Aug. 7, 1935) in Otis Ferguson, *The Film Criticism of Otis Ferguson*, ed. Robert Wilson (Philadelphia: Temple University Press, 1971), p. 85.

205 **"Disney is as free . . ."** Clipping, [n.d.], 8 MWEZ, n.c. 17,901, New York Public Library for the Performing Arts.

205 **Indifferent to money.** See Pringle, "Mickey's Father," p. 28; "Profound Mouse," p. 38; Arthur Mann, "Mickey Mouse's Financial Career," *Harper's* 168 (May 1934), p. 714.

205 **"he could swear . . ."** Kinney, *Disney and Other Animated Characters*, p. 149.

205 **"played the role . . ."** Quoted in Randy Bright, *Disneyland: The Inside Story* (New York: Harry N. Abrams, 1987), p. 190.

206 **"There's just one thing . . ."** Quoted in Bob Thomas, *Walt Disney: An American Original* (New York: Hyperion, 1994), p. 192.

206 **"Well he knew . . ."** Colvig to Larry Morey, Dec. 29, 1937, Colvig, Pinto, Personal Folder, Roy O. Disney Corr. A-C (1929–51), A2993, WDA.

206 ***The Golden Touch.*** Kinney, *Disney and Animated Characters*, p. 52; Ben Sharpsteen, interview by Don Peri, Mar. 5, 1975, p. 2, WDA.

206 **Unprepossessing.** Culhane, *Talking Animals*, p. 109; Milton Kahl quoted in Hubler, *Disney*, p. 338; Skolsky, "Mickey Mouse," p. 173.

207 **Killing owl.** Churchill, "Disney's Philosophy," p. 9.

207 **Moods.** Kinney, *Disney and Animated Characters*, p. 157; Bill Peet quoted in Thomas and Johnston, *Illusion of Life*, p. 379.

207 **"apt to rip a storyboard . . ."** Thomas and Johnston, *Illusion of Life*, p. 379.

207 **"The big part of my career . . ."** Quoted in Hubler, *Disney*, p. 479.

207 **Osmosis.** Ben Sharpsteen, Answers to Questions Submitted by Dave Smith, Sept. 1974, p. 13, WDA.

207 **"Of all the things . . ."** Animator Paul Carlson quoted in Amy Boothe Green and Howard Green, *Remembering Walt: Favorite Memories of Walt Disney* (New York: Hyperion, 1999), p. 209.

207 **"best gag mind . . ."** Huemer, *Recollections*, p. 49.

208 **"Of all the studio chiefs . . ."** Quoted in Mosley, *Disney's World*, p. 278.

208 **"would do a rough outline . . ."** Ward Kimball, interview by Rick Shale, pp. 23–24, WDA.

208 **"And he would be the leader . . ."** Ibid.

208 **Walt wrote all the dialogue.** Ben Sharpsteen, interview by Don Peri, Apr. 16, 1974, p. 7, WDA.

208 **"Walt was always very . . ."** Betsy Richmond, "Remembering Walt: Ollie Johnston," Apr. 1986, p. 1, WDA.

208 **Eric Larson claimed . . .** Larson interview by Rasmussen, Feb. 22, 1978, p. 3, WDA.

208 **Chesterfield butts.** Kinney, *Disney and Animated Characters*, p. 72. In the 1930s Walt also smoked Lucky Strikes.

208 **"He could be brutal."** Quoted in Jim Korkis, "The Story of Jack Hannah," *Persistence of Vision*, no. 8 [1995], p. 35.

208 **Homer Brightman.** Leo Salkin quoted in Solomon, *Enchanted Drawings*, p. 57.

209 **"If Walt said to me . . ."** Charles Solomon, *The Disney That Never Was: The Stories and Art from Five Decades of Unproduced Animation* (New York: Hyperion, 1995), p. 16.

209 **"kind of trance."** Green and Green, *Remembering Walt*, p. 110.

209 **"Y'know this old guy would come snufin' . . ."** Thomas and Johnston, *Illusion of Life*, pp. 99–100.

209 **"You'd have the feeling . . ."** Ibid., p. 41.

209 **"supersalesman."** Kimball, "Wonderful World of Disney," p. 266.

209 **Unique sensitivity.** Larson interview by Rasmussen, p. 3.

210 **"He oftentimes didn't know . . ."** Quoted in Eliot, *Dark Prince*, p. 91.

210 **Setting up table.** Thomas and Johnston, *Illusion of Life*, p. 37.

210 **"forte was the supervision . . ."** Ben Sharpsteen, interview by Don Peri, Feb. 6, 1974, p. 12, WDA.

210 **"A lot of the guys . . ."** Maurice Rapf quoted in Patrick McGilligan and Paul Buhle, *Tender Comrades: A Backstory of the Hollywood Blacklist* (New York: St. Martin's Press, 1997), p. 522.

210 **"little things . . ."** Quoted in Barrier, *Hollywood Cartoons*, p. 70.

210 ***The Country Mouse.*** Hubler, *Disney*, pp. 187–88.

210 **Mickey's tail.** Frank Reilly, "The Walt Disney Comic Strips," *Cartoonist Profiles*, Winter 1969, p. 14.

210 **"People don't realize . . ."** Solomon, *Disney That Never Was*, p. 20.

210 **"I think the outstanding thing . . ."** Barrier, *Hollywood Cartoons*, p. 70.

210 **"greatest gift."** Anonymous employee quoted in Watkin, *Disney*, p. 19.

210 **"I don't want just . . ."** Frank Thomas quoted in Green and Green, *Remembering Walt*, p. 100.

210 **"He was very excited . . ."** Greene and Greene, *Man Behind the Magic*, p. 91.

211 **Walt as conductor.** Ruth Waterbury, "What Snow White's Father Is Doing Now," *Liberty*, Nov. 26, 1938.

211 **Pollen.** "Pollen Man," *The New Yorker*, Nov. 1, 1941, pp. 14–15.

211 **"We all had egos . . ."** Steve Hulett, "A Star Is Drawn," *Film Comment*, Jan.–Feb. 1979.

211 **"He could disarm people . . ."** Ben Sharpsteen, interview by Don Peri, April 26, 1974, p. 5, WDA.

211 **"That was what Walt's . . ."** Bob Broughton, interview by author.

211 **"Of all the things I've done . . ."** Miller, *Story of Disney*, p. 125.

212 **"When he'd come into a room . . ."** Huemer, *Recollections*, p. 95.

211 **"awe."** Jim Korkis, "Close Encounters of the Walt Kind," *POV* 1, no. 3, (Spring 1993), p. 49.

211 **"He had an overwhelming power . . ."** Green and Green, *Remembering Walt*, p. 87.

212 **"You talk as if . . ."** Hubler, *Disney*, p. 229.

212 **"I couldn't understand it."** Anonymous quoted in Michael Fessier, Jr., "Legacy of a Last Tycoon," *LAT*, Nov. 12, 1967.

SIX || Folly

214 **Rentals 50 percent higher.** "Mickey Mouse and the Bankers," *Fortune*, Nov. 1934, p. 94.

214 **Economics of shorts.** Memo, Bill Garity to Roy, Jul. 12, 1935, Roy O. Disney Corr. re: Trips, 1934–1935 Folder, Roy O. Disney Corr., Disney, Roy O.—Personal & Trips (1934–41), A2995, WDA.

214 **Double bills.** Irving Lesser to Roy, April 28, 1931, Irving Lesser Folder, Roy O. Disney Corr., G-Lo (1930–41), A2996, WDA.

214 **$600,000 profit.** "Mickey Mouse and Bankers," p. 94.

214 **"The first decade . . ."** Quoted in Lawrence Edward Watkin, *Walt Disney*, unpub. ms., n.d., p. 149, WDA.

214 **"The short subject was just a filler . . ."** Walt Disney, interview by Pete Martin, Reels 6 & 7, pp. 48–49, A2681, WDA.

214 **"I think that Walt was impatient . . ."** Steve Hulett, "A Star Is Drawn," *Film Comment*, Jan.–Feb. 1979.

214 **"[W]e sensed we had gone . . ."** Walt Disney, "Growing Pains," *American Cinematographer*, Mar. 1941, p. 140.

215 **The idea of producing a feature . . .** Walt Disney interview by Martin, Reels 6 & 7, p. 43.

215 ***Alice in Wonderland.*** Fulton Brylawski (attorney) to Roy, Jun. 6, 1932, Misc. File, WDA.

215 **Schuster prodding on *Bambi*.** M. Lincoln Schuster to Walt, May 1, 1933, Si, D.V.'s letters, 1931–33 Folder, Walt Disney Corr., 1930–1934, P-U, A1505, WDA.

215 **"Schenck talked like they . . ."** Roy to Walt, George [Morris], Gunther [Lessing], May 10, 1933, Roy O. Disney—1933 Folder, Roy O. Disney Corr., Disney, Roy O.—Personal & Trips (1930–33), A2994, WDA.

215 **Walt's fear.** [Lessing?] to Roy, Oct. 21, 1933, Disney, Roy O.—1933 Folder, Roy O. Disney Corr., Disney, Roy O.—Personal & Trips (1934–41), A2995, WDA.

215 **Suggestions.** Hobart Bosworth to Walt, Nov. 2, 1932, B—D.V.'s letters, 1931–1933, Walt Disney Corr., 1930–1934, A-C, A1502, WDA; [?] to Symon Gould, May 9, 1933, O—D.V.'s letters, 1931–1933, Walt Disney Corr., 1930–1934, J-O, WDA.

215 **Mary Pickford and *Alice*.** Pickford to Walt, Apr. 19, 1933; Walt to Pickford, April 27, 1933; Pickford to Walt, May 24, 1933, Misc. File, WDA.

216 **Registering *Snow White*.** Roy to Lucille Benedict, May 22, 1933, Roy O. Disney—1933 Folder, Roy O. Disney Corr., Disney, Roy O.—Personal & Trips (1930–33), A2994, WDA.

216 **"[I]t was well-known . . ."** Disney, "Growing Pains," p. 140.

216 **"I had sympathetic . . ."** Quoted in Richard Greene and Katherine Greene, *The Man Behind the Magic: The Story of Walt Disney* (New York: Viking, 1991), p. 80.

216 ***Snow White* play.** *Brooklyn Eagle*, Feb. 27, 1938; Paul Hollister, *Man or Mouse: The Story of Walt Disney, So Far*; unpub. ms., 1955, chap. 8, p. 2, WDA.

216 ***Snow White* screening.** Walt to J. Searle Dawley, Jan. 4, 1944, D Folder, Walt Disney Corr., 1944, A-E, A1530, WDA; Walt to Frank L. Newman, Feb. 21, 1938, Misc. File, WDA; Harry Tytle, *"Walt's Boys": An Insider's Account of Disney's Golden Years* (Royal Oak, Mich.: Airtight Seals Allied Production, 1997), p. vii. See also Karen Merritt, "The Little Girl/Little Mother Transformation: The American Evolution of 'Snow White and the Seven Dwarfs,' " in *Storytelling in Animation: The Art of the Animated Image*, ed. John Canemaker (Los Angeles: AFI, 1988), pp. 2:105–21; and Brian Burnes, Robert W. Butler, and Dan Viets, *Walt Disney's Missouri: The Roots of Creative Genius*, ed. Donna Martin (Kansas City, Mo.: Kansas City Star Books, 2002), pp. 62–63.

216 **"stories that tell about . . ."** Bruno Bettelheim, *The Uses of Enchantment: The Meaning and Importance of Fairy Tales* (New York: Alfred A. Knopf, 1975), pp. 7–8.

217 **Freudian interpretation.** Peter Brunette, "Snow White and the Seven Dwarfs," in *The American Animated Cartoon: A Critical Anthology*, ed. Gerald Peary and Danny Peary (New York: E. P. Dutton, 1980), pp. 72–73.

217 **Cultural interpretation.** Steven Watts, *The Magic Kingdom: Walt Disney and the American Way of Life* (Boston: Houghton Mifflin, 1997), p. 83.

217 **Winthrop Ames play.** Memo, Gunther Lessing to Walt, Re: Ames Version—Snow White, Apr. 7, 1937, Inter-Office Communications, Walt Disney Corr., 1936–1937, E-L, A1512, WDA; Merritt, "Little Girl," pp. 110–11.

217 **Jessie Braham White.** *Snow White and the Seven Dwarfs* by Jessie Braham

White, Snow White Continuities, gag suggestions, etc., 1934 dupes, *Snow White and the Seven Dwarfs,* Continuities, gag suggestions, etc., Jan. 1937—undated, Box 3, A1736, WDA.

217 **"We had a business meeting . . ."** [Lucille Benedict?] to Roy, May 19, 1933, Roy O. Disney—1933 Folder, Roy O. Disney Corr., Disney, Roy O.—Personal & Trips (1930–33), A2994, WDA.

217 **"Walt was such a wonderful . . ."** Dick Huemer, "The Battle of Washington," *Funnyworld,* no. 22 (Winter 1980), p. 24.

218 **Telling Pfeiffer.** Walter Pfeiffer, interview by Bob Thomas, Apr. 26, 1973, WDA.

218 **"He was a spellbinder."** Joe Grant, interview by author.

218 **Anderson's recollection of meeting.** Richard Holliss and Brian Sibley, *Walt Disney's* Snow White and the Seven Dwarfs *and the Making of the Classic Film* (New York: Simon & Schuster, 1987), p. 7; Charles Solomon, *Enchanted Drawings: The History of Animation* (New York: Alfred A. Knopf, 1989), pp. 57–58; Jay Horan, *Video Interview with Ken Anderson, Bill Cottrell and Herb Ryman,* Sept. 15, 1983, pp. 18–19; Martin Krause and Linda Witkowski, *Walt Disney's* Snow White and the Seven Dwarfs: *An Art in Its Making* (New York: Hyperion, 1994), pp. 25–26, 42.

218 **"That one performance . . ."** Robert De Roos, "The Magic Worlds of Walt Disney," *National Geographic,* Aug. 1963, in *Disney Discourse: Producing the Magic Kingdom,* ed. Eric Smoodin (New York: Routledge, 1994), p. 59.

218 **"We saw it at first as Walt's folly."** Joe Grant, interview by author.

218 **"may take the edge off . . ."** 1934 letter quoted in Richard G. Hubler, *Walt Disney,* unpub. ms., pp. 248–49, RHC.

219 **Worry about emotional investment.** "Mouse & Man," *Time,* Dec. 27, 1937, pp. 19, 21.

219 **Concern whether Walt could focus.** Frank Thomas quoted in Krause and Witowski, *Walt Disney's* Snow White, p. 43.

219 **"we will destroy it."** Douglas W. Churchill, "Now Mickey Mouse Enters Art's Temple," *NYT Magazine,* Jun. 3, 1934, pp. 12–13.

219 **"foreign countries were yelling . . ."** Lessing to Roy, Jul. 15, 1935, Roy O. Corr. Re trips: 1934–1935 Folder, Roy O. Disney Corr, Disney, Roy O.—Personal & Trips (1934–41), A2995, WDA.

219 **Meeting with Whitney, Zanuck, Schenck.** Roy to Walt, Lessing, Nov. 2, 1933, Disney, Roy O.—1933 Folder, Roy O. Disney Corr., Disney, Roy O.—Personal & Trips (1934–41), WDA.

219 **Schenck pulling out.** Roy Disney, interview by Richard Hubler, Feb. 20, 1968, p. 15, WDA.

219 **"We've bought the whole damned sweepstakes."** "Mouse & Man."

220 **First outlines.** Manuscript, Aug. 9, 1934, Snow White—Walt's Notes on continuities, *Snow White and the Seven Dwarfs,* Sweatbox Notes, Seq. 13A—16A, Misc. files (financial, promotion, etc.) Punch Sheets—French Version, Box 7, A1733, WDA. This is the first outline on file at the studio.

220 **Suggestions for script.** "Suggestions and Notes on 'Snowwhite' " Conference Oct. 3, 1934, by Harry Bailey, Snow White—Story Meetings, Oct. 1934–Nov. 1934 Folder, *Snow White and the Seven Dwarfs,* Story Meetings Oct. 1934–1937, Box 1, A1731, WDA. The notes are dated Oct. 12, 1934.

220 **Naming dwarfs.** Manuscript [Snow White], Aug. 9, 1934, Snow White—Continuities, gag suggestions, etc. July–Sept. 1934, *Snow White and the Seven Dwarfs*, Continuities, gag suggestions, etc., Jul. 1934–Dec. 1936, Box 2, A1737; "Suggestions and Notes on 'Snowwhite,' " Conference Oct. 9, 1934, by Harry Bailey, Snow White—Story Meetings, Oct. 1934–Nov. 1934 Folder, *Snow White and the Seven Dwarfs*, Story Meetings Oct. 1934–1937, Box 1, A1731, WDA.

220 **"Rather than spend too much . . ."** Snow White (tentative outline), Oct. 22, 1934, SW—Continuities, gag suggestions, etc. 1934 dupes, *Snow White and the Seven Dwarfs*, Continuities, gag suggestions, etc., Jan. 1937—undated, Box 3, A1736, WDA.

221 **Soundstage meeting.** "Suggestions and Notes on 'Snowwhite' " Sound Stage Meeting, Oct. 30, 1934, Snow White—Story Meetings, Oct. 1934–Nov. 1934 Folder, *Snow White and the Seven Dwarfs*, Story Meetings Oct. 1934–1937 Box 1, A1731, WDA.

221 **"Try to give . . ."** Outline, Snow White and the Seven Dwarfs, Nov. 2, 1934, Snow White Continuities, gag suggestions, etc. Nov. 1934, *Snow White and the Seven Dwarfs*, Continuities, gag suggestions, etc., Jul. 1934–Dec. 1936, Box 2, A1737, WDA.

221 **"At the start . . ."** Quoted in Krause and Witkowski, *Walt Disney's* Snow White, p. 19.

222 **"defective thyroid."** Roy Disney interview by Hubler, Feb. 20, 1968, p. 7.

222 **"matters accumulate . . ."** Memo, Walt to Ben [Sharpsteen], Dave [Hand], [Wilfred] Jackson, June 1, 1935, Inter-Office Communications, Walt Disney Corr. 1935, He-R, Z1509, WDA. Sharpsteen, Hand and Jaxon were left in charge of the animation side.

222 **"Everyone aboard . . ."** Roy to Gunnie [Lessing], George [Morris], and Mitch [Francis], [Jun. 7, 1935], Roy O. Corr. Re trips: 1935–1934 folder, Roy O. Disney Corr., Disney, Roy O.—Personal & Trips (1934–41), A2995, WDA.

222 **"We weren't used to the celebrities . . ."** Edna Disney, Aug. 20, 1968, RHC, Box 14, Folder 52.

222 **Dinner with Rothschilds.** Bob Thomas, *Building a Company: Roy O. Disney and the Creation of an Entertainment Empire* (New York: Hyperion, 1998), pp. 100–101.

222 **Crowds in London.** *LAT,* Jun. 13, 1935.

222 **"hundred pressmen . . ."** Paul Holt, "His Brother Dispels a Load of Illusions," *London Daily Express,* Jun. 13, 1935, Scrapbook, WDA.

222 **"Big Shot."** Roy Disney interview by Hubler, Feb. 20, 1968, pp. 9–10.

223 **League of Nations reception.** Walt to Ted Patrick, *Holiday,* Feb. 1, 1956, Ho Folder, Walt Disney Corr., 1956, G-L, A1563, WDA.

223 **Mussolini bragged . . .** Hubler, *Disney,* p. 206.

223 **"tired but happy."** Tel. Walt Disney Prods. to Roy Disney, Aug. 5, 1935, Roy O. Disney Corr. Re trips: 1934–1935, Roy O. Disney Corr., Disney, Roy O.—Personal & Trips (1934–41), A2995, WDA.

223 **"got such a welcome . . ."** *LAT,* Aug. 12, 1935.

223 **"Walt has been royally . . ."** Roy to Mr. and Mrs. Elias Disney, Jul. 1, 1935, Roy O. Disney Corr. Re trips: 1934–1935 Folder, Roy O. Disney Corr., Disney, Roy O.—Personal & Trips (1934–41), A2995, WDA.

223 **"You tell Doc . . ."** Hubler, *Disney,* p. 207.

223 **"When a dispatch . . ."** *LAT,* Aug. 12, 1935.

223 **"I found that all over . . ."** *Los Angeles Examiner,* Aug. 11, 1935.

224 **Alternate weeks.** Memo, Walt to Sears, Oct. 12, 1935, Inter-Office Communications, Walt Disney Corr., 1935, He-R, A1509, WDA.

224 **"our one chance . . ."** Memo, Walt to Roy, Dec. 2, 1935, Subject: UA Contract, Inter-Office Comm., Walt Disney Corr., 1935, A1509, WDA.

224 **"Have some birds . . ."** Story Meeting on SNOW WHITE, Oct. 31, 1935, Snow White—Story Meetings, Oct. 1935–Dec. 1935 Folder, *Snow White and the Seven Dwarfs,* Story Meetings Oct. 1934–1937, Box 1, A1731, WDA.

224 **"I've had continuity all wrapped . . ."** Walt to Sidney Franklin, Dec. 19, 1935, Misc. File, WDA.

224 **Scenes to Bill Tytla.** Memo to Bill Tytla, Dec. 4, 1935, Inter-Office Comm., Walt Disney Corr., 1935, A1509, WDA.

225 **"I can't be satisfied . . ."** Carmen Maxwell to Walt, Aug. 10, 1934, M, D.V.'s letters, 1934 Folder, Walt Disney Corr., 1930–1934, J-O, A1504, WDA.

225 **Art Babbitt.** John Canemaker, "Art Babbitt: The Animator as Firebrand," *Millimeter,* Sept. 1975, pp. 8–12, 42; Klaus Strzyz, "Art Babbitt," *Comics Journal,* no. 120 (March 1988), pp. 77–87; Michael Barrier, *Hollywood Cartoons: American Animation in Its Golden Age* (New York: Oxford University Press, 1999), p. 83.

225 **Dick Huemer.** Richard Huemer, *Recollections of Richard Huemer,* unpub. ms., 1969, pp. 1, 45, Special Collections, Young Research Library, UCLA.

225 **Grim Natwick.** "Snow White Animator," *Cartoonist Profiles* 1, no. 4 (Fall 1969), pp. 14–15; John Canemaker, "Grim Natwick," *Film Comment,* Jan.–Feb. 1975, pp. 57–61.

226 **"I'm a Cossack!"** Huemer, *Recollections,* p. 188.

226 **"hovered over his drawing board . . ."** Grim Natwick, "Animation," *Cartoonist Profiles,* no. 40 (Dec. 1978), p. 42.

226 **"He expresses a keen desire . . ."** Roy to Walt, May 26, 1933, Roy O. Disney—1933 Folder, Roy O. Disney Corr., Disney, Roy O.—Personal & Trips (1930–33), A2994, WDA.

226 **"to bring a stranger in . . ."** Sharpsteen to Tytla, Dec. 2, 1934, Ben Sharpsteen Folder, Walt Disney Corr., 1930–1934, P-U, A1505, WDA.

226 **"on-again off-again romance."** Bill Tytla, interview by George Sherman, *Cartoonist Profiles,* August 1970, p. 12.

226 **Forces and Forms.** Frank Thomas and Ollie Johnston, *The Illusion of Life: Disney Animation* (New York: Hyperion, 1981), p. 539.

226 **Pluck discarded drawings.** Natwick, "Animation," p. 42.

227 **"the idea was like a chain letter . . ."** Ham Luske, Notes, ca. 1956, WDA.

227 **Reitherman background.** John Canemaker, *Walt Disney's Nine Old Men and the Art of Animation* (New York: Disney Editions, 2001), pp. 32–33.

227 **"kind of guy . . ."** Sweatbox Notes, *Bambi,* Sept. 1, 1939, *Bambi*—Story Meetings, 1939, *Bambi* Production Materials—Story Meeting Notes, Sweatbox Notes, Corr., Research, 3267, WDA.

227 **Eric Larson.** Canemaker, *Nine Old Men,* pp. 56–58; Eric Larson, interview by Mica Prods., [n.d.], pp. 1–5, WDA.

227 **Ward Kimball.** Canemaker, *Nine Old Men,* pp. 88–93; Ward Kimball, interview by Christopher Finch and Linda Rosenkrantz, May 10, 1972, pp. 1–4, WDA; Marc Eliot, *Walt Disney: Hollywood's Dark Prince* (New York: Carol Pub-

lishing Group, 1993), p. 88; Ward Kimball, "The Wonderful World of Walt Disney," in *You Must Remember This*, ed. Walter Wagner (New York: G. P. Putnam's Sons, 1975), pp. 264–65.

228 **"He never did what was expected."** Thomas and Johnston, *Illusion of Life*, p. 171.

228 **"looked for an opportunity . . ."** Ben Sharpsteen, Answers to Questions Submitted by Dave Smith, Sept. 1974, p. 10, WDA.

228 **Milt Kahl.** Canemaker, *Nine Old Men*, pp. 132–36; Milt Kahl, Mica Prods., Nov. 3, 1983, p. 7, WDA.

228 **Frank Thomas.** Canemaker, *Nine Old Men*, pp. 170–74; John Canemaker, "Sincerely Yours, Frank Thomas," *Millimeter*, Jan. 1975, pp. 16–17.

228 **Ollie Johnston.** Canemaker, *Nine Old Men*, pp. 208–13.

229 **Marc Davis.** Ibid., pp. 266–71.

229 **"Attended classes . . ."** Marc Davis, interview by Bob Thomas, May 25, 1973, p. 1, WDA.

229 **"The qualification . . ."** Ben Sharpsteen to Director of Art Instruction, Pratt Institute, Jun. 6, 1934, Ben Sharpsteen Folder, Walt Disney Corr., 1930–1934, P-U, A1505, WDA.

229 **Response to recruitment.** Richard Schickel, *The Disney Version: The Life, Times, Art and Commerce of Walt Disney*, 3rd ed. (1968; repr., Chicago: Elephantine Paperbacks, 1997), p. 172; Memo, Vern Caldwell to Walt, Re: Talent Publicity, Nov. 15, 1939, Caldwell, Vernon, Folder, Walt Disney Corr., Inter-Office, 1938–1944, C, A1626, WDA.

229 **"the Depression was the greatest thing . . ."** Marc Davis, interview, May 21, 1968, RHC, Box 14, Folder 51.

229 **"It looked like a real utopia . . ."** Quoted in Canemaker, *Nine Old Men*, p. 243.

230 **From in-betweener to master animator.** *Official Report of the Proceedings of the National Labor Relations Board, In the Matter of Walt Disney Prods., Inc. and Arthur Babbitt*, Los Angeles, Oct. 9, 1942, p. 231.

230 **"goddamn poor working habits . . ."** Shamus Culhane, *Talking Animals and Other People* (New York: St. Martin's Press, 1986), pp. 110–11.

230 **Training.** Marc Davis, interview by Bob Thomas, Fall 1989, WDA; Frances Osborne (Walt Disney Productions) to Don Graham, Feb. 8, 1935, G, Walt Disney Corr., 1935, A1508, WDA.

230 **"[i]ntensive lectures . . ."** Quoted in John Canemaker, "Disney Design—1928–1979: How the Disney Studio Changed the Look of the Animated Cartoon," *Millimeter*, Feb. 1979, p. 107.

230 **"tied up in some way . . ."** Memo, Walt to Roy Scott. Re: Tuesday night shows, Sept. 18, 1935, Inter-Office Communications, Walt Disney Corr., 1935, He-R, A1509, WDA.

230 **Analyzing film.** Thomas and Johnston, *Illusion of Life*, p. 72.

230 **"Put in simple terms . . ."** Quoted in Canemaker, "Disney Design," p. 106.

231 **"to discuss with them . . ."** Thomas and Johnston, *Illusion of Life*, pp. 71–72.

231 **"Immediately following these talks . . ."** Memo, Walt to Don Graham, Dec. 23, 1935, cited in Culhane, *Talking Animals*, p. 117.

231 **"Caricature Class."** Memo, Walt to Don Graham, Jan. 10, 1936, Inter-Office Communications, Walt Disney Corr., 1936–1937, E-L, A1512, WDA.

231 **Expanding courses.** Don Graham, *The Art of Animation*, unpub. ms., n.d., p. 7, WDA.
231 **Excursions to zoo.** Culhane, *Talking Animals*, pp. 133–36.
231 **"I am convinced . . ."** Memo, Walt to Graham, Dec. 23, 1935, quoted in ibid., p. 119.
231 **"A creative structure . . ."** I. Klein, "When Walt Disney Took Another Giant Step!" *Cartoonist Profiles*, no. 33 (March 1977), p. 75.
231 **"like a marvelous big Renaissance craft hall."** Quoted in Richard Holliss and Brian Sibley, *The Disney Studio Story* (New York: Crown Publishers, 1988), p. 26.
231 **"Walt's idea . . ."** Boris Morkovin, Technique and Psychology of the Animated Cartoon, Studio Course, Nov. 14, 1935–Feb. 5, 1936, Beginners' Class, 1935–1936, WDA.
231 **"Shock is the soul of the gag."** Dr. Boris Morkovin, "Psychology of a Gag," [n.d.], p. 2, WDA.
231 **"You must train your imagination . . ."** Ibid., p. 11.
232 **"an ideal way to promote . . ."** Memo, Walt to Dr. Morkovin, Oct. 10, 1935, Inter-Office Communications, Walt Disney Corr., 1935, He-R, A1509, WDA.
232 **"[A]n hour a week under Ted Sears . . ."** George Turner to Walt, Jan. 24, 1935, ibid.
232 **"thinking animation character . . ."** Graham, *Art of Animation*, p. 12.
232 **"analyzing people . . ."** Ward Kimball to Thorkil Rasmussen, Feb. 23, 1978, quoted in Canemaker, *Nine Old Men*, p. 96.
232 **"[Y]ou watch these . . ."** Thomas to Christopher Finch, May 17, 1972, quoted in ibid., p. 198.
232 **"It came to a [point] . . ."** Larson interview by Mica Prods., pp. 13–14.
232 **Luske taking off tie.** Canemaker, *Nine Old Men*, p. 59.
233 **"Ham was studying . . ."** Thomas and Johnston, *Illusion of Life*, p. 107.
233 **"We saw every ballet . . ."** Holliss and Sibley, *Disney's* Snow White, p. 17.
233 **"perfect time . . ."** Canemaker, *Nine Old Men*, p. 273.
233 **"It is possible . . ."** Memo, Walt to Paul Hopkins, Nov. 25, 1935, Re: Production Notes on Snow White, Snow White Prod. Notes, Nov. 25, 1935, *Snow White and the Seven Dwarfs*, Continuities, gag suggestions, etc., Jul. 1934–Dec. 1936, Box 2, A1737, WDA.
233 **"If he gave Grumpy to Tytla . . ."** Krause and Witkowski, *Walt Disney's* Snow White, p. 31.
234 **"two months of experimental animation . . ."** Quoted in Holliss and Sibley, *Disney's* Snow White, p. 31.
234 **Walt assigned.** Memo, Walt to Paul Hopkins, Nov. 25, 1935.
234 **Harry Bailey.** Huemer, *Recollections*, p. 200.
234 **Cottrell as director.** Bill Cottrell, interview by Jay Horan, Aug.–Oct. 1983, p. 109, WDA.
234 **"all the key animators . . ."** David Dodd Hand, *Memoirs* (Cambria, Calif.: Lighthouse Litho, 1990), p. 77.
235 **Characters versus scenes.** See Barrier, *Hollywood Cartoons*, pp. 150–51.
235 **"I need 300 artists . . ."** Holliss and Sibley, *Disney Studio Story*, p. 28.
235 **Walt never thanked him.** Ben Sharpsteen, interview by Dave Smith, Oct. 21, 1974, p. 20, WDA.

235 **Seven hundred initial applicants.** George Drake to Walt, Apr. 4, 1936; Apr. 18, 1936; Apr. 19, 1936, Drake, George, Folder, Walt Disney Corr., 1936–1937, A-D, A1511, WDA.

236 **Cost of New York recruitment.** Memo, Edward M. Francis to Walt, Jun. 12, 1936, Re: Costs—New York Art School, Inter-Office Communications, Walt Disney Corr., 1936–1937, E-L, A1512, WDA.

236 **Resentments.** Sharpsteen interview by Smith, p. 21.

236 **Twenty-two of over two thousand.** Carter Ludlow to Roy, May 16, 1936; Ludlow to Louis Sobol, Jun. 17, 1936, Ludlow, Carter—1936 Folder, Roy O. Disney Corr., Lu-Mi, (1930–1939), A2997, WDA.

236 **Most hated man at Disney.** Canemaker, *Nine Old Men*, p. 59.

236 **"George had huge ears . . ."** Jay Horan, *Video Interview with Ken Anderson, Bill Cottrell and Herb Ryman*, Sept. 19, 1983, p. 73, WDA.

236 **"During that one month . . ."** Bill Peet, *Bill Peet: An Autobiography* (Boston: Houghton Mifflin, 1989), n.p.

236 **"so far in advance . . ."** Robert D. Feild, *The Art of Walt Disney* (New York: Macmillan, 1942), p. 78.

236 **"mythical sun . . ."** Grim Natwick, "Animation," *Cartoonist Profiles* (June 1979), p. 74.

236 **"Each new picture contained . . ."** Thomas and Johnston, *Illusion of Life*, p. 145.

237 **"We were part of a thing . . ."** Dick Huemer, "With Disney on Olympus," *Funnyworld*, no. 17 (Fall 1977), p. 38.

237 **"It wasn't that you had to do . . ."** Quoted in Thomas and Johnston, *Illusion of Life*, p. 146.

237 **"the whole studio grew like Topsy."** Quoted in Krause and Witkowski, *Walt Disney's* Snow White, p. 24.

237 **Expansion.** David R. Smith, "Disney Before Burbank: The Kingswell and Hyperion Studios," *Funnyworld*, no. 20 (Summer 1979), pp. 36–38; Thomas and Johnston, *Illusion of Life*, pp. 141–42; Jimmy Johnson, *Inside the Whimsy Works: My Thirty-Seven Years with Walt Disney Productions*, unpub. ms., 1975, p. 3, WDA.

237 **"any structure that was near . . ."** Thomas and Johnston, *Illusion of Life*, p. 142.

237 **"occupied all of the living rooms . . ."** Peet, *Autobiography*, p. 95.

238 **Twelve buildings.** Walt Disney, *Autobiography*, 1939, 5th installment, p. 6, WDA; Memo, George Morris to Roy O. Disney, Re: insurance, April 30, 1937, Board of Fire Underwriters of the Pacific, Roy O. Disney Corr., A-C (1929–51), A2993, WDA.

238 **"a beautiful plant."** John Canemaker, "Vlad Tytla: Animation's Michelangelo," in *The American Animated Cartoon: A Critical Anthology*, ed. Gerald Peary and Danny Peary (New York: E. P. Dutton, 1980), p. 85.

238 **Courtyard.** Henry F. Pringle, "Mickey Mouse's Father," *McCall's*, Aug. 1932, pp. 7, 28.

238 **"small municipal kindergarten . . ."** Janet Flanner, "Boom Shot of Hollywood," *Harper's Bazaar*, Nov. 1, 1936.

238 **"quaint, cozy look . . ."** Peet, *Autobiography*, p. 80.

238 **"In the first place . . ."** Culhane, *Talking Animals*, p. 113.

238 **"The desk furniture was something!"** Ward Kimball, interview by Christopher Finch and Linda Rosenkrantz, May 10, 1972, p. 8, WDA.

238 **"maybe an Ivy League campus . . ."** Tytle, "*Walt's Boys,*" p. 7.

238 **Average age.** Clipping [1934], no title, Scrapbook, WDA.

238 ***The Mickey Mouse Melodeon.*** Kinney, *Walt Disney and Other Animated Characters: An Unauthorized Account of the Early Years at Disney's* (New York: Harmony Books, 1988), pp. 50–51.

239 **Baseball.** Peet, *Autobiography,* p. 99; Kinney, *Disney and Animated Characters,* p. 21.

239 **Pranks.** Thomas and Johnston, *Illusion of Life,* p. 120; Ward Kimball, interview about Walt Kelly, May 25, 1964, p. 4, WDA; Bill Justice, *Justice for Disney* (Dayton, Ohio: Tomart Publications, 1992), p. 106; Canemaker, *Nine Old Men,* p. 136; Culhane, *Talking Animals,* p. 146; Milt Kahl, interview by Mica Prods., Nov. 3, 1983, pp. 6–7, WDA.

239 **"psychiatrist's heaven."** Arthur Miller, "Walter in Wonderland," *LAT Magazine,* Sept. 4, 1938.

239 **"If this is not a crazy house . . ."** Ferdinand Horvath, Jun. 1, 1933, quoted in John Canemaker, *Before the Animation Begins: The Art and Lives of Disney Inspirational Sketch Artists* (New York: Hyperion, 1996), p. 27.

239 **"too much visiting . . ."** Memo, Walt to All Prod. Employees, May 20, 1935, Inter-Office Communications, Walt Disney Corr., 1935, He-R, A1509, WDA.

239 **"Why don't you get some of that . . ."** Thomas and Johnston, *Illusion of Life,* p. 145.

239 **Drinking.** Canemaker, *Nine Old Men,* p. 93; Kinney, *Disney and Animated Characters,* p. 75.

239 **"Maybe more ideas . . ."** Kinney, *Disney and Animated Characters,* p. 170.

239 **Stag films.** Kimball interview about Kelly, p. 8.

239 **Pornographic cartoons.** Kimball interview by Finch and Rosenkrantz, p. 7.

240 **"dipping your pen . . ."** Kinney, *Disney and Animated Characters,* p. 37.

240 **"Ben Sharpsteen."** Ibid.

240 **At least thirty-five couples.** Tytle, "*Walt's Boys,*" p. 11.

240 **"sexual intercourse."** Canemaker, *Nine Old Men,* p. 154.

240 **"Walt's big happy family."** Sidney Skolsky, "Mickey Mouse—Meet Your Maker," *Hearst's International Cosmopolitan,* Feb. 1934, p. 172.

240 **"Dad wanted to take care . . ."** Amy Boothe Green and Howard E. Green, *Remembering Walt: Favorite Memories of Walt Disney* (New York: Hyperion, 1999), p. 68.

240 **No time clock.** Douglas W. Churchill, "Disney's 'Philosophy,' " *NYT Magazine,* Mar. 6, 1938, p. 23.

240 **Sick leave.** Jim Korkis, "Excuse Me, But Have You Heard of Paul Murry?" *POV,* no. 5, p. 24.

240 **Vacations.** George Morris to Roy, May 17, 1933, Roy O. Disney—1933 Folder, Roy O. Disney Corr., Disney, Roy O.—Personal & Trips (1930–33), A2994, WDA.

241 **"I want you to take . . ."** Walt to Bill Garity, July 6, 1934, Garity, William E., Personal File, Roy O. Disney Corr., G-Lo (1930–41), A2996, WDA.

241 **Salaries.** Culhane, *Talking Animals,* p. 14; Klaus Strzyz, "Art Babbitt," *Comics Journal,* no. 120 (March 1988), p. 78.

241 **Salary adjustments.** Memo, Walt to Paul Hopkins, May 10, 1937, Inter-Office Communications, Walt Disney Corr., 1936–1937, E-L, A1512, WDA. Walt asks Hopkins to check on assistants in the special effects department whose time records are not complete and "to size up them and [place] a valuation on their ability and make whatever salary adjustments are necessary."

241 **"His ambition is to pay . . ."** Douglas W. Churchill, "How Mickey Mouse Enters Art's Temple," *NYT Magazine*, Jun. 3, 1934, p. 13.

241 **" 'You know, Joe' . . ."** Quoted in Eliot, *Dark Prince*, p. 115.

241 **"pioneer in more things . . ."** [Jan. 26, 1938], Otis Ferguson, *The Film Criticism of Otis Ferguson*, ed. Robert Wilson (Philadelphia: Temple University Press, 1971), p. 211.

241 **Left-wing praise.** Gregory A. Waller, "Mickey, Walt and Film Criticism from *Steamboat Willie* to *Bambi*," in Peary and Peary, *Animated Cartoon*, p. 55.

242 **"physically unable . . ."** Memo, Paul Hopkins to Walt, Nov. 7, 1936, Inter-Office Comm., Walt Disney Corr., 1936–1937, E-L, A1512, WDA.

242 **Only as good as last scene.** Thomas and Johnston, *Illusion of Life*, p. 235.

242 **"I have never found . . ."** *Bambi* Story Meeting, April 5, 1939, pp. 21–22, quoted in Steven Watts, *The Magic Kingdom: Walt Disney and the American Way of Life* (Boston: Houghton Mifflin, 1997), p. 186.

242 **"I believe it will help me . . ."** Jack King to Walt, May 31, 1933, K, D.V.'s Letters, 1931–33 Folder, Walt Disney Corr., 1930–1934, J-O, A1504, WDA.

242 **"Ben realizes he is not talented."** Quoted in Hubler, *Disney*, p. 327.

242 **"He's OK."** Quoted in Watts, *Magic Kingdom*, p. 197.

242 **"son of a bitch . . ."** Hubler, *Disney*, p. 327.

243 **"The verbal beatings . . ."** Ibid., p. 328.

243 **"I was constantly called upon . . ."** Ben Sharpsteen, interview by Richard Hubler, Oct. 29, 1968, p. 26, WDA.

243 **Bonus plan.** Walt Disney, interview by Pete Martin, Reels 6 & 7, p. 42.

243 **"to be repaid . . ."** Roy to Walt, Aug. 31, 1935, Roy O. Corr. Re trips: 1934–1935 Folder, Roy O. Disney Corr., Disney, Roy O.—Personal & Trips (1934–41), A2995, WDA.

243 **"I was always trying . . ."** Deposition of Walt Disney, Jun. 19, 1942, Superior Court, California, No. 471865, Babbitt case, Walt Disney Corr., Inter-Office, 1938–1944, A-B, A1625, WDA, p. 37.

243 **Details of bonus plan.** Memo, Bill Garity, Apr. 8, 1936, Babbitt case, Walt Disney Corr., Inter-Office Communications, 1938–1944, A-B, A1625, WDA.

243 **"Nobody liked it really . . ."** Ben Sharpsteen, interview by Don Peri, Feb. 6, 1974, p. 21, WDA.

243 **Redoing work of poorer animators.** Thomas and Johnston, *Illusion of Life*, p. 153.

244 **"Some sort of magic light . . ."** Ward Kimball, interview by Richard Hubler, May 21, 1968, p. 33, WDA.

244 **"I definitely intend . . ."** Ed Strickland to Walt, n.d., St Folder, Walt Disney Corr., 1936–1937, S-Z, A1514, WDA.

244 **"night and day . . ."** Quoted in Krause and Witkowski, *Walt Disney's* Snow White, p. 31.

244 **"It was the love of his life . . ."** Hubler, *Disney*, p. 308.

244 **"Open with dancing . . ."** Discussion on Entertainment Sequence of "Snow

White," [Jan. 1936], 10–12 p.m., Snow White Story Meetings, Jan. 1936–Jul. 1936 folder, *Snow White and the Seven Dwarfs*, Story Meetings Oct. 1934–1937, Box 1, A1731, WDA.

245 **"[H]e was telling it all the time . . ."** Eric Larson, interview by Mike Bonifer, p. 18, WDA.

245 **"Every time he'd come into a room . . ."** Eliot, *Dark Prince*, p. 101.

245 **Three or four dozen times.** Greene and Greene, *Inside the Dream*, p. 50.

245 **"Whether he used the idea . . ."** Sharpsteen interview by Hubler, Oct. 29, 1968, p. 25.

245 **"It would be good for her . . ."** Story Conference on Seq. 3B, Snow White Alone in the Woods, Sat., Jun. 27, 1936, 8:45 to 1:00 p.m., Story Meetings, Jan. 1936–Jul. 1936 folder, *Snow White and the Seven Dwarfs*, Story Meetings—Oct. 1934–1937, Box 1, A1731, WDA.

245 **"[S]he is stooped over . . ."** Story Conference on Seq. 3A, Snow White and the Huntsman in the Woods, ibid.

246 **"Let him break . . ."** Seq. 11A Lodge Meeting, Story Conference, Dec. 7, 1936, 9:00 to 12:30, ibid.

246 **"I like good comedy . . ."** Story Conference on Snow White Spook Seq. (4D), May 21, 1936, ibid.

246 **"his fanny in the last half . . ."** Seq. 3D, House Cleaning, *Snow White and the Seven Dwarfs*, Sweatbox Notes, Seq. 1b–10B, Box 6, A1732, WDA.

246 **"Dopey could come in . . ."** Story Conference Seq. 4A & 4B (Dwarfs in the Mine and Marching Home), Nov. 2, 1936, 9:00 a.m. to 11:50, Snow White—Story Meetings, Nov. 1936 only folder, *Snow White and the Seven Dwarfs*, Story Meetings, Oct. 1934–1937, Box 1, A1731, WDA.

246 **"It was often difficult . . ."** Thomas and Johnston, *Illusion of Life*, p. 113.

246 **"What we are trying to do . . ."** Dwarfs Personality Meeting, Dec. 29, 1936, Snow White—Story Meetings, Dec. 16–31, 1936 Folder, *Snow White and the Seven Dwarfs*, Story Meetings, Oct. 1934–1937, Box 1, A1731, WDA.

246 **"everyone who had ever been associated . . ."** Joseph Barbera, *My Life in 'toons: From Flatbush to Bedrock in Under a Century* (Atlanta: Turner Publishing, 1994), p. 44.

247 **"It is my opinion . . ."** Quoted in Thomas and Johnston, *Illusion of Life*, p. 97.

247 **"all walking on tiptoes . . ."** George Sherman, "Bill Tytla Interview," *Cartoonist Profiles* (Aug. 1970), p. 12.

247 **"There is a lot of stuff . . ."** Bill Tytla, "Handling of Dwarfs in *Snow White*," Action Analysis Class, Dec. 10, 1936, p. 4, WDA.

247 **"I think they're afraid . . ."** Note, Ted Sears, n.d., Inter-Office Communication, S.W. Notes (things to watch), SW Continuities, gag suggestions, etc., *Snow White and the Seven Dwarfs*, Continuities, gag suggestions, etc., Jan. 1937, Box 3, A1736, WDA.

247 **"The one thing I don't want . . ."** Eric Larson and Ham Luske, Training Course Lecture Series, "Analysis and Handling of Animal Characters in Snow White" [1937], Undated Soup Eating Seq. folder, *Snow White and the Seven Dwarfs*, Story Meeting, Oct. 1934–1937, Box 1, A1731, WDA.

248 **"It was funny . . ."** Frank Thomas quoted in Krause and Witkowski, *Walt Disney's* Snow White, p. 44.

248 **Factions.** David R. Smith, "Ben Sharpsteen . . . 33 Years with Disney," *Millimeter*, Apr. 1975, p. 40.

248 **"I don't know what they're looking for."** Canemaker, *Nine Old Men*, pp. 176–177.
248 **"bunch of Cinderellas."** Ibid., p. 177.
248 **"we have come to the conclusion . . ."** Sears to Klein [Nov. 1933] quoted in I. Klein, "When Walt Disney Took Another Giant Step!" *Cartoonist Profiles*, no. 33 (Mar. 1977), p. 74.
248 **"I guess we could do better . . ."** Clark to Thomas and Johnston, Sept. 14, 1978, quoted in Canemaker, *Nine Old Men*, p. 18.
248 **Complaints about Natwick.** Memo, Paul Hopkins to Walt, Re: Grim Natwick, Aug. 22, 1935, Inter-Office Communications, Walt Disney Corr., 1935, He-R, A1509, WDA. According to Hopkins, Natwick had been delivering only 35 percent of his quota footage in the shorts.
248 **Natwick versus Luske.** See Barrier, *Hollywood Cartoons*, pp. 199–200.
249 **Natwick's scorn.** See animationartist.com/columns/DJohnson/FourFaces/fourfaces.html. Johnson believes that Walt retained Luske's early animation of Snow White encountering the dwarfs' cottage, most likely because it would have been prohibitively expensive to scrap it all, but that he inclined toward Natwick's and Campbell's drawings.
249 **"Snow White was a sweet and graceful . . ."** Canemaker, "Grim Natwick," *Film Comment*, Jan.–Feb. 1975, p. 59.
249 **Twenty-six scenes.** Barrier, *Hollywood Cartoons*, p. 193.
249 **Mute Dopey.** Untitled sheet. Nov. 25, 1935, Snow White Continuities, gag suggestions, etc., Sept.–Nov. 1935, *Snow White and the Seven Dwarfs*, continuities, gag suggestions, etc., Jul. 1934–Dec. 1936, Box 2, A1737, WDA.
249 **"happy sort of fellow."** Snow White Dwarfs' Personalities, Dec. 3, 1935, Snow White continuities, gag suggestions, etc., Dec. 1935, A1737, WDA.
249 **Deafy jettisoned for Sneezy.** See Snow White Continuities, gag suggestions, etc. Jan.–Feb. 1936 Folder, *Snow White and the Seven Dwarfs*, Continuities, gag suggestions, etc., Jul. 1934–Dec. 1936, Box 2, A1737, WDA. In Fred Moore's Leica reel notes he refers to Sneezy, though Dozey is used instead of Sleepy.
249 **James Gleason.** Gleason to Walt, Aug. 30, 1935, G, Walt Disney Corr., 1935, A1508, WDA.
249 **"[H]e did all these inspirational movements . . ."** Kimball interview by Bonifer, p. 29.
250 **"characteristics of the dwarfs."** Story Conference, Personalities of the Seven Dwarfs, Nov. 3, 1936, 7:30 p.m. to 10:00 p.m., Snow White—Story Meetings, Nov. 1936 only folder, *Snow White and the Seven Dwarfs*, Story Meetings, Oct. 1934–1937, Box 1, A1731, WDA.
250 **"he forgot we were there."** Thomas and Johnston, *Illusion of Life*, p. 398.
250 **"[T]he animators themselves don't know yet . . ."** Tytla, "Handling of Dwarfs in 'Snow White,' " p. 8.
250 **"[W]e have got to have characteristics . . ."** Story Conference, Personalities of the Seven Dwarfs, Nov. 17, 1936, 7:30 p.m. to 10:00 p.m., Show White—Story Meetings, Nov. 1936 only folder, *Snow White and the Seven Dwarfs*, Story Meetings, Oct. 1934–1937, Box 1, A1731, WDA.
250 **"To me, Erny . . ."** Handwritten notes on Snow White Dwarfs' Personalities, Dec. 15, 1936, Snow White—continuities, gag suggestions, etc., Dec. 1936 Folder, *Snow White and the Seven Dwarfs*, Continuities, gag suggestions, etc., Jul. 1934–Dec. 1936, Box 2, A1737, WDA.

250 **"superficial mannerism."** Story Conference Discussion on Personalities of Dwarfs, Nov. 17, 1936, 7:30 p.m. to 10:00 p.m., Snow White—Story Meetings, Nov. 1936 only folder, *Snow White and the Seven Dwarfs*, Story Meetings, Oct. 1934–1937, Box 1, A1731, WDA.

250 **"I think you have to know these fellows . . ."** Story Conference on Characteristics and Personalities of the Seven Dwarfs, Dec. 15, 1936, 7:00 p.m. to 10:30 p.m., Story Meetings, Dec. 1–15, 1936 Folder, *Snow White and the Seven Dwarfs*, Story Meetings, Oct. 1934–1937, Box 1, A1731, WDA.

251 **"He is, like Doc . . ."** Handwritten Notes on Snow White Dwarfs' Personalities, Dec. 15, 1936, Snow White—continuities, gag suggestions, etc. Dec. 1936 folder, *Snow White and the Seven Dwarfs*, Continuities, gag suggestions, etc., Jul. 1934–Dec. 1936, Box 2 A1737, WDA.

251 **"Harlan has a characteristic . . ."** Ibid.

251 **Stepin Fetchit.** Story Conference, Personalities of the Seven Dwarfs, Nov. 17, 1936, 7:30 p.m. to 10:00 p.m., Snow White—Story Meetings, Nov. 1936 only folder, *Snow White and the Seven Dwarfs*, Story Meetings, Oct. 1934–1937, Box 1, A1731, WDA.

251 **Moore's descriptions.** Story Meeting on Discussion of Dwarfs Personalities and Characteristics, Dec. 8, 1936, 7:00 p.m. to 10:00 p.m., Story Meetings, Dec. 1–15, 1936 folder, *Snow White and the Seven Dwarfs*, Story Meetings, Oct. 1934–1937, Box 1, A1731, WDA.

251 **"we are depending upon . . ."** Snow White Dwarfs' Personalities, Dec. 3, 1935, Snow White continuities, gag suggestions, etc., Dec. 1935, A1737, WDA.

251 **Name Dopey.** Diane Disney Miller, as told to Pete Martin, *The Story of Walt Disney* (New York: Holt, 1956), p. 138.

251 **"Dopey has some Harpo . . ."** Story Conference, Discussion on Personalities of Dwarfs, Nov. 17, 1936, 7:30 p.m. to 10:00 p.m., Snow White—Story Meetings, Nov. 1936 only folder, *Snow White and the Seven Dwarfs*, Story Meetings Oct. 1934–1937, Box 1, A1731, WDA.

252 **"The boys couldn't seem to get him . . ."** Holliss and Sibley, *Disney Studio Story*, p. 15.

252 **"He is slow at figuring things out . . ."** Discussion on Dopey, Dec. 9, 1936, Story Meetings, Dec. 1–15, 1936 Folder, *Snow White and the Seven Dwarfs*, Story Meetings Oct. 1934–1937, Box 1, A1731, WDA.

252 **"I think the thing . . ."** Story Conference on Characteristics and Personalities of the Seven Dwarfs, Dec. 15, 1936, WDA.

252 **Inviting Eddie Collins.** Story Meeting on Discussion of Dwarfs' Personalities and Characteristics, Dec. 8, 1936, WDA.

252 **"in a way like Pluto."** Snow White Dwarfs' Personalities, Dec. 3, 1935, WDA.

252 **"You know the way a dog . . ."** Holliss and Sibley, *Disney Studio Story*, p. 15.

252 **"Details that Are to Be on Dwarfs . . ."** Jan. 8, 1937, SW continuities, gag suggestions, etc. Jan.–Feb. 1937, *Snow White and the Seven Dwarfs*, Continuities, gag suggestions, etc., Jan 1937—undated, Box 3, A1736, WDA.

253 **"She read the lines."** Bill Cottrell, interview by Jay Horan, Aug.–Oct. 1983, p. 8, WDA.

253 **Removing false teeth.** Krause and Witkowski, *Walt Disney's* Snow White, p. 36.

253 **150 girls.** "Andrea Caselotti," in Dave Smith, *Disney A to Z: The Updated Official Encyclopedia* (New York: Hyperion, 1998), p. 92.

253 **Virginia Davis.** "The Virginia Davis Interview," *Hogan's Alley*, no. 2 (Summer 1995), p. 110.

253 **"She sounds to me . . ."** Walt Disney interview by Martin, Reels 6 & 7, pp. 53–54.

253 **Caselotti's first tracks.** Sound Dept. Daily Report, Jan. 20, 1936, Snow White Sound Reports, *Snow White and the Seven Dwarfs*, Sweatbox Notes, Seq. 13A–16A, Misc. Files (financial, promotion, etc.), Punch Sheets French Version, Box 7, A1733, WDA.

254 **"not rhymed or definite beat . . ."** Snow White—General Treatment of Dialogue, Action, and Music [1935], Snow White—Story Meetings, Oct. 1935–Dec. 1935 Folder, *Snow White and the Seven Dwarfs*, Story Meetings Oct. 1934–1937, Box 1, A1731, WDA.

254 **"I don't like the Cab Calloway . . ."** Seq. 8A—Entertainment Conf., Jan 18, 1936, 2–4 p.m., Snow White Story Meetings, Jan. 1936–Jul. 1936 Folder, *Snow White and the Seven Dwarfs*, Story Meetings Oct. 1934–1937, Box 1, A1731, WDA.

254 **"You're Never Too Old to Be Young."** Snow White Entertainment Seq., 8A, Jan. 6, 1936, 9–12 a.m., Snow White Story Meetings, Jan. 1936–Jul. 1936 Folder, *Snow White and the Seven Dwarfs*, Story Meetings, Oct. 1934–1937, Box 1, A1731, WDA.

254 **"blowing on bottles and jugs . . ."** Thomas and Johnston, *Illusion of Life*, p. 198.

254 **"Bashful could half talk . . ."** Story Meeting on Seq. 8A (Entertainment), March 31, 1937, 8:30 a.m. to 12:15 p.m., Snow White—Story Meetings—Feb.–Mar. 1937 Folder, *Snow White and the Seven Dwarfs*, Story Meetings, Oct. 1934–1937, Box 1, A1731, WDA.

254 **One track lacked rhythm.** Walt's Criticisms and Discussion of 5B, 6A Rerecorded Track, Seq. 5B, SW Tells Dwarfs to Wash, *Snow White and Seven Dwarfs*, Sweatbox Notes, Seq. 1b–10B, Box 6, A1732, WDA.

254 **"The Silly Song."** Snow White—dialogue: songs, 1937, *Snow White and the Seven Dwarfs*, Dialogue and Songs, 1934–1937 undated duplicate, Box 5, A1735, WDA.

254 **"It's still that influence . . ."** Seq. 8A—Entertainment Meeting, Feb. 16, 1937, Snow White—Story Meetings, Feb.–Mar. 1937 Folder, *Snow White and the Seven Dwarfs*, Story Meetings, Oct. 1934–1937, Box 1, A1731, WDA.

255 **Complaints on paints.** Edward M. Francis to F. R. Miller, Jul. 16, 1935, Miller, F. R., Folder, Roy O. Disney Corr., Lu-Mi (1930–1939), A2997, WDA.

255 **Its own binder.** Stephen Worth and Lew Stude, "Vintage Notes: The Care and Restoration of Vintage Animation Cels," *POV* 1, no. 2 (Winter 1992), p. 13.

255 **Spectraphotometer.** *New York Daily Mirror*, Feb. 26, 1938.

255 **twelve hundred distinct pigments.** Robert Feild, *The Art of Walt Disney* (New York: Macmillan, 1942), p. 270.

255 **Technicolor chart.** Leonard Maltin, *The Disney Films*, 3rd ed. (New York: Hyperion, 1995), pp. 9–10.

255 **"They got colors everywhere . . ."** Effects on Seq. 3C & 3D, Sweatbox Session, Dec. 1, 1936, 1:00 p.m. to 5:30 p.m., Snow White—Story Meetings, Dec.

1–15, 1936 Folder, *Snow White and the Seven Dwarfs*, Story Meetings, Oct. 1934–1937, Box 1, A1731, WDA.

255 **"For *Snow White*, . . ."** Mike Barrier, "Screenwriter for a Duck: Carl Barks at the Disney Studio," *Funnyworld*, no. 21 (Fall 1979), p. 12.

256 **"He'd just sit all day . . ."** Eric Larson, interview by Steve Hulett, Apr. 19, 1978, p. 2, WDA. For more on Hurter, see John Canemaker, *Before the Animation Begins: The Art and Lives of Disney Inspirational Sketch Artists* (New York: Hyperion, 1996), pp. 9–25.

256 **Fifty to one hundred sketches.** Steve Hulett, "A Star is Drawn," *Film Comment* (Jan.–Feb. 1979), p. 13.

256 **"I remember quite clearly . . ."** Larson interview by Hulett, p. 2.

256 **"all prop coloring, . . ."** Background Meeting with Layout Men on Snow White, Nov. 23, 1936, Story Meetings, Nov. 1936 only folder, *Snow White and the Seven Dwarfs*, Story Meetings, Oct. 1934–1937, Box 1, A1731, WDA.

256 **"Albert knows the character . . ."** Conf., Dec. 1, 1936, in Robin Allan, *Walt Disney and Europe* (Bloomington, Ind.: Indiana University Press, 1999), p. 46.

257 **Paper and texture.** See Krause and Witkowski, *Walt Disney's* Snow White, p. 164; Christopher Finch, *The Art of Walt Disney: From Mickey Mouse to the Magic Kingdoms*, rev. ed. (New York: Harry N. Abrams, 1993), p. 67.

257 **"He was afraid . . ."** Miller, *Story of Disney*, p. 137.

257 **Ken Anderson's tests.** David Smith, "New Dimensions—Beginnings of the Disney Multiplane Camera," in *The Art of the Animated Image: An Anthology*, ed. Charles Solomon (Los Angeles: American Film Institute, 1989), pp. 40–42.

258 **Iwerks's multiplane.** Ibid., p. 40.

258 **Operation of multiplane.** Bob Broughton, interview by author; Thomas and Johnston, *Illusion of Life*, p. 307.

258 **Painfully slow.** Memo: Sam Armstrong to Walt Disney/Paul Hopkins, Re: The Old Mill, Multiplane Prod., March 30, 1937, Inter-Office Communications, Walt Disney Corr., 1936–1937, E-L, A1512, WDA.

258 **"It was always my ambition . . ."** "Mouse & Man," *Time*, Dec. 27, 1937, pp. 19–21.

258 **"an audience could be swept up . . ."** Thomas and Johnston, *Illusion of Life*, p. 78.

259 **Eric Larson on *The Old Mill*.** Eric Larson, interview by Mica Prods., [n.d.], pp. 11–12, WDA.

259 **"Even in the eyes of the Studio . . ."** Feild, *Art of Disney*, p. 274.

259 **"[T]he big studios . . ."** Roy to Elias and Flora Disney, Apr. 6, 1936, quoted in Thomas, *Building a Company*, p. 105.

259 **"competitive cartoons . . ."** Memo, Walt to Roy. Nov. 29, 1935, Sub: UA Contract, Inter-Office Comm., Walt Disney Corr., 1935, A1509, WDA.

259 **"I don't want to make any money . . ."** Memo, Lessing to Roy, Jun. 15, 1936, Roy O. Disney—Trip to NY, May 1936, Apr. 1937, Roy O. Disney Corr., Disney, Roy O.—Personal & Trips (1934–41), A2995, WDA.

259 **Television rights.** Dudley McClure, "Television Prospects Cause Disney to Join Forces with RKO," *Oregon Sunday Journal*, Mar. 15, 1936.

260 **"[P]ersonally I have seen enough . . ."** *LAT*, Mar. 3, 1936.

260 **"to make at least half . . ."** Memo, Walt to Roy, Dec. 4, 1936, Inter-Office Communications, Walt Disney Corr., 1936–1937, E-L, A1512, WDA.

260 **First cels sent to ink and paint.** Press Release, Snow White Publicity folder, Press Releases, 1951, WDA.

260 **"Many felt that to have . . ."** Hand, *Memoirs*, p. 77.

260 **Dwarfs entering cottage.** See Seq. 4D, Spooks, *Snow White and the Seven Dwarfs*, Sweatbox Notes, Seq. 1b–10B, Box 6, A1732.

260 **Sweatboxing scenes.** Walt Disney Desk Diaries, 1937, A3084, WDA.

260 **"tremendous pressure"** Ollie Johnston interview by author.

261 **"We gotta get the picture out!"** Frank Thomas to John Canemaker, March 18, 1998, quoted in Canemaker, *Nine Old Men*, p. 21.

261 **"My criticism is all impersonal . . ."** Conf. of Assistant Directors on Feature Procedure, Feb. 3, 1937, Story Meetings, Feb–March 1937 folder, *Snow White and the Seven Dwarfs*, Story Meetings, Oct. 1934–1937, Box 1, A1731, WDA.

261 **Putting a stopwatch on Walt.** Hand, *Memoirs*, p. 76.

261 **"We must avoid taking up the time . . ."** Conference of Assistant Directors on Feature Procedure, Feb. 3, 1937, WDA.

261 **Pep talk.** Memo, George Groepper (layout and in-between) to Walt, Jan. 29, 1937, Inter-Office Communications, Walt Disney Corr., 1936–1937, E-L, A1512, WDA.

261 **"This picture is a tremendous thing."** Conference of Assistant Directors on Feature Procedure, Feb. 3, 1937, WDA.

261 **"The work now being planned . . ."** Bill Tytla, Action Analysis Class, Jun. 8, 1937, quoted in Thomas and Johnston, *Illusion of Life*, p. 548.

262 **Live action models.** Ward Kimball interview by Bonifer, p. 28; Canemaker, *Nine Old Men*, p. 245; Snow White continuities, gag suggestions, etc., March-April 1936 Folder, *Snow White and the Seven Dwarfs*, Continuities, gag suggestions, etc., Jul. 1934–Dec. 1936, Box 2, A1737, WDA.

262 **"I think you can use . . ."** Story Meeting on Discussion of Dwarfs' Personalities and Characteristics, Dec. 8, 1936, WDA.

262 **"Stress the point . . ."** Story Meeting on Discussion of Seven Dwarfs Personalities, Nov. 24, 1936, 7:30 p.m. to 10:00 p.m., Snow White—Story Meetings, Nov. 1936 only folder, *Snow White and the Seven Dwarfs*, Story Meetings, Oct. 1934–1937, Box 1, A1731, WDA.

262 **"he did not want any animators . . ."** Ben Sharpsteen, interview by Don Peri, Mar. 26, 1975, p. 12, WDA.

262 **"Live action is what . . ."** Luncheon Meeting on Production, F-1, Snow White, Feb. 18, 1937, Story Meetings, Feb.–Mar. 1937 Folder, *Snow White and the Seven Dwarfs*, Story Meetings, Oct. 1934–1937, Box 1, A1731, WDA.

262 **Child actors.** Meeting on Seq. 10A—Dwarfs Leave for Mine, March 16, 1937, *Snow White and the Seven Dwarfs*, Story Meetings, Oct. 1934–1937, Box 1, A1731, WDA.

263 **"There is a lot of Snow White . . ."** Ibid.

263 **Photostats of Queen.** Seq. 7A, Queen Changes to Witch, *Snow White and the Seven Dwarfs*, Sweatbox Notes, Seq. 1b–10B, Box 6, A1732, WDA.

263 **"I want this definitely left out . . ."** Walt to Roy Scott, May 15, 1937, Inter-Office Communications, Walt Disney Corr., 1936–1937, E-L, A1512, WDA.

263 **"snapped up."** Sweatbox Session, Dwarfs Finish Bed—Animals Warn them, Jul. 13, 1937, *Snow White and the Seven Dwarfs*, Sweatbox Notes, Seq. 13A–16A, Misc. Files (financial, promotion, et.) Punch Sheets French Version, Box 7, A1733, WDA.

263 **"I don't think it has . . ."** The Meeting and the Bed (Dick Creedon), Nov. 15, 1936, *Snow White* continuities, gag suggestions, etc., Nov. 1936 Folder, *Snow White and the Seven Dwarfs*, Continuities, gag suggestions, etc., July 1934–Dec. 1936, Box 2, A1737, WDA.

263 **"Take out all the superfluous . . ."** Story Conference Notes on Snow White F-1 (Building Seq.), Feb. 1, 1937, Snow White—Story Meetings, Feb.–Mar. 1937 Folder, *Snow White and the Seven Dwarfs*, Story Meetings, Oct. 1934–1937, Box 1, A1731, WDA.

263 **"created a feeling of tension . . ."** Culhane, *Talking Animals*, p. 179.

264 **You fellows are all trying . . ."** Meeting of Dwarf Animators, Jun. 8, 1937, Snow White—Story Meetings, Apr.–Oct. 1937 Folder, *Snow White and the Seven Dwarfs*, Story Meetings, Oct. 1934–37, Box 1, A1731, WDA.

264 **"finish the details . . ."** Sweatbox Session, Dwarfs Finish Bed—Animals Warn them, Jul. 12, 1937, *Snow White and the Seven Dwarfs*, Sweatbox Notes, Seq. 13A–16A, Misc. Files (financial, promotion, etc.) Punch Sheets French Version, Box 7, A1733, WDA.

264 **Nude Snow White.** Kimball, "Wonderful World of Walt Disney," p. 269.

264 **Animation lightboards.** Marc Davis to Richard Williams, n.d., quoted in Canemaker, *Nine Old Men*, p. 1.

264 **Two twelve-hour shifts.** Broughton interview.

264 **"ideal achievement."** Cy Young to Walt, Sept. 17, 1938, XYZ Folder, Walt Disney Corr., 1938–1939, U-Z, A1520, WDA.

264 **"I suggest that you get down . . ."** Memo, Walt to Bob Kuwahara, Jun. 22, 1937, Inter-Office Communications, Walt Disney Corr., 1936–1937, E-L, A1512, WDA.

264 **Borrowed ink and paint girls.** Memo, George Morris to Roy, Oct. 23, 1937, Roy O. Disney—Trip to NY, Sept. 1937–38 Folder, Roy O. Disney Corr., Disney, Roy O.—Personal & Trips (1934–41), A2995, WDA.

264 **"With all this additional help . . ."** Roy to Lessing, Oct. 2, 1937, ibid.

265 **"UNEXPECTED BUSINESS . . ."** Tel. Walt to Feg Murray, Jul. 16, 1937, Mo Folder, Walt Disney Corr., 1936–1937, M-R, A1513, WDA.

265 **"THE SUPER COLOSSAL SNOW WHITE . . ."** Tel. Walt and Lilly to Margaret and Hal Roach, Sept. 28, 1937, Ro Folder, ibid.

265 **$250,000 estimate.** Disney, "Growing Pains," p. 140.

265 **"Our only difficulty . . ."** Roy to Walt, Aug. 31, 1935, Roy O. Corr. Re Trips: 1934–1935 Folder, Roy O. Disney, Corr., Disney, Roy O.—Personal & Trips (1934–41), A2995, WDA.

265 **Bank of America loans.** Memo, Herb Lamb to Walt, Re: Financial Status, Feb. 8, 1941, Lamb Folder, Walt Disney Inter-Office Corr., 1938–1944, L-M, A1629, WDA.

265 **"I had to mortgage . . ."** *New York Post*, Jun. 20, 1938.

265 **"Roy was very brave . . ."** Disney, "Growing Pains," p. 140.

265 **Joe Rosenberg.** Mitchell Gordon, "Case of the Unretiring Mr. Rosenberg," *Wall Street Journal*, Feb. 14, 1968.

266 **"Joe, if Disney does this thing . . ."** Miller, *Story of Disney*, p. 143. See also Walt Disney interview by Martin, Reels 6 & 7, Reel 7, p. 1.

266 **"a bunch of SOB's."** Roy Disney, interview by Richard Hubler, Jun. 18, 1968, RHC, Box 14, Folder 52.

266 **$20,000 a week.** B. R. Crisler, "Film Gossip of the Week," *NYT,* May 30, 1937, sec. 10, p. 3.

266 **"we are confident . . ."** Memo, Roy to Walt, Apr. 1, 1937, Re: Misc., Inter-Office Corr., Walt Disney Corr., 1938–1939, I-Me, A1517, WDA.

266 **Rosenberg screening.** Miller, *Story of Disney*, pp. 140–41.

266 **"innocent and unsophisticated."** Green and Green, *Remembering Walt*, p. 77.

266 **"[D]espite the fact that most of the audience . . ."** Walt to Depinet, Sept. 4, 1937, RKO–NY Folder, Walt Disney Corr., 1938–1939, Q-T, A1519, WDA.

267 **359 respondents.** Snow White Screening Questionaires, *Snow White and the Seven Dwarfs*, Sweatbox Notes, Seq. 13A–16A, Misc. Files (financial, promotion, etc.), Punch Sheets—French Version, Box 7, A1733.

267 **"If you were trying to sell an idea . . ."** Thomas and Johnston, *Illusion of Life*, p. 152.

267 **"Obviously, my reaction . . ."** *Newsweek*, Jun. 28, 1999, p. 42.

267 **"I am so glad you are so enthusiastic . . ."** Kay Kamen to Roy, Aug. 31, 1937, Kay Kamen Folder, WDA.

267 **"plenty of money."** Memo, Lessing to Roy, Re: "Snow White" etc., Sept. 14, 1937, Roy O. Disney—Trip to NY, Sept. 1937–38 Folder, Roy O. Disney Corr., Disney, Roy O.—Personal & Trips (1934–41), A2995, WDA.

267 **"Ned says your investment . . ."** M. H. Aylesworth to Walt, A Folder, Walt Disney Corr., 1936–1937, A-D, A1511, WDA.

268 **"He keeps on hollering . . ."** I. Klein, "Some Close-Up Shots of Walt Disney During the 'Golden Years,' " *Funnyworld*, no. 23 (Spring 1983), p. 48.

268 **Sharpsteen contract.** Memo, Walt to Roy, Feb. 18, 1937, Inter-Office Communications, Walt Disney Corr., 1936–1937, E-L, A1512, WDA.

268 **Salary adjustments.** Memo, George Morris to Walt, Apr. 19, 1937, Morris, George, Walt Disney Inter-Office Corr., 1938–1944, L-M, A1629; Memo, Walt to George Morris, Re. Salary Adjustments, Apr. 21, 1937, Inter-Office Communications, Walt Disney Corr., 1936–1937, E-L, A1512, WDA.

268 **Averaging half the footage.** Memo, Paul Hopkins to Walt, Aug. 7, 1937, Inter-Office Communications, Walt Disney Corr., 1936–1937, E-L, A1512, WDA.

268 **Footage per day.** Snow White—Cost Statistics, [n.d.] Snow White—Animation Cost Analysis, *Snow White and the Seven Dwarfs*, Sweatbox Notes, Seq. 13A–16A, Misc. Files (financial, promotion, etc.), Punch Sheets—French Version, Box 7, A1733.

268 **Not ready for Christmas.** Memo, Lessing to Roy, Re: "Snow White" etc., Sept. 14, 1937, Roy O. Disney—Trip to NY, Sept. 1937–38 Folder, Roy O. Disney Corr., Disney, Roy O.—Personal & Trips (1934–41), A2995, WDA.

268 **Final animation, cels, photography.** Press Release, Snow White Publicity File, Press Releases, 1951, WDA. Though the press release lists the final animation date as November 8, another document suggests it was finished on November 11. See *Snow White and the Seven Dwarfs*, Seq. 16A, Back to Life, Away with Prince, *Snow White and the Seven Dwarfs*, Sweatbox Notes, Seq. 13A–16A, ibid.

268 **"It had gotten around . . ."** John Province, "Bill Peet Unleashed," *Hogan's Alley*, Hogan/interviews/peet/peet.asp.

269 **"There is going to be a lot of sympathy . . ."** Story Conference Notes—Seq. 15A (Dwarfs Weeping at S.W.'s Bier), July 27, 1937, Snow White—Story

Meetings—Apr.–Oct. 1937 Folder, *Snow White and the Seven Dwarfs*, Story Meetings, Oct. 1934–1937, Box 1, A1731, WDA.

269 **"concentrating on Grumpy . . ."** Story Conference Notes on Snow White, Seq. 10B, 14J, 15A, May 1, 1937, *Snow White and the Seven Dwarfs*, Sweatbox Notes, Seq. 13A–16A, Misc. Files (financial, promotion, etc.), Punch Sheets—French Version, Box 7, A1733, WDA. Also Thomas and Johnston, *Illusion of Life*, p. 477.

269 **"The movement on the dwarfs . . ."** Sweatbox Session, Aug. 18, 1937, Snow White—Story Meetings—Apr.–Oct. 1937 Folder, *Snow White and the Seven Dwarfs*, Story Meetings, Oct. 1934–1937, Box 1, A1731, WDA.

269 **"is actually tearing out his heart . . ."** Meeting of Dwarf Animators, Jun. 8, 1937, Snow White—Story Meetings, Apr.–Oct. 1937 Folder, *Snow White and the Seven Dwarfs*, Story Meetings, Oct. 1934–1937, Box 1, A1731, WDA.

269 **"as if they knew in their minds . . ."** Seq. 4D, Spooks, *Snow White and the Seven Dwarfs*, Sweatbox Notes, Seq. 1b–10B, Box 6, A1732, WDA.

269 **Bemoaned that the Magic Mirror.** *Snow White and the Seven Dwarfs*, Sweatbox Notes, Seq. 1b–10B, Box 6, A1732, WDA.

269 **"she was carrying . . ."** Sweatbox Session, Seq. 13A, Sept. 23, 1937, Snow White, Seq. 13A—Snow White Making Pies, *Snow White and the Seven Dwarfs*, Sweatbox Notes, Seq. 13A–16A, Misc. Files (financial, promotion, etc.), Punch Sheets—French Version, Box 7, A1733, WDA.

269 **Moore and Grumpy's finger.** Frank Thomas quoted in Green and Green, *Remembering Walt*, p. 67.

269 **"When anybody sings, . . ."** F-1 Snow White Meeting on Seq. 10A—Dwarfs Leave for Mine, March 116, 1937, Snow White—Story Meetings, Feb.–Mar. 1937, *Snow White and the Seven Dwarfs*, Story Meeting, Oct. 1934–1937, Box 1, A1731, WDA.

269 **"Watch to keep it . . ."** Story Meeting on Seq. 8A (Entertainment), Mar. 31, 1937, 8:30 a.m. to 12:15 p.m., Snow White—Story Meetings—Feb–Mar. 1937 Folder, *Snow White and the Seven Dwarfs*, Story Meetings, Oct. 1934–1937, Box 1, A1731, WDA.

270 **"We've worked hard . . ."** Quoted in Maltin, *Disney Films*, p. 32.

270 **"There were some things . . ."** J. P. Shanley, "King of Disneyland," *NYT*, Dec. 5, 1954.

270 **"I said forget it."** Roy Disney interview by Hubler, June 18, 1968.

270 **"Disney's Folly."** Miller, *Story of Disney*, p. 145.

270 **"I want everybody to be sold . . ."** Memo, Walt to Roy, Feb. 25, 1937, Inter-Office Communications, Walt Disney Corr., 1936–1937, E-L, A1512, WDA.

271 **Chaplin's offer.** Memo, Roy to Walt, Re: "Snow White" Campaign, Mar. 31, 1937, Inter-Office Corr., Walt Disney Corr., 1938–1939, I-Me, A1517, WDA.

271 **"invaluable service."** Walt to Chaplin, May 31, 1938, Ch Folder, Walt Disney Corr., 1938–1939, A-De, A1515, WDA.

271 **Pomona preview.** Bill Cottrell, interview by Bob Thomas, Jun. 6, 1973, Cottrell, Bill, Folder; Ben Sharpsteen, Answers to Questions Submitted by Dave Smith, Sept. 1974, p. 1, WDA.

271 **Animators tacking posters.** Ken Anderson, interview by Bob Thomas, May 15, 1973, p. 13, WDA.

271 **Man on train platform.** Miller, *Story of Disney*, p. 145.

271 **"AM CONVINCED ALL OUR FONDEST HOPES . . ."** Tel. Chaplin to Walt, Dec. 21, 1937, Snow White (First Nite Congratulations, etc.) Folder, Walt Disney Corr., 1938–1039, Q-T, A1519, WDA.

272 **"Well, it's been a lot of fun . . ."** Walt Disney, interview at *Snow White* Premiere, Dec. 21, 1937, Carthay Circle, WDA.

272 **"I believe everyone . . ."** Peet, *Autobiography*, n.p.

272 **"They even applauded . . ."** Steve Hulett, "A Star is Drawn," *Film Comment* (Winter 1979).

272 **"highlight."** Greene and Greene, *Man Behind the Magic*, p. 83.

272 **"Clark Gable and Carole Lombard . . ."** Krause and Witkowski, *Walt Disney's* Snow White, p. 47.

272 **"thunderous ovation."** Peet, *Autobiography*.

272 **"I don't know how we did it."** Canemaker, "Grim Natwick," p. 60.

272 **Congratulations.** Hunt Stromberg to Walt, Dec. 29, 1937; Tel. Harman-Ising Studios to Walt, Dec. 22, 1937; Nat Levine to Walt, Dec. 27, 1937, Snow White (First Nite Congratulations, etc.) Folder, Walt Disney Corr., 1938–1939, Q-T, A1519, WDA.

273 **I WISH I COULD MAKE PICTURES . . ."** Tel. DeMille to Walt, Feb. 1, 1938, Walt Disney Corr., 1938–1939, A-De, A1515, WDA.

273 **"It's probably too soon . . ."** Joe Rosenberg to Walt, Dec. 23, 1937, B Folder, Walt Disney Corr., 1936–1937, A-D, A1511, WDA.

273 **"Let your fears be quieted . . ."** *NYT*, Jan. 14, 1938, p. 21.

273 **"an authentic masterpiece . . ."** "Mouse & Man."

273 **"among the genuine artistic achievements . . ."** [Jan. 26, 1938] Ferguson, *Film Criticism*, p. 209.

273 **"happiest event since Armistice."** *NYT*, Feb. 8, 1940, p. 18.

273 **"he thought Metro Goldwyn . . ."** Hal Sloane to Walt, Jan. 5, 1937 [actually 1938], Sloane, Hal, Folder, Walt Disney Corr., 1938–1939, Q-T, A1519, WDA.

273 **"miniature communist society."** *Daily Worker*, Jan. 15, 1938.

273 **"Wars are being fought . . ."** Frank Nugent, "One Touch of Disney," *NYT*, Jan. 23, 1938, sec. 11, p. 5.

274 **Technical achievement.** Feild, *Art of Disney*, pp. 2–3.

SEVEN || Parnassus

276 ***Snow White* grosses.** Picture Income—Current Theatre Returns Folder, *Snow White and the Seven Dwarfs*, Sweatbox Notes, Seq. 13A–16A, Misc. Files (financial, promotion, etc.), Punch Sheets—French Version, Box 7, A1733, WDA.

276 **General release figures.** Memo, George Morris to Walt, Aug. 1, 1938, Morris, George E., Folder, Walt Disney Corr., Inter-Office Corr., 1938–1944, A1629; Summary of Income Statements from Dec. 31, 1934, to Oct. 2, 1943, Morris, George E., Folder, Inter-Office Corr., 1938–1944, L-M, A1629, WDA.

277 **Highest-grossing.** *NYT*, May 2, 1939, p. 29.

277 **Seen by more people.** Diane Disney Miller, as told to Pete Martin, *The Story of Walt Disney* (New York: Henry Holt, 1956), pp. 146–47.

277 **"They came in their hundreds . . ."** C. A. Lejeune, "Dopey is Adopted by John Bull," *NYT*, Sept. 18, 1938, sec. 10, p. 3.

277 **Foreign grosses.** Cable First-Run Daily Gross Receipts, Paris, Picture Income—Current Theatre Returns Folder, *Snow White and the Seven Dwarfs*, Sweatbox Notes, Seq. 13A–16A, Misc. Files (financial, promotion, etc.), Punch Sheets—French Version, Box 7, A1733, WDA.

277 **Dutch boycott.** *NYT*, Feb. 5, 1939, sec. 9, p. 4.

277 **Forty-nine countries.** Ibid.

277 **Snow White products.** Ibid.

277 **Commissioned play.** Memo, Erwin Verity to Hal Thompson, Re: Audience Reactions Lists, Apr. 7, 1938, Snow White playlet, Snow White and the Seven Dwarfs, Sweatbox Notes, Seq. 13A–16A, Misc. Files (financial, promotion, etc.), Punch Sheets—French Version, Box 7, A1733, WDA.

277 **"if I listen in . . ."** Memo, Walt to Roy, Re: Radio Show, Jan. 10, 1938, Radio Folder, Walt Disney Corr., Inter-Office, 1938–1944, R-S, A1631, WDA.

277 **Selling cels.** Richard Holliss and Brian Sibley, *Walt Disney's* Snow White and the Seven Dwarfs *and the Making of the Classic Film* (New York: Simon & Schuster, 1987), p. 66.

277 ***NYT* editorial.** "Topics of the Times," *NYT*, May 2, 1938, p. 16.

277 **"it is quite within the bounds . . ."** Memo, Gregory Dickson to Walt, Re: Academy Award, Jan. 25, 1938, Inter-Office Communications, Walt Disney Corr., 1936–1937, E-L, A1512, WDA.

278 **Academy Award presentation.** Mason Wiley and Damien Bona, *Inside Oscar: The Unofficial History of the Academy Awards* (New York: Ballantine Books, 1987), p. 90. See also Transcript, WDA.

278 **"Conditions for us . . ."** Elias to Walt, Aug. 25, 1933, D, D.V.'s Letters, 1931–33, Walt Disney Corr., 1930–1934, D-I, A1503, WDA.

278 **"Roy is very generous . . ."** Elias to Ray Disney, Feb. 21, 1933, Elias Disney Box, WDA.

278 **DeSoto car.** Ruth Disney Beecher quoted in Katherine Greene and Richard Greene, *Inside the Dream: The Personal Story of Walt Disney* (New York: Roundtable Press, 2001), p. 69.

278 **Flora ordered to rest.** Flora Disney to Raymond Disney, Jan. 21, 1933, Disney Family: Genealogy, Etc., A2383, WDA.

278 **Elias's failing health.** "Disney Family Settled in Huron County in 1848," *Goderich Signal Star*, Jul. 7, 1999, p. A4; the article was originally published in 1938.

278 **"We have a tremendous load . . ."** Letter quoted in Bob Thomas, *Building a Company: Roy O. Disney and the Creation of an Entertainment Empire* (New York: Hyperion, 1998), p. 115.

279 **"We wish we could sell . . ."** Flora to Irene Campbell, Dec. 10, 1931, Perkins, Mrs. Jessie, Folder, P File, Walt Disney Corr., 1956, M-R, A1564, WDA.

279 **"I think it's a great day . . ."** "Disney Family Settled in Huron County."

279 **"Severest Critic."** Mrs. Walt Disney as told to Isabella Taves, "I Live With a Genius," *McCall's*, Feb. 1953, p. 40.

279 **"I can't stand the sight"** Quoted in Frank Rasky, "80 Million a Year from Fantasy," *Star Weekly* (Toronto), Nov. 14, 1964.

279 **"He demanded a lot . . ."** Mrs. Walt Disney, interview by Richard Hubler, Apr. 16, 1968, Disney, Lillian, WDA.

279 **Discussed divorce.** Marc Eliot, *Walt Disney: Hollywood's Dark Prince* (New York: Carol Publishing Group, 1993), p. 113. Though Eliot did not provide an annotation, he did conduct an interview with William Cottrell, Walt's longtime employee and by 1938 the husband of Lillian's sister, Hazel; in a note to the author, Eliot confirmed that Cottrell was the source.

279 **"He was very close to Lilly . . ."** Dolores Voght, interview by Richard Hubler, RHC, Box 17, Folder 57.

280 **"Mother was a well contained . . ."** Richard G. Hubler, *Walt Disney*, unpub. ms., 1968, pp. 766–67, RHC.

280 **Sharon Mae.** Sharon Brown, interview by Richard Hubler, Jul. 9, 1968, RHC, Box 14, Folder 51.

280 **Picking up Sharon.** Diane Disney Miller, interview by author.

280 **"I do not care . . ."** Walt to Mike Cowles, *Look*, Jul. 25 and Jul. 29, 1955, Li Folder, Walt Disney Corr., 1955, E-L, A1558, WDA.

280 **Another adoption.** A note in Walt's Desk Diary for March 8, 1938, indicates a 9:45 a.m. appointment at the Hall of Justice for "Adoption." It is impossible to say whether this related to Sharon or to another adoption.

280 **Hair loss treatments.** Sidney Skolsky, "Tintypes," *New York Daily Mirror*, Jan. 13, 1938.

280 **Polo injury.** Mrs. Walt Disney interview by Hubler.

281 **Westcott accident.** *LAT*, Oct. 28, 1935, Oct. 30, 1935, Oct. 31, 1935; *Hollywood Reporter*, Oct. 28, 1935. See also Harry Tytle quoted in Hubler, *Disney*, pp. 271–72. Tytle believes that Westcott's helmet strap snapped his neck, though he died of a skull fracture.

281 **Roy quitting polo.** Memo, Roy to Dolores Voght, Dec. 2, 1935, Inter-Office Communications, Walt Disney Corr., 1935, A1509, WDA.

281 **Quitting polo.** Walt to Polo Committee, Riviera Country Club, May 21, 1938; Walt to Mr. L. L. Morrison, May 21, 1938, Misc. Files, WDA.

281 **Badminton.** Walt Disney, interview by Pete Martin, Reels 6 & 7, Reel 7, WDA, p. 30.

281 **"[W]hen the Studio began . . ."** Quoted in Amy Boothe Green and Howard E. Green, *Remembering Walt: Favorite Memories of Walt Disney* (New York: Hyperion, 1999), p. 28.

281 **Spencer Tracys.** See for example Walt to Spencer Tracy and Louise Tracy, Jun. 24, 1936, T Folder, Walt Disney Corr., 1936–1937, S-Z, A1514, WDA.

281 **"Walt was a hard guy . . ."** Ward Kimball, "The Wonderful World of Walt Disney," in *You Must Remember This*, ed. Walter Wagner (New York: G. P. Putnam's Sons, 1975), p. 264.

281 **"friendly, . . ."** Harry Tytle, *One of "Walt's Boys": An Insider's Account of Disney's Golden Years* (Royal Oak, Mich.: Airtight Seals Allied Products, 1997), p. 223.

282 **"[H]e really didn't have time . . ."** Mrs. Walt Disney interview by Hubler.

282 **"little time for actual recreation."** Walt to Mrs. Grace L. Stenderup, Folded Hills Ranch, Feb. 4, 1939, St Folder, Walt Disney Corr., 1938–1939, Q-T, A1519, WDA.

282 **"might just as well have brought along tables . . ."** Quoted in Eliot, *Dark Prince*, p. 82.

282 **"He didn't know anything else . . ."** Dave Hand, interview by Michael Barrier, in Didier Ghez, *Walt's People* (Xlibris, 2005), p. 1:93.

282 **"I've lived with it too much . . ."** Walt Disney interview by Martin, Reel 11, p. 49.

283 **Diane asking for autograph.** Miller, *Story of Disney*, p. 5.

283 **"I thought that my father . . ."** *Walt Disney: An Intimate History of the Man and His Magic*, CD-ROM, Pantheon Productions, 1998.

283 **"They used to love to go . . ."** Walt Disney interview by Martin, Reels 9 & 10, pp. 67–68.

283 ***Alice in Wonderland.*** Memo, Gunther Lessing to Walt, Re: *Alice in Wonderland*, Nov. 26, 1937, Inter-Office Communications, Walt Disney Corr., 1936–1937, E-L, A1512, WDA; *NYT*, May 23, 1938.

283 ***Peter Pan.*** Roy to Lessing, Apr. 22, 1938, Disney, Roy O.—Trip to Europe, 1938 Folder, Roy O. Disney Corr., Disney, Roy O.—Personal & Trips (1934–41), A2995, WDA; Jim Korkis, "Disney's Pre-Production Peter Pan," *POV* 1, no. 2 (Winter 1992), p. 47.

283 **"still wears the look . . ."** *NYT*, Jun. 12, 1938, sec. 10, p. 4.

283 ***Snow White* costs.** Snow White—Cost Statistics [n.d.], Snow White—Animation Cost Analysis, *Snow White and the Seven Dwarfs*, Sweatbox Notes, Seq. 13A–16A, Misc. Files (financial, promotion, etc.), Punch Sheets—French Version, Box 7, A1733, WDA. This document also lists the cost of every employee on the film and the hours he spent on it.

283 **$2.3 million debt.** Memo, Herb Lamb to Walt, Re: Financial Status, Feb. 8, 1941, Lamb Folder, Walt Disney Inter-Office Corr., 1938–1944, L-M, A1629, WDA.

284 **"Roy brought Mr. Giannini . . ."** I. Klein, "Reminiscences," *Cartoonist Profiles*, 1, no. 7 (Aug. 1970), p. 17.

284 **Revolving fund.** Memo, Lessing to Roy, Re: Misc. Goings On, Apr. 27, 1938, Disney, Roy O.—Trip to Europe, 1938 Folder, Roy O. Disney Corr., Disney, Roy O.—Personal & Trips (1934–41), A2995, WDA.

284 **"We already took the last drop . . ."** Memo, Lessing to Roy, Re: Future Product Distribution, May 4, 1938, ibid.

284 **Bonuses.** Memo, Morris to Roy, May 2, 1938, ibid; *New York Post*, Jun. 29, 1938.

284 **"They deserve it."** Ed Sullivan, "Hollywood," *New York Daily News*, Aug. 10, 1938.

284 **Five-day week and Lake Narconian announcement.** Memo, Morris to Roy, May 2, 1938.

284 **Lake Narconian.** Dick Huemer, "Thumbnail Sketches," *Funnyworld*, Fall 1979, p. 42; Bob Broughton, interview by author; Leonard Mosley, *Disney's World: A Biography* (New York: Stein & Day, 1985), p. 167.

285 **"prolonged applause."** *NYT*, Jun. 23, 1938, p. 25

285 **Music Hall.** *NYT*, Jul. 3, 1938, sec. 9, p. 3.

285 **Trophy case.** Frank Nugent, "This Disney Whirl," *NYT*, Jan. 29, 1939, sec. 9, p. 5.

285 **"We have to prove to the public . . ."** Walt to W. G. Van Schmus, May 27, 1938, Misc. File, WDA.

285 **"he was afraid . . ."** Douglas W. Churchill, "Walt Disney Sighs for More Whirls," *NYT*, Jan. 9, 1938, sec. 10, p. 5.

285 **"taking literally . . ."** Sweatbox Session, *The Autograph Hound*, July 8, 1938, *Autograph Hound* Folder, RM 25, WDA.

286 **Adding employees.** Walt Disney, "Growing Pains," *American Cinematographer,* Mar. 1941, p. 141.

286 **"horrible deal."** Ham Luske, Notes, ca. 1956, WDA.

286 **"years of confusion . . ."** Disney, "Growing Pains," p. 141.

286 **"The only way . . ."** Studio Profit Sharing Plan (Minutes), Jan. 30, 1940, Walt Disney Productions, Mar. 31, 1942, Walt Disney Productions, Walt Disney Corr., Inter-Office, 1938–1944, D, A1627, WDA.

286 **Changing the company name.** Memo, Roy to Walt, Re: Corporate Name, Oct. 20, 1938, Disney, Roy O., Folder, Walt Disney Corr., Inter-Office, 1938–1944, D, A1627, WDA. See also *LAT,* Sept. 30, 1938.

287 **Decision to build new studio.** Memo, Morris to Roy, May 2, 1938, Disney, Roy O.—Trip to Europe, 1938 Folder, Roy O. Disney Corr., Disney, Roy O.—Personal & Trips (1934–1941), A2995, WDA.

287 **"It looks as though . . ."** Memo, Morris to Roy, May 21, 1938, ibid.

287 **Lessing urged Roy to return.** Memo, Lessing to Roy, Re: Return to Studio, May 21, 1938, ibid.

287 ***Los Angeles Times* report.** *LAT,* Jun. 18, 1938.

287 **"You know how I got . . ."** Studio Profit Sharing Plan (Minutes), Jan. 30, 1940.

287 **Joe Rosenberg's response.** Memo, George Morris to Walt, May 26, 1938, Morris, George E., Folder, Walt Disney Corr., Inter-Office, 1938–1944, A1629, WDA.

288 **Kem Weber.** See David Gebhard and Harriete Von Breton, *Kem Weber: The Moderne in Southern California, 1920–1941* (Santa Barbara: University of California Press, 1969).

288 **"comfort of mind . . ."** "Walt Disney Studios," *California Arts and Architecture,* Jan. 1941.

288 **"Walt planned out very carefully."** Ben Sharpsteen, interview by Richard Hubler, Oct. 29, 1968, p. 4, WDA.

288 **"He'd say, 'How about if . . .' "** Quoted in Thomas, *Building a Company,* p. 133.

289 **Frank Thomas designing animation table.** Milt Kahl, interview by Christopher Finch and Linda Rosenkrantz, May 18, 1972, p. 19, WDA.

289 **New desks.** Bill Justice, *Justice for Disney* (Dayton, Ohio: Tomart Publications, 1992), p. 30.

289 **Humidity and temperature controls.** Paul Hollister, *Man or Mouse: The Story of Walt Disney, So Far,* unpub. ms., 1955, chap. 9, p. 4, WDA.

289 **Meeting with Franklin.** Sidney Franklin to Walt, Apr. 20, 1935; Walt to Franklin, Sept. 13, 1935, Misc. File, WDA.

289 **MGM offer.** Franklin to Walt, Dec. 10, 1935; Memo, Roy to Walt, Feb. 27, 1936, Franklin, Sidney A., Folder, Walt Disney Corr., 1936–1937, E-L, A1512, WDA.

289 ***Bambi* synopsis.** Bianca Majolie, Synopsis, May 13, 1937, BAMBI—Continuities, Dave Hand, *Bambi* Production Materials—Story Meeting Notes, Sweatbox Notes, Corr., Research, A3267, WDA.

289 **"The staff looked hopefully to Walt . . ."** Frank Thomas and Ollie Johnston, *Walt Disney's "Bambi"* (New York: Stewart, Tabori & Chang, 1990), p. 113.

290 **"possibilities with animals."** Story Conference on *Bambi,* Sept. 11, 1937,

Bambi—Story Meetings, 1937–38, *Bambi* Prod. Materials—Story Meeting Notes, Sweatbox notes, Corr., Research, A3267, WDA.

290 **Sept. 4 story conference.** Story Conference on *Bambi*, Sept. 4, 1937, ibid.

290 **Story of hare.** Larry [Morey] and Ted [Sears] comments, Summing up the Meeting Held with Sydney [*sic*] Franklin on Oct. 20, 1937, Bill Cottrell Notes & Drafts, Oct. 1937, ibid.

290 **"[I]t showed us a new dimension . . ."** Thomas and Johnston, *Disney's "Bambi,"* pp. 116–17.

290 **Session with Franklin.** Story Conference on *Bambi*, Dec. 15, 1937, *Bambi*—Story Meetings, 1937–38, *Bambi* Production Materials—Story Meeting Notes, Sweatbox Notes, Corr., Research, A3267, WDA.

291 **Announcement postponing film.** *LAT*, Dec. 15, 1937.

291 **"just busting his guts . . ."** Quoted in Mosley, *Disney's World*, p. 177.

291 **instructing Lessing.** Memo, Walt to Gunther Lessing, Sept. 15, 1937, Inter-Office Communications, Walt Disney Corr., 1936–1937, E-L, A1512, WDA.

291 **"I think the thing to do . . ."** Story Meeting, Dec. 3, 1937, Story Meetings, 1937–1938 Folder, *Pinocchio*, Story Material, A2961, WDA.

291 **" 'Crank it out' . . ."** Jack Kinney, *Walt Disney and Other Assorted Characters: An Unauthorized Account of the Early Years at Disney's* (New York: Harmony Books, 1988), pp. 108–109.

292 **Visiting Roy E. Disney.** Greene and Greene, *Inside the Dream*, p. 62.

292 **Hurrying the process.** Story Meeting, Dec. 11, 1937, Story Meetings 1937–1938 Folder, *Pinocchio*, Story Material, A2961, WDA; Walt Disney, "Pinocchio—How Now?" *NYT*, Feb. 4, 1940, sec. 9, p. 4.

292 **Peet's recollection of story sessions.** Bill Peet, *Bill Peet: An Autobiography* (Boston: Houghton Mifflin, 1989), pp. 100–107.

292 **Walt at story sessions.** See Story Meetings 1937–1938 Folder, *Pinocchio*, Story Material, A2961, WDA.

293 **"I want to feel it . . ."** Story Meeting, Seq. 10 (Pinocchio Walks Into Ocean Searching for Geppetto), May 19, 1938, ibid.

293 **"*Pinocchio* was a picture . . ."** Thomas and Johnston, *Disney's "Bambi,"* p. 113.

293 **"[W]e were pretty cocky . . ."** Ward Kimball, interview by Mica Prods., aired Jul. 1, 1984, pp. 21–22, WDA.

293 **"In fact, Walt confidently predicted . . ."** Studio Profit Sharing Plan (Minutes), Jan. 30, 1940, WDA.

293 **Sharpsteen and *Pinocchio*.** Luske, Notes, ca. 1956; Ken Anderson, interview by Bob Thomas, May 15, 1973, p. 14, WDA.

293 **Sharpsteen's analysis.** Ben Sharpsteen, Answers to Questions Submitted by Dave Smith, Sept. 1974, p. 13, WDA.

293 **"We've tried to take care . . ."** Sweatbox Notes, *Bambi*, Sept. 1, 1939, *Bambi*—Story Meetings, 1939, *Bambi* Prod. Materials—Story Meeting Notes, Sweatbox notes, Corr., Research A3267, WDA.

293 **"We went through . . ."** Story Meeting Notes, Nov. 29, 1939, ibid.

294 **"One difficulty . . ."** Story Meeting, Dec. 3, 1937, Story Meetings 1937–1938 Folder, *Pinocchio*, Story Material, A2961.

294 **Enlarging role of Blue Fairy.** Ibid.

294 **Pinocchio like Charlie McCarthy and Harpo Marx.** Story Meeting, Jan. 6,

1938, Story Meetings 1937–1938 Folder, *Pinocchio,* Story Material, A2961, WDA.

294 **Walt was displeased.** Christopher Finch, *The Art of Walt Disney: From Mickey Mouse to the Magic Kingdom* (New York: Harry N. Abrams, 1993), p. 77.

294 **Ham Luske's suggestion.** Mosley, *Disney's World,* p. 179.

294 **"[A]fter six or eight months . . ."** Kimball interview by Mica, pp. 21–22.

294 **Revised synopsis.** *Pinocchio* Synopsis, June 22, 1938, General Synopsis, Jun. 22, 1928, Folder, *Pinocchio,* Story Material, A2961, WDA.

294 **"We said, 'Here's . . .'"** Sweatbox Notes, *Bambi,* Sept. 1, 1939, *Bambi—*Story Meetings, 1939, *Bambi* Production Materials—Story Meeting Notes, Sweatbox Notes, Corr., Research, A3267, WDA.

295 **In a single typical day in February . . .** Feb. 4, 1938, Walt Disney Desk Diaries, 1938, Walt Disney Desk Diaries, 1934–1943, A3084, WDA.

295 **"sheer fantasy . . ."** Walt Disney, "Mickey Mouse Presents," in *We Make the Movies,* ed. Nancy Naumburg (New York: W. W. Norton, 1937), p. 270.

295 **Meeting Stokowski at Chasen's.** Abram Chasins, *Leopold Stokowski: A Profile* (New York: Hawthorn Books, 1979), pp. 168–69; John Culhane, *Walt Disney's* Fantasia (New York: Harry N. Abrams, 1983), pp. 15, 81.

295 **Yen Sid.** Steven Watts, *The Magic Kingdom: Walt Disney and the American Way of Life* (Boston: Houghton Mifflin, 1997), p. 96.

296 **"It is the picture . . ."** Story continuity, Nov. 6, 1937, cited in ibid., pp. 84, 96.

296 **"Of course you know . . ."** "Three Disney Channel Stars Remember Walt," *Disney Channel Magazine,* Feb. 1984.

296 **"plucky, put upon . . ."** Introduction to *The Art of Mickey Mouse,* ed. Craig Yoe and Janet Morra Yoe, in John Updike, *More Matter* (New York: Alfred A. Knopf, 1999), p. 205.

296 **"Our dilemma . . ."** Kimball, "Wonderful World of Walt Disney," p. 276.

296 **"Mickey Mouse was a nothing . . ."** Friz Freleng, *Recollections of Friz Freleng,* unpub. ms., 1969, p. 34, Special Collections, Young Research Library, UCLA.

296 **Developing Mickey.** Kinney, *Disney and Animated Characters,* p. 108; Ben Sharpsteen, interview by Dave Smith, Oct. 21, 1974, p. 23, WDA.

297 **"Now that's the way . . ."** Frank Thomas and Ollie Johnston, *The Illusion of Life: Disney Animation* (New York: Hyperion, 1981), p. 126.

297 **"body is to be drawn . . ."** Quoted in ibid., p. 551.

297 **"counter movements . . ."** Ward Kimball, interview by Steve Hulett, p. 5, WDA.

297 **"traveled this ontogenetic pathway . . ."** Stephen Jay Gould, "A Biological Homage to Mickey Mouse," in *The Panda's Thumb: More Reflections in Natural History* (New York: W. W. Norton, 1980), pp. 97–104.

297 **"I think people think of Mickey . . ."** Quoted in Charles Solomon, *The Disney That Never Was: The Stories and Art from Five Decades of Unproduced Animation* (New York: Hyperion, 1995), p. 38.

297 **"his vitality, . . ."** Updike, *More Matter,* p. 204.

297 **"We got tired . . ."** Walt's annotations on Bob Thomas, *Walt Disney,* ms., pp. 54–55, WDA.

298 **Not rehabilitating Mickey.** Culhane, *Disney's* Fantasia, p. 13; Sharpsteen interview by Smith, pp. 10–11.

298 **"It would be difficult . . ."** Chester S. Cobb, Handwritten Notes, n.d., *Sorcerer's Apprentice*—Chester Cobb suggestions, *Fantasia* Story Meetings, etc., A1782, WDA.

298 **"What would you think . . ."** Stokowski to Walt, Nov. 26, 1937, St Folder, Walt Disney Corr., 1938–1939, Q-T, A1519, WDA.

298 **"we should try to follow . . ."** Memo, Walt to Otto Englander, Aug. 31, 1937, Inter-Office Communications, Walt Disney Corr., 1936–1937, E-L, A1512, WDA.

298 **"all steamed up."** Walt to Gregory Dickson, Oct. 26, 1937, St Folder, Walt Disney Corr., 1938–1939, Q-T, A1519, WDA.

298 **"you have no more . . ."** Stokowski to Walt, Nov. 2, 1937, St Folder, ibid.

299 **"avoid slapstick gags."** "The Sorcerer's Apprentice," SPECIAL NOTICE, Nov. 15, 1937, *Sorcerer's Apprentice*, Transcripts—Extra Copies Folder, *Fantasia* Story Meetings, etc., A1782, WDA.

299 **"I have never been more . . ."** Walt to Stokowski, Nov. 18, 1937, St Folder, Walt Disney Corr., 1938–1939, Q-T, A1519, WDA.

299 **Exploiting divorce.** Walt to Gregory Dickson, Dec. 27, 1937, Inter-Office Communications, Walt Disney Corr., 1936–1937, E-L, A1512, WDA.

299 **Recording at night.** James Algar quoted in Culhane, *Disney's* Fantasia, p. 16.

299 **Bath towels.** Ibid.

299 **"sizable portion . . ."** Chasins, *Stokowski*, p. 171.

299 **New contract.** Memo, Roy to Walt, Re: Mr. Stokowski and the Musical Feature, Feb. 22, 1938, Inter-Office Corr., Walt Disney Corr., 1938–1939, I-Me, A1517, WDA.

299 **Sharpsteen's analysis.** Sharpsteen interview by Smith, p. 11, WDA.

299 **Preventing animators' boredom.** Story Meeting on "The Nutcracker Suite," Mar. 2, 1939, Story Meetings 1939, *Fantasia*, Story Meetings, etc., A1782, WDA.

300 ***Flower Ballet.*** Notes on General Story Meeting, May 11, 1935; Dick Creedon to Halvenson and Rickard, *Flower Ballet*, Sept. 10, 1936; Conference on "Flower Ballet," Sept. 24, 1936, *Fantasia*—"Flower Ballet"—dated meetings & continuities, *Fantasia* Story Meetings, etc. A1782, WDA.

300 **"I can't get into a rut . . ."** *LAT*, Feb. 21, 1941.

300 **"This is not the cartoon medium."** Story Meeting, Dec. 8, 1938, Concert Feature—Meetings, 1938, *Fantasia*, Story Meetings, etc., A1782, WDA.

300 **"[I]t's a continual fight . . ."** Ibid.

300 **"[W]e're not making . . ."** Story Meeting, Dec. 23, 1938, ibid.

301 **"[T]hey're worried about the high-brow . . ."** Story Meeting, Nov. 11, 1938, ibid.

301 **"I wouldn't worry . . ."** Story Meeting, Nov. 17, 1938, ibid.

301 **"There are things in that music . . ."** Story Meeting, Nov. 8, 1938, ibid.

301 **"just the ordinary guy . . ."** Roy O. Disney, interview by Richard Hubler, Nov. 17, 1967, p. 15, WDA.

301 **"Even if the thing's a flop . . ."** Story Meeting Notes, Nov. 29, 1939, *Bambi*—Story Meetings, 1939, *Bambi* Production Materials—Story Meeting Notes, Sweatbox Notes, Corr., Research A3267, WDA.

301 **"I am up to my neck . . ."** Walt to Deems Taylor, Aug. 4, 1938, T Folder, Walt Disney Corr., 1938–1939, Q-T, A1519, WDA.

302 **Across the street from pornographic film studio.** John Canemaker, *Walt Disney's Nine Old Men and the Art of Animation* (New York: Disney Editions, 2001), pp. 274–75.

302 **Resentful.** Thomas and Johnston, *Disney's "Bambi,"* p. 126.

302 **Walt seldom appeared.** Marc Davis, interview by Bob Thomas, Fall 1989, WDA.

302 **"riding herd . . ."** Memo, Lessing to Roy, Re: Misc. Goings On, Apr. 27, 1938, Disney, Roy O.—Trip to Europe, 1938 Folder, Roy O. Disney Corr., Disney, Roy O.—Personal & Trips (1934–41), A2995, WDA.

302 **Discontent and dread.** Thomas and Johnston, *Disney's "Bambi,"* pp. 107, 135.

303 **Parents' new home.** Memo, Roy to Walt, Re: New Home for Mother and Dad, Sept. 22, 1938, Disney, Roy O., Folder, Walt Disney Corr., Inter-Office, 1938–1944, D, A1627, WDA.

303 **"We better get this furnace fixed . . ."** Ruth Disney Beecher, interview by David Smith, Nov. 4, 1974, Beecher, Ruth, Folder, WDA.

303 **Flora's death.** Ibid. Also Ted Beecher, interview by Dave Smith, Nov. 4, 1974, WDA.

303 **"installation of the furnace showed . . ."** Quoted in Thomas, *Building a Company,* p. 126.

304 **Parents touring Forest Lawn.** Hubler, *Disney,* p. 842.

304 **"You should have seen . . ."** Glenn Puder, interview by author.

304 **"I don't want to talk . . ."** Richard Greene and Katherine Greene, *The Man Behind the Magic: The Story of Walt Disney* (New York: Viking, 1991), p. 86.

304 **"Jiminy."** The first reference to this name that I could find is Story Meetings, Seq. 3—Pinocchio Meets Fox and Cat—Taken to Theatre; Seq. 7—Fox and Cat Take Pinocchio to Pleasure Island, Sept. 13, 1938, Story Meetings 1938–39 folder, *Pinocchio,* Story Material, A2761, WDA.

304 **"vibra harps . . ."** Story Meetings, Oct. 21, 1938, ibid.

304 **"His little laugh . . ."** Story Meetings, Dec. 8, 1938. ibid.

304 **"[T]he general outline seems . . ."** Ibid.

305 **Jiminy as narrator.** Story Meeting, Jan. 16, 1939, ibid.

305 **Jiminy and Uncle Ed.** Mosley, *Disney's World,* pp. 181–82.

305 **"God, he did such . . ."** Ward Kimball, interview by Thorkil Rasmussen, Feb. 23, 1978, p. 5, WDA.

305 **"sort of halfway thing."** Kimball interview by Mica, pp. 32–33.

305 **"felt the character needed to be . . ."** Quoted in Charles Solomon, *Enchanted Drawings: The History of Animation* (New York: Alfred A. Knopf, 1989), p. 63.

305 **Kahl animating Pinocchio.** Ollie Johnston to John Canemaker, Mar. 19, 1998, in Canemaker, *Nine Old Men,* pp. 137–38; Milt Kahl, interview by Mica Prods., Nov. 3, 1983, p. 42, WDA.

306 **Even Fred Moore was impressed . . .** Charles Solomon, "An Afternoon with Ollie Johnston, Frank Thomas and Pinocchio," *Animation World,* no. 3 (July 1998).

306 **"[i]t all gives us . . ."** Walt to Otto Englander, Dec. 4, 1937, Inter-Office Communications, Walt Disney Corr., 1936–1937, E-L, A1512, WDA.

306 **Model dept.** Quoted in Greene and Greene, *Inside the Dream,* p. 61.

306 **Filming inanimate objects.** Thomas and Johnston, *Illusion of Life,* p. 329.

306 **Twenty women in the airbrush department.** Ibid., p. 271.
306 **"We must keep from going broke . . ."** Meeting on Color Tests, Mar. 29, 1939, Story Meetings, 1938–39, *Pinocchio*, Story Material, A2961, WDA.
306 **"[T]his was an era . . ."** Frank Thomas, interview by Bob Thomas quoted in Watts, *Magic Kingdom*, p. 106.
306 **"change the history . . ."** Ollie Johnston, interview by author.
307 **"We've always wanted to do . . ."** Story Meeting on "The Nutcracker Suite," Mar. 2, 1939, Story Meetings 1939, *Fantasia*, Story Meetings, etc., A1782, WDA.
307 **Securing releases.** Stokowski to Walt, Jun. 10, 1938, St Folder, Walt Disney Corr., 1938–39, Q-T, A1519, WDA.
307 **Considering music.** Notes from Story Meetings, Sept. 8, 1938, "Moto Perpetuo" (Perpetual Motion), Sept. 15, 1938; Story Meeting, Sept. 10, 1938; Hal Thompson, "Siegfried," Sept. 12, 1938, Extra Copies (*Nibelungen Ring*); Memo, Mary Goodrich to John [Rose], Jun. 9, 1938; Story Meeting, Sept. 14, 1938; Story Meeting, Sept. 26, 1938, *Fantasia*, Story Meetings, etc., A1782, WDA.
308 **"swooping through the halls . . ."** Shamus Culhane, *Talking Animals and Other People* (New York: St. Martin's Press, 1986), p. 197.
308 **"What is loud . . ."** Robyn Flans, "Joe Grant," *Disney News*, Fall 1970, p. 31.
308 **Harpo Marx.** Culhane, *Disney's* Fantasia, p. 16.
308 **"blowing the top off . . ."** Story Meeting, Nov. 17, 1938, *Concert Feature*—Meetings, 1938, *Fantasia*, Story Meetings, etc., A1782, WDA.
308 **Soundstage concert.** Sept. 29, 1938, *Concert Feature*—Meetings, Sept. 1938, ibid.
308 **"until all hands were red."** Jimmy Johnson, *Inside the Whimsy Works: My Thirty-Seven Years with Walt Disney Productions*, unpub. ms., 1975, p. 11, WDA.
308 **"I don't know what more . . ."** Story Meeting, Sept. 30, 1938, *Concert Feature*—Meetings, Sept. 1938, *Fantasia*, Story Meetings, etc., A1782, WDA.
309 **"We're searching here . . ."** Story Meeting, Nov. 11, 1938, ibid.
309 **"It is like pruning . . ."** Meeting on Sound Stage—Beethoven's Symphony no. 6, n.d., ibid.
309 **"if the spirit of the music . . ."** Story Meeting, *Fantasia*, Room 232, Sept. 13, 1938, ibid.
309 **Not everything had to connect.** Story Meeting, Oct. 24, 1938, *Concert Feature*—Meetings, 1938, *Fantasia*, Story Meetings, etc., A1782, WDA.
309 **"I know everybody has the tendency . . ."** Story Meeting, Dec. 23, 1938, ibid.
309 **"story annoys you."** Story Meeting on *Fantasia*, Sept. 28, 1938, ibid.
309 **three-dimensional effect.** Story Meeting on *Fantasia*, Sept. 26, 1938; Sept. 28, 1938, ibid.
309 **Perfume.** Story Meeting, Sept. 14, 1938, ibid.
310 **"It would be quite a sensation . . ."** Story Meeting, Sept. 26, 1938, ibid.
310 **"We don't want to follow . . ."** Story Meeting, "Toccata and Fugue," Nov. 8, 1938, ibid.
310 **"a sort of mad musician . . ."** Story Meeting, Sept. 10, 1938; "Night on Bald Mountain," Story Meeting, Sept. 29, 1938, *Concert Feature*—Meetings, Sept. 1938, *Fantasia*, Story Meetings, etc., A1782, WDA.
310 **"Cydalise."** Story Meeting, Sept. 30, 1938, *Concert Feature*—Meetings, Sept. 1938; Story Meeting, Oct. 17, 1938, *Concert Feature*—Meetings, 1938; Story

Meeting, Nov. 2, 1938, *Concert Feature*—Meetings, 1938, *Fantasia*, Story Meetings, etc., A1782, WDA.

310 **"Dance of the Hours."** Story Meeting on *Fantasia*, Sept. 29, 1938; Story Meeting, Oct. 17, 1938, ibid.

311 **Belcher live action.** Nov. 9, 1938, Walt Disney Desk Diaries, 1938, Walt Disney Desk Diaries, 1934–1943, A3084, WDA; Memo, Jack Caldwell to Dick Huemer, Re: "Dance of the Hours," Oct. 27, 1938; Story Meeting, Nov. 2, 1938, *Concert Feature*—Meeting, 1938, *Fantasia*, Story Meetings, etc., A1782, WDA.

311 **"The Nutcracker Suite."** Story Meeting on *Fantasia*, ["Nutcracker Suite"], Sept. 28, 1938, *Concert Feature*—Meetings, Sept. 1938, *Fantasia* Story Meetings, etc., A1782, WDA.

311 **Reconsidering "Nutcracker."** Brief Synopsis of "Nutcracker Suite," Nov. 1, 1938, *Concert Feature* Meetings, 1938, *Fantasia*, Story Meetings, etc., A1782, WDA; Story Meeting, *Concert Feature*—"Nutcracker Suite"—Chinese Dance, Nov. 25, 1938, *Concert Feature*—Meetings 1938 folder, *Fantasia*, Story Meetings, etc., A1782, WDA.

311 **"[T]here's something very valuable . . ."** Story Meeting, *Concert Feature*—"Nutcracker Suite"—Chinese Dance, Nov. 25, 1938.

312 **"something of a prehistoric theme . . ."** Story Meeting, Sept. 13, 1938, *Concert Feature*—Meetings, Sept. 1938, *Fantasia*, Story Meetings, etc., A1782, WDA.

312 **"The happy ending again!"** Story Meeting on *Fantasia*, Sept. 30, 1938, ibid.

312 **"as though the studio had sent . . ."** John Hubley quoted in Culhane, *Disney's* Fantasia, p. 120.

312 **H. G. Wells.** Story Meeting, Sept. 23, 1938, WDA.

312 **Didn't want to antagonize Christian fundamentalists.** John Hubley quoted in Culhane, *Disney's* Fantasia, p. 126.

312 **"That's what I see . . ."** Story Meeting, Sept. 23, 1938, WDA.

313 **Striking primitive themes.** Story Meeting, Oct. 3, 1938, WDA.

313 **"It will be safer . . ."** Ibid.

313 **"Something like the last . . ."** Story Meeting, Oct. 19, 1938, *Concert Feature*—Meetings, 1938, *Fantasia*, Story Meetings, etc., A1782, WDA.

313 **"If you had selected any other . . ."** Deems Taylor to Stuart [Buchanan], Feb. 22, 1939, T Folder, Walt Disney Corr., 1938–1939, Q-T, A1519, WDA.

314 **Restrictions.** Chasins, *Stokowski*, pp. 175–76.

314 **"Mr. Stokowski is a little difficult . . ."** Memo, Stuart Buchanan to Walt, Mar. 27, 1939, Buchanan, Stuart, Walt Disney Corr., Inter-Office, 1938–1944, A1625, WDA.

314 **Stokowski happier with recordings.** Chasins, *Stokowski*, p. 172.

314 **Already over budget.** Memo, Herb Lamb to Walt, Re: Production and Cost Report, Nov. 16, 1938, Lamb, Herb, Folder, Walt Disney Corr., Inter-Office, 1938–1944, L-M, A1629, WDA. By this point the studio had spent $650,739.06.

314 **"There's certain guys . . ."** Sweatbox Notes, *Bambi*, Sept. 9, 1939, *Bambi*—Story Meetings, 1939, *Bambi* Production Materials—Story Meeting Notes, Sweatbox Notes, Corr., Research, A3267, WDA.

314 **"These people had come . . ."** Memo, William B. Levy to Walt, Oct. 31, 1939, Levy, Wm. B., Folder, Walt Disney Corr., Inter-Office, 1938–1944, L-M, A1629, WDA.

314 **Dividends of extra time.** Sweatbox Notes, Sept. 1, 1939, *Bambi*—Story

Meetings, 1939, *Bambi* Production Materials—Story Meeting Notes, Sweatbox Notes, Corr., Research A3267, WDA.

315 **"jell so well."** Sweatbox Notes, Sept. 9, 1939, ibid.

315 **"The whole damn thing . . ."** Milt Kahl, interview by Bob Thomas, May 14, 1973, p. 14, WDA.

315 **"You had people trying to outdo . . ."** Quoted in Steve Hulett, "A Star is Drawn," *Film Comment*, Jan.–Feb. 1979.

315 **"We worked every night . . ."** Quoted in Eliot, *Dark Prince*, pp. 122–23.

315 **"It's the toughest job . . ."** Walt to Van Schmus, Oct. 20, 1939, Misc. File, WDA.

316 **Contest submissions.** F#4—Title Contest—Key File, Walt Disney Corr., Inter-Office 1938–1944, S-Z, A1632, WDA.

316 **"It isn't the word alone . . ."** Hal Horne to Paul Stuart Buchanan, May 26, 1939, F#4—Title Contest—Key File, Walt Disney Corr., Inter-Office 1938–1944, S-Z, A1632, WDA. To my knowledge, the first time the word *Fantasia* appears in relation to the film is in a desk diary entry on Apr. 20, 1938, for a sweatbox session of "dance of fawns."

316 **"by trying to find what we want . . ."** Stokowski to Walt, Oct. 20, 1939, St Folder, Walt Disney Corr., 1938–1939, Q-T, A1519, WDA.

316 **"no artists."** Quoted in Jules Engel, interviewed by Lawrence Wechsler and Milton Zolotow, Los Angeles Art Community Group Portrait, UCLA, 1985, p. 21.

316 **"you're going to have people . . ."** Ibid.

316 **"wild abstraction."** Story Meeting on "Toccata and Fugue," Feb. 28, 1939, Story Meetings—1939, *Fantasia*, Story Meetings, etc. A1782, WDA.

316 **"You bring figures in . . ."** Story Meeting Notes—"Toccata and Fugue," Aug. 21, 1939, ibid.

316 **"This is more or less picturing . . ."** Ibid.

317 **"It's like something you see . . ."** Story Meeting on "The Nutcracker Suite," Mar. 2, 1939, Story Meetings—1939, *Fantasia*, Story Meetings, etc., A1782, WDA.

317 **"[T]here's a theory . . ."** Story Meeting on "Toccata and Fugue," Jun. 5, 1939, ibid.

317 **"things must be big . . ."** Story Meeting on "Toccata and Fugue," Mar. 3, 1939, ibid.

317 **"We don't get too serious . . ."** Meeting on Sound Stage—Beethoven's Symphony No. 6, Aug. 8, 1939, ibid.

317 **Walt was so eager to proceed . . .** Ibid.

317 **Quarrel over "Pastorale."** *Concert Feature* Meeting with Stokowski, Jul. 14, 1939; Meeting on Sound Stage—Beethoven's Symphony No. 6, Aug. 8, 1939, Story Meetings—1939, *Fantasia*, Story Meetings, etc., A1782, WDA.

318 ***Bambi* schedule.** Telephone conversation between Dave Hand and Perce Pearce, Mar. 29, 1939, *Bambi*—Correspondence, Perce Pearce, *Bambi* Production Materials, Story and Meeting Notes, Sweatbox Notes, Corr., Research, A3267, WDA.

318 **Walt's new instructions.** Ibid.

318 **"best animal animators . . ."** Meeting, Apr. 5, 1939, *Bambi*—Story Meetings, 1939, ibid.

318 **"There is no formula . . ."** Ibid.

318 **"[W]e've found that out . . ."** *Bambi*—First Four Reels (Meeting Notes—Sound Stage—Aug. 31, 1939), ibid.

319 **"they have a very analytical . . ."** Sweatbox Notes, *Bambi*, Sept. 1, 1939, ibid.

319 **Kahl, Larson, Thomas controlling animation.** Sweatbox Notes, *Bambi*, Sept. 9, 1939, ibid.

319 **New *Bambi* schedule.** Ibid.

319 **"There would be a disaster . . ."** Ibid.

319 **"It's wise to move easy . . ."** Ibid.

319 **"sacks of wheat."** Eric Larson, interview by Mica Prods., n.d., pp. 18–19, WDA.

319 **Deer film and live deer.** Walt to George Schaefer, RKO, Nov. 1, 1939, RKO Hollywood Folder, Walt Disney Corr., 1938–1939, Q-T, A1519, WDA; Thomas and Johnston, *Illusion of Life*, p. 342; Richard Huemer, *Recollections of Richard Huemer*, unpub. ms., 1969, p. 103, Special Collections, Young Research Library, UCLA; Thomas and Johnston, *Disney's "Bambi,"* p. 130.

320 **Lebrun's anatomy classes.** Thomas and Johnston, *Illusion of Life*, pp. 336–37, 339–40; Larson interview by Mica, p. 20.

320 **Centralizing Thumper.** Sweatbox Notes, *Bambi*, Sept. 1, 1939, *Bambi*—Story Meetings, 1939, *Bambi* Production Materials—Story Meeting Notes, Sweatbox Notes, Corr., Research, A3267, WDA.

320 **"[N]ow the first part . . ."** Thomas and Johnston, *Disney's "Bambi,"* p. 148.

320 **"Say we open up . . ."** Story Meeting Notes, Nov. 22, 1939, *Bambi*—Story Meetings, 1939, *Bambi* Production Materials—Story Meeting Notes, Sweatbox Notes, Corr., Research, A3267, WDA.

321 **"He has never been on ice before."** Meeting Notes, Dec. 11, 1939, ibid.

321 **Consulting three times a week.** *Discussion of New Burbank Disney Studio by Frank Crowhurst*, interview by Gerrit Roelof, Apr. 16, 1940, p. 15, WDA.

321 **"All was nebulous . . ."** Ibid.

321 **Ground-breaking.** New Studio Building (Misc. Folder), Walt Disney Corr., Inter-Office, 1938–1944, NoQ, A1630, WDA.

321 **"It is going to save the studio . . ."** Memo, Roy to William Garity and Frank Crowhurst, Re: Studio Building Program, Jan. 19, 1939, New Studio Building Folder, Walt Disney Corr., Inter-Office, 1938–1944, N-Q, A1630, WDA.

321 **Debating economies.** Discussion of New Studio Unit Set-Up, Oct. 24, 1938—Sweatbox 4, New Studio Building (Misc.), ibid.

322 **RFC loan.** Memo, George Morris to Roy, Jun. 9, 1939; Roy to George Morris, Jun. 25, 1939, Disney, Roy O.—Trip to New York, June, July 1939 Folder, Roy O. Disney Corr., Disney, Roy O.—Personal & Trips (1934–41), A2995, WDA.

322 **Diane and Sharon yelling.** Meeting Notes, Dec. 11, 1939, *Bambi*—Story Meetings, 1939, *Bambi* Production Materials—Story Meeting Notes, Sweatbox Notes, Corr., Research, A3267, WDA.

322 **"I thought he would be excited . . ."** Quoted in Thomas, *Building a Company*, p. 127.

322 **"What else is it good for?"** J. P. McEvoy, "Walt Disney Goes to War," *This Week*, Jul. 5, 1942, p. 16.

322 **"Give me the plans, . . ."** *Discussion of New Burbank Disney Studio*, p. 2.

322 **Colors and campus.** Ibid., pp. 6–7, 16.

322 **Quail, doves, rabbits . . .** Cash Shockley (head paint foreman) to Marty Sklar, Jul. 26, 1968, RHC, Box 27, Folder 107.

323 **"[I]t wasn't until . . ."** Bill Cottrell, interview by Jay Horan, Aug.–Oct. 1983, p. 72, WDA.

323 **Size of Burbank compared to Hyperion.** Estimate on New Studio Cost, No. 3—Nov. 4, 1938, New Studio Building Misc. Folder, Walt Disney Corr., Inter-Office, 1938–1944, N-Q, A1630, WDA.

323 **Animation Building.** Robert D. Feild, *The Art of Walt Disney* (New York: Macmillan, 1942), pp. 80–82, 85–86; Justice, *Justice*, pp. 28–29.

323 **Snack bar.** Ollie Johnston quoted in Thomas, *Building a Company*, p. 133.

323 **Gymnasium.** Justice, *Justice*, pp. 116–17.

323 **Noontime show.** Paul Hollister, "Genius at Work: Walt Disney," *Atlantic Monthly* 166, no. 6 (Dec. 1940), pp. 689–701.

323 **"swank hotel."** Walt to Mike May, Jan. 18, 1940, May. C.A. (Mike) Folder, Walt Disney Corr., 1945–1946, L-P, A1535, WDA.

323 **Housing on the lot.** Joe Grant quoted in Green and Green, *Remembering Walt*, p. 118.

323 **"The whole atmosphere . . ."** Clipping, *LAT*, n.d. [Dec. 1940, Jan. 1941], WDA.

324 **"walk across the lawns . . ."** Sam Robins, "Disney Again Tries Trailblazing," *NYT Magazine*, Nov. 3, 1940, p. 6.

324 **"[Y]ou can't help feeling . . ."** Hollister, "Genius at Work."

324 **"Everyone seemed happy . . ."** Fay Adler to Walt [rec. March 11, 1941], A Folder, Walt Disney Corr., 1940–1941, A-B, A1520, WDA.

324 **"collegiate atmosphere . . ."** Anthony Bower, "Snow White and the 1,200 Dwarfs," *Nation*, 152 (May 10, 1941), p. 565.

324 **"Everything looked so nice . . ."** Justice, *Justice*, p. 28.

324 ***"you will cause discontent!"*** Quoted in Hollister, *Man or Mouse*, chap. 8, p. 7.

324 **Impersonality.** Quoted in Watts, *Magic Kingdom*, p. 207.

324 **Attempts at greater efficiency.** Johnson, *Whimsy Works*, Chap. 2, p. 5.

324 **"When Disney began to get . . ."** Art Babbitt quoted in Charles Glenn, "Disney Strike Leader Tells of New Kind of 'Animation,' " *LA Labor* [July 1941], 1941 Strike Press Clippings, Disney Studio Strike, 1941 (from Main Files), A1683, WDA.

325 **"line of demarcation . . ."** Bill Melendez quoted in Solomon, *Enchanted Drawings*, pp. 62–63.

325 **"[I]t was his thought . . ."** Memo, George Morris to Roy, Jan. 26, 1939, Disney, Roy O.—Trip to NY, January 1939 Folder, Roy O. Disney Corr., Disney, Roy O.—Personal & Trips (1934–1941), A2995, WDA.

326 **" 'Pinocchio tops any . . ."** *LAT*, Feb. 4, 1940.

326 **"happiest event since the war."** *NYT*, Feb. 8, 1940.

326 **"brings the cartoon . . ."** "It's a Disney," [Mar. 11, 1940] in Otis Ferguson, *The Film Criticism of Otis Ferguson*, ed. Robert Wilson (Philadelphia: Temple University Press, 1971), p. 289.

326 **"infallible."** *New York Herald Tribune*, Feb. 8, 1940.

326 **"any worries you may have had . . ."** Memo, Stuart Buchanan to Walt, Feb. 8, 1940, *Pinocchio* (First Nite Congratulations) Folder, Walt Disney Corr., 1938–1939, A1518, WDA.

327 **"Everything from my viewpoint . . ."** Roy to Walt, Feb. 10, 1940, Disney, Roy O., Folder, Walt Disney Corr., Inter-Office, 1938–1944, D, A1627, WDA.

327 **"severe loss."** Memo, George Morris to Roy, Apr. 24, 1940, cited in "Outline of Points that May Come Up in Walt Disney's Deposition," Jun. 6, 1942, Babbitt Case Folder, Walt Disney Corr., Inter-Office, 1938–1944, A-B, A1625, WDA.

327 **"[T]he expression was at the Music Hall . . ."** Ben Sharpsteen, interview by Richard Hubler, Oct. 9, 1968, WDA, p. 6.

327 **"bleakest vision . . ."** Finch, *Art of Disney*, p. 88.

327 **Walt blamed *Gone with the Wind*.** Sam Robins, "Disney Again Tries Trail-blazing," *NYT Magazine*, Nov. 3, 1940, p. 19.

327 ***Pinocchio* overseas.** Thomas Brady, "Hollywood Makes Little Ones Out of Big Ones," *NYT*, July 21, 1940, sec. 9, p. 3; Walt Disney interview by Martin, Reels 6 & 7, Reel 7, p. 21, WDA.

327 **$2 million gross.** Reel by Reel Sweatbox Notes, Mar. 10, 1941, BAMBI NOTES (Complete by Seq) of REVISIONS Resulting from March showings, 1941, *Bambi* Production Materials—Story Meeting Notes, Sweatbox Notes, Corr., Research, A3267, WDA.

327 **"Pinocchio lacked . . ."** *LAT*, Jan. 12, 1941.

328 **"Man is in the forest!"** Charles Solomon, "Historical Perspective," *Animation* (Summer 1992), pp. 31–33.

328 **"We would like to pull you in . . ."** *Bambi*, Seq. 4.3 (BAMBI MEETS FALINE ON THE MEADOW), Jan. 9, 1940, *Bambi*—Story Meetings, 1940, *Bambi* Production Materials—Story Meeting Notes, Sweatbox Notes, Corr., Research, A3267, WDA.

328 **"These pictures represent . . ."** BAMBI—SEQ. 11, Feb. 1, 1940, *Bambi*—Story Meetings, 1940, ibid.

328 **Fifteen months.** BAMBI—SEQ. 12.0 (Story Meeting Notes), Feb. 27, 1940, *Bambi*—Story Meetings, 1940, ibid.

328 **"I wanted a special show."** COLOR LEICA MEETING, BAMBI—"Raindrop Sequence" 2.4, Apr. 22, 1940, ibid.

328 **RCA and Fantasound.** Walt to Sarnoff, May 24, 1939; Sarnoff to Walt, Jun. 14, 1939; Tel. Roy to Walt, Jun. 27, 1939, Radio Corp. of America (David Sarnoff) Folder, Walt Disney Corr., 1938–1939, Q-T, A1519; Memo, Roy to Walt, Jul. 6, 1939, Re: RCA Projection Equipment for *Fantasia*, Roy O. Folder, Walt Disney Corr., Inter-Office, 1938–1944, A1627, WDA.

329 **"There was complete silence."** Hand, *Memoirs*, p. 72.

329 **Generous salary.** *Motion Picture Daily*, Jan. 7, 1936. Walt's 1934 salary was listed at $78,000. Chaplin received $143,000, Bing Crosby $104,499, and Mae West $339,266.

329 **Salaries.** John H. Crider, "Disney Cartoons Go 'Big Business," *NYT*, Mar. 14, 1940, p. 28.

329 **"I could buy . . ."** Arthur Miller, "Walter in Wonderland," *LAT Magazine*, Dec. 4, 1938.

329 **"I belong to this studio."** Ibid.

330 **As early as 1928 . . .** Edwin Schallert, "Busy Future Outlined," *LAT*, Feb. 2, 1953.

330 **"We don't have to answer . . ."** Douglas W. Churchill, "Disney's 'Philosophy,' " *NYT Magazine*, Mar. 6, 1938, p. 23.

330 **Waiting after *Snow White*.** Memo, Herb Lamb to Walt, Re: Financial Status, Feb. 8, 1941, Lamb Folder, Walt Disney Interoffice Corr., 1938–1944, L-M, A1629, WDA.

330 **Profit and loss.** Crider, "Cartoons," p. 28; *NYT,* Dec. 21, 1940, p. 25.

330 **Finances.** Hollister, *Man or Mouse,* chap. 6, pp. 12–14.

330 **"I suggest we give these boys . . ."** Ibid., p. 14.

331 **$45,000 per short.** Summary of Income Statements from Dec. 31, 1934, to Oct. 2, 1943, Morris, George, Folder; Roy to Bob Carr, John Ross, Re: Definition of Picture Costs, Jul. 2, 1941, Disney, Roy O., Walt Disney Interoffice Corr., 1938–1944, L-M, A1627, WDA.

331 **"[Y]ou spend a hell of a lot . . ."** Memo, George Morris to Roy, Jun. 16, 1939, Disney, Roy O.—Trip to NY, Jun.–Jul. 1939 Folder, Roy O. Disney Corr., Disney, Roy O.—Personal & Trips (1934–41), A2995, WDA.

331 **Terms of stock issue.** Roy to Walt, Feb. 16, 1940, Disney, Roy O., Walt Disney Corr., Inter-Office, 1938–1944, D, A1627, WDA; *NYT,* April 2, 1940.

332 **"It will seem a little odd . . ."** Quoted in "History in the Making," *Current History,* Apr. 1940, p. 7.

332 **Fred Moore visit.** Fred Moore to Walt, Mar. 26, 1940, Kidder, Peabody Co. Folder, Walt Disney Corr., 1940–1941, G-M, A1523, WDA.

332 **"If you sell any of it, . . ."** Walt Disney interview by Martin, Reel 12, pp. 23–24.

333 **"It's there."** BAMBI—SEQ. 12.0 (Story Meeting Notes), Feb. 27, 1940, *Bambi*—Story Meetings, 1940, *Bambi* Productions Materials—Story Meeting Notes, Sweatbox Notes, Corr., Research, A3267, WDA.

333 **"He let me know very emphatically . . ."** Sharpsteen, Answers to Questions Submitted by Smith, p. 14.

333 **"The reason we brought it in . . ."** Quoted in Leonard Maltin, *The Disney Films,* 3rd ed. (New York: Hyperion, 1995), p. 50.

333 **"And listening to him tell . . ."** Ward Kimball, interview by Mica Prods., aired Jul. 1, 1984, pp. 23–24, WDA.

333 **"I was one of the 'poor boys.' . . ."** "Bill Peet Unleashed," interview by John Province, n.d., *Hogan's Alley,* http://cagle.msnbc.com/hogan/interviews/peet/peet.asp.

334 **"[i]t was in the nature . . ."** George Sherman, "Bill Tytla," *Cartoonist Profiles* (Aug. 1970), p. 12.

334 **Efficiencies.** Michael Barrier, *Hollywood Cartoons: American Animation in its Golden Age* (New York: Oxford University Press, 1999), p. 310.

334 **Idea for *The Reluctant Dragon*.** *LAT,* Nov. 19, 1940.

334 **"The answer [to the financial crisis] . . ."** Meeting on Benchley Picture, May 7, 1940, Benchley—*A Trip Through the Studio* Folder, Box: *Reluctant Dragon, Dumbo, Saludos Amigos, Victory Through Air Power, Three Caballeros,* A2829, WDA.

334 **Laying out the story.** *A Trip Through the Studio* (Benchley Picture), May 21, 1940, ibid.

335 **"I don't think you should have *any* . . ."** Ibid.

335 **"The thing we should play up . . ."** Memo, Walt to Al Perkins, Re: Benchley Short, May 6, 1940, ibid.

335 **"Walt gave me a completely free hand . . ."** Quoted in Maltin, *Disney Films,* p. 48.

335 **Watching a rough cut.** Walt Disney Desk Diaries, Oct. 30, 1940, entry, 1940, WDA.

335 **"very revolutionary type . . ."** Ward Kimball, interview by John Canemaker, Jul. 7, 1973, WDA.

336 **"All remaining sequences . . ."** Memo, Pearce to Walt, Re: BAMBI Report, Jun. 8, 1940, *Bambi* Corr., Perce Pearce, *Bambi* Prod. Materials—Story and Meeting Notes, Sweatbox Notes, Corr., Research, A3267, WDA.

336 **"the dread of Man . . ."** BAMBI—SEQ. 8.0 (Story Meeting Notes), Jun. 15, 1940, *Bambi*—Story Meetings, 1940, ibid.

336 **"He's hunting for his mother . . ."** BAMBI—SEQ. 13, 14,15, Story Meeting Notes, Jun. 14, 1940, ibid.

336 **"Walt was demanding eloquence . . ."** Thomas and Johnston, *Disney's "Bambi,"* pp. 142–43.

336 **Skunk and Owl.** Sweatbox Notes, *Bambi*, Sept. 9, 1939, *Bambi*—Story Meetings, 1939, *Bambi* Production Materials—Story Meeting Notes, Sweatbox Notes, Corr., Research, A3267, WDA.

336 **"I'd like to see us find things, . . ."** BAMBI—SEQ. 11, Feb. 1, 1940, *Bambi*—Story Meetings, 1940. He makes a similar comment at a story meeting on Feb. 3.

337 **"possibly the most important day . . ."** Thomas and Johnston, *Disney's "Bambi,"* p. 160.

337 **"That's great stuff . . ."** BAMBI—Animation Review, Seq. 2.1, 2.2, 4.3, Mar. 1, 1940, *Bambi*—Story Meetings, 1940, *Bambi* Production Materials—Story Meeting Notes, Sweatbox Notes, Corr., Research, A3267, WDA.

337 **"It's your picture. . . ."** Thomas and Johnston, "*Disney's Bambi,*" p. 160.

337 **Take a trip.** BAMBI—Animation Review, Seq. 2.1, 2.2, 4.3, Mar. 1, 1940.

337 **"This is opening up something . . ."** Ibid.

338 **"He needs broader things."** Sweatbox Notes, *Bambi*, Sept. 1, 1939, *Bambi*—Story Meetings, 1939, *Bambi* Prod. Materials—Story Meeting Notes, Sweatbox Notes, Corr. Research, A3267, WDA.

338 **"They have absolute confidence in us. . . ."** Memo, Roy to Walt, Jul. 5, 1940, Memos to and from Walt, 1940–1943 folder, Roy O. Disney Inter-Office Corr., Disney, Roy O.—trips to Disneyland (1954–61), A3002, WDA.

338 **"we are using our best . . ."** Walt to Stoky, July 29, 1940, Stokowski, Leopold, Folder, Walt Disney Corr., 1945–1946, R-Z, A1526, WDA.

338 **One cameraman . . .** Thomas and Johnston, *Illusion of Life*, p. 307.

338 **Watching dailies.** Bob Broughton (cameraman), interview by author.

339 **"Yes, it is true."** John Canemaker, "Art Babbitt," *Cartoonist Profiles* (Dec. 1979), p. 11.

339 **"We are portraying . . ."** "Ave Maria," Meeting Notes, Feb. 8, 1940, "Ave Maria"—Meeting Notes, *Fantasia* Story Meetings, etc., A1782, WDA.

339 **"There's still a lot of Christians . . ."** Story Meeting, Dec. 8, 1938, *Concert Feature*—Meetings, 1938, *Fantasia*, Story Meetings, etc., A1782, WDA.

339 **"feeling that you are inside a cathedral . . ."** "Ave Maria," Meeting Notes, Jan. 12, 1940, "Ave Maria"—Meeting Notes, ibid.

339 **Down to the dissolves.** "Ave Maria" notes dictated by Jaxon on changes suggested with Walt, Jun. 25, 1940, "Ave Maria"—Meeting Notes, ibid.

339 **It took six days.** Thomas and Johnston, *Illusion of Life*, pp. 265–66; Broughton interview.

339 **Getting Stokowski to play.** Broughton interview.

340 **"It's a lousy job."** "Ave Maria," Meeting, Aug. 2, 1940, "Ave Maria"—Meeting Notes, *Fantasia* Story Meetings, etc., A1782, WDA.

340 **Earthquake.** Broughton interview.

340 **Motorcycle idling.** Thomas and Johnston, *Illusion of Life*, p. 541.

340 **"something that will arrest the attention . . ."** Stokowski to Walt, Nov. 16, 1940; Walt to Stokowski, Nov. 18, 1940, Stokowski, Leopold, Folder, Walt Disney Corr., 1945–1946, R-Z, A1536.

340 **"slow money maker . . ."** Meeting on Benchley Picture, May 7, 1940, Benchley—A Trip Thru the Studio Folder, Box: *Reluctant Dragon, Dumbo, Saludos Amigos, Victory Through Air Power, Three Caballeros*, A2829, WDA.

340 **Financing and releasing *Fantasia* themselves.** Roy to Walt, Feb. 16, 1940, Disney, Roy O., Walt Disney Corr., Inter-Office, 1938–1944, D, A1627, WDA.

340 **"bang-up financing program . . ."** M. H. Aylesworth to Walt, Dec. 27, 1939, A Folder, Walt Disney Corr., 1938–1939, A-De, A1515, WDA.

341 **Hal Horne's second thoughts.** Hal Horne to Roy, Jul. 9, 1940, Horne, Hal, Folder, Walt Disney Corr., 1942–1943, D-H, A1527, WDA.

341 **RKO contract.** Memo, Roy to Walt, Re: Feature Contracts, August 2, 1940, D Folder, Walt Disney Inter-Office Corr., 1938–1944, D, A1627, WDA.

341 **Distributing themselves.** Roy to Walt, Dec. 5, 1940, Disney, Roy O., ibid.

341 **Weight of Fantasound.** Roy to Walt, Oct. 23, 1940, Re: Sound Equipment, ibid.

341 **Installation of Fantasound.** *NYT*, Nov. 1, 1940, p. 32. A jurisdictional dispute ensued between two unions, one claiming priority because the Broadway was an old theater and the union *maintained* equipment, the other claiming priority because the Broadway had been refurbished and the union *installed* new equipment. The dispute jeopardized the premiere. Though it was finally resolved, it meant that the theater was still being wired on the day of the premiere.

341 **Leaving for New York.** Dolores Voght to C. W. May, Nov. 2, 1940, May, C.A. (Mike), Folder, Walt Disney Corr., 1945–1946, L-P, A1525; Walt to Daisy Beck, Feb. 15, 1941, Misc. File, WDA.

341 **"only goes to show . . ."** Walt to Neysa McMein, Nov. 2, 1940, Mc Folder, Walt Disney Corr., 1940–1941, G-M, A1523, WDA.

341 **"I don't know how much money . . ."** Theodore Straus, "A Sorcerer, Not an Apprentice," *NYT*, Nov. 17, 1940, sec. 9, p. 4.

341 **"We're selling entertainment . . ."** *New York World-Telegram* quoted in Culhane, *Disney's* Fantasia, p. 29.

342 **Patronesses.** *NYT*, Oct. 28, 1940, p. 14.

342 **"gala premiere"** Walt to Daisy Beck, Feb. 15, 1941, Misc. File, WDA.

342 **"motion picture history was made . . ."** *NYT*, Nov. 14, 1940, p. 28.

342 ***Times* editorial.** *NYT*, Nov. 15, 1940, p. 20.

342 **Olin Downes.** *NYT*, Nov. 14, 1940, p. 28; Nov. 17, 1940, sec. 9, p. 7.

342 **"his first mistake."** "Both Fantasy and Fancy," [Nov. 25, 1940,] in Ferguson, *Film Criticism*, p. 317.

343 **"The forces of evil . . ."** Harry Raymond, "A Dissenting Report on Disney's 'Fantasia,' " *Daily Worker*, Dec. 6, 1940.

343 **Dorothy Thompson.** "On the Record," *NY Herald Tribune*, Nov. 25, 1940, p. 8.

343 **"couldn't have been sweeter."** Walt to Mike May, Nov. 19, 1940, May, C.A. (Mike), Folder, Walt Disney Corr., 1945–1946, L-P, A1535, WDA.

343 **Writing Stokowski.** Walt to Stokowski, Nov. 18, 1940, Misc. File, WDA.

343 **"The premiere audience was . . ."** Edwin Schallert, "Fantasia Acclaimed as Cinema Masterpiece," *LAT,* Jan. 30, 1941.

344 **"an earthquake in motion picture history."** Arthur Miller, "The Art Thrill of the Week," *LAT,* Feb. 2, 1941.

344 **"There is nothing . . ."** *LAT,* Feb. 2, 1941.

344 **"big experience,"** Robins, "Disney Again Tries Trailblazing," p. 7.

344 **"suicidal."** Walt to Dudley Crafts Watson (Art Institute of Chicago), May 20, 1941, W Folder, Walt Disney Corr., 1940–1941, S-Z, A1525, WDA.

344 **"disappointment"** Roy O. Disney, interview by Richard Hubler, Nov. 17, 1967, p. 16, WDA.

344 **"He said something to the effect . . ."** Quoted in Solomon, *The Disney That Never Was,* p. 153.

344 **"Every time I've made a mistake . . ."** Walt Disney interview by Martin, Reel 11, p. 42.

344 **Stravinsky's visit.** Igor Stravinsky and Robert Craft, *Expositions and Developments* (Garden City, N.Y.: Doubleday & Co., 1962), p. 166.

344 **Stormed out.** Quoted in *Champaign-Urbana Courier,* Mar. 3, 1949, in Culhane, *Disney's* Fantasia, p. 117.

345 **"Doesn't sound bad . . ."** "Disney Backward Masking," *POV,* no. 6–7 [1995], p. 4.

345 **"Doesn't sound as if . . ."** *LAT,* Jan. 11, 1941.

345 "WILL FINISH THIS WEEK . . ." Tel. Roy to Walt, Nov. 30, 1940, Disney, Roy O., Walt Disney Corr., Inter-Office, 1938–1944, D, A1627, WDA.

345 **Broadway Theater.** Memo, Paul Scanlon to Dolores Voght, Re: *Fantasia,* Mar. 11, 1941, *Fantasia*—Distribution, Walt Disney Corr., Inter-Office, 1938–1944, F-K, A1628, WDA. Thomas M. Pryor, "By Way of Report," *NYT,* Nov. 24, 1940, sec. 9, p. 4.

345 **Net profits at Boston, Los Angeles, San Francisco.** *Fantasia:* Results of All Engagements Where *Fantasia* is Being Shown as of W/E Apr. 5, 1941, Disney, Roy O., Walt Disney Corr., Inter-Office, 1938–1944, D, A1627, WDA.

345 **"I see no reason . . ."** Roy to Walt, Dec. 5, 1940, ibid.

345 **"[W]e were frightened."** Story Meeting Future *Concert Feature,* May 14, 1940, *Concert Feature II* (Sequel), *Fantasia,* Story Meetings, etc., A1782, WDA.

346 **"The prospective patron . . ."** *Hollywood Citizen-News,* Jan. 20, 1941, quoted in Solomon, *Disney That Never Was,* p. 130.

346 **Remake the film each year.** Disney, "Growing Pains," p. 141.

346 **"From all the talk . . ."** Stokowski to Walt, Dec. 27, 1940, Stokowski, Leopold, Folder, Walt Disney Corr., 1945–1946, R-Z, A1536, WDA.

346 **"stir up musical circles."** Story Board Meeting on "Insect Ballet," Dec. 23, 1940, *Concert Feature II* (Sequel), *Fantasia,* Story Meetings, etc., A1782, WDA.

346 **"Peter and the Wolf."** Ibid.; Walt Disney interview by Martin, Reels 9 & 10, p. 39.

346 **Economies.** Story Meeting on "Ride of the Valkyries" and "Swan of Tuonela," Jan. 27, 1941, *Concert Feature II* (Sequel), *Fantasia,* Story Meetings, etc., A1782, WDA.

347 **"Humoresque."** Story Meeting, *Fantasia* Alternates, "Mushrooms," Mar. 29, 1941, ibid.

347 **Exceeding loan limit.** Memo, Herb Lamb to Walt, Feb. 22, 1941, Lamb, Herb, Folder, Walt Disney Corr., Inter-Office, 1938–1944, L-M, A1629, WDA.

347 **"It is my opinion . . ."** Roy to Walt, Re: *Fantasia*, Apr. 8, 1941, Disney, Roy O., Walt Disney Corr., Inter-Office, 1938–1944, D, A1627, WDA.

347 **"down to the smallest town . . ."** Ibid.

347 **Modified sound system.** *NYT*, Apr. 27, 1941, sec. 9, p. 4.

347 **Telling Stokowski.** Roy to Walt, Mar. 18, 1941, Re: Stokowski *Fantasia*, Disney, Roy O., Walt Disney Corr., Inter-Office, 1938–1944, D, A1627, WDA; Ed Plumb to Stokowski, Mar. 28, 1941, Stokowski, Leopold, Folder, Walt Disney Corr., 1945–1946, R-Z, A1526, WDA.

347 **"I frankly don't know . . ."** Memo, Walt to Roy, Apr. 28, 1941, ibid.

347 **"We must remember . . ."** Memo, Walt to Roy, Nov. 24, 1941, Memos to and from Walt, 1940–1943 Folder, Roy O. Disney Inter-Office Corr., Disney, Roy O.—Trips to Disneyland (1954–1961), A3002, WDA.

348 **"I'm fearful . . ."** Roy to Walt, Re: Studio Situation, Oct. 18, 1941, ibid.

348 **"[T]he segments would now be thought of . . ."** Memo, Herb Lamb to those listed, Re: *Fantasia* Alternates Change, April 1, 1941, Lamb, Herb, Folder, Walt Disney Corr., Inter-Office, 1938–1944, L-M, A1629, WDA.

348 **"I am sure I will be . . ."** Walt to Stokowski, Jan. 26, 1942, Stokowski, Leopold, Folder, Walt Disney Corr., 1945–1946, R-Z, A1526, WDA.

348 **"That damn thing . . ."** "Pollen Man," *The New Yorker*, Nov. 1, 1941, pp. 14–15.

348 **"What war?"** Jack Hannah quoted in Jim Korkis, "Jack Hannah in His Own Words," *POV*, no. 8, [1995], p. 48.

EIGHT || Two Wars

349 **Belt-tightening.** Memo, Roy to Walt, et al., Apr. 30, 1940, Memos to and from Walt, 1940–1943 Folder, Roy O. Disney Inter-Office Corr., Disney, Roy O.—Trips to Disneyland (1954–61), A3002, WDA.

349 **Reinstating merit raises.** Memo, Walt to Roy, Dec. 14, 1940, Hugh Presley—Personnel Dept. Folder, Walt Disney Corr., Inter-Office, 1938–1944, N-Q, A1630, WDA.

350 **Raising salaries gradually.** Memo, Walt to Herb Lamb, Re: Process Lab Salary Scale, Mar. 3, 1941, Lamb, Herb, Folder, Walt Disney Corr., Inter-Office, 1938–1944, L-M, A1629, WDA.

350 **Pretax profit and bonuses.** *NYT*, Feb. 7, 1941, p. 33; Walt Disney, Speech to Disney Staff, Feb. 10, 1941, WDA.

350 **"You never win with bankers."** Phone conversation, Walt with Dwight Cooke, Henry Souvaine, Inc. [Feb. 26, 1941], Souvaine, Henry Inc., Folder, Walt Disney Corr., 1942–1943, Q-S, A1529, WDA.

350 **"Between the two . . ."** Clipping [Mar. 1941], Joe Rosenberg to Walt, March 11, 1941, Ro Folder, Walt Disney Corr., 1940–1941, N-R, A1524, WDA.

350 **"I know the bank is nervous . . ."** Memo, Roy to Walt, Re: OUR OVERALL POSITION, Mar. 11, 1941, Memos to and from Walt, 1940–1943 Folder, Roy O. Disney, Inter-Office Corr., Disney, Roy O.—Trips to Disneyland (1954–61), A3002, WDA.

351 **Splicer.** Memo, Walt to Bob Cook, Feb. 26, 1941, C Folder, Walt Disney Corr., Inter-Office, 1938–1944, C, A1626, WDA.

351 **Dream about empty Burbank.** Joe Grant, interview by author.

351 **"Walt began to become disengaged . . ."** Wilfred Jackson, interview by Steve Hulett, Jul. 25, 1978, WDA.

351 **"seemed to have trouble . . ."** Harry Tytle, *One of "Walt's Boys": An Insider's Account of Disney's Golden Years* (Royal Oak, Mich.: Airtight Seals Allied Products, 1997), p. 15.

351 **Seldom engaged in small talk.** Frank Reilly, "The Walt Disney Comic Strips," *Cartoonist Profiles* (Winter 1969), p. 18.

351 **No one barged in on Walt.** Milt Kahl, interview by Christopher Finch and Linda Rosenkrantz, May 18, 1972, p. 19, WDA.

351 **"You could put your arm . . ."** Quoted in Bob Thomas, *Building a Company: Roy O. Disney and the Creation of an Entertainment Empire* (New York: Hyperion, 1998), p. 3.

352 **"[h]e'd stuck with Disney . . ."** Marc Eliot, *Walt Disney: Hollywood's Dark Prince* (New York: HarperCollins, 1994), p. 90.

352 **"He was one of the first . . ."** Quoted in Charles Solomon, *Enchanted Drawings: The History of Animation* (New York: Alfred A. Knopf, 1989), pp. 86–87.

352 **Iwerks writing Walt.** Iwerks to Walt, Jul. 26, 1940, Memo, Caldwell to Walt, Re: UB IWERKS, Aug. 8, 1940, Caldwell, Vernon, Folder, Walt Disney Corr., Inter-Office, 1938–1944, C, A1626, WDA.

352 **Rehiring Iwerks.** Ben Sharpsteen, interview by Don Peri, Feb. 6, 1974, p. 35, WDA; Ben Sharpsteen, interview by David Smith, Nov. 17, 1971, WDA; Memo, Ben Sharpsteen to Walt, Re: U.B. Iwerks, Aug. 12, 1940, Sharpsteen, Ben, Folder, Walt Disney Corr., Inter-Office, 1938–1944, R S, A1631, WDA; Ub Iwerks int., ca. 1956, WDA.

353 **"I always knew that he was . . ."** Ben Sharpsteen, interview by Don Peri, March 5, 1975, p. 8, WDA.

353 **"weeding out marginal people."** Tytle, *One of "Walt's Boys,"* p. 142.

353 **"Personally, I am greatly shocked . . ."** Hazel Sewell to Walt, May 12, 1938; Walt to Hazel, May 13, 1938, Se Folder, Walt Disney Corr., 1938–1939, Q-T, A1519, WDA.

353 **"The reason that you have not been . . ."** Memo, Walt to Carlos [Manriquez], Jan. 20, 1936, Walt Disney Corr., Inter-Office, 1936–1937, E-L, A1512, WDA.

353 **"like a Dutch uncle . . ."** Gunther Lessing to Roy, May 19, 1937, Roy O. Disney—Trip to New York, May 1936, April 1937, Roy O. Disney Corr., Disney, Roy O.—Personal & Trips (1934–41), A2995, WDA.

353 **"He is just a clown . . ."** Memo, Walt to Roy, Aug. 14, 1937, Colvig, Pinto—Personal, Roy O. Disney Corr., A-C (1929–1951), A2993, WDA.

353 **One storyman was fired . . .** Ward Kimball, interview by Rick Shale, Jan. 29, 1976, p. 23, WDA.

353 **Average age of animators.** Douglas Gomery, "Disney's Business History: A Reinterpretation," in *Disney Discourse: Producing the Magic Kingdom*, ed. Eric Smoodin (New York: Routledge, 1994), p. 74.

354 **Division among employees.** Jack Kinney, *Walt Disney and Other Assorted Characters: An Unauthorized Account of the Early Years at Disney's* (New York: Harmony Books, 1988), p. 148.

354 **"my boys."** Shamus Culhane, *Talking Animals and Other People* (New York: St. Martin's Press, 1986), pp. 236–37.

354 **Psychology book.** *Deposition of Walt Disney*, Jun. 19, 1942, Superior Court, Calif., No. 471865, Babbitt Case, Walt Disney Corr., Inter-Office, 1938–1944, A-B, A1625, WDA.

354 **"Usually each of us . . ."** Frank Thomas and Ollie Johnston, *The Illusion of Life: Disney Animation* (New York: Hyperion, 1981), pp. 105–6.

354 **"God help you . . ."** Bob Thomas, *Walt Disney: An American Original* (New York: Hyperion, 1994), p. 15.

354 **"But if we don't try . . ."** Ibid., p. 189.

354 **"You learned early on . . ."** Quoted in Leonard Mosley, *Disney's World* (New York: Stein & Day, 1985), p. 188.

354 **"Everybody with any sense . . ."** Bob Broughton (camera operator), interview by author.

354 **"No one person . . ."** Quoted in Thomas and Johnston, *Illusion of Life*, p. 303.

354 **"don't mention anybody . . ."** Dave Hand, interview by Michael Barrier, in Didier Ghez, *Walt's People*, (Xlibris, 2005), p. 1:68.

354 **"Being left off the credits . . ."** Bill Peet, *Bill Peet: An Autobiography* (Boston: Houghton Mifflin, 1989), pp. 108–9.

355 **"If there's going to be any awards . . ."** Bill Melendez, interview by author.

355 **"touch-me-nots."** Tytle, *One of "Walt's Boys,"* p. 69.

355 **"He's a genius at using . . ."** Anonymous in Richard G. Hubler, *Walt Disney*, unpub. ms., 1968, p. 8, RHC.

355 **Salaries.** Memo, H. J. Presley to Herb Lamb, Re: Personnel Report, Dec. 14, 1939, Lamb, Herb, Folder, Walt Disney Corr., Inter-Office, 1938–1944, L-M, A1629, WDA.

355 **"soreheads."** Sharpsteen interview by Peri, p. 22.

355 **Tensions.** Ward Kimball, interview by John Canemaker, Jul. 7, 1973, WDA; Ward Kimball, interview by Richard Hubler, May 21, 1968, p. 34, WDA.

355 **"If I gave one person . . ."** Walt Disney interview by Martin, Reel 12, p. 27.

355 **"Their practicing could be heard . . ."** Animator Paul Murry quoted in Jim Korkis, "Excuse Me, But Have You Heard of Paul Murry?" *POV*, no. 5, p. 24.

355 **Penthouse Club.** Bob Thomas, *Building a Company*, p. 144.

356 **Organizing Iwerks.** Culhane, *Talking Animals*, p. 86.

356 **Fleischer studio strike.** Leslie Cabarga, "Strike at the Fleischer Factory," in *The Animated American Cartoon: A Critical Anthology*, ed. Gerald Peary and Danny Peary (New York: E. P. Dutton, 1980), pp. 201–6; Solomon, *Enchanted Drawings*, p. 80.

356 **Herbert Sorrell's organizing.** Herbert Knott Sorrell, *You Don't Choose Your Friends: The Memoirs of Herbert Knott Sorrell*, Oral History Project, 1963, pp. 66–68, Special Collections, Young Research Library, UCLA.

356 **Unionization at Disney.** *Official Report of the Proceedings Before the National Labor Relations Board, In the Matter of Walt Disney and Arthur Babbitt*, Oct. 8, 1942, pp. 1–155, Babbitt Case, Walt Disney Corr., Inter-Office, 1938–1944, A-B, A1625, WDA.

357 **Lessing in Mexico.** Gunther Lessing, *My Adventures During the Madero-Villa Mexican Revolution*, unpub. ms., 1963, WDA.

358 **"Dopey."** Roy O. Disney, interview by Richard Hubler, Nov. 17, 1967, pp. 18–19, WDA.

358 **Elias Disney being attacked.** "Disney Biography, 50th Wedding Anniversary of Mr. and Mrs. Elias Disney," Disney Family: Genealogy, Etc., A2383, WDA.

358 **"During the preliminary seminars . . ."** Culhane, *Talking Animals*, p. 224.

358 **Fainting inker.** Quoted in Eliot, *Dark Prince*, p. 136.

358 **"[s]queeze Disney's balls . . ."** Ibid., p. 138.

358 **Federation meeting and plan.** Handbill, Open Meetings; Mimeo, The Impartial Chairmanship Plan [Feb. 7, 1941], Federation of Screen Cartoonists—Handbills and Bulletins, Disney Studio Strike 1941 (from Main Files), A1683, WDA.

358 **SCG charges and Disney retaliation.** *NYT*, Feb. 4, 1941, p. 19; Memorandum to Mr. Walt Disney [1942], Babbitt Case, Walt Disney Corr., Inter-Office, 1938–1944, A-B, A1625, WDA.

358 **Herbert Sorrell.** Sorrell, *You Don't Choose*, pp. 1–26.

359 **February 10, 1941, Speech.** Talk Given by Walt to All Employees, Feb. 10 and 11, 1941, Disney, Walt, Speeches, Strike (Feb. 10, 1941, May 27, 1941), TR 91 3, WDA.

360 **"sob story."** Klaus Strzyz, "Ward Kimball," *Comics Journal*, no. 120 (March 1988), p. 91.

360 **"benevolent and understanding father."** David Swift quoted in Leonard Mosley, *Disney's World* (New York: Stein & Day, 1985), p. 193.

360 **"This speech recruited more . . ."** Anthony Bower, "Snow White and the 1,200 Dwarfs," *Nation* 152 (May 10, 1941), p. 565.

360 **Meeting with Lamb.** Luncheon Meeting, Feb. 12, 1941, Lamb, Herb, Folder, Walt Disney Corr., Inter-Office, 1938–1944, L-M, A1629, WDA.

361 **"I became all confused."** Walt Disney interview by Martin, Reels 6 & 7, Reel 7, p. 29.

361 **"We were disappointed in him."** Anonymous quoted in Richard Schickel, *The Disney Version: The Life, Times, Art and Commerce of Walt Disney*, 3rd ed. (1968; repr. Chicago: Elephant Paperbacks, 1997), p. 256.

361 **"almost a pathetic character."** Charles Glenn, "Exploding Some Myths About Mr. Walt Disney," *Daily Worker*, Feb. 17, 1941.

361 **"stars in their eyes . . ."** Bill Hurtz quoted in Leonard Maltin, *Of Mice and Magic: A History of American Animated Cartoons* (New York: Plune), p. 23.

361 **Babbitt at meeting.** *In the Matter of Walt Disney Prods. and Arthur Babbitt, Decisions of the National Labor Relations Board*, NLRB, Case no. C-2415, Mar. 31, 1943.

361 **Cross-check.** Exposure Sheet (Disney Unit of SGC) [March 1941]; The Animator, April 1941, Handbills (distributed during strike), Disney Studio Strike 1941 (from Main Files), A1683, WDA.

361 **O'Rourke.** Handbill, Special Announcement, Mar. 14, 1941, Federation of Screen Cartoonists—Handbills and Bulletins, Disney Studio Strike 1941 (from Main Files), A1683, WDA.

361 **Austerity plan.** *Official Report of the Proceedings Before the NLRB, In the Matter of Walt Disney Prods., Inc., and Arthur Babbitt*, Los Angeles, Oct. 9, 1942, pp. 156–312, Babbitt Case, Walt Disney Corr., Inter-Office, 1938–1944, A-B, A1625, p. 241.

362 **Eliminating food service.** Roy, [draft speech,] Mar. 22, 1941, Disney, Roy O., Walt Disney Corr., Inter-Office, 1938–1944, D, A1627, WDA.

362 **"Let us now be assured . . ."** Ibid.

362 **"Munich."** Anthony O'Rourke to Walt, Apr. 14, 1941, O'Rourke, Anthony, Folder, Walt Disney Corr., Inter-Office, 1938–1944, L-M, A1629, WDA.

362 **"get out the much-needed production . . ."** Memo, Walt to All Employees, Apr. 15, 1941, Handbills (distributed during strike), Disney Studio Strike 1941 (from Main Files), A1683, WDA.

362 **"laid at the door . . ."** *Variety*, Apr. 30, 1941.

362 **"In our entire history . . ."** Draft letter, Walt to Eleanor Roosevelt, May 2, 1941, Ro Folder, Walt Disney Corr., 1940–1941, N-R, A1524, WDA.

362 **American Society of Screen Cartoonists.** *LAT*, May 23, 1941, Strike Press Clippings, Disney Studio Strike 1941 (from Main Files), A1683; Handbill: "But Mr. Babbitt . . ." [May 15, 1941] Federation of Screen Cartoonists—Handbills and Bulletins, Disney Studio Strike 1941 (from Main Files), A1683, WDA.

363 **"I don't care if you keep . . ."** *Official Report of the Proceedings Before the NLRB*, pp. 159–60.

363 **"electricity between us."** John Canemaker, "Art Babbitt: The Animator as Firebrand," *Millimeter*, Sept. 1975, p. 10.

363 **"one person who seems to push . . ."** Tytle, *One of "Walt's Boys,"* p. 93.

363 **Indiscreet.** Canemaker, "Art Babbitt," p. 42.

363 **"My attitude was . . ."** Ibid.

363 **Affair with Marjorie Belcher.** Eliot, *Dark Prince*, p. 102.

363 **"I was letting myself in . . ."** *Official Report of the Proceedings Before the NLRB*, p. 151.

363 **"He was a fighter."** Strzyz, "Ward Kimball," p. 95.

363 **"stiff, old-fashioned stuff."** Memo, Walt to Jaxon, Mar. 3, 1941, J Folder, Walt Disney Corr., Inter-Office, 1938–1944, F-K, A1628, WDA.

363 **Arresting and jailing Babbitt.** Strzyz, "Ward Kimball," p. 79.

364 **"mind your own goddamn business."** *Official Report of the Proceedings Before the NLRB*, p. 154.

364 **"It is Babbitt . . ."** Memo, Lessing to Walt, May 1, 1941, Gunther Lessing Memo/*Variety* Apr. 30, 1941, Disney Studio Strike 1941 (from Main Files), A1683, WDA.

364 **"blitzkrieg."** Blitzkrieg, Handbills (distributed during strike), ibid.

364 **May 27, 1941, speech.** Walt's Talk to Studio Personnel in the Theatre, May 27, 1941, [dated Oct. 14, 1942], Disney, Walt, Speeches Strike (Feb. 10, 1941, May 27, 1941), TR 91–3, WDA.

364 **"went over with a bang . . ."** Lessing to Walt, May 27, 1941, O'Rourke, Anthony, Folder, Walt Disney Corr., Inter-Office, 1938–1944, L-M, A1629, WDA.

364 **Babbitt firing.** *Official Report of the Proceedings Before the NLRB*, p. 174.

365 **"Cars stopped all the way . . ."** Strzyz, "Ward Kimball," p. 92.

365 **"Walt Disney, you should be ashamed . . ."** Quoted in Eliot, *Dark Prince*, p. 153.

365 **Walt beaming.** Strzyz, "Ward Kimball," p. 93.

365 **Later that afternoon . . .** Jack Kinney, *Disney and Animated Characters*, pp. 137–38.

365 **Number of strikers.** Thomas Brady, "Whimsy on Strike," *NYT*, Jun. 29, 1941, sec. 9, p. 3.

365 **Guild estimate.** *Hollywood Reporter*, May 28, 1941.
365 **"indoctrinated by Disney . . ."** Bill Melendez, interview by author.
366 **"malcontents."** Walt to Westbrook Pegler, Aug. 11, 1941, P Folder, Walt Disney Corr., 1940–1941, N-R, A1524, WDA.
366 **"good old days when we had . . ."** Leland Payne to Walt, Jun. 25, 1941, P Folder, Walt Disney Corr., 1940–1941, N-R, A1524, WDA.
366 **"It hurt him."** Quoted in Mosley, *Disney's World*, p. 195.
366 **"Commie sons-of-bitches."** Strzyz, "Ward Kimball," p. 94.
366 **"Commies moved in . . ."** Quoted in Paul Hollister, *Man or Mouse: The Story of Walt Disney, So Far*, unpub. ms., 1955, chap. 10, p. 7, WDA.
366 **"[M]oney was never the basic . . ."** Roy Disney, interview by Richard Hubler, Jun. 18, 1968, RHC, Box 14, Folder 52.
366 **Walt showed photographs . . .** Walt Disney interview by Martin, Reels 6 & 7, Reel 7, p. 34.
366 **O'Rourke and Tenney.** Draft note [suggested by A. O'Rourke, Jun. 3, 1941,] Walt to Assemblyman Jack B. Tenney, O'Rourke, Anthony, Folder, Walt Disney Corr., Inter-Office, 1938–1944, L-M, A1629, WDA.
366 **Herbert Sorrell dossier.** Report, Communist Infilltration of Screen Cartoonists Guild, Oct. 30, 1944, FBI, Screen Cartoonists Guild Folder, #10-22533.
366 **"I had a lot of people . . ."** Walt Disney interview by Martin, Reels 9 & 10, p. 50.
367 **Dave Hilberman's Communism.** John Canemaker, "David Hilberman," *Cartoonist Profiles* (Dec. 1980), p. 19.
367 **William Pomerance.** Report, FBI Communist Infiltration of Screen Cartoonists Guild, Oct. 30, 1944, FBI, Screen Cartoonists Guild File, #10-22533.
367 **"something out of *The Grapes of Wrath*."** Hubler, *Disney*, p. 365.
367 **Picket signs.** Untitled clipping, Aug. 5, 1941, 8-MWEZ: n.c., 17,901, New York Public Library for the Performing Arts; Photograph, Disney Studio Strike 1941 (from Main Files), A1683, WDA.
367 **"most unique picket line . . ."** Quoted in *Screen Actor*, Jun. 1941, 1941 Strike Press Clippings, Disney Studio Strike 1941 (from Main Files), A1683, WDA.
367 **Leon Schlesinger.** Sorrell, *You Don't Choose*, pp. 69–70.
367 **"very jaunty."** Strzyz, "Ward Kimball," pp. 81–82.
367 **Walt at the entrance.** Quoted in Amy Boothe Green and Howard Green, *Remembering Walt: Favorite Memories of Walt Disney* (New York: Hyperion, 1999), p. 118.
368 **"mighty uncomplimentary things."** Richard Huemer, *Recollections of Richard Huemer*, Special Collections, Young Research Library, UCLA.
368 **Jack Kinney recalled.** Kinney, *Disney and Animated Characters*, p. 138.
368 **Fifty policemen.** Sorrell, *You Can't Choose*, pp. 68–69.
368 **Lessing hung in effigy.** *LAT*, Jun. 6, 1941.
368 **"flying squadron."** *Variety*, May 29, 1941.
368 ***The Reluctant Dragon.*** "Preview Off," [*Variety*] 1941, *Variety*, Jul. 7, 1941, Strike Press Clippings, Disney Studio Strike 1941 (from Main Files), A1683; "One the Line," Jul. 25, 1941, Handbills (distributed during strike), Disney Studio Strike 1941 (from Main Files), A1683, WDA.
368 **June negotiations.** See *Hollywood Reporter*, Jun. 20, 1941, Jun. 25, 1941;

Motion Picture Daily, Jun. 12, 1941, Jun. 25, 1941; *Variety*, Jun. 25, 1941, Jun. 27, 1941; *Hollywood Citizen News*, Jun. 26, 1941; *Los Angeles Daily News*, Jun. 7, 1941; *Los Angeles Evening Herald and Express*, Jun. 11, 1941, Jun. 17, 1941.

368 **"we feel very much . . ."** Walt to Paul Hollister, Jun. 30, 1941, Ho Folder, Walt Disney Corr., 1940–1941, G-M, A1523, WDA.

368 **"deadwood."** *Los Angeles Evening Herald and Express*, Jun. 2, 1941.

369 **Disbanding the studio.** Joe Grant, interview by Michael Barrier, www.michaelbarrier.com/Interviews/Grant/interview_joe_grant.htm.

369 **Walt and Tytla.** George Sherman, "Bill Tytla," *Cartoonist Profiles* (August 1970), p. 14.

369 **Bioff meeting.** Eliot, *Dark Prince*, pp. 156–57; Sorrell, *You Can't Choose*, pp. 71–72; Strzyz, "Ward Kimball," p. 81; *Variety*, Jul. 2, 1941.

370 **"[H]e honestly tried to settle it . . ."** Walt to Westbrook Pegler, Aug. 11, 1941, P Folder, Walt Disney Corr., 1940–1941, N-R, A1524, WDA.

370 **Lessing reaction.** *LAT*, Jul. 15, 1941.

370 **Doc Giannini's involvement.** Sorrell, *You Can't Choose*, pp. 70–71.

370 **Settlement terms.** *NYT*, Aug. 7, 1941, p. 15; *Los Angeles Daily News*, Aug. 6, 1941.

371 **"I went from $32.50 . . ."** Broughton interview.

371 **"catastrophe."** Walt to Pegler, Aug. 11, 1941.

371 **"godsend."** Ibid.

371 **Nelson Rockefeller and coordinator.** Cary Reich, *The Life of Nelson Rockefeller: Worlds to Conquer, 1908–1958* (New York: Doubleday, 1996), pp. 166–73, 181–85, 214.

372 **Meeting with coordinator.** "Walt Disney: Great Teacher," *Fortune*, Aug., 1942, p. 93.

372 **Roy meeting Whitney.** Roy [dictated to Marian Collins] to Walt, Jun. 18, 1941, Disney, Roy O., Walt Disney Corr., Inter-Office, 1938–1944, D, A1627, WDA.

372 **"Lets try to bring the show down . . ."** Roy to Walt, undated [June 1941], ibid.

372 **"combined 'business and pleasure' . . ."** Walt to Jack Fugit, Jul. 31, 1941, Walt Disney Corr., 1940–1941, F, A1522, WDA.

372 **"We don't know whether we'll have . . ."** Ben Sharpsteen, interview by Don Peri, Feb. 6, 1974, p. 28, WDA.

372 **"We landed for refueling . . ."** Quoted in Jay Horan, *Video Interview with Ken Anderson, Bill Cottrell and Herb Ryman*, Sept. 15, 1983, p. 7, WDA.

372 **"Mainly we were wined . . ."** Frank Thomas to Bob Thomas, May 10, 1973, quoted in John Canemaker, *Walt Disney's Nine Old Men and the Art of Animation* (New York: Disney Editions, 2001), p. 185.

373 **Palace Hotel.** Cottrell quoted in *Video Interview with Ken Anderson, Bill Cottrell, and Herb Ryman*, p. 12; Bill Cottrell, interview by Richard Hubler, Mar. 12, 1968, WDA.

373 **"dances and feasting and drinking."** Quoted in Hubler, *Disney*, p. 373.

373 **Lillian observed . . .** Mrs. Walt Disney as told to Isabella Taves, "I Live With a Genius," *McCall's*, Feb. 1953, p. 106.

373 **"goddamned tired . . ."** Cottrell quoted in Hubler, *Disney*, p. 376.

373 **"so worn out . . ."** Walt to Colonel Gil Proctor, May 21, 1943, P Folder, Walt Disney Corr., 1942–1943, I-P, A1528, WDA.

373 **Ordered off the boat.** Cottrell interview by Hubler.

373 **"In all we were gone . . ."** Walt to Daisy Beck, Nov. 27, 1941, Misc. File, WDA.

373 **Layoff list.** *Variety*, August 18, 1941.

374 **"hat in hand . . ."** David Dodd Hand, *Memoirs* (Cambria, Calif.: Lighthouse Litho, 1990), p. 81.

374 **Settling the layoffs.** Memo, [Hal] Adelquist to Walt, Re: Layoff and Reorganization, Oct. 15, 1941, Reports sent to Walt in New York, Oct. 23, 1941; Memo, George Morris to Roy, Re: Resume of Events, Oct. 16, 1941, Reports sent to Walt in New York, Oct. 23, 1941; Roy to Walt, Aug. 20, 1941, Disney, Roy O., Walt Disney Corr., Inter-Office, 1938–1944, D, A1627, WDA.

374 **Number of employees.** *LAT*, Sept. 16, 1941.

374 **"We are definitely in a period . . ."** Memo, Roy to Walt, Re: Studio Situation, Oct. 18, 1941, Reports sent to Walt in New York, Oct. 23, 1941, Walt Disney Corr., Inter-Office, 1938–1944, D, A1627, WDA.

374 **"completely lost and heartbroken . . ."** Ruth Disney Beecher to Mr. Kersey Jackson, Feb. 17, 1939, Disney Family Canada Corr., Disney Family: Genealogy, etc., A2382, WDA.

374 **"remarkable physical condition . . ."** Dr. Thomas M. Hearn to Roy, Dec. 19, 1938, Disney, Walt, Personal Folder, Walt Disney Corr., 1938–1939, De-I, A1516, WDA.

374 **"really a lost person."** Walt Disney interview by Martin, Reel 11, p. 15.

375 **Elias's death.** Roy to Walt, Sept. 21, 1941, Disney Family General Folder, Disney Family: Genealogy etc., A2383, WDA.

375 **Telegram of Elias's death.** Bill Cottrell quoted in Steven Watts, *The Magic Kingdom: Walt Disney and the American Way of Life* (Boston: Houghton Mifflin, 1997), p. 22.

375 **Cross of lilies.** Roy to Walt, Sept. 21, 1941.

375 **"I believe that by the time . . ."** Ibid.

376 **Roy's estimates.** Memo, Roy to J. H. Rosenberg, Oct. 8, 1941, Disney, Roy O., Walt Disney Corr., Inter-Office, 1938–1944, D, A1627, WDA.

376 **"executive committee."** Roy to Walt, Re: Studio Situation, Oct. 18, 1941, Memos to and from Walt, 1940–1943 Folder, Roy O. Disney Inter-Office Corr., Disney, Roy O.—Trips to Disneyland (1954–61), A3002, WDA.

376 **Nine features in two years.** Walt Disney, "Growing Pains," *American Cinematographer*, Mar. 1941, p. 141.

377 ***Peter Pan* instead of *The Wind in the Willows*.** Memo, Walt to Roy, Nov. 24, 1941, Memos to and from Walt, 1940–1943 Folder, Roy O. Disney Inter-Office Corr., Disney, Roy O.—Trips to Disneyland (1954–61), A3002, WDA.

377 **Economies.** Memo, Roy to Walt, Re: Studio Situation, Oct. 18, 1941, Reports Sent to Walt in New York October 23, 1941, Disney Inter-Office Corr., 1938–1944, D, A1627, WDA.

377 **"It was like being in another world!"** Hand, *Memoirs*, p. 82.

377 **"My wife used to accuse me . . ."** Hubler, *Disney*, p. 487. The probable source of the quote is Ward Kimball.

377 **"From all the reports I get . . ."** Roy to Walt, Re: Studio Situation, Oct. 18, 1941, WDA.

377 **"Sometimes you've got to kind of build . . ."** Walt Disney interview by Martin, Reels 6 & 7, Reel 7, pp. 45–46.

377 **"He was aloof; . . ."** Quoted in Michael Barrier, *Hollywood Cartoons: American Animation in its Golden Age* (New York: Oxford University Press, 1999), pp. 383–84.

378 **"We were doing a lot of crazy . . ."** John D. Ford, "An Interview with John and Faith Hubley," in Peary and Peary, *The Animated American Cartoon*, p. 184.

378 **"He felt betrayed."** Quoted in Richard Holliss and Brian Sibley, *The Disney Studio Story* (New York: Crown Publishers, 1988), p. 44.

378 **"almost broke Walt's heart."** Ham Luske, Notes, ca. 1956, WDA.

378 **"only out of pure sympathy."** Klaus Strzyz, "Ward Kimball," *Comics Journal*, March 1988, p. 94.

378 **"very hard-nosed place."** Kinney, *Disney and Animated Characters*, p. 139.

378 **"praise accomplishes nothing . . ."** Memo, Walt to Frenchy, Jun. 1, 1935, Inter-Office Communications, Walt Disney Corr., 1935, He-R, A1509, WDA.

378 **"[W]e always said . . ."** Ward Kimball, interview by Richard Hubler, May 21, 1968, pp. 3–4, WDA.

378 **Bianca Majolie vomiting.** Bill Peet quoted by John Canemaker in Katherine Greene and Richard Greene, *Inside the Dream: The Personal Story of Walt Disney* (New York: Roundtable Press, 2001), p. 68.

378 **"Don't be afraid of me."** Huemer, *Recollections*, p. 171.

378 **"He had a way . . ."** Kinney, *Disney and Animated Characters*, p. 152.

379 **Ken Anderson burning Walt's mustache.** Ken Anderson, interview by Bob Thomas, May 15, 1973, pp. 17–18, WDA.

379 **"You'd go to a meeting . . ."** Quoted in Hubler, *Disney*, p. 326.

379 **"carefully and deliberately."** Thomas and Johnston, *Illusion of Life*, pp. 198–99.

379 **"[H]is whole approach . . ."** Kimball interview by Hubler, p. 27, WDA.

379 **Babbitt's return and termination.** *In the Matter of Walt Disney Prods. and Arthur Babbitt, Decisions of National Labor Relations Board*, Mar. 31, 1943, pp. 904–6; *Official Report of the Proceedings Before the National Labor Relations Board, In the Matter of Walt Disney Prods. and Arthur Babbitt*, Oct. 9, 1942, p. 213.

380 **"difficult person . . ."** Memorandum to Mr. Walt Disney [from Gunther Lessing], n.d., Babbitt Case, Walt Disney Corr., Inter-Office, 1938–1944, A-B, A1625, WDA.

380 **NLRB ruling.** *In the Matter of Walt Disney Prods. and Arthur Babbitt, Decisions of the NLRB*, Mar. 31, 1943, pp. 892–95.

380 **"It used to be, . . ."** John Cowles, Jr., interview by author.

380 **Walking five abreast down the hallways.** Strzyz, "Ward Kimball," p. 95.

380 **"never forgave us . . ."** Quoted in Solomon, *Enchanted Drawings*, p. 71.

380 **"esprit de corps . . ."** Culhane, *Talking Animals*, p. 236.

381 **"most genial, . . ."** *NYT*, Oct. 24, 1941, p. 27.

381 **"I have never seen anything . . ."** "Two for the Show," (Oct. 27, 1941) in Otis Ferguson, *The Film Criticism of Otis Ferguson*, ed. Robert Wilson, (Philadelphia: Temple University Press, 1971), p. 392.

381 **"bill of very inferior goods."** Westbrook Pegler, "Fair Enough," *LAT*, Dec. 5, 1941.

381 **"highest achievement yet reached . . ."** Alexander Woollcott to Walt, Jan. 12, 1942; Walt to Woollcott, Jan. 30, 1942, Wi Folder, Walt Disney Corr., 1942–1943, T-Z, A1530, WDA.

381 **Walt grumbling about *Dumbo* credit.** Huemer, *Recollections*, p. 154.

381 **"facetious."** Williston Rich to Walt, Dec. 16, 1941, T Folder, Walt Disney Corr., 1940–1941, S-Z, A1525, WDA.

381 **December 7.** Walt Disney interview by Martin, Reels 6 & 7, Reel 7, p. 47; Bill Justice, *Justice for Disney* (Dayton, Ohio: Tomart Publications, 1992), p. 37.

382 **Kamen in Washington.** Kamen to Walt, Dec. 6, 1941; Kamen to Walt, Dec. 13, 1941, Kay Kamen (Government & Commercial films) Folder, Walt Disney Corr., Inter-Office, World War II, A-K, A1633.

382 **"essential purpose."** Walt to Norman Thomas, Jul. 15, 1938, T Folder, Walt Disney Corr., 1938–1939, Q-T, A1519, WDA.

382 **"An engineer or other . . ."** Memorandum on Use of Animated Cartoon Medium for Technical Training Films in Defense Industry, From: Walt Disney Prods., To: Those Responsible for Training Labor in the Defense Industries, Mar. 14, 1941, Isador Lubin Papers, Box 93, FDR Library.

382 **April 3 Conference.** Luncheon and Conference, April 3, 1941; Walt to Aviation Film Comm., Apr. 10, 1941, Industrial Training Films, Walt Disney Corr., Inter-Office, 1938–1944, C, A1626, WDA; *New York Post*, Apr. 7, 1941.

383 **Canadian contract.** Richard Shale, *Donald Duck Joins Up: The Walt Disney Studio During World War II* (Ann Arbor, Mich.: UMI Research Press, 1982), p. 16; Memo, SAT to Walt, May 8, 1941, Re: Rivet Job Cost, Industrial Training Films, Walt Disney Corr., Inter-Office, 1938–1944, C, A1626, WDA.

383 **Caldwell in Washington.** Caldwell to Bob Carr and [Jack] Rose, May 14, 1941, Caldwell, Vernon, Folder, Walt Disney Corr., Inter-Office, 1938–1944, C, A1626, WDA.

383 **Service representative and defense committee.** Walt Disney Desk Diaries, Oct. 21, 1940, entry, WDA; Jock Lawrence to Walt, Nov. 14, 1940, Association of Motion Picture Producers Folder, Walt Disney Corr., 1940–1941, A-B, A1520, WDA.

383 **"Miraculous! . . ."** Bob Carr to Walt, Aug. 2, 1941, Canadian Govt. War Films (John Grierson, Film Commissioner), Walt Disney Corr., Inter-Office, World War II, A-K, A1633, WDA.

383 **Henry Sell.** Walt to Kamen, Dec. 3, 1941, Kay Kamen (Government & Commercial films) Folder, Walt Disney Corr., Inter-Office, World War II, A-K, A1633, WDA.

383 **December 8 call.** Shale, *Donald Duck*, pp. 22–23. Though Shale cites a transcript of this conversation, I was unable to locate it in the Disney Archives. See also Kamen to Walt, Roy, Bob Carr, Dec. 13, 1941, Kay Kamen (Government & Coommercial films) Folder, Walt Disney Corr., Inter-Office, World War II, A-K, A1633, WDA.

383 **Wings on building.** Frank Thomas and Ollie Johnston, *Walt Disney's "Bambi"* (New York: Stewart, Tabori & Chang, 1990), p. 186.

384 **"what John Barrymore . . ."** Morgenthau Diary, n.d., no. 493, pp. 12–13, FDR Presidential Library.

384 **Meeting with Morgenthau.** Walt Disney interview by Martin, Reels 6 & 7, Reel 7, pp. 51–53; Joe Grant, interview by author.

384 **Letter of agreement.** Memo, George Buffington to Secretary Morgenthau, Dec. 19, 1941, Treasury Dept. (Income Tax Film), Walt Disney Corr., Inter-Office, World War II, L-Z, A1634, WDA.

384 **Animated in a week.** Memo, Adelquist to Walt, Re: Animation Casting, Dec. 30, 1941, Walt Disney Corr., Inter-Office, 1938–1944, A, A-B, A1625, WDA.

384 **Morgenthau meeting.** Dick Huemer, "The Battle of Washington," *Funnyworld*, no. 22 (Winter 1980), pp. 22–24; Diane Disney Miller, as told to Pete Martin *The Story of Walt Disney* (New York: Holt, 1956), pp. 174–75; Walt to Morgenthau, Jan. 13, 1942, Treasury Dept (Income Tax Film), Walt Disney Corr., Inter-Office, World War II, L-Z, A1634, WDA.

385 **"We slept on the job."** Walt Disney interview by Martin, Reels 6 & 7, Reel 7, p. 53.

385 **"This is the fastest time . . ."** Tel. Walt to George Buffington, Jan. 20, 1942, Treasury Dept. (Income Tax Film), Walt Disney Corr., Inter-Office, World War II, L-Z, A1634, WDA.

385 **"Finally he turned around . . ."** Quoted in Hubler, *Disney*, pp. 401–2.

385 **"greatly excited . . ."** Memo, George Morris to Roy, Jan. 26, 1942, Morris, George E., Folder, Walt Disney Corr., Inter-Office, 1938–1944, A1627, WDA.

385 **Success of *The New Spirit*.** Arthur Mayer, War Activities Comm., Motion Picture Industry, Mar. 17, 1942, to George Buffington, Treasury Dept. (Income Tax Film), Walt Disney Corr., Inter-Office, World War II, L-Z, A1634; George Gallup to Buffington, April 28, 1942, Gallup Poll Folder, Walt Disney Corr., Inter-Office, 1938–1944, F-K, A1628, WDA.

385 **House opposition to appropriations for *The New Spirit*.** *Congressional Record*, House, 77th Cong., 2nd sess., Feb. 6, 1942, p. 1095; Feb. 9, 1942, pp. 1128, 1110. *LAT*, Feb. 10, 1942. See also Shale, *Donald Duck*, pp. 29–31.

386 **Loss on *The New Spirit*.** Walt to Senator Sheridan Downey, Mar. 19, 1943, Do Folder, Walt Disney Corr., 1942–1943, D-H, A1527, WDA.

386 **"out of pocket costs."** Memo, Roy to Walt, Re: Treasury Dept. Film, Jan. 30, 1942, Treasury Dept. (Income Tax Film), Walt Disney Corr., Inter-Office, World War II, L-Z, A1634, WDA.

386 **Kansas City visit.** "A Loving Cup to Disney," *Kansas City Star*, Feb. 14, 1942; "Mickey Mouse a Local Boy," *Kansas City Star*, Feb. 13, 1942.

387 **"I'm going to make these South American . . ."** "Pollen Man," *The New Yorker*, Nov. 1, 1941, pp. 14–15.

387 **"just as broad appeal . . ."** Roy to Walt, Nov. 14, 1941, Disney, Roy O., Walt Disney Corr., Inter-Office, 1938–1944, D, A1627, WDA.

387 **Lobbying by Selznick.** See Walt to Selznick, Jan. 30, 1942; Selznick to Whitney, Feb. 3, 1942; Whitney to Selznick, Feb. 12, 1942, Selznick to Whitney, Feb. 17, 1942, National Records Center, Suitland, Md., Record Group 229, Box 216, Misc. Disney, cited in Shale, *Donald Duck*, p. 44.

387 **"If the 12 South American . . ."** Memo, Walt to Roy, Re: Shorts Production Program, Apr. 2, 1942, Memos to and from Walt, 1940–1943 Folder, Roy O. Disney, Inter-Office Corr., Disney, Roy O.—Trips to Disneyland (1954–1961), A3002, WDA.

387 **"my bad photography . . ."** Walt to Selznick, Jul. 23, 1942, cited in Shale, *Donald Duck*, p. 44.

388 **"Maybe the development above . . ."** Walt to Kamen, Dec. 3, 1941, Kay Kamen (Government & Commercial Films) Folder, Walt Disney Corr., Inter-Office, World War II, A-K, A1633, WDA.

388 **Capra and Walt.** Walt Disney interview by Martin, Reel 8, pp. 15–16; Capra

to Walt, Mar. 4, 1942, Army Dept.—Capra Project, Walt Disney Corr., Inter-Office, World War II, A-K, A1633, WDA.

388 **"deal directly with the Axis menace . . ."** Tel. Jock Whitney to Walt, n.d. [1942], Coordinator of Inter-American Affairs, Walt Disney Corr., Inter-Office, World War II, A-K, A1633, WDA.

388 **Insignia.** See Shale, *Donald Duck*, p. 85; Bob Carr to Kamen, Re: Insignia Licensing, Jan. 12, 1942, Kay Kamen (Government & Commercial films) Folder, Walt Disney Corr., Inter-Office, World War II, A-K, A1633, WDA.

388 **"There is nothing at the moment . . ."** Fred L. Moore to Walt, Jan. 30, 1942, Moore, Fred (Misc. Corr.) Folder, Walt Disney Corr., 1942–1943, I-P, A1528, WDA.

388 **More than cost.** Memo, Roy to Walt, Re: Curtiss-Wright People, Jan. 30, 1942, Curtiss-Wright Folder, Walt Disney Corr., 1942–1943, A-C, A1526, WDA.

389 **Navy contracts.** William Garity to George Morris and Roy, May 11, 1942; Roy to Walt, May 12, 1942, Navy Forming Operations, Walt Disney Corr., Inter-Office, World War II, L-Z, A1634, WDA.

389 **"which can be heard in the halls."** J. C. Hutchinson to Walt, Sept. 9, 1942; Tel. Walt to Hutchinson, Sept. 11, 1942, Ho Folder, Walt Disney Corr., 1942–1943, D-H, A1527, WDA.

389 **"Walt more or less . . ."** Quoted in Greene and Greene, *Inside the Dream*, p. 79.

389 **"Disney is fearful . . ."** Inter-Office Communications, Kuhn to Morgenthau, Mar. 6, 1942, Morgenthau Diary, #505, FDR Library.

390 **Dispute over financing *Education for Death*.** Ferdinand Kuhn, Jr., to Morgenthau, Mar. 24, 1942, Morgenthau Diary 510, #208, FDR Library.

390 **Crossing the line into propaganda.** Roy to Walt, Re: Four Propaganda Subjects, Jul. 9, 1942, Disney, Roy O., Walt Disney Corr., Inter-Office, 1938–1944, D, A1627, WDA. This note says that Roy has contracted for four films with the Coordinator's Office to be completed on Oct. 1, Nov. 1, Dec. 1, and Jan. 1 respectively.

390 **"in the background."** Memo, Roy O. Disney, Feb. 16, 1942, Reader's Digest Folder, Annex, WDA.

390 **"Der Fuehrer's Face."** Oliver Wallace as told to Ralph Parker, "How I Wrote the Fuehrer's Face," *Dispatch from Disney's*, I, 1943; Tel. Roy to Walt, Oct. 5, 1942, Disney, Roy O., Walt Disney Corr., Inter-Office, 1938–1944, D, A1627, WDA; Shale, *Donald Duck*, pp. 62–63.

391 **Propaganda films.** Donald M. Niles, War Films Coordinator, to Francis Alstock, Nov. 3, 1942, Education for Death Folder, 2743, WDA.

391 **Major Alexander de Seversky.** "Victory Through Air Power," *Reader's Digest*, Jul. 1942, *Victory Through Air Power* Folder, Walt Disney Corr., Inter-Office, 1938–1944, S-Z, A1632, WDA.

391 **Seversky biography.** *New York Post Daily Magazine*, Jul. 7, 1943.

391 **Theories of de Seversky.** "Victory Through Air Power," *Reader's Digest*, Jul. 1942, *Victory Through Air Power* Folder, Walt Disney Corr., Inter-Office, 1938–1944, S-Z, A1632, WDA.

391 **Fifth best-selling book.** Alice Payne Hackett, *Seventy Years of Bestsellers, 1895–1965* (New York: R. R. Bowker, 1967).

392 **Criticisms of de Seversky.** *Philadelphia Record*, May 3, 1942; *Washington Post*, Apr. 26, 1942; *New York Daily News*, Apr. 20, 1942; *NYT*, May 3, 1942, Excerpts of Critics' Comments on Seversky's Book, *Victory Through Air Power*—Misc. Treatments, Drafts, *Reluctant Dragon, Dumbo, Saludos Amigos, Victory Through Air Power, Three Caballeros*, A2829, WDA.

392 **"The thing that I felt . . ."** Walt Disney interview by Martin, Reels 9 & 10, p. 30.

392 **"definitely eliminate my name . . ."** Tel. Walt to Leo Samuels, May 4, 1942, quoted in Shale, *Donald Duck*, p. 68.

392 **Navy dissuading him.** Walt Disney interview by Martin, Reels 9 & 10, p. 31.

392 **"The whole point with Seversky, . . ."** Frank Wead (Navy Department Bureau of Aeronautics), Jul. 10, 1942, W Folder, Walt Disney Corr., 1942–1943, T-Z, A1530, WDA.

392 **Navy promise to give studio so much business.** Kamen to Walt, Re: Navy, Sept. 19, 1942, Kay Kamen (Government & Commercial Films) Folder, Walt Disney Corr., Inter-Office, World War II, A-K, A1633, WDA.

392 **John Thatch.** Shale, *Donald Duck*, p. 70; Erwin Verity, interview by Dave Smith and Rick Shale, Jan. 19, 1976, p. 2, WDA.

392 **"sold completely. . . ."** Marc Davis, interview by Bob Thomas, May 25, 1973, p. 14, WDA.

392 **"became a sort of Mecca . . ."** Interview, *Victory Through Air Power* Folder, Walt Disney Corr., Inter-Office, 1938–1944, S-Z, A1632, WDA.

393 **"refreshing and interesting."** Roy to Walt, Jul. 21, 1942, Re: Major de Seversky, Disney, Roy O., Walt Disney Corr., Inter-Office, 1938–1944, D, A1627, WDA.

393 **"the sooner VICTORY THROUGH AIR POWER . . ."** Jack Sayers (Audience Research Institute) to Perce Pearce, Sept. 24, 1942, *Victory Through Air Power* Folder, Walt Disney Corr., Inter-Office, 1938–1944, S-Z, A1632, WDA.

393 **"Seversky would come in . . ."** Jay Horan, *Video Interview with Ken Anderson, Bill Cottrell and Herb Ryman*, Sept. 15, 1983, p. 3, WDA.

393 **"We have got to build it up . . ."** Bombing of Tokyo—And General Overall Discussion of Picture, Sept. 10, 1942, 3B-1, Seversky Meetings, *Reluctant Dragon, Dumbo, Saludos Amigos, Victory Through Air Power, Three Caballeors*, A2829, WDA.

393 **"If we're going to get stuck . . ."** Global Problems Story Meeting, Sept. 11, 1942, Afternoon Session, Seversky Meetings, ibid.

393 **"bastard picture."** Ibid.

393 **"[W]e can show torpedoes . . ."** United Press International, Aug. 5, 1942, *Victory Through Air Power* Folder, Walt Disney Corr., Inter-Office, 1938–1944, S-Z, A1632, WDA.

394 **"You bomb the heart of the octopus . . ."** Meeting Notes—Narration & Dialogue from 50-Ton Load Seq. to End of Picture, Sept. 22, 1942, *Victory Through Air Power*—Misc. Treatments, Drafts, *Reluctant Dragon, Dumbo, Saludos Amigos, Victory Through Air Power, Three Cabelleros*, A2829, WDA.

394 **"The basic idea is big."** Memo: Walt to Pearse [*sic*], Dave [Hand], Sherriff, Aug. 27, 1943 [?]; *Victory Through Air Power*—I, ARI, Sept. 2, 1942, *Victory Through Air Power* Folder, Walt Disney Corr., Inter-Office, 1938–1944, S-Z, A1632, WDA.

394 **"I've scarcely been in my office . . ."** Walt to Walter Wanger, Oct. 23, 1942, Motion Picture Society for the Americas, Walt Disney Corr., 1944, F-N, A1531, WDA.

394 **Walt's complaints.** Overall Meeting, *Victory Through Air Power,* Nov. 10, 1942, Seversky Meetings, *Reluctant Dragon, Dumbo, Saludos Amigos, Victory Through Air Power, Three Cabelleros,* A2829, WDA.

394 **"There is a little too much optimism . . ."** Overall Running, *Victory Through Air Power,* Nov. 27, 1942, ibid.

394 **"We had better whip it . . ."** Comments on Running of #2015, *Saludos Amigos,* May 6, 1942, *Saludos—*Meetings—Notes, ibid.

395 **"Everybody in our office is . . ."** Fran Alstock to Walt, Jul. 30, 1942, Coordinator of Inter-American Affairs, Walt Disney Corr., Inter-Office, World War II, A-K, A1633, WDA.

395 **"quite exceeds . . ."** Nelson Rockefeller to Walt, Jul. 30, 1942, ibid.

395 **Deterring other studios from gremlin films.** Shale, *Donald Duck,* p. 83.

395 **Roy's complaint.** Roy to Walt, Jul. 28, 1942, Disney, Roy O., Walt Disney Corr., Inter-Office, 1938–1944, D, A1627, WDA.

395 **"very very heavy villains."** Story Meeting on Gremlins, Aug. 20, 1943, Gremlins Story (Data and Material), Walt Disney Corr., Inter Office, 1938–1944, F-K, A1628, WDA.

395 **No one seemed to know what a gremlin should look like.** Ward Kimball, interview by Rick Shale, Jan. 19, 1976, p. 7, WDA.

396 **Meeting with RAF fliers.** T. Hee quoted in Hubler, *Disney,* pp. 395–96.

396 **"Definitely, the GREMLINS . . ."** Walt to Stalky [Dahl], Dec. 18, 1943, Gremlins Story (Data and Material), Walt Disney Corr., Inter-Office, 1938–1944, F-K, A1628, WDA.

396 **$150,000 from Bank of America.** Memo, George Morris to Roy, Re: Resume of Events, Oct. 16, 1941, Reports sent to Walt in New York, Oct. 23, 1941, Walt Disney Corr., Inter-Office, 1938–1944, D, A1627, WDA.

396 **Economies on *Bambi*.** Memo, George Goepper to Walt, Re: *Bambi* Footage, Apr. 29, 1941, Goepper, George, Walt Disney Corr., Inter-Office, 1938–1944, F-K, A1628, WDA. See also Meeting in Walt's Office, Mar. 3, 1941, BAMBI NOTES (Complete by Seq.) of REVISIONS Resulting from March showings, 1941, *Bambi* Production Materials—Story Meeting Notes, Sweatbox Notes, Corr., Research A3267, WDA.

396 **"Frank, I know it hurts . . ."** Frank Thomas and Ollie Johnston, *Walt Disney's "Bambi"* (New York: Stewart, Tabori & Chang, 1990), pp. 181–82.

396 **"losing something."** Sharpsteen interview by Peri, p. 4.

396 **Slashing the film.** Thomas and Johnson, *Disney's "Bambi,"* p. 183.

396 **"There was not much excitement . . ."** Ibid., p. 186.

397 **"Here I am, Bambi!"** Ibid.

397 **Dropping roadshow plans.** Memo, Dave Hand to Walt, Re: Dave Hand's Unit, Oct. 17, 1941, Reports sent to Walt in New York, Oct. 23, 1941, Walt Disney Corr., Inter-Office, 1938–1944, D, A1627, WDA.

397 **Gallup survey.** David Ogilvy (associate director, Audience Research Institute) to Roy, Aug. 22, 1942, *Bambi—*Exploitation and Publicity, Walt Disney Corr., Inter-Office, 1938–1944, A, A1625, WDA.

397 **"BAMBI deals are coming in . . ."** Memo, Roy to Walt, Re: *Bambi,* Sept. 3,

1942, Memos to and from Walt, 1940–1943 Folder, Roy O. Disney, Inter-Office Corr., Disney, Roy O.—Trips to Disneyland (1954–61) A3002, WDA.

397 **"musical circle of Hollywood."** Comments During First Theater Running, Mar. 7, 1941, BAMBI NOTES (Complete by Seq.) of REVISIONS Resulting from March showings, 1941, *Bambi* Production Materials—Story Meeting Notes, Sweatbox Notes, Corr., Research, A3267, WDA.

397 **Frank Churchill.** Carolyn Churchill to Walt, May 24, 1942, C Folder, Walt Disney Corr., 1942–1943, A-C, A1526, WDA.

397 **"In his search for perfection . . ."** *NYT*, Aug. 13, 1942.

397 **"entirely unpleasant."** Manny Farber, "Saccharine Symphony—Bambi," in Peary and Peary *The American Animated Cartoon*, p. 90.

398 **Young Diane** Diane Disney Miller, interview by author; Don Eddy, "The Amazing Secret of Walt Disney."

398 **Exchange with Raymond J. Brown.** Brown to Walt, Jun. 17, 1942; Walt to Brown, Jun. 17, 1942, O Folder, Walt Disney Corr., 1942–1943, I-P, A1528, WDA.

399 **Brown controversy.** Howard Kemp to Walt, Sept. 6, 1942; Walt to Harry Leeding, Sept. 11, 1942; VC [Vern Caldwell] to Walt, [Sept. 1942], *Bambi* (Controversial Letters), Walt Disney Corr., Inter-Office, 1938–1944, A, A1625, WDA.

399 **"our friends in the Music Hall . . ."** Roy to George Morris, Aug. 19, 1942, Disney, Roy O., Walt Disney Corr., Inter-Office, 1938–1944, D, A1627, WDA.

399 **Lost roughly $200,000.** To: Board of Directors From: George Morris, Oct. 21, 1943, Walt Disney Productions, ibid.

399 **"Living with BAMBI . . ."** Walt to Jimmy Starr, Jul. 9, 1942, St Folder, Walt Disney Corr., 1942–1943, Q-S, A1529, WDA.

399 **Identification badges.** Walt to Uncle Robert, Aug. 10, 1942, D Folder, Walt Disney Corr., 1942–1943, D-H, A1527, WDA.

399 **Visiting draft boards.** Walt Disney interview by Martin, Disc 9, WDA.

400 **Almost 28 percent of the staff.** Hedda Hopper, "Disney Outlines Postwar Plans," *LAT*, Feb. 20, 1944.

400 **Commandeering bedroom off Walt's office.** Erwin Verity, interview by Dave Smith and Rick Shale, Jan. 19, 1976, p. 18, WDA.

400 **Firing rockets off the roof.** John Hench, interview by Leonard Maltin, *On the Front Lines: The War Years*, DVD (Buena Vista Home Entertainment, 2004).

400 **Wartime economizing.** Marc Davis quoted in Solomon, *Enchanted Drawings*, p. 119; Memo, George Morris to Walt, Re: Lockheed Leases, July 19, 1942, Morris, George E., Folder, Walt Disney Corr., Inter-Office, 1938–1944, A1629; Jim Fletcher, artist, quoted in Green and Green, *Remembering Walt*, p. 120; Walt Disney interview by Martin, Reel 8, p. 14.

400 **"You were just going to be locked in . . ."** Mike Barrier, "Screenwriter for a Duck: Carl Barks at the Disney Studio," *Funnyworld*, no. 21 (Fall 1979), p. 14.

400 **"mental equipment."** Carl Nater, "Walt Disney Studio—A War Plant," *Journal of the Society of Motion Picture Engineers*, vol. 42, no. 3 (Mar. 1944), p. 173.

400 **"We must throw out entirely . . ."** Memo, Adelquist to Walt, Jan. 13, 1942, Walt Disney Corr., Inter-Office, 1938–1944, A folder, A-B, A1625, WDA.

400 **"I really believe that Walt . . ."** "Walt Disney: Great Teacher," *Fortune*, Aug. 1942, p. 156.

400 **Charged average of $12 per foot.** Thomas F. Brady, "Donald Doesn't Duck the Issue," *NYT,* Jun. 21, 1942, sec. 8, p. 3; Nater, "Disney Studio," pp. 172–73.

401 **Pay cut.** Walt to Walt Disney Productions, May 28, 1943, Walt Disney Productions, Walt Disney Corr., Inter-Office, 1938–1944, D, A1627, WDA.

401 **Meeting with Rosenberg.** Memo, Roy to Walt, Jan. 28, 1942, Memos to and from Walt, 1940–1943 Folder, Roy O. Disney, Inter-Office Corr., Disney, Roy O.—Trips to Disneyland (1954–61), A3002; Memo, George Morris to Walt, Jan. 28, 1942, Morris, George E., Walt Disney Corr., Inter-Office, 1938–1944, A1629, WDA.

401 **"This past year . . ."** Walt to Uncle Robert, Aunt Charlotte, Dec. 28, 1942, D Folder, Walt Disney Corr., 1942–1943, D-H, A1527, WDA.

401 **300,000 feet of film.** Theodore Straus, "Donald Duck's Disney," *NYT,* Feb. 7, 1943, sec. 2, p. 3.

401 **Over 75 percent of studio's output.** *LAT,* May 17, 1942.

401 **"one of the great teachers . . ."** "Walt Disney: Great Teacher," p. 93.

401 **"At times it seemed we slipped . . ."** Tytle, *One of "Walt's Boys,"* p. 43.

401 **Dr. Earnest Hooten.** David M. Little (Harvard University) to Walt, Feb. 15, 1943, H Folder, Walt Disney Corr., 1942–1943, D-H, A1527, WDA.

402 **"I hope it has all the success . . ."** Gilbert Seldes to Walt, Jan. 15, 1943, Se Folder, Walt Disney Corr., 1942–1943, Q-S, A1529, WDA.

402 **"one of the happiest missions . . ."** *NYT,* Feb. 13, 1943, p. 8.

402 **"depresses me."** James Agee, *Agee on Film* (New York: Universal Library, Grosset & Dunlap, 1969), p. 1:29 [Feb. 20, 1943].

402 **"mingled pride and sadness . . ."** Cited in Watts, *Magic Kingdom,* p. 246.

402 **"outstanding achievement . . ."** Nelson Rockefeller to Walt, May 20, 1943, Seminar (for South American Countries), Walt Disney Corr., Inter-Office, 1938–1944, R-S, A1631, WDA.

402 **Threat to tear down theater.** Kyle Crichton, "Riot from Rio," *Collier's,* Dec. 19, 1942, p. 90.

402 **"completely adored . . ."** Gladys Arnold to Walt, Oct. 9, 1943, A Folder, Walt Disney Corr., 1942–1943, A-C, A1526, WDA.

402 **Complaints.** Shale, *Donald Duck,* pp. 48–49.

403 **"It's important."** Straus, "Duck's Disney," p. 3.

403 **Walt and Skouras.** *Victory Through Air Power* Meeting, Feb. 24, 1943, *Victory Through Air Power* Folder, Walt Disney Corr., Inter-Office, 1938–1944, S-Z, A1632, WDA.

403 **"[d]iwide the attention."** Leonard Maltin, *The Disney Films,* 3rd ed. (New York: Hyperion, 1995), pp. 63–64.

404 **"I am sure we are going to raise . . ."** Memo: Roy to Walt, May 11, 1943, *Victory Through Air Power* Folder, Walt Disney Corr., Inter-Office, 1938–1944, S-Z, A1632, WDA.

404 **Pearce and Seversky.** Walt to Roy, May 15, 1943, ibid.

404 **"most powerful and vital document . . ."** Tel. Mary and Albert Lasker to Walt, July 2, 1943, ibid.

404 **"truly great production."** Tel. Hearst to Walt, Jul. 2, 1943, ibid.

404 **Nelson Rockefeller.** Rockefeller to Walt, Jul. 10, 1943, ibid.

404 **Reaction at preview.** David E. Weshner (Disney publicity) to Walt, July 13, 1943, ibid.

404 **Reviews.** *Christian Science Monitor,* Jul. 19, 1943; *Wall Street Journal,* Jul. 20, 1943; *NYT,* July 26, 1943; *NYT,* Jul. 25, 1943; Agee, *On Film,* p. 43; *Daily Worker,* Jul. 21, 1943.

404 **"Response enthusiastic."** Tel. Vern Caldwell to Walt, July 9, 1943, *Victory Through Air Power* Folder, Walt Disney Corr., Inter-Office, 1938–1944, S-Z, A1632, WDA.

404 **Arnold's screenings.** Vern Caldwell to Walt [Jul. 1943], ibid. According to Paul F. Anderson, "The Artist and the Aviator," unpub. ms., 2005, the navy recruited a former admiral, Harry Ervin Yarnall, to mount a counteroffensive against the film, basically by promoting the navy's own theories of military success.

405 **Showing *Victory* to FDR.** John Gunther, *Taken at the Flood* (New York: Harper Bros., 1960), p. 285.

405 **"I was assured . . ."** De Seversky to Elsa Maxwell, Dec. 9, 1947, Se Folder, Walt Disney Corr., 1947–1948, N-S, A1539, WDA.

405 **"Whether it makes money . . ."** Walt to Upton Close, Jul. 9, 1943, C Folder, Walt Disney Corr., 1942–1943, A-C, A1526, WDA.

405 **"There wasn't any doubt . . ."** Woolie Reitherman, interview by Christopher Finch and Linda Rosenkrantz, May 9, 1972, p. 4, WDA.

405 **Costs of *Victory*.** Paul L. Pease to de Seversky, Feb. 27, 1958, S Folder, Walt Disney Corr., 1958, Q-Z, A1572; To: Board of Directors, From: George Morris, Oct. 22, 1943, Walt Disney Productions, Walt Disney Corr., Inter-Office, 1938–1944, D, A1627, WDA.

405 **$500,000 in film projects.** Memo, Cottrell/Cutting to Walt, Re: Educational Program, Feb. 5, 1943, Mexico and Central America Folder, Walt Disney Corr., Inter-Office, 1938–1944, A1629, WDA. The memo added that $100,000 of the appropriation "might be more or less wasted on experimentation."

406 **Mazatlán.** *LAT,* Oct. 10, 1943; *NYT,* Oct. 10, 1943.

406 **Edict requiring personal approval.** Tytle, *One of "Walt's Boys,"* p. 47.

406 **Hiring John Sheehan.** Minutes of Board of Directors, Sept. 7, 1943, Morris, George E., Folder, Walt Disney Corr., Inter-Office, 1938–1944, A1629, WDA.

406 **Commercials.** Memo, Jack Sheehan to Those Concerned, Re: Project Priority List, Jul. 1, 1944, J. V. Sheehan Folder, Walt Disney Corr., Inter-Office, 1938–1944, R-S, A1631; Kamen to Walt and Roy, Re: National Dairy Products Corp., Jul. 13, 1943; Kamen to William Reydel, Feb. 25, 1942, Kay Kamen (Government & Commercial Films) Folder, Walt Disney Corr., Inter-Office, World War II, A-K, A1633, WDA.

406 **Foote, Cone & Belding.** Memo, Roy to Walt, Re: Our Foote, Cone & Belding Association, Oct. 23, 1944, Walt Disney 1941–1945 Folder, Roy O. Disney Inter-Office Corr., Disney, Roy O.—Trips to Disneyland (1954–61), A3002, WDA.

406 **Vacillating on commercials.** Tytle, *One of "Walt's Boys,"* p. 99; Walt to Carol Irwin, Young & Rubicam, Oct. 8, 1943, Ho Folder, Walt Disney Corr., 1942–1943, D-H, A1527, WDA.

406 **Ninety-four percent.** Hedda Hopper, "Disney Outlines Postwar Plans," *LAT,* Feb. 20, 1944.

406 **Output June 1943.** Tytle, *One of "Walt's Boys,"* p. 43.

407 **"If every American . . ."** Walter Wanger, "Mickey Icarus, 1943," *Saturday Review of Literature,* Sept. 4, 1943, in Smoodin, *Disney Discourse,* p. 46.

407 **"We all have to adjust . . ."** Walt to Nina Cauger, Jun. 25, 1942, Ted Cauger Collection.

407 **"And I didn't want to walk away . . ."** Greene and Greene, *Inside the Dream*, p. 79.

407 **Walt attempting to interest Roy in combinations.** Memo, Roy to Walt, Re: Mickey Mouse/*Wind in the Willows* Combined, Oct. 28, 1943; Memo, Roy to Walt, Re: Studio Product, Nov. 10, 1943, Memos to and from Walt, 1940–1943 Folder, Roy O. Disney Inter-Office Corr., Disney, Roy O.—Trips to Disneyland (1954–61), A3002, WDA. Also Memo, Paul Pease to Walt and Roy, Oct. 4, 1943, Paul Pease Folder, Walt Disney Corr., Inter-Office, 1938–1944, N-Q, A1630.

408 **Sundays with the girls.** Diane Disney Miller quoted in Thomas, *Walt Disney*, p. 5; Green and Green, *Remembering Walt*, p. 32; Diane Disney Miller, interview by author.

408 **Taffy.** Walt to Janet Bishop, Jan. 30, 1942, F Folder, Walt Disney Corr., 1942–1943, D-H, A1527, WDA.

408 **"brings me off my high horse."** Walt to Norman Rockwell, Dec. 31, 1941, Ro Folder, Walt Disney Corr., 1940–1941, N-R, A1524, WDA. Rockwell had done portraits of the girls.

408 **"Last Sunday was the first time . . ."** Walt to Deems Taylor, Apr. 25, 1944, T Folder, Walt Disney Corr., 1944, S-Z, A1533, WDA.

408 **"openness."** Hubler, *Disney*, p. 703.

408 **Dave Hand's resignation.** Hand, *Memoirs*, p. 82.

409 **Roy showing *Caballeros* material to Rockefeller.** Memo, Roy to Walt, Mar. 27, 1944, T Folder, Walt Disney Corr., 1944, S-Z, A1533, WDA.

409 **Walt wired Vern Caldwell.** Tel. Walt to Caldwell, Jul. 13, 1943, Caldwell, Vernon, Folder, Walt Disney Corr., Inter-Office, 1938–1944, C, A1626, WDA.

409 **"IT MOVES WITH THE TEMPO . . ."** Tel. Walt to Rockefeller, Nov. 10, 1944, *The Three Caballeros* Folder, Walt Disney Corr., 1945–1946, R-Z, A1536, WDA.

409 **"one bit of animation I'm proud of."** Ward Kimball, interview by Rick Shale, Jan. 29, 1976, pp. 34–35, WDA.

409 **"whole wave of preposterous actions . . ."** Thomas and Johnston, *Illusion of Life*, pp. 522, 524.

409 **Agee,** *On Film*, p. 141 [Feb. 10, 1945].

409 **Deming on *Caballeros*.** Barbara Deming, "The Artlessness of Walt Disney," *Partisan Review* 12, no. 2 (Spring 1945), pp. 226–31.

410 **Kamen overhearing RKO grumbling.** Memo, Kamen to Roy, Feb. 2, 1945, Kay Kamen (Government & Commercial Films), Walt Disney Corr., Inter-Office, World War II, A-K, A1633, WDA.

410 **$900,000 in 11 weeks.** Memo, William D. Levy to Roy, Re: Billings, May 15, 1945, Roy Disney Folder, Walt Disney Corr., Inter-Office, 1945–1952, A-L, A1635, WDA.

410 **"one of the greatest creators . . ."** Cited in Memo, Jack Cutting to Walt, Jan. 10, 1944 [*sic*], Jack Cutting Folder, ibid.

410 **"best thing Disney has made . . ."** Memo, Cutting to Walt, Apr. 2, 1945, ibid.

410 **Reducing debt.** Memo, George Morris to Walt, Re: Financial Report, May 10, 1943, Morris, George E., Folder, Walt Disney Corr., Inter-Office, 1938–1944, A1629, WDA.

410 **Bank of America suggestions.** Memo, Jonathan Bell Lovelace to Walt, Roy, Re: Walt Disney Productions, Preferred Stock, Oct. 21, 1944, L Folder, Walt Disney Corr., 1944, F-N, A1531, WDA.

410 **"Do we want to maintain . . ."** Memo, Roy to Walt, Mar. 31, 1945, Roy Disney Folder, Walt Disney Corr., Inter-Office, 1945–1952, A-L, A1635, WDA.

411 **"lost faith in me."** Walt Disney interview by Martin, Reels 9 & 10, Reel 10, p. 14.

411 **Train ride with Nate Blumberg.** Memo, Walt to Roy, Mar. 16, 1942, Memos to and from Walt, 1940–1943, Roy O. Disney, Inter-Office Corr, Disney, Roy O.—Trips to Disneyland (1954–61), A3002, WDA.

411 **Walt prodding Roy on rereleasing *Snow White*.** Tel. Walt to Roy, Jul. 1, 1943, Disney, Roy O., Walt Disney Corr., Inter-Office, 1938–1944, D, A1627, WDA.

411 **"exceptional gross."** Vern Caldwell to Walt, Dec. 14, 1943, RKO (NY) Folder, Walt Disney Corr., 1951–1952, R-S, A1540, WDA.

411 **"your production problems."** Memo, Roy to Walt, Feb. 11, 1944, Disney, Roy O., Folder, Walt Disney Corr., Inter-Office, 1938–1944, D, A1627, WDA.

411 **"SNOW WHITE really seems hot."** Memo, Roy to Walt, Mar. 27, 1944, T Folder, Walt Disney Corr., 1944, S-Z, A1533, WDA.

412 **$50 million of savings bonds.** *LAT,* May 6, 1946.

412 **Between 150 and 300 hours of films.** Hollister, *Man or Mouse,* chap. 15, p. 12.

412 **"For Christ's sake . . ."** Quoted in Charles Solomon, *The Disney That Never Was: The Stories and Art from Five Decades of Unproduced Animation* (New York: Hyperion, 1995), p. 119.

412 **"created a greater sensation . . ."** Memo, Jack Cutting to Walt, Jan. 23, 1945, Jack Cutting Folder, Walt Disney Corr., Inter-Office, 1945–1952, A-L, A1635, WDA.

412 **"most effective work . . ."** Nelson Rockefeller to Walt, May 17, 1946, Ro Folder, Walt Disney Corr., 1945–1946, R-Z, A1536, WDA. Paul F. Anderson in "The Artist and the Aviator" credits *Victory Through Air Power* with changing military tactics and putting greater emphasis on air power. Among other things he cites the decision by Secretary of the Navy Frank Knox, shortly after the film's premiere, to consolidate the arms of the navy air corps.

NINE || Adrift

413 **"I am now hoping . . ."** Walt to Ruth, Dec. 5, 1945, D Folder, Walt Disney Corr., 1945–1946, A-K, A1534, WDA.

413 **Projects.** *LAT,* Feb. 18, 1945; Charles Solomon, *The Disney That Never Was: The Stories and Art from Five Decades of Unproduced Animation* (New York: Hyperion, 1995), p. 172; *NYT,* Mar. 10, 1946, sec. 2, p. 3; Hedda Hopper, "Disney Outlines Postwar Plans," *LAT,* Feb. 20, 1944. Walt had announced the coproduction of Hans Christian Andersen in 1941. See *LAT,* Mar. 28, 1941.

414 **Radio program.** Memo, Jack Reeder to Walt, Re: Research Work on a Possible Disney Radio Show, Oct. 22, 1945, John Reeder Folder, Walt Disney Corr., Inter-Office, 1945–1952, M-Z, A1636, WDA.

414 **"motion picture business was gonna . . ."** Walt Disney, interview by Pete Martin, Reels 9 & 10, p. 23.

414 **"I think we have a great future . . ."** Walt to Lieutenant Lee Blair, USNR, Dec. 4, 1945, Bi Folder, Walt Disney Corr., 1945–1946, A-K, A1534, WDA.

414 **"100% toward building up . . ."** Walt to Arch A. Mercey (motion picture consultant, Office of War Mobilization and Reconversion), May 10, 1946, M Folder, Walt Disney Corr., 1945–1946, L-P, A1535, WDA.

414 **Dali and Walt.** Richard G. Hubler, *Walt Disney*, unpub. ms, 1968, p. 691, RHC; Walt to Dali, Feb. 19, 1944; Dali to Walt, Feb. 21, 1944, D Folder, Walt Disney Corr., 1944, A1530, WDA.

415 **Dali deal.** Memo, Jack Lavin to Walt, Re: Salatore [*sic*] Dali, Nov. 2, 1945, L Folder, Walt Disney Inter-Office Corr., 1945–1952, A-L, A1635, WDA. Dali was to receive $10,000 and two round-trip railway tickets from New York to Los Angeles. He also demanded "equal billing" to everyone but Walt Disney.

415 **"NEW FRESH POSSIBILITIES . . ."** Dali to Walt, Sept. 20, 1945, Walt Disney Corr., 1945–1946, D Folder, A-K, A1534, WDA.

415 **"We await with great hope . . ."** Ibid.

415 **"The thing I resent most . . ."** Arthur Miller, "Dali and Disney Plan Something Definitely New," *LAT*, Apr. 7, 1946.

415 **Scarching country for fine artists.** Ibid.

416 **"The night of our meeting . . ."** Dali to Walt, n.d. [1946], D Folder, Walt Disney Corr., 1945–1946, A-K, A1534, WDA.

416 **"in fact, they spilled out . . ."** Walt to Fleur Cowles, Jun. 10, 1957, Da Folder, Walt Disney Corr., 1957, A-D, A1566, WDA.

416 **"[I]t will become . . ."** Gala Dali to Walt, Jun. 2, 1946, D Folder, Walt Disney Corr., 1945–1946, A-K, A1534, WDA.

416 **"We are not going to let . . ."** Walt to Dalis, Jun. 11, 1946, ibid.

416 **Floyd B. Odlum.** *NYT*, Sept. 30, 1945, sec. 2, p. 1.

416 **"After the war was over . . ."** Roy O. Disney, interview by Richard Hubler, Nov. 17, 1967, p. 7, WDA.

416 **"the typical, tightfisted . . ."** Shamus Culhane, *Talking Animals and Other People* (New York: St. Martin's Press, 1986), p. 140.

417 **Roy visiting animators.** David Dodd Hand, *Memoirs* (Cambria, Calif.: Lighthouse Litho, 1990), p. 72.

417 **"quite a screamer."** Walt Disney interview by Martin, Reels 9 & 10, p. 40.

417 **"It seemed like quite a chore . . ."** Ibid., pp. 37, 40.

417 **"Walt had a way of telling . . ."** Frank Thomas and Ollie Johnston, *The Illusion of Life: Disney Animation* (New York: Hyperion, 1981), p. 274.

417 **"just talking."** Wilfred Jackson, interview by David Smith, May 14, 1971, WDA.

417 **"suddenly shift course . . ."** Harry Tytle, *One of "Walt's Boys": An Insider's Account of Disney's Golden Years* (Royal Oak, Mich.: Airtight Seals Allied Production, 1997), p. 87.

417 **"did not like people being too close . . ."** Marc Davis, interview by Richard Hubler, May 21, 1968, RHC, Box 14, Folder 51.

417 **"habit of taking . . ."** Richard Huemer, *Recollections of Richard Huemer*, unpub. ms., 1969, p. 130, Special Collections, Young Research Library, UCLA.

418 **"We are all disorganized . . ."** Ben Sharpsteen, interview by Richard Hubler, Oct. 29, 1968, p. 32, WDA.

418 **Inventory of studio equipment.** Anonymous quoted in Hubler, *Disney*, p. 29.

418 **"The most prevalent complaint . . ."** Tytle, *One of "Walt's Boys,"* p. 58.

418 **"A studio cannot be run . . ."** Robert B. Sherman and Richard M. Sherman, *Walt's Time: From Before to Beyond*, ed. Bruce Gordon, David Mumford, and Jeff Kurtti (Santa Clarita, Calif.: Camphor Tree Publishers, 1998), p. 158.

418 **"I am convinced . . ."** Memo, Walt to Roy Williams, Re: Donald's Cure, Mar. 21, 1943, W Folder, Walt Disney Corr., Inter-Office, 1938–1944, S-Z, A1632, WDA.

418 **Rise in overhead as a percentage of studio cost.** DeBord to Walt and Roy, Dec. 7, 1944, DeBord, Edward, Folder, Walt Disney Corr., Inter-Office, 1938–1944, D, A1627, WDA.

418 **DeBord's recommendations.** DeBord to Roy, Aug. 28, 1944; DeBord to Walt, Oct. 19, 1944, ibid.; Memo, DeBord to Walt, Re: Directors Bonus Plan, Apr. 20, 1945, DeBord Engineering Folder, Walt Disney Corr., Inter-Office, 1945–1952, A-L, A1635; Minutes of Adjourned Meeting of Board of Directors, Jun. 13, 1944, Morris, George E., Folder, Walt Disney Corr., Inter-Office, 1938–1944, A1629, WDA.

419 **Finding and hiring Reeder.** Vern Caldwell to Walt, n.d. [Apr. 1945], R Folder, Walt Disney Corr., 1945–1946, R-Z, A1536; Roy to Walt, Jun. 19, 1945, Roy Disney Folder, Walt Disney Corr., Inter-Office, 1945–1952, A-L, A1635, WDA.

419 **Management committee.** Roy to John F. Reeder et al., Oct. 10, 1945, Roy Disney Folder, Walt Disney Corr., Inter-Office, 1945–1952, A-L, A1635, WDA.

419 **Reorganization.** Memo, Walt to Those Listed, Re: Organization Changes, Dec. 7, 1945, John Reeder Folder, Walt Disney Corr., Inter-Office, 1945–1952, M-Z, A1636, WDA; *LAT*, Sept. 11, 1945.

419 **"Nine Old Men."** Harry Tytle, interview by author; Ollie Johnston, interview by author; Thomas and Johnston, *Illusion of Life*, p. 159; Shamus Culhane, *Talking Animals and Other People* (New York: St. Martin's Press, 1986), p. 244.

420 **Ambivalence.** Tytle, *One of "Walt's Boys,"* p. 50.

420 **Fretting about Leahy and Reeder.** Ibid., p. 49.

420 **Not attending management committee meetings.** Ibid., pp. 50–51.

420 **Walt's eruption.** Ibid., p. 75. Harry Teitel, later Tytle, kept a diary for the years he worked at the Disney studio. This comes from an entry on Apr. 8, 1946, quoting Bill Anderson who had attended the meeting.

421 **Reeder's recommendations.** Report [Jack Reeder], Aug. 19, 1946, Layoff (Aug. 1946), Walt Disney Corr., Inter-Office, 1945–1952, A-L, A1635, WDA.

421 **"in the mechanical, though not the spiritual."** Tytle, *One of "Walt's Boys,"* p. 56.

421 **"The new people were interposed . . ."** Jimmy Johnson, *Inside the Whimsy Works: My Thirty-Seven Years with Walt Disney Productions*, unpub. ms., 1975, chap. 3, pp. 1–2, WDA.

421 **Losing interest in shorts.** Tytle, *One of "Walt's Boys,"* p. 83.

422 **Chip and Dale.** Jim Korkis, "Jack Hannah in His Own Words," *POV*, no. 8 [1995], p. 44; Bill Justice, *Justice for Disney* (Dayton, Ohio: Tomart Publications, 1992), p. 47. They were named, according to Hannah, by his assistant, Bea Selke, after Chippendale furniture.

422 **"[G]radually people forgot . . ."** Thomas and Johnston, *Illusion of Life*, p. 280.

422 **"of weeding out marginal talent."** Memo, Ken Peterson to Walt, Re: Weeding Out, July 5, 1946, P Folder, Walt Disney Corr., Inter-Office, 1945–1952, M-Z, A1636, WDA.

422 **"Chopin" of animators.** Quoted in John Canemaker, *Walt Disney's Nine Old Men and the Art of Animation* (New York: Disney Editions, 2001), pp. 175–76.

422 **"dissatisfation" and "torment."** Ibid.

422 **"giving him a bad deal."** Ward Kimball, interview by Steve Hulett, p. 6, WDA.

423 **"to look crude."** Ibid.

423 **"had not followed . . ."** Canemaker, *Nine Old Men*, p. 16.

423 **"lacked the ability . . ."** Ben Sharpsteen, Answers to Questions Submitted by Dave Smith, Sept. 1974, pp. 18–19, WDA.

423 **"psychologically fragile."** Frank Thomas, interview by author.

423 **"We're through with caviar."** "Father Goose," *Time*, Dec. 27, 1954, p. 46.

424 **"Walt was a bear . . ."** Bill Peet, *Bill Peet: An Autobiography* (Boston: Houghton Mifflin., 1989), p. 123.

424 **"prodigious" sighs.** Lawrence Edward Watkin, *Walt Disney*, unpub. ms., n.d., p. 14, WDA.

424 **ARI.** Tytle, *One of "Walt's Boys,"* pp. 28–29; Leo Salkin, "Disney's 'Pigs is Pigs': Notes from a Journal, 1949–1953," in *Storytelling in Animation: The Art of the Animated Image*, ed. John Canemaker (Los Angeles: AFI, 1988), p. 2:13.

424 **Never previewed for children.** Bob Thomas, *Walt Disney*, ms. annotated by Walt Disney, p. 39, WDA. This may have led to the mistaken impression that Walt did not like children. In fact, he would frequently respond to children's letters personally—advising prospective young animators on what they might do to enter the profession.

424 **Twenty separate evaluations.** Jack Sayers (ARI) to Card Walker, Dec. 7, 1948, Audience Research Corr., 1948–1949, Roy O. Disney Corr., A-C (1929–1951), A2993, WDA.

424 **Shorts and quality.** Tytle, *One of "Walt's Boys,"* pp. 76–77.

424 **"I had a strong conviction . . ."** Diane Disney Miller, as told to Pete Martin, *The Story of Walt Disney* (New York: Holt, 1956), p. 190.

425 **"in order to complete the PACKAGE . . ."** Memo, Jacques Roberts to Walt, Nov. 4, 1944, Swing Street Package, R Folder, Walt Disney Corr., Inter-Office, 1938–1944, R-S, A1631, WDA.

425 **"didn't feel warmly . . ."** Marc Davis, interview by Bob Thomas, May 25, 1973, p. 7, WDA.

425 **"[W]e at the studio . . ."** Ben Sharpsteen, interview by Don Peri, Mar. 26, 1975, p. 33, WDA.

425 **"experience in precipitate ups and downs."** *NYT*, Apr. 28, 1946, sec. 2, p. 1.

425 **"tacky."** James Agee, *Agee on Film* (New York: Universal Library, Grosset & Dunlap, 1969), p. 1:198 [Apr. 27, 1946].

425 **"burst out laughing, . . ."** T. Hee quoted in Hubler, *Disney*, pp. 38–40.

426 **Made with shorts crews.** Memo, Walt to Sharpsteen, Re: Mickey Feature, May 6, 1940, Sharpsteen, Ben, Folder, Walt Disney Corr., Inter-Office, 1938–1944, R-S, A1631, WDA.

426 **Jimmy Macdonald as Mickey Mouse.** Jim Macdonald, interview by Richard Hubler, Aug. 13, 1968, p. 3; Julia Joslin, "Mickey's Other Voice," *Disney News*, Summer 1988, p. 43.

426 **Eisenstein on *Make Mine Music*.** *Eisenstein on Disney*, ed. Jay Leyda, trans. Alan Upchurch (London: Methuen, 1988), pp. 63–65.

426 **Schickel's analysis.** Richard Schickel, *The Disney Version: The Life, Times, Art and Commerce of Walt Disney*, 3rd ed. (1968, repr. Chicago: Elephant Paperbacks, 1997), p. 13.

427 **"Suppose you visit a friend."** Hermine Rich Isaacs, "The Films in Review," *Theatre Arts*, June 1946, pp. 343–45.

427 **"pack of greyhounds . . ."** Al Eugster quoted in Leslie Iwerks and John Kenworthy, *The Hand Behind the Mouse* (New York: Disney Editions, 2001), p. 133.

427 ***Ali Baba*.** Clipping, Sept. 4, 1938, MWEZ, n.c. 19,000, New York Public Library for the Performing Arts; Danny Peary "Reminiscing with Walter Lantz," in *The Animated American Cartoon: A Critical Anthology*, ed. Gerald Peary and Danny Peary (New York: E. P. Dutton, 1980), p. 195.

427 **"Disney is the Tiffany . . ."** Quoted in Charles Solomon, *Enchanted Drawings: The History of Animation* (New York: Alfred A. Knopf, 1989), p. 94.

428 **"Making cartoons is like delivering milk."** Joseph Barbera, *My Life in 'toons: From Flatbush to Bedrock in Under a Century* (Atlanta: Turner Publishing, 1994), p. 54.

428 **"He didn't care."** Huemer, *Recollections*, p. 46.

428 **Mintz ordered his staff . . .** I. Klein, " 'Screen Gems' Made of Paste: Memories of the Charles Mintz Studio," *Funnyworld*, no. 20 (Summer 1979), p. 41.

428 **Walter Lantz had no story department.** Leo Salkin quoted in Solomon, *Enchanted Drawings*, p. 89.

428 **"We showed those Disney guys . . ."** Quoted in Culhane, *Talking Animals*, p. 235.

428 **Fred Quimby.** Barbera, *Life in 'toons*, pp. 65, 84.

429 **Termite Terrace.** Bill Melendez, interview by author.

429 **"looked and stank . . ."** Culhane, *Talking Animals*, p. 246.

429 **Floors, oil, and holes.** Melendez interview.

429 **Walls.** Michael Maltese quoted in Joe Adamson, "Well, for Heaven's Sake! Grown Men!" *Film Comment*, Jan.-Feb. 1975, p. 18.

429 **"Pew, . . ."** Ibid.

429 **"Walt spent more . . ."** Quoted in Solomon, *Enchanted Drawings*, p. 149.

429 **Footage.** Ibid., p. 104.

429 **"always smelled of Parma Violet."** Ibid., p. 153.

430 **"Jeethus Christh, . . ."** Chuck Jones, *Chuck Amuck: The Life and Times of an Animated Cartoonist* (New York: Avon Books, 1989), pp. 89–90.

430 **"[H]is wallet spoke."** Quoted in Michael Barrier, *Hollywood Cartoons: American Animation in its Golden Age* (New York: Oxford University Press, 1999), p. 335.

430 **"they're not renegades . . ."** Joe Adamson, *Tex Avery: King of Cartoons* (New York: DaCapo Press, 1975), p. 160.

430 **"cute stuff."** Maltese quoted in Adamson, "Well, for Heaven's sake!," p. 18.

430 **"The Warner Bros. animators didn't have . . ."** Melendez interview.

430 **"We were laughing . . ."** Chuck Jones quoted in Stefan Kanfer, *Serious Busi-*

ness: The Art and Commerce of Animation in America from Betty Boop to "Toy Story"* (New York: Scribner, 1997), p. 95.

430 **"directors, animators, and writers were indeed a laboratory . . ."** Jones, *Chuck Amuck*, p. 65.

430 **"We did our thing . . ."** Reg Hart, "Interview with Friz Freleng," *Griffithiana*, no. 34 (Dec. 1988), p. 35.

430 **"I need a feature cartoon . . ."** Ibid., p. 74.

431 **"many of us wished . . ."** Jack Kinney, *Walt Disney and Other Animated Characters: An Unauthorized Account of the Early Years at Disney's* (New York: Harmony Books, 1988), p. 130.

431 **"It was like admiring the kind of dame . . ."** Quoted in Barrier, *Hollywood Cartoons*, p. 402.

431 **"jealous of how funny . . ."** Quoted in Solomon, *Enchanted Drawings*, p. 107.

432 **"shaken the American people loose . . ."** David M. Kennedy, *Freedom from Fear: The American People in Depression and War, 1929–1945* (New York: Oxford University Press, 1999), p. 857.

432 **"pain in the ass . . ."** Reitherman to Frank Thomas and Ollie Johnston, Jan. 17, 1979, quoted in Canemaker, *Nine Old Men*, pp. 44–45.

432 **"a way to get into live action, . . ."** Quoted in Solomon, *Enchanted Drawings*, p. 185.

433 **Negotiating with Harris family and preparing stories.** Memo, Roy Disney and John Ross (story editor) to Walt and Production Board, Re: Uncle Remus Material, May 23, 1939; Memo, George Stallings to Walt, Re: Uncle Remus, Sept. 8, 1939, *Song of South* Corr. Folder, Walt Disney Corr., 1947–1948, N-S, A1539, WDA.

433 **"to get an authentic feeling . . ."** Clipping, *Variety*, Nov. 5 or 6, 1940, C.A. (Mike) May Folder, Walt Disney Corr., 1945–1946, L-P, A1535, WDA.

433 **"big enough in caliber . . ."** Memo, Roy to Walt, Jun. 21, 1944, Walt Disney 1941–1954 Folder, Roy O. Disney Inter-Office Corr., Disney, Roy O.—Trips to Disneyland (1954–61), A3002, WDA.

433 **"insatiable."** Quoted in Patrick McGilligan and Paul Buhle, *Tender Comrades. A Backstory of the Hollywood Blacklist* (New York: St. Martin's Press, 1997), p. 522.

433 **"vicious piece of hocus pocus."** *Chattanooga Tennessee Times*, Sept. 15, 1944, Caldwell, Vernon, Walt Disney Corr., Inter-Office, 1938–1944, C, A1626, WDA.

433 **"nigger pile" and "picaninny."** Story Conference on Snow White—Last Part of Seq. 6A, June 23, 1936, Snow White Story Meetings, Jan. 1936–Jul. 1936 folder, *Snow White and the Seven Dwarfs*, Story Meetings—Oct. 1934–1937, Box 1, A1731, WDA; Walt to Mike May, Apr. 19, 1945, May, C.A. (Mike) Folder, Walt Disney Corr., 1945–1946, L-P, A1535, WDA.

433 **Crows understanding prejudice.** Michael Wilmington, "Dumbo," in *American Animated Cartoon*, p. 81.

433 **Black centaurette.** Story Meeting, Oct. 17, 1938 [afternoon], *Concert Feature*—Meetings, 1938, *Fantasia*, Story Meetings, etc., A1782, WDA. This was excised for subsequent releases.

434 **"Between the negro haters . . ."** Caldwell to [Perce] Pearce, Jun. 19, 1944, Caldwell, Vernon, Walt Disney Corr., Inter-Office, 1938–1944, C, A1626, WDA.

434 **Bill Kupper and *Stormy Weather*.** Memo, William B. Levy to Roy, Re: "Uncle Remus," Jun. 26, 1944, Disney, Roy O., Folder, Walt Disney Corr., Inter-Office, 1938–1944, D, A1627, WDA.

434 **"That's exactly why I want you . . ."** McGilligan and Buhle, *Tender Comrades*, p. 521.

434 **Rapf's changes.** Maurice Rapf, Notes on Uncle Remus [1944], *Song of South* Corr. Folder, Walt Disney Corr., 1947–1948, N-S, A1539, WDA.; McGilligan and Buhle, *Tender Comrades*, p. 524.

434 **"I can't find a damn thing . . ."** Memo, Lessing to Walt, Re: Uncle Remus Sequence A, Nov. 9, 1944, *Song of South* Corr. Folder, Walt Disney Corr., 1947–1948, N-S, A1539, WDA.

435 **Hattie McDaniel.** Hattie McDaniel to Walt, Jun. 9, 1947, ibid.

435 **Walter White.** Walt to Walter White, Jul. 25, 1944, ibid.

435 **Breen's friend's comments.** Memo, Francis Harmon to Joseph Breen, Jul. 31, 1944, MPPDA folder, Walt Disney Corr., 1945–1946, L-P, A1535, WDA.

435 **Dr. Alain Locke.** Dr. Alain Locke to Walter Wanger, Sept. 4, 1944, *Song of South* Corr. Folder, Walt Disney Corr., 1947–1948, N-S, A1539, WDA.

435 **"cause serious trouble . . ."** Memo, Arch Reeve to Joseph I. Breen and Will Hays, Aug. 18, 1944, ibid.

435 **Clarence Muse.** Report on Foreign-Inspired Agitation Among American Negroes in Los Angeles Field Division [1945], File #100-14872, Walt Disney, FBI.

435 **Muse's vendetta.** Rapf quoted in McGilligan and Buhle, *Tender Comrades*, p. 524.

436 **Contacting Robeson.** Memo, Earl Rettig to Walt, Feb. 20, 1941; Earl Rettig to Rudolph Polk, Columbia Management, Feb. 20, 1941, Earl Rettig Folder, Walt Disney Corr., Inter-Office, 1938–1944, R-S, A1631, WDA.

436 **Apologizing to Robeson.** Tel. Walt to Sheridan Gibney, Mar. 2, 1943, G Folder, Walt Disney Corr., 1942–1943, D-H, A1527, WDA.

436 **Finding James Baskett.** Walt to Jean Hersholt, Jan. 30, 1948, Academy of Motion Picture Arts & Sciences Folder, Walt Disney Corr., 1951–1952, A-Ch, A1544, WDA.

436 **Estimated cost of refitting soundstage.** Memo, Dick Pfahler to Those Listed, Re: Equipment for Live Action, Oct. 9, 1945, Dick Pfahler Folder, Walt Disney Corr., 1945–1952, M-Z, A1636, WDA.

436 **Lovelace's suggestion.** Jonathan Bell Lovelace to Walt, Sept. 18, 1944, *Song of South* Corr. Folder, Walt Disney Corr., 1947–1948, N-S, A1539, WDA.

436 **$390,000 for Goldwyn's services.** Memo, Fred Leahy to Walt, Jan. 22, 1948, L Folder, Walt Disney Corr., 1945–1952, A-L, A1635, WDA.

436 **"atmospheric shots."** Walt to Joseph Breen, Dec. 11, 1944, MPPDA Folder, Walt Disney Corr., 1945–1946, L-P, A1535, WDA.

437 **Scolding Jackson.** Wilfred Jackson quoted in Barrier, *Hollywood Cartoons*, p. 389.

437 **"We all sat there . . ."** Jackson quoted in Hubler, *Disney*, p. 504.

437 **Retitled *Song of the South*.** Walt to Wright Bryan (editor of *Atlanta Journal*), Jun. 11, 1946, *Song of South* Corr. Folder, Walt Disney Corr., 1947–1948, N-S, A1539, WDA. Walt told the Harrises that there were so many "uncles" on various radio programs for young people that the film might be misconstrued as being "entertainment exclusively for children."

437 **"almost all of the animators . . ."** Marc Davis, interview by Bob Thomas, May 25, 1973, p. 16, WDA.

437 **"kind of a high . . ."** Milt Kahl, interview by Mica Prods., Nov. 3, 1983, p. 28, WDA.

437 **"SAW WALT DISNEY'S SONG OF THE SOUTH . . ."** Ned Depinet to John Reeder, Jul. 31, 1946, John Reeder Folder, Walt Disney Corr., Inter-Office, 1945–1952, M-Z, A1636, WDA; Ned E. Depinet to Robert Mochrie, Jul. 31, 1946, *Make Mine Music* Folder, Walt Disney Corr., 1945–1946, L-P, A1535, WDA. Caldwell had forwarded the letter to Walt with his comments on the bottom.

437 **"highest potential."** Bill Levy to Roy, Nov. 18, 1946, *Song of South* Corr. Folder, Walt Disney Corr., 1947–1948, N-S, A1539, WDA.

438 **"More and more, Walt Disney's craftsmen . . ."** *NYT*, Nov. 28, 1946.

438 **$3.3 million gross.** Roy to Walt, Jan. 21, 1947, Roy Disney Folder, Walt Disney Corr., Inter-Office, 1945–1952, A-L, A1635, WDA.

438 **"idyllic master-slave relationship . . ."** *NYT*, Nov. 28, 1946.

438 **"insult to minorities."** *NYT*, Dec. 24, 1946.

438 **Picketing.** *NYT*, Dec. 14, 1946.

438 **"You stopped being Walt Disney, . . ."** Billy Rose, "Pitching Horseshoes," *PM*, Dec. 17, 1946.

438 **Maurice Rapf agreed with attackers.** McGilligan and Buhle, *Tender Comrades*, p. 523.

438 **"tallies with the reputation . . ."** Phineas J. Biron, "Strictly Confidential," *Messenger*, Jan. 3, 1947 quoted in Steven Watts, *The Magic Kingdom: Walt Disney and the American Way of Life* (Boston: Houghton Mifflin, 1997), p. 276.

438 **"the best actor, I believe, . . ."** Walt to Ruth, Dec. 5, 1945, D Folder, Walt Disney Corr., 1945–1946, A-K, A1534, WDA.

438 **Bert Williams record.** Walt to James Baskett, Jul. 28, 1947, B Folder, Walt Disney Corr., 1947–1948, A-H, A15137, WDA.

438 **"almost wholly without direction"** Walt to Jean Hersholt (president, Motion Picture Academy), Jan. 30, 1948, Academy of Motion Picture Arts & Sciences Folder, Walt Disney Corr., 1951–1952, A-Ch, A1544, WDA.

439 **"friend in deed . . ."** Margaret Baskett to Walt, Aug. 20, 1948, ibid.

439 **"Let's do *anything* . . ."** Walt Disney interview by Martin, Disc 9, WDA.

439 **"It would, of course, be a new departure . . ."** Walt to James Mason, Feb. 7, 1947, M Folder, Walt Disney Corr., 1947–1948, I-M, A1538, WDA.

439 **"kick in the teeth . . ."** Miller, *Story of Disney*, p. 80.

439 **"When he came back to animation . . ."** Quoted in Katherine Greene and Richard Greene, *Inside the Dream: The Personal Story of Walt Disney* (New York: Roundtable Press, 2001), p. 95.

440 **Studio on rebound.** *NYT*, Jan. 10, 1947.

440 **Loan from RKO.** Tytle, *One of "Walt's Boys,"* p. 57.

440 **"always seemed to be a little worried."** Quoted in Canemaker, *Nine Old Men*, p. 45.

440 **"Walt looked at him . . ."** Anonymous quoted in Hubler, *Disney*, p. 24.

440 **"Look, you're letting this place . . ."** Quoted in Bob Thomas, *Building a Company: Roy O. Disney and the Creation of an Entertainment Empire* (New York: Hyperion, 1998), p. 160.

440 **Health.** George L. Williams to Walt, Jul. 10, 1947, W Folder, Walt Disney Corr., 1947–1948, T-Z, A1540; Dr. Barclay E. Noble to Walt, Jan. 18, 1945, N

Folder, Walt Disney Corr., 1944, F-N, A1531; Walt to Jessie Perkins, Mar. 24, 1949, P Folder, Walt Disney Corr., 1949–1950, H-Q, A1542; Walt Disney Desk Diaries, May–Jun., 1948, WDA.

440 **"I'd give a lot for a little . . ."** Walt to Herb Disney, Dec. 8, 1947, D Folder, Walt Disney Corr., 1947–1948, A-H, A1537, WDA.

441 **"central figure in the corporate reclamation . . ."** Jackson Lears, "The Mouse That Roared," *New Republic*, Jun. 15, 1998, p. 29.

441 **"If no one [else] was in the room . . ."** Quoted in Barrier, *Hollywood Cartoons*, p. 395.

442 **Tyrolean jacket.** Frank Nugent, "This Disney Whirl," *NYT*, Jan. 29, 1939, sec. 9, p. 5.

442 **"pied ensemble."** Paul Hollister, "Genius at Work: Walt Disney," *Atlantic Monthly* 166, no. 6 (Dec. 1940), pp. 689–701.

442 **Dashing.** Quoted in Hubler, *Disney*, p. 759.

442 **"He turned himself from a cartoonist . . ."** Robert Hughes, "Disney: Mousebrow to Highbrow," *Time*, Oct. 15, 1973, p. 88.

442 **"critiques of the social order . . ."** Watts, *Magic Kingdom*, p. xvi.

443 **"careless, temperamental artist."** Walt to Helen Hughes Dulany, Dec. 5, 1933, D. D.V.'s Letters, 1931–33, Walt Disney Corr., 1930–1934, D-I, A1503, WDA.

443 **"The late forties was the time . . ."** Anonymous quoted in Schickel, *Disney Version*, p. 282.

443 **Trip to Goderich.** Walt Disney Party [1947], Walt Disney, 1941–1954 Folder, Roy O. Disney, Inter-Office Corr., Disney, Roy O.—Trips to Disneyland (1954–61), A3002, WDA; "Walt Disney Visits Home of His Forebears in Goderich District," *Goderich Signal Star*, Jun. 19, 1947; Walt to Uncle Robert, Aug. 7, 1947, D Folder, Walt Disney Corr., 1947–1948, A-H, A1537, WDA; "Walt and his Philosophy," interview by Fletcher Markle, Canadian Broadcasting Co., [Sept. 1963], *ReView*, JAN. 1978, p. 81.

444 **"It is not visionary . . ."** Memo, Roy to Walt, Re: Saturday Night Broadcast "For This We Fight," Jul. 27, 1943, Radio Program—"For This We Fight" Folder, Walt Disney Corr., 1942–1943, Q-S, A1529, WDA.

444 **Negotiations with *Encyclopaedia Britannica*.** Tel. William Benton to Walt, Apr. 5, 1944, *Encyclopaedia Britannica* Films Folder, Walt Disney Corr., A-E, 1944, A1530, WDA.

444 **"Probably the worst student . . ."** Walt to Disney Beck Fellers, Dec. 11, 1944, F Folder, Walt Disney Corr., 1944, F-N, A1531, WDA.

444 **Visiting Stanford.** Donald B. Tresidder to Walt, Mar. 21, 1945, T Folder, Walt Disney Corr., 1945–1946, R-Z, A1536, WDA.

444 **"He would make entertainment . . ."** Jimmy Johnson, *Inside the Whimsy Works: My Thirty-Seven Years with Walt Disney Productions*, unpub. ms., 1975, chap. 2, p. 11, WDA.

444 **"We can't be boring."** Ben Sharpsteen, interview by Richard Hubler, Oct. 29, 1968, p. 17, WDA.

444 **"certainly take a long time . . ."** Memo, Roy to Walt, Dec. 15, 1944, C Folder, Walt Disney Corr., 1944, A1530, WDA. See also Wendell Chapman to Walt, Dec. 6, 1944, ibid.

445 **"This is one of God's creatures . . ."** Mrs. Ted Cauger, interview by author.

445 **"to eventually make films . . ."** Memo, Carl Nater to Jack Sheehan, Dec. 26, 1944, Carl Nater Folder, Walt Disney Corr., Inter-Office, 1938–1944, N-Q, A1630, WDA.
445 **Sharpsteen approaching Walt.** Sharpsteen interview by Hubler, pp. 18–20.
445 **Millottes' offer of photos.** Walt to A. Milotte, Dec. 17, 1940, Me Folder, Walt Disney Corr., 1940–1941, G-M, A1523, WDA.
445 **"You know—mining, fishing . . ."** J. P. McEvoy, "McEvoy in Disneyland," *Reader's Digest*, Feb. 1955, p. 23.
445 **"Too many mines. . . ."** Ibid., p. 23.
446 **"[W]hatever it ran . . ."** Sharpsteen interview by Hubler, p. 23.
446 **"to see some of the things . . ."** Roy to Ruth, Aug. 15, 1947, B Folder, Walt Disney Corr., 1947–1948, A-H, A1537, WDA.
446 **"They all say, . . ."** McEvoy, "Disneyland," p. 23.
446 **"It knocks the people . . ."** Quoted in Iwerks and Kenworthy, *The Hand Behind the Mouse*, p. 169.
446 **"tell him to hit RKO . . ."** Ben Sharpsteen, interview by Don Peri, Mar. 26, 1975, WDA, p. 34.
446 **"[W]herever we saw a change . . ."** Quoted in Hubler, *Disney*, p. 554.
447 **"hoping it was the end."** Walt Disney interview by Martin, Disc 9, WDA.
448 **"Many of the things he advocated . . ."** Letter quoted in Bob Thomas, *Building a Company*, p. 121.
448 **Attacked by Irish kids.** McGilligan and Buhle, *Tender Comrades*, p. 523.
448 **Voted for Roosevelt.** Walt Disney interview by Martin, Reel 12, p. 28.
448 **"[A] long time ago . . ."** Walt to Neysa McMein, Aug. 13, 1940, Mc Folder, Walt Disney Corr., 1940–1941, G-M, A1523, WDA.
448 **"I don't go in for bill-board patriotism."** Memo, Walt to Bob Carr, Jun. 8, 1940, C Folder, Walt Disney Corr., Inter-Office, 1938–1944, C, A1626, WDA.
448 **"He was very apolitical . . ."** Joe Grant, interview by author.
448 **Walt attending Bund meetings.** Quoted in Marc Eliot, *Walt Disney: Hollywood's Dark Prince* (HarperCollins, 1994), p. 129.
449 **Jay Stowitts.** Anne Holliday, "Stowitts," QAR: Artist Page, queerarts.org/archive/jan_98/stowitts/biography.html
449 **"the greatest personage . . ."** Stowitts to Walt, Nov. 25, 1938, St Folder, Walt Disney Corr., 1938–1939, Q-T, A1519, WDA.
449 **Riefenstahl's visit.** Leni Riefenstahl, *Leni Riefenstahl: A Memoir* (New York: St. Martin's Press, 1987), pp. 239–40.
449 **"let 'em fight . . ."** *Los Angeles News*, Sept. 15, 1935.
449 **Left-wing causes.** Thomas L. Harris (executive director of the National Council of American Soviet Friendship) to Walt, Oct. 20, 1943, N Folder, Walt Disney Corr., 1942–1943, I-P, A1528, WDA; Jessica Smith (editor of, *Soviet Russia Today*) to Walt, Oct. 7, 1942, Si Folder, Walt Disney Corr., 1942–1943, Q-S, A1529, WDA; Associated Colleges to Walt, Mar. 4, 1943, A Folder, Walt Disney Corr., 1942–1943, A-C, A1526, WDA; *Daily Worker*, Jan. 13, 1944.
450 **Lauding Max Eastman.** Walt to A. L. Cole (general manager of *Reader's Digest*), Jul. 2, 1943, *Reader's Digest* Folder, Walt Disney Corr., 1944, O-R, A1532, WDA.
450 **Hollywood Republican Committee.** *Daily Worker*, Sept. 7, 1942.

450 **UCLA writers' conference.** Report, League of American Writers, FBI, Oct. 25, 1943, #100-5377.

450 **Organizing anti-Communist group.** Memo for SAC, Re: Metro-Goldwyn-Mayer, Dec. 1, 1943, FBI, Motion Picture Alliance, #62-2481-1; Subject: Recommendations for Membership, MPA, Dec. 14, 1943, FBI, Motion Picture Alliance, #62-2481-4.

450 **First meetings of MPA.** Walt Disney Desk Diaries, 1944; "Film Group Will Fight Communism," AP, Feb. 5, 1944; Report: Communist Infiltration of the Council of Hollywood Guilds and Unions, Sept. 21, 1944, FBI, #LA100-22299.

451 **Letter to Reynolds.** *Variety*, Mar. 15, 1944.

451 **Rumors on Dies.** *Daily Variety*, May 17, 1944.

451 **SWG meeting.** To: Director FBI, Re: Motion Picture Alliance for the Preservation of American Ideals, FBI, May 10, 1944, #62-2484-65.

451 **"[T]he public pronouncements . . ."** Elmer Rice, "Strictly Personal," Nov. 11, 1944, p. 18.

451 **An informant told the FBI . . .** To: Director, Re: Motion Picture Alliance for the Preservation of American Ideals, FBI, May 10, 1944.

451 **Wanger and Walt.** Wanger to George Leighton, MPA, May 26, 1944; Wanger to Walt, May 29, 1944; Walt to Wanger, Jul. 28, 1944; Wanger to Walt, Jul. 31, 1944, Walter Wanger Folder, Walt Disney Corr., 1944, S-Z, A1533, WDA.

452 **Supporting Dewey.** Receipt, Republican Finance Committee of Southern Calif. of the 1944–46 Republican State Central Commission of California, Oct. 2, 1944, Republican Party Campaign, 1944 Folder, Walt Disney Corr., 1944, O-R, A1532, WDA.

452 **"I'm sorry I can only give money."** Walt to K. F. Morgan, Oct. 14, 1946, Mo Folder, Walt Disney Corr., 1945–1946, L-P, A1535, WDA.

453 **HUAC appearance.** Stenographic Transcript of Hearings Before the Committee on Un-American Activities, vol. 5, Oct. 24, 1947 (Washington, D.C.: Washington Reporting Service), pp. 717–30; *Washington Daily News*, Oct. 24, 1947.

453 **"as effective as that of any witness."** H. A. Smith to Gunther Lessing, Oct. 28, 1947, Un-American Activities Committee Folder, Walt Disney Corr., 1947–1948, T-Z, A1540, WDA.

453 **League investigation.** Anna Lord Strauss to Walt, Oct. 29, 1947, ibid.

453 **"several women . . ."** *LAT*, Oct. 29, 1947.

454 **Lessing's investigation.** Memo, Gunther Lessing to Walt, Oct. 29, 1947, Un-American Activities Committee Folder, Walt Disney Corr., 1947–1948, T-Z, A1540, WDA.

454 **"recommend your organization . . ."** Lessing to Anna Lord Strauss, Nov. 20, 1947, ibid.

454 **"I would have no hesitancy . . ."** Walt to William A. Knost (chairman of the American Legion Hollywood Post No. 43), Dec. 24, 1947, ibid.

454 **Waldorf meeting.** Tel. Walt to Eric Johnson (president of the MPAA), Nov. 19, 1947, ibid.

454 **"Blacklisting me would have been embarrassing."** McGilligan and Buhle, *Tender Comrades*, pp. 522–23.

454 ***Alert.*** N. H. Partridge, Jr., to Walt, Mar. 22, 1949, A Folder, Walt Disney Corr., 1949–1950, A-G, A1541, WDA.

454 **Cooperating with FBI.** See R. C. Hood, SAC, to Walt, Dec. 16, 1949, F Folder, ibid.; R. C. Hood, SAC, to Walt, Dec. 21, 1948, Ho Folder, Walt Disney Corr., 1947–1948, A-H, A1537, WDA; Administrative, n.d., FBI, LA #140-1847.

454 **Peddler in *Pigs*.** Rabbi J. X. Cohen to Walt, Jun. 14, 1933; Roy to Cohen, Jun. 21, 1933, A Folder, 1932–1933, Roy O. Disney Corr., A-C (1929–51), A2993, WDA; J. B. Kaufman, "Three Little Pigs—Big Little Picture," *American Cinematographer*, Nov. 1988, pp. 43–44.

455 **"This proves that we are not prejudiced."** Memo, Kay Kamen to Roy, Aug. 13, 1935, Inter-Office Communications, Walt Disney Corr., 1935, He-R, A1509, WDA.

455 **"cheap kike."** Roy to Lucille [Benedict], May 11, 1933, Roy O. Disney 1933 Folder, Roy O. Disney Corr., Disney, Roy O.—Personal & Trips (1930–33), A2994, WDA.

455 **Walt grousing about Jews.** Ted Caugcr, interview by author.

455 **"coon voices" and "garlic eaters."** Story Meeting, Jan. 18, 1939, Story Meetings, 1938–1939, *Pinocchio*, Story Material, A2761, WDA.

455 **"I think she is intelligent . . ."** Walt to Ruth, Jan. 22, 1943, D Folder, Walt Disney Corr., 1942–1943, D-H, A1527, WDA.

455 **"Some of the most influential people . . ."** Quoted in Amy Boothe Green and Howard E. Green, *Remembering Walt: Favorite Memories of Walt Disney* (New York: Hyperion, 1999), p. 00. He made the same statement in an interview with the author.

455 **More Jews . . .** Diane Disney Miller, interview by author.

456 **"very conservative guy."** McGilligan and Buhle, *Tender Comrades*, p. 523.

456 **Tytle telling Walt.** Harry Tytle, interview by author.

456 **Jewish-themed film.** Memo, Roy to Walt, Re: Little Songs on Big Subjects, Dec. 24, 1947, Walt Disney, 1941–1954 folder, Roy O. Disney Inter-Office Corr., Disney, Roy O.—Trips to Disneyland (1954–61), A3002, WDA.

456 **Man of the Year.** Dr. Irving Leroy Ress to Walt, Dec. 15 1955, B'nai B'rith Folder, Walt Disney Corr. 1955, A-B, A1556, WDA.

456 **"He wasn't a troublemaker, . . ."** Quoted in Eliot, *Dark Prince*, p. 138.

456 **"Okay, Davy Boy, . . ."** Quoted in Leonard Mosley, *Disney's World: A Biography* (New York: Stein & Day, 1985), p. 207.

456 **Swift and Disney cordiality.** David Swift to Walt, Dec. 14, 1964, S Folder, Walt Disney Corr., 1964, Radziwill-Z, A1604; Walt to Swift, Jun. 15, 1961, C Folder, Walt Disney Corr., 1961, A-Christmas, A1586, WDA.

457 **Smoke Tree anti-Semitism.** Harry Tytle, interview by author.

457 **Asking Josie Mankiewicz to leave.** Peter Davis (widower of Josie Mankiewicz), conversation with author.

457 **Sharpsteen anti-Semitism.** Art Davis, interview by Paul Anderson, Paul Anderson Collection.

457 **"There is every possibility . . ."** Memo, Mar. 22, 1944, Motion Picture Alliance File, FBI, #62-2404-87.

457 **MPA and anti-Semitism.** Memo, SAC, Re: Motion Picture Society for the Preservation of American Ideals, Mar. 13, 1944, #62-2404-39; Memo, SAC, Re:

Motion Picture Society for the Preservation of American Ideals, Mar. 24, 1944, #62-2404-40; Memo, SAC, Re: Motion Picture Society for the Preservation of American Ideals, Mar. 22, 1944, #62-2404-47, Motion Picture Alliance File, FBI.

458 **Another reorganization.** Memo, Leahy to Walt, Dec. 3, 1947, Attached: Cartoon Feature Production, L Folder, Walt Disney Corr., Inter-Office, 1945–1952, A-L, A1635, WDA.

458 **"We knew that it would never endure."** Ben Sharpsteen, interview by Don Peri, May 2, 1974, WDA, pp. 1–2.

458 **Leahy losing authority.** Tytle, *One of "Walt's Boys,"* p. 52.

458 **"[W]e have never considered it . . ."** Walt to Mrs. Elbert Dwinell, Feb. 22, 1937, Do Folder, Walt Disney Corr., 1936–1937, A-D, A1511, WDA.

459 **Failure of *Melody Time*.** Hubler, *Disney*, p. 404; Memo, Roy to Walt, Re: Distribution, Sept. 10, 1948, Roy Disney Folder, Walt Disney Corr., Inter-Office, 1945–1952, A-L, A1635, WDA.

459 **Roy was insistent.** John Province, "Bill Peet Unleashed," *Hogan's Alley*, http://cagle.msnbc.com/hogan/interviews/peet/peet.asp.

459 **"very, very teetered."** Woolie Reitherman, interview by Christopher Finch and Linda Rosenkrantz, May 9, 1972, pp. 4–5, WDA.

459 **Margaret O'Brien.** Memo, Roy to Walt, Re: Distribution, Sept. 10, 1948.

459 **Vote on *Cinderella*.** Jimmy Johnson, *Inside the Whimsy Works*, chap. 3, p. 3.

459 **Competing to see which might finish first.** Card Walker quoted in Greene and Greene, *Inside the Dream*, p. 94.

459 **Reitherman and *Cinderella*.** Reitherman interview by Finch and Rosenkrantz, p. 5.

460 **"*Cinderella* really brought back . . ."** Ben Sharpsteen, interview by Don Peri, Mar. 5, 1975, pp. 11–12, WDA.

460 **"important."** Milt Kahl, interview by Mica Prods., WDA.

460 **"to see whether the scenes . . ."** Quoted in Greene and Greene, *Inside the Dream*, p. 95.

460 **Certain directorial perspective.** Frank Thomas, interview by author.

460 **"your feet were nailed . . ."** Solomon, *Enchanted Drawings*, p. 188.

460 **"have to be done with a great deal . . ."** Walt to Margaret Hedda Johnson, Jun. 26, 1947, J Folder, Walt Disney Corr., 1947–1948, I-M, A1538, WDA.

460 **Mary Blair's design.** Ben Sharpsteen, interview by Don Peri, Apr. 26, 1974, pp. 1–2, WDA.

460 **Reimagining scenes.** Tytle, *One of "Walt's Boys,"* p. 41.

461 **ARI surveys.** Walt Disney Desk Diaries, Nov. 1, 1948. These sessions ran right through 1949.

461 **Sharpsteen's report.** Memo, Ben [Sharpsteen] to Walt, Nov. 23, 1948, Ben Sharpsteen Folder, Walt Disney Corr., Inter-Office, 1945–1952, M-Z, A1636, WDA.

461 **"sort of like a little puppy dog."** Tommie Wilck, interviewed by Richard Hubler, Aug. 13, 1968, p. 22, WDA.

461 **Too much homework.** Greene and Greene, *Inside the Dream*, p. 57.

461 **"He would collect all my drawings . . ."** Greene and Greene, *Man Behind the Magic*, p. 103.

461 **Sharon's school plays.** Ibid.

461 **Diane and opera.** Quoted in Hubler, *Disney*, p. 792; Diane Disney Miller interview by author.

461 **"And he would listen."** Quoted in Bob Thomas, *Walt Disney: An American Original* (New York: Hyperion, 1994), p. 5.

462 **Spanking Sharon.** Sharon Brown, interview by Richard Hubler, July 9, 1968, RHC, Box 14, Folder 51.

462 **Diane and Palm Springs.** Bob Thomas, *An American Original*, p. 5.

462 **"Well, you are."** Diane Disney Miller interview by author.

462 **"picture of patience."** Brown interview by Hubler, RHC, Box 14, Folder 51.

462 **Diane's first menstruation.** Watts, *Magic Kingdom*, p. 356.

462 **Burma Trail.** Diane Disney Miller interview by author.

462 **Acting at Smoke Tree.** Mrs. Walt Disney, interview by Richard Hubler, Apr. 16, 1968, RHC, Box 14, Folder 52.

463 **"no other dog . . ."** Walt Disney interview by Martin, Reel 11, pp. 57–58.

463 **Duchess at the studio.** Paul Smith and Hazel George, interview by David Tietyen, Aug. 29, 1978, pp. 7–8, WDA.

463 **Hazel George's background.** Hazel George, interview by John Canemaker, Jan. 4, 1995, WDA, transcribed by author.

463 **Hazel George and Walt.** Ibid.; Thomas, *Walt Disney*, p. 8.

464 **Asking Kimball to railroad fair.** Ward Kimball, interview by Mica Prods., aired Jul. 1, 1984, WDA, p. 67.

464 **"just sat there, . . ."** Quoted in Mosley, *Disney's World*, p. 217.

464 **"We were like little kids, . . ."** Greene and Greene, *Man Behind the Magic*, p. 104. See also Michael Broggie, *Walt Disney's Railroad Story* (Pasadena, Calif.: Pentrex, 1997), p. 77.

464 **"lands."** Karal Ann Marling, "Imagineering the Disney Theme Parks," in *Designing Disney's Theme Parks: The Architecture of Reassurance*, ed. Karal Ann Marling (New York: Flammarion, 1997), p. 45.

464 **On the trip out.** Broggie, *Railroad Story*, p. 62.

464 **"He was very preoccupied . . ."** Ward Kimball, interview by Richard Hubler, May 21, 1968, pp. 40–41, WDA.

464 **"Walt was reliving his youth."** Quoted in Broggie, *Railroad Story*, p. 81.

465 **"No matter what plans I made . . ."** Mrs. Walt Disney, as told to Isabella Taves, "I Live With a Genius," *McCall's*, Feb. 1953, p. 103.

465 **"just a hobby . . ."** *LAT*, Jun. 23, 1955.

465 **Urging Lillian.** Lillian Disney, foreword to Broggie, *Railroad Story*, n.p.

465 **Planted the seed.** Broggie, *Railroad Story*, pp. 52, 56.

465 **Walt at "steam up" party.** Ward Kimball, introduction to ibid., p. 12.

465 **Train piston.** Hubler, *Disney*, p. 774.

465 **"I bought myself a birthday . . ."** Walt to Ruth, Dec. 8, 1947, B Folder, Walt Disney Corr., 1947–1948, A-H, A1537, WDA.

466 **According to one visitor . . .** John Hench quoted in Hubler, *Disney*, p. 773.

466 **"This is an electric train. . . ."** Marling, *Theme Parks*, p. 40.

466 **Ollie Johnston's railroad.** Broggie, *Railroad Story*, p. 99.

466 **Dick Jackson.** Ibid., pp. 95–96.

466 **"Personally, I envy you . . ."** Walt to William Jones, May 14, 1948, Miniature Railroad Folder, Walt Disney Corr., 1947–1948, I-M, A1538, WDA.

466 **Richard Jones's inquiries.** See Miniature Railroad Folder, ibid.

466 **Little engines.** Irene Lewis (Little Engines) to Walt, [Sept.] 19, 1948, ibid.
466 **Central Pacific 173.** Walt to William "Casey" Jones, Nov. 17, 1948, ibid.
466 **As Roger Broggie told it . . .** Broggie, *Railroad Story*, pp. 126–27.
466 **"if it can be had at . . ."** Walt to Jones, Nov. 17, 1948.
467 **"boxcars."** Broggie, *Railroad Story*, p. 127.
467 **At workshop with Duchess and Sharon.** Diane quoted in Green and Green, *Remembering Walt*, p. 44; Brown interview by Hubler.
467 **"rookie machinist."** Broggie, *Railroad Story*, p. 127.
467 **"You know, it does me some good . . ."** Green and Green, *Remembering Walt*, p. 31.
467 **"Hey, I think I found . . ."** Quoted in Christopher Finch, *The Art of Walt Disney: From Mickey Mouse to the Magic Kingdoms* (New York: Henry Abrams, 1975).
467 **"If he took his family . . ."** Miller, *Story of Disney*, p. 157.
467 **Trial runs at studio.** Walt to Jack Cutting, Jan. 5, 1949, Co Folder, Walt Disney Corr., 1949–1950, A-G, A1541, WDA.
467 **"wholly, almost weirdly, . . ."** Bosley Crowther, "The Dream Merchant," *NYT*, Dec. 16, 1966, p. 40.
468 **"He left the reins . . ."** Quoted in Leonard Maltin, *The Disney Films*, 3rd ed. (New York: Hyperion, 1995), p. 88.
468 **Throwing Bill Anderson out of meeting.** Tytle, *One of "Walt's Boys,"* p. 42.
468 **"figments of a small boy's imagination."** Quoted in Maltin, *Disney Films*, p. 88.
468 **"He knew he had a problem."** Card Walker, interview by Richard Hubler, Jul. 2, 1968, p. 10, WDA.
469 **"No good, certainly, can come . . ."** Mr. Harper, "After Hours," *Harper's*, Jun. 1948, pp. 573–74.
469 **"this is not intended . . ."** Walt to George Schaefer, Mar. 27, 1941, RKO (Hollywood), Walt Disney Corr., 1940–1941, N-R, A1524, WDA.
470 **"As soon as Walt rode . . ."** Anonymous quoted in Greene and Greene, *Inside the Dream*, p. 91.
470 **"very upset."** Ben Sharpsteen, interview by Don Peri, Mar. 5, 1975, p. 10, WDA.
470 **"Well, I'll tell you, Milt. . . ."** Hazel George, interview by David Tietyen, p. 25, WDA.
470 **British rules on film imports.** *LAT*, Jun. 18, 1948.
470 **Agreement with France.** *NYT*, Aug. 23, 1948.
470 **Impounded funds.** Memo, Roy to Paul Pease, Ray Keller, Re: Blocked Currency, Sept. 1, 1949, Roy Disney Folder, Walt Disney Corr., Inter-Office, 1945–1952, A-L, A1635, WDA.
470 **"I did them in summer . . ."** Walt Disney interview by Martin, Reel 8, p. 22.
470 **"in excellent spirits . . ."** Memo, Roy (quoting July 5 letter from Bill Levy in London), July 8, 1949, *Treasure Island* Corr. Folder, Walt Disney Corr., 1949–1950, R-Z, A1543, WDA.
470 **"fantastically wonderful sunshine."** Memo, Roy (quoting July 11 letter from Cyril James), Re: *Treasure Island*, July 14, 1949, ibid.
471 **"seems pleased with everything."** Alvin Manuel to Jack Lavin, Jul. 20, 1949, ibid.

471 **Provisions.** Memo, Dolores Voght to Steve Keller (New York office), Jun. 8, 1949, K Folder, Walt Disney Corr., 1949–1950, H-Q, A1542, WDA.

471 **Driscoll problem.** Memo, Fred Leahy to Walt, Re: *Treasure Island,* Jun. 1, 1949; Memo, Roy to Walt, Re: Bobby Driscoll—TREASURE ISLAND, Sept. 6, 1949, *Treasure Island* Corr. Folder, Walt Disney Corr., 1949–1950, R-Z, A1543; *LAT,* Sept. 28, 1949.

471 **Involvement in *Treasure Island.*** Tel. Walt to Pearce, Jan. 10, 1950; Tel. Walt to Leahy, Jan. 12, 1950; Tel. Walt to Perce Pearce, Fred Leahy, Jan. 18, 1950, *Treasure Island* Corr. Folder, Walt Disney Corr., 1949–1950, R-Z, A1543, WDA.

472 **Profits for *Treasure Island.*** Memo, Roy to Walt, Re: Live Action Production, Feb. 1, 1951, Roy Disney Folder, Walt Disney Corr., Inter-Office, 1945–1952, A-L, A1635, WDA.

472 **"We are not forsaking . . ."** Walt to Douglas Fairbanks, Jr., Dec. 27, 1950, F Folder, Walt Disney Corr., 1949–1950, A-G, A1541.

472 **"The prestige and dignity of the name . . ."** Kay Kamen to Walter Granger, Jr., Apr. 9, 1947, G Folder, Walt Disney Corr., 1947–1948, A-H, A1537, WDA.

472 **Roughly $100 million in goods.** Frank Nugent, "The Million Dollar Mouse," *NYT Magazine,* Sept. 21, 1947, p. 61.

472 **Donald Duck foods.** Kay Kamen to Walt, Oct. 29, 1948, K Folder, Walt Disney Corr., 1947–1948, I-M, A1538, WDA.

472 **Five-millionth Mickey Mouse watch.** "The Mighty Mouse," *Time,* Oct. 25, 1948.

472 **$1.25 million in profits.** Memo, Roy to Walt, Re: General Notes, Jul. 10, 1950, Walt Disney 1941–1954 Folder, Roy O. Disney Inter-Office Corr., Disney, Roy O.—Trips to Disneyland (1954–61), A3002, WDA; Irving Wallace, "Mickey Mouse and How He Grew," *Collier's,* Apr. 9, 1949, p. 36.

472 **Whitman Publishing deal.** Memo, Roy to Walt, Jan. 7, 1948, Roy Disney Folder, Walt Disney Corr., Inter-Office, 1945–1952, A-L, A1635, WDA.

472 **"very happy."** Walt to Mr. and Mrs. Isidore Goldstein, Nov. 16, 1949, G Folder, Walt Disney Corr., 1949–1950, A-G, A1541, WDA.

473 **Kamen's letter to Vice President Robert Heide and John Gilman,** "The Master of Marketing," http://scoop.diamondgalleries.com/scoop_article.asp?ai=1317&si=124.

473 **"new high in our history."** Memo, Roy to Walt, Re: General Notes, Jul. 10, 1950, Roy Disney Folder, Walt Disney Corr., Inter-Office, 1945–1952, A-L, A1635, WDA.

473 **Appointing O. B. Johnston.** Jimmy Johnson, *Inside the Whimsy Works,* chap. 2, pp. 25–26.

473 **Music-publishing division.** Ibid., chap. 5, p. 4.

473 **"some ups and downs . . ."** Memo, Roy to Walt, Re: General Notes, Jul. 10, 1950, Roy Disney Folder, Walt Disney Corr., Inter-Office, 1945–1952, A-L, A11635, WDA.

473 **"[N]o matter what you were talking about, . . ."** Ward Kimball, interview by Richard Hubler, May 21, 1968, pp. 41–42, WDA.

473 **"he lived here, . . ."** Milt Kahl, interview by Bob Thomas, May 14, 1973, p. 11, WDA.

473 **His secretary recalled . . .** Anonymous [Dolores Voght], interview by Richard Hubler, RHC, Box 17, Folder 64.

473 **"sort of a wedding anniversary present . . ."** Walt to Jessie Perkins, Nov. 16, 1949, P Folder, Walt Disney Corr., 1949–1950, H-Q, A1542, WDA.

474 **"All in all, I think it is going to be . . ."** Ibid.

474 **Diane and Lillian had found a site . . .** Lillian quoted in Hubler, *Disney*, p. 619.

474 **Seeing the property at Holmby Hills.** Ibid.; Harold Janss to Walt, May 24, 1948, J Folder, Walt Disney Corr., 1947–1948, I-M, A1538, WDA; Broggie, *Railroad Story*, pp. 107–9.

474 **Advantage of property.** Diane Disney Miller interview by author.

474 **Closing the deal.** Bank of America Loan Application, Feb. 15, 1949, WDA.

475 **"didn't make the kind of money . . ."** Diane Disney Miller interview by author.

475 **Laying track.** Walt to Casey Jones, May 3, 1950; Walt to Geraldine (Mrs. Casey) Jones, Nov. 9, 1950, Jones, William (Casey), Folder, Walt Disney Corr., Railroad 1958, A–J, A1668, WDA.

475 **"And she'd sit and look at me . . ."** Walt Disney interview by Martin, Reel 11, pp. 57–58. See also Don Eddy, "The Amazing Secret of Walt Disney," *American Magazine*, Aug. 1955, p. 113.

475 **"fix these huge goopy things . . ."** Ward Kimball, "The Wonderful World of Walt Disney," in *You Must Remember This*, ed. Walter Wagner (New York: G. P. Putnam's Sons, 1975), p. 274.

475 **"weird concoctions."** Quoted in Greene and Greene, *Inside the Dream*, p. 120.

475 **"means of keeping . . ."** Walt to Mrs. Jack Cutting, Apr. 3, 1951, Co Folder, Walt Disney Corr., 1951–1952, Co-G, A1545, WDA.

476 **Cost of railroad.** Walt Disney Permanent Railroad Installation at Home, Mar. 5, 1951, A Folder, Walt Disney Corr. Miniatures, 1948–1956, A-Z, A1667, WDA.

476 **"We spent the first half-year . . ."** Mrs. Walt Disney, "Genius," p. 103.

476 **Dali on the train's perfection.** Walt to Fleur Cowles, Jun. 10, 1957, Da Folder, Walt Disney Corr., 1957, A-D, A1566, WDA.

476 **"Walt is not an artist."** Quoted in Irving Wallace, "Mickey Mouse and How He Grew," *Collier's*, Apr. 9, 1949, p. 36.

476 **"businesslike."** Cowles interview.

476 **More unpredictable.** Tytle, *One of "Walt's Boys,"* p. 111.

477 **"Boys, if *Cinderella* . . ."** Richard Huemer, *Recollections*, UCLA, Special Collections, Young Research Library, p. 150.

477 **"The finished picture is not everything . . ."** Walt to William I. Nichols, *This Week*, Nov. 18, 1949, N folder, Walt Disney Corr., 1949–1950, H-Q, A1542, WDA.

477 **"That was just a picture."** Walt Disney, interview by Pete Martin, Disc 9, WDA.

477 **"unstinting praise from all"** Tel. Bill Levy to Walt, Nov. 10, 1949, *Cinderella* folder, Walt Disney Corr., 1949–1950, A-G, A1541, WDA.

477 **Reception to *Cinderella*.** Michael Curtiz to Walt, Jan. 16, 1950; Hal Wallis to Walt, Feb. 13, 1950; Walter Wanger to Walt, Jan. 9, 1950, ibid.

477 **"I feel stronger than ever . . ."** Roy to Walt, Apr. 12, 1950, *Treasure Island* Corr. Folder, Walt Disney Corr., 1949–1950, R-Z, A1543, WDA.

478 ***Cinderella* gross.** Hubler, *Disney*, p. 484.

TEN || City on a Hill

480 **"troubled feast."** William E. Leuchtenberg, *A Troubled Feast: American Society Since 1945*, updated ed. (Boston: Little, Brown, 1983).

480 **"The fundamental problems . . ."** Quoted in ibid., p. 4.

480 **"in factories, . . ."** J. Howard McGrath quoted in William Chafe, *The Unfinished Journey: America Since World War II*, 3rd ed. (New York: Oxford University Press, 1995), p. 99.

480 **"to the existentialist dilemma . . ."** Ibid., p. 136.

481 **"If people would think more of fairies . . ."** Mr. Harper, "After Hours," *Harper's*, Jun. 1948, p. 573.

481 **"problems become too hectic."** Walt to Ruth, Dec. 4, 1952, B Folder, Walt Disney Corr., 1951–1952, A-Ch, A1544, WDA.

481 **Soliciting miniatures.** See William Rast, R Folder, Walt Disney Corr., 1947–1948, N-S, A1539; Dorothy Voght to Edith Perry Mason; Miles Kimball; Pueblo Gift Shop, etc., Nov. 19, 1948, Miniature Railroads Folder, Walt Disney Corr., 1947–1948, I-M, A1538; Walt to Beth Martin, Sept. 9, 1949, Martin, Beth, Folder, Walt Disney Corr., Miniatures, 1948–1956, A-Z, A1667; Kate G. Kamen to Walt, Sept. 15, 1949, K Folder, Walt Disney Corr., 1949–1950, H-Q, A1542; Walt to Elizabeth Pijuet, Sept. 30, 1949, P Folder, Walt Disney Corr., ibid., WDA.

482 **"I become so absorbed . . ."** Walt to M. L. Gordon (S. E. Overton Co.), Apr. 18, 1951, O Folder, Walt Disney Corr., Miniatures, 1948–1956, A-Z, A1667, WDA.

482 **Buttonholing Ken Anderson.** Jay Horan, *Video Interview with Ken Anderson, Bill Cottrell and Herb Ryman*, Sept. 19, 1983, pp. 38–41, WDA; Richard G. Hubler, *Walt Disney*, unpub. ms., 1968, RHC, p. 620.

482 **Archetypal American scenes.** Ken Anderson Sketches for Granny's Cabin Folder, Walt Disney, Herb Lamb Reports, 1940–1941, Miniatures, Dancing Man, Etc., A1673, WDA.

482 **Hiring Ebsen.** Contract, Buddy Ebsen, Feb. 12, 1951, E Folder, Walt Disney Corr., 1951–1952, Co-G, A1545, WDA. He was paid $150.

482 **Analyzing Ebsen's dance.** Broggie quoted in Paul F. Anderson, "A Great Big Beautiful Tomorrow: Walt Disney & World's Fairs," *POV*, no. 6–7 (1995), p. 85.

482 **Figure's pants.** Milt Kahl, interview by Mica Prods., Nov. 3, 1983, Reel 6, p. 31, WDA.

482 **"The quintessential product . . ."** Jackson Lears, "The Mouse that Roared," *New Republic*, Jun. 15, 1998, p. 27.

482 **"it always takes a lot of time . . ."** Walt to William Stensgaard, Jan. 15, 1951, St Folder, Walt Disney Corr., 1951–1952, R-S, A1548, WDA.

483 **Spent $24,000.** Walt Disney's Americana in Miniature, Mar. 5, 1951, A Folder, Walt Disney Corr., Miniatures, 1948–1956, A-Z, A1667, WDA.

483 **Miniatures on approval.** See Martin, Beth, Folder, ibid.

483 **Pot-bellied stoves.** Walt to Beth Martin, Jan. 22, 1952; Feb. 21, 1952; Mar. 4, 1952; Mar. 12, 1952, ibid.

483 **Showing Disneylandia.** Walt to William Stensgaard, Nov. 29, 1951, St Folder, Walt Disney Corr., 1951–1952, R-S, A1548, WDA; Karal Ann Marling, "Imagineering the Disney Theme Parks," in *Designing Disney's Theme Parks: The Architecture of Reassurance*, ed. Karal Ann Marling (New York: Flammarion, 1997), pp. 50–51.

483 **Granny Kincaid's cabin.** *Los Angeles Daily News*, Nov. 28, 1952; Walt to Beulah Bondi, Dec. 3, 1952, Cabin Miniatures Folder, Walt Disney Corr., Miniatures, 1948–1956, A-Z, A1667, WDA.

483 **"Why does he do it?"** Walt to Hedda Hopper, Dec. 19, 1952, Ho Folder, Walt Disney Corr., 1951–1952, H-L, A1546, WDA.

484 **"One of these days . . ."** Quoted in Charles Solomon, *Enchanted Drawings: The History of Animation* (New York: Alfred A. Knopf, 1989), p. 191.

484 **"He'd see families . . ."** Quoted in Amy Boothe Green and Howard E. Green, *Remembering Walt: Favorite Memories of Walt Disney* (New York: Hyperion, 1999), p. 147.

484 **"he always wanted to build . . ."** Don Eddy, "The Amazing Secret of Walt Disney," *American Magazine*, Aug. 1955, p. 114.

484 **Wilfred Jackson at *Snow White* premiere.** Wilfred Jackson, interview by David Smith, May 14, 1971, WDA.

484 **"just something to show people . . ."** Ben Sharpsteen, interview by Don Peri, Feb. 7, 1975, p. 6, WDA.

484 **Dick Irvine remembered . . .** Hubler, *Disney*, p. 626.

484 **John Hench recalled . . .** Quoted in Marling, "Imagineering," p. 52.

484 **Mentioning train ride to Tytle.** Harry Tytle, *One of "Walt's Boys": An Insider's Account of Disney's Golden Years* (Royal Oak, Mich.: Airtight Seals Allied Production, 1997), p. 125. The exact date was Apr. 19, 1948.

484 **"enough to pay . . ."** Ward Kimball to Walt, Jul. 12, 1948, K Folder, Walt Disney Corr., 1947–1948, I-M, A1538, WDA.

485 **"While I know the whole plan . . ."** Walt to William "Casey" Jones, Aug. 19, 1948, Miniature Railroads Folder, ibid.

485 **Description of village.** Untitled for Dick Kelsey, Aug. 31, 1948, Miniature Railroads Folder, ibid.

485 **Riverboat and merry-go-rounds.** Walt to Colonel D. O. Elliott (Corps of Engineers), Oct. 15, 1948, ibid.; Walt to Jack Cutting, Jan. 5, 1949, Co Folder, Walt Disney Corr., 1949–1950, A-G, A1541, WDA.

485 **"To tell the truth, . . ."** Walt to Hank O'Leary (Atchison, Topeka and Santa Fe Railway Co.), Oct. 15, 1948, Miniature Railroads Folder, Walt Disney Corr., 1947–1948, I-M, A1538, WDA.

486 **"I'm going to move on . . ."** Paul Smith and Hazel George, interview by David Tietyen, Aug. 29, 1978, p. 29, WDA.

486 **Rights to *Alice*.** *NYT*, May 20, 1938.

486 **Huemer on Huxley.** Richard Huemer, *Recollections of Richard Huemer*, unpub. ms., 1969, pp. 121–22, Special Collections, Young Research Library, UCLA.

486 **"There is no story in the book."** Bob Carr to Ralph Parker, Apr. 20, 1943, Ralph Parker Folder, Walt Disney Corr., Inter-Office, 1938–1944, N-Q, A1630, WDA.

486 **"You could hear him . . ."** Quoted in "Growing Up Disney," *People*, Dec. 21, 1998, p. 55.

486 **"especially sophisticated people."** Ben Sharpsteen, interview by Don Peri, p. 13, WDA.

487 **Replacing *Alice* with *Peter Pan*.** Walt Disney, interview by Pete Martin, Reels 9 & 10, p. 46.

487 **"self-cancelling effect . . ."** Quoted in Leonard Maltin, *The Disney Films*, 3rd ed. (New York: Hyperion, 1995), p. 103.

487 **"too much sameness."** Tytle, *One of "Walt's Boys,"* p. 41.

487 **"trapped into making . . ."** Quoted in Peter Bart, "The Golden Stuff of Disney Dreams," *NYT*, Dec. 5, 1965, sec. 2, p. 13.

487 **"We just didn't feel a thing, . . ."** Walt Disney interview by Martin, Disc 12, WDA.

487 **Rival production.** *NYT*, Jul. 3, 1951. See also Memo, Roy to Walt (Paris), Jul. 16, 1951, Roy Disney Folder, Walt Disney Corr., Inter-Office, 1945–1952, A-L, A1635, WDA. Roy wrote of the judge's decision: "It was a terrible shock to me. I couldn't believe such a thing was possible."

487 **Went blank.** Walt to Victor Young, Mar. 9, 1951, XYZ Folder, Walt Disney Corr., 1951–1952, T-Z, A1549, WDA.

487 **"Watching this picture . . ."** *NYT*, Jul. 30, 1951.

487 **only $2 million.** Hubler, *Disney*, p. 484.

487 **"merely suggestions."** Walt to Perce [Pearce] and Larry [Watkin], Jan. 12, 1951, *Robin Hood* (Correspondence, Details, etc.) Folder, Walt Disney Corr., 1951–1952, R-S, A1548, WDA.

488 **"[T]his is important . . ."** Walt to Pearce, Apr. 19, 1951, ibid.

488 **Regaling family with plans.** Lillian Disney, Foreword, in Michael Broggie, *Walt Disney's Railroad Story* (Pasadena, Calif.: Pentrex, 1997), n.p.

488 **"his conversation about it at home . . ."** Diane Disney Miller, as told to Pete Martin, *The Story of Walt Disney* (New York: Holt, 1956), p. 199.

488 **Goff plans.** See Marling, "Imagineering," pp. 39, 52.

488 **"[E]very time you had a meeting . . ."** Milt Kahl, interview by Bob Thomas, May 14, 1973, p. 12, WDA.

488 **"Walt just carried on and on . . ."** Donn Tatum quoted in Randy Bright, *Disneyland: Inside Story* (New York: Harry N. Abrams, 1987), p. 54.

488 **Lillian being "afraid" of the park.** Quoted in Green and Green, *Remembering Walt*, p. 150.

488 **Justifying park as TV studio.** Roy Disney to Harlan Hobbs, Aug. 24, 1951, Ho Folder, Walt Disney Corr., 1951–1952, H-L, A1546, WDA.

488 **John Cowles's architectural drawings.** John Cowles, Jr., interview by author.

488 **Presentation to Burbank Parks and Recreation Committee.** "Walt Disney Plans Park for Children," *LAT*, Mar. 24, 1952; Marling, "Imagineering," pp. 52, 54.

489 **Searching for a coach.** Larry Lansburgh to Walt, Mar. 29, 1952, Carriages, Coaches, Carousels, Etc., Folder, Walt Disney Corr., Inter-Office, 1958–1959, A-Do, A1645, WDA.

489 **Owen Pope.** Dolly and Owen Pope, interview by Bob Mathieson, Jan. 25, 1980, Pope, Owen and Dolly, Folder, WDA.

489 **"A Trip Through Disneyland."** Memo, Ben Sharpsteen to Walt, Re: Non-

theatricals, Aug. 17, 1951, Ben Sharpsteen Folder, Walt Disney Corr., Inter-Office, 1945–1952, M-Z, A1636, WDA.

489 **"I don't recall a specific occasion . . ."** Bill Cottrell, interview by Jay Horan, Aug./Oct. 1983, p. 86, WDA.

489 **"as busy as the proverbial 'ten cats on a tin roof' "** Memo, Walt to Pearce, Oct. 1, 1952, *Knighthood* Folder, Walt Disney Corr., 1951–1952, H-L, A1546, WDA.

490 **Development and money spent on Peter Pan.** Roy to Walt, Jul. 9, 1942, Disney, Roy O., Walt Disney Corr., Inter-Office, 1938–1944, D, A1627; Memo, Ralph Parker to Walt, Jul. 2, 1943, Attached: Alphabetical List of Stories on Which We Have Worked and Placed in Reserve, Ralph Parker Folder, Walt Disney Corr., Inter-Office, 1938–1944, N-Q, A1630, WDA.

490 **"too heavy, . . ."** Memo, Roy to Walt, Mar. 27, 1944, T Folder, Walt Disney Corr., 1944, S-Z, A1533, WDA.

490 **Cary Grant.** Memo, Jack Lavin to Walt, Re: Cary Grant, Jul. 22, 1946, L Folder, Walt Disney Corr., Inter-Office, 1945–1952, A-L, A1635, WDA.

490 ***Don Quixote.*** Memo, Roy to Walt, Nov. 3, 1950, Walt Disney, 1941–1954 Folder, Roy O. Disney, Inter-Office Corr., Disney, Roy O.—Trips to Disneyland (1954–61), A3002, WDA.

490 **"Y'know, I've been thinking of Cinderella."** Jack Kinney, *Walt Disney and Other Animated Characters: An Unauthorized Account of the Early Years at Disney's* (New York: Harmony Books, 1988), pp. 173–74.

490 **Peter Pan live action.** Jim Korkis, "Disney's Pre-Production Peter Pan," *POV* 1, no. 2 (Winter 1992), p. 48.

490 **"Some of these Peter Pans look like hell."** Milt Kahl, interview by Mica Prods., Nov. 3, 1983, p. 8 into A, WDA.

491 **Bill Peet's analysis.** Quoted in Solomon, *Enchanted Drawings*, p. 192.

491 **"I think you're beginning to get him."** Quoted in Michael Barrier, *Hollywood Cartoons: American Animation in Its Golden Age* (New York: Oxford University Press, 1999), pp. 551–52.

491 **"frankly and boldly created . . ."** *NYT*, Feb. 12, 1953, p. 23.

491 **"I might say that Roy is wearing . . ."** Walt to Kathryn Gordon, Mar. 17, 1953, Gr Folder, Walt Disney Corr., 1953–1954, G-K, A1552, WDA.

491 **Ken Peterson memo.** Memo, Ken Peterson to Walt, Dec. 2, 1953, Ken Peterson Folder, Walt Disney Corr., Inter-Office, 1953–1955, M-P, A1639, WDA.

492 **Roy's suggestion about rights to Walt's name.** Memo, Roy to Walt, Re: Your Personal Situation, Sept. 14, 1951, Disney, Roy, Folder, Walt Disney, Inter-Office Corr., 1945–1952, A-L, A1635, WDA; Bill Cottrell, interview by Jay Horan, Aug.–Oct. 1983, p. 37, WDA.

493 **WED-Walt Disney Productions deal.** *Variety*, Jun. 17, 1953; Minutes of Annual Meeting of Stockholders, Feb. 3, 1953; Minutes of a Special Meeting of the Board of Directors, Mar. 24, 1953, Walt Disney Productions Board Meetings Folder, Walt Disney Corr., Inter-Office, 1953–1955, D-L, A1638, WDA.

493 **One angry stockholder.** *NYT*, Jun. 18, 1953; *LAT*, Aug. 28, 1953.

494 **"I want you to work on Disneyland . . ."** Quoted in Steven Watts, *The Magic Kingdom: Walt Disney and the American Way of Life* (Boston: Houghton Mifflin, 1997), p. 435.

494 **"When he actually got into Disneyland, . . ."** Cottrell interview by Horan, p. 67.

494 **"hook, line and sinker."** W. L. Pereira (Pereira and Luckman) to Walt, Apr. 10, 1952, Pereira and Luckman Folder, Walt Disney Corr., Inter-Office, 1953–1955, M-P, A1639, WDA.

494 **Dr. Chales Straub.** [Marty Sklar,] *The WED Story*, first draft, Mar. 2, 1964, WED Enterprises Folder, Walt Disney Corr., Inter-Office, 1960–1964, Tryon-Z, A1652, WDA.

494 **"very much like doing a set . . ."** Wade Rubottom quoted in *Disneyland News*, Jul. 1955.

495 **Goff in Europe.** Walt to Harper Goff, Mar. 20, 1951, Ho Folder, Walt Disney Corr., 1951–1952, H-L, A1546, WDA.

495 **Roy investigating rides.** Memo, Cyril James, London Office, to Roy, Re: "Rotor" Carnival Concession, Oct. 5, 1951, London Office Folder, ibid.

495 **Harper Goff's excursions.** Memo, Harper Goff to Walt, Re: Georgia Trip, Jan. 28, 1952, O Folder, Walt Disney Corr., 1951–1952, N-P, A1547; Memo, Harper Goff to Walt, Apr. 16, 1953, G Folder, Walt Disney Corr., Miniatures, 1948–1956, A-Z, A1667; Memo, Bill Hyland to Walt/Roy, Re: Tour re "Disneyland," Jan. 8, 1953, Property: Prospects, Etc.—Disneyland Folder, Walt Disney Corr., Inter-Office, 1956–1957, Disneyland J, A1642, WDA.

495 **Walt's whirlwind.** Richard W. Fewel (Fewel & Co. Investment Securities) to Walt, May 19, 1953, F Folder, Walt Disney Corr., Miniatures, 1948–1956, A-Z, A1667; Walt to Ivan L. Colins, May 1, 1953, ibid.; Memo, WED Enterprises to Walt, RE: Disneyland Meeting with John Gostovich (general manager of A.F. Gilmore Co. & Farmers Market), Nov. 6, 1953, Disneyland General, Walt Disney Corr., Inter-Office, 1953–1955, D-L, A1638, WDA.

495 **"[W]e'd measure the width . . ."** Quoted in Green and Green, *Remembering Walt*, p. 152.

495 **"The dream's wide open . . ."** Quoted in Randy Bright, *Disneyland: The Inside Story* (New York: Harry N. Abrams, 1987), p. 48.

495 **"We would write our ideas . . ."** Quoted in Hubler, *Disney*, pp. 627–28,

495 **Exhausted from days of planning.** Broggie, *Railroad Story*, p. 204.

495 **"as a hobby."** Robert DeRoos, "The Magic Worlds of Walt Disney," *National Geographic*, Aug. 1963.

496 **"The first scheme you had . . ."** Quoted in Katherine Greene and Richard Greene, *The Man Behind the Magic: The Story of Walt Disney* (New York: Viking, 1991), p. 124.

496 **Walt redrawing layout.** Hubler, *Disney*, p. 782.

496 **"Dammit, I love it here."** Quoted in Bob Thomas, *Walt Disney: An American Original* (New York: Hyperion, 1994), p. 305.

496 **"I thought that was why he enjoyed . . ."** Cottrell interview by Horan, p. 73.

496 **"sandbox."** Katherine Greene and Richard Greene, *Inside the Dream: The Personal Story of Walt Disney* (New York: Roundtable Press, 2001), p. 131.

497 **"Here you see mixturesque beauty . . ."** Quoted in Neil Harris, "Expository Expositions" in Marling, *Theme Parks*, p. 26.

497 **"child of Hollywood out of Kansas."** Anonymous quoted in ibid.

497 **"This is scene one . . ."** Anonymous quoted in Marling, *Theme Parks*, p. 60.

497 **"One could take every feature . . ."** Christopher Finch, *The Art of Walt Disney: From Mickey Mouse to the Magic Kingdoms* (New York: Henry Abrams, 1975), p. 158.

497 **Western town.** Marling, *Theme Parks*, pp. 103, 105.

497 **Jungle cruise.** Bright, *Inside Story*, p. 69.

498 **"We want everyone to feel . . ."** The Disneyland Story, Sept. 3, 1954, Disneyland, 1954–1961 Folder, Roy O. Disney, Inter-Office Corr., Disney, Roy O.—Trips to Disneyland (1954–61), A3002, WDA.

498 **"We enter the land of Disney . . ."** Leo E. Litwak, "A Fantasy That Paid Off," *NYT Magazine*, Jun. 27, 1965, p. 27.

498 **"[W]hen you enter DISNEYLAND . . ."** Disneyland Story.

498 **John Hench's analysis of Disneyland's appeal.** Bright, *Inside Story*, p. 48.

498 **"architecture of reassurance."** Marling, *Theme Parks*, p. 83.

499 **"the road map . . ."** Quoted in Van Arsdale France, *Window on Main Street: 35 Years of Creating Happiness at Disneyland Park* (Nashua, N.H.: Laughter Publications, 1991), p. 111.

499 **"The symbolism is almost too perfect . . ."** Richard Schickel, *The Disney Version: The Life, Times, Art and Commerce of Walt Disney*, 3rd ed. (1968; repr., Chicago: Elephant Paperbacks, 1997), p. 48.

499 **"There's an American theme . . ."** *LAT*, Jul. 9, 1957.

499 **"So the Disney parks . . ."** Margaret J. King, "Disneyland and Walt Disney World: Traditional Values in Futuristic Form," *Journal of Popular Culture* 15, no. 1 (Summer 1981), p. 131.

500 **"found themselves completely submerged . . ."** Watts, *Magic Kingdom*, p. 392.

500 **"looking into the advisability . . ."** Walt to Terry Turner (RKO), May 15, 1952, Property: Prospects, Etc., Disneyland Folder, Walt Disney Corr., Inter-Office, 1956–1957, Disneyland J, A1642, WDA.

500 **"Burbank city did not want . . ."** Cowles interview.

500 **Hunting for properties.** Card Walker quoted in Hubler, *Disney*, p. 623; Walt to Kathryn Gordon, Mar. 17, 1953, Gr Folder, Walt Disney Corr., 1953–1954, G-K, A1552, WDA; Memo, Roy to Walt, Oct. 29, 1952, Disney, Roy, Folder, Walt Disney Corr., Inter-Office, 1953–1955, D-L, A1638; Memo, Nat Winecoff and Dick Irvine to Walt, Re: Disneyland Sight [*sic*] Survey, May 23, 1953, Disneyland Property: Prospects, Etc., Folder, Walt Disney Corr., Inter-Office, 1956, A1642, WDA.

500 **Price and Disney.** Marling, *Theme Parks*, p. 62; Hubler, *Disney*, pp. 632–33; Greene and Greene, *Inside the Dream*, p. 106; Minutes of a Special Meeting of the Board of Dirs., Jun. 8, 1953, Walt Disney Productions—Board Meetings Folder, Walt Disney Corr., Inter-Office, 1953–1955, D-L, A1638, WDA.

500 **SRI survey.** Harrison Price, Stewart and Rollins, Final Report, "An Analysis of Location Factors for Disneyland," Aug. 28, 1953, Stanford Research Institute, History Room, Anaheim Public Library.

501 **"My wife kept complaining . . ."** "The World of Walt Disney," *Newsweek*, Dec. 31, 1962, p. 49.

501 **"limit of my personal borrowing ability."** Walt to Dr. William C. Bowers, Jan. 31, 1951, Bi Folder, Walt Disney Corr., 1951–1952, A-Ch, A1544, WDA.

501 **Smoke Tree.** Walt to Jessie [Perkins], Apr. 2, 1952, Perkins, Mrs. Jessie, Folder, Walt Disney Corr., 1951–1952, N-P, A1547; Will Dean to Walt, Mar. 3, 1953, Si folder, Walt Disney Corr., 1955, S-Z, A1560; Walt to John J. Mitchell, Feb. 10, 1954, Me Folder, Walt Disney Corr., 1953–1954, L-O, A1553, WDA.

501 **Disneyland Boosters and Backers.** Bright, *Inside Story,* p. 53.

502 **"he'd always suddenly . . ."** Walt Disney interview by Martin, Reels 9 & 10, p. 68.

502 **"wondered where the money was coming from, . . ."** Don Eddy, "The Amazing Secret of Walt Disney," *American Magazine,* Aug. 1955, p. 114.

502 **"thinking considerable."** Roy (in New York) to Walt, Mar. 21, 1952, Roy Disney Folder, Walt Disney Corr., Inter-Office, 1945–1952, A-L, A1635, WDA.

502 **Camden television demonstration.** Ralph Austrian to Walt, Aug. 7, 1956, A Folder, Walt Disney Corr., 1956, A-B, A1561, WDA.

502 **FCC license.** A. H. Weiler, "By Way of Report," *NYT,* Oct. 14, 1945, sec. 2, p. 3; Memo, Roy to Walt, Re: Television, Mar. 5, 1946, Roy Disney Folder, Walt Disney Corr., Inter-Office, 1945–1952, A-L, A1635, WDA.

503 **TV sets for executives.** Memo, Roy to Walt, Re: Television Receivers, Mar. 19, 1947, ibid.

503 **"day and night."** John Crosby, "Radio and Television," *New York Herald Tribune,* Dec. 13, 1954.

503 **"Television is the coming thing."** Paul Smith and Hazel George, interview by David Tietyen, Aug. 29, 1978, p. 32, WDA.

503 **"take full advantage . . ."** Thomas M. Pryor, "Disney Will Spend Millions on Films," *NYT,* Jun. 20, 1952, p. 19.

503 **"We wouldn't have the pressure . . ."** Memo, Roy to Walt, Re: Television Show, Sept. 4, 1951, Roy Disney Folder, Walt Disney Corr., Inter-Office, 1945–1952, A-L, A1635, WDA.

503 **As early as March 1950.** Memo, Roy to Walt, Re: Television Show, Mar. 17, 1950, Walt Disney, 1941–1954 Folder, Roy O. Disney, Inter-Office Corr., Disney, Roy O.—Trips to Disneyland (1954–61), A3002, WDA; Tytle, *One of "Walt's Boys,"* p. 113.

503 **"tremendous send-off."** Memo, Roy to Walt, Re: Television, Aug. 30, 1950, Roy Disney Folder, Walt Disney Corr., Inter-Office, 1945–1952, A-L, A1635, WDA.

503 **"you think in terms of pouring . . ."** Memo, Roy to Walt, Re: Proposed Television Show with Coca-Cola, Sept. 15, 1950, ibid.

503 **"Walt Disney can take over television . . ."** *NYT,* Dec. 26, 1950, p. 24.

503 **A Gallup poll.** Cited in Watts, *Magic Kingdom,* p. 367.

504 **Discussing a series.** Tytle, *One of "Walt's Boys,"* p. 114. Tytle dates the first meeting Mar. 30, 1951.

504 **Meeting with Stein.** Memo, Roy to Walt, Re: Jules Stein, May 4, 1951, Walt Disney, 1941–1954 Folder, Roy O. Disney, Inter-Office Corr., Disney, Roy O.—Trips to Disneyland (1954–61), A3002.

504 **"octopus."** Ward Kimball, interview by Richard Hubler, May 21, 1968, p. 48, WDA.

504 **Television sponsorship discussions.** Memo, Roy to Walt, Jul. 10, 1952; Memo, Roy to Walt, Jul. 17, 1952, Walt Disney, 1941–1954 Folder, Roy O. Disney, Inter-Office Corr., Disney, Roy O.—Trips to Disneyland (1954–1961), A3002, WDA.

505 **"my own private venture . . ."** Walt to Kathryn Gordon, Mar. 17, 1953, Gr Folder, Walt Disney Corr., 1953–1954, G-K, A1552, WDA.

505 **Asked to make a pilot.** Ray Stark (Famous Artists Corp.) to Walt, Jan. 6,

1953, Foster, Norman, Folder, Walt Disney Corr., 1955, E-L, A1558; Cottrell interview by Horan, pp. 83–85.

505 **Roy's discussions.** Memo, Roy to Walt, Re: TELEVISION, Jul. 31, 1953, Walt Disney, 1941–1954 Folder, Roy O. Disney, Inter-Office Corr., Disney, Roy O.—Trips to Disneyland (1954–1961), A3002, WDA.

506 **Cottrell's suggestions.** Walt Disney, 4TV Shows, First Draft Outline, Sept. 30, 1953, Bill Cottrell Folder, Walt Disney Corr., Inter-Office, 1953–1955, A-C, A1637, WDA.

506 **"Walt was very 'hot' . . ."** Tytle, *One of "Walt's Boys,"* p. 125.

506 **Ryman's session.** Horan, *Video Interview* pp. 31–34; Lucille Ryman Carroll quoted in Paul F. Anderson, "A Brush With Disney . . . Herb Ryman," *POV* 1, no. 2 (Winter 1992), p. 29. In this version Walt added, "This is my dream."

507 **Goldenson's recollection.** Leonard H. Goldenson, *Beating the Odds*, with Marvin J. Wolf (New York: Charles Scribner's Sons, 1991), pp. 122–23.

507 **ABC's situation.** See Christopher Anderson, *Hollywood TV: The Studio System in the Fifties* (Austin, Tex: University of Texas Press, 1994), pp. 138–40.

507 **Paley stood them up.** Harry Ackerman (vice-president in charge of network programs, CBS) to Walt, Feb. 24, 1954, C Folder, Walt Disney Corr., 1953–1954, C-F, A1551, WDA.

508 **"They see tremendous tie-in value . . ."** Memo, Nat [Winecoff] and Dick [Irvine] to Walt, Re: Report on Trip, Dec. 30, 1953, Disneyland General, Walt Disney Corr., Inter-Office, 1953–1955, D-L, A1638, WDA.

508 **Goldenson's deal for financing.** Goldenson, *Beating*, pp. 123–24.

508 **Fierce negotiations.** Walter Ames, "Disney Signs Agreement for TV," *LAT*, Apr. 3, 1954. Ames said that the Disneys broke off negotiations when an ABC executive prematurely leaked the agreement to a trade paper and negotiations resumed by phone later that week. See also Paul Hollister, *Man or Mouse: The Story of Walt Disney, So Far*, unpub. ms., 1955, chap. 22, p. 5, WDA. Hollister says that Roy negotiated with ABC executives Robert Kintner and Sid Markley for two days.

508 **"ABC needed the television show . . ."** Speech at Tenth Anniversary of Disneyland, Jul. 17, 1965, quoted in France, *Window*, n.p.

508 **Paid by Walt himself,** Walt Disney interview by Martin, Reels 9 & 10, p. 70.

508 **SRI report on financing.** C.V. Wood (Stanford Research Institute), "Disneyland Financial Planning Analysis," Jan. 25, 1954, St Folder, Walt Disney Corr., 1953–1954, P-S, A1554, WDA.

509 **Increasing credit line.** Minutes of Special Meeting of the Board of Directors, Mar. 29, 1954, Walt Disney Productions—Board Meeting Folder, Walt Disney Corr., Inter-Office, 1953–1955, D-L, A1638, WDA.

509 **Financing.** Status Report—Disneyland—5-10-54, Disneyland General, Walt Disney Corr., Inter-Office, 1953–1955, D-L, A1638; Memo, Paul Pease, Roy Disney, Sidney Markley, E. H. Waldewitz, C. V. Wood, Dick Leonard to Members of the Board of Directors of Disneyland, Re: Projection of Disposition of Disneyland, Inc., First Mortgage Bonds, Jun. 23, 1954, Walt Disney Corr., Inter-Office, 1953–1955, P Folder, M-P, A1639; Minutes of Special Meeting of Board of Directors, May 13, 1955; Minutes of Special Meeting of Board of Directors, Apr. 30, 1954, Walt Disney Productions Board of Directors Meetings Folder, Walt Disney Corr., Inter-Office, 1953–1955, D-L, A1638; Schickel, *Disney Version*, p. 313.

509 **"rotund little man . . ."** Jimmy Johnson, *Inside the Whimsy Works: My Thirty-seven Years with Walt Disney Productions*, unpub. ms., 1975, chap. 3, p. 4, WDA.
509 **"first move by a leading film studio . . ."** Thomas M. Pryor, "Hollywood Double Entente," *NYT*, Apr. 11, 1954, sec. 2, p. 5.
509 **"an entirely new concept . . ."** Quoted in Thomas M. Pryor, "Disney and A.B.C. Sign TV Contract," *NYT*, Apr. 3, 1954, p. 19.
510 **TV meeting.** Notes on TV Meeting—Mar. 19, 1954, TV Notes and Meeting Folder, Walt Disney Corr., Inter-Office, 1953–1955, R-Z, A1640.
510 **Meeting with Kintner and ABC executives.** Notes on TV Meeting—Mar. 22, 1954, ibid.
510 **"You—you be the producer . . ."** Quoted in Lorraine Santoli, *The Official Mickey Mouse Club Book* (New York: Hyperion, 1995), p. 16.
511 **"delighted."** Tel. Kintner to Walt, Apr. 19, 1954, ABC—Robert E. Kintner Folder, Walt Disney Corr., 1955, A-B, A1556, WDA.
511 **Kintner watching premiere.** Hollister, *Man or Mouse*, chap. 22, p. 7.
511 **"[I]f the evening's promise . . ."** *NYT*, Oct. 29, 1954, p. 34.
511 **"will prove a dominant figure . . ."** *Variety*, Nov. 3, 1954.
511 ***Disneyland* ratings.** Memo, Card Walker to Those Listed, Re: Nielsen Report, Nov. 11, 1956, Walker, Card, Folder, Walt Disney Corr., Inter-Office, 1956–1957, Sunderland-Z, A1644; Press Release, ABC, Jun. 23, 1955, Sandy Cummings, ABC, Walt Disney Corr., Inter-Office, 1953–1955, A-C, A1637, WDA.
511 **One-half of ABC's billings.** Anderson, *Hollywood TV*, p. 141.
511 **"an American institution."** "A Wonderful World," *Newsweek*, Apr. 18, 1955, p. 62.
512 **Agreement to appear not more than three times.** Memo, Roy to Walt, RE: ABC Contract Television, May 11, 1954, Disney, Roy, Folder, Walt Disney Corr., Inter-Office, 1953–1955, D-L, A1638, WDA.
512 **Walt's self-assessment.** Meeting of May 26, 1954, TV Notes & Meetings Folder, Walt Disney Corr., Inter-Office, 1953–1955, R-Z, A1640, WDA.
512 ***Time* cover story.** "Father Goose," *Time*, Dec. 27, 1954, pp. 42–46.
513 **"*the* change in his life."** Ward Kimball, interview by Richard Hubler, May 21, 1968, p. 21, WDA.
513 **"I smoke and I drink . . ."** Marty Sklar, http://disney.go.com/disneyatoz/familymuseum/index.html.
513 **"You could see how he grew . . ."** Quoted in Green and Green, *Remembering Walt*, p. 145.
513 **"letting people know . . ."** Quoted in ibid., p. 30.
513 **"played the role . . ."** Quoted in Bright, *Inside Story*, p. 190.
513 **"most flagrant example . . ."** Lears, "Mouse that Roared," p. 33.
513 **"In the last analysis, . . ."** Schickel, *Disney Version*, p. 44.
514 **"Walt Disney's stuff is good enough . . ."** Thomas Hart Benton to Walt, Mar. 19, 1946, D Folder, Walt Disney Corr., 1945–1946, A-K, A1534, WDA.
514 **"And the first one we pulled out . . ."** Quoted in Paul F. Anderson, "Walt Disney's Davy Crockett," *POV*, no. 5, p. 26.
514 **"Yeah, but what does he *do*?"** Bill Walsh, interview by Leonard Shannon, Apr. 9, 1974, p. 8, WDA.
514 **Auditioning Fess Parker.** Greene and Greene, *Inside the Dream*, p. 115.

514 **Parker gave himself thirty-six months.** Mark Hawthorne, "Fess Parker," *Disney News*, Winter 1989, p. 38.

514 **Writing the "Ballad of Davy Crockett."** Bill Walsh quoted in Christopher Finch, *The Art of Walt Disney: From Mickey Mouse to the Magic Kingdoms* (New York: Harry N. Abrams, 1975), p. 137.

515 **Bill Walsh and the song.** Quoted in Hubler, *Disney*, p. 587.

515 ***Disneyland*'s audience.** Sandy Cummings to Walt, Dec. 28, 1954, Sandy Cummings Folder, Walt Disney Corr., Inter-Office, 1953–1955, A-C, A1637, WDA. The actual rating was 44.4, which made *Disneyland* the fifth-highest-rated program on television at the time.

515 **"ABC couldn't believe it. . . ."** Quoted in Anderson, "Disney's Davy Crockett," p. 38.

515 **Compared it to Mickey Mouse.** Walt Disney interview by Martin, Disc 10, WDA.

515 **Even in political circles.** Watts, *Magic Kingdom*, pp. 319–20.

515 **Parker in Washington.** Quoted in ibid., p. 313.

515 **"And wherever he goes . . ."** Memo, Card Walker to Walt, Re: Davy Crockett—Fess Parker Tour, Jun. 4, 1955, Card Walker Folder, Walt Disney Corr., Inter-Office, 1953–1955, R-Z, A1640, WDA.

515 **"And it was an extremely emotional . . ."** Quoted in Anderson, "Disney's Davy Crockett," p. 38.

515 **"[s]ooner or later he will either . . ."** Memo, Bill Anderson to Walt, Re: Fess Parker, May 1, 1956, Anderson, Bill, Folder, Walt Disney Corr., Inter-Office, 1956, A1641, WDA.

516 **$750,000 budget.** Memo, Bill Anderson to Walt, Re: 954-1955 *Disneyland* Television Show, Jan. 29, 1955, Anderson, Bill, Folder, Walt Disney Corr., Inter-Office, 1953–1955, A-C, A1637, WDA.

516 **Bear zipper.** Greene, and Greene, *Inside the Dream*, p. 116.

516 **"The people of the U.S. . . ."** "Davy's Time," *Time*, May 30, 1955, pp. 9–10.

516 **"hero-hunger."** J. P. Telotte, *Disney TV* (Detroit: Wayne State University Press, 2004), p. 35.

516 **"Walt Disney, with his instinctive feel . . ."** Watts, *Magic Kingdom*, p. 317.

517 **Walt initiating *Man in Space*.** Ward Kimball, interview by Mica Prods., aired July 1, 1984, p. 39, WDA.

517 ***Our Friend the Atom*.** Marian to Walt, Jun. 10, 1956, E Folder, Walt Disney Corr., 1956, C-F, A1562; Walt to Mr. J. E. Thorin, Armour Research Foundation, Jul. 2, 1956, A Folder, Walt Disney Corr., 1956, A-B, A1561, WDA.

518 ***Disneyland* budgets.** Memo, Bill Anderson to Walt, Re: 1954–1955 *Disneyland* Television Shows, Jan. 29, 1955, Anderson, Bill, Folder, Walt Disney Corr., Inter-Office, 1953–1955, A-C, A1637, WDA.

518 **Portland Cement Association.** Memo, Carl Nater to Walt, Mar. 15, 1956, Nater, Carl, Folder, Walt Disney Corr., Inter-Office, 1956–1957, K-Secrets, A1643, WDA.

518 **Hiring ad agency.** Memo, Roy to Walt, Re: Confidential Report, Oct. 23, 1944, Disney, Roy O., Folder, Walt Disney Corr., Inter-Office, 1938–1944, D, A1627, WDA.

518 **"By and large, they are all . . ."** Memo, Roy to Walt, Sept. 13, 1948, Roy Disney Folder, Walt Disney Corr., Inter-Office, 1945–1952, A-L, A1635, WDA.

518 **Negotiating with RKO.** Memo, Roy to Walt, Nov. 9, 1950, Walt Disney, 1941–1954 Folder, Roy O. Disney, Inter-Office Corr., Disney, Roy O.—Trips to Disneyland 1954–61), A3002, WDA.

519 **"They had a lot of liabilities . . ."** Quoted in Hubler, *Disney*, p. 488.

519 **Asked to take over studio to thwart Hughes.** Bob Thomas, "Disney Tells of Plans," *Los Angeles Herald Express*, Sept. 16, 1955.

519 **RKO balked at distributing shorts.** Memo, Roy to Walt, Re: Short Subjects, RKO, Jun. 5, 1952, Roy Disney Folder, Walt Disney Corr., Inter-Office, 1945–1952, A-L, A1635, WDA.

519 **"complete liquidation . . ."** Walt to Roy, Jul. 2, 1952, Walt Disney, 1941–1954 Folder, Roy O. Disney, Inter-Office Corr., Disney, Roy O.—Trips to Disneyland (1954–61), A3002, WDA.

519 **Roy's plan.** Memo, Roy to Walt, Aug. 4, 1952, ibid.

519 **"so important to them . . ."** Memo, Roy to Walt, Re: General, Jul. 31, 1953, Walt Disney, 1941–1954 Folder, Roy O. Disney, Inter-Office Corr., Disney, Roy O.—Trips to Disneyland (1954–61), A3002, WDA.

519 **Leaving RKO.** *NYT*, Sept. 21, 1954, p. 24.

519 **"my big brother Roy's project . . ."** Walt to Donald M. Merserau, *Box Office*, Nov. 26, 1954, Me Folder, Walt Disney Corr., 1953–1954, L-O, A1553, WDA.

520 **"It was shot for TV, . . ."** Walt to Elmo and Lorraine Williams, Mar. 17, 1955, Wi Folder, Walt Disney Corr., 1955, S-Z, A1560, WDA.

520 **Kirk Douglas case.** *NYT*, Aug. 2, 1956, p. 49; *LAT*, Dec. 11, 1956; Tytle, *One of "Walt's Boys,"* pp. 119–20; Memo, Walt to Gunther Lessing, Re: Kirk Douglas Case, May 1, 1957, L Folder, Walt Disney Corr., Inter-Office, 1956–1957, R-Secrets, A1643, WDA.

520 **"It makes me a little sad . . ."** Kirk Douglas to Walt, May 11, 1959, Do Folder, Walt Disney Corr., 1959, Di-G, A1575, WDA.

520 **"turning point."** Anderson, *Hollywood TV*, p. 141.

520 **"I am not sure just where . . ."** Benjamin Kalmenson, *U.S. vs Twentieth Century Fox, et. al*, Oct. 31, 1955, quoted in ibid., p. 154.

520 **Kintner's rhapsody.** Robert Kintner to Walt Disney, Dec. 16, 1954, A Folder, Walt Disney Corr., 1953–1954, A-B, A1550, WDA.

521 **By one account . . .** Hollister, *Man or Mouse*, chap. 22, p. 12.

521 **Outlines for first hundred shows.** Memo, Adelquist to Walt, Re: *Mickey Mouse Club* Show, Feb. 19, 1955, Hal Adelquist TV Folder, Walt Disney Corr., Inter-Office, 1953–1955, A-C, A1637, WDA.

521 **"those kinds with tightly curled hairdos."** Walsh quoted in Finch, *Art of Disney*, pp. 362–63; Walsh quoted in Santoli, *Official Mickey Mouse*, pp. 29–30.

521 **"The talented kids . . ."** Memo, Walt to Hal Adelquist, Apr. 15, 1955, Hal Adelquist TV Folder, Walt Disney Corr., Inter-Office, 1953–1955, A-C, A1637, WDA.

521 **"We've got to let Walt discover you."** Santoli, *Mouse Club Book*, pp. 23–24.

521 **"fat and funny lookin'."** Ibid.

522 **Inventing the hat.** Ibid., p. 25.

522 **"We would discuss an idea . . ."** Quoted in Hubler, *Disney*, p. 591.

522 **"disastrous."** *NYT*, Oct. 4, 1955, p. 71.

522 **131 children.** *MM Club* Reactions, Oct. 4, 1955, *Mickey Mouse Club* Reactions Folder, Roy to Jack Wrenn, City Hall, Marceline, Jul. 24, 1956, M Folder, Walt Disney Corr., 1956, M-R, A1564, WDA.

522 **"only show Babe Paley . . ."** Jimmie Dodd to Walt, Feb. 27, 1956, Do Folder, Walt Disney Corr., 1956, C-F, A1562, WDA.

522 **About $3 million.** Roy Disney to Robert Kintner, Jan. 20, 1956, ABC Robert Kintner Folder, Walt Disney Corr., 1956, A-B, A1561, WDA.

522 **"damned serious and direct orders."** William C. Park to Ed Ettinger (public relations), Aug. 12, 1955, *Mickey Mouse Club*—Newsreel folder, Walt Disney Corr., Inter-Office, 1953–1955, M-P, A1639, WDA.

523 **$2.4 million to the park.** Memo, Paul Pease to Walt, Feb. 10, 1955, P Folder, ibid.

523 **"This avalanche of work . . ."** Quoted in Hubler, *Disney*, p. 580.

523 **"Those were the days . . ."** Ward Kimball, interview by John Canemaker, Jul. 7, 1973, WDA.

523 **"[T]he difference was . . ."** Milt Kahl, interview by Christopher Finch and Linda Rosenkrantz, May 18, 1972, p. 9, WDA.

523 **Davis drawing new plans.** Marling, *Theme Parks*, p. 63.

523 **"through a fascinating jumble . . ."** J. P. McEvoy, "McEvoy in Disneyland," *Reader's Digest*, Feb. 1955, pp. 25–26.

524 **Expeditions.** Preliminary Report from Wm. H. D. Cottrell, Jun. 25, 1954, to WED Enterprises, Disneyland, Inc., Bill Cottrell Folder, Walt Disney Corr., Inter-Office, 1953–1955, A-C, A1637; Memo, Ron Miller to C. V. Wood, Jr., Jul. 7, 1954, Disneyland (Amusement Parks Other than D.L.) Folder, Walt Disney Corr., Inter-Office, 1958–1959, A1645, WDA.

524 **"While we were planning . . ."** Quoted in Dick Adler, "Hippos Revenge," *Los Angeles Magazine*, Sept. 1990, pp. 90–91.

524 **No one with experience.** France, *Window*, p. 36.

524 **"the most winning and likable . . ."** R. C. Linnell, "Personal Experiences, Observations and Opinions Relative to Thematic Parks," Aug. 1, 1960, C.V. Wood Folder, Walt Disney Corr., 1961, M-Z, A1589, WDA.

524 **Using charm to coax.** France, *Window*, p. 17.

524 **"Walt reacted to him . . ."** Harrison "Buzz" Price, *Walt's Revolution! By the Numbers* (Orlando, Fla.: Ripley Entertainment, 2003), p. 136.

524 **"trapped."** Disney, Disneyland Tenth Anniversary Speech quoted in ibid., p. 37.

524 **Disneyland offices.** Ibid., p. 52.

524 **Laying out foundations and framing.** William T. Wheeler (structural engineer), "Report on Structural Design of Disneyland Anaheim, Calif.," Aug. 15, 1955, W Folder, Walt Disney Corr., 1955, S–Z, A1560, WDA.

525 **Sandy soil.** Martin A. Sklar, *Walt Disney's Disneyland* (New York: Disney Productions, 1974), n.p.

525 **Labor problems.** Horan, *Video Interview*, p. 43, WDA; Bright, *Inside Story*, pp. 92–93.

525 **"He walked over every inch . . ."** Ward Kimball, "The Wonderful World of Walt Disney," in *You Must Remember This*, ed. Walter Wagner (New York: G. P. Putnam's Sons, 1975), p. 272.

525 **"Walt's approach was to say, . . ."** Quoted in Greene and Greene, *Inside the Dream*, p. 107.

525 **"You know, I've spent . . ."** Goff quoted in Betsy Richman, "Harper Goff Remembers," *Disney News*, Summer 1986, p. 33.

525 **Crying when he said it.** Robin Allan, "Harper Goff," in *Walt's People*, ed. Didier Ghez (Xlibris, 2005), p. 1:229.

526 **"By the time Joc gets through . . ."** Bright, *Inside Story*, p. 68.

526 **"Joe's Ditch."** Ibid., p. 76.

526 **Giving Popes choice of house.** Dolly and Own Pope, interview by Bob Mathieson, WDA.

526 **Walt visiting Arrow Development.** Memo, George Whitney to Walt, Dec. 21, 1954, George Whitney Folder, Walt Disney Corr., Inter-Office, 1956–1957, Sunderland-Z, A1644, WDA. See also Whitney to C. V. Wood, Sept. 9, 1954; Whitney to Walt, July 27, Aug. 11, Aug. 17, Aug. 19, 1954.

526 **Pressuring for a train.** Walt to Frederic Shaw (architect), Feb. 10, 1954, Si Folder, Walt Disney Corr., 1955, S-Z, A1560; Kimball quoted in Marc Eliot, *Walt Disney: Hollywood's Dark Prince* (New York: HarperCollins, 1994), p. 246.

526 **"he would hate to be the one . . ."** Jack DeVol, Jan. 15, 1954, Disneyland—General, Walt Disney Corr., Inter-Office, 1953–1955, D-L, A1638, WDA.

527 **"greatly enthused."** Nat Winecoff to Robert Kintner [1954], A Folder, Walt Disney Corr., 1953–1954, A-B, A1550, WDA.

527 **"never in his life . . ."** Memo, Roy to Walt, Re: Standard Oil of Calif., Jul. 15, 1954, Disney, Roy, Folder, Walt Disney Corr., Inter-Office, 1953–1955, D-L, A1638, WDA.

527 **Lessees.** Disneyland Lessee Rent & Participation Status [Dec. 1955], C. V. Wood, Jr., Folder, Walt Disney Corr., Inter-Office, 1953–1955, R-Z, A1640, WDA.

527 **Spiraling costs.** Joe Fowler quoted in Bright, *Inside Story*, p. 92.

527 **Financing.** Memo, Paul Pease to Roy/Walt, RE: Disneyland, Jun. 13, 1955, P Folder, Walt Disney Corr., Inter-Office, 1953–1955, M-P, A1639, WDA.

527 **"Look, the thing . . ."** Green and Green, *Remembering Walt*, p. 16.

527 **Gustaf Tenggren watercolor.** Marling, *Theme Parks*, pp. 123–24.

527 **Canal Boats of the World.** Bright, *Inside Story*, pp. 116–17.

528 **"Toward the opening . . ."** Quoted in Michael Broggie, *Walt Disney's Railroad Story* (Pasadena, Calif.: Pentrex, 1997), p. 121.

528 **"[W]e don't hire for jobs here . . ."** Van France quoted in Kevin Wallace, "The Engineering of Ease," *The New Yorker*, Sept. 7, 1963, p. 114.

528 **"[Y]ou can't go on stage . . ."** Ibid., p. 122.

528 **Dress code.** Tytle, *One of "Walt's Boys,"* p. 131.

528 **"Walt doesn't like fat guys."** Charley Thompson quoted in France, *Window*, p. 50.

528 **Strikers on Walt's antipathy toward blacks.** Bill Melendez, interview by author.

528 **CORE request.** *NYT*, July 26, 1963.

528 **"It is calculated . . ."** Leo E. Litwak, "A Fantasy That Paid Off," *NYT Magazine*, Jun. 27, 1965, p. 25.

528 **"Simonized Coney Island."** Wallace, "Engineering of Ease," p. 104.

529 **"people are going to be embarrassed . . ."** Jack Lindquist (Disneyland executive) quoted in Green and Green, *Remembering Walt*, pp. 124–25.

529 **ABC sold out advertising.** Tel. James A. Stablie (ABC) to Roy, Mar. 10, 1955, ABC General Folder, Walt Disney Corr., 1956, A-B, A1561, WDA.

529 **crews rehearsing.** *NYT*, Jul. 3, 1955, sec. 2, p. 7.

529 **9,500 people.** News memo to Disneyland Lessees, May 16, 1955, Disneyland 1954–1961 folder, Roy O. Disney, Inter-Office Corr., Disney, Roy O.—Trips to Disneyland (1954–61), A3002, WDA.

529 **"just like a little kid."** Quoted in Green and Green, *Remembering Walt*, p. 155.

529 **Harrison Ellenshaw.** Quoted in Scott M. Richter, "Peter Ellenshaw and Harrison Ellenshaw," *Disney News*, Fall 1994, p. 64.

529 **"world's biggest toy . . ."** "Father Goose," p. 42.

530 **"[H]e would stop . . ."** Grenade Curran quoted in Paul F. Anderson, "The Apple Box Incident," *POV* 1, no. 1 (Jul. 17, 1992), p. 31.

530 **"We had a tent set up, . . ."** Walt Pfeiffer, interview by Christopher Finch and Linda Rosenkrantz, Jul. 5, 1972, WDA.

530 **Anniversary party.** Greene and Greene, *Man Behind the Magic*, pp. 126–27.

530 **Walt waiting for guests.** France, *Window*, p. 28.

530 **Hollywood Bowl.** *LAT*, Jul. 11, 15, 1955; Memo, Bill Walsh to Walt, Re: Work Sheet, Jul. 12, 1955, Bill Walsh Folder, Walt Disney Corr., Inter-Office, 1953–1955, R-Z, A1640, WDA.

530 **three thousand workers . . .** Richard Holliss and Brian Sibley, *The Disney Studio Story* (New York: Crown Publishers, 1988), p. 69.

531 **"Walt put on a mask . . ."** Ken Anderson in Jay Horan, *Video Interview with Ken Anderson, Bill Cottrell and Herb Ryman*, Sept. 15, 1983, p. 26, WDA.

531 **"Just about everyone was worried . . ."** Quoted in France, *Window*, p. 30.

531 **Counterfeiting tickets.** Bright, *Inside Story*, p. 96.

531 **28,000 people had fought their way.** France, *Window*, p. 30.

531 **heels stuck.** Bob Broughton, interview by author.

532 **"Either you let me through here . . ."** Art Linkletter quoted in Greene and Greene, *Inside the Dream*, pp. 122–23.

532 **Seventy million Americans.** News Memo to Disneyland Lessees, Aug. 19, 1955, Disneyland Publicity Folder, Walt Disney Corr., Inter-Office, 1956–1957, Disneyland J, A1642, WDA.

532 **Director was so frazzled.** France, *Window*, p. 27.

532 **"things weren't going quite well."** Glenn Puder, interview by author.

532 **"I have never seen a happier man."** Quoted in "Growing Up Disney," *People*, Dec. 21, 1998, p. 56.

532 **"tear streaming down his cheek."** Green and Green, *Remembering Walt*, p. 153.

532 **Watching fireworks.** Greene and Greene, *Inside the Dream*, p. 126.

532 **"Walt's dream is a nightmare."** Bright, *Inside Story*, p. 107.

532 **"I think that everyone . . ."** *Disneyland, USA*, Disney Enterprises, DVD.

533 **"Walt Disney's cartoon world . . ."** "Disneyland," *McCall's*, Jan. 1955, p. 8.

533 **"Mr. Disney has tastefully . . ."** *NYT*, Jul. 22, 1955, p. 22.

533 **"cute movie set is what . . ."** Notes on TV Meeting, Mar. 22, 1954, TV Notes & Meetings Folder, Walt Disney Corr., Inter-Office, 1953–1955, R-Z, A1640, WDA.

533 **"success of Disneyland was primarily based . . ."** Ben Sharpsteen, interview by Don Peri, Feb. 7, 1975, p. 4, WDA.

533 **Scale.** Walt to William Rast, Nov. 21, 1957, R Folder, Walt Disney Corr., 1957, P-Z, A1568, WDA.

533 **"made the street a toy."** Quoted in Marling, *Theme Parks*, p. 79.
533 **"[P]eople like to think . . ."** Ibid., p. 80.
533 **"You know, tyrants in the past . . ."** Ken Anderson in Horan, *Video Interview*, p. 64.
534 **"key frames."** Bright, *Inside Story*, p. 156.
534 **"kind of live action cross dissolve."** Quoted in Green and Green, *Remembering Walt*, p. 156.
534 **Acting out guests' reactions.** Marling, *Theme Parks*, p. 64.
534 **"that Good triumphs over Evil . . ."** Yi Fu Tuan with Steven D. Hoelscher, "Disneyland: Its Place in World Culture," in ibid., p. 198.
534 **Scolding publicist.** Bright, *Inside Story*, p. 115.
534 **"I want them to feel . . ."** Quoted in Sklar, *Disneyland*.
534 **"less an amusement park . . ."** Gladwin Hill, "The Never Never Land Khrushchev Never Saw," *NYT*, Oct. 4, 1959, sec. 2, part 2, p. 11.
535 **"Something in the Disney parks, . . ."** Greil Marcus, "Forty Years of Overstatement," in Marling, *Theme Parks*, p. 203.
535 **"When Walt built Disneyland, . . ."** Quoted in Green and Green, *Remembering Walt*, p. 102.
535 **John Hench and order.** Quoted in Marling, *Theme Parks*, p. 82.
535 **"single descriptive word . . ."** Walter Annenberg to Walt, Sept. 10, 1956, A Folder, Walt Disney Corr., 1956, A-B, A1561, WDA.
535 **"where, in this most elaborate . . ."** Wallace, "Engineering of Ease."
536 **"You're always so absorbed . . ."** Walt Disney interview by Martin, Disc 10.
536 **"He knew everything . . ."** Quoted in Green and Green, *Remembering Walt*, p. 159.
536 **Lillian said he knew where every nail . . .** Greene and Greene, *Inside the Dream*, p. 124.
536 **"ironing out some little problems."** Walt to Feg Murray, Jul. 29, 1955, Disneyland Premiere Folder, Walt Disney Corr., 1955, C-D, A1557, WDA.
536 **Spending most of his time at the park.** Walt to Robert A. Day, Dec. 1, 1955, D folder, ibid.
536 **"You know, Joe . . ."** Quoted in Green and Green, *Remembering Walt*, p. 164.
536 **Autographs.** Walt to Mrs. Max Hill, Dec. 1, 1961, A Folder, Walt Disney Corr., 1961, A-Christmas, A1586, WDA.
536 **"If the trip is seven minutes . . ."** France, *Window*, pp. 44–45.
536 **Stuffing oranges.** Bo Foster quoted in Green and Green, *Remembering Walt*, p. 160.
536 **Appear at night.** James Haught, Jr., quoted in ibid., p. 157.
536 **"He practically lived there."** Quoted in Greene and Greene, *Man Behind the Magic*, p. 138.
537 **Standing at the window.** Sherry Alberoni quoted in Eliot, *Dark Prince*, p. 254.
537 **Attendance.** Gladwin Hill, "A World Walt Disney Created," *NYT Magazine*, Jul. 31, 1955; Gladwin Hill, "Disneyland Reports on Its First Ten Million," Feb. 2, 1958, sec. 2, Part 2, pp. 1, 7; News Memo to Disneyland Lessees, Aug. 17, 1955, Disneyland 1954–1961 Folder, Roy O. Disney, Inter-Office Corr., Disney, Roy O.—Trips to Disneyland (1954–61), A3002; News Memo to Disneyland Lessees, Oct. 8, 1955, Disneyland Publicity Folder, Walt Disney Corr., Inter-

Office, 1956–1957, Disneyland J, A1642, WDA; "How to Make a Duck," *Time,* Jul. 29, 1957, pp. 76, 78.

537 **Ticket book.** News Memo to Disneyland Lessees, Oct. 8, 1955, Disneyland Publicity Folder, Walt Disney Corr., Inter-Office, 1956–1957, Disneyland J, A1642, WDA.

538 **Circus ambition and failure.** Walt to Gil Conlin, Mar. 9, 1960, Walt Disney Corr., 1960, C, A1581; Walt to John H. Harris (Ice Capades), Mar. 19, 1958, Harris, John, Folder, Walt Disney Corr., 1958, H-P, A1571, WDA.

538 **"it is not unique enough . . ."** Park Operations Commission, Meeting Minutes, Dec. 13, 1955, Disneyland Operations Committee Folder, Walt Disney Corr., Inter-Office, 1953–1955, D-L, A1638, WDA.

538 **Alpine Skyway.** Memo, Jack Sayers to Walt, Re: Chair Lift, Nov. 18, 1955; F. A. Picard to C. V. Wood, Dec. 1, 1955, Von Roll (Picard) Folder, Walt Disney Corr., 1956, S-Z, A1565, WDA.

538 **House of Tomorrow.** Walt to Edgar Monsanto Queeny, Dec. 2, 1955; Walt to Ralph F. Hansen (manager of market development, Monsanto), Jan. 10, 1956, Hansen to Walt, Jan. 20, 1956, Monsanto Folder, Walt Disney Corr., 1956, M-R, A1564, WDA; *Popular Science,* Apr. 1956.

538 **Cottrell's reappraisal.** Memo, Walt to Bill Cottrell, Feb. 2, 1956, Cottrell, Bill, Folder, Walt Disney Corr., Inter-Office, 1956–1957, A-Disney, A1641, WDA.

538 **Expansion.** *LAT,* May 13, 1956.

538 **Snow on Main Street.** Joe Fowler quoted in Dave Hooper, "WDW Disneyana Convention, 1992," *POV* 1, no. 2 (Winter 1992), p. 56.

538 **Fear of Wood's cadre.** France, *Window,* p. 50.

539 **Assuming duties of general manager.** Bulletin, Jan. 19, 1956, C. V. Wood, Jr., Folder, Walt Disney Corr., Inter-Office, 1953–1955, R-Z, A1640, WDA.

539 **Meeting of Disneyland Policy and Planning Committee,** Minutes of Disneyland Policy and Planning Committee, Feb. 8, 1956, Mar. 22, 1956, Apr. 17, 1956, Disneyland Policy & Planning Committee Folder, Walt Disney Corr., Inter-Office, 1956–1957, Disneyland J, A1642, WDA.

539 **"I feel what's wrong . . ."** Walt Disney interview by Martin, Reels 9 & 10, Reel 10, p. 16.

539 **"[W]e can talk something over . . ."** Ibid., p. 64.

539 **"synopsis" meeting.** Memo, Bob Sunderland to Walt, Re: Synopsis Meeting, Feb. 28, 1956, Sunderland, Bob, Folder, Walt Disney Corr., Inter-Office, 1956–1957, Sunderland-Z, A1644, WDA.

539 **"Walt says in effect, . . ."** Ben Sharpsteen, interview by Dave Smith, Oct. 21, 1974, p. 15, WDA.

540 **The conundrum.** Ben Sharpsteen, interview by Peri, Feb. 6, 1974, p. 38, WDA.

540 **"There was a general feeling of nervousness . . ."** Richard Fleischer, *Just Tell Me When to Cry: A Memoir* (New York: Carroll & Graf, 1993), p. 104.

540 **"with the total respect . . ."** Charles Shows, *Walt: Backstage Adventures with Walt Disney* (Huntington Beach, Calif.: Windsong Books International, 1979), pp. 24, 52.

540 **"Fear, in fact, . . ."** Joan Scott, "Ordeal by Disney," *Film Comment,* Dec. 1987, pp. 52, 54.

540 **"These seem to be . . ."** Memo, Ben Sharpsteen to Walt, Oct. 2, 1956, S Folder, Walt Disney Corr., Inter-Office, 1956–1957, K-Secrets, A1643, WDA.

540 **"steel springs inside a silk pillow."** Don Eddy, "The Amazing Secret of Walt Disney," *American Magazine* (Aug. 1955), p. 111.

540 **"[A]ll the dead wood . . ."** Memo, Walt to Lessing, Mar. 13, 1952, Gunther Lessing Folder, Walt Disney Corr., Inter-Office, 1945–1952, A-L, A1635, WDA.

540 **"I feel he is still on our payroll, . . ."** Memo, Walt to Bill Anderson, Feb. 3, 1956, Anderson, Bill, Folder, Walt Disney Corr., Inter-Office, 1956–1957, A-Disney, A1641, WDA.

541 **"Because of world market conditions . . ."** To Whom It May Concern, Oct. 12, 1948, J Folder, Walt Disney Corr., 1947–1948, I-M, A1538, WDA.

541 **"dead wood."** Harry Tytle, interview by author.

541 **Hal Adelquist.** Adelquist to Walt, Jul. 8, 1957, A Folder, Walt Disney Corr., 1957, A-D, A1566, WDA.

541 **Laying off Jack Kinney.** Tytle, *One of "Walt's Boys,"* pp. 142–43.

541 **"I do not believe we are justified, . . ."** Elly Horvath to Walt, Apr. 19, 1956; Walt to Mrs. E. Horvath, Apr. 23, 1956, Ho Folder, Walt Disney Corr., 1956, G-L, A1563, WDA.

541 **"In the ominous silence, . . ."** Scott, "Ordeal by Disney," p. 56.

541 **Walt and Bill Peet.** Ward Kimball, interview by Richard Hubler, May 21, 1968, pp. 25–26, WDA.

542 **"Once you get in Walt's doghouse, . . ."** Bill Peet, *Bill Peet: An Autobiography* (Boston: Houghton Mifflin, 1989), p. 158.

542 **"blasted him up one side . . ."** Fleischer, *Just Tell Me When*, p. 105.

542 **"I'm talking. . . ."** Quoted in Leonard Mosley, *Disney's World* (New York: Stein & Day, 1985), p. 240.

542 **"You have to have a humble attitude, . . ."** Tytle, *One of "Walt's Boys,"* p. 164.

542 **"You were being patted on the head . . ."** Quoted in Lawrence Edward Watkin, *Walt Disney*, unpub. ms., n.d., p. 32, WDA.

542 **"As time went on, . . ."** Quoted in Bob Thomas, *Building a Company: Roy O. Disney and the Creation of an Entertainment Empire* (New York: Hyperion, 1998), p. 3.

542 **"because they brought in people . . ."** Eric Larson, interview by Steve Hulett, Apr. 19, 1978, p. 5, WDA.

542 **"lovable genius."** Louella O. Parsons, "Walt Disney, The Lovable Genius Who Never Grew Up," *Los Angeles Examiner*, Pictorial Living Section, Jan. 9, 1955.

543 **"our wonderful life together."** Watts, *Magic Kingdom*, p. 354.

543 **"[S]he used to be provoked . . ."** Roy O. Disney, interview by Richard Hubler, Feb. 20, 1968, p. 5, WDA.

543 **"possessive."** Quoted in Hubler, *Disney*, p. 765.

543 **"Well, it keeps Walt from playing . . ."** Kimball, "Wonderful World," p. 281.

543 **Walt and the kid.** Quoted in Green and Green, *Remembering Walt*, pp. 16–17.

543 **"That situation all but caused . . ."** Walt to T. Hee, Jan. 17, 1957, He-Hn Folder, Walt Disney Corr., 1957, E-O, A1567, WDA.

543 **"attached to one of those flying saucers . . ."** Mrs. Walt Disney, as told to Isabella Taves, "I Live With a Genius," *McCall's*, Feb. 1953, p. 39.
543 **"I've always been worried. . . ."** Quoted in Hubler, *Disney*, p. 257.
544 **"You listen to your wife, huh?"** I. Klein, "Some Close-Up Shots of Walt Disney During the 'Golden Years,' " *Funnyworld*, no. 23 (Spring 1983), p. 48.
544 **"how henpecked he is."** Mrs. Walt Disney, "Genius," p. 39.
544 **"Heavens, Mother had quarrels . . ."** Hubler, *Disney*, p. 768.
544 **"In fact, she usually . . ."** Hedda Hopper, "Poppins' Success Depresses Disney," *LAT*, Jan. 1, 1965.
544 **"But how would you like . . ."** Tytle, *One of "Walt's Boys,"* p. 96.
544 **"She was sort of unconscious . . ."** Quoted in Hubler, *Disney*, p. 763.
544 **"Madam Queen."** Lillian quoted in ibid., p. 761.
544 **Diane thought** Diane Disney Miller, interview by author.
544 **"always had his arm around her."** Ibid.
544 **Rumba or mambo lesions.** Green and Green, *Remembering Walt*, p. 23.
544 **"Here's your Christmas present."** Mrs. Lillian Disney Truyens, interview by Bob Thomas, Apr. 19, 1973, Disney, Lillian, WDA.
544 **Box of radios.** Lucille Martin (secretary, NFFC Convention), Jul. 21, 2000.
545 **Daily schedule.** Dolores Voght in Hubler, *Disney*, p. 208.
545 **"He would always touch it . . ."** Quoted in Broggie, *Railroad Story*, p. 105.
545 **"ran full tilt into the side of the garage. . . ."** Quoted in Hubler, *Disney*, p. 781.
545 **"I was wearing myself out . . ."** Bill Davidson, "The Fantastic Walt Disney," *Saturday Evening Post*, Nov. 8, 1964.
545 **"I feel you take them . . ."** Walt Disney interview by Martin, Reel 11, pp. 58–59.
546 **"He was furious."** Quoted in Hubler, *Disney*, p. 546.
546 **Duchess's blanket.** Eddy, "Amazing Secret," p. 113.
546 **"always on the go."** Walt to Ruth, Dec. 5, 1951, D Folder, Walt Disney Corr., 1951–1952, A-Ch, A1544, WDA.
546 **"Heretofore with the association of only girls . . ."** Walt to Jessie Perkins, Oct. 12, 1951, Perkins, Mrs. Jessie, Folder, Walt Disney Corr., 1951–1952, N-P, A1547, WDA.
546 **Walt suggesting Diane marry Ron Miller.** Diane Disney Miller, as told to Pete Martin, "My Dad, Walt Disney," *Saturday Evening Post*, Nov. 17, 1956, p. 27.
546 **"wonderful boy . . ."** Walt to Herb Disney, Apr. 28, 1954, D Folder, Walt Disney Corr., 1953–1954, C-F, A1551, WDA. Herbert's wife Louise had died of cancer, and Herbert himself had gotten remarried just a month before Diane.
546 **Diane's wedding.** *LAT*, May 10, 1954.
546 **"Diane pulled a name . . ."** Walt to Bob Stevenson, Nov. 28, 1961, S Folder, Walt Disney Corr., Inter-Office, 1960–1964, N-Tatum, A1651, WDA.
546 **Naming Christopher.** Greene and Greene, *Man Behind the Magic*, p. 135.
546 **"custodian of his grandson."** Diane quoted in Hubler, *Disney*, p. 771.
547 **"it gets a bit hectic . . ."** Walt to Ruth, Dec. 5, 1956, B Folder, Walt Disney Corr., 1956, A-B, A1561, WDA.
547 **"[w]hat with our new granddaughter . . ."** Walt to Mrs. Tom Deane, Tracy Clinic, Tracy, John, Clinic Folder, Walt Disney Corr., 1956, S-Z, A1565, WDA.

547 **"in writing such a story . . ."** Walt to Cameron Shipp, Jun. 7, 1950, Se Folder, Walt Disney Corr., 1949–1950, R-Z, A1543, WDA.

547 **Paul Hollister.** Ted Weeks (*Atlantic Monthly*) to Walt, Mar. 30, 1955, *The Atlantic Monthly* Folder; Paul Hollister to Roy, Jul. 18, 1955, Paul Hollister Folder; Memo, Roy to Walt, Re: Paul Hollister's Manuscript MAN OR MOUSE, Nov. 10, 1955, Paul Hollister Folder; Paul Hollister to Walt, Apr. 26, 1956, Paul Hollister Folder, Walt Disney Corr., 1956, S-L, A1563, WDA.

548 **"I can't get any money . . ."** Diane quoted in Greene and Greene, *Inside the Dream*, p. 10.

548 ***The Story of Walt Disney.*** Pete Martin to Diane, Feb. 18, 1957; Walt to Ben Hibbs (editor of *Saturday Evening Post*), Oct. 2, 1956, *Sat. Eve. Post* folder, Walt Disney Corr., 1957, P-Z, A1568, WDA.

548 **"just sails through her classes."** Walt to Ruth, Dec. 8, 1947, B Folder, Walt Disney Corr., 1947–1948, A-H, A1537, WDA.

548 **"she'd rather ride horses . . ."** Ibid.

548 **"personality seemed to be hidden . . ."** Walt to Mrs. J. Burton Vasche, Mar. 9, 1954, P Folder, Walt Disney Corr., 1953–1954, P-S, A1554, WDA.

548 **"loves" it.** Walt to Perce Pearce, Feb. 15, 1955, Perce Pearce Folder, Walt Disney Corr., Inter-Office, 1953–1955, M-P, A1639, WDA.

548 **"I really just didn't like it."** Sharon Brown, interview by Richard Hubler, Jul. 9, 1968, RHC, Box 14, Folder 51.

549 **"after this one stint, . . ."** Walt to Ruth, Dec. 5, 1956, B Folder, Walt Disney Corr., 1956, A-B, A1561, WDA.

549 **So hastily arranged Roy did not attend.** Memo, Roy to Walt, Apr. 14, 1959, Disney, Roy, Folder, Walt Disney Corr., Inter-Office, 1958–1959, A-Do, A1645, WDA.

549 **"shook like a man with a fever."** Quoted in Hubler, *Disney*, p. 772.

549 **"This isn't your dance yet. . . ."** Quoted in ibid.

549 **Thelma Howard.** Duane Noriyuki, "Thelma Howard's Legacy of Hope," *LAT*, Oct. 24, 1994; "Saving Grace," *People*, Nov. 21, 1994; Greene and Greene, *Inside the Dream*, p. 136.

549 **Biff's.** Miller, "My Dad, Walt Disney," p. 132.

549 **"If it ever comes . . ."** Eddy, "Amazing Secret," p. 112.

550 **"He didn't trust women or cats."** Quoted in Hubler, *Disney*, p. 481.

550 **"great suspicion of women."** Quoted in ibid, p. 482.

550 **"more at ease with women . . ."** Paul Smith and Hazel George, interview by David Tietyen, Aug. 29, 1978, p. 41, WDA.

550 **"I love Mickey Mouse . . ."** Ward Kimball, "The Wonderful World of Walt Disney," in *You Must Remember This*, ed. Walter Wagner (New York: G. P. Putnam's Sons, 1975), p. 281.

550 **"wild time at nights."** Ken Anderson, interview by Bob Thomas, May 15, 1972, pp. 29–30, WDA.

551 **"He looked at everything."** Quoted in Green and Green, *Remembering Walt*, p. 138.

551 **"Every time I would take a mouthful . . ."** Greene and Greene, *Inside the Dream*, p. 135.

551 **Lillian and Thelma not laughing loudly enough.** Tommie Wilck, interview by Richard Hubler, Aug. 13, 1968, p. 25, WDA.

551 **Bed time.** Bill Davidson, "The Latter Day Aesop," *TV Guide*, May 27, 1960; Brown interview by Hubler.

551 **Getting up at night.** Mrs. Walt Disney, interview by Richard Hubler, Apr. 16, 1968, RHC, Box 14, Folder 52; Truyens interview by Thomas.

551 **"wouldn't get off his back."** Bob Broughton, interview by author.

551 **Four Oscars.** Patty Disney quoted in Green and Green, *Remembering Walt*, p. 19.

551 **Rehiring Phyllis Hurrell.** Wilck interview by Hubler, pp. 14–16.

551 **"Goddamn it . . ."** Milt Kahl, interview by Richard Hubler, Feb. 27, 1968, p. 21, WDA.

552 **"I don't want any publicity at all."** Walt to Mr. and Mrs. Louis Lighton, Aug. 8, 1957, L Folder, Walt Disney Corr., 1957, E-O, A1567, WDA.

552 **"[w]e were more than glad . . ."** Walt to Ruth, Dec. ?, 1957, B Folder, Walt Disney Corr., 1957, A-B, A1566, WDA.

552 **"inviolable rule . . ."** Walt to Alma Taylor, Jan. 19, 1961, T Folder, Walt Disney Corr., 1961, M-Z, A1589, WDA.

553 **"has to go on."** Quoted in Tytle, *One of "Walt's Boys,"* Sept. 17, 1953, p. 80.

553 **"something to keep . . ."** Quoted in Solomon, *Enchanted Drawings*, p. 201.

553 **Storymen importuning.** Tytle, *One of "Walt's Boys,"* p. 88.

553 **"it didn't seem possible . . ."** Wilfred Jackson, interviewed by Richard Hubler, Mar. 26, 1968, WDA.

553 **"You had to ask Walt . . ."** Quoted in Solomon, *Enchanted Drawings*, p. 194.

553 **"You're not in any trouble."** Frank Thomas quoted in John Canemaker, *Walt Disney's Nine Old Men and the Art of Animation* (New York: Disney Editions, 2001), p. 203.

553 **Prodding Walt.** Milt Kahl, interview by Christopher Finch and Linda Rosenkrantz, May 18, 1972, p. 16, WDA.

553 **"farmed-out" Memo:** Harry Tytle to Walt, Re: Progress Report, Jan. 11, 1957, Tytle, Harry, Folder, Walt Disney Corr., Inter-Office, 1956–1957, Sunderland-Z, A1644, WDA.

554 **"[w]hat the hell . . ."** Paul Smith and Hazel George, interview by David Tietyen, Aug. 29, 1978, p. 41, WDA.

554 **Reissues earned as much as 90 percent . . .** Quoted in Solomon, *Enchanted Drawings*, p. 171.

554 **"It was very modern . . ."** Quoted in John D. Ford, "An Interview with John and Faith Hubley," in *The Animated American Cartoon: A Critical Anthology*, ed. Gerald Peary and Danny Peary, (New York: E. P. Dutton, 1980), p. 190.

554 **"revolution."** John Hubley, "Evolution of a Cartoonist," *Sight and Sound*, Winter 1961–62, p. 17.

554 **Formation of Poster Service.** John Canemaker, "David Hilberman," *Cartoonist Profiles* (Dec. 1980), p. 21; Solomon, *Enchanted Drawings*, pp. 211–14; Barrier, *Hollywood Cartoons*, pp. 507–11.

555 **"our camera is closer . . ."** Barrier, *Hollywood Cartoons*, p. 512.

555 **"It was simply . . ."** Canemaker, "Hilberman," p. 19.

555 **"[O]ur approach was a painterly . . ."** Jules Engel, interview by Lawrence Wechsler and Milton Zolotow, *Los Angeles Art Community: Group Portrait*, UCLA, 1985, p. 67.

555 **"They thought they were dead."** Bill Melendez, interview by author.

555 **"Warner Bros. humor."** Bill Scott quoted in Barrier, *Hollywood Cartoons*, p. 522.

555 **"wry gimace . . ."** David Fisher, "Two Premieres: Disney and UPA," in Peary and Peary, *Animated Cartoon*, p. 180.

555 **"The big change . . ."** Quoted in Patrick McGilligan and Paul Buhle, *Tender Comrades: A Backstory of the Hollywood Blacklist* (New York: St. Martin's Press, 1997), p. 297.

556 **"may prove as resounding . . ."** Quoted in Solomon, *Enchanted Drawings*, p. 214.

556 **"new cult is forming . . ."** Fisher, "Two Premieres," pp. 178–79, 182.

556 **"There isn't enough money . . ."** Walt Disney interview by Martin, Reel 1, p. 8.

556 **"We had a lot of product . . ."** Quoted in Hubler, *Disney*, p. 237.

557 **"[E]verybody said you'll never . . ."** Ward Kimball, interview by Christopher Finch and Linda Rosenkrantz, May 10, 1972, pp. 13–14, WDA.

557 **"In style a clean steal . . ."** *Time*, Dec. 7, 1953.

557 ***Lady and the Tramp* history.** Story History of Lady, Aug. 12, 1943, Ralph Parker Folder, Walt Disney Corr., Inter-Office, 1938–1944, N-Q, A1630, WDA.

557 **"distasteful."** Memo, Joe Grant, Dick Huemer to Walt, Re: Comments on the Ward Green [*sic*] script, Oct. 5, 1943, Greene, Ward, Folder, Walt Disney Corr., 1953–1954, G-K, A1552, WDA.

557 **"Tramp."** Ward Greene, "Happy Dan, the Whistling Dog, and Miss Patsy, the Beautiful Spaniel," p. 16, ibid.

557 **"I should confine my efforts . . ."** Walt to Ward Greene, Jul. 25, 1944, King Features Syndicate Folder, Walt Disney Corr., 1951–1952, H-L, A1546, WDA.

557 **Roy encouraging *Lady*.** Memo, Roy to Walt, Re: Lady, May 20, 1952, Disney, Roy, Folder, Walt Disney Corr., Inter-Office, 1953–1955, D-L, A1638, WDA.

557 ***Lady* missing date.** Memo, Bill Anderson to Walt, Re: Production Status Report, Mar. 1, 1954, Bill Anderson Folder, Walt Disney Corr., Inter-Office, 1953–1955, A-C, A1637, WDA.

558 **"tackled the project . . ."** Quoted in Hubler, *Disney*, p. 435.

558 **"our most ambitious cartoon feature, to date."** Walt to Dodie Smith, Dec. 19, 1957, Si Folder, Walt Disney Corr., 1957, P-Z, A1568, WDA.

558 **"Make them [the characters] as real . . ."** Quoted in Leonard Maltin, *The Disney Films*, 3rd ed. (New York: Hyperion, 1995), p. 156.

558 **"When I first saw his stuff, . . ."** Quoted in John Canemaker, *Before the Animation Begins: The Art and Lives of Disney Inspirational Sketch Artists* (New York: Hyperion, 1996), p. 162.

558 **"I had to fight myself . . ."** Quoted in ibid, p. 160.

558 **"moving illustration, . . ."** Eric Larson, interview by Thorkil Rasmussen, Feb. 22, 1978, p. 6, WDA.

558 **Didn't care how long it took.** Eric Larson to Mike Barrier, Oct. 27, 1976, quoted in Canemaker, *Nine Old Men*, pp. 74–75.

559 **"overall story board discussion."** Memo, Ken Peterson to Walt, Re: Sleeping Beauty, Feb. 25, 1955, Ken Peterson Folder, Walt Disney Corr., Inter-Office, 1953–1955, M-P, A1639, WDA.

559 **"He wouldn't have story meetings."** Milt Kahl, interview by Bob Thomas, May 14, 1973, p. 2, WDA.

559 **Staff and trainees.** Memo, Ken Peterson to Walt, Re: Casting Report, May 23, 1955, ibid.

559 **Half as quickly.** Memo, Harry Tytle to Walt, Re: Cartoon Production, Mar. 30, 1956, Tytle, Harry, Folder, Walt Disney Corr., Inter-Office, 1956–1957, Sunderland-Z, A1644, WDA.

559 **By January 1957 . . .** Memo, Ken Peterson to Walt, Re: Sleeping Beauty, Jan. 30, 1957, P Folder, Walt Disney Corr., Inter-Office, 1957, K-Secrets, A1643, WDA.

559 **Budget of the film had soared.** Tytle, *One of "Walt's Boys,"* p. 41.

559 **"[Y]ou had to do . . ."** Don Bluth quoted in Canemaker, *Nine Old Men*, p. 75.

559 **"a noticeable, marked difference."** Tytle, *One of "Walt's Boys,"* p. 219.

559 **Dick Huemer agreed.** Huemer, *Recollections*, pp. 154–55.

559 **"ringmaster directing . . ."** Peet, *Autobiography*, p. 150.

559 **"They measured the width of the line . . ."** Don Bluth to John Canemaker, Dec. 2, 1998, quoted in Canemaker, *Nine Old Men*, p. 75.

560 **Red blotch.** Ibid., p. 196.

560 **"downfall."** Ibid., p. 73.

560 **"Will be a bonanza . . ."** Memo, Card Walker to Walt, Re: Sleeping Beauty, Non-Critical, Apr. 11, 1957, ARI Reports, Walt Disney Corr., Inter-Office, 1956–1957, A-Disney, A1641, WDA.

560 **[I]t got monotonous."** Ben Sharpsteen, interview by Don Peri, Mar. 5, 1975, p. 12, WDA.

560 **Dick Huemer thought it was Walt's lack of involvement.** Quoted in Hubler, *Disney*, p. 486.

560 **"how heavy the animation was . . ."** Milt Kahl, interview by Mica Prods., Nov. 3, 1983, WDA, Reel 6, p. 15.

560 **$900,000 loss.** Memo, Roy to Walt, Re: Year-end Closings, Oct. 7, 1960, Disney, Roy, Folder, Walt Disney Corr., Inter-Office, 1960–1964, A-Disney Aircraft, A1648, WDA.

560 **Loyalty oaths.** Barrier, *Hollywood Cartoons*, pp. 533–34.

560 **Union harassment.** Melendez interview.

561 **One producer had a dictum . . .** John Canemaker, *Felix: The Twisted Tale of the World's Most Famous Cat* (New York: DaCapo Press, 1996), p. 150.

561 **"secret weapon."** Joseph Barbera, *My Life in 'toons: From Flatbush to Bedrock in Under a Century* (Atlanta: Turner Publishing, 1994), p. 115.

ELEVEN || Slouching Toward Utopia

562 **Earnings per share.** Michael Gordon, "Disney's Land," *Wall Street Journal*, Feb. 4, 1958, p. 1.

562 **"Sales and net profits have enjoyed . . ."** George Adamy (portfolio adviser), "Walt Disney Prods.," A Folder, Delafield and Delafield, Sept. 1958, Walt Disney Corr., 1958, A-C, A1569, WDA.

562 **"[w]ring every possible profitable squeal . . ."** Gordon, "Disney's Land," pp. 1, 12.

563 **Income breakdown.** Adamy, "Walt Disney Prods."

563 **Merging and revamping.** Memo, Roy to Walt, Oct. 7, 1960, Walt Disney, 1955–1961 Folder, Roy O. Disney Inter-Office Corr., Disney, Roy O.—Trips to Disneyland (1954–61), A3002, WDA.

563 **$70 million in revenue.** Memo, Mel Melton to Walt, Re: Financial Highlights, Dec. 5, 1961, M Folder, Walt Disney Corr., Inter-Office, 1960–1964, Herald-M, A1650, WDA.

563 **"For the first time . . ."** Art Buchwald, "The Banks Owe Disney Now," *New York Herald Tribune*, Sept. 17, 1961.

563 **ABC renewals.** Contract, Jan. 15, 1957, American Broadcasting Co. Folder, Walt Disney Corr., 1957, A-D, A1566, WDA.

563 **"which will be unequaled . . ."** Tel. Walt to K. G. Manuel, (vice-president of AC Sparkplugs), May 20, 1957, G Folder, Walt Disney Corr., 1957, E-O, A1567, WDA.

563 **"Walt's finely focused intensity . . ."** Robert B. Sherman and Richard H. Sherman, *Walt's Time: From Before to Beyond*, ed. Bruce Gordon, David Mumford, and Jeff Kurtti (Santa Clarita, Calif.: Camphor Tree Publishers, 1998), p. 13.

563 **Walt and the Z.** "A Disney Animator Looks Back," *Disney News*, Fall 1985, p. 25.

564 **"will never be finished."** Walt Disney, interview by Pete Martin, Reels 9 & 10, p. 69.

564 **"my baby."** Gereon Zimmerman, "Walt Disney: Giant at the Fair," *Look*, Feb. 11, 1964, p. 32.

564 **"working, planning and developing it."** Walt to Mrs. Max Hill, Dec. 1, 1961, A Folder, Walt Disney Corr., 1961, A-Christmas, A1586, WDA.

564 **"getting out of the hole."** Anne K. Okey, "Jack Lindquist," *Disney News*, Summer 1993, p. 41.

564 **$5.5 million expansion.** Memo, Ed Ettinger to Walt, Re: Press Meeting-Thursday, Dec. 4, 1958, Dec. 2, 1958, Ed Ettinger Folder, Walt Disney Corr., Inter-Office, 1958–1959, Dover-M, A1646, WDA.

564 **"And Walt got all the way up . . ."** Marc Davis, interview by Bob Thomas, May 25, 1973, p. 23, WDA.

564 **Liberty Street.** Karal Ann Marling, "Imagineering the Disney Theme Parks," in *Designing Disney's Theme Parks: The Architecture of Reassurance*, ed. Karal Ann Marling (New York: Flammarion, 1997), p. 90; Paul F. Anderson, "A Great Big Beautiful Tomorrow: Walt Disney & World's Fairs," *POV*, no. 6–7 (1995), p. 60; Memo, Bill Mahoney to Those Listed, Re: Liberty Street, Feb. 11, 1959, Bill Mahoney Folder, Walt Disney Corr., Inter-Office, 1958–1959, Dover-M, A1646, WDA.

564 **Costumed characters.** Memo, Tommy Walker to Dick Irvine, Re: Disney Characters Project, Mar. 22, 1961, Disneyland 1954–1961 Folder, Roy O. Disney, Inter-Office Corr, Disney, Roy O.—Trips to Disneyland (1954–61), A3002, WDA. It was more synergy that animator Bill Justice was asked to help design the costumes.

564 **a $7 million expansion.** *NYT*, Feb. 8, 1962, p. 19.

565 **Buying additional land.** Memo, Jack C. Sayers to Walt, Re: Property Around Disneyland, Aug. 7, 1956, Memo, Fred Schumacher to Jack Sayers, Re: Land Acquisition Program, Oct. 28, 1957, Jack Sayers Folder, Walt Disney Corr.,

Inter-Office, 1956–1957, K-Secrets, A1643; Price to Walt, Nov. 18, 1957, P-Q folder, Walt Disney Corr., 1957, P-Z, A1568, WDA.

565 **"You never know when you'll bump . . ."** Kevin Wallace, "The Engineering of Ease," *The New Yorker*, Sept. 7, 1963, p. 106.

565 **"We looked forward to Disneyland . . ."** *NYT*, Nov. 13, 1961.

565 **"I am told that in Indonesia . . ."** John Foster Dulles to Walt, Jun. 19, 1956, Do Folder, Walt Disney Corr., 1956, A-B, A1561, WDA.

565 **One African president . . .** *LAT*, Jun. 23, 1960.

565 **Mrs. Khrushchev's request.** *NYT*, Sept. 22, 1959, p. 16.

566 **Khrushchev's anger.** *NYT*, Sept. 20, 1959, p. 1.

566 **"If you want to go on with the arms race, . . ."** Harrison Salisbury, "Premier Angered," *NYT*, Sept. 20, 1959, p. 1.

566 **"deprived of the pleasure . . ."** *NYT*, Sept. 22, 1959, p. 21.

566 **Milestone Award.** *NYT*, Oct. 25, 1956, p. 39; *LAT*, Feb. 18, 1957.

566 **Olympics.** *NYT*, Nov. 5, 1958, p. 50; *NYT*, Nov. 26, 1959, p. 58.

566 **President's Committee on Education.** *NYT*, Apr. 20, 1956; Walt to Shane McCarthy (executive director of the President's Council on Youth Fitness), Apr. 18, 1957, P-Q Folder, Walt Disney Corr., 1957, P-Z, A1568, WDA.

567 **People to People.** *NYT*, Nov. 9, 1961, p. 1.

567 **Tullytown, Pennsylvania.** Clipping, "School to Be Named for Walt Disney," [1953,] T Folder, Walt Disney Corr., 1953–1954, T-Z, A1555, WDA. It was dedicated on Sept. 25, 1955.

567 **Honorary degrees.** Richard G. Hubler, *Walt Disney*, unpub. ms., 1968, p. 22, RHC; *LAT*, Jun. 3, 1963.

567 **Museum of Modern Art.** Richard Griffith to Walt, Nov. 11, 1957, and Card Walker to Richard Griffith, Nov. 26, 1957, Me-Mz Folder, Walt Disney Corr., 1957, E-O, A1567, WDA.

567 **Nobel Prize campaign.** Lillian Gish to Walt, Jul. 27, 1962, G Folder, Walt Disney Corr., 1962, Committees—H (Misc.), A1591, WDA.

567 **Fires.** Walt to Bob Stevenson, Nov. 28, 1961, S Folder, Walt Disney Corr., Inter-Office, 1960–1964, N-Tatum, A1651, WDA.

567 **"magnetic field."** Ken Anderson, interview by Bob Thomas, May 15, 1973, p. 1, WDA.

567 **"His eyes are dull . . ."** Edith Efron, "Still Attacking His Ancient Enemy—Conformity," *TV Guide*, Jul. 17, 1965, p. 11.

567 **"unearthly quality."** Jack Alexander, "The Amazing Story of Walt Disney," *Saturday Evening Post*, Oct. 31, 1953, p. 84.

568 **Mercedes.** Ivan Stauffer to Walt, May 26, 1965, S Folder, Walt Disney Corr., N-S, A1611, WDA.

568 **"out cuss a drunken pirate!"** Charles Shows, *Walt: Backstage Adventures with Walt Disney* (Huntington Beach, Calif.: Windsong Books International, 1979), pp. 71–72.

568 **Young Walt Disney's eyes.** Clipping, Maria Winn, "Front Views and Profiles," *Chicago Tribune* [Aug. 1943], Wi Folder, Walt Disney Corr., 1942–1943, T-Z, A1530, WDA; Henry F. Pringle, "Mickey Mouse's Father," *McCall's*, Aug. 1932, p. 28.

568 **"bright."** Quoted in Amy Boothe Green and Howard E. Green, *Remembering Walt: Favorite Memories of Walt Disney* (New York: Hyperion, 1999), p. 60.

568 **"kind of cheerful merriment . . ."** Ibid., p. 76.

568 **"appeared to be under the lash . . ."** Aubrey Menen, "Dazzled in Disneyland," *Holiday*, Jul. 1963.

568 **"I function better . . ."** Van Arsdale France, *Window on Main Street: 35 Years of Creating Happiness at Disneyland Park* (Nashua, N.H.: Laughter Publications, 1991), p. 33.

568 **"I've got to have a project . . ."** Ollie Johnston, interview by Christopher Finch and Linda Rosenkrantz, Jun. 2, 1972, p. 27, WDA.

568 **"there are only a certain number . . ."** Robert Kintner to Walt, Feb. 23, 1956, ABC—Robert E. Kintner Folder, Walt Disney Corr., 1956, A-B, A1561, WDA.

568 ***Zorro* problems.** Tel. Card Walker to Leonard Goldenson, Jul. 10, 1957, Walker, Card, Folder, Walt Disney Corr., Inter-Office, 1956–1957, Sunderland-Z, A1644, WDA.

568 **Pressure for Westerns.** Walt Disney interview by Martin, Reels 1 & 2, p. 17.

568 **"approximately one hour of your time."** Memo, Card Walker to Walt, Re: Meeting on *Walt Disney Presents*, Jul. 27, 1959, Card Walker Folder, Walt Disney Corr., Inter-Office, 1958–1959, N-Z, A1647, WDA.

569 **Roy's proposals.** Memo, Roy to Walt, Re: ABC Contracts, Feb. 20, 1959, ABC—General Folder, Walt Disney Corr., 1959, A-Ca, A1573, WDA.

569 **"I think they are a bunch . . ."** Ibid.

569 **"In all common sense . . ."** Memo, Roy to Walt, Re: Leonard Goldenson, Jun. 19, 1959, Walt Disney, 1955–1961 Folder, Roy O. Disney, Inter-Office Corr., Disney, Roy O.—Trips to Disneyland (1954–61), A3002, WDA.

569 **"it seems to us you are not as eager . . ."** Roy to Leonard Goldenson, Mar. 27, 1959, ABC—General Folder, Walt Disney Corr., 1959, A-Ca, A1573, WDA.

569 **"[M]y brother figured, . . ."** Quoted in France, *Window*, p. 79.

569 **"[D]o what you think's necessary."** Roy Disney, interview by Richard G. Hubler, Jun. 18, 1968, RHC, Box 14, Folder 52.

569 **ABC buyout.** Memo, Roy, Re: ABC Case, Jun. 6, 1960, A Folder, Walt Disney Corr., 1960, A-B, A1580, WDA.

570 **"drift."** Tel. Card Walker and Donn Tatum to Walt (in London), Aug. 11, 1960, National Broadcasting Co. Folder, Walt Disney Corr., 1960, N-O, A1584, WDA.

570 **"get this deal."** Quoted in Katherine Greene and Richard Greene, *Inside the Dream: The Personal Story of Walt Disney* (New York: Roundtable Press, 2001), p. 118.

570 **NBC deal.** *Variety*, Dec. 2, 1960.

570 **"most important and far-reaching . . ."** *Variety*, Aug. 10, 1960.

570 **"I shouldn't have listened."** Cecil Smith, "Disney's New Magic Wand," *LAT*, Aug. 20, 1961.

570 **"I never saw such an overnight change . . ."** Anonymous quoted in Bill Davidson, "The Latter-Day Aesop," *TV Guide*, May 20, 1961.

570 **"Newton Minow can relax."** *New York Herald Tribune*, Sept. 25, 1961.

571 **Selling televisions.** Card Walker to Walt, [Sept. 1961,] Walt Disney Folder, Walt Disney Corr., 1961, Comm. to Disneyland, A1587, WDA; Memo, Card Walker to Roy/Walt, Oct. 5, 1961, Card Walker, 1960–62 Folder, Walt Disney Corr., Inter-Office, 1960–1964, Tryon-Z, A1652, WDA.

571 **"whole atmosphere is pleasing . . ."** Memo, Roy to Walt, Re: TELEVISION,

Nov. 15, 1961, Walt Disney, 1955–1961 Folder, Roy O. Disney, Inter-Office, Corr., Disney, Roy O.—Trips to Disneyland (1954–61), A3002, WDA.

571 **"You know, Rush, . . ."** Rush Johnson, interview by author.

571 **Farm in Ellis, Kansas.** "Walt and His Philosophy," interview by Fletcher Markle (CBCS), *ReView*, Jan. 1978, p. 81.

571 **Child care centers.** William F. Brandt (director of public relations, Bozell & Jacobs) to Walt, Mar. 21, 1957; Card Walker to Walt, Apr. 22, 1957, B Folder, Walt Disney Corr., 1957, A-D, A1566, WDA.

571 **Arrow Development stake.** Memo, Bill Cottrell to Walt, Re: Progress Report—WED, Mar. 15, 1960, Harrison Price Folder, Walt Disney Corr., Inter-Office, 1960–1964, N-Tatum, A1651, WDA.

572 **Relocating the train and building convention center.** Memo, Edsel Curry to Walt, Re: Relocation of Viewliner—Newport Dunes, Dec. 18, 1958; Memo, Curry to Walt, Re: WED Projects, Aug. 20, 1958, Co Folder, Walt Disney Corr., Inter-Office, 1958–1959, A-Do, A1645, WDA.

572 **Smoke Tree development.** Memo, Bob Clark to Walt, Re: Smoke Tree Development Program, Feb. 7, 1958; Memo, Edsel Curry to Walt, Re: Plot Plan—Smoke Tree Frontage Property, Dec. 29, 1958, Smoke Tree Ranch—1958 Folder, Walt Disney Corr., 1958, Q-Z, A1572, WDA; Walt to board of directors, Smoke Tree Ranch, Nov. 11, 1963, Smoke Tree Folder, Walt Disney Corr., 1963, O-Z, A1598, WDA.

572 **$277,000 stock interest.** Memo, Dolores [Voght] to Walt, Aug. 25, 1961, Walt Disney Folder, Walt Disney Corr., 1961, Comm. to Disneyland, A1587, WDA.

572 **"We wasted a million dollars . . ."** Quoted in Hubler, *Disney*, p. 734.

572 **"The data pointed out a crying need . . ."** Quoted in ibid., pp. 439–40.

572 **"government looks favorably . . ."** Memo, Buzz Price to Mickey Clark, Re: Mammoth, Jun. 25, 1963, Harrison Price Folder, Walt Disney Corr., Inter-Office, 1960–1964, N-Tatum, A1651, WDA.

572 **Mineral King.** Harrison Price to Hon. Hugh M. Burns, California Senate, Nov. 29, 1963, ibid.

573 **Aspen.** Draft, An Analysis of Development Opportunities in Aspen, Colorado, n.d., Aspen Development Opportunities Folder, Walt Disney Corr., Special Projects, 1961–1965, Aspen-Hallmark, A1660, WDA; Bob Hicks (ERA) to Walt, Jan. 18, 1963, Harrison Price Folder, Walt Disney Corr., Inter-Office, 1960–1964, N-Tatum, A1651, WDA.

573 **"I am so excited . . ."** Jules Stein to Walt, March 3, 1959, St Folder, Walt Disney Corr., 1959, Sp-Z, A1579, WDA.

573 **Vacation Village.** Memo, Jack Sayers to Those Concerned, Re: Monterey Project, Jun. 3, 1963, Jack Sayers Folder, Walt Disney Corr., Inter-Office, 1960–1964, N-Tatum, A1651, WDA.

573 **Hallmark development.** Richard Irvine to J. C. Hall, Oct. 19, 1962; Buzz Price to Irvine, Nov. 20, 1962; Price to Irvine, Mar. 6, 1963; Hallmark Project Folder, Walt Disney Corr., Special Projects, 1961–1965, Aspen-Hallmark, A1660, WDA.

573 **Niagara Falls.** Memo, Card [Walker] to Walt/Roy, Sept. 25, 1963, Niagara Falls Projects Folder, Walt Disney Corr., Special Projects, 1961–1965, New York-Pratt, A1662, WDA.

573 **City of the Arts.** "The Walt Disney Seven Arts City," WED Enterprises,

Inc., [1958,] Chouinard Folder, Walt Disney Corr., 1958, A-C, A1569, WDA; "Seven Arts City," n.d., Chouinard—City of Arts Folder, Walt Disney Corr., 1959, Ch-De, A1574, WDA; Memo, Harrison A. Price to Walt, Re: Lincoln Center, May 5, 1960, Harrison Price Folder, Walt Disney Corr., Inter-Office, 1960–1964, N-Tatum. A1651, WDA.

574 **"one entire village . . ."** Walt to William Pereira, May 13, 1960, Chouinard—City of Arts Folder, Walt Disney Corr., 1960, C, A1581, WDA.

574 **Nabisco cartoon.** Memo, Roy to Walt, Re: National Biscuit Picture, Jul. 25, 1938, Inter-Office Corr., Walt Disney Corr., 1938–1939, I-Me, A1517, WDA.

574 **"something that will impress . . ."** Robert Warner to Walt, Jan. 17, 1957, B Folder, Walt Disney Corr., 1957, A–D, A1566, WDA.

574 **"hit not only of the American Pavillion . . ."** Ralph Adams to Jack Sayers, May 5, 1958, Jack Sayers—1958 Folder, Walt Disney Corr., 1958–1959, N-Z, A1647; Robert Warner to Dolores Voght, Apr. 19, 1958, Bob Warner Folder, Walt Disney Corr., 1959, Sp-Z, A1579, WDA.

574 **Moscow Fair.** Anthony Guarco (acting director, Motion Picture Services USIA) to Walt, Aug. 18, 1959, U.S. Government Folder, ibid.

575 **Meeting with Moses.** Memo, Sayers to Those Concerned, Aug. 15, 1960, Jack Sayers 1960–62 Folder, Walt Disney Corr., Inter Office, 1960–1964, N-Tatum, A1651, WDA.

575 **Meeting executives of companies.** Memo, Jack Sayers to Those Concerned, Jul. 25, 1960, Walt Disney, 1955–61 Folder, Roy O. Disney, Inter-Office Corr., Disney, Roy O.—Trips to Disneyland (1954–61), A3002, WDA.

575 **Jack Sayers's touring.** Memo, Jack Sayers to Those Concerned, Dec. 23, 1960, Jack Sayers 1960–62 Folder, Walt Disney Corr., Inter-Office, 1960–1964, N-Tatum, A1651, WDA.

575 **Ford and GE.** Memo, Jack Sayers to Those Concerned, Re: General Electric, Sept. 22, 1960, ibid.

575 **"It will help us. . . ."** Quoted in Green and Green, *Remembering Walt*, pp. 169–70.

575 **Bill Cottrell's analysis.** Bill Cottrell, interview by Jay Horan, Aug.-Oct. 1983, p. 51, WDA.

575 **"trial balloon."** Quoted in Paul F. Anderson, "A Great Big Beautiful Tomorrow: Walt Disney & World's Fairs," *POV*, no. 6–7 (1995), p. 30.

576 **A series of underground wheels.** Ibid., pp. 32–33.

576 **Ford demonstration.** Ibid., p. 41.

576 **GE budget.** Tel. Dick Irvine and Jack Sayers to Walt, Sept. 1, 1961, Walt Disney Folder, Walt Disney Corr., 1961, Comm. to Disneyland, A1587, WDA.

576 **"Don't you think you might have asked . . ."** Cottrell interview by Horan, pp. 43–45.

577 **GE rejecting historical approach.** William Cottrell to James Weldy (GE), Aug. 2, 1962, General Electric Folder, Walt Disney Corr., Special Projects, 1961–1965, Aspen-Hallmark, A1660, WDA.

577 **"I spent my whole life . . ."** Anderson, "Great Big," p. 63.

577 **"All right, gentlemen, what I want . . ."** Jack Spiers quoted in Green and Green, *Remembering Walt*, p. 174.

577 **"refrigerator show."** Quoted in Randy Bright, *Disneyland: The Inside Story* (New York: Harry N. Abrams, 1987), p. 176.

577 **Walt climbing the stage.** Anderson, "Great Big," pp. 65–66.

577 **Jumping into the tub.** Ibid., p. 68.

577 **"Walt had his foot in everything."** Ibid., p. 69.

577 **"There was more of Walt . . ."** Ibid., p. 68.

578 **Meeting with Department of Commerce.** Charles Luckman to Walt, Oct. 2, 1962; George Rothwell to Roy, Sept. 17, 1962, New York World's Fair Folder, Walt Disney Corr., 1962, Helen-N, A1592, WDA.

578 **Monorail.** Anderson, "Great Big," pp. 109–10.

578 ***One Nation Under God* showings and reaction.** Memo, Jack Sayers to Those Concerned, Re: One Nation Under God Presentation, Jun. 7, 1961, Jack Sayers 1960–62 Folder, Walt Disney Corr., Inter-Office, 1960–1964, N-Tatum, A1651; Marvin Stone (director, Industrial Section, New York World's Fair), Jun. 13, 1961; Memo, Sayers to Those Concerned, Re: "One Nation Under God," Jul. 31, 1962, New York World's Fair Folder, Walt Disney Corr., 1962, Helen-N, A1592. WDA.

578 **Moses's lobbying.** Anderson, "Great Big," pp. 89–90.

578 **"too important to the Fair . . ."** Ibid., p. 90.

578 **"I'd like to not be able . . ."** Ibid., p. 61.

579 **Chinatown.** Memo, Dick Irvine to Walt, Re: Notes on Chinatown Meeting of Oct. 1, Oct. 2, 1959, Audio-Animatronics Folder, WDA.

579 **Coining *Audio-Animatronics*.** Memo, David Mumford to Dave Smith, Re: Origin of "Audio-Animatronics," Mar. 20, 1985, ibid.

579 **Ub Iwerks erected head.** Ken Anderson in Jay Horan, *Video Interview with Ken Anderson, Bill Cottrell and Herb Ryman*, Sept. 19, 1983, p. 47, WDA.

579 **"you can't have human beings . . ."** Herb Ryman in ibid., pp. 49–50.

579 **Reading about Lincoln.** Jack Alexander, "The Amazing Story of Walt Disney," *Saturday Evening Post*, Oct. 31, 1953.

579 **"It was all right for you . . ."** Norris Leap, "Disney Has One Success Secret," *LAT*, Sept. 25, 1960.

579 **"It seemed that we were getting into areas . . ."** Blaine Gibson quoted in Bright, *Inside Story*, p. 172.

579 **"We're making the legend of Pygmalion . . ."** Hubler, *Disney*, p. 33.

579 **"and cocked his eyebrow, . . ."** Quoted in Anderson, "Great Big," p. 92.

580 **Buying patent.** Memo, Neal E. McClure to Walt, Re: Audio-Animatronics, Jun. 14, 1962, Mc Folder, Walt Disney Corr., Inter-Office, 1960–1964, Herald-M, A1650, WDA.

580 **"All we have to do . . ."** Murray Schumach, "Disney Animation Uses Polaris Tape," *NYT*, Jun. 20, 1963, p. 30.

580 **"weigh half as much . . ."** Anderson, "Great Big," p. 88.

580 **Rising Lincoln.** Memo, Irvine to Walt, Re: Status Report, Jul. 19, 1961, Dick Irvine Folder, Walt Disney Corr., Inter-Office, 1960–1964, Herald-M, A1650, WDA.

580 **Secret room.** Neil Gallagher (machinist) quoted in Anderson, "Great Big," p. 87.

580 **Moses at the studio.** Memo, Dick Irving–Jack Sayers to Walt, Re: Mr. Moses' Visit, Apr. 23, 1962, New York World's Fair Folder, Walt Disney Corr., 1962, Helen-N, A1592; Bright, *Inside Story*, pp. 169–70.

581 **"overwhelmed."** Anderson, "Great Big," pp. 90–91.

581 **"look with great favor . . ."** Memo, Jack Sayers to Those Concerned, Apr.

18, 1963, Fair Projects Folder, Walt Disney Corr., Special Projects, 1961–1965, Aspen-Hallmark, A1660, WDA.

581 **Commission convened and negotiations.** Memo, Jack Sayers to Those Concerned, May 20, 1963, Jack Sayers Folder, Walt Disney Corr., Inter-Office, 1960–1964, N-Tatum, A1651; Memo, Fred Schumacher (projects manager) to Card Walker, Re: Lincoln Figure, Jul. 29, 1963, Illinois Exhibit for New York Fair Folder, Walt Disney Corr., Special Projects, 1961–1965, Illinois-National, A1661, WDA.

581 **"best business proposition . . ."** Tel. Walt to Moses, Jul. 26, 1963, ibid.

581 **Criticisms.** Jack Mabley, *Chicago's American*, Nov. 4, 1963.

581 **"Imagine you're in the presence . . ."** *Chicago Daily News*, Nov. 20, 1963.

582 **"I'll make those decisions."** Bright, *Inside Story*, p. 177.

582 **"one more piece of real estate."** Quoted in Anderson, "Great Big," p. 99.

582 **"It's a small world . . ."** Quoted in ibid., p. 105.

582 **Mobilization.** Karal Ann Marling, "Imagineering the Disney Theme Parks," in *Designing Disney's Theme Parks: The Architecture of Reassurance*, ed. Karal Ann Marling (New York: Flammarion, 1997), p. 132; Anderson, "Great Big," p. 99.

583 **"We would put Walt . . ."** Quoted in Anderson, "Great Big," p. 107.

583 **"You know, Bill . . ."** Bill Peet, *Bill Peet: An Autobiography* (Boston: Houghton Mifflin, 1989), p. 172.

583 **Delegating more responsibility.** Robert De Roos, "The Magic Worlds of Walt Disney," *National Geographic*, Aug. 1963.

583 **"They won't be able to handle it, . . ."** Quoted in Leonard Mosley, *Disney's World* (New York: Stein & Day, 1985), p. 276.

583 **Adding third soundstage.** Minutes of Special Meeting of Board of Directors, Apr. 3, 1953, Walt Disney Productions—Board Meeting Folder, Walt Disney Corr., Inter-Office, 1953–1955, D-L, A1638, WDA; Paul Hollister, *Man or Mouse: The Story of Walt Disney, So Far*, unpub. ms., 1955, chap. 17, p. 3, WDA. Hollister puts the cost at $600,000.

583 **Studio expansion.** Michael Gordon, "Disney's Land," *Wall Street Journal*, Feb. 4, 1958, p. 12.

583 **Golden Oak Ranch.** *LAT*, Apr. 9, 1959; Memo, Dick Pfahler to Those Concerned, Mar. 2, 1964, P Folder, Walt Disney Corr., Inter-Office, 1960–1964, N-Tatum, A1651, WDA.

584 **Firing Ward Kimball.** Marc Davis to Robin Allan, Jun. 11, 1985 in John Canemaker, *Walt Disney's Nine Old Men and the Art of Animation* (New York: Disney Editions, 2001), p. 121.

584 **"I'm the boss of everything . . ."** DeRoos, "Magic Worlds."

584 **"I'm not the perfectionist anymore."** *Baltimore News-Post*, May 1959, in " 'Disney's No Comic Character': Burris Jenkins in Disneyland," *The E Ticket*, Fall 2002, p. 40.

584 **"It was run from the top down . . ."** Shows, *Backstage Adventures*, p. 75.

585 **"Walt would never let any person get in . . ."** Quoted in Hubler, *Disney*, p. 413.

585 **"I think he is a find."** Memo: Walt to Bill Anderson, Jun. 29, 1956, Bill Anderson Folder, Walt Disney Corr., Inter-Office, 1956, A1641, WDA.

585 **Discovering Hayley Mills.** Bill Anderson, interview by Bob Thomas, May 17, 1973, WDA.

586 **"His live movies have become . . ."** Dr. Max Rafferty, "The Greatest Pedagogue of Them All," *LAT*, Apr. 19, 1965.

586 **Grosses.** Memo, Card [Walker] to Walt: Re: Doris Day Pictures, May 29, 1962, Card Walker, 1961–62 Folder, Walt Disney Corr., Inter-Office, 1960–1964, Tryon-Z, A1652, WDA.

586 **"one of the funniest . . ."** Tel. Walt to Russell Downing, Radio City Music Hall, Sept. 28, 1960, D Folder, Walt Disney Corr., 1960, D-H, A1582, WDA.

586 **Crying at *Pollyanna*.** Quoted in Mosley, *Disney's World*, p. 260.

586 **"Our part in things . . ."** "The World of Walt Disney," *Newsweek*, Dec. 31, 1962, p. 48.

587 **"We're making corn, Peter."** Quoted in Green and Green, *Remembering Walt*, p. 99.

587 **"These avant garde artists . . ."** Efron, "Still Attacking," p. 13.

587 **"infinite possibilities."** Richard Schickel, *The Disney Version: The Life, Times, Art and Commerce of Walt Disney*, 3rd ed. (1968; repr., Chicago: Elephant Paperbacks, 1997), pp. 306–7, 94.

587 **"I feel that wit . . ."** Bill Roberts to Walt, Apr. 27, 1960, R Folder, Walt Disney Corr., 1960, P-Z, A1585, WDA.

587 **"they have had the opportunity . . ."** Tel. Bill Anderson to Walt, Jun. 5, 1963, Bill Anderson Folder, Walt Disney Corr., Inter-Office, 1960–1964, A-Disney Aircraft, A1648, WDA.

587 **"I do not want my name attached . . ."** Tel. Walt to William Anderson, Apr. 23, 1962, Mills, John, and Family Folder, Walt Disney Corr., 1965, K-M, A1610, WDA.

587 **"That's the kind of film . . ."** Ron Miller quoted in Katherine Greene and Richard Greene, *Inside the Dream: The Personal Story of Walt Disney* (New York: Roundtable Press, 2001), p. 137.

587 **"it set me to thinking . . ."** Memo, Walt to Roy, May 31, 1963, Roy Disney Folder, Walt Disney Corr., Inter-Office, 1960–1964, A-Disney Aircraft, A1648, WDA.

588 **"a lot of yelling and screaming . . ."** Quoted in Bob Thomas, *Building a Company: Roy O. Disney and the Creation of an Entertainment Empire* (New York: Hyperion, 1998), p. 256; Ron Miller, interview by author.

588 **"I tried to explain . . ."** Ibid., p. 257.

588 **Pancake House.** Anderson, *Hollywood TV*, p. 36.

588 **"Nobody had to ask anyone . . ."** Quoted in Greene and Greene, *Inside the Dream*, p. 131.

589 **Monies paid in fiscal year 1960.** *Variety*, Apr. 18, 1961.

589 **Negotiating with Loyd Wright.** Memo, Roy to Walt, Re: Your Personal Contract with W.D.P., Nov. 11, 1960, Roy Disney Folder, Walt Disney Corr., Inter-Office, 1960–1964, A-Disney Aircraft, A1648, WDA.

589 **"You could hear them . . ."** Quoted in Hubler, *Disney*, p. 459.

589 **Car door slam.** Quoted in Thomas, *Building a Company*, p. 161.

589 **"We work for years . . ."** Jimmy Johnson, *Inside the Whimsy Works: My Thirty-Seven Years with Walt Disney Productions*, unpub. ms., 1975, chap. 1, p. 2, WDA.

589 **"Roy's great ambition in life, . . ."** Quoted in Greene and Greene, *Man Behind the Magic*, p. 70.

589 **"striving father, . . ."** Harry Tytle, *One of "Walt's Boys": An Insider's Account of*

Disney's Golden Years (Royal Oak, Mich.: Airtight Seals Allied Productions, 1997), p. 14.

590 **"Walt would tell him, . . ."** Walter Pfeiffer, interview by Bob Thomas, Apr. 26, 1973, WDA.

590 **Rivalry between Roy E. and Ron Miller.** Tytle, *One of "Walt's Boys,"* p. 19.

590 **"That was the first time . . ."** Quoted in Thomas, *Building a Company*, p. 261.

590 **"None of us would be here . . ."** Ibid., p. 262.

591 **Terms of contracts.** *Variety*, Apr. 18, 1961.

591 **"It is wonderful to smoke . . ."** Walt to Roy, Jun. 24, 1961, D Folder, Walt Disney Corr., 1961, Comm. to Disneyland, A1587, WDA.

591 **Peace pipe atop portrait.** Johnson, *Whimsy Works*, chap. 2, p. 3.

591 **Reviewing and auditing Chouinard.** Memo, Mickey Clark to Walt, Re: Progress Report No. 1, Chouinard Art Institute, Sept. 27, 1956; Price Waterhouse [unsigned] to Walt, Oct. 2, 1956; Memo, Clark to Walt, Re: Chouinard Art School, Jan. 22, 1957; Memo, Mickey Clark to Walt, Re: Chouinard Art Institute, Dec. 13, 1957, Chouinard Art Institute Folder, Walt Disney Corr., 1957, A-D, A1566; Memo, Mickey Clark to Walt, Oct. 3, 1956, Clark, Mickey, Folder, Walt Disney Corr., Inter-Office, 1956–1957, A-Disney, A1641, WDA.

592 **"We could get the best instructors . . ."** Walt to Hopkins, Re: Prof. Robert Feild, Feb. 28, 1939, Feild, Robert, Folder, Walt Disney Corr., Inter-Office, 1938–1944, F-K, A1628, WDA.

592 **"You have to do something . . ."** Tommie Wilck quoted in Hubler, *Disney*, p. 808.

592 **"Walt was obsessed with the idea . . ."** Quoted in Hubler, *Disney*, p. 278.

592 **"He wanted to build that school!"** Quoted in Green and Green, *Remembering Walt*, p. 184.

592 **"I want people to come there . . ."** Quoted in Hubler, *Disney*, p. 749.

592 **"we had schools of music, . . ."** Millard Sheets, Los Angeles Art Community: Group Portrait, interview by George M. Godwin, 1977, pp. 341–42, Special Collections, Young Research Library, UCLA.

592 **"so the students who were studying fine arts . . ."** Quoted in Greene and Greene, *Inside the Dream*, p. 176.

593 **"I don't mean teach *drawing*, . . ."** Green and Green, *Remembering Walt*, p. 185.

593 **"He was losing interest . . ."** Libby Slate, "Marc Davis," *Disney News*, Fall 1992, p. 26.

593 **"[I]f you see fit . . ."** Walt to Joseph P. Kennedy, Apr. 26, 1961, Joseph P. Kennedy Folder, Walt Disney Corr., 1965, K-M, A1610, WDA.

593 **"It doesn't have a wienie!"** Anderson, "Great Big," p. 69.

593 **Walt didn't see prototype.** Memo, Tommie [Wilck] to Walt, Sept. 6, 1963, Walt Disney Folder, Walt Disney Corr., 1963, Congratulatory-H (Misc.), A1596, WDA.

593 **"We were living off of black coffee . . ."** Quoted in Anderson, "Great Big," p. 107.

593 **"it is very gratifying . . ."** Memo, Roy to Walt, Re: New Orleans Square, May 15, 1964, Roy Disney Folder, Walt Disney Corr., Inter-Office, 1960–1964, A-Disney Aircraft, A1648, WDA.

594 **Royal Dano and Lincoln.** Bob Gurr quoted in Anderson, "Great Big," p. 94.

594 **"Oh, yeah, [Walt] was upset, . . ."** Marc Davis, interview by Bob Thomas, May 25, 1973, p. 25, WDA.

594 **"You never saw such a stack . . ."** Ruthie Tompson, presentation at the National Fantasy Fan Club (NFFC) Convention, Jul. 21, 2000.

594 **"Well, I guess we've prolonged this . . ."** Anderson, "Great Big," p. 97.

594 **"Ladies and gentlemen, . . ."** Bright, *Inside Story*, p. 173.

595 **"This is not a toy."** *Chicago Daily News*, Apr. 21, 1964.

595 **Other accounts attributed the difficulties . . .** Anderson, "Great Big," pp. 97–98.

595 **Operating on April 30.** *Chicago Sun-Times*, Apr. 30, 1964; *Chicago Tribune*, Apr. 30, 1964.

595 **"Do you suppose God is mad . . ."** Quoted in Hubler, *Disney*, p. 686.

595 **"Dad cried . . ."** Quoted in Greene and Greene, *Inside the Dream*, p. 157.

595 **Checkup and rest.** *LAT*, May 13, 1964.

595 **First season attendance.** Steven C. Van Voorhis (manager, New York World's Fair Operation, GE) to Members of Executive Office, Nov. 6, 1964, General Electric Folder, Walt Disney Corr., Special Projects, 1961–1965, Aspen-Hallmark, A1660, WDA.

595 **"always its ultimate destination."** Walt to Ralph Newman, Nov. 10, 1964, Illinois Exhibit for New York Fair Folder, Walt Disney Corr., Special Projects, 1961–1965, Illinois-National, A1661, WDA.

595 **"chuckling, really enjoying it."** Robert B. Sherman and Richard M. Sherman, *Walt's Time: From Before to Beyond*, ed. Bruce Gordon, David Mumford, and Jeff Kurtti (Santa Clarita, Calif.: Camphor Tree Publishers, 1998), p. 39.

595 **Joe Grant and *Mary Poppins*.** Joe Grant, interview by Michael Barrier, www.michaelbarrier.com/Interviews/Grant/interview_joe_grant.htm.

595 **Roy contacting Travers.** Memo, Perce Pearce to Roy, Re: *Mary Poppins*, Jan. 6, 1944, P Folder, Walt Disney Corr., Inter-Office, 1938–1944, N-Q, A1630; Memo, Roy to Walt, Re; *Mary Poppins* Stories, Jan. 24, 1944, T Folder, Walt Disney Corr., 19444, S-Z, A1533, WDA.

596 **Roy meeting Travers and Walt willing to fly to Arizona.** Memo, Roy to Walt, Jan. 20, 1944, Disney, Roy O., Walt Disney Corr., Inter-Office, 1938–1944, D, A1627; Walt to Mrs. P. L. Travers, Feb. 24, 1944, T Folder, Walt Disney Corr., 1944, S-Z, A1533, WDA.

596 **Roy phoned again in March.** Memo, Roy to Walt, Mar. 27, 1944, T Folder, Walt Disney Corr., S-Z, A1533, WDA.

596 **Script approval.** Memo, Bill Dover to Walt, Re: *Mary Poppins* Stories, Feb. 4, 1959, Bill Dover Folder, Walt Disney Corr., Inter-Office, 1958–1959, Dover-M, A1646, WDA.

596 **Travers's terms.** Memo, Frank Waldheim to Bill Dover, Re: *Mary Poppins*, Apr. 20, 1959; Memo, Bill Dover to Walt, Re: *Mary Poppins*, Jul. 3, 1959, Bill Dover Folder, Walt Disney Corr., Inter-Office, 1958–1959, Dover-M, A1646, WDA.

596 **"Amelia Earhardt [*sic*] type."** Memo, Roy to Walt, Re: *Mary Poppins* Stories, Jan. 24, 1944.

596 **Not a fan of Walt Disney's work.** Brian Sibley quoted in Greene and Greene, *Inside the Dream*, p. 147.

596 **Travers's treatment.** Walt to Travers, Jul. 29, 1960; Walt to Travers, Feb. 13, 1961, Pamela Travers Folder, Walt Disney Corr., 1964, Radziwill-Z, A1604, WDA.

596 **"benefit of your reactions . . ."** Walt to Travers, Feb. 13, 1961, ibid.

597 **"Mary Poppins project is so important . . ."** Travers to Walt, Apr. 13, 1961; Tel. Walt to Travers, Apr. 14, 1961, Pamela Travers Folder, Walt Disney Corr., 1964, Radziwill-Z, A1604, WDA.

597 **Signing and retracting.** Memo, Bill Dover to Walt, Re: "Mary Poppins"—Pamela Travers, May 2, 1961, Walt to Travers, May 18, 1962, Pamela Travers Folder, Walt Disney Corr., ibid.

597 **"When we sat down . . ."** Sherman and Sherman, *Walt's Time*, p. 40.

597 **"we will make use of it . . ."** Walt to Pamela Travers, Mar. 21, 1963, Pamela Travers Folder, Walt Disney Corr., 1964, Radziwill-Z, A1604, WDA.

597 **Mary Martin.** Walt to Travers, Mar. 31, 1961; Tel. Walt to Mary Martin, Mar. 8, 1961, ibid.

597 **Julie Harris.** Memo, [Bill] Dover to Walt, Re: *Mary Poppins*, Oct. 6, 1961, Bill Dover, 1960–1962 Folder, Walt Disney Corr., Inter-Office, 1960–1964, Disney Foundation-H (Misc.), A1649; Walt to Julie Harris, Mar. 26, 1962, H Folder, Walt Disney Corr., 1962, Committees-H (Misc.), A1591, WDA.

597 **Julie Andrews.** Walt to Julie Andrews, Feb. 26, 1962, Andrews, Julie, Folder, Walt Disney Corr., 1964, A-C (Misc.), A1599, WDA.

598 **Special operation.** Walt to Julie Andrews, Oct. 31, 1962, ibid.

598 **"mutiliating the story."** Travers to Walt, May 21, 1962, Pamela Travers Folder, Walt Disney Corr., 1964, Radziwill-Z, A1604, WDA.

598 **"Walt had rooms of storyboards . . ."** Quoted in Greene and Greene, *Inside the Dream*, p. 150.

598 **"There wasn't a sad face . . ."** Quoted in Paul F. Anderson, "Walt's World," *POV* 1, no. 3 (Spring 1993), p. 9.

598 **"making sure that everybody was happy . . ."** Quoted in Greene and Greene, *Inside the Dream*, p. 151.

599 **"like a big kid."** Tracy Watson, "Karen Dotrice," *Disney News*, Winter 1994, p. 47.

599 **"I think it's going to be one of our best."** Walt to Ruth, Dec. 5, 1963, B Folder, Walt Disney Corr., 1963, A-B, A1594, WDA.

599 **"chickenfeed."** Iwerks quoted in Hubler, *Disney*, p. 457.

600 **"Jolly Holiday."** Sherman and Sherman, *Walt's Story*, p. 42.

600 **"The animator would fuss and complain . . ."** Frank Thomas and Ollie Johnston, *The Illusion of Life: Disney Animation* (New York: Hyperion, 1981), pp. 526–27.

600 **"terrific."** Tel. Walt to Bill Anderson, Oct. 17, 1963, Bill Anderson Folder, Walt Disney Corr., Inter-Office, 1960–1964, A-Disney Aircraft, A1648, WDA.

600 **Showing film to exhibitor.** Hubler, *Disney*, p. 535.

600 **"You have made a great many . . ."** Goldwyn quoted in Sherman and Sherman, *Walt's Story*, p. 60.

600 **"The whole picture is . . ."** Pamela Travers to Walt, Sept. 1, 1964, Pamela Travers Folder, Walt Disney Corr., 1964, Radziwill-Z, A1604, WDA.

600 **Travers expressing her disappointment.** Caitlin Flanagan, "Becoming Mary Poppins," *The New Yorker*, Dec. 19, 2005, p. 46. Flanagan also recounts a

story from Richard Sherman where Travers, having had to wangle an invitation to the premiere, cornered Walt afterward and complained about the animated sequence. To which Walt allegedly said, "Pamela, that ship has sailed." But this is highly unlikely given Travers's communication with Walt.

600 ***Poppins*'s gross.** Memo, Card Walker to Walt, Re: *Mary Poppins*, Mar. 10, 1966, Card Walker Folder, Walt Disney Corr., Inter-Office, 1965–1966, Retlaw-Z, A1655, WDA; Schickel, *Disney Version*, p. 28.

600 **Moscow showing.** Memo, Card Walker to Walt, Re: *Mary Poppins*—Moscow, Ned Clarke letter, 7/11/65, July 19, 1965, Card Walker Folder, ibid.

601 **"That lovely statue . . ."** Julie Andrews to Walt, [Apr. 29, 1965,] Andrews, Julie, Folder, Walt Disney Corr., 1964, A-C (Misc.) A1599, WDA.

601 **"Knowing Hollywood, . . ."** Walt to Julie Andrews, Apr. 29, 1965, ibid.

601 **"With the business . . ."** Hedda Hopper, "Rumored Sell-Out Denied by Disney," *LAT*, Feb. 13, 1965.

601 **"I'm on the spot."** Efron, "Still Attacking," p. 14.

601 **"[w]hen we got in the car . . ."** Marc Davis, interview by Bob Thomas, May 25, 1973, pp. 27–29, WDA; Hubler, *Disney*, p. 609.

601 **Fair attendance.** Memo, Frank Stanek to Marty Sklar, May 9, 1968, Re: NY World's Fair: Attendance Figures, RHC, Box 17, Folder 57.

602 **"If This is Architecture, . . ."** *Life*, Jul. 31, 1964.

602 **Winston Churchill.** Bill Cottrell, interview by Jay Horan, Aug.–Oct., 1983, p. 52, WDA.

602 **Sayers's meetings.** Memo, Jack Sayers to Walt, Aug. 31, 1965, Jack Sayers Folder, Walt Disney Corr., Inter-Office, 196501966, Retlaw-Z, A1655, WDA.

602 **Recruiting General Potter.** Memo, Card Walker to Walt, Re: General Potter, Jan. 18, 1965, Walt Disney Corr., N-S, A1611, WDA.

602 **"testing ground."** Quoted in Anderson, "Great Big," p. 30.

603 **SRI study on New Jersey.** SRI, [Report on New Jersey Theme Park], [1958,] Harrison Price Folder, Walt Disney Corr., Inter-Office, 1960–1964, N-Tatum, A1651, WDA.

603 **"*that* audience is not responsive."** Harrison Price quoted in Hubler, *Disney*, p. 722.

603 **"Walt is interested . . ."** Memo, Vincent Jefferds to Walt, Re: Disneyland-Type Park in Brasilia, May 31, 1960, J Folder, Walt Disney Corr., Inter-Office, 1960–1964, Herald-M, A1650, WDA.

603 **Inception of St. Louis Project.** Brian Burnes, Robert W. Butler, and Dan Viets, *Walt Disney's Missouri: The Roots of Creative Genius*, ed. Donna Martin (Kansas City: Kansas City Star Books, 2002), p. 142.

603 **Terms of St. Louis Project.** Draft letter, Walt Disney Productions to Civic Center Redevelopment Corp., St. Louis, Nov. 5, 1963, General Electric Folder, Walt Disney Corr., Special Projects, 1961–1965, Aspen-Hallmark, A1660, WDA.

603 **St. Louis attractions.** Memo, Art Dept. to Whom It May Concern, Re: Walt Disney–St. Louis Project, Nov. 27, 1963, St. Louis Project Folder, Walt Disney Corr., Special Projects, 1961–1965, Premiere-Walt, A1663, WDA.

603 **Announcing second Disneyland.** Peter Bart, "Walt Disney Eyes a 2nd Disneyland," *NYT*, Jul. 3, 1964, p. 13.

604 **"St. Louis project is only in the talking stage."** Walt to Jack Williams, Jr.,

(*Waycross* [Ga.] *Journal-Herald*), Jul. 1, 1964, Disneyland General Folder, Walt Disney Corr., 1964, Disney-Gifts, A1601, WDA.

604 **Losing interest.** Burnes, Butler, and Viets, *Disney's Missouri*, pp. 147, 151; Memo, Mel Melton to Walt, Re: Project St. Louis, Apr. 28, 1964, St. Louis Project Folder, Walt Disney Corr., Special Projects, 1961–1965, Premiere-Walt, A1663, WDA.

604 **"Florida would be better . . ."** Phil Meyer, "Florida Disneyland?" *Miami Herald*, Aug. 9, 1959.

604 **City of Tomorrow.** An Economic Master Plan for the City of Tomorrow, Dec. 17, 1959, Project West Folder, Walt Disney Corr., 1960, P-Z, A1585, WDA.

604 **Roy reconnoitered.** Robert Price Foster, *The Founding of a Kingdom*, unpub. ms., 1992, p. 7, WDA.

604 **"influence RCA's plans."** Card Walker to Walt, May 26, 1960, Walt Disney, Inter Co. Memos Folder, Walt Disney Corr., Inter-Office, 1960–1964, A-Disney Aircraft, A1648, WDA.

604 **"It just wasn't working."** Bill Cottrell interview by Horan, Aug.–Oct. 1983, p. 61, WDA.

604 **"It was that Disneyland, . . ."** Quoted in Hubler, *Disney*, pp. 722–23.

605 **"We are more enthusiastic . . ."** Memo, Donn Tatum to Walt, Re: Florida, Jun. 1, 1961, Donn Tatum Folder, Walt Disney Corr. Inter-Office, 1960–1964, N-Tatum, A1651, WDA.

605 **Convening executives.** Foster, *Founding*, p. 11.

605 **"What do you want to do that for?"** Mrs. Walt Disney interview by Richard Hubler, Apr. 16, 1968, Disney, Lillian, Folder, WDA.

605 **"We would carefully select a third party . . ."** Memo, Card Walker to Walt/Roy, Re: Discussion Outlined for New Project, Sept. 13, 1963, Card Walker, 1960–62 folder, Walt Disney Corr., Inter-Office, 1960–1964, Tryon-Z, A1652, WDA.

605 **Walt's decision.** Bob Thomas, *Walt Disney: An American Original* (New York: Hyperion, 1994), p. 334.

605 **November trip.** Foster, *Founding*, pp. 9–10.

606 **Flying in Gulfstream.** Ibid., pp. 27–28.

606 **Foster in Florida.** Ibid., pp. 38–45; Memo, Bob Foster to Walt, Re: Project Future Present Status, May 7, 1964, Florida—Inter-Office Memos Folder, Walt Disney Corr., Walt Disney World, A-Z, A1666, WDA.

606 **Roy's negotiations.** Foster, *Founding*, pp. 67–73.

606 **"our own constitutional convention."** Ibid., p. 143.

606 **Recognized by waitress.** Card Walker quoted in Greene and Greene, *Inside the Dream*, p. 165.

606 **"There are so many things . . ."** *News-Journal*, Daytona Beach, Apr. 11, 1965, B Folder, Walt Disney Corr., 1965, A-B, A1605, WDA.

606 **Already purchased 27,400 acres.** Memo, Bob Foster to Those Listed, Re: Project Future, Apr. 26, 1965, Florida—Inter-Office Memos Folder, Walt Disney Corr., Walt Disney World, A-Z, A1666, WDA.

606 **"sell you on the idea . . ."** Memo, Roy to Walt, Aug. 3, 1965, Roy Disney Folder, Walt Disney Corr., Inter-Office, 1965–1966, A-I, A1653, WDA.

607 **"He looked like I had thrown a bucket . . ."** *Orlando Sentinel*, Jul. 28, 2003.

607 **"WE SAY: 'MYSTERY' INDUSTRY IS DISNEY."** *Orlando Sentinel*, Oct. 24, 1965.

607 **News conference.** *NYT*, Nov. 16, 1965; Press Release: Walt Disney Outlines Preliminary Concepts for his Disney World, Nov. 15, 1965, Florida—Press Releases Folder, Walt Disney Corr., Walt Disney World, A-Z, A1666, WDA; *Variety*, Nov. 24, 1965; C. E. Wright, "East Coast Disneyland to Rise Near Orlando," *NYT*, Nov. 21, 1965, sec. 10, p. 3.

608 **"We want something educational . . ."** *NYT*, Nov. 16, 1965.

608 **"lousy" job.** Peter Blake, "The Lessons of the Parks," in Christopher Finch, *The Art of Walt Disney: From Mickey Mouse to the Magic Kingdoms* (1973; New York: Harry N. Abrams, 1993), p. 431.

608 **Walt didn't set foot on the property.** Foster, *Founding*, pp. 155–56.

608 **Not a member of central committee.** Minutes of Dec. 9, 1965, Florida Operating Comm. Meeting, Florida—Florida Operating Committee Folder, Walt Disney Corr., Walt Disney World, A-Z, A1666. Walt did sit on the eleven-member Operating Committee, but it was the four-man Central Committee that served as the park's secretariat.

608 **"Walt instinctively resists . . ."** Bart, "Disney Eyes a 2nd," p. 13.

608 **Riding in the train from the Chicago Railroad Fair . . .** Kimball quoted in Michael Broggie, *Walt Disney's Railroad Story* (Pasadena, Calif.: Pentrex, 1997), p. 68.

608 **City planning books.** Marling, *Theme Parks*, pp. 146–47; Green and Green, *Remembering Walt*, p. 175.

608 **"Why should I run for mayor . . . ?"** Ray Bradbury, interview by author.

609 **"Walt was intrigued . . ."** Quoted in Hubler, *Disney*, pp. 724–25.

609 **"It was the real wienie."** Quoted in Marling, *Theme Parks*, p. 154.

609 **"living, breathing community."** Quoted in Blake, "Lessons of Parks," p. 448.

609 **20,000 residents, 60,000 residents, 100,000 residents . . .** ERA (Economics Research Associates), "An Economic Master Plan for Project Future," Oct. 13, 1965, Florida—E.R.A. Reports Folder, Walt Disney Corr., Walt Disney World, A-Z, A1666, WDA; R. O. Stratton (manager of program development, GE), Transportation Aspects of "Community of Tomorrow" in GE-Disneyland Pavilion, Mar. 18, 1966, M Folder, Walt Disney Corr., Inter-Office, 1965–1966, J-Reddy, A1654; Stratton to O.V. Melton (president, WED), Dec. 1, 1965, Florida—Inter-Office Memos Folder, Walt Disney Corr., Walt Disney World, A-Z, A1666, WDA.

609 **"It will worry about . . ."** Blake, "Lessons of Parks," p. 448.

609 **EPCOT government.** See Steven Mannheim, *Walt Disney and the Quest for Community* (Burlington, Vt.: Ashgate, 2002), pp. 113–14.

609 **"Walt expected things . . ."** Quoted in Hubler, *Disney*, p. 718.

610 **"overwhelming."** Robert Moses, "EPCOT: Walt Disney's Legacy," *Newsday*, Apr. 29, 1967, p. 14.

610 **Corporate partners.** R. O. Stratton to O. V. Melton, Dec. 1, 1965, Florida—Inter-Office Memos Folder, Walt Disney Corr., Walt Disney World, A-Z, A1666; Memo, Joe Potter to Tommie Wilck, Re: Pittsburgh Trip, Jan. 5, 1966, P Folder, Walt Disney Corr., Inter-Office, 1965, J-Reddy, A1654; Memo, Jack Sayers to Walt, Re: RCA, Feb. 2, 1966, Jack Sayers Folder, Walt Disney Corr., Inter-Office, 1965–1966, Retlaw-Z, A1655, WDA.

610 **Becket's design.** Marvin Davis quoted in Marling, *Theme Parks*, p. 149.
610 **Plans scribbled on napkin.** Hubler, *Disney*, p. 726.
610 **"sketching away with a big pencil . . ."** Bob Gurr quoted in Greene and Greene, *Inside the Dream*, p. 169.
611 **"I vividly remember . . ."** Quoted in ibid., p. 169.
611 **Resigning from MPA.** Walt to MPA, Feb. 9, 1956; Borden Chase (executive committee, Motion Picture Alliance) to Walt, Feb. 29, 1956; Memo, Gunther Lessing to Dolores Voght, Feb. 6, 1956, Mo Folder, Walt Disney Corr., 1956, M-R, A1564, WDA. Lessing, a board member himself, had apparently urged Walt to resign after the attack on the Writers Guild of America (on which he had not been consulted), "not only because the need for such an organization had ceased to exist, but it is, in my opinion now a vehicle for Ward Bond to throw his weight around," naming a notoriously red-baiting actor. The MPA called Walt's resignation a "bombshell" and asked him to reconsider. He didn't.
612 **Strong-arming contributions.** Michael Barrier, "Ward Kimball," in *Walt's People*, ed. Didier Ghez (Xlibris, 2006), pp. 2: 116–17.
612 **Goldwater support.** Memo, Bill Anderson to Walt/Roy, Re: Republican Campaign Contributions, Oct. 26, 1964, Bill Anderson Folder, Walt Disney Corr., Inter-Office, 1960–1964, A-Disney Aircraft, A1648; Walt to Holmes Tuttle, Sept. 11, 1964, T Folder, Walt Disney Corr., 1964, Radziwill-Z, A1604; Walt to Barry Goldwater, Jul. 31, 1964; Goldwater to Walt, Aug. 9, 1964, G Folder, Walt Disney Corr., 1964, Disney-Gifts, A1601, WDA.
612 **"taking up the gun . . ."** Walt to Di, Oct. 2, 1964, M Folder, Walt Disney Corr., 1964, M-R (Misc.), A1603, WDA.
612 **"Talk to enough people . . ."** Herbert Gold, "Nobody's Mad at Murphy," *NYT Magazine*, Dec. 13, 1964, p. 52.
612 **Lillian and Democrats for George Murphy.** Lillian to Wayne Griffin, Aug. 18, 1964, G Folder, Walt Disney Corr., 1964, Disney-Gifts, A1601, WDA.
612 **"I had my little fling . . ."** Peter Bart, "The Golden Stuff of Disney Dreams," *NYT*, Dec. 5, 1965, sec. 2, p. 13.
612 **"one person no country could find fault with."** Note to Walt, Mar. 3, 1965, Tournament of Roses Folder, Walt Disney Corr., 1966, Speaking Requests-Z, A1620, WDA.
612 **"revered and honored . . ."** Bart, "Golden Stuff," p. 13.
612 **Presidential Medal of Freedom.** Charles Ridgway quoted in Green and Green, *Remembering Walt*, p. 82.
612 **Fellow honorees.** *NYT*, Jul. 4, 1964, pp. 1, 10.
613 **"almost everything objectionable."** Frances Clark Sayers, "Walt Disney Accused," interview by Charles M. Weisenberg, *F.M. and Fine Arts*, Aug. 1965.
613 **"Disneyland is presented as imaginary . . ."** Jean Baudrillard, *Selected Writings*, ed. Mark Poster (Stanford, Calif.: Stanford University Press, 1988), p. 172.
613 **"disappointment in expectations."** Godfrey Hodgson, *America in Our Time: From World War II to Nixon, What Happened and Why* (New York: Random House, 1976), p. 38.
614 **"How's this for the cover . . ."** Gene Lester quoted in Hubler, *Disney*, pp. 697B–98.
614 **Re-evaluation of Disney's films.** Douglas Brode, *From Walt to Woodstock: How Disney Created the Counterculture* (Austin, Tex.: University of Texas Press,

2004). This is one of the most original and interesting studies of Walt Disney's work, and it is practically unique in presenting Disney as a closet liberal.

615 **"mournful sigh."** Peet, *Autobiography*, p. 171.

615 **"[A]nd he drew a curtain . . ."** Marc Davis, interview by Richard Hubler, May 21, 1968, RHC, Box 14, Folder 51.

616 **"He may have consumed . . ."** Quoted in Greene and Greene, *Remembering Walt*, p. 85.

616 **"[S]tarting at five o'clock . . ."** Ward Kimball, interview by Richard Hubler, May 21, 1968, p. 24, WDA.

616 **"That was quite a long way . . ."** Jack Kinney, *Walt Disney and Other Animated Characters: An Unauthorized Account of the Early Years at Disney's* (New York: Harmony Books, 1988), p. 160.

616 **Drinking diet.** Tommie Wilck, interview by Richard Hubler, Aug. 13, 1968, WDA.

616 **Hollywood Stars.** Louella Parsons, "Walt Disney, The Lovable Genius Who Never Grew Up," *Los Angeles Examiner Pictorial Living*, Jan. 9, 1955.

616 **Los Angeles baseball team.** Walt to Bob Reynolds, Pres. (president, Los Angeles Angels), Feb. 2, 1965, R Folder, Walt Disney Corr., N-S, A1611, WDA.

616 **"go to your head."** Walt to Nels Hokanson, Apr. 2, 1964, H Folder, Walt Disney Corr., 1964, H-Mc, A1602, WDA.

616 **Passion for lawn bowling.** [Tommie Wilck] to Walt, Feb. 16, 1965, Smoke Tree Folder, Walt Disney Corr., N-S, A1611; Itinerary, Sept. 11, 1964, Walt Disney Folder, Walt Disney Corr., 1964, Disney-Gifts, A1601, WDA.

616 **Australian vacation.** Walt to Max and Emily Schwab, May 4, 1966, S Folder, Walt Disney Corr., 1966, N-Smoke Tree, A1619, WDA.

617 **"badly."** Sharon Brown, interview by Richard Hubler, Jul. 9, 1968, RHC, Box 14, Folder 51.

617 **150 hours.** Hubler, *Disney*, p. 703.

617 **"I'm thrilled to have a male heir . . ."** Walt to Bob Stevenson, Nov. 28, 1961, S Folder, Walt Disney Corr., Inter-Office, 1960–1964, N-Tatum, A1651, WDA.

617 **"We'd play on the lawn . . ."** Quoted in Greene and Greene, *Inside the Dream*, pp. 170–71.

618 **"Feed the Birds."** Sherman and Sherman, *Walt's Time*, p. 49.

618 **"The guy just has a sincere desire . . ."** Memo, Charles Levy to Joe Reddy, Re: Dick Schickel, Sept. 9, 1966, R Folder, Walt Disney Corr., 1966, N-Smoke Tree Ranch, A1619, WDA.

618 **"As far as I'm concerned . . ."** Walt to Hobart Lewis (executive editor, *Reader's Digest*), Sept. 15, 1966, R Folder, Walt Disney Corr., 1966, N-Smoke Tree Ranch, A1619, WDA.

618 **"I don't know how much time . . ."** Reverend Glenn Puder, interview by author.

618 **Credit for *Lt. Robin Crusoe, U.S.N.*** Green and Green, *Remembering Walt*, p. 135.

618 **Marceline Project.** Memo, Harrison Price/Bill Cottrell to Walt, Re: Marceline Project, Oct. 25, 1965; Memo, Buzz Price/Mickey Clark/Bill Cottrell to Rush Johnson, Re: Marceline Project, Nov. 1, 1965, Marceline, City of, Folder, Walt Disney Corr., 1966, J-M, A1618, WDA.

619 **Mineral King.** *LAT*, Nov. 6, 1965; *NYT*, Dec. 18, 1965.

619 **Visiting Disneyland.** Walt Disney, interview by Hooper Fowler, *Look*, Jan. 1964, p. 2, WDA.

619 **"It looks just like home."** *NYT*, July 26, 1966.

619 **Regale his secretaries.** Lucille Martin, presentation at the NFFC Convention, Jul. 21, 2000.

619 **"[W]ith that kind of a start . . ."** Memo, Roy to Walt, Aug. 20, 1965, Walt Disney Folder, Roy O. Disney, Inter-Office Corr., Disney, Roy O.—Trips to Disneyland (1954–61), A3002, WDA.

619 **Loans and donations.** Walt to Brigadier General C. B. Drake, Apr. 4, 1966, D Folder, Walt Disney Corr., 1966, Christmas Thank Yous—Disney Birthday, A1615, WDA.

619 **Listening to an opera.** Walt to Blanche Seaver, Aug. 15, 1966, S Folder, Walt Disney Corr., 1966, N-Smoke Tree Ranch, A1619, WDA.

619 **Streamlining the system.** Canemaker, *Nine Old Men*, p. 50.

620 **Bill Peet complained.** Peet, *Autobiography*, p. 165.

620 **Xerography.** Bill Tytla to Walt, Mar. 4, 1956, T Folder, Walt Disney Corr., 1956, S-Z, A1565, WDA; Leslie Iwerks and John Kenworthy, *The Hand Behind the Mouse* (New York: Disney Editions, 2001), pp. 192–93.

620 **"It was the first time . . ."** Marc Davis, interview by Bob Thomas, Fall 1989, WDA.

620 **"spoils the beauty . . ."** Eric Larson, interview by Christopher Finch and Linda Rosenkrantz, Jul. 25, 1972, p. 7, WDA.

620 **"Then he had second thoughts."** Quoted in Charles Solomon, *Enchanted Drawings: The History of Animation* (New York: Alfred A. Knopf, 1989), p. 266.

620 **"require drastic steps . . ."** Memo, Ken Peterson to Walt, Re: *Sword in the Stone*, Jan. 4, 1961, Ken Peterson Folder, Walt Disney Corr., Inter-Office, 1960–1964, N-Tatum, A1651, WDA.

621 **"He was interested in a picture . . ."** Milt Kahl, interview by Bob Thomas, May 14, 1973, p. 6, WDA.

621 **"It would take about ½ hour."** Memo, Woolie [Reitherman] to Walt, Re: *Jungle Book*, Apr. 20, 1966, R Folder, Walt Disney Corr., Inter-Office, 1965–1966, J-Reddy, A1654, WDA.

621 **Walt thought the audience wouldn't identify . . .** Michel Fessier, Jr., "Legacy of a Last Tycoon," *LAT*, Nov. 12, 1967.

621 **"When Walt heard Phil's test . . ."** Frank Thomas and Ollie Johnston, *The Illusion of Life: Disney Animation* (New York: Hyperion, 1981), p. 407.

621 **"I'm making this trip . . ."** Walt to Mrs. Eugene Hill-Smith, Apr. 29, 1966, H Folder, Walt Disney Corr., 1966, H-I, A1617, WDA.

621 **"enough work to keep . . ."** Price quoted in Hubler, *Disney*, p. 722.

622 **Ailments.** Tommie Wilck quoted in Hubler, *Disney*, pp. 829–30; Dr. Edward W. Boland to Walt, Jun. 22, 1959, Bi Folder, Walt Disney Corr., 1959, A-Ca, A1573; Walt to Ruth, Dec. 6, 1960, B Folder, Walt Disney Corr., 1960, A-B, A1580, WDA.

622 **"I am in the process . . ."** Walt to Hayley Mills, Oct. 1, 1963, Mills, John, and Family Folder, Walt Disney Corr., 1965, K-M, A1610, WDA.

622 **Polo injury.** Walt to Floyd Odlum, Dec. 15, 1951, O Folder, Walt Disney Corr., 1951–1952, N-P, A1547, WDA; Roy O. Disney, interview by Richard Hubler, Nov. 17, 1967, p. 25, WDA.

622 **Trip with Ellenshaw.** Mosley, *Disney's World*, pp. 241–43.

622 **"it got so bad . . ."** Quoted in Hubler, *Disney*, p. 830.
622 **"He constantly complained . . ."** Marc Davis interview by Hubler, May 21, 1968, p. 6.
622 **"gimpy" and "pooped."** Quoted in Hubler, *Disney*, pp. 837–38.
622 **"lush."** Mosley, *Disney's World*, pp. 276–77. See also Paul Smith and Hazel George, interview by David Tietyen, Aug. 29, 1978, p. 27, WDA; Hazel George, interview by John Canemaker, Jan. 4, 1995, WDA.
622 **"Here is the same man . . ."** Ward Kimball, interview by Rick Shale, p. 24, WDA.
623 **"His proud head . . ."** Shows, *Backstage Adventures*, p. 197.
623 **Diffusion filters.** Robert De Roos, "The Magic Worlds of Walt Disney," *National Geographic*, Aug. 1963.
623 **"Whenever Father gets depressed . . ."** Diane Disney Miller, as told to Pete Martin, *The Story of Walt Disney* (New York: Holt, 1956), p. 114.
623 **"get the hell back to work."** Ryman quoted in Hubler, *Disney*, p. 842.
623 **"fierce reaming out."** Harrison "Buzz" Price, *Walt's Revolution! By the Numbers* (Orlando, Fla.: Ripley Entertainment, 2003), p. 62.
623 **"[l]ongevity seems to run . . ."** Walt to Aunt Jessie, Apr. 20, 1951, Perkins, Jessie, Folder, Walt Disney Corr., 1951–1952, N-P, A1547, WDA.
623 **"normal for my age."** Walt to Hayley Mills, Feb. 3, 1966, M Folder, Walt Disney Corr., 1966, J-M, A1618, WDA.
624 **"Just about the most interesting . . ."** Walt to Captain Martin D. Carmody (11th Naval District, San Diego), Jul. 28, 1965, C Folder, Walt Disney Corr., 1965, C-Christmas, A1606, WDA.
624 **"It's something I've always wanted . . ."** Walt to Thomas Meek (Harris, Upham & Co.), Jun. 14, 1966, M Folder, Walt Disney Corr., 1966, J-M, A1618, WDA.
624 **"We're just going to cruise . . ."** Walt to Kay Clark, Jun. 22, 1966, C Folder, Walt Disney Corr., 1966, B-Christmas, A1614, WDA.
624 **"at each other's throats . . ."** Quoted in Hubler, *Disney*, p. 7.
624 **Rehearsing EPCOT presentation.** Marling, *Theme Parks*, p. 150.
624 **Arguing with Kahl.** Ollie Johnston, interview by Richard Hubler, RHC, Box 17, Folder 57.
624 **"I don't know, fellows, . . ."** Schickel, *Disney Version*, p. 360.
624 **Charging Tytle with lowering costs.** Memo, Harry Tytle to Walt, Jul. 22, 1966, Harry Tytle Folder, Walt Disney Corr., Inter-Office, 1965–1966, Retlaw-Z, A1655, WDA.
624 **GE merger.** Walt to Dave Burke (GE), Sept. 16, 1966; Agenda for Oct. 3 Conference, n.d., G Folder, Walt Disney Corr., 1966, Disney Personal—Gifts, A1616, WDA.
625 **"You could just see him sag."** Herbie Hughes (chief of rigging), interview, WDA.
625 **" 'D' date."** Memo, Roy to Walt, Oct. 24, 1966, Roy Disney Folder, Walt Disney Corr., Inter-Office, 1965–1966, A-I, A1653, WDA.
625 **"When I get out of the hospital . . ."** Quoted in Green and Green, *Remembering Walt*, p. 192.
626 **"I'm not going over there to die."** Quoted in Katherine Greene and Richard Greene, *The Man Behind the Magic: The Story of Walt Disney* (New York: Viking, 1991), p. 167.

626 **"They took an x-ray . . ."** Quoted in Greene and Greene, *Inside the Dream*, pp. 177–78.

626 **Official press release.** *NYT*, Nov. 9, 1966, p. 42.

626 **"I just can't picture him . . ."** Diane Disney Miller interview by author.

626 **Sharon and school play.** Miller, *Story of Disney*, p. 131.

626 **"burned more furniture . . ."** Quoted in Hubler, Disney, p. 199.

626 **"He would forget to put them out."** Quoted in Green and Green, *Remembering Walt*, p. 83.

626 **Switching to a pipe.** Grant interview by Barrier, www.Michaelbarrier.com/Interviews/Grant/interview_joe_grant.htm.

626 **Lessing lobbying Walt.** Memo, Gunther Lessing to Walt, Feb. 5, 1957, L Folder, Walt Disney Corr., Inter-Office, 1956–1957, K-Secrets, A1643, WDA.

626 **"I didn't tell her *how* . . ."** Fulton Burley quoted in Green and Green, *Remembering Walt*, pp. 200–201.

627 **"When I timidly asked . . ."** Quoted in Mosley, *Disney's World*, p. 275.

627 **The day before the operation.** Diane quoted in Greene and Greene, *Inside the Dream*, p. 178; interview by author.

627 **Doctor's announcement.** "Growing Up Disney," *People*, Dec. 21, 1998, p. 56.

627 **Roy exploded.** Greene and Greene, *Man Behind the Magic*, p. 167.

627 **"what the elements essential . . ."** Spec McClure to Tommie Wilck, Dec. 7, 1966, McClure, Spec (David C.), Folder, Walt Disney Corr., 1966, J-M, A1618, WDA.

627 **Tytle's visit.** Tytle, *One of "Walt's Boys,"* p. 213.

627 **"Welcome to the club."** Ron Miller quoted in Green and Green, *Remembering Walt*, p. 194.

627 **"Several papers carry . . ."** Memo, Cyril Edgar to Ned Clark, Nov. 11, 1966, Walt Disney Folder, Roy O. Disney, Inter-Office Corr., Disney, Roy O.—Trips to Disneyland (1954–61), A3002, WDA.

628 **"He's going to be okay."** Ruth to Madeline [Wheeler], Nov. 26, 1966; Madeline Wheeler to Ruth, Dec. 1, 1966, B Folder, Walt Disney Corr., 1966, B-Christmas, A1614, WDA.

628 **Press release.** *LAT*, Nov. 23, 1966.

628 **Demanding Tommie Wilck . . .** Tommie Wilck interview by Bob Thomas, WDA.

628 **"You'd think I was going to die . . ."** Tytle, *One of "Walt's Boys,"* p. 213.

628 **"he was gaining strength."** Sharpsteen, interview by Don Peri, Feb. 6, 1974, p. 42, WDA.

628 **"[H]is voice took on enthusiasm . . ."** Quoted in Hubler, *Disney*, p. 838.

628 **"laughed like hell."** Marc Davis interview by Hubler, May 21, 1968, p. 7, WDA.

628 **"Goodbye, Marc."** Ibid., Greene and Greene, *Man Behind the Magic*, p. 167.

628 **"I had a scare, Hib."** Green and Green, *Remembering Walt*, p. 196.

628 **"We decided he was doomed."** Quoted in Mosley, *Disney's World*, pp. 293–94.

628 **"There's something I want to tell you."** Thomas, *American Original*, p. 352.

629 **"He looked defeated . . ."** Quoted in Hubler, *Disney*, p. 841.

629 **"Just heard that Walt . . ."** Edna and Roy to Walt and Lilly, Nov. 22, 1966, Roy Disney Folder, Walt Disney Corr., Inter-Office, 1965–1966, A-I, A1653, WDA.

629 **"As far as my problem . . ."** Walt to Kay Clark, Nov. 23, 1966, C Folder, Walt Disney Corr., 1966, B-Christmas, A1614, WDA.

629 **Lillian clung to hope.** Mrs. Walt Disney interview by Hubler, April 16, 1968, RHC, Box 14, Folder 52.

629 **"I don't think he accepted it."** Kimball interview by Hubler, p. 23.

629 **Walt told Ron Miller . . .** Hubler, *Disney*, p. 833.

629 **$3.75 million.** Memo, Mickey Clark to Walt, Feb. 22, 1965, Mickey Clark Folder, Walt Disney Corr., Inter-Office, 1965–1966, A-I, A1653, WDA.

629 **$12 million profit.** Memo, Roy to Walt, Oct. 24, 1966, Walt Disney Folder, Roy O. Disney, Inter-Office Corr., Disney, Roy O.—Trips to Disneyland (1954–61), A3002, WDA.

629 **Will.** Last Will and Testament of Walter E. Disney, Mar. 18, 1966, bk. 1809, p. 108.

630 **"The last thing he said to me was . . ."** Quoted in Hubler, *Disney*, p. 834.

630 **"Hope this finds you . . ."** Tel. Roy to Walt, Dec. 5, 1966, Roy Disney Folder, Walt Disney Corr., Inter-Office, 1965–1966, A-I, A1653, WDA.

630 **Ellenshaw painting.** Mosley, *Disney's World*, p. 294; Greene and Greene, *Man Behind the Magic*, p. 168.

630 **"Somehow that would make him *not* die."** Quoted in Hubler, *Disney*, pp. 834–35; Diane Disney Miller, interview by author.

630 **"I know he's going to get better."** Diane quoted in Greene and Greene, *Inside the Dream*, p. 179.

630 **Bob Brown's visit.** Mrs. Walt Disney interview by Hubler, Apr. 16, 1968, RHC, Box 14, Folder 52.

630 **"Uncle Roy was standing . . ."** Quoted in Greene and Greene, *Inside the Dream*, pp. 179–80.

631 **"Now Daddy, now you won't . . ."** Diane quoted in http://disneygo.com/disneyatoz/familymuseum/collection/insidestory; Diane Disney Miller, interview by author.

631 **"Cardia arrest . . ."** Certificate of Death, no. 7097-050719, Registrar-Recorder, Los Angeles County.

631 **"I took care of Walt . . ."** Patty Disney quoted in Green and Green, *Remembering Walt*, p. 197.

631 **"I knew that he was very sick."** Martin, presentation at NFFC Convention.

631 **"The death of Walt Disney . . ."** Roy O. Disney, statement, Walt Disney Productions, Roy Disney Folder, Walt Disney Corr., Inter-Office, 1965–1966, A-I, A1653, WDA.

631 **"Why are you dragging your feet?"** Mosley, *Disney's World*, p. 290.

631 **"Fancy being remembered . . ."** Ibid., p. 296.

631 **"Marvin, Walt's dead."** Quoted in Marling, *Theme Parks*, p. 154.

631 **"All of it, . . ."** *NYT*, Dec. 16, 1966, p. 46.

632 **"Aesop with a magic brush, . . ."** *LAT*, Dec. 16, 1966, sec. 2, p. 4.

632 **"Disney was dead, . . ."** *Time*, Dec. 23, 1966, p. 71.

633 **Funeral.** Diane Disney Miller, interview by author.

633 **"sacred memorial . . ."** Forest Lawn Brochure, Disney, Walt Death Folder, WDA.

SELECTED BIBLIOGRAPHY

A NOTE ON SOURCES

What follows is by necessity a highly selected bibliography intended only to suggest sources for those who would like to pursue their interest in Walt Disney. It is limited because there are hundreds of books on Walt Disney, his films, and his theme parks, and the number continues to grow apace. There are also thousands of articles on him. The quantity, which rivals that of an American president, is arguably larger than that of any other figure in the popular culture and is a testament to his reach and influence, but to list them all is beyond the scope of this biography's bibliography. Any exhaustive bibliography would easily fill a volume of its own, and it has: Kathy Merlock Jackson has published *Walt Disney: A Bio-Bibliography* (Greenport, Conn.: Greenwood Press, 1993), and Elizabeth Leebron and Lynn Gartley have published *Walt Disney: A Guide to References and Resources* (Boston: G. K. Hall, 1979). Anyone interested in serious Disney study would be well advised to consult these books.

I attempted to read all the extant Disney literature—books and articles—and I cite many of these sources in the endnotes. This volume, however, is based primarily on my examination of documents at the Walt Disney Archives (herein WDA) and at other repositories, and these sources are referenced in the endnotes so that readers can see the materials on which I based my conclusions and so that future investigators can find those materials. Scholars are fortunate that Walt, who practically from childhood had an inflated sense of his own importance, seemed to keep everything, even a postcard he drew for his mother when he was a boy, and the archive has retained nearly all of this detritus. When I embarked on this project, I endeavored to read every letter, memo, story meeting transcript, financial ledger, chart, desk diary, annotation, and doodle in the collection in chronological order so that I would be in the moment with Walt, experiencing as best I could what he was feeling and thinking at the time and over time. There are, needless to say, tens if not hundreds of thousands of these items. I do not know whether I succeeded in reading them all—the archive continually springs surprises—but I was told that only David Smith, the longtime archivist, and I have even made the attempt. It took years, and I can only hope that the reader will feel rewarded by the effort.

Other major sources for this biography are the recollections of those who knew Walt Disney. I conducted dozens of interviews, typically two to three hours in length. Diane Disney Miller, Walt's only surviving daughter, not only submitted to a lengthy interview but graciously and generously sent me her observations and answered questions as I reviewed the manuscript. As for the interviews with Walt's employees, I had a slight disappointment. I quickly discovered that those who had worked most intimately with him were now gone, that those who survived knew him only glancingly (Walt would have turned one hundred on December 5, 2001), and that as the studio expanded he so compartmentalized himself that no one really could be considered a true intimate. Nearly all of those I interviewed—even remarkable individuals like the animators Frank Thomas and Ollie Johnston, who were mainstays of the studio—had, when one considers how long they toiled there, surprisingly few personal encounters with Walt. (One employee I interviewed who had logged several decades at the studio and occupied a position of some importance could scarcely recall more than a few times he met individually with Walt.) Fortunately the archive houses dozens if not hundreds of interviews with Disney family members and studio employees, including those who worked most closely with him in the early years, and while no single interview provides or could be expected to provide an all-illuminating revelation, taken together they yield as vivid a portrait of Walt Disney as we are likely to get. Again, I have tried diligently to read all of these transcripts and listen to the tapes when transcripts do not exist, and they are extensively referenced in the endnotes, though not in the Bibliography.

Of special note is one particular set of interviews. Shortly after Walt's death Roy O. Disney commissioned a biography of his brother and hired Richard G. Hubler, a veteran journalist who had written a recent biography of Cole Porter and had ghost-written Ronald Reagan's autobiography, *Where's the Rest of Me?* Under studio auspices, Hubler interviewed dozens of employees as well as Roy O., Sharon, Diane, and the reticent Lillian. Though Roy was deeply disappointed with the manuscript and ultimately deemed it unpublishable, the interviews are a precious trove for any Disney biographer. I have generally cited the source for these interviews as RHC, for the Richard Hubler Collection at Boston University, though they are also available at the Disney Archives and I have used that citation when full transcripts were available at RHC.

When Walt coaxed Diane to "write" his biography, he recruited Pete Martin, another veteran journalist, to assist her. Martin conducted long interviews with Walt and his family that serve as the basis for *The Story of Walt Disney.* These interviews have been transcribed and the transcripts are available at the archive, but I listened to the audio as well and found discrepancies and omissions between the original tapes and the transcriptions. I have referenced the book itself in my notes whenever possible because it is easily accessible to readers. I have referenced the transcriptions in the notes where they elaborate upon something in Diane Disney Miller's text because they are, theoretically at least, also available to scholars. Finally, I have referenced the audio disks themselves, which are not readily available, only when they bear information not included in the book or the transcript. In any case, these interviews may be the single most valuable source in gaining a sense of what Walt was actually thinking: Walt's version of events in his own voice.

In addition to these materials, there are accounts of Walt and the studio, published and unpublished, by Disney employees including Dave Hand, Jack Kinney, Bill

Justice, Harry Tytle, and Robert Price Foster, who was responsible for heading the operation to buy the land for Disney World. Though one must always make allowances for recollections and the vicissitudes of memory, these memoirs add substantially to the record.

Any Disney biographer is also indebted to animation journals, especially *Millimeter, Funnyworld,* and *Cartoonist Profiles.* Several articles of particular interest are listed in the Bibliography, but many others of value are not because to do so would, again, lengthen the Bibliography beyond what would be practical or portable. Any serious investigator would be rewarded by poring through these publications, which obviously are not limited to the animations of Walt Disney. The greatest debt for Disney specialists, however, is to Paul Anderson's *Persistence of Vision* (herein *POV*), published irregularly when Paul thinks an issue is ready. One cannot say enough about what Paul and *POV* have contributed to Disney scholarship, and one cannot even try to reference single articles or single issues in a bibliography because they are all essential. Indeed, the number on the New York World's Fair titled "A Great Big Beautiful Tomorrow" (1995) remains the single best source on Disney's involvement in the fair.

Though he is long gone, Walt Disney remains a work in progress. One suspects that his films and theme parks will supply fodder for endless rumination, analysis, and confrontation on issues like the meaning of America, capitalism, mass culture, fabrication, history, and even gender values, and that attitudes toward him will be a barometer for shifting moods about all of these things for years and perhaps decades to come. No bibliography can capture the full measure of this debate, which is why one will have to keep amending the list as the arguments over Walt Disney and his legacy continue to rage.

BOOKS

Allan, Robin. *Walt Disney and Europe: European Influences on the Animated Feature Films of Walt Disney.* Bloomington: Indiana University Press, 1999.

Anderson, Christopher. *Hollywood TV: The Studio System in the Fifties.* Austin, Tex.: University of Texas Press, 1994.

At Home in Ellis County, Kansas, 1867–1992, vol. 1. Hays, Kan.: History Book Committee, 1991.

Bain, David, and Bruce Harris. *Mickey Mouse: Fifty Happy Years.* New York: Harmony Books, 1977.

Barbera, Joseph. *My Life in 'toons: From Flatbush to Bedrock in Under a Century.* Atlanta: Turner Publishing, 1994.

Barrier, Michael. *Hollywood Cartoons: American Animation in Its Golden Age.* New York: Oxford University Press, 1999.

Bettelheim, Bruno. *The Uses of Enchantment: The Meaning and Importance of Fairy Tales.* New York: Alfred A. Knopf, 1975.

Blitz, Marcia. *Donald Duck.* New York: Harmony Books, 1979.

Bright, Randy. *Disneyland: The Inside Story.* New York: Harry N. Abrams, 1987.

Brode, Douglas. *From Walt to Woodstock: How Disney Created the Counterculture.* Austin: University of Texas Press, 2004.

Broggie, Michael. *Walt Disney's Railroad Story.* Pasadena, Calif.: Pentrex, 1997.

Bryman, Alan. *Disney and His Worlds.* New York: Routledge, 1995.

———. *The Disneyfication of Society.* London: SAGE, 2004.

Burnes, Brian, Robert W. Butler, and Dan Viets. *Walt Disney's Missouri: The Roots of Creative Genius*, ed. Donna Martin. Kansas City: Kansas City Star Books, 2002.

Canemaker, John. *Before the Animation Begins: The Art and Lives of Disney Inspirational Sketch Artists.* New York: Hyperion Books, 1996.

———. *Felix: The Twisted Tale of the World's Most Popular Cat.* New York: Da Capo Press, 1996.

———. *Paper Dreams: The Art and Artists of the Disney Storyboards.* New York: Disney Editions, 1999.

———. *Walt Disney's Nine Old Men and the Art of Animation.* New York: Disney Editions, 2001.

Capra, Frank. *The Name Above the Title: An Autobiography.* New York: Macmillan, 1971.

Chasins, Abram. *Leopold Stokowski: A Profile.* New York: Hawthorn Books, 1979.

Cotter, Bill. *The Wonderful World of Disney Television: A Complete History.* New York: Disney Editions, 1997.

Crafton, Donald. *Before Mickey: The Animated Film, 1898–1928.* Cambridge, Mass.: MIT Press, 1982.

Culhane, John. *Walt Disney's* Fantasia. New York: Harry N. Abrams, 1983.

Culhane, Shamus. *Talking Animals and Other People.* New York: St. Martin's Press, 1986.

Eisenstein, Sergei. *Eisenstein on Disney.* Edited by Jay Leyda, translated by Alan Upchurch. London: Methuen, 1988.

Eliot, Marc. *Walt Disney: Hollywood's Dark Prince.* New York: Carol Publishing Group, 1993.

Feild, Robert. *The Art of Walt Disney.* New York: Macmillan, 1942.

Finch, Christopher. *The Art of Walt Disney: From Mickey Mouse to the Magic Kingdoms*, rev. ed. New York: Harry N. Abrams, 1993.

Fleischer, Richard. *Just Tell Me When to Cry: A Memoir.* New York: Carroll & Graf, 1993.

Foresman, Sherry. *The History of the Disney Family.* Des Moines, Ia.: Foresman, 1979.

France, Van Arsdale. *Window on Main Street: 35 Years of Creating Happiness at Disneyland Park.* Nashua, N.H.: Laughter Publications, 1991.

Gebhard, David, and Harriete Von Breton. *Kem Weber: The Moderne in Southern California, 1920–1941.* Santa Barbara: University of California Press, 1969.

Ghez, Didier, ed. *Walt's People*, vol. 1. Xlibris, 2005.

———. *Walt's People*, vol. 2. Xlibris, 2006.

Giroux, Henry A. *The Mouse that Roared: Disney and the End of Innocence.* Lanham, Md.: Rowman & Littlefield, 1999.

Goldenson, Leonard H., with Marvin J. Wolf. *Beating the Odds.* New York: Charles Scribner's Sons, 1991.

Green, Amy Boothe, and Howard E. Green. *Remembering Walt: Favorite Memories of Walt Disney.* New York: Hyperion Books, 1999.

Greene, Katherine, and Richard Greene. *The Man Behind the Magic: The Story of Walt Disney.* New York: Viking, 1991.

———. *Inside the Dream: The Personal Story of Walt Disney.* New York: Roundtable Press, 2001.

Hand, David Dodd. *Memoirs.* Cambria, Calif.: Lighthouse Litho, 1990.

History of Marceline, 1888–1988, Centennial Edition. Marceline, Mo., 1988.

Holliss, Richard, and Brian Sibley. *Walt Disney's* Snow White and the Seven Dwarfs *and the Making of the Classic Film.* New York: Simon & Schuster, 1987.

———. *The Disney Studio Story.* New York: Crown Publishers, 1988.

Iwerks, Leslie, and John Kenworthy. *The Hand Behind the Mouse.* New York: Disney Editions, 2001.

Jackson, Kathy Merlock, ed. *Walt Disney Conversations.* Jackson: University of Mississippi, 2006.

Jones, Chuck. *Chuck Amuck: The Life and Times of an Animated Cartoonist.* New York: Avon Books. 1989.

Justice, Bill. *Justice for Disney.* Dayton, Ohio: Tomart Publications, 1992.

Kanfer, Stefan. *Serious Business: The Art and Commerce of Animation in America from Betty Boop to Toy Story.* New York: Charles Scribner's Sons, 1997.

Kinney, Jack. *Walt Disney and Other Animated Characters: An Unauthorized Account of the Early Years at Disney's.* New York: Harmony Books, 1988.

Koszarski, Richard. *An Evening's Entertainment: The Age of the Silent Feature Picture, 1915–1928.* Berkeley: University of California Press, 1990.

Krause, Martin, and Linda Witkowski. *Walt Disney's* Snow White and the Seven Dwarfs: *An Art in Its Making.* New York: Hyperion Books, 1994.

Lutz, Edwin G. *Animated Cartoons: How They Are Made, Their Origin and Development.* 1920; reprint Bedford, Mass.: Applewood Books, 1998.

Maltin, Leonard. *Of Mice and Magic: A History of American Animated Cartoons,* rev. ed. New York: Plume, 1987.

———. *The Disney Films,* 3rd ed. New York: Hyperion Books, 1995.

Mannheim, Steven. *Walt Disney and the Quest for Community.* Burlington, Vt.: Ashgate Publishing, 2002.

Marceline, Missouri: Past and Present Progress and Prosperity. 1913; reprint Walsworth Publishing, 1975.

Marion, Frances. *Off With Their Heads! A Serio-Comic Tale of Hollywood.* New York: Macmillan, 1972.

Marling, Karal Ann, ed. *Designing Disney's Theme Parks: The Architecture of Reassurance.* New York: Flammarion, 1997.

McGilligan, Patrick, and Paul Buhle. *Tender Comrades: A Backstory of the Hollywood Blacklist.* New York: St. Martin's Press, 1997.

Merritt, Russell, and J. B. Kaufman. *Walt in Wonderland: The Silent Films of Walt Disney.* Baltimore: Johns Hopkins University Press, 1993.

Miller, Diane Disney, as told to Pete Martin. *The Story of Walt Disney.* New York: Holt, 1956.

Mosley, Leonard. *Disney's World: A Biography.* New York: Stein & Day, 1985.

Peary, Gerald, and Danny Peary. *The American Animated Cartoon: A Critical Anthology.* New York: E. P. Dutton, 1980.

Peet, Bill. *Bill Peet: An Autobiography.* Boston: Houghton Mifflin, 1989.

Price, Harrison "Buzz." *Walt's Revolution! By the Numbers.* Orlando, Fla.: Ripley Entertainment, 2003.

Ramsaye, Terry. *A Million and One Nights.* New York: Simon & Schuster, 1926.

Reichenbach, Harry, as told to David Freedman. *Phantom Fame: The Anatomy of Ballyhoo.* New York: Simon & Schuster, 1931.

Sammond, Nicholas. *Babes in Tomorrowland: Walt Disney and the Making of the American Child.* Durham, N.C.: Duke University Press, 2005.

Santoli, Lorraine. *The Official Mickey Mouse Club Book.* New York: Hyperion Books, 1995.

Schickel, Richard. *The Disney Version: The Life, Times, Art and Commerce of Walt Disney,* 3rd ed. Chicago: Elephant Paperbacks, 1997.

Shale, Richard. *Donald Duck Joins Up: The Walt Disney Studio During World War II.* Ann Arbor, Mich.: UMI Research Press, 1982.

Sherman, Robert B., and Richard M. Sherman. *Walt's Time: From Before to Beyond,* ed. Bruce Gordon, David Mumford, and Jeff Kurtti. Santa Clarita, Calif.: Camphor Tree Publishers, 1998.

Shows, Charles. *Walt: Backstage Adventures with Walt Disney.* Huntington Beach, Calif.: Windsong Books International, 1979.

Sklar, Martin A. *Walt Disney's Disneyland.* New York: Disney Productions, 1964.

Smith, Dave. *Disney A to Z: The Updated Official Encyclopedia.* New York: Hyperion Books, 1998.

Smith, David, with Steven B. Clark. *Disney: The First 100 Years.* New York: Disney Editions, 2003.

Smoodin, Eric, ed. *Disney Discourse: Producing the Magic Kingdom.* New York: Routledge, 1996.

Solomon, Charles. *Enchanted Drawings: The History of Animation.* New York: Alfred A. Knopf, 1989.

———. *The Disney That Never Was: The Stories and Art from Five Decades of Unproduced Animation.* New York: Hyperion Books, 1995.

Susman, Warren I. *Culture as History: The Transformation of American Society in the Twentieth Century.* New York: Pantheon, 1984.

Telotte, J. P. *Disney TV.* Detroit: Wayne State University Press, 2004.

Thomas, Bob. *Walt Disney: An American Original.* 1976; reprint New York: Hyperion, 1994.

———. *Building a Company: Roy O. Disney and the Creation of an Entertainment Empire.* New York: Hyperion, 1998.

Thomas, Frank, and Ollie Johnston. *The Illusion of Life: Disney Animation.* New York: Hyperion Books, 1981.

———. *Walt Disney's "Bambi": The Story and the Film.* New York: Stewart, Tabori & Chang, 1990.

Tietyen, David. *The Musical World of Walt Disney.* Milwaukee: H. Leonard Publishing, 1990.

Trethewey, Richard L. *Walt Disney: The FBI Files.* Pacifica, Calif.: Rainbo Animation Art, 1994.

Tytle, Harry. *One of "Walt's Boys": An Insider's Account of Disney's Golden Years.* Royal Oak, Mich.: Airtight Seals Allied Production, 1997.

Wasko, Janet. *Understanding Disney: The Manufacture of Fantasy.* Malden, Mass.: Blackwell Publishers, 2001.

Watts, Steven. *The Magic Kingdom: Walt Disney and the American Way of Life.* Boston: Houghton Mifflin, 1997.

ARTICLES AND ESSAYS

Adamson, Joe. "With Walt on Olympus: An Interview with Dick Huemer." *Funnyworld,* Fall 1977.

Alexander, Jack. "The Amazing Story of Walt Disney." *Saturday Evening Post,* Oct. 31, 1953.

Apple, Max. "Uncle Walt." *Esquire,* Dec. 1983.

Barrier, Mike. " 'Building a Better Mouse': Fifty Years of Disney Animation." *Funnyworld*, Fall 1979.

———. "Screenwriter for a Duck: Carl Barks at the Disney Studio." *Funnyworld*, Fall 1979.

Berland, David I. "Disney and Freud: Walt Meets the Id." *Journal of Popular Culture*, Spring 1982.

"Big Bad Wolf." *Fortune*, Nov. 1934.

Brockway, Robert W. "The Masks of Mickey Mouse: Symbol of a Generation." *Journal of Popular Culture*, Spring 1989.

Brunette, Peter. "Snow White and the Seven Dwarfs." In *The American Animated Cartoon: A Critical Anthology*. Edited by Gerald Peary and Danny Peary. New York: E.P. Dutton, 1980.

Canemaker, John. "Sincerely Yours, Frank Thomas." *Millimeter*, Jan. 1975.

———. "Grim Natwick." *Film Comment*, Jan.–Feb. 1975.

———. "Art Babbitt: The Animator as Firebrand." *Millimeter*, Sept. 1975.

———. "Vladimir William Tytla (1904–1968): Animation's Michelangelo." *Cinefantastique*, Winter 1976.

———. "Disney Design, 1928–1979: How the Disney Studio Changed the Look of the Animated Cartoon." *Millimeter*, Feb. 1979.

———. "David Hilberman." *Cartoonist Profiles*, Dec. 1980.

Charlot, Jean. "But Is It Art? A Disney Disquisition." *American Scholar*, Summer 1939.

Churchill, Douglas W. "How Mickey Mouse Enters Art's Temple." *NYT Magazine*, Jun. 3, 1934.

———. "Disney's Philosophy." *NYT Magazine*, Mar. 6, 1938.

Culhane, John. "A Mouse for All Seasons." *Saturday Review of Literature*, Nov. 11, 1978.

Dale, Kittie. "Disneyland, Ks., Had Its Historic, Exciting Moments." *Ellis Review*, 1972.

Davidson, Bill. "The Fantastic Walt Disney." *Saturday Evening Post*, Nov. 8, 1964.

De Roos, Robert. "The Magic Worlds of Walt Disney." *National Geographic*, Aug. 1963.

Deming, Barbara. "The Artlessness of Walt Disney." *Partisan Review* 12, no. 2 (Spring 1945).

"Disney Family Settled in Huron County in 1848." *Goderich Signal Star*, Jul. 7, 1999.

Disney, Mrs. Walt, as told to Isabella Taves. "I Live With a Genius." *McCall's*, Feb. 1953.

Disney, Walt. "The Cartoon's Contribution to Children." *Overland Monthly and Outwest Magazine*, Oct. 1933.

———. "The Marceline I Knew." *Marceline News*, Sept. 7, 1938.

———. "Growing Pains." *American Cinematographer*, Mar. 1941.

———. "A Roving Mouse Landed Me in a Hole!" *New York Enquirer*, May 5, 1957.

———. "Newspaperboys, Ah, How Well I Remember!" *Family Weekly*, Oct. 14, 1961.

Eddy, Don. "The Amazing Secret of Walt Disney." *American Magazine*, Aug. 1955.

Efron, Edith. "Still Attacking His Ancient Enemy—Conformity." *TV Guide*, Jun. 17, 1965.

"Father Goose." *Time*, Dec. 17, 1954.

Fessier, Michael, Jr. "Legacy of a Last Tycoon." *Los Angeles Times*, Nov. 12, 1967.

Flans, Robyn. "Joe Grant." *Disney News*, Fall 1970.

Ford, John D. "An Interview with John and Faith Hubley." In *The American Animated Cartoon: A Critical Anthology*. Edited by Gerald Peary and Danny Peary. New York: E. P. Dutton, 1980.

Gardner, John. "Saint Walt: The Greatest Artist the World Has Ever Known, Except for Possibly, Apollonius of Rhodes." *New York*, Nov. 12, 1973.

Glenn, Charles. "Exploding Some Myths About Mr. Disney." *Daily Worker*, Feb. 17, 1941.

Gordon, Mitchell. "Case of the Unretiring Mr. Rosenberg." *Wall Street Journal*, Feb. 14, 1968.

Gould, Stephen Jay. "A Biological Homage to Mickey Mouse" in *The Panda's Thumb: More Reflections in Natural History*. New York: W.W. Norton, 1980.

"Growing Up Disney." *People*, Dec. 21, 1998.

Halevy, Julian. "Disneyland and Las Vegas." *Nation*, Jun. 7, 1958.

Hart, Reg. "Interview with Friz Freleng." *Griffithiana*, no. 34 (Dec. 1988).

Hirsch, M. J., Jr. "Mouse Minter." *Advertising and Selling*, Jul. 18, 1935.

Hiss, Tony, and David McClelland. "The Quack and Disney." *The New Yorker*, Dec. 19, 1975.

Hollister, Paul. "Genius at Work: Walt Disney." *Atlantic Monthly* 166 (Dec. 1940).

Huemer, Dick. "Thumbnail Sketches." *Funnyworld*, Fall 1979.

———. "The Battle of Washington." *Funnyworld*, Winter 1980.

Hughes, Robert. "Walt Disney: From Mousebrow to Highbrow." *Time*, Oct. 15, 1973.

Hulett, Steve. "A Star Is Drawn." *Film Comment*, Jan.–Feb. 1979.

Jackson, Kathy Merlock. "Mickey and the Tramp: Walt Disney's Debt to Charlie Chaplin." *Journal of American Culture*, Dec. 2003.

Jamison, Barbara Berch. "Of Mouse and Man, or Mickey Reaches 25." *NYT Magazine*, Sept. 13, 1953.

JWM. "Walt Disney, Showman and Educator, Remembers Daisy." *CTA Journal*, Dec. 1955.

Kaufman, J. B. "Three Little Pigs—Big Little Picture." *American Cinematographer*, Nov. 1988.

Kimball, Ward. "The Wonderful World of Walt Disney." In *You Must Remember This*. Edited by Walter Wagner. New York: G.P. Putnam's Sons, 1975.

King, Margaret J. "Disneyland and Walt Disney World: Traditional Values in Futuristic Form." *Journal of Popular Culture* 15, no. 1 (Summer 1981).

———. "The Recycled Hero: Walt Disney's Davy Crockett." In *Davy Crockett: The Man, the Legend, the Legacy*. Edited by Michael A. Lofaro. Knoxville: University of Tennessee Press, 1985.

Klein, I. "Golden Age Animator Vladimir (Bill) Tytla." *Cartoonist Profiles*, Aug. 1970.

———. "Reminiscences." *Cartoonist Profiles*, Aug. 1970.

———. "The Disney Studio in the 1930s." *Cartoonist Profiles*, 1974.

———. "When Walt Disney Took Another Giant Step!" *Cartoonist Profiles*, Mar. 1977.

———. "I. Klein." *Cartoonist Profiles*, Sept. 1978.

———. " 'Screen Gems' Made of Paste: Memories of the Charles Mintz Studio." *Funnyworld*, Summer 1979.

———. "Some Close-Up Shots of Walt Disney During the 'Golden Years.' " *Funnyworld*, Spring 1983.

Lawrance, Lowell. "Mickey Mouse—Inspiration from Mouse in K.C. Studio." *Kansas City Journal-Post*, Sept. 8, 1935.

Lears, Jackson. "The Mouse that Roared." *New Republic*, Jun. 15, 1998.

Litwak, Leo E. "A Fantasy That Paid Off." *NYT Magazine*, Jun. 27, 1965.
Low, David. "Leonardo da Disney." *New Republic*, Jan. 5, 1942.
Mann, Arthur. "Mickey Mouse's Financial Career." *Harper's*, May 1934.
McEvoy, J. P. "Walt Disney Goes to War." *This Week*, Jul. 5, 1942.
Menen, Aubrey. "Dazzled in Disneyland." *Holiday*, Jul. 1963.
Merritt, Karen, and Russell Merritt. "Mythic Mouse." *Griffithiana*, Dec. 1988.
"Mickey Mouse and the Bankers." *Fortune*, Nov. 1934.
Miller, Arthur. "Walter in Wonderland." *Los Angeles Times*, Dec. 4, 1938.
———. "Dali and Disney Plan Something Definitely New." *Los Angeles Times*, Apr. 7, 1946.
"Mouse and Man." *Time*, Dec. 27, 1937.
"Mr. and Mrs. Disney." *Ladies' Home Journal*, Mar. 1941.
Muir, Florabel. "Animated Cartoons Going Over Big." *New York Sunday News*, Dec. 1, 1929.
Nater, Carl. "Walt Disney Studio—A War Plant." *Journal of the Society of Motion Picture Engineers* 42, no. 3 (Mar. 1944).
Natwick, Grim. "Animation." *Cartoonist Profiles*, Dec. 1978.
———. "Animation." *Cartoonist Profiles*, June 1979.
Nugent, Frank. "The Slapstick Professor." *New York Times*, May 5, 1935.
———. "Disney Is Now Art—But He Wonders." *NYT Magazine*, Feb. 26, 1939.
———. "The Million Dollar Mouse." *NYT Magazine*, Sept. 21, 1947.
Peet, Creighton. "Mickey Mouse's Miraculous Monkey Shines." *Literary Digest*, Aug. 9, 1930.
Peri, Don. "Roy Williams: An Interview." *Funnyworld*, Fall 1977.
"Pollen Man." *The New Yorker*, Nov. 1, 1941.
Pringle, Henry F. "Mickey Mouse's Father." *McCall's*, Aug. 1932.
"Profound Mouse." *Time*, May 15, 1933.
Rafferty, Dr. Max. "The Greatest Pedagogue of Them All." *Los Angeles Times*, Apr. 19, 1965.
Rasky, Frank. "80 Million a Year from Fantasy." *Star Weekly* (Toronto), Nov. 14, 1964.
Reilly, Frank. "The Walt Disney Comic Strips." *Cartoonist Profiles*, Winter 1969.
Robbins, L. H. "Mickey Mouse Emerges as Economist." *NYT Magazine*, Mar. 10, 1935.
Robins, Sam. "Disney Again Tries Trailblazing." *NYT Magazine*, Nov. 3, 1940.
Salkin, Leo. "Disney's 'Pigs is Pigs': Notes from a Journal, 1949–1953." In *Storytelling in Animation: The Art of the Animated Image*, vol. 2. Edited by John Canemaker. Los Angeles: AFI, 1993.
Santora, Phil. "A Kid from Chicago." New York *Daily News*, Sept. 30, 1964.
Schickel, Richard. "Ruler of the Magic Kingdom." *Time*, Dec. 7, 1998.
Scott, Joan. "Ordeal by Disney." *Film Comment*, Dec. 1987.
Scully, Vincent. "If This Is Architecture . . ." *Life*, Jul. 31, 1964.
Seldes, Gilbert. "Mickey Mouse Maker." *The New Yorker*, Dec. 19, 1931.
———. "Disney and Others." *New Republic*, Jun. 8, 1932.
———. "No Art, Mr. Disney." *Esquire*, Sept. 1937.
Shanley, J. P. "King of Disneyland." *New York Times*, Dec. 5, 1954.
Sherman, George. "Bill Tytla." *Cartoonist Profiles*, Aug. 1970.
Skolsky, Sidney. "Mickey Mouse—Meet Your Maker." *Hearst's International Cosmopolitan*, Feb. 1934.
Slate, Libby. "Marc Davis." *Disney News*, Fall 1992.

Smith, David R. "Ub Iwerks, 1901–1971." *Funnyworld*, Spring 1972.
———. "Ben Sharpsteen . . . 33 Years with Disney." *Millimeter*, Apr. 1975.
———. "Up to Date in Kansas City." *Funnyworld*, Fall 1978.
———. "Disney Before Burbank: The Kingswell and Hyperion Studios." *Funnyworld*, Summer 1979.
———. "New Dimensions—Beginnings of the Disney Multiplane Camera." In *The Art of the Animated Image: An Anthology*. Edited by Charles Solomon. Los Angeles: American Film Institute, 1989.
Solomon, Charles. "Historical Perspective." *Animation Magazine*, Summer 1992.
Strzyz, Klaus. "Art Babbitt." *Comics Journal*, Fall 1969.
———. "Art Babbitt." *Comics Journal*, Mar. 1988.
———. "Ward Kimball." *Comics Journal*, Mar. 1988.
Syring, Richard H. "One of the Great Geniuses." *Silver Screen*, Nov. 1932.
Thompson, Dorothy. "On the Record." *New York Herald Tribune*, Nov. 25, 1940.
Trillin, Calvin. "Disney World, Fla." *The New Yorker*. Nov. 6, 1971.
Updike, John. "Introduction to *The Art of Mickey Mouse*." In John Updike, *More Matter*. New York: Alfred A. Knopf, 1999.
"Virginia Davis Interview." *Hogan's Alley*, no. 2 (Summer 1995).
Wallace, Irving. "Mickey Mouse and How He Grew." *Collier's*, Apr. 9, 1949.
Wallace, Kevin. "The Engineering of Ease." *The New Yorker*, Sept. 7, 1963.
Waller, Gregory A. "Mickey, Walt and Film Criticism from *Steamboat Willie* to *Bambi*." In *The American Animated Cartoon: A Critical Anthology*. Edited by Gerald Peary and Danny Peary. New York: E.P. Dutton, 1980.
"Walt Disney Accused." Frances Clark Sayers, interview by Charles M. Weisenberg. *F.M. and Fine Arts*, Aug. 1965.
"Walt Disney Studios." *California Arts and Architecture*, Jan. 1941.
Wanger, Walter. "Mickey Icarus, 1943: Fusing Ideas with the Art of the Animated Film." *Saturday Review of Literature*, Sept. 4, 1943.
Waterbury, Ruth. "What Snow White's Father Is Doing Now." *Liberty*, Nov. 26, 1938.
"The Wide World of Walt Disney." *Newsweek*, Dec. 31, 1962.
"A Wonderful World." *Newsweek*, Apr. 18, 1955.
Woolf, S. J. "Walt Disney Tells Us What Makes Him Happy." *NYT Magazine*, July 10, 1938.

UNPUBLISHED MANUSCRIPTS AND ARTICLES

Anderson, Paul F. *The Artist and the Aviator: Victory Through Air Power*. 2005.
Discussion of New Burbank Disney Studio. Frank Crowhurst, interview by Grant Roelof. Apr. 16, 1940. WDA.
Disney, Walt. *Autobiography*. 1934. WDA.
———. *Autobiography*. 2nd, 3rd, 5th installments. 1939. WDA.
Early Chicago Residences of the Elias Disney Family. Commission on Chicago Historical and Architectural Landmarks. [1991.]
Foster, Robert Price. *The Founding of a Kingdom*. 1992. WDA.
Freleng, Friz. *Reflections of Friz Freleng*. 1969. Special Collections, Young Research Library, UCLA.
Graham, Don. *The Art of Animation*. n.d. WDA.

Hollister, Paul. *Man or Mouse: The Story of Walt Disney, So Far.* 1955. WDA.

Hubler, Richard G. *Walt Disney.* RHC. 1968.

Huemer, Richard. *Recollections of Richard Huemer.* 1969. Special Collections, Young Research Library, UCLA.

Johnson, Jimmy. *Inside the Whimsy Works: My Thirty-Seven Years with Walt Disney Productions.* 1975. WDA.

Jungmeyer, Jack. "The Marceline Farm Days in the Boyhood of Walt Disney." Dec. 20, 1954. WDA.

Lessing, Gunther. *My Adventures During the Madero-Villa Mexican Revolution.* 1963. WDA.

Los Angeles Art Community: Group Portrait. Jules Engel, interview by Lawrence Wechsler and Milton Zolotow. 1985. UCLA.

Perkins, Jessie Call. *The History of the Call Family.* December 1947. WDA.

Pesmen, Louis. Untitled ms. [1971]. WDA.

Sorrell, Herbert Knott. *You Don't Choose Your Friends: The Memoirs of Herbert Knott Sorrell.* 1963. Special Collections, Young Research Library, UCLA.

Watkin, Lawrence Edward. *Walt Disney.* n.d. WDA.

ACKNOWLEDGMENTS

When one works on a project as big as this one for as many years as it has taken me to accomplish it, one accumulates many debts along the way, but I have one major creditor: Howard Green. Among scholars, the Walt Disney Company has gained the unenviable reputation of being an impregnable corporate fortress, about as forthcoming as the old Soviet Kremlin. *No one* gains full access, I was warned by numerous individuals who had tried, unless one is serving the company's agenda. Those people didn't account for Howard Green. Howard Green is the longtime vice-president for studio communications at the Disney company, though the crisp austerity of that title is misleading. Howard is no button-down bureaucrat. He is an enthusiast, a historian, an astute critic, a facilitator, and a good and generous friend—someone who would have fit comfortably into the old, informal Hyperion enclave. His friendship has been one of the great rewards of my writing this book. When I first met Howard at the studio years ago at the inception of this project, I was braced for a maze of restrictions and a pile of provisos, including the proviso that I write approvingly of Walt Disney. Instead, I got a simple injunction: Write a serious book. I have tried to do so, but I couldn't have done so without the assistance of Howard, who opened the extensive Disney archives to me and introduced me to Disney animators, Disney scholars, old Disney employees, and acquaintances of Walt. It should be noted that having done all this, Howard did not require me to submit the manuscript to the studio for approval, and I haven't. I received cooperation. I did not seek nor did I receive a company imprimatur.

Another individual who deserves special praise is Roy E. Disney, Roy O. Disney's son and Walt Disney's nephew. I was told that Roy E. was instrumental in facilitating studio cooperation for this book. At the same time, he never attempted to influence what I was writing.

Having been loosed in the Disney Archives, where I would spend thousands upon thousands of hours working my way through Walt Disney's correspondence and reading tens of thousands of other documents as well as watching Disney films and listening to Disney recordings, I was aided and abetted by three other extraordinary individuals whom I am now privileged to call friends. Dave Smith founded the archives in 1971 and has headed them ever since. In the Disney community Dave is a legend—the primary fount of Disney information. He was never less than generous in sharing that information with me, in answering all questions, large and small, and in ferreting out any material that I requested and even some that I didn't know enough about to request. The archives manager, Robert Tieman, is also a published Disney authority. Robert, a self-professed curmudgeon, once took umbrage at an article that described him as cheery, so he will no doubt be offended when I say how much I appreciated his willingness to answer the numerous questions with which I pelted him daily, his forays to the annex to find material that was not readily available, and—dare I say it—the dry good humor with which he tolerated me even after years of my pestering him for Disney arcana. Robert's drollery leavened those long ten-hour days in the archives. Last but by no means least is Rebecca Cline, the assistant archivist. Rebecca not only answered questions, fetched material, Xeroxed documents, assisted my photo research, and took me on a tour of the studio, including Walt's office, she also patiently listened whenever I discovered what I thought was some golden nugget of information and listened even more patiently as I expatiated on some new theory of Walt that I was formulating. Just as Robert's drollery helped me through those long lunchless days, so did Becky's kindness and unfailing good nature. One couldn't ask for a better companion or a more decent human being. In addition to everything else they did, Dave, Robert, and Rebecca all read the manuscript and provided comments that made this a better book than it would otherwise have been. Thanks are due as well to Brian Hoffman of the archives, and Shelly Graham at the Disney Photo Library, who assisted in the photo research and scanned the images, and Margaret Adamic, who provided legal clearances.

I also received encouragement and assistance from the community of Disney scholars—and it is a community. Virtually all of them offered to help, welcoming me into their ranks and sharing their interviews, their documents, their contacts, and their insights. I owe thanks to Michael Danley, Katherine and Richard Greene, J. B. Kaufman, Jeff Kurtti, Les Perkins, Alex Rannie, Rick Shale, and above all Paul F. Anderson, the editor and publisher of the indispensable Disney journal *Persistence of Vision,* who not only provided material from his own extensive archives and supplied his informed perspectives on various issues but gave me a personal guided tour of Walt Disney's Los Angeles. I benefited greatly from his expertise and counsel.

In Marceline, Missouri, Kaye Malins escorted me through her house, which was once the Disney farmhouse, let me roam the acreage, and recounted Walt's trips to the area. Dan Viets, another Disney scholar, not only accompanied me on my visit to Marceline but gave me a tour of Disney sites in Kansas City, from the old Disney house on Bellefontaine to the Laugh-O-Gram offices in the now-empty McConahy Building. Dan even pried a large piece of plywood off the McConahy door so we could stand, albeit precariously, in Walt's old business quarters. Barbara Babbitt, Art Babbitt's widow, pored through her photo collection to provide me with images of her husband.

I am also indebted to the many Disney employees, family members, and acquaintances who submitted to lengthy interviews or provided information. Of them I would single out for special thanks three individuals: the late Harry Tytle, who worked at the studio for over thirty years, most of them in an executive capacity, and kept a daily journal that he was kind enough to let me peruse; Diane Disney Miller; and again Roy E. Disney.

I have not tallied the number of archives and libraries I visited or with which I corresponded, including presidential libraries, local historical societies, and even church offices, though to list them all would take several pages at least. The staffs of each of them have my deepest gratitude. My own local library, the Amagansett Free Library in the sublime community of Amagansett, New York, filled dozens of requests for books with unflagging good cheer, often surprising me at how quickly the staff managed to locate even the most obscure volumes. For these efforts, and for not taking no for an answer, librarian Judith Wolfe deserves special praise.

A basic hardship of writing a book over the time it took me to write this one is financial. The John Simon Guggenheim Memorial Foundation provided a fellowship that lifted that burden slightly. I am grateful for the honor and the stipend.

Over the years my friends have listened to me talk about Walt Disney, too kind to manifest the boredom they must have felt. Robert Solomon provided guidance; David Suter offered insights; Elizabeth Bassine read the manuscript with a keen eye; Bob Spitz, a superb biographer in his own right, commiserated, advised, and supported; Craig Hoffman gave me a place to stay in California, a substitute family, and unwavering moral support; Ann and Ed Dorr were another home-away-from-home on my many visits to Los Angeles when I was holed up in the archives; Marty Kaplan and my colleagues at the Lear Center at the University of Southern California provided intellectual sustenance; and Phil Rosenthal and Monica Horan were good friends during my extended stays.

At Alfred A. Knopf, my publishing home, my editor Jon Segal, with whom I have now done three books, was a model of old-fashioned stewardship. He read, he probed, he encouraged, he promoted and advocated, he lauded what he regarded as the book's strengths and sought to have me correct what he saw as its deficiencies. His editing improved the book immeasurably. He was also uncommonly patient, appreciating how long it takes to gather data, especially when one does the research single-handedly, as I do, and to craft a book. Above all, he cared both about the quality of the book and about its fate. In a world of corporate implacability, one couldn't ask for more.

I am also indebted to Jon's assistant, Ida Giragossian, who once again performed so many thankless but necessary tasks and who served as wrangler in getting the manuscript through production; to Gabrielle Brooks, my publicist, who seems genuinely to love the books she champions, which is why her authors genuinely love her; to the incomparable Mel Rosenthal, who scrutinized the manuscript with his unfailing eye and engaged me in long, fruitful debates on style and grammar; to Soonyoung Kwon for her sensitive design of the book; and to Barbara de Wilde, who designed her third jacket for me with her usual inventiveness and brilliance. Finally, like everyone at Knopf, I am grateful to Sonny Mehta for the standards he sets and the support he provides. Anyone working at Knopf has some sense of the mission that the Disney animators felt in the studio's heyday.

In my career I have only had one agent, which testifies to how wonderful my agent is professionally as well as how much I adore her personally. For twenty-five years now Elaine Markson has been a source of encouragement, reassurance, understanding, and calm. She reads acutely, she defends ferociously, she intervenes diplomatically, and she supports enthusiastically. I cannot imagine doing a book without her.

As much as this book has been the product of dozens if not hundreds of individuals, it finally belongs to my family, who often had to suffer through the research and writing of it and who certainly sacrificed for it. I hope they think that it was worth it since the gratitude I can extend to them—to my wife, Christina, my daughters Laurel and Tänne (to whom this book is dedicated), and my mother—is certainly insufficient. I love my work, but I live for them.

Needless to say, I take full responsibility for what appears on these pages, even though, like Walt Disney, I had an army of people to help. My profoundest hope is that I have justified their faith in me and in this project.

INDEX

PHOTOGRAPHIC CREDITS

All photographs and illustrations are courtesy of Disney Enterprises, Inc. © Disney Enterprises Inc. except for the following:

The Academy of Motion Pictures Arts and Sciences: Pat A. Powers
AP Photos: Walt testifying before HUAC
Barbara Babbitt: Art Babbitt and strike photo
Bettmann/CORBIS: Walt and Christopher; Stokowski and Walt
Getty Images: Walt and Kay Kamen

A NOTE ABOUT THE AUTHOR

Neal Gabler is the author of *An Empire of Their Own: How the Jews Invented Hollywood,* for which he won the Los Angeles Times Book Prize for History; *Winchell: Gossip, Power and the Culture of Celebrity,* which was a finalist for the National Book Critics Circle Award and was named the nonfiction book of the year by *Time* magazine; and *Life the Movie: How Entertainment Conquered Reality,* which has been assigned on college campuses across the country. Mr. Gabler has been a recipient of a Guggenheim Fellowship, and he is a senior fellow at the Norman Lear Center for the Study of Entertainment and Society at the Annenberg School for Communications at the University of Southern California. He was born in Chicago and lives with his wife in Amagansett, New York.

A NOTE ON THE TYPE

This book was set in Janson, a typeface long thought to have been made by the Dutchman Anton Janson, who was a practicing type-founder in Leipzig during the years 1668–1687. However, it has been conclusively demonstrated that these types are actually the work of Nicholas Kis (1650–1702), a Hungarian, who most probably learned his trade from the master Dutch typefounder Dirk Voskens. The type is an excellent example of the influential and sturdy Dutch types that prevailed in England up to the time William Caslon (1692–1766) developed his own incomparable designs from them.

Composed by North Market Street Graphics,
Lancaster, Pennsylvania

Printed and bound by R. R. Donnelley & Sons,
Harrisonburg, Virginia

Designed by Soonyoung Kwon